ONE THIRD OF OUR TIME?

AN INTRODUCTION TO RECREATION BEHAVIOR AND RESOURCES

ONE THIRD OF OUR TIME?

AN INTRODUCTION TO RECREATION BEHAVIOR AND RESOURCES

Michael Chubb
Michigan State University

Holly R. Chubb
Recreation Resource Consultants

Cartography by
Sherman Hollander

John Wiley & Sons, Inc.
New York   Chichester   Brisbane   Toronto

Production Manager: Rose Mary Hirsch
Designer: Rafael Hernandez
Photo Research by Flavia Rando/Picturebook
Photo Editor: Stella Kupferberg
Illustrations: John Balbalis
Copy Editor: Ellen MacElree

Library of Congress Cataloging in Publication Data

Chubb, Michael.
    One third of our time?

    Bibliography: p.
    Includes index.
    1. Recreation — United States. 2. Recreation —
Psychological aspects. 3. Natural resources —
United States. I. Chubb, Holly R., joint author.
II. Title.
GV53.C43   790′.0973   80-25131
ISBN 0-471-15637-X

To our daughter, Saralee, who lived with us during the four years when this book completely dominated our lives and who somehow managed to remain both cheerful and supportive in spite of the fact that her sacrifices far exceeded our own. Thank you, Saralee, for your love and your understanding; this book would never have been completed without your help.

PREFACE

This book is designed to fill a serious gap in the recreation literature. Currently, no introductory textbook deals comprehensively, systematically, objectively, and in a balanced manner with both the behavioral and the resource aspects of recreation. Present introductory texts tend to fall into two groups: those that assume their readers will follow a career in recreation programming (administering recreation activity programs) and those that assume the readers will proceed to a career in recreation resource management. Many books deal with only one part of the recreation spectrum such as local government-operated recreation programs in urban settings or the so-called resource-based recreation in national parks and other less developed areas. Some are primarily "how-to-do-it" books, and others tend to preach a particular philosophy rather than discuss recreation on a purely objective basis. There is simply no comprehensive introductory recreation textbook like those written for beginning courses in other applied sciences.

GENESIS AND GOALS
This book had its beginnings in my search for better materials with which to teach an introductory course. Existing textbooks had the drawbacks previously mentioned and most had few or no useful illustrations, especially diagrams that clearly demonstrated concepts and interrelationships or maps that showed significant distributions. During the same period, and after a number of years working full time on recreation research involving extraurban resources, I became involved in three in-depth surveys of recreation behavior and resources in urban impacted areas. These experiences convinced me that the main mission of the recreation profession should be to develop research methods, planning techniques, facilities, programs, management procedures, and personnel that best serve the needs of all citizens rather than just the desires of certain highly vocal or particularly active groups.[1] Such a mission demands a much wider interdisciplinary approach to the provision of recreation experiences than is espoused by many recreation professionals and organizations.

Our goal, therefore, is to provide a textbook that will give beginning students or practitioners seeking careers in a wide variety of recreation or recreation-related fields (such as recreation activity programming, recreation resource management, forestry, fisheries and wildlife management, tourism, recreation geography, landscape architecture, and urban planning) a broad understanding of the nature and scope of recreation behavior and resources on which they can build their subsequent specializations. Recreation professionals, whatever their ultimate career goals, should have a basic knowledge of all kinds of recreation behavior, resources, and programs, from the urban core to the wilderness, if they are to meet the increasingly diverse demands placed upon them by the complex social and political environments in which they operate. They can then appreciate the contributions and problems of the various resources and agencies that make up the recreation environments with which they interact professionally. Such an appreciation helps them understand the context in which important decisions are

[1] Michael Chubb, "Recreation Use Surveys and the Ignored Majority," in *Proceedings of the State Outdoor Recreation Planning Workshop*, Bureau of Outdoor Recreation, U.S. Department of the Interior, Ann Arbor, Mich., 1971; and *Recreation in the Lansing Model Cities Area: A Study of Spare Time Behavior and Attitudes*, Recreation Resource Consultants, East Lansing, Mich., 1972.

made and encourages a cooperative approach to problems that are of mutual concern to two or more recreation agencies. Cooperative approaches will be of increasing significance as changing conditions make closer cooperation among different recreation providers more economically and socially desirable or, in some cases, obligatory. More important, a holistic understanding of the significance of recreation and the various factors that affect participation makes it more likely that recreation professionals will appreciate the full individual and social implications of providing or not providing specific kinds of experiences in a particular way to a given population. Without this understanding, recreation programs can be unimaginative, stereotyped, unbalanced, or even inappropriate and actually discriminatory for certain portions of the population.

Developing a comprehensive, interdisciplinary textbook of this type has been very difficult. Reviewing and keeping abreast of the extensive recreation-oriented literature pertaining to all the disciplines proved extremely time-consuming. Having to condense our findings into one book of reasonable size became a major challenge. In addition, since there are few studies that discuss recreation behavior or resources in broad-brush, interdisciplinary terms, we had to collect data from a variety of published and unpublished sources and interpret this information in the light of personal experiences in order to produce generalized discussions. In many cases, such syntheses resulted in the development of new concepts and perspectives. However, it is these fresh insights that made the project personally worthwhile; we

hope that they will help bring all who share our conviction that a broad approach is essential one step nearer to a full understanding of recreation behavior and resources.

CONTENT AND USAGE

The material omitted from this book far exceeds the topics that were included. In particular, we deliberately refrained from including material concerning the practical aspects of recreation administration, resource management, or activity programming because such topics are covered in detail in special courses that most recreation students are required to take later in their programs. Instead, have focused on the basic historic, behavioral, and resource topics that form a firm foundation on which more specific courses on recreation philosophy, research, planning, design, administration, management, programming, and career development can be based.

This book may be used in a number of different ways. We hope that instructors will teach their courses in a manner that will permit all the principal concepts and facts in both the behavioral and resource sections to be adequately covered. Instructors in different disciplines can adjust the emphasis to suit their area of specialization. For example, activity-programming oriented courses can give special emphasis to topics such as the psychological, physical health, and social significance of recreation (Chapter 3); the social and personal factors affecting participation (Chapters 5 and 7); the nature and extent of participation (Chapter 8); private and commercial resources (Chapters 11

and 12); local and regional government resources (Chapter 13); professional resources (Chapter 17); and problems and future trends (Chapter 18). Other topics can be given less emphasis or, when appropriate, assigned for individual reading and study.

Similarly, instructors teaching courses in other fields can give emphasis to those topics that they consider fundamental but still expose their students to the interdisciplinary approach. Geographers can focus on topics such as land use, population factors, social attitudes, resource availability, transportation, perceptions, territoriality, participation patterns, carrying capacity, undeveloped resources, commercial resources, energy supply impacts, and international trade implications. The accompanying table suggests areas of special emphasis for a number of disciplines.

Another approach is to use the book as a text for a two-course sequence. The first course could include the introduction, historical perspective, significance of recreation, and recreation participation chapters (Parts One and Two); the second course would then cover the resource and future chapters (Parts Three and Four). The disadvantage of this arrangement is that some students would not be required to take both courses (even if the first course was made a prerequisite for the second) and, therefore, would not be exposed to both the behavioral and resource materials.

We have taken special pains to secure illustrations that are effective teaching aids. Each of the more than 160 photographs was selected by us personally from the hundreds supplied by the Wiley picture editors, and the many others we obtained from individuals, chambers of commerce, or recreation enterprises and agencies. We devised the 37 diagrams especially to clarify important concepts or relationships.

The 37 maps were designed cooperatively with our cartographer, Sherman Hollander, who then went far beyond the call of duty in his painstaking preparation of the excellent final drawings. Many illustra-

tions have explanatory captions that turn them into minilessons.

The listing of concepts and problems at the beginning of each chapter indicates the nature of the main topics included in it. There-

Suggested Areas of Special Emphasis for Several Disciplines
(The numbers in parentheses are page numbers)

Recreation Activity Programming	Recreation Resource Management	Tourism Management	Recreation Geography	Urban and Regional Planning
Amount of participation (49)	Amount of participation (49)	Educational significance (57)	Economic significance (75)	Social significance (61)
Psychological significance (51)	Social significance (61)	Political significance (69)	Land use (80)	Economic significance (75)
Educational significance (57)	Land use (80)	Economic significance (75)	External economic factors (88)	Land use (80)
Health significance (59)	Economic and population factors (86)	Economic and population factors (86)	Population factors (110)	Economic and population factors (86)
Social significance (61)	Social factors (119)	Accessibility, resources, and transportation (152)	Social attitudes (130)	Accessibility, resources, and transportation (152)
External social factors (119)	Accessibility, resources, and transportation (152)	Nature and extent of participation (229)	Resource availability (153)	Nature and extent of participation (229)
Personal factors (188)	Nature and extent of participation (229)	Undeveloped recreation resources (296)	Transportation (159)	Undeveloped recreation resources (296)
Nature and extent of participation (229)	Nature of resources (286)	Commercial recreation resources (365)	Perceptions (190)	Private recreation resources (324)
Private organization resources (337)	Undeveloped resources (296)	National resources (510)	Territoriality (214)	Commercial recreation resources (365)
Quasi-public organizations (347)	Local and regional resources (413)	Performing arts resources (571)	Participation patterns (251)	Local and regional resources (413)
Camps, hotels, and resorts (386)	State and provincial resources (462)	Museums and collections (590)	Resource classification (287)	Multilevel resources (546)
Local and regional agencies (413)	National and multilevel resources (509)	Energy supply implications (653)	Carrying capacity (291)	Cultural resources (562)
Performing arts resources (571)	Professional resources (619)	Economic trends and issues (675)	Undeveloped resources (296)	Administration (620)
Professional resources (619)	Resource trends and issues (653)		Hierarchy of enterprises (407)	Problems, trends, and the future (652)
Social trends and issues (689)			Distribution of public resources (416)	

fore, it functions to some extent as an index and also provides students and instructors with a checklist of important themes that should be assimilated and understood by reading the chapter and attending related lectures. The discussion topics at the end of each chapter have been designed to encourage readers to relate the main issues raised in the chapter to their own environments and experiences.

Students will find the further readings section at the end of each chapter useful for identifying sources of additional information. All of the publications listed are usually available in college libraries. The extensive bibliography at the end of this book lists many other sources that can provide further information.

METRIC UNITS AND APPROXIMATIONS

Wherever appropriate, numerical values are given in metric units followed by the English measurement system equivalent in parentheses. If the numerical value is a precise measurement, then the metric and English system values correspond within the limits imposed by arithmetic rounding. However, if a measurement is imprecise (such as the approximate length of a trail) or is expressed as a rough range of values, then the metric and English equivalents are rounded to a similar degree in order to avoid giving an unwarranted impression of precision for one of the sets of values. For example, neighborhood parks in many new communities are said to be 5 to 10 hectares or 10 to 25 acres in size; the precise equivalent of this acreage range would be 4.05 to 10.13 hectares. Values have also been rounded in many of the tables; in the case of percentages, slight adjustments have often been made so that the columns add up to 100 percent.

USER REACTIONS SOLICITED

We invite those who discover any errors or omissions in this book to write to us and point them out. We also welcome other comments, particularly about the overall arrangement and coverage of the various topics. Suggestions from instructors and students who have used this book in introductory courses will be especially appreciated.

Michael Chubb

ACKNOWLEDGMENTS

This book would not have been possible without the encouragement and assistance of many wonderful people. We are particularly appreciative of the substantial direct and indirect contributions made by the following individuals and organizations:

- The many faculty members who participated in my education, especially Raleigh Barlowe, former Chairperson of the Department of Resource Development, Michigan State University; Charles E. Doell, Superintendent Emeritus of the Minneapolis Park Commission; Leslie M. Reid, Head, Department of Recreation and Parks, Texas A&M University; and Louis F. Twardzik, Chairperson, Department of Park and Recreation Resources, Michigan State University.
- Colleagues in the departments of Geography, Park and Recreation Resources, and Resource Development at Michigan State University who provided understanding and encouragement. We particularly appreciated the support of Dr. Lawrence M. Sommers, former Chairperson of the Department of Geography at Michigan State University who initially pointed out the professional disadvantages of pursuing such a lengthy task but encouraged us once we had decided to proceed. His successor, Dr. Gary Manson, was also most solicitous even when it appeared that the project would never end!
- The many staff members at John Wiley & Sons who worked on editing and publishing this book. We are especially grateful to Publisher Andrew E. Ford, Jr., whose enthusiastic response to our ideas launched the project, and to Wayne Anderson, Editor—Recreation and Parks, who subsequently kept us going by showing great patience and faith in the value of our work even when it became more arduous and time-consuming than any of us had ever imagined.
- The reviewers selected by the publisher who helped determine the structure and quality of this book— Tony A. Mobley, Consulting Editor, and Richard A. Conover of Clemson University; Craig Finney of California State University at Northridge; Susan D. Hanlon of Florida State University; and John H. Schultz of the University of Minnesota.
- My brother, D. Peter Chubb of Rustington, Sussex, England, who provided extensive information and many potential illustrations from Great Britain and other parts of Europe.
- The hundreds of professionals in dozens of public agencies, quasi-public organizations, and commercial enterprises who answered questions and supplied materials. We are especially appreciative of the assistance of the following organizations and individuals:

U.S. Department of Agriculture—Rupert M. Cutler, Forest Service—Robert Prausa, George H. Stankey, and Tom Steele
U.S. Department of the Interior National Park Service—Priscilla R. Baker, Bureau of Land Management—Darrell E. Lewis
Parks Canada—John A. Carruthers
State and provincial park and recreation agencies—British Columbia, Robert E. Pfister and J. B. L. Walter; California, William C. Dillinger; Colorado, Bernie G. Bovee and Robert G. Carlson; Kentucky, Carl Stout; Michigan, Jim Hane and Larry Miller; New York, Harold J. Dyer; Ontario, Ron J. Vrancart; and Texas, Paul E. Schlimper.
Local and regional agencies— Cheyenne, David R. Romero; Metropolitan Dade County, Bill Bird and W. Howard Gregg; Delta Township, Mark Graham; DuPage County Forest Preserve, Howard C. Johnson and Lance Loucks; East Bay Regional Park District, Christian Nelson; Evansville, Vern Hartenburg; Gaston County, Carl M. Baber, Jr.; Huron-Clinton Metropolitan Authority, Robert L. Bryan; Kansas City, Frank Vaydik; Town of Madison, H. Clark Schroeder; Meridian Township, Glen Ziegler; Milwaukee, Robert Mikula; Muskingum Watershed Conservancy

District, Thomas K. James; New York City, Joseph P. Davidson; Riverside County, Dick Simons; Sioux City, Paul A. Morris; Terrebonne Parish, E. Jay Ellington; Metropolitan Toronto, Frank E. Kershaw; Metropolitan Toronto and Region Conservation Authority, Brian E. Denney; and Willamalane District, Mary Ellen Leach.

- Recreation resource managers in both urban and extraurban locations who have helped us understand the pragmatic aspects of providing recreation opportunities by showing us the resources under their care and sharing their experiences.
- The many students who, in taking courses with me or serving as research assistants, have contributed to my knowledge and appreciation of recreation by reacting to concepts

and materials or introducing me to new ideas and resources. I am particularly grateful to Douglas M. Crapo and Ronald W. Hodgson for expanding my interest in survey research methods, to William D. Martin for helping me become involved in inner-city recreation problems, and to Theresa N. Westover for her assistance and encouragement during the final two years of this book's preparation.

M. C.

CONTENTS

PART 4
THE FUTURE

ONE THIRD OF OUR TIME?

AN INTRODUCTION TO RECREATION BEHAVIOR AND RESOURCES

INTRODUCTION

Rafting Pennsylvania's Youghiogheny River, like most recreation activities, is a complex experience that depends for its success on many personal and external factors ranging from equipment and weather suitability to individual skills and participant compatibility.

1

INTRODUCTION: NATURE AND SCOPE

CONCEPTS & PROBLEMS

The Importance of Recreation
Interdisciplinary Foundation
Seven Major Themes
The Significance of Perception
Multiple Role Perception
The Definition of Recreation
Recreation Environments Are
  Complex
Understanding Behavior Is
  Crucial

THE IMPORTANCE OF RECREATION

Recreation plays many vital roles in modern living (Figure 1.1). For individuals, it is a life-sustaining essential. Active recreation maintains and restores bodily vitality and muscular ability. This is increasingly important

Figure 1.1 **Paley Park, a minipark in midtown Manhattan, is a restful green retreat for employees from nearby shops and offices. Even brief periods of relaxation while talking to friends, solving a crossword puzzle, strumming a guitar, or reading a book help people to survive the pressures of their daily routines.**

as more people spend larger portions of their time in sedentary occupations and walk less. Recreation reduces the stresses of the crowded conditions and hectic pace in urban areas. For many who spend their days at repetitive or impersonal tasks, it is the only aspect of life that provides excitement and fulfillment. Recreation is also used in medical treatment to help people overcome physical and mental disabilities.

Recreation is equally beneficial to society as a whole. It offers opportunities for people to get to know and appreciate others in their own communities. Recreational travel can develop understanding and strengthen relationships within and between nations. Recreation is also a valuable educational tool; people learn more easily if education is enjoyable. In addition, recreation can lead to increased environmental awareness and understanding as people hike, camp, and enjoy their surroundings.

Finally, recreation is of great economic importance. Vast sums of money are spent on *recreation goods* (television sets, reading material, sports equipment, and vehicles) and on *recreation services* (professional sports admissions, entertainment, tours, and resorts). Many people are employed in these and related businesses. Much land is used for recreation activities either exclusively or in combination with other uses such as agriculture or forestry. This raises the value of such property.

Recreation is therefore of great significance to both individuals and society. Paradoxically, however, there is sometimes a reluctance to support public recreation programs. Individuals collectively spend billions of dollars every year on personal enjoyment yet local governments are inclined to cut public recreation budgets more readily than budgets for other services.[1] The media and government agencies emphasize the social and economic significance of recreation but universities rarely support recreation programs as generously as other applied sciences. No other human activity is as complex and yet relatively little attention is given to recreation research and planning.

THE NATURE AND PURPOSES OF THIS BOOK

This book is based on the conviction that recreation is an essential part of life. It is as important to human welfare as nutrition or education and therefore deserves the same level of careful, unemotional, and objective study.

We believe that the study of recreation must be interdisciplinary in nature. Recreation professionals must understand the motivations and feelings of participants as well as the social, political, and physical factors that affect their recreation environments. A basic knowledge of the psychology and sociology of recreation is therefore as important as understanding methods for developing facilities, managing land, organizing programs, or administering an agency. Professionals must also appreciate the way in which the various components of a recreation environment interact. They should have a basic knowledge of all types of recreation—public, quasi-public, commercial, and private—from the urban core to the remote wilderness. Today's complex problems require an understanding that is both interdisciplinary and geographically expansive.

In the past, the various recreation professions operated independently of one another. Many cities had recreation departments that were separate from their park departments and the two agencies often competed for funds and recognition. Fortunately, this division between the land managers and those responsible for recreation services is disappearing. Most cities now have combined departments. In 1966, the National Recreation and Park Association was formed in the United States by merging both groups' professional organizations. More recently, college recreation departments have added resource courses while land management-oriented academic programs have started to include behavioral courses.

Traditional boundaries are also disappearing in recreation employment. Land-managing agencies are hiring social scientists and professionals skilled in developing recreation services. Persons with land management training are now employed in organizations that are primarily concerned with recreation programs. The U.S. National Park Service sends its new rangers to urban units such as those in Washington or New York as a test of their ability to work with large numbers of people.

Many North American recreational professionals have also been rather provincial in their outlook. They have shown little interest in problems and solutions outside their own immediate geographic areas.

[1] This has certainly proved to be the case recently in California. See Chapter 18.

But the preeminence of Canada and the United States in many aspects of recreation— especially research and planning— is being challenged. Nations such as Australia, France, Great Britain, Japan, the Netherlands, New Zealand, and West Germany are expanding research and developing innovative recreation programs. It is important, therefore, that recreation professionals develop a basic understanding of conditions and achievements in other nations.

Therefore, this book has been written with both an interdisciplinary and an international perspective. It is intended to fill a void in the recreation literature by providing a broad introduction to recreation in a manner similar to introductory textbooks in other disciplines. It provides an overview of the essential components of recreation and forms a solid foundation on which to build any one of a variety of career specializations. However, resources and programs that are most significant in providing opportunities for large numbers of people have been emphasized.

Seven major themes have been woven into the chapters that follow. They include:

- The *magnitude* and *diversity* of recreation participation.
- The importance of considering peoples' *attitudes* when identifying and understanding recreation behavior.
- The need to see recreation as *a series of interacting complex systems.*
- The great *diversity of resources* used for recreation.
- The huge *economic impact* of recreation.
- The *rapid changes* taking place in some facets of recreation compared to the *timeless aspects* of other facets.
- The need for careful *research,* cooperative *planning,* imaginative *adminis-*

tration, and intelligent *management* in all aspects of recreation opportunity provision.

The main purpose of this book is to foster a greater understanding of these themes so that tomorrow's recreation opportunities may be even better than those available today.

RECREATION TERMINOLOGY

THE MEANING OF 'RECREATION"

Webster defines *recreation* as "refreshment of strength and spirits after toil: diversion; . . ."[2] The *Oxford Dictionary* says recreation is "the action of recreating (oneself or another), or fact of being recreated, by some pleasant occupation, pastime or amusement."[3] Obviously dictionary definitions cover a wide range of activities; depending on a person's desires and perceptions, refreshment of strength or spirits can be achieved in countless ways. For instance, refreshment may result from running in a marathon race, sleeping late on a Sunday morning, reading to children, hunting rabbits, gambling at a race track, digging in a garden, watching television, eating in a restaurant, window shopping, repairing a car, or going to church.

Nevertheless, activities like those listed above may not always be perceived as recreational even when undertaken during what appears to be free time. A person who is anxious to do something

[2] *Webster's Seventh New Collegiate Dictionary,* G. & C. Merriam Company, Springfield, Mass., 1971.
[3] *The Oxford English Dictionary,* Clarendon Press, Oxford, 1933.

else may regard reading to children or digging in the family garden as unwelcome duties. On the other hand, activities such as eating or drinking can be partly or largely recreational although they fulfill essential bodily needs. It is equally difficult to distinguish between the sexual and recreational components of events involving both males and females such as social dancing or beach activities. Participation in religious events, especially major festivals, also presents a problem. Besides those participating because of spiritual motivations, there are many who take part as a social duty, some who regard attendance as beneficial to their business or career, and others who simply enjoy the ritual or social interaction.

Some writers use a list of activities to help them define recreation. This approach has its limitations. It is necessary to know each person's perception of an activity before it can be classified as recreation, work, duty, bodily necessity, or spiritual experience; recreation activity listings will therefore differ from individual to individual. In addition, an individual may perceive an activity differently at various times. Taking a dog for a walk may be largely recreational on a fine spring morning but may have no recreational component on a cold, rainy night (Figure 1.2).

The model in Figure 1.3 illustrates the problems involved in classifying a human activity. Each of the five main activity roles has been represented by a circle. Any one of these roles can become completely or partly superimposed on an activity depending on how the participant perceives involvement. The crucial factor is the *attitude* of the participant. Sometimes more than

Figure 1.2 Only the person walking a dog in Central Park, New York City, on a chilly rainy evening knows how the experience is perceived. It could be work, recreation, a duty, a bodily necessity, or a mixture of two or more of these roles depending on the participant's attitude.

one role can be superimposed at one time as shown in Figure 1.4. This is a case of *multiple role perception* which is discussed further in Chapter 8.

LIMITATIONS IMPOSED BY SOME DEFINITIONS

Some writers attempt to establish narrow definitions for the word recreation. Limited definitions are obviously easier to interpret, simpler to apply philosophically, and provide arguments for restricting professionally directed recreation to activities that are considered acceptable. In fact, some professionals maintain that they have a responsibility to foster participation in certain types of recreation and

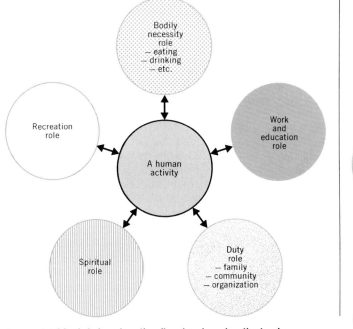

Figure 1.3 Model showing the five basic roles that a human activity can assume; one or more roles is assumed depending on the way in which the participant perceives the activity.

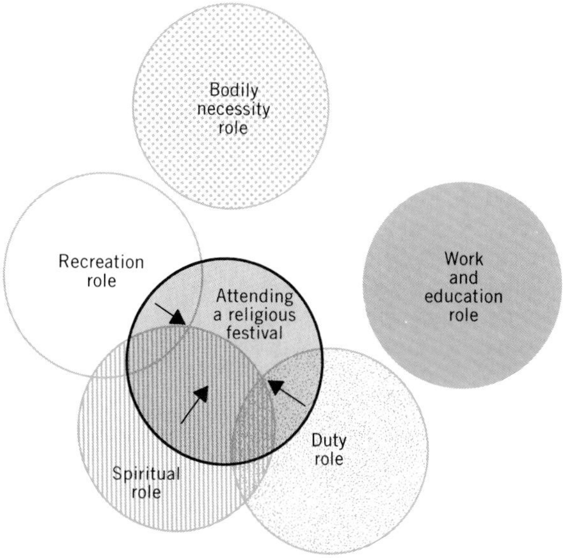

Figure 1.4 An example of multiple-role perception; an individual perceives attending a religious festival as partly a spiritual experience, partly a duty, and partly a recreation experience.

discourage participation in activities that they consider less desirable. A limiting definition is regarded as essential to these philosophies.

Limitations are frequently imposed by the use of restrictive adjectives. Some authors state that an activity has to be "constructive,"[4] or "uplifting," or of "high quality" to be included in what they call recreation. They exclude what they term "amusements," "time fillers," or "loafing." Apparently they feel that a participant cannot be refreshed unless the activity is beneficial to mind or body in a way that is acceptable to them. Playing a pinball machine, sleeping in the sun, reading a comic book, or tearing around a gravel pit on a noisy motorcycle are not recreation according to definitions limited in this manner. Obviously the application of such restrictive adjectives is very subjective and not based on whether or not the participant is actually refreshed.

Another commonly used stipulation is that an activity must be socially acceptable in order to be considered recreation. This is a reasonable requirement as long as it is applied as a broad general principle. An antisocial act will make a normal person psychologically uncomfortable and therefore will hardly be a refreshing recreation experience. However, "social acceptability" is not easy to define. First, public attitudes change; for instance, the acceptability of casino gambling varies from time to time and from place to place. Second, the limits of social acceptability are often ill-defined. Playing bingo for

prizes is considered a form of gambling and thus is illegal in many jurisdictions. When religious groups use the game as a means of raising funds, does such sponsorship make the game socially acceptable even in a location where it is technically illegal?[5] Apparently it does since law enforcement agencies often ignore bingo in these situations.

Several authors stipulate that an activity must be engaged in "from choice" or "voluntarily" or "without compulsion" to be considered recreation. This implies that if people participate in an activity because it is a part of their job or education, or because it is a duty, they cannot be refreshed by the experience! However, observation shows that many people do get refreshment from required physical education and sports programs in schools or military service. And some obtain recreation experiences from certain aspects of their work.

Attempts to create limited definitions by using restrictive adjectives, stipulations of social acceptability, or requirements that participation be completely voluntary are counterproductive. Recreation is a widely used word and efforts to convert it into a specialized technical term are unlikely to either change dictionary definitions or common usage.

A DEFINITION OF RECREATION

In this book, the word recreation is used in its broadest dictionary

sense. We consider recreation to be *any type of conscious enjoyment.* It can take place at any time and at any location. It may include activities that are normally thought of as basic bodily functions, activities that are usually considered psychologically abnormal, or even activities that damage objects, the individual, or society. The only criterion is whether or not *the participant perceives the activity as recreational.*

It does not follow that the use of a broad definition will have undesirable effects. The question of what kinds of recreation activities are offered by public or private organizations is still a matter of policy to be decided by appropriate groups in society. Adherence to traditional restrictive definitions of recreation can be a serious handicap especially when providing recreation experiences for special groups. The absence of arbitrary restrictions fosters a wider professional perspective. It encourages the provision of a diversity of enjoyable opportunities appropriate to the needs of all groups in a society.

OTHER IMPORTANT TERMS

Definition of the word *leisure* presents problems that are in some respects the same as those discussed previously for recreation.[6] *Webster's* states leisure is "freedom provided by the cessation of activities; especially time free from work or duties."[7] The *Oxford Dictionary* defines it as "the state of having time at one's own disposal; time which can be spent as one pleases;

---

[4] Some societies condone quite *destructive* activities such as cockfighting, boxing, American football, or shooting animals and birds.

[5] In the case of fund-raising bingo games, there is also the question of whether or not a player perceives participation as a duty. No doubt most players enjoy the experience but some might not go if they did not feel an obligation to the sponsoring organization (Figure 11.6).

[6] For a good discussion see Geoffrey Godbey, *Recreation, Park and Leisure Services,* W. B. Saunders, Philadelphia, 1978.

[7] *Webster,* op. cit.

free or unoccupied time."[8]

Some recreation professionals use *leisure* and *recreation* as if they were interchangeable, ignoring dictionary definitions and common usage. Other professionals and sociologists attempt to establish narrower meanings. They define leisure as the "productive," "creative," or "contemplative" use of free time. On the other hand, the word "leisure" is not commonly used by some segments of society. Many people, especially the disadvantaged, feel that only the affluent have leisure; they use the words *free time* or *spare time* instead. In this book, we use the word leisure in its broadest dictionary sense and alternate it with the terms free time, spare time, or **discretionary time** to provide variety.

Outdoor recreation is another term that causes difficulty. During the 1960s and early 1970s, it was widely used in both technical writings and the popular press. It was also made part of the title of many government agencies. In the process, some recreation professionals started to give the term a restricted meaning. They used it to describe only those types of recreation that normally take place outside urban areas. Outdoor activities such as backyard games and barbecues, basketball in city parks, and professional sports events were excluded. For example, Public Law 85-470, the Outdoor Recreation Resources Review Act, specifically excluded "recreation facilities, programs, and opportunities usually associated with urban development such as playgrounds, stadia, golf courses, city parks, and zoos when defining outdoor recreation resources." A current textbook defines outdoor recreation as "those recreational activities which occur in an outdoor (natural) environment and which relate directly to that environment" and makes it clear that only relatively undeveloped environments such as state and national parks are included.[9] However, the public, the press, and many recreation professionals use outdoor recreation in its dictionary sense to mean any type of recreation activity that takes place outside a building in urban as well as rural settings.

Avoidance of urban recreation problems by outdoor recreation specialists and agencies became an issue in the late 1960s and early 1970s. Citizens asked why these professionals and agencies were not doing more to assist urban outdoor recreation. A number of changes resulted. In the United States, the federal Bureau of Outdoor Recreation became more involved with city recreation. Many states dropped the word outdoor from the titles of their state recreation plans and recreation agencies, and began to provide more assistance to urban recreation. However, the term outdoor recreation is still widely used, and the nonurban interpretation lingers in some instances.[10]

Another difficulty with the phrase outdoor recreation is the growing frequency with which some activities are taking place both indoors and outdoors. Tennis, American football, soccer, and baseball are played indoors as well as outdoors. In some cases, facilities have retracting roofs so that an event can change from indoors to outdoors quite rapidly.

Because of these problems, we do not use the phrase outdoor recreation in this book. Urban and extraurban recreation are differentiated by explicit wording.

ORGANIZATION OF THIS BOOK

When attempting to describe recreation and the environments in which it takes place, it is difficult to know where to begin. Every recreation environment is a complex set of interlocking components as shown in Figure 1.5. Some components such as physical condition, recreation preferences, education, and income are primarily characteristics of the participant. Others are largely external, such as the nature and extent of public and commercial recreation resources. Some components do not fall neatly into either group. For instance, a major factor in participation is mobility or lack thereof. Mobility depends on personal characteristics of the participant, such as physical condition and income, as well as on aspects of the external environment, for example, the availability and condition of roads and vehicles. Since all the components interact, no component is necessarily more important than another. However, understanding human behavior is the key to understanding recreation. Therefore, the factors that affect participation will be discussed before examining the nature of recreation participation and the role of recreation resources.

The arrangement of topics in

---

[8] *The Oxford English Dictionary,* op. cit.

[9] Clayne R. Jensen, *Outdoor Recreation in America,* Third Edition, Burgess, Minneapolis, 1977, p. 8.

[10] In Britain and some other English-speaking nations, the word countryside is often used in connection with recreation that takes place away from urban areas. The term does not have the same meaning and extensive usage in North America.

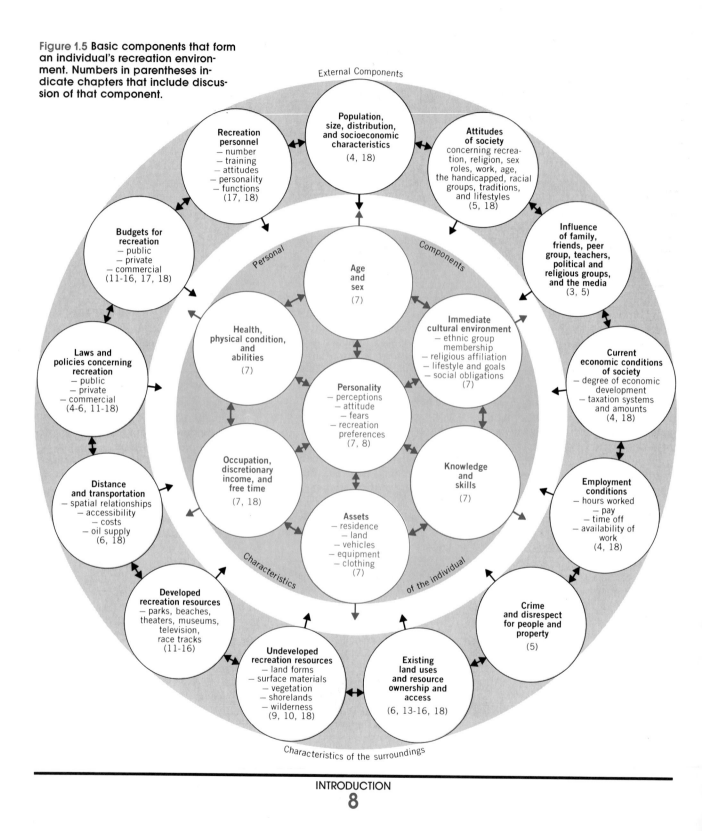

Figure 1.5 Basic components that form an individual's recreation environment. Numbers in parentheses indicate chapters that include discussion of that component.

External Components

Recreation
personnel
— number
— training
— attitudes
— personality
— functions
(17, 18)

Population,
size, distribution,
and socioeconomic
characteristics
(4, 18)

Attitudes
of society
concerning recrea-
tion, religion, sex
roles, work, age,
the handicapped, racial
groups, traditions,
and lifestyles
(5, 18)

Budgets for
recreation
— public
— private
— commercial
(11-16, 17, 18)

Personal

Components

Influence
of family,
friends, peer
group, teachers,
political and
religious groups,
and the media
(3, 5)

Laws and
policies concerning
recreation
— public
— private
— commercial
(4-6, 11-18)

Age
and
sex
(7)

Health,
physical condition,
and
abilities
(7)

Immediate
cultural environment
— ethnic group
membership
— religious affiliation
— lifestyle and goals
— social obligations
(7)

Current
economic conditions
of society
— degree of economic
development
— taxation systems
and amounts
(4, 18)

Personality
— perceptions
— attitude
— fears
— recreation
preferences
(7, 8)

Distance
and transportation
— spatial relationships
— accessibility
— costs
— oil supply
(6, 18)

Occupation,
discretionary
income, and
free time
(7, 18)

Knowledge
and
skills
(7)

Employment
conditions
— hours worked
— pay
— time off
— availability of
work
(4, 18)

Assets
— residence
— land
— vehicles
— equipment
— clothing
(7)

Characteristics

of the individual

Developed
recreation resources
— parks, beaches,
theaters, museums,
television,
race tracks
(11-16)

Crime
and disrespect
for people and
property
(5)

Undeveloped
recreation resources
— land forms
— surface materials
— vegetation
— shorelands
— wilderness
(9, 10, 18)

Existing
land uses
and resource
ownership and
access
(6, 13-16, 18)

Characteristics of the surroundings

Figure 1.6 Organization of the topics in this book.

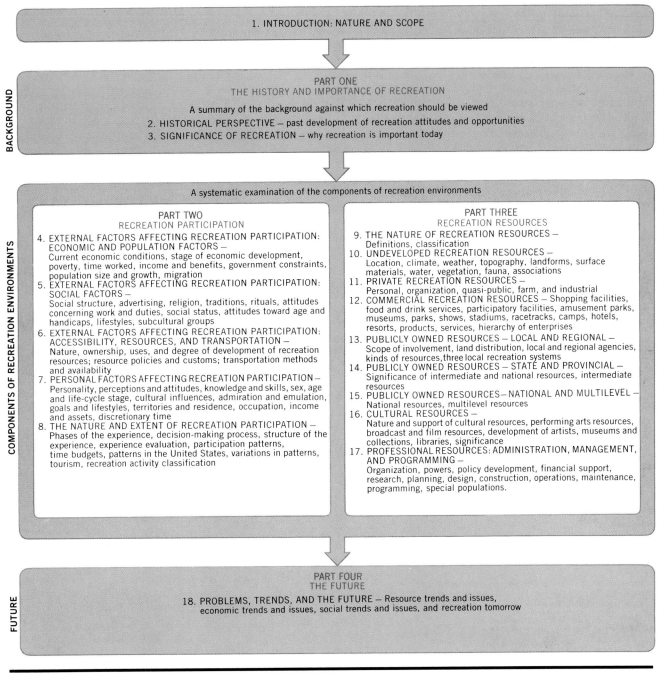

BACKGROUND

COMPONENTS OF RECREATION ENVIRONMENTS

FUTURE

1. INTRODUCTION: NATURE AND SCOPE

PART ONE
THE HISTORY AND IMPORTANCE OF RECREATION

A summary of the background against which recreation should be viewed
2. HISTORICAL PERSPECTIVE — past development of recreation attitudes and opportunities
3. SIGNIFICANCE OF RECREATION — why recreation is important today

A systematic examination of the components of recreation environments

PART TWO
RECREATION PARTICIPATION
4. EXTERNAL FACTORS AFFECTING RECREATION PARTICIPATION: ECONOMIC AND POPULATION FACTORS — Current economic conditions, stage of economic development, poverty, time worked, income and benefits, government constraints, population size and growth, migration
5. EXTERNAL FACTORS AFFECTING RECREATION PARTICIPATION: SOCIAL FACTORS — Social structure, advertising, religion, traditions, rituals, attitudes concerning work and duties, social status, attitudes toward age and handicaps, lifestyles, subcultural groups
6. EXTERNAL FACTORS AFFECTING RECREATION PARTICIPATION: ACCESSIBILITY, RESOURCES, AND TRANSPORTATION — Nature, ownership, uses, and degree of development of recreation resources; resource policies and customs; transportation methods and availability
7. PERSONAL FACTORS AFFECTING RECREATION PARTICIPATION— Personality, perceptions and attitudes, knowledge and skills, sex, age and life-cycle stage, cultural influences, admiration and emulation, goals and lifestyles, territories and residence, occupation, income and assets, discretionary time
8. THE NATURE AND EXTENT OF RECREATION PARTICIPATION — Phases of the experience, decision-making process, structure of the experience, experience evaluation, participation patterns, time budgets, patterns in the United States, variations in patterns, tourism, recreation activity classification

PART THREE
RECREATION RESOURCES
9. THE NATURE OF RECREATION RESOURCES — Definitions, classification
10. UNDEVELOPED RECREATION RESOURCES — Location, climate, weather, topography, landforms, surface materials, water, vegetation, fauna, associations
11. PRIVATE RECREATION RESOURCES — Personal, organization, quasi-public, farm, and industrial
12. COMMERCIAL RECREATION RESOURCES — Shopping facilities, food and drink services, participatory facilities, amusement parks, museums, parks, shows, stadiums, racetracks, camps, hotels, resorts, products, services, hierarchy of enterprises
13. PUBLICLY OWNED RESOURCES — LOCAL AND REGIONAL — Scope of involvement, land distribution, local and regional agencies, kinds of resources, three local recreation systems
14. PUBLICLY OWNED RESOURCES — STATE AND PROVINCIAL — Significance of intermediate and national resources, intermediate resources
15. PUBLICLY OWNED RESOURCES—NATIONAL AND MULTILEVEL — National resources, multilevel resources
16. CULTURAL RESOURCES — Nature and support of cultural resources, performing arts resources, broadcast and film resources, development of artists, museums and collections, libraries, significance
17. PROFESSIONAL RESOURCES: ADMINISTRATION, MANAGEMENT, AND PROGRAMMING — Organization, powers, policy development, financial support, research, planning, design, construction, operations, maintenance, programming, special populations.

PART FOUR
THE FUTURE
18. PROBLEMS, TRENDS, AND THE FUTURE — Resource trends and issues, economic trends and issues, social trends and issues, and recreation tomorrow

this book is shown in Figure 1.6. It is divided into four parts. Part One summarizes the context in which current participation takes place; it describes the historical development of recreation and discusses the reasons why recreation is so significant in today's world. Parts Two and Three are a systematic examination of the components that form recreation environments. Chapters 4 to 6 in Part Two outline the economic population, social, resource accessibility, and transportation factors that affect participation. Chapter 7 summarizes the role of individual participation characteristics. Then the structure and basic patterns of participation are described in Chapter 8.

Part Three examines the various resource components of the recreation environment. Chapter 9 explores the nature of recreation resources; Chapter 10 is concerned with undeveloped resources such as topography, water, and vegetation. Privately owned and commercial recreation resources are described in Chapters 11 and 12. Chapters 13 to 15 are devoted to a summary of publicly owned recreation resources at the local, intermediate, and national levels. Chapter 16 describes cultural resources and their sources of support. Chapter 17 examines some of the professional resources necessary to provide recreation opportuni-

ties—administrative, research, planning, design, and operations and maintenance skills. It concludes with an overview of professionals' contributions in conducting recreation programs. Part Four describes current resource, economic, and social trends and issues, and examines their probable impact on recreation in the future.

USING THIS BOOK

Each of the following chapters is a summary of the most important ideas concerning a particular topic. Brief suggestions concerning readings that supply more details are included at the end of each chapter. These have been limited to books and journals that can readily be obtained through most college libraries. An extensive bibliography at the back of this book includes a wider range of significant sources some of which are less readily available. The footnotes indicate other pertinent materials but are restricted to sources that were used directly. All words in the text that are printed in color using a bold-faced type are defined in a glossary of terms that also appears at the back of the book.

In reading the chapters it is important to remember that this book is an introduction to a deceptively complex field of study. As is the case with an introductory book in

any discipline, it is only a beginning. There are many textbooks and journal articles that discuss details of each of the main topics mentioned. Those wishing to become really competent in the field as a whole or in any of its specialized subdivisions will naturally wish to undertake much more extensive studies.

In addition to more extensive reading, visits to recreation resources and discussions with professionals are essential for a good understanding of recreation. Unfortunately, many people do not make contact with recreation outside their own sphere of participation and develop a narrow egocentric outlook. Periodic visits to a wide range of recreation resources including some during periods of heavy use are essential for those who wish to develop a broader more objective perspective. The serious student will supplement class experiences with appropriate personal visits and contacts.

Unlike many sciences, the study of recreation is quite new and is based on comparatively little empirical data. This means that it is a rapidly changing field. Therefore, we must all be prepared to modify our beliefs and methods of solving problems in the light of new information and ideas as they emerge.

DISCUSSION TOPICS

1. Should the academic study of recreation be based on an interdisciplinary foundation, or is it desirable for students in some disciplines to study recreation only within their proposed specialization?
2. Is it practical or desirable for recreation professionals to contend that both recreation and leisure have much more restricted meanings than those given in dictionaries?
3. Is the term outdoor recreation necessary or can we dispense with it in order to avoid confusion?
4. Does Figure 1.5 adequately convey the number of factors involved and the complexity of typical recreation environments?

An excellent general discussion of recreation is contained in the 1965 edition of the *Encyclopaedia Britannica* (unfortunately, a similar article does not appear in later editions). A chapter entitled "Play, Recreation, and Leisure" provides a good review of various traditional interpretations of these words in Richard Kraus' textbook *Recreation and Leisure in Modern Society* published in New York by Appleton-Century-Crofts in 1978. Geoffrey Godbey and Stanley Parker present a thoroughly modern view of recreation in *Leisure Studies and Services: An Overview* published in 1976 by Saunders of Philadelphia. Six traditional concepts of leisure and a complex sociological model are discussed in Max Kaplan's 1975 textbook *Leisure: Theory and Policy* published in New York by Wiley.

PART ONE

THE HISTORY AND IMPORTANCE OF RECREATION

A twentieth century audience watches a classical Greek drama in the 2300-year-old theater built into a hillside at Epidaurus, 60 kilometers (40 miles) southwest of Athens.

2

HISTORICAL PERSPECTIVE

Recreation, like other aspects of human behavior, is constantly changing. Attitudes and participation patterns continually evolve. Major changes are still taking place. An appreciation of the historical development of recreation helps us understand present behavior and probable future trends.

During early human social development, recreation was an integral part of everyday activities. Enjoyment could take place at any

Figure 2.1 An artist's impression of how a performance may have appeared to an Athenian sitting in an upper-row seat in the Theater of Dionysus 2300 years ago.

time if conditions were favorable. Hunting, fishing, and gathering food were fun when participants were favored with good health, fine weather, and plenty of game, fish, or berries. Recreation was spontaneous; it just happened. As society evolved, games associated with everyday activities developed and art forms such as utensil ornamentation and rock paintings emerged.

Later, recreation became more formal and class differences developed. Tribal rulers arranged recreation experiences to suit their preferences. They could hunt, feast, or play games at will while others performed necessary subsistence activities. Eventually, specialized occupations and land uses developed. The first recreation resource managers were probably those who guarded game animals reserved for a ruler and assured his hunting pleasure by driving the game toward the hunting party. Those who were not in privileged positions enjoyed hunting and other pleasurable activities if and when they were permitted to do so.

The development of agriculture widened the gap between the ruling classes and the rest of the population. It demanded intensive labor and encouraged the growth of larger settlements. Both these trends resulted in more arduous, monotonous work and less free time for the laboring classes.

RECREATION IN EARLY CIVILIZATIONS: 5000 B.C. to A.D. 300

During the Egyptian, Assyrian, and Babylonian civilizations, recreation became more diverse. Hunting, horse racing, wrestling, boxing, archery, and other martial competitions were popular; music, dancing, and drama flourished. Those in the ruling classes competed with one another in providing lavish entertainment. Numerous free men as well as slaves were employed in providing these recreation opportunities.

Many activities, especially elaborate festivals, were associated with religious events. Drinking and gambling were common and of special importance to the laboring classes. Lands set aside for recreation became more extensive. Large formal gardens were constructed with pools and vegetation arranged in geometric designs. The most famous were the Hanging Gardens of Babylon, which appeared to be suspended when seen from a distance because of their terraced arrangement.

During this era, recreation developed in a similar manner on the Indian subcontinent and in China. Advanced forms of games, sports, drama, and music together with elaborate ornamental gardens, hunting preserves, and zoological exhibits were common. However, differences in religion and philosophy resulted in some variation in attitudes toward recreation. For example, the Chinese believed that landscape features such as the sky, mountains, seas, rivers, and rocks were materializations of spirits. They had a great reverence for natural landscapes and reproduced them in their gardens and other artistic works. Gardens were built primarily for personal contemplation and enjoyment rather than as displays of affluence and grandeur.

When the Greek civilization reached its peak about 500 B.C., the desirability of various types of recreation became an important issue.

The ruling class (about 20 percent of the population) had been freed from work by the use of slaves but depended on the military capabilities of its free citizens for defense against ever-present aggressors. Physical fitness and athletic ability were considered a necessity and therefore an obligation to the state. Extensive sports programs, elaborate athletic facilities, and frequent competitions developed. Originally, participation was widespread and on a high philosophical level. Later, sponsorship of athletes by the affluent began and eventually many sports events involved professionals performing before spectators.

It was in this context that the Greeks developed what is known as their *leisure ethic*. They considered the intelligent use of free time to be the main purpose of life. Activities that had constructive qualities such as music or philosophical contemplation were acceptable. Those activities normally undertaken by the masses for refreshment after work were considered inappropriate. Aristotle and other philosophers argued about the acceptability of various activities and probably experienced much enjoyment in doing so! Nevertheless, Greek cities usually had extensive gardens, parks, open-air theaters, gymnasiums, and other recreation facilities; therefore, the citizens enjoyed a wide range of activities in spite of philosophical attempts at restriction.

Dramatic performances were frequent and elaborate. Every city of any size and reputation had an open-air theater (Figure 2.1). Presentations were a combination of ritual, pageant, music, drama, and religious teachings. Their primary purpose was not so much to entertain or initiate social change as to relieve tension through the sharing of ritualistic experiences. Performances lasted from dawn until dark. Members of the audience brought mats and pillows for comfort as well as food and wine for refreshment between plays.

The Romans were more pragmatic. In the early days of the empire, they encouraged individual citizen participation in athletics for health and military reasons. Free individuals did not take part in music, dancing, and drama as much as they had during the Greek civilization. These activities were primarily the responsibility of professionals and slaves. Hunting and fishing continued to be popular activities. Better transportation and security resulted in travel to baths, resorts, athletic events, and cultural attractions. Some trips were taken primarily to see foreign wonders such

as the pyramids in Egypt.

As the Roman Empire grew rich from its conquests and colonies, a large urban middle class developed. This politically significant group was not rich but had considerable free time. The work day finished early every afternoon and they enjoyed some 200 holidays each year. Emperors attempted to keep people content by providing free food and entertainment.

By A.D. 350, the population of Rome numbered more than 1 million, and the provision of public recreation had become a major government function and expense. There were frequent parades, chariot races, horse races, exhibitions of various forms of combat, and huge feasts. Unfortunately, the people constantly demanded new and more exciting kinds of entertainment. The nature of many of the events gradually changed from

athletic contests to bloody spectacles involving animals, and finally, humans. Professional gladiators fought to the death. Slaves and prisoners were maimed or killed in a variety of combat or carnivorous animal events.

Inhuman performances reached a peak following the construction of the Colosseum arena in A.D. 80. Its opening was celebrated by a series of spectacles lasting 100 days that included land and sea battles with thousands of combatants (Figure 2.2). Later, the arena was modified to facilitate performances involving large numbers of wild animals. The Colosseum became the hub of life in Rome, and large arenas were constructed in most of the provincial towns throughout the Roman world. In addition to various types of arenas, the typical city included open-air theaters, numerous public baths, gymnasiums, courts for ball games, and a limited number of gardens and parks.

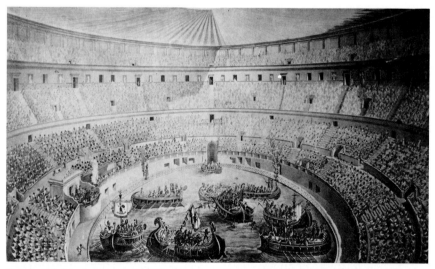

Figure 2.2 An archaeologist's impression of one of the naval battles staged in the Colosseum in A.D. 80 during the opening celebrations. This 60,000-seat structure was the most elaborate and versatile spectator facility ever built.

THE MIDDLE AGES: A.D. 500 to A.D. 1350

The fall of the Roman Empire, the long period of intermittent warfare that followed, and the spread of Christianity had a profound effect on recreation throughout the Western World. The Catholic church taught that the main purpose of living was to prepare the soul for salvation. The human body, with its weaknesses for food, drink, and other pleasures, was regarded as a handicap that had to be overcome. The Roman lifestyle was seen as the exact opposite of that required of Christians.

As the monasteries expanded

during the following centuries, more people lived under the Catholic system of hard labor, good works, and self-deprivation. The rigor with which these principles were observed depended on the particular sect and the attitudes of local church and secular leaders. Many people led relatively drab lives filled with hard work and religious duties. Others, particularly some of the rulers and clergy, participated in a wide range of recreation activities. Social drinking, gambling, secular music, and theatrical performances were officially regarded as sinful but many frequently took part in such activities in connection with religious festivals!

Despite the criticism of Roman excesses, hunting was a major activity of the ruling classes including many clergy. Kings, nobles, and bishops established game reserves and spent large sums of money on hunting and falconry. Hunting by the nobility was justified as being compatible with church teachings because it produced food, was physically arduous, and was better than idleness! In contrast, many of the limited activities enjoyed by the poor were criticized or even banned as immoral time wasters. Restrictive guidelines or laws affecting recreation behavior were frequently motivated by practical considerations rather than religious fervor. Kings and religious leaders desired maximum citizen participation in work or military training. Their concern for the number of days worked was justified. The Church had established the Sabbath as a day of rest and had also designated many other days as religious festivals, which kept the peasants from the fields. Craftsmen enjoyed additional holidays; in fact, they only worked

about 200 days a year by the late Middle Ages.

A number of important traditions were reestablished or initiated during this period. The Protestant work ethic, which emerged centuries later, had its origins in the concept that work was necessary and beneficial to the soul. Since work was good, recreation was bad, and certain activities such as gambling and social drinking were considered to be particularly undesirable. Hunting was regarded as a privilege of the aristocracy. Wild animals, birds, and fish were considered the property of the landowners. In most cases, peasants were not permitted to take game under any circumstances. Only the nobility participated in tournaments, jousting, and other events on horseback. The privately owned open "common land" within or adjacent to the villages that was used to contain farm animals at night or in time of danger became regarded as semipublic land available for community activities. During the early Middle Ages, these activities were primarily religious festivals. Later, village commons were used for dancing, games, and various types of traveling performances.

THE RENAISSANCE AND REFORMATION ERA: 1350–1700

During the period between A.D. 1300 and A.D. 1500, the power of the Catholic church declined. Europe came under the control of powerful monarchs and their supporting nobilities. Two opposing movements then began to influence society. First, reduction in the power of the Church permitted a reawakening of interest in the arts

and other forms of recreation. Literature, drama, music, painting, and ballet flourished under the sponsorship of nobles and royalty. Theaters and opera houses were built and numerous troupes of actors, singers, musicians, and dancers became established. Participation in many forms of active recreation increased. The affluent became intrigued with formal ballroom dancing, tennis, and other ball games. The working class favored football (a primitive form of soccer), prizefights (boxing), cock fighting, and bear baiting.

However, the worldliness of the Catholic clergy, a pleasure-seeking aristocracy, and widespread drinking, gambling, and participation in cruel sports promoted the second major movement—the Protestant Reformation. It began in the early 1500s and involved the establishment of a number of new Christian sects that disassociated themselves from the Catholic church. Their religious beliefs varied but generally included strict enforcement of Sunday as a day of worship and rest, restrictions on alcoholic beverages, gambling, and social dancing, and strong adherence to the work ethic. Many were extreme in their opposition to most forms of recreation including all sports, theatrical performances, pretty clothing, nonreligious poetry and music, and books that did not have a serious religious or educational purpose. Some would not even permit children to play because it encouraged idleness and diverted them from religious activities.

Besides participating in few activities themselves, the Protestants exerted strong moral and legal pressures on the rest of the population in communities where they were

Figure 2.3 A small corner of the geometrically shaped formal gardens at the Palace of Versailles on the outskirts of Paris. Originally designed by André Lenôtre for the Sun King, Louis XIV, the gardens were copied extensively and created a new landscape style. They are now one of France's most visited tourist attractions.

strong. In Britain, for example, they succeeded in having a series of laws passed that restricted commerce and recreation on Sundays. However, many ignored or avoided these restrictions. The rich were able to do much as they pleased on their estates, and the urban poor were left largely to their own devices. The middle class, which contained the majority of the Protestants, and those living in small communities were affected most.

Although the construction of recreation entities was much more extensive during this period than in the Middle Ages, most of it was private development undertaken by the aristocracy. Theaters and opera houses were generally built by and for the ruling classes. Numerous formal gardens and landscaped parks were constructed as part of private estates. A few of these gardens and parks were open to the public on a regular basis but most were closed or open only on special occasions. The gardens were generally complex rectangular designs on flat or terraced land and were comprised of clipped hedges and trees, shallow pools, masonry work, and graveled areas (Figure 2.3). The affluent continued to hunt extensively, and hunting reserves became more numerous and better defined. It is fortunate that so many gardens, estates, and preserves were established during this period of population increase and agricultural expansion; a good number are now public open spaces (Figure 2.4).

The Renaissance also produced limited improvements in urban design. Broad avenues and public squares were included in some of the new areas that developed outside the old walled cities. A few public parks or play areas began to appear as towns grew larger and residents had more difficulty in reaching pasture land for games and public events.

North America was colonized during this era. A good proportion of the early settlers, especially those in New England, belonged to Protestant sects that disapproved of idleness and most forms of recreation. Some communities passed laws prohibiting any activities on Sundays except those that were spiritual or essential for basic subsistence. Laws forbidding participation at any time in activities such as card games, mixed dancing, and theatrical performances were also common. However, the degree to

which Puritan taboos were observed and the nature of these restrictions varied considerably from place to place. Many men regularly enjoyed hunting, fishing, marksmanship contests, horse racing, and cricket. Taverns were well patronized and often provided opportunities for card playing or watching cockfighting, bear baiting, or boxing. Fairs and festivals frequently included square dancing and athletic or musical contests

Attitudes and laws were least restrictive in the southern colonies. Fewer settlers held Puritan beliefs and more landowners had sufficient wealth to employ indentured servants and hired hands. A relatively wealthy aristocracy developed, especially with the introduction of slave-operated plantations. They enjoyed gambling, hunting, and all

types of games but laws often specifically prohibited participation by the working class in such activities.

Puritan attitudes and the absence of large urban areas resulted in little attention being given to the provision of public recreation facilities until well after the American Revolution. Public common land existed in many settlements, particularly in New England, but recreation was not the original objective (Figure 2.5). Similarly, some city planners included squares or other open areas in their designs in order to create more attractive and impressive urban environments rather than to provide specific on-site recreation opportunities. Nevertheless, the squares laid out under the direction of William Penn in Philadelphia and James Oglethorpe in Savannah, together with the plazas resulting from Spanish settlement of the Southwest, subsequently had a considerable effect on recreation. Similar open spaces were included in many other urban designs. Often as the cities grew larger, they were the only public lands available for recreation in downtown areas.

Survival needs and democratic attitudes led to more liberal hunting and fishing laws in North America than in Europe. Early evidence of this was the Massachusetts Great Ponds Act of 1641. It decreed that all ponds over 10 acres in extent were open for public use including fishing and waterfowl hunting. Other early New England laws indicated a democratic approach to the protection of woodlands and wildlife.

During the almost 6000 years summarized in the preceding paragraphs, recreation attitudes and participation went through many changes. However, the situation at

Figure 2.4 Londoners enjoy spring sunshine in St. James Park, one of the 10 parks in the center of the city that is still technically the private property of the British Royal Family. In the late seventeenth century, King Charles II converted it into a French formal garden and opened it to the public. In 1827, the park was changed to an informal design.

Figure 2.5 Set aside by the original settlers as "a commons" for public grazing purposes, the Boston Common is now a 20-hectare (50-acre) green oasis next to the downtown business and government districts in Boston, Massachusetts. Boating facilities and the band shell where the Boston Pops performs its July 4 concert are in Charlesbank Park in the foreground.

the end of the period was basically the same as at the beginning; only the ruling classes were able to enjoy a wide range of opportunities. In spite of the earlier Greek and Roman development of public recreation, there were virtually no lands or programs specifically dedicated to this purpose in later periods. The common people had to be content with some social drinking, a little gambling, an occasional festival, and such other amusements as they could themselves devise. The next 250 years

produced many revolutions—including one in recreation attitudes, behavior, and policies.

THE SECOND RECREATION REVOLUTION

The dramatic changes in recreation that occurred between 1700 and the present time constitute the *second recreation revolution.* The first revolution took place during the Greek and Roman eras when participation in a wide range of activities ceased

to be the privilege of a very small ruling class and became the right of many. A similar radical change has taken place during the last 300 years; a wide variety of activities, including many that were previously the prerogative of the rich, have become available to a majority of citizens.

So many significant events took place during the second recreation revolution, that it is difficult to discuss them briefly. The main events will be shown in a series of chronological charts and systematically summarized in the text. Emphasis will be given to changes in the United States, since they frequently foreshadowed similar happenings elsewhere. Federal legislation and actions are mentioned most often because they provide indications of national attitudes. However, many parallel events took place in lower levels of government, in private organizations, and in business. Social changes and advances in recreation services are not listed as frequently; they are not as well documented as developments associated with parks and other tangible recreation resources.

The second recreation revolution has been divided into seven stages as shown in Figure 2.6. Although these phases are based on developments in the United States, many other nations have gone through similar stages as industrialization and social changes altered attitudes and behavior. Some nations have experienced much less involvement by government agencies (Stage 4). Others have had relatively limited mechanization of recreation (Stage 6). Some emerging nations are going through similar transitions much more quickly than the United States because of rapid industrialization.

STAGE 1 – THE PRELUDE: 1700–1840

Seventeenth century Puritan attitudes toward work and recreation continued to have a major effect during the early 1700s. Their influence was greatest where the strict Protestant sects were strong. But changes were slowly taking place (Table 2.1). Some of the growing middle class followed the lead of the wealthy and enjoyed forbidden

activities such as plays, dances, and sporting events. Urban centers grew in size so that more people lived in environments where pressures to conform were weaker. Both domestic and international travel increased, speeding up the diffusion of new ideas and fashions. Even in New England, card playing became widespread and attendance at concerts became respectable. Theatrical

THE SECOND RECREATION REVOLUTION
1700 TO THE PRESENT

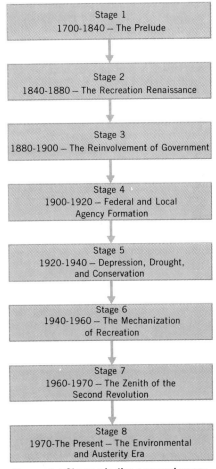

Figure 2.6 **Stages in the second recreation revolution.**

productions were still regarded as evil in strongly Protestant areas, but readings and commentaries on plays began to be included in educational lecture programs.

Attitudes toward undeveloped resources were also changing. The "wilderness" was previously regarded as something that had to be conquered. Protestant theology tended to represent it as an earthly hell that Christians had a duty to subdue by clearing and farming. During the eighteenth century, Romanticism—the view that a primitive life and undeveloped scenery are valuable in themselves—grew with the popularity of the writings and authors such as Rousseau and Byron. Later, some American writers developed a romantic approach to the wilderness.

Newspaper stories, magazine articles, lectures, poetry, and novels on the unsettled parts of North America were in demand. Interest reached a climax with the Lewis and Clark exploration of the Northwest and the discovery of the wonders of the Yellowstone region in the Rocky Mountains. Although public sentiments and policies supported private development and settlement of the wilderness, ideas such as Catlin's suggestion of a national park to preserve Indian culture started to attract attention.

At the same time, the Industrial Revolution was taking place. It began in the late eighteenth century with the development of the steam engine and textile machines. By the early 1800s, steam locomotives and steam boats were revolutionizing transportation and travel, and stimulating the development of large industrial cities. Rapid industrialization took place in parts of Britain, northern Europe, and the north-

Table 2.1 Stage 1 of the Second Recreation Revolution—
The Prelude: 1700–1840

Date	Event
	STAGE 1—THE PRELUDE 1700–1840
Early 1700s	— "Taking the waters" and enjoying entertainment at spas (hot springs) is fashionable, especially in Europe.
	— Taking "the Grand Tour" of Europe is popular, particularly with the English.*
	— Romanticism—value of simple life and wilderness—promoted by writers such as Rousseau and Byron.
1700's—1800s	— Gradual spread of literacy and the reading habit in Europe; commercial libraries flourish; over 800 mechanics' institutes with small libraries formed in British industrial towns.*
1776–1783	— American War of Independence—a period of austerity and restraint for most Americans.
Late 1700s	— **Steam engine and textile machines developed—industrial revolution begins.**
1789–1799	— French Revolution—spreads idea of individual freedom to pursue happiness.*
1791	— L'Enfant, supervised by Washington and Jefferson, designs the City of Washington with much open space.
Early 1800s	— **Steam locomotive, steamboat, and telegraph developed accelerating the industrial revolution.**
	— Rapid influx of emigrants from Europe—speeds up urbanization in the Northeast.
	— 14- to 18-hour workday and 6-day week leave little free time for recreation activities.
	— Puritan influence continues to have an effect on recreation but theater and sports draw large crowds.
1803	— Jefferson completes the Louisiana Purchase—Mississippi to the Rocky Mountains area added to the U.S.
1805–1806	— **Lewis and Clark expedition explores the Northwest—Coulter returns to discover Yellowstone.**
1812–1814	— War of 1812—the U.S. declares war on Britain—the British burn Washington.
1815	— Battle of Waterloo—ends wars of the Napoleonic era in Europe.*
1820s	— Hotels expand in White and Catskill mountains; appreciable numbers of tourists visit Niagara Falls.
	— Writers such as Cooper (The Pioneers—1823) and Bryant (The Forest Hymn—1825) provide a romantic view of the American wilderness.
1821	— Florida is ceded to the U.S. by Spain following the Seminole Wars.
1830	— **William IV becomes King in Britain—extensive reforms begin—slavery abolished in British Empire, Factory Act passed, trade unionism starts.** *
1832	— Congress reserves land in Arkansas for public spa—later becomes Hot Springs National Park.
1833	— Catlin letters on Indian culture in New York paper; propose preservation by "a Nation's park."
1835	— Reed and Matheson suggest Niagara Falls should be considered "the property of civilized mankind."
1837	— Queen Victoria begins her reign in Britain—lasts until 1901—period of comparative tranquility.*

* Events occurring outside the United States.

eastern United States.

The Protestant work ethic was strong, especially in the northeastern part of North America. Men, women, and children worked 14 to 18 hours a day for six days a week. Working conditions were harsh and often dangerous. Not since the days of the Roman slaves had so many people worked so hard for such long hours. Industrialized cities and towns grew rapidly. Immigrants from Europe arrived in North America in increasing numbers and worked hard in factories and fields to fulfill their dreams of prosperity.

But reform movements were gaining strength. The American and French Revolutions encouraged democratic thinking. Britain abolished slavery in her colonies, improved working conditions in factories, and provided the environment in which the first trade unions developed. It was the prelude to much more radical change.

STAGE 2—THE RECREATION RENAISSANCE: 1840–1880

The early part of the Victorian era saw some strengthening of Puritan attitudes toward recreation especially those concerning the theater and activities permissable on Sundays. Religious leaders joined employers in opposing shorter working hours because more free time would only be used for "sinful activities." Women (at least those in the middle and upper classes) were considered frail and in constant need of protection from physical exertion. Unmarried ladies were protected from contact with men. As a result, women in the middle and upper classes participated in relatively few kinds of recreation activities.

Recreation experienced a renaissance in spite of these restrictive trends in some segments of society (Table 2.2). Workers in the expanding cities sought substitutes for the family and for community amusements of their home towns and rural areas. With less social pressure to conform, they patronized various types of commercial recreation and paid less attention to observing the Sabbath. Feelings of personal independence were encouraged by the growth of democracy and labor unions. Bars, beer gardens, dance halls, amusement parks, and a variety of stage shows became common in urban areas. Entrepreneurs disguised theatrical performances as lecture programs in order to make them more socially acceptable. So the door to more varied recreation opportunities gradually opened—at least in the cities.

The success of urban theaters and commercial recreation may have helped reverse the attitudes of some religious leaders. Whatever the reasons, the "Muscular Christianity" movement of the middle 1800s endorsed physical fitness as a character builder and therefore compatible with Christian principles. This prepared the way for several other significant changes. Respectable people could now take part in sports and athletics or watch others doing so. Athletic and sports clubs grew more numerous, and professional sports teams were organized.

Table 2.2 Stage 2 of the Second Recreation Revolution—
The Recreation Renaissance: 1840–1880

STAGE 2—THE RECREATION RENAISSANCE: 1840–1880

Date	Event
Middle 1800s	— Industrialization, immigration, and urbanization continue at a rapid pace.
	— **Muscular Christianity movement develops—leaders say physical fitness is compatible with teachings.**
	— Physical activity is more acceptable to strict Protestants—walking, rowing, and skating grow.
	— Public library movement grows in United States, Canada, and Britain with the passage of library legislation, formation of library associations, and gifts from philanthropists such as Andrew Carnegie.
1841	— In Britain, Thomas Cook arranges first train excursion—begins organized mass movements of less affluent to recreation resources, especially one-day rail trips to "the seaside."
1853	— **New York City authorizes purchase and development of Central Park; designed by Olmsted and Vaux.**
	— In France, Fontainebleau reserve is established near Paris.*
1860	— National Association of Baseball Players starts league of 50 clubs and charges admission.
1860s	— Boys' Clubs founded in Hartford, Connecticut. YMCAs start to offer substantial recreation programs.
1861–1865	— American Civil War—expanded recreation knowledge, participation, and travel.
1864	— **Congress grants Yosemite Valley to California for state-operated park.**
1865	— **Ratification of the Thirteenth Amendment abolishes slavery in the United States.**
1867	— United States purchases Alaska from Russia for $7.2 million.
	— Canada is formed from New Brunswick, Nova Scotia, Ontario, and Quebec by the British North America Act.*
1869	— First railroad across North America completed—starts era of long-distance train tourism.
1870	— **Washburn-Langford-Doane party explores Yellowstone region and decides to press for public ownership and use rather than seek commercial opportunities.**
	— Bicycling begins to be a widely practiced recreation activity.
1871	— Olmsted advocates systems of interrelated parks for cities.
1872	— **Congress sets aside a vast area around Yellowstone as a national "pleasuring ground."**
	— Arbor Day started in Nebraska—results in much tree planting nationwide.
	— In Britain, Cook leaves with group of clients for the first round-the-world tour.*
1875	— Fort Mackinac in Michigan designated as the first federal military park.
	— American Forestry Association formed—assisted in creation of public forests and parks.
1877	— Twenty cities in the United States have organized municipal park systems.
1879	— **Australia established "The National Park" (later Royal National Park) near Sydney.***

*Events occurring outside the United States.

Attitudes toward women were changing. Participation in croquet, lawn tennis, golf, archery, roller skating, and ice skating was no longer considered unladylike. However, women still had to wear heavy, hot clothing from neck to toe (Figure 2.7) and they were not expected to take part vigorously. Gradually, women began to participate in a greater range of social events with men.

Wars during this period also had an effect on recreation. Much larger numbers of men were beginning to be involved in such conflicts, and many were conscripts rather than professional soldiers or volunteers. Young men from conservative communities were exposed to sports, games, and attitudes toward recreation that were unfamiliar to them. Recreation became a frequent activity for many who previously had enjoyed few opportunities.

Workers still endured a long work week, but their productivity was beginning to have an effect on recreation opportunities. Railroads developed rapidly and started to provide recreational travel at modest cost. Rail transportation also permitted theatrical companies, circuses, and other forms of entertainment to move around much more readily. Sporting goods, books, and periodicals became widely available. The bicycle provided recreation directly and also made many other forms of recreation more readily accessible to the less affluent.

Several factors contributed to the expansion of reading as a recreation experience. Literacy continued to spread, especially late in the period when compulsory universal education was adopted. Since a better educated working

Figure 2.7 **Although women took part in vigorous activities in the late 1800s, they were handicapped by dress requirements. Men could take off their coats to play tennis but women struggled to participate in corsets, tight bodices, and voluminous skirts that swept the ground.**

force was required for industrial production, schools, technical institutes, and libraries were politically popular. Public libraries were promoted by social reformers and temperance advocates as stimulators of honesty, hard work, and sobriety. Philanthropists contributed substantial sums for the building and support of libraries; the Andrew Carnegie foundation alone donated £2 million for library construction in Britain and more than $42 million for similar purposes in the United States and Canada. However, the majority of library users preferred reading novels for fun to studying nonfiction books in order to advance their moral well-being or technical knowledge as advocated by most library promoters. The rec-

reational purposes of public libraries were not endorsed by many advocates until the early 1900s.

Cities and towns started to develop managed park systems. Previously, most urban publicly owned open space was in the form of relatively small commons or squares together with boulevards or malls in more sophisticated communities. Picnics and sports events were usually held on private land outside the urban areas— often a pasture bordering a lake or river. In Europe, the lack of publicly developed recreation space was less serious. Large areas of open land around public buildings often remained vacant, and the extensive grounds associated with the homes of the aristocracy were frequently made available for public use by permission of the owner, by purchase, or by seizure. Rapid urbanization and industrial expansion often made it difficult for urban dwellers to reach open space outside developed areas. Some cities started to acquire larger parks in order to provide opportunities that had previously been obtained in the open countryside.

In some cases, the romantic attitude toward landscape also had an influence. New York City's Central Park is the classic example of the combined influences of urbanization and Romanticism. Certain New York civic leaders and newspaper writers were disturbed by the rapid northward growth of the city on Manhattan Island. They warned the citizens that eventually no large expanse of accessible open space would be left unless a major public park was created. After much debate, the city decided to purchase 340 hectares (840 acres) of rocky swampland just north of its boundaries. A design competition was conducted, and Frederick Law Olmsted and Calvert Vaux won first prize. Their plan involved the imitation of natural landscapes rather than the geometric design approach. It brought the rural landscape to the urban dweller and provided opportunities to walk, ride, drive (horsedrawn vehicles), boat, and ice skate in a sylvan environment (Figure 2.8). Opponents feared it would be improperly used by irresponsible citizens but Olmsted drew up strict regulations and a special police force was employed to enforce them.

Widespread acclaim of Central Park's aesthetic and functional features resulted in it being the prototype for many other grandly landscaped North American parks. Olmsted's professional reputation was firmly established and he was engaged to design a succession of parks including Prospect Park in Brooklyn, Fairmount Park in Philadelphia, Riverside and Morningside Parks in New York, Mount Royal Park in Montreal, Belle Isle Park in Detroit, and South Park in Chicago. Central Park's success undoubtedly resulted in many cities constructing larger and more elaborately landscaped parks than would have been built otherwise.

Two other precedent-setting events occurred during this period. John Muir and other Californians persuaded Congress to grant Yosemite Valley and the Mariposa Grove of giant sequoia trees to the State of California for preservation and enjoyment by the public. This took place in 1864, after Central Park had been built. Olmsted influenced the Yosemite legislation and became the area's first custodian.

The second major event was the exploration of the Yellowstone backcountry by a group of Montana businessmen led by H. D. Washburn and N. P. Langford. They traveled through it in 1870 in order to see the reported natural wonders and assess its potential for commercial enterprises. After seeing the area, they agreed among themselves that it deserved permanent preservation as a national reserve. Langford lobbied for the necessary federal legislation, two federal parties explored the area, Representative Clagett introduced his parks bill in 1871, and the bill was passed by Congress in 1872. It established a 648,000-hectare (1.6-million acre) reserve "as a public park or pleasuring ground for the benefit and enjoyment of the people."[1] Cornelius Hedges, a lawyer with the Washburn party, has traditionally been credited with persuading the group that public preservation rather than commercial exploitation was the morally right course of action. However, there were obviously many previous events that contributed to this decision and created the atmosphere in which it became politically possible. No doubt Romanticism, the congressional reservation of the Arkansas hot springs, the writings of

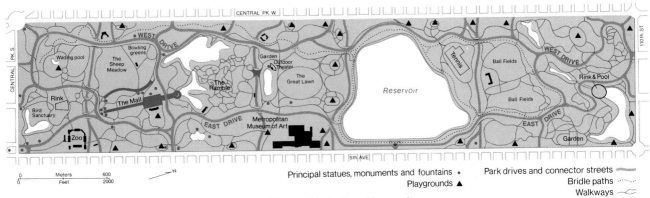

Figure 2.8 Map showing Central Park in New York City as it is today. Many of Olmsted and Vaux's classic features including the informal shapes, separated circulation systems, extensive meadow areas, and meandering water bodies are still evident despite the intrusion of monuments, playgrounds, sports facilities, and a number of inappropriate buildings. (Source: Drawn from a New York City Department of Parks and Recreation plan.)

[1] An Act to Set Apart a Certain Tract of Land Lying Near the Headwaters of the Yellowstone River as a Public Park, *Statutes at Large 17*, 32 (1872).

people such as Catlin, Bryant, Cooper, Olmsted, and Muir, and the creation of the Yosemite reserve all contributed.

Whatever the chain of circumstances, the Yellowstone act created several major precedents. Its passage indicated that rapid private exploitation of resources was not necessarily the best public policy. It established the political feasibility of setting aside a large area of public land for protection and public enjoyment as part of a national heritage. Finally, the Yellowstone act made the federal government responsible for this large, remote reserve. These precedents prepared the way for many other recreation and conservation measures, including the creation of the American national park system and similar systems developed by other nations.

The period from 1840–1880 was therefore an era of "recreation renaissance." Social restrictions on recreation participation were reduced, particularly for women. Opportunities for a variety of recreation experiences expanded, especially in urban areas. Nevertheless, perhaps the most significant change was the beginning of increased government involvement in the provision of recreation opportunities.

STAGE 3 – THE REINVOLVEMENT OF GOVERNMENT: 1880–1900

Between the fall of the Roman Empire and the beginning of this period there had been virtually no continuing public programs to provide recreation for the average citizen. Some of the medieval rulers and aristocracy periodically pro-

vided sports events or entertainments to encourage allegiance or as a gesture of goodwill. Later, urban officials used limited amounts of public money or donations to maintain public squares and provide municipal support for festive occasions. The idea of using substantial amounts of tax funds for the development of recreation facilities and provision of recreation opportunities for the general public was therefore quite revolutionary.

As Table 2.3 shows, a succession of events took place between 1880 and 1900, which reestablished government involvement in recreation on a major scale. In the United States, the development and expansion of urban park systems was particularly prominent. More than 80 cities formally organized park systems. Children's play areas known as sand gardens were provided and, in some cases, staffed at public expense. New York City began a major park and playground expansion program costing $1 million, required new schools to include playground space, and built recreation piers along its river frontages. Boston established the first metropolitan park system with a 5-mile-long ring of park land designed by Olmsted. Illinois passed a law permitting the establishment of local park districts involving more than one municipality. The first county park system was formed in New Jersey. In Britain, the national government made the first grants for local sports fields and indoor swimming pools.

A major factor in the growth of local government and private organization involvement in recreation during this stage was the emergence of a number of influential individuals and associations.

These individuals and organizations were dedicated to improving the opportunities for people to take part in recreation and physical education activities that could be considered beneficial to their character and physical health. Most of their efforts were concentrated on helping the urban disadvantaged, and usually there was a strong moralistic attitude toward recreation or physical educational activities. Provision of such programs was advocated primarily as a means of combating antisocial behavior such as drinking, gambling, and juvenile delinquency. Such individuals and organizations contributed greatly to the provision of recreation opportunities being accepted as a necessary function of government. Their arguments that recreation and physical education reduced social problems resulted in increasing amounts of public and private funds being devoted to such programs. At that time, arguing that recreation opportunities should be offered just to provide pleasure would have carried little if any weight.

Joseph Lee was probably the most influential leader who emerged during this period. He played a key role in developing playgrounds in Boston and later became a nationally known advocate of public recreation programs. In 1906, he helped found the Playground Association of America (which eventually developed along with several other organizations into the National Recreation and Park Association). Lee served as president of the association for 10 years. He also assisted in the development of the National Recreation School and was one of its principal instructors.

Another person who played a

Table 2.3 Stage 3 of the Second Recreation Revolution—
The Reinvolvement of Government: 1880–1900

STAGE 3—THE REINVOLVEMENT OF GOVERNMENT: 1880–1900

Date	Event
Late 1800s	— **Physical education and sports now accepted as part of education at all levels.**
	— YMCA now a major supplier of physical recreation opportunities—has 260 large gymnasiums in the U.S.
	— **British Parliament authorizes grants to local government for playing fields and indoor pools.***
1880	— 700 prominent people in U.S., Canada, and Britain sign petition urging preservation of Niagara Falls.
1884	— Bill introduced in British Parliament to preserve public access to open lands in Scotland.*
1885	— American Association for Health, Physical Education and Recreation founded.
	— **New York State appropriates $1.5 million for the purchase of a Niagara Falls preserve after a fierce battle in the legislature; also establishes the Adirondack Forest Preserve.**
	— Idea of sandpiles for children to play in introduced from Germany. Sand garden movement in U.S. started with installation of sandpiles at a mission and a nursery in Boston.
	— Canada establishes Rocky Mountain (later Banff) as its first national park.*
	— **English manufacturer introduces "safety bicycle" with small wheels and a chain drive; it became the first practical, personally owned mechanical form of transportation available to the masses.**
1886	— In Canada, Ontario government approves the creation of a provincial park at Niagara Falls.*
	— U.S. Army starts to patrol Yellowstone preserve and begins to develop a basic road system.
1888	— **New York City Playground Law appropriates $1 million for playgrounds and parks.**
1889	— Jane Addams opens famous Chicago settlement house. Its recreation facilities were expanded in 1882 to include a model playground with sandboxes and facilities for handball and indoor baseball.
1889–1895	— Minnesota begins its state park system by acquiring two historic sites and Itasca Park.
1890s	— "The Gay 90s" includes a boom in professional sports and commercial recreation.
	— **Joseph Lee emerged as an influential advocate of recreation. Helped set up playgrounds in Boston after seeing the lack of opportunities and boys arrested for playing in the streets. Opened model playground in 1898 with a boys' section, sports section, and individual gardens as well as children's facilities.**
	— New York City law requires new schools to have playground space.
	— Several flora and fauna preserves established in Belgian Congo and South Africa.*
	— Sequoia, Yosemite, General Grant (Kings Canyon), and Mt. Ranier national preserves established.
1891	— **Yellowstone Timberland Reserve approved—first federal land set aside for forestry purposes.**
1892	— A total of 100 cities in U.S. have municipal park systems.
	— **The nation's first metropolitan park system is established in Boston.**
	— Sierra Club founded by John Muir—encourages appreciation and protection of mountain environments.
1893	— Illinois passes law permitting establishment of local park districts.
1894	— New Zealand creates Tongariro National Park, its first national preserve.
	— New York State constitutional amendment allows state funds to be used for purchase of forest preserves.
1895	— **Essex County, New Jersey establishes the nation's first county park system.**
	— National Trust established as a charity in Britain in order to buy beautiful areas to serve as "open air sitting rooms for the poor."*
1897	— New York City builds recreation piers into its rivers.

*Events occurring outside the United States.

major role in establishing recreation services as a function of local government was Luther H. Gulick. He was a physician who first became involved in physical education instruction at what is now Springfield College, Massachusetts. Later, he was supervisor of physical education programs for the YMCA. Then he was appointed director of physical education for the New York City school system and founded the first public school athletic league. In 1906, Gulick provided leadership for the national conference of recreation, park, and school administrators that voted to form the National Playground Association and also elected him to be its first president. Like Lee, Gulick profoundly influenced the development of recreation in America by his speeches, lectures, and writing.

State and provincial government involvement also began to take place. A major legislative battle was fought in New York State concerning the purchase of lands for a Niagara Falls state reservation. The Province of Ontario decided the only speedy solution to the problem of uncontrolled commercial exploitation at Niagara was the creation of a provincial reserve. Several other states acquired historical sites or small parks which later became part of state park systems. The forest-conservation movement also began to enjoy success at both the state and federal levels. Although recreation was generally not a

stated purpose, the state and federal forest reserves created at this time subsequently became important recreation resources.

Progress with recreation and conservation programs at the national government level was steady but not spectacular. Canada established its first national parks, and a number of important areas including Yosemite and Mount Ranier were added to the American national park system. Since no federal park agency had been established, the U.S. Army was responsible for the protection and operation of Yellowstone.

Relaxation of social restrictions on recreation participation continued. Physical training and sports were now an integral part of educational curricula at all levels in both Europe and North America. The

YMCA and other quasi-public groups were major providers of physical recreation opportunities (Figure 2.9). Many religious sects developed educational and recreational programs at their places of worship. Professional sports organizations increased. Other commercial recreation resources flourished, particularly saloons, dance halls, amusement parks, and vaudeville. Mass participation in a wide variety of activities had begun.

STAGE 4—LOCAL AND FEDERAL AGENCY DEVELOPMENT: 1900–1920

At the beginning of the new century, the average workday was down to 10 hours but most people still worked six days each week. A few employers, however, were beginning to give a half-holiday on Saturday and a two-week summer vacation.

Although some 800 American cities had municipal park systems, only about a dozen were using public funds to provide recreation services. The idea of using tax money to provide leaders and programs was slow in gaining acceptance among politicians and taxpayers despite the fact that such services were said to reduce delinquency and citizens were worried about the effects, particularly on young people, of urban commercial recreation and its associated liquor and vice.

Urban park systems continued to grow—quite dramatically in some cases. A $5 million neighborhood park bond issue was approved with an 83 percent majority in Chicago although conservative leaders such as Marshall Field campaigned against it.

Figure 2.9 A drawing made in 1870 shows the gymnasium in use at the Young Men's Christian Association (YMCA) Building in New York City. Reading and meeting rooms were the other principal amenities provided at such facilities.

Quasi-public groups, particularly the Boy Scouts and Boys' Clubs, expanded and provided opportunities for youth in many cities. The provision of recreation leaders and programs at military camps and factories during World War I showed the value of such services and resulted in some expansion of civilian programs after the war.

Development of state and provincially administered recreation showed little progress during this period. Some states in the Northeast and Midwest added a few parks to their systems but progress was slow. The national park system was expanding and people often expected the federal government to include sites in it that were more suitable for development as state parks. Modest expansion of state forest systems occurred.

More spectacular advances were made at the federal level (Table 2.4). These were in some measure because of the dedication and vigor of President Theodore Roosevelt, an enthusiastic outdoorsman. The first national wildlife refuge was created in Florida. Passage of the Antiquities Act enabled historic and scientific sites to be reserved as national monuments by presidential proclamation. Formation of the U.S. Forest Service created a precedent for the establishment of other federal, professional land-managing agencies. President Roosevelt added many new areas to the national forest system displeasing some conservative factions. He signed proclamations establishing 33 new forest preserves just a few hours before signing a bill that transferred establishment authority to the Congress. The Weeks Act was passed authorizing the actual purchase of private land in the headwaters of streams for addition to the forest preserves. This was primarily intended to aid in maintaining stream flow during drought in the eastern part of the nation.

During this period, the recreational value of the national forests began to be recognized. Many sites for seasonal homes and resorts were leased. Increased automobile ownership stimulated recreation use and resulted in management problems. The U.S. Forest Service carried out several minor and one system-wide recreation survey. Some Forest Service personnel began to fear that recreation developments would eventually preclude true wilderness experiences. As a result, Carhart and Leopold developed the idea of preserving choice scenic areas with only minimal development of trails.

Some new national reserves were added during the early part of this period but it was not until 1916 that Congress established the National Park Service and officially recognized that a national park system had gradually developed. Appropriations for the new service were meager in the early years. Because of this and the previous absence of any administrative agency other than the U.S. Army, most national parks and monuments were largely undeveloped and poorly protected.

This era included the first major boom in the production and sales of a manufactured item used primarily for recreation. The phonograph caught the public's imagination and, by 1919, Americans were spending more on phonographs and records than on books, magazines, sporting goods, and musical instruments. Changing attitudes, larger discretionary incomes, mass production, and modern selling techniques made this possible. The phonograph boom paved the way for subsequent mass consumption of recreation merchandise such as radios, television sets, boats, and camping equipment.

Ownership and use of automobiles also increased but not as rapidly as the phonograph. Henry Ford introduced the mass-produced Model T in 1909. However, it sold for $950 at that time, which put it beyond the budget of the average working man. By 1916 the price had dropped to $360 but World War I and the lack of good roads retarded the growth of motoring.

Silent motion pictures projected on a screen started to spread across North America in 1905. Two years later, daily audiences totaled more than 250,000. By 1910, there were over 10,000 theaters in the United States showing films to 10 million customers each week. The era of relatively cheap mass entertainment had begun.

STAGE 5 – DEPRESSION, DROUGHT, AND CONSERVATION: 1920–1940

The period between the two wars was a period of contrasts (Table 2.5). On the one hand, many factors contributed to the expansion of participation in recreation. The average working day at the beginning of the period had dropped to nine hours, and many worked a five-and-a-half-day week. Large numbers of people in urban areas were beginning to have significant amounts of free time and discretionary income. Car ownership and usage increased dramatically in the middle 1920s, especially in the

Table 2.4 Stage 4 of the Second Recreation Revolution — Federal and Local Agency Formation: 1900–1920

STAGE 4 — FEDERAL AND LOCAL AGENCY FORMATION: 1900–1920

Date	Event
Early 1900s	— The Free Time Revolution begins; most employees work 10 hours rather than 12 or 14 each day, and a few have Saturday afternoons off. The idea of paid summer vacations has been introduced.
	— A total of 12 cities in the U.S. are using public funds to provide recreation services.
	— **Boys' Clubs, Boy Scouts, Girl Scouts, and many other youth and service clubs flourish.**
1900	— New York and New Jersey form an interstate compact to preserve the scenic Hudson Palisades.
1901	— **Theodore Roosevelt becomes President — believes in values of recreation and conservation.**
1902	— Almost 800 cities in U.S. have organized municipal park systems.
	— Congress passes the Reclamation Act — starts reservoir-building irrigation program in the West.
1903	— Luther Gulick organizes Public School Athletic League in New York City.
	— **Chicago voters approve $5 million bond issue for the development of neighborhood parks.**
	— Roosevelt establishes Pelican Island, Florida, as the first national wildlife refuge.
1904	— City of Los Angeles sets up a Board of Playground Commissioners to administer all its playgrounds.
1905	— **Congress authorizes creation of U.S. Forest Service; Agricultural Secretary Wilson suggests "greatest good for the greatest number" as a guiding philosophy for the national forests.**
	— First projected motion picture shown at The Nickelodeon theater in McKeesport, Pennsylvania.
1906	— Playground Association of America formed — became Playground and Recreation Association of America (PRAA).
	— Antiquities Act passed — Devil's Tower and Petrified Forest are designated first national monuments.
1907	— Roosevelt adds 33 new forest preserves by signing last-minute proclamations as Congress takes back power.
1908	— **Ford Motor Company introduces its Model T car and mass produces it revolutionizing transportation.**
	— White House State Governors' Conservation Conference recommends formation of a national park service.
1909	— North American Conservation Conference adopts conservation principles for the continent.
	— Eleven states have state forests totaling 1.2 million hectares (3 million acres).
1910–1920	— Numerous studies are made of recreation problems in the cities especially the moral aspects of commercial recreation.
	— Phonograph and phonograph records sales boom heralding a new era in consumer spending.
1910–1937	— **Joseph Lee is president of the PRAA (later NRA); his lectures, writings, and founding of the National Recreation School result in the unofficial title of "Father of American Recreation."**
1911	— New Jersey passes first state act permitting formation of several types of local government recreation agencies.
	— Congress passes Weeks Act — authorizes purchase of headwater lands for national forests.
	— National Education Association endorses use of schoolgrounds for recreation purposes.
1914–1918	— World War I — federal War Camp Community Service provides recreation at bases.
1916	— **Congress creates the National Park Service and puts it in charge of 15 parks and 21 monuments.**
1917	— First issue of *Parks and Recreation* magazine published by American Institute of Park Executives.
1918	— One-third of men examined for the U.S. Army are found to be physically unfit.
	— British Education Act authorizes local school authorities to provide playing fields and physical education centers.*
	— National Commission on Secondary Education recommends school involvement in local recreation programs.
	— U.S. Forest Service makes first national forest recreation survey.
	— PRAA created the National Physical Education Service to promote mandatory physical education in public schools.
1918–1920	— More workers get Saturday afternoon off; they start to have "a weekend" that can be used more effectively for recreation especially as Sunday restrictions decrease.
1919	— Community Services, Inc., is developed from War Camp Service to provide civilian services.
	— U.S. Forest Service personnel develop wilderness concept and apply it at Trappers Lake, Colorado.
	— Ratification of 18th Amendment to U.S. Constitution outlaws manufacture and sales of alcoholic beverages.

*Events occurring outside the United States.

Table 2.5 Stage 5 of the Second Recreation Revolution—
Depression, Drought, and Conservation: 1920–1940

STAGE 5—DEPRESSION, DROUGHT, AND CONSERVATION: 1920–1940

Date	Event
Early 1920s	— Average worker spends 9 hours on the job and works 5½ days each week; many urban workers have significant amounts of discretionary income as well as more free time.
	— Mass-produced cars at lower prices expand ownership—Model T ford now costs only a little over $300.
	— **Radio broadcasting begins; 5000 radios in U.S. in 1920; jumps to 5 million by 1924.**
1920	— PRAA forms Bureau of Colored Work to promote recreation facilities and programs for black urban residents.
	— Several bills in Congress provide grants for state programs aiding physical education in schools.
1920–1926	— Community recreation schools offer one-month course in recreation services.
1921	— **National Park Service revives interest in state parks at National Conference on State Parks.**
	— U.S. Forest Service and Ontario government jointly establish Quetico-Superior Roadless Area.
1922	— Congress provides first funds ($10,000) specifically for national forest recreation developments.
1924	— President Coolidge calls National Conference on Outdoor Recreation.
	— U.S. Forest Service designates first national forest primitive (semiwilderness) area.
1925	— British National Playing Fields Association formed; adopts open-space standard of 5 acres per 1000.*
	— PRAA does two-year, $50,000 study of local park administration and acreage and forms a research department.
1926	— PRAA becomes National Recreation Association (NRA).
	— Nearly 1700 cities have park systems totaling over 100,000 hectares (250,000 acres).
1927–1929	— Introduction of films with sound tracks raises weekly movie audience to over 100 million.
1929	— In USSR, 300-ha (750-acre) Park of Culture and Rest is opened in Moscow.*
	— **Great Depression; one-third labor force unemployed; recreation needed more but funded less.**
	— 980 cities now have city departments that provide recreation services for citizens.
1929–1941	— NRA receives a $500,000 grant from Laura S. Rockefeller Memorial fund; greatly expands work.
Early 1930s	— Park management or recreation land-use courses started at several universities.
	— **Dust bowl conditions on Great Plains help stimulate support for conservation measures.**
1932	— First International Recreation Congress held in Los Angeles during Olympic Games.
	— Recreation authorized as a major use and occasionally a paramount use of national forests.
	— Mass trespass on private hill land by Britons seeking public access ends in arrest and prison for some.*
1933	— **Franklin D. Roosevelt becomes president at height of depression; Congress cooperates with him to start massive program to make work and provide recreation opportunities.**
	— All national parks, monuments, and some other areas consolidated into national park system under NPS.
1934	— Japan establishes eight areas as its first national parks.*
1935	— British government and local authorities form Central Council of Recreative Physical Training.*
1936	— Congress authorizes nationwide survey by Park Service of all recreation facilities except national forests.
	— Lake Mead and Blue Ridge Parkway established—first national recreation area and first national parkway.
	— Courses in recreation services begin at several universities and colleges.
1937	— **Wildlife Restoration (Pittman-Robertson) Act passed by Congress; federal taxes imposed on firearms and ammunition and earmarked for state wildlife management programs.**
	— British Physical Training and Recreation Act gives financial aid to school and community sports programs.*
	— Congress establishes Cape Hatteras as the first national seashore.
Late 1930s	— Young people form their own "cellar clubs" in cities—over 6000 established in New York alone.
1938	— Society of Recreation Workers formed (later became American Recreation Society).
	— **Fair Labor Standards Act passed by Congress—40 hours set as desirable industrial work week.**
1939	— World War II begins in Europe.

*Events occurring outside the United States.

United States as roads were improved and the price of cars decreased. More people traveled farther from home on weekend excursions and vacation trips as the paving of roads made both urban and extraurban recreation resources more accessible. Radio followed the pattern of the phonograph with ownership in the United States rising rapidly from 5000 in 1920 to more than 5 million by 1924.

On the other hand, it was an era of world economic depression that resulted in great suffering, particularly in the major industrial nations. A minor depression in the early 1920s was followed by a period of relative prosperity. Then came the stock market crash of 1929 and the Great Depression, which was only ended by economic mobilization at the beginning of World War II. When President Franklin D. Roosevelt took office in 1933, the average income in the United States was half the 1929 level and 15 million people were unemployed. A major factor causing the depression to be so severe in the United States was the development of a lifestyle that included much recreation spending. Consequently, since industry in the United States was much more consumer-oriented than in Britain or France, sudden reductions in consumer spending had more serious effects.

This period also included contrasting social changes. Attitudes toward recreation generally relaxed even further. Baseball became recognized as the national game in the United States. American football, both professional and collegiate, drew increasingly large crowds as did horse racing, dog racing, automobile racing, and prize fighting. New or reintroduced activities such as "the talkies" (motion pictures with sound), contract bridge, crossword puzzles, and dance marathons were welcomed enthusiastically and spread rapidly to even remote locations. The first motion picture with a human voice on the sound track was released in 1928. One year later, 110 million admissions to movie shows were being sold *each week* and annual receipts exceeded $1 billion. The involvement of women in a great variety of arduous jobs during World War I had helped reduce many of the remaining Victorian constraints on women's recreation. Female swimmers, campers, hikers, and bicycle riders could now participate vigorously and in much more sensible clothing.

But appearances were deceptive. A strong Puritan influence still existed. Women continued to encounter conservative attitudes toward their participation in competitive sports. When American women entered track-and-field events in the 1928 Olympic Games, there was a storm of protest from all the major American women's athletic groups including the Women's Athletic Section of the American Physical Education Association.[2] The prevailing attitude of many female physical education and recreation leaders was that women should take part in games and certain kinds of athletics but not in a competitive manner. Another indication of the Puritan undercurrents was the passage of the Prohibition Amendment to the U.S. Constitution.

The most significant recreation event during this period was the development of President Roosevelt's "New Deal" program to create jobs and recreation opportunities. Massive federal funding supported the design and construction of a wide range of public works including recreation facilities at all levels of government. Cities received help with the construction of libraries, recreation centers, swimming pools, ornamental gardens, and parkways. Picnic shelters, roads, bridges, campgrounds, trails, cabins, and ranger stations were built in state and national parks and forests (Figure 2.10). Writers, musicians, actors, artists, and recreation specialists were given work and produced various forms of recreation experiences from murals in public buildings to entertainment in parks. For example, the Federal Theater Project gave work to 14,010 people, which resulted in the presentation of 924 productions and the broadcast of 6000 radio plays. For admissions ranging from five cents to one dollar, over 30 million people saw these live presentations. Many had not attended live dramatic performances previously.

The Roosevelt depression-fighting programs had a profound and lasting effect on recreation. The design of parks and recreation facilities advanced greatly under the supervision of professionals employed by the National Park Service and other agencies. By the end of the 1930s, thousands of city, state, and national parks were well equipped with good-quality facilities. Understanding and rapport developed between many recreation professionals in different levels of government where previously there had been little contact. The first large-scale recreation-facility inventories and user studies were carried out.

[2] Later it became the American Association for Health, Physical Education and Recreation.

Figure 2.10 Federally funded Works Progress Administration (WPA) and Civilian Conservation Corps (CCC) projects employed tens of thousands of unemployed men during the depression. Here workers put the finishing touches to a WPA funded picnic pavilion at Comstock Park in the City of Lansing, Michigan, in August 1936.

Not all the effects of the depression on recreation were good. Reduced tax collections produced cuts in local government appropriations for parks and recreation. Recreation services were reduced or eliminated at a time when large numbers of people were unemployed and in need of recreation opportunities that involved little or no expenditures. Federal programs provided some opportunities but did not fill the gap in many locations. Unemployed youth in major cities were particulary in need of recreation services. To satisfy this need, many groups of young people formed private clubs in the late 1930s using disused basements and other space they could borrow or appropriate.

State park systems began to grow quite rapidly again after a period of comparative stagnation. Stephen T. Mather, the Director of the National Park Service, arranged for a National Conference on State Parks in 1921. At that meeting, he pointed out that the Park Service had difficulty just acquiring and administering areas of prime *national* significance. It would never be able to purchase and develop all the lesser sites that had been recommended for inclusion in the national park system by politicians and interested citizens. Mather suggested that these sites should be state parks. Many states began or expanded existing state park systems during the years that followed. Later in this period, state park system development was further stimulated by the various New Deal pub-

lic works programs mentioned earlier.

At the federal level, great progress was made in developing the national park system and establishing sound management policies. Congress enlarged the horizons for the system in 1925 by authorizing the development of parks in the southern Appalachian Mountains and at Mammoth Cave, Kentucky. Acquisition was to be by donation; all previous parks and monuments had been created from public domain lands. A series of congressional acts in the middle 1930s greatly expanded the size and scope of the system. In 1933, all national parks, monuments, military parks, battlefield parks, the National Capital Parks, and many national cemeteries and memorials were consolidated into an enlarged system. Two years later, the Historic Sites Act authorized the establishment and protection of national historic sites and federal assistance with several cooperative programs. Three new types of national park system units were initiated when Congress established the Lake Mead National Recreation Area in California, the Blue Ridge Parkway along the Appalachian Mountains, and the Cape Hatteras National Seashore in North Carolina. The Park Service was also instructed to make a nationwide study of all publicly owned parks and recreation facilities (except those in the national forests) in order to provide information for nationwide recreation planning.

The U.S. Forest Service also expanded its recreation activities considerably in this period. In 1921, a large area of interconnecting lakes and streams along the Minnesota-Ontario boundary was jointly designated by the United States and Ontario as a roadless area. A year later, the first funds were appropriated by Congress for the development of public recreation facilities in the national forests. The sum was quite small ($10,000) and some felt this was a result of lobbying by Stephen Mather who feared competition with the national parks. In 1924, the first national forest primitive (semiwilderness) area was designated in New Mexico. Finally, in 1932, the Chief of the Forest Service gave instructions that recreation was to be considered a major use, and occasionally a paramount use, of all national forests.

The Roaring Twenties and the Great Depression were therefore periods of major change in recreation, especially in the United States. The European industrial nations experienced somewhat similar changes in recreation attitudes and behavior but not to the same extent. Since Europeans had less discretionary income and showed more restraint in the adoption of innovations, smaller proportions of the populations were affected. No other nation carried out massive public programs to combat unemployment like those used in the United States. Therefore, it was adoption of public policies rather than just affluence that produced the extensive recreation facilities characteristic of American national, state, and local parks at the end of the 1930s. In addition, employment of large numbers of recreation leaders on government payrolls had firmly established recreation services as a public function.

Thus affluence, industrial specialization in consumer goods, rapid acceptance of innovations, the adoption of policies for government

participation in recreation services, and the impact of the depression make-work programs all contributed to the status of recreation in the United States at the end of the 1930s. In Europe, public recreation facilities were confined almost exclusively to the urban areas, and most recreation services were provided by educational, quasi-public, or private organizations.

STAGE 6 – THE MECHANIZATION OF RECREATION: 1940–1960

World War II brought the development of recreation almost to a halt. Expansion of park systems ceased. Skeleton staffs tried to keep up with basic protection and maintenance duties. Recreational travel was largely eliminated. In Europe especially, coastal beaches were closed to the public and strewn with barricades, mines, and fortifications. Inland parks, forests, and other remote areas were used for military bases and training grounds. City parks often contained air raid shelters, antiaircraft guns, and temporary buildings. Large numbers of both professional leaders and volunteers assisted with recreation programs for the military and in factories. More than 40,000 people were members of the Special Services Division of the U.S. Army alone.

At the end of the war there was a rapid increase in recreation participation (Table 2.6). In the United States and Canada where no widespread destruction demanded attention and the economies were strong, participation quickly returned to prewar levels and then shot ahead. Many people's horizons had been enlarged by travel in the military or employ-

ment in industry. Returning military personnel and factory workers often had money saved. As the production of automobiles and other consumer goods started to catch up with demand, people began to travel as never before.

In 1946, Congress held hearings on the creation of a federal recreation service. The idea of the federal government being permanently involved in providing all types of recreation opportunities did not receive political support, and the proposal was abandoned. However, urban park departments continued to restore facilities and expand their programs.

The Civil Rights Movement began to have a significant effect on all kinds of recreation during the 1950s. Although the national focus was on achieving equality in education and employment opportunity and in desegregating resources such as buses, lunch counters, and other urban facilities, a number of important recreation-oriented events also took place. The first crack in the "color bar" that prevented black athletes from playing for major professional sports teams occurred when the Brooklyn Dodgers brought Jackie Robinson up from their farm team in 1947. A series of legal test cases were initiated including one against the state of Maryland for racial segregation in state parks. Courageous black citizens asserted their right of equal access to recreation opportunities by attempting to use segregated beaches, swimming pools, commercial parks, and the traditionally "white sides" of town squares. Some public and commercial facilities closed to avoid integration but the battle was gradually being won in Congress and in the courts.

Table 2.6 Stage 6 of the Second Recreation Revolution—
The Mechanization of Recreation: 1940–1960

Date	Event
\multicolumn{2}{}{STAGE 6—THE MECHANIZATION OF RECREATION: 1940 to 1960}	

STAGE 6—THE MECHANIZATION OF RECREATION: 1940 to 1960

Date	Event
1941	— **U.S. enters World War II; many military and voluntary agencies provide recreation at home and abroad; defense plant programs lead to formation of National Industrial Recreation Association.**
	— Recreation experiences and expansion of horizons by travel during war result in greater expectations.
1944	— Congress passes Flood Control Act; authorizes recreation developments at Corps of Engineers impoundments.
1945	— Downer report recommends sites for Britain's first national parks and suggests 12 other possible areas.*
Late 1940s	— Many parks, swimming pools, libraries, and other recreation structures developed as war memorials.
	— Pentup desire to travel and enjoy life puts pressure on recreation resources as cars, boats, and trailers become available again.
	— **Television broadcasting and ownership of sets grow rapidly in U.S., Canada, and parts of Europe.**
1946	— Congress holds hearings on possible creation of federal recreation service but no action taken.
1947	— Jackie Robinson becomes the first black to play for a major professional sports team in the U.S.
1948	— **Water Pollution Control Act authorizes federal aid to state and local pollution projects.**
1949	— **British National Parks and Access to the Countryside Act passed; starts national park program.***
	— President Truman signs aircraft restrictions for Superior National Forest canoe area.
1950	— Average work week is about 40 hours; most workers have two-day weekend so trips can start on Friday night.
	— **Federal Fish Restoration (Dingell-Johnson) Act taxes tackle to aid state sport fishing programs.**
1954	— U.S. Supreme Court ban on racial segregation in schools paves way for end of discrimination in recreation.
Middle 1950s	— **Civil Rights Movement grows; test cases include state park segregation case against Maryland.**
1956	— Congress creates Bureau of Sports Fisheries and Wildlife; undertakes federal fish and wildlife programs.
	— **National Park Service begins "Mission 66" to restore and improve national park system.**
	— International Recreation Association founded (now World Lesiure and Recreation Association).
1957	— **Forest Service begins "Operation Outdoors" to restore and improve its recreation facilities.**
	— **European Economic Community (Common Market) formed—stimulates recreation with reductions in border formalities, improved transportation, and socioeconomic progress.***
1958	— **Congress appoints Recreation Resources Review Commission to examine nation's recreation needs.**
	— **Federal Aid Highway Act starts massive federal aid for nationwide system of high-speed highways.**
	— Congress authorizes construction of the National Cultural Center for the Performing Arts (Kennedy Center).
	— Bureau of Land Management (BLM) policy to sell or lease public domain land for recreation approved.
	— French High Commissariat for Youth and Sports set up in Ministry of Education.*
1959	— British Recreation Grounds Act provides loans to help local governments buy recreation land.*
	— Clawson's classic article "The Crisis in Outdoor Recreation" appears in *American Forests* magazine.

*Events occurring outside the United States.

However, the most widespread change that took place in the 15 years following World War II was the mechanization of recreation. It had begun before the war with increasing use of the automobile for trips to beaches, parks and, in some cases, for cross-country vacations. In the 1950s, shorter working hours, prosperity, social desirability, and the pentup urge to travel resulted in recreation movements of middle- and lower-income people on an unprecedented scale. Use of regional parks, county parks, state parks, national park system areas, and national forest recreation sites near population centers increased dramatically. Attendance at many areas grew at an annual rate of 15 to 20 percent. More and more campers began to use trailers of increasing size and complexity. Boating expanded both in the number and size of boats and in terms of the boats' capabilities. Outboard motors became standard equipment. The average horsepower of motors increased dramatically as waterskiing flourished, and larger boats at reasonable prices made long-distance cruising possible for more people. The majority of boats now had to be transported on specially built trailers or kept at marinas rather than carried on the tops of cars.

Other forms of mechanical recreation began to develop in the late 1950s. Motorcycle riding started to become popular again with young people in North America, and there was an increase in the off-highway use of these vehicles. Canadian manufacturers developed the snowmobile primarily for work applications and for use by hunters and fisher-persons. However, as the machines became smaller, faster, and cheaper, people began buying and riding them just for enjoyment.

By the end of this period, a new type of recreation-resource user had become common throughout Canada and the United States. Previously the typical camping family had spent two continuous weeks at one park or forest usually in midsummer. During this vacation, they squeezed into one or possibly two tents, cooked over a wood fire, and shared some simple equipment while fishing from the shore or less frequently from a small rowboat. Now many families slept in large cabin trailers, sometimes setting up a separate tent for the children, and

erected an awning over the picnic table area to provide shade and protection during rainy weather. Meals were prepared with propane or gasoline stoves. Larger quantities of garbage resulted from the use of prepared foods and beverages in cans or bottles. Small rowboats were replaced with larger craft powered by outboard motors. Many campers used these power boats for waterskiing or cruising often to the discomfort of those who wished to fish. An increasing number started to drive to a park or forest campground for a number of camping weekends at other times in the year in addition to their regular camping vacation. Attendance increased both at peak periods and throughout the season.

This great increase in the use of public recreation resources, combined with the impact of mechanical equipment and the limited development and maintenance of the 1940s, produced disturbing results. Recreation professionals pointed out that if the trends of the 1950s continued, many recreation facilities would be destroyed by overuse. The United States National Park Service sought to remedy the situation in 1956 by starting "Mission 66" — a 10-year restoration and improvement program. "Operation Outdoors" was a similar campaign initiated by the U.S. Forest Service.

Then in 1958, one of the most significant events in the history of public involvement in recreation took place. At the urgings of Joseph Penfold, President of the Izaak Walton League of America, and other concerned conservationists, Congress appointed a committee of its members and several prominent persons to study the situation. The act established the purposes of the

Commission in the following terms:

> . . . in order to preserve, develop, and assure accessibility to all American people of present and future generations such quality and quantity of outdoor recreation resources as will be necessary and desirable for individual enjoyment, and to assure the spiritual, cultural, and physical benefits that such outdoor recreation provides; in order to inventory and evaluate the outdoor recreation resources and opportunities of the Nation, to determine the types and location of such resources and opportunities which will be required by present and future generations; and in order to make comprehensive information and recommendations leading to these goals available to the President, the Congress, and the individual States and Territories, there is hereby authorized and created a bipartisan Outdoor Recreation Resources Review Commission.[3]

The following year, American Forests published an article by Dr. Marion Clawson, a resource economist with Resources for the Future, entitled "The Crisis in Outdoor Recreation."[4] This classic article documented the widening gap between recreation participation and available developed resources. It had a widespread impact on re-

[3] An Act for the establishment of a National Outdoor Recreation Resources Review Commission, *Statutes at Large 72*, Part 1, 238 (1958).

[4] Marion Clawson, "The Crisis in Outdoor Recreation," *American Forests, 65*, 3, 22–31 (March 1959).

source professionals and members of conservation organizations.

A number of unrelated federal acts passed during this period had substantial effects on recreation. The Flood Control Act of 1944 permitted the Army Corps of Engineers to undertake the development of recreation facilities at its reservoirs. Federal aid for state and local water pollution control was authorized in 1948; it was the first major step in the long fight to reduce domestic and industrial pollution of the nation's waterways. In 1950, the Fish Restoration and Management Act (commonly known by the names of its congressional sponsors, Dingell and Johnson) imposed a federal tax on fishing equipment, which was earmarked for sport fishery improvement. The most far-reaching measure was the 1958 Federal-Aid Highway Act that authorized large grants for the proposed interstate highway system. These events and those described earlier all set the stage for the decade that followed and helped make it the most remarkable 10 years of the second recreation revolution.

STAGE 7 – THE ZENTH OF THE SECOND RECREATION REVOLUTION: 1960–1970

Many factors combined to make this a remarkable period for recreation. In the United States it was a prosperous era with high employment, high discretionary incomes, and great aspirations. Democratic presidents working with largely Democratic congresses produced a flood of social, conservation, and recreation legislation (Table 2.7).

The presentation and implementation of the 28-volume Outdoor Recreation Resources Review Commission[5] report was probably the most important recreation event of the era. It recommended major extensions of federal involvement in recreation and stimulated a series of advances in recreation research, planning, facility construction, and program development. President Kennedy presented a special message to Congress endorsing most of the report's recommendations. A major suggestion was the establishment of a federal Bureau of Outdoor Recreation to coordinate and assist with extraurban recreation at all levels; it was formed immediately. Later, the recommended Land and Water Conservation Fund was set up to provide grants for the stimulation of state and local recreation program expansion. Many other acts, policies, and events of this era resulted from the influence of the ORRRC reports.

At the local government level, development of recreation facilities and programs did not progress as fast as at the state and federal levels. Attempts to initiate substantial federal government assistance for urban recreation had failed in 1946. The act authorizing the Outdoor Recreation Resources Review Commission specifically excluded consideration of urban recreation although some mention of city problems was included in the reports. However, the problems of providing recreation opportunities in populated areas continued to grow. During the 1950s and 1960s, there was a great increase in single-family-residence construction in the suburbs and surrounding rural areas. Many suburbs became separate cities and developed their own

[5] Abbreviated to ORRRC in many future references.

park and recreation departments. Even so, rapid growth, poor planning, high land values, escalating construction costs, and the demand for other services often created difficulties. Some new municipalities and many of the enlarged older cities were not able to provide adequate recreation opportunities for the sprawling populations.

At the same time, many inner-city park and recreation departments were also experiencing difficulties. Movement of middle-income and some lower-income citizens to the suburbs and an influx of poor– often unemployed– people hastened urban decay and reduced tax receipts. In many cases, city parks and recreation centers became overused, undermaintained, and vandalized. Most cities did not have the means to mount a "Mission 66" type of attack on such problems. However, a series of acts concerning urban planning and development were passed by Congress. Several of these provided grants to assist with the planning and acquisition of urban open space. Others provided limited help with community facilities and programs. Unfortunately, attitudes toward urban recreation and opposition by some conservation groups resulted in city park and recreation systems receiving little financial assistance from the Land and Water Conservation Fund during the early years of the program.

Spectacular progress was made during this era at the state level. Many of the heavily populated states approved substantial bond issues to help finance the expansion of state park systems and other state recreation facilities. Matching grants from the Land and Water Conservation Fund were used to

Table 2.7 Stage 7 of the Second Recreation Revolution—
The Zenith of the Revolution: 1960–1970

STAGE 7—THE ZENITH OF THE SECOND REVOLUTION: 1960–1970

Date	Event
1960	— **Multiple Use Sustained Yield Act makes recreation one of the main objectives of national forests.**
	— British Wolfenden Committee says sport is an essential part of life and a delinquency control; Albermarle Report recommends improvements in youth services including recreation.*
	— California publishes two-volume recreation plan that analyzes resources and participation.
Early 1960s	— New York and Wisconsin voters pass multimillion dollar bond issues to increase and improve state-operated recreation facilities.
1961	— Congress passes Housing Act with $50 million for state and local purchase of urban open space.
	— U.S. Travel Service created in Department of Commerce to promote foreign tourism in America.
1962	— **Outdoor Recreation Resources Review Commission report recommends substantial federal aid to recreation; President Kennedy presents a special message to Congress on conservation and endorses most of the ORRRC recommendations.**
	— **Federal Bureau of Outdoor Recreation established to coordinate, assist, and stimulate recreation.**
	— First World Conference on national parks held in Seattle, Washington.
1963	— U.S. Supreme Court says municipal facilities may not be racially segregated.
	— U.N. Conference on International Travel and Tourism attended by 600 delegates from 84 nations.*
	— **Civil Rights Act forbids discrimination at all types of public and commercial facilities.**
	— **Land and Water Conservation Fund passes; aids federal, state, and local park developments.**
	— **Wilderness Act authorizes creation of a national wilderness system and designates 3.7 million ha (9 million acres) of national forest land as the first wilderness areas.**
	— Land Law Review Commission appointed to review U.S. federal land policies.
	— Economic Opportunity Act provides jobs and training for youth—often involves recreation facilities.
	— California voters pass a $150 million bond issue to improve their state park system.
	— World Recreation Congress in Japan—500 delegates from 32 nations attend.*
	— French Commission on Leisure for All recommends park system covering 6 percent of the nation.*
Middle 1960s	— Tourism now tops list of international trade items in terms of value.
1965	— **89th Congress called "Conservation Congress" because it passes 51 conservation bills.**
	— **President Johnson gives Congress message and holds White House Conference on Natural Beauty.**
	— Demonstration Cities and Metropolitan Development Act includes demonstration recreation program grants.
	— National Foundation for the Arts and Humanities gives grants for cultural developments.
	— Highway Beautification Act includes grants for highway aesthetics and recreation opportunities.
	— **National Recreation and Park Association (NRPA) formed by merger of several organizations.**
	— United States now has almost 2400 municipal park systems covering 325,000 ha (800,000 acres).
1966	— President forms cabinet-level Recreation Advisory Council to coordinate all federal recreation programs.
1968	— Congress establishes four "permanent" three-day weekend holidays.
	— National Advisory Commission on Civil Disorders say lack of recreation opportunities was a major complaint.
	— Architectural Barriers Act requires access for the handicapped to all federally aided public facilities.
	— **Wild and Scenic Rivers Act authorizes national program of protecting undeveloped rivers.**
	— **National Trail System Act begins natural system of riding and hiking trails.**
	— **British Parliament passes Countryside Act expanding the national government's role in rural recreation.***
	— **National Environmental Policy Act requires federal agencies to report environmental impact of their projects and sets up Council on Environmental Quality to coordinate national environmental program.**
	— National Recreation and Park Association begins the *Journal of Leisure Research*.

* Events occurring outside the United States.

expand acquisition and development budgets. Large numbers of picnic areas, campgrounds, beaches, boat-launching sites, and other types of facilities were built.

Congress passed many other important recreation measures during this period. Four permanent three-day-weekend national holidays were created by designating particular days instead of the same date every year. The Multiple Use Sustained Yield Act of 1960 formally established recreation as one of the five management purposes of the national forests. The National Wilderness Act designated 3.7 million hectares (9 million acres) of the national forests as the first national wilderness areas. Congress also inaugurated a 10-year review of the rest of the nation's federal lands to identify all other potential wilderness areas. The first national lakeshore (Pictured Rocks), Wolf Trap Farm Park for the Performing Arts, several new national seashores and recreation areas, and a number of other units were added to the national park system. A national wild and scenic rivers program and a national trail system program were also begun.

President Johnson, largely in response to Mrs. Johnson's urgings, threw his support behind a major program of landscape beautification. He delivered a precedent-setting message to Congress on the topic and promoted projects ranging from extensive plantings of flowers and shrubs in Washington to the removal of highway advertising and the screening of junk yards.

Racial segregation at municipal facilities was struck down as unconstitutional by the U.S. Supreme Court in 1963. The Civil Rights Act of 1964 made racial discrimination illegal at all types of public and commercial recreation facilities. Major disturbances including looting and arson occurred in the black neighborhoods of some large U.S. cities; lack of recreation opportunities was a major grievance. Additional recreation programs were subsequently provided in many cases, but many inner-city areas continued to be deficient in recreation opportunities.

The mechanization of recreation continued. The development of four-lane, high-speed highways in much of North America and Europe stimulated long-distance automobile travel and the movement of various types of recreation equipment. Boats and motors, camping trailers, and motor homes grew bigger, more sophisticated, and more expensive. Large sums were invested in ski tows, snow-making equipment, and snow-grooming machines at winter resorts. Snowmobile production in North America rose from about 10,000 units a year in the early 1960s to more than half a million by the end of the decade. Japanese motorcycles captured the world's markets and became the dominant "trail bikes" for off-highway use in North America. "Dune buggy" and four-wheel-drive vehicle sales expanded, especially in the West where there were large areas of open lands available for off-highway travel. Aircraft replaced ocean liners as the main means of transatlantic travel, and large numbers of tourists and skiers started flying to the resort areas of the world.

The recreation professions also advanced significantly during this period. Formation of the National Recreation and Park Association in 1965 was an important milestone. Five previously separate organizations—the American Association of Zoological Parks and Aquariums, American Institute of Park Executives, American Recreation Society, National Conference on State Parks, and National Recreation Association—agreed to amalgamate. Other groups joined later. This merger was a major breakthrough in the movement to develop understanding and cooperation between the various professional groups associated with recreation.

This then was the decade when the recreation revolution reached its zenith in North America. No doubt participation will still continue to increase and many innovations in equipment and behavior will appear in the future. However, it is unlikely that such an important series of events and so many rapid and radical changes in recreation legislation, attitudes, and behavior will occur again in such a short period. Some of these events and changes will be discussed more extensively in later chapters.

STAGE 8—THE ENVIRONMENTAL AND AUSTERITY ERA: 1970 TO THE PRESENT

Although the conservation movement grew strong and many environmentally oriented programs were started during the first 70 years of the twentieth century, environmental problems did not become continuous topics of widespread public concern until the late 1960s. Then, a combination of circumstances including growing problems with population, food and energy supplies, increasing pollution, and the war in Vietnam produced a major awakening, especially among young people. As a result, the status of recreation changed. It no longer occupied the favored position it had enjoyed during the zenith of the revolution. A particular recreation facility or program could now be either "good" or "bad" depending on one's interpretation of a desirable environment. People started using environmental arguments when objecting to proposed recreation developments.

The 1973 embargo on exports of oil by certain petroleum-producing nations and the accompanying energy crisis drew added attention to the environmental issues involving recreation (Table 2.8). Travel was curtailed by actual fuel shortages, fear of shortages, or reductions in permissable highway speeds. Sunday automobile travel was banned for a period in the Netherlands. Considerable reduction in recreation participation occurred at some locations such as Florida's tourist areas.

The middle 1970s was also a period of economic recession. This situation together with the petroleum shortage reduced purchases of cars and some other recreation goods. Sales of motor homes and larger travel trailers dropped substantially but rose again slowly once it became clear that gasoline rationing was unlikely. Public recreation programs were also reduced by the recession. High unemployment, lower revenues from business and income taxes, larger welfare costs, reluctance to raise taxes, and inflation resulted in budgetary problems. Cutbacks were generally largest in recreation maintenance and operation funds. The national park system and many state and local park systems suffered severe staff cuts.

Nevertheless, participation increased again following the energy crisis and reached new records during the U.S. bicentennial celebrations.

The energy crisis and the recession also contributed to increased participation in walking, hiking, and cycling in both Canada and the United States. This movement began in the 1960s with the desire for a simpler lifestyle by many young people. It blossomed with the development of greater environmental awareness and a reawakening of interest in the health benefits of physical activity. Participation in jogging and various sports also increased. Tennis experienced phenomenal growth. In spite of this trend toward more physical recreation, interest in mechanical recreation continued to grow. Even the bicycle boom appeared to be partly inspired by a love for equipment; any bicycle with less than 10 speeds was considered old-fashioned. A new craze was the modification and ornamentation of utility vans. Sale of these vehicles increased sharply as young people equipped them with a great variety of furnishings and sound equipment. At the same time, millions of people installed two-way citizens band (CB) radios in their vehicles and used them primarily for recreation purposes.

The early 1970s were also significant as the turning point in federal government participation in urban recreation. Although considerable progress had been made during the previous decade in providing federal funds for urban open space, the accessibility of most kinds of public recreation tended to be lowest for poor inner-city residents. Some aid for public recreation services in urban areas had

been provided but it was comparatively small and involved a number of different programs. Urban leaders and professional groups continued to agitate for additional federal support and several conferences on this topic took place. Following the urban disturbances of the 1960s and the growth in the congressional power of the cities, it appeared likely that more federal aid to urban recreation would be forthcoming.

Interior Secretary Hickel submitted the long overdue nationwide recreation plan to the Nixon administration in 1970. It was rejected, allegedly for being excessively costly and too urban oriented. The following year, President Nixon announced the Legacy of Parks program, which was designed to speed up the acquisition of vital recreation lands, especially near urban areas. National park system acquisitions were accelerated and two urban national recreation areas named Gateway East and Golden Gate were established in New York and San Francisco. In spite of austerity budgets, the Legacy of Parks program continued into 1974 when President Nixon signed the Cuyahoga Valley National Recreation Area bill. Some opposition to the urban aspects of the program began to develop in the middle 1970s when it became apparent that the high land costs and operational expenses of such areas would be met, at least in part, by curtailing other aspects of the national parks program.

In 1972, the federal government started a revenue-sharing program whereby substantial amounts of federal tax money were returned to local governments in order to bolster public services. Some of this

Table 2.8 Stage 8 in the Second Recreation Revolution—
The Environmental and Austerity Era: 1970 to The Present

STAGE 8—THE ENVIRONMENTAL AND AUSTERITY ERA: 1970 TO THE PRESENT

Date	Event
1970	— Land Law Review Commission report recommends larger recreation role for federal lands.
	— Administration rejects Hickel's nationwide plan, "The Recreation Imperative," because of cost and urban emphasis.
1971	— Alaska Native Claims Settlement Act gives 18 million ha (44 million acres) to native peoples and authorizes expansion of the national forests and national park system areas in the state.
	— U.S. Forest Service starts program of greater public involvement in its decision-making processes.
	— **President Nixon announces "Legacy of Parks" accelerated acquisition program for national park lands.**
1972	— **Title IX of Education Act requires equal opportunities for both sexes in school and college sports.**
	— **Water Pollution Control Act decrees all waters must be safe for fishing and swimming by 1983.**
	— **U.S. national park centennial marked by adding 14 units including two "Gateway" recreation areas.**
	— **Coastal Zone Management Act provides coastal planning and zoning funds—more recreation studies.**
	— Federal revenue-sharing funds given to local governments—some used for recreation purposes.
	— Bureau of Outdoor Recreation holds public hearings around the nation on revised nationwide plan.
1973	— **Oil-exporting nations' embargo and other factors produce fuel shortages in developed nations.**
	— Rehabilitation Act bans bias against handicapped in federally funded jobs or programs and building access.
	— Release of administration's nationwide recreation plan entitled "Outdoor Recreation: A Legacy for America."
1974	— Education for All Handicapped Children Act requires education in least restrictive environment possible.
	— Forest and Rangeland Renewable Resources Planning Act orders periodic national forest resource assessment.
	— **Congress authorizes Big Cypress and Big Thicket National Preserves and Cuyhago Valley National Recreation Area.**
	— Eastern Wilderness Areas Act adds 16 areas in eastern national forests to national wilderness system.
	— Outdoor Recreation Research Needs Workshop sponsored by Bureau of Outdoor Recreation.
	— U.S. Park Service revises policies in direction of more preservation, less development, and limitations on use.
	— Housing and Community Development Act provides grants for urban projects including recreation.
	— California voters approve $250 million bond issue for parks, recreation, and wildlife projects.
1975	— Florida passes Growth Management Act, which permits local control of overdevelopment.
	— Governors of states in the Delaware River Basin veto Tocks Island Dam.
	— Federal Aid Highway Act provides $10 million for the construction of demonstration bikeways.
	— Community Services Act provides summer recreation for children of low-income families.
1976	— **Congress approves experimental voluntary four-day week and staggered hours for federal employees.**
	— **Federal Land Policy and Management Act orders intensive multiple-use management of BLM lands.**
	— Congress decides against dams in Hell's Canyon and establishes national recreation area.
1977	— President Carter's message to Congress advocates more protection of barrier islands, wetlands, and rivers.
1978	— **Congress raises minimum mandatory retirement age to 70 and drops it for most federal employees.**
	— U.S. court gives physically qualified girls right to compete with boys in interscholastic contact sports.
	— **National Parks and Recreation Act starts $1.2 billion improvement of urban and national parks.**
	— 527,000 ha (1,300,000 acres) of western national forest designated by Endangered American Wilderness Act.
	— **Alaska lands bill fails in Congress so President Carter proclaims 23 million ha (56 million acres) as national monuments and withdraws similar area of national resource lands from use.**
	— Congress reduces controls on domestic airline fares and routes to increase competition and reduce fares.
	— **Californians pass Proposition 13 cutting local property taxes and reducing recreation services.**
	— **New government in Iran, reduced oil production in other exporting nations, and higher prices result in gasoline shortages, higher fuel costs, and less recreational travel in many nations.**
1979	— Californians pass Proposition 4 tying government expenditure increases to population and cost of living changes.
1980	— Designated "The Year of the Coast"; legislation, is introduced in Congress to protect underdeveloped barrier islands by cutting federal support for development of parks and wildlife refuges.
	— National Park Service submits *The State of the Parks* report on depreciation of system's resources.

money was spent on recreation but generally the amounts were small compared to the size of the problems. More aid came in the form of the 1974 Housing and Community Development Act, which provided 100 percent grants for certain types of municipal improvements including recreation facilities and services. In 1975, Congress passed the Community Services Act, which supplied grants for summer recreation programs for children of low-income families. Therefore, considerable advances were made in federal assistance to urban recreation although a major direct assault on the problem by the federal government has still not occurred.

Increased attention to environmental problems affected recreation in several other ways. For example, it reduced the effort made to improve recreation opportunities. Conservation-oriented organizations, citizens' groups, and public agencies found the proliferation of environmentally important public hearings, legislation, and administrative procedures often took time previously used for recreation matters. Similarly, a smaller proportion of natural resource agency budgets were spent on recreation as environmental programs increased. Requirements that environmental impact statements be submitted and approved before major projects could be started also had an effect. In many cases, these requirements were beneficial to recreation but sometimes projects were delayed or abandoned.

On the other hand, there were many environmental events of the early 1970s that were directly or indirectly beneficial to recreation. The federal Coastal Zone Management Act of 1972 and supporting legisla-

tion and administrative action by state governments resulted in greater efforts to conserve shoreline resources. These resources are extremely important for many recreation activities and essential to the production of fish and wildlife. Likewise, efforts to reduce water and air pollution, begin land-use planning programs, and reexamine forestry practices were generally beneficial to recreation.

A change in direction occurred when the Democratic administration of President Carter took office in 1977. Environmentally-oriented rather than business-oriented persons were appointed to a number of key positions. Cecil D. Andrus, well known as an environmental crusader while governor of Idaho, was appointed secretary of the interior placing him in charge of national parks, wildlife refuges, public domain lands, and many environmental programs. Rupert Cutler, resource development professor and wilderness activist, became assistant secretary of agriculture responsible for the U.S. Forest Service and many other conservation-oriented programs in that department.

During his first month in office, President Carter proposed a five-year program to protect and restore the national parks by providing additional land acquisition funds for recently approved parks, rehabilitating older parks, and increasing the number of staff. Later he presented an environmental message to Congress. The message was very broad covering pollution and health, energy and the environment, the urban environment, natural resources, the national heritage, and the global environment. A major theme was the reduction of federal government bureaucracy

and inertia in environmental matters. Actions specifically affecting recreation were orders to control off-highway vehicle damage on federal lands, review barrier island conservation, and encourage protection of floodplains and wetlands. The message also proposed designation or enlargement of 10 wilderness areas, expansion of the National Wild and Scenic Rivers System, and designation of three national scenic trails. However, the emphasis was on coordinating environmental planning and action rather than on developing new programs or areas.

A series of events in 1978 made it a remarkable year for action by the U.S. government in the field of recreation. Representative Phillip Burton, the influential chairman of the House of Representatives Subcommittee on Parks and Insular Affairs, brought together a large number of congressional and administration proposals and created an omnibus parks bill. Known as the National Parks and Recreation Act, it passed through Congress relatively easily because it included provisions for new or improved recreation opportunities in many parts of the nation. The act approved more than 150 recreation projects in 44 states costing some $1.2 billion. The major projects authorized were:

- A five-year, $650 million program to refurbish or extend recreation resources and programs in inner-city neighborhoods.
- Grants of up to $155 million for federal and state acquisition of property for the proposed Santa Monica Mountains National Recreation Area along the California Coast just west of Los Angeles.
- Initial land purchases costing $25 mil-

lion for a proposed Pine Barrens National Reserve in southern New Jersey.

- Addition of 19 other new units to the national park system.
- Funds for the purchase of lands needed to enlarge 29 existing units of the national park system and for facility development in 34 units.
- Transfer of the controversial Mineral King Valley (long desired by the Walt Disney Corporation for a major ski resort) from the Sequoia National Forest to Sequoia National Park.
- Designation of some 800,000 hectares (2 million acres) within eight national park system units as part of the national wilderness system and another 49,000 hectares (120,000 acres) as potential wilderness additions.
- Addition of eight new segments totaling 385 kilometers (620 miles) to the national wild and scenic rivers system and the study of 17 other rivers for possible inclusion in the system.

The first-mentioned project, known as the Urban Park and Recreation Recovery Program, was the first federal combined assault on both recreation resource and services problems in urban areas. It focused on improving close-to-home opportunities in economically disadvantaged large cities, especially for minority and low- and moderate-income residents.

Adoption of such a wide range of recreation legislation in any one year is uncommon but a number of other events made 1978 even more unusual. Congress approved the Endangered American Wilderness Act adding more land to the national wilderness system than was added at any one time since the passage of the original Wilderness Act in 1964. Three other acts designated some 500,000 hectares (1,250,000 acres) of new wilderness in Montana, authorized a study

of almost 400,000 hectares (1 million acres) of potential wilderness in that state, and added 17,000 hectares (43,000 acres) to the Boundary Waters Canoe Area wilderness in Minnesota.

But the most spectacular (though not necessarily most important) development came at the end of the year. Throughout 1978, Congress had debated the merits of various bills designed to establish a number of national parks, forests, and wildlife refuges in Alaska. The House of Representatives passed such a measure but a similar bill died in the Senate when the Alaskan senators vehemently opposed it. President Carter then took action to prevent development of the most unique areas in the lands being considered for these various kinds of reserves until Congress could examine the matter further. He used his powers under the 1906 Antiquities Act to proclaim 17 national monuments with a total area of 23 million hectares (56 million acres). The president also authorized the secretary of the interior to designate 16 million hectares (40 million acres) as national wildlife refuges under the Federal Land Policy and Management Act of 1976. Similarly, the secretary of agriculture took action to prevent mineral entry or state selection of the lands in certain national forest areas. The presidential creation of the new national monuments was the largest single addition to the national park system ever made. The land added was equal to $1\frac{3}{4}$ times the total area of the system at that time.

The final years of the 1970s were not without their problems, however. Voters in California passed Proposition 13, which substantially cut property taxes result-

ing in serious reductions in local government recreation services. Interruption of oil exports from Iran following the overthrow of the Shah was followed by reduction of production in some other exporting nations and a series of oil price increases. These events had widespread effects in many of the developed nations including shortages of gasoline, reduction in recreational travel, increased inflation, and economic recession. The implications of these events are discussed more extensively in Chapter 18.

Therefore, although recreation progressed significantly in the United States during the 1970s, it no longer enjoyed the prominent position it occupied previously. It had come to be considered an essential aspect of living, an important function of government, and a significant market factor in business. However, it now had to compete directly with other resource uses, economic demands, social needs, and environmental requirements. Much of the magic and emotionalism of the revolution was over.

Most nations have not experienced a recreation revolution of the same intensity as the revolutions in the United States and Canada. West Germany appears to be at or near a zenith that may come closer to the American and Canadian experience than any other major nation. Other advanced European nations, Japan, Australia, and New Zealand, are at or near zeniths that will be more modest because of economic or resource limitations. Less developed nations may be decades or centuries from reaching their zeniths. Differences in culture, social goals, and economic development control the nature and timing of changes in recreation opportunity supply.[6] Current world resource,

[6] These differences are discussed in subsequent chapters.

economic and political problems suggest that few in any nations are likely to reach zeniths that will be comparable with those of the United States, Canada, and West Germany.

This chapter has outlined the historical development of recreation. Chapter 3 will explain why recreation is such an important aspect of life today.

DISCUSSION TOPICS

1. Articles in the popular press often give the impression that people living today in advanced industrial nations have more free time than people enjoyed at any previous time. Is this a correct impression?
2. The Protestant movement resulted in restrictions on recreation participation but also aided recreation because of its encouragement of democracy and social reform. How did these two effects interact and contribute to today's recreation environments?
3. If the Washburn party had not explored the Yellowstone area in the summer of 1870 would the various national park systems of the world exist today?
4. Why can the period from 1840 to 1880 be termed "the recreation renaissance?"
5. Explain why the old expression "Every cloud has a silver lining" is applicable to the history of recreation during the Great Depression.
6. Would the United States and Canada have reached the zenith of the second recreation revolution if a second great depression had occurred in the years following World War II?

FURTHER READINGS

A first-rate professional review of the historical development of recreation is contained in Part Two of Richard Kraus' textbook *Recreation and Leisure in Modern Society* published in 1971 by Appleton-Century-Crofts, New York. A 35-page booklet entitled *America's Park and Recreation Heritage: A Chronology* by Carlton S. Van Doren and Louis Hodges published in 1975 by the United States Department of the Interior, Bureau of Outdoor Recreation, Washington, is an excellent summary and study guide. It also contains a good historical bibliography. *A History of Recreation: America Learns to Play* by Foster Rhea Dulles and published in 1965 by Appleton-Century-Crofts is a fascinating, detailed account of the growth of recreation in the United States. Although it is the product of much careful research by a skilled historian, it is quite light and often humorous. It should be required reading for everyone interested in recreation. An equally readable account of how the 10 Royal Parks became London's most heavily used public green space is *Royal Parks for the People* by Hazel Thurston published in Newton Abbot by David & Charles in 1974.

More information on the history of the extraurban aspects of recreation in the United States can be obtained from *Recreational Use of Wild Lands* by C. Frank Brockman and Lawrence C. Merriman, Jr., a textbook published by McGraw-Hill, New York, in 1973. A continuing series of articles entitled "History and Archives" in the *Journal of Physical Education and Recreation* provides a wealth of information and sources; the series started in the February 1968 copy. *Parks and Recreation* magazine has published many historical articles; the series "Play for America" by Richard F. Knapp that appeared from August 1972 to January 1974 provides a good summary of the development of recreation services and the associated professional groups. Material from this series is included in a book by Knapp and Charles E. Hartsoe entitled *Play for America: The History of the National Recreation Association: 1906–1965* published by the National Recreation and Park Association in 1979.

3

SIGNIFICANCE OF RECREATION

The goal of this chapter is to establish the importance of recreation in today's complex world. Many people— especially those who are strongly influenced by the work ethic— do not recognize its significance. To these people, recreation is a pleasant but nonessential activity over which the demands of work, education, and social obligations always take precedence. Rec-

Figure 3.1 **Young people get acquainted as they share a book and a joke on the steps of an apartment house in Harlem, New York City. Recreation is often the common bond that brings individuals together and promotes social cohesiveness.**

reation, however, is not a distinctly separate activity that can be treated as a nonessential and relegated to last place when assigning money, time, or skills. Instead it is a crucial and integral part of human existence that is woven through and around other human activities such as working, learning, performing social duties, eating, drinking, and sleeping. The right amount of recreation can provide cohesiveness to individual lives, bring people together, and contribute to the strength of society (Figure 3.1).

It is important to understand the significance and many facets of recreation's role in modern society before examining its components in detail. A knowledge of the size and impact of this role helps develop an appreciation of the complicated context in which any recreation activity, facility, or program exists. No person is an island and no aspect of a recreation environment occurs by itself. All aspects of recreation—participation, resources, policies, programs, conflicts, and management problems—must be visualized in the broader context of recreation's significance in the life of the individual and society. The student of recreation who wishes to remain objective must maintain this broad viewpoint whatever professional specialization is eventually followed. Without this perspective, the relative importance and implications of the particular recreation activities or programs with which the student is involved cannot be fully understood.

Some aspects of the significance of recreation can be easily shown. For example, estimates of the number of people attending major sports events, going to national parks, or watching television

programs are readily available. On the other hand, information concerning use of urban park systems, activities at home, or dispersed recreation in forest areas is often absent or incomplete. The psychological and social values of recreation are also hard to measure, and therefore information on these topics is usually based on opinion rather than extensive scientific evidence. Even data on recreation's economic impact are fragmentary. Nearly every aspect of the significance of recreation needs further investigation.

In examining the significance of recreation, it is tempting to focus on the benefits and scarcely mention or even ignore costs and detrimental effects. Most writers concentrate almost exclusively on its positive aspects. Some attempt to avoid the problem of negative effects by defining recreation narrowly. Nevertheless, even recreation that is "constructive," "uplifting," or "of high quality," can have detrimental results. An objective examination shows that recreation, like all other human activities, does involve costs to the individual and society. These costs may be of several different types. Some such as entrance fees or expenditures for recreation goods or facilities are monetary. Others involve psychological, physical, or social costs; for example, when death or severe injury results from contact sports, boating, swimming, or vehicle accidents associated with recreation. Environmental or social costs occur when a recreation environment is used inappropriately or excessively. Whatever the nature or magnitide of these costs, their existence must be recognized and taken into account when making decisions regarding personal

participation and public or private sponsorship of recreation.

Besides remembering that recreation has costs as well as benefits, the complexity of the relationships involved must also be kept in mind. The ways in which a recreation activity is significant tend to overlap rather than fall neatly into one or two of the several categories discussed in this chapter. People's involvement in a specific activity can be significant to some degree in all of the categories mentioned, although it is used as an example in connection with only one category. These groupings, therefore, must not be regarded as mutually exclusive and tightly defined analytical areas. Instead, they are convenient headings that make it possible to review a complex continuum in a systematic manner. For the participant, there is no artificial division of the experience into such groupings; usually the activity is enjoyed for its own sake with little or no thought for the precise nature of the benefits and costs involved.

RECREATION AS A HUMAN RIGHT

A number of legislative bodies have legally established the importance of recreation by passing laws or declarations that protect the right of citizens to participate in leisure activities. This legislation may now appear to be unnecessary in many developed nations but it should be remembered that, until quite recently, "idleness" was considered sinful by large numbers of people living in these countries. Even now, some religious and conservative groups in the advanced nations and many more people elsewhere in the world do not regard recreation as a necessity of life and resist government attempts to provide recreation opportunities. Legislation that establishes recreation as a human right is therefore both an indication of its importance and a reminder that negative attitudes still exist.

A key document establishing people's rights to recreation is the U.N. Universal Declaration of Human Rights adopted by the General Assembly in 1948. In it, the member nations agreed that everyone has "the right to rest and leisure, including reasonable limitation of working hours and periodic holidays with pay," and ". . . the right freely to participate in the cultural life of the community, to enjoy the arts and to share in scientific advancement and its benefits."[1] Many nations have referred to the declaration when drafting or redrafting their constitutions, and some may have been prompted by it to include provisions regarding recreation. The declaration is also cited frequently in U.N. debates and written materials as the standard that should be observed by all nations.

The constitutions of the developed non-Communist nations generally do not contain specific references to recreation. In the second paragraph of the American Declaration of Independence, adopted in 1776, the representatives of the 13 colonies affirmed their belief that the pursuit of happiness is a God-given, inalienable right. The U.S. Constitution contains no direct references to recreation or happiness. However, the use of public funds for recreation purposes has been successfully defended in court as

being justified by Section 8 of Article 1. It authorizes the collection of taxes by Congress to "provide for the common defense and general welfare" of the country. This clause is the constitutional foundation on which federal government and state and local government involvement in recreation are based. Two-thirds of the individual state constitutions authorize the state government to undertake "general welfare" programs. Some follow the Declaration of Independence and give the citizens the right to "alter or abolish" a government that fails to secure happiness for its people.

It would be nice to assume that the absence of specific guarantees of rights to recreation in the constitutions of non-Communist democratic nations indicates that the right was so well established it was considered unnecessary to mention it specifically. On the contrary, a long hard battle had to be fought against powerful business interests and some conservative and religious groups by organized labor, reformers, or recreation professionals in order to obtain reduced working hours, paid holidays and vacations, or authority to spend public moneys on the provision of recreation opportunities. In the 1920s, for instance, industrialists spoke against the reduction of factory hours because of the demoralizing effect that more free time would have on the workers. Court suits were brought against public bodies that used taxes to pay for parks or recreation programs. The battle continues today. In government bodies where conservative elements predominate, park and recreation budgets are usually smaller and are generally the first to be reduced in time of fiscal difficulty.

In contrast, the Communist nations generally have strong constitutional protection for citizen rights to free time and recreation based on Karl Marx's ideas concerning the relationships between reduction in working hours and freedom, recreation, and the development of the individual. The clauses concerning recreation often follow the lead provided by Article 119 of the Fundamental Law of the Union of Soviet Socialist Republics. It states that:

> rest and leisure is ensured by the establishment of a seven-hour day for industrial, office, and professional workers, the reduction of the working day to six hours for arduous trades and to four hours in shops where conditions of work are particularly arduous; by institution of annual vacations with full pay for industrial, office, and professional workers, and by placing a wide network of sanatoriums, holiday homes and clubs at the disposal of the working people.[2]

Most of the other Communist constitutions, including that of the People's Republic of China, contain similar stipulations regarding working hours and also guarantee rights to participation in cultural programs. The Polish constitution is the most specific in terms of the opportunities and resources to be provided. It states that citizens in both urban and rural areas have the right to develop their creative talents and benefit from the development of workers' vacation programs and

[1] United Nations, *Human Rights: A Compilation of International Instruments of the United Nations,* United Nations, New York, 1978.

[2] Jan F. Triska, ed., *Constitutions of the Communist-Party States,* The Hoover Institute on War, Revolution and Peace, Stanford University, 1968, p. 59.

tourism and the provision of health resorts, sports facilities, recreation centers, clubs, parks, libraries, books, newspapers, radio, cinemas, theaters, and museums.

Unfortunately, such clauses in national constitutions do not ensure that citizens will indeed enjoy the benefits of more free time and extensive state-provided recreation opportunities. Most of the Communist countries have had to retain longer working hours in order to reach industrial and agricultural production targets, and the growth of recreation facilities and programs has often been slow. State control of athletic programs, cultural activities, personal travel, and other aspects of recreation has also reduced freedom of choice.

Many nations do not have constitutional guarantees of this kind, and some governments still have negative attitudes toward shorter working hours and substantial public recreation expenditures. In order to provide guidelines in these cases, representatives from 16 international recreation organizations, under the leadership of the International Recreation Association (now World Leisure and Recreation Association), adopted a Charter for Leisure in 1970 (Table 3.1).

The signatory organizations represent a large number of recreation professionals and influential lay persons from around the world. Although it had no legal status, the charter is influencing official attitudes toward recreation and may eventually lead to the passage of more comprehensive legislation by the United Nations, individual nations, and political units within nations.

[3] Ibid., p. 343.

AMOUNT OF PARTICIPATION

A very tangible indicator of the significance of recreation is the amount of participation that takes place. In the more developed nations, evidence of massive participation in many kinds of activities is often obvious. Stores are crammed with recreation merchandise; television antennas sprout from rooftops; major items of recreation equipment such as swimming pools, boats, and camping vehicles are common in people's yards; and traffic jams form at sports events, park entrances, and along highways leading to resort areas (Figure 3.2).

The magnitude of participation is frequently expressed as estimates of the number of times or number of days people take part in one activity or in a group of activities. Information of this kind comes from data on the sale of admission tickets, counts of people entering facilities, or questionnaires concerning places visited or time spent on recreation activities. Some examples of

Figure 3.2 Despite high fuel prices, French highway A-7 between Paris and the Riviera becomes jammed with traffic when city dwellers go for their traditional summer vacation in July. One-third of the noncommercial vehicles are carrying luggage on roof racks or towing trailers.

Table 3.1 Internationally Developed Charter for Leisure

Charter for Leisure
developed and approved by 165 international organizations in 1970

Article 1

Every man has a right to leisure time. This right comprises reasonable working hours, regular paid holidays, favourable traveling conditions and suitable social planning, including reasonable access to leisure facilities, areas and equipment in order to enhance the advantages of leisure time.

Article 2

The right to enjoy leisure time with complete freedom is absolute. The prerequisites for undertaking individual leisure pursuits should be safeguarded to the same extent as those for collective enjoyment of leisure time.

Article 3

Every man has a right to easy access to recreational facilities open to the public, and to nature reserves by lakes, seas, wooded areas, in the mountains and to open spaces in general. These areas, their fauna and flora, must be protected and conserved.

Article 4

Every man has a right to participate in and be introduced to all types of recreation during leisure time, such as sports and games, open-air living, travel, theatre, dancing, pictorial art, music, science and handicrafts, irrespective of age, sex, or level of education.

Article 5

Leisure time should be unorganized in the sense that official authorities, urban planners, architects, and private groups of individuals do not decide how others are to use their leisure time. The above-mentioned should create or assist in the planning of the leisure opportunities, aesthetic environments and recreation facilities required to enable man to exercise individual choice in the use of his leisure, according to his personal tastes and under his own responsibility.

Article 6

Every man has a right to the opportunity for learning how to enjoy his leisure time. Family, school, and community should instruct him in the art of exploiting his leisure time in the most sensible fashion. In schools, classes, and courses of instruction, children, adolescents, and adults must be given the opportunity to develop the skills, attitudes, and understandings essential for leisure literacy.

Article 7

The responsibility for education for leisure is still divided among a large number of disciplines and institutions. In the interests of everyone and in order to utilize purposefully all the funds and assistance available in the various administrative levels, this responsibility should be fully coordinated among all public and private bodies concerned with leisure. The goal should be for a community of leisure. In countries, where feasible, special schools for recreational studies should be established. These schools would train leaders to help promote recreational programs and assist individuals and groups during their leisure hours, in so far as they can without restricting freedom of choice. Such service is worthy of the finest creative efforts of man.

SOURCE: "Charter for Leisure," *Journal of Health, Physical Education and Recreation, 42,* 2 (1971).

indicators that show the magnitude and diversity of recreation participation are listed in Table 3.2. Similar data could be presented for thousands of other situations in the developed nations around the world.

The bulk of recreation participation, however, in both the developed countries and developing nations is not of this type. Most recreation experiences take place in or close to home and involve everyday pleasures such as relaxing, chatting with family or friends, or playing simple games. This type of recreation participation is generally not measured because it does not involve travel, large expenditures of money, or the use of public or commercial lands and facilities. Nevertheless, these common activities are the most important ones because they occur with such frequency and have the greatest psychological and social significance.

On the average, people spend

about one-third of their time on some form of recreation. The actual proportion depends on the individual as well as on the social and economic environments in which the person lives. Therefore, recreation is of great significance both in terms of the numbers of people participating and because of the large amount of time involved.

PSYCHOLOGICAL SIGNIFICANCE

Authorities generally agree that participation in some form of recreation is a psychological necessity for most people. Unfortunately, it is difficult to conclusively demonstrate the psychological benefits or detrimental effects of recreation. Researchers cannot readily differentiate between the effects of recreation and other influences unless the individuals are in a controlled environment such as a school, hospital, or other type of institution. Similarly, it is impossible to categorize recreation activities according to their potential to produce specific psychological effects. One person may derive a particular psychological benefit from one type of recreation experience while another may require a completely different type of experience to achieve the same effect. In addition, a recreation experience usually produces not one but a variety of psychological reactions in the same participant. Sometimes, these reactions are a mixture of positive and negative effects making it very difficult to determine the net result. For these reasons, it can be said that all forms of recreation have psychological significance but whether a particular recreation experience has positive or negative effects depends largely on the perceptions of the individual participant.

RELAXATION
Perhaps the most important psychological benefit obtained from recreation is relaxation. Relaxation provides a respite from life's worries and pressures, relieves feelings of tension and fatigue, and restores mental efficiency. Most people need it after a day's work, following an emotionally disturbing experience, or part way through a long period of involvement in one task. Individuals with jobs that are emotionally demanding often seek relaxing experiences before beginning work.

Some people achieve relaxation through physical activity—jogging, playing golf, or disco dancing, for example. Others find that intense mental activity—reading a thought-provoking book, playing a game of bridge or chess, or working on a crossword puzzle, for instance—can have a relaxing effect. But for a great many individuals, relaxation comes not from physical or mental activity but from an absence of it—dozing on a couch, daydreaming while lying in the sun, or passively watching a situation comedy on TV.

Unhappily, not all spare time experiences prove relaxing. For example, taking a vacation trip to relieve stress may not always do so. Unforeseen problems arising from overcrowding, bad weather, an accident, or the antisocial or unpleasant behavior of others may actually add to a person's feelings of tension, making relaxation impossible. Sometimes, the problem lies not with the recreation activity but with the individual. Some persons try to crowd so many activities into one short period that there is no time

for relaxation. Others are prevented from relaxing because they are burdened with serious personal problems or work-ethic-based feelings of guilt concerning recreation.

SELF-REALIZATION
Recreation can provide valuable opportunities for self-realization. Everyone needs to have an adequate sense of personal worth; it provides the self-confidence that enables people to develop their full potential and withstand life's many pressures, problems, and disappointments. Once, the work ethic created a social environment in which most people sought and, in many cases, found purpose and self-esteem in their work. Now, specialization, automation, and the sheer volume of work have made a higher proportion of the available jobs unsatisfying and impersonal.

Because of time constraints and work loads, fewer and fewer people can take pride in "a job well done." So many individuals work on just one small part of a product or process that they can gain little satisfaction from their limited and repetitive contributions. But people without work also face a loss of self-esteem, and the numbers of these people continue to grow. Therefore, recreation is of great significance because through it, the unemployed and retired as well as many employed persons can find opportunities for the self-realization that they cannot or do not obtain from work.

Recreation can provide feelings of personal worth in many different ways. Examples include:

- Activities in the arts that provide opportunities for persons to create something original (Figure 3.3).

Table 3.2 Indicators of Recreation Participation Magnitude

Indicators of the Magnitude of Recreation Participation[a]

About 50 million Americans play a musical instrument for pleasure; of these, 18 million play the piano and 15 million play the guitar.

Over 1 million people visit the beaches and amusement park at Coney Island on a typical hot summer Sunday.

Annual attendance at Broadway plays is about 10 million; attendance at live plays throughout the United States is 100 million.

About 16 million Americans buy hunting licenses and 26 million purchase fishing licenses.

Over 760 million phonograph records are purchased in the United States every year.

About 57 percent of all American households have one or more pets including 46 million dogs and 26 million cats; 42 million households keep tropical fish.

The American *per capita* annual consumption of beverages includes 359 cans of soft drinks; 85 l (22.4 gal) of beer; 7 l (1.85 gal) of wine; and 7.6 l (2 gal) of hard liquor.

More than 20 million Americans collect postage stamps as a hobby.

Las Vegas, Nevada, famous for casino gambling and big-name entertainment, attracts over 10 million visits annually.

6 million American boys and girls aged 7 to 19 play soccer; almost 5 million people attend American Soccer League games.

Collectively, Americans are estimated to spend 100 billion hours a year watching programs on 145.7 million working television sets.

Around 25 million people in the United States play tennis regularly and another 8 million play racquetball.

People see a movie in a U.S. theater on about 1 billion occasions each year; attendance at Soviet movies is over 4 billion.

Over 1 billion people around the world watched at least part of the 1976 Olympics Games on television.

Two out of every five Americans participate in one or more craft activities.

More than 50 million Americans go boating in over 10 million pleasure boats.

The television program "The Muppet Show" is watched regularly in 107 nations by more than 235 million people.

Nearly 20 million Americans jog regularly; about 50,000 individuals have competed in at least one marathon event.

Millions of Americans every year enjoy an evening of dancing in one of 20,000 discotheques located throughout the country.

Around 50 percent of all American households have some type of garden.

[a] Data are for the late 1970s.

- Membership in service-, religious-, and youth-oriented organizations involving opportunities for individuals to enjoy helping others and making unique contributions to programs and projects that are perceived by society as important.
- Participation in high-risk sports, outdoor adventure programs, and athletics that present opportunities for individuals to face personal challenges, compete with others, and experience success and feelings of exhilaration.
- Involvement in collecting hobbies that provide opportunities for persons to develop feelings of pride, worth, and accomplishment while acquiring, studying, and displaying certain kinds of materials.
- Attending discussion groups, lectures, workshops, and classes that include intellectual stimulation, increase competency in skill areas, or develop self-confidence.

In addition, many people achieve self-realization in a solitary manner. By engaging in certain activities — reading, research, jogging, travel, quiet contemplation, visiting a museum — they fulfill some personal goal or achieve higher levels of self-discovery or self-improvement.

Participation in recreation activities does not automatically assure

Table 3.2 Indicators of Recreation Participation Magnitude

Indicators of the Magnitude of Recreation Participation [a]

Attendance at major sporting events of all kinds is over 250 million in the United States alone.

About 17 million tourists visit New York City and around 3 million visit San Francisco every year.

More than 100 million Americans swim as a recreation activity; over 1 million in-ground and 3 million above-ground private swimming pools are now in use in the yards of American homes.

The 3 dozen major amusement parks in the United States attract around 80 million visitors a year.

Not counting people who watched the game in bars and clubs, 105 million Americans saw some or all of the Super Bowl XIV football game on television; this surpassed the final segment of "Roots," which was watched by about 98 million people.

Around 250 million visits are made each year to units of the U.S. national park system.

About 25 million Americans use citizens band (CB) radios for pleasure.

Over 1 billion copies of *TV Guide* are purchased by people every year.

Thoroughbred horse racing is the most popular spectator sport in the United States attracting about 45 million people.

American museums are visited by over 300 million persons a year.

More than 20 million Americans travel outside the country on vacation trips every year.

Over 60 million Americans take a summer vacation by automobile or recreation vehicle to locations within the United States.

One-third of all adult Americans smoke, consuming 605 billion cigarettes a year.

Every day, around 25,000 Americans buy one of Harold Robbins' novels; total sales now exceed 200 million copies.

One-fourth of all shoe sales in the United States involves the purchase of one of the hundreds of styles of athletic shoes.

Around 28 million Americans rollerskate either out-of-doors or at one of 6000 rinks; skate sales average 300,000 pairs a month.

Central Park in New York City is used by an estimated 12 million people a year.

There are over 400 million radios in working order in the United States, and Americans purchase about 40 million new ones every year.

Some 1.2 million Americans annually go on a river or ocean cruise.

Over 100 million Americans watch all or part of one of the televised New Year's Day parades; the most famous one — the Tournament of Roses Parade — is seen in person by more than 1 million people lining the parade route.

[a] Data are for the late 1970s.

self-realization, however. For example, self-esteem can actually be diminished if individuals fail to achieve the level of success in a chosen activity that they anticipated for themselves or that others expected of them. This is particularly true in the case of competitive events, programs that teach skills, and activities involving social relationships such as parties and dances. The unemployed and retired also may find it difficult, if not impossible, to achieve self-realization through participation in recreation activities since they offer no monetary compensation. Unfortunately, many people feel that an activity's importance depends on the amount of money a person receives for doing it. These kinds of problems present a special challenge to persons responsible for conducting recreation programs.

ESCAPE MECHANISM

For growing numbers of people, recreation is important because it offers temporary relief from unpleasant realities in their personal lives that they find difficult or impossible to bear. By immersing

Figure 3.3 Painting a vase during a retirement-home art class provides pleasure and a feeling of personal worth for this participant.

themselves in the make-believe world of books, magazines, games, music, sports, motion pictures, television, bars, or discotheques, or by losing themselves in daydreaming, they escape from their problems. In so doing, they regain the emotional or physical strength they need to carry on. For others, recreation provides escape from boredom, thereby protecting their mental health. This is particularly true in the case of people subjected to the monotony associated with unemployment, retirement, imprisonment, repetitive types of work, or confinement because of health problems, bad weather, or long, severe winters (Figure 3.4).

Unfortunately, participation in escapist activities seldom solves the problems that originally made it necessary to try to escape. If the problems are only minor or temporary in nature, there is little danger involved in seeking this form of relief. But when the problems appear to be permanent and insurmountable, escape through recreation can cease to be an occasional and harmless activity and become instead a regular way of life. When this occurs, some individuals suffer serious disorientation or lose touch with reality altogether.

One of the most common and most dangerous methods of escaping reality is the consumption of alcohol or the use of other drugs. When used in moderation, these methods seem to provide some people with temporary relief from tension and anxiety. However, dependence on these substances often leads to overindulgence and the creation of serious psychological and physical problems that only reduce the individual's ability to cope. Similarly, participation in gambling activities offers excitement and a respite from the problems of everyday living. But for persons who become addicted, misery rather than pleasure is the price they and the people who care about them must pay for their excessive involvement.

In the case of children and young people—especially those who retreat more or less permanently into the dream worlds of comics, television, magazines, motion pictures, drugs, and alcohol—the results can be particularly tragic. Some never learn the essential lessons of life and end up unable to deal with its complexities or to relate to people around them. Others —particularly those individuals who watch excessive amounts of television—develop distorted views of the real world. For example, many who watch programs containing a high incidence of violence, natural disasters, and human suffering come to view their environments as much more dangerous than they really are. Others who gravitate toward programs with happy endings find real life confusing and increasingly disappointing because the people they know and meet are not nearly as pleasant, understanding, or reliable as the ones who inhabit television's make-believe communities.

THERAPEUTIC PSYCHOLOGICAL SIGNIFICANCE

The therapeutic value of recreation is well known to members of the medical profession. By involving patients in recreation activities, recreation therapists are able to help

Figure 3.4 Inmates in the Attica state prison in New York play chess through the bars to while away the hours.

introspection, relieve boredom, lessen anxiety, and provide opportunities to socialize or release pent-up emotions. In centers specializing in the treatment of young children, the availability of good recreation opportunities is considered equally important to the provision of proper medical care (Figure 3.5).

Recreation is also gaining acceptance as an effective type of preventive medicine. Individuals are advised by their doctors to include more or different forms of recreation in their schedules to reduce the likelihood of emotional as well as physical problems. In West Germany, for instance, a "cure" of three to four weeks on one of the islands situated off the coast of Friesland is frequently prescribed for a great variety of ailments. During their stay, "patients" enjoy total

dispel the threat of isolation and social rejection, encourage the timid, disarm the aggressive, motivate the lethargic, calm the restless, and divert the melancholic individuals under their care.[5] Consequently, recreation serves as a valuable tool in the rehabilitation of the mentally retarded, the emotionally disturbed, the juvenile delinquent, the criminal, the drug addict, the alcoholic, the disabled, and the elderly. Where well-run recreation programs form a part of general hospital environments, results may also be impressive; for instance, patient drug requirements may be decreased by as much as 50 percent, and the length of hospitalization may be shortened appreciably. Involvement in recreation activities can minimize

[5] See Chapter 17.

Figure 3.5 Young patients in the Sidney Farber Cancer Institute in Boston, Massachusetts, have fun playing games in a home-like atmosphere. Well-run recreation programs in health care institutions can have substantial therapeutic benefits for patients of all ages.

relaxation, peace, absence of noise and distractions, and freedom from anxiety and pressure. Health insurance benefits pay for these vacations, including the cost of all medical services, participation in a wide variety of recreation activities, lodging, and food. The premise is that mental and physical health can be preserved or restored while problems are minimal, thus averting the likelihood of more serious illness, inability to work, and expensive medical treatment later on.

However, people do not have to be under medical care to benefit from the therapeutic effects of recreation. They themselves or relatives or friends may recognize that their mental health is endangered and that participation in a recreation activity is likely to be of assistance. Examples of ways in which people use recreation to restore emotional balance or avoid the development of emotional problems include the following.

- Individuals who have recently moved or been bereaved or divorced join social or hobby clubs to make new friends and dispel chronic loneliness.
- A person who is going through some type of personal crisis seeks comfort and peace in aesthetic experiences such as watching a sunset, viewing a work of art, reading a poem, or listening to soothing music.
- An introverted individual acquires a knowledge of certain recreation activities to use as a source of topics for conversation and to help build self-confidence and gain acceptance in social situations.
- People who feel obliged to repress their emotions at work or in their personal relationships find harmless outlets for their aggressive feelings by watching contact sports on television, by facing and meeting the challenges inherent in high-risk activities, by participating vigorously in sports, or by

engaging in a variety of simple activities like kicking a ball around a backyard, going for a ride on a bicycle or motorcycle, or shooting at a target.
- Isolated, lonely individuals keep their television sets turned on all day long, since the people in the television programs provide a link to the outside world and serve as surrogate companions (Figure 3.6).

Another form of recreation that can be beneficial for those who feel isolated is keeping pets. It can be especially therapeutic for children, the elderly, the sick, and the disabled. These people frequently feel frustrated, lonely, and very insignificant because they either live alone in comparative isolation or must continuously take orders from or be physically dependent on others. Pets can make them feel needed

and important. In addition, the loving relationship that frequently develops between these people and their pets can help them survive what is often a very difficult period.

Not all recreation activities are therapeutically beneficial, however. Some activities can encourage behavior and produce reactions that may threaten rather than bolster a person's emotional balance. Some psychologists, for example, question the cathartic value of watching violent sports or movies. They suggest that feelings of aggression are not satiated in many instances; instead, the experience can encourage aggressive behavior, either during or immediately following the activity. They also feel that spectators at sports events who lose control often are left with feelings of shame, guilt,

Figure 3.6 Individuals isolated by age, infirmities, or other circumstances often play their television sets all day long for companionship.

increased anger, or resentment (especially if their team loses) that magnify rather than relieve their feelings of frustration. Similarly, participants in competitive games and sports who become obsessed with the need to win—or the fear of losing—may find that their recreation experience escalates tensions and increases aggravation instead of providing the period of relaxation that they seek.

Weekends, holidays, and vacations are eagerly awaited by the majority of people and are generally regarded as psychologically beneficial. Unfortunately, they can also be awaited with anxiety or fear, disliked while in progress, and regretted in retrospect. Vacations, or indeed any extended period away from the job, can be ordeals for workaholics. On the other hand, weekends and holidays may be stressful for people who must work or catch up on personal duties and chores if they perceive them as times when they *should* be enjoying recreation. Vacations that do not fulfill expectations or resolve certain personal or interpersonal problems as anticipated can also be very disappointing.

Traditional festivals may be extremely unhappy occasions for people who have unrealistic expectations. Christmas, for example, can be a particularly traumatic period, primarily because its image as a time of festivity, gift exchanges, feasting, and family warmth and togetherness has been idealized and promoted ad nauseam by advertisers, merchants, writers, and television producers. For persons who have lost loved ones through divorce or death, who are temporarily separated or alienated from family and friends, or who have few friends or little money to be used on gift purchases or entertainment, this period can be a time for feelings of guilt, shame, self-hate, loneliness, frustration, disappointment, sadness, or even acute depression. For those who enjoy the Christmas season, it is hard to realize that, at one of the supposedly happiest times of the year, the suicide rate rises and crisis clinics are swamped with calls for help.

EDUCATIONAL SIGNIFICANCE

Recreation plays an important role in education. It may be a direct role — some forms of recreation impart useful knowledge or develop physical and mental skills. It can also be an indirect role — recreation settings are often used to enhance learning processes. But in either case, the key element is enjoyment. Learning from a recreation activity or in a recreational atmosphere can be such a pleasant experience that it occurs without effort or, in some cases, without an awareness that it is even taking place. Because of this, recreation seldom receives the credit it deserves for its contributions to education. Nevertheless, the average person acquires far more knowledge and skills through participation in recreation activities than through formal education. One reason for this is that the learning-through-recreation process begins as soon as people are old enough to play and continues through their entire lifetimes. Television, for example, now has a major influence on people of all ages. Although it is only one of a vast array of educationally significant recreation resources, television will receive special emphasis throughout this section because of its great impact, both positive and negative.

DEVELOPMENT OF SKILLS

In the available space, even a rudimentary coverage of all the ways in which participation in recreation activities can teach skills is impossible. The few examples that follow give only an indication of the scope and nature of recreation's contributions.

Children develop language skills as they communicate with others during play, hear and sing songs, read or listen to stories and poems, participate in word games, see or take part in plays and puppet shows, listen to the radio, and watch television. Young TV viewers, for example, tend to develop richer vocabularies at an earlier age than children who are not exposed to TV. Programs like "Sesame Street" (currently watched in about 9.5 million American homes including 90 percent of the low-income households with young children in the inner-city neighborhoods of Chicago, New York, and Washington) develop basic cognitive, perceptual, and reasoning skills, which help lay a foundation for a successful learning experience in the classroom. Art activities help individuals of all ages develop perception and motor skills, and are—according to some behavioral scientists—essential to brain development during the childhood years.

Schools are taking advantage of young people's passion for television to strengthen language skills. Asked to read scripts as they watch television programs at home, children who do not read well often develop a keen desire to improve. Many are motivated to read books, some for the first time. Writing skills improve as youngsters write about the scripts or certain aspects of the telecasts. Better readers develop creative writing skills as they seek to improve the scripts or prepare original ones. Also, opportunities to speak before a group occur during informal discussions about the mechanics of the presentation or the staging of parts of the show.

Counting, calculating, and other mathematical and reasoning skills are improved or developed through activities such as hopscotch, Monopoly, bingo, dice games, cribbage or other card games and through the development of an understanding of sports scores and statistics. Motor skills are acquired during participation in recreation activities such as bicycling, dancing, and sports and while playing games like jacks and jumprope. Many toys also aid physical development. Adult participation in sports activities, in playing musical instruments, and in learning craft and hobby techniques maintains and perfects motor skills already acquired and also develops new ones.

ACQUISITION OF KNOWLEDGE

The ways in which recreation contributes to the acquisition of factual knowledge are many and varied. Physical recreation activities between periods of intensive study, for instance, provide relaxation and restore the ability to concentrate. Recreation activities such as social events, outings, and sports that are offered by clubs and other organizations may lead people to participate in experiences that are largely educational and that they might otherwise avoid. For example, sports programs in schools can mo-

tivate some students to come to school regularly or to continue their schooling after they have reached the mandatory minimum age for leaving school.

When learning experiences in the classroom take place in a recreational atmosphere that stimulates interest and a receptive attitude, more is learned and the knowledge is retained longer. For example, reading, writing, and arithmetic programs that capitalize on young people's enthusiasm for sports have successfully motivated some less successful students, especially those in certain inner-city schools. When teachers develop lesson plans based on sports and present the materials in competitive game formats, children previously considered to be nonachievers have become interested in these programs. Many have quickly acquired basic skills and facts that they have either refused to learn or found too difficult to understand in ordinary school classes. Better yet, their curiosity has been aroused and, in many cases, they apply their newly acquired knowledge to afterschool activities thereby accelerating the learning process.

Education also regularly takes place as a natural outcome of participation in recreation activities. Stamp collectors, for example, often become fascinated by the events or places depicted in their stamps and, as a result, seek and absorb a great many historical or geographical facts. Similarly, rock collectors learn geology, birdwatchers become knowledgeable about ecology, and people who operate pleasure boats on large bodies of water find out about coastal morphology, tides, currents, and meteorology. Travel can be highly educational as well as

recreational whether it involves exploration of environments close to home or sightseeing in a national park or a foreign country (Figure 3.7).

Recreation experiences at relatively undeveloped locations are increasingly important as more people spend their lives in urban environments. Knowledge about tree growth, pond life, or the effects of wave action on a shoreline can be obtained in the classroom but understanding is usually limited without the opportunity to stroll through a forest, visit a pond, or explore a beach. Television also expands people's visual perceptions of environments with which they are personally unfamiliar.

However, recreation has its limitations as an aid to learning. It can, for example, have a distracting influence; the educational goals on a nature-study field trip may not be achieved because of the sheer excitement and enjoyment of the experience unless the leader can control behavior and provide adequate direction. Similarly, students in a classroom may become so preoccupied with thoughts of personal recreation activities — the prospect of a Saturday night party or a social engagement or the recollection of yesterday's football game, for instance — that concentration is reduced and learning is impaired.

Some forms of recreation often have such appeal that they take precedence over activities that would probably be educationally superior if undertaken instead. For instance, activities that are diverting and not mentally stimulating are often preferred by physically exhausted workers, harried housewives, or students feeling the pressures of school work. Television

Figure 3.7 During a conducted tour with a National Park Service ranger-interpreter, families visiting Mesa Verde National Park in southwestern Colorado learn about the history of the Pueblo Indians and how they built their cliff dwellings.

programs with little intellectual challenge are frequently chosen under these circumstances. Educators consider this to be potentially harmful, especially for young people. Watching television reduces participation in pursuits that could result in personal growth and intellectual development such as reading, letter writing, playing games, working on hobbies, or taking part in family conversations. As has already been pointed out, television can improve verbal skills in younger children. Sometimes, however, there is very little comprehension of what the words actually mean, and some of the acquired speech patterns are not desirable. Excessive television viewing can also produce a decline in the ability to pay attention and a passive attitude and dulling effect that are not conducive to learning at any time.

DEVELOPMENT OF LEARNED BEHAVIOR

Many recreation activities provide experiences that aid in the development of desirable character traits and attitudes that enable people to learn and to function successfully in modern society. Participation in games, sports, and various clubs and organizations can help people discover the value of good leadership, cooperation, and observance of rules. The importance of being responsible and carrying out duties properly can be instilled in the minds of those who go camping, canoeing, and mountain climbing with others.

However, such activities do not automatically produce desirable effects. If leadership attitude, direction, and control are inadequate or inappropriate, negative traits such as dishonesty, selfishness, disdain

for rules, lack of respect for authority, or contempt for others may develop instead. In the worst cases, a general corruption of attitudes and character may result that is detrimental to the individual as well as to society. Unfortunately, there have been many examples of this in little league, high school, college, and professional sports.

SIGNIFICANCE FOR PHYSICAL HEALTH

The physical effects of recreation on humans are generally easier to identify and measure than the psychological effects. Anyone who is inactive for a long period because of hospitalization or desk work soon becomes personally aware of the value of regular exercise. Rapid tiring and shortness of breath when physical activity is attempted, a lack of muscle tone, and a general feeling of not being up to par mentally or physically are usually experienced. People need a reasonable amount of regular physical activity to maintain their optimum physiological condition.

Walking and hard physical labor in the home or fields once provided sufficient exercise for most of the world's people. Today, mechanization, the increase in sedentary jobs, extensive use of motorized transportation, and the popularity of television as a spare-time activity have resulted in large numbers of people not having sufficient exercise in their daily routines. Obesity has become a major problem. In the United States, as many as 65 million people weigh far more than they should for optimum health. In addition, 1 million persons a year die of cardiovascular disease, and another 23 million are afflicted with its disabling effects. Although it has not been proven that exercise by itself can actually prevent obesity or heart disease, it can improve the heart's efficiency, increase the respiratory system's capabilities, strengthen muscles (including the heart muscle), develop stamina and vitality, and help reduce body fat if the individual also adopts sensible eating habits. Persons who have exercised regularly also stand a better chance of surviving heart attacks. Recreation activities that are considered most effective as aids in weight control and the conditioning of the cardiovascular, musculatory, and respiratory systems include: aerobic, disco, and square dancing; bicycling and cross-country skiing; handball and racquetball; ice- and roller-skating; jogging and running; jumping rope; and vigorous swimming.

The real significance of recreation in relation to physical health is that it can be such a pleasant experience. People could obtain all the physical activity they require for the maintenance of good health by regularly performing formal exercises. Unfortunately, the majority of people find such routines boring and laborious, especially if they do them alone. Vigorous recreation, on the other hand, can provide opportunities for social contacts and participation in enjoyable activities that are often so engrossing that the physical effort required by the participant is scarcely noticed.

Participation in active forms of recreation may also have considerable therapeutic value. It can reactivate bodies that have deteriorated during long illnesses. It can help elderly persons who have spent a number of years in nursing homes, or other environments where they were encouraged to lead sedentary lives, to regain their mobility and become capable of taking care of themselves again. Physical activity can also play a preventive role; people who regularly engage in active forms of recreation are more likely to retain their vigor, physical capabilities, and health as they age. Physical activity can also be valuable in the treatment of disease; for instance, regular exercise is now considered as important as diet and insulin in the control of diabetes mellitus, since it increases the cellular uptake of glucose even in the absence of insulin. And finally, for many persons with physical handicaps, participation in certain kinds of recreation activities can produce remarkable results. Gymnastics, for example, are used to help children overcome severe balance and coordination problems. Swimming, dancing, arts and crafts, and a variety of games and sports are just a few of the recreation activities that are utilized in therapeutic programs designed to develop the physical capabilities of patients.

Forms of recreation that are not physically demanding can also contribute to the maintenance of good health. For example, medical science does not fully understand the role of the sun's rays in maintaining human health but it appears that light is a vital ingredient. As more of the world's people spend a majority of their time sheltered in homes, schools, factories, and offices rather than exposed to full-spectrum light, recreation activities that take place out-of-doors assume added importance.

Recreation also contributes to people's well-being by providing opportunities for socializing. Taking part in a recreation experience with other people often leads to the development of new friendships; engaging in recreation activities with family members or friends frequently strengthens interpersonal relationships. These results can be very beneficial; scientific studies indicate that individuals with strong family ties, a number of good friends, or active affiliation with one or more organizations are more resistant to disease, accidents, and suicide than persons who by choice or circumstance lead socially isolated lives.

All forms of recreation are not physically beneficial of course. Excessive television watching, for instance, has already been mentioned as one of the factors contributing to people's poor physical condition, since it robs individuals of opportunities to be physically active. Nevertheless, this example can also be used to point out that it is not the recreation activity— in this case, television watching— that usually causes harm but instead the way in which the individual participates— in this particular instance, viewing television *excessively*. This fact should be kept in mind when examining Table 3.3, which lists some of the recreation activities that can be physically harmful under certain circumstances. Ignorance, carelessness, an obsessive desire to win, overindulgence, or lack of necessary skills and a refusal to take proper precautions, obey rules, or utilize recommended protective devices account for most of the deaths, illnesses, and injuries described. Many of the recreation-related discomforts (muscular aches and pains), disabilities (slipped spinal discs, joint inflammations, pinched nerves), and even deaths (often from heart attacks and falls) occur as a result of excessive demands being placed on out-of-condition or overweight bodies. Most of these afflictions could be avoided if more individuals were sensible and practiced moderation when beginning physically demanding recreation activities.

SOCIAL SIGNIFICANCE

Recreation is socially significant in many ways. Its effects are felt by every strata of society from the family and neighborhood level to the national and international levels. Often the effects are predominantly beneficial; sometimes they are not. Occasionally, they are so powerful that they challenge society and, in some instances, force it to change in response.

INDIVIDUAL AND FAMILY PARTICIPATION

People's individual recreation lifestyles have a considerable impact on those around them. The nature and scope of this impact on friends, relatives, fellow employees, and casual contacts depend on a number of factors. Some individuals are quite solitary in the type of recreation they select and in the way they interact with others. An unmarried person may stay up late to work on a hobby, read a book, or see a television program and never mention it to anyone, including fellow employees. In this case, the social impact is limited to subtle effects on the individual's behavior; he or she might be more relaxed and easier to get along with or cranky and uncooperative because of lack of sleep. On the other hand, a more outgoing person may devote considerable time to discussing personal recreation experiences with family members or associates. This can be socially constructive, providing mutual enjoyment and strengthening interpersonal relationships. Discussions of past or anticipated social, cultural, and sports events play a major role in social interaction.

Sometimes, however, the results of these discussions are not beneficial. Bragging about certain recreation possessions or accomplishments, intolerance for other people's points of view about particular activities, or boring repetitions of personal experiences may destroy rather then build interpersonal relationships. The classic examples of this are when a former athlete constantly relives personal moments of glory or a traveler insists on recounting old vacation experiences with the aid of frequently seen, poor-quality slides or movies.

The social impact of a person's recreation lifestyle is usually limited to a relatively few friends and acquaintances, but it can have a much wider effect. For instance, executives who enjoy satisfying recreation experiences are more likely to be pleasant and considerate employers than executives who are unfulfilled by their free-time activities. This may result in improved working conditions, better fringe benefits, and higher pay for hundreds of employees. In turn, these advantages may have beneficial social effects on the employees' families and other people in the communities in which they live. Similarly, the recreation lifestyles of politicians and bureaucrats can have far-reaching social effects. For example, the relaxation that British Prime Minister Winston Churchill achieved through landscape painting during the critical periods of World War II may have had a considerable effect on world history. Not only did it help him to personally withstand tremendous pressures but also it may well have influenced his decision-making capabilities, which were of the utmost importance to the outcome of the war.

Unfortunately, the social effects of an individual's recreation lifestyle can also be very negative. Poor losers or perfectionists returning from a golf game in which they played poorly or the opponent played better may be abusive to those around them. Some dissatisfied participants may operate automobiles with belligerence and, in doing so, may cause traffic accidents. Inconsiderate motorcyclists, snowmobilers, or boaters can cause considerable harm to the environment and distress to people living or camping nearby. Disgruntled gun owners may shoot at power-line insulators, thereby interrupting electric power supplies; this can endanger people's lives and inconvenience whole communities.

Of all of the social effects that recreation can produce, its impact on the family may be the most important because, in the majority of countries, the family is considered to be the foundation of society. When recreation brings family members closer together, it can be a powerful influence for good (Figure 3.8). For example, when everyone in a family cooperates in preparing for and participating in a picnic, the result is far more than just momentary pleasure for each individual. The event may be of real social benefit if family members become better acquainted with

Table 3.3 Examples of the Adverse Effects of Selected Recreation Activities in the United States

Activity	Adverse Effects	Frequent Causes
1. Around Home and Entertainment Activities		
Keeping pets	— Over 1 million bites and scratches need medical help each year. — Diseases transmitted to humans; dogs may carry 40 diseases.	— Ignorance of safe pet-handling methods; provocation. — Failure to control pets; exposure to animal feces.
Growing house plants; gardening	— Illness or death from eating or touching poisonous plants— common with young children. — Strains, sprains, cuts, amputations, eye injuries.	— Curiosity and ignorance; allergies. — Improper lifting or equipment use, particularly lawn mowers.
Celebrations— especially July 4 and Christmas	— House fires cause many injuries and some deaths at Christmas; some electrocutions. — 6000 serious injuries from fireworks a year despite government control of design and sales.	— Dry Christmas trees; faulty tree-light wiring. — Misuse of fireworks; use of fireworks by young people; homemade fireworks.
Smoking, drinking alcohol, use of other drugs	— Lung cancer and heart attacks; alcohol addiction is third most serious health problem— 200,000 deaths a year; 4 out of 10 hospitalizations involve alcohol-related illness; 1.5 million drug addicts; harmful to unborn babies, may alter personality.	— Lack of understanding of effects; prolonged heavy use; operating vehicles or machinery while influenced by alcohol or drugs.
Snacking; preference for snack foods	— Contributes to dental cavities, obesity, high blood pressure, heart disease, diabetes, nutritional deficiencies, decreased vitality, and increased susceptibility to illnessess.	— Overindulgence; high salt, fat, and sugar content; eating only snack foods by preference; skipping meals to eat snacks during recreation without getting fat.
Hobbies— ceramics, painting, woodworking, photography, lapidary	— Poisoning, burns, cuts, fractures, infections, and eye injuries or amputations from toxic substances, dusts, flying particles, or cutting tools.	— Ignorance, carelessness, lack of skill, poor ventilation, failure to use protective gear, inadequate warnings issued with products.
Playing radio, stereo; going to rock concerts, discotheques	— Temporary or permanent hearing loss; tinnitus (a permanent sensation of sound in the ears).	— Prolonged exposure to sounds of 100 decibels or more (individuals, rock concerts, and discotheques often use 100 to 140 db).
Playing with toys	— 600,000 hospital-treated injuries a year involving swallowing parts, being wounded by sharp points and edges, and suffering toy-related falls and collisions; 40,000 children a year hurt on backyard play equipment.	— Toy unsuited to child's age or abilities; faulty manufacture; improper or unsupervised use.
Bicycling	— 1000 deaths and 1 million injuries; 500,000 require medical treatment.	— Careless or reckless cycling; unsuitable surfaces or hazardous conditions; wrong size bicycle.
2. Sports and Fitness Activities		
Tackle football	— 1.5 million injuries a year; 50 percent of all high school male athletic injuries; 90 percent of professional players injured in typical season.	— Bodies insufficiently developed; poor condition; insufficient training; inadequate protective equipment; disregard for rules; aggressive play.

Table 3.3 Examples of the Adverse Effects of Selected Recreation Activities in the United States

Activity	Adverse Effects	Frequent Causes
2. Sports and Fitness Activities (continued)		
Skiing	— 500,000 skiers injured a year; broken bones, sprains, cartilage tears common.	— Poor condition; insufficient skills or experience; faulty equipment; taking risks; crowded slopes.
Jogging, golfing racket sports, softball, bowling	— 20 million injuries a year; most common are sprains, strains, inflammation, fractures, tendon ruptures, and dislocations causing pain and loss of movement; racket sports annually responsible for 8000 serious eye injuries.	— Poor condition; improper equipment; excessive or irregular participation; poor techniques; inadequate protective equipment.
3. Water-Oriented Activities		
Fishing, swimming, boating, water skiing, hiking near water, etc.	— Drownings or death by hypothermia; 7000 fatalities in 1978; injuries and illnesses from exposure to contaminated water, sharp objects, and organisms that injure or transmit disease; eye, ear-canal, and fungus infections common.	— Lack of judgment or mastery of basic swimming, boating, fishing, or survival techniques; panicking; refusal to wear safety devices or heed warnings; use of alcohol or drugs; going barefoot; poor backyard pool security.
4. High-Risk Activities		
Skydiving, white water travel, hang gliding, scuba diving, etc.	— Numerous accidents; high incidence of permanent injury or death; 10,000 fatalities a year.	— Poor physical condition; inadequate preparation or equipment; recklessness; lack of judgment, skills, or knowledge; use of alcohol or other drugs.
5. Other Outdoor Activities		
Using playground equipment	— 150,000 children are seriously injured at playgrounds each year: cuts, bruises, concussions.	— Unsafe or broken equipment; hard surfaces; poor supervision; reckless or aggressive behavior.
Sunbathing; prolonged exposure to sun and heat	— Burns, eye injury, premature skin aging, skin cancer, heat exhaustion, fatal heat stroke; 6000 skin cancer deaths a year; 300,000 new cases annually.	— Overexposure to sun's ultraviolet light or excessive heat; poor physical condition; improper clothing; dehydration; skin cancer risk greatest for fair complexions.
Automobile driving	— 50,000 deaths a year; by 1976, 25 million had died from auto-related injuries worldwide; many accidents occur while driving for recreation purposes.	— Alcohol or other drugs is a factor in at least half of all accidents; ignorance of drugs' effects; careless or reckless driving; speeding; failure to use safety devices.
Nature study, camping, hiking, wild foods, foreign travel	— Falls and stepping on harmful objects; illnesses from poor foods or water; discomfort, illness, occasional death from plants (poison ivy, pollens), insects (mosquitoes, wasps, ticks), and other organisms (scorpions, snakes, jellyfish, bears)	— Improper clothing and footwear; going barefoot; failure to avoid harmful plants and animals; allergies; provocation of animals; lack of judgment, knowledge, or preparation.
Picnicking, food festivals, potluck suppers and banquets, restaurants, etc.	— Discomfort, serious illness, or death from insect stings or contaminated foods; about 19,000 hospital cases of food poisoning each year; another 200,000 probably affected.	— Insects attracted to foods; improperly prepared and stored food.

Figure 3.8 A family picnic at a small lake in Ulster County, New York State, provides a relaxed atmosphere for the strengthening of interpersonal relationships.

each other and feelings of family solidarity are strengthened. Pleasant activities of this kind can help a family withstand both internal and external pressures. Recreation experiences are also valuable when they result in improved communication between husband and wife or parents and children. They may prevent the development of family or wider social problems that commonly arise when these relationships become weak or unsatisfactory.

Unfortunately, recreation can also have a weakening or destructive effect on family unity. Some of the most common examples include:

• Undue emphasis on the purchase of recreation goods; acquisition sometimes becomes an end in itself with additional family members getting a job or working over time in order to afford them.

• Excessive devotion of one spouse's time to a particular activity that may be highly rewarding to the individual concerned but may exclude the other spouse and result in deterioration of the marriage.

• Allocation of most of a family's discretionary income to one recreation activity that is enjoyed by some but not all family members; not only does this prevent participation by other family members in activities of their choice but also it can cause division of the family and produce a buildup of resentment or antagonism on the part of the family members who are forced to either take part or be left out completely.

In addition, some recreation activities are more likely than others to prove harmful both to the individual and to the family as a whole. These include the consumption of alcohol, gambling, and television watching. All are said to add a little spice to people's humdrum lives

and, in moderation, this is often the case. Unfortunately, these activities can easily become addictive and it is then that the problems begin.

Alcohol is well known for its ability to negatively affect the personality, health, and behavior patterns of heavy drinkers to the detriment of the individual and eventually all family members. Over 10 million Americans currently find it impossible to control their alcohol consumption. For some 9 million Americans, the urge to gamble is so strong that it takes precedence over family, job, and self-respect. The ordeal that results often lasts a lifetime as the compulsive gambler depletes the family's financial resources, goes heavily into debt, becomes secretive and irritable, abuses or is indifferent to other family members, periodically suffers acute depression or attempts suicide, or turns to crime to pay gambling debts. In comparison, television seems harmless enough. But, in excess, it too can divide families if individuals go off by themselves to see favorite programs or retreat into themselves even when they are sitting with other family members watching the same show.

RECREATION-BASED AFFILIATIONS

Another important social aspect of recreation is the role it plays in bringing unrelated people together. Many individuals in modern society find it difficult to make meaningful social contacts beyond their own family units. Young people who have moved away from home; single, widowed, and divorced adults; and retired couples usually find it easier to meet new friends through participation in recreation activities than by any other means, including contacts made at work. Taking part in programs and events sponsored by a church organization, private club or association, or local parks and recreation department is the best or only means of finding a mate for a growing number of people.

At one time, membership in recreation-oriented organizations was primarily the prerogative of the affluent. Now, in the developed nations, people from all walks of life form and take an active part in a wide variety of associations. This is especially true in more densely populated areas. These organizations include orchestras, choral groups, and drama societies and a diversity of clubs ranging from social clubs, benevolent organizations, and hobby and craft societies to associations for cyclists, skiers, and hunters. Through participation in various events such as trips, socials, festivals, concerts, shows, and parades, individuals in these groups, neighborhoods, or even entire cities become involved and gain a sense of unity. Class and social distinctions are forgotten, at least to some degree, and are replaced with feelings of common purpose and mutual pride.

Participation in well-run, recreation-oriented organizations can produce other socially desirable results. Individuals, especially young people, can discover the nature and value of democratic processes and come to accept a variety of behavior patterns, social obligations, and taboos. This acceptance helps people function successfully and happily as family members and as part of society. Recreation-oriented groups may also consolidate the wishes of individuals and success-

fully pass them on to the general public, government agencies, or company representatives. In this way they can initiate constructive community action and foster civic pride. Tangible benefits to society such as new or better-equipped parks, community centers, libraries, and instructional programs in the arts are often the final result.

Of even greater importance perhaps are the beneficial effects of these organizations on community vitality and cohesion. For instance, participation in the arts is currently expanding rapidly. Citizen support for activities such as the formation of local arts councils, presentation of community-sponsored film programs and concerts, and the construction of cultural centers is widespread. Many of these projects owe their success to total community dedication with hundreds of people contributing their time and financial support. During the process, individuals find creative, personally satisfying ways to serve their community, intergroup relationships are improved, and the community itself becomes a more attractive place in which to live.

Formation of and membership in recreation-oriented organizations does not always produce socially beneficial results of course. Organization members sometimes strongly disagree about the merits of a particular project or the methods to be followed in achieving certain results. When such disagreements lead to outbursts of anger and the harboring of permanent resentments, the result is disharmony and division rather than unity. Similarly, events sponsored by ethnic or special-interest groups do not always improve relationships with outsiders. Sometimes they can appear threat-

ening or be taken as challenges to other groups, causing alienation and tension within the community. Occasionally, they lead to outbreaks of hostility that result in property damage and serious injury to some of the participants and innocent bystanders.

IMPACT ON SOCIETY AS A WHOLE

The effects of recreation on the individual and family have a cumulative impact on society as a whole. As mentioned earlier, recreation helps individuals learn society's rules and appreciate the need to observe them. It therefore plays an important role in the preservation of social order. The contributions of recreation to the prevention of delinquency and crime are especially valuable. It is generally recognized that children, teenagers, and adults are less likely to engage in antisocial acts if their environments contain adequate, attractive, and readily accessible recreation opportunities. Even in rural areas, increasing numbers of communities are developing teenage recreation programs to combat rising behavioral problems resulting from boredom, increased mobility, and reduced parental control. Similarly, recreation can play a significant role in the rehabilitation of lawbreakers; unfortunately, many correctional institutions currently do not have the space or funding available to provide adequate recreation opportunities.

Recreation can help society survive during difficult periods. Public libraries, for example, were a haven during the depression era for the unemployed and are a refuge for many who are out of work today. They are a safe, comfortable place to spend time and find opportunities for socializing, self-improvement, and entertainment without charge. The arts are also a valuable source of comfort and fulfillment in troubled times. In Seattle, for example, when the Boeing Corporation laid off 50,000 workers in 1970 and the city's unemployment rate reached 17 percent, just surviving became the main purpose in life. Individuals who had been completely immersed in their work suddenly found themselves facing an uncertain future. Many discovered the pleasures of the parks, libraries, and museums; attendance at free concerts, film showings, and art fairs soared. In response to this show of interest, Seattle established its first fully staffed and funded Municipal Arts Commission. The Seattle Symphony also had its first completely sold out season. Apparently, many jobless families found so much solace in the music that they sacrificed other "essentials" in order to retain their symphony memberships.

On the other hand, recreation also contributes to social disorder. Some recreation facilities encourage socially undesirable behavior by providing gathering places that are attractive to antisocial groups and suitable locations for criminal activity. Theft, vandalism, assault, prostitution, and drug dealing have become serious problems, particularly in certain urban parks. Much of the social value of these facilities is lost because most citizens are afraid to use them. Voters in some communities have become so disillusioned by this antisocial behavior that they have rejected proposals for new parks and playgrounds. Crime is also negatively affecting recreation at extraurban locations. Many state

parks, national parks, and national forest areas now have crime problems of the type previously only found in crowded urban environments.

Society has also been subjected to an increase in recreation-associated "white collar" crime. One example is the fraudulent marketing techniques employed in the sale of recreation products or vacation experiences. Dishonest practices in the sale of recreation properties such as cottage sites have also become a serious social problem. A few years ago, as many as 9 out of 10 land developers violated the law by dispensing inaccurate, incomplete, or misleading information to the buying public. Better government controls and increased buyer awareness are reducing the harm caused by these fraudulent practices but it is estimated that one in five developers still uses somewhat deceptive procedures.

Society also faces user-conflict problems in connection with recreation resources. Farmers and persons owning property near beaches, lakes, or streams are frequently annoyed and sometimes threatened by hunters, fisherpersons, and other recreating trespassers. Other common sources of conflict associated with recreation include: the fouling of public parks by people walking their dogs; the use of parks for heavy drinking, loud radio playing, vehicle cruising, and other boisterous activities that interfere with some people's ability to enjoy the amenities; and the desire of two or more incompatible groups of recreation users to enjoy the same limited resources (for example, small inland lakes, scenic rivers, and trails).

Earlier in this section it was

pointed out that recreation can bring people together. This aspect of recreation can act as a powerful unifying force not only within a nation but also on an international level. For instance, opportunities to participate in international athletic competitions, sporting events, and cultural exchanges increase contacts between people from many different societies. The interchanges that take place are often helpful in removing cultural barriers and promoting mutual feelings of respect that bring unity to peoples of the world community. Similarly, within a nation, recreation can be used to increase contacts between the general public and special populations (the elderly, mentally and physically handicapped, economically disadvantaged, and people with various emotional problems). In so doing, many of these people who have been isolated and uninvolved can be drawn into the mainstream of community life and helped to become more productive members of society.

Again, it must be remembered that the results are not always positive. Interchanges during recreation can alienate people as well as bring them closer together. Sometimes, this is the result of personality or cultural differences over which society has little control. However, it can be because of a lack of organization, supervision, or direction. Organizations offering opportunities for people to meet and interact can ensure that these interchanges are beneficial to the individuals concerned and to society in general by insisting on strong and sensitive leadership whether the persons involved are paid professionals or volunteers.

On a broader scale, recreation

can also be divisive. Although the formation of recreation-oriented organizations unites individuals with similar interests, it can also isolate them from the rest of society and reinforce their differences and prejudices. Similarly, sports, children's camps, and youth-oriented organizations separated the sexes, at least until very recently. In the same way, recreation programs designed for one particular age or cultural group tend to fragment rather than unify society.

Recreation can affect society in many other ways. Its contributions to health are of major significance. A lack of physical or mental fitness reduces a society's ability to defend itself. Poor health negatively affects a citizen's potential to contribute to society in an economic, physical, cultural, intellectual, and leadership capacity. In addition, society loses economically because of the costs of medical and family welfare services. Illness alone is said to cost about $250 billion a year in the United States. If, as some studies suggest, a high proportion— perhaps 50 percent— of illnesses could be avoided or minimized by people controlling their weight, getting adequate exercise, and limiting their use of cigarettes, alcohol, and other drugs, the impact of recreation would be considerable. However, whether the results of recreation are beneficial or detrimental to a population's health depends largely on the choices the majority of citizens make. The involvement of large numbers of people in physically active and emotionally satisfying forms of recreation has a very positive impact on the maintenance and restoration of good physical and mental health. Conversely, the involvement of millions of people in

recreation activities that involve drinking, smoking, and consuming excessive amounts of high-calorie snack foods is likely to have negative effects. Recreation-related injuries and fatalities also have a negative impact. Obviously, it is in the best interests of society to provide attractive alternatives to potentially destructive forms of recreation and to offer the leadership, guidance, and instruction that will allow more people to participate in recreation activities without running the risks of serious adverse effects.

Another important aspect of recreation that affects society is its ability to create employment opportunities. In many cities and extraurban resort areas, large proportions of the population work in hotels, restaurants, shops, and a wide variety of sports, cultural, and entertainment facilities. Many others are employed in the construction or maintenance of recreation resources or the manufacture or repair of recreation goods. In economically depressed areas and underdeveloped nations, tourism frequently provides a source of sorely needed revenue to improve existing social conditions. At the same time, however, the influx of large numbers of tourists can have a destructive effect on the environment, the lifestyles, and the culture of the permanent population.

The setting aside of land for recreation purposes can also have significant nonrecreational advantages to society. Urban parks, for example, have a definite effect on the environment in the immediate area especially when covered with large trees. The greenery reduces temperatures and the sun's glare, acts as a barrier to noise, traps dust, and lowers the levels of other air

pollutants. In some cases, trees can also act as wind barriers. Recreation land is sometimes important to society because it protects environmentally significant areas from development. This can be particularly important in the case of areas that are subject to flash flooding or severe erosion. Recreation resources that include wetlands which are major aquifer-recharge areas or important stream sources may preserve community water supplies. Coastal parks and citizen interest in protecting water areas for swimming, fishing, and boating often prevent the filling or pollution of wetlands and estuaries that are essential breeding and nursery areas for commercially important fish and shellfish. Other recreation lands— especially the larger, more remote national parks and wilderness areas — preserve glacial formations, rare species of flora and fauna, and natural habitats that are of great scientific significance. Similarly, many resources of historical or cultural significance would not be preserved for present and future generations if they were not also of recreational value. At the same time, of course, the use and overuse of such resources for recreation purposes causes damage that in some cases is irreversible. The threat of forest fire and its accompanying detrimental effects is also increased by the presence of recreation participants who are careless with their campfires, cigarettes, and matches.

RECREATION PRODUCES SOCIAL CHANGE

Recreation can actually stimulate changes in society. It can affect a society's belief and change its social structure.

Impact on Society's Beliefs. Since recreation occupies a steadily increasing portion of people's time, it has a growing ability to influence attitudes and behavior.

If a large enough portion of the population regularly engages in recreation activities that foster attitudes or behavior patterns that differ considerably from those that currently prevail, the attitudes and behavior of the rest of the population may begin to change. Some examples of American social attitudes and values that have been influenced by recreation include:

- Changes in attitudes toward race, especially those concerning the place of black citizens in society; the status of internationally famous black performers such as Marian Anderson (Figure 3.9), exceptional athletes like Jackie Robinson (the first black to play major league baseball), and television programs such as "Roots" (seen by 130 million Americans during its original broadcast in 1977) have helped reduce racial prejudice.
- Improvement in attitudes toward women and their role in society; the increasing participation of women in demanding or dangerous competitive sports (tennis, gymnastics, long-distance running, downhill skiing, race car driving, skydiving) and their considerable achievements are forcing society to change its long-standing beliefs regarding women's physical capabilities and to remove some of the traditional restrictions that have barred females from many activities and occupations.
- Changes in attitudes toward social values and mores; participation in certain recreation activities, exposure to peer pressure during recreation, the lifestyles of favorite athletes and entertainers, and the influences of the broadcast, record, and film media have all had a tremendous effect on the way large numbers of Americans behave and choose to live.

Although many of these changes in values and mores have been beneficial, a considerable number are detrimental to society. These include the growing acceptance of pornography, prostitution, and participation in casual sex (especially among the very young); gambling; the use of alcohol, marijuana, and other drugs; and violent and various other antisocial patterns of behavior.

Effect on Social Structure. Recreation also contributes to changes in the structure of society. It has done much to remove social barriers by creating numerous opportunities for individuals from different backgrounds to meet, get to know each other and, in many cases, become good friends. It has also helped reduce class distinctions. The media—television in particular—has played a major role in this regard, making a wide range of cultural experiences accessible to individuals regardless of their position in society. It has greatly increased people's knowledge and expanded their horizons. Consciously or subconsciously, it has affected the way they speak, dress, and behave. When the long-term effects of intermingling and interacting with different kinds of people during recreation are added, changes often take place that can obliterate most or all

Figure 3.9 A vast crowd and large radio audience hear black contralto Marian Anderson present her symbolic concert at Washington's Lincoln Memorial on Easter Sunday, 1939, after the Daughters of the American Revolution prevented her from performing in Constitution Hall because of her race. Widely reported by the press and movie newsreels, this incident brought home to millions of Americans the insidious and unconstitutional nature of racism.

of an individual's class-related characteristics.

Another factor that blurs class distinctions is the tendency for particular recreation activities to be less and less associated with specific social classes. At one time, as Chapter 2 pointed out, recreation choices were very much dependent on membership in a particular stratum of society with a few activities considered appropriate only for the lower classes and a great many activities reserved almost exclusively for the upper classes. Today, participation in any recreation activity generally depends only on personal preference and the ability to pay the necessary costs. Unfortunately, the latter requirement is often just as limiting and divisive as social restrictions used to be. And so, it can be said that recreation has helped destroy one kind of class structure only to replace it with another kind, this time a division of citizens according to their buying power.

POLITICAL SIGNIFICANCE

Recreation is of considerable political significance at all levels of government. Its importance varies according to its status in a region or country. Generally, recreation plays a larger role in the internal and external politics of a nation as it proceeds through the various stages of development. However, tourism-related matters can become major political issues in relatively underdeveloped societies.

INTERNAL POLITICAL SIGNIFICANCE

The political roles of recreation within a nation depend largely on its form of government. Totalitarian governments frequently use recreation as a political tool to make indoctrination palatable and mold citizen attitudes and behavior patterns. Basic ideologies and concepts of citizenship are taught through government involvement in recreation programs of all kinds and for all ages. Government agencies are in charge of every facet of the recreation experience from nursery school play and youth organization activities to adult sports and vacation programs. They also control the nature and content of cultural opportunities.

The political value of recreation can also be increased by controlling the nature of the facilities themselves. For example, Communist countries often provide sports, camping, and vacation opportunities for their citizens at facilities designed for large homogeneous groups rather than for individuals or family units. This can foster acceptance of communal life and de-emphasize the importance of the individual or strong family ties.

Generally, in democracies such as Canada, the United States, and the countries of Western Europe, the internal political aspects of recreation are low key and less evident. This does not mean that they do not exist. All governments consider it expedient to stimulate feelings of pride, patriotism, and a sense of common purpose in the populace. This is done in a variety of ways including the government funding of cultural resources and programs and the designation and celebration of national holidays.

Local-, intermediate-, and national-level politicians often find that the promise or provision of new recreation facilities and programs can be counted on to appeal to a substantial number of voters, thereby contributing to the success of their election campaigns. For instance, during the 1976 campaign for the U.S. presidency, political commentators suggested that President Ford's announcement of a $1.5 billion federal park program was politically motivated. The announcement came one month before election day at a time when public opinion polls indicated that the other presidential candidate, Mr. Carter, was pulling ahead of Mr. Ford (Figure 3.10). Critics maintained that the announced program was not new, but a compilation of existing proposals, many of which were already under congressional consideration.

Governments also regulate or ban certain forms of recreation for political reasons. This is often the case when one form of government is overthrown and replaced with another, or when the government wishes to change its ideological direction. For example, Mao Zedong's Cultural Revolution in the People's Republic of China included a purge of many art forms and recreation activities, especially those that were closely identified with earlier political regimes or with Western civilization. Curtailment of these activities not only eliminated any tendency they might have had to perpetuate no longer acceptable attitudes or patterns of behavior but also it made way for the introduction of art forms and activities designed to foster the new ideologies.

A major change in leadership or direction, however, is not required for the introduction of censorship or restrictive regulations concerning recreation. Specific activities may receive censure at any time a government feels that they

Figure 3.10 **Nationally syndicated editorial page cartoonist Jeff MacNelly's drawing suggests President Ford's $1.5 billion federal parks program announcement near the end of the 1976 presidential campaign was a political ploy intended to extinguish candidate Jimmy Carter's apparent lead in popularity.**

Reprinted by permission of the Chicago Tribune—New York News Syndicate.

threaten a nation's well-being. Any form of recreation that is apt to foster discontent or disunity, challenge the social or political system, dilute or destroy a nation's culture, or interfere with the achievement of national goals may fall into this category. Examples include:

- Certain recreation-related consumer goods such as television sets and automobiles; mass production of such items may interfere with the nation's commitment to increase its manufacturing of essentials and export goods, encourage private rather than communal recreation patterns, increase the demand for services (roads), or cause discontent (television viewers discovering the disparities between their living conditions and those of people in other areas or nations).
- Recreation activities that are unique to one particular subculture or region;

some governments regard these as undesirable because they are divisive and may reinforce lifestyles that are considered inappropriate.
- Recreational travel by citizens internally or abroad; opportunities to see how other people live and to exchange ideas with persons of other regions and nationalities are sometimes restricted because it is feared such experiences may cause discontent.
- Mass influxes of foreign tourists; these may be discouraged or prohibited because they have the potential to disrupt the lives of citizens, overtax the nation's resources, and pollute or destroy native culture.
- Artists and printed or recorded works from foreign countries; these may introduce ideas or encourage lifestyles that the government deems undesirable, interfere with the development of the nation's culture, or break down barriers between nations that

governments wish to preserve because they are considered politically useful.

These last mentioned recreation resources—books, radio and television programs, motion pictures, records, performing artists—are considered especially dangerous because they have such a tremendous impact on youth. These items are often almost impossible to control once limited entry is permitted.

Canada, for example, has regulated broadcasting and publishing operations to try to reduce the negative effect that American magazines and television programming are having on the preservation and development of a uniquely Canadian culture. Television programming of American origin, however, remains a serious problem. A large proportion of the population lives close enough to the border to be able to receive American broadcasts, and the spread of cable television stations is increasing the ability of American networks to reach those who live in more remote locations.

Even governments that decide to take a more aggressive approach sometimes find total control is beyond their reach. A number of governments that consider modern pop-rock music a decadent and undesirable art form, for example, formerly banned records and tours by Western artists who perform this type of music. Nevertheless, the performers and their material have become well-known to large numbers of young people in some of these countries. This was accomplished by surreptitiously listening to foreign broadcasts and obtaining black market recordings, sheet music, and publications featuring news about the performers and their music. Gradually, some of these nations have found it politically expedient to yield to public pressure. For example, approved forms of pop-rock music can now be played openly in the Soviet Union at restaurants and dances, and selected foreign artists have been allowed to present rock concerts at designated locations since 1977.

Finally, recreation can be a useful tool for political factions and special interest groups wishing to obtain concessions from their governments. Knowing how significant recreation is to the economy of a region or nation and how important it is to ordinary citizens, these special groups sometimes attempt to impede recreation in order to gain political power. Examples include:

- Farmers being urged in 1978 by leaders of the American Agriculture Movement to close their lands to fisherpersons, hunters, and other recreation seekers; it was hoped this would lead to manufacturers of recreation goods, retailers, tourist facility operators, and members of sportsperson's clubs petitioning the government to guarantee better prices for farm crops.
- Businesses, associations, and individuals being encouraged by supporters of the Equal Rights Amendment to vacation or hold conventions only in states that ratified the amendment; the dollar losses to tourist-oriented businesses and city economies (estimated to currently exceed $100 million) were expected to result in local political pressures being placed on state legislatures to adopt the amendment.
- The bombing campaign begun by the Basque separatist organization in Spain during the summer of 1979 and directed specifically at tourism-related facilities (air terminals, railroad stations, festivals, beach resorts, res-

taurants, state-run hotels); the intention was to disrupt the economically important Spanish tourist industry forcing the government to release imprisoned Basque terrorist suspects and grant Basque independence.

There is not much doubt that recreation will be used more frequently for political purposes if it continues to grow in economic importance. Tourism can be disrupted fairly easily and result in widespread economic discomfort. In Spain, for example, tourism at the usually crowded Mediterranean beach resorts was reduced by as much as 40 percent during July 1979.

INTERNATIONAL POLITICAL SIGNIFICANCE

Governments also use recreation for international political purposes. They attempt to nurture national pride and achieve world prestige through successful participation in international sports and athletic events or by sending cultural exhibits, films, groups of performing artists, or theatrical companies to other nations. In some cases, art forms distributed abroad such as motion pictures, television programs, exhibits, books, plays, and dance presentations are largely propaganda designed to impress or indoctrinate people in other nations rather than just to provide enjoyment.

Contacts between nations in a setting that is recreational can nurture feelings of good will. For example, a sport was used to initiate détente between the People's Republic of China and the United States. In 1971, following two years of U.S. government overtures, a team of American table tennis players was invited to compete with

a Chinese team in Peking. A few American correspondents were permitted to accompany them. This was the first time since the establishment of the Communist government that Americans had been admitted into China, and this so-called "Ping-Pong diplomacy" was followed by further lessening of tension and the beginning of more normal diplomatic and trade relationships.

Sports are also being used by major political powers as part of their efforts to win favor with the citizens of Third World nations. At least half the population in many of these countries is under 20 years of age, and therefore sports programs are an ideal way to reach the hearts and minds of the people. A highly respected foreign coach can shape the thinking and ideology of large numbers of young, impressionable athletes. Frequently, the coach's influence also reaches native coaches, the families of the athletes, local officials, and the general public. In 1975, the Soviet Union assigned 7000 sports coaches and technicians to Third World nations to help develop sports programs. The United States has a budget of about $250,000 a year for international athletic exchanges; using these funds, a total of 76 American teams visited other nations in 1975.

World political pressure brought about by sports boycotts and exclusions undoubtedly helped ease racial discrimination in the Union of South Africa. The negative reaction of many nations to the apartheid policy of the government resulted in the exclusion of South African athletes and sports teams from many international events, including the Olympic Games. South Africa was unhappy about these exclusions since the majority of white South Africans value acceptance by the world, particularly in the world of sport. Therefore, to appease the protesters, the government began to allow some racially mixed teams in international competition. By 1976, enough citizens were questioning apartheid's negative effects on sports to cause the Ministry of Sports to adopt modest measures of integration including certain multiracial sporting events in South Africa.

The Significance of the Olympic Games. Unfortunately, international recreational events have often been used as forums for political struggles. This is a particularly serious problem in the case of the Olympic Games and threatens their survival. Now that television audiences of more than 1 billion persons watch the Games, some groups are regarding the event as the world's largest political stage.

DEVELOPMENT OF THE OLYMPIC GAMES AS A POLITICAL FORUM

The Olympic Games, the world's foremost amateur competition, began as a festival in classical Greece. Hostilities and jealousies were temporarily set aside to permit a time for the enjoyment and glorification of sport. Corruption, commercialism, and excessive national pride gradually destroyed their meaning and the Games were abolished in A.D. 393. They were revived, however, in 1896 as a means of keeping the spirit of amateur sport alive. At the time, the International Olympic Commission (IOC)

was formed and charged with providing an opportunity at four-year intervals for the world's outstanding amateur athletes to meet and compete not as representatives of their individual countries but as individuals.

Gradually, use of the Olympic Games for political purposes increased:

- The 1936 Games, held in Berlin, were used as a showcase for Naziism; German Chancellor Adolf Hitler left the stadium rather than congratulate a medal-winning black athlete (the American runner, Jesse Owens).
- An official count of the number of medals awarded each country was instituted in 1952; from then on, competition between nations rather than individuals received emphasis.
- At the 1968 Games in Mexico City, military forces were used to prevent student organizations from disrupting the proceedings for political purposes; two black American sprinters used clenched-fist salutes when on the victory stand to protest the living conditions of blacks in American ghettos and, by this act, drew the world's attention to the real political potential of the Olympic Games.
- At the 1972 Games in Munich, West Germany, terrorists attempted to use the political potential of the Games to gain the release of 200 Arabs from Israeli prisons. They were unsuccessful but, unfortunately, this act of terrorism resulted in the murder of 11 Israeli athletes who had been used as hostages.
- In 1974, the president of the International Olympic Committee made the following appeal:

On behalf of the International Olympic Committee, I appeal to every single sportsman and woman not to come to the Olympic Games if they wish to make use of sport for political purposes. . . . We all have our own beliefs; we all have our friends and enemies; but the aim of the Olympic Movement is to subjugate these in the fellowship which is enshrined in the intertwining Olympic rings representing the five continents of the world wedded together in sport, peace, and friendship. If this is not accomplished, then the Olympic Movement and all sport, whether amateur or professional, is doomed. Instead of progressing toward the common ideals, we shall retreat into barbarism.[6]

In spite of, or perhaps because of the events at the previous Games, the 1976 Olympics at Montreal, Canada, were exploited for political purposes to a degree never attempted at previous meets. First, the host country, Canada, surprised the world and set a precedent by denying admittance to the athletes from Taiwan as long as they insisted on competing as "the Republic of China." Canada justified this action on the ground that it recognized the Communist mainland as the Republic of China and could not similarly recognize the Nationalist Government on Taiwan. However, Taiwan had already been officially accepted into the competition under the name Republic of China by the IOC, the

[6] Chris Basher, "Montreal: The XXI Olympiad," *1977 Britannica Book of the Year,* Encyclopaedia Britannica, Inc., Chicago, 1977.

body that is solely responsible for accreditation. According to Olympic rules, the host country is bound to permit free access to the Olympic site for all IOC approved participants.

Since Canada was in error according to Olympic rules, the Nationalist Government refused to give in. Canada continued to insist that the team could not use the name Republic of China but compromised somewhat by announcing that their flag and national anthem would be used during the presentation ceremony if any of the athletes from Taiwan won a medal. Since this was still not acceptable to the Nationalist Government, the 42 competitors went home. Some commentators suggested that this confrontation was caused by pressure from the People's Republic of China coupled with Canada's need to continue exporting large quantities of wheat to that country.

A second political crisis developed during the 1976 Olympic Games concerning New Zealand's participation. In this case, the controversy arose because a New Zealand rugby football team was touring South Africa. As a result, 16 African nations threatened to withdraw unless New Zealand athletes were barred from the Games. (Many nations will not compete against South African teams because of the government's apartheid policies.) The IOC refused to comply with this demand, and New Zealand's athletes continued to take part. A total of 24 nations then withdrew in protest and the Games proceeded without another 655 competitors, several of whom were potential gold medal winners.

The incidents at the 1976 Games were minor skirmishes compared to the confrontations that developed concerning the 1980 Olympics in Moscow. Preparations were proceeding relatively smoothly at the end of 1979. The Soviet government appeared anxious to avoid political disputes like those that had plagued the previous Games because it would be the first time the prestigious event had been held in a Communist nation. Then, in late December, the Russians moved more than four army divisions into Afghanistan ostensibly to oust the pro-Soviet but uncooperative president and quell a growing Muslim rebellion. Western nations, the People's Republic of China, Muslim countries, and a number of other Third World nations condemned the Soviet action. Many nations believed strong countermeasures were warranted because it was the first time since 1945 that Russian troops had been used to seize a nation not previously under direct Soviet control. Some feared that the move was the first step toward Soviet dominance of the Persian Gulf petroleum-producing region by establishing naval or air bases in the area or undertaking a similar intervention in Iran.

A U.N. Security Council resolution calling for immediate withdrawal of foreign troops from Afghanistan was vetoed by the Soviet Union. Seventeen Muslim and Third World nations then introduced a U.N. General Assembly resolution deploring the Soviet intervention and calling for withdrawal; it passed 104 to 18 with 18 nations abstaining and 12 delegates absent. This unusually strong condemnation of Russia was largely the result of 78 Third World nations voting in favor while only 9 voted no, 18 abstained, and 10 were absent.

It was in this context that the question of participation in the 1980 Moscow Olympic Games became a matter of worldwide concern. Saudi Arabia announced that it would not take part. President Carter proposed that the United States not participate and that the Games be moved to another nation or cancelled if Soviet troops were not withdrawn from Afghanistan by mid-February. This was seen as a much more effective inducement for the Soviets to withdraw than the other steps that he ordered. The latter included increasing U.S. military forces in the Middle East, starting cooperative defense programs with the People's Republic of China, reviving military equipment deliveries to Pakistan, banning Russian fishing in American waters, and halting the sale to the Soviet Union of advanced technological items and 17 million metric tons of much needed grain. Analysts felt that the Soviet government would view the possible failure of the Games as a much greater threat because it was counting on gaining international respectability and great propaganda benefits from saturation coverage of a successful Olympics by the world's media. They suggested that the substitution of "free world games" or even a boycott by a substantial number of nations would produce a loss of face both at home and abroad, which would be difficult to counteract. So the threat of nonparticipation in an international recreation event became a strategic weapon that was apparently viewed as being potentially more powerful than military movements, alliances with arch enemies, or economic sanctions.

As it turned out, the 1980 Olympic Games did not prove as

effective a political weapon as the United States had hoped. Although 65 nations stayed away from the Games, only 36 of these had actually intended to send athletes. The Games took place in Moscow as scheduled and the Soviet Union declared the boycott attempt a failure since so many athletes and nations — 6000 competitors representing 81 countries — had chosen to participate.

However, the Games did not produce nearly the benefits the Soviet Union had expected. Around 2300 athletes were missing from nations that represented 73 percent of the gold medals won by non-Communist countries during the 1976 Games. The absence of important sporting nations such as Argentina, Canada, Japan, Kenya, Norway, the People's Republic of China, the United States, and West Germany definitely affected the level of competition in most of the 22 sports. Much of the prestige and opportunities for propaganda that the Soviet Union had hoped to gain were also lost as 16 teams from competing countries either refused to take part in any of the ceremonies or chose not to display their national flags or use their national anthems, attendance at the Games by foreign visitors dropped from an expected 300,000 to less than 150,000, and the saturation television coverage afforded previous summer Olympic Games did not materialize. Although NBC had paid over $87 million for the privilege, the network decided not to broadcast the Games as planned. As a result, Americans did not have access to live telecasts and the coverage that was provided generated little interest. Similarly, the opening ceremonies, a three-hour, carefully

orchestrated spectacle, was not seen live in Canada or 15 nations of Western Europe.

Whether the decision to boycott has any effect on the situation in Afghanistan, it is definitely encouraging a reassessment of what the Games have become. This may result in steps being taken to de-emphasize the political aspects of the event (it has already been proposed that all visible signs of national involvement such as flags and anthems should be banned) and to reorganize the Games as competitions between *individuals* (people should be allowed to enter individually rather than through their nation's Olympic committees). It has also been proposed that the IOC arrange for the establishment of a permanent, neutral site (possibly Greece) for the Games to avoid any future problems with either visas or boycotts.

If these types of political confrontations continue in the future, the Olympic Games will never again be a contest of the world's best athletes. Unless the IOC finds ways to depoliticize the Games and strengthen enforcement of its rules, host countries will exclude nations whom they do not recognize, and causes of all types will be promoted by demonstrations, threats, and boycotts.

Another indication of the increasing political significance of the Olympic Games is the tremendous efforts to win medals now being made by a number of governments. Several nations have initiated substantial government-funded programs to find and train the best possible athletes. The German Democratic Republic (East Germany) undertook such a program in preparation for the 1976 (and

subsequent) Olympic Games. Its goal is to produce outstanding athletes who will demonstrate the superiority of their society and way of life by remarkable achievements in international competition. The program so far has been eminently successful; in the 1976 Summer Olympics, the German Democratic Republic won a total of 90 medals (compared to the Soviet Union's 125 and the United States' 94). Special emphasis on the training of women for swimming events produced some astonishing results. East German women completely dominated this event winning 10 out of the 11 titles and breaking 8 world records.

This politically oriented emphasis on the winning of medals to build national prestige is stimulating other governments to do likewise. Even some of the smallest nations have begun such programs. If the current trend continues, future Olympic Games will be dominated by professionals who are selected, trained, and supported by the state rather than by amateurs who are selected by sports associations and who excel because of the dedication, skill, and self-sacrifice of themselves, their families, and their coaches. Just as in professional sport, success will generally depend on the level of financial support.

It was probably inevitable that national achievement would receive added emphasis as instant communications made it possible for more than a billion television viewers, radio listeners, and newspaper readers to become personally engrossed in the Games. An additional 800 million persons will probably have an interest in future Games because of the entry of the People's Republic of China and other nations into the 1980 Olympics. If so, well over half of the world's people may be directly involved to some degree. Never before has the interest of so many individuals been focused on a single event.

Therefore, although purists' complaints about the loss of individual amateur emphasis are justified, the politicization of the Olympic Games may create the greatest opportunity to date for recreation to contribute to human welfare. If security against terrorist activity can be assured and political confrontations minimized, future Games will be beneficial to the world community in four ways.

First, the Olympics will provide more recreation for a greater number of people than any other event in history as they anticipate, view, read about, and discuss the competitions. Second, the viewing of the Games on television will stimulate interest in the outside world and greatly expand knowledge of the world community; this will occur even though political propaganda may be injected into the commentaries and biased coverage created by program editing. Third, if massive media coverage has its usual effect, the Games will become the greatest universal stimulus to individual participation in vigorous recreation that the world has ever known and the benefits to physical and mental health should be proportionately large. Finally, the Games will provide a highly visible forum where some of the ambitions, frustrations, and aggressions of nations can be released in a relatively harmless way by appearing on world television, winning a medal, establishing a new world record, or even scoring political points with limited boycotts.

Of course, there will be negative aspects of an expanded and politicized Olympic program. These will probably include: athletes damaged emotionally by extreme pressures to excel both at home and at the Games themselves; an overemphasis on sports programs to the detriment of other vital social and environmental concerns; and the inevitable harm to the pride of some participating nations. The challenge to humanity— especially the tens of thousands of professionals associated with sports and athletics— is to make sure that the benefits far exceed the costs.

SIGNIFICANCE OF GOVERNMENT INVOLVEMENT

The involvement of various levels of government in recreation has already been mentioned in connection with human rights, psychological importance, education, physical health, social benefits, and political significance. It will also be discussed in several subsequent chapters.

The degree to which a government becomes responsible for the provision of recreation opportunities depends on a nation's level of economic development. As a country progresses economically, greater needs for public recreation develop, and more funds for government programs become available. In Chapter 2, ways in which the national, state, and local governments of the United States became increasingly involved in recreation following the recreation renaissance were described. Since that time, land, facilities, programs, and employees have gradually been added until recreation is now a major component of American government. Because the recreation functions of government are not always assigned to separate administrative units or included as distinct budget items, it is impossible to provide complete statistics indicating the full magnitude of involvement. However, some indicators of the present magnitude of government recreation-oriented activities in the United States are given in Table 3.4. The governments of a number of the other developed nations are becoming more extensively involved as their countries progress into the more advanced stages of the recreation revolution.

ECONOMIC SIGNIFICANCE

Recreation has tremendous economic significance, especially in the developed nations where so many recreation activities involve travel and the purchase of numerous goods and services (Figure 3.11). In the United States, for example, Florida alone receives more than 35 million recreation-oriented visits by out-of-state residents annually.

These visitors generate some 600,000 jobs and add 3/4 billion dollars to state tax revenues while spending a total of about $16 billion. This amount is more than the gross national products of Ireland ($11 billion), New Zealand ($15 billion), or Portugal ($15.5 billion). On a national scale, tourism is currently America's third largest industry, generating revenues of $215 billion (about 9 percent of the GNP).

It is not uncommon for people in developed nations to spend more money on recreation than on any

Table 3.4 Indicators of the Magnitude of Government Involvement

Indicators of the Magnitude of Government Involvement in Recreation in the United States

More than 80 federal government agencies, commissions, and councils operate over 300 separate "outdoor recreation-related" programs.

Local, state, and federal government support for cultural facilities and programs exceeds $1 billion annually.

The eight federal agencies that manage land for recreation have 301 million ha (760 million acres) under their jurisdiction, much of which is used for concentrated or dispersed recreation.

These federal agencies spend an average of over $600 million a year for capital costs and maintenance associated with their recreation programs employing over 12,000 permanent employees and more than 6000 person-years of seasonal help in the process.

The federal government spends about $10 million each year on encouraging foreign tourists to visit the United States.

The National Park Service, one of the eight agencies involved in the management of land for recreation, has an annual budget of over $350 million and employs more than 7600 permanent staff to administer its 12 million ha (30 million acres) of land.

A total of $475 million in federal revenue-sharing grants and Department of Housing and Urban Development block grants was spent on state and local recreation and cultural programs between 1972 and 1975.

State government agencies manage over 18 million ha (45 million acres) of land for recreation purposes and spend nearly $675 million annually in their management.

The National Endowment for the Arts allocated $27 million in federal money to be used as matching funds by 75 arts organizations in 23 states in 1978.

States have issued $2.8 billion worth of bonds for recreation land acquisition and development since 1960.

In 1976, Congress amended the Land and Water Conservation Fund Act so that as much as $10.8 billion in federal grants may be made available for state and federal recreation and historic preservation programs during the period 1978–1989.

Local governments have 4.5 million ha (11 million acres) of recreation land and spend about $2.5 billion annually on "outdoor recreation" programs.

The California state legislature recently provided $25 million in matching funds to aid local government agencies in acquiring and developing public recreation areas.

The state park systems of the United States employ over 45,000 people and spend over $700 million a year in managing some 4 million ha (10 million acres) of land.

other single item, including housing, food, clothing, health care, or education. In the United States, total annual recreation-related expenditures are said to be as high as $218 billion or an average of about $990 per capita. Even this estimate is probably far lower than it should be because it is difficult to identify all purchases of this kind. Money spent on items such as television sets, sports equipment, camping gear, children's toys, and theme park or movie theater admission tickets is fairly easy to measure. Items of this type are usually included in recreation-related expenditure estimates. On the other hand, it is extremely difficult to determine what proportion of the money spent on items such as food, housing, furniture, clothing, automobiles, and gasoline, or on the construction and maintenance of streets and highways, shopping centers, and churches, should be considered a recreation-related expenditure. Items such as these are usually excluded from estimates of recreation-related expenditures. In spite of such omissions, the economic impact is still enormous; some indicators of its magnitude are given in Table 3.5.

Recreation is also a major source of employment. It is almost as difficult to estimate the total number of people whose income is recreation-related as it is to determine recreation-related expenditures, and for the same reasons. It is fairly easy to determine the number of people who are directly involved full time or part time in the provision of recreation services (over 5 million Americans) or in the manufacture, distribution, sales, repair, or construction of recreation goods and facilities. It is also possible to obtain a reasonably accurate estimate of the number of individuals who are employed by the various levels of government to provide recreation programs or resources on a full-time or seasonal basis (about 400,000 persons in the United States). Estimating the number of people whose work is indirectly related to recreation is much more difficult. These people might be involved in the production or distribution of materials needed by the recreation industry (agricultural products, energy, lumber, paper), in the manufacture or construction of products that are not considered primarily recreational but nevertheless are used for recreation purposes (private homes, automobiles), or in the provision of services that help people take part in recreation activities (public transportation system employees, babysitters). The number of people employed in these kinds of jobs must be in the tens of millions.

Another way in which recreation is economically significant is its impact on a nation's balance of payments. The balance can be negative; the nation may spend more money abroad than it receives in payments from other nations. Currently, the United States is an example of this situation. Part of the problem in America's case is due to the fact that it imports more recreation-related products than it manages to sell abroad. Foreign items that are purchased extensively by the American consumer for recreation purposes include petroleum, television sets, cameras, stereos, athletic shoes, bicycles, motorcycles, and ski equipment.

In addition, the United States suffers economic losses from international tourism. Not only are there more Americans who travel abroad each year than there are visitors from foreign countries but also American tourists spend more during their travels, thereby adding to the balance-of-payments deficit by between $1 and $3 billion a year. This amount, however, is considerably less than it used to be because of the recent growth in international travel to the United States. Larger numbers of people are choosing the United States as a destination, and are staying longer, traveling greater distances during their visits, and

Figure 3.11 Recreation's economic impact is particularly evident in the City of Miami Beach, Florida, where dozens of hotels and their swimming pools, sundecks, and tennis courts have been crowded onto a narrow barrier island. A $25 million renovation of the pool and grounds has just been completed at the Fontainebleau Hilton (curved building). The 300-foot-wide beach has been pumped into place as part of a $65 million U.S. Army Corps of Engineers sand replenishment project.

Table 3.5 Indicators of Recreation Expenditures Magnitude

Indicators of the Magnitude of Recreation Expenditures in the United States[a]

About $15 billion a year is spent on the purchase of radios, television sets, stereo equipment, and other electronic merchandise.

Americans spend about $20 billion a year at fast-food restaurants such as McDonald's, Burger King, and Kentucky Fried Chicken.

About $5 billion a year is spent on the care and feeding of over 700 million pets.

Americans annually pay about $2 billion in admission fees to spectator events.

About 14.5 million households pay a monthly fee averaging $7 to have their TV sets hooked up to cables that transmit as many as 36 channels; of these households, 4 million pay an extra $8 to $10 a month to receive a package of movies, sports, and specials.

Each year, Americans spend an average of $90 per child on the purchase of toys; annual retail sales exceed $5 billion with dolls, road-racing sets, and electronic games each accounting for sales of about $500 million.

During their annual visits to 35 state and 2350 local fairs, Americans spend $1 billion.

Box office receipts in New York's Broadway theater district exceed $135 million a year and generate additional expenditures of over $300 million for restaurant meals, drinks, and hotel accommodations.

Annual expenditures on travel trailers, campers, motor homes, and other recreation vehicles exceed $4 billion.

Annual expenditures on hobby supplies total well over $1 billion.

Gambling costs Americans $60 billion year; Atlantic City's Resorts International Casino alone grosses $200 million a year.

Phonograph record and tape sales total between $3 and $4 billion a year.

Over $6 billion a year is spent on pleasure boating for boats, accessories, repairs, dockage fees, and fuel.

Americans spend $1 billion a year on the purchase of bicycles, accessories, and parts.

More than 17 million tourists visit New York City every year spending an estimated $2.5 billion.

Box office receipts at movie theaters exceed $2 billion a year.

Americans spend over $11.5 billion on books, magazines, and newspapers every year.

The vistor to a major amusement park spends an average of $12; total expenditures exceed $900 million a year.

Discotheques gross over $6 billion a year.

[a] Data are for the late 1970s.

spending more on goods to take home.

Unfortunately, nations that continuously have large balance-of-payments deficits also generally experience other financial problems. These include increased inflation of consumer goods and services and devaluation of their currencies in comparison to the stronger currencies of other nations. This too has happened to the United States. In some cases, if the negative effects of tourism and the purchase of foreign goods become very serious, a country may find it necessary to restrict its imports and regulate the amount of money its citizens may spend on foreign travel.

For some nations, of course, tourism can be a tremendous economic asset. Many nations gain much more than they lose from the annual recreation-related movement of about 266 million people who spend around $65 billion during their international travels (1978 figures). Britain, for instance, in spite of the growth in the number of its citizens traveling abroad (11.1 million in 1977), attracted larger numbers (11.5 million) of freer spending visitors from overseas who contributed $6 billion to the economy. This resulted in a net gain of $2 billion and many economically ben-

Table 3.5 Indicators of Recreation Expenditures Magnitude

Indicators of the Magnitude of Recreation Expenditures in the United States[a]

Americans spend over $55 billion a year on domestic travel for pleasure; foreign travel expenditures exceed $11 billion.

One billion copies of the 35¢ *TV Guide* magazine are purchased every year.

Americans spend about $17 billion a year on the purchase of sporting goods.

The purchase and installation of in-ground swimming pools costs home owners $2.5 billion a year.

Annual expenditures on running-related merchandise total more than $300 million a year, two-thirds of which are spent on shoes.

Annual soft drink sales exceed $11 billion; expenditures on alcoholic beverages exceed $12 billion.

Sales of hunting and fishing licenses total more than $340 million a year.

Americans spend over $250 million on the purchase of houseplants each year.

Annual expenditures on minor sports accessories include $15 million for fog-resistant plastic ski goggles and $12 million for headbands.

A record crowd of 70,000 paid just under $6 million to attend the 1978 Muhammed Ali–Leon Spinks fight at New Orlean's Superdome.

Skiing expenditures including travel, lodging, equipment, clothing, and lift tickets exceed $2 billion a year.

Americans annually spend over $4 billion on the purchase of newspapers and an equal amount on books.

American adults smoke an average of 200 packs of cigarettes a year for which they spend $18 billion.

Government sources estimate that Americans spend as much as $4 billion on pornographic materials and entertainment.

Americans annually spend over $700 million on the purchase of time-shared units at resorts with the price of a unit averaging about $4000 for one week's use per year.

Do-it-yourself projects account for about $30 billion of the annual $55 billion home improvement expenditure total; of these projects, about 75 percent are estimated to be nonessential in nature and are being undertaken by homeowners to improve or expand the recreational and aesthetic qualities of their home or yard.

Amateur photographers in the United States spend over $3 billion a year on cameras, film, and other accessories and materials.

[a] Data are for the late 1970s.

---

eficial side effects; it was estimated, for example, that 1.5 million jobs were directly related to international tourism.

Some of the smaller nations receive proportionally larger benefits. Most that rely on tourism as their primary source of income are favored with good beaches and climatic conditions. The Bahamas, for instance, with a population of less than 250,000 and a land area of 13,000 square kilometers (5000 square miles), attracts almost 1 million tourists a year, excluding cruise ship visitors. Tourism contributes well over $400 million to the nation's economy, thereby generating 70 percent of the GNP, 60 percent of government revenues, and 40 percent of the employment opportunities.

There are many other ways in which recreation has an economic impact. Some of these include:

- The effect on property values; land that is of value for recreation or is near recreation resources continues to bring considerably higher prices than similar land elsewhere — homes near parks, golf courses, lakes, or rivers are usually worth more.
- The generation of government revenues through taxes that are frequently paid in connection with recreation; these include sales taxes

derived from the purchase of goods and services, income taxes on wages earned in recreation-related jobs, property taxes from private and commercial properties that are partly or totally recreation-oriented, business and corporate taxes on recreation-related enterprises, gasoline taxes, and special taxes on amusements, restaurant meals, and hotel accommodations.

- The effect of recreation resources in attracting businesses and industries to locate in one area rather than another.
- The public relations value to companies of supporting cultural institutions or sponsoring sports programing and competitive events; the economic significance of associating a company's name with recreation resources is hard to determine but it can improve a company's image and increase profits.
- The beneficial effects of recreation participation on large numbers of individuals; such effects can increase productivity at work and save society and industry the costs of dealing with even more vandalism, crime, absenteeism, accidents, mental illnesses, physical ailments, and premature deaths brought on by boredom, suppressed emotions, loss of self-esteem, stress, and poor physical condition.

In addition, recreation has become extremely valuable to the publishing, newspaper, broadcasting, and advertising industries. It is impossible to estimate its actual worth but even a casual glance at the magazine and nonfiction sections in book stores, the content of daily newspapers, programs on television, or advertisements in magazines gives some idea of recreation's great value in attracting people's attention and selling merchandise.

Sometimes, however, recreation results in costs rather than benefits to individuals, society, or industry. Examples include:

- The lost wages and the costs of medical treatment that individuals and their families bear because of injuries sustained during recreation and the costs of damages to property incurred as a result of recreation activities.
- The decreased productivity of workers either through unnecessary absenteeism, inattentiveness, or lethargy at times of the year closely associated with recreation; examples are the opening of the baseball, fishing, or hunting seasons or the two-week holiday period around Christmas and New Year's.
- The economic repercussions of people relocating to be close to recreation amenities; such migrations can reduce the tax base in communities that lose population, depriving some of much needed revenue, while the influx of people into small communities may cause equally serious financial problems if the newcomers demand substantial improvements in public facilities and services.

There are also the high costs that industry and society must pay to solve some of the problems that are a direct result of recreation. These include the $500 million in public money that is spent each year on dog-related problems (picking up and disposing of strays, removing feces from public places, compensating farmers for livestock killed by dogs). Other examples are the $1 billion spent each year by the U.S. Coast Guard on small pleasure boat rescue operations and the $15 billion a year it is estimated problem drinkers cost employers in sick pay, accidents, lost production, and—especially in the case of foremen and executives—bad judgment.

RECREATION AS A LAND USE

In many of the developed nations, a greater proportion of the earth's surface is used for recreation than for any other purpose. This is because people in advanced societies have the time, money, and inclination to engage in a wide variety of recreation activities that require large areas of land.

Hunting is one of the most expansive recreation land uses. Land owners and their guests hunt on private farms, ranches, and woodlands. Individuals or small groups often lease private lands for hunting purposes; this is a particularly common practice in Europe. Much of the vast expanses of public lands in Canada and the United States are used extensively for hunting. Other activities that usually involve large areas are pleasure driving, hiking, skiing, snowmobiling, nature study, boating, fishing, and waterskiing. In some cases, especially pleasure driving and sightseeing, the property owners or controlling agencies may not even be aware that their land is supplying recreation opportunities.

Most land that is used intensively for recreation lies in or near urban areas. It includes city streets, shopping centers, schoolyards, public park systems, and a wide range of commercial recreation facilities from restaurants and movie theaters to marinas and amusement parks. However, as explained in Chapters 8 and 11, the land that receives the vast majority of recreation use is the land on which people actually live (Figure 3.12).

It is not easy to estimate the total area of land and water in a nation that is used for recreation. Values are usually available for intensively used public recreation lands but information on much of the dispersed use of other public lands and most of the recreation on

Figure 3.12 In some cases, the dominant role of private residences as recreation resources is clearly evident. Six portable swimming pools and much lawn furniture are visible in this photograph of backyards in Brooklyn, New York City.

private lands is usually inadequate. Table 3.6 gives an indication of the amount of land used for recreation in the United States. From these figures it is clear that at least 20 percent of the nation is either designated primarily as recreation land or used intensively for recreation. An additional 40 percent or more is used extensively for recreation. In the more highly developed European countries, the proportion of the land used for recreation is probably even higher. Although public hunting is not as prevalent in Europe as in the United States and Canada, traditional public access to footpaths through agricultural lands and private forests, moorlands, and hill country results in widespread recreation use of nonpublic lands in

the form of walking, hiking, scenic viewing, and nature study.

A second significant aspect of recreation as a land use is the rate at which changes are taking place. These changes are particularly pronounced in the United States where increased participation and affluence have produced rapid expansion of many types of recreation land. Public parks at the local, state, and federal levels have been expanded considerably. Commercial recreation enterprises have grown in both number and size of land holdings. However, the most spectacular changes have been in the growth of second home and retirement home communities. These are spreading over hundreds of square miles particularly in areas with cli-

matic or water resource advantages that facilitate recreation participation. These developments are so numerous and expansive they have become a major environmental problem especially where fragile wetlands or shorelines are involved. The amount of dispersed recreation use taking place on both public and private lands is growing rapidly because the increasing use of boats, canoes, motorcycles, snowmobiles, trucks, and four-wheel-drive vehicles has made many areas much more accessible.

RECREATION AS A CATALYST OF CHANGE

As is the case with so many things, the total significance of recreation to society is more than the sum of its individual parts. It is important as a human right, because of the magnitude of participation, and by reason of its psychological, physical, social, governmental, political, economic, and land-use consequences. In areas of the world where these effects are most evident, recreation is having a much more extensive impact than can be attributed to the total effect of each factor acting separately. Instead, the various influences combine and, in so doing, become a force that modifies the nature of whole societies. Traditional lifestyles are being altered, basic behavior patterns and beliefs are being changed, and governments are being forced to redirect their activities. Recreation is acting as one of the most powerful catalysts of change that the world has ever known.

Therefore, recreation is significant to us all not only because it is a major component of everyday life

Table 3.6 Proportion of U.S. Land Area Used for Recreation

Type of Land	Kinds of Resources Included	Estimated Area[a]
Public lands used primarily for recreation	City, county, and regional parks; state and national parks; parts of state forests, national forests, and other federal lands.	1,295,000 sq km (500,000 sq mi) 14 percent of the nation.
Public lands where recreation is one of several uses or a secondary use	Remainder of state and national forests, Bureau of Land Management lands, wildlife refuge lands, and reservoir areas.	1,766,380 sq km (682,000 sq mi) 18 percent of the nation.
Commercial recreation enterprises	Restaurants, bars, billiard halls, theaters, bowling centers, amusement parks, commercial golf courses, campgrounds, guest ranches, summer resorts, etc.	Unknown. 85,000 rural enterprises occupied 93,080 sq km (35,940 sq mi) or 2.6 percent of the nation in 1965. Total is much larger.
Nonprofit recreation resources and commercial lands used incidentally for recreation	Private and quasi-private groups such as country clubs, swimming clubs, hunting clubs, conservation clubs; youth, religious, and civic groups; land-holding industries, unposted farm land, industrial recreation land.	1,889,900 sq km (729,700 sq mi) 20 percent of the nation.
Private personal recreation lands	Areas used for recreation around private residences; vacation homes, and private extraurban lands used only for recreation of family and friends.	Unknown. Large and very significant.

[a] Data developed from U.S. Department of the Interior, Bureau of Outdoor Recreation, *Outdoor Recreation: A Legacy for America*, U.S. Government Printing Office, Washington, 1973.

that helps hold society together but also, paradoxically, because it is acting as such a potent catalyst of change. Decisions concerning recreation facilities and programs affect not only today's participants but also future generations as well. Our actions as consumers, voters, political representatives, or recreation professionals have long-term as well as immediate consequences. This should be kept in mind as the mechanics of recreation behavior and the provision of opportunities are examined in the chapters that follow.

DISCUSSION TOPICS

1. Is it necessary for all state, provincial, and national constitutions to contain clauses guaranteeing recreation as a basic human right?
2. Are all the psychologically significant aspects of recreation of equal importance?
3. What are the social effects of your own personal recreation behavior? Give examples of both the positive and negative social effects of recreation in your home community.
4. Is politics really detrimental to international sports and athletics? Justify your answer. "If "yes," how could political influences be eliminated?

5. How can recreation be both a major component of everyday life that helps hold society together and, at the same time, a catalyst that facilitates change?

FURTHER READINGS

Information on the significance of recreation is scattered through many sources and is very incomplete. Many basic textbooks have sections that mention some aspects of the significance of recreation. In the second edition of their book *Recreation in American Life,* published in 1972 by Wadsworth in Belmont, California, Reynold Carlson, Theodore Deppe, and Janet MacLean summarize the importance of recreation in the first chapter. Richard Kraus includes chapters on "Recreation and Human Values" and "Recreation and Social Functions" in *Recreation and Leisure in Modern Society* published in New York by Appleton-Century-Crofts in 1971. These and many other textbooks have useful chapters on the economic significance of recreation.

However, since recreation's impact on society changes rapidly both in nature and magnitude, a full appreciation of the present significance of recreation is only achieved by studying current events. Much up-to-date information can be obtained by regularly reading periodicals such as *Parks and Recreation,* published by the National Recreation and Park Association, the *Journal of Physical Education and Recreation* issued by the American Alliance for Health, Physical Education, Recreation, and Dance, or *Recreation Canada,* journal of the Canadian Parks/Recreation Association. Other good sources of current data are newspapers and newsmagazines although the information is often scattered through materials that are not concerned with recreation. Useful articles are found in local newspapers, in major national newspapers such as the *New York Times* (especially the Sunday edition), and in magazines such as *U.S. News and World Report, Time, Newsweek,* and *Business Week.*

More than 11,000 men and women of varying ages and backgrounds run across the Verrazano Narrows Bridge at the start of the New York City Marathon. Foot races are just one of the many recreation activities that take place on urban streets and roads.

4

EXTERNAL FACTORS AFFECTING RECREATION PARTICIPATION: ECONOMIC AND POPULATION FACTORS

CONCEPTS & PROBLEMS

Infinite Complexity
Ever-Changing Relationships
Stages in Economic Development
Three Economic Sectors
The Handicap of Poverty
Work Impact
Discretionary Income
Government Curbs and Stimuli
Thresholds and Dispersions
Asymmetrical Population Patterns
Four Population Growth Phases
Population Migration

Figure 4.1 Many factors contribute to the skiing experience in Colorado's Rocky Mountains including society's attitudes toward skiing, transportation availability, climate, topography, public ownership of mountain lands, commercial facility development, and the individual's motivations, economic status, and physical abilities.

The nature and extent of recreation participation depends on many features of an individual's recreation environment. In Chapter 1, these factors were divided into two groups— external components and personal components (Figure 1.5). The external components include the economic situation, employment patterns and conditions, taxes and government regulations, population characteristics, various social factors, and recreation resource accessibility. The personal components are the participant's personality and attitudes, knowledge and skills, sex, age, personal characteristics, occupation, discretionary income, personal possessions, and time available for recreation. In Part Two, the nature of these various factors and their effect on participation will be explored.

As each of these factors is examined, remember that the various components have been artificially separated and labeled so that some of their characteristics and affects on participation can be identified. In reality, however, these are never completely separate items but are really part of a continuum. Each identified component in the recreation environment model is actually a subsystem in which numerous components interact. Each of these extremely complicated subsystems in turn overlap other equally complex subsystems and all are inextricably interwoven. Similarly, the division into personal and external components is an arbitrary one; most of an individual's personal characteristics are, to some extent at least, functions of the external environment.

The great range in the size of recreation environments is another important feature that must be kept in mind when exploring the factors that affect participation. Some people have very confined recreation environments. Those who live in thinly populated, remote parts of undeveloped nations, for instance, may have little contact with the outside world. In such cases, the influences of the recreation environment may consist almost exclusively of those provided by family members, the farm, a relatively few neighbors, and a nearby hamlet. The only outside influences may be an occasional visitor on official business or a few items that are available for sale or barter at the village market or store.

In contrast, many people in developed societies now live in recreation environments that extend around the world. For example, consider two skiers at a resort in the Rocky Mountains (Figure 4.1). To get there, they traveled on an aircraft built in Seattle and based in New York that operates on fuel refined in New Jersey from Saudi Arabian crude oil. They ride up the mountain on a Swiss chairlift wearing ski clothing made in the United States and boots from Japan fitted with Austrian skis. The snow has been produced from moisture that evaporated from the Pacific Ocean. The quality of their experience depends to a great extent on the characteristics of this snow and the terrain it covers. But it is also dependent on the skiers' current physical condition, on their skills, and on the way they are treated by resort employees and other skiers. In the evening, they enjoy a meal highlighted by steaks from cattle raised in Colorado and wines produced in France. They dance to music recorded by artists of several nationalities and talk with people from many different states and backgrounds. They finish their day watching a late-night television movie photographed largely in Europe involving actors and film technicians from many countries. The film is running through projection equipment in New York and is reaching their bedroom television set over a complex network of cables, microwave relays, and transmitters.

At first, this situation may appear to be a far-fetched example. However, these kinds of complex recreation environments are becoming increasingly common as activities in the developed nations involve more long-distance travel and a greater dependency on specialized goods and services. Think of the complexity of the environments in which millions of people in dozens of countries watch or listen to the World Cup soccer final. But complexity is not restricted to recreation environments associated with ski resorts or major sports events. There is a tendency today for all types of recreation activities to become more complicated as aspirations grow, social conflicts increase, and more people are prepared to spend time and money in securing what they perceive to be a desirable experience.

In dividing a complex recreation environment into components, attributing too much importance to one or a few factors must also be avoided. For example, some sources give the impression that increases in population, discretionary income, personal mobility, and free time are solely responsible for the recent growth of extraurban recreation participation in the developed nations. Obviously, these factors have been important but many other components in the recreation environment contributed. A steady increase in the supply of recreation resources also played an important role. And a major factor has been the decision by millions of people to spend their extra time and money on certain kinds of recreation such as pleasure driving, swimming, fishing, and camping. Under different circumstances, increases in population, discretionary income, personal mobility, and free time could produce, instead, a much greater surge of participation in indoor activities or even nonrecreational activities such as the development of business enterprises. Therefore, cultural and social factors such as perceptions, attitudes, and advertising are as significant as more people, money, mobility, and free time, or the availability of resources. No doubt, there are many other factors that also contribute; all must be given equal attention.

The external and personal factors that affect recreation participation also differ in the degree to which their influence changes with time. Some factors are quite stable having basically the same influence for a long time. For example, the effect of an individual's personality on participation in certain recreation activities remains fairly constant. In contrast, the influence of other factors may vary greatly. Economic conditions may change from prosperity to recession within a few months; governments suddenly may impose or modify hunting, drinking, or gambling regulations; the opening of a new highway can completely alter the accessibility of a resource; or an accident or illness can suddenly change a person's physical condition and ability to take part in certain recreation activi-

ties. The manner and degree of interaction between the recreation environment and the participant is therefore constantly changing.

Everyone interested in recreation should have a basic understanding of the factors that affect participation and how they interact. Recreation planners and administrators must be especially well informed, since they have to take these factors into account when planning future facilities and programs. Estimating probable future population size, distribution, socioeconomic characteristics, and recreation preferences is particularly important in long-range planning, especially when large sums of money or extensive undeveloped resources are to be committed to recreation.

Unfortunately, little is known about the precise way in which participation is affected by these various factors. Researchers have devoted much time to investigating the relationships between participation and some of the more convenient factors such as age, occupation, income, and education, hoping to develop straightforward methods of predicting future needs for recreation opportunities. Originally, it was hypothesized that participation is directly proportional to one or several of these factors. If this proved to be correct, it would then be relatively easy to predict the magnitude of future participation by extrapolation, since national censuses regularly provide information concerning these variables. Unfortunately, the relationships have not proved to be as strong as hypothesized, and most researchers now agree that participation is controlled by a much more complicated set of factors than was initially suspected.

Therefore, when considering the various factors that affect recreation participation, it is essential to recognize the artifical nature of the division into components, the great range in size and complexity of recreation environments, the fact that all components of an environment can affect participation, that the influence of most factors can change with time, and that comparatively little is known about the quantitative relationships between the factors and participation.

In Part Two, the various factors that affect participation will be discussed in some detail. This opening chapter is devoted to economic and population factors. Chapter 5 explores the effect of social influences while Chapter 6 considers the other main external factor—resource accessibility, including transportation. Personal characteristics and attributes that influence recreation opportunities are summarized in Chapter 7. Part Two concludes with Chapter 8, which examines the nature of participation including an examination of the various phases of an experience and differences in activity patterns.

EXTERNAL ECONOMIC FACTORS

The economic condition of the individual participants, the surrounding community, the region, the nation, and the entire world play a major role in determining recreation participation. In this section, the discussion of external economic factors has been divided into the groups shown on the left in Figure 4.2; the personal economic factors listed at the top right are discussed in Chapter 7.

ECONOMIC CONDITIONS

When considering the impact of economic conditions on recreation, it is important to remember that they vary within countries as well as among countries. In the United States and Canada, two of the world's most affluent nations, there are depressed areas where economic development has been retarded. These areas are not confined to the ghettos of large cities. There are also many small towns and rural areas that are economically depressed. Like less developed nations, many of these enclaves have few people employed in manufacturing and service industries, low per capita incomes, limited public services, and less sophisticated recreation systems. The existence and characteristics of these economically disadvantaged areas must be taken into consideration when planning, developing, and administering recreation programs.

Stages in Development.
Economic development is easier to describe and understand if it is viewed as a series of stages. W. W. Rostow, a well-known economist and historian, suggested a five-stage system which provides a useful framework for discussing the impact of economic development on recreation. Rostow's five stages and their principal characteristics[1] are:

• *Traditional society* — relatively unchanged for a long time; a land-owning aristocracy and traditional customs dominate social, economic, and political life; most of the people work in agriculture; output per person cannot be increased within the present system; the majority live a hand-to-mouth existence; some traditional societies are extremely poor and large numbers of people frequently suffer from malnutrition, periodic famines, and epidemics.

[1] W. W. Rostow, *The Stages of Economic Growth,* Cambridge University Press, New York, 1960. Experts do not agree on the appropriateness of this or other systems that define the stages of economic development.

Figure 4.2 **Organization and interrelationships of main factors affecting an individual's economic status.**

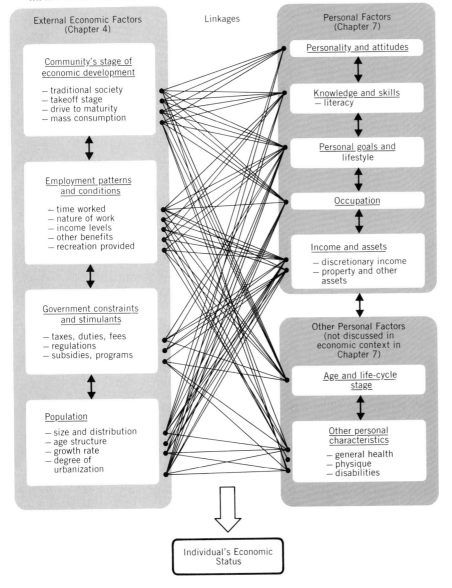

MAIN FACTORS AFFECTING AN INDIVIDUAL'S ECONOMIC STATUS

- *Preconditions for takeoff*—new ideas and goals come from outside or within the society; leaders see that change is possible and desirable for personal or social purposes; this stage may last for many decades.
- *Takeoff stage*—the leaders in favor of change amass sufficient political and economic power to begin to overcome resistance; new capital and technology start to alter production methods and the structure of the economy; manufacturing and service industries begin to expand; usually lasts only two or three decades.
- *The drive to maturity*—industrialization proceeds; economic growth occurs in all sectors of the economy but the emphasis gradually changes from heavy industry to sophisticated manufacturing involving a multitude of products; can last 50 or 60 years.
- *High mass consumption*—the economy reaches its full potential and produces large quantities of consumer goods and services; emphasis tends to change to satisfying social and cultural needs and desires.

It must be remembered that since these stages are only arbitrary divisions of a continuum, there are no well-defined boundaries between them.

In recent years, it has become common to refer to the highly developed nations as the "haves" and the remaining nations as the "have nots." The haves consist of the wealthy nations in the high-mass-comsumption stage plus those countries that have almost finished their drive to maturity.

One group of haves in the Northern Hemisphere consists of the world's 24 wealthiest nations (Canada, the United States, most countries of Western Europe, Japan, the Soviet Union, and the main Communist countries of Eastern Europe), which contain about 1.1 billion of the world's 4 billion

people and earn approximately 67 percent of the world's income. The remaining haves are mostly in the Southern Hemisphere, include about 600 million people, and earn about 22 percent of the world's income. The have nots, consisting of the nations in the first three stages together with those in the very early stages of the drive to maturity are also called the Third World.[2] This group consists of two-thirds of the world's nations, contains 2.3 billion people, and earns about 11 percent of the world's income. The countries that are still in the traditional stage are sometimes called the *Fourth World* in order to indicate that their extreme poverty sets them apart even from the other Third World nations. These 45 countries have an annual per capita output of less than $300.

A society does not necessarily keep moving through these five economic stages without interruption. The process may begin and then stop at a certain stage for an extended period. The stage at which a society currently exists depends on the nature of the society, its resources, and the type and magnitude of outside influences. Changes in government or external economic conditions can retard or accelerate development. For example, rapidly increasing oil prices have provided a serious setback to developing nations that do not have their own oil supplies.

As a society goes through these economic development stages, the distribution of the labor force within the various economic sectors changes. In a traditional society, most individuals work in the

[2] Originally this term referred to all nations other than the highly developed western nations and the Communist bloc.

primary sector—the extractive industries such as agriculture, fishing, hunting, and timber cutting. Few are involved in the *secondary sector*—the manufacturing of goods for sale to others. An equally small number are in the *tertiary sector*—providing services such as retail sales and education. In traditional societies, those in the primary sector usually have very low incomes.

During subsequent stages of development, the proportions change (Figure 4.3). Employment in the primary sector decreases as mechanization of these industries occurs. At the same time, the proportion in the secondary sector grows with the expansion of manufacturing. Employees earn higher per capita incomes as productivity increases. The society becomes more affluent. More money is spent on services and the tertiary sector expands.

The proportion of the labor force involved in producing recreation goods and services is small in a traditional society. After the takeoff stage it grows slowly at first but then more rapidly during the drive to maturity as workers have more money to spend on recreation. In the high-mass-consumption stage, more than half of the labor force may become directly or indirectly involved in producing recreation opportunities.

Effect on Recreation. A society's level of development plays a critical role in determining the nature and extent of recreation participation because it affects so many interconnected factors. For example, as a nation or region changes from an undeveloped to a developed state:

- People do not have to spend as much of their time struggling to sat-

Figure 4.3 **Hypothetical changes in labor force distribution between sectors during economic development.**

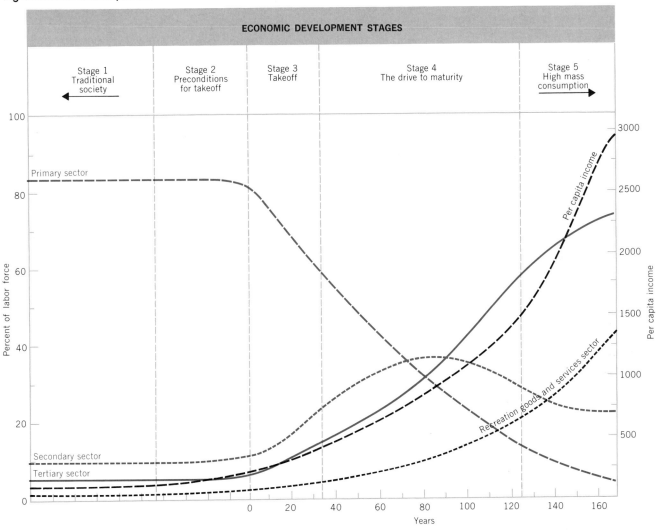

isfy their basic food and shelter needs; they have more time for other activities including recreation.

- Food supplies and health services improve resulting in better physical and mental health and increased longevity; people who are healthier and live longer can take part in a wider range of recreation activities and have more time and energy to do so.

- Income increases and eventually reaches a stage where money is left over and can be used for recreation expenditures.

- Education improves expanding the range of activities in which people can take part.

- Industries and businesses are developed increasing the availability of products and facilities that expand

recreation opportunities.

- Communications systems are developed extending the range of recreation possibilities.

- Transportation improves making recreational travel possible and reducing the cost of recreation goods.

- Government programs at various levels may now be expanded to include the establishment and operation of recreation facilities such as parks, community centers, and libraries.

The impact of economic development on recreation is therefore cumulative. At first, little progress appears to be made but gradually all the interconnecting factors begin to complement one another and change takes place more and more rapidly.

In most traditional societies, the majority of the people are poor agriculturalists with few recreation resources at their disposal other than the land and water around them. Recreation consists primarily of conversation, storytelling, singing, dancing, music, and simple games and sports. These people do not travel far; most activities take place at home, within, or close to their own village (Figure 4.4).

Figure 4.4 Abouré children playing a checkers-like game near their home in the village of Yaou, Ivory Coast, West Africa. Most recreation in traditional societies consists of conversations, storytelling, singing, dancing, feasting, and simple games in or close to participants' homes.

During the takeoff stage, this pattern starts to change. Transportation improves bringing outside influences and goods. New activities begin to spread through the society. More travel takes place.

As industrialization occurs during the drive to maturity, per capita income increases, the standard of living rises, and larger proportions of the population are able to spend part of their income on recreation. Recreation activities change rapidly. Traditional patterns are often partially or largely replaced with activities such as listening to the radio, seeing motion pictures or television programs, watching or taking part in modern sports, bicycle or motorcycle riding, and reading books or magazines.

In the high-mass-consumption stage, the majority of the population has access to a full range of modern activities. Most own a number of items of recreation equipment, are able to use a variety of recreation services, and travel much more extensively than people did in any of the previous stages.

However, economic development can have negative as well as positive effects on recreation. If growth is allowed to proceed in an unplanned manner with no thought for its impact on people or the environment, participation in many activities may actually be reduced. This has happened in many of today's developed nations. Water pollution from industrial, commercial, and residential sources, for example, has robbed people of millions of opportunities to wade, swim, fish, or just sit and relax by lakes, streams, and rivers. Although millions of people enjoy high living standards in these countries, there are also large numbers who have

been bypassed by prosperity. Some of these people, especially those who live in urban slums, appear to have fewer carefree moments and more limited recreation environments than many of those who live in undeveloped societies. The challenge to society, therefore, is to find the levels and patterns of economic development that provide the best compromise between economic well-being and a desirable environment.

Development Patterns. An appreciation of the distribution of economic development levels . makes it easier to understand the nature and problems of recreation at various locations. This is particularly important for those who are involved in tourism or in aiding developing regions. Without this appreciation it is sometimes hard to understand why less developed nations and regions have difficulty providing necessary tourist amenities or protecting magnificent undeveloped recreation resources.

World distribution of economic development levels is shown in Figure 4.5. The map is based on interpretation of several factors including population growth rate, per capita income, per capita energy supply, and the proportion of the labor force in the various economic sectors. These are broad generalizations founded on averages for entire nations; within each nation there are usually areas that are more developed or less developed than the average. In some cases, a comparatively small portion of a country's population has reached the takeoff stage while many millions still live a largely traditional existence. As a result, such nations will take much longer to complete the takeoff stage.

Figure 4.5 **World distribution of economic development stages. Stages are based on infant mortality rates, death rates, illiteracy, per capita income, and dominant economic sector.**

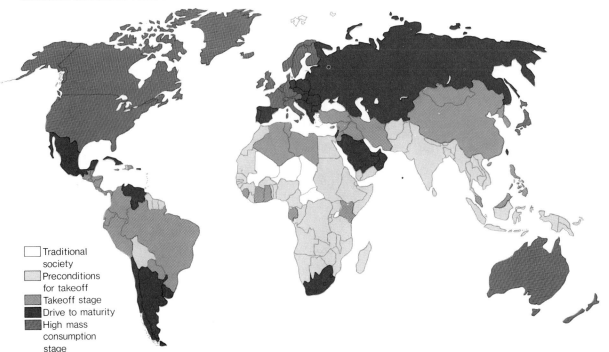

Legend:
- ☐ Traditional society
- ☐ Preconditions for takeoff
- ▨ Takeoff stage
- ■ Drive to maturity
- ▦ High mass consumption stage

As the map shows, the majority of the nations that are still in the traditional society stage are concentrated in Africa and southern Asia. Most of these countries have high birth rates and high death rates. Seventy percent or more of their labor forces are in agriculture, 10 percent or less in manufacturing, and 20 percent or less in service industries. Per capita incomes are only a few hundred dollars a year and illiteracy is high.

Countries in the midst of developing the conditions necessary for economic takeoff are located in South and Central America and in a band across North Africa, the Middle East, and Asia. These nations generally have about two-thirds of their labor force in agricul-

ture but their manufacturing and service industries are expanding. They also show other symptoms of development such as more advanced transportation systems and more advanced technologies than the nations in the previous group. Countries such as India and China have been included in this group because they have achieved many of the advances necessary for takeoff although their population problems have not been solved.

The Soviet Union, several nations in Eastern Europe, Spain, Portugal, Mexico, and a number of nations in South America are now at various stages in the drive to maturity. Most have less than 50 percent of their labor forces in agriculture and about 30 percent in both man-

ufacturing and services. Per capita incomes are three or four times higher than in the nations in the traditional society stage.

The nations in the high-mass-consumption stage are Canada, the United States, the remainder of Western Europe, Japan, Australia, and New Zealand. Most have 25 percent or less of their labor forces in agriculture, 30 to 50 percent in manufacturing, and 40 to 60 percent in the service sector. Per capita incomes are two to four times as large as the nations still in the drive to maturity stage. These countries have high standards of living involving the manufacturing of large supplies of recreation goods and the provision of elaborate public and commercial recreation services.

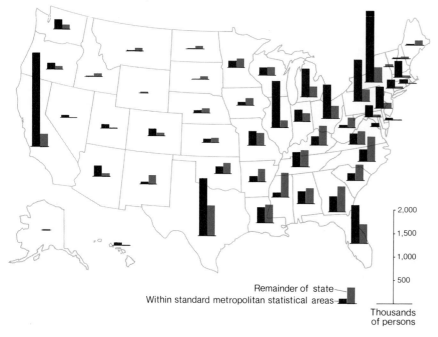

Figure 4.6 Number of Americans with incomes below the official poverty levels in standard metropolitan statistical areas and the remainder of each state in 1975. (Source: Data from U.S. Department of Commerce, *Current Population Reports — Consumer Income, 1976.*)

Remainder of state
Within standard metropolitan statistical areas

2,000
1,500
1,000
500

Thousands
of persons

The Handicap of Poverty.
But even the more affluent nations have people who have not benefited from economic development as much as others and are handicapped by poverty. The United States, for example, still has about 25 million individuals or over 11 percent of the population with incomes below the official poverty level.[3] In order to understand the significance of poverty statistics, it is important to know not only the number of poor people and how they are distributed but also the proportion of poor in a given population. In Figure 4.6, the *numbers of people* below the poverty level in

[3] The government's definition of the poverty level is the minimum amount a family needs to buy the basic necessities.

standard metropolitan statistical areas and the number living in the rest of each state are shown by the size of the columns. The urban poor are concentrated in the Washington to Boston "megalopolis," in the cities of the Ohio-Michigan-Illinois manufacturing region, and in Florida, Texas, and California. On the other hand, there are large numbers of poor outside the metropolitan areas in most of the states in a region extending from New York to Florida in the east and Michigan to Texas in the west.

When the poverty data are expressed as the *percentage of families* below the poverty level, a different pattern emerges (Figure 4.7). All of the states in the Southeast, plus predominantly agricultural

states in the upper Mississippi Valley, and some parts of the Southwest stand out as having higher proportions of poor people. The poorest areas in the nation are concentrated in six regions: an inland belt running along the Atlantic and Gulf Coast from near Richmond, Virginia, to the Mexican border; the lower Mississippi Valley; the coal mining regions of Tennessee, Kentucky, and West Virginia; the Ozark regions of Oklahoma, Arkansas, and Missouri; portions of North and South Dakota; and an area in southern Colorado and northern New Mexico.

These distributions affect participation in several ways. Locations with large numbers of poor people present a special challenge to public and quasi-public recreation agencies especially in areas with inadequate public transportation systems. People with low incomes depend on public and quasi-public recreation opportunities for recreation outside the home to a greater extent than do the more affluent. The poor do not have the recreation rooms, landscaped backyards, automobiles, recreation vehicles, seasonal homes, and other amenities that enhance the recreation environments of those with higher incomes. Unfortunately, the less affluent often do not take part in public and quasi-public opportunities as much as those with higher incomes because the poor often lack the education, clothing, transportation, and knowledge of facilities and programs that are conducive to participation. Places with many poor people need large-scale special programs to facilitate their participation. However, in areas where the proportion of poor is high (Figure 4.7), the amount of locally raised money available per capita for public and quasi-public recreation programs is generally small. As we will see later, some of the locations with the highest proportions of low-income people have the most inadequate state and local government recreation programs.

Current Economic Atmosphere. Recreation participation patterns can change quite rapidly if a society experiences substantial alterations in economic conditions. During periods of economic recession and depression, for instance, living costs escalate and unemployment and layoffs increase. The unemployed and the underemployed have little or no money to spend on anything but essentials. Those still working usually reduce their discretionary expenditures because they are worried about the future. Participation in more costly recreation activities—foreign travel, resort vacations, expensive restaurant meals, many forms of commercial entertainment—declines. Consequently, the need for inexpensive recreation opportunities in and close to home increases. This need was recognized during the Great Depression of the 1930s when almost one-third of the U.S. labor force was out of work. Unemployed entertainers, musicians, and recreation specialists were hired, usually with federal funds, and a wide range of recreation activities was provided in local parks and community centers.

In more recent periods of economic decline, the impact on recreation has not been as great. Generally, the proportions of unemployed have been smaller and unemployment benefits from government and other sources larger. In addition, many people have had higher discretionary incomes, and these have provided a buffer during periods of financial difficulty. Instead of eliminating recreation activities, these people have often chosen to save less or postpone other expenditures. Even the people who have had to reduce their spending have considered recreation an essential rather than a luxury. Many of these people have compromised by substituting less expensive recreation activities and, often, they have reduced their household expenditures rather than abandon their recreation participation patterns.

Differences in economic conditions between nations can also change recreation behavior. For example, an economic recession in Britain in the early 1970s resulted in the value of the pound sterling decreasing relative to other currencies. As a result, tourism in Britain increased 12 percent in 1975 at a time when world tourism barely grew at all. The following year, lured by the relative cheapness of the package tours and merchandise, over 10 million foreign visitors spent more than $3 billion in Britain. In some cases, inflation can have the same effect. Inflated vacation costs at home are believed to have contributed to the surge in overseas travel by the Japanese during the recession of the middle 1970s. They found they could get as much or more for their money abroad and at the same time gain the excitement and prestige of a foreign trip.

EMPLOYMENT PATTERNS AND CONDITIONS

The work people do has a considerable impact on their recreation

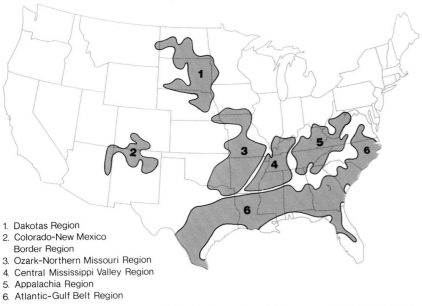

1. Dakotas Region
2. Colorado-New Mexico Border Region
3. Ozark-Northern Missouri Region
4. Central Mississippi Valley Region
5. Appalachia Region
6. Atlantic-Gulf Belt Region

Figure 4.7 Main regions of the United States where high proportions of the families have incomes below official poverty levels. (Source: **Data from a map in Stanley D. Brunn and James D. Wheeler, "Spatial Dimensions of Poverty in the United States."** Geografiska Annaler, **53, 1 (1971, Series B.)**

participation. The number of hours they work, when they work, the paid holidays and vacations to which they are entitled, the nature of their job, and the pay and other benefits that they receive all affect the nature and amount of recreation opportunities available to them.

Time Worked. Reduction of the average workweek for many workers to 40 hours or less has been a major factor in expanding recreation opportunities. As Table 4.1 shows, a typical factory worker currently has about four times as much free time as in the late 1800s. The 5-day, 40-hour week now in effect for the majority of workers in the developed nations provides more than 50 hours of free time each week if the employee has no other obligations. Some union contracts provide for a considerably shorter workweek, and a 35-hour week will probably be the standard for unionized industrial workers by the middle 1980s. Nevertheless, if the average number of hours actually worked by all types of workers is calculated, it is considerably more than 40 hours each week. In fact, the total has changed very little in the past 30 years. This is because many unionized employees choose to work overtime in order to earn more money. In addition, large numbers of nonunionized employees and most self-employed persons work more than 40 hours. Nevertheless, an increasing proportion of the labor force has the option of working fewer than 40 hours each week.

Changes in the distribution of working hours also affect recreation participation. In Victorian times, many workers could only participate in more time-consuming activities on holidays. They had little free

Table 4.1 The Free-Time Revolution: Reduction of the Industrial Workweek Since 1850

Period	Typical Industrial Workweek[a]		Weekly Free Time (hours)[b]	Percent Increment	Percent Increase From 1800s
Late 1800s	6 days of 12 to 14 hr	= 78 hr	13	—	—
Early 1900s	6 days of 10 hr	= 60 hr	31	138	138
1920s	5½ days of 9 hr	= 50 hr	41	32	215
1950s	5 days of 8 hr	= 40 hr	51	24	292
1980s	5 days of 7 hr	= 35 hr	56[c]	10	331

[a] Most agricultural workers and many in service and professional occupations still work considerably more than 40 hours per week.
[b] Assuming eight hours for sleep and three hours for other essential activities each day.
[c] One third of the week.

time during the six-day workweek, and many activities were taboo on Sundays. Relaxation of Sunday restrictions followed by the introduction of the half-day on Saturday, and then the full Saturday holiday, greatly increased recreation possibilities. The creation of the "weekend" gave people the opportunity to regularly enjoy excursions and other activities requiring more than a day to complete.

Now, alternatives to the standard 8 A.M. to 5 P.M. five-day workweek are being introduced. These include *flexitime* where employees arrange their own 40-hour weekly work schedule around a core time during the middle of the day. Developed in Munich in 1967 at the Messerschmidts Belkow Co., the flexitime concept has spread faster than any other management innovation in recent years. Over 50 percent of the West German, 30 percent of the French, and 40 percent of the Swiss work force are now on some form of flexitime. The British government adopted variable hours for a half million civil servants, and a similar number of American workers choose their own hours. Altogether, some 10 million

workers in 10 countries now have some control over their work schedule.

One variation of flexitime is the four-and-a-half-day week where employees arrange their 40 hours so that Friday afternoon is left free. Some industries are experimenting with four 10-hour days so that either Friday or Monday is free creating a regular three-day weekend. Others are trying three 12-hour days arranged so that the four-day weekend always includes Sunday. If compressed workweeks that create three- and four-day weekends become common, recreation participation patterns will change as dramatically as they did earlier with the adoption of the two-day weekend.

Earned time, which means that workers can go home whenever they fulfill the production quota set for the full working day, is another scheme that in some cases allows industrious workers to leave their jobs two, three, or even four hours before the end of their shifts and still be paid for eight. Workers in one American plant using this system enjoy increased participation in many activities—fishing, gardening, playing with their children after work, tinkering with cars, and taking courses offered at the factory in subjects such as ceramics and guitar playing.

American employers are, on the whole, pleased with flexible time programs; they report a substantial reduction in absenteeism and tardiness, a considerable increase in employee morale, an improved ability to attract and retain well-qualified, high-caliber employees and, in many cases, a rise in production and profits or a boost in efficiency and quality of work. The decrease in absenteeism is especially gratifying to employers. Staying home from work presently involves the loss of more than 100 million hours of working time per week and gives rise to a great deal of unnecessary cost and inefficiency.

Another aspect of work that controls recreation participation is the period during the day when the work takes place. In the United States, a large number of factories, businesses, and public services like hospitals operate around the clock. Many commercial establishments including stores and hotels are open from early morning until late at night or do not close at all. Some services such as bank check clearing offices and trash collection in central city areas operate primarily at night. As a result, more than 13.5 million employees have to work hours other than 8 A.M. to 5 P.M., and some work on weekends.

Those who are on afternoon, night, or weekend shifts are often recreationally disadvantaged. Much of their free time occurs when others are working or their children are in school. Those who work the evening shift miss many family recreation activities, social events, concerts, sporting events, and television programs. In addition, most public and commercial recreation facilities are geared to people working in the daytime. Some establishments such as racket sports facilities and bowling alleys are beginning to stay open at night to accommodate those who work evening shifts and wish to follow the accepted pattern of recreating after work (Figure 4.8). An even larger proportion of workers is likely to be asked to accept evening, night, and weekend shifts in the future as increased amounts of all types of work are done by costly machines. Society will change to some degree to accommodate this trend but the workers involved will still be affected when wishing to participate in many social events and outdoor activities that require daylight.

Mediterranean and Latin American countries that observe the custom of the siesta have a work schedule that gives workers time off in the middle of the afternoon. For example, the traditional workday for retail and business employees in Greece started at 8 A.M. and continued until 2 P.M. Stores and offices would then close while workers went home for a large lunch and long nap, visited their lovers, or enjoyed the beach during the hottest part of the day. They then returned to shops and offices from 5 P.M. to 8 P.M. Consequently, social events seldom began before 10 P.M. and often lasted until 2 or 3 A.M.

In 1977, the Greek government tried to change the workday to 9 A.M. to 5:30 P.M. in an effort to conform to western European ways in preparation for membership in

Figure 4.8 **Bowling centers in communities wih sufficient potential customers to warrant it often operate round-the-clock to accommodate those who find it inconvenient or impossible to bowl during the more traditional afternoon and evening hours.**

the European Economic Community. Unlike some workers in Latin American cities who are actively seeking the abandonment of the siesta, the Greeks were generally resentful. Midafternoon, for many of the 9 million Greek citizens, is when the family gathers to share good food and conversation. Some complained that the only time the family could get together socially under this new routine was on Sunday. Single workers without family ties missed the opportunities provided by siesta for relaxation, visiting with friends, or enjoying the sun along the waterfront. Others reported that their good times spent socializing in the evening were also suffering. They said they were so tired after the long uninterrupted working period that they did not have the energy to go out as usual; instead, they stayed at home and went to bed early or watched TV. The fact that the workweek, under the new system, had been reduced from 48 to 43 hours seemed unimportant. During the first half of a three-month trial period, wildcat strikes erupted and customers stayed away in protest. The government was forced to concede defeat, at least temporarily, and allow the shops to return to the split-shift schedule.

Up to this point, we have been discussing time worked on the basis of the eight-hour day. Millions of workers in both the developed and developing nations still work many more than 40 hours a week. Even in the United States, it is estimated that one-quarter of the nonfarm labor force spends more than 40 hours on the job; about 18 percent work at least 49 hours per week. A six-day workweek is fairly common for employees and proprietors of family owned retail stores and other

small businesses, and also for farmers and their helpers. Homemakers may find that they have short intermittent breaks during the day that are suitable for watching television, reading, or sunbathing, but not long enough for many other pursuits. Small children at home or meal preparation may also restrict their activities to those that can be enjoyed in or near the home. Many managers, executives, teachers, and other professionals catch up on their routine paper work, prepare new work, or study professional materials in the evenings or on weekends. Generally, unionized industrial workers have more free time available for recreation than service and white collar employees.

Holidays and Vacations.
Time available for recreation has also increased substantially since 1900 because of changes in holiday and vacation arrangements. In the Victorian era, there were virtually no public holidays as we know them today. Only Sunday and other days of religious significance were widely observed. Now a great variety of holiday and vacation arrangements exists. Most nations have a number of one-day national holidays scattered throughout the year, and many require that workers receive pay for these days as well as for an annual vacation. Ten paid employee holidays a year is currently common in American businesses. However, some industrial workers enjoy as many as 20 holidays in addition to their three to five weeks of annual paid vacation.

Some communities or regions also schedule holidays to provide opportunities for residents to take part in recreation activities of local significance. For instance, many

employees have paid time off during New Orleans' Mardi Gras or the Calgary Stampede. In some portions of the United States where many employees and employers go deer hunting every year, it is common for industries and offices to operate on a reduced scale or even close down completely during the first part of the deer season. Employees at one firm in Michigan's Upper Peninsula actually have a clause in their contract allowing them to take up to five days each year for deer hunting.

Most teachers have several holidays during the school year, one or two weeks at Christmas and Easter, and five or more weeks in the summer. However, teachers usually put in long hours during the school year and some find it is economically essential or professionally desirable to work or further their own education during the summer. On the other hand, some farmers, doctors, and small businessmen find it difficult to take any holidays or vacations. For example, small dairy farmers with no hired help or relatives who can periodically take their place find it impossible to take even a weekend off because the cows must be milked every morning and evening.

Others are limited in the kinds of recreation activities they can undertake because of the seasonality of their work. This is the case with many who work in agriculture, construction, or recreation services in parts of the world where one or more seasons are unfavorable. In Canada and the northern parts of the United States, for instance, many areas experience less than six months of warm weather. During this period, many farmers, agricultural workers, road construction workers, and resort employees work from dawn to dusk seven days a week. Construction work and even cultivation and harvesting are sometimes carried out with the aid of artificial light to make the most of the short season.

People in these types of situations do not have time for the evening, weekend, and vacation activities during the summer to which most people look forward. Some can make up for this, of course, by taking vacations during the winter and traveling to warmer areas. Unfortunately, those with low incomes usually cannot afford to compensate in this manner; many have to make their summer earnings last through the rest of the year.

The advent of paid vacations lasting several weeks has greatly increased the range of activities in which workers may participate. Coupled with more discretionary income, lengthy vacations have made it possible for large numbers of working, middle-class citizens to travel widely (Figure 4.9). The availability of large blocks of free time also enables some people to undertake projects that would otherwise be difficult or impractical; these include building a boat, summer cottage, or recreation room. Others use the time for concentrated periods of gardening or artistic creativity.

One problem with lengthy vacations is that some employers have difficulty maintaining reasonable levels of productivity during the months that are most popular for vacations. In some cases, this is solved by completely closing businesses or factories for several weeks. When this is done during an already busy vacation period, it may contribute to problems with peak loads at certain recreation facilities. Many employers prefer to stagger their workers' vacations so that operations can proceed without interruption. Consequently, many employees are not able to take their vacations at the most popular time or at the time they prefer. This may prevent some people from taking part in their favorite recreation activities if participation is only possible at other times during the year. Nevertheless, most employees in the developed nations have much

Figure 4.9 A middle-class family admires the gigantic presidential likenesses carved into a mountain face at Mount Rushmore National Memorial while on a summer trip in the West.

longer vacations than their predecessors and are able to take them at reasonably convenient times.

Nature of the Work. The type of work and the conditions under which it is done influence recreation behavior. In societies where most workers are engaged in arduous labor such as hand cultivation of crops, lumbering without mechanical equipment, or non-mechanized mining, construction, or heavy manufacturing, the majority are unlikely to spend their evenings participating in rigorous activities. Conversely, where many people are in sedentary occupations, there is likely to be considerable interest in active recreation following work such as jogging, bicycling, tennis, or team sports.

On the other hand, many people's ability to participate in some forms of recreation are limited by the effects of their work. Sedentary occupations, for instance, can reduce stamina over a period of time and cause people to stop taking part in strenuous activities. Although safety precautions and working conditions are improving, some workers are still being injured by improper lifting techniques, falls, or other kinds of accidents. Others are seriously affected by chemicals or dusts. In both cases, workers are usually prevented from participating in some forms of recreation temporarily or permanently because of the effects of their work-related injuries.

Although work generally becomes less arduous physically as societies become more highly developed, it often becomes more psychologically taxing. Automation and specialization, for instance, frequently result in repetitious, tedious jobs. The fragmentation of the ma-

jority of production and secretarial work also denies the worker a sense of overall responsibility and accomplishment. This often results in feelings of dissatisfaction and frustration. The demands of modern production schedules can also produce tensions and feelings of despair; some workers continually struggle against time or heavy work loads without any real hope of relief. For many, the loss of personal identity can be psychologically damaging; people find themselves part of a crowd of faceless workers with every move dictated by a clock, machine, or supervisor. Others in supervisory or executive positions find the responsibility of directing complicated, modern factories, businesses, or government services equally debilitating.

Therefore, the physical fatigue formerly experienced by the majority of workers is frequently replaced in modern society with boredom, frustration, and psychological exhaustion. Recreation activities are often selected expressly as an antidote for these effects. Some people find relief by taking part in contrasting activities; people with boring, undemanding jobs, for instance, often look for free time activities that are exciting or physically or intellectually challenging. Others with frustrating jobs find temporary relief through the anesthetic effects of television, alcohol, or drugs. Those with demanding jobs seek relaxation through hobbies and activities like fishing and gardening. And large numbers of people who work at solitary, sedentary jobs find volleyball, softball, or bowling offer opportunities for physical exercise as well as social interaction both during the game and afterward.

In some cases it is the location

of the job that influences recreation selection. Those who work at home, on their own farm, or at their own resort frequently desire a change of environment when taking part in a recreation activity. For instance, a parent who has been alone with little children all day or all week may feel a desperate need to get out of the home environment. He or she may wish to go to a discotheque, bar, or sports event that offers stimulation and involves interaction with other adults. Unfortunately, the other parent's work may involve contact with many people in a noisy bustling environment. So while one desires an "evening out" in the midst of a crowd, the other anticipates a "nice, quiet evening at home" with a good book or a hobby.

The attitudes and behavior of employers and fellow employees can contribute to a person's selection of recreation activities. Some employers have a considerable influence on their employees' recreation behavior, encouraging them to follow recreation patterns that they feel are desirable for business purposes. Executives and sales persons are often expected to join particular clubs, play certain sports, or be seen at certain cultural or social events. Other employees play on company sports teams or actively participate in physical fitness programs at the urgings of management or co-workers. Participation in these cases may be regarded as a duty but can also be highly pleasurable. Employers can also affect workers' recreation choices and lifestyles by the kinds of recreation facilities they provide. And finally, if members of a firm establish a pattern of inviting each other to social events such as pool-side cocktail parties or barbeques, this type of recreation is likely to be accepted and emulated by new employees as they join the firm.

Occupations affect recreation in many other ways. People who have public images to maintain such as ministers, politicians, and their families, or professional people such as teachers, doctors, and lawyers, frequently feel obliged not to participate in certain activities in order to avoid criticism and the risk of offending anyone connected with their work. Persons who have gained fame and wide recognition through their work—athletes, politicians, musicians, actors, and actresses—may find their opportunities to participate in many activities severely curtailed or spoiled by the effects of public adulation. Wherever they go they are instantly recognized and often find it becomes difficult or impossible to enjoy simple pleasures such as a walk in a park or a meal in a restaurant because people will not leave them alone. They may also feel obligated to avoid recreation activities that might lead to an injury that would interfere with their work.

Income and Benefits. The amount of income and the fringe benefits, if any, that people receive have a major influence on recreation participation. The key factor is not the gross income received by the individual or household; instead, it is the amount of *discretionary income.* This is the money left over after the basic costs of existence such as taxes, housing, food, transportation to work, and health care have been paid. Since discretionary income depends partly on the lifestyle, obligations, and advantages of the individual, these aspects will be discussed more exten-

sively in Chapter 7. Even so, higher gross income generally means more discretionary income.

During the past century, the growth in the relative purchasing power of people in the developed nations and in some of the developing nations has had a substantial impact on recreation behavior. In these countries, the wages earned by most employees increased much faster than the cost of the necessities of life. As a result, living standards rose and the majority have had more discretionary income. From time to time and particularly in recent years, inflation has reduced purchasing power but, by and large, the majority of people in the more advanced nations are much better off than in the past.

The wages paid in a particular society depend on many factors. If the demand for a product or service is low, employers will have difficulty maintaining wage levels let alone increasing them. Increased demand, on the other hand, will produce higher profits and an ability to raise wages and expand fringe benefits. Similarly, increased productivity may make higher wages possible. The activities of labor unions often result in increased wages and fringe benefits. Government minimum wage regulations may raise the wages for low-paying jobs, and in doing so, force wages at higher levels to also be increased.

Unfortunately, minimum wage laws usually lead to fewer unskilled workers, young people in particular, being employed, since employers are reluctant to pay what they consider high wages for what they feel will be relatively low productivity. This only increases the number of young people who have unlimited free time but virtually no discre-

tionary income. It also produces a secondary recreation effect in that many of these people engage in antisocial acts in an attempt to pass time or obtain merchandise or spending money. These acts often interfere with the recreation experiences or opportunities of other people.

The amount of money earned by people also varies greatly. Sexual and racial discrimination can result in women and minority group individuals being paid less. In addition, those who grow up in disadvantaged families generally have lower incomes in later life because their opportunities and expectations have been limited. In the United States, for example, 25 percent fewer male high school graduates from the bottom economic quarter of the population go to college than those from the top economic quarter even when the graduates compared are of equal academic ability. In the case of female high school graduates, 35 percent fewer continue their education. As a result, the children of families in the top 20 percent of the socioeconomic pyramid have average incomes that are 75 percent higher than those coming from the bottom 20 percent. The distribution of income groupings in the U.S. population is shown in Figure 4.10.

The fringe benefits provided for workers by employers are an important aspect of income. In many cases they are services that employees would have to buy from their wages if the employers did not pay for them. Therefore, those who receive substantial fringe benefits generally have higher discretionary income than those who do not. In several European countries, however, agreements between manage-

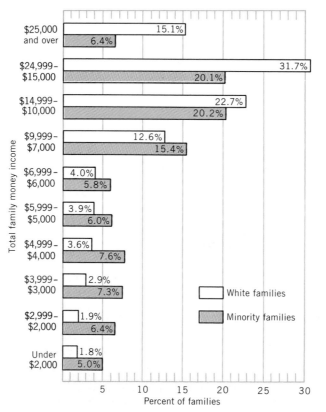

Figure 4.10 Distribution of U.S. minority and white families among income groups in 1975. A total of 53.5 percent of minority families had an income of $10,000 or less compared to only 30.7 percent of white families. (Source: U.S. Bureau of the Budget, Current Population Reports, Series P-60, No. 103.)

ment and the labor unions provide a special fringe benefit that often has a direct effect on recreation. In West Germany, for instance, at the beginning of their annual vacation, workers and civil servants receive an extra two week's salary in addition to their regular wages for the vacation period. Italian workers also receive a substantial vacation bonus. For those who find it difficult to save for vacations, this payment expands their vacation oppor-

tunities. It provides the necessary extra cash to make an away-from-home vacation feasible and, in many cases, encourages travel to locations in foreign countries.

Fringe benefits cost American employers about $400 billion each year, an amount equal to about one-third of total employee wages. These benefits fall into two groups. First, there are wages paid for time not worked; these include vacations, holidays, coffee breaks, and

rest periods, together with time off for sick leave, bereavements, jury duty, and military commitments. Total costs of such benefits average more than $35 per employee each week including some $13 for paid vacations and $9 for paid holidays. In the second group are profit-sharing payments and employer contributions for benefits such as pensions, life and health insurance, social security, and unemployment compensation. These total about $63 per employee each week.

Some firms are adopting flexible benefit plans known as the *cafeteria system.* Each employee chooses from several benefit options; these include various combinations of life insurance, dental coverage, vision and hearing care, prescription drug coverage, maternity benefits, lump sum death benefits, or additional days of vacation. Recreation participation is affected because the employees either take more vacation time or select benefits that eliminate or reduce the need to pay for certain services from their wages, which in effect increases discretionary income.

And finally, there are two special types of fringe benefits—incentive programs and perquisites. These schemes result in employees enjoying a wide variety of recreation experiences that they might otherwise not be able to afford. The benefits provided are substantial. American businesses, for instance, spend some $2.6 billion a year on incentive programs. Such programs are designed to motivate employees to work harder and therefore help the company compete more successfully with rival firms and increase profits. These schemes reward outstanding workers with cash or prizes. The latter include television sets, sailboats, and travel packages that provide winners and their spouses with luxury weekends in cities like Las Vegas, New York, or Los Angeles or one-week vacations in locales like Honolulu, Tokyo, London, and Rome.

Companies that provide *perquisites* consider them to be an effective means of recruiting and retaining key personnel, building company loyalty and morale, and providing employees with experiences that can relieve stress or improve physical condition. Perquisites, which currently are not taxed, often replace and are preferable to pay increases which are fully taxable. For lower-level employees they range from the use of company-owned recreation facilities to discounts on company products or free travel for transportation industry workers. At the management levels, perquisites often include substantial entertainment allowances, private club memberships, and sabbatical leaves. Some executives enjoy the use of cars, airplanes, yachts, hotel suites, company leased box seats at performing arts facilities, enclosed suites at sports stadiums, and resort facilities such as hunting lodges, fishing camps, and ski condominiums. Since companies do not reveal the full extent of the privileges provided, no accurate estimates of their value are available but it is suggested that perquisites probably amount to billions of dollars annually.

Recreation Programs. In the developed nations, an increasing number of industries, businesses, institutions, governments, and labor unions are providing recreation opportunities for employees and their families. These range from minor contributions of money or goods for sports teams and social events to costly facilities such as athletic complexes, community centers, and vacation resorts. Some employers and unions hire extensive full-time recreation staffs to organize sports schedules, cultural programs, social events, and a variety of weekend and vacation trips. Private corporations in the United States now spend more than $3 billion a year on employee recreation and education programs.

Employee facilities and programs can influence recreation participation in several ways. Workers and their families may be introduced to recreation activities and resources with which they might otherwise not become familiar. Participation in activities that are already part of a worker's recreation lifestyle tends to increase because it is easier to take part more frequently when facilities are at the place of work. Finally, workers may not use resources at or near their homes as frequently if they prefer the facilities or camaraderie at the office or factory.

Women and Young People. The proportion of women working outside the home has an impact on recreation behavior. When married women, especially those with young children, work long hours at arduous jobs, they are less likely to have the time or inclination to undertake vigorous activities or lead very active social lives. In a family situation where both partners work in tiring jobs, many household chores are likely to be put off until the weekend. Under those circumstances, a family may find it difficult to take part in any of the weekend recreation activities that require large blocks of time. Where both partners have jobs that involve rotating shifts, it may even become difficult to arrange any time for recreation together except during annual vacations.

On the other hand, women working may have many positive effects on recreation participation. Single women can be independent when earning instead of having to rely on their families for support. In many modern societies, they feel as free as single men to establish their own households, buy cars and recreation merchandise, go on vacation trips, and generally create their own recreation lifestyles (Figure 4.11). The number of single women working therefore has a direct effect on the number of women participating in many kinds of activities especially those that take place in urban areas.

In families where the wife

Figure 4.11 Two young women rest beside a fountain in Arles while on a camping tour of southern France. Changes in social attitudes together with more and better paying jobs for women have greatly increased the recreation opportunities open to them.

works, this additional income can also affect recreation behavior. Some women earn enough to hire people to come in while they are at work to care for the children and, in some cases, do the housework. If her work is enjoyable and not too arduous, the working wife may actually be less tired and have more time and energy for recreation than if she had stayed at home. Millions of families in the United States have gone from low-income to middle-income, or middle-income to relatively high-income status because of the wife's earnings. Many families use the extra income for recreation purposes such as the purchase of recreation equipment and vacations.

Young people, on the other hand, are finding it increasingly difficult to obtain jobs. This is the result of a combination of factors including the high birth rates in the 1950s, economic recessions increasing the numbers of unemployed, moonlighting by older workers already fully employed, larger numbers of married women entering the work force, higher minimum wages, and the low demand for workers with few marketable skills and little or no experience. This lack of skills is not always the problem, however. Some young people are finding themselves overqualified for the jobs that are available. Italy and Britain in particular are turning out university graduates in fields already saturated with job applicants. Some find employment in unrelated fields or end up doing menial work. Many refuse to work at jobs they consider beneath them and simply give up searching for employment.

Unfortunately, many young people who fail to find work within a reasonable length of time develop attitudes and lifestyles that make them unsuitable for work when jobs do develop. As a result, individuals who are not hired during the initial search for employment tend to remain unemployed. Unemployment among young people has been described as the industrial world's gravest problem. In 24 of the richest nations, over 7 million unemployed young people are looking for work or, in despair, have adopted a life of apathy or antisocial behavior. In Canada, France, Italy, the United States, and other nations of the industrialized West, 40 percent of the unemployed are people under 25 years of age. In Britain, the number of jobless teenagers increased tenfold in a decade and, in the United States, over 16 percent of the teenagers who seek work do not find a job.

High employment among young people means they do not have much or any money to spend on recreation. This limits participation and encourages delinquency. Absence of an assured income may also contribute to the postponement or rejection of marriage, which in turn reduces the proportion of the population involved in the recreation patterns characteristic of young families.

Retirement. The age at which people retire determines to some degree the nature, extent, and location of recreation participation by older people. If retirement takes place at a reasonable age and the retirees are in good health and have adequate amounts of discretionary income, they may have many years to do much as they please. In the developed nations, the numbers of people in this situation have been increasing. For instance, the number of American workers retiring before 65 has more than tripled in the past decade, and 62 is currently the average retirement age. Participation by older people in community recreation activities and programs, hobbies, clubs, and travel has shown major increases as a result.

Reasons for these changes include the adoption of mandatory retirement, government pension plans, higher income levels during the working years that have allowed more people to accumulate some savings, increased longevity, and improved health. A major contributing factor has been the recent adoption by some industries of special retirement plans that allow employees to retire not at a specified age but after a set number of years of service. One of these—the "30-and-out plan"—now applies to most workers in American automobile manufacturing plants. Although not obligatory, this plan does permit any employee to retire with full pension after 30 years of service. Under this scheme, many workers are qualifying for retirement at 47 or 48 years of age.

Although substantial numbers of Americans are seizing the opportunity to retire and enjoy themselves while they are still young and healthy, many are choosing not to do so. In fact, it is not expected that the average retirement age will drop much further in the United States, at least for another generation. Some authorities predict that the trend might even be reversed. Reasons for this include:

- Fear of the impact of rapid inflation on pensions and the realization that retirement can mean radically reduced standards of living.
- Desire to raise retirement benefits by working longer.

Apprehension about retirement and the changes in lifestyles that result. Desire or need of the self-employed to continue working as long as health permits.

Decision of some individuals to continue working periodically as consultants or to turn lifetime skills and hobbies into enjoyable postretirement revenue-producers.

The federal government's raising of the minimum permissible mandatory retirement age from 65 to 70 and the removal of all age limits for most federal employees.

The federal government action was taken in 1978 in response to increased public discontent with forced retirement policies.

However, it is economically advantageous to the nation if people work longer. Longevity and population age structures are resulting in the number of retirees increasing much faster than the number of employed workers. For example, there were 31 social security beneficiaries in the United States for every 100 workers in 1977; by A.D. 2030, there will be more than 50. In addition, inflation and resultant increases in pension payments, plus the fact that people are living and drawing pensions longer, are resulting in retirees receiving much more money than they contributed. Therefore, although it will cause more unemployment problems, especially among young people just entering the job market, there are indications that Americans may eventually be encouraged or even required to retire later than they do now.

GOVERNMENT CONSTRAINTS

Taxes, duties, fees, and regulations imposed by governments have a widespread constraining effect on recreation. Some taxes such as personal income taxes, social security taxes, property taxes, and sales taxes apply to large proportions of a nation's population and reduce the money people have left for recreation. The impact of these taxes depends on the way in which they are calculated and the income level of the individual or family. Whether or not these taxes are imposed, and if so, the tax rates, exemptions, and deductions that are permitted vary considerably from place to place.

Income and Social Security Taxes. European income and social security taxes are generally much higher than similar Canadian or American taxes. For example, a family with two children on the average pays income and social security taxes equal to about one-third of its income in the nations with extensive social and health programs such as Denmark, Sweden, and the Netherlands while an equivalent family in the United States or Canada would pay about one-sixth. However, the taxpayers in these European countries receive more social services and, therefore, have to budget less for health care and other forms of security. In many cases, lower-income Europeans receive family allowances and other cash benefits that also offset the higher tax rates. Nevertheless, the net effect is that the middle and upper classes in these nations have less discretionary income than they do in Canada or the United States. A few developed nations have much lower tax rates—for example, France and Japan, respectively, collect 11 and 10 percent of workers' wages in national income taxes. This leaves the workers with more discretionary income but, at the same time, they also receive less adequate social services.

The tax exemptions and deductions that are permitted can affect the availability of recreation resources. These also vary considerably from nation to nation. For instance, most countries consider it desirable for citizens to own their own homes and try to make it easier for them to do so by allowing them to deduct all interest payments on their income tax returns or, in a few nations like Austria, by permitting the deduction of the principal payments as well. In addition, many nations of Western Europe provide tax-exempt or bonus savings plans that act as incentives to save enough money for a downpayment. In many cases, if it were not for these measures, people of modest income would never be able to have their own homes and the greater opportunities for certain kinds of recreation that home ownership provides.

Of equal significance are the laws concerning tax exemptions for donations. U.S. laws are far more generous in this regard and, as a result, philanthropy by individuals as well as corporations is encouraged. This is particularly beneficial to nonprofit cultural organizations and institutions that often depend on these private donations to survive or to improve their programs and facilities. Because of this effect, the tax exemption laws can be said to enhance the cultural environment of the entire nation, affording many more cultural opportunities to the citizens than they otherwise might have had.

Consumer Taxes. Another type of taxation—consumer taxes—is also higher in most of the other nations of the world than in the

United States. For example, value-added taxes on services as well as goods, sales taxes on merchandise, and special luxury or excise taxes and duties on commodities such as photographic equipment, stereos, alcoholic beverages, and tobacco cost consumers two and three times as much, not only in most of the European countries but in Canada as well. These taxes are especially important because they frequently have a direct effect on recreation behavior. A good example is taxes on automobile fuels.

Gasoline and diesel fuel taxes vary greatly from country to country and are imposed for a variety of purposes. Some fuel taxes are levied for road construction and maintenance purposes and thus are similar to a user fee. Sometimes, they are regarded as a source of general revenue or used to discourage fuel consumption, especially where petroleum products are imported. In Europe and most of the rest of the world, motor fuel taxes have been much higher than in the United States and Canada; the combined federal-state tax on gasoline in the United States, for instance, averages 12 cents a gallon in comparison to $1.54 in Italy, $1.02 in West Germany, and 69 cents in Britain.[4] In addition, motorists in these nations pay more for the gasoline itself. In the United States, the price of gasoline has been kept at artificially low levels because originally much of the oil was produced within the country, competition between companies was fierce, large markets and high consumption reduced distribution costs, and taxes were generally levied only to build and sustain the highway system rather than produce revenue for other purposes. The availability of plentiful and relatively cheap gasoline has until recently[5] encouraged Americans to buy big cars, travel trailers, motor homes, and boats.

The operating costs and taxes on motor vehicles and accessories in the United States are also relatively low. No national taxes are paid directly on the car at the time of sale although federal taxes on tires are reflected in the list price. Most of the individual states charge sales taxes ranging from 2 to 7 percent. In many nations of Europe, however, automobiles are treated as luxury items and taxed at much higher rates. Yearly road fund taxes — the equivalent of North American license fees — are also much higher and increase much faster with horsepower. As a result, it is considerably more expensive to own and operate a car in Europe, and this has several effects. First, Europeans have to be more affluent before they feel able to afford a car or they must be willing to make larger sacrifices elsewhere in their budgets to do so. Second, higher operating costs encourage them to buy smaller cars and drive less. Consequently, recreation behavior in Europe is less automobile-oriented and there are fewer recreation vehicles, especially large ones.

Other kinds of consumer taxes have similar effects on recreation behavior depending on their magnitude. For example, the 4 or 5 percent sales tax charged by many American states is relatively minor and generally does little to change recreation participation patterns. On the other hand, high taxes such as those often imposed on commodities regarded as luxury items may affect some people's ability to purchase them. This is sometimes the intention of governments. Examples include:

- High taxes on alcoholic beverages to limit consumption, thereby reducing the incidence of alcohol-related social problems.
- Luxury taxes on nonessential items to discourage consumer spending in general, thereby reducing inflation.
- The imposition of heavy import duties on foreign goods to raise money or to discourage their purchase, thereby protecting domestic industries and improving the nation's balance of trade.

Such taxes often make it financially impossible for some people to buy certain recreation products or as much of a particular recreation item as they would like. They also force large numbers of people to buy domestic products that, in some instances, may be inferior to or far more expensive than their imported equivalents.

Some governments tax recreation directly with taxes on admission tickets to concerts, plays, movies, or other performances. Others tax restaurant meals and all types of overnight accommodations. Such taxes are usually not more than 10 percent but they can discourage participation by poorer people, especially those with larger families. Revenues from taxes on performances and accommodations are often used to pay for general government services rather than being dedicated specifically to the support of recreation. About 100 countries impose an entry or departure tax on the foreign visitor to help finance the cost of airport facilities. In

[4] 1979 figures.

[5] See Chapter 18, "Energy Supply Implications."

some nations like the United States, the charges are added to the air-fares whether they are international or domestic flights. These taxes are mostly an inconvenience rather than a deterrent to travel but they do contribute to the overall costs; for instance, the domestic air tax in the United States is 8 percent of the price of the ticket, and the departure tax in Australia is $11.50.

Some taxes, licenses, and fees are imposed in order to provide or maintain recreation facilities or programs. For instance, the 10 percent federal excise tax on fishing tackle and the 11 percent tax on firearms and ammunition, paid by American fisherpersons and hunters, are used for fish and wildlife management. In addition, fisherpersons and hunters have to buy state hunting and fishing licenses. Those who wish to hunt birds such as ducks and geese also purchase a federal migratory bird stamp. Some states also require the purchase of a special stamp for trout or salmon fishing. Admission fees are charged at many federal, state, provincial, and local recreation facilities. Additional fees are often charged for special services such as camping, boat launching, swimming, or the use of sports equipment. Governments have also used special taxes on cigarettes or gasoline to raise money for park facilities.

Although special taxes, licenses, and user fees appear to be a fair way of financing public recreation programs, they reduce the spontaneity of participation and discourage the less affluent from taking part. Fishing license fees, for example, may be regarded as nominal by avid fisherpersons but may be sufficient to discourage casual anglers. Cheaper short-term licenses

have been devised to solve this difficulty but there is still the inconvenience of finding a license vendor. License requirements are particularly discouraging to would-be participants traveling through several nations, states, or provinces in a relatively short period of time.

Property Taxes. Finally, there are the effects of property taxes. This is the one type of tax affecting people's recreation behavior that is higher in the United States than elsewhere. Generally, property taxes are two or three times higher than they would be for equivalent properties in any of the countries of Europe. In addition, at least until recently,[6] property taxes in the United States have been climbing an average of over 10 percent a year. These taxes influence recreation participation in several ways.

When residential property taxes are high, people tend to buy smaller lots and houses or live in condominiums, apartments, or house trailers. This may restrict or eliminate activities such as gardening, having pets, or engaging in any hobbies that require substantial work or storage space. High property taxes also discourage homeowners from making recreation improvements such as the building of swimming pools or recreation rooms. Rapid increases in local property taxes also affect homeowners' recreation behavior. Some American families, in an effort to meet the rising costs of home ownership, are reducing their expenditures on nonessentials and trips away from home, and purchases of recreation equipment are often postponed or eliminated. Others

[6] See Chapter 18, "Changing Government Roles."

seek additional income; the wife may go to work at least part-time or the husband takes on a second job. Less free time is available for recreation as a result.

The hardest hit, however, are the elderly and others living on fixed incomes. Growing numbers are having to sell their homes and suffer the trauma of leaving familiar surroundings. Many settle for less comfortable, even austere, living arrangements where very few of their former recreation opportunities are available or possible. Meanwhile, many homeowners vent their frustration and demonstrate their concern over rising tax rates by defeating local government bond issues and millage proposals. Local authorities are finding it difficult in some communities to obtain sufficient funds for the acquisition or development of parks, the continuation of sports, arts, and extracurricular recreation programs in schools, or the operation of recreation programs.

There are other ways in which high property taxes affect recreation participation. Around many American cities, there are large areas of what appears to be abandoned farm land. High property taxes based on potential value for development have led farmers to sell these lands to speculators rather than continue farming. Speculators can afford to hold the land for many years because of the tax laws and the large profits that can be made when the land is eventually used for building purposes. As a result, urban dwellers lose the pleasure of seeing active agricultural landscapes much earlier than is necessary. On the other hand, these belts of vacant open space are often used extensively by hik-

Figure 4.12 This vertical air photograph shows evidence of much recreation use in Orion Township just north of Pontiac, Michigan. Trails through disused fields indicate extensive use by motorcycles or other off-highway vehicles. Dredged channels behind residences improve lake access for water recreation.

ers, snowmobilers, motorcyclists, and persons interested in nature study (Figure 4.12).

High local property taxes also discourage private and commercial recreation facilities in and around cities where they are most needed. Since many commercial recreation enterprises such as tennis clubs, drive-in movie theaters, golf driving ranges, miniature golf facilities, campgrounds, and race tracks operate on relatively low profit margins, they frequently find they cannot afford to stay in business when property taxes rise. Some go out of business and the property is sold and converted to residential or commercial uses. Others move further out into the country where taxes are lower. This may make them more accessible to some suburban and rural residents but their availability to people in the urban core may be completely lost, especially if they are no longer accessible by public transportation.

Regulations and Resources. Along with the various taxes and fees, governments impose a great variety of regulations that influence recreation behavior. Examples of these are included in Table 4.2. Although many government regulations are restrictive, some stimulate recreation participation.

So far, this section has dealt mainly with taxes and regulations that governments impose. But there are many other ways in which governments affect recreation participation. Public parks and recreation programs are provided by a variety of government agencies. Subsidies are provided for museums, sports facilities, cultural centers, broadcasting systems, libraries, tourist facilities, educational institutions, roads,

Table 4.2 Examples of Government Regulations Affecting Recreation Participation

Fish and game regulations specify the locations and dates when fishing and hunting may take place and control the kinds and numbers of fish and game that may be taken.

Regulations regarding the speed of vehicles on streets and highways determine how long it will take to reach a recreation resource or whether or not a particular resource can be reached at all during a specific time such as a weekend or vacation.

Gun control laws and local ordinances may make it more difficult for individuals to own or use hunting and target firearms.

Controls setting maximum bank mortgage interest rates and zoning ordinances can affect people's ability to purchase or build houses or seasonal homes and influence the nature and scope of the dwelling's recreation amenities.

Laws requiring boaters to wear life jackets, motorcyclists to wear helmets, or tent fabrics to be fireproofed make participation safer but increase the cost or, in the case of some boating and cycling enthusiasts, detract from the enjoyment of the experience.

Strict health regulations safeguard people's health but make it more difficult for private organizations to hold fund-raising events featuring the serving of food or for small family-run restaurants, bars, resorts, and campgrounds to continue to operate.

Daylight saving time laws increase opportunities for participation in recreation activities that take place out-of-doors in the evenings; such laws are in effect in all but a few places in the United States, Canada, and Europe at least during the warm-weather months.

Laws governing the use of two-way radios for nonbusiness purposes restrict the use of such radios for pleasure in Britain and permit the development of the citizens band (CB) radio as a popular hobby in the United States.

Environmental protection laws restrict the development of certain kinds of recreation resources, enhance the aesthetic qualities of others, and restore the water quality of some so that water-dependent activities can resume.

Government-imposed curfews interfere with the recreation lifestyles of people, especially young people for whom the curfews are often intended as a means of control.

Laws limiting the amount of currency a citizen may take out of the country can restrict or eliminate foreign travel.

Government-imposed marketing controls affect consumer costs as well as the availability of certain recreation products.

Regulations requiring the completion of safety courses and age restrictions for the operation of motorized vehicles may prohibit the use of cars, motorboats, snowmobiles, or recreation vehicles by some individuals.

Government-imposed regulations reserving use of certain parks, sports facilities, programs, restaurants, hotels, theaters, or means of transportation for one segment of the population limit the recreation opportunities of the excluded individuals; conversely, laws prohibiting the exclusion of people because of race, color, or sex increase the opportunities of certain individuals.

Regulations concerning public access determine the extent of recreation that can take place on land or bodies of water on or adjacent to private property; Swedish laws that protect the individual's right to cross another person's land allow people to camp for one night on private property, boat on private waters, use water from private wells, or pick wild berries, flowers, and mushrooms on privately owned land without obtaining the owner's permission.

Regulations governing the use of public lands and recreation facilities determine the kinds of activities that can take place and limit participation to certain times and locations.

Federal and state laws that regulate the design and size of fireworks that can be manufactured or that restrict the types that can be sold or used have reduced the firework-related injury rate in the United States but also have limited people's use of fireworks.

The Morse code proficiency requirement for amateur radio licenses has discouraged millions of would-be hams from participating in the hobby.

Local and intermediate government ordinances concerning noise (stereos, parties), smoking or drinking in public places, use of city streets (skateboarding, playing games), and use of residential yards (storing of travel trailers, keeping livestock, rebuilding vehicles) limit people's recreation behavior.

and many other structures and organizations associated with recreation. Much of Part Three is devoted to an examination of the role of government in providing recreation opportunities.

POPULATION FACTORS

The number of people living in a recreation environment and their basic characteristics have a significant effect on the nature and amount of recreation participation that takes place.

POPULATION DISTRIBUTION

If the rate at which people take part in recreation activities remains constant, then the total amount of participation that occurs in an area will vary directly with population size. Large populations generate large amounts of participation that may cause problems if accessible recreation resources are insufficient. User dissatisfaction, conflicts, and actual physical depreciation of the resources may result.

On the other hand, a large population is sometimes an important stimulus to the provision of recreation opportunities. For example, business interests will not develop a commercial recreation facility if the potential market is too small to provide an adequate return on investment. As a result, commercial recreation opportunities in small towns are often limited because the population is not large enough to support facilities such as movie theaters or bowling alleys. Similarly, a community has to reach a certain size before it can finance special public facilities like a swimming pool or in-

door ice arena. Small communities cannot offer as great a variety of recreation programs because there are too few potential participants to form sports leagues for groups of various ages and abilities, special interest clubs and classes, or activity programs for special populations. On a larger scale, a metropolitan area must have a population of sufficient size before a full-time symphony orchestra or a professional sports team is financially feasible. Similarly, only nations with large populations can support major motion picture or television production studios.

The number of people needed before a facility, program, or service can be justified is called the **threshold population.** This number varies with the activity involved, the degree to which it is subsidized from public or other funds, and the affluence of the participants. Based on the minimum number of persons needed, facilities, programs, or services can be arranged in a series of groupings or a hierarchy. This concept will be discussed further in Chapter 12.

Population density and dispersion also have significant effects on participation. Some parts of nations contain so many people that most of the land is needed for town sites, agriculture, or wood growing, and large areas devoted primarily to recreation like North American national parks are not feasible. This is especially true in the densely populated parts of Pakistan, India, Bangladesh, and the People's Republic of China (Figure 4.13). In these areas there are many sizable urban areas but the majority of the population still lives in rural villages. Intensive subsistence agriculture occupies most of the land and the

majority of the people's time and energy. Educational and recreational opportunities are limited.

Outside Southeast Asia, the densely populated areas are generally urbanized and most of the residents have higher incomes. Urbanization is proceeding rapidly in both the developed and developing nations. As Figure 4.14 shows, more than 60 percent of the residents of Australia, New Zealand, North America, Europe, and the Soviet Union now live in urban areas. By the year 2000, the proportion is expected to reach 75 percent. In the Third World countries, the shift to urban living is equally dramatic; only one-sixth of the population lived in urban areas in 1960 but by 1979, the proportion had risen to one-third. This trend is also expected to continue. On a worldwide basis, it is estimated that at least 50 percent of the population will be urban dwellers by 2000. At least 50 cities will have populations of over 5 million, 22 of which will exceed 10 mill on.[7] Most of these huge urban areas will be located in the less developed nations. Mexico City is expected to reach 32 million; other megacities will include Calcutta and Bombay in India, Peking and Shanghai in the People's Republic of China, and Sao Paulo in Brazil.

Urbanization has varying effects on recreation participation depending on the resultant population densities. In the older industrial towns and cities of Europe, Canada, and the United States, many people live close together in tenements, apartment buildings, and row houses (Figure 3.12). Most of

[7] Currently, the largest urban area is New York with a population of 16 million.

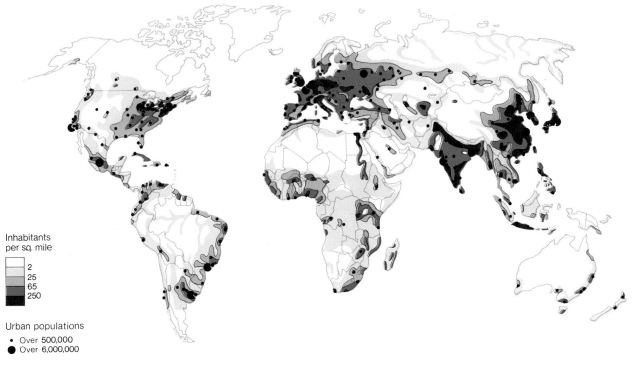

Figure 4.13 World distribution of population and major cities. Densely populated regions offer more urban recreation opportunities but fewer extraurban opportunities. Much of the world's international tourism involves travel between major cities.

Inhabitants per sq. mile

- 2
- 25
- 65
- 250

Urban populations
- Over 500,000
- Over 6,000,000

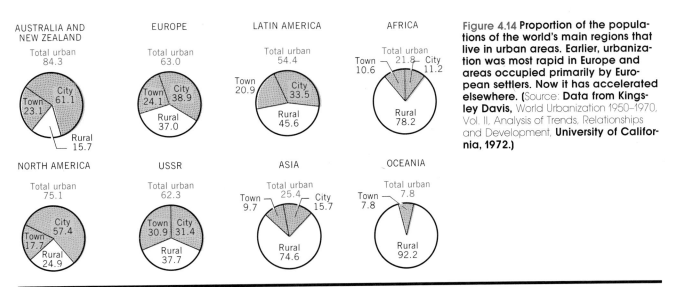

AUSTRALIA AND NEW ZEALAND
Total urban 84.3
City 61.1
Town 23.1
Rural 15.7

EUROPE
Total urban 63.0
Town 24.1
City 38.9
Rural 37.0

LATIN AMERICA
Total urban 54.4
Town 20.9
City 33.5
Rural 45.6

AFRICA
Total urban 21.8
Town 10.6
City 11.2
Rural 78.2

NORTH AMERICA
Total urban 75.1
City 57.4
Town 17.7
Rural 24.9

USSR
Total urban 62.3
Town 30.9
City 31.4
Rural 37.7

ASIA
Total urban 25.4
Town 9.7
City 15.7
Rural 74.6

OCEANIA
Total urban 7.8
Town 7.8
Rural 92.2

Figure 4.14 Proportion of the populations of the world's main regions that live in urban areas. Earlier, urbanization was most rapid in Europe and areas occupied primarily by European settlers. Now it has accelerated elsewhere. (Source: Data from Kingsley Davis, World Urbanization 1950–1970, Vol. II, Analysis of Trends, Relationships and Development, University of California, 1972.)

these communities developed with little thought for open-space needs. Those cities that grew to a fair size before the public park movement began generally have little open space in their older sections unless parks and other types of green space have been created recently by urban renewal programs. As a result, people living in these areas usually have to travel some distance to reach larger parks and special amenities such as zoos. Where older sections do have a number of well-distributed small parks and squares, they are readily available to large numbers of people. This may also mean that a neighborhood park has sufficient residents within easy walking distance to justify activities such as a summer playground program or a senior citizens center.

In contrast, people are often so dispersed in modern suburban areas, it is necessary to include an impractically large area to obtain the threshold population needed to justify a facility or program. This dispersion problem is particularly serious in American and Canadian housing developments where each house lot is 0.1 hectare (¼ acre) or more in size. In such circumstances, it is impractical to provide supervised playground or neighborhood park facilities within acceptable distances of all residences.

The large number of people concentrated in cities contributes to the attractiveness of urban areas for many people. While a majority move into cities because of jobs, many consider additional recreation opportunities an added or even primary incentive. Not only do cities have the necessary population for high-threshold sports and cultural activities but also they make it pos-sible for people to establish recreation-associated relationships more easily. There are enough people to form viable groups for all types of social, sports, and hobby activities. Ethnic clubs, sports groups of all kinds, collectors' organizations interested in everything from antiques to zithers, and a great variety of social groups flourish in large cities. A variety of constantly changing social contacts and recreation opportunities is always available for those who desire them. Of course, urban areas also have their disadvantages. Large numbers of people may compete for limited resources resulting in crowded parks and beaches and long waits for theater seats, sports tickets, or tennis courts. Those who seek more pristine locations for recreation activities out of doors find they have to travel farther and farther as populations grow and cities expand.

The manner in which population is dispersed on a state, provincial, or national scale is also significant. For example, some political units such as France or the states of Mississippi, Alabama, and Georgia in the United States, have moderately sized populations that are relatively evenly distributed. This means that large portions of these populations have reasonably good access to rural recreation opportunities such as fishing, hiking, or pleasure driving.

Some political units have **asymmetrically distributed populations.** Such distributions are caused by a variety of climatic, topographic, soil, and historical circumstances. Two-thirds of the United States' 220 million population is concentrated in the eastern one-third of the nation, especially in the northeastern states (Figure 4.15).

As a result, many extraurban recreation resources in the northeast are overcrowded or have been destroyed. On the other hand, the western two-thirds of the country is relatively lightly populated and contains many places where residents and visitors can enjoy recreation in comparatively undeveloped environments. Similarly, Canada's population is concentrated primarily in a narrow belt in southern Ontario and Quebec. Most Soviet citizens live in the western quarter of the nation, and the majority of the population of South America is within 500 kilometers (300 miles) of the coast (Figure 4.13). Australia is an extreme example with 11 million of its 13 million people living in a narrow band around its southeastern and eastern coastlines. Some of the relatively unpopulated areas of these nations are already used to some degree for recreation. Other locations have considerable recreation potential and will become increasingly important nationally and internationally if transportation improves their accessibility. Many nations are attempting to expand their national parks and other types of reserves and recreation areas in such regions while there is still an opportunity to do so.

Asymmetrical distribution of population results in a greater variety of recreation opportunities than would otherwise exist in some of the more densely populated smaller nations. In the Netherlands, for instance, with an average population density of 332 people per square kilometer, (860 persons per square mile), there are sandy areas in the northeastern provinces of Drenthe and Overijssel that are lightly populated and used for forestry and dispersed recreation. Likewise, neighboring

Figure 4.15 Population distribution in Canada and the
United States. Vast areas of the western United States and
northern Canada have very low population densities.

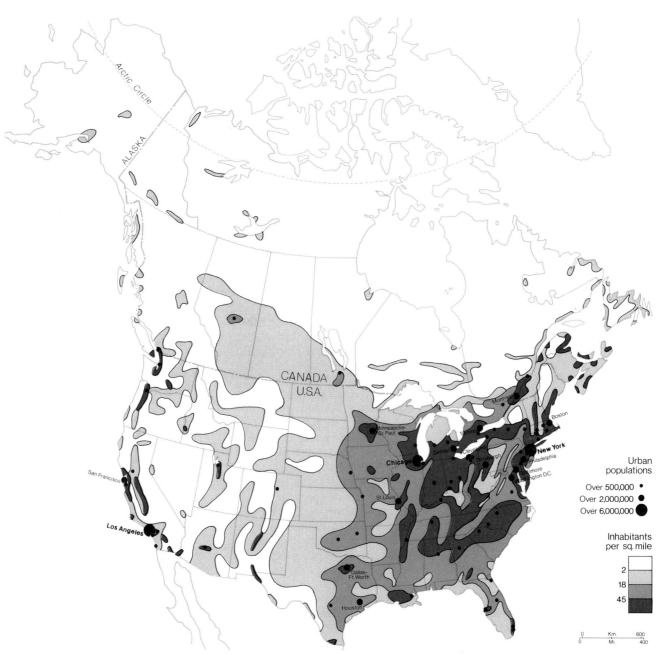

Belgium has comparatively few people in the wooded upland Ardennes, and tourism is now this region's major source of income. Britain's 56 million people are concentrated in the southeast and the industrialized Midlands, leaving large, quite thinly populated areas in the counties of Devon, Cornwall, and Yorkshire, in the Lake District, in Wales, and in large portions of Scotland. These areas provide opportunities for a great variety of dispersed recreation and are the location of most national parks and many other recreation amenities.

Many political units within nations exhibit asymmetrical distributions with similar recreational implications. Michigan is the classic example in the United States with most of its 9 million residents living in the southern third of the state and enjoying the wide range of opportunities presented by the more sparsely populated but accessible northern two-thirds. Other examples are the states of California and New York, and the province of Ontario in Canada.

POPULATION GROWTH

The rate at which a population is growing can have a major impact on recreation participation. Typically, a nation's population growth pattern goes through several phases corresponding roughly to the economic development stages described earlier. In a traditional society, birth and death rates are relatively high and fluctuate considerably because of periodic famines and epidemics; consequently, the population remains fairly constant (Figure 4.16) and is usually comparatively small. In some cases,

food and medical aid from developed nations or international organizations reduce the impact of famine and disease, allowing populations to increase. The true preconditions for takeoff (Stage 2) begin to occur, however, when a country starts to develop its own capabilities to combat famines and epidemics. Birth and death rates begin to stabilize with the death rate at a somewhat lower level. The population starts to increase. During the takeoff stage, the death rate slowly decreases as innovations such as better water supplies, traveling health teams, and improved varieties of crops are introduced. The birth rate remains high so the population increases rapidly. The birth rate begins to drop during the drive to maturity as economic development raises the standard of living and education and medical services improve; as a result, the population growth rate starts to decrease. The final stage, characteristic of a fully developed nation in the high-mass-consumption stage, has relatively low birth and death rates; the population grows slowly or remains static.

Because of these growth characteristics, the populations in the have-not nations tend to be young. In many of the developing countries almost 40 percent of the citizens are under 15 years of age, a factor that, along with the current high birth rates, threatens to double their populations by 2000. If present trends continue, the have-not nations may contain well over 4 billion people or 80 percent of the world's population by that time.

Not only are more of the world's people being crowded into the developing nations but also there are indications that some of these countries are destined to be-

come poorer and less able to provide for their growing populations as time goes by. A great many may never have the opportunity to progress through the various stages of economic development for several reasons. These include:

- Escalating oil prices that force countries without petroleum resources of their own to use more and more of their limited revenues to buy oil.
- The economic slump that has reduced the demand by other nations for the products they have to sell.
- Inflation in the industrialized nations that is increasing the costs of goods the Third World countries must purchase from them.
- The growing tendency toward protectionism on the part of the more affluent nations, making it increasingly difficult for developing countries to market their products abroad.

Already, these factors are causing considerable deterioration in the economies of the Third World nations. To pay for the imports they need, they have accumulated debts of over $250 billion; just paying the interest on these debts consumes more than 12 percent of the value of their exports. Debts now are equal to almost 25 percent of their total output and, in a number of cases, nations are finding it difficult to obtain any more credit or maintain present living standards or levels of industrial and agricultural production.[8]

Clearly, these countries must concentrate on raising food production, providing health and educational services, and improving their balance-of-payments situations. Few can afford to spend more than token amounts on recreation unless the expenditures result in direct

[8] See Chapter 18, "International Trade."

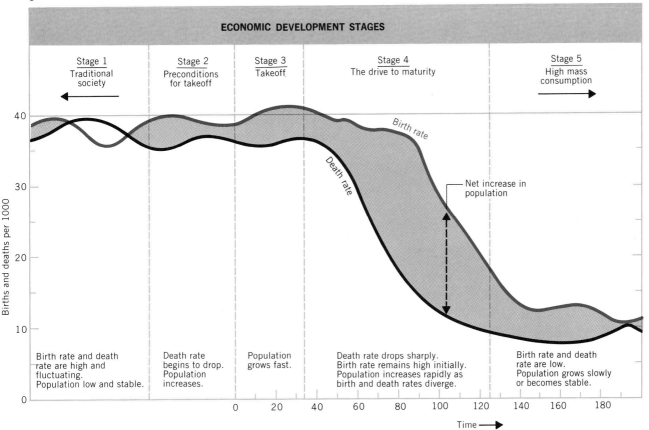

Figure 4.16 Diagram of typical birth and death rate changes during economic development. If population grows very rapidly during the takeoff or drive to maturity stages, development may be retarded.

economic benefits. Often, national parks and other reserves have been designated in these nations but funds for their development, administration, and protection are meager or nonexistent. However, some are developing or expanding tourist facilities in order to increase their foreign exchange earnings. The recreation needs of the general population are therefore of very low priority. The situation will probably become worse where populations

continue to expand rapidly, placing even greater stresses on unstable economies.

Population growth in the have nations is expected to remain relatively slow as birth rates continue to drop and the proportion of older people increases. However, the developed world will have substantially more people, including considerable numbers of immigrants from the more crowded and economically disadvantaged nations. This

larger population will place additional pressures on existing recreation resources and result in increased demand for recreation opportunities from both public and commercial providers.

MIGRATION AND URBANIZATION

Permanent movement of people to new homes and jobs is another factor that affects recreation. Migration

Figure 4.17 Children play on an abandoned car in a disintegrating neighborhood of the South Bronx, New York City. Recreation opportunities usually decrease as urban cores decay because of vandalism, crime, the age of facilities, low tax revenues, and the flight of commercial recreation facilities to the suburbs.

from rural areas into the cities continues in most nations as people are forced off the land by population growth and enticed by prospects of jobs or a more exciting existence. In Canada and the United States, and to some extent in Europe, this migration has contributed substantially to the temporary movement to the countryside that takes place on weekends and vacations. Much of this travel is recreational in nature as recent arrivals in urban areas seek to return to the countryside. Many, even second-generation city dwellers, leave to visit relatives or

friends or recreate in an environment familiar to themselves or their parents.

The second phase of urbanization takes place as city dwellers become more affluent and the center of cities becomes overcrowded and starts to decay. The affluent then move out from the urban core and join prosperous migrants from other locations to form continually expanding suburbs. New, less affluent migrants replace them in the inner city and the proportion of low-income and unemployed persons increases.

In many American urban centers, this process gradually produced "hollow cities." The older central business district and surrounding residential areas disintegrated leaving a landscape comprised of empty lots, dilapidated residences, poorly maintained commercial property, burnt-out buildings, and trash-filled streets (Figure 4.17). The city center ceased to be the focus for urban recreation with well-patronized stores, restaurants, movie theaters, concert halls, and other facilities. Most of these amenities left with the flight to the suburbs. Crime increased. Public facilities such as libraries, recreation centers, and parks were increasingly difficult and expensive to protect, maintain, and operate. Finally, the inner city became almost a no-man's-land except during the business hours of the commercial establishments that remained.

A third phase of urbanization is now well underway in the United States. Many people are moving out of the larger urban centers and into smaller cities and towns. Metropolitan areas such as New York, Cleveland, Pittsburgh, Detroit, St. Louis, Newark, and Philadelphia have been losing more residents than they gain. Even some of the more affluent suburban areas near New York are becoming less populated. For a growing number of people, the disadvantages of the big metropolitan areas — commuting to work, traffic congestion, high taxes, and crime — are apparently outweighing the advantages. One reason for this migration is that many of the smaller centers now have improved amenities such as better stores, shopping malls, cultural opportunities, and TV reception.

This reverse migration is having a considerable impact on recreation participation. It is increasing pressure on recreation resources in the cities and towns to which people are going. This sometimes causes problems initially but it also helps some places reach the threshold populations needed for the development of new facilities and programs. Some migrants move with the expectation of participating more frequently in activities in the surrounding countryside. As a result, public and private lands are receiving increased use particularly for picnicking, swimming, fishing, hunting, motorcycling, and snowmobiling.

Some of these migrants are going comparatively short distances and settling in and around smaller urban centers while large numbers are moving considerable distances to settle in other states. The most remarkable change has been the reversal of the previous movement into the industrial northeast and

northcentral regions. During the 1970–1979 period, three states — New York, Rhode Island, and Pennsylvania — as well as the District of Columbia, actually had population losses. Most of the other states of the Northeast and Midwest recorded only modest growth. The West and South, on the other hand, had massive increases with about 4 million of the 15 million new citizens coming from these northern regions. The states recording the largest population increases were California (2.7 million), Texas (2.2 million), and Florida (2 million). The highest percentage gains were Nevada (43.6 percent), Arizona (38 percent), Wyoming (35 percent), Alaska (34 percent), Florida (30.5 percent), and Utah (29 percent).

There is strong evidence that one reason for this change in population movement is the recreation opportunities that are available in the southern and western regions.

Many of the migrants mention the recreation advantages of a less densely populated location, a warmer climate, or a coastal, desert, or alpine environment. Although a good number of those going to Florida, Arizona, and California are retirees, many moving to these and the other states are young families. These migrants will have a substantial effect on recreation now and in the future. In arid western states like Arizona, migrants are substantially increasing the growth rate in areas that are environmentally fragile. In some locations, water resources are limited and additional residents will make existing conflicts between recreation and other water uses even more serious.

These then are the main ways in which external economic factors and population factors influence participation in recreation. In the next chapter the effects that social customs and attitudes have on recreation behavior will be examined.

DISCUSSION TOPICS

1. At which of the five stages of economic development is the region where you currently live? Where are the nearest examples of regions that have reached each of the other four stages? What are the main differences between each of these five regions with respect to recreation opportunities and participation?
2. Who are the people in your community who suffer from the handicap of poverty? What impact does poverty have on their recreation opportunities?
3. What effect do working hours, shift work, vacations, nature of the work, income, and other employment-related factors have on the recreation opportunities available to you, your family, parents, other relatives, and acquaintances? Are there differences in the impact of these factors between your community and others with which you are familiar?
4. What effect do local, state or provincial, and federal government taxes, regulations, and financial programs have on your own recreation behavior or that of your family and acquaintances?
5. How have population size, dispersion, growth rates, and migration patterns affected recreation in areas with which you are familiar? What effect will present population trends in these areas probably have on future recreation participation?

FURTHER READINGS

Although much has been published on the economic impact of recreation on communities, most sources provide limited information on the effect of economic factors on participation. Many surveys have included investigations of the relationships between income levels and participation. Some examples of these data are included in Chapter 8. Population size and growth are discussed in recreation textbooks but population dispersion and migration are mentioned infrequently. The best sources of general information on work and population factors are books written by sociologists including Max Kaplan's *Leisure Theory and Policy* published in New York by Wiley in 1975 or *Of Time, Work and Leisure* written in 1962 by Sebastian de Grazia and published in New York by Doubleday-Anchor. In order to find appropriate passages in books or journals, it is usually necessary to search the index for suitable references under headings such as "disadvantaged," "economic," "income," "migration," "occupation," "population," "poverty," and "work," as well as under "fringe benefits," "leisure," "recreation," "retirement," and "vacations."

5

EXTERNAL FACTORS AFFECTING RECREATION PARTICIPATION: SOCIAL FACTORS

Recreation participation is strongly influenced by the way people are organized into groups, such as families, associations, communities, and nations, and by the ideas, princi-

Figure 5.1 Driving on the beach is traditional at Daytona Beach where 23 miles of sand are designated as a Florida state highway. More recently, college students started taking spring break in the area. Social group pressures, curiosity, sunshine, warmth, and stories of unrestrained revelry have attracted as many as 600,000 students for the annual rites.

ples, and laws adopted by these groupings. Some of these influences are readily observed. Others are subtle and not easily recognized. Many are so intricately woven into our everyday lives that we neither see them as factors controlling behavior nor realize how much these influences vary from group to group. Most of us accept our own lives as the norm and expect everyone who looks like us to think and behave in the same way. Conversely, we are sometimes surprised when those who look or sound substantially different have the same desires or behavior patterns.

The social factors that affect recreation behavior are complex. Although they have been organized into 14 topics in this book, actually their influences overlap and interact; often it is difficult to determine where the effects of one factor begin and the impact of another ends. For example, the social factors associated with traditional mass participation events and rituals such as the annual spring migration of young people to Daytona Beach, Florida (Figure 5.1) are numerous and intricately interrelated. This should be kept in mind as the social factors are discussed in the sections that follow.

SOCIAL INSTITUTIONS

Most people wish to be accepted by and feel a part of the society in which they live. To achieve these goals, they learn the rules of the social institutions that surround them and conform to those rules so that they fit in. In this way, the behavior patterns of people are molded by the beliefs and requirements of each of the various social groups to which they belong.

SOCIAL STRUCTURE

The way in which a society is organized affects recreation participation patterns. If the society in which they live has a strong nuclear family structure, then people usually take part in more family group activities than people who live in societies where the family unit is weak. Similarly, both informal and formal organization on larger scales, such as social classes, cliques, youth gangs, tribes, neighborhoods, church congregations, villages, and cities, influence behavior. Here are some examples of the effects of social structure:

- Elderly people often control or influence the recreation behavior of adults and children in traditional extended families.
- Participation in recreation activities as a family group has been decreasing in modern societies, especially where both parents work and young people move away from home at an early age.
- In Communist countries, state-organized youth groups or workers' cadres often replace the family as the social structure within which recreation takes place; recreation patterns change accordingly.
- Although division into social classes based on family history is decreasing in the developed nations, some groups such as yacht clubs, opera guilds, and country clubs still tend to be identified with certain income levels, professions, or religious affiliations.
- In predominantly Catholic regions, the parish is often the dominant social unit; for example, in Canada's Province of Quebec, snowmobile clubs and their trail systems are often organized on a parish basis (Figure 5.2).
- Single persons, childless couples, widows, and widowers often feel out of place in situations where families

make up the majority of recreation facility users; as a result, they may avoid recreation resources used extensively by families.
- College and university students constitute a separate stratum in society and have recreation participation patterns that differ substantially from other young people.

Recreation also has an effect on social structure. In modern societies, young people often leave home in order to recreate as they choose; in doing so, they reduce or eliminate nuclear or extended families. People frequently join recreation organizations without other family members. Sometimes these organizations become the dominant social structures in people's lives, and the friendships founded in common recreation interests become the most influential of all personal interrelationships.

INFLUENCE OF FAMILY AND FRIENDS

In societies where the family is a well-developed part of the social structure, the recreation attitudes and preferences of parents, brothers, and sisters may have a considerable effect on an individual's recreation behavior. The influence of grandparents is generally small in most highly developed nations because fewer people grow up in extended families. In the United States, however, many grandparents in traditional black, Chicano, or farm families have remained in closer contact with extended family members, are well respected, and have continued to play a more influential guiding role.

People are most impressionable and learn most readily from those with whom they come

Figure 5.2 **Portion of the Province of Quebec's official snowmobile trail map for a rural area 60 kilometers (40 miles) southeast of Quebec City. Most of these trails are developed, maintained, and operated on a parish basis by parish snowmobile clubs.** (Source: Drawn from Quebec Ministère des Transports, "Sentiers de Motoneige—Quebec Trois-Riviers" map, Quebec, Quebec, 1974.)

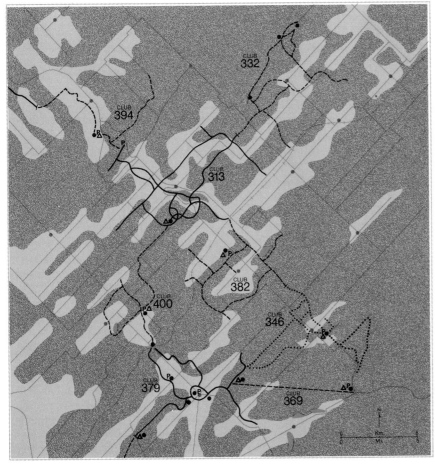

• Shelters   —— Roads   • Villages
△ Restaurants   ⚏ Club trails
P Parking   ▓ Wooded areas

of the family are nonconformists who encourage each other to develop individualistic lifestyles, the children are more likely to feel free to explore recreation opportunities other than those most frequently undertaken by the society in which they live.

Early exposure to certain types of activities often sets the pattern for recreation behavior as adults. General preferences such as a love for outdoor activities, a passion for sports, an interest in the arts, or a fondness for social events are frequently developed in childhood. These patterns may be major factors influencing recreation choice throughout life. Individuals are also introduced to specific activities during childhood, which they may continue to enjoy as adults. Beginning some of the activities that require the mastery of certain skills at this age can have definite advantages. Usually, children are less afraid of failure or injury, and therefore people can more readily acquire the necessary skills as children than at any other stage in life. In fact, if individuals do not have an opportunity to learn the rudimentary skills associated with activities such as playing musical instruments, painting, swimming, or social dancing, while children, they may be too embarrassed or apprehensive to learn them later on.

Sometimes, of course, a child does not share a parent's enthusiasm for a particular activity. Participation then becomes a duty or matter of compulsion. Subsequently, the individual as an adult may reject not only that activity but all others that possess similar negative connotations. Frequently, the child's aversion stems not so much from a personal dislike of the activity but

into close contact during their childhood and teenage years. Attitudes and skills developed at that time often remain with individuals for life and are even passed on to their children. If the parents and other members of the family are close-knit and highly supportive of the

society in which they live, the prevailing lifestyle of that society is likely to be accepted by the children. The children will then limit their recreation to activities that are considered appropriate by the majority of the people in that society. On the other hand, if the members from a general lack of readiness. Especially in modern societies, there is considerable pressure for children to mature quickly. This often results in young people being introduced to recreation experiences too soon. This premature exposure can be emotionally damaging when children are unable to satisfy their parents' unrealistic expectations. In some cases, permanent physical injury that limits a child's recreation participation in the future may also result.

One activity in which parents play an increasingly important role is the development of an enthusiasm for reading. In societies where television has become a major free-time activity, children may never develop a positive attitude toward reading unless parents nurture their children's desire to read—give them books as gifts, read to them regularly when they are young, keep a home library of interesting reading materials, read themselves and talk with their children about what they have read, and introduce them at an early age to the opportunities offered by their community library. This can have far-reaching effects on the children's recreation opportunities as adults, since adequate reading and language skills are necessary for the enjoyment of a variety of recreation activities.

The home environment can also affect recreation behavior in more subtle ways. The manner in which a child is treated by all members of the household molds the developing personality. Current and future participation is highly influenced by personality traits such as timidity, gregariousness, aggressiveness, and inquisitiveness. As adults, individuals tend to select recreation opportunities that are most compatible with their personalities.

Children often derive basic attitudes concerning the roles of the sexes from their home environments. Most women who are prominent in sports attribute their achievements, at least partly, to parents who introduced them to sports, never questioned their right as females to participate, supported their competitiveness, and encouraged them to excel. Parents of handicapped children often play a special role in the development of both skills and attitudes that affect the individuals' participation patterns as children and throughout life. Loving, patient, and supportive parents who are willing and able to devote large amounts of time can help to minimize the handicap. This type of assistance encourages the development of a positive outlook and the confidence and determination that enables the individual to accept the limitations of the handicap and yet participate in recreation to the fullest possible extent.

Other people with whom the individual comes in contact may also contribute to the development of recreation preferences. Friends in the neighborhood or at school, parents of friends, relatives visited periodically, school teachers, as well as youth group leaders and coaches may all have a lasting effect, and not always in direct proportion to the length of encounter. Peer group influences during the adolescent years can be particularly significant, since they sometimes supplant family member influences completely and determine not only the activities a young person chooses but also how he or she takes part.

Sometimes a single experience such as a camping trip with a scout troop or a visit to a museum as part of a classroom field trip can have a lifelong impact. These experiences, however, can be negative as well as positive. A child who is frightened during a swimming or camping experience, humiliated by a sarcastic sports coach, or bored by a long concert may develop a strong and permanent aversion for the activity involved. Anyone introducing young people to recreation in general or trying to develop their interest in one activity in particular has a tremendous responsibility (Figure 7.6).

ADVERTISING AND OTHER COMMERCIAL ACTIVITIES

Commercial advertising and sales promotion techniques have a major impact on recreation participation in societies where it is accepted as an integral part of everyday life. In fact, it may now be the single most powerful influence to which some people are exposed, especially those who watch television extensively. Vast sums of money are spent on the promotion of goods and services in newspapers and magazines, and on billboards, radio, and television. An increasingly large proportion of this advertising is recreation-oriented. Business interests stimulate recreation participation by:

- Setting up store displays that encourage the purchase of recreation clothing, equipment, and services.
- Holding special demonstrations or shows of boats, vehicles, camping gear, photographic equipment, hobby materials and techniques, or other recreation-related products and activities.
- Promoting the sale of recreation opportunities, goods, and services by elaborate advertising in the print and electronic media.

- Advertising nonrecreational products in recreation settings that are meant to stimulate sales but, unintentionally, reinforce prospective buyers' positive attitudes toward recreation in general or one recreation activity in particular.
- Arranging for recreation goods and services to be mentioned or used in films, television shows, and newspaper or magazine articles.
- Emphasizing the importance of recreation through advertisements of labor-saving devices that suggest the time saved by their purchase and use can become extra time for recreation activities.
- Selling recreation goods or services such as seasonal homes or vacation trips by mail or telephone advertising.
- Giving recreation goods or services as promotional gifts or prizes in contests.
- Sponsoring recreation events ranging from children's neighborhood pet shows and tourism-promoting films to professional football games on television.

The effects of such commercial activities on recreation participation are tremendous.

The attitudes, tastes, behavior, and opportunities of millions of people are being changed by advertising whether they are aware of it or not. It is a multimillion dollar snowball becoming larger and more complex as it rolls along. As people are encouraged to participate more often and try different recreation activities, they constitute a larger, highly specialized market which in turn attracts more manufacturers, vendors of services, retailers, and of course, more advertisers. In a relatively short period of time, people may be persuaded to abandon former recreation lifestyles for new patterns of behavior, or to accept new recreation products, activities, or services as necessities rather than luxuries. They are made to feel "old fashioned" if they cling to their "outdated" lifestyles or products. They are also made to feel disadvantaged if they do not have many of these constantly promoted items and opportunities. Everything from family room bar equipment to vacations in exotic locations are included in the barrage of sales messages.

There are other kinds of commercial promotions that are more subtle yet can have far-reaching effects. For example, a number of women's and men's magazines promote certain recreation-oriented lifestyles as being desirable. Articles describe appropriate clothes to wear, places to visit, and recreation activities in which to participate. Sometimes such publications become involved in elaborate promotional schemes with producers of specific goods and services. For instance, a national magazine helped lure between 600,000 and 1 million college students to Daytona Beach for the 1976 spring break by publishing articles, initiating on-campus promotions, and arranging for an exposition by manufacturers of products with special appeal to this age-group to take place in Daytona Beach during that period.

Unfortunately, the recreation experiences promoted by magazines and advertisers do not always live up to the expectations induced by the articles and advertisements. In the case of the Daytona Beach promotion, the sun was there to greet the expectant visitors just as all of them had anticipated. So was the promised freedom from nearly every middle-class constraint that had already attracted substantial participants to the area in previous spring breaks. However, for many of the newcomers, the promised numerous opportunities to meet attractive members of the opposite sex and enjoy continuous partying, camaraderie, and other sensual pleasures failed to materialize.

This is one of the unfortunate aspects of advertising. Many advertisers are not really interested in participant satisfaction with the promoted recreation experience. They are primarily concerned with making money and furthering their own interests or the interests of those they represent. In their desire to achieve these goals, the advertisers may create false impressions. When the advertising seems to almost guarantee a certain result that is not forthcoming, people may have their dreams shattered and become so disillusioned that they never attempt to take part again in recreation activities of that nature. In some cases, their participation in recreation activities in general may also be affected as a result of the negative attitudes and loss of self-esteem brought on by a totally unhappy experience. Worst of all, perhaps, those who are induced to take part in activities or buy products in which they have little real interest are deprived of alternative opportunities. If they had not been influenced by advertising, these people might have used their free time or discretionary income to better advantage.

Advertisers have also been accused of being irresponsible because of the manner in which they promote the large-scale sale of recreation products such as camping equipment, snowmobiles, or off-highway vehicles in areas where the supply of resources suitable for their use is inadequate. Naive consumers may enthusiastically buy a product and then become discouraged and frustrated when they discover that

Table 5.1 The Influence of Religious and Political Doctrines: Examples of Their Effects on Recreation

Doctrine or Practice	Influence on the Individual	Influence on Society
1. Work, education, and service to others are meritorious; recreation is justifiable only to restore the individual for more work, education, or service	— Feeling of guilt when not working, learning, serving, or performing religious duties. — Participates less than really wishes. — Avoids opportunities that occur outside scheduled free time. — Satisfaction for supporters of doctrine.	— Public agencies and commercial enterprises may be regulated so that they provide only approved activities at "appropriate" times.
2. Particular days or hours of the day are sacred or special and must be reserved for religious or political observances— for example, Christian Sundays, Christmas Day; Jewish Saturdays, Passover; Muslim prayers several times each day, Friday services; Communist May Day.	— Provision of time off from work. — Guilt feelings for some of those who do not observe doctrine. — Pressure to conform on those who recreate during prescribed times. — Boredom or frustration for those who cannot recreate when they wish, especially if their personal religion or political affiliation demands abstinence at a time other than that of the dominant religion or political doctrine— for example, Jews in predominantly Christian communities. — Frustration for those who do not observe doctrine but have friends who do; becomes difficult or impossible to find enough participants for a game or other group activity.	— Closing of industry, businesses, government offices, and schools at specified times. — Closing of public and commercial recreation facilities such as tennis courts, bars, theaters, libraries, stores, and recreation centers. — Legal or social prohibition of games or noisy activities such as target shooting or hunting during sacred periods. — Sunday is observed as a holiday even in the Soviet Union. — Christmas Day is a national holiday in the majority of the world's nations even in some where efforts have been made to discourage its observance.
3. Mandatory or expected commitment of adherents' time or money to the cause.	— Gives satisfaction to those who are willing and able to contribute as required; can be recreational. — Causes anxiety and conflict where individuals wish to use time and money for other purposes such as recreation. — Some commit most or all of their spare time and money to the organization leaving little or no time or money for recreation.	— Maintains religious or political organization as a significant force in the community. — May or may not strengthen social structure.
4. Identification or prohibition of some recreation activities as "bad" while others are approved as "good." Banning of specific films, books, music, writers, or artists. Disapproval of certain games, sports, and pastimes. Religions often ban gambling and alcoholic drink; some prohibit social dancing or the viewing of films, television, or any other pictorial materials.	— May not be able to undertake activity desired. — Where alcoholic beverages are competely prohibited, entrepreneurs may avoid community as a site for restaurants, bowling alleys, and other commercial facilities— some opportunities may be denied to all citizens. — Feeling of guilt if banned opportunities are desired. — Banned items may be made more attractive, especially to young people.	— Standards of morality are established including moral aspects of recreation. — Laws passed banning or regulating specific activities. — Censorship procedures or controls to exclude "undesirable" items or persons are set up. — Criminal element may become involved in provision of banned opportunities.

Table 5.1 The Influence of Religious and Political Doctrines: Examples of Their Effects on Recreation (Continued)

Doctrine or Practice	Influence on the Individual	Influence on Society
5. Provision of approved recreation opportunities by religious or political group for the benefit of individuals—emphasis is often on physical activities.	— Opportunities provided that otherwise would not be available—disadvantaged are often especially benefited. — Members of some religious or political groups have improved opportunities. — Participation without guilt or with little guilt since activity is sponsored by an approved group.	— Communities may not have to spend as much tax money on providing public recreation opportunities. — Social structure may be less segregated along political or religious lines if all may participate without distinction. — Religious and political segregation may be emphasized if only organization members are permitted to participate.
6. Provision of opportunities or use of recreational events as a means of spreading religious or political beliefs. Some groups include indoctrinal material in youth group programs, concerts, plays, literature, and art. Others use athletes and half-time programs at sports events to reach and influence people.	— More opportunities of different kinds are available. — Participation may be discouraged or experiences spoiled because individual resents being indoctrinated. — Persons with dependent personalities may live happier lives because they do not have to make as many decisions for themselves.	— Communities may become better places in which to live because of increased religious or political activity. — If religious or political doctrines are repressive, basic freedoms may be reduced. — Communities may turn away from recreation activities that become associated with undesirable doctrines.

the new activity cannot be enjoyed as planned. These purchasers find themselves facing three alternatives. They can give up the activity and sell the equipment or store it to enjoy at some future date when a move to another location improves the opportunity for its use. They can travel considerable distances to reach suitable resources. Or they can try to use the equipment in nearby areas where the necessary resources are not available. In the latter situation, they may trespass on private property, much to the consternation of the landowner, or use public areas illegally. This may result in unsafe conditions for themselves and others, conflicts with legitimate resource users, or damage to the environment.

RELIGIOUS AND POLITICAL INFLUENCES

Most religious and many political organizations are concerned with all facets of human life and therefore teach doctrines that affect recreation participation in a variety of ways. Some doctrines affect recreation participation by designating certain recreation activities as "good" or "evil." Other doctrines influence participation indirectly by specifying how followers should behave or spend their time and money. The nature of these teachings and the degree to which they are followed vary greatly even within the same religious sect or political party. They generally fall into one of the six classes listed in Table 5.1.

The work ethic continues to af-

fect attitudes and influence behavior in large portions of the developed world. The degree to which this doctrine persists depends largely on the religious and cultural heritage as well as the homogeneity of the population. In the United States, for example, its influence is strongest in predominantly Protestant small town and rural areas where it continues to influence personal as well as community attitudes and behavior. In such areas, people tend to work longer and harder, and less emphasis is given to providing recreation facilities and programs.

A Christian belief that has widespread influence is the observance of Sunday as a day of worship and rest. At one time, laws prohibiting commercial activities on

Sundays (or blue laws as they came to be called in the United States) were passed in many Christian communities to ensure the proper conduct of citizens on the Sabbath. Gradually, the laws lost much of their religious meaning but were supported and retained as a legal means of assuring that workers had a common day of rest. Nevertheless, especially in areas where they are most restrictive and strictly enforced, they affect the recreation opportunities of large numbers of people by prohibiting all but the most essential kinds of business on Sundays. Stores, restaurants, theaters, sports facilities, and most other commercial recreation enterprises are closed. Tourists who are unaware of the laws can be greatly inconvenienced if they need meals, gasoline, or other supplies, or if they schedule visits to the area's shops or cultural facilities on a Sunday. In urban locations, such restrictions can be especially hard on lonely people who live by themselves in small apartments or hotel rooms (Figure 5.3). Since public and quasi-public recreation facilities also tend to close, these people may have no place to go in bad weather except a religious institution, which may only be open for a few hours. Men and women who live at home or in boarding houses where many kinds of activities are restricted, or where visits by members of the opposite sex are forbidden, often find Sunday the most desolate day of the week.

The effects are not necessarily negative of course. In many communities, these regulations ensure that the staffs of most public and private enterprises have an opportunity to use one day each week as they see fit. Certainly, there are sit-

Figure 5.3 The Sunday closing of neighborhood cafés is hard on people who depend on them for social and entertainment opportunities. This café's name is particularly apt on Saturday night when lonely users realize they will have no place to go on Sunday.

uations where all the members of a household would seldom have the same day free and be able to do things together if it were not for Sunday closing laws. Generally, Canada and Britain have more restrictive laws than the United States. However, about half of the states and many local jurisdictions throughout the United States impose some kind of ban on Sunday commerce.

Religious groups appear to be more successful in controlling alcohol consumption than political organizations. Where large proportions of the population are strict adherents to Buddhist, Muslim, or fundamentalist Protestant faiths, communities or nations generally have the most restrictive and effective alcoholic beverage customs and laws. In the United States, a crusade by the Women's Christian Temperance Union and a period of prohibition have led to a variety of liquor laws and regulations, many of which still remain in effect in areas where temperance and religious organizations are strong. Some are state laws; most are county, township, or city ordinances. All serve the same purpose; by making it difficult for all or some of the population to obtain alcoholic beverages, it is hoped that the levels of consumption can be controlled. The regulations range from almost no restrictions to the complete banning of all beer, wine, and spirit sales.

Regulations that sharply curtail the hours when places serving alcoholic beverages can remain open, that impose higher drinking-age requirements, or that prohibit the sale of liquor by the drink have the greatest effect on recreation participation. In some areas, there are fewer recreation facilities of certain kinds because proprietors of establishments such as restaurants, nightclubs, discotheques, bowling centers, spectator sports facilities, and resorts often will not locate in places that forbid or severely restrict sales. They believe that they cannot make an adequate profit or attract sufficient customers if they are not allowed to serve alcoholic drinks.

Similarly, facilities that cater primarily to a young clientele may close when the legal drinking age is raised and business decreases. Some may remain open but undergo substantial changes in decor, menu offerings, and entertainment formats in order to attract an older clientele. In either case, the 18- to 20-year-olds may have lost more than just their drinking rights. For many young people, especially in college communities, the facilities offered opportunities to meet people, listen to music, dance, or perform before an audience of peers. Even in situations where they are still admitted, the atmosphere that made these facilities such attractive meeting places may no longer exist. Unless new facilities are provided that offer the same kinds of recreation opportunities in a nondrinking environment, this age-group is likely to find itself increasingly disadvan-

taged. When such groups attempt to relocate their socializing activities to public places like streets, shopping center parking lots, and parks they usually find they are equally unwelcome there. This situation is unlikely to improve in the near future since the movement to lower the legal drinking age has now been reversed. Twenty-eight states liberalized their laws between 1970 and 1975; by 1979, however, six states had raised the drinking age again and at least 12 more were proposing to do so.

Gambling is another aspect of recreation that is opposed on moral grounds by many religious groups, fundamentalist Protestants in particular. In regions where these groups remain strong, legalized gambling is generally prohibited. But even in these areas, games such as bingo are often permitted as a means of raising money for church programs and other charitable purposes. Generally, the United States is more restrictive in its attitudes toward legal gambling than any other developed Western nation with the exception of Canada. But this appears to be changing for several reasons. Powerful business interests favoring gambling are spending large sums of money to secure the support of political leaders and voters. Increasing numbers of citizens are willing to condone gambling operations if they are likely to generate public revenues and prevent further tax increases. And in most areas, larger numbers of people are regarding gambling as harmless entertainment rather than a moral sin. As a result, legalized gambling is spreading rapidly (Figure 5.4) and is likely to continue to grow in spite of occasional setbacks in regions where antigambling sentiment prevails. Al-

ready, the considerable success as public revenue earners of 14 state-run lotteries and Atlantic City's commercial casinos is causing at least 15 other states to consider liberalizing their gambling policies.

Political doctrines can have considerable impact on recreation participation in both the democratic and totalitarian nations. In the democratic countries, the most significant issue is the degree of government involvement with recreation. Some nations, states, provinces, and local governmental units follow policies of minimal involvement. Others are engaged in many kinds of recreation programs ranging from support of the arts to the acquisition and protection of remote national parks. In the past, the governments that participated least in such programs were generally the ones that followed the most conservative doctrines. However, involvement in many jurisdictions is now becoming more a matter of political expediency than political doctrine as voters become concerned about the provision of public recreation opportunities (Figure 3.10).

In the Communist nations, political doctrines can affect all kinds of recreation participation. Not only do these governments control public park and recreation programs but also they restrict travel by both citizens and foreign visitors and direct the nature, policies, finances, and programs of art galleries, theaters, orchestras, museums, libraries, broadcasting systems, resorts, transportation systems, and tourist organizations. Manufacturing and importing is also controlled so that the nature and availability of all recreation goods from books and recordings to television sets and automobiles depend on government

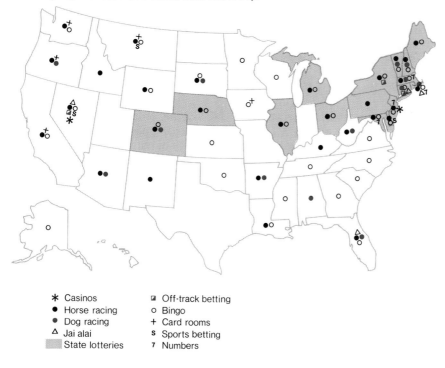

Figure 5.4 **Distribution of forms of gambling operated or legalized by the various states in the United States. States with no legalized gambling or only bingo are predominantly those with high proportions of rural residents and strong conservative protestant churches.** (Source: **Data from George Moneyaun, "Governments Bet on Gambling," Christian Science Monitor article reprinted in** The State Journal, **Lansing, Mich., April 17, 1977 and "Gambling: The Newest Growth Industry," special report,** Business Week, **2539, June 26, 1978).**

✳ Casinos	◰ Off-track betting
● Horse racing	○ Bingo
● Dog racing	+ Card rooms
△ Jai alai	ˢ Sports betting
State lotteries	⁷ Numbers

policies. In addition, individuals and families frequently do not own their place of residence; the state owns the buildings and the surrounding lands, and people have little opportunity or incentive to develop personal recreation environments to suit their own needs.

Generally, the Communist nations that have followed the Maoist doctrines of the People's Republic of China have had the most restrictive recreation policies. Until recently, most recreation activities that could be readily identified with the Western world or earlier Chinese regimes were banned or discouraged by government policies. Activities were limited to ones considered supportive of Chinese Communist ideology and goals, and most programs appeared to outsiders to be largely propagandist. Undesirable recreation ranged from tennis, social dancing, and foreign literature and music to traditional Chinese opera that had long been a central part of the recreation lifestyles of the masses. Before the Cultural Revolution, daily speech had been filled with expressions taken from these productions, and no major public ceremony or celebration was considered complete without an operatic presentation.

In early 1977, however, under the leadership of Chairman Hua Guo-feng, restrictions were relaxed. Since then, the Chinese people have once again had access to many formerly banned recreation experiences including the music of Beethoven and other Western classical composers, the works of Shakespeare and contemporary American authors, foreign movies, and a few of the traditional operas whose themes are considered acceptable. Provincial stage shows and plays are starting to give less emphasis to propagandist material, and a few of them even include a touch of romance, strictly taboo under earlier doctrines. More foreign tourists (1 million in 1979) are being granted permission to visit selected parts of the country and, for the first time in many years, the Chinese people are being permitted to talk to them. Whether this trend toward the relaxation of restrictions will continue, however, is not yet clear. The government has expressed concern over some of the results of the new permissiveness, and a return to a more restrictive regime may have already begun.

TRADITIONS, RITUALS, AND HABITS

Recreation participation patterns are often the result of long-established social customs. Some patterns have their origin in religious festivals; others in annual celebrations of important historical events. Many traditions have developed because of a combination of circumstances. For example, the traditional British family's summer excursion to *the seaside* had its beginnings in the mid-eighteenth century when the affluent followed the example of George III and adopted ocean bath-

Figure 5.5 Many Britons continue to take their vacations at seaside resorts. Here at Eastbourne on the English Channel, they may take part in all the traditional activities including strolling along the Grand Parade, listening to band concerts (center), going for boat trips, or seeing a show at the pier (upper right).

ing as a health measure. The introduction of relatively cheap rail transportation in the middle 1800s and the fact that Britain is a small island permitted the annual seaside trip to become a national institution.

Today, the seaside is still featured in 75 percent of all British vacations. Millions of families travel to seaside resort areas during July and August, often returning to the same location year after year (Figure 5.5). Many follow the same ritual each time. In fact, the traditional and ritualistic aspects of the trip appear to be an essential ingredient for most of the participants. Even crowding seems to be accepted as

an integral part of the experience.

Traditional and ritualistic recreation events like the British seaside holiday become cherished parts of an individual's or family's lifestyle. Many of these experiences are linked to a particular season. Although the activity itself may soon lose its novelty as the season progresses, the first occasion on which it can be done is exciting and takes on a special meaning. For example, children in colder regions wait eagerly for the first snowfall so that they can build snowmen or try out ice skates and sleighs. Then, just as impatiently, they long for the snow to depart so that they can ride bikes

and fly kites. Similarly, adults look forward to the first football game of the fall season or the opening of trout fishing in the spring. Other examples of traditions, rituals, and habits that affect recreation participation include:

- National holidays such as the fourth of July celebrations in the United States; these often involve parades, community concerts, picnics, and firework displays.
- The four-day Thanksgiving holiday in the United States, which has become more than a time set aside for remembering one's blessings; it is regarded as the one time in the year when families should try to get to-

gether for a visit and a feast that features traditional foods.

- State or provincial holidays such as Pioneer Day in the state of Utah or the separate anniversary days for each of the provincial districts in New Zealand; these holidays may feature activities like rodeos, sports events, parades, and regattas.
- The ritual of *paseo* (promenading through the main part of town or around the central plaza in the early evening) that provides a pleasant opportunity for meeting friends, exchanging gossip, or making new acquaintances in Spain and many Spanish-speaking nations.
- Religious festivals such as the Hindu spring festival of Holi that includes singing and dance performances and great merriment in the streets with participants throwing colored powders and water at one another.
- Habitual patterns of personal behavior such as attending a movie, going for a walk, visiting a library, eating at a restaurant, buying a book or record, telephoning a friend or relative, seeing a favorite television series, or spending an evening at a bar, billiards parlor, or bowling center on a more or less set schedule.
- Local rituals that have become well-established such as the informal gathering of a large crowd in New York's Times Square every December 31 to celebrate the start of another year.

Whatever the origin of these behavioral patterns, they do affect the nature, extent, and timing of recreation participation. They are often instrumental in determining peak use of certain facilities and should be considered in designing amenities and organizing programs. An appreciation of traditions, rituals, and habits is essential in understanding recreation behavior.

SOCIAL ATTITUDES

The prevailing attitudes of a society play a role in determining how a person's sex, age, ethnic origin, and handicaps affect recreation participation. Many of these attitudes are restrictive and reduce the range and number of recreation opportunities available to certain individuals. The majority are not founded on fact; often they are nothing more than prejudices and myths that have sprung up and been perpetuated over a long period of time. Unfortunately, they have gained status by becoming part of a society's cultural heritage and, as such, have often been accepted without question.

SEX ROLES AND CHARACTERISTICS

Attitudes concerning the everyday role of males and females and their respective recreational capabilities are major factors influencing participation. Both sexes are disadvantaged by some of these attitudes but females suffer most because a far greater proportion of the attitudes affecting their recreation behavior are restrictive in nature.

Attitudes Toward Work. In most modern societies, the accepted roles for each sex still tend to follow traditional patterns. The man is generally perceived as the aggressive breadwinner while the woman is seen in the more passive role of homemaker and mother. When married women with children follow the traditional roles conscientiously, they usually have little time for recreation. Cleaning up following the evening meal, bathing and attending to the needs of the children, preparing the next day's lunch kits for family members who eat away from home, ironing and mending clothes, sewing, or knitting take up much of each evening. Large portions of weekends are spent preparing meals, keeping the house in order, shopping, and caring for the children. When the family shares a recreation experience by going on a picnic, taking a vacation, or celebrating Christmas, wives often work even harder than usual making all the necessary preparations. Of course, some of these duties may be pleasurable but there is much truth in the old saying, "Man may work from sun to sun, but the woman's work is never done." Most mothers would be delighted if they could just work a 40-hour week!

In contrast, the traditional male working day is much shorter. Many married men put in their eight hours at their place of employment, come home, eat supper, and then spend the evening as they choose. Helping with household chores or child care is often not regarded as part of the male role. Some men justify this uneven distribution of after-supper duties by pointing out that the man works hard all day while the woman has a chance to relax between chores. But this pattern of duties often persists even when the woman also has a full-time job outside the home. Many married women who work perform all the regular household and child care tasks that they were unable to do while at work during the evenings and on weekends. Strict adherence to the traditional roles means that married women generally have far less free time than their husbands and that their available free time is much more fragmented.

The traditional roles of the sexes also affect the amount of time girls have for recreation. In earlier times, boys and girls both took an active part in the daily family routine. Everyone helped and there were tasks assigned to each member of the family unit according to age, capability, and sex. Girls helped their mothers with the housekeeping and care of the younger children while boys fetched water, chopped firewood, cleaned out the ashes from the fireplace or furnace, or helped their fathers with repairs, care of livestock, or work in the fields. In a modern urban family situation where the husband works away from home, few chores remain that are perceived by society as being suitable for boys. Some are expected to help with a few tasks like lawn cutting, shoveling snow, and car washing but many have no household duties to perform. Most girls, on the other hand, are expected to help with all types of homemaking tasks. As a result, boys generally enjoy more free time than girls.

Choice of Activity. Society also discriminates against females by controlling their movements outside the home and restricting their choice of friends and activities. Even in highly developed societies, parents often observe the traditional taboos. Going out with male friends is closely controlled and in some families may actually be prohibited. Certain kinds of recreation activities and locations are forbidden, and girls and women are expected to return home at a reasonable hour. Moving away from home to live alone or with a friend may be out of the question if you are a young woman but quite acceptable if you are a man. Of course, in some environments, there are good reasons for girls and women being protected more than boys and men, but the attitudes of society are often unreasonable and discriminatory in

the case of the older teenagers and young women.

Even as an independent adult, a woman finds her recreation opportunities affected by the fact that she is female. In many communities, it is not safe for a woman to travel alone especially after dark. Therefore, a woman may not be able to participate in any activities or events that take place in certain locations or end late at night. Women also find themselves unwelcome in many organizations and clubs, and in some commercial establishments such as bars or pool halls that cater, by custom, to a male clientele. Even women golfers — despite the fact that there are well over 3 million of them — face these kinds of discriminatory situations. Some private golf clubs ban women and many others severely curtail their hours of play. On public golf courses where supposedly there is no discrimination, female golfers often find themselves barely tolerated or actually derided by male golfers. And finally, some of the best tournaments are still closed to women.

For some women, these societal inequities do not end with marriage. Their husbands automatically assume the protective role once occupied by the parents and determine how much money their wives should spend or which recreation activities they should undertake. In some cases, the husband insists that his wife join him in his preferred recreation pursuits whether she wishes to or not. This unhappy situation can work the other way around of course but it is far less common and not nearly as socially acceptable. A husband who helps with the housework and constantly does things his wife wants him to

do is pitied and considered "henpecked" by society while a wife who conforms to her husband's wishes is praised and considered a "model wife."

Attitudes concerning women's participation in recreation were most restrictive during the Victorian era. Females were believed to have weak physiques and delicate constitutions that required protection from any form of physical or emotional stress. Genteel ladies were expected to avoid exposure to the sun and refrain from strenuous activity. Physically and emotionally competitive sports, in particular, were considered potentially dangerous to female physiques and personalities.

Regrettably, many Victorian biases persist. At least until very recently, girls in general have neither been expected nor encouraged to show a keen interest in playing contact sports, climbing trees, building forts, going on long hikes or bike rides, wrestling, or any of the other rough-and-tumble activities that are supposed to be favorite pastimes of boys. In fact, whenever such interests have been shown, participation has tended to be discouraged or prohibited as unseemly behavior. Consequently, most females have not had and still do not have the opportunity to develop the physical strength that would enable them to participate successfully with males in many sports and other outdoor activities. Only the occasional "tomboy" persists in playing "boys' games" thereby developing the stamina and skills that enable her to keep up with boys during the teenage years. No wonder fewer women than men participate regularly as adults in vigorous recreation activities.

The belief that females are much less interested in sports and other physically arduous activities is so well-established that society accepts without question the inequities that it has produced. Female sports programs in schools and universities usually have had much smaller budgets than the male programs. Facilities and equipment for female participants have generally been inferior, coaches have been paid less, and male events have had precedence in scheduling. Most municipal recreation programs have also provided a much greater number of opportunities for males than for females. Cities, for instance, often provided an abundance of softball, baseball, basketball, football, soccer, or hockey teams for boys and men but few sports teams for girls and women.

Some may contend that increased sports opportunities for females are not warranted because of lack of participation. There is increasing evidence, however, that female sports programs will flourish if they are supported by both community enthusiasm and adequate funding, facilities, coaching, and administrative services. The classic example is the Iowa high school basketball program for girls. Most of the state's 500 high schools have girls' basketball teams competing in a statewide elimination schedule. The final playoff games take place before crowds of 15,000 spectators in Des Moines while more than 2.5 million fans in nine states watch the games on television (Figure 5.6). The Veterans Memorial Auditorium where the final games are played is sold out weeks in advance, and hotel space is booked as much as a year ahead. Not only is the basketball program self-supporting but

Figure 5.6 Teams competing in the Iowa girls' high school basketball play-off tournament are introduced to 15,000 fans packing the Veterans' Memorial Auditorium in Des Moines and a large television audience. The success of this program indicates that the relative absence of women's sports in other areas is largely a matter of discriminatory attitudes.

also it provides funds for other sports activities for girls. Interestingly enough, this unique program is not a new development; the first state championship was held in 1919, and participation and enthusiasm have been growing ever since.

Societal attitudes toward female participation in strenuous activities may finally be changing. A major step toward eliminating sexual discrimination in American school and college recreation programs was undertaken in 1972 with the passage of Title IX of the amendments to the federal Education Act. This made it illegal to discriminate against any person who wishes to participate in an educational program or activity that receives federal financial assistance.

Although opposition by male-dominated organizations has resulted in the adoption of relatively weak enforcement procedures for Title IX, many improvements have taken place. Schools and colleges are increasing budgets for women's sports and improving the facilities, coaching, and the status of the staff involved. Coeducational physical education classes and gym teams are increasing, thereby equalizing the opportunities for young people to develop their physical capabilities and acquire sports-related skills. Schools are also expanding the number and kinds of sports programs available to females. For instance, high school basketball program opportunities increased by 39 percent between 1976 and 1978 with the addition of 2000 programs.

Many girls' teams in traditionally male sports such as soccer have been organized. And, where the institution only has one team in a particular sport, females are now being granted the opportunity to try out for previously all-male teams in sports such as baseball and volleyball. Because of the increased opportunities, the number of girls taking part in interscholastic sports programs grew by more than 600 percent between 1971 and 1979. There are now 2.1 million female participants. Similar improvements have also taken place in intramural and youth league sports programs that regularly use school facilities.

Of course, Title IX does not *guarantee* girls an opportunity to play on boys' teams. Although it does not require it, Title IX allows segregation by sex in contact sports (defined as basketball, boxing, football, ice hockey, rugby, and wrestling). But this limitation has been successfully challenged. In 1974, two female Ohio middle school students competed for and were awarded positions on their school's interscholastic all-male basketball team. The Board of Education excluded them from participating with boys by reason of their sex but complied with the Title IX regulations by creating a separate girls' basketball team. The girls felt this would not provide them with an equal opportunity to develop skills because it would lack the challenges provided in the much more competitive all-boys team and league. So, a suit was filed on their behalf in U.S. District Court against the Ohio High School Athletic Association and state officials. The Association's rule prohibiting mixed gender interscholastic athletic competition in contact sports was the reason for the girls' exclusion.

Federal Judge Carl Rubin issued a decision in their favor ruling that both the Ohio and federal regulations forbidding coeducational sports were unconstitutional. This decision resulted in mixed reactions. Some athletic organization officials said it would interfere with the development of good female teams and encourage males who did not make their own teams to try out for and possibly dominate female teams. Others, especially some of the male sports columnists and football coaches, were openly derisive of the ruling as they envisaged women trying to compete with men on professional football teams.

However, Judge Rubin did not expect many women to abandon their participation in sports activities with other women and compete on an equal basis with stronger and better trained men in sports such as football and boxing. All he was concerned about was their right to try to do so if they felt physically qualified. In his ruling he said:

> It has always been traditional that "boys play football and girls are cheerleaders." Why so? Where is it written that girls may not, if suitably qualified, play football? There may be a multitude of reasons why a girl might elect not to do so. Reasons of stature or weight or reasons of temperament, motivation, or interest. This is a matter of personal choice. But a prohibition without exception based upon sex is not. It is this that is both unfair and contrary to personal rights contemplated in the Fourteenth Amendment to the United States Constitution.

> It may well be that there is a student today in an Ohio high school who lacks only the proper coaching and training to become the greatest quarterback in professional football history. Of course the odds are astronomical against her, but isn't she entitled to a fair chance to try?[1]

This decision is ensuring that many more females will have a reasonable opportunity to participate in good quality sports programs in the future.

Although cases of sexual discrimination in sports receive the most publicity, there are many other situations where women's participation in recreation is hampered as a result of sexual prejudice. Many activities have traditionally been regarded as "manly"; as a result even when women have the desire or ability to participate, it is often considered inappropriate for them to do so. Sometimes participation is prohibited; more often, women are simply made to feel unwelcome and uncomfortable when they try to take part. These activities include visiting bars unescorted, playing pool or certain card and dice games, riding motorcycles, or going hunting. Women have also found it difficult to achieve recognition as first-class amateur or professional musicians; for instance, until quite recently, major orchestras and bands have been largely male. There are still very few female conductors.

Finally, females are less likely to be introduced to recreation activ-

[1] Yellow Springs Board of Education *v.* Ohio High School Athletic Association, C-3-76-205, U.S. District Court, Southern District of Ohio, Western Division (1978).

ities that are mentally challenging. It is not uncommon to find people who believe females are just naturally inferior in their abilities to reason, concentrate, or deal with problems analytically and unemotionally. Consequently, they are seldom encouraged to pursue recreation activities such as debating, bridge, or chess. And yet, in spite of this neglect, at least half of the students involved in elementary school chess club programs, and many of the best players, are girls. Nevertheless, defenders of the myths concerning the female's ability or interest in such pursuits point out that there are very few girls in high school or adult chess clubs. Unfortunately, they seldom ask the girls why they drop out as they mature. The majority leave clubs because it is socially expedient to do so. They find that when they lose a game, male opponents act in a patronizing and superior manner. When they win, the males become angry, sarcastic, and upset. Neither situation enhances their relationships with members of the opposite sex.

It would be inappropriate to end a description of social attitudes toward the selection of activities without pointing out that boys and men also are affected by sexual stereotyping. Males are generally expected to be athletic, strong, self-sufficient, ambitious, competitive, aggressive, brave, unemotional, gregarious, and "born leaders," and participation in recreation activities that develop these traits is encouraged. Young men who show strong preferences for passive, introspective, solitary, or sedentary activities (such as reading, classical music, painting, nature study, and creative hobbies) and who dislike and avoid participation in activities

like team sports, hunting, fishing, and "hanging out with the boys" are often urged to change their patterns of behavior. Cooking, sewing, knitting, ballet, and playing with dolls or younger brothers and sisters are activities that are seldom encouraged, since they are regarded as suitable only for girls. Even the U.S. Post Office recently felt it necessary in promoting the sale of stamps to advertise the fact that stamp collectors can be very manly individuals (Figure 5.7).

The insistence on the development of certain personal characteristics that are considered appropri-

Figure 5.7 The U.S. Post Office used this full-page color advertisement in a national magazine to emphasize that stamp collecting is a manly hobby. The narrative identifies the player as Dave Rowe, a 2.03 meter (6 foot, 8 inch) 127 kilogram (280 pound) defensive tackle on the Oakland Raiders professional football team.

ate for males, and the repression of those that are not, also has its effects on recreation participation. Just as females find it difficult to be successful in or get enjoyment from some sports, games, and adventure activities because they have never had the opportunity to develop aggressive and competitive traits or learn self-sufficiency, so males are sometimes hampered in the pursuit of certain recreation experiences. They may find it hard to develop warm, loving relationships with other people or to appreciate certain cultural or aesthetic experiences. They have been programmed to play the role of the macho male so successfully that they are no longer capable of being gentle, expressing emotion, or enjoying experiences that appeal to the senses.

ATTITUDES CONCERNING AGE

Participation in recreation is affected by society's attitudes concerning the appropriateness of taking part in various activities at different ages. Some activities are considered appropriate for children, some for teenagers, some for adults, and others for older people. Individuals are expected to "act their age" and those who do not are often criticized or considered eccentric.

In the case of children, both the amount of time devoted to recreation and the types of opportunities available are determined by social attitudes. These attitudes vary considerably. Some societies place a great deal of importance on giving children almost unlimited opportunities to play; in other societies where children must contribute to the family's support as soon as possible, play is a luxury available only to the youngest individuals. In some societies structured recreation activities may be considered most helpful to good child development; in others, unrestricted play may be regarded as essential to personality growth. Passive indoor activities may be discouraged and active outdoor games encouraged. Group play may be seen as socially beneficial, and solitary, introspective activities may be frowned on.

Societies often determine the ages at which young people can begin certain activities by organizing recreation programs for different age-groups, by regulating the sale of items to minors (cigarettes, alcohol, books, and magazines), by denying young people access to resources (facilities that permit gambling or serve alcohol, adult book stores, theaters showing films with adult themes), or by placing age restrictions on participation (use of firearms for hunting or the operation of motor vehicles and boats).

But just as often society's restrictive influence can be indirect or even unintentional. People may voluntarily limit their recreation participation by avoiding activities that they feel are socially unacceptable for their particular age-group (Figure 5.8). This social custom of linking certain activities with certain age-groups can be particularly confining in the case of teenagers. In their desire to gain recognition as a separate group, they may avoid any activities that society deems particularly appropriate for either younger or much older people. For instance, they may avoid participation in any of the games and activities that are commonly enjoyed by children, even if the urge to do so is strong. Similarly, they may go through a

Figure 5.8 Young adults take part in a sandcastle-building contest on the beach at San Diego, California. Until recently, sand play was perceived as exclusively a children's activity, thereby limiting the value of beaches as resources. The breakdown of traditional age barriers often expands recreation opportunities.

stage when they stop watching television, keeping pets, sewing or cooking, or even taking part in family parties and outings because they perceive them as activities closely associated with being parents or being much younger or older members of the family group. They may be especially reluctant to engage in activities such as knitting, gardening, reading newspapers, or relaxing in rocking chairs or porch swings—activities that society may be perceived as prescribing for old folks!

Conventional societal controls usually lessen when young people begin to work or go to college. The peer group continues to be a major influence, especially regarding participation in some of the less socially acceptable recreation activities. But for many young people, it is the

least restricted period of their lives. It is a time for living away from home, exploring some of the less common recreation activities, giving or attending parties, frequenting drinking and dancing establishments, or going away alone or with friends on recreation trips. Even the social attitudes restricting recreation participation according to age and sex may to a large extent have little effect because many young, single people have become determined to free themselves from the confines of these arbitrary restrictions (Figure 5.8).

When young people get married, they usually begin to move out of this period of maximum recreation freedom. Under the extended family system in less developed societies, there may be periods when comparatively little extra responsibility is placed on young husbands, and their recreation behavior continues much as before. The majority of young families in developed nations, however, tend to live away from their parents and shoulder full responsibility almost immediately. Marital, parental, social, community, and work responsibilities usually decrease the amount of time available for recreation. In addition, social pressures to take part in family types of recreation often reduce or eliminate participation in the activities typical of the young unmarried worker and college student.

Some individuals attempt to prolong this latter state as long as possible by remaining single or childless. However, they soon begin to find their age makes them less acceptable in many of the recreation environments frequented by the younger workers and college students. At the same time, they often feel out of place with family groups. As a result, many seek involvement in informal groups of single people or childless couples, or join clubs and programs that are designed around their special needs and interests.

In most developed nations, recreation during middle age focuses primarily on the family unit. Husbands and wives often participate in separate activities but the majority of recreation activities on weekends and during vacations involves the family group; families that do not follow this pattern are often considered unusual and are sometimes openly criticized by a society that encourages family togetherness. The nature of the activities undertaken also tends to change with the age of the children; for instance, many parents find it difficult to participate in events away from home or travel as much as they would like when the children are small. The degree to which social constraints restrict the recreation activities of young and middle-aged families is controlled largely by their economic situation. More affluent families are able to pay other people to fulfill some of their family or social responsibilities and do not have to be as preoccupied with the need to maintain or improve their incomes.

Although recent law changes are making it easier for people to continue to work beyond age 65, the majority of older Americans are still choosing to retire at 65 or earlier. For these people, recreation takes on a new significance. Unfortunately, many people in this age-group are prevented from enjoying their free time or feel obliged to restrict their recreation choices because of social attitudes. One of these influential attitudes regards the value of work. Although there has been some softening of this attitude, a great many people in the United States still believe that individuals derive their social importance and personal satisfaction from the work they do and how well they do it. For this reason, many older people prefer to put off retirement as long as possible; they feel society will no longer respect or appreciate them once they no longer have a regular paid job. Others who do retire are sometimes unable to obtain any satisfaction from most kinds of recreation; they restrict their participation to the few recreation choices that allow them to continue to feel wanted and of service to the community.

Another social attitude that influences recreation choice concerns the comparative values of youth and old age. In some societies, the acquisition of wisdom and age are closely linked and older people are well respected. In other societies, such as the United States, where large proportions of the population have been under 25, youth has become an ideal and the act of growing old has been regarded as an unfortunate and dreaded event. In fact, at its zenith, there was a tendency to regard anyone over 30 as past their prime! However, this attitude is also beginning to change because the aging of the post World War II baby boom generation, the low birth rate, and increased longevity are producing a steady increase in the proportion of older citizens. Unfortunately, the change has not come quickly enough for some; many older people are so afraid of being treated like social outcasts that they feel compelled to "act young." As long as health permits, they avoid certain behavior patterns or activities and take part instead only in those forms of recreation that society considers youthful.

Senility is a condition associated with advancing age, which has a serious effect on recreation participation. All forms of senility were previously considered natural and inevitable. Now, some types are regarded as debilitating forms of social conditioning. It is increasingly apparent that many older persons are suffering from learned helplessness and intellectual neglect rather than disease or age-related physical deterioration. In many cases where old people in nursing homes have been exposed to stimulating, progressive environments and have received the encouragement and support of friends, family, group counseling, and interested, well-trained physical and recreation therapists, deterioration has been reversed and dependency reduced to a remarkable extent.

Society's neglect of older people includes many instances where their recreation needs are ignored or not recognized. Many facilities have been built that are difficult for the elderly to reach or enter. Vandalized benches are removed from parks and not replaced. Neighborhood parks are neglected in favor of less accessible, larger areas where youth-oriented active forms of recreation predominate. Programs in community centers and retirement homes often consist primarily of activities that amuse and pacify rather than reinvolve and stimulate.

ATTITUDES TOWARD THE HANDICAPPED

As many as 50 million Americans are deaf, visually impaired, wheelchair confined, orthopedically disabled, mentally retarded, institutionalized, homebound, or emotionally disturbed. All of these citizens are to some extent excluded from full participation in recreation because of the limitations imposed by their handicaps. However, the attitude of society toward the handicapped and their capabilities has proved to be an even greater limitation. The President's Commission on Olympic Sports reported that:

This attitude is generally one of ignorance, apathy, lack of awareness, or antagonism. This attitudinal barrier is multidimensional as it involves not only the sensitivities of the general public toward the physi-cally and mentally disabled, but also the perceptions of the handicapped toward themselves.[2]

This situation has affected the recreation lifestyle of the handicapped in a number of ways.

Ignorance about the underlying causes of certain handicaps and their possible effects has led to a lack of understanding or sensitivity on the part of large portions of the general public. All too often, the handicapped are stared at, whispered about, pitied, patronized, ridiculed, abused, ignored, or rejected when they try to take part in recreation activities. These reactions frequently make the handicapped or their parents so uncomfortable that they give up trying to use certain recreation facilities or to participate in some of the recreation programs that are open to the general public whether they are actually excluded or not.

Fear and superstition are also factors that affect people's recreation. This is particularly sad for individuals who suffer disorders or diseases whose effects can be controlled. For example, the seizures associated with epilepsy can be completely controlled in the majority of cases by proper medication. But the social stigma attached to this and many other conditions is not eliminated with treatment, and individuals who have them often find themselves rejected by family members and almost completely expelled from the mainstream of the society in which they live.

Even common diseases can

[2] President's Commission on Olympic Sports, *Final Report of the President's Commission on Olympic Sports 1975–1977*, U.S. Government Printing Office, Washington, 1977.

have this effect. Cancer strikes 700,000 Americans a year, many of whom face the same kind of lack of understanding and alienation from, or even abandonment by, friends and relatives. Society has tended to equate cancer with death to such an extent that some people are uneasy around anyone with the disease. In spite of all evidence to the contrary, some people are afraid it may be contagious. The dread of cancer does more than condemn cancer patients to loneliness and social rejection, however. This unreasonable fear also prevents many individuals from seeking medical help when they notice one of the warning signs. If it is not a malignancy, they have worried needlessly and reduced their ability to enjoy themselves for an extended period of time. If it is cancer, they have affected their chances of being cured and have possibly cheated themselves of many years of life and all the recreation experiences that they would have contained. Unfortunately, their needless death only serves to perpetuate the myth concerning the incurability of cancer, and therefore the social stigma attached to the disease grows even stronger.

Ignorance about the capabilities of handicapped individuals also has a negative effect. Handicapped persons are often discouraged or prohibited from taking part in certain recreation activities because it is erroneously believed that they would find participation harmful, too difficult, or uninteresting as a result of the limitations imposed by their handicaps. Even the terminology used by society to describe people with handicaps is negative and, therefore, psychologically harmful. First, it divides society into two groups setting those who happen to have some distinguishing characteristic apart from the mainstream of society. Second, it makes value judgments about their capabilities; this not only affects the attitudes of nonhandicapped persons toward the handicapped, it can also influence how handicapped individuals feel about themselves. Just as senility in the elderly is often a form of social conditioning, so the self-pity and feelings of helplessness that many handicapped persons experience can be a conditioned response to negative social attitudes.

Recognizing this fact, some of the handicapped are rejecting terms in common usage and suggesting that words that convey a more positive image be used instead. They recommend substituting "wheelchair user" for "person confined to a wheelchair," "characteristic" for "disability," "challenge" for "problem," and "handicapper" for "disabled."[3] In this way, they expect to reduce society's emphasis on the condition and its limiting effects and direct attention instead to the individual who may be experiencing a particular characteristic but is neither defined nor controlled by its effects.

Many people also tend to link any form of visible handicap with other forms, especially a loss of mental acuity or sexuality. This leads to uncomfortable situations when handicapped people try to participate in a recreation activity or develop close interpersonal relationships. For example, even highly intelligent individuals with handicaps are sometimes treated in a conde-

[3] Eric A. Gentile and Judy K. Taylor, "Images, Words and Identity," Michigan State University Handicapper Program, East Lansing, Mich., 1977.

scending manner and, when a friend or relative is present, may find themselves ignored completely. This can be most unpleasant when a handicapped adult is out on a date or on a family outing, and clerks, ticket sellers, or waiters choose to discuss their choice of merchandise, seats, or food not with them but with their dates, wives, or even their children. It is little wonder that some of the handicapped have trouble developing self-esteem or that others prefer to isolate themselves and keep contacts with the outside world to a minimum!

The tendency to underestimate the competency of the handicapped or to overprotect them affects their recreation in a less direct way. Until very recently, for instance, handicapped children were likely to be institutionalized or taught either at home or in special classes. Not only did this set them apart from the mainstream of society at an early age but also it denied them many of the educational and social opportunities afforded the rest of society. Because the handicapped have generally received less education and social orientation than other citizens, they have been less likely to work or have worked for less than the average wage. As a result, even today, more than one-third of the handicapped Americans are in the poverty category compared to only one-fifth of the total population. This in turn determines the amount and kinds of recreation they can afford.

Antagonism also has negative effects. Again, largely because of ignorance, many people have avoided working, living, or recreating with the handicapped. They have preferred that such people be

isolated in institutions, special workshops, and separate recreation programs and facilities. This seems especially true in the case of the retarded, emotionally disturbed, or mentally ill. Even today when attempts are being made to provide a more normal lifestyle for these people, portions of the general public refuse to have anything to do with them, resisting efforts such as mainstreaming in schools or the establishment of halfway houses in their neighborhoods. Such antagonistic attitudes cannot be regulated by law and as long as they persist, there will never be equality of employment, housing, or recreation opportunities for the handicapped.

Recreation opportunities for the handicapped are also reduced by apathy and a lack of awareness of their special needs. This is especially true for people who have difficulty walking or who are confined to wheelchairs. Although most physical barriers could be avoided, society has generally shown little concern for the problems of these people. Sidewalks and curbs, stairs and steps, bus and subway system designs, narrow and revolving doors, and the height of door knobs, elevator buttons, drinking fountains, telephones, and toilet facilities restrict the mobility of those in wheelchairs. Public buildings such as museums and libraries, national monuments, and parks are frequently the worst offenders with endless steps, no places provided at building entrances where the handicapped can easily leave or enter vehicles, and long distances to walk or travel by wheelchair from parking lots to the facilities. (Figure 5.9).

Costs of correcting these errors are often high but considerable progress is being made in the

Figure 5.9 A handicapped library user begins the arduous and time-consuming task of descending a flight of steps to the main floor. Despite recent efforts, many recreation resources are still not readily accessible to wheelchair users who often forego participating rather than suffer the indignities and hazards of being helped by others.

United States. The Rehabilitation Act of 1973 requires these modifications and directs that new federally aided construction provide access to the handicapped. Improvements are also being made in the education of the handicapped. The 1974 Education for All Handicapped Children Act requires that public school authorities seek out and identify handicapped children before they are old enough to go to school. These children must then be educated with their nonhandicapped peers to the maximum extent possible. This includes being given access to all of the school programs that are available to nonhandicapped children such as art,

music, library, and physical education. Such legislation cannot force individuals to change their attitudes but it increases people's awareness of the handicapped's problems, reduces the number of physical barriers, and helps the handicapped obtain equal education employment opportunities. Gradually, many of the physical and social barriers that turned the handicapped into second class citizens are being removed.

OTHER DISCRIMINATORY ATTITUDES

Individuals do not have to possess one of the debilitating physical or mental handicaps discussed in the

previous section to be discriminated against. In some cases, it is only necessary for an individual to be slightly different from society's perception of what is "normal." Certain standards of physical size, appearance, and ability gradually become accepted by a society, and those who do not meet these standards are often deprived of opportunities.

For example, some people with special characteristics are disadvantaged because they are too few in number to form a valuable market for certain goods and services or to band together to demand their rights. Since they are usually a minority and dispersed throughout the population, society is often not intentionally discriminatory; the general public quite often is simply unaware that problems exist. Some examples of this kind of discrimination are:

- Recreation clothing and equipment are often not adjustable nor made in appropriate sizes for people who are much shorter, taller, larger, or smaller than the accepted norm; even though women are not numerically a minority they are disadvantaged because the myth that women have little interest in or aptitude for certain recreation activities has discouraged manufacturers from making equipment to fit them.
- Shelves in stores and lockers, handrails on buses, or rungs on bar stools are out of reach for short people.
- Some models of automobiles and recreation vehicles, bunks in campers, or the distance between rows of seats in theaters are ill-suited to tall people.
- Many items of recreation equipment (golf clubs, baseball gloves, camera shutter releases, decks of cards, bolt action rifles, some stringed instruments, scissors, and other tools), and instructions for some activities (knitting for instance), are designed

primarily for right-handed people, thereby placing left-handed individuals (10 percent of the population) at a disadvantage when trying to use them.

Some manufacturers do produce goods designed to accommodate the needs of these special groups, but usually they are either much higher priced or require special ordering, which may involve waits of weeks or even months.

Social attitudes concerning people who differ in any appreciable way from the accepted norm are frequently negative and, as a result, the recreation opportunities for such individuals are often diminished. Some examples of this type of discrimination are:

- People who are overweight, disfigured, divorced, widowed, or who have remained single after a certain age, finding that society does not welcome their participation in many kinds of recreation activities, especially social events.
- Society's right-handed bias causing individuals with left-handed tendencies considerable grief; efforts by parents and teachers to destroy this natural characteristic can cause emotional stress and inhibit the development of good physical coordination while those who do not change are subjected to psychologically damaging remarks and jokes about their left-handedness and "clumsiness" (especially when attempting recreation activities designed for right-handed people).
- In recreation activities, including sports, where no attempt is made to organize participation according to size, individuals who are below or above average size and height often find it embarrassing or impossible to compete.
- In a society that considers tall men and petite women ideal, short men and tall women can be disadvantaged

when it comes to going out with members of the opposite sex or taking part in any social events like parties and dances.

Sadly, these social biases are so pervasive that very few people are conscious of them except the victims themselves. Yet, because of them, millions of people must suffer disparaging nicknames, teasing, rejection, or abuse.

In an effort to avoid unkind treatment, many individuals limit their recreation participation. For example, overweight persons give up swimming; short boys stop asking girls to go out with them; homely individuals turn down invitations to parties; and small people stop trying to take part in athletics or team sports. What makes this particularly tragic is that it is so unnecessary. One glance at a crowd of ordinary, everyday people proves how very few individuals there are who satisfy the requirements for the ideal physique. But people seldom compare themselves with ordinary citizens. They look instead to the magazines and television advertisements, fashion models, professional athletes, movie stars, and beauty queens for an indication of acceptability. Since these "ideal" individuals are seldom anything but tall, strong, and handsome (men), or petite, slim, and beautiful (women), the victims themselves help perpetuate the myth.

SOCIAL STATUS AND ADULATION

People are often motivated to buy certain recreation goods or engage in particular recreation activities in order to gain social status. The number of people seeking recognition through such activities appears to be increasing. This may be because social class and occupation are becoming less significant factors in determining status, especially in the industrialized nations.

Individuals of all ages seek and achieve status through the possession of recreation merchandise. Children who are the first in their family, neighborhood, or school class to own a newly introduced and heavily promoted toy find themselves the source of much admiration and envy. Often, in the case of the more commonly owned possessions such as bicycles and sports equipment, it is the model or manufacturer that counts. At a very early age, children learn how important it is not just to acquire certain items but also to be sure that they are the right kinds of items if they are to earn the adulation of peers. As people get older, the same kinds of rules apply. Possessing a huge and powerful "box," the term young urban Americans use to describe the large portable transistor radio-cassette tape players that many of them carry, currently establishes their identity and earns them the attention and admiration of other young people. Purchasing a fairly unique and usually expensive item such as a large boat, a customized van, or a sports car has the same effect for the older adult.

Some seek status through membership in organizations such as country clubs, opera guilds, yacht clubs, or elite hunting and fishing organizations. These groups provide comfortable retreats for the rich and influential where they may meet others like themselves and take part in a wide range of recreation activities in an environment and a manner that provides status.

Membership is often limited to people from a particular group. Some are all-male or all-female; others include only persons of the same ethnic background, religion, social standing, or special interest. However, there are some indications of change. Those that have no non-white members— even as token members— are being nudged into accepting blacks as guests, and many all-male clubs are making provisions for women to at least be admitted as visitors at specified times and places or for special events. And so, gradually, many of these institutions are losing some of the exclusive characteristics that gave them their status value.

For some people, taking part in a particular sport or going on vacation to a location that has status is very important. Many people gain status by regularly attending and supporting community cultural events such as performances by the resident orchestra, opera, or ballet organizations, or exhibitions sponsored by the local art museum or gallery. Young people achieve recognition among their peers through attending concerts by currently popular performers. Evidence of attendance such as a souvenir program, a photograph taken personally during the performance, the performer's autograph or, best of all, an article of clothing that belonged to the star increases the prestige that can be acquired through participation in such activities. In some social groups, reading a particular book, attending a certain play, seeing a recent movie, going to an exclusive discotheque, or riding on a particular amusement park roller coaster is highly regarded.

Traditionally, the upper class in society creates an enviable lifestyle

and in so doing establishes the criteria by which status can be achieved. Members of the middle and working classes then aspire to emulate them. Golf, tennis, sailing, European tours, ski vacations, and Caribbean cruises, are all examples of activities generally associated with the socially elite. Recently, however, these activities have become accessible to anyone having the necessary time, money, and inclination and, because of this, they have lost much of their original status. On the other hand, people have come to look to the best-known celebrities in the sports and entertainment fields for guidance in their choice of recreation lifestyles. Many persons are ardent fans of these people and emulate their behavior in an effort to be like them, to acquire some of their glamor, or to personally attract some of the same kind of adulation that they commonly receive. As a result, many individuals have taken up activities such as tennis, backgammon, and using cocaine at parties not because the upper classes enjoy them but because they are currently popular with motion picture and television personalities.

During the last two decades, there has also been a growing interest in the behavior of certain antiestablishment segments of society. To many people, their lives took on a special glamor and attractiveness because such segments seemed to enjoy a free and exciting lifestyle they had never known. Gradually, some of their preferences have been adopted by people of all income and education levels. Denim jeans, vans, motorcycles, and the use of marijuana have even become status symbols for some members of the so-called upper class.

Status-seeking affects the recreation opportunities of whole populations because it contributes to changes in recreation participation patterns including the creation of short-lived fads. A new or reintroduced recreation activity, product, or environment is adopted by a few. For a combination of reasons, it rapidly becomes fashionable. People flock to participate, buy, or visit the resource or area but, in so doing, they cause its status value to fall. Participation, ownership, or attendance decreases, and the activity, product, or destination is abandoned or becomes relatively insignificant as people move on to seek new forms of status-giving recreation. However, during the period when it is most popular, a fad encourages a large number of people (including many individuals who are not status-minded) to try activities, products, resources, and locations that they otherwise would not have tried. If these people enjoy their experiences, they may continue their involvement, thereby contributing to the survival and establishment of a new recreation participation pattern. In this way, many activities, resorts, and kinds of recreation equipment have now become permanent parts of the recreation environment because of the initial support of status-seeking individuals.

A special form of status-seeking occurs in connection with athletics, sports, music, and the performing arts. Some people who participate in these activities do so primarily because they desire the adulation of those who see them perform. Being watched by others, hearing the cheers and applause, receiving congratulations afterward, reading and hearing reports in the media, and preparing a scrapbook of mementos are all important incentives to participation. How a society recognizes its performers and athletes plays a significant role, therefore, in determining the participation patterns of those who seek adulation.

Finally, it is not always essential to actually possess a recreation item or engage in a certain activity to achieve status. Some resources have such impact that it is only necessary to give the *impression* that one has a status item or partakes in a status activity to create a personal image that is socially advantageous. For example, individuals who do not take part in sports or athletics of any kind wear expensive warm-up suits and athletic shoes to shop in and to use during park outings, or they appear at beaches or ski resorts in suitable swim or ski attire. Automobile owners buy dummy citizens band radio antennas for their cars. People who spend most of their time indoors, or who have neither the time nor money for midwinter vacations in warm weather locations, maintain year-round tans at one of the nation's 1000 sun-lamp tanning salons; they believe a tan provides status because it denotes health, affluence, and an abundance of free time. Aspiring socialites decorate their homes with books, pianos, or hobby collections in which they have no real interest. And urban office workers (who may never leave the city) wear hiking boots and rugged outdoor clothing to work and social occasions in order to appear part of the hiking, camping, and rugged outdoorsman subculture.

SOCIALLY APPROVED LIFESTYLES

The lifestyles that a society considers acceptable or desirable play a major role in determining recreation participation patterns. If people live in a reasonably favorable environment and are part of a society that puts little emphasis on material possessions, they may have a considerable amount of time in which to play. The classic example is the original lifestyle of the Polynesian peoples; they lived a life of comparative ease because their limited aspirations could be satisfied from nearby resources with relatively little effort.

In contrast, most of the world's modern societies aspire to a much more sophisticated and materialistic way of life. Many of the citizens live in relatively unfavorable locations where it would be difficult or impossible to subsist on the local resources even if they wanted to do so. Therefore, most of the people in the developed nations and many of the people in the undeveloped nations can only obtain the goods and services that they need or desire by exchanging much of their time and energy for goods produced elsewhere. This leaves less time for recreation than in the case of the original Polynesians.

At least until recently, American society has encouraged its members to aspire to lifestyles characterized by professional employment and a sizable gadget-filled house on a large lot in the suburbs, with two large late-model automobiles providing unlimited transportation. To achieve this lifestyle, many have been willing to take additional jobs or even borrow large sums of money thereby further reducing their free time or the proportion of their salaries that could be used for recreation. Often the only locations that were considered socially or environmentally desirable for such residences were considerable distances from urban centers. Spending one or two hours a day traveling to work became an accepted part of the ideal lifestyle. If, instead, society had endorsed an inner-city lifestyle where people lived close to their work and shopping facilities, then urban communities and the recreation environments of the inhabitants would be completely different.

Society also has considerable impact on people's recreation environments when it influences marriage and household composition. In the past, the majority of societies accepted the household as normally consisting of a married couple, a number of children, and possibly one or more dependent relatives. Today in the developed societies, children are still desired and for the most part considered an asset, but they are also recognized as a financial burden. In addition they are very time-consuming, especially for parents who no longer have relatives or friends nearby to share in their care.

But a society's lifestyle aspirations change with time, which is certainly the case in the United States. Although these lifestyles still predominate, alternate lifestyles are now emerging and gaining respectability. For instance, the suburban single-family-dwelling lifestyle with all it entails is becoming less of an ideal. A growing number of people are moving into condominiums and apartments to have more time for recreation, and some are choosing urban locations to put them closer to work, nearer to a wide range of urban recreation activities including cultural events, and to decrease their dependency on the private automobile. It is becoming increasingly acceptable to remain single or childless to maintain the playboy or playgirl type lifestyle characterized by travel and participation in a wide variety of the more expensive recreation activities. And finally, if circumstances permit, people are choosing to relocate to more favorable environments such as Colorado or the sunbelt states that facilitate the pursuit of outdoor recreation-oriented lifestyles even if it means a loss of income or an abandonment of long-standing social and cultural ties. Only a few years ago, society would have looked down on or criticized these non-traditional lifestyles.

CULTURAL AND SUBCULTURAL GROUPS

The cultural and subcultural groups to which a person belongs are an important aspect of the person's recreation environment. Each nation has its own set of cultural characteristics, some of which may directly affect recreation. For example, although Canada has been strongly influenced by the United States, it has its own unique culture. The dominant sport is ice hockey rather than football or baseball, and Canadian football has its own distinct rules. Lacrosse, the traditional game of the North American Indians, and curling, a winter sport that originated in Scotland and was introduced by Scottish soldiers in 1759, are enjoyed extensively in Canada while they are not well-known in the United States. Canadians follow a pattern of national holiday celebrations and Wednesday afternoon store closings that are much closer to the British than the American pattern. Publicly owned radio, television, and docu-

mentary film production in Canada also follow British practices quite closely. National government involvement in the preservation and encouragement of national and regional cultures has been much more extensive in Canada than the United States. These and many other factors result in a subtle blending of European and North American cultures expressed in a uniquely Canadian way.

In addition to variations in the activities undertaken and the attitudes toward government involvement in recreation, some cultures have different approaches to participation. The Chinese, for example, tend to place less emphasis on winning than on the observance of good manners. Participants in the World Table Tennis Tournaments cannot understand (and sometimes become quite indignant) when they sense that a game is being deliberately forfeited by the talented Chinese players in order to allow another team to savor the thrill of winning.

People of British extraction and those who have been influenced by British culture generally espouse a strict ethic of good sportsmanship. It calls for participants to show appreciation for good performances by opponents in sports events and to try to be good losers as well as gracious winners. People of Latin temperament, on the other hand, tend to let their personal emotions show more openly. Players and spectators at sports events often express very partisan feelings, and it is not uncommon for members of opposing teams as well as coaches, referees, or spectators with different views to be verbally abused, threatened, or even physically assaulted.

This means that the same ac-

tivity can have different characteristics from one culture to another. For example, a game may be played in one nation in a relatively quiet and restrained environment while in another country the conduct of both players and spectators turns it into a noisy, violent, emotionally charged experience. As a result of these cultural differences, people may find that they do not enjoy taking part in a favorite activity when they move into an area dominated by another culture. Difficulties also occur when teams from different cultures meet in international competition.

Another important cultural characteristic that has a major influence on recreation participation is the way in which societies perceive time. Adherence to customary clock times and planned schedules is common in the United States and Canada. It is less prevalent in Europe, Japan, and elsewhere in modern societies. In less developed nations, it is largely absent; people tend to do things when they have the opportunity or when they feel like it. The natural rhythms of the sun, seasons, and the human life-cycle are the primary constraints.

Adherence to customary clock times affects people's recreation in many ways. Time can be a tyrant since individuals plan and undertake recreation activities according to specific clock times rather than their desires. Even when no clock or other indicator of time is visible, people are still aware of clock time and regulate their behavior accordingly. Participants often stop enjoying an engrossing activity because they sense that it is the conventional time to eat a meal or go to bed. Similarly, people will not begin a recreation activity if it appears that they cannot complete it or have a reasonably worthwhile experience before being required to turn to something else at a set time. During an activity, participants are often conscious of the passage of time and, as a result, they often fail to relax and enjoy the experience fully. Instead, they try to get as much done as possible in the prescribed time or they interrupt their activity periodically to find out what time it is. In either case, the quality of the experience suffers. Of course, there are occasions when it is important that appointments be kept, but often it is only social conditioning that makes a person adhere to rigid schedules.

Adherence to set schedules can be equally detrimental to recreation enjoyment. Individuals who are accustomed to following personally developed or group developed schedules often find it difficult to adapt to unexpected delays or disruptions. If it rains on a day when fishing, gardening, or some other outdoor activity is planned, they are apt to be miserable and wander restlessly around, frequently looking out and wondering when the rain will stop. Some people worry about the valuable time they are losing from the planned activity but seem unable to use it effectively for an alternative pleasurable activity. On the other hand, when work or duty routines are unexpectedly disrupted or when people must wait an extended period of time for transportation or appointments, they find it impossible to take recreational advantage of these unplanned free moments.

Observance of customary clock times also affects recreation because it creates problems with peak use of recreation facilities. For example,

Figure 5.10 This extensive lineup formed outside a Manhattan, New York City, movie theater that was showing the movie *Star Wars*: People often wait for extended periods because they insist on seeing attractions during peak attendance times.

restaurant customers often wait before being seated because they follow the social custom that decrees a certain limited period is the correct time to enjoy a restaurant meal. Similarly, people frequently waste time waiting because they insist on attending a movie in the evening, playing tennis in the afternoon, or visiting amusement parks or beaches on peak periods (Figure 5.10). Of course, some individuals cannot go at any other time and others prefer to go when facilities are crowded because of increased possibilities for social interaction. But many could avoid these periods if they felt free to do so. Most would find their recreation experiences enhanced because resources would be less crowded and, in many cases, better maintained.

In less developed societies, people value free time because it

provides opportunities to be inactive. "Doing nothing" can be a valuable, enjoyable recreation activity that is both relaxing and restorative. Be that as it may, attitudes toward time and the "proper" use of it make it difficult for many people in developed societies, particularly in the United States and Canada, to participate in this form of recreation. Spouses, parents, friends, neighbors, or the individual's own conscience often make people feel guilty if they lie in hammocks, bask in the sun, or sit idly on park benches for any length of time. Professionals and textbooks contribute to the problem by insisting that "recreation is activity as opposed to idleness."[4] As a result, some individuals find they have to seek out-

[4] D. C. Weiskopf, *A Guide to Recreation and Leisure,* Allyn and Bacon, Boston, 1975.

of-the-way resorts or travel abroad to less developed locations and more relaxed societies in order to escape this active recreation ethic.

Subcultural groups within nations also exhibit differences in their preferred recreation activities and the manner in which they participate. These differences are frequently of great importance in recreation planning and management. Examples of subcultural groupings that have a major effect on recreation behavior are:

- *Subcultures of poverty* — comprise a small proportion of the population in some nations and include most of the population in others; they range from the people in the ghettos or barrios in urban centers and dispersed groups of low-income servants and migrant workers to the majority of farmers and peasants in depressed agricultural areas.
- *Subcultures of place* — are produced because the location in which people live or grow up affects their attitudes and behavior; consciously or unconsciously they become attached to one or more places such as their neighborhoods, schools, towns, counties, states, provinces, or regions.
- *Subcultures of religion* — each religious group (Eastern Orthodox, Jewish, Muslim, Roman Catholic, various Protestant sects, and others) forms its own subculture.
- *Subcultures of ethnic origin* — some ethnic groups (certain Scottish, German, Finnish, and Chinese groups, for example) maintain separate identities and distinct behavioral patterns.
- *Subcultures of age* — young children, teenagers, the middle-aged, and the elderly, for instance, often form separate subcultures.
- *Subcultures of principal activity* — these include groups such as students, persons who do the same kind of work, the unemployed, the independently wealthy, and retired individuals.

- *Subcultures of marital status* — single, married, divorced, and widowed people tend to constitute groups with similar behavioral characteristics.
- *Subcultures of politics* — Democrats, Republicans, Liberals, Progressive Conservatives, Labour, Socialists, Communists, and other parties form distinct groups.
- *Subcultures of lifestyle and special interests* — people who are part of groups such as women's movements, communes, homosexuals, youth gangs, hunters, surfers, and citizens band radio enthusiasts often exhibit similar participation patterns.

Membership in several of these groupings is inescapable and, therefore, most individuals are influenced by the mores and behavior patterns of more than one subculture. Little conflict arises from this plurality of influences, however, since membership in one subculture will usually take precedence over others. Some may have only occasional or very limited impact on the individual.

Belonging to a subculture can affect an individual's recreation behavior in several ways. Within a subculture, the individual is influenced by the beliefs and behavior of the other members. Since some of these influences are so intangible and so well-integrated into everyday life that they are accepted without question, most individuals within a subculture — often without even being aware of it — tend to behave in much the same way. They unconsciously favor certain kinds of recreation experiences and take part in activities in a similar manner.

In some subcultures, however, there is such a keen desire to retain a unique identity, to perpetuate certain attitudes and behavior patterns, and to try to avoid contamination by outside ideas and practices that

guidelines and rules are well-established and carefully taught. This is especially true of ethnic, religious, and some special interest groups. Membership in these subcultures often requires a strict adherence to clearly specified behavior patterns. Members of these groups may have access to many unique recreation opportunities because of their membership, but they may also feel obliged to refrain from many of the recreation opportunities open to them through memberships in other subcultures connected to age, place, or principal activity.

The attitudes of society toward the various subcultures contained within it are also of major significance. When a group is large enough to be dominant, the community or nation usually accepts some or all of its recreation behavior patterns as the norm although there may be little demand made on nonmembers to conform. Sometimes, however, the majority group may seek to alter or control the behavior of one or even all of the minority groups. In the United States, for example, the white majority in the southern states restricted or prohibited the use, by black citizens, of bars, restaurants, theaters, public libraries, parks, and other recreation facilities until civil rights demonstrations as well as legislative and legal action by the federal government initiated a change in the 1960s. Elsewhere in the United States, the blacks were also treated unfairly, but generally the discrimination was less pervasive and not as severe.

Nevertheless, discrimination against this subcultural group continues in many subtle ways. For instance, neighborhoods with high percentages of black and other minority populations sometimes receive smaller allocations of funds for recreation programs than do heavily white neighborhoods. Although black athletes dominate professional basketball and football teams and constitute one-fifth of major league baseball players, very few are ever appointed to leadership positions. For example, in football, center, free safety, and quarterback positions are still largely reserved for whites, and in baseball, blacks are concentrated in the outfield. In spite of their high numbers and outstanding performances in professional sports, blacks hold few administrative and head coaching jobs. Similar discriminatory practices and unequal representation exist in amateur sports, the arts, and a great many private clubs and recreation organizations. Unfortunately, these forms of discrimination are much more insidious and difficult to eradicate than the earlier more obvious ones, and it may be a long time before black Americans actually achieve full equality in terms of recreation opportunity or recreation-related employment.

Discrimination against subcultural groups is not limited to the United States but occurs in many other parts of the world. One of the most serious situations is in South Africa where a white minority controls a black, Indian, and mixed-race majority. The recreation opportunities open to these groups are strongly influenced by restrictive regulations requiring them to live in specific locations or by controls on travel and the use of buses, taxis, and trains. Some of the recreation resources such as sporting events, restaurants, theaters, and opera houses have recently been desegregated, but others like cinemas,

parks, beaches, bars, and hotels mostly continue to operate as segregated facilities. Many of India's more than 80 million Harijans ("untouchables") are still unable to go where they wish and associate with whom they please because of caste prejudice, although the Indian Constitution adopted in 1955 specifically forbids this discrimination. Even in Sweden that previously prided itself on its civil liberties, there have been instances where racial antagonism has reduced recreation opportunities. Skirmishes between Swedish youths and Turkish immigrants have occurred, and some restaurants and discotheques are reported to have refused admittance to African and American blacks.

Societal attitudes toward a subculture can also negatively influence the recreation opportunities available to its members even where there is no conscious intention to discriminate. If recreation planners and managers have erroneous ideas concerning the recreation preferences of subculture members, they may provide inappropriate facilities and programs. This has often proved to be the case because many planners and managers base their opinions on the preferences of their *own* subculture instead of conducting surveys, making observations, and consulting knowledgeable community leaders in the neighborhoods concerned.

CRIME AND DISRESPECT FOR PEOPLE AND PROPERTY

Crime and other antisocial acts are major constraints on recreation participation. They reduce people's op-

portunities in a multitude of ways in both rural and urban environments. Many of these constraints are subtle and not readily visible to law enforcement agencies or recreation professionals. Nevertheless, these completely unnecessary limitations on people's freedom to enjoy themselves as they please often determine recreation lifestyles.

Older neighborhoods in many of the world's larger cities have high crime rates. American cities, especially New York and Chicago, have areas where residents are virtual prisoners in their apartments, especially at night. Considered as easy prey, the elderly are particularly affected; some are afraid to take a stroll down a street, go to a neighborhood store, use a community center, sit in a park, or even visit friends who live in the same building (Figure 5.11). Many are unwilling or financially unable to move to safer and more congenial neighborhoods. Some are living in the neighborhoods in which they grew up and raised their families, and to move away from friends, places of worship, and the merchants that they have known for so long is unthinkable. So they remain, even though these amenities have become largely inaccessible to them. Fear of robbery, assault, or rape is affecting the recreation environments of people of all ages in many different environments. The northern half of New York's Central Park is avoided by many park users. Even bird-watching groups concentrate their activities in the more open and heavily used southern half although the northern portion has more interesting birds and animals now that it is lightly used. Some groups are escorted by a police officer on a motor scooter to

Elderly in Terror of Crime

The Bronx, a borough of the City of New York, has more than a quarter of a million residents over 60 years of age. Many have been victims of crime at least once, some many times. As many as 25 elderly people have been murdered there in one year. They try to protect themselves from robbery and violence by barricading their tiny apartments and venturing out as infrequently as possible. One 87 year old widow described how she arranged for protection by a male escort carrying a knife and a cane in order to go to a nearby supermarket each week for a few groceries. When asked how she passed the time, she said: "Oh, I have things to keep me busy. I read, and I like to watch television, especially Henry Fonda movies. I used to go to the senior citizens' center, but I don't go anymore, because some kids started following me. Once they tried to give me a dead cat."

Her fears were, unfortunately, not groundless—almost every elderly person at the senior citizen recreation center had been mugged at least once and one 80 year old man was attacked three times in one week. She also had friends who had been injured by youths throwing bottles and stones at them when they tried to spend a few hours sitting in the sun in a nearby park.[5]

[5] Judy Klemesrud, "Many Elderly in the Bronx Spend Their Lives in Terror of Crime," *The New York Times*, November 12, 1976.

Figure 5.11 In some cities, elderly people travel in groups even in daylight because they are afraid of being abused or robbed. In this case, a group stays close together as they leave the Mount Eden Center in the Bronx, New York City.

discourage binocular snatchers. Central Park and many other urban and suburban recreation facilities are quickly abandoned as night falls. This is doubly unfortunate, since most working people can only use the parks in the evenings during the week, and green spaces are often the only places for many inner-city residents to find respite from summer heat.

Because of the risk of crime or unpleasant experiences, people in some cities avoid public transportation at night. This often limits their opportunities to those that are nearby. Children are instructed to play at home or in areas of parks where they can be readily seen. Some young children living in high-rise apartments seldom if ever have the opportunity to play outside.

Like the elderly, women of all ages are disadvantaged by fear of crime. Many avoid traveling anywhere alone or being out-of-doors after dark. Most stay away from localities that might place them in danger. A growing number take courses in self-defense in order to preserve at least some of their freedom and independence. Because of the risk of being molested, women often do not participate alone or even in groups in activities such as jogging, visiting urban parks, attending outdoor concerts and special events, fishing, camping, or taking sightseeing vacations on their own either in their own country or abroad.

Even in daylight hours, an increasing number of parks, beaches, and other facilities are becoming uninviting, especially to older people and families, because of the likelihood of criminal and antisocial behavior. Permissive attitudes of society have resulted in increased public drunkenness, drug use, rowdiness, fighting, littering, and vandalism. The peace and quiet expected by many park visitors is often broken by the inconsiderate playing of loud radio and tape recorder music or the frequent and intentionally noisy arrival and departure of individuals cruising the areas in cars or on motorcycles. Some people are avoiding sports events and public performances of youth-oriented musical groups because of the thoughtless, often dangerous, behavior that takes place.

Drinking drivers discourage many from participating in activities that necessitate driving during periods that are perceived as being particularly risky; people know that the majority of automobile accidents are alcohol-related, especially those that occur late at night or on holidays such as New Year's Eve. Vandalism to all types of recreation resources ranging from the smashing of washroom fixtures in urban parks to the spraypainting of obscenities on rocks in national parks does millions of dollars worth of damage each year and results in the depreciation or loss of untold recreation opportunities.

Theft is another crime that is having a major effect on participation. Although theft has always been somewhat of a problem in cities, people were seldom bothered in rural areas. In Canada and the United States, beach visitors went swimming and left their belongings including radios, car keys, and wallets unattended, campers left their campsites and valuable equipment

for days at a time without taking any special precautions, and boat owners did not feel it necessary to remove outboard motors or fishing gear when docking boats overnight. Now, recreation-related items of many kinds are popular targets for thieves in both urban and extraurban locations. Often the victims are those who can least afford to lose a treasured recreation item. Young people have their bicycles stolen and burglars take television sets, radios, and phonographs from the dwellings of the poor. Members of these groups often find it economically impossible to replace such losses.

Automobile thefts have grown to almost epidemic proportions in some American communities. Wheels, tires, hub caps, tape decks, radios, and other accessories are also frequently stolen. People living in neighborhoods where such thefts are common find it difficult or impossible to keep a respectable car in working order. As a result, many of their recreation opportunities, especially the chance to drive out of the urban area and enjoy activities in more rural environments, are greatly reduced or even eliminated.

Travelers both at home and abroad have their vacations ruined by the theft of money, credit cards, or passports from their persons, luggage, cars, or hotel rooms. Some locations have such bad reputations that tourists avoid them altogether or make very brief and very apprehensive visits.

Besides reducing people's recreation opportunities because of violence and the actual theft of belongings, documents, or money, crime affects participation in several other ways. Examples include the following.

- Sometimes an individual will forego an experience to watch a group's possessions or car while the rest participate in an activity.
- Students may leave their bicycles or stereo equipment at home rather than risk having it stolen from a dormitory or apartment.
- Tourists may carry everything of value with them wherever they go despite the weight and resulting fatigue in order not to leave items such as purses, cameras, or portable radios unattended in automobiles, campgrounds, or hotel rooms.
- Large sums that might otherwise be spent on recreation are used instead to buy theft and vandalism insurance, alarm systems, and protective fences, window grills, and door locks and chains.

Some people solve the problem by not buying any of the things that are most susceptible to theft. They make do with old, cheap bicycles and cars, never buy equipment such as cameras, car radios, or tape decks, and take some comfort in the knowledge that they own nothing that anyone would want to steal. In the process, they are depriving themselves of the enjoyment these possessions might bring.

But perhaps the greatest recreational loss resulting from crime and antisocial behavior is the loss of tranquility and the accompanying reduction in the quality of the experience. True refreshment only comes when participants are able to relax and become fully immersed in the enjoyment of the activity. That elderly lady in the Bronx apartment, for instance, would have difficulty getting deeply involved in a Henry Fonda movie on television if she hears noises outside her window. Tourists cannot fully enjoy sightseeing when they are constantly worrying about pickpockets, someone breaking into their cars, or the unruly behavior of a group of youths. It takes much of the fun out of gardening if one has to be anxious about the possibility of vandals damaging the trees, trampling or uprooting the flowers, or stealing the vegetables. And it may not be worth going to a sports event or concert if participants worry during much of the event about the possibility of being hurt by thrown objects or of being molested in the parking lot or on the way home. Obviously, many recreation opportunities could be restored or enhanced and participation and enjoyment increased by taking whatever steps are necessary to liberate people from the tyranny of crime and antisocial behavior.

CIVIL DISORDER AND WAR

One of the factors determining the living conditions and therefore the recreation opportunities of large numbers of people in a given community, region, nation, or group of nations is the threat or actual outbreak of violence between groups of people. On a small scale, gang wars and conflicts between groups of people with different religious or political beliefs, or ethnic or racial backgrounds, can completely disrupt the daily lives of the people involved. Such disturbances also affect the mobility of others and turn schools, streets, subways, community recreation centers, playgrounds, and parks as well as commercial recreation resources such as bars, sports facilities and amusement parks into no-man's lands where residents and tourists alike are afraid to go. Recreation opportunities are reduced even more when

programs, facilities, or events are discontinued, closed, or cancelled in an effort to avoid further trouble. Similarly, the imposition of curfews or restrictive policies regarding the use of public and private facilities may help control the outbreaks of violence but may also decrease people's recreation opportunities. Finally, the destruction of public and private property that occurs during these disturbances damages or destroys many recreation resources that may or may not be repaired or replaced.

On a larger scale, the complete breakdown of relationships between politically opposed groups of citizens or people of different nationalities that culminate in the outbreak of civil disorders or wars can have the most serious effects both during the conflicts themselves and afterward as nations go through a recovery period. This type of strife is costly not only in terms of human casualties and suffering but also in terms of property and environmental damage as well as economic losses. Nor are the effects confined solely to the nations that are directly involved. The economies and well-being of many countries suffer from the interruption of normal international patterns of trade and communication and from the costs of bolstering their own defense systems or supplying aid to one or more of the warring countries.

These commitments can have a considerable effect on the economic well-being of a country. Part of the current economic success of Japan, for example, is attributable to the fact that Japan has been denied the right to rearm since the end of World War II. This has proven a tremendous advantage in a world where most nations reserve

large portions of their national budgets for various kinds of military spending. Currently, the world's nations spend some $400 billion a year on military defense, invest another $30 billion in weapons research, and employ 91 million people in the armed services or military-related occupations. All of these endeavors drain the nations' financial resources and divert funds from domestic programs that might solve social and environmental problems or provide additional recreation opportunities.

Some conflicts have widespread effects on recreation. An example is the recent upheaval in Iran that resulted from the overthrow of the regime of Shah Mohammed Reza Pahlavi. Initially, this interrupted the flow of crude oil from Iran to many nations. In the United States, it represented a loss of 5 percent of the nation's total supply (see Chapter 18). Some localized gasoline and heating oil shortages occurred, and airlines had to cancel hundreds of flights. Long after the resumption of oil production in Iran, the U.S. economy continued to suffer from a reduction in the size of oil shipments and a sharp increase in oil prices. Fear of gasoline shortages persisted, and the price of gasoline, heating oil, airline tickets, and hundreds of items that utilize petroleum or petroleum derivatives in their manufacture or distribution continued to rise. Although it was not completely to blame, the revolution in Iran and its effect on gasoline supplies were contributing factors in the decisions of large numbers of Americans to cancel or alter their vacation plans in the summer of 1979.

Of course, these effects are inconsequential compared to the personal, economic, and environmental consequences of the fighting that takes place in countries actually embroiled in civil or international wars. Thousands of lives may be lost or disrupted; numerous homes, farms, industries, natural resources, recreation facilities, and transportation systems may be damaged or destroyed; and the economies of the nations may be severely taxed or completely drained. Win or lose, it takes years for the nations involved to overcome the debilitating effects of waging war. And finally, for those peoples who suffer defeat, life under a new regime means many changes. Whether recreation opportunities eventually are reduced, altered, or increased depends largely on the ideology and policies of the new form of government.

THE EFFECT ON TOURISM

Tourism is often severely affected by the presence of global conflict. In times of internal conflict or foreign wars, nonessential travel is often forbidden or impossible, and the facilities that cater to tourists are sometimes closed, destroyed, or converted to other uses. During the recovery period, little effort may be directed toward reactivating the tourist industry, at least until essential services and facilities have been restored and rebuilt. Sometimes, however, a nation whose economy has been ravaged by the effects of war may give top priority to the rehabilitation of the tourist industry, particularly if it can be expected to draw large numbers of foreign visitors and thereby earn hard currency. This does not always occur, however, since tourists are sometimes reluctant to vacation in an area that has a past history of conflict. It takes many years to rebuild a thriving tourist trade, and even then, people remain wary and cancel their visits at the first indication of unrest. Because of the recent rapid increase in foreign pleasure travel these disruptive effects are being felt by larger portions of the world's people. Conflicts that are presently taking place in or between some 30 nations and are threatening to erupt in several more will have a negative impact on tourism in those areas for years to come.

This completes the review of the social factors that influence recreation behavior. Chapter 6 discusses the role of resource availability and transportation in making recreation opportunities accessible to potential participants.

DISCUSSION TOPICS

1. How does community-wide adherence to religious or political doctrines affect your recreation behavior or the recreation participation of individuals or families with whom you are familiar?
2. What roles do traditions, habits, and rituals play in the recreation participation patterns of your family, of other families that you know, and of communities in which you have lived?
3. In what ways do social attitudes toward the roles of the sexes influence the recreation opportunities open to males and females in communities with which you are familiar? Are these attitudes and influences changing? If so, what effect will these changes have in the future?
4. Does intentional or unintentional discrimination against the handicapped or other subcultural groups limit the recreation opportunities available to them in your community or other communities in which you have lived? How can these situations be improved?
5. What effects do crime, other antisocial activities, and conflicts have on your own recreation opportunities, on the opportunities open to your family, or on those available to others in your community? What could be done to change the situation?

FURTHER READINGS

Geoffrey Godbey and Stanley Parker consider a number of the external social aspects of recreation participation in their book *Leisure Studies and Services: An Overview* published in Philadelphia by W. B. Saunders in 1976. Section II of their book examines some of the influences of work, education, religion, age, sex, and the family. *Leisure: Theory and Policy* by Max Kaplan, published in 1975 by John Wiley & Sons of New York, is a sociological textbook and provides much pertinent information concerning social groupings and their influence on recreation behavior. Although written 20 years ago, Sebastian de Grazia's *Of Time, Work and Leisure,* published in New York by the Twentieth Century Fund in 1962, is still the most readable general review of sociological influences. It should be required reading for all recreation professionals because of the insights and challenges that it provides. Added perspectives on social factors affecting recreation participation in American urban core areas can be obtained from a collection of readings entitled *Recreation and Leisure Service for the Disadvantaged,* edited by John A. Nesbitt, Paul D. Brown, and James F. Murphy and published in 1970 by Lea & Febiger of Philadelphia.

Nevertheless, since the attitudes and behavior of modern societies are continually changing, some of the facts and ideas in those books can rapidly become outdated. In order to keep abreast of such changes, it is necessary to read appropriate articles in the professional recreation journals mentioned earlier, in sociological journals, in newspapers, and in newsmagazines. Personal observation and discussions with recreation participants and recreation program managers are also essential for a good understanding of current social influences.

6

EXTERNAL FACTORS AFFECTING RECREATION PARTICIPATION: ACCESSIBILITY, RESOURCES, AND TRANSPORTATION

CONCEPTS & PROBLEMS

Opportunity Accessibility
Resource Availability
Transportation Availability
The Dominance of Climate
Resource Ownership
Riparian or Appropriation Laws
Nonrecreational Resource Uses
Impact of Resource Policy
Recreation Environment Growth
Cars Give Freedom of Access
The Vicious Circle in Public
    Transportation

Figure 6.1 The crucial role of transportation was demonstrated in 1980 during the first few days of the XIII Olympic Winter Games at Lake Placid, New York. Spectators had to park in peripheral lots up to 25 kilometers (15 miles) from the events because parking space in the village was limited. When the shuttle bus system proved inadequate, thousands waited for 90 minutes or more in the bitter cold, missing the events they had paid much money and traveled great distances to see.

In examining external factors affecting participation, consideration of opportunity accessibility has been left until last because it is a more complex concept. *Accessibility* depends primarily on external factors, but it is also affected by a number of personal factors. The latter include personality, sex, age, attitude, physical condition, and personal possessions; these will be discussed in Chapter 7. External factors already described in Chapters 4 and 5 such as income levels, hours worked, length of vacations, religious influences, attitudes toward the role of the sexes, crime, and aids provided for the handicapped also influence the nature and extent of opportunities open to individuals. However, two major external aspects of opportunity accessibility have not been discussed in detail; they are recreation resource availability and transportation availability (Figure 6.1). This chapter is devoted to these two important participation determinants. Transportation availability is given emphasis; discussion of recreation resources is limited to the main factors that control availability, since Part Three provides detailed descriptions of the nature and extent of such resources.

The accessibility of recreation opportunities is a key factor in participation. If all other external and personal factors favor people taking part in an activity but problems with access to the necessary recreation resources makes participation impossible, the favorable external and personal factors are of no consequence. Yet, overall accessibility is often scarcely mentioned in recreation literature, as attention is focused on population size, amount of free time, income, and the general mobility of populations. Researchers have also frequently ignored the subject in developing techniques for predicting recreation behavior. Nevertheless, access is the final deciding factor in determining whether or not participation in a particular activity can take place irrespective of other external and personal factors.

RESOURCE AVAILABILITY

Almost all recreation activities require one or more external resources. The majority involve the use of land that has been modified by human action. Many include the use of some type of manufactured item. The **availability** of such recreation resources depends on the nature of the undeveloped resources present in an area, on resource ownership, on the degree to which they are developed, on the carrying capacity of the resources, and on their distribution.

UNDEVELOPED RESOURCES

The combination of undeveloped resources existing in a given area determines, to a large extent, the recreation activities that can occur there. Extremely arid regions with resources limited to air, sky, gravel, and rock may be scenically valuable and suitable for use by various types of off-highway vehicles but are generally inhospitable to other activities. On the other hand, areas with large numbers of good-quality lakes are often suitable for a wide range of activities, including seasonal homes, swimming, waterskiing, sailing, fishing, and nature study. People who live near coastlines that consist of mixtures of headlands, bays, beaches, and estuaries are able to enjoy similar diverse opportunities. Flat areas may be suitable for certain types of automobile racing, the building of airports, and many other kinds of recreation facilities. However, rolling, hilly, or mountainous land is generally more satisfactory for a broad range of extraurban recreation activities, especially tobogganing, downhill skiing, rock climbing, and hang gliding. The geologic history of some locations has resulted in abundant and varied materials for rockhounds and lapidarists, whereas other places offer little or nothing.

The dominant undeveloped resource factor, however, is climate. Participation in most outdoor activities is affected to some extent by weather patterns. Some regions are not cold enough for snow or ice, therefore skiing, tobogganing, snowmobiling, and outdoor ice skating are impossible. Other areas are too hot, at least in the middle of the day, for strenuous activities. Similarly, rain, clouds, wind, and other daily and seasonal aspects of weather conditions are often the crucial factors that decide if and when people may enjoy activities outside.[1]

Humans are not always willing to abstain from activities that are made difficult or impossible by the limitations of an undeveloped environment. Modern technology is now utilized to modify environments to mitigate or overcome such limitations. Bulldozers and scrapers are used to build artificial ski hills. Sand is pumped onto shorelines to create beaches. Channels are dug so that boats can reach docks and

[1] See Chapter 10.

Figure 6.2 **Boat access to Heron Island National Park at the south end of Australia's Great Barrier Reef would be difficult or impossible in larger boats without the channel cut through the reef. This sightseeing, interpretive, and research area is part of the Queensland state park system.**

marina facilities (Figure 6.2). Snow-making machines are employed to compensate for inadequate precipitation. Enclosed stadiums are erected to free professional sports such as football, baseball, and soccer from the dictates of the weather. Be that as it may, most outdoor activities, including many involving extensive development, are still dependent on the basic nature and magnitude of undeveloped resources.

OWNERSHIP, POLICIES, AND CUSTOMS

Participation in recreation activities is frequently affected by resource-ownership patterns. Citizens in Canada and the United States, for example, are fortunate to have large areas of publicly owned land open to them for a wide range of recreation uses. In addition, most fish and game are public property and can be legally taken by any person who does not trespass and who has an appropriate license— these can generally be purchased with little difficulty and for quite nominal fees. In contrast, many European nations have a smaller proportion of public lands. Most game belongs to the landowners, and others may hunt only as invited guests or fee-paying patrons. In some countries, mem-bership in a hunting club and successful completion of preparatory instruction and examinations is required before a person may go hunting. Therefore, hunting in Europe is primarily an activity of the affluent, especially landowners and business people. In the United States and Canada, hunters come from all levels of society, including the poor. In the same way, fishing for species such as salmon and trout is affected by differences in land- and fish-ownership laws as well as government and landowner policies.

Resource ownership, laws, and public policies have a similar impact on participation in other recreation activities. In Europe, many people obtain recreation experiences from privately owned agricultural or wooded areas because traditional pathways that run across private land are open to walkers, bicyclists, and equestrians. A very different situation exists in Canada and the United States where few such rights-of-way exist. Attempts by state, provincial, and local governments to establish new rights-of-way through private lands for recreation trails are generally costly procedures—land or easements have to be purchased and arrangements made for construction, fencing, and maintenance at public expense.

In some cases, differences in ownership or laws within nations also affect participation. In the United States, most publicly owned less developed land is in the West, far from the majority of the population. This situation tends to encourage many outdoor activities such as backpacking, horseback riding on trails, and off-highway vehicle use in the West but discourages them in the East. On the other hand, laws regarding the ownership of water resources in the West differ from those in the East and are less favorable to recreation participation. In the East, the *riparian doctrine* permits each landowner along a waterway to use water for normal purposes, provided the flow is not decreased sufficiently to interfere with similar uses downstream. Water-resource ownership in the West is governed by the *appropriation doctrine,* which allows water rights to be acquired by those who first own land along a waterway and declare their intention of using the water. As a result, virtually all the water in some of these rivers

has been appropriated for irrigation or other purposes, leaving little or no water for downstream recreation and other uses.

There are many other resource laws, policies, and customs that influence recreation participation. Public regulations concerning hunting and fishing seasons; the species and number of fish or game that can be taken; the cost of fishing, hunting, and boat licenses; the use of horses or vehicles on public lands; or the age at which young people may camp in public parks unaccompanied by adults affect the accessibility of opportunities. Policies followed by private landowners often control public access to resources. In the past, many farmers and ranchers in Canada and the United States have been tolerant of those who picnic, camp, hunt, snowmobile, or otherwise use or cross their lands for recreation purposes. More are now installing no-trespassing signs as pressures on the land grow and problems with littering, vandalism, and rowdiness increase.

EXISTING RESOURCE USES

The nonrecreation uses to which resources are put have both immediate and delayed effects on recreation participation. The recreation use of an estuary or river for swimming, fishing, and sailing, for instance, may be directly affected if there is much ship or barge traffic that produces substantial wakes. Such wakes can be dangerous to swimmers and waders, especially small children, and may discourage small-boat sailing as well as fishing from the shore or from boats. The use of such waters by shipping also depreciates the recreation environ-

ment when it is accompanied by erosion, dredging of channels, dumping of dredged materials, and the discharge of oil and other substances.

Agricultural practices can have an impact on many types of recreation. Depending on the location and the circumstances, the conversion of pasture to grain crops may increase populations of pheasants and deer. On the other hand, the removal of hedgerows and patches of woodland can reduce certain wildlife populations. Agricultural practices that result in sizable amounts of fertilizers or eroded soil being washed into waterways and lakes produce excessive growth of algae, decreased oxygen levels, and other conditions detrimental to fish species preferred by fisherpersons. Pesticides and other chemicals used in agriculture and elsewhere also find their way into the waters and may harm fish. In some locations, contamination of the waters may be so severe that fisherpersons are advised not to eat their catches or the area is closed to fishing. Pesticides have also affected the populations of many birds that people enjoy hunting or seeing—some species, including the American eagle, are becoming endangered.

Forestry practices can have similar effects. Poor log skidding, yarding, and haul-road-construction techniques may greatly accelerate erosion and damage fisheries by depositing large amounts of silt in streams and lakes. Areas that have been logged may spoil people's aesthetic enjoyment. On the other hand, logged areas generally produce more wild flowers, berries, and game animals (such as deer) than do uncut forests. In addition, logging haul roads and skidways provide access to areas that were relatively inaccessible. Naturalists, berrypickers, and hunters, therefore, generally find logged areas provide more recreation opportunities than uncut mature woodlands.

Land close to American cities is often unused for many years because speculators buy it and await a profitable opportunity to sell it to developers; during this period, it is frequently used far more extensively for recreation than when it was cultivated. In urban and suburban areas, lands near airports, expressways, railroads, and some types of factories may be so noisy that most people find them unsuitable locations for any kind of recreation activity. Nearby residents may also find it difficult to engage in social or contemplative recreation activities inside their homes. Similarly, areas that have odor problems because they are adjacent to sewage-treatment plants, chemical plants, pulp mills, improperly operated garbage dumps, or extensive animal feedlots may be virtually unusable for recreation purposes.

Mining and quarrying can also affect recreation participation. If the large, rocky areas of open pits or tailing dumps are not rehabilitated, a virtual biologic desert may result and persist for many years. Such environments usually offer few recreation opportunities. Acid wastes from open-pit coal mines can also reduce the availability of opportunities by polluting nearby streams. On the other hand, mines and quarries can be valuable recreation resources, especially in relatively flat areas. Some abandoned open-pit mines make attractive parks or hunting, fishing, or camping areas, especially if ponds or lakes have been created. Old quarries may be

developed into spectacular gardens such as the famous Rock Gardens in Hamilton, Ontario, Canada. Amateur lapidarists, mineralogists, and paleontologists often collect interesting materials at mine dumps and in quarries. Some quarries and sandpits are used extensively by off-highway motorcyclists, and many motorcycling organizations stage races and hillclimbs at such locations. Sandpits may also be good sites for rifle ranges.

DEVELOPED RESOURCES

The availability of most recreation opportunities is dependent on the nature, extent, and accessibility of developed recreation resources. In some cases, a prominent original feature of the landscape is turned into a recreation resource by the development of facilities. For example, a trail is built to a hitherto almost inaccessible scenic area, allowing people to visit the site on foot or horseback; a small boat harbor is constructed, making recreational boating feasible along a stretch of rugged coastline; ski runs are cut through the timber and a chairlift is installed on a mountain slope, making downhill skiing possible; or bringing in large quantities of sand turns a shallow, silted lake into an attractive environment for swimming and beach-oriented activities.

In other cases, the original features of a site are less important; opportunities are created by building structures such as recreation centers, tennis courts, libraries, theaters, and night clubs, and they become the primary recreation resource. The degree to which resources are developed for recreation depends on many previous

and current factors, including public policies, budgets, and the number and abilities of the people involved.

Resource policies that affect recreation participation are established by a variety of people. Private landowners make decisions regarding the use of their residence yards, farms, and woodlands. Politicians, park board members, and voters decide on the nature and extent of park systems. Administrators and managers set policies regarding the development and operation of lands and facilities. Health boards and fire departments establish rules that control the use of both indoor and outdoor resources. Examples of policies that influence participation are:

- Policies concerning priorities— wilderness-type experiences or developed-facility activities; landscape preservation or installation of high-capacity roads, parking lots, and buildings; sports fishing or commercial fishing; restricted use or multiple use of resources; development of resort-type facilities for the affluent or public parks for lower income people.
- Policies regarding the nature and extent of facilities that are developed at particular locations— parking areas, picnic areas, playgrounds, tennis courts, toilet facilities, campsites, roads, boat-launching ramps, athletic facilities, swimming pools, libraries, discotheques, resorts.
- Policies concerning the times that resources will be open to the public— seasons, days of the week, daily opening and closing hours.
- Policies regarding fees— whether to charge for admission and, if so, how much; whether to offer reduced rates for groups, children, students, families, older persons, season ticketholders, or on special days; whether to charge tourists more than residents; whether to make the facility self-supporting by adjusting fees to cover costs.

- Policies regulating admission— whether to admit everyone or only those of certain ages, sex, affiliation, or qualifications; whether to restrict use to children accompanied by adults, women with escorts, people in cars, residents of the municipality, or individuals in appropriate attire (those wearing shoes, ties and jackets, bathing caps, lifejackets, etc.).
- Policies providing for access of participation by special groups— the handicapped, the aged, young people, individuals with certain ethnic or religious backgrounds, people with specific qualifications and skills.
- Policies concerning the manner in which resources may be used— prohibition of motor vehicles, motorcycles, motors on boats, picnicking, swimming, overnight camping, building fires, hunting, fishing, collecting specimens, taking photographs, playing radios, feeding animals, traveling off the trail.

Setting policies that will provide the optimum number of desirable quality recreation experiences for intended participant groups is one of the most important responsibilities of those who administer recreation resources.

The amount of money available for the acquisition, development, and operation of recreation resources is often as important as policies in determining the nature and extent of participation. Where budgets are inadequate, some of the following limitations on participation may occur: the area of land available for recreation is insufficient; resources such as lakes, beaches, and fishing streams remain largely inaccessible to the general public; development of facilities and programs is limited; police protection, safety measures, maintenance and professional staff are inadequate; facilities deteriorate and vandalism increases. On the other

hand, if a public agency, private organization, or commercial enterprise has sufficient funds, it can plan its facilities and programs so that they facilitate participation.

With adequate support, appropriate areas of suitable land may be acquired at locations where recreation opportunities are needed; well-designed and suitably constructed facilities can be built; an adequate number of appropriately trained persons can be hired to carry out all necessary administrative, operational, and maintenance work; the proper equipment and supplies can be purchased so that employees may perform their assignments correctly, efficiently, and safely; information or advertising campaigns can be conducted to inform people of the availability of opportunities; brochures, maps, and other materials can be provided to assist visitors in understanding and enjoying the resources.

Nearly all recreation activities depend to some extent on the contributions of people. These contributions may be made by individuals as part of their regular assignments while working for a recreation agency or enterprise. Other contributions can take place as an incidental part of work for organizations that are not directly concerned with recreation or as a part of purely volunteer activities. The quality of such efforts often affects participation, for instance:

- A poorly informed, disinterested person answering telephone enquiries at a city park and recreation department will discourage some people from taking part in the department's programs.
- Insensitive recreation center supervisors, swimming instructors, resort managers, camp directors, or volun-

teer leaders may discourage use of their facilities, participation in their programs, or even instill in participants a lasting dislike for the activity concerned.
- Well-trained, enthusiastic librarians dedicated to helping people use the library to the fullest extent will stimulate the use of all types of library resources.
- Park rangers, forest organization personnel, or local sporting goods store employees can do much to help people use less developed resources to better advantage by suggesting routes to follow and problems to avoid when backpacking, horseback riding, motorcycling, rock collecting, fishing, or canoeing; uninformed or surly individuals can cause people to get into dangerous situations, go elsewhere, or abandon their plans altogether.

Organizations that provide recreation opportunities should therefore make a point of only choosing well-qualified staff and volunteer leaders who understand and have empathy with the various kinds of people being served.

The availability of many opportunities depends on the size of an area's population. When the population exceeds the threshold number needed to pay the costs (either through taxes or admission fees), a community may contain publicly owned resources such as libraries, tennis courts, and swimming pools or commercially operated facilities such as bowling alleys, movie theaters, and discotheques. The variety of both public and privately operated recreation opportunities tends to increase with population size. More specialized facilities and recreation professionals are provided as larger numbers of potential participants make this possible. Thus people who live in a large city are likely to have chances to take part in more kinds of recreation than residents of a smaller community.

The degree to which opportunities are made known to potential participants by word of mouth, signs, advertising, news broadcasts, and articles in newspapers or magazines is often a major factor in accessibility. If people are completely unaware of an opportunity, it is inaccessible to them. If they know vaguely that it exists but cannot find out readily when, where, or how to participate, the opportunity will remain largely unavailable. Commercial recreation establishments are well aware of the need to reach potential clients, but public, quasi-public, and private organizations often fail to inform citizens adequately about their facilities and programs. City park and recreation departments frequently rely almost exclusively on newspaper advertising to inform citizens of their programs. But more than three-quarters of the poorer, less educated households may remain unaware of city recreation programs if only newspaper advertising is used. On the other hand, there are some situations where the briefest mention of an opportunity in the right place can immediately contribute substantially to accessibility. For example, just the inclusion of a green area and the label, national park, on maps used by motorists can rapidly produce a flood of potential visitors, even if the area is still undeveloped.

Finally, the availability of recreation opportunities also depends on the development or refinement of recreation equipment. Such items as bicycles, ice skates, skis, snowmobiles, roller skates, scuba gear, automatic cameras, tennis rackets,

Figure 6.3 An Owens-Corning ® advertisement points out that the development of fiberglass made it possible to reduce surfboard weight from as much as 40 kilograms (90 pounds) when made of redwood to less than 7 kilograms (15 pounds). This has made surfboards easier to transport and less dangerous when surfers are hit by loose boards.

Fiberglas has helped rocket sales of surfboards 9,900 percent. How much would it boost sales of your product?

For centuries, just a few natives surfed. By 1940, only 1,000 people a year were up to buying (or *carrying*) the 90-lb. redwood boards being sold.

Then came surfboards made with Fiberglas.* Smoother. Brighter. And under 15 pounds. Presto! Instant fun. Instant lifestyle. Instant sales—now coasting at 100,000 boards a year.

*T.M. Reg. O.C.F. for reinforcements for plastics.

Fiberglas reinforcement, added to plastic, can be engineered into a materials "system" with almost any desired characteristic.

Products like room air conditioners and fishing trawlers benefit from the same strength, lightness, and water resistance that improved surfboards. Other products like circuit breakers and oilfield line pipe are better because they're more moldable, electrically nonconductive, more resistant to corrosion, or less expensive.

Would a Fiberglas materials system make *your* product better? We'll help you find out. Write O.R. Meeks, Owens-Corning Fiberglas Corp., Fiberglas Tower, Toledo, Ohio 43659.

Owens-Corning is Fiberglas FIBERGLAS

musical instruments, television sets, and a great variety of toys and games have all— through their invention and subsequent improvement— enriched the lives of many participants. Innovations that have had major impacts on recreation are the discovery and mass production of such materials as nylon, aluminum, fiberglass, and thermoplastics as well as the development and manufacture of transistors and magnetic tape. For instance, fiberglass-reinforced plastics are used extensively in the manufacture of such recreation items as skis, fishing rods, protective sports equipment, pool cues, sports car bodies, skateboards, powerboats, sailboats, snowmobiles, all-terrain vehicles, hang glider frames, stadium seats, basketball backboards, many types of gymnastic equipment, rackets, golf clubs, bowling scoring equipment, motorhome bodies, and playground equipment (Figure 6.3). Modern materials and mass production methods have made a major contribution to the availability of all kinds of opportunities from skateboarding on city sidewalks to backpacking in remote wilderness areas.

TRANSPORTATION DEVELOPMENT IMPACT

As economic development occurs and recreation environments become more complex, transportation comes to play an increasingly significant role in participation. In modern societies, most recreation experiences away from the place of residence involve the use of some form of mechanical transportation. The dispersed nature of many modern communities, especially those in Canada and the United States, result in most trips to libraries, parks, and other local recreation resources being made by bicycle, automobile, or public transportation. Those who do not have access to suitable transportation are often unable to participate in the majority of recreation opportunities available in their community and the surrounding area.

It is only about 140 years since rapid changes in transportation began to contribute to the Second Recreation Revolution[2] in the developed nations. Up to that time, the large majority of people were limited to walking as a means of reaching a recreation resource; only the more affluent could afford to ride horses or travel in horsedrawn vehicles. As a result, most people's recreation environments were confined to those resources they could reach on foot during time free from work. This limited the average person's recreation environment to a radius of about 16 kilometers (10 miles) on Sundays, and other holidays and to only 5 or 6 kilometers (3 or 4 miles) on workday evenings.

Then, in the early 1800s, the Industrial Revolution produced steam-powered boats and locomotives, and the average person's recreation environment slowly began to expand. By the end of the century, railroad and steamboat travel had become widespread in parts of Europe and the northeastern portion of North America. Eventually, even comparatively low-income people could afford some of the excursions to sports events or resorts. The recreation environment had increased to a radius of 80 to 150 kilometers (50 to 100 miles) on Sundays and holidays. In many cities, horsedrawn tramcars were introduced, expanding the radius both in the evenings and on weekends. But, for the most part, workers living in small communities and farm laborers continued to walk.

The first practical means of individual transportation that became available to the less affluent was the safety bicycle introduced by an English manufacturer in 1885. Depending on the quality of the roads available, it increased the radius of people's recreation environment to 15 kilometers (10 miles) or more of an evening and 50 kilometers (30 miles) or more of a Sunday or holiday. When railroads started to carry bicycles as cheaply as passenger baggage, the bicycle owner began to enjoy great flexibility in recreational travel. By the early 1900s, millions of bicycles had been sold. City streets, parks, and nearby country roads became quite crowded with bicycles on Sundays and holidays as people enjoyed their newfound personal mobility.

The automobile was a relatively expensive novelty at first and had comparatively little impact on most people's recreation environments until after World War I. Mass production then brought car ownership within the reach of the middle class, and road improvements made cars a practical means of transportation away from the cities. The depression prevented the automobile from becoming a major method of individual transportation for lower-income workers until after World War II. Depending on highway and traffic conditions and in the absence of other forms of transportation, the family car currently provides an

[2] See Chapter 2.

evening recreation environment radius of 50 kilometers to 100 kilometers (30 to 60 miles) and a one-day holiday radius of 150 kilometers to 250 kilometers (100 to 150 miles).

During the first half of the twentieth century, public transportation in the cities expanded. Electric tramcars, buses, and subways flourished and suburban or interurban electric train systems were developed. In many cities, these systems were extensive and fares were relatively low so that public transportation became the principal means of travel to recreation resources. Many systems made it possible for inner-city residents to reach facilities such as beaches, lakes, or amusement parks outside the city limits.

Water transportation's role in recreation also expanded during the late 1800s and the first half of the twentieth century. Ferries carried large numbers of tourists and one-day trippers across water barriers such as the English Channel. In many cases, the boat trip itself was the main recreation experience. Cruises of a few hours, all day, or several days were common from seaside resorts and harbors on the Great Lakes and on other large inland lakes and rivers. Fares were often low enough to permit participation by lower income people. Transatlantic and other long-distance voyages by the more affluent reached their peak after World War II but started to decline as costs rose and air travel became cheaper.

Although the Wright brothers made their famous first flight with a heavier-than-air machine in 1909 and commercial aviation was well underway by the middle 1930s, the full impact of the airplane on recreation is still to come. Since World War II, air travel has become a major factor in the flow of tourists both nationally and internationally, but most people who travel by air are in the middle and upper classes. However, special no-frill charter and package rates have begun to make air travel available to people with more modest incomes.

Air travel has increased the accessibility of certain kinds of activities such as vacations at ski areas and warm-climate resorts to a much wider range of people. For example, it has been particularly helpful to segments of the population who experience difficulty getting away from their jobs for long periods. Professional people, farmers, and those who run small businesses can now spend a weekend or week at a resort 1500 kilometers (1000 miles) away and use only a few hours of their vacation time in traveling. Previously, they would have spent four or five days traveling by car or train.

The great expansion of people's recreation environments that has taken place in the last 140 years is summarized in Figure 6.4. It is based on average conditions in the more populated areas of Europe and the northeastern portions of the United States and Canada. Another way of looking at the impact of transportation innovations is to consider the tremendous reductions in travel times that have occurred in the 140-year period (Figure 6.5). Irrespective of how it is viewed, transportation changes coupled with economic development are shrinking space and completely changing the accessibility of recreation opportunities for those living in the more advanced nations. Since 1950, the number of Americans traveling abroad (excluding trips to Canada and Mexico) has risen from about 650,000 a year to more than 8 million. During the same time, the number of people visiting the United States from overseas rose from 230,000 to over 5 million. Similar mass movements are occurring between other developed nations and groups of developed nations. The same kinds of changes will take place elsewhere in the world as other countries' economies and transportation systems are developed.

CURRENT TRANSPORTATION METHODS

The relative importance of various methods of transportation in providing access to recreation opportunities varies considerably. In some locations, walking is still of great significance. Elsewhere, public transportation, private cars, boats, or aircraft may dominate. Often, more than one method is used. People take public transportation to a point close to their intended destination and then walk. Some take bicycles along as they travel by car, train, or plane to use them as transportation later on. The "fly-drive" form of vacation is used frequently to combine the speed of air travel with the convenience of a car at the destination. It is therefore important for those involved in recreation planning or management to be well acquainted with all forms of transportation and the manner in which they interact.

WALKING
In spite of all the modern developments in transportation, walking

Figure 6.4 Typical changes in the size of people's recreation environments that occurred as transportation improved in developed areas of Europe and northeastern North America. Similar changes take place today as nations advance economically only usually they take place more quickly.

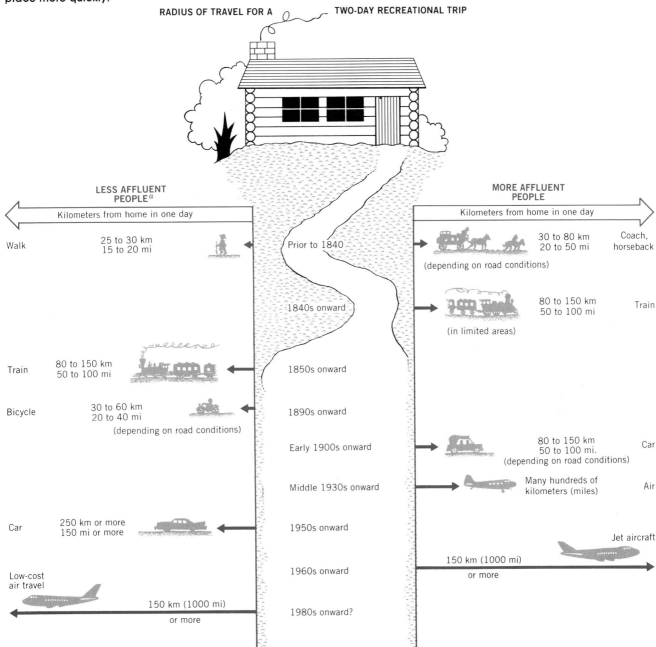

RADIUS OF TRAVEL FOR A   TWO-DAY RECREATIONAL TRIP

LESS AFFLUENT PEOPLE[a]

Kilometers from home in one day

Walk	25 to 30 km / 15 to 20 mi	
Train	80 to 150 km / 50 to 100 mi	
Bicycle	30 to 60 km / 20 to 40 mi (depending on road conditions)	
Car	250 km or more / 150 mi or more	
Low-cost air travel	150 km (1000 mi) or more	

MORE AFFLUENT PEOPLE

Kilometers from home in one day

Prior to 1840

30 to 80 km / 20 to 50 mi (depending on road conditions) — Coach, horseback

1840s onward

80 to 150 km / 50 to 100 mi (in limited areas) — Train

1850s onward

1890s onward

Early 1900s onward

80 to 150 km / 50 to 100 mi. (depending on road conditions) — Car

Middle 1930s onward

Many hundreds of kilometers (miles) — Air

1950s onward

1960s onward

150 km (1000 mi) or more — Jet aircraft

1980s onward?

[a]Until the twentieth century many workers seldom had two consecutive days off from work. Some did not begin two-day weekends until the 1940s.

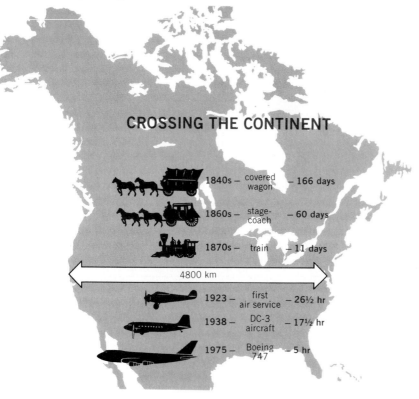

Figure 6.5 Reduction in the time needed to cross the North American continent. The 4800 kilometers (3000 miles) between New York and San Francisco can now be crossed in one-fiftieth of the time it took 100 years ago and one-fifth of the time needed 50 years ago.

CROSSING THE CONTINENT

1840s — covered wagon — 166 days

1860s — stage-coach — 60 days

1870s — train — 11 days

4800 km

1923 — first air service — 26½ hr

1938 — DC-3 aircraft — 17½ hr

1975 — Boeing 747 — 5 hr

continues to be an important factor for opportunity accessibility and a major recreation activity in itself. Walking is often the only available method of reaching recreation resources away from home for most inhabitants of less developed countries, and many of the lower income people in developed nations. It is also the chosen method of travel for growing numbers of more affluent citizens who are concerned about physical fitness or the preservation of the environment. Unfortunately, facilities for walkers are often absent in some of the developed countries. In the United States

and Canada, for instance, almost all of the rural roads and some of the suburban residential streets lack developed sidewalks or pathways. In many cases, walkers can only reach suburban and rural parks or other recreation facilities by walking on the edge of the road surface itself or by struggling over rough roadside terrain; even the entrance drives into parks often do not have sidewalks or pathways. Under such circumstances, people are often discouraged or prevented from walking to nearby recreation resources.

As mentioned earlier, the general absence of public footpaths

across private land means that walking and hiking opportunities in the rural areas of Canada and the United States are also more limited than in Europe. In England and Wales alone, for instance, 225,000 kilometers (140,000 miles) of footpaths provide access to virtually every stretch of the countryside. Distances between interesting landscape features are also greater in much of North America, especially in the flatter areas of the Midwest, Great Plains, and Great Basin. In addition, most parts of the United States and Canada lack the little-traveled, winding country lanes of Europe because rectangular land-survey systems were used in laying out the majority of the states and provinces. European rural roads, on the other hand, provide many aesthetically pleasing opportunities for walking and hiking that complement the network of public footpaths (Figure 6.6). The use of such roads and pathways is also encouraged by the ready access to many rural areas provided by local buses and trains.

In urban areas, the feasibility of sightseeing on foot is frequently determined by the age of the city. In old cities, which developed before the automobile, places of interest are commonly grouped together, thereby facilitating walking tours. Again, good public transportation systems can encourage walking if such systems make it easy to move between locations where walking tours are feasible.

RIDING HORSES
Although horses, ponies, mules, and donkeys have ceased to be a primary method of transportation in developed nations, they are still of importance for recreation. Many

Figure 6.6 **Two hikers set out in the early morning along a winding country road through Britain's Lake District. One in jest bears the "L" sign that British law requires on vehicles being driven by "learners."**

people ride horses purely for the pleasure derived from doing so and not for transportation. Others regard riding as a dual purpose activity—they like riding and it also provides transportation to or through desirable recreation environments. To a minority, riding itself is not particularly pleasurable. In fact, it may even be a frightening experience to some, but they will tolerate this method of transportation in order to reach a special recreation resource.

Whether the riding experience is regarded as a means of transportation or as a source of pleasure, it gives access to recreation resources that many individuals would otherwise be unable to visit. In Grand Canyon National Park, for example, thousands of persons who would be physically incapable of hiking down to the bottom of the canyon and then up again are able to experience its marvels by taking the concessionaire-operated mule trips. Similarly, riding animals provide access to dozens of national parks, forests, wilderness areas, archaeological sites, and wildlife reserves located elsewhere in the United States and other parts of the world. Larger numbers of people are likely to use this method of access to more remote recreation resources as areas where vehicle travel is prohibited increase in number and a growing proportion of the population consists of healthy and reasonably affluent older citizens.

CYCLING

The bicycle is the most common mechanical means of transportation in the world today. Total worldwide production exceeded 36 million bicycles a year in 1970 and is now about 50 million. Even in the United States, where it is not considered a primary means of transportation, about 95 million bicycles are now in use.

For young people, old people, and the poor, bicycles are often the only available means of transportation other than walking. Children experience their first taste of independent mobility when they are given tricycles or bicycles. Their recreation environment expands tremendously as they get older and are given more freedom to leave the home territory. Eventually, they can use their bicycles to visit nearby parks and playgrounds, reach friends' homes or neighborhood stores, travel to sports and other community events, go fishing, explore surrounding neighborhoods and rural areas, visit museums and zoos, get books from the library, or even go on long-distance camping trips (Figure 6.7).

In some nations, especially where fewer people have automobiles, adults also use bicycles extensively for recreational travel. In parts of Europe, for example, families cycle to the beach or into the countryside for weekend picnics and outings. In the United States and Canada, the adult use of bicycles is increasing, but most recreational cycling is undertaken for its exercise value and occurs on nearby streets or in parks without any particular destination in mind. In some communities, however, adults are beginning to use their bicycles to reach local recreation resources on a more or less regular basis. For instance, older people in retirement communities located in the southern portions of the United States use bicycles and adult tricycles extensively. If they do not have

a car or are unable to drive, a bicycle or tricycle can substantially increase the radius of their recreation environments and enable them to preserve a measure of independence.

Participation in recreational cycling and the use of bicycles for transportation to recreation resources depend partly on the availability of suitable roads or bicycle trails. As in the case of walking and hiking, conditions are generally more favorable for cycling in Europe than in North America because of the shorter distances between places of interest, the large number of country roads that receive comparatively little motor traffic, and the prevalence of separate

bicycle paths in both urban and rural areas. In addition, European drivers are more accustomed to cyclists so that bicycling is somewhat less hazardous on roads and streets in Europe. Severe winter weather in much of Canada and the United States, on the other hand, makes bicycling impossible or difficult for several months each year and contributes to the rougher condition of roads, especially the edges of paved roads where cyclists usually travel.

However, this situation is changing, Gradually, Americans are being provided with the facilities they need to make the bicycle a more useful means of regular transportation. About 96,540 kilometers (60,000 miles) of bicycle paths

Figure 6.7 **The availability of bicycles made it possible for these New York City teenagers to spend a pleasant summer afternoon together dangling their feet in the water of Conservatory Pond in Central Park.**

have now been constructed throughout the United States, and public support for cycling facilities is growing. The federal government made $6 million available to communities in 1976 for the development of bikeways and some 500 different projects resulted. Legislation passed in 1978 suggested that $20 million a year for four years be appropriated for bikeways so programs to expand the network are expected to grow. Meanwhile, attempts are being made to solve the other major problems of would-be cyclists—the transportation of their bicycles to suitable departure points and their storage at the places of destination. In some cities, buses are being equipped with special bike racks and safe-storage facilities are being provided at outlying subway stops, downtown parking lots, and work places. It is unlikely that the bicycle will ever reach the prominent transportation position that it has achieved in many other countries, but, at least, it now has an excellent chance of becoming a viable good-weather choice for millions of Americans. And, most important, the bicycle will ever reach the promfull potential as an important link to the outside world for those who have no other means of transportation.

PERSONAL MOTORIZED TRANSPORTATION

During the revival of popular interest in environmental problems that occurred in the early 1970s, it became fashionable to attack the motor vehicle as the arch villain. Of course, the way people have chosen to develop and use motor vehicles has contributed substantially to many environmental problems, in-

cluding energy shortages, air pollution, decline in public transportation facilities, urban sprawl, and other land-use problems. Be that as it may, the automobile and other motorized vehicles have also contributed in many ways to the improvement of people's environments, especially their recreation environments.

Role of Private Vehicles.
Like the bicycle, the privately owned motor vehicle enhances people's recreation environments, primarily because it provides freedom to travel. Previously, those with modest or low incomes were confined to recreation opportunities in the home or within walking, bicycling, or public transportation range. They were often restricted in the time they could devote to an activity away from home by the constraints of distance or the limitations of public transportation schedules. Reliance on walking, bicycling, or public transportation also limited participation in activities that required the transportation of a substantial amount of supplies or recreation equipment. The affluent, on the other hand, could go where they wanted, when they wanted, and rent or purchase virtually any type of recreation good or service after they got there.

The production of relatively low-cost motor vehicles did more to democratize recreation than any other development of the twentieth century. Behind the wheel of a privately owned vehicle, distinctions of age or position tend to disappear. Drivers and passengers feel liberated and are able to break away from the frustrations of their personal lives and the limitations of their everyday environments. They

feel they can do what they want to do rather than what the community or their social position allows. But it does more than provide a means of escape; rich or poor, a car is a magic carpet that transports its occupants to the attractions of the outside world.

Ownership or access to a motor vehicle enlarges and improves people's recreation environments because it provides:

- Freedom to go to urban and extraurban recreation resources that cannot be reached readily by other means.
- Freedom to live on farms, ranches, or at other dispersed locations but still to be able to take part regularly in recreation activities in nearby communities such as borrowing books from a library, seeing movies, attending social and sporting events, and belonging to clubs and hobby groups.
- Freedom to have more private recreation experiences—people with cars at their disposal can readily travel through a large recreation resource such as a forest until they find an unoccupied or less crowded area.
- Freedom for families with young children and pets to take part more readily in activities such as seeing a movie, shopping, going to the beach, camping, or traveling long distances to visit relatives or sightsee; helpful items such as baby carriages, food, toys, camping gear, and other personal belongings can be carried; children can sleep en route or during such activities as a movie at a drive-in theater; and expenses for meals and accommodations can be reduced or avoided.
- Freedom for the handicapped to reach nearby and distant recreation resources; public transportation is often inaccessible to those in wheelchairs or who have difficulty walking or climbing stairs.
- Freedom to take part in certain activities that require special equipment; traveling by bicycle or by public

transportation is usually not practical for those who wish to take a harp, boat, surfboard, hang glider, horse, or snowmobile with them, and it is decidedly inconvenient for those who bring home large antiques, heavy rock specimens, a deer carcass, or an ice chest full of fish they have caught.

- Freedom from fear (at least to some extent) when wishing to take part in a recreation opportunity in an area or at a time of day when antisocial acts such as rapes and muggings are more likely to occur.
- Freedom to use more time for recreation; other means of transportation frequently take longer to cover a given distance and public transportation often stops running early in the evening, but people with their own transportation can stay to hear the end of a concert, enjoy all of a social event, or see the sun set and the moon rise.
- Freedom to have a place of one's own. A vehicle is cherished by many young people (especially those from large families) because, for the first time, they have a defined personal territory where they can feel secure, entertain friends, and behave as they wish.
- Freedom to express one's individuality. Selection of a particular kind of vehicle is often the first, and sometimes the only, major decision a person has an opportunity to make. In some cases, opportunities to be creative occur as individuals rebuild vehicles, paint them in special color schemes, and add accessories or furnishings.
- Freedom (when on a sightseeing trip) to visit only preferred locations with the ability to stay as long as desired, instead of being tied to the places and times specified by a tour guide or transportation company.
- Freedom for unsponsored sports teams to compete with teams in other areas or for groups of performers and members of social or hobby clubs to take part in events at distant locations.

In addition, modern motor vehicles equipped with heaters and air conditioners encourage participation in recreation activities during weather that would otherwise make travel uncomfortable or impossible. Automobiles are especially valuable to people living in cold, snowy climates because they eliminate the extended period of social isolation that used to occur in past times; people with properly equipped cars are able to visit neighbors and take part in community recreation events in all but the most severe weather.

Although the privately owned motor vehicle has made tremendous positive contributions to our recreation environments, these gains are not without cost. Besides the estimated 250,000 traffic deaths and 7 million serious injuries that occur throughout the world each year, there are the well-known environmental problems of air pollution, energy and other kinds of resource depletion, and the use of large land areas for roads. The noise, fumes, and dangers of heavy traffic can interfere with one's participation in or enjoyment of bicycling and walking for pleasure, windowshopping, relaxing in urban parks, or engaging in outdoor activities around the place of one's residence. Young children may not even be allowed to play outside if they live in areas where traffic is heavy and the houses are not fenced or set back from the street.

The availability of the private automobile and the construction of highways has also generated suburban sprawl, and this, in turn, has adversely affected some people's recreation. For example, individuals who live in suburban areas but cannot afford a car or are not allowed to drive may have extremely limited

recreation environments. And, those who continue to live in urban neighborhoods may find their general living conditions deteriorating and their recreation opportunities decreasing as the tax base erodes and the population on which commercial recreation enterprises depended for support becomes poorer and smaller.

Specific recreation opportunities are also lost because of the prevalence of motor vehicles and the way in which they are used. For instance, valuable recreation land that could have provided additional recreation opportunities is frequently devoted to large parking lots or used for roads and highways. Unless automobile use is banned, valuable beach lands such as those at Daytona Beach in Florida (Figure 5.1) can become busy roadways; or, unique resources such as the main valley in Yosemite National Park in California can become so crowded with vehicles that the aesthetic experiences people hope to enjoy are depreciated or even destroyed. In addition and most ironically of all—considering that automobiles have played such a major role in the expansion of people's recreation environments—millions of hours of potential recreation time are lost each year because work schedules, customs, driving habits, and inadequate road systems result in millions of people regularly spending significant portions of their free time in traffic jams or driving slowly along badly congested roads.

Vehicle and Road Distribution. To appreciate the role that motor vehicles play in recreation, particularly tourism, it is important to understand the great differences that exist in various parts of the world in the numbers of vehicles available and the condition and distribution of roads. There are now more than 271 million passenger cars in use throughout the world. Generally, the nations that are more economically advanced have more cars in proportion to their populations than less developed countries. This is not true in the case of the Communist countries. Table 6.1 shows that the Soviet Union and China have a much smaller proportion of cars than might be expected from their position on the economic development ladder. This is because both nations have followed political policies of making producer goods instead of consumer goods such as automobiles. In contrast, Brazil has a relatively high proportion of cars as a result of generally favorable policies toward consumer-goods importation and production. However, the recreation benefits of motor vehicles are not unknown to people in Communist nations. Public desire for more consumer goods, including cars, has stimulated policy changes in the Soviet Union and some eastern European nations. In Russia *automobilizatsiya* (automobilization) is proceeding with surprising speed. In 1970, there were less than 1 million privately owned automobiles in operation; by 1977, the number had grown to well over 5 million.

Russians are showing the same proclivity for owning and using cars for recreation as people in the non-Communist nations. Unfortunately, the Soviet highway and service systems are not able to support the influx of private cars. Most of the 1.4 million kilometers (860,000 miles) of highways are poorly graded and 90 percent of the system is un-

Table 6.1 Number of Passenger Cars in Use and Number of Persons per Car for Selected Nations

Nation	Number of Cars in Use (Thousands)	Number of Persons per Car
United States	109,003	2
New Zealand	1,210	3
Canada	8,870	3
Australia	5,284	3
France	16,230	3
West Germany	19,180	3
United Kingdom	14,355	4
Japan	18,476	6
South Africa	2,169	12
Brazil	6,349	18
Mexico	2,641	25
Soviet Union	5,660	46
Kenya	84	171
Bolivia	23	208
India	800	782
Bangladesh	20	4,028
China	50	17,328

SOURCE: Developed from United Nations, "Motor Vehicles in Use," *1978 Statistical Yearbook*, United Nations, New York, 1979, and "World Transportation," 1979 Britannica Book of the Year, Encyclopaedia Britannica, Inc., Chicago, 1979.

paved. Of Soviet roads, 7 out of 10 become impassable during the spring thaw and many urban roads carry twice their intended traffic volumes. The normal highway features found in the West such as road signs, safety barriers, lighting in urban areas, roadside rest areas, and centerline markings are largely absent. There are few service stations, almost two-thirds of the drivers have had no formal training, and drunken driving is a serious problem. As a result, automobile crashes are numerous and the fatality rate is high.

Figure 6.8 shows the world distribution of roads suitable for ordinary motor vehicles. The main portion of the United States, a narrow strip across southern Canada, most of western Europe, and a large part of India are generally highly accessi-

ble by car. Turkey, the European part of the Soviet Union, Japan, New Zealand, and the southeastern portion of Australia are moderately well provided with roads. Relatively open networks of motorable roads exist in Argentina, Uruguay, Paraguay, eastern Brazil, and parts of Mexico; the rest of Latin America is largely inaccessible by ordinary car. The southern two-thirds of Africa has few roads and much of the northern third cannot be reached by conventional automobiles. The southern two-thirds of Asia has a sparse road network (except for India and Japan), and the northern third, like most of Alaska and northern Canada, lacks roads. The western two-thirds of Australia has no motorable roads in the interior desert areas and only a few roads around the periphery.

Figure 6.8 Distribution of world's main highways. Areas more than 100 kilometers (60 miles) from these roads are generally inaccessible by ordinary motor vehicle. In less developed regions, only the areas immediately adjacent to these roads may be accessible.

Effect of Road Type. The nature of a region's highways as well as the density of the highway network affects the accessibility of recreation opportunities. Most of the world's motorable roads follow routes established decades or centuries before motor vehicles became common. Many wind through the countryside connecting places that were early settlements. In the days of travel on foot, by wagon, or on horseback these routes were reasonably satisfactory. Today, they are both an advantage and disadvantage to recreation participation.

The narrow, winding, indirect roads found in areas settled before the use of rectangular survey systems and the advent of the automobile are a recreation resource in themselves (see Chapter 15). They tend to be quieter, since they discourage fast through traffic, particularly heavy trucks, and the areas they traverse are often much less developed. The pastoral landscapes they go through and the small communities they connect provide many recreation opportunities for residents as well as tourists. Even the ones that have been straightened and widened to form main routes or facilitate the use of modern snowplow equipment often have great appeal to people who

are in no hurry and who seek a relaxing and more interesting driving experience en route to a particular destination.

On the other hand, regions that only have winding, indirect roads, which frequently pass through towns and villages, are difficult to traverse quickly and are both frustrating and annoying to those who are anxious to reach a recreation resource some distance away. Now that such large areas of North America and Europe are served by modern high-speed, controlled-access highways, it is sometimes difficult to realize what an obstacle areas with older road systems can be. However, there are still many areas lying between high-speed highways and regions where such highways have not been built. In such situations, the accessibility of some types of recreation opportunities may be reduced for both residents and potential visitors. If, for example, travel by motor vehicle averages only 50 kilometers (30 miles) an hour instead of the 90 kilometers (55 miles) an hour or more achieved on high-speed highways, people are then only able to travel about 150 kilometers (90 miles) on a Friday evening instead of 265 kilometers (165 miles). This more than triples the total area that may be reached in three hours or less thereby greatly expanding the number of accessible opportunities.

The building of high-speed highways in Europe, Japan, and North America has also had a profound effect on long-distance travel. In the United States, the National System of Interstate and Defense Highways was planned as a 68,400-kilometer (42,500-mile) network connecting more than 90 percent of the nation's cities with populations over 50,000 (Figure 6.9). More than 92 percent of the planned mileage is now open to traffic. It is possible to drive the 4867 kilometers (3025 miles) from New York to San Francisco on Interstate Highway 80 and encounter less than 150 kilometers (100 miles) of older, two-lane highway.

In Europe, the high-speed, controlled-access highway had its

Limited access highways
Other major highways

Figure 6.9 Limited-access highways in the United States and Canada have greatly increased the accessibility of many recreation resources by reducing the time required to reach them. The dense network in the northeast has contributed to the accessibility of local and regional resources as well as those at greater distances. (Source: Developed from, U.S. Department of Transportation, "The National System of Interstate and Defense Highways" map, Washington, D.C., 1977).

beginnings with Hitler's autobahns. Today, the German network connects with similar systems in Belgium, the Netherlands, Switzerland, and Italy (Figure 6.10). Austria and the United Kingdom do not have as extensive networks, but most of the heavily traveled, congested areas are serviced by such highways. France has built a north-south highway (Figure 3.2) with connections into Belgium and along the Mediterranean to Italy and Spain. The other main French expressway runs southwesterly from Paris along the route to Bordeaux and Madrid. Smaller, but significant, systems are being developed in Greece, Sweden, and Denmark. Limited stretches of high-speed, controlled-access highways have been built to improve access to some major cities in Portugal, Spain, Norway, and Finland. In eastern Europe, a 10,000-kilometer (6200-mile) high-speed highway system, which will extend from the Baltic to the Mediterranean Sea, is scheduled for completion in 1990. The system will include roads in Poland, Czechoslovakia, Hungary, Romania, Yugoslavia, and Bulgaria. It will connect with similar highways in the German Democratic Republic, Austria, Italy, Greece, and Turkey.

These highways have reduced travel time substantially. In Europe, the distances involved in recreational travel are generally shorter than in North America, but towns, villages, side roads, and other features that slow traffic are usually encountered more frequently. The reduction in travel time has, therefore, been just as spectacular in Europe, in spite of shorter distances. The 450-kilometer (280-mile) drive from London to the

Figure 6.10 Western Europe's expanding system of motorways (limited-access highways) coupled with growing car ownership has radically changed recreation participation patterns. Large numbers of automobile tourists and campers from northern and central locations are now driving to the French, Italian, or Spanish Mediterranean coasts and other resort areas.

Lake District, for example, used to take 10 to 12 hours but can now be completed in 5 to 6 hours. In the United States, the 2110-kilometer (1310-mile) drive from Chicago to Yellowstone National Park took the average vacationing family 4 or 5 days in the 1950s because of the speed limits and traffic problems when passing through settlements and the difficulty of passing slow-moving vehicles on two-lane highways. Now the trip can be made in 3 days by using interstate highways. This makes a trip to the Yellowstone area feasible for a person with only 8 to 10 days of vacation, whereas, previously, it was necessary to have 12 to 14 days to make it worthwhile.

In a similar manner, the interstate system has brought the recreation resources of Florida, the gulf coast, and the Pacific coast several days closer to motorists who live in the Northeast. In Canada, the 1175-kilometer (730-mile) Mac-Donald-Cartier Freeway has reduced travel times in the more heavily populated areas of southern Ontario and Quebec, whereas Highway 400, running north from Toronto, helps relieve some of the congestion produced by weekend traffic flowing to and from the cottage and resort areas to the north.

As for the future of the world's highway systems, it is becoming apparent that in some countries at least, development has reached its zenith. For example, public opposition and rising construction costs may make it impossible to complete the American interstate highway system as originally planned. Citizens are concerned about the disruption of neighborhoods or communities as well as the loss of agricultural and recreation lands,

especially in suburban areas. Completion of the remaining 7 percent of the American interstate highway system will cost an amount equal to at least one-third of the $104 billion already spent on the network. It appears doubtful that more than another 5 or 6 percent will be built. Meanwhile, large portions of the nation's 6.1 million kilometers (3.8 million miles) of streets and highways (including many of the older sections of the interstate) and at least 20 percent of the highway bridges have deteriorated sufficiently to need extensive repairs or even replacement. It is estimated that simply maintaining the nation's roads at 1975 levels of quality will require annual expenditures of $22 billion over the next few years. This estimate does not take into consideration the likely effects of inflation.

Similar situations are presently facing many other nations, especially those whose roadways are subjected to heavy truck traffic, periodic freeze-and-thaw cycles, and the use of salt to remove ice during cold-weather months. In the developed countries, it appears likely that future highway programs will concentrate on the maintenance, reconstruction, and improvement of existing roadways rather than the expansion of highway networks. In the less developed nations, especially those in Africa, large expenditures will continue to be made on building new roads that give access to isolated regions and connect with road systems of adjacent countries.

Intercontinental Highways. Another type of road that will probably affect recreation participation substantially in the future is the intercontinental highway. The first organized example of this is the

Pan-American Highway, which may eventually permit motorists to travel all the way from Fairbanks, Alaska, to Tierra del Fuego at the southernmost tip of South America, a distance of 30,600 kilometers (19,000 miles). Only about 160 kilometers (100 miles) in Colombia and Panama remain unbuilt, but problems with terrain and the control of hoof and mouth disease (a catastrophic sickness affecting cattle) may delay completion indefinitely. Until that time, travelers must move their cars around the gap by ship.

Most of the Pan-American Highway has only two lanes (much is unpaved), and it often runs through quite remote regions with little or no services. In some of the countries there are problems with border-crossing formalities and lawlessness. Therefore, even when completed, it will be many years before it will have the same impact as the opening of a new high-speed highway across a nation such as France or the United States would have. However, it does promise to open the door to intercontinental travel by American and Canadian motorists. If conditions improve and sufficient numbers take advantage of the opportunity, the highway may eventually have a significant impact on tourism in Latin America.

Although no construction program comparable to the Pan-American Highway has taken place, a few private motorists and some tourists in commercial buses are traveling by road from Europe through the Middle East to India. Some tours and private parties, usually in four-wheel-drive vehicles are also crossing the Sahara and visiting nations in central and southern Africa. It is unlikely that such Europe-to-Asia and across-Africa routes will become busy tourist routes, however, until some of the nations involved become more politically stable and the roads and services are improved.

Other Vehicles. Throughout this discussion of the role of roads and privately owned motor vehicles in making recreation opportunities accessible, the emphasis has been on four-wheeled vehicles. Other kinds of motor vehicles are also important, especially in some of the less highly developed nations. Mopeds and other types of motor-scooters are used extensively in parts of Europe and Southeast Asia, especially in the cities. Motorcycles are also widely used for both urban and rural transportation. In Canada and the United States, motorcycles are the most common form of motorized two-wheel transportation. This is partly because the use of motorscooters (mopeds) on public roads was generally discouraged or prohibited until recently. However, an easing of safety requirements and approval of their use in a growing number of states together with gasoline price increases and supply problems has resulted in a rapid increase in sales. Approximately 1 million mopeds are currently in regular use as a means of transportation in the United States compared to 4 million in Japan and 25 million in Europe.

Two-wheel motor vehicles have the disadvantages of being more hazardous to the operator than four-wheel vehicles. They are also miserable to use in wet weather and difficult or impossible to ride under snowy or icy conditions. Therefore, they will always tend to be more numerous in warmer climates. Even so, motorscooters and motorcycles are making

a valuable contribution to the accessibility of recreation opportunities. Low-income people find them particularly useful because they cost much less than automobiles and also are cheaper to operate and store.

PUBLIC TRANSPORTATION

Bus, streetcar, subway, and railroad systems are extremely important components of many people's recreation environments. This may not always be apparent to the casual observer because, except in the case of long-distance buses, the transit vehicles in which participants ride are usually not parked outside recreation resources. Nevertheless, millions of people all over the world depend on mass transit to reach recreation opportunities. In the cities, they may ride only a few blocks or as much as 30 kilometers (20 miles) to see a movie, go shopping or window-shopping, visit friends, attend a sports event, or reach a zoo, park, beach, concert, or museum. Some cities have public transit systems that extend outside the urbanized area and provide access to recreation resources in the surrounding countryside. However, the nature and extent of mass transit systems vary greatly so that the degree to which they make recreation opportunities accessible changes radically from place to place.

These differences are particularly great in the United States. An increasing proportion of the population own automobiles and prefer to use them for transportation to work as well as for trips to recreation destinations. As a result, total ridership on existing mass transit systems has declined substantially

since World War II, whereas costs have steadily risen. Public support for the maintenance or extension of present services or the building of new systems where none previously existed is also limited. Although more than 25 million Americans regularly use public transportation, this is only equal to the number that did so in 1905 and is less than half the 1950 ridership.

Urban Transit Systems. The situation in New York City, although not necessarily typical, illustrates the recreational importance and problems of urban transportation systems. The Metropolitan Transit Authority in that city operates both an electric subway and a diesel bus system (Figure 6.11). Subway trains operate on more than 25 different routes, covering 375 kilometers (231 miles), and the bus system has a total of 217 routes (43 in and out of Manhattan alone). Residents of downtown Manhattan, for example, can reach all of the nearby public, quasi-public, commercial, and private recreation resources relatively easily by bus, subway, or a combination of the two. They can also travel to more distant resources such as the Aqueduct Race Track (horseracing), the Bronx Zoo, the Brooklyn Botanic Gardens, Coney Island, Gateway East National Recreation Area, Shea Stadium — home of the New York Mets (baseball team) and the New York Jets (football team); and Yankee Stadium — home of the New York Yankees (baseball team). The farthest they can go on the city's subway is to Pelham Bay Park (in the Bronx) on Long Island Sound or to Rockaway Beach (in Brooklyn) on the Atlantic Ocean. Both are about 15 miles in a straight line from downtown Man-

Figure 6.11 Dozens of major recreation resources in the New York area can be reached by subway train or bus. This map shows many of the best known of these resources and the main public transportation routes that give access to them.

Bus routes
Subway system
Major parks

hattan, but the distance actually traveled is much more. Residents in the city's four boroughs other than Manhattan travel in the opposite direction to reach downtown recreation resources. Connecting buses in adjacent municipalities, long-distance buses, and commuter trains extend the range of mass transit to areas beyond the city limits.

Unhappily, the Metropolitan Transit Authority has been experiencing difficulties that have decreased the effectiveness of the system in making recreation resources accessible. The postwar rapid growth of private car ownership and use, higher fares, and mounting problems with unruly behavior and crime have produced a decrease in ridership from 3.3 billion in the late 1940s to about 1.5 billion currently. This situation has created a vicious circle. Decreased ridership means lower revenues. Lower revenues and increased costs necessitate fare increases. Higher fares discourage riders, especially the less affluent who could benefit most from low-cost transportation to the recreation destinations provided by the system. Financial problems have also prompted the Metropolitan Transit Authority to reduce the frequency of service, particularly at night and on weekends. Passenger protection, station maintenance, and the replacement of vehicles have also been cut back. All of these measures have a greater negative impact on the use of the system for travel to recreation resources than they do on its use for getting to work.

But even new transit systems are in trouble if they are expected to be largely self-supporting. The new Metrorail system in Washington, D.C., has increased its weekday ridership to about 270,000 now that 55 kilometers (34 miles) of its planned 161-kilometer (100-mile) system is in operation. Even though this exceeds expectations, fares still cover only half the operating costs. At first, this system functioned mostly as a commuter service for residents, but, with its operating schedule recently extended to midnight and weekends, it is also a tremendous asset to tourists. From the national airport located on the outskirts of Alexandria, Virginia, for example, riders can be transported inexpensively to the Pentagon in 5 minutes, the Capitol in 9 minutes, the Smithsonian Institution complex in 13 minutes, and the midtown area in 15 minutes. Access is provided to all of the major points of interest in the area, including the White House; the John F. Kennedy Center for the Performing Arts; Arlington National Cemetery; and the Robert F. Kennedy Stadium, home of the Redskins (professional football team). Already, it has proved its worth as a support system for people wishing to attend evening football games by staying open beyond midnight to get the fans home and by operating additional trains to handle the crowds. Although there was talk of trimming the system to 97 kilometers (60 miles) because of escalating costs, it is now intended to complete the five-line network, which will serve the citizens and visitors not only in the District of Columbia but in the nearby suburbs of Virginia and Maryland as well. At a revised estimated cost of $7 billion, Metrorail may become the single most expensive public works project in American history.

With costs like these, 80 per-

cent of which are usually borne by the federal government, it would seem unlikely that any more high-capacity, heavy-rail urban transportation systems will be built once the ones that are currently in various stages of development are completed. As a consequence, some areas such as New York; Washington, D.C.; San Francisco; Miami; Buffalo; Atlanta; and Baltimore will have above- or below-ground rail systems at their citizens' disposal, whereas other areas such as San Diego and Honolulu may not. However, this will not necessarily mean that the citizens of cities without subway systems will have a lower level of recreation resource accessibility. Quite the contrary in some cases. Rail systems are rigid and generally afford access at only a few widely spaced stations; therefore, especially in communities with dispersed populations, the rehabilitation and expansion of existing bus and tram systems can sometimes provide better service for much larger proportions of the community's citizens. Unfortunately, the cost of equipment and operation of surface transit lines is also high and many cities are finding it financially impossible to develop adequate systems.

Smaller cities and towns are also experiencing difficulties with their public transportation systems. During the last 30 years, privately owned bus systems in some communities have gone bankrupt as ridership decreased, leaving the residents without any kind of inexpensive service. In other cities and towns, municipally owned bus systems now depend heavily on public subsidies to pay for their deficits and the purchase of new equipment. In a number of commu-

nities, service is being curtailed rather than expanded in an effort to cut costs. Less affluent citizens in communities with terminated or reduced bus services usually find it more difficult to reach basic recreation facilities such as parks, libraries, movie theaters, and downtown shopping areas.

Many factors influence the effectiveness of an urban transit system in making recreation opportunities accessible to a population. For a system to be successful it should:

- Project a positive image through media advertising and other types of public relations activities that demonstrate the advantages of using the transit system for travel to recreation destinations.
- Provide safe, protected, and well-maintained vehicles, stations, shelters, and other facilities so that people of all ages and both sexes can confidently travel on the system at all times.
- Serve the entire population so that no one has to walk a long distance to reach a transit stop; this is particularly important for elderly and handicapped persons and in climates that have extended periods of severe weather.
- Have a fare schedule that is low enough not to discourage use of the system by lower income citizens, especially families with several children or persons living on social security payments.
- Schedule sufficiently frequent service during the evenings and on weekends to eliminate long waits; this is particularly important at locations with extensive recreation resources.
- Provide express service to important recreation destinations and appropriate numbers of extra vehicles during peak recreation travel periods.

A system can be even more effective if, in addition, it connects with systems in neighboring municipalities or with extraurban transportation systems.

Lighted, protected, and reasonably priced park-and-ride parking lots at the ends of main transit routes enable and encourage people from surrounding rural areas to use transit systems for trips to downtown recreation resources. Special racks or bus trailers can facilitate the transportation of equipment such as skis or bicycles and, as a result, expand the recreation benefits that can be derived from the system. Unfortunately, many of the better recreation facilities and opportunities lie on the periphery of cities just beyond the limits of bus or subway lines serving the metropolitan area. Extending routes to include these important recreation areas or making connections with neighboring systems that do serve them can expand recreation environments considerably for urban residents.

Unfortunately, all of these innovations and operating policies require funding that present levels of ridership and public subsidies fail to provide. Whether the gasoline shortages and escalating costs continue to encourage more people to use public transportation regularly remains to be seen. Ridership doubled during the spring of 1979, but, by fall, only about 10 percent of the new riders were still using public transportation. In any case, fares alone can never finance adequate systems, since operating costs are rising at such alarming rates. Unlike most other nations where mass transit has been considered a priority item for years, governments at all levels in the United States have only recently begun to recognize the value of good public transportation systems. They are still largely

undecided about the forms they should take and the levels of public funding they should receive. However, many state and local governments are beginning to make considerable progress toward formulating plans for the development of systems suitable to their particular circumstances. And the federal government is gradually de-emphasizing the importance of the private automobile and highway network in its national transportation policy. Although levels of aid remain low in comparison to need, there is a trend toward higher levels of support that may bode well for the future of urban transit systems in the United States.

Extraurban Trains. As in the case of motorable roads, most of the world's railroad lines are concentrated in the more densely populated areas of the highly developed nations (Figure 6.12). Rail lines are quite widely spaced in the western part of the United States. Canada's railroads are concentrated in a narrow belt across the southern portion of the country. Soviet railroads are most dense in the European portion of the nation, but its network is much less dense than the networks in much of the rest of Europe and the eastern United States. There are few railroad lines in the Soviet portions of Asia. Japan, New Zealand, and the more developed portions of Australia, South Africa, Argentina, and Brazil have relatively dense railroad networks. India is unique among the less developed nations in that it has a railroad network that covers most of its territory. Mexico and China have relatively open networks covering only part of their territories. Most of the rest of the world is

without rail service, except in the vicinity of major cities.

As in the case of urban transit systems, travel by trains outside towns and cities in the developed nations has decreased roughly in proportion to the increased ownership and use of private cars. In 1929, 77 percent of all long-distance travel by mechanical transportation in the United States was by steam railroads. Now only about 1 percent of Americans travel by train and just 3 percent go by bus. In other nations, the reductions have not been as great because of the smaller proportion of privately owned automobiles.

In the United States, large-scale freight hauling by road coupled with the rapidly increasing costs of operations, rebuilding of deteriorating track, replacement of rolling stock, along with the virtual disappearance of passengers has led to the bankruptcy of many railroads or the severe curtailment of passenger services during the last three decades. In an effort to preserve passenger service, Congress established the National Railroad Passenger Corporation— known as Amtrak— in 1970. Two-thirds of the passenger trains were discontinued, a series of appropriations were provided to pay for track rental, new rolling stock, and other improvements, and the corporation was instructed to become self-supporting by 1976.

This has not proven possible; it is very expensive to rehabilitate and operate a national passenger rail travel system, especially in a country such as the United States where distances are great and people have become unaccustomed to using trains. To do it properly, Amtrak would have needed far more

Figure 6.12 Distribution of the world's principal railroads. Only Europe, the Ganges Valley in India, Japan, the eastern half of the United States, and a narrow belt across southern Canada have extensive dense networks of railroad lines. Most of the developing nations have few or no railroads to help provide access to recreation resources.

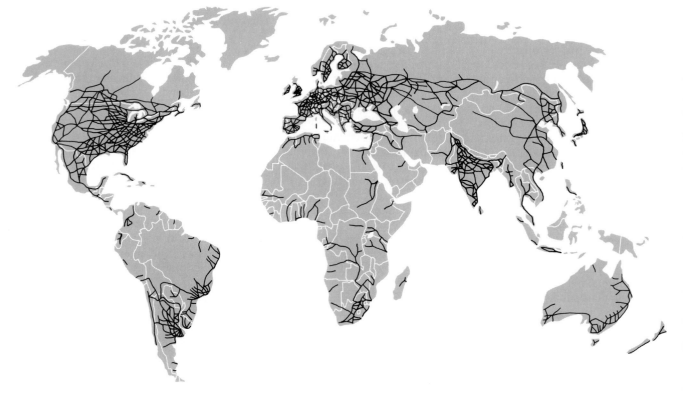

than the $4.2 billion in subsidies it received in its first eight years of operation. To its critics, such funding (amounting to a $2 subsidy for every $1 paid by a passenger) is considered exorbitant and unjustified, especially in a period of fiscal restraint.

Actually, it is very frugal in comparison to the support that other systems receive. Annual subsidies in Japan amount to almost that much and the Japanese system has less than half the track mileage to maintain. Of course, there are basic differences; the amount of

service provided in passenger miles is twenty times as high on Japanese trains and the equipment and service are much better. Proponents of the Amtrak system maintain, however, that similar service could be provided on American trains if adequate funding were made available.

Instead, in an effort to hold down costs and still fulfill its responsibilities to the residents of about 500 cities and towns along some 44,250 kilometers (27,500 miles) of track, Amtrak has found it necessary to compromise on the quality of its service. Finances have been

insufficient to cover the costs of upgrading previously neglected roadbeds, replacing antiquated equipment, and developing punctual, fast, and comfortable trains. Nevertheless, Amtrak has accomplished a great deal in eight years. The worst sections of roadbed have been repaired, about 25 percent of the rolling stock has been replaced, and ridership has been raised from 16 million in 1972 to 19 million in 1978. Although it still represents an insignificant proportion of all intercity traffic, it is a good beginning and one that promises to get better.

For instance, during the 1979 period of petroleum shortages, Americans rediscovered trains and total ridership increased to 21.4 million. Moreover, this figure could have been much higher; at the height of the crisis, passengers stood in the aisles on the most desirable runs and many potential customers were turned away.

In spite of its recent successes, the future of Amtrak is not bright. Plans to reduce its mileage by 43 percent and discontinue 24 of its trains and routes (as an economy measure to save $1.4 billion in federal subsidies over a five-year period) were announced in early 1979. Since that time, opposition has managed to reduce these cutbacks to about 20 percent of the system and, for the time being, no region of the country will be left without at least one major train. Several states, including California, are planning to provide partial funding for some of the routes that operate within their borders. But there is no indication of strong support for the development of an adequate nationwide long-distance passenger rail service. At best, it would seem that only the corridor routes operating between cities such as San Diego and Los Angeles, Chicago and Detroit, or linking Boston, Philadelphia, New York, and Washington will survive.

If this is the case, many of the opportunities to travel by train to recreation resources such as New England ski resorts, southern Florida resort communities, or national parks like Yellowstone, Grand Canyon, and Yosemite will disappear. Many smaller communities scattered across America will be deprived of their last regularly operated connecting link to other communities. American and foreign travelers alike will lose the chance to view some of America's most spectacular scenery or watch a cross section of rural and small-town America go by. The railroad's recreation function will be reduced to that of an expanded urban mass transit system transporting people between a limited number of large metropolitan communities for a day of shopping, a visit to friends, or an evening's entertainment.

Other nations are having similar financial difficulties with their rail passenger systems. Canada, for instance, amalgamated its two transcontinental passenger railroads into a new government-sponsored organization called Via Rail in 1978 after several years of operating with $200-million deficits. Unlike Amtrak, however, Via Rail is not expected to become self-supporting, nor has it suffered a massive elimination of routes. No doubt some of the trains with limited ridership will eventually be dropped, but the government has promised not only to replace them with buses but also to integrate all rail, air, and bus routes, thereby making it possible to make use of a combination of public transportation services. The system intends to emphasize intercity, short-haul, high-density service, but daily transcontinental service will continue and the use of trains as a leisurely, inexpensive means of becoming familiar with one region, province, or the entire nation is being promoted in Canada as well as in the United States and Europe.

Elsewhere in the world, all the major railroads are government owned. They are also unprofitable, although the deficits differ considerably from nation to nation, depending on ridership levels and the type of service being provided. The Japanese National Railways, for instance, have accumulated deficits of $20 billion over the last few years. However, in the process, service has been upgraded and expanded to include an 1100-kilometer (700-mile) high-speed electric train system (Shinkansen) that links Tokyo and Fukuoka on the southernmost island of Kyushu. Including stops, travel time averages 160 kilometers (100 miles) per hour. In spite of such heavy deficits, the Japanese government has decided to extend the Shinkansen line to northern Honshu. It also decided to raise subsidies rather than fares after a fare increase in 1976 reduced ridership by as much as 34 percent on some lines. This commitment to the provision of efficient, relatively inexpensive rail service is encouraged, of course, by high levels of use, but the commitment also serves to strengthen the use of trains as a primary means of travel. The Shinkansen trains have carried over 1.3 billion passengers during their 14 years of operation, and, on a per capita basis, the Japanese use trains an average of 64 times a year for a total distance of about 1930 kilometers (1200 miles).

European railroads are also continuing to expand, although every effort is being made to control deficits. Passenger trains have been discontinued on many branch lines, and some lines have been closed completely, but main lines still offer frequent passenger service. National and international modernized high-speed trains link most large cities, especially in France, West Germany, and Italy. Britain has developed high-speed lines linking London with Bristol, south Wales, and Edinburgh.

The number of passengers carried is much higher on European trains than on trains in the United States and Canada. France, for instance, had a ridership in 1978 of 683 million. Again, it is partly a matter of providing comfortable, efficient service that encourages train use. But new customers are also being lured in a variety of ways, most of which are intended to encourage recreation-oriented travel.[3] Examples include:

- Providing efficient train service to airports as well as major cities, thereby readily enabling tourists to combine air and rail travel.
- Promoting train use by the handicapped through the provision of special facilities and services on the trains as well as at stations.
- Providing motorail services, which allow travelers to transport their automobiles on flatcars, thereby allowing them to sleep or relax en route but still have the use of their vehicles when they reach their destinations. These services are most common on the overnight international lines that bring people from the northern portions of western Europe to vacation at the various resort areas of the Mediterranean coast.
- Adding special "entertainment coaches," which give passengers access to such recreation experiences as jukebox music, pinball games, exhibitions, shows, and tourist information programs as they travel.
- Providing facilities that readily permit people to transport their horses, bicycles, camping equipment, skiing, and other recreation gear to desirable locations where they can use them for recreation activities (Figure 6.13).
- Initiating discount schemes such as special family fares, off-peak-hour

and off-season rates, and short-term railpass systems, which provide unlimited train-travel privileges at considerable savings to those who purchase the pass before going to Europe.

Two of these short-term railpass offerings—Eurailpass and the even cheaper Eurail Youthpass—are encouraging growing numbers of North American tourists to use trains as their primary or only means of traveling from place to place during their one- to three-month visits to 16 different western European countries.

Such programs are especially useful in making recreation resources in out-of-the-way places accessible to tourists who are less inclined to be venturesome in their modes of travel. They also make it

possible for students on limited budgets to visit many more recreation resources during their visits; some plan their itineraries so that they sleep on the trains, thereby extending their budgets even further. And finally, many of the passes give access—either without charge or at sharply reduced rates—to many other forms of travel, including selected bus routes, steamers, ferries, and cruise boats.

Unlike the future of passenger trains in North America, the situation seems very hopeful in Europe. The railroads appear to be managing to survive the peak years of automobile use more or less intact. They are currently gaining strong public support as the most logical way to provide transportation for large numbers of people and at the

[3] Many of these methods are also being utilized by Canadian and American railroads, but they do not have the same effect because they are much less common and far less aggressively promoted.

Figure 6.13 It takes only 15 minutes by electric train for residents of Zurich, Switzerland, to reach the slopes and forests of the Uetliberg. Local train services are a significant part of many European recreation environments.

same time conserve energy or utilize forms of energy other than petroleum. They are also continuing to be competitive in both time and cost with other forms of transportation, including air travel. The relatively short distances between many places of interest is also a distinct advantage. For example, some high-speed trains are being scheduled to operate between major cities during meal times; this permits passengers to utilize their travel time for eating, thereby using less of their day for travel. The fact that most of the stations are located in the heart of a city—close to business and shopping districts, places of entertainment, and major cultural resources—also gives European trains an advantage over other forms of travel.

In some of the other nations such as the Soviet Union, China, and India where highway networks are not as well developed and automobile ownership is limited, railroads continue to be a primary means of transportation. Over $23 billion has been committed to the improvement of rail service in the Soviet Union in recent years, including the development of a high-speed passenger line between Moscow and Leningrad. China has undertaken a massive modernization program, which includes electrification of its core services, double tracking of main routes, and the construction of six new ones. India's railways are also expanding and are used extensively by residents traveling short as well as long distances to visit relatives and friends, participate in festivals, take recreation trips to cities, or go to resorts in the Himalayan foothills. Foreign tourists also use the trains of these nations for their journeys,

since road transportation is often slow or not readily available.

In the developing nations, railroads generally have little impact on the recreation of the majority of the people because so few lines exist. This situation appears unlikely to change radically in the future. Because of the high cost and inflexibility of railroads in comparison to road transportation, emerging nations will probably go directly to extensive highway networks and avoid the railroad expansion phase that was typical of earlier development patterns. However, those lines that do exist often carry many passengers—both residents and foreign visitors—who are traveling for recreation purposes.

Extraurban Buses. Although extraurban bus travel has decreased considerably in the developed nations that have high levels of automobile ownership, it still is an important means of recreational touring and travel to recreation destinations. In the United States and Canada, regularly scheduled buses are used extensively for both short- and long-distance trips to recreation resources. Often the bus is the only means of travel open to those who do not have access to a car or who do not wish to drive to a particular destination. For the less affluent and older people who have given up driving, buses provide a relatively inexpensive, convenient means of travel between cities, towns, and some smaller centers if they happen to be on a bus route.

Unfortunately, regularly scheduled extraurban buses are generally limited to main highways. Consequently, they only provide access to recreation resources along such routes and these are predominantly

urban in nature. Extraurban recreation resources are seldom serviced unless they are on a main highway or are major attractions that generate sufficient use to warrant a side trip. Travelers on regularly scheduled buses in Canada and the United States must often hitchhike, walk, or take long, expensive taxi rides to reach recreation resources. Many units of the national and state park systems as well as most national forest, national wildlife refuge, Corps of Engineers facilities, and large numbers of regional parks and private attractions are not serviced. Where such extraurban resources are reached by a bus route, the service is usually infrequent. This often makes it impossible for the bus traveler to visit such resources without staying overnight. If there are no suitable accommodations in the vicinity, only those who bring their own camping gear can enjoy these areas.

Nevertheless, other than hitchhiking, scheduled buses are the cheapest practical way of traveling longer distances to visit a number of recreation resources; the bicycle is not a feasible alternative in most situations because of long distances, poor road conditions, time constraints, or possible problems with bad weather. Unlimited bus travel passes reduce the cost of transportation for those who wish to visit many recreation attractions over a large area in a relatively short time. They are often used by foreign tourists anxious to see as much as possible on a limited budget.

Chartered and tour buses also provide access to many opportunities but are proportionally less important than they once were. Private groups charter buses for purposes such as visiting exhibitions, going to amusement parks, taking sports teams to away games, traveling to ski and beach resorts, or attending concerts, theater performances, or professional sports events. However, the people taking part are generally more affluent than bus-trip participants used to be. Rising charter prices and the acquisition of cars by lower income groups have made group bus trips less financially attractive, especially if one wage earner has to buy seats for several family members. The cost of the gasoline used in making the trip by car is usually the only cost that is counted when making the comparison, so that automobile travel appears to be cheaper. Of course, many groups use chartered buses not for the sake of economy but because of the opportunities for conviviality during the trip, the convenience of no one having to bother with the responsibility of driving or parking, and, sometimes, the freedom to enjoy alcoholic beverages en route.

Tour operators run bus trips to specific destinations for recreation purposes such as visits to major sports events; to Nashville (world center for country music); to Las Vegas for gambling; to Washington, D.C.; or to the Canadian National Exhibition in Toronto. Buses are also used for tours where the travel portion of the trip is regarded as the primary recreation experience. Such trips range from fairly short tours that visit a succession of places in a period of four or five days to month-long safaris. Examples of the latter are tours that include all the famous attractions of California and Arizona, the Pacific Northwest, or the Canadian Rocky Mountain area. Many of these tours are now relatively expensive and appeal pri-

marily to older people and others who do not wish to drive or plan their own trips.

Like other means of public transportation, extraurban bus systems are in financial difficulty. In the United States, ridership on regularly scheduled services dropped by 20 percent in a 10-year period, whereas costs of equipment and fuel escalated. By 1977, service to 1800 small communities, many of which were served by no other form of public transportation, had been abandoned; service had been sharply reduced on dozens of other routes; and some of the nation's 1000 private bus companies were facing bankruptcy.

However, a combination of several factors has halted the decline and may actually reverse it. Gasoline shortages and the rising costs of automobile travel have begun to make buses far more attractive not only to students, the poor, and retired people on fixed incomes (who made up two-thirds of the ridership until recently) but also to the more affluent. Ridership between the 15,000 communities served has grown from 332 million passengers in 1977 to an estimated 340 to 350 million in 1979. The number of buses is being increased where the demand is highest, and they are being made cleaner, safer, and more comfortable to retain their new customers. A campaign is also underway to improve and relocate bus terminals, many of which have become dirty, dilapidated, and surrounded by rundown neighborhoods that most people avoid. Congressional authorization of $160 million in grants for the construction of intermodal transportation centers is expected partially to solve this problem. It will stimulate the devel-

opment of modern, safe facilities that interurban bus companies will share with mass transit companies and, in some locations, with airlines and Amtrak.

Finally, the first direct federal subsidies and taxation changes are promising some relief to buslines that need it most. In 1978, Congress authorized the spending of $30 million in subsidies each year for four years to keep certain money-losing rural routes in operation. In numbers of people served, these routes are relatively unimportant, since they account for only 30 percent of the total ridership. However, they serve most of the 14,000 communities that have no other regularly scheduled form of public transportation.

In many parts of Europe, regularly scheduled extraurban bus services are still significant components of recreation systems. Such services are particularly well developed in economically advanced areas with relatively large, dispersed populations. In the more populated regions of Great Britain, for instance, buses run regularly between many of the cities and towns, often following quite circuitous routes through the countryside to provide service to scattered villages. Shorter distances, denser populations, and a smaller proportion of people owning automobiles make such service more feasible than in Canada or the United States.

Recreation resources are much more accessible to the person without a car in places that have such rural bus services. Most European national and regional parks can be reached by bus and some bus routes run through the parks themselves. Other recreation resources, including forest areas, nature reserves, historic sites, and remote beaches are frequently within relatively short distances of bus stops. In many locations, the bus system complements the footpath, road, and railway systems so that it is possible to go out on one form of public transportation, walk considerable distances on footpaths or side roads, and return by means of a different route on another form of public transportation.

A great range of bus tours is offered in western European countries. A larger proportion of the population than in the United States and Canada participates in such tours because of lower car-ownership rates, the higher prices of gasoline, and problems of driving on congested streets and highways. Some tours are of only a few hours' duration around a city or through the countryside to well-known sightseeing locations. At the other end of the spectrum are international bus tours lasting several weeks and visiting many countries. The typical glass-topped sightseeing bus used for tours is a common sight on European highways.

In less developed nations, buses are often the only form of public transportation available over vast regions. Many people living in such regions are accustomed to walking long distances and only use buses on special occasions. As economic conditions improve, more are able to afford the cost of bus service to go to festivals or sporting events in local towns or to see the sights of nearby cities.

Water Transportation. Long-distance transportation of passengers by water declined drastically in the 1960s because airline fares became equal to, or cheaper

than, boat fares. In the late 1950s, more than 1 million people crossed the Atlantic Ocean by ship each year, now less than one-tenth of that number do so. Most of the big transatlantic liners have been scrapped, turned into cruise ships, or sold for other purposes. There were similar declines in long-distance water-borne passenger traffic elsewhere in the world. The only places where water transportation of passengers over considerable distances is still thriving are locations where the alternative air transportation is absent, where people wish to take vehicles with them, where the trip itself offers some exceptional recreation experiences, or where the majority of potential passengers are unable to pay air fares.

One water route that is still used heavily, in spite of air travel being cheaper, is the Inside Passage to Alaska (Figure 14.12). It is possible to drive all the way to Alaska through Canada, but some 1800 kilometers (1120 miles) of the 2445-kilometer (1520-mile) Alaska Highway is gravel-surfaced and can be impassable in bad weather. In order to make Alaska more accessible, the state operates a ferry system from Seattle, Washington, to Haines and Skagway, Alaska. This voyage of over 1600 kilometers (1000 miles) takes about three and a half days and involves sailing through some of the most magnificent coastal scenery in the world. People use the Alaska Marine Highway, as it is known, both to see the scenery and because it is the easiest way to take a motor vehicle to Alaska. An increasing number of cruise ships are also using the Inside Passage. A private company, British Columbia Ferries, also operates a passenger and vehicle

ferry over the southern portion of the route.

There are many other locations where ferry trips of various lengths provide important links in recreation transportation systems. Some trips offer little in terms of scenery compared to the Inside Passage to Alaska, but they may be a recreation experience as well as transportation for those who seldom travel by boat. Examples of some recreationally significant ferry services in North America are: the Vancouver and Seattle ferries to Victoria on Vancouver Island; the Los Angeles area ferry to Catalina Island; the Tobemory Ferry across the entrance to Ontario's Georgian Bay; ferries across Lake Champlain between New York State and Vermont; the Liberty Island and Staten Island ferries in New York harbor; New England ferries to offshore islands such as Martha's Vineyard and Nantucket; ferries between New Brunswick and Prince Edward Island; and ferries between Nova Scotia and Newfoundland. Elsewhere in the world, ferries play important recreation roles in carrying people between the United Kingdom and France, Belgium, the Netherlands, West Germany, Sweden, and Norway; across the Irish Sea; across various parts of the Mediterranean, particularly between the mainland and islands such as Majorca, Corsica, Sardinia, Sicily, and the Greek islands; and, through Japan's Inland Sea. There are thousands of other ferry routes to islands or across lakes, estuaries, and rivers that enable people to reach otherwise inaccessible recreation resources or locations that would be more expensive or take much longer to reach by other means.

New technology is changing

Figure 6.14 Cars and passengers bound for Calais, France, wait to board a British hovercraft after it has been driven up onto its ramp at Ramsgate, England. Powered by four large gas turbine (jet) engines, these craft can carry up to 254 passengers and 30 cars across the English Channel at speeds up to 128 kilometers (80 miles) per hour.

some of the constraints that formerly controlled the feasibility of water transportation. The use of hovercraft, which ride on a cushion of air (Figure 6.14), and hydrofoil boats, which skim over the waves on submerged wings, has increased speeds dramatically and largely eliminated seasickness and other problems experienced in moderately rough weather. Hydrofoil boats are in use as ferries between Niagara Falls and Toronto and between Miami and Freeport (in the Bahamas), for trips across the English Channel and across the Irish Sea, for travel between Hong Kong and Canton, for cruises from Vienna to Budapest along the Danube River, and to take people from the Japanese main island of Honshu to the resorts on Sado Island.

The *Finnjet*, currently the largest hydrofoil in service, is now operating between Finland and West Germany. Although it is 215-meters (700-feet) long, carries 1532 passengers and 350 cars, has a casino, discotheque, nightclub, two swimming pools, and three restaurants, the *Finnjet* travels at 56 kilometers (35 miles) per hour and covers the distance between Helsinki and Travemünde in 22 hours instead of the 44 hours required by a conventional ferry. People currently are willing to pay considerably more for the speed or novelty offered by hydrofoils and hovercraft. It is likely that costs per passenger will gradually decrease, speeds will rise, and various forms of advanced watercraft will play an even larger part in making recreation resources accessible in the future.

There are many other forms of water travel that involve varying proportions of transportation and recreation, depending on the objectives of those using the service. Now that operators have overcome the image of cruises being for those who are older, affluent, and inactive, for instance, more people are traveling on cruise ships. Smaller numbers of people are traveling as paying passengers on freighters or coastal vessels. A growing number of people are taking cruises on inland waters on smaller boats and barges. Since, in most of these cases, it is the voyage itself and the amenities on board rather than the destinations that are the main attraction, cruises will be discussed as commercial recreation resources in Chapter 12.

Privately owned watercraft are of considerable importance in providing access to recreation opportunities. Some seasonal homeowners use boats to reach their properties on islands, along saltwater shorelines, across lakes, or on rivers. Fisherpersons use their boats for transportation from one fishing spot to another. Hunters often travel across lakes, along rivers, or through wetland channels to find suitable hunting environments. Similarly, birdwatchers, shell collectors, swimmers, scuba divers, and campers frequently use water transportation to reach favorable locations for their activities.

Air Transportation. Air travel is radically changing the accessibility of more distant recreation opportunities. Primarily, this is because it saves time, but, in doing so, it can also reduce the costs of many kinds of experiences. For example, it is now feasible for people with quite modest incomes to fly from Great Britain to one of the Mediterranean resort islands or from Chicago or Toronto to the Caribbean for a week-long vacation. Previously, just getting there by car or train and then by boat took four or more days of vacation time and involved considerable expenditures on food and lodging. Under those circumstances, such trips were beyond the reach of most people.

Air travel today is often cheaper than any other form of travel, with the possible exception of walking or bicycling. In fact, some of the lowest air fares would probably prove lower than the cost of walking or bicycling if the price of shoes, special clothing, bicycle parts, and additional food and overnight accommodations were included in the calculations. Nevertheless, as recently as 1977, air travel accounted for only 10 percent of all travel in the United States. In addition, most of the persons who were traveling by air for recreation purposes were relatively affluent, having an average household income of $25,400. And finally, a relatively small proportion of the population was doing most of the flying; 45 percent of the nation's population had never flown.

Since that time, the situation has changed dramatically; today only 35 percent of the adult population have yet to fly, and air travel accounts for 12 percent of all travel. More significantly, most of the increase—a rise from 223 million passengers in 1976 to an estimated 300 million in 1979—involves people who previously did not consider flying as a viable alternative to other forms of transportation. In a substantial number of cases, they had not previously considered a long-distance trip as being economically feasible under any circumstances. These new customers include: elderly widows going to see their grandchildren; teenagers, college students, and retired couples starting out to explore another region or a different continent; young couples with children going to visit relatives or to enjoy an away-from-home travel experience; and a diversified group of less affluent individuals with special interests in such activities as skiing, hiking, bicycling, skin diving, golfing, fishing, and hunting.

The reasons for this upsurge in air travel and the changes in air-passenger age and income are numerous and complicated. Obviously, the trend toward increased use of air travel was already well established in 1977; air travel had been growing more or less steadily since the early 1960s when it involved 49 million passengers, most of whom were affluent or traveling for business purposes on expense accounts. Reasons for this growth included increases in discretionary income and free time among the general population; an overall reduction in the fear of flying; heavy promotion of air travel as a safe, convenient, and not overly expensive alternative to other forms of transportation; the tremendous improvements in both equipment and every aspect of service; the deterioration of rail and bus services; and the introduction of low-cost charter flights and reduced fares for non-peak-hour or off-season travel. However, two changes took place in 1977 that were to revolutionize the industry.

The first change involved the U. S. Government's decision to begin the deregulation of air travel. Previously, airlines were tightly controlled by national and international regulations. Internationally scheduled airlines generally agreed on fares among themselves, but these only went into effect following the approval of the governments concerned. Many airlines such as the principal British scheduled airlines were (and continue to be) government operated. But even privately owned airlines had little economic or decision-making freedom. In the United States, the Civil Aeronautics Board (CAB) controlled almost all aspects of operation, including routes flown, frequency of flights, services offered, and fares charged. Initially, this had been most helpful in protecting the infant industry and assuring the development and maintenance of airline service to smaller communities, which otherwise would have been bypassed as too unprofitable. But the controls were also reducing competition among airlines and keeping air fares at higher levels than would have occurred under a competitive system.

Deregulation has had spectacular results. Starting in 1977, airlines were permitted to lease aircraft to tour operators for advance-booking charters. Passengers were required to buy their tickets 30 to 45 days in advance, but they paid up to 40 percent less than regular economy-class fares. Previously, charter-fare passengers had to either belong to an organization or purchase a package that included hotel accommodations, but these restrictions were lifted. In addition, Texas International Airlines was allowed to operate some of its flights as minimum service (no-frills) flights at half the usual price. The company's passenger traffic increased 700 percent and flights that were previously 70 percent empty became 75 percent full as people discovered they could travel cheaper by air than by bus. The company was also pleased to find that few passengers diverted to cheap flights from regular flights; most minimum-service flight passengers were people who would not have flown at the regular fare rate. After this initial success, other airlines introduced similar cutrate services.

The other major change came in the middle of 1977 when a small, privately owned British charter operation, Laker Airways, was granted permission to operate a low-cost Skytrain service between London and New York. Skytrain consisted of a regularly scheduled one-class, no-frills service with tickets sold a few hours in advance of takeoff time on a first-come, first-served basis. The tickets were also one-way, eliminating another requirement of charter fares— round-trip tickets that predetermine the length of stay. Meals, drinks, and movies were available as optional extras, but passengers were free to bring their own food. This innovative service was important not only because it gave hundreds of thousands of people in Europe as well as the United States and Canada an opportunity to visit another continent at bargain prices but also because it proved there was a market for cutrate services (Figure 6.15). Later, Laker Airways was permitted to make Skytrain flights between London and Los Angeles and sell confirmed seats for the next flight to those who were left in line following the sale of all seats on a current flight. Skytrain led to other airlines offering cheap standby fares and special promo-

tional fares not only on transatlantic flights but also on Canadian and American long-distance domestic flights as well.

Whether this trend will continue is still unclear. The deregulation that has occurred in North America has not taken place elsewhere. In fact, the continued high cost of air travel in Europe has contributed to more less-affluent Europeans flying to North America for a vacation. In many cases, it is cheaper for them to fly the Atlantic than it is to fly between two Euro-

Figure 6.15 Would-be passengers read, nap, converse, play games, and watch the world go by as they wait at London's Gatwick Airport for the first Laker Airways no-reservations, low-cost transatlantic flight in September 1977. In order to compete, other companies began cut-rate fares for those willing to let the airline assign them to a particular flight.

pean cities. Internationally, the greatest impact has been on North Atlantic flights, although prices for special charter or promotional flights to almost any destination have shown some extensive reductions from time to time. Obviously, the very low, discount fares of the late 1970s could not continue indefinitely. Sharply escalating labor and fuel costs and the need to replace and expand their equipment have already forced the airlines to raise their fares several times. However, it is unlikely that the structure of air fares will ever return to what it was. Millions of less-affluent people have had a taste of flying and will wish to do so again. And the airlines have also discovered that profits can be higher if they keep prices low and airplanes filled.

However, airplanes are never going to replace cars, trains, or buses as a means of everyday transportation for the masses. Cost is not the only factor controlling their use. A major influence is how readily people can use air services. The air-transport industry in the United States is built on a framework of scheduled and charter services provided by short-, medium-, and long-haul carriers in the domestic, continental, and intercontinental fields. Major airlines have tended in the past to concentrate on the large cities, except where required by government regulations to serve smaller population centers. Some communities are connected to major airports by small airlines, but low profits on such routes mean that many places have no regular service. People who live in such communities either have to ask friends or relatives to drive them to the nearest airport or use public transportation or taxis. In some

Figure 6.16 The dominance of the North Atlantic international routes, the domestic and international routes in Europe, and the domestic routes in North America is shown by this map of principal air routes. Cities outside these areas such as Caracas, Rio de Janeiro, Nairobi, Cairo, Bombay, Singapore, and Tokyo stand out as important travel centers.

cases, it takes them as long to get to an airport and board the plane as it does to fly 1000 miles or more. The effectiveness of air transportation in making opportunities available, therefore, depends to a large extent on where a person lives in relation to airports used by scheduled and unscheduled airlines.

It is not as easy to represent air transportation opportunities on a map as it is to represent roads and railroads because air routes change from time to time and much air travel is on unscheduled routes. Figure 6.16 shows the distribution of the world's principal scheduled commercial air routes. As one

would expect, air transportation tends to be best developed in the nations with advanced economies and especially in regions with substantial populations. The areas with the most extensive services are the eastern half and the west coast regions of the United States and the industrial portions of western Europe. More than one-third of the world's total air traffic, 7 of the 11 leading airlines, and 9 of the 10 most heavily used airports are in the United States. Unscheduled commercial air services are an important means of travel to many recreation resources, especially in areas where other forms of trans-

portation are scarce or absent. Small aircraft, for example, are used extensively to transport fisherpersons and hunters in Alaska and some of the more remote areas of Canada.

An increasing number of individuals are taking up private flying, both as a means of transportation and as a recreation activity. There are now more than 750,000 active private pilots in the United States and their number is expected to double within a decade. Many of these pilots never own a plane; they rent one when they wish to fly and can afford to do so. Nevertheless, a growing proportion of pilots purchase aircraft, either on their own or with one or more friends, since some simple two-seaters cost little more than the highest priced automobiles. In addition, with proper maintenance, small planes can last 20 or 30 years and maintain good resale value, making them a better investment in the long run than many automobiles. Light aircraft can also be faster and use less gasoline than a car if conditions are favorable. A small, but growing, number of people use light planes to expand their recreation environments by flying to resorts, hunting and fishing locations, sporting events, and other cities. They are able to participate in recreation activities in several different locations during one weekend or visit a much wider range of recreation resources during an annual vacation. Many also take part in various flying events— fly-ins, dawn patrols, treasure hunts, spot-landing contests, and poker runs— and acquire a national circle of friends as they attend distant races and conventions.

Private flying in other nations is more strictly regulated and proportionately more expensive. As a result, there are fewer private pilots and aircraft. In Europe, for instance, there are 510 private pilots per 1 million population compared with 3300 per 1 million in the United States. Canada and Australia have

3200 and 2800 per 1 million respectively.

TRANSPORTATION OF RECREATION GOODS

The nature and extent of a nation's transportation system affects the supply of recreation goods and, hence, the availability of associated opportunities. In the United States, for example, it is not just the size of the consumer market that has made recreation goods widely available at comparatively lower prices than in other countries. A major factor has been the transportation system, especially long-distance trucking, which has made it possible to move large volumes of merchandise swiftly and at reasonable cost. As a result, retailers in cities and towns and even in many smaller communities across the nation are able to sell a wide range of recreation goods. Automobiles, boats, snowmobiles, camping vehicles, fishing equipment, cameras, film, television sets, swimsuits, books, table games, and other items are readily available. If the exact item is not on hand, it can usually be ordered through the retailer or from a mail-order catalog and delivered quickly and inexpensively by the transportation system. Without reliable, efficient networks of rail, truck, and air services, markets would be local or regional at best and the benefits

of mass production and large-scale marketing would be reduced.

The transportation of many other kinds of items also affects recreation experiences. Restaurant menus would be much less varied and interesting and the quality of foods would decrease without good transportation systems. Increasing amounts of high-value perishable items such as seafood and Chinese vegetables are being moved by air. Refrigerated trucks carry perishables from producing areas, ports, and airports to wholesalers. Smaller trucks distribute foods to the restaurants. Many restaurant chains have central warehouses where bulk food from wholesalers is divided into appropriately sized quantities or actual portions, packaged, and then shipped in company trucks to the individual units. Dozens of other products that people take for granted such as soft drinks, beer, ice cream, gasoline, newspapers, and cigarettes are readily obtainable because transportation is available for their distribution.

This concludes our review of the various aspects of resource and transportation availability that influence recreation participation. Further discussion of the effect of distance and methods of transportation are included in Chapters 8 and 18. In the next chapter, the role of personal factors is considered.

DISCUSSION TOPICS

1. How does the availability of recreation resources affect participation patterns in communities with which you are familiar? What impact has modern technology had on the availability of resources in these areas?

2. What effect do the policies of public and private organizations or individuals have on the availability of recreation resources in communities that you know? Can you suggest any policy changes that would increase the availability of recreation resources?

3. What roles do walking, riding horses, and cycling play in the accessibility of recreation resources in your community? Is it desirable and feasible to change these roles? If so, how could such changes be effected?
4. How do the ownership of motor vehicles and the nature and distribution of highways affect the accessibility of recreation opportunities in communities with which you are familiar?
5. What is the impact of mass transit on access to recreation resources in your community? Could its impact be improved? If so, how?

FURTHER READINGS

Although a number of recreation textbooks include some mention of the mechanics of policymaking, none provides a systematic discussion of the effects of various policies on recreation participation. Some good examples of policy issues commonly encountered by urban park and recreation departments are included in Chapters 9, 10, and 11 of *Elements of Park and Recreation Administration* by Charles E. Doell and Louis F. Twardzik, published in Minneapolis by Burgess in 1979. Marion Clawson and Jack L. Knetsch outline some major public policy issues concerning recreation in the final chapter of their book, *Economics of Outdoor Recreation,* which was published in Baltimore by The Johns Hopkins University Press in 1966. An excellent way to become familiar with the intricacies of recreation policies is to attend meetings of park and recreation boards, natural resources commissions, or legislative committees where the advantages and disadvantages of various policies are debated.

Recreation textbooks generally include only brief mention of the role of transportation. Two British books contain more references than most; they are J. Allan Patmore's 1970 book, *Land and Leisure,* published in Newton Abbot, Devon, by David & Charles, and *Recreational Geography* edited by Patrick Lavery and published in New York by John Wiley in 1974. General background information on transportation can be obtained from encyclopedias. Usually, it is necessary to look under such headings as engineering projects as well as transportation. News, business, and travel magazines often include articles on the effects of transportation on recreation.

7

PERSONAL FACTORS AFFECTING PARTICIPATION

Every individual is very much a product of the various environments in which he or she has lived. Each person is affected by those environments, both physically and psychologically. Yet, no two people are exactly the same; each of us has somewhat different reactions to the same stimuli. Some get tired or thirsty before others when playing sports or hiking. The water seems too cold for swimming to one indi-

Figure 7.1 **Shyness is a personal characteristic that seriously limits many people's recreation opportunities.**

vidual and just right to another. Colors, landscapes, and works of art are enjoyed differently— or not at all by those who are colorblind. Some love the taste of chocolate, others dislike it. One person prefers loud music, whereas the next person complains that it produces pain. An odor may bring pleasure to some and be unpleasant or even result in allergic reactions in others. Similarly, individuals react differently to psychological stimuli.

This chapter reviews the main groupings of personal characteristics that influence people's recreation behavior (Figure 7.1). These personal factors combine with the external factors discussed in the previous chapters to form the recreation environment in which decisions concerning participation are made. Within the constraints imposed by these internal and external factors and stimulated by many of them, the individual develops recreation *motivations*— inner urges that prompt him or her to behave in a particular way with regard to recreation. These motivations result in personal *preferences* for certain kinds of recreation experiences. When a group of people make a decision regarding collective recreation participation, it is usually a compromise that is based on their individual motivations and preferences as constrained by various external factors.

In the description of personal factors that follows, basic characteristics such as personality and skills will be discussed first, followed by factors such as income and discretionary time, which are strongly linked to external influences. However, all the aspects of an individual's personal recreation environment are significant and any one

can be crucial, depending on the circumstances.

PERSONALITY

People's personalities influence not only their choice of recreation activities and the amount and patterns of participation but also play a major role in determining how much enjoyment is obtained. Personality is more important in giving meaning to an experience than any of the other personal characteristics. Since personality plays such a pivotal role, it has been placed at the center of the personal components in the recreation environment diagram (Figure 1.5).

Dissimilar personalities will have completely different reactions to the possibility of taking part in a given activity. To outgoing persons, an activity may be welcomed as a chance to try something new and exciting, to make new friends, to obtain new insights, to learn new skills, or to share talents with others. Shy, insecure people, on the other hand, may dread any unfamiliar, unstructured situation because they fear rejection and are unduly concerned with the evaluation of their performance by others (Figure 7.1).

Of all the personality traits, shyness is perhaps the most significant, both in terms of its influence on people's recreation lifestyles and the number of people it affects. Almost everyone experiences shyness at one time or another, but about 40 percent of the population considers their bouts of shyness frequent and severe enough to affect the quality of their lives negatively. Of course, shyness is not a characteristic a person is born with; it is an acquired trait that seems most prevalent in societies such as the United

States, where a strong emphasis is placed on individual and personal achievement. However, once shyness (or indeed any other personal characteristic) has been acquired, it becomes a factor that must be dealt with on the personal level.

Shyness takes several forms. Shy introverts blush, stammer, do not easily initiate a conversation or make decisions, avoid eye contact, and appear generally ill at ease in most social situations. Shy extroverts, on the other hand, manage to cover up their shyness (at least in certain environments), and to people who do not know them well, they may appear outgoing and at ease. However, shyness takes over and discomfort is experienced as soon as they are no longer in an environment where they can excel or play an adopted role. Many performers— athletes, comedians, performing artists— fall into this category. Shy bullies have another method of handling their problem; they remove the threat of evaluation by taking the offensive and keeping people at a safe distance with aggressive, domineering behavior. Unfortunately, in all of these cases, a barrier has been erected that effectively prevents other people from getting close. Worse yet, people are often alienated by shy people because they misinterpret their behavior as snobbishness, condescension, boredom, prudishness, attention-seeking, self-conceit, buffoonery, or even hostility.

Shyness affects recreation participation in a variety of ways. Shy people often avoid any kind of recreation activity involving high levels of socialization or verbal communication. Some live in virtual isolation without friends or normal sexual relationships. Others may be so anxious about the possibility of failure that they have difficulty deciding to participate. They may seek and depend on the advice and encouragement of relatives, associates, professional counselors, or the media. Often they will dare to take part only if someone they know also decides to participate. Others may avoid the problem of having to make decisions and risk failure by clinging to a limited number of familiar activities rather than exploring new possibilities. If they do feel a break from their normal routine is desirable, they may restrict themselves to activities that are well organized and highly structured. Passive activities, where the individual can be a spectator or otherwise play an inconspicuous role, may also be preferred.

Some individuals can become so timid, lonely, or insecure that they dread free time. Intentionally or subconsciously, they may avoid it by spending long hours at work or by prolonging their routine household jobs to keep themselves busy. Others may drift into escapist or self-destructive habits such as complete inactivity during free time, daydreaming, the use of alcohol or other drugs, or various forms of antisocial behavior.

However, shyness is not the only personality trait that plays a role in determining recreation participation. For example:

- Perfectionists may become frustrated and disillusioned with activities in which they have difficulty excelling or in group activities where other participants do not strive for the same level of excellence.
- Gentle individuals may avoid contact sports as either participants or spectators and may dislike hunting, fishing,

violent movies and television programs, or activities involving boisterous crowds.
- Domineering, egotistical people may seek group activities that permit them to exert control over others, but they may find many social experiences unsatisfactory because of the negative reaction of other participants to their dictatorial attitudes.
- Those with secure, introspective, or creative personalities may welcome solitary activities during which they can relax, explore their individuality and potential, or develop and renew themselves.
- Frustrated, tense, or angry individuals may find release in vigorous activities, violent television programs, contact sports, hunting, war games, or destructive antisocial pursuits.
- Competitive, aggressive personalities may find many routine activities boring and seek situations where they can either compete against themselves or the environment or where they feel adequately challenged by participants of equal ability.
- Those who have gregarious personalities and like to be with people favor the sociability of parties, club activities, discotheques, cruises, and heavily used parks, beaches, and resorts.
- People who crave group adulation prefer activities in which they feel they can excel and seek group situations that present ample opportunities to demonstrate their talents.
- Individuals of high intelligence may search for mental challenges in their recreation and select stimulating activities like championship chess, difficult puzzles, discussion groups, or the study of philosophy or foreign languages.
- People who are insecure about their place in society tend to choose activities that they believe will establish or enhance their social status; they participate in certain organizations, sports, and forms of entertainment, and plan their vacations at locations that they believe will raise or confirm their social standing.

However, it is dangerous to jump to conclusions regarding the relationship between personality and participation in certain activities.

Personality traits do not have to determine people's recreation lifestyles. Especially in the last few years, many traits that were previously regarded as permanent handicaps have come to be considered conditions that can be modified; many individuals have managed, either alone or with professional help, to rid themselves of most of the restrictions imposed by such traits. This is especially important to those who are responsible for organizing recreation programs. A growing number of people are taking part in activities for which their personalities do not prepare them. Not everyone who signs up for an adventure program is fearless, and many individuals who come to a social event are not the poised, gregarious types they seem to be. Program directors need to be aware of this and do all they can to help people feel comfortable in the recreation roles they have chosen for themselves.

PERCEPTIONS AND ATTITUDES

Perceptions and attitudes play a major role in determining whether or not individuals participate in recreation, and, if so, how much they enjoy their experiences. Like personality traits, people's perceptions and attitudes are products of their total environment. All the stimuli received throughout life mold the individual's outlook and feelings. These stimuli, in turn, are controlled by the person's personality, sex, age, health, cultural background, upbringing, education, environment, occupation, and social contacts. It is not surprising, therefore, that each individual's perceptions of recreation and attitudes toward participation in various activities tend to be unique. Recognizing that individuals have different perceptions and attitudes is important when providing any type of public, private, or commercial recreation activity.

The directors of the Coleman Company showed that they appreciated this fact in an advertisement for folding camping trailers (Figure 7.2). Each member of a hypothetical family is shown developing different ideas concerning the advantages of trailer ownership. The elimination of any problems connected with finding overnight accommodations appeals to the husband. He also perceives the camper as being economical and easy to tow; he looks forward to setting up camp in scenic locations where he can pursue his hobby of photography. His wife sees a folding camper as bringing the family together without creating difficult or time-consuming housekeeping problems for her. The children visualize a camping vacation that will facilitate their own special outdoor interests.

PERCEPTIONS

Perception is not just a matter of seeing things visually. People perceive the world around them with each of their five senses and develop mental impressions based on an interpretation of all of the stimuli they receive. Often these mental images are stored and seemingly forgotten for weeks or years. Sometimes, parts of the image become hazy and feelings become less in-

Figure 7.2 **This advertisement for camping trailers points out that each member of a family may have different perceptions and attitudes concerning the advantages of owning a camper and going on a camping vacation.**

Affordable, fun, family vacations.

Dad thinks of the Coleman <u>folding camper</u> as a way to get away from it all and relax on <u>4-inch foam beds</u>. It folds up small, so it tows <u>and stows easy</u> and <u>saves gas</u>, too. Towing a Coleman takes less than one extra gallon of gas for 100 miles of highway travel, <u>and any car can tow one</u>. When they're ready to stop, it folds out to create living space in the great outdoors for the whole family (where there's always a vacancy, free of charge!).

Mom says it brings the <u>family together</u>. And the <u>built-in kitchen</u> makes camping easy for her.

Susie . . . she just likes to watch nature through those great <u>big camper windows</u> and listen to the crickets chirp at night.

Billy gets to fish in the

stream beside their campsite because they don't need fancy park facilities for their Coleman.

Ruff chases rabbits (of course).

It's an <u>affordable American Dream</u> for any family. In fact, Coleman's <u>low, everyday prices can fit a camper into any camper's budget</u>. It's a Coleman Folding Camping Trailer.

Buy your Coleman now, and get a double sleeping bag and two pillows FREE!

Perfect for overnight stops, this matching bag and pillow set is designed especially to fit the wing beds of any Coleman Camper.

See us for your Coleman Camper now, and get your sleeping bag and pillows FREE! This is a limited-time offer, so come in today!

Seven magnificent folding camping trailers for '77.

![Coleman] **Folding Camping Trailers**
the camper's camper

(Dealer Imprint Area)

tense with the passage of time. Frequently, another stronger image alters the earlier one or becomes dominant replacing the first impressions. At times, many related images are received, merge, and form little more than vague impressions.

On the other hand, a single impression may be so intense and dramatic when it is received that it is impossible to change or forget. It remains strong and vivid, affecting other images both related and unrelated during an entire lifetime. It may be a positive image that is recalled with increasing warmth over the years and that encourages the individual to seek situations consciously or unconsciously that may recreate the pleasurable experience or produce a similarly happy feeling under a quite different set of circumstances.

Perceptions of Recreation Experiences. Many of our attitudes toward recreation activities are affected by childhood experiences. For instance, as a child, a woman had spent a summer at the seashore with her grandparents. She remembers many details of the happy experience, but especially the great thrill she felt in seeing the ocean for the first time and being able to explore a seashore environment. She also recalls how nice it was to be with her grandparents because, unlike her parents at home, the grandparents did not require her to eat meals or go to bed at set times or scold her if she got dirty or wandered off alone. The relaxed, permissive atmosphere was, in fact, what she enjoyed most of all. From this time on, she perceives the marine environment as fascinating and restorative and visits

it whenever possible. She has taken up shell-collecting as a hobby and has recently become active in a local organization that is fighting for the preservation of a nearby estuary threatened by industrial development. As an adult, she has largely abandoned the restrictive lifestyle of her parents and tries instead to live, particularly during her free time, in a less scheduled, more carefree manner. She looks forward to taking her son on a similar seashore vacation as soon as he is old enough and hopes that she can make the experience as relaxed and memorable for him as it once was for her.

Unfortunately, it is frequently the unhappy images that dominate. A frightening event or uncomfortable experience may prove impossible to forget and lead an individual to avoid participation not only in the activity during which the unhappy incident occurred but also in associated activities as well. For example, people who have been camping during an extended period of cold, wet weather may never go camping again and perceive it and other extraurban recreation activities as undesirable, both for themselves and others.

Poor experiences with people may also create lasting negative attitudes. For example, a domineering, sarcastic, insensitive, or inept sports coach, music teacher, youth group leader, or recreation program director may produce not only a permanent dislike for the activity concerned but also a loss of self-confidence, which produces a reluctance to take part in other activities requiring the learning of new skills. A lack of acceptance by other participants in a group activity may have a similar effect.

Circumstances, equipment, or facilities may also produce negative perceptions and attitudes. For instance, crowded conditions at a beach on a holiday weekend may leave some visitors with such unfavorable impressions that they never attempt to go to that beach again. Similarly, poor service from a particular recreation product or facility — an outboard motor that is unreliable and hard to start, poor skiing equipment, a leaky tent, seats at a concert located where the acoustics are poor — may produce such unsatisfactory recreation experiences that they cause disillusionment and a negative image of the activities themselves.

People's attitudes vary greatly, since everyone has a different collection of stored images. The same activity may be perceived very differently by a set of twins, a husband and wife, or two recreation professionals. A day-long canoe trip down a well-known river with relatively mild rapids may, for example, be perceived in the following ways by a number of participants:

- Members of a large party of teenagers on the traditional high school spring outing for seniors look forward to it as an exciting adventure, which provides lots of opportunities for beer drinking, sunbathing, contacts with the opposite sex, and horseplay in the water when canoes collide or capsize. Since the river environment is secondary to the social experience and the experience can be manipulated and controlled by the participants themselves, the trip for the majority of participants is a great success.
- A budding photographer anticipates outstanding pictures of tumbling water and picturesque shorelines. Since he finds the scenery much less spectacular than visualized from the

tourist literature, his trip is quite disappointing.

- Pleasant childhood memories of exciting canoe trips with her father inspire a vacationing urban resident to rent a canoe and take her family down the river. Because problems are more numerous and pleasures far fewer than on those recollected trips, she finds the experience much less satisfying than expected.
- The apprehensive husband of the above woman is canoeing for the first time; he is relieved when the trip is over, since he had visions of punctured or overturned canoes—resulting in drownings or injuries—every time the canoe grated against the bottom or passed through rough water.
- The teen age children of the above couple cannot wait to get back home to enjoy social activities with their friends. They perceive the canoe trip as a boring waste of time and a childish activity undertaken as an involuntary family duty, so that they hate every minute of the trip.
- A student interested in local history has read much about the early days in the region. Since he enjoys imagining, during the trip, how the original explorers felt as they traveled down the river, he savors every moment of an experience that has become a glorious mixture of reality and fantasy.
- Two experienced canoeists from another part of the country are taking the trip because of the river's local reputation as a fine canoeing river. Although they regard the experience as enjoyable, they are disappointed in the river itself because they judge the experiences offered by a higher set of standards than most local canoeists.
- Two wilderness lovers have visualized a relatively unspoiled and tranquil setting for their trip rather than a river crowded with noisy users and marred with beer cans and other litter. However, since they see a rare species of orchid en route, they perceive the trip as well worthwhile.

Similarly, people approach other recreation activities with a great variety of images in their minds. These images may be very different from those that recreation professionals believe to be the main sources of user attitudes.

Perceptions of Work and Free Time. Although perceptions of actual activities or locations are important determinants of recreation behavior, the way individuals view all aspects of life often play an even more significant role. For instance, a critical factor is a person's perception of his or her work responsibilities. If household tasks or employment outside the home are regarded as onerous duties to be performed in the least possible time and with the least expenditure of effort, then the individual is likely to perceive recreation as a means of escape or an opportunity for personal fulfillment. Such people usually take every possible opportunity to engage in recreation, both during working hours and after work. Some regard recreation not as relief but as their main purpose in life.

On the other hand, a person who sees his or her work as a valuable opportunity for personal achievement and fulfillment may regard recreation as relatively unimportant. Some may emphasize their work almost to the exclusion of what most people perceive as typical free-time pursuits. Others may not regard work so positively but prefer it to free time because they view the available recreation opportunities as unsatisfactory. Similarly, an individual's perception of family, social, religious, educational, civic, and health-care responsibilities will affect recreation participation and behavior.

People's perceptions of free time also influence how they use it. If free time is regarded as a privilege, it is likely that the individual will try to use it wisely and develop a program of recreation activities that is perceived as personally beneficial and socially constructive. Others may see free time mainly as a chance to escape temporarily from the physical and mental environments associated with work and routine duties. They regard it as an opportunity rather than a privilege, paying little heed to what they do as long as it provides what they perceive as a much-needed change of pace. They spend every possible moment simply "trying to get away from it all."

Some see free time as neither privilege nor opportunity but rather as an empty space that, if left unfilled, becomes intimidating. In their anxiety to fill the vacuum, they often appear to lose much of the benefit that can be derived from recreation. They work so hard at playing it almost becomes another job. Rush is substituted for relaxation and physical and mental exhaustion for refreshment. They tear from one social event to another or spend much of their weekend time fighting highway traffic to spend a few extra hours at a distant Shangri-la. Similar recreation behavior patterns may arise from a perception of free time as a precious commodity. Every spare moment must be crammed with activity to be sure it is not wasted.

Others perceive time when they do not have to work as a well-earned right and consider such time a private possession, which can and should be used exactly as they wish. These people may ignore many or all of their family responsi-

Figure 7.3 **This man will probably return home refreshed after snoozing away a warm afternoon on a calm lake. The boat serves as an extension of his home territory permitting him to relax in an isolated yet familiar environment.**

bilities and spend most off-duty hours sleeping, sitting in bars, watching television, or immersed in a favorite sport or hobby. Family and friends complain that they can seldom persuade them to take part in other activities.

For some, however, free time is none of these things. It is simply a means to an end. It is time to be used effectively to achieve optimum refreshment of mind and body (Figure 7.3). In pursuit of this goal, these individuals tend to develop a well-balanced recreation lifestyle.

Perceptions of People and Places. The images individuals have of places, people, and organizations are also key factors in participation. Potential participants are less likely to take part in activities if they have a poor image of the location, person, or group involved in providing the opportunity. For instance, some individuals have very positive and romantic images of

New York and eagerly look forward to visiting the city. Others have developed extremely negative perceptions of the city because of the way they have interpreted newspaper reports about its traffic and economic and crime problems. They will never consider visiting New York, even though they might like to take advantage of its many excellent recreation opportunities, including museums, restaurants, stores, sports facilities, and Broadway plays. Similarly, people perceive individual program organizers, coaches, instructors, and performers or particular public, private, or commercial organizations either favorably or unfavorably.

Such perceptions are often founded on biased or limited information. Sometimes they are based on nothing more than a single incident, which is either personally experienced or reported by an acquaintance. This is particularly true

in the case of commercial recreation resources. One surly employee, an error in a bill or reservation, or poor service by an inexperienced clerk or waiter can produce a negative image, which may not necessarily be correct, but, nonetheless, the customer is upset or disenchanted and never comes back. Similarly, many people tend to judge neighborhoods, communities, states, provinces, and even nations on the basis of superficial information and observances.

Although such judgments depend on one or more aspects of the external environment, they are largely a product of individual interpretation of these external factors. Each person's perceptions of a particular situation tends to be somewhat different. For example, an introverted person may be quite unnerved and decide not to use the library facilities again if a librarian is unusually abrupt and unhelpful when asked for assistance in finding a book. A more extroverted person may think little of it and simply persist in demanding the librarian's help; he or she may also complain to the library director about the employee's unpleasant behavior, but the incident will not be taken personally nor will it affect the person's positive perceptions of the library facility.

ATTITUDES

People develop attitudes toward recreation participation based on interpretation of their own perceptions supplemented by information received from others. For instance, if an individual already has a favorable image of a particular activity and is then encouraged to participate by friendly, helpful people, the experience will likely be enjoyable and his or her attitude will be positive. On the other hand, a person may perceive an activity favorably but develop a negative attitude toward it because of the disagreeable behavior of others. Similarly, individuals who are made to feel guilty about the amount of time they spend on favorite activities such as golf or bowling may cease to participate and develop negative attitudes concerning the activities they once found so enjoyable.

Many attitudes start taking shape at an early age. As discussed in Chapter 5, parents, brothers, sisters, other relatives, friends, and teachers all play a major part in developing attitudes. Even so, studies are tending to disprove the belief that recreation attitudes and behavior patterns developed in childhood always remain dominant in adults. Individuals appear to be freeing themselves from attitudes developed in their early years much more easily than in the past. About half of adult recreation participation may now involve activities and patterns of behavior acquired as adults. However, in some instances, this only means that influences from new sources have become much more powerful than previous ones.

Many personal factors modify people's attitudes. Age and physical condition, for example, can radically alter a person's outlook; tobogganing may appear to be tremendous fun at 12, rather childish at 18, a family duty at 35, and downright dangerous by the time a person reaches 60. Attitudes also change with the acquisition of skills and knowledge.

Attitudes, however, are often hard to alter once they become firmly established. Individuals frequently resist change and instead seek reinforcement of existing beliefs. They hold onto their attitudes by avoiding discussions, television programs, and any written materials that are apt to present conflicting ideas or opinions. Often, the attitudes that are most resistant to change are the ones that are based on highly emotional perceptions of the nature, effect, or value of certain activities. They may be founded on very narrow views of the situation with little regard for basic facts.

Some of the most vociferous foes of hunting, for instance, appear to base their views on emotional rather than objective interpretations of wildlife management policies. Frequently, they have quite unrealistic perceptions of animal population origins, sizes, and environmental relationships. On the other hand, there are many hunters who are equally emotional and irrational about suggested gun regulations or proposed changes in game management such as legalizing the hunting of does and fawns. A similar situation involves motorcycling, with people at one extreme having completely negative feelings toward the sport and the people who participate in it; at the other extreme are the avid motorcyclists who believe that any attempt to regulate use is both unnecessary and an infringement of basic liberties.

In the case of both hunting and motorcycling, there are large numbers of people, including participants, whose perceptions and attitudes lie somewhere between these extremes. But they tend to be inconspicuous compared to those on the emotional fringes. As a result, many prospective participants, the general public, and some recreation managers and administrators tend to perceive the conspicuous vocal minorities as being representative of the majority. This is most unfortunate not only because it reinforces biased attitudes but also because it tends to discourage participation in potentially satisfying sports and, in some instances, leads to discriminatory policies and overly restrictive management decisions.

In recent years, personal attitudes toward recreation opportunities that involve risk of injury or death have become important participation determinants. At one time, most recreation participants tended to avoid activities that were considered dangerous. Recreation primarily involved relaxation, moderate physical exertion, or sportsmanlike competition. Those who undertook the more challenging or dangerous activities were often admired but at the same time were regarded as somewhat abnormal, irresponsible attention-seekers. During the past two decades, however, participation in many challenging and high-risk activities has been growing steadily, especially in the United States. Mountaineering, hotdogging (acrobatic downhill skiing), scuba diving, hang gliding, parachute jumping, spelunking (exploring caves), adventure experiences in the wilderness, and various forms of gasoline-powered vehicle racing are no longer activities undertaken by just a few daredevils (Figure 7.4). Sports such as surfing, white-water canoeing, downhill skiing, off-highway motorcycling, and snowmobiling are attracting substantial numbers of participants. An increasing proportion of these participants seek the ultimate thrill by undertaking such activities in a manner involving maximum risk. The possibil-

Figure 7.4 **A hang gliding enthusiast takes advantage of the height and up-drafts of Devil's Dyke, a ridge of chalk hills in southern England. Hang gliding was one of the high-risk activities that became prominent in the 1970s.**

ity of physical injury also appears to be less of a deterrent to children; for example, many youngsters admit that part of the appeal of skate-boarding is the danger involved.

Psychologists have suggested a variety of theories to account for the increasing numbers that have positive attitudes toward partici-pation in higher risk activities. Some feel that individuals generally have a basic need for the kinds of stimu-lation and satisfaction that come from facing and successfully meet-ing a challenge. They suggest that modern living fails to provide ade-quate challenges so that more peo-ple are seeking such opportunities in their free-time pursuits. Others

say that many participants are driven toward these activities be-cause they provide one of the few socially acceptable outlets for ag-gression available in peacetime. A few express concern that an in-crease in boredom-suicidal tenden-cies are contributing to the change.

Whatever the reasons for parti-cipation might be, it is doubtful that such substantial numbers would be forming positive attitudes toward taking part if other factors were not making it attractive or easy to do so. A nucleus of individuals who have an urgent need to prove themselves, discover their limita-tions, and experience thrills is, no doubt, having a powerful influence

on others. Participation in most of the high-risk activities is also en-couraged because this type of rec-reation is frequently featured in the press, electronic media, and all forms of advertising. High discre-tionary incomes, more free time, and easier accessibility to the neces-sary resources together with better and more affordable equipment have also made taking part in such sports feasible. Finally, the wide-spread formation of participant clubs and instructional programs has exposed increasing numbers to challenge activities and made it pos-sible to acquire the requisite skills readily. Therefore, it is important to remember when assessing the value of people's attitudes in determining recreation participation patterns that there are always external factors in-volved. Although an individual's de-cision to participate is a very per-sonal action, the opportunity to take part is likely influenced by or dependent on a number of factors over which the individual has rela-tively little control.

KNOWLEDGE AND SKILLS

It is often said that knowledge is power and that it can set people free. This is particularly true in the case of free-time activities; knowl-edge *is* recreation power. People with a reasonably good basic edu-cation have a much better opportu-nity to participate in a wide range of recreation activities than those who have had little education. Indi-viduals who have a good education plus additional knowledge and skills associated with specific recreation activities— an understanding of the rules of a game, proficiency in play-ing a musical instrument, or training in playing a sport—are free to take part to the fullest extent and with maximum ease and personal satisfaction. Yet, less than one-half of all Americans are said to have the educational proficiency needed to deal successfully with the complexities of modern living and one-fifth of the population is functionally incompetent. This means that almost 30 million Americans over the age of 18 are unable to read and fully understand advertisements, restaurant menus, driver's tests, roadmaps, bus schedules, or newspaper and magazine articles; they also lack minimal proficiency in problem-solving skills and find it impossible to calculate correct change, follow anything but the simplest verbal instructions, write letters, address envelopes, write checks, or prepare shopping lists. Substantial numbers are similarly handicapped in the other developed nations and worldwide, one-third of the adult population (800 million people) cannot read, write, or do a simple calculation in written form.

Being unable to read, write, and calculate can severely limit recreation participation. In less developed nations, illiteracy may have very little effect if there are few opportunities for activities that involve such skills. In highly developed countries, however, those who are illiterate or poorly educated are at a severe disadvantage. Many recreation activities require reading, writing, language, or calculation skills; some examples are:

- Reading a newspaper for pleasure or to obtain information on recreation events—such as movies, concerts, plays, exhibitions, sports, and festivals—or to learn about recreation goods and services for sale from the display and classified advertisements.
- Reading a television or radio program guide to know when programs of interest are scheduled and on which station they will be broadcast.
- Interpreting sports scores and statistics.
- Understanding more sophisticated movies, television programs, plays, lectures, and literature.
- Playing such games as cribbage, scrabble, or Monopoly; working crossword and many other kinds of word or mathematical puzzles.
- Understanding many comic books and cartoons.
- Reading magazines, paperback books, best sellers, classics, poetry, and other forms of literature.
- Using a roadmap that involves reading, interpretation of spatial relationships, and simple mathematics.
- Writing and reading letters from relatives or friends; ordering recreation goods from catalogs; asking for tourist information and maps by mail.
- Reading and interpreting instructions necessary for activities such as cooking, knitting, crafts, do-it-yourself projects, or assembling hobby kits or recreation equipment.
- Reading flyers, posters, and newspaper announcements concerning public or private recreation programs.

This inability to find out about upcoming community recreation programs is particularly tragic because many of the functionally incompetent are economically disadvantaged and in need of such opportunities. Unless organizations take pains to use television, radio, vehicles with public-address systems, community leaders, oral announcements in schools and places of business, and other means of verbal communication, illiterate people even miss the many recreation opportunities in which they would have no trouble participating.

Associated with illiteracy and of equal concern is the growing inability or unwillingness of young people to concentrate on studies or, indeed, any endeavor requiring perseverance and self-discipline. An increasing number avoid challenges and settle for whatever pursuits are the least demanding; they choose a short book instead of a longer one, a comic book instead of a printed book, or, better still, the superficial viewing of the least demanding program available on television.

Such habits are affecting not only their educational and employment opportunities but also their recreation lifestyles. Some activities—the playing of musical instruments, participation in sports and games, or the pursuit of a hobby or craft—require the acquisition of skills to be truly satisfying experiences. Many young people find it unpleasant, difficult, or impossible to exert the effort necessary for the learning of these skills. As a result, they lose interest quickly or do not even attempt to take part in such activities. Unfortunately, these patterns often persist; as adults they tend to try only the recreation activities that seem to make few demands and offer instant gratification.

Industry is well aware of this trend and has been quick to take advantage. Paint-by-number kits, cameras that only require the pressing of one button, condensed books, guided tours, electronic organs, and sports equipment or instructional programs that promise immediate enjoyment and success —seemingly without effort—attract growing numbers of participants. Sadly, many of these individuals get little satisfaction from the simplified activity; instead of becoming interested and deeply involved, they soon become bored, drop out, and move on to something else. For instance, more than 75 million people in the United States are casual photographers. The majority, however, do not progress past the instant-camera stage and, consequently, do not become involved in any of the more demanding technical and artistic aspects of the art of photography. As a result, they have little opportunity to be creative or to discuss the finer points of the hobby with other participants.

Even those who accept the need to expend effort pursuing competence in recreation activities are affected by the trend toward superficial involvement. They find themselves trying to take lessons, play games, undertake hobbies, or go on trips with restless individuals who want to get on to the main activity whether or not they are sufficiently prepared. Some of these individuals then proceed to take part in such a way that it ruins the experience for those who are skilled or better prepared.

Language and dialect differences also limit people's recreation environments. In the United States, about 8 million people do not speak English as their primary language, and, of these, 5 million have trouble speaking or understanding any English. These people are likely to be recreationally disadvantaged all of their lives because of their inability to communicate adequately in a variety of recreation situations. With more than 2 million Spanish-speaking people in this predicament, some communities are providing Spanish-speaking staff, Spanish language recreation programs, and instruction in English to help bridge the gap (Figure 7.5). But many people of Hispanic and other backgrounds live in locations where little or no language assistance is provided; they often find it easier to give up and restrict their recreation activities to those they can provide for themselves rather than struggle to overcome both the linguistic and cultural barriers that make it so difficult to participate in community recreation events.

Dialects can cause similar problems with understanding and communication. Some dialects bear so little resemblance to the original languages from which they have developed that they almost have the same effect as a foreign language. Poor urban blacks in the United States, for example, have developed a form of English that is largely incomprehensible to those who have not lived in areas where it is the common means of communication. This dialect is so well established in some areas that children have difficulty making the transition to standard English in school. A special series of readers and tape recordings is now being used in an effort to bridge this language gap. The amount of black vernacular decreases and the proportion of standard English increases through the series so that the students are able to use stan-

Figure 7.5 Basketball is one of several organized activities offered in Spanish as part of the recreation program in Hartford, Connecticut. Although the coach, Rolan Axelson, is not Hispanic, he is fluent in Spanish and therefore is able to instruct this Hispanic group in the language with which they are most comfortable. Not only does this make the program more enjoyable for the participants, it is also easier for them to learn the skills necessary to improve their game.

dard textbooks when they finish the program. The same kinds of problems can occur with other dialects and languages. There is a growing concern over the rights of minority groups to be taught in the language with which they are most familiar. And certainly there is justification for it. However, it is also a fact that those who go through such language-bridging programs when they are young will be better able to take advantage of all the opportunities that are part of the dominant culture's heritage. Of course, these include a wide range of recreation programs, activities, and events.

ECONOMIC AND TIME IMPLICATIONS

Education also affects recreation participation because of its economic implications (see Chapter 4). Most educationally disadvantaged individuals are not able to secure well-paying jobs, especially if they also have a language or dialect disadvantage. On the other hand, a better education and language proficiency usually mean more discretionary income and, therefore, a wider range of recreation opportunities. Such abilities can also result in individuals getting more recreation goods or services for their money because they can take advantage of sales, avoid interest payments, and be more astute at budgeting.

On the other hand, choosing to obtain a trade school, community college, or university education can, temporarily at least, reduce recreation opportunities. As education costs escalate, many middle-class families curtail all nonessential spending to provide funds for their children's education. Growing num-

bers of young people are also assuming part or all of the costs of obtaining trade skills or a college education. As a result, recreation participation for parents, students, and all other members of the family may be limited for a considerable length of time. The need for sizable expenditures on higher education usually occurs when most parents with modest incomes have just reached the stage when their discretionary incomes are beginning to increase. Most often, they are in their middle forties and in reasonable health. Without the burden of education costs, they would at last be financially able to travel, start new activities and hobbies, or make major recreation equipment purchases. Unfortunately, many find that health problems and diminishing vigor prevent them from realizing the same recreation potential once their children have finished college and they have again accumulated the necessary money.

In addition, teenagers and young people who choose to obtain more education are often economically dependent on their families for much longer than would otherwise be the case. Because of this dependence, the nature and amount of their recreation participation, especially expenditures, are sometimes limited and may be influenced by their parents. At the same time, however, many students are temporarily relieved of much of the adult work and family or community responsibilities that those who do not continue their education assume at an earlier age. Therefore, to some extent at least, they may have the time and freedom to participate in some activities for a longer period of time than would otherwise be possible.

SOURCES AND IMPACT

In addition to providing basic reading, writing, and arithmetic skills, education can contribute substantially in other ways to people's ability to participate in recreation. Attitudes toward recreation can be altered by programs and courses offered by elementary schools as well as colleges. Those who learn while young that recreation is a valuable and meaningful part of everyday life are more likely to engage freely and enthusiastically in recreation as adults. They will realize and accept the need to set aside time for recreation activities throughout their lives. Schools can be especially helpful in expanding people's recreation horizons. Well-designed courses and extracurricular programs can successfully introduce interested students to art, crafts, music, dance, drama, nature study, games, and sports. Many are providing opportunities to develop recreation skills that will be useful throughout life— swimming, dancing, tennis, golf, backpacking, boating, skating, horseback riding, bowling, skiing, bridge, chess, and so on. Such programs are often more valuable to the average person than some of the more traditional team sports in which relatively few participate after leaving school. For instance, part of the substantial increase in swimming participation evident in many parts of the United States, Canada, and Europe is believed to be a direct result of swimming instruction in the schools.

School courses and extracurricular programs involving recreation are especially important because they reach individuals at a stage in life when they can most easily accept and learn new ideas, physical skills, and habits without as much embarrassment, fear of failure, or injury as in later life. There is also a better chance that people will remember and automatically observe safety rules if they learn them in a school situation. Many recreation-related accidents could be avoided if participants were better informed and aware of possible dangers. More knowledge and increased skills also contribute to the recreation experience if they improve the chance of success and instill confidence in the participant.

Be that as it may, the impact of school and college programs depends to a large extent on the individual. Although some physical education is still required in most schools, the majority of other recreation-oriented programs and all extracurricular activities are a matter of choice. A potential lifetime of participation in an activity such as music, art, drama, chess, or a sport may be lost because a student dislikes a particular instructor or the course does not fit into a schedule or fulfill requirements for graduation. Unhappily, most students make decisions regarding the recreation-oriented aspects of their school programs on their own with little or no investigation or counseling.

An encouraging development is the increasing number of opportunities for adults to learn how to use their free time more effectively. Some colleges and local government parks and recreation departments now offer courses or individualized programs on this topic. They also provide courses that teach specific recreation skills or that offer insights into a wide range of recreation activities and resources.

But people can obtain recreation-opportunity information and develop skills in many informal ways. Frequently, these sources include: libraries; television and radio programs; newspaper articles; the many specialized arts, crafts, hobby, sports, and travel magazines; how-to-do-it books and records; hunting, fishing, and tourist literature and guidebooks; and demonstrations or exhibits staged by various organizations. Much information and many skills, however, are obtained from personal contacts with relatives, neighbors, friends, and acquaintances who are willing to share their talents and knowledge. As never before, large numbers of the world's people are able to expand their recreation horizons and capabilities throughout their entire lives if they choose to take advantage of the wide range of sources and opportunities that are available to them.

SEX

The sex of the individual imposes some physical constraints on participation in certain recreation activities. The female body is generally shorter, smaller, lighter, composed of a higher proportion of fat, more flexible and loosely jointed, narrower in the shoulders, broader in the hips, and with shorter extremities in relationship to the trunk. Because of such characteristics, some women may have difficulty doing such things as spanning more than an octave on a piano, playing bar chords on a thick-necked guitar, or carrying as heavy loads as men do during canoeing or backpacking expeditions.

Some of these differences give women an advantage in gymnastics and certain competitive sports such as long-distance running, swim-

ming, and cycling. However, they may place women at a disadvantage in sprinting, wrestling, football, and any activity requiring long-distance throwing. But this does not mean that women should not take part in such activities; it only indicates that it would be unfair to expect the average woman to compete successfully on equal terms with the average man in situations where differences in arm length, shoulder power, or sheer size would play a crucial role in deciding the outcome. On this basis, of course, it is equally inappropriate for men or women of different body characteristics to compete together unless special rules or handicaps are employed.

The myths about women's lack of stamina[1] or susceptibility to injuries have been disproved. As more women are taking part in competitive sports, it is becoming clear that physiologically women may be somewhat better suited to activities that require endurance and that, given proper conditioning, training, and equipment they suffer no higher injury rates or more serious injuries than men. On the other hand, men are also disadvantaged in some situations. Many lack the overall agility and coordination of women, which is such an asset in gymnastics and dance. With larger hands, men find some of the movements required in many hobby-and-crafts activities frustrating and difficult. However, social conditioning and lack of practice in using

[1] Girls taking part in the Iowa high school basketball program are still not allowed to run over half the length of the court or dribble more than twice at one time because they continue to play under special rules established in 1920 when the sport as played by boys was considered too strenuous for girls.

anything but their large muscles may be more to blame for apparent clumsiness than any physiological differences.

Nevertheless, the sex of the individual often makes a considerable difference to recreation lifestyles. As explained in Chapter 5, society's sex-role stereotyping largely determines not only the kinds of recreation that are open to people but also the manner and environment in which they participate and the amount of time that they can use for recreation activities. Fortunately, an increasing number of individuals—men and women—are finding the courage to revolt against society's arbitrary constraints and take part in any kind of recreation activity that interests them.

This is not always easy; many who try to take part in activities not normally associated with persons of their sex face censure and ridicule. Some are temporarily blocked from doing so by traditions, regulations, and laws that seem insurmountable. But tremendous progress is being made. Men are freer than they have ever been to react emotionally in recreation situations, to become intimately involved with the care of their children, to engage in the household arts (cooking, sewing), and to take part in dance and the visual arts. As for women who have traditionally been more constrained, the changes are even more dramatic.

Women are now coaching men's sports teams; competing in marathons; driving race cars; riding thoroughbreds in races; powerlifting; playing hockey, soccer, softball, baseball, basketball, and football on mixed as well as all-female teams; climbing mountains; serving as sports journalists; competing with men in rifle-shooting events; conducting or playing in major orchestras; and getting their pilot's licenses and qualifying as flight instructors. They are proving that they are able not only to excel at such sports as golf, tennis, skating, and gymnastics but can also attract large and respectful audiences while doing so. The latter fact is perhaps one of the most important achievements so far, since it is destroying the traditionally condescending attitudes toward women in sports. These attitudes have long discouraged women from participating and denied them adequate financial support or coverage in the media.

Of course, it should be pointed out that the proportion of women participating in many of the activities mentioned is still small as is the case with men engaging in activities formerly considered inappropriate for the male sex. But it is not sheer numbers that count. What matters is the simple fact that individuals are doing these things, enjoying doing them, and doing them well. By so doing, they are making it increasingly difficult for society to perpetuate the myths and the constraints that have prevented their participation in the past. At the same time, they are making it easier for everyone to choose recreation lifestyles to suit themselves rather than to suit society.

AGE AND LIFE CYCLE

An individual's physical, mental, intellectual, and social abilities to participate in recreation vary with age and stage in the life cycle. The degree to which these abilities are developed at a particular age depends on heredity and the intellectual, social, and physical environments in which a person has lived. The primary value of recreation to the individual also changes with age. Especially in childhood, recreation *introduces* the individual to a host of experiences and *develops* mental and physical powers. For the teenager, recreation provides opportunities for *exploration* of tastes and talents. Young workers and college students find it a medium for *adventure*. During the middle years, it *sustains* individuals and families as they combat the pressures of life. In early retirement, it can *maintain* important physical and mental capabilities. And, finally, during the later years, it can provide much *consolation*.

Children are able to participate with great energy, at least for short time periods. They generally have the physical flexibility to attempt gymnastics, diving, and other sports more easily than older people. Often they are able to accept and learn new ideas and skills faster than adults. Sometimes, however, attempting new activities too soon can lead to disappointment, frustration, or injury because the child is not sufficiently developed either physically or mentally. In addition, children are often disadvantaged by having to use facilities and equipment or participate in programs that are designed without consideration for their size, strength, and other limitations.

During their teens, most young people are pleased to find that they can take part successfully in almost all types of physical activities. They are no longer too short, too light, or too weak for most adult activities. Individual human bodies, however, mature at different rates and some young people may become actively involved in demanding sports before they are ready. Until the middle teens, for instance, the ligaments of the joints and the bone-growth centers may be susceptible to serious injury. For this reason, it is often recommended that sports involving violent contact or jumping from heights be avoided until at least the age of 15.

Adolescence is a time for exploration. Young people need to establish their identities and test their capabilities; they do so by participating in clubs, athletics, and social events. They also strive to expand their horizons through involvement in reading, discussion, a variety of hobby activities, dance, music, and art lessons. They strengthen their capabilities and build self-confidence through the acquisition and perfection of the skills required for many games, sports, and extraurban recreation activities. They practice the social graces and learn how to relate to members of the opposite sex during group activities, at parties, and by going out together.

When individuals become workers or college students, their physical capabilities and energy are usually at a peak. Most seek a wide assortment of recreation opportunities and continue to develop various recreation skills. Freedom from parental and social restraints together with control over increasingly large amounts of money make it the age for adventure. Commercial recreation establishments of all kinds provide social opportunities, excitement, and outlets for energy. Participation in strenuous sports, social events, going out with the opposite sex, activities associated with their school or place of work, and travel to distant places are common. Interest in high-risk activities such as motorcycle racing, skiing,

and mountain climbing is at its peak.

Married persons with children often find their recreation patterns disrupted and restricted. Some resent the change from the more glamorous and adventuresome lifestyle they enjoyed as single workers or college students. Others welcome the stable, noncompetitive, and predictable recreation patterns of family life. They appreciate being able to develop close personal relationships with family members and enjoy recreation experiences undertaken as a family unit. Introducing children to various kinds of recreation activities may be both satisfying and challenging (Figure 7.6). Participation in strenuous and high-risk sports gradually decreases; this occurs not only because of the time committed to family activities but also because of increased feelings

of responsibility and decreasing vigor.

On the other hand, skills developed through years of practice make some sports, hobbies, and games even more enjoyable. Mental acuity may be at its height and years of acquired knowledge may have developed a deeper appreciation for the arts. However, a lack of discretionary income may restrict involvement in many types of recreation both during the early years of marriage when money is being used to acquire a house and furnishings as well as later on when the children are going to college. Families in these situations develop recreation participation patterns that focus on the home. Common activities are television-watching, reading, playing games, and gardening. Trips away from home tend to be visits to friends and relatives, to less

Figure 7.6 A father teaches his son to ride a bicycle. Introducing children to new recreation activities can be a challenging but pleasurable experience for parents.

expensive commercial facilities, or to local museums, zoos, shopping centers, parks, and special community events. Visits are also made to parks and other public lands within a half-day's drive for picnicking, swimming, fishing, or camping purposes. Recreation sustains both the individuals separately and the family as a whole during this period in the life cycle that is often challenging and stressful.

Married persons without children and those with children who have become financially independent may find themselves with the best of all worlds. They may possess the same freedom from responsibilities that single adults have as well as the companionship, support, and love of a spouse that married persons with children enjoy. Unlike the elderly, they are more likely to enjoy reasonably good health. Many also have fewer responsibilities and more discretionary income than people in any of the other stages. There are many exceptions, of course, but life during this stage can be a very satisfying time that involves some or all of the recreation experiences of all the other age groups.

Freed from parental and peer-group pressures, members of these special groups can indulge themselves and take part unselfconsciously in activities associated with all age levels. They may have the time and the money to explore many recreation opportunities they missed as children or single adults. They may not be quite as agile or as foolhardy as the younger age groups, but they may be able to afford to take part in some adventurous activities in such a manner that they can avoid most of the risks. It is during this midlife stage that

many people enjoy the pleasures of owning expensive recreation goods such as boats, recreation vehicles, stereos, cameras, and sports equipment; dining at exclusive restaurants; attending concerts and the theater in the best seats; having season tickets to the games of a local sports team; belonging to a private country club; taking a vacation during the winter as well as the summer; and going on fairly frequent get-away weekends to nearby cities or resorts.

Physiological changes that affect recreation participation occur with advancing age. As the human body gets older, it gradually becomes less flexible and endurance is reduced. The effect of diseases and injuries over the years may also restrict involvement in some activities. Arteriosclerosis can lead to the debilitating condition of senility and further limit the ability to participate. However, with improved preventive medicine techniques and remarkable progress in the treatment of disease, large numbers of individuals can look forward to years of comparatively good health in which to enjoy a great variety of recreation activities.

As retirement provides more time, people often have an increased interest in the pursuit of such activities as travel, reading, gardening, hobbies, games, and the enjoyment of newspapers, magazines, radio, and television. Although participation in more strenuous sports may not be feasible for most, there are many activities such as bicycling and swimming that can be undertaken to provide enjoyment and beneficial exercise. For retirees, recreation is often an important factor in maintaining physical and mental capabilities. One of

the toughest struggles facing many older people, especially those living alone, is the battle against loneliness. There is an urgent need to communicate and to be able to share ideas and problems. Community centers can provide opportunities for older people to meet and assuage their feelings of isolation in the sharing of pleasant recreation activities.

Finally, recreation often becomes an important source of comfort and pleasure to the infirm or sick during their later years. Although their ability to participate may be extremely limited, their days may be brightened by a visitor, an interesting book, a social event, or a radio or television program. How these postretirement years are spent, however, is largely determined by factors over which elderly people have little control. They can fight the discriminatory policies and attitudes that threaten their freedom to work or play as they please, but they cannot overcome inadequate pensions and inflation, which, in far too many cases, takes away most of their recreation opportunities and makes it a struggle just to survive.

OTHER PERSONAL CHARACTERISTICS

All men and women are not created equal. There are many personal characteristics and conditions that influence recreation participation besides those associated with sex and age (Table 7.1). As explained earlier, much of the negative impact of these factors on participation is a result of social attitudes or neglect. For example, if society wishes to reduce the effect of differences—such as body size—on

Table 7.1 Effects of Personal Differences and Disabilities on Recreation Participation[a]

Type of Difference or Disability	Difference or Disability: May[b]
Personal Appearance	
— 50 million men, 60 million women, and 10 million children are overweight by a total of 1.4 billion pounds; of these, 65 million are considered obese — 7.3 percent of adult males are under 165 cm (5 ft 5 in.) and 6.8 percent of females are under 152 cm (5 ft) — 3 percent of adults are excessively tall, 193 cm (6 ft 4 in.) for males and 178 cm (5 ft 10 in.) for females — 10 percent of the population is left-handed — 20 million people have physical characteristics that society considers ugly	— influence recreation choices and behavior patterns — interfere with ability to take part in some activities — hinder development of positive self-image, affecting willingness to participate and manner in which one takes part in many kinds of recreation activities, particularly social activities — lead to emotional problems (in the case of obese people, physical ailments) that further limit participation — be psychologically harmful and interfere with good motor-skill development if left-handed individual is forced to become right-handed
Impaired Eyesight	
— 15 million Americans have severe visual impairments — 1.3 million Americans, including 43,000 school-age children, are blind — around 5 percent of all children age three to five have eye defects serious enough to eventually impair eyesight — defective color vision is a problem for 4 percent of males and 0.4 percent of females	— reduce mobility — individual cannot find way in unfamiliar locations without help and should not, or cannot, drive a vehicle, guide a boat, or fly aircraft — make it difficult or impossible to watch television, appreciate scenery or art, play sports, or go hunting or fishing — cause problems with correspondence, reading books, or using cameras — make many hobbies difficult, unsatisfying, frustrating, or impossible — present problems with driving, artistic activities, identifying rock specimens or bird and animal species, and reduce the aesthetic appeal of scenery and works of art
Impaired Hearing	
— 14.5 million Americans suffer some form of hearing disorder — over 2 million Americans, including 246,000 school-age children, are deaf — 36 million adults are afflicted with tinnitus (sensations of sound in the ears)	— cause problems in social situations; hinder or prevent conversations, especially in groups or on the telephone — reduce or remove pleasures of radio, television, films, concerts, plays, lectures, religious services, or dancing — inhibit or prevent aesthetic appreciation of bird songs or other sounds of nature — cause difficulties when playing games that involve calling out scores or instructions (tennis, football) — interfere with enjoyment of many experiences and impede relaxation and sleep
Impaired Manual Dexterity or Mobility	
— afflictions resulting from chronic or prolonged illness, arthritis, rheumatism, cerebral palsy, asthma, anemia, and cardiovascular diseases probably affect 14 percent of all Americans — 30 million people, including 250,000 children, have arthritis — 700,000 persons are afflicted with cerebral palsy	— make individual incapable of caring for self with consequent loss of self-esteem and withdrawal from social contacts — make writing letters, turning the pages of a book, cooking, hobbies, playing musical instruments, and gardening difficult or impossible — mean that strenuous activities are impossible and less arduous activities such as walking, driving, hobbies, table games, or attending sports and social events may also be exhausting, difficult, or impossible — result in children finding that common activities are tiring, frustrating, or beyond their capabilities.

Type of Difference or Disability	Difference or Disability: May[b]
Impaired Intellectual or Emotional Capacity — 3 percent of population is mentally retarded, including 1 million school-age children — 1 million school-age children are learning disabled — 8 million school-age children have severe psychological problems — each year, about 250,000 Americans are so depressed they attempt suicide	— make participation in any type of recreation activity unsatisfactory or impossible if the individual is incapable of participating in a "normal" manner or is experiencing severe emotional problems — result in newspapers and many books, television programs, films, sports, and table games providing little or no pleasure to the individual
Impaired Voice, Speech, or Language — 20 million Americans are affected in some way by stuttering; by loss of speech due to strokes and disease; by speech articulation and voice disorders; by difficulty in developing normal speech patterns (e.g., those who have been profoundly deaf from birth) includes 1 million stutterers and 3.5 million school-age children.	— make individual unable or reluctant to take part in conversations or any activity involving much oral communication (e.g., shopping, drama, singing, debates, social events, citizens band radio, hobby clubs) — reduce self-confidence and lead to avoidance of recreation activities that involve contacts with strangers or large groups of people
Physical Disabilities — 11.5 million Americans are permanently disabled as a result of birth defects, injury, strokes, and other degenerative diseases— includes 500,000 in wheelchairs and 3 million who use canes, braces, crutches, and walkers — the disabled include 3.5 million veterans and 300,000 school-age children — at any given time, some 12.5 million people are temporarily disabled	— cause loss of mobility and restrict or prevent participation in many activities — limit access (particularly for those in wheelchairs) to many recreation resources, facilities, and programs — reduce access to public transportation, further limiting mobility and access to recreation environments — result in loss of independence because of inability to take care of basic needs; inhibit participation in some activities and restrict participation in others to times when the assistance of another person is available
Allergic Reactions — at any given time, 15 percent of Americans may be suffering from an allergic reaction to pollens, foods, stings, cold, etc.; as high as 30 percent may be affected by an allergy at least once in their lifetimes — 50 percent of the population is susceptible to allergic reactions following contact with plants such as poison ivy	— encourage or force individuals to avoid outdoor activities all year or during certain periods if allergic to pollens or other seasonal allergens — result in inability to drive vehicle, attend social events, engage in sports, watch television, read, or concentrate on games and hobbies if sneezing, eye irritation, congestion, itching, or swelling become severe or if using medication that produces drowsiness — mean enjoyment of meals and social events is reduced because person cannot eat seafoods or foods containing chocolate, nuts, eggs, sugar, or milk products — preclude persons allergic to animal danders from having pets
— 2 million people have allergic reactions to insect stings	— prompt susceptible individuals to avoid activities such as gardening and eating outdoors which increase risk of insect stings
— some individuals have an allergic reaction (respiratory problems, faintness, itchiness, hives) to cold temperatures	— forces sufferers to avoid exposure to cold; activities such as swimming, skating, skiing, or hiking in cold weather are unpleasant or dangerous

Table 7.1 Effects of Personal Differences and Disabilities on Recreation Participation[a] (Continued)

Type of Difference or Disability	Difference or Disability: May[b]
Impaired Taste or Smell — afflicts 2 million Americans — affects most people temporarily as result of upper respiratory infections, allergies	— deprive person of most of the pleasures associated with the preparation and consumption of food and drink — prevent enjoyment of the aroma of flowers, perfumes, or seashore or woodland environments — sometimes result in loss of appetite, depression, weight loss, physical deterioration, or a general reduction in zest for living
Oral Problems — fear of dentists, lack of money for dental services, and ignorance about the value of good dental care result in millions of Americans suffering the negative effects of decayed, impacted, or abnormal teeth — 50 percent of Americans over 75 years of age have lost all their teeth	— limit ability to eat or enjoy some favorite foods — reduce self-confidence in social situations, resulting in avoidance of, or rejection by, other people, especially members of the opposite sex — may contribute to health problems that further limit participation
Addiction — 10 million Americans are alcoholics — 1.5 million are drug addicts; includes 400,000 heroin addicts — 5.3 million teenagers have drinking problems; one out of every nine high school seniors are daily marijuana users	— interfere with ability or desire to take part in many activities — increase hazards of activities involving motorized vehicles and equipment or requiring good judgment to avoid dangerous situations (scuba diving, mountain climbing, skiing) — lead to physical ailments, emotional problems, or injuries that further restrict participation

[a] All data is for the United States.
[b] In all these cases, the attitudes and neglect of society have as great an effect on participation as the disability itself. See Chapter 5.
Source: Developed from numerous newspaper and magazine articles, television programs, and government or association reports.

sports and athletic competitions, it can do so by organizing appropriate age and size classes or by making recreation goods adjustable and in a variety of sizes. Even so, there are limits beyond which measures to accommodate differences are not feasible. In a small community, for instance, it will not be possible to form youth sports teams for each age and size group and some compromises will have to be made. The challenge is for organizers of recreation programs to find the compromises that provide the highest levels of satisfaction for the largest proportions of individuals in the community.

The degree to which personal characteristics and conditions affect an individual's participation also depends to a large degree on personal recreation preferences and aspirations. A teenage boy who has always dreamed of becoming a basketball star but stops growing at 165 centimeters (5 feet 6 inches) will probably perceive his height as a constraint. On the other hand, a girl who hoped to be a ballet dancer would probably regard a height of close to 180 centimeters (6 feet) as a handicap. Similarly, an individual whose main pleasure is playing the guitar will be more devastated by the onset of severe

rheumatoid arthritis than someone whose chief delight is watching sports on television.

The normal personal characteristics that may effect an individual's ability to take part in specific recreation activities include differences in height, weight, bone and muscular structure, body proportions, coordination, stamina, memory, imagination, and personality. For instance, height, especially the proportions of leg and torso, can be real assets in such sports as basketball. Weight and body structure can be important factors in wrestling. Shorter, slight individuals may be disadvantaged in both basketball and wrestling but find these characteristics assets in equestrian and spelunking activities. Some individuals are built more rigidly than others and therefore risk injury in gymnastics and wrestling; others are too flexible and frequently suffer dislocations of knees, elbows, and shoulders when they engage in contact sports. A lack of coordination can limit both participation in, and enjoyment of, many recreation activities such as skating, baseball, and painting. Poor memory or an inability to concentrate places individuals at a distinct disadvantage in many team sports, games (such as chess and cards), or activities (such as drama, music, or dance). A rich imagination is an asset in the creative activities of art and writing. Personality traits affect both the individual's choice of recreation and the ability to participate. The position in the family according to birth order may also influence recreation participation. For instance, firstborn and lastborn children are often treated differently and, as a result, they may develop personality traits and recreation preferences not found in the other children.

Some of these factors—height for example—are primarily a matter of inherited characteristics that the individual cannot change to any great extent. Others, such as weight and personality traits can more readily be controlled or modified by the individual. However, such changes may only come about with determined effort and considerable encouragement and support from others. Recreation agencies should be prepared, therefore, to assist people who wish to overcome characteristics of this kind by the provision of sensitive personnel and appropriate programs.

In addition to the normal range of differences in personal characteristics, many people suffer from conditons—both physical and psychological—that may restrict or preclude recreation participation or enjoyment. One of the most serious conditions, both because of its debilitating effects and the sheer numbers of people who are afflicted, is a chronic irrational fear of specific objects, organisms, or situations. These phobias (as such fears are called) affect at least 50 million Americans. Depending on the neurosis, the afflicted individual may be unable to participate in most water-dependent activities, keep a pet or be near certain kinds of animals, travel in an airplane, or take part in any activities involving crowds, public speaking, high places, or confined spaces. Some find participation difficult or impossible if it requires leaving the home environment. Many people feel their excessive fears are unique personal weaknesses rather than common disorders. Consequently, they never discuss their problems with anyone. Instead, they make lame excuses for their behavior and severely limit their opportunities rather than seek the therapy that could help them overcome their phobias.

Severe emotional distress is another common condition that interferes with people's enjoyment of a full spectrum of recreation experiences. According to a recent report by the President's Commission on Mental Health, about 25 percent of Americans suffer severe emotional distress at any one time. Of these, some 15 percent (32 million persons) actually receive treatment for mental problems each year and another 5 percent are estimated to have diagnosable mental illness

needing professional care. Nevertheless, all of the 25 percent are considered to have psychological problems severe enough to impair their lives at least to some extent. Many of these conditions are fortunately temporary in nature and can be successfully treated. Emotional distress is not confined to the adult population. Millions of young people suffer periodically from acute feelings of depression and hopelessness. Between 250,000 and 500,000 attempt to end their lives each year and at least 5000 succeed, making suicide the third most common cause of childhood death.

Similarly, for every 100 persons (excluding those in nursing homes or other institutions), there are 175 short-term acute illnesses or other debilitating conditions every year. Of these, over 50 percent are upper respiratory conditions and about 18 percent are due to injuries. Nearly 20 million people undergo some form of surgery every year. Although these afflictions are not permanent, adult Americans have to restrict their activities for an average of 17 days each year while recovering from their effects; children usually are similarly indisposed for even longer periods of time.

Many other conditions are permanent but can be mitigated through the use of various mechanical aids. For example, over 50 percent of the population in the United States have visual limitations requiring corrective lenses. This condition can be largely overcome if people can afford and are willing to wear glasses. Nevertheless, corrective lenses are frequently an inconvenience when taking part in recreation activities. They are a distinct disadvantage in many hobbies and outdoor activities and are potentially dangerous in some sports. Similarly, more than 14 million individuals have impaired hearing. Many of these conditions can be improved with hearing aids, but they are not effective in every recreation situation.

However, many chronic conditions—including impaired hearing and eyesight—are so serious that they substantially affect people's ability to participate in recreation activities (see Table 7.1). Of course, the impact of these conditions can often be reduced. Drugs control pain, injections mitigate debilitating effects, physical therapy improves motor functions, and technological advances provide helpful mechanical aids. However, such treatments and devices are frequently inaccessible to low-income and older people. Consequently, they may continue to suffer maximum impairment of their recreation environments.

The proportion of the population that suffers from chronic ailments varies considerably from place to place. In many of the poorer nations, malnutrition and disease have resulted in large proportions of the population suffering from physical and mental limitations, even where the majority are young people. Diseases almost unheard of elsewhere afflict people in enormous numbers, for example, malaria (produces fever, chills, headache, weakness, and, in about 10 percent of the cases, death)—150 million cases a year with one-fourth of the adult population of Africa suffering recurrent bouts of the disease; schistosomiasis or snail fever (leads to liver and spleen damage and chronic heart disease)—200 million cases a year; filariasis

(causes swelling and inflammation or blindness)—300 million cases a year. In the more advanced nations, the numbers of persons with disabilities are smaller but still substantial. For example, there are presently more than 47 million people in the United States who suffer from one or more chronic impairments that can affect recreation participation. Of these, 5.6 million (1 out of every 8 persons in this category) are school-age children. And every day, 700 American babies are born with serious birth defects.

The age structure of a community or nation also determines the proportion of the population that is disabled. Obviously, a society that contains a high proportion of older people is likely to have a greater number of persons suffering from permanent disabilities associated with aging. For example, of the 22 million Americans currently over 65 years of age, 1 million are in nursing homes, 1 million are confined to their own homes because of disabilities, and over 2 million need help or have difficulty getting around. About 23 percent of the 7 million elderly individuals (over 75 years of age) are limited in their activities; another 23 percent suffer the effects of heart conditions; and a further 23 percent are affected by hypertension. Arthritis afflicts at least 38 percent of the elderly; 14 percent are in chronic poor health; 30 percent have developed bothersome hearing impairments; 50 percent have lost all their teeth; and of those who have visual disability—about 60 percent—only 15 percent can achieve 20/20 vision even with visual correction. Since the proportion of older people is increasing in the United States, the number and percentage of citizens

with activity limitations such as these will also continue to grow. As a result, the need to provide suitable recreation opportunities for the disabled will become an even greater challenge in the future for recreation professionals and for society as a whole.

CULTURAL AND SUBCULTURAL INFLUENCES

Personal reactions to the influences of culture and subcultures play a significant role in determining recreation behavior. As mentioned earlier, there are some cultural and subcultural influences that are accepted by the great majority of people who are members of such groups. Many other cultural and subcultural influences are not as widely accepted. An individual's decision depends largely on how the advantages or disadvantages of acceptance are perceived.

Some find that the dominant subculture in which they grew up is too confining; they move away from the home environment at the first opportunity and quickly abandon all of the customs and patterns of behavior learned as a part of the subculture. Even so, such individuals usually retain some of the attitudes and perceptions acquired as a child and are still, perhaps subconsciously, influenced by them. Others, who perceive membership in a particular subculture as desirable and beneficial, will continue to respect and adhere to its behavioral guidelines, even if they move away. Many of the subculture's cherished activities and customs may have to be abandoned, however, simply because they are no longer available or feasible. Nevertheless, the subcultural ties remain strong and traditional activities continue to be enjoyed whenever practical. Sometimes the activities of the new environment are adapted to resemble the old ones, and the attitudes of the old subculture still strongly influence the manner in which these individuals participate. Even in modern mobile societies, subcultural influences can remain strong. The degree to which individuals retain or reject the mores and behavioral patterns of the subcultures to which they have been exposed must be considered in recreation planning.

RELIGIOUS AFFILIATIONS

As pointed out in Chapter 5, religious and ideological doctrines have a widespread effect on the nature and availability of recreation opportunities in many societies. Religion and ideology are also important aspects of each individual's personal recreation environment.

In spite of major social changes during the past century, membership in religious groups remains relatively high. Religious affiliation continues to be an important factor in people's use of free time. Of American adults, for example, 40 percent attend church or synagogue services in an average week. More than 130 million people, or over 60 percent of the population, are members of religious organizations to which they donate some $12 billion a year. Figure 7.7 shows the distribution of this membership among various major religious groups in the United States and Canada.

An individual's recreation environment may be substantially affected by a decision to join a religious group or continue a religious

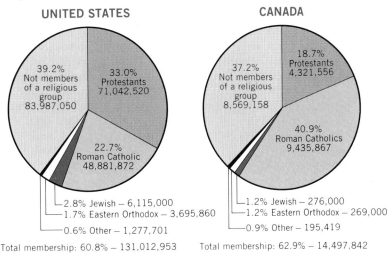

Figure 7.7 **Estimated proportion and number of persons affiliated with various religious groups in the United States and Canada. Membership criteria differ. Catholic and some Protestant churches count all baptized persons, including infants. Other groups count only those who join formally as teenagers or adults.** (Source: **Developed from Constant H. Jacquet, Jr. (ed.),** Yearbook of American and Canadian Churches 1977. **Abingdon, Nashville, Tenn., 1977, pp. 239–243.)**

UNITED STATES

39.2% Not members of a religious group 83,987,050

33.0% Protestants 71,042,520

22.7% Roman Catholic 48,881,872

2.8% Jewish — 6,115,000
1.7% Eastern Orthodox — 3,695,860
0.6% Other — 1,277,701

Total membership: 60.8% — 131,012,953

CANADA

37.2% Not members of a religious group 8,569,158

18.7% Protestants 4,321,556

40.9% Roman Catholics 9,435,867

1.2% Jewish — 276,000
1.2% Eastern Orthodox — 269,000
0.9% Other — 195,419

Total membership: 62.9% — 14,497,842

affiliation begun in childhood. Sometimes this decision is made largely on the basis of personal conviction with only minor external cultural and subcultural influences. Often it involves considerable social pressure from family, friends, and the community in general. And sometimes it is made for social, business, or political reasons.

Whatever the reason for joining, religious-group membership affects an individual's recreation participation in several ways. It may provide recreation opportunities as part of the organization's programs, especially if there are social or athletic facilities. Some people find they have better opportunities for satisfactory social experiences in the company of fellow members; ethnic churches in particular may function

as community centers where members spend most of their free time. Young people wishing to meet compatible members of the opposite sex may also find participation in church activities very helpful.

Membership can also have a limiting effect. Members may choose to abstain from certain activities regarded as undesirable by the religious group. Participation in weekend religious services can take precedence over participation in certain kinds of recreation activities. For instance, an individual who faithfully takes part in weekend services may be unable to become involved on weekends in camping, travel, or other activities such as fishing, hunting, visiting relatives, or skiing at locations requiring more than several hours' travel time. Persons who belong to stricter religious groups that prohibit many types of recreation on the Sabbath may not be able to participate in those activities at all if they are not held on another day when persons are free to participate.

Some members may regard religious observances and other activities of the organization such as fund-raising drives and social events as duties rather than things they really wish to do. Consequently, they derive little or no pleasure from them. Under those circumstances, the time and money devoted to religious-group membership can be said to reduce the time and money that the individual could use for recreation. Obviously, the attitude of the individual toward participation in a religion and adherence to its doctrines is the critical factor determining the effect of membership. People who are happy with their religious affiliations are unlikely to feel recreationally deprived no matter how restrictive the religious ideology may be; they will consider their recreation lifestyle adequate and be content.

The effect of membership in political groups is similar to that of religious-organization membership. Usually the restrictive influence is not as great, but some people spend much time and money on political activities. Political organizations in Communist countries often provide rigid guidelines for desirable recreation patterns of behavior and expect considerable commitments of time and effort to political activities. As in the case of religion, the attitude of the individual determines whether or not such activities have a recreation component and, if so, how proportionally significant it is.

ETHNIC GROUPS

Belonging to a particular ethnic or racial group can affect an individual's recreation potential in several ways. Minority ethnic and racial groups often lack many of the opportunities available to other people in their community or nation. For instance, as a whole, North American Indian, Hispanic, and black citizens in the United States are more poorly educated, housed, and employed than other citizens. Unemployment among blacks is particularly serious; in some locations it is double the rate for whites with more than 60 percent of black teenagers unable to find work. This chronically high rate of joblessness has resulted in the creation of a minority within a minority whose members cluster in big city slums to form a subculture that lives almost without hope in an environment founded on welfare payments, crime, drugs, and alcohol. Individuals born into this subculture become a part of the cycle of deterioration. Many grow up in extreme poverty with no father present, an unemployed mother, and possibly a sister or brother in jail. The world of work is unknown to them and when they graduate from an inadequate school program, often emerging as functional illiterates, their chance to obtain a decent job and escape from the bleak environment that surrounds them is almost nil. As far as recreation opportunities are concerned, they are likely to be severely restricted not only by the lack of income and education but also because there may be few facilities available in the immediate neighborhood. Obviously, in such cases, there are definite advantages to being born into a different ethnic or racial subculture.

Of course, membership in a particular ethnic or racial group can also have many advantages besides those of economic or educational opportunity. Members may have access to a wide variety of recreation experiences and activities, both within the family unit and the community, that outsiders never have. These range from the way family members care for each other and the traditions they share to the social events, cultural programs, and sports activities available at the local church, community center, school, or other commercial facilities. Often there are also special foods, handicrafts, art, literature, music, dances, sports, games, and traditional celebrations that members share with all others of their nationality or race as part of their special cultural heritage.

Members may also inherit certain physical characteristics that tend to occur more frequently among those of a particular racial or ethnic group. Some, such as the debilitating diseases that have been shown to be genetically linked to particular groups and races (Tay-Sachs disease among Jews, sickle cell anemia among blacks) may be completely negative in their effect on the individual's recreation participation. Other inherited differences may present advantages as well as disadvantages. For instance, the fact that orientals are generally somewhat shorter in stature and more lightly built than whites may make basketball or football less attractive as sports choices, at least if the other competitors are whites; but it may also provide better opportunities for orientals to excel in such sports as gymnastics.

Similarly, some scientists attribute physical characteristics associated with race as part of the reason black athletes currently dominate several sports in the United States and are virtually absent in others. There may be some truth in this; a greater proportion of American blacks have lighter trunks, larger builds, larger hands, longer and heavier limb bones, and less body fat. These characteristics are generally advantageous in activities that involve running, jumping, and ball handling such as basketball, baseball, and American football but may be a disadvantage in swimming. However, it should be pointed out there are also social and personal reasons for black athletic excellence that may be of even greater significance. Many minority groups— Irish, Jews, Italians, as well as blacks— have traditionally used the sports and entertainment fields both as a means of escaping from ghettos and as a way of gaining acceptance into the mainstream of society. With opportunities to succeed in trades, business, and the professions largely closed to them, higher proportions of individuals in these minority groups have tended to focus all their energies on achievement in sport, music, comedy, theater, or dance.

Whatever the reasons, there is no doubt that blacks constitute a much larger proportion of some American athletic groups than would be expected, considering they only make up 11 percent of the total population. For instance, 65 percent of the players in the National Basketball Association are black (Figure 7.8) as are 42 percent of the players in the National Football League and 19 percent of those in baseball's Major Leagues. They also dominate intercollegiate athletics with numbers in far greater

Figure 7.8 Maurice Lucas of the Portland Trail Blazers professional basketball team goes up to score against the New York Knicks. More than two-thirds of the players and most of the stars in the National Basketball Association's teams are black.

proportion than the percentage of black students would suggest. Of 30 medals awarded to United States track and field athletes at the Montreal Olympic Games in 1976, 24 were won by black athletes. All the gold medals won by Americans in boxing at these Games were won by blacks. The image of the star athlete in America is increasingly a black image.

So, some black persons as well as individuals from other cultural or subcultural groups may have advantages or disadvantages' depending on the nature of the activity, in which they wish to participate. Be that as it may, it is still largely the individual who decides whether or not to use the advantages or try to overcome the disadvantages.

ADMIRATION AND EMULATION

Another powerful stimulant to participation is admiration for others who undertake certain recreation activities. This can be a very personal feeling and have nothing to do with the urge to gain social status or wealth. Many young people, for instance, start acting like a parent, older brother or sister, other relative, teacher, or friend and begin taking part in some of the activities in which these persons are involved, not for any personal gain, but simply because the young people respect and admire them and hope to be like them someday. Feelings of insecurity and a lack of self-confidence also encourage people— adults as well as children— to emulate the behavior of others. Where the role model is a famous person, however, it is impossible to be sure that at least some dreaming of possible fame and fortune is not mixed with the admiration.

In any event, the wish to emulate admired persons does influence the choice of recreation activity and the way in which an individual participates. For example, the number of young girls enrolled in gymnastics programs in the United States increased more than tenfold in the 1971–1976 period. Those were the years when a succession of young female gymnasts (Cathy Rigby, Olga Korbut, and Nadia Comaneci) were featured on television as they performed and excelled in international competitions.

In addition to athletes, people admire and emulate a wide range of public figures. For instance, the rapid growth of golf in the 1950s was believed, at least partly, to be the result of President Eisenhower's enthusiasm for the game. In Great Britain, the recreation activities of the Royal Family have considerable impact. Film, nightclub, and television personalities as well as singers and musicians often have international influence as their personal beliefs and activities are reported in newspapers and magazines around the world. Sometimes the differences between these performers' public images or performing roles and their private lifestyles are forgotten or confused. Consequently, it may be the glamorous activities they engage in as part of their work or the behavior patterns they assume in one or all of their acting roles that are admired and emulated. In some cases, the emulation of well-known personalities can have negative effects. For instance, Evel Knievel's motorcycle-jumping exploits produced a rash of injuries when imitated by children riding their bicycles.

GOALS AND LIFESTYLES

As they mature, most people develop a series of long-range personal aspirations and goals. However, not all of them will prove practical. Many, due to circumstances beyond the individual's control, will be unattainable. And others will be abandoned from time to time as the individual changes and replaces them with quite different ones.

Some people's goals are primarily focused on recreation. Such goals can exert a lifetime influence on the use of free time and discre-

tionary income as an individual seeks to attain them. These aspirations may range from visiting a number of famous places or climbing a particular mountain to winning a certain athletic event, developing artistic skills, or becoming proficient on one or more musical instruments. Such goals often become a consuming passion to the exclusion of all other recreation pursuits. Some individuals gladly make concessions in choice of occupation, place of residence, and marital status to follow their dream.

A growing number of individuals are adopting such lifestyles; recreation rather than work is their main concern. Some follow a work-play-work lifestyle and consider it a great way to live. Such people may work for six months, save as much as they can, and then take off for a resort area for an uninterrupted period of sunning, sailing, surfing, scuba diving, or skiing. When their money runs out, they seek full-time employment again. Others, in their dedication to certain interests such as the theater, skiing, or exploring the wilderness accept low-paying or menial jobs so that they can live in surroundings where personal involvement is possible year round or, at least, for the duration of a particular season.

More people are compromising on their lifestyles and adopting the work pattern known as job-sharing, or twinning. This involves two workers agreeing to divide one full-time job between them. Sometimes they perform complementary tasks; in other cases, they merely divide the hours. Older people find job-sharing makes it possible to ease gradually into retirement. Handicapped people who find a full-time job a bit too much for them

are able to work halftime. Students can attend school and still earn an income. Job-sharing is especially appealing to parents who find the arrangement allows both wife and husband to pursue a career and share equally in housekeeping and child-rearing responsibilities. For many, however, it is simply a good method of having more time for desired recreation activities and earning enough money to live at the same time.

At the other end of the spectrum are people who choose a particular job as their main goal and central interest in life. All other activities are secondary to this goal and, wherever possible, complementary. For instance, activities may be undertaken that are likely to provide opportunities to meet, become friends with, and impress influential people; to develop and sustain the image of success as perceived for that particular occupation; or to improve work-related skills, build self-assurance and poise, or increase general knowledge.

A fairly representative example of this work-oriented lifestyle is the one followed by many ambitious business executives. Typically, they belong to exclusive country clubs where they play golf or tennis regularly and attend a variety of social functions. They own attractive suburban homes in select neighborhoods and communities where friends and business associates can be graciously entertained around the swimming pool and barbecue area in summer or in the well-equipped bar and gameroom during the winter. They support community organizations such as the local opera guild and college football team and take an active part in religious and service organization affairs. Some attend evening college courses on a fairly regular basis to expand skills and conversational abilities. These activities may provide such persons with considerable enjoyment, but they are nevertheless often perceived as essential parts of a successful executive's lifestyle.

Another increasingly common work-oriented lifestyle occurs when older married women decide to pursue careers. For instance, it is not at all unusual nowadays to find a middle-aged mother and housewife attending evening classes at a high school or college to fulfill her ambition to become professionally qualified in a chosen field. Although she will readily admit that it complicates her life and leaves little free time for anything else, she considers the sacrifices worthwhile. Recreation opportunities for the rest of the family are also reduced, but her husband and children may be very proud of her accomplishments and do everything they can to encourage her to continue with her plans. On their part, this may involve taking on many of the routine household tasks, foregoing some recreation activities, taking part in many other activities without her presence, and making do with less discretionary income because of the costs of babysitting, tuition, books, and transportation.

A large number of American households are living highly work-oriented lives. Besides the business executive and educationally motivated lifestyles mentioned, people who are conscientious doctors, teachers, or other professionals or those who operate family shops, businesses, farms, or resorts often have little time for anything but work. Whether they consider themselves recreationally deprived or not depends on their attitudes toward their work and the satisfactions they receive from it.

Most people's goals are neither completely work oriented nor purely recreation oriented; generally, the goals are a compromise between the desire to enjoy life and the practical demands of earning a living. Neither do most people have well-defined goals. Instead, they live, more or less, on a day-to-day basis, taking advantage of work and recreation opportunities as they come along and patterning their behavior after the lifestyle prevalent in their neighborhood or community.

Until recently, the traditional lifestyle in the United States and other developed nations has been the nuclear family (consisting of two parents and several children) living by themselves in a house or apartment with the husband's earnings supporting the entire household. The general goals of those living this lifestyle have usually been to earn enough to be able to pay for all of the basic needs, to enjoy reasonably good health, to have some children and have them turn out well, and to be well respected in the community.

At one time, most people tended to accept the situation into which they were born along with its associated lifestyle; they aspired to educational levels and types of employment that were not very different from those of their parents or the people in the surrounding neighborhood, and, unless something unusual happened, they remained in the same community or general area. Their recreation lifestyles, too, were quite similar to those they had known as children or were those of current friends, neighbors, or co-workers who shared the same environment. Generally, they expected little change and considered themselves very fortunate if, during their lifetimes, they were able to attain a few privileges that their parents had never enjoyed. A few with special talents, determination, or luck usually managed to break free and change their way of life substantially, but they were the exceptions.

This situation is changing, at least for the people with above-subsistence incomes. Such people are not as resigned to the lifestyle that fate has decreed for them. In growing numbers, they are setting out to make life better for their children; or the children are taking it upon themselves to reject the past and change their futures. Lifestyles that differ from those of parents, community, or the traditional husband-working/wife-at-home/several-children model are being adopted much more widely, and recreation behavior patterns are changing accordingly.

Many more people are choosing to remain single, others are marrying much later in life, and a substantial number are living together without marrying. Both those who marry young and those who wait until they are older are tending to have fewer children. An increasing number are deciding to have no children at all. Because of these changes, the proportion of the population that is free to pursue the activities of youth — playing sports, attending parties, or traveling extensively — is expanding rapidly.

Another major lifestyle change has been the marked increase in the mobility of households. In the United States, mobility reached a peak in the 1950s and 1960s when over 20 percent of the nation's households moved each year. This rate has now declined somewhat, but it is still high. The urge to move is not restricted to young or single adults but is distributed throughout the entire population. Even older people are tending to leave their former neighborhoods following retirement. Many are moving not once but several times as their health or finances change. Some go only a few kilometers to live in an apartment or retirement home in another part of their community. Others travel thousands of kilometers to take up residence in retirement communities or lead a nomad existence after buying a travel trailer in which to live. These various kinds of moves occur for a variety of reasons. Motives for moving include reducing the size of one's residence, being closer to children or grandchildren, having better access to health-care facilities, or living in a more salubrious or safer environment.

For most of the other age groups, moves involve promotions or job changes that in themselves affect established patterns of recreation participation. In many cases, relocation may also mean separation of grown children from their parents and other relatives. When third generation children are involved, there is the added loss of opportunity for the development of mutually beneficial grandparent-grandchildren relationships. Similarly, friendships are interrupted when families move, and, even though new ones may replace them, they never seem quite the same as the ones that were left behind. Sometimes the moves entail a dramatic change of environ-

ment—from rural area to large city, from alpine area to coastal region, or from a cold climate to a warm one. Although such changes are often welcome and, in fact, may have prompted the decision to move, they still have negative as well as positive effects on the recreation opportunities and behavior patterns of each family member. Finally, moves may involve the expenditure of considerable amounts of time and money, both of which might otherwise have been spent on recreation. However, these losses may be immaterial for those who earn a higher salary, work fewer hours, receive a longer paid vacation, or live close to favorite recreation resources as a result of their moves.

People are choosing to make many other kinds of changes in the traditional lifestyle. For example, three of every five wives—28.4 million women—are working full- or part-time. The marriages of four out of ten couples—older people as well as young people—are ending in divorce. Four out of every five of these people are also choosing to marry again. In cases where the new husband and wife both have custody of children from former marriages, the result is a reconstituted family consisting of a number of unrelated young people. Another nontraditional kind of household is being created by couples who have embraced a homosexual lifestyle. A growing number of women are raising children alone and holding down full-time jobs as heads of their households. In some families, the traditional role of the sexes has been reversed and the wife is the principal or even the sole wage earner, whereas the husband assumes most of the household duties

including the care of the children. Older adults, sometimes with families to support, are dropping out of professions they no longer find satisfying and pursuing new careers. This often entails a major change of direction, which involves going back to college and changing almost every aspect of an earlier lifestyle. All of these personally-chosen or family-chosen changes are altering people's recreation environments.

TERRITORIES AND RESIDENCE

The way in which a person perceives surrounding space and chooses locations in which to undertake life's various activities has a substantial impact on recreation. Although such perceptions and choices are conditioned by the environments in which the individual has lived, they are still very personal. Each individual's viewpoint is different and every decision is unique.

TERRITORIES

Most people are highly aware of conditions in the space around them. This awareness results in the establishment of definite territories. Sometimes the boundaries of these territories are expressed in tangible forms such as fences, no-trespassing signs, graffiti, or closed doors. In other situations, there are no visible indications of boundaries. Nevertheless, they still exist in people's minds and a trespasser may cause a sense of uneasiness, a defensive reaction, an expression of hostility, or even an eruption of violence. The extent of these territories depends on a number of factors, including the activities concerned; the ownership of the land or the facility; the culture, personality, and perceptions of the person or persons claiming jurisdiction; and relationships to the persons or people who may seek to invade the territory.

Personal Space. On the smallest scale, everyone has a sense of interpersonal distance, which they consider appropriate and try to maintain in an effort to feel secure and comfortable. This becomes a personal portable space in which an individual lives. At social events, people stand a certain distance apart when talking or they space their chairs at definite intervals when in conversation with one another, depending on the size of their personal boundaries. If others move inside this invisible boundary, the person may feel threatened; on the other hand, if people stay too far beyond it, the individual may feel rejected. The success or failure of interpersonal relationships depends largely on the nature of each individual's personal space, their attitudes toward those who interact with this space, and the manner in which such interaction takes place.

Usually, people are adaptable, adjusting their personal space requirements to changing situations. As the environment becomes more crowded, individuals— although it may make them somewhat uncomfortable to do so— usually reduce the size of their personal space. When situations become overcrowded, most people survive by acting as nonpersons; they lose facial expression, avoid eye or body contact, and keep body movement to a minimum. These adaptions allow people to share crowded buses, elevators, and sidewalks. At concerts, parades, movies, or sports events people may also feel discomfited by

the close proximity of strangers, but they feel less threatened because everyone tends to face the same direction. Once the activity begins, each individual relates to the performers, and, to a large extent, is able to disregard the presence of the other spectators. However, some people are unable to overcome their need for a sizable amount of personal space and, as a result, may forego all recreation activities that require close contact with other persons.

Home Territory. In addition to personal space, most people need some form of home territory. To the majority, it is the room, apartment, or house where they live. Some people seldom leave their home territory and feel most secure there. Others may regard it as little more than a place to sleep, store personal belongings, or pick up mail. Most, however, expect the home territory to provide at least a reasonable amount of protection, privacy, and security to satisfy basic personal needs and to be a suitable site for a number of social functions.

The majority of people in developed societies perceive the home territory as their exclusive domain and resent others invading it without invitation or permission. When sharing living quarters, an individual may regard a particular room, a corner of a room, or certain pieces of furniture as personal territory. A family living in a house often considers the entire yard as well as parts of the adjacent public right-of-way as home territory. Similarly, in the western world, most farmers and other owners of large tracts perceive their properties as private domains. In contrast, the North

American Indian culture was based on the concept that no one could own land and present-day socialist and Communist nations follow policies of partial or complete public ownership.

Recreation participation is affected in many ways by the attitude that home territory is a private domain. Because it is regarded as a no-man's-land between home territories, open space between buildings in urban areas is often underutilized, even in locations where recreation space is lacking. Some people treat nearby public park areas as extensions of their home territories. They resist changes being made in them that they personally dislike or they oppose programs being initiated that are apt to attract outsiders.

Many like to carry the secure feeling obtained from being on home territory with them when they participate in recreation away from home. This is one of the reasons that automobiles, recreation vehicles, and boats are so popular; they function as an extension of the home territory (Figures 7.3 and 10.5). Thus there is no need to leave home psychologically when one sees a movie at a drive-in theater or visits a national park in a trailer.

Even a place to lie on a beach (Figure 9.2), a table at which to sit in a restaurant or library, the area around a campsite at a public park, or a whole valley in a wilderness area may be perceived as an extension of the home territory. If people find it disturbing to share territories with others, the carrying capacity of the resource will be much less than if they are prepared to share. Where farmers and other private landowners have strong territorial feelings, they are likely to prevent rather than encourage use of their property by hunters, hikers, berry-pickers, and others seeking recreation opportunities.

However, although land-use problems do exist at public parks and on private properties, conflicts are surprisingly few. Boundaries on a personal, family, subcultural group, and even national level are maintained to avoid strife rather than promote it. The establishment of territorial rights is a highly successful system of space sharing that allows different individuals, groups, and nations to coexist.

Place of Residence. Selection of residence locations and types are major factors in determining the availability of recreation opportunities. As will be discussed in detail in Part Three, geographic location affects the nature and accessibility of opportunities. Some recreation activities are not universally available because special conditions such as a particular climate or type of topography are required. Other opportunities are unavailable because they have not been provided by private enterprise or government. In some cases, opportunities may exist but be inaccessible because the individual's mobility is limited.

Personal mobility is not just a matter of physical health and the availability of transportation; several psychological components are also involved. There is a bonding mechanism by which an individual's relationship to the home territory is defined. The bond may be with the territory itself, with other persons within it, or with both the territory and the persons. If the bond is very strong, the individual may tend to

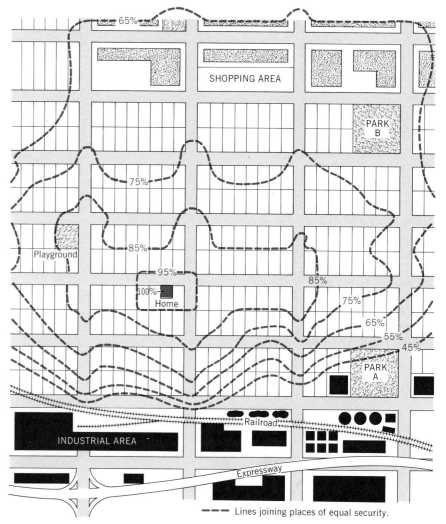

Figure 7.9 **Hypothetical distribution of levels of security around home territory for a family living near an industrial area. Real or imagined dangers or just a feeling of uneasiness can make one area less hospitable than another. Positive experiences and familiarity that result from frequent visits raise feelings of security in the shopping area.**

--- Lines joining places of equal security.

remain close to home. If the bond is primarily to other persons, then the individual may feel quite comfortable exploring areas a long distance from the home territory if accompanied by these persons. Therefore, the distance people can travel from their home territories without feeling insecure depends on the nature and strength of their bonds and on how they perceive the intervening environments.

For example, consider a hypothetical family living in a small city

(Figure 7.9). This family feels 100 percent secure when on home territory inside the residence or in the surrounding yard. The immediate neighborhood is perceived as familiar and hospitable; there is a feeling of joint possession along with the other residents. All members of the family move easily through the neighborhood and feel comfortable when involved in recreation activities there. As geographic distance increases, however, the sense of security decreases. It drops off most rapidly in the direction of an older industrial section to the south. In the opposite direction, an area of stores and small businesses provides a greater feeling of security at the same distance. Consequently, the family is more likely to use Park B than Park A, although the latter is closer to their residence. However, the older teenagers in the family are not as strongly bonded to the home territory. They are more secure at greater distances from the residence and tend to venture farther afield, especially in the company of each other.

Some individuals are so reluctant to go any distance from the home territory they never take a vacation away from the residence, neighborhood, or home community. Many of those who do travel try to reduce the separation from the home territory and the accompanying feeling of isolation as much as possible. They may do this by taking personal belongings that are reminders of home such as family photographs or pets. Often they take relatives or friends. While away, telephone calls, postcards, and letters to relatives, friends, and neighbors can help retain a sense of contact with the home territory. Travel arrangements made through

a local travel agent may also provide a feeling of security. All-inclusive tours, especially if escorted, may help by keeping contacts with the unknown to a minimum. Seeing well-known landmarks that have become familiar through movies, travel brochures, and guidebooks at home can also reduce feelings of strangeness, and make the home territory appear less distant.

In the past, most people had little to say in the location and nature of the home territory to which they became psychologically attached. If their place of birth was a farm, village, or poor urban neighborhood, they were likely to grow up and live there for the rest of their lives. Now an increasing proportion of the population is choosing the neighborhood in which it wishes to live. For many, this has meant moving from the city to the suburbs. One of the advantages often mentioned is the availability of open space and parks; yet even the older children spend most of their time playing around their residences or in the streets rather than in nearby parks or open spaces. The bond to the home territory appears to remain strong even in the more salubrious suburban environment.

Most people's choice of residence location is influenced by their place of employment, the general appearance of a neighborhood, and the type and cost of housing available. Some also take the quality of schools or the proximity of shopping areas into consideration. A few consider recreation as a primary factor in neighborhood selection, for example, some dedicated golfers try to live near a golf course and large-boat owners often seek resi-

dences with river or estuary frontage suitable for mooring their craft. On the other hand, recreation is a growing influence in the selection of the geographic region of residence with significant numbers of people moving to areas that have warmer climates or mountain or seashore recreation opportunities nearby.

When an individual or family chooses a residence location, their future recreation environment and feasible participation patterns have been determined whether or not they are aware of it. If a downtown urban location is chosen, a wide range of commercial and cultural activities are usually available. Good transportation systems may make travel to these amenities and those on the outskirts of the city relatively easy. On the other hand, open space may be scarce and crowded. Participation in activities such as hunting or snowmobiling, which require large areas of relatively undeveloped resources, may be impossible.

If a suburban location is chosen, local commercial and cultural recreation opportunities may be poorly developed, whereas those in the downtown area are too far away to be easily reached. Public parks, sports programs, and indoor recreation facilities may be well developed, but the absence of good public transportation can make it almost impossible to participate without access to an automobile. Recreation involving relatively undeveloped resources in the countryside beyond the suburbs is closer. However, these areas are often crowded, necessitating longer trips for some types of experiences. The larger residential lots of the suburbs and better environmental conditions usually permit added activities on the home territory such as keeping pets, playing games, gardening, sunbathing, or swimming.

At the same time, a general lack of diversity often exists, especially in the newly developed suburbs. This may have an adverse effect. Young people may grow up in a protected, but isolated, environment where they have little contact at home or school with people from different backgrounds. Older people may be nonexistent. Families may be very much alike in age structure, income, and outlook. Even their houses and possessions may lack individuality. As a result, the environment of these young people may be boring and their social lives completely divorced from reality and outside stimulation.

When a rural location is selected, many of the recreation amenities of urban areas can only be enjoyed infrequently. It may be difficult, for example, to take part regularly in organizations such as hobby clubs or cultural groups. Playing on sports teams or borrowing books from a good library may not be feasible. In more remote areas, television and radio reception may be poor or even impossible. On the positive side, the rural resident has easy access to many opportunities associated with undeveloped resources. It may be possible to go fishing, snowmobiling, camping, skiing, or hunting on or very close to the home territory. Lower prices may allow people to buy more land so that they can keep horses or other large pets, grow most of their own fruits and vegetables, build a tennis court, or excavate a swimming, fishing, and boating pond. Many rural residents also find it easy to have large

items of recreation equipment on their land such as motor homes, big boats, workshops, horse trailers, or even light aircraft. Residence-lot sizes and municipal regulations often make this impossible in urban and suburban locations.

The selection of a particular neighborhood within a downtown area, suburb, or rural area also affects participation. In both urban and rural environments, the social attitudes of others already living in the area can be very important. For instance, if the neighbors tend to keep to themselves, newcomers who would like an active neighborhood social life are bound to be disappointed. Similarly, if cliques exist based on race, religion, in-

come, place of employment, recreation interests, or other factors, participation in the social life of the neighborhood may be difficult or impossible. In contrast, many neighborhoods contain a high proportion of friendly people who get along well socially and regularly plan and enjoy a variety of neighborhood recreation events (Figure 7.10).

Although it is difficult for an individual or family to discover some of the social limitations before actually living in a neighborhood, they can usually see most of the physical characteristics fairly easily. Neighborhoods and residences vary in the quality of their environment for sunbathing; enjoying an attractive view; gardening; jogging, bicycling;

Figure 7.10 A cul-de-sac in a California subdivision is an ideal location for a Fourth of July block party. Thirty-three families took part in the celebrations that included a parade and fireworks.

playing in the streets; making use of a playground or park; going for a walk; keeping a car clean; studying nature; having a pet; going to church; buying an evening newspaper, hamburger, or ice cream cone; enjoying peace and quiet; operating an amateur radio transmitter; storing possessions out-of-doors; or sitting on the porch and watching passersby. However, even physical factors change according to time of day, day of the week, or season of the year, and the behavior and attitudes of residents as well as local ordinances can reduce or eliminate opportunities that seemed available on a brief visit to the neighborhood. This often leads to disappointment and frustration when conditions restrict or prevent participation later on.

Type of Residence. The type of shelter in which individuals have to live or choose to live has a substantial impact on their recreation opportunities. The homeless person, whether a wanderer by choice, a poor person who cannot afford the price of a room, someone in military service, or an elderly or sick person who has been placed in an institution or hospital is unable to participate in many common activities. Often they are not able to have any recreation items, except small things they can keep with them. People in institutions, for example, are usually not permitted to have their own plants or pets, radios and television sets are frequently restricted, and, in some cases, even small items such as candy and magazines disappear before they can be enjoyed. Under these circumstances, individuals may have no recreation opportunities except those they can create within

themselves or the few activities provided by the institution. Often, they lose any sense of a home territory; they may be almost totally dispossessed and disadvantaged.

Persons who do have rooms where they can do as they wish are able to participate in a much wider range of activities. There is room for many recreation items from pictures on the walls to a television set in the corner. Friends can be brought home for quiet conversation, a game of cards, a musical session, or maybe a little lovemaking. However, many who rent rooms are faced with restrictions concerning noise, cooking, pets, attaching items to the walls, or the gender and hours of visitors. Those who live in boarding houses find that their recreation participation is influenced by such factors as inflexible meal hours, the times that the house television set or piano may be used, and what kinds of hobbies are permitted. A person's choice of a rented room or boarding house can, therefore, greatly affect the range of available recreation opportunities.

People who rent apartments or houses may also face restrictions. They may not be able to have pets, install an outside television antenna, park a recreation vehicle, or set up a workshop. However, renters usually have the advantage of having to spend far less of their potential recreation time on maintenance work than homeowners. Some modern apartment complexes provide recreation facilities for the use of tenants such as swimming pools, playgrounds, tennis courts, saunas, and club houses with indoor gameroom and meeting-room facilities.

Those who choose to buy a house face a bewildering number of

choices in addition to the question of location. Many of these choices affect recreation participation. If the house is new or older and poorly maintained, it will take time and money to do the necessary development or restorative work. A larger, more expensive house will provide more space for entertaining, hobbies, and games such as table tennis and pool, but the added financial strain may limit the family's ability to buy recreation goods or go on vacation. A large property can provide space for games, sports, picnics, gardening, children's play equipment, and other activities, but it may require so much care that it is difficult to find time to enjoy these advantages.

A two- or three-story house may provide better separation of activities where the family is large and individuals simultaneously expect to enjoy such activities as music practice, reading, playing games, and entertaining friends. People who indulge in workshop hobbies may find homes with basements particularly useful. A multitude of home features can facilitate or enhance recreation. These include patios, which encourage meals out-of-doors; garages and sheds, which provide places to store recreation vehicles, motorcycles, snowmobiles, boats, and other larger pieces of recreation equipment; and balconies and flat roofs, which can be suitable for sunbathing, sitting outside, or growing miniature gardens.

A relatively new option is now available in many parts of the United States and Canada. It is the condominium form of housing, where the resident owns the actual living unit but shares the surrounding land, its features, and the costs of upkeep with the other condominium owners (see p. 342). In this way, the owner is freed from the outside maintenance and development work associated with owning a single-family dwelling but, at the same time, has more room in, and control over, the living unit than is usually the case in apartments. Most of these complexes have communal recreation facilities similar to high-priced apartment projects. A growing number are designed for those who like a particular type of recreation activity such as skiing, golf, boating, tennis, or ocean-beach-oriented recreation (Figure 7.11).

The individual or family can, therefore, enhance or restrict recreation opportunities when selecting a housing unit, picking a neighborhood, or selecting an urban, suburban, or rural location. Perhaps the two most important factors influencing recreation participation that are determined by the selection of a residence location are the amount of personal and communal space that will be available and the degree to which the neighborhood is secure from crime. Adequate space and freedom from fear make many recreation opportunities available to people even in low-income areas.

OCCUPATION

The kind of work that individuals choose affects their recreation participation. Even so, few people in the past have chosen occupations because of the recreation opportunities they permit or encourage. Instead, jobs were selected for the most part to please parents or because they were readily at hand, paid good wages, offered self-satisfaction, or provided status. Today, however, more people in developed societies are making employment-related decisions based on a career's potential for recreation. For example, they may favor jobs that have longer vacations, flexible working hours, company-provided recreation opportunities, or involve locations suitable for preferred recreation activities. Higher educational levels and an increasing proportion of jobs in the tertiary sector (education, finance, health, recreation, repair, retail) permit a larger proportion of employees to make such decisions.

Some try to obtain work that they perceive as being largely or partially recreational — such as jobs in the entertainment, professional

Figure 7.11 **The Lakeway World of Tennis condominium complex near Austin, Texas, is a combined resort and residential development. It is partly owned by the World Championship Tennis organization.**

sports, tourism, resort management, or fisheries and wildlife fields. Often, however, they are disappointed by the competition for the available positions, relatively low incomes, or the large amount of routine office work involved. A small minority manage to find an occupation where most of their working time is spent on activities that they perceive as largely recreational in nature, but even this situation can prove disappointing if there is a lack of variety and challenge.

An increasing number of workers are trying to strike a reasonable balance among salary, working conditions, and free time when selecting an occupation. They look for jobs that provide reasonable rewards but avoid constraints on recreation participation such as evening or weekend shifts. Some seek positions such as teaching, which are seasonal or offer long vacations. Evening or night shifts are sometimes attractive to those who wish to spend much time on such daytime activities as fishing or golfing. Others find the flexitime approach is desirable because it enables them to play a game of tennis or golf when facilities are less crowded or go to work later on the morning following a late-night social or cultural event. Then, there are those who select jobs that have a good potential for overtime so that they can earn more money for recreation goods and vacations.

In some instances, workers are influenced in their selection of a job by other features they perceive as recreationally advantageous. Airline and railroad personnel often regard their travel privileges as recreation fringe benefits. Some people take traveling sales representative jobs partly because of the opportunity to travel and enjoy many recreation opportunities at no cost to themselves. An increasing number of employees choose employment with firms because they provide recreation benefits in the form of company-sponsored sports teams, social events, or recreation facilities (Figure 11.12).

PERSONAL INCOME AND ADVANTAGES

The amount of money an individual or family has to spend after paying for the essentials of life is a major factor controlling recreation participation. It affects all aspects of recreation behavior from the time that can be spent on activities and the recreation resources that can be acquired to the services that can be purchased and the distances that can be traveled. However, there are many people who have personal advantages that are not reflected in their incomes. They have access to opportunities for which they make no direct payment. The nature and extent of their participation may therefore resemble individuals with much higher incomes.

DISCRETIONARY INCOME

Discretionary income is that income left after people pay for what are regarded by their particular culture to be the basic essentials needed to operate an average household. Two households can have the same gross incomes but entirely different discretionary incomes, depending on their respective compositions and obligations. For example, consider two middle-class families with the same gross incomes. Family A consists of the parents and a teenager who plans to continue working for a local firm after graduating from high school. They live in an urban apartment. It is well maintained and the taxes and heat are included in the rent so that the family has few other housing costs. They consider the health insurance, life insurance, and pension programs provided as fringe benefits by the wage earner's company to be adequate and have purchased no additional coverage. They do not own a car and use public transportation to travel around the city.

Family B consists of the parents and three children. They live in a modest suburban house, but their housing costs, including mortgage payments, taxes, utilities, and maintenance are considerably more than those of Family A. Public transportation is poorly developed in their suburb so that a car is regarded as a necessity to travel to work and to go shopping. As a result, their transportation costs are more than twice those of Family A, even though A spends a sizable amount on transportation during their annual vacation. The food and clothing costs for Family B are greater than those for Family A (even though their tastes are simpler and less expensive) because of the two extra children. The two older children are doing well in school and the parents hope that both will go on to college; they are trying to set aside a little money each month to make this dream possible. The wage earner in Family B is self-employed and pays directly for health insurance and retirement. Family B also spends a sizable amount on life insurance premiums because of the responsibility they feel towards the three children. Family B pays somewhat less income taxes than Family A because of the added deductions for extra dependents, house interest, and taxes. Overall, Family A has several thousand dollars more discretionary income each year than Family B. Because of this, Family A can afford to spend more on recreation, both during the year and during an annual vacation.

Sometimes individuals or families have such large financial commitments in comparison to their incomes that they have little or no discretionary income left to use for recreation. Often, the reasons for this are beyond people's control. Some individuals would work if they could, but they are unable to find employment; others have low-paying jobs. As the population ages, a growing number of people are trying to manage on pensions and social security benefits, which provide only a portion of the amount of money they earned before retirement. Inflation, another factor over which people have no control, makes it even harder for people with low incomes to meet their basic expenses. In addition, people frequently have one or more types of external financial obligations that reduce discretionary income such as contributions to the support of relatives, alimony payments, or medical expenses.

But in many cases, the apparent lack of discretionary income is due to decisions people have chosen to make. They choose the kind of housing they will live in, the quantity and quality of furnishings and appliances they will own, the types of transportation they will use, the style of clothing they will wear, the number of children they will have, the educational opportunities they will provide, and the levels of health care and other forms of security they feel will be appropriate.

People who are active members of religious organizations often elect to make substantial contributions to such organizations, especially when funds are being raised for renovations or a new building. Others believe in a variety of causes and charitable organizations and decide to donate considerable sums of money for their support. In many cases, the money they spend is either a completely voluntary expenditure or is far more than would be needed to acquire the essentials. For instance, the home or vehicle may offer much more than basic shelter or transportation. Therefore, at least this unnecessary portion of their costs can be said to be a use of discretionary income.

Whether these decisions and expenditures are also looked upon as recreational depends to a large extent on whether they are made to please oneself. Instead, they may be the result of subtle pressures from relatives, friends, peers, members of an organization, or advertisers. Only the people involved really know. But there are signs that a growing number of people are questioning their motives for living the way they do and are choosing to spend their discretionary income as they see fit, not as is expected of them. For these people, this may mean a condominium, apartment, house trailer, or older house rather than a new single-family dwelling, a less ostentatious automobile, fewer costly (but inessential) appliances and gadgets, and, as a result, they have considerably more money to be used directly on recreation.

PERSONAL ASSETS AND ADVANTAGES

Earnings from current employment or social security and pension payments are not the only assets and sources of wealth that affect recreation participation. Some people may have quite low levels of conventional earnings but enjoy recreation opportunities normally experienced only by those with much higher incomes. For instance, individuals with affluent friends, parents, or other relatives often have considerable advantages. Besides the monetary or material gifts they may be given from time to time, they may also have the periodic use of these people's vacation homes, boats, vehicles, and sporting equipment. People who inherit farms, ranches, or other nonurban lands or who belong to rural families frequently enjoy opportunities that others have to pay for in admission fees or licenses. Much walking, riding, motorcycling, snowmobiling, picnicking, swimming, camping, hunting, fishing, berry-picking, and mushroom-gathering takes place on privately owned land of this nature. Some individuals, who would never be able to afford seasonal homes at today's prices, inherit cottages acquired by relatives 30 or 40 years earlier when land was relatively cheap and construction costs were comparatively low.

Others have personal assets that may not be of direct value recreationally but still increase the potential for recreation. For example, some inherit money, stocks, bonds, or valuable objects, thereby expanding discretionary income. Assets of these kinds may also enable people to select less arduous work, take time off without pay, or retire before they reach normal retirement age.

The individual's or family's ability to manage money is also an important factor, both in the case of the earned income and inherited wealth. Some are able to enjoy more and better recreation opportunities than others in their income group simply because they use their money wisely. By avoiding extravagances and saving their money to buy items on sale or for cash instead of by installments, they make their funds go further. In effect, they increase their discretionary income by practicing good fiscal management.

PERSONAL POSSESSIONS

The kinds of personal possessions people own or can borrow influence their recreation behavior patterns. In fact, recreation interests and skills are often developed because of the availability of certain kinds of recreation equipment rather than as a result of innate desires. Children, in particular, may be disadvantaged by the absence of even the most mundane recreation items. For example, when a six- or seven-year-old boy playing at a new minipark was asked how he liked swimming in the portable swimming pool, which had been there all summer, he replied without hesitation, "Ain't got no swimsuit."

Often there is no need for formal instruction or encouragement; the mere existence of a piece of equipment and the opportunity to use it is enough to spark an interest in a recreation activity. For instance, a child who has access to a saw, hammer, nails, and a variety of wood scraps may become interested and eventually quite skilled in carpentry. This may lead to involvement in related hobbies in adult life. The child who grows up without informal opportunities of this kind is

much less likely to ever participate in such activities. Similarly, the child who lives in an environment that contains a fishing rod, a piano, a garden area and gardening tools, or a football is more likely to become interested in fishing, music, gardening, or playing football. Of course, participation by a parent, relative, or neighbor can, and often does, increase a child's interest in an activity. In some cases, formal or informal instruction is necessary if the child's initial involvement is to be successful and pleasurable rather than frustrating and disappointing. Nevertheless, the chance to choose an activity and then do it on one's own has special appeal. Nothing can replace the thrill of coming across a disused guitar in a storage area and trying to learn how to play a few chords or heading for the backyard or vacant lot with a shovel, some old boards, and a few tools to begin the construction of a fort or tree house.

Whether or not a person has access to a motor vehicle is of major significance to people's recreation environments. If a vehicle is not available and no public transportation serves an area, individuals who live there can only travel as far as they can walk, unless someone with a vehicle offers them a ride. However, possession of an automobile can mean much more than just a convenient source of transportation. This is especially true in the case of older teenage males who are beginning to go out with girls. Having a car at their disposal can provide status, build confidence, and make them more attractive to certain members of the opposite sex, even if the money they have to spend is limited.

The type and condition of a

vehicle is also important because it dictates to some extent the kinds of recreation activities for which it may be used. For example, if the vehicle is old, it may be unwise to use it for an extensive vacation trip. A small car may not carry all the members of a large family plus luggage or camping gear. Some sports cars may have great appeal for recreation driving on good roads but be unsuitable for touring because of a lack of luggage space and a low ground clearance. Small vehicles may have neither the weight nor the power to permit the safe towing of camping trailers or boat trailers. Conventional station wagons offer considerable space but often lack the load-carrying capability and headroom to make them entirely satisfactory for people who wish to sleep in them or carry gear on a roof rack. Many are turning to trucks and vans because of their greater interior space, load-carrying capacity, and durability. Manufacturers have increased the number of special models of trucks and vans they produce as well as the amount of recreation-oriented advertising they buy to capitalize on this growing market (Figure 7.12).

Similarly, people's choices of camping equipment affect where they can go camping and this in turn, often determines what activities can be undertaken. If a large travel trailer or motorhome is chosen, for instance, it may be impossible to travel extensively because of the high cost or the shortage of fuel. Large vehicles of this kind cannot be taken on many rough or narrow backroads and are prohibited on some parkways and park roads and in some campgrounds. They are also difficult or impossible to use or park in many downtown

Figure 7.12 During the 1970s, the proportion of American and Canadian vehicle buyers that selected trucks, vans, and other "work" vehicles in order to use them for recreation grew tremendously. This advertisement capitalizes on that trend by depicting a recreation environment and showing camping and fishing gear in the truck although recreation is not mentioned in the text.

areas. On the other hand, small truck-mounted campers do not use excessive amounts of gasoline and travel easily over most backroads. These vehicles can be used in the majority of campgrounds and often at any convenient location alongside a road or on open land. Truck campers are particularly popular with American and Canadian hunters, fisherpersons, and rockhounds, because they make it possible to reach relatively inaccessible back-country areas and camp comfortably, even if the weather is wet or cold.

There is also a great range of tents— from large family tents that weigh as much as 22.5 kilograms (50 pounds) to one-man, backpacking tents that weigh 2.25 kilograms (5 pounds) or less. The height of a tent, its stability in windy weather, and the water-, wind-, and insect-resistance of its construction, all determine how comfortable an occupant will be under adverse conditions. Sleeping bags used in camping also vary greatly in their weight and insulating qualities. Therefore, the selection of camping equipment involves a number of important decisions that will determine how many can go camping, under what conditions they will remain comfortable, and how far they will be able to carry the equipment.

A person's decision whether or not to have a pet— and, if so, what kind— also has many implications for recreation. Obviously, pets provide much pleasure and companionship, but they also interfere with participation in many activities. For example, some owners move to rural areas so that they can afford sufficient land and have the opportunity to keep a horse; in doing so, they may have to do without some other forms of recreation not only because of the nonurban location in which they have to live but also because of the costs of horse ownership. People who own rambunctious dogs may find gardening impractical, particularly if they fence their yards and let the dogs run free. Unless owners have friends or relatives who will look after their pets while they are away, they may have to place them in kennels at considerable expense or go away for short periods only. If they take their pets with them, they may be unable to stay at many hotels and motels or camp in some parks. Pets can also limit owners' movements between nations because of disease-control regulations.

Reasonably affluent people in the developed nations have many other kinds of possessions that influence their recreation behavior—radios, stereo equipment, cameras, television sets, books, games, musical instruments, hobby materials and craft tools, hunting and fishing equipment, boats, bicycles, various sports equipment, and special clothing and footwear. In fact, some individuals have so many possessions that their care leaves little time for their intended recreation use. Others spend so much money on their purchases or maintenance that they have little or no money left over to pay for the lessons, gasoline, travel expenses, or accessories such as tapes and records, film, and antennas or cable hookups that would make their use possible or far more enjoyable. Some families are going heavily into debt to acquire a vast array of expensive recreation possessions. Many of these same households are also suffering a severe loss of free time as wives take part- or full-time jobs or husbands work overtime or get a second job either to pay their debts or to earn enough money to purchase even more recreation goods and services.

In contrast, poor people, especially those in the developing nations, may have very few recreation possessions. Consequently, the range of recreation opportunities open to them may be quite small. These opportunities generally involve traditional pastimes, for instance, conversation with friends, playing cards, strolling through the village or city, having a drink in the local tavern, singing, or dancing. Under such circumstances, simple possessions such as a few chairs on which to sit in front of a cottage, a pack of cards, some presentable clothes, a homemade musical instrument, or a mongrel dog may bring more joy to their owners than costly and sophisticated possessions bring to the affluent.

TIME AVAILABLE FOR RECREATION

The amount of time a person has available for recreation is another critical controlling factor. It depends on the time required for work; the time devoted to social obligations; the time needed for the bodily necessities such as eating, sleeping, and personal care; and the manner in which the individual perceives and organizes his or her free time. The way in which an individual allocates time between these various functions is called a **time budget.**

WORK LIFESTYLE

In Chapter 4 the influence that the external aspects of a person's occupation—number of hours worked per day and week, particular shift, type of work, holidays—have on recreation were discussed. There are some other aspects of occupation that also affect the time available for recreation that are controlled, at least to some extent, by the individual. For example, the choice of job together with the selection of a place of residence control the amount of time that will be spent each day on traveling to and from work. The time workers devote to travel increased as older downtown residential areas declined and suburbs extended farther into the countryside. Millions of individuals now spend over an hour in work-related travel each day and some 500,000 Americans commute distances of 160 kilometers (100 miles) or more. Some of this time may have recreation value for those who are able to just relax or enjoy a conversation, newspaper, magazine, book, or radio program while traveling. For many, however, it has no recreation potential but instead is merely a boring routine or an emotionally and physically exhausting struggle through heavy traffic. Those who spend two hours in travel each working day are losing approximately one-fifth of their weekly potential recreation time by doing so. Unfortunately, commuting considerable distances to work appears to be widely accepted as a necessity or the price a person must pay for living where they want, and few people strenuously explore possible alternatives.

In an effort to keep ahead of inflation or earn additional discretionary income, increasing numbers of Americans are seeking part- or even full-time employment in addition to their regular work. Multiple jobholding—or moonlighting as it is called—now involves 5 percent (8.7 million) of the total employed. Of these, 20 percent report that they enjoy the second job and find it personally gratifying. Others obtain little personal satisfaction but look forward to the nonessentials that they intend to purchase with the additional income. These workers consider it a good use of free time and are content with the arrangement. The majority of moonlighters, however, feel that the second job is simply an economical necessity—to meet regular expenses or pay off debts—so that they must drive themselves to earn extra money by sacrificing opportunities for rest, relaxation, and recuperation.

People have some control over several other aspects of their occupations that affect the amount of time they have left for recreation. Most employees and self-employed persons decide whether or not they will always work hard, work after hours, take all the vacation time available to them, or stay away when they feel unwell, when weather conditions make travel difficult, or when they have something they would rather do. Decisions of this kind depend to a large extent on how individuals perceive their jobs. This, in turn, is connected to their personalities. When people see their jobs as merely a source of income, take no pride in their work, and feel no responsibility to society or employers, they are likely to come in late, leave early, take days off on the slightest pretext, and loaf as much as possible.

On the other hand, many office workers, teachers, and other professionals work late or take work home with them in the evenings or on weekends. No doubt, some enjoy doing so because they are interested in their work and prefer it to any recreation activity they might otherwise be doing; in fact, the work may *be* their recreation. Others do it only because they feel they must to meet employer expectations, reach goals they have set themselves, secure a promotion, or increase their income. In many cases, however, they do not really have to work after hours. They could achieve the primary goals of their jobs within regular working hours if only they managed their time better. Some are willing to exchange their freedom to do as they wish in the evenings for recreation time while at work. They take extended coffee breaks and lunch hours or spend much time in social conversation in the office or on the telephone. Others allow easy and unessential jobs to occupy much of their normal working hours. Different work habits or a change of job could provide these individuals with more off-the-job free time if they wanted it.

SOCIAL OBLIGATIONS
People usually have a number of social obligations in addition to their occupations. One of every four American adults, for example, commits considerable amounts of time and money to religious groups, fund-raising and volunteer organizations, political activities, parent-teacher associations, youth programs, service clubs, or civic duties and organizations. Although social pressures are often a motivating factor, a desire to belong also encourages people to assume a variety of functions within their communities. Whether or not this involvement is wholly or partly recreational, or entirely duty, is de-termined, of course, by the individual's perceptions of the different obligations and the benefits to be derived from fulfilling them.

In less developed societies, many people—related and unrelated—share their total existence in a complex network of mutual obligations and responsibilities established by custom. It is common for three generations to live, work, and play together in close proximity to other members of the society and with continual concern for each other's welfare. In developed societies, many of these obligations have become primarily a matter of individual conscience and are extensive or limited according to the individual's need and desire to relate to other people.

Obligations to immediate family or friends form the basis for a large proportion of the off-work activities undertaken by many individuals. Some find such experiences thoroughly enjoyable and look upon them as recreation. Others regard them mainly as social duties and perform them with varying degrees of dislike, boredom, or resentment. People who are members of large families and continue to live in the area where most of their relatives reside often find their discretionary time severely limited by various family obligations. Some families turn weekly dinners and the celebration of special holidays throughout the year into fixed rituals. It becomes very difficult for an individual or household to avoid such obligations without giving offense.

Examples of social obligations, common in developed societies, that may or may not be pleasurable but that require the use of discretionary time, are:

- Telephoning, visiting, or writing letters to relatives or friends.
- Husbands and wives helping each other with maintenance of the household.
- Assisting children with their homework or other school projects.
- Taking children, relatives, or friends to school, the doctor's office, a shopping center, another person's house, or other locations.
- Discussing a problem with a relative, neighbor, or friend.
- Making appropriate responses to events such as births, deaths, marriages, illnesses, promotions, and graduations by calling on the telephone, writing letters, ordering flowers, buying and sending gifts, or making personal visits.
- Helping neighbors by loaning tools; assisting with sewing, hobby, construction, or house-repair projects; or minding pets, plants, or gardens while they are away.
- Babysitting for relatives, friends, or neighbors.
- Engaging in recreation activities selected by the family, relatives, or friends that are not preferred by the individual.

THE USE OF DISCRETIONARY TIME

From the earlier discussions of both external and personal occupational and social factors, it is clear that individual time budgets vary greatly. Some individuals who work less than 35 hours a week, live close to their jobs, and have no social obligations may have more than 90 hours of discretionary time each week, much of which can be spent on recreation. The unemployed, young people, retired persons, and the wealthy often have much more. At the other end of the spectrum are hard-working people with two jobs and extensive social obligations who have little or no discretionary

time. Of course, this does not necessarily mean that they are unhappy; they may enjoy their work and their obligations and be perfectly content with their way of life.

For the majority of people in modern societies, however, there are about 50 to 60 hours each week that are not committed to work or nonrecreational social obligations. This means that about one-third of their time is available for discretionary activities *not counting holidays and vacations*. How individuals choose to use these hours is perhaps the most important of all the factors that play a part in determining recreation participation patterns. There are many external influences that can affect an individual's choice, but it is still largely a personal matter.

First, the individual controls, to some extent, the amount of time spent on bodily necessities—sleeping, preparing meals, eating, drinking, washing, shaving, caring for clothing, and dressing. Some people keep these down to an absolute minimum, especially if they have developed an ability to organize so that little time is "wasted." Others are so meticulous in their personal habits or so disorganized that they spend much of their free time on these activities. A few have mastered the art of living in a leisurely manner and of obtaining as much pleasure as possible from all of life's experiences, including the basic everyday routines. But for the majority, most recreation takes place in the time that remains after work, duty, and the bodily necessities have been accommodated.

The manner in which individuals use their remaining free time for recreation depends largely on how they perceive that time and the

uses to which it can be put. These perceptions are often the result of social conditioning (see p. 143), but a growing number of individuals, especially in the United States and Canada, are breaking away from socially acquired behavior patterns and using free time as they see fit. They are taking part in activities when they wish and for as long as they wish instead of adhering to set times or customary schedules. And most important, they are abandoning the active recreation ethic and are exploring inactivity as a viable alternative.

Americans and Canadians who try loafing tend to do so initially on an away-from-home vacation. Usually, they find that adjustment takes several uncomfortable days but gradually the guilty feelings about "wasted time" disappear. From then on, time takes on a new and wonderful dimension and they find themselves thoroughly enjoying the experience of "doing nothing." Often these individuals come back to their daily routines truly refreshed and change their regular recreation patterns of behavior to include some less structured, less demanding, and less active pursuits. They maintain that their recreation is not as purposeful as it was, but it has become more valuable as they begin to see what the word, re-creation, really means.

The length of time available for participation in recreation can also influence the quality of the experience. For growing numbers of people in the developed world, it is not easy to shed the cares and pressures of work and modern living. In fact, there is growing evidence that, to be able to relax, many people now need a longer weekend than the present two days. No doubt, this is partly a result of many individuals having to devote all or part of their Saturdays to shopping, household obligations, or home maintenance. Whatever the reasons, there are indications that the block of uninterrupted free time provided by the four-and-a-half-day or four-day week is more valuable to people psychologically than the shorter daily periods of nonworking time associated with the five-day workweek. The extended vacation is also of increasing importance. For many people, it provides the only period during the year in which they can truly unwind and engage in activities such as hobbies, do-it-yourself projects, and travel without feeling pressed for time or burdened with routine responsibilities.

This finishes the consideration of the factors that influence people's recreation behavior. The next chapter concludes this series of chapters on participation by examining the nature of recreation experiences and patterns of participation.

DISCUSSION TOPICS

1. In what ways do the personalities of people you know correlate with their attitudes regarding various types of recreation?
2. What roles have literacy, language, and the learning of recreation skills played in making recreation opportunities available to you? Would your recreation behavior patterns change appreciably if you were suddenly illiterate?
3. Compare the ways in which membership in subcultural groups has affected your recreation lifestyle with the effects that membership in similar or different subcultural groups have had on the recreation lifestyles of members of your family and other people that you know.
4. What kinds of personal goals and lifestyles do you feel are most likely to give you an optimum recreation lifestyle on a long-term basis?
5. How do work and social obligations affect your recreation opportunities and the opportunities of others with whom you are acquainted? How could you or the other individuals that you mentioned change these work and social obligations so that more desirable recreation lifestyles could be achieved?

FURTHER READINGS

The Psychology of Leisure by John Neulinger published in Springfield, Illinois, by Charles C. Thomas in 1974 includes a more detailed discussion of many personal factors that affect participation.. Chapter 4, "Leisure in the Social-Psychological Context," and Chapter 5, "The Formation of Leisure Attitudes," are particularly pertinent. Max Kaplan's *Leisure: Theory and Policy* contains many references to personal factors. The most important passages are Chapter 4, "Conditions: Objective Aspects of the Individual Situation," and the first part of Chapter 5 "Selections: External, Internal, and Mediating Factors." A useful general discussion of how people view the world around them is Yi-Fu Tuan's *Topophilia: A Study of Environmental Perception, Attitudes, and Values* published in Englewood Cliffs, New Jersey, by Prentice-Hall in 1974.

The *Journal of Leisure Research* and *Society and Leisure* (published by the European Centre for Leisure and Education, Prague, Czechoslovakia) include articles concerning the relationships between specific external or personal factors and participation. Similar articles occasionally appear in a number of other journals, including those published for professionals in geography, landscape architecture, planning, psychiatry, psychology, and sociology.

8

THE NATURE AND EXTENT OF RECREATION PARTICIPATION

The four previous chapters described the main components of recreation environments. This chapter explains how these factors influence people's recreation decisions and discusses the nature of the recreation experience, the magnitude of participation, and the classification of experiences.

Figure 8.1 Spectators at a professional baseball game show emotions ranging from elation to boredom revealing motivations extending from avid support of the home team to accompanying someone else as a duty.

The concept that recreation motivations are influenced by external and personal environmental factors that result in people choosing specific activities was introduced at the beginning of Chapter 7. Recreation researchers and planners are particularly interested in motivations and decisions because they are the key to understanding why people participate in specific activities. If the mechanism by which individuals and groups decide to participate can be understood, then recreation planners and managers will be able to do a better job of providing or helping people find appropriate recreation opportunities. This is especially important when resources become crowded and managers seek ways of diverting people to other activities or locations.

Unfortunately, it is not easy to unravel the process by which an individual decides to participate. Consider the people at the baseball game in Figure 8.1. Although many are probably strong supporters of the home team, a great variety of different factors caused them to be spectators on that particular day. No doubt there are many present who are not season ticketholders and are attending more as a matter of chance. Included in this group would be some who did not want to go to work and felt that seeing the game was better than walking the streets or sitting in a bar. Others may be lonely individuals, especially some of the retirees, who enjoy the social experience as much as, or even more than, the game itself. Some are troubled people who can temporarily forget their worries by becoming emotionally involved in the game. A large number are there because they accompanied an avid fan, but they would probably

choose to do something else if they were in a position to do so. In the case of young couples, neither person may be a strong supporter of the team, but baseball provides a fairly cheap alternative to the traditional movie when inviting someone out for an afternoon or evening.

Even among the regular fans, there are many variations in the process by which individuals decide to go to games. In some families, there is a tradition of supporting the home team. Others become involved because fellow workers are strong supporters and they wish to be accepted by them. In some cases, individuals go because it gives them status. They become local experts on the game and are always ready with a statistic or personal reminiscence whenever the topic of baseball comes up. Then there are some who vicariously participate in the game. Mentally, sometimes almost physically, they pitch, bat, catch, and run as if they were actually playing; it is much more than a spectator sport to them. Obviously then, people attend such games for a variety of reasons, some of which may have very little to do with baseball. A good number of those who live within a reasonable distance might attend even if the event involved a completely different sport or was some type of concert or show.

It is unwise, therefore, to jump to conclusions concerning the reasons for people's participation in a recreation activity. Planners and managers have to be particularly careful that they do not assume everyone has the same perceptions, attitudes, motivations, and preferences. Even where it is possible to interview adequate samples of participants, it is not easy to discover

the true reasons for an individual's taking part. In many cases, a skillful psychologist would find it difficult to pin down the exact reasons, even with the aid of a long, detailed personal interview. One of the major problems involved in investigating the reasons why people participate is the difficulty of readily understanding the nature of the experience for each individual.

THE NATURE OF THE EXPERIENCE

To the casual observer, an individual's participation in an activity may appear to be a simple matter. In reality, however, it is usually complex, consisting of a number of separate *experience phases* that entail various depths of involvement and different degrees of satisfaction.

PHASES OF THE EXPERIENCE

Each recreation experience is composed of 11 phases (Figure 8.2). In some cases, the experience may be relatively simple, take little time, and entail minimal involvement in most, or even all, of the phases. Other experiences are long and complicated processes in which several or all of the phases are well developed and of considerable importance.

Awareness Phase. An experience begins the moment an individual becomes aware that a particular recreation opportunity exists. This awareness may come from many sources, including:

- Growing up in a family where someone takes part.
- Hearing about it from family members, other relatives, friends, coworkers, or fellow students.

- Seeing someone participate—in the community, on television, at the movies, or at a concert, exhibit, or sports event.
- Seeing or hearing the activity mentioned or advertised in newspapers or magazines or on radio or television.
- Becoming aware of the necessary equipment or available facilities at someone's home, while traveling, or at a store or exhibit.
- Reading about the activity in a book, catalog, mailed announcement, or on a poster.

The experience need not proceed beyond this awareness phase immediately. In some cases, the individual will not even consider the possibility of taking part personally. Consequently, awareness may not develop into a decision to participate for many days, weeks, months, or even years.

Initial-Decision Phase. During the initial-decision phase, individuals decide whether or not they would like to participate. The initial decision may be in the form of an immediate reaction on becoming aware of the opportunity. This is often the case with young people who react instinctively when given a chance to take part. Others may think about the opportunity for a long time before making up their minds. The decision may be positive or negative, or the individual may postpone a decision temporarily or indefinitely. Where the postponement is temporary, it is usually a matter of obtaining additional information or advice. Indefinite postponements may be the result of indecisiveness, not having the necessary time or money to take part, or deciding to wait until other circumstances become more favorable.

Exploratory Phase. Even when people decide that they wish to participate, a period of investigation or consultation with others often follows. This may involve obtaining permission from parents or arranging for time off with an employer. Often it is a matter of assembling information, such as where and when to go or what equipment to buy. If the activity cannot be done alone, this phase may involve a search for a suitable partner. If the individual is apprehensive about participating, the explorations may include a search for reassurance, especially from those who have already taken part in the activity.

Sometimes people do not proceed beyond this phase. In some cases, they have no intention or hope of doing so. They write and obtain tourist literature, attend lectures or slide presentations, visit retail outlets to see and discuss certain recreation products, or talk to people who participate in that particular sport, hobby, or activity. Such individuals obtain pleasure from these investigations and enjoy taking part vicariously in the activity. Therefore, what appears to be an exploratory phase is actually the main experience for them.

Final-Decision Phase. Although individuals may hold onto dreams of participating for years, most people make a final decision relatively soon. Sometimes circumstances force them to decide promptly. If someone invites a person to take part in a game or go to a social event, an immediate response may be almost mandatory. Deadlines for ticket sales for a concert or for signing up as a team participant may also make it impossible to postpone a decision.

All of these preliminary phases may provide pleasurable experiences. The exploratory process may be particularly enjoyable, especially if it involves the reading of interesting literature concerning the proposed activity or when it includes demonstrations by people who are pleasant and enthusiastic. The final decision to participate may, in itself, be an exhilarating experience.

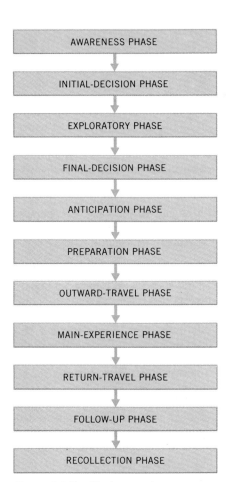

Figure 8.2 The 11 phases of a recreation experience. The length and significance of each phase varies considerably from activity to activity and from individual to individual.

AWARENESS PHASE

INITIAL-DECISION PHASE

EXPLORATORY PHASE

FINAL-DECISION PHASE

ANTICIPATION PHASE

PREPARATION PHASE

OUTWARD-TRAVEL PHASE

MAIN-EXPERIENCE PHASE

RETURN-TRAVEL PHASE

FOLLOW-UP PHASE

RECOLLECTION PHASE

Figure 8.3 **At the spring opening of Cedar Point Amusement Park, Sandusky, Ohio, an excited group of young people run toward the newly installed Giant Wheel so that they will be among the first riders. The ride itself lasted only a few minutes but the anticipation phase may have lasted hours, days, or even many months.**

Anticipation Phase. Anticipation is often an extremely important part of the recreation experience. Children can hardly wait for Christmas and look forward eagerly to its arrival. Teenagers spend hours happily talking about an upcoming social event or rock concert that they plan to attend. They may also discuss possible problems and spend much time wondering what the actual experience will be like. People of all ages become excited about forthcoming vacations. At the same time, however, they may be somewhat apprehensive about certain aspects of the trip. In many cases, the anticipation phase may be as important as the main experience. For instance, thinking about an amusement park ride can be as thrilling as the ride itself (Figure 8.3). Unfortunately, it may lead to disappointment if the experience does not meet these expectations.

The length of the anticipation phase can vary greatly. Sometimes people start reacting to the thought of taking part as soon as they first become aware of an opportunity. Anticipation then continues through all the subsequent phases until participation actually begins. Others try to avoid becoming too enthusiastic during the early stages because of the possibility of disappointment if circumstances prevent participation. Some individuals try to control their apprehensions by thinking about the main experience as little as possible. Others postpone the final decision to participate until the last possible moment to reduce the anticipation phase to a minimum. A few individuals, at least to the casual observer, appear not to experience any of the emotions commonly associated with the anticipation phase. However, looking forward to an event is a very personal matter and no one can ever know exactly how another person feels.

Preparation Phase. Getting ready for many activities appears to be a simple matter, involving little or no physical preparation. Even so, prospective participants may have to prepare themselves psychologically if they are apprehensive about taking part. Some worry about how well they will perform when invited to take part in a social event or in an activity involving skills or requiring physical agility. Preparation for these individuals includes convincing themselves that they will have a reasonable chance of being successful. If they are unable to do this, they will probably change their minds at the last moment and decide not to participate.

Many activities involve considerable physical preparation. Food has to be prepared for social events, family occasions, picnics, and camping trips. Shopping, cleaning, sewing, washing clothes, ironing, repairing equipment, and packing may be included in getting ready for vacations, camping, boating, skiing, birthday parties, or other social events. Planning for the intended activity sometimes involves considerable advance preparation such as engaging a babysitter, making reservations, writing invitations or requests for information, developing an itinerary, obtaining necessary travel or medical documents, or arranging for care of the home.

The preparation phase may provide little or no enjoyment; it can even discourage an individual from participating. This frequently happens when unforeseen circumstances make the preparations more difficult than anticipated. Perhaps the regular babysitter is not available and several telephone calls to other possible sitters prove unsuccessful. Or reaching a bicycle needed for the main experience involves moving a lot of materials piled up in front of it and repairing a leak in the back tire. The individual, in these cases, may simply decide that the necessary preparations are too much bother and give up in disgust. Usually, however, anticipation of the main experience helps a person survive this phase even if it involves a series of unpleasant chores.

On the other hand, the preparation phase may provide great satisfaction or excellent opportunities for social interaction. For example, a person may spend many days repairing a boat in preparation for a summer of sailing, fishing, or waterskiing. The activity may not be an end in itself; yet, the individual takes great pride in the project and is stimulated by the challenges involved. Similarly, preparing food for a family reunion may be most enjoyable if the individual is a good cook and knows from experience that the effort will be appreciated. The activity will be further enhanced if it is done in the company of compatible individuals who have not seen each other for some time. The renewal of friendships and the exchange of gossip then becomes a secondary recreation experience almost as pleasurable as the main experience itself.

Up to this point, the phases that occur *before* any movement toward the activity site takes place have been discussed. For some activities, these preliminary phases may be relatively inconspicuous. For example, a teenager is invited to go on a bike ride by a friend who is passing by on a new bicycle. The individual agrees and leaves immediately with the friend, or so it seems. Nevertheless, all of the preliminary phases have occurred. The awareness phase took place when the invitation was extended. The initial-decision phase consisted of the quick positive response. The exploratory phase involved a glance at a watch to make sure that there was enough time. The time check showed that there was sufficient time, and this permitted the final positive decision to be made. However, no noticeable action occurred to indicate that this had happened. The anticipation phase was not readily apparent either, but both teenagers were inwardly pleased. One looked forward to showing off a new acquisition, the other hoped to be given an opportunity to ride a 10-speed bicycle for the first time. The preparation phase was also minimal. The teenager who had been invited to go on the ride went to the garage, got out a bicycle, took a few seconds to pinch the tires to see that they were adequately inflated, and bent over to tie a shoelace before joining the owner of the new 10-speed bicycle at the bottom of the driveway.

Outward-Travel Phase. The outward-travel phase may be barely noticeable if the activity takes place in or around the participant's residence. In the case of the cyclist mentioned above, it consisted of traveling the short distance between the garage where the bicycle was stored and the street where the friend was waiting. In many other cases, travel to the activity site is a primary component and plays a variety of roles in the total experience.

Finding a means of transportation can be difficult and can be a major consideration in the initial-decision, exploratory, final-decision, and preparation phases. The outward-travel phase may be unpleasant or hazardous. In fact, the likelihood of problems arising in connection with the travel phase can sometimes result in a last-minute decision not to participate. This phase can also be an enjoyable adventure in itself; some may look forward to it as a pleasant secondary recreation experience. And, in the case of tours or cruises, the travel itself can be a major part of the main experience.

Main-Experience Phase.
The main experience can be short or long and may or may not be continuous. Many experiences are broken into segments. Commercial television and radio stations interrupt their programs with advertising, for example. Some athletic events and concerts include periods of little or no activity, which may be frustrating to impatient persons. Nevertheless, interruptions may provide welcome opportunities for social interaction or consuming refreshments, which become secondary activities that are complementary to the main experience. Touring usually involves a series of major and minor experiences interspersed with periods of travel, preparation, and attention to basic bodily needs.

Return-Travel Phase. Travel back to the residence is often a new or altered experience. On longer trips, the return route may be different and prove more interesting or scenic than the outward journey. With the main goal accomplished, return travel may also be a more relaxed, enjoyable activity. Some-

times anticipation of the main experience has been replaced with looking forward to the familiarity and comfort of home. It can be an unhappy phase if the main experience was exceptionally pleasurable and the participants dislike the idea of returning to normal routines. It may also be unpleasant if the main experience proved unsatisfactory because of bad weather, an accident, illness, criminal activity, or poor behavior by someone connected with the experience. Some people have to rush because they leave themselves too little time to get home comfortably. Tiredness sometimes makes people irritable and may turn the homeward journey into a negative experience.

Traveling home is usually less exciting than the outward journey if the same route is followed. However, the use of a different means of transportation may be all that is required to make the return trip memorable. Taking a taxi instead of the subway may provide a much-needed psychological lift. Or, in the case of long-distance travel, returning by air, train, or boat may become an important recreation experience, especially if the individual has not used these means of transportation before. The addition of a new and attractive individual to the group or a change in interpersonal relationships, either during this phase or earlier in the main experience, may prove stimulating. For example, blind dates that turn out well may result in the return-travel phase becoming the main experience as the individuals talk to each other, discover mutual interests, and delight in each other's company on the way home. The outcome of the main experience — if it is good — may also have a positive

effect. The individual or group, during this phase, may actually enjoy a "natural high" as they bask in the afterglow of a successful main experience.

Follow-up Phase. The follow-up phase consists of cleaning up following the experience, getting over any physical effects, recovering from excitement or other psychological reactions, and readjusting to regular routines. For many activities, it is a minor part of the total experience, such as turning off the television set, returning a book to the library, or putting away a game or a piece of sports equipment. Other activities may require a formal expression of appreciation or the care or repair of equipment.

This phase becomes more time consuming and complicated as activities increase in sophistication. Washing dishes and restoring the house to order can be a major task following a large party. Follow-up activities after a long camping trip can last for days. Clothing and bedding has to be washed and put away. Souvenirs must be sorted and films sent for processing. Excess food and cooking equipment must be cleaned up and stored. Accumulated mail has to be processed and a host of personal, family, and social duties resumed. Participants may also have to recover from fatigue, jet lag, sunburn, strained muscles, or perhaps more serious injuries or illnesses.

The follow-up phase is the one most likely to be disliked or dreaded, but it is usually undertaken philosophically as the price that must be paid for the experience. On the other hand, cleanup chores done in the company of others may be quite enjoyable as the highlights of the main experience are recalled and discussed.

Recollection Phase. For many people, the recollection phase is of primary importance. Some value it almost more than the main experience because recollection can continue for months or even years, whereas the experience itself may occupy only a fleeting moment. This is clearly shown by the intensity with which people collect and treasure souvenirs, such as photographs, autographs, specimens (shells, rocks, driftwood), and all sorts of manufactured memorabilia imprinted with the names of personalities, resorts, or landmarks.

Recollection takes a numer of different forms. It may be a purely personal matter if the individual only retains mental images and enjoys recalling them without anyone being aware of it. Others enjoy looking through photographs or souvenirs by themselves. A few keep diaries to assist recall. Many like to involve other people in the process. They talk to others about their experiences, show their photographs and souvenirs to visitors and co-workers, or put on color slide programs for friends and relatives.

Such activities are sometimes more than just a matter of recollection. They may emerge as separate main recreation experiences. For instance, photographers may devote a great deal of time and effort to the processing and displaying of the photographs they took on vacation, rockhounds may spend months creating jewelry out of the rock specimens they collected, and children may enjoy playing with their souvenirs or acting out some of their experiences. The amount of pleasure that is derived from the recollection component depends on the individual.

These, then, are the 11 phases of the recreation experience. The way in which they interact will be discussed further in a later section. The next section examines the decision phases in more detail.

THE DECISION-MAKING PROCESS

The process by which a person decides to take part in a recreation activity is complex. In some situations, the final decision follows the initial decision within a matter of minutes or even seconds. Under other circumstances, years may elapse between the initial and final decisions. Whatever the time span involved, a multitude of influences play a part in the decision. All of the external and personal factors that form the individual's recreation environment are involved. Some factors play a major role, whereas others have only a limited influence.

Motivation. If potential participants are to go through the various preliminary phases of a recreation experience and participate, they first must be stimulated by some form of personal motivation. In some cases, motivation may play a major role in the awareness phase. For instance, individuals who already have some motivation to engage in a particular activity are likely to notice a newspaper advertisement or become aware of a radio or television announcement concerning the activity. Those who do not have such an inner urge may physically "see" or "hear" such advertisements or announcements but fail to receive the message or respond to it.

Motivation is necessary before people can make the initial decision to participate. Individuals who are insufficiently motivated are also less likely to try to overcome problems encountered in the phases leading up to the main experience. Some will not proceed past the exploratory phase, not being sufficiently interested to find out when or how to participate. Many drop out at the preparation stage because the urge to take part is not strong enough to sustain them through the mundane activities involved in getting ready.

Although it is easy to understand the important role of motivation in recreation behavior, it is usually difficult to discover the exact mechanism by which a particular motivation developed. The process is outlined in Figure 8.4. As shown, everyone develops basic life goals in accordance with their personalities, perceptions, and attitudes toward the environment in which they live. While developing these goals, everyone also establishes a general recreation orientation. Some become oriented toward urban — others toward extraurban — recreation. Some develop inclinations toward solitary activities indoors, whereas others gravitate toward group activities that can be enjoyed out-of-doors. Meanwhile, the adoption of basic life goals influences the choice of a recreation lifestyle that may be work oriented, physically active, primarily social, or mostly pleasure seeking. This choice, in turn, leads to the selection of general recreation preferences (sports, social activities, creative pastimes) and also to the formation of more specific recreation goals (meeting new people, having fun, developing certain skills).

The selection of these general

areas of interest— acting within the limits set by the individual's personal characteristics (sex, age, physical condition, and mental and physical abilities) and in accordance with the individual's established general recreation orientation and lifestyle— interacts with past and present stimuli from the external environment to produce recreation motivations. Some of these external influences are general in nature and encourage the adoption of certain patterns of recreation behavior. Examples are the effect of national attitudes concerning the importance of different kinds of activities, cultural experiences, or behavior, and subcultural group orientations toward particular recreation participation patterns.

Other external factors often act as powerful, direct stimuli to participation in one specific activity. Radio, television, newspaper, and magazine features provide many such influences. Advertisers of rec-

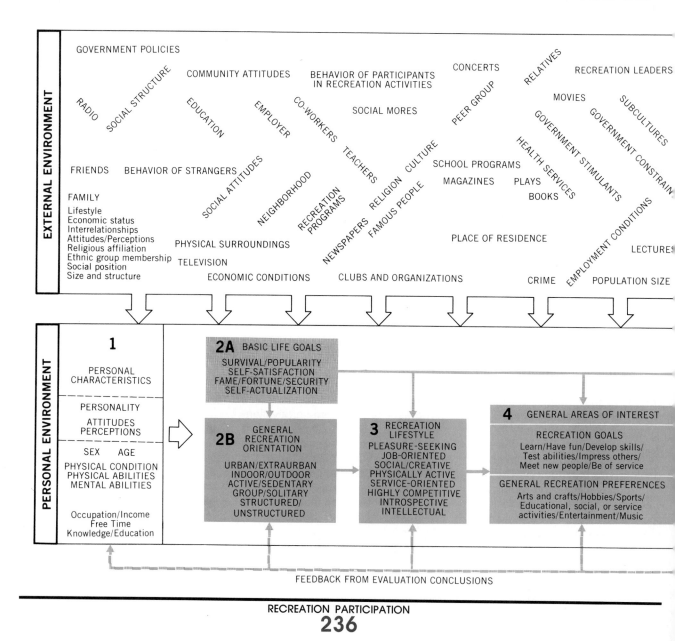

reation goods and services attempt to provide the motivation needed for people to buy their products. Sometimes advertisements contain quite subtle stimuli. Other advertisements leave nothing to chance and try to create a specific motivational thought process in a potential participant's mind (Figure 8.5).

When this system of personal and external stimuli motivates individuals sufficiently to consider participating in recreation, the decision-making process takes place. It occurs when a specific opportunity to participate arises or when, over a period of time, individuals consider the activities in which they might participate if circumstances permit. To understand how individuals decide whether or not to take part in an activity, it is helpful to think of the process as a *decision tree* with four basic stages, as shown in Figure 8.6. The relative importance of each of these stages varies from individual to individual and from situation to situation.

Stage 1: Assessment of Relative Value. When they become aware of a new recreation opportunity, most people first decide how personally valuable taking part in that type of activity would be. In the hypothetical example used in Figure 8.6, the process starts with the announcement that guitar instruction is being added to the program of a neighborhood recreation center. Some individuals immediately dismiss the idea of participating, since it does not fall within their general recreation orientation. Others may briefly regard it as a possibility but reject the idea because other available activities are more likely to satisfy their motivational needs. The remainder feel guitar playing has a higher potential value than other possible activities and decide that they would definitely like to learn to play. Some become excited and deeply committed; they rank the activity far ahead of any other alternatives. Others develop various degrees of commitment, ranging downward to those who are only marginally interested because guitar playing falls near the boundary of their recreation orientation, but they decide to "give it a try."

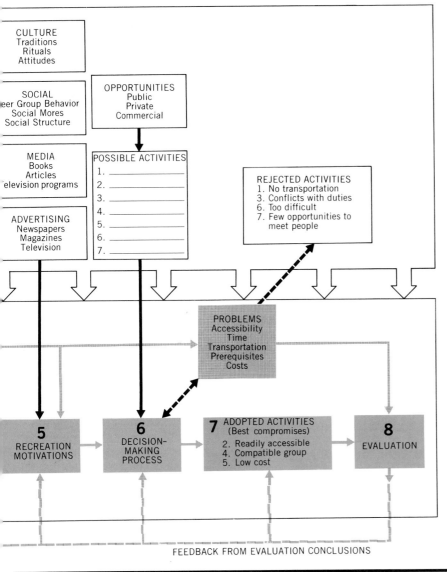

Figure 8.4 Diagram showing the participation process including the development of recreation motivations (Hypothetical).

FEEDBACK FROM EVALUATION CONCLUSIONS

This initial stage in the decision process is a crucial one. People decide on the basis of their existing perceptions of the activity. Sometimes these perceptions are inaccurate. As a result, they either lose the chance of taking part in an activity that could be of value to them or soon become disappointed when the experience does not meet their expectations. This can be most discouraging to professionals who are trying to introduce new recreation activities. In some cases, educational programs may be necessary to make sure that prospective participants understand the nature of the activities to be offered. This is particularly important in situations where people have only one chance to select an activity.

Stage 2: Assessment of Probable Satisfaction. Once people decide that an activity is of more value to them than any of the alternatives, they usually evaluate the offered opportunity. They decide whether or not it is likely to provide the degree of satisfaction necessary to make participation worthwhile. In the case of guitar instruction, some may decide that the program would probably not be a satisfactory experience because the proposed class size might make it difficult to obtain individual help. Thus they assess other methods of learning to play a guitar and conclude that it would be better to enroll in a course offered by their community college or in a class arranged by a local music store.

Stage 3: Assessment of Personal Suitability. Those who arrived at affirmative decisions during the first two stages then normally assess the experience on the basis of how comfortable they are likely to feel if they participate. Personality plays a pivotal role at this stage. Extroverts are unlikely to have any reservations. They expect the instruction classes will be fun because of social interaction opportunities and chances to show off, especially if they have had some previous guitar experience. Shy individuals, on the other hand, will worry about the possibility that they will be uncomfortable. They may

Figure 8.5 Advertisers often try to motivate people to purchase recreation products by providing stimuli that interest individuals with a variety of recreation orientations. This sophisticated Radio Corporation of America advertisement tries to illustrate the need for a portable television set to people in five different subgroups.

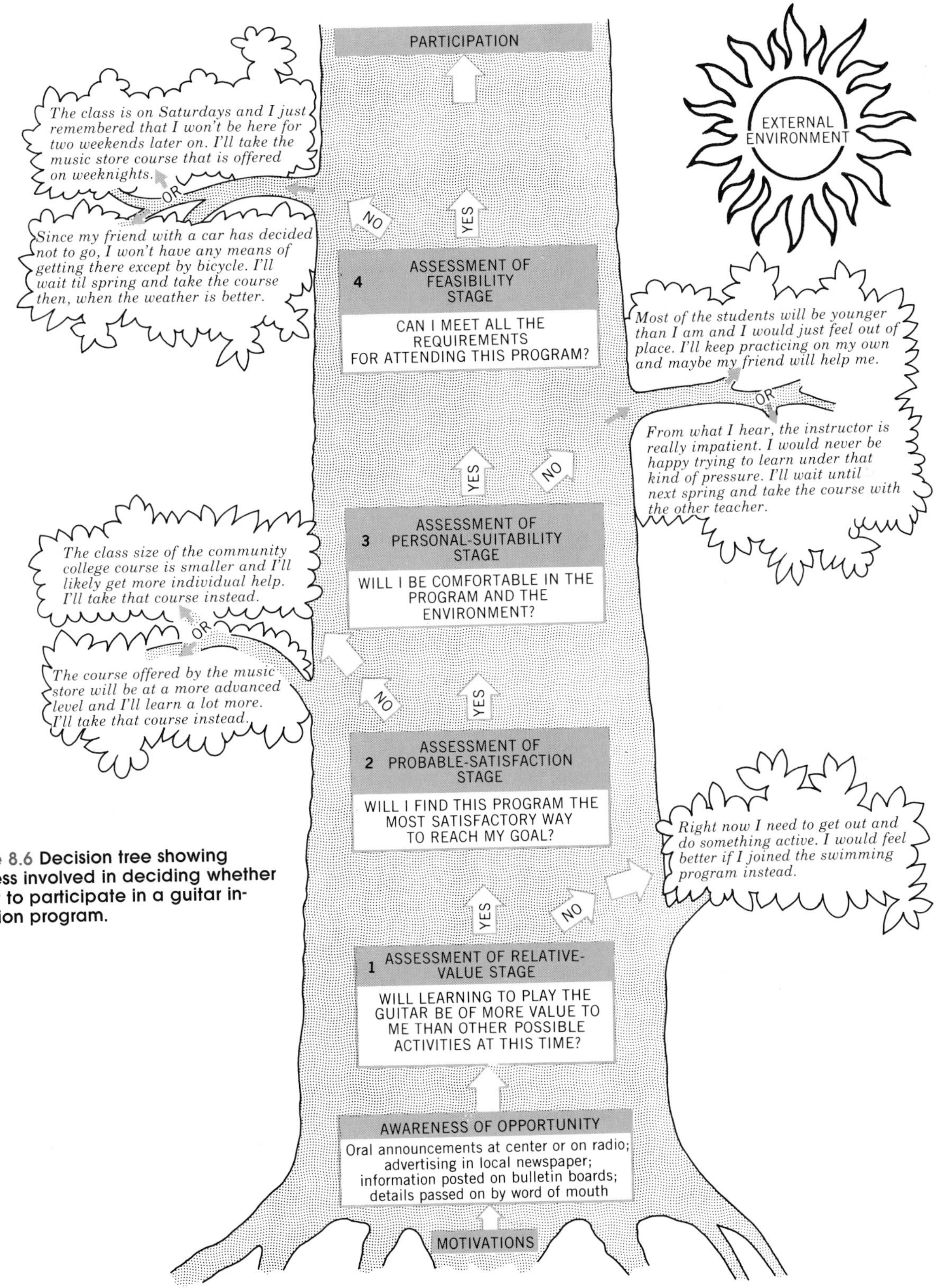

PARTICIPATION

The class is on Saturdays and I just remembered that I won't be here for two weekends later on. I'll take the music store course that is offered on weeknights.

OR

Since my friend with a car has decided not to go, I won't have any means of getting there except by bicycle. I'll wait til spring and take the course then, when the weather is better.

NO   YES

4   ASSESSMENT OF FEASIBILITY STAGE

CAN I MEET ALL THE REQUIREMENTS FOR ATTENDING THIS PROGRAM?

EXTERNAL ENVIRONMENT

Most of the students will be younger than I am and I would just feel out of place. I'll keep practicing on my own and maybe my friend will help me.

OR

From what I hear, the instructor is really impatient. I would never be happy trying to learn under that kind of pressure. I'll wait until next spring and take the course with the other teacher.

YES   NO

3   ASSESSMENT OF PERSONAL-SUITABILITY STAGE

WILL I BE COMFORTABLE IN THE PROGRAM AND THE ENVIRONMENT?

The class size of the community college course is smaller and I'll likely get more individual help. I'll take that course instead.

OR

The course offered by the music store will be at a more advanced level and I'll learn a lot more. I'll take that course instead.

NO   YES

2   ASSESSMENT OF PROBABLE-SATISFACTION STAGE

WILL I FIND THIS PROGRAM THE MOST SATISFACTORY WAY TO REACH MY GOAL?

Right now I need to get out and do something active. I would feel better if I joined the swimming program instead.

YES   NO

1   ASSESSMENT OF RELATIVE-VALUE STAGE

WILL LEARNING TO PLAY THE GUITAR BE OF MORE VALUE TO ME THAN OTHER POSSIBLE ACTIVITIES AT THIS TIME?

AWARENESS OF OPPORTUNITY

Oral announcements at center or on radio; advertising in local newspaper; information posted on bulletin boards; details passed on by word of mouth

MOTIVATIONS

Figure 8.6 Decision tree showing process involved in deciding whether or not to participate in a guitar instruction program.

wonder, for instance, if the instructor will expect each person to play individually and whether or not other class members will ridicule their efforts. Other personality traits may be similarly involved in people's assessment of their personal suitability for the experience.

Stage 4: Assessment of Feasibility. The final stage is an assessment of whether or not the individual can meet all the other requirements necessary for participation. Factors considered may be the time that an opportunity occurs, its cost, transportation availability, and equipment needs. Some people may make affirmative decisions at each of the three earlier stages and then realize that it is impossible for them to take part because of constraints of this type.

Variations in the Process. The four stages described appear to be involved in most participation decisions. However, they need not occur in the exact sequence shown. Generally, the first step has to be the decision regarding the activity's value relative to motivational needs. Following that, however, the sequence may change, depending on the circumstances. For example, a person might decide that the guitar instruction program is of sufficient value to participate and then immediately see that its scheduled time makes participation impossible. Similarly, assessment of personal suitability may occur as the second stage rather than the third.

Frequently, decision making does not take place in a series of four separate stages. Instead, the individual mulls over the main issues and reaches a decision that is more intuitive than carefully reasoned. Sometimes people say that they

"don't feel like taking part" but are unable to give specific reasons. Others do not need time to consider an opportunity; they give an immediate answer. Often such quick decisions are the result of having made the same or similar decisions in the past.

Whatever the process, participation decisions are often very personal. This is because all of the personal factors affecting recreation discussed in Chapter 7 play a part in the process. Some of these factors may appear to dominate when a particular choice is made, but the others still play their part. Personality, perceptions, and attitudes are especially significant. Each person's external recreation environment also plays an important role. It is the ever-present background that molds many of the personal characteristics and provides the context in which each decision is made. Since the combination of personal and external environmental factors is different for each person, the pattern of participation decisions made by each individual is unique. In addition, many of the external environmental factors and personal factors are continually changing. Therefore, participation decision making is a dynamic rather than a static process.

Multiple Alternatives. In many cases, the potential participant does not merely decide between taking part and not taking part. Most people, especially the more affluent, have a number of alternatives from which to choose. Three hypothetical examples that show how the motivational process plays a part in the decision-making process are outlined in Table 8.1. In the first example, the individual

has developed a basic goal of discovering his or her personal capabilities but is oriented away from competitive activities. A strong motivation to take part in a creative activity results in, and is satisfied by, the selection of a woodworking class.

In the second example, a medical checkup convinces the individual of the dangers of being overweight and in poor physical condition. The doctor recommends regular exercise to help control the weight problem and improve general health and life expectancy. Formal exercises are not considered a viable alternative; the thought of doing boring exercises alone and spending additional time at home is uninviting. Instead, the individual resolves to find an activity that requires the necessary physical effort but is fun and can be enjoyed with others. This provides the necessary motivation to consider a number of alternatives and finally begin to swim regularly.

In the third case, the person's basic goal is to regain a feeling of belonging after breaking off a romance and moving to a new community. This goal results in an orientation toward social activities. In turn, this orientation provides motivation to take part in programs involving participants of similar age and interests, many of whom are members of the opposite sex. Membership in a singles club is selected as the alternative most likely to fulfill these needs.

Recreation Choices. By means of this decision-making process, potential participants select alternatives that are perceived as the best compromises under a given set of circumstances. Such choices are frequently called preferences by authors. This word is misleading because participants usually do not have the opportunity to choose from the full spectrum of recreation activities. Often the range of alternatives from which a person selects an activity is limited. The individual may long to explore certain activities but can only choose from a few that are actually available. Of these few, some may not prove to be financially feasible and others will not lie within the physical capabilities of the individual. Even in choosing between the few activities that are feasible, the prospective participant may not select the one that is most preferred; instead, the final choice may be another compromise in which a less desirable activity is selected simply because the activity happens to be the most feasible of the available alternatives. It is therefore a choice from among the feasible activities and not necessarily any indication of what the individual would most prefer to do.

There are several other reasons why participation in an activity should not be considered to indicate a definite preference for that activity over all possible alternatives. In some cases, people are not aware of all the alternatives open to them; these individuals do not have a chance to "prefer" opportunities with which they are not familiar. In other situations, individuals make what appear to be purely recreational choices but are, in fact, partly or entirely motivated by work or duty considerations. For example, a business person may join a club, learn to play golf, or buy a large cabin cruiser primarily to make or enhance business contacts. Similarly, many people only participate in an activity because they feel it is

their social duty to take part. Given a free choice, they would do something quite different. Much holiday travel and the resultant participation in family sightseeing, restaurant meals, picnicking, or camping activities fall into this category. In such cases, participation cannot be considered an indication of personal preference for either a specific recreation activity or location.

Because of these problems, relatively little is known about people's true recreation preferences. Only where in-depth interviews investigate individual motivations and decisions is it possible to begin to understand why certain people take part in particular activities. Most recreation-user studies concentrate on determining the nature and extent of participation rather than investigating motivations and decisions. Since the term, preferences, may tend to create a false impression, the word, *choices,* will be used when indicating activities in which people decide to participate.

THE STRUCTURE OF THE EXPERIENCE

The structure of people's individual recreation experiences varies considerably. Although they may appear to participate in the same activity, their experiences can differ greatly. Unequal amounts of time may be spent on the experience phases. Main and secondary experiences can be combined in a variety of ways. In some cases, work or duty may intermingle with a recreation experience and, in addition, individual levels of involvement may vary greatly.

Combinations of Phases.
The various experience phases are

the basic building blocks from which the total experience is constructed. Individuals or groups create their own unique recreation experiences by combining phases in a multitude of different ways. The length of time devoted to each phase is often regulated to suit the participant. Those who enjoy the anticipation and preparation phases may make their final decisions early so that they can obtain maximum satisfaction from these phases. Conversely, those who dislike getting ready often do a minimum of preparation at the last minute. Similarly, some may allocate much time to the travel, follow-up, or recollection phases, whereas others do not.

Participants also affect the relative impact of each phase through the amount and kind of personal effort that they make. One individual may spend much time preparing for a trip but not obtain commensurate benefits. Another person may take less time but achieve more satisfaction because of greater or better directed efforts. In many cases, knowledge and skill are involved in deciding what amounts of time and effort are needed for each phase. Counseling by recreation professionals or experienced friends can often help people choose appropriate levels of effort for the various phases.

Combinations of Experiences.
In addition to variations in the time and effort devoted to the various phases of an experience, people's recreation behavior differs because of the different ways experiences are combined to form participation patterns. Comparatively few experiences are enjoyed as separate entities. In some cases, the main experience is coupled to sec-

Table 8.1 Hypothetical Examples of the Participation Process for Three Individuals

Steps in Process	Individual ➥ Number 1	Individual ➥ Number 2	Individual ➥ Number 3
1. Personal Characteristics (those that affect current choice of activity)	— Self-sufficient, secure, inquisitive — Single, no nonwork duties — Welcomes constructive relationships but often prefers to be alone — Finds work intellectually satisfying, creatively unfulfilling	— Gregarious, easygoing, nonaggressive nature — Seldom leaves chair in undemanding desk job; has family and home duties — Middle-aged, feeling effects of sedentary life; presently overweight and in poor physical condition	— Somewhat reserved, insecure nature; welcomes support from other people; feels isolated if alone very long — Unable to relate recreationally to older co-workers — Works overtime on weekends for more spending money
2a. Basic Life Goal	— Self-Actualization	— Survival (new goal; result of doctor's warning at checkup) — Self-Satisfaction (original goal)	— Security — Be accepted by others
Creates desire to	— Learn strengths and weaknesses — Explore own capabilities — Realize full potential — Develop individuality — Understand self	— Improve physical condition — Develop stamina — Increase life expectancy — Enjoy pleasurable experiences	— Be loved and needed by someone — Be recognized as important — Achieve reasonable amount of status — Develop a safe, familiar environment
2b. General Recreation Orientation	— Urban, indoor — Solitary, two persons, or small group with similar interests	— Urban or extraurban, depending on circumstances — Group — Outdoor in summer or during vacation; indoor for social events	— Indoor and outdoor; no preference — Urban and extraurban in familiar situations — Social
Tends to be	— Sedentary; unstructured	— Sedentary (must change)	— Active; structured
3. Recreation Lifestyle	— Noncompetitive; self-centered — Highly creative; introspective	— Noncompetitive; pleasure seeking — Social; leisurely	— Noncompetitive; pleasure seeking — Social; physically active
Tends to be	— Somewhat intellectual	— Family oriented	— Conventional
Recreation goals	— Try different experiences — Discover personal interests — Continue activities of interest to full extent of capability	— Have fun — Relax — Be with pleasant people — Do things for and with family	— Be accepted, liked, appreciated, and respected by others — Develop close mutually supportive relationships with a few special people — Feel comfortable in recreation situations
Recreation preferences	— Art, crafts, hobbies, music, reading, creative writing, lectures, exhibits, games like chess and puzzles	— Family outings, social events, club membership, sports events, card parties, camping, fishing, hunting	— Social activities, noncompetitive team sports, membership in organizations, sharing experiences with a friend
External factors	— Announcements of evening college, quasi-public agency, and community recreation programs	— Doctor's warning about health; friend's invitation to jog; possible solution suggested by family	— Co-workers recommend recreation programs at work; notice of youth group meeting in church calendar; newspaper article about singles club

(left margin, rotated:) 4. General Areas of Interest   5. Specific

Table 8.1 Hypothetical Examples of the Participation Process for Three Individuals (Continued)

Steps in Process	Individual ➡ Number 1	Individual ➡ Number 2	Individual ➡ Number 3
Motivating Factors — Personal factors	− Present activities boring; needs challenge − Wishes to try something new − Job unfulfilling at the moment; needs outlet for creativity	− Need to assuage guilt feelings developed from talk with doctor − Real desire to look, feel better − Wants to relieve family's fears	− Need to find young people with similar interests in unfamiliar community, escape feeling of loneliness, meet compatible member of opposite sex with whom to share free time
6. Decision-making Process — Possibilities considered	(1) college − watercolor painting (2) quasi-public − folk guitar (3) community program − woodcarving	(1) with friend − jog in neighborhood (2) with son − tennis in nearby park (3) with spouse − "swim and trim" class	(1) employee bowling, volleyball teams (2) church youth organization program (3) community singles club social events
Advantages	(1) excellent instructor; interesting opportunity and real challenge (2) new, demanding, and exciting experience; cheap way to test interest, ability (3) new activity; held on best night; complements other artistic hobbies	(1) no lessons; can begin right away; will not disrupt schedule; before work with friend (2) group lessons; courts nearby; Saturday mornings; practice possible before work; son will play (3) remembers swimming as fun; class for age-group; can do all year, on outings	(1) easy access; likes bowling and volleyball; friendships with co-workers aided (2) participants of similar age and background; well organized; activities familiar; friendly group (3) social emphasis and smaller special interest groups give chance to meet people and help run events
Disadvantages	(1) does not satisfy desire for different experience; might better continue developing sketching skills (2) at first class discovers group too large, much younger, more eager for good time than skills; teacher well qualified but disorganized (3) not as appealing as guitar; permits little originality − all work on same projects to learn skills	(1) jogging on city streets unpleasant, boring, and dangerous; hard on feet (2) people at lessons competitive and motivated to excel; son plays well and should not play just for exercise; no other practice partner available (3) classes interfere with other activities; indoor pool not appealing; appearance and lack of skills embarrassing	(1) most participants older, married, with other interests; tendency to discuss work, gossip; highly competitive (2) weekend activities conflict with work; group small and most members of opposite sex already involved with someone; must take part in entire program to belong (3) large group somewhat intimidating; few activities of interest except social events; difficult to attend without car
Decision	(1) negative − not sufficiently motivated (2) regretfully negative − take private lessons later (3) positive − format acceptable; will do original work at home	(1) negative − harder than expected; feels ridiculous (2) negative − too competitive and no practice partner available (3) positive − better than expected; may even be fun; more important than cards or club activities it interferes with	(1) negative − feels too young and inadequate (2) negative − may take part in the future if work schedule changes (3) positive − not as comfortable as church group but passable; will try to gain support for desired activities

ondary experiences that form various sequential patterns. In other instances, more than one experience takes place simultaneously. Frequently, sequential and simultaneous patterns are combined.

Sequential patterns often take on the form of rituals, for instance, the typical evening out with dinner at a restaurant followed by a movie, play, or concert and then some refreshments on the way home. Similarly, a family's day at the beach may habitually consist of a stop at a snack bar for ice cream or a soft drink as a secondary experience during the outward-travel phase, a swim on arrival, a picnic lunch, games on the beach, and another swim before departure.

Simultaneous experiences appear to be increasing with advances in technology. People watch television while they eat, drink, or work on hobbies such as knitting. Pleasure driving often includes listening to the car radio. Sometimes more than two activities are attempted simultaneously, for example, people often sunbathe, read a magazine, and play background music on a portable radio at the same time.

Some of the most complex combinations of experiences occur during vacations. A family on an automobile camping trip, for example, may obtain pleasure from a wide variety of activities. During a single day, they may enjoy the following recreation experiences:

- Cooking a pancake breakfast on a campstove.
- Observing small animals, birds, and interesting plants around the campsite.
- Enjoying the countryside as they travel.
- Visiting a famous national historic site, taking photographs, and learning

about the historic event from exhibits.
- Eating a picnic lunch in a nearby town park.
- Playing briefly on the playground equipment at the park.
- Enjoying the countryside again as they continue on their trip.
- Reading pamphlets obtained from the visitor center at the historic site and discussing what had been seen and heard.
- Picking and eating wild berries alongside the road.
- Shopping for groceries and souvenirs in a town.
- Playing with a toy purchased as a souvenir.
- Stopping at a farm to buy eggs and talking to the farm family about their farm and the area.
- Finding a campground, selecting a campsite, and setting up camp.
- Exploring the campground area and talking to other campers about their experiences.
- Building a campfire, eating a meal prepared over the fire, and relaxing with a family singalong until the fire dies down.
- Listening to the unfamiliar night sounds as they fall asleep.

Experience mixtures of this type are commonly a part of family vacations.

In this example, the structure of the day's activities is complicated in a number of ways. Some of the experiences started months ago with the decision to take the trip; the preparation and anticipation phases began at that time. The visit to the historic site and the route taken through the countryside were both preplanned. Other activities such as the berrypicking, use of the playground, and the purchase of souvenirs were undertaken spontaneously. Thus the awareness, initial-decision, exploratory, final-decision, anticipation, and preparation phases took no more than a few minutes.

The length of the main experience varies from two or three minutes in the case of watching animals and birds around the campsite in the morning to several hours when visiting the historic site, viewing the countryside, or reading the pamphlets and discussing the historic events later on in the afternoon. In addition, viewing the countryside, reading the historic materials, partaking in the discussions, eating the berries, and enjoying the souvenirs are activities that overlap and at certain times take place simultaneously. The trip through the countryside is also interrupted periodically by other activities, such as stopping at the farm for eggs. Similarly, the follow-up and recollection phases differ substantially for the various experiences.

An added complication is that individual members of the family perceive and experience each activity differently. This is partly dependent on age, sex, and role in the family group, but it is also a function of personal perceptions, attitudes, motivations, and preferences. Each of the activities will have produced little or no satisfaction for at least one member of the family, and each individual may have found a different activity the most enjoyable experience of the day.

Much recreation participation involves complex mixtures of experiences like those described in the example of the family camping trip. In fact, many people appear to agree with the old adage, "variety is the spice of life," when they select recreation opportunities. This is especially true in the case of families or other groups when it is necessary to try to accommodate the recreation interests of a number of different people. From the wilderness to the urban commercial recreation resource, the most heavily used entities are those that provide a variety of experiences. Examples of facilities of this type are:

- Commercial theme parks that include a variety of rides, animal exhibits, shows, live entertainment, demonstrations, eating places, and souvenir shops.
- Summer resorts that provide swimming, boating, waterskiing, and a range of other opportunities, such as fishing, tennis, golf, restaurants, bars, and live entertainment.
- Major hiking trails that offer a great variety of rolling terrain, scenic views, interesting flora, and other fascinating things to look at.
- Commercial tours that involve visits to several kinds of tourist attractions and include opportunities for a number of different activities each day.

Many of the world's heavily used urban parks (Figure 8.7) are popular because users are able to under-

Figure 8.7 Few urban parks offer a wider range of recreation opportunities than Mexico City's 1050-hectare (2600-acre) Chapultepac park. Three lakes add to its attractiveness and benches, pathways, and rental boats make it possible for people to enjoy these water resources in a variety of ways. Other common activities include picnicking, going to the amusement park, using the playground equipment, visiting museum exhibits, and attending the free concerts, programs, and classes held on Sundays for adults as well as children.

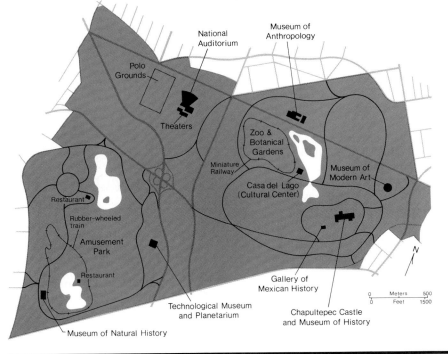

take a variety of activities during their visits.

Multiple-Role Situations. A discussion of recreation experience structure is not complete without mention of situations where a participant fulfills two or more basic human activity roles at the same time. These are of two types. The first, where a single activity is perceived by the participant to fulfill two or more roles, was introduced in Chapter 1. As Figure 1.4 shows, attendance at a religious festival can be partly a religious experience, partly a duty, and partly recreation. Other examples of multiple-role situations are:

- Enjoying the walk or drive to work on a fine spring morning.
- Obtaining pleasure from painting one's room or home.
- Finding some aspects of one's job to be thoroughly enjoyable.
- Visiting relatives as a matter of duty but finding the experience pleasurable.
- Taking part in a required school field trip and enjoying much of the experience.
- Enjoying therapeutic exercises prescribed to overcome a physical disability resulting from an accident.

Often it is difficult, if not impossible, to know how much of an activity that also fulfills a work, duty, religious, or bodily necessity role is actually recreational. Certainly, it makes understanding the structure of some recreation experiences a formidable task. Recreation professionals who direct activity programs should be aware of this problem and understand how individual perceptions of the roles played during participation may affect attitudes and behavior.

The second kind of situation (where participants fulfill two or more roles) is when they perform a nonrecreation activity at the same time as a recreation activity. At one time, little distinction was made between the various aspects of human existence. Gradually, however, the five human roles (Figure 1.3) became largely separate, at least in more industrialized societies, and individuals began to regard recreation as a separate activity. Relieving the monotony of repetitive, arduous tasks by singing or talking continued to be acceptable behavior, but this was condoned mostly because it increased productivity. When the work demanded concentration, however, people were expected to give the task their undivided attention. Today, "mixing business with pleasure" is far more common and many people no longer regard the addition of another activity as a distraction or an indication of disinterest in the job at hand. Even when doing complicated tasks, growing numbers of people see it as an ideal way to cram a little more recreation into their busy lives. Examples include: workers gossiping and joking while on the job, students listening to music on the radio while studying, or people watching television while eating a meal.

The problems associated with people fulfilling more than one role at the same time are of particular concern to those who conduct and interpret recreation surveys. For example, when individuals are asked to record the hours that they spend on recreation activities, some report so many hours of television-watching that it does not seem possible that they do anything else! Further investigation usually reveals that they habitually leave the television set turned on all day as a background for other activities but actually devote little time to viewing as a primary activity. Other persons report a schedule almost devoid of recreation. In reality, however, they may enjoy many recreation experiences but, because no time was set aside exclusively for recreation, they fail to acknowledge its existence.

Multiple-Purpose Trips. Finally, there is the question of *multiple-purpose trips*. This is a major obstacle in measuring the extent and economic impact of tourism. Increasing numbers of people travel for purposes other than recreation but include recreation activities in their itineraries (Figure 8.8). Busi-

Figure 8.8 This Boeing aircraft advertisement in a weekly newsmagazine encourages businesspersons to think in terms of multipurpose trips that involve engaging in recreation in the company of their spouses as a secondary activity. The company wishes to fill more aircraft seats (and hence sell more aircraft) but it is also affecting people's recreation behavior.

ness and professional people take their spouses and sometimes the whole family on business trips or to conventions. People participate in recreation while investigating a job opportunity and living conditions in another locality. Visits to relatives are also commonly incorporated into vacation trips and may or may not be recreational, depending on how the visitor perceives the experience. The structure of these types of experiences is often difficult to investigate properly because it is impossible to find out what proportion of the time and costs should be counted as recreational.

All of these aspects of participation—relative length and importance of each phase, personal involvement in each phase, sequence of experiences, simultaneous experiences, combinations of experiences, multiple-role situations, and multiple-purpose trips—may play a part in determining the nature of an experience. Recreation professionals should keep this in mind as they approach their work, whether it involves research, planning, administration, contact with participants, or maintenance.

EVALUATION OF THE EXPERIENCE

People's evaluations of their recreation experiences play an important role in determining present and future participation patterns. If participants find an experience does not provide expected levels of satisfaction, they will usually reduce or terminate their involvement. In addition, people who have unsatisfactory experiences are likely to be reluctant to take part again and may also discourage others from participating.

Evaluation of an experience takes place in stages. The preparation phase, the outward-travel phase, and the follow-up phase tend to be evaluated as they take place. Then a final judgment is made during the recollection phase, which may continue for several months or even longer. The final evaluation may be altered by the passage of time and the fading of memories or by the effect of later experiences.

Usually, the final evaluation is based on the participant's general level of satisfaction with all phases of the experience. However, there are situations where one event during a single phase can determine the satisfaction level for the entire experience. For example, a couple may enjoy preparing for a party at their home and be delighted with the success of the event. On the following day, however, their satisfaction may fade as they spend hours cleaning up. If the large food stain on the new carpet cannot be removed and a bad cigarette burn is discovered on a cherished coffee table, the entire experience may assume a negative image in their minds. On the other hand, an individual playing in a basketball championship may be extremely disappointed when the team loses the final game but still have a very high level of satisfaction because of an outstanding personal performance.

The level of satisfaction that an experience provides is largely dependent on the expectations of the individual concerned. Some people are easy to please and will be satisfied with an average experience. Others expect much more and will be dissatisfied unless they get it. Expectations are often based on previous experiences as well as the

reputation of a particular opportunity. If people have been accustomed to skiing under ideal conditions in the Rocky Mountains or the Alps, they are unlikely to be completely satisfied with skiing in the Great Lakes area or in Britain.

Some people develop unreasonably high expectations for certain kinds of experiences, particularly special events, such as concerts by famous stars, extended vacations, and visits to well-known national parks or wilderness areas. Such events frequently represent a large emotional investment as well as substantial commitments of time, money, and effort. Consequently, participants develop unrealistic visions of an idyllic experience. They accept the fact that things sometimes go wrong in daily life but somehow expect these special occasions to be perfect. When difficulties do arise, their dream is shattered. Minor problems may seem to be major catastrophes. As a result, individuals tend to overreact, becoming highly emotional and, in some cases, irrational. Even when everything goes well, however, activities have been planned, awaited, and thought about for so long, the actual experience cannot possibly live up to the participants' dreams.

Part of the problem is the unrealistic images of experiences often projected by commercial advertising, tourist literature, magazine photographs, and travel films. All, quite naturally, wish to create a good impression, so only the best is shown. Historic sites, scenic drives, beaches, swimming pools, campgrounds, and restaurants are usually depicted with one or two groups of users enjoying an ideal experience in immaculately maintained surroundings. Pictures of national

Figure 8.9 People often develop unrealistic expectations because rosy images presented by the media or promotional materials do not reflect reality. The upper view of Dovedale Gorge in the Peak District National Park (one of Great Britain's most famous scenic locations) is the cover photograph from a commercially published booklet called the Dovedale Guide. Similar pictures frequently appear in magazines and tourist literature. The lower photograph shows the gorge as most people see it complete with crowded pathways, refreshment stands in operation, and so many people trying to cross the stepping stones it is difficult to stop the flow and go in the other direction.

parks and wilderness areas often show few or no users at all (Figure 8.9). Many vacationers, commercial tour participants, and wilderness users, therefore, do not anticipate traffic jams, overflowing parking areas, poorly maintained and overcrowded picnic areas and visitor centers, packed campgrounds, long lines at restaurants, or numerous hikers on wilderness trails. No doubt they feel that the truth-in-advertising laws ought to be extended to include the promotion of recreation opportunities.

Satisfaction can also be affected by a person's state of mind.

Individuals who are harassed or depressed may find it impossible to enjoy an experience of any kind; yet, unfortunately, they are the very people who most need to do so. Conversely, individuals who are happy and relaxed are likely to be able to enjoy themselves, at least to some extent, in almost any kind of recreation situation.

Conclusions concerning different aspects of the experience are fed back into various phases of the participation process (Figure 8.4). The feedback may go only as far as one of the decision-making stages if the conclusion concerns the relative

value, satisfaction, suitability, or feasibility of a specific activity. However, if the participant concludes that a whole grouping of activities will not provide satisfactory experiences, the feedback may cause a change in the individual's general recreation orientation. In some cases, the impact of participation may be so great that it results in an alteration of basic life goals or even basic attitudes and perceptions. However, such far-reaching changes usually occur only after a number of similar experiences confirm an initial impression regarding a particular group of activities or a certain recreation orientation.

THE QUALITY EXPERIENCE

Although there are sometimes considerable differences among individuals' expectations and reality, many enjoy what they perceive to be *quality experiences.* Activities that are undertaken spontaneously for sheer fun are most often remembered as quality experiences. Such activities are usually an end in themselves and involve no pressures, ulterior motives, long-term goals, or preconceived expectations.

People who most frequently enjoy quality experiences are those who have the perceptions and attitudes necessary to grasp such opportunities wherever and whenever they occur. Children and teenagers often have this knack. Young persons interested in nature study, for instance, can enjoy almost wilderness-type experiences in vacant lots or along open drainage ditches right in their own neighborhoods. Engrossed in their own observations of plant and animal life, they do not seem to notice nearby houses, power lines, passing cars, or even

the trash at the site. In fact, in some ways, these areas may be preferable to wilderness environments because they are accessible and can be visited and explored in a leisurely fashion during all four seasons of the year.

It is important, therefore, to avoid thinking that unique remote environments, superlative facilities, or internationally famous artists are prerequisites for quality experiences. The demand for such resources often exceeds the supply. In addition, energy shortages are aggravating the problem in the case of unique resources located in or near urban centers. Therefore, every effort should be made to provide quality experiences in or close to people's home environments. Both public and private providers of recreation experiences can help accomplish this goal by striving to turn neighborhood recreation opportunities into high-quality experiences.

For some individuals, it is the element of surprise that sets one experience apart from another—a surprise birthday party, the chance meeting with an old friend during attendance at a social event, or the unexpected sighting of a particular plant, bird, or animal during a camping trip. Winning a game may be a great thrill to a novice chess or tennis player. Creative activities can produce quality experiences, whether the projects are commonplace or quite spectacular. Painting a car may be highly rewarding to one individual, whereas painting a beautiful landscape picture is an everyday occurrence to another. Growing magnificent orchids in a greenhouse may be less satisfying for one person than producing a few vegetables on a va-

cant lot in the inner city is for another. The joy comes from the attitude of the participant rather than the nature, rarity, or expense of the resources involved.

The quality of an experience is seldom based on the time that it occupies. Appreciating the beauty of a particular scene may take only a moment but may be remembered for months or even years. Nevertheless, having enough time for an activity can be important. A person who cannot complete an activity because of insufficient time may become frustrated and feel that the whole experience has been spoiled. Just having enough time to take it easy while on vacation may turn the simple pleasures of sleeping late and loafing into memorable experiences.

Since recreation enjoyment is such a personal matter and depends on so many factors, it is not feasible to draw up a set of precise specifications for a quality recreation experience. However, it is evident that individuals are most likely to enjoy a good number of quality experiences if their recreation lifestyles include the following features:

- Sufficient and appropriately distributed free time to permit total involvement, relaxation, and enjoyment of the selected experiences.
- Emphasis on relaxed enjoyment of one or a few activities at any one time rather than a rush to experience many different activities or repeat one kind of activity as often as possible in the available time.
- Selection of a well-balanced recreation lifestyle drawn from several of the main types of activity groupings— social, physical, cultural, creative, exciting, relaxing, and entertaining activities.
- Cultivation of the curiosity, desire, and courage needed to stimulate and

enable the individual to try new activities, meet new people, explore new places, consider and accept new ideas, and increase awareness, knowledge, and skills.

- Development and retention of positive attitudes that give people, places, programs, and recreation activities a chance to prove their worth.
- An openness that enables an individual not only to love and help others but also to accept affection and support.

In addition, a philosophic approach to life that fosters reasonable expectations and encourages the participant to get the most out of each recreation opportunity favors high-quality experiences.

Obviously, the characteristics and attitudes of prospective participants play major roles in the search for quality recreation experiences. However, it is the privilege and responsibility of parents, teachers, friends, recreation professionals, governments at all levels, performers, operators of recreation facilities, and providers of recreation equipment to create the best possible environment in which an individual may seek and, hopefully, find such experiences.

PARTICIPATION PATTERNS

Although the external and personal factors affecting participation vary from individual to individual and produce motivations and choices that are highly personal, recognizable *participation patterns* emerge because substantial numbers of people take part in approximately the same way. Recreation planners, administrators, and managers must have a basic understanding of these patterns so that they can provide appropriate opportunities. They also

need to know how participation patterns are changing so that facilities suitable for people's future needs may be planned in advance.

PARTICIPATION-DATA PROBLEMS

Unfortunately, it is not easy to carry out reliable recreation surveys. Quite large numbers of people must be asked many detailed questions if accurate information on numerous recreation activities is to be obtained. This is an expensive proposition. As a result, comparatively few detailed surveys are performed on a national or regional scale. Consequently, reliable quantitative information on recreation participation patterns for nations or regions is scarce. Often the only available information is many years old and may no longer be applicable because of rapidly changing conditions.

In some places, smaller units of government such as states, provinces, and counties have made quite frequent recreation surveys. Such studies often provide valuable information on behavior patterns, but they must be used cautiously. Usually, their findings are only valid for the population and area included in the survey. For instance, some locations have an above-average supply of recreation resources, residents take advantage of the high accessibility of opportunities, and, as a result, participation is higher than elsewhere. This is true in the case of states such as Michigan and Minnesota. They have boating participation rates that are about twice the United States national average because of the ready accessibility of large areas of boatable water. Obviously, it would be

erroneous to use the national rates for Michigan and Minnesota or vice versa.

There are also problems in interpreting the data included in many recreation survey reports. For example, reports frequently contain tables that show the numbers of hours or the percentages of people's time that are spent participating in various forms of "outdoor recreation." At first sight, it appears possible to compare the values contained in tables of this kind for different nations, states, provinces, or other geographic units. Unfortunately, investigation usually shows that the values cannot be compared because different survey methods were used. Often the activities included are not defined in the same manner, and the key questions are asked differently, thus making comparisons invalid.

Finally, there are no reliable international, national, or large-scale regional studies that have investigated all types of recreation participation in detail. Most surveys focus on a single activity, such as camping, boating, or hunting, or on one of the following four topics: "outdoor recreation" (usually excluding outdoor activities in urban environments); tourism (especially its economic impact); the use of local government parks and recreation programs; or time-budget studies. This last kind of survey requires people to keep diaries that show how much time they spend on all types of daily activities. Such studies can provide good information concerning the time people devote to recreation, but they are expensive and difficult to administer on a large scale. In addition, it is also usually impractical to obtain detailed data concerning the types of recreation activities undertaken at various locations.

Therefore, when reading statistics on recreation participation patterns, it is important to know the following facts concerning the data to interpret them correctly:

- The year in which the data were collected; often five or more years elapse between the time a survey is conducted and publication of the data so that significant changes may have occurred in the interim.
- The dates and conditions under which the survey was conducted; some data may only be representative of short periods (such as the summer months) and differ considerably from year-round information.
- The exact nature of the population represented by the information; often data are only representative of segments of populations, for instance, a sample of students in a physical education and recreation class does not represent all students or information obtained from campers using public parks and forests is unlikely to be identical to information obtained from those who usually camp at private facilities.
- The definitional boundaries that were explicitly set or implied by the study procedures; the respondent, researcher, and reader definitions of terms such as recreation, leisure, outdoor recreation, neighborhood, pleasure-driving, and hiking may differ considerably. This may lead the researcher to misinterpret the responses or the reader to misinterpret the final data.
- The definition of any units used in the survey or analysis; a visitor-day, for example, may be counted as a total of 24 hours of actual use in one case or as a total of four quarter days of varying lengths in another study.

Surveys can also be biased by the wording of questions and by the manner and order in which they are asked. In addition, respondents do not necessarily give accurate information, especially if they sense an opportunity to please an interviewer or if the question concerns a topic (such as the number of hours spent in drinking establishments) that involves social mores. Unfortunately, the casual reader is usually unable to detect such problems.

RECREATION TIME-BUDGETS

When visualizing recreation participation patterns in the United States, Canada, and many of the other developed nations, it is tempting to think primarily in terms of the millions of people who visit national parks, crowd into state or provincial parks, or go hunting, thereby getting the impression that most recreation takes place at extraurban locations. Nothing could be further from the truth. Although the number of people taking part in extraurban recreation has increased substantially, such participation is only a small fraction of total participation. The majority of recreation experiences still occur in or near the participant's home. However, since most of these experiences take place on private land, they are difficult to measure and no public agency regularly gathers such information.

Multinational Time-Budget Study. The only major study that makes it possible to compare the use of time for recreation in a number of different cultural, political, and economic situations is the Multinational Comparative Time-Budget Research Project carried out in the middle 1960s.[1] Household

[1] Alexander Szalai (ed.), *The Use of Time: Daily Activities of Urban and Suburban Populations in Twelve Countries,* Mouton, The Hague, 1972.

interviews were conducted in 12 nations—the United States, 3 countries in Western Europe, the Soviet Union, 6 countries in Eastern Europe, as well as Peru in South America. A total of 27,860 time-budgets were obtained for sample days in the lives of people who were members of urban or suburban households. Only households that contained at least one adult between 18 and 65 years of age and that had at least one member working in a nonagricultural job were included. The majority of the households sampled were located in medium-sized industrial cities. The data are not representative, therefore, of the total population of each of the 12 nations but should be typical of a large, growing, and influential portion of people in these nations.

Although the multinational time-budget study is more than 10 years old and does not include every segment of the populations sampled, it provides useful insights into people's use of time for recreation. It is still relevant because time distribution among work, personal needs, and the other main time-budget categories has probably changed comparatively little for people living in industrial cities of the type investigated in the study.[2] Such persons now comprise even larger proportions of these nation's populations. The survey data also shows the differences in recreation behavior among homemakers, employed women, and employed

[2] Robinson's comparison of the American data in the multinational study with similar data gathered in 1975 revealed that the basic patterns had not changed substantially. John P. Robinson, *Changes in American's Use of Time: 1965–1975, A Progress Report,* Cleveland State University, Cleveland, Ohio, 1977.

men. Detailed information on the hours spent on various recreation activities makes useful comparisons among nations possible. In some cases, these differences can be linked to cultural, social, economic, or political dissimilarities, or to variations in the supply of opportunities.

General Time-Budget Patterns. A good impression of how the time of urban residents is distributed can be obtained by examining the multinational project data for France, the United States, and the Soviet Union. The French data were based on 2805 interviews in 6 cities scattered across northern France. The American estimates came from 1243 respondents in 44 metropolitan areas and were designed to be representative of urban areas nationwide. The 2891 interviews in the Russian sample were all from the city of Pskov, which is located in the western portion of the Soviet Union near the Baltic Sea.

Figure 8.10 consists of a set of three time-budget graphs for each of three nations. They show the percentage of time spent on nine activity groupings during the average working day by homemakers, employed women, and employed men in each sample. Perhaps the most noticeable characteristic of these graphs is the similarity of the patterns for each class of person (homemakers, employed women, and employed men) in all three nations. This similarity of the working day for the three groups of people persists in the data for the other nine countries. It is remarkable that the patterns are so alike considering the differences that exist among these nations in cultures, traditions, eco-

nomic structures, political systems, and degrees of economic development.

The amounts and patterns of sleep are basically the same in all the graphs in Figure 8.10 and were found to vary little in the samples for all 12 nations. Meal patterns differ much more extensively. The French respondents spent the most time eating (98 minutes a day), followed by the Americans (60 minutes), and the Russians (48 minutes). Since more workers in France go home for a midday meal than in America or Russia, the graphs for the French workers show increases in travel, home and family activities, and recreation during the middle part of the day. The French and American work patterns are similar, except that the French tend to work longer afternoons. The Russian workers in the sample have somewhat shorter working hours than either the French or the Americans. The American homemaker spends about one hour less a day on household duties than do French and Russian homemakers. The 868-page report contains extensive statistical analyses and discussion of the differences in time allocated to work, travel, and household activities.

Recreation Time. Since activities other than work were recorded by the name of the activity without any indication of whether the participant considered it to be recreation or duty, it is impossible to know the full extent of recreation in the lives of the multinational project respondents. In Figure 8.10, some of the time shown on the graphs as being used for eating and traveling should be considered recreation. In addition, the home and family care category includes food

preparation, gardening, animal care, reading to children, indoor and outdoor games with children, shopping, and other activities that are often recreation. The category we call personal care and duties (labeled semi-leisure in the study) includes attending classes, going to lectures, taking part in political activities, studying, and participating in civic organizations, all of which can be recreational, at least to some extent, depending on the circumstances.

The group of activities in Figure 8.10 included in the category, other recreation, are those listed in Table 8.2, except for television viewing and other mass media (listening to the radio and reading books, magazines, and newspapers), both of which are shown separately on the graphs. No doubt some of these other recreation activities could also be regarded as duties by some respondents, especially sewing, knitting, conversing, writing letters, and certain social events. Nevertheless, the majority of the participants would consider most of the time spent on these activities to be recreation.

The most outstanding feature of the recreation patterns shown in Figure 8.10 is the dominance of the mass media in the free-time behavior of each of the three classes of respondents in all three nations. Use of the media in the home (watching television, listening to the radio, and reading books, magazines, and newspapers) accounted for one-third or more of all free time. (In the study, free time was defined as the time left after work, household tasks, child care, and physiological and other personal-care activities have been accommodated.) The distribution of partici-

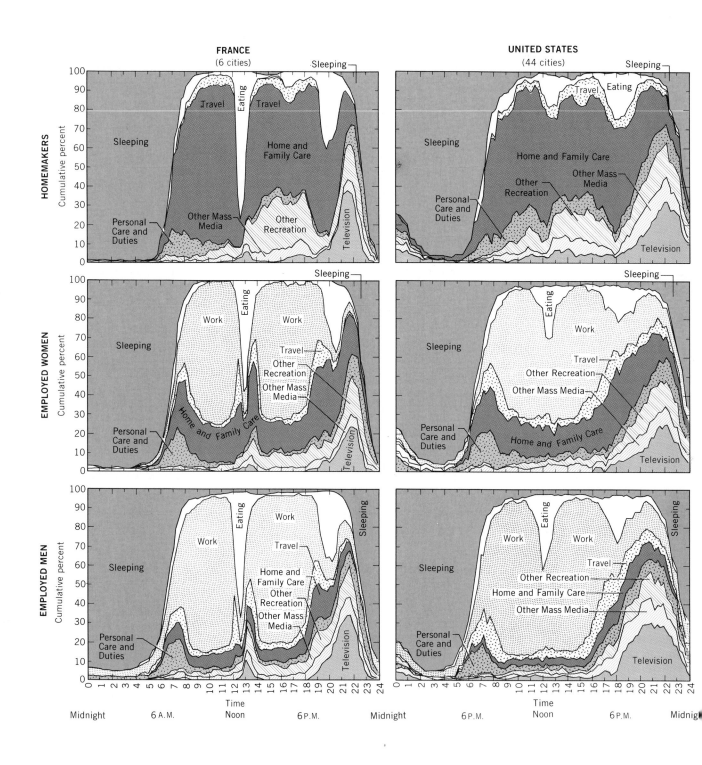

FRANCE
(6 cities)

UNITED STATES
(44 cities)

HOMEMAKERS
Cumulative percent

EMPLOYED WOMEN
Cumulative percent

EMPLOYED MEN
Cumulative percent

Time
Midnight 6 A.M. Noon 6 P.M. Midnight

Time
6 P.M. Noon 6 P.M. Midnight

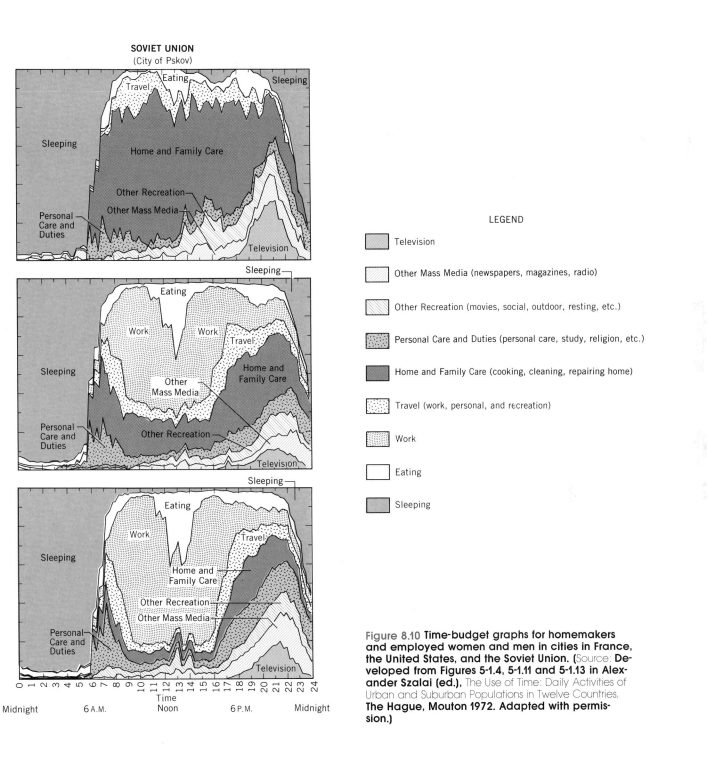

SOVIET UNION
(City of Pskov)

LEGEND

Television

Other Mass Media (newspapers, magazines, radio)

Other Recreation (movies, social, outdoor, resting, etc.)

Personal Care and Duties (personal care, study, religion, etc.)

Home and Family Care (cooking, cleaning, repairing home)

Travel (work, personal, and recreation)

Work

Eating

Sleeping

Figure 8.10 **Time-budget graphs for homemakers and employed women and men in cities in France, the United States, and the Soviet Union. (**Source: **Developed from Figures 5-1.4, 5-1.11 and 5-1.13 in Alexander Szalai (ed.),** The Use of Time: Daily Activities of Urban and Suburban Populations in Twelve Countries, **The Hague, Mouton 1972. Adapted with permission.)**

Table 8.2 Average Time per Day per Respondent Spent on Identifiable Recreation Activities[a] and Percent of Respondents That Participated

	French Cities (N=2805)		American Cities (N=1243)		Russian City (N=2891)	
	Average Minutes per Day per Person	Percent of Individuals Participating	Average Minutes per Day per Person	Percent of Individuals Participating	Average Minutes per Day per Person	Percent of Individuals Participating
Group I						
Attend sports event	0.4	0.5	1.0	0.7	0.6	0.4
Circus, dancing, nightclub	2.6	1.6	4.4	3.0	2.0	1.4
Movies	2.7	1.8	3.2	2.0	15.5	14.6
Theater, concert, opera	0.5	0.5	0.4	0.4	2.9	1.7
Museums, exhibitions	—	0.2	0.2	0.3	0.2	0.2
Visit to or from friends	16.3	24.5	39.4	36.3	4.6	7.5
Party or visit to or from friends plus meal	8.2	10.9	15.0	16.1	4.3	3.5
Visit to café, bar, or tearoom	4.1	8.6	2.7	4.0	0.6	0.6
Attend other kinds of receptions	0.1	0.1	0.8	1.0	0.1	0.1
Travel connected with this group	9.3	23.7	12.0	29.7	12.7	23.1
Group II						
Sports practice and exercise	1.4	2.5	5.5	5.7	3.6	18.4
Excursions, hike, hunt, fish	1.1	0.7	1.3	0.8	3.5	1.2
Take walks	10.2	14.1	1.1	2.4	10.2	15.9
Technical hobbies, collecting	2.9	3.5	1.7	1.9	0.8	0.8
Needlework, sew, knit	14.0	15.9	7.0	7.7	5.4	5.8
Sculpture, paint, pottery, write	0.3	0.2	0.8	1.2	0.4	0.3

[a] Depending on the perception of the participant, excludes some activities that may or may not be recreation such as eating, gardening, playing with children.

pation in the media activities tended to be similar in each of the three nations, except that the French devoted considerably less time to them, both during the week and on their days off. Russian homemakers participated more extensively in these activities—especially reading books—than either their French or American counterparts. However, only 8 percent of the Russian women were not employed so that the high participation by the homemakers did not raise the average values substantially.

Television viewing occupied the largest portion of time devoted to the media in each of the three nations, for all three classes of persons, and for both working days and days off. In France, approximately half of the sample household members watched television as a primary activity at least once a day, resulting in a per capita average of 58 minutes daily viewing (Table 8.2). In the American sample, just over two-thirds watched, producing a per capita average of 92 minutes compared to one-third

Table 8.2 Average Time per Day per Respondent Spent on Identifiable Recreation Activities[a] and Percent of Respondents That Participated (Continued)

	French Cities (N=2805)		American Cities (N=1243)		Russian City (N=2891)	
	Average Minutes per Day per Person	Percent of Individuals Participating	Average Minutes per Day per Person	Percent of Individuals Participating	Average Minutes per Day per Person	Percent of Individuals Participating
Group II (Continued)						
Sing, play instrument	0.2	0.4	0.9	1.1	0.7	0.9
Indoor social games	3.3	4.1	5.1	5.3	3.4	7.8
Other pastimes	0.9	1.8	2.3	3.8	0.5	0.4
Travel connected with this group	2.9	7.8	1.7	6.0	2.2	3.9
Group III						
Listen to radio[b]	5.0	12.2	3.6	8.2	9.7	23.0
Watch television	58.1	54.1	91.6	70.3	38.5	35.7
Listen to records	0.7	1.5	0.9	1.7	0.4	0.8
Read books[b]	6.8	12.3	5.3	7.1	29.3	36.2
Read magazines[b]	3.7	9.1	6.4	11.3	5.2	11.9
Read newspapers[b]	14.4	40.0	23.8	48.6	15.1	42.2
Conversations, including telephone	16.7	41.9	18.4	41.2	8.2	25.2
Write private correspondence	4.0	12.2	5.9	12.3	4.4	13.4
Relax, think, do nothing	12.6	29.7	4.0	10.5	6.4	17.6
Travel connected with this group	0.1	0.4	—	0.2	1.1	4.3
Subtotal—other media	29.9	—	39.1	—	59.3	—
Subtotal—other recreation	115.5	—	135.7	—	94.7	—
Total minutes per day	203.5	—	266.4	—	192.5	—

[b] Listening to the radio and reading books, magazines, and newspapers are shown as other mass media in Figure 8.9.

SOURCE: Adapted from Tables 2–1.1 and 2–1.2 in Alexander Szalai (ed.), *The Use of Time: Daily Activities of Urban and Suburban Populations in Twelve Countries,* The Hague, Mouton, 1972.

viewing an average of 39 minutes in Russia. These differences roughly correspond to the proportions of respondents owning television sets, namely, 65 percent in the French sample, 97 percent in the American cities, and 52 percent in Pskov.

Reading newspapers was the second most important media activity in terms of the proportions of sample household members participating. The percentage taking part was high in all three nations with 40 percent in the French, 49 percent in the American, and 42 percent in Russian households. The average per capita time spent daily on the activity was 14, 24, and 15 minutes respectively. However, these values for all respondents mask major differences in participation rates among the groups. In all cases except one, the percentage taking part, the average time spent, and the percent of free time used to read the newspaper were higher for employed men than for employed women or homemakers (Table 8.3). The one exception was homemakers in the United States

Table 8.3 Percent Participating, Average Time, and Percent of Identifiable Free Time Involved in Newspaper Reading as a Primary Activity

Day and Group	French Cities			American Cities			Russian City		
	Percent of Group[a]	Minutes per Day[b]	Percent of Free Time[c]	Percent of Group[a]	Minutes per Day[b]	Percent of Free Time[c]	Percent of Group[a]	Minutes per Day[b]	Percent of Free Time[c]
Workdays (Weekdays for Homemakers)									
Homemakers	37.6	11	4.9	48.9	18	5.8	31.9	9	3.8
Employed women	26.6	8	6.7	36.9	12	6.7	32.2	10	6.3
Employed men	50.2	18	11.2	54.1	22	10.4	65.2	23	9.3
Homemakers	21.4	6	1.7	64.8	39	7.9	13.3	4	1.0
Employed women	24.5	8	2.6	44.2	22	5.5	29.8	12	3.4
Employed men	42.5	17	3.7	60.2	37	7.2	61.2	29	5.3
Average day (all respondents)	39.9	14	5.7	48.6	24	7.9	42.2	15	6.1

[a] Percent of group participating.

[b] Average minutes spent per day per person.

[c] Percent of average free time for that group and day. Free time is total time devoted to recreation, excluding recreation involved in certain household, civic, and educational activities.

SOURCE: Developed from Table 2–2 in Alexander Szalai (ed.), *The Use of Time: Daily Activities of Urban and Suburban Populations in Twelve Countries*, The Hague, Mouton, 1972.

on Sunday; the large size of American Sunday newspapers may have contributed to this situation. From the data it is clear that newspapers are an important recreation resource for a large proportion of urban populations. Some may read them for business information, but the majority obviously find newspapers a major source of enjoyment. Homemakers and employed women would probably spend more time reading newspapers if they had more free time.

The values in Table 8.2 reveal a number of other significant patterns, for instance:

- In the French and American cities, conversations with people in the home or on the telephone occupied second or third place, both in terms of the proportion participating and the time spent on the activity; conversations were of much less importance in the Russian households.

- Visits to or from friends were next in importance in the American and French cities but quite low on the list in Pskov.
- Reading books was of much greater importance in the Russian households than in either the French or American households; no doubt the availability of television sets and television programs influenced this situation.
- Relaxing, thinking, and doing nothing were approximately twice as important in the French households as in the Russian households and three times as important as in the American households.
- The proportion of Russian respondents going to movies was over seven times the proportion of the French and American respondents who went.
- As one might expect, going for a walk occupied a much more prominent position in the French and Russian recreation time-budgets than in the American ones.
- The proportion of the respondents in

Pskov that took part in sports and exercise was three times greater than the proportion in the American sample and over seven times the proportion in the French situation.

Many of these national differences would be affected by the supply of opportunities as well as by cultural differences and government policies, but data on opportunity accessibility are not provided.

When the participation data in Table 8.2 are regrouped into three categories—recreation at home, recreation in the neighborhood, and recreation beyond the neighborhood—the dominance of activities at home is clearly demonstrated (Table 8.4). In all three samples, more than two-thirds of people's recreation time was spent on activities in or around their residences. (No doubt some of the time devoted to hobbies, the arts, music, and other activities in that group took place away from home, but the proportion was likely quite small.) Actually, the proportion of recreation time spent at home was probably considerably larger than this because the coding system used did not permit enjoyable occasions involving education, gardening, animal care, playing with children, shopping, and other house and family activities to be counted as recreation. In the case of the American urban populations, it is likely that approximately 90 percent of their recreation time was and still is spent at home.

In Table 8.4, division of the other activities into neighborhood and outside the neighborhood is more arbitrary. Some of the sports activities or visits to cafés and bars may have taken place outside the neighborhood. However, the travel times shown for Groups I and II are quite small and are more likely to be associated with going to sports events, movies, theaters, or muse-

Table 8.4 Proportion of Identifiable Time Spent on Recreation Activities at Home, in the Neighborhood, and at Some Distance from Home

Activity Location	French Cities (N=2805)		American Cities (N=1243)		Russian City (N=2891)	
	Average Minutes per Day per Person[a]	Percent of Free Time[b]	Average Minutes per Day per Person[a]	Percent of Free Time[b]	Average Minutes per Day per Person[a]	Percent of Free Time[b]
Activities at Home						
Media activities, records, conversation, correspondence, relax, do nothing (Group III minus travel)[c]	122.0	60.0	159.9	60.0	117.2	60.9
Visits with friends plus parties and meals with friends (from Group I)	24.5	12.0	54.4	20.4	8.9	4.6
Technical hobbies, sew, knit, arts, music, indoor games, other pastimes (from Group II)	21.6	10.6	17.8	6.7	11.2	5.8
Subtotal	168.1	82.6	232.1	87.1	137.3	71.3
Activities in Neighborhood						
Visit café or bar;	4.1	2.0	2.7	1.0	0.6	0.3
receptions (from Group I)	0.1	0.1	0.8	0.3	0.1	0.1
Sports practice and exercise;	1.4	0.7	5.5	2.1	3.6	1.9
take walks (from Group II)	10.2	5.0	1.1	0.4	10.2	5.3
Travel (from Group III)	0.1	0.1	–	–	1.1	0.6
Subtotal	15.9	7.9	10.1	3.8	15.6	8.2
Activities Outside Neighborhood						
Sports events;	0.4	0.2	1.0	0.4	0.6	0.3
circus, dancing, nightclub, movies, theater, concert, opera, museum, exhibits;	5.8	2.9	8.2	3.1	20.6	10.7
travel (from Group I)	9.3	4.6	12.0	4.5	12.7	6.6
Excursions, hike, hunt, fish;	1.1	0.5	1.3	0.5	3.5	1.8
travel (from Group II)	2.9	1.4	1.7	0.6	2.2	1.1
Subtotal	19.5	9.6	24.2	9.1	39.6	20.5
Total—all activities	203.5	100.1	266.4	100.0	192.5	100.0

[a] Time is average number of minutes per day per person in urban households that met study criteria.

[b] Percent of total time devoted to recreation, excluding recreation involved in certain household, civic, and educational activities.

[c] The groups referred to are the three classes of activities used in the original study and shown as Groups I, II, and III in Table 8.2.

SOURCE: Developed from data in Table 8.2.

Table 8.5 Indications of the Proportion of Identifiable Free Time Spent on Extraurban Recreation and Active Recreation Out-of-Doors

Activity Groupings	French Cities (N=2805)		American Cities (N=1243)		Russian City (N=2891)	
	Average Minutes per Day per Person[a]	Percent of Free Time[b]	Average Minutes per Day per Person[a]	Percent of Free Time[b]	Average Minutes per Day per Person[a]	Percent of Free Time[b]
Extraurban ("Outdoor") Recreation						
Excursions, hike, hunt, fish	1.1	0.5	1.3	0.5	3.5	1.8
Travel (from Group II)	2.9	1.4	1.7	0.6	2.2	1.1
Total	4.0	2.0	3.0	1.1	5.7	2.9
Active Recreation Out-of-Doors (*Add to extraurban values above*)						
Attend sports events	0.4	0.2	1.0	0.4	0.6	0.3
Sports practice and exercise	1.4	0.7	5.5	2.1	3.6	1.9
Take walks	10.2	5.0	1.1	0.4	10.2	5.3
Total	16.0	7.9	10.6	4.0	20.1	10.4

[a] Time is average number of minutes per day per person in urban households that met study criteria.
[b] Percent of total time devoted to recreation, excluding recreation involved in certain household, civic, and educational activities.
SOURCE: Developed from data in Table 8.2

ums; going on excursions; or going on hiking, hunting, or fishing trips. It is highly probably that some of the time included in the activities outside the neighborhood should be included in the neighborhood values.

Finally, the data in Table 8.4 make it possible to draw some tentative conclusions regarding the proportion of time devoted to recreation in less developed environments. Excursions, hunting, and fishing are most likely to have taken place outside the urban environment. No doubt much of the travel in connection with Group II in Table 8.2 was associated with the excursions and the hiking, hunting, and fishing trips. Therefore, combining these two groups (Table 8.5) provides an estimate of the maximum amount of time that is likely to have been spent on extraurban recreation (the limited group of activities often called outdoor recrea-

tion in the literature). The totals indicate that the American respondents devoted no more than 1.1 percent of their recreation time to these types of activities, whereas the French and Russian household members spent more actual time and a higher percentage of their recreation time on them. No doubt all these values would have been somewhat higher if some of the sample days had occurred during the summer vacation period.

A broader spectrum of activities that takes place primarily out-of-doors can be included by adding the time spent on sports practice, exercise, walks, and sports events to the values calculated for extraurban recreation (Table 8.5). Even with this wider definition, it only comprises 4 percent of the American respondents' recreation time-budget, 7.9 percent in the case of the French households, and 10.4 percent for the Russian sample. The

French and Russian values are higher primarily because of the substantial amount of time devoted to walking. No doubt some of this walking was done in local parks but much must have occurred along city streets; such walking is usually not included in estimates of "outdoor recreation" participation. In addition, a good portion of spectator sports and participation in sports and exercise probably took place indoors in all three cases. The proportion of total recreation time spent on these activities would also decrease considerably if the pleasurable experiences associated with education, gardening, pet care, looking after children, shopping, and other home and family activities were included as recreation.

Many other aspects of recreation behavior can be understood better by examination of the extensive tables in the Multinational Comparative Time-Budget Research Project. More frequent and more extensive studies of this kind are required if recreation professionals are to understand the complex patterns of recreation participation. As can readily be seen from the multinational study, it is necessary to know more than whether or not a person took part in an activity. Information indicating whether or not an activity was perceived as recreational, the total time spent on all kinds of pleasurable activities, and the locations where recreation activities took place is needed to understand fully the magnitude, structure, and patterns of participation.

PATTERNS IN THE UNITED STATES

Professionals and others interested in recreation have difficulty in obtaining an accurate impression of the full scope of recreation participation. On the one hand, relatively little-known studies such as the multinational time-budget survey show that most free time is spent at home watching television, conversing with friends and relatives, or reading newspapers, books, and magazines. On the other hand, the media, government agencies, and many professional journals bombard the public with large-sounding estimates of the total number of tourists, the number of spectators attending sports events, the rapid growth in disco dancing, or the environmental impact of the increasing numbers of wilderness users. This preoccupation with recreation away from home is not suprising. Such a statistic as "Americans spend 20 percent of their recreation time visiting with friends" is less likely to make the headlines than

"250 million visit our national parks." In addition, researchers are generally not conducting participation investigations at levels between broad-brush time-budget studies on the one hand and detailed site-specific or activity-specific surveys undertaken by government agencies and commercial interests on the other hand. Consequently, little quantitative information is available concerning recreation in the home or immediate neighborhood.

This section brings together data from many sources to describe American participation patterns in some detail. More quantitative surveys of recreation behavior are routinely or periodically carried out in the United States than in any other nation. The American experience often provides indications of recreation trends that may occur in other countries as economic development and diffusion of technological innovations take place. The information problems described earlier and the many gaps in the information make it necessary to use qualitative generalizations as well as numerical data.

Understanding Recreation Data. In attempting to obtain a balanced view of recreation participation, it is important to remember constantly that numerical information can be deceptive. On the one hand, participation in many activities seems to remain relatively constant, whereas participation in other activities shows what appears to be tremendous increases.

For example, well-established activities such as television-viewing, stamp and coin collecting, swimming, camping, and fishing appeal to large numbers of people and

continue to attract many new participants. Their annual growth rate, however, is relatively slow and does not show the extremely large percentage increases exhibited by such new or revived activities as disco dancing or roller-skating. Three factors contribute to this situation.

First, the number of people participating in well-established activities is already huge so that very large numbers of new participants are required to produce a substantial increase. In contrast, only a few hundred thousand additional participants in a new activity may result in a spectacular percentage increase.

Second, some people are continually dropping out of the older activities for various reasons, whereas, at the same time, many others are just beginning to take part. The actual changes taking place may be quite large, but the resultant net percentage growth in participation may be small. On the other hand, comparatively few may drop out of a new activity during its early stages; it normally takes some time for the novelty to wear off and for people to decide to give up an activity they personally advocated or in which they have recently invested substantial amounts of time, effort, or money. There is also considerable social and peer group pressure encouraging new and continued participation as more and more individuals become caught up in the excitement generated by the new activity and its enthusiastic supporters.

Third, established activities have well-developed support systems that help keep participation relatively stable. When many individuals have taken part in a particular activity over a long period of time, it actually becomes a part of the culture. As a result, it is easy and natural for young people and newcomers to follow and accept the culture's prevailing recreation participation patterns. Once involved in well-established activities, there is also a tendency to continue to take part as long as circumstances permit. People generally feel comfortable continuing to do something that they—and possibly their parents before them—have done for quite a long time. Suppliers of opportunities and manufacturers of recreation goods also contribute to an activity's stability. Public and private investments in equipment, facilities, and programs are often substantial. It is neither economically feasible to make frequent changes, nor is it possible to make radical changes overnight.

In contrast, the new fast-growth activities lack stability. In the United States, for example, skateboarding, soccer, and the operation of citizens band (CB) radios all experienced sudden, proportionally large changes in participation in the 1970s. However, the starting interest levels were very low and these activities had few of the support systems necessary to thrive. All three survived the introductory stage and managed to build support and sustain public interest with varying degrees of success.

Soccer appears to be gathering momentum as more people at many levels—youth groups, schools, amateur clubs, and professional teams—are showing an interest in the sport and cooperating in the improvement of players, facilities, and coaching, and the promotion of spectator support (Figure 8.11). The game also appeals to a broad spectrum of society—men,

women, boys, and girls—and this in itself may ensure its survival. On the other hand, the initial growth in enthusiasm for CB radios slowed somewhat in the late 1970s. Then the gasoline shortages in 1979 created another surge of interest similar to that of 1973–1974, which helped to stimulate the craze originally. The fact that relatively few people are abandoning the hobby and are continuing to use their sets an average of over 14 hours a week for at least 39 weeks of the year would indicate this activity is achieving stability. Skateboarding, however, may not endure. Although it has acquired a support

system that includes 200 skateboard parks, three national magazines, and the International Skateboarding Association, it has not been able to broaden its appeal to either girls or older people. In the late 1970s, the young people who were so enamored of the sport began deserting their skateboards for rollerskates. Without an influx of new participants, sales of boards and accessories plummeted from $166 million in 1977 to $64 million in 1978. Only time can tell whether these three activities are just passing fads or are destined to become accepted, permanent parts of the American recreation environment.

Figure 8.11 Young people's interest in soccer is growing in North America particularly where recreation agencies are providing well-run programs at readily accessible, neighborhood facilities. These youngsters playing in a school sportsfield are part of the 650 boys and 100 girls six years of age and older who take part in the Washington, D.C., Department of Recreation soccer programs that are offered both during the summer and after school and on Saturdays during the fall.

It should also be remembered that media accounts and government reports concerning the growth and diversity of recreation participation do not mean that the majority of individuals take part in a great variety of activities. On the contrary, most people explore relatively few activities during a lifetime and spend the majority of their recreation time on only two or three. In fact, the multinational time-budget project indicated that average persons in the highly developed nations may actually spend most of their free time on fewer activities than typical individuals in some of the less developed nations. This is partly the result of so much time being spent on the media and entertaining friends at home. But whatever the range of activities involved, individuals and families generally settle into recreation routines centered on two or three activities that remain relatively constant. Usually, this pattern is altered only by a substantial change in lifestyle such as marriage, the arrival of children, ill health, or a radical change in environment, amount of free time, or discretionary income.

In addition, it is important to keep the following points in mind when reading statistical information on recreation participation:

- The range of activities included in the data may be limited, for instance, statistics concerning "outdoor recreation" may not include those activities on which most people spend the majority of their time out-of-doors (gardening and other backyard activities, walks in the neighborhood, etc.).
- Recreation statistics only reflect the behavior characteristics of the kinds of people, places, times of day, days of the week, or months of the year included in the survey.

- Facility attendance figures do not distinguish between one time and repeat participants so that they do not indicate the *proportion* of a population taking part.
- Statistics concerning the number or percent of persons who participate can be deceptive if the time period is long and a person only has to take part once to be counted. For example, published figures may show that a high percentage of people enjoyed swimming during a particular year, but further investigation discloses that a substantial proportion did not go more than once or twice and that a small number actually did the bulk of the swimming.
- Increases in participation over time are not necessarily the result of more participation per person; some increases are partly caused by population growth, changes in recordkeeping practices, or the inclusion of data from new areas in attendance estimates.

Therefore, before using recreation participation statistics, it is important to be completely familiar with the basis on which they were gathered.

Time Distribution. If the multinational time-budget data for adult urban Americans are rearranged in order of the percentage of recreation time spent on various activity groupings, the histograms shown in Figure 8.12 are obtained. They indicate that most people choose activities that are well known and readily accessible. Although American urban populations generally enjoy one of the widest ranges of recreation opportunities of any comparable group in the world, the majority spend nearly all of their recreation time on a few activities at home. They select activities with which they are already familiar, that they feel comfortable

doing, that other people around them enjoy, and that require a minimum of effort. Consequently, these Americans devote about three-quarters of their primary recreation time to watching television, listening to the radio, taking part in social visits, reading, communicating with family members, relaxing, thinking, and doing nothing.

Some recreation professionals may find this disturbing. Certainly, the lack of physical exercise and the large proportion of people who are overweight that is part of this pattern have become serious national problems. On the other hand, the considerable time spent on social visiting, family communication, and reading is undoubtedly a very positive feature. Unfortunately, there is evidence that the proportion of time spent on television-viewing has increased at the expense of the other activities, especially reading.

Television and Radio. The dominant position of television and radio is only partly revealed by Figure 8.12. In addition to the almost 36 percent of primary recreation time devoted to the broadcast media, television and radio occupy a daily average of about two hours and one hour respectively per adult as secondary activities. About 80 percent of the respondents watched television and over 50 percent listened to the radio as secondary activities. Most of this television viewing occurred while taking part in other recreation activities (43 percent) or carrying out household duties (39 percent). About 28 percent of radio listening as a secondary activity occurred while at work, more than 35 percent during household duties, and over 12 percent while traveling.

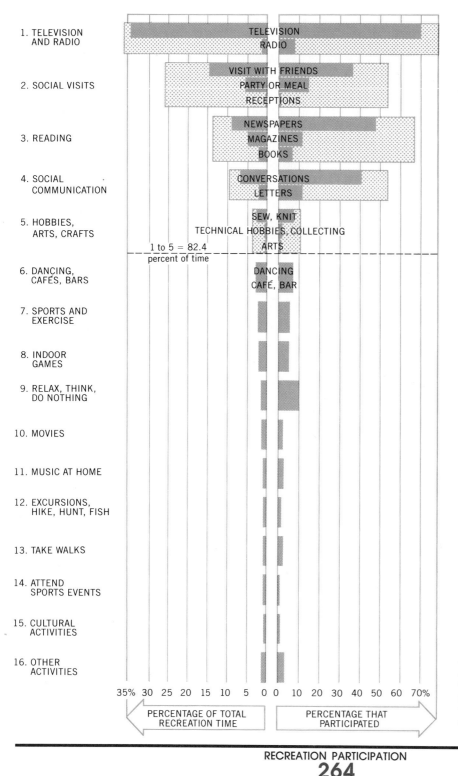

1. TELEVISION AND RADIO
2. SOCIAL VISITS
3. READING
4. SOCIAL COMMUNICATION
5. HOBBIES, ARTS, CRAFTS
6. DANCING, CAFÉS, BARS
7. SPORTS AND EXERCISE
8. INDOOR GAMES
9. RELAX, THINK, DO NOTHING
10. MOVIES
11. MUSIC AT HOME
12. EXCURSIONS, HIKE, HUNT, FISH
13. TAKE WALKS
14. ATTEND SPORTS EVENTS
15. CULTURAL ACTIVITIES
16. OTHER ACTIVITIES

1 to 5 = 82.4 percent of time

TELEVISION / RADIO
VISIT WITH FRIENDS / PARTY OR MEAL / RECEPTIONS
NEWSPAPERS / MAGAZINES / BOOKS
CONVERSATIONS / LETTERS
SEW, KNIT / TECHNICAL HOBBIES, COLLECTING / ARTS
DANCING / CAFÉ, BAR

35% 30 25 20 15 10 5 0 0 10 20 30 40 50 60 70%

PERCENTAGE OF TOTAL RECREATION TIME

PERCENTAGE THAT PARTICIPATED

Crime and comedy serials, Hollywood movies, special feature programs, and major sports events attract peak television audiences. Almost one of every two Americans (over 100 million people) watches at least part of the Super Bowl (the final game of the professional football season). The 14 daytime soap operas (domestic tragedies aimed specifically at homemakers) attract a steady daily audience of over 30 million. Many soap opera fans watch or listen for several hours each weekday as a primary or secondary activity. Some hate to miss a single episode and subscribe to a magazine that helps them keep abreast of the twists and turns of the complicated plots.

Social Visits. Social visits follow the broadcast media in order of importance, occupying about 21 percent of primary recreation time. Well over one-third of adult urban Americans take part on more than a casual basis in visits to friends, parties and meals with friends, and special social occasions. Unlike television and radio, social visits are not considered significant as secondary activities.

The survey does not indicate what proportion of these social activities may have involved relatives or business associates and, therefore, may have been duty or work rather than recreation. No informa-

Figure 8.12 **Percentage of persons participating and percentage of total primary recreation time spent on principal recreation activities by urban, adult Americans.** (Source: **Developed from 1965 multinational survey data in Alexander Szalai (ed.), The Use of Time: Daily Activities of Urban and Suburban Populations in Twelve Countries, The Hague, Mouton, 1972.**)

tion was obtained on the activities undertaken during such visits. Most of the time appears to be devoted to conversation and meals.

Reading. Reading newspapers, magazines, and books is third in order of importance, taking up over 13 percent of the time spent on primary recreation activities (Figure 8.13). On the average, almost half of adult urban Americans read newspapers although, as Table 8.3 indicated, the proportion varies depending on the day of the week and whether the individual is a homemaker, employed female, or employed male.

The proportion of time and the percentage of people who read newspapers on more than a casual basis has declined a little since the time-budget study was conducted. For instance, weekday circulation of daily newspapers fell from 63.1 to 60 million copies per day between 1973 and 1978, and the number of people reading a daily newspaper is reported to have decreased 7 percent. The decline is largely the result of competition from television and the fact that an increasing proportion of the population has grown up in a television-dominated culture.

Newspaper publishers are trying to reverse this trend by promotional campaigns and changes in newspaper content. Human interest stories, gossip columns, pictorial coverage of special events, and summary articles are being featured rather than in-depth analyses of national and international news. Because potential customers are said to be more concerned with their own interests than national events or international affairs, more space is being assigned to consumer ad-

Figure 8.13 **Reading newspapers and magazines is a particularly important activity for farm families especially if they live in areas where television reception is limited or impossible.**

vice, self-improvement topics, reports on upcoming events, and articles about lifestyles, recreation activities, and tourist resources. Even the staid, formerly business-oriented *New York Times* has added more graphics and special magazine-style sections on food, sports, recreation, and home improvements.

At the present time, nearly 1800 daily newspapers, 7500 weekly papers, and 640 Sunday papers are published in the United States with circulations of 60, 35, and 51 million. Newspaper publishing is the nation's third largest industry employing almost 400,000 people and earning more than $14 billion a year from advertising and newspaper sales.

Although young people currently appear to be buying fewer newspapers, they are purchasing a

disproportionate and increasing number of magazines. Several general-interest magazines that were once American institutions have gone out of business; nonetheless, magazine circulation has risen from 147 million in 1950 to more than 260 million. There are now over 10,000 different magazines published in the United States; 336 new ones started publishing in 1978 alone. Those that seek a broad audience tend to concentrate on trivia, gossip, the latest societal trends, news of the arts and entertainment world, and sex. Special-interest publications focus on specific recreation activities such as antique collecting, arts and crafts, boating, camping, fishing, travel, photography, and television viewing.

Americans are also buying more books although today's customers favor paperback editions of novels and other materials with mass audience appeal. In 1977, for example, over 531 million paperbacks were sold; these purchases represented more than half of the total $4.6 billion spent by Americans during that year on all kinds of books. The top sellers are often books that have recently been made into successful movies or television programs or scripts from popular movies that have been quickly turned into book form.

Although tastes in reading material may have changed, book sales do indicate that Americans are continuing to read during their spare time despite the inroads of television. A recent study conducted for the book industry seems to substantiate this. In a 1978 survey of 1450 adults, it was found that 10 percent had read more than 25 books in a six-month period, 15 percent had read 10 to 25 books, and 30 percent had read 1 to 10 books. However, the survey also discovered that nearly half the adults had read no books at all; of these, 39 percent had read only newspapers, or magazines and 6 percent had read nothing. According to recent American Booksellers Association estimates, only 5 to 6 percent of the American public are currently regular book buyers.

Conversation and Personal Letters. Conversation (including talking on the telephone) and writing personal letters make up the group of activities that is fourth in importance. Employed women spent about 40 percent more time, and homemakers over twice as much, on conversation as a primary activity than the employed men. Conversation is especially important as a secondary activity with an ad-

ditional $2\frac{1}{2}$ hours per person being devoted to it each day. Two-fifths of this occurs at work, one-fifth during meals, and another fifth during primary recreation activities, especially television viewing and active sports or exercise. Working men recorded 25 percent more conversation as a secondary activity than working women, and 87 percent more than homemakers. When the primary and secondary figures are combined, the percentage participating is about the same for all three groups, but the men spend about 57 percent more time on conversation than the homemakers.

Little is known about personal letter writing as a recreation activity. No doubt duty is often involved, but many people obtain much enjoyment from it. With 12 percent of the respondents participating in letter writing as a primary activity and spending an average of six minutes per day per person on it, the United States is among the top three letter-writing nations according to the multinational study.

Hobbies, Arts, and Crafts. The fifth position in Figure 8.12 is occupied by hobbies, arts, and crafts, which take 3.6 percent of people's recreation time. The proportions of urban adults participating (7.7 percent in sewing or knitting, 1.9 percent in collecting and technical hobbies, and 1.2 percent in the arts and creative writing) appears to be small and to contradict other figures. For example, it is commonly reported that 40 percent of American adults take part in some form of craft and 33 percent collect stamps, coins, or some other item. This apparent discrepancy is because only a small proportion of hobbyists and collectors spend suf-

ficient time on a day-2-day basis for their participation to become prominent in time-budget studies.

Whether or not they spend much time participating, the number who take part in hobbies, arts, and crafts, appears to be increasing. No doubt this is partly because of higher discretionary incomes and more free time, but it is probably also the result of a growing need for self-actualization. Pottery, ceramics, woodworking, painting, glassblowing, making jewelry, embroidery, and needlepoint are all gaining new participants. Increased interest in pioneer crafts has stimulated the growth of whittling, making candles, caning chairs, quilting, weaving, and making handcrafted toys and musical instruments. On a larger scale, more people are involved in restoring furniture, houses, and old cars. The most commonly collected items in the United States are stamps, coins, antiques, bottles, rocks, fossils, shells, butterflies, guns, dolls, Indian artifacts, baseball cards, and comic books. Most collectors spend relatively little time on their hobby, except during vacation periods or when they acquire new items or display their collections. Yet, many casual collectors enjoy their collections continually by keeping them on display in their living quarters. Some collectors, however, spend every spare moment on their hobbies and continually add to their collections by going to special stores, attending shows, and purchasing or exchanging through the mail. Participants enjoy the excitment and surprises associated with searching for new items, the personal contacts with those who share their interests, and the satisfaction of owning and displaying a growing collection.

Technical hobbies that attract the most participants in the United States are rebuilding and modifying cars, photography, amateur radio operating, building model railroads, and various other forms of model building. Obviously the depth to which participants become involved varies greatly. In photography, for example, the majority of those who take photographs know little about how the cameras or films work. To these people, photography is not really a technical hobby as much as a souvenir-collecting hobby or art form. At the other end of the spectrum are amateur photographers who do their own color developing and enlarging or even build their own cameras.

Dancing, Cafés, Bars. The sixth group in order of the total amount of time involved is visiting dancehalls, nightclubs, cafés, bars, and other similar commercial establishments. (In the survey, work-connected restaurant meals were not considered recreational and were not included in this category.) In Figure 8.12, this is the first group of activities that takes place outside the home and it only appears when more than 82 percent of the total time for primary activities has already been attributed to activities in or around the home.

Participation in this group of activities is expanding. The advent of television, the decline of ballroom-style dancing, and the adoption of informal life and clothing styles during the 1960s kept commercial entertainment participation at a lower level than might be expected, given the substantial rise in discretionary incomes. Similarly, growth in the patronage of fast-food establishments tended to retard the development of cafés and restaurants. However, a swing toward a more sophisticated nightlife was underway by the middle 1970s. Although fast-food restaurant chains remained well patronized, more elaborate restaurants increased their business substantially. Restaurants specializing in particular kinds of food became more numerous. Nevertheless, dancing to full-sized bands and live entertainment by comedians and other performers remained relatively limited. Proprietors cannot provide the quality of television music and entertainment to which people have become accustomed for prices patrons are willing to pay.

The environment proved favorable for the rapid growth of discotheques. Expanding in the United States from 3000 to 20,000 establishments in the 1974–1979 period, discotheques have been opened to appeal to a variety of groups. Although furnishings, lighting, and sound systems require a substantial initial investment, operating costs are moderate so that admission charges for the less elaborate ones can be quite low compared to other forms of entertainment. In addition to the cost factor, people are attracted to discotheques for a number of reasons. They offer excellent opportunities for social interaction, vigorous exercise, fun, escape from reality, and the achievement of self-actualization.

Sports, Exercise, and Walking. The seventh grouping in order of time spent per urban adult is participation in active sports and exercise. This group excludes hiking and forms of exercise associated with extraurban activities such as excursions to the beach or hunting, fishing, and camping. If the proportion taking walks (the thirteenth group in Figure 8.12) is added to the proportion participating in sports and exercise, it appears likely that between 8 and 10 percent of the adult urban population takes part in active recreation on a regular basis. This may appear low in view of the publicity given increased participation in jogging, bicycling, tennis, and other sports. For example, a 1977 *U.S. News & World Report* article reported that, "The rush of Americans to participant sports rolls along unchecked."[3] An accompanying table showed participants in 25 sports adding up to almost 700 million (Table 8.6). Again the apparent contradiction is largely because the multinational time-budget study de-emphasizes the infrequent short-term participant's contribution.

Surveys that count everyone who takes part, even if they only spend a few minutes on one occasion, tend to give a false impression of the importance of activities. The values can be more distorted if young people of school age are included. Since a large proportion go swimming, use bicycles for transportation, or become involved at least once in neighborhood versions of many sports such as basketball, softball, or football, their inclusion can raise the numbers of participants substantially.

In the case of participation in sports and exercise, the evidence indicates that a relatively small part —perhaps 10 or 15 percent— of the adult population takes part quite frequently and for appreciable

[3] "How Americans Pursue Happiness," *U.S. News & World Report,* May 23, 1977.

Table 8.6 Twenty-five Sports in the United States with the Most Participants

Sport	Millions of Participants[a]
1. Swimming	103.5
2. Bicycling	75.0
3. Fishing	63.9
4. Camping	58.1
5. Bowling	44.4
6. Pool/billiards	35.8
7. Boating	35.2
8. Table tennis	32.2
9. Tennis	29.2
10. Softball	27.3
11. Basketball	25.8
12. Ice skating	25.8
13. Hunting	20.5
14. Golf	16.6
15. Baseball	15.7
16. Football	14.9
17. Water skiing	14.7
18. Snow skiing	11.0
19. Motorbiking/ motorcycling	9.7
20. Snowmobiling	9.2
21. Jogging	8.5
22. Sailing	7.3
23. Archery	5.5
24. Handball	5.3
25. Racquetball	2.7

[a] Number of persons who participated at least once in 1976.
SOURCE: "The Boom in Leisure," *U.S. News & World Report,* May 23, 1977. Copyright © 1977 by *U.S. News & World Report.* Reprinted by permission.

periods of time. Many in this group also participate in several different activities. Another 35 to 40 percent undertake sports or exercise irregularly and for limited lengths of time. The remaining 50 percent get virtually no vigorous exercise at all.

Swimming is at the top of the list of sports in terms of the number who take part at least once. However, swimming for many people involves wading and playing in the water or sunbathing near the water so that its exercise value for many people may be quite limited. Cycling is second in terms of total participants, but, again, a relatively small proportion of adult cyclists use the bicycle for regular vigorous exercise. Few take more than an occasional brief, leisurely ride around neighborhood streets. Nevertheless, bicycle ownership and use expanded tremendously in the 1970s. It remains to be seen if a more bicycle-oriented generation and improved bicycle paths will result in more frequent and longer distance cycling by adults in the future.

Jogging and other types of running gained many adult participants during the 1970s, but the proportion that continues to take part regularly is relatively small. Those who do run reasonable distances suggest that it is impossible to run and worry at the same time. They also contend that running produces a feeling of euphoria that is achievable in no other way. Long-distance running is drawing a surprising number of participants. At one time, only a select group of more affluent male athletes took part in long-distance running. Now changes in people's perceptions and attitudes have resulted in participation by a much broader cross section of the population including substantial numbers of women, older people, less affluent individuals, and people who previously have not taken part in athletic activities. A growing number of these runners eventually take part in an organized competition; for instance, 80,000 entries were received for the 320 marathon events held throughout the United States during 1979, and 11,553 persons competed in the New York City Marathon alone (p. 85).

Walking for pleasure, although not usually referred to as a sport, is sufficiently like jogging to be included in this group. As in the case of some of the other activities, there are problems in defining and measuring walking for pleasure so that statistics vary. However, it appears to be more important in terms of the amount of time devoted to it than any of the active sports. This is remarkable, since most walking takes place in urban environments, many of which do not have particularly favorable conditions for safe or pleasant walking experiences.

Tennis and racquetball (more like handball and played indoors with a short racquet) have attracted many who seek strenuous physical exercise but prefer a social or competitive atmosphere to more solitary activities such as jogging. The number of tennis players increased by 45 percent between 1973 and 1976. Racquetball, starting from a much smaller base, is growing even more quickly; participation has increased from 50,000 to 8 million since 1970. It is a fast, hard game that is easier to learn than tennis and provides a maximum of exercise in a minimum of time. Age and sex differences have less impact than in tennis so that a wider range of people can enjoy playing together.

Other Home Activities. Indoor games continue to provide pleasure regularly for about 5 percent of urban adults. Chess, checkers, backgammon, Monopoly, bridge, and other card games are still prominent, but many new table and video games are also played.

Pool, billiards, and table tennis are common activities, especially in larger ranch-style houses with basement recreation rooms.

The multinational time-budget study showed that the relaxing, thinking, and doing-nothing group of activities was ninth in order of the amount of time involved. However, over 10 percent of the respondents spent their time in that way, which is larger than the percentage who read books.

Regular participation in musical activities (including listening to records, singing, and playing an instrument) occupied less than 1 percent of urban adults' recreation time and involved less than 3 percent of those included in the multinational study. No doubt these proportions are somewhat higher today with the growth in ownership of musical instruments, phonographs, and tape recorders. Certainly, the percentages would increase considerably if teenagers were included, since many of them spend more time listening to records, singing, and playing musical instruments than adults. Some authorities estimate that 23 percent of the U. S. population are amateur musicians who play regularly, and 11 percent sing in choirs or choral societies. Whatever the level of participation, millions find music is a special form of release. It is usually very different from all other activities, and participants can immerse themselves completely in listening, singing, or playing.

There are a number of other activities included in the multinational study that occur primarily at home, which can be pleasurable, but were not considered recreational. For example, urban adult Americans were shown to spend an average of 3 minutes per day on gardening and pet care, and 12.2 percent of this group were more than casually involved in such activities. In any event, more than half of American households now have gardens, the 700 million pets outnumber the human population by almost three to one, and large sums of money are spent on pet and garden supplies or services. Similarly, there are other activities, such as making home improvements, that can be recreational although they are usually not included in recreation statistics.

Movies and Cultural Events.

Going to a movie was tenth in terms of time regularly spent on recreation activities by urban adults for an average of 3.2 minutes per day per person or 1.2 percent of the total time. Of this group, 2 percent were shown to be regular moviegoers. However, casual and regular movie attendance now exceeds 1 billion a year at the nation's 16,000 motion picture theaters.

Attendance at live theater performances, concerts, and operas, as well as at museums and exhibitions is last in the ranking of activities shown in Figure 8.12. Again, it is a situation where many people participate once or twice a year, but comparatively few take part on a regular basis. Over 300 million visits to museums occur each year, with more than 80 million people going one or more times. About 62 million attend one or more live theater performances every year. The corresponding figures for other kinds of performances are: popular music, 55 million; classical music, 25 million; opera, 10 million; and ballet or other dance programs, 20 million.

Attending Sports Events.

More Americans are interested on a day-to-day basis in following sports happenings than in any other activity. Millions turn to the sports section first when reading newspapers; articles and statistics on sports personalities and events often occupy 10 or more pages in the larger daily newspapers. Coverage of sports events attracts large audiences on radio and television. In response to this interest, American television networks devoted over 1000 hours to sports programming in 1976, including substantial coverage of the Montreal Olympic Games.

The great majority of sports involvement consists of television viewing, radio listening, newspaper or magazine reading, conversation, or thinking. As the multinational study showed, attending sports events ranks quite low in terms of regular participation. Less than 1 percent of urban adults went to sports events on a regular basis. Nevertheless, attendance is substantial and continues to increase, as shown in Table 8.7. Intercollegiate sports events receive the enthusiastic support of the general public as well as the student population. College football (Figure 8.14) now occupies fourth place behind thoroughbred racing, automobile racing, and professional baseball, with college basketball attendance in sixth place. In addition, millions of spectators watch a great variety of other events, including school sports, sports programs, operated by municipal recreation departments, quasi-public agency sports, private company team sports competitions, and many private organization events—from motorcycle hill-climbs to country club tennis tournaments.

Table 8.7 Growth in Attendance at the Main Commercial and College Sports Events from 1966 to 1976

Sports Event	Attendance (Millions)		Percent Increase
	1966	1976	
1. Thoroughbred racing	40.9	51.2	25%
2. Auto racing	39.0	50.0	28%
3. Major league baseball	25.2	32.6	29%
4. College football	25.3	32.0	26%
5. Harness racing	23.2	30.7	32%
6. College basketball	17.0	25.5	50%
7. Greyhound racing	11.1	19.0	71%
8. Professional football	7.7	15.0	95%
9. Major league hockey	3.1	14.4	365%
10. Minor league baseball	10.1	11.3	12%
11. Professional basketball	2.3	8.5	270%
12. Professional wrestling	4.8	5.0	4%
13. Minor league hockey	2.9	4.9	69%
14. College hockey	0.8	3.4	325%
15. Professional boxing	1.7	3.2	88%
16. Professional soccer	(negligible)	2.8	—
17. Professional golf	1.5	2.3	53%
18. Professional tennis	(negligible)	2.2	—
Total	216.6	314.0	45%

SOURCE: "The Boom in Leisure," *U.S. News & World Report,* May 23, 1977. Copyright © 1977 by *U.S. News & World Report.* Reprinted by permission.

civic, and community organizations is considered pleasurable by many volunteers; about 25 percent of Americans take part in some type of volunteer service.

Activities Away from Home. Travel away from the home community for recreation purposes is highly seasonal. The majority of such travel takes place during the summer months when

Figure 8.14 **More than 70,000 spectators (equivalent to almost 5 percent of the state's population) crowd into the University of Nebraska's Memorial Stadium in Lincoln for an intercollegiate football game. Support for intercollegiate football has grown spectacularly in a number of less populated states; it provides a sense of identity on a nationwide scale for residents of areas which lack other attributes that are regularly of national significance.**

Other Activities in the Community. There are a number of other activities that people undertake within their communities that may provide considerable pleasure but are seldom included in recreation statistics. Many people enjoy windowshopping, especially in modern shopping centers or areas that have concentrations of specialty shops. About 20 million adult Americans attend part-time instructional programs at colleges, community centers, churches, retirement homes, and hospitals. A substantial portion of this self-improvement effort is not connected in any way with employment but is the result of a basic desire to learn something new or take part in a stimulating experience. Service to church, charitable, children are not at school. As the multinational study data demonstrate, a comparatively small proportion of the American urban adult population regularly leaves the home community during other times of the year for excursions, hunting, fishing, hiking, and similar outdoor pursuits. However, the proportion of people who are taking vacations at other times in the year or traveling away from home for winter sports is increasing.

Although many surveys have included questions concerning recreational travel, comparatively little is known about nationwide patterns. Bureau-of-the-Census data on travel by households indicate that about 12 percent of trips over 161 kilometers (100 miles) are for "outdoor recreation" purposes; such trips involve 9 percent of the total long-distance mileage traveled (Table 8.8). Sightseeing and entertainment are the main purpose of some 13 percent of household trips in excess of 161 kilometers. Almost 60 percent of household long-distance travel is in order to visit friends and relatives or for business purposes. Many of the trips to visit friends or relatives as well as the business travel probably have a recreation component.

When the "outdoor recreation" and sightseeing categories are combined, the Census data indicate that American households took about 118 million person-trips of over 161 kilometers for purely recreation purposes in 1972. Since there were about 67 million households at that time, this is equivalent to 1.8 person-trips per household. This indicates that a large proportion of the population never take a trip of more than 161 kilometers because millions of households

Table 8.8 Purposes and Transportation Mode of All Types of Trips Over 160 Kilometers by U.S. Residents

Characteristic	Person-Trips[a] (in Millions)		Person-Miles[b] (in Billions)	
	Number	Percent	Number	Percent
Purpose of trip				
Visiting	176	38.4	143	38.7
Business	93	20.2	81	22.0
"Outdoor recreation"	57	12.4	33	9.0
Sightseeing and entertainment	61	13.3	57	15.3
Other	72	15.7	55	14.9
Total	459		369	
Means of transportation				
Automobile/truck	391	85.2	252	69.4
Bus	8	1.8	5	1.5
Train	2	0.4	2	0.5
Air	54	11.8	100	27.6
Other	4	0.8	4	1.0
Total	459		363	

[a] A person-trip is counted each time a person takes a trip.
[b] One person traveling to and back from a place 1 mile away constitutes 2-person miles.
SOURCE: Adapted from 1972 data in U.S. Department of Commerce, Bureau of the Census, *The Statistical Abstract of the United States*, U.S. Government Printing Office, Washington, D.C., 1976, p. 222.

commonly go on many weekend trips to seasonal homes or take several long vacation trips each year. Most trips that involve recreation as either a primary purpose or as a secondary goal in combination with visits to relatives or business activities take place by privately owned automobile. The Census data on travel show that 85 percent of all person-trips were by automobile or truck, almost 12 percent by air, almost 2 percent by bus, and less than 0.5 percent by train (Table 8.8). Automobile and truck travel amounted to 69 percent of the distance covered, whereas air travel accounted for almost 8 percent.

Although complete quantitative information is not available concerning the recreational travel patterns of Americans, long-distance recreational travel can be characterized in the following general terms:

- A large proportion of such travel occurs as people drive to visit relatives and friends on weekends and during vacations; Thanksgiving and Christmas are especially important.
- California, Texas, Florida, New York, Michigan, Pennsylvania, Illinois, Ohio, and Wisconsin (in approximately that order) recorded the largest number of person-trips each year by nonresidents; however, many of these trips have been solely for business or to visit friends or relatives, whereas others involve travelers passing through the state to other destinations.
- Cities that attract large numbers of visitors include New York City, Los Angeles, Washington, San Francisco, Chicago, and New Orleans.

- The more than 30 major theme parks are primary attractions, especially Disneyland near Los Angeles and Disney World in central Florida.
- The U. S. Travel Service lists the five natural wonders that Americans most *wish* to visit as the canyon in Grand Canyon National Park, Arizona (Figure 9.1); the thermal areas in Yellowstone National Park (especially the geyser, Old Faithful), Wyoming; the cataracts at Niagara Falls, New York; the giant sequoia and redwood forests, California; and, the highest mountain in North America, Mount McKinley, Alaska. However, this does not mean these places are the most visited natural wonders; more accessible resources such as the Great Smoky Mountains National Park on the North Carolina-Tennessee border, or Everglades National Park in Flordia attract much larger numbers of travelers than any of the top five, except Niagara Falls.
- The U. S. Travel Service also lists the top five constructed wonders that Americans most *wish* to visit as the Golden Gate Bridge, San Francisco; the carved heads of four U. S. Presidents[4] at Mount Rushmore National Memorial, South Dakota (Figure 4.9); the Astrodome sports and convention complex, Houston, Texas; the Statue of Liberty National Monument, New York City; and the Hoover Dam on the Colorado River between Arizona and Nevada. Again, there are a number of constructed attractions that actually draw larger numbers of visitors because they are more accessible than some of the top five attractions; more people visit the Lincoln Memorial in Washington, D.C., for example, than the Statue of Liberty.
- Complexes of attractions (developed, undeveloped, or combinations of both) are popular destinations for travelers. Families in particular like to have a range of opportunities open to them within a relatively small area; examples of popular complexes are Disney World (Figure 12.6) and other attractions near Orlando, Florida; Great Smoky Mountains National Park and the associated developments in Gatlinburg, Tennessee; and Cape Cod National Seashore as well as the commercial and private resources at Cape Cod in Massachusetts.
- Special events, services, or products often stimulate visits by travelers; examples are country music tours and shows in Nashville, Tennessee; winery tours in northern California; gambling in Las Vegas, Nevada; or Pennsylvania Dutch food and handicrafts in Pennsylvania.

Chambers of commerce and tourist organizations are well aware of the drawing power of these various types of attractions and try to develop and publicize such opportunities in a manner that will be most attractive to the greatest number of potential visitors.

Americans also travel abroad in large numbers. In 1973, a record number—24.7 million person-trips—were made to foreign destinations, including Canada, Mexico, and the Caribbean. The oil crisis and economic recession decreased the number going to other countries in 1974 and 1975, but foreign travel increased again in subsequent years.

More than 50 percent of American trips abroad are to Canada and about 14 percent are to Mexico. These trips are often separated from travel statistics for several reasons. A substantial proportion are brief visits to border towns that have few of the characteristics normally associated with foreign travel. Such visits seldom last longer than a few hours and frequently emphasize shopping, dining at a restaurant, or visiting relatives or friends rather than sightseeing or attending a special event. Most Americans visit even the more distant Canadian destinations in their own cars rather than using public transportation. And finally, much of the travel is either for business purposes or involves nonrecreational journeys on a Mexican or Canadian highway in order to reach another destination in the United States. An example of the latter is the high incidence of Americans traveling from Detroit to Buffalo through Southern Ontario.

The growth of American travel to other parts of the world is shown in Figure 8.15. The effect of growing affluence and cheaper air travel is reflected in the rapid increases that occurred after 1960. Total overseas travel to foreign countries increased by 100 percent between 1965 and 1970, compared to 60 percent between 1960 and 1965 and 21 percent between 1970 and 1975. About one-half of overseas foreign travel is now to Europe and the Mediterranean, and one-third to the Caribbean and Central America. Although Europe and the Mediterranean region continued to be the main destination, the number going to other places has continued to grow at a relatively steady rate. No doubt part of this change is the result of increased business travel, but more Americans are also going to resorts in the Caribbean and South America or on tours to the Soviet Union, China, Africa, India, Japan, and to Australasia.

Over 1 million Americans take part annually in ocean or river cruises, many of which cater to special interests. The Caribbean remains the most frequent destination, but cruises, such as those via

[4] George Washington, Thomas Jefferson, Abraham Lincoln, and Theodore Roosevelt.

Figure 8.15 Number of American residents who traveled overseas to foreign countries from 1955 to 1978. Not included: travel to Canada and Mexico; cruise ship travelers: travel by military personnel, other government employees and dependents; and U.S. citizens resident abroad. (Source: Developed from data in, The Statistical Abstract of the United States, U.S. Department of Commerce, Bureau of the Census, Government Printing Office, Washington, D.C., 1976, p. 223, and U.S. Travel Service, "American Travel Abroad by Geographic Destination 1970-1978," Washington, D.C., undated.)

the Inside Passage to Alaska, through the Panama Canal, and along the coast of Mexico are increasing in popularity. A growing number of people are taking longer voyages— for example, voyages to the South Pacific, China, and even around the world, a cruise that may take 10 months to complete.

Summer Recreation Patterns. Since the majority of the American population lives in areas that have only three or four months of warm weather, summer recreation behavior patterns are of particular importance. June, July, and August are the peak attendance months at most outdoor facilities. Agencies and commercial suppliers often operate with small staffs and many facilities or programs are closed or discontinued during the remainder of the year. Therefore, the summer months are frequently considered separately when compiling participation data and in planning and managing recreation resources.

The 1972 National Recreation Survey involved personal interviews with members of 4029 randomly selected households distributed throughout the 48 contiguous states. One respondent, 12 years of age or older, was randomly selected from each household. Although the introductory statement identified "outdoor recreation" as the subject of the survey and defined it as "any recreation activity which takes place outdoors,"[5] the interview focused on extraurban recreation. Whether it was intentional or not, respondents' thinking was directed toward recreation in less-developed environments by the list of possible "outdoor activities" that was handed to them before the first question was asked. This list began with camping, hunting, fishing, riding motorcycles off the road, and driving four-wheel vehicles off the

[5] "Appendix A, An Economic Analysis," a supplement to U. S. Department of the Interior, Bureau of Outdoor Recreation, *Outdoor Recreation: A Legacy for America,* U.S. Government Printing Office, Washington, D.C., 1974, p. 1–52.

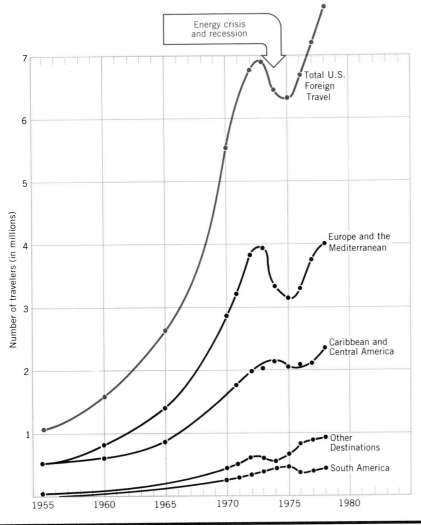

road. Item 11, walking for pleasure, stipulated that the walks had to be more than 30 minutes in length. Some activities that are more frequently experienced in urban environments were included such as bicycling, outdoor pool swimming, tennis, and going to outdoor sports events, but these appear later in the list. Common outdoor activities such as playing in the street, gardening, or relaxing outside on lawn chairs or park benches are not mentioned. The response, therefore, was probably biased toward extraurban recreation and, in particular, toward those activities that appeared on the list.

The data from the 1972 National Recreation Survey cannot, therefore, be considered an indication of total nationwide participation even though they are labeled, "Summer 1972 Recreation Activities,"in the nationwide plan[6] and elsewhere. In reality, the information is for extraurban activities and a few selected urban outdoor activities. Within these limits, the 1972 National Recreation Survey shows that swimming at beaches, lakes, and rivers, together with fishing, sightseeing, picnicking, walking for pleasure (over 30 minutes), and playing outdoor games and sports (other than tennis or golf) probably occupy the most time (Figure 8.16). Driving for pleasure and camping at developed sites are probably also in the top 10 activities in terms of time spent on them but the survey did not obtain this information, since it did not include total participation data.

[6] U.S. Department of the Interior, Bureau of Outdoor Recreation, *Outdoor Recreation: A Legacy for America*, U. S. Government Printing Office, Washington, D.C., 1973, p. 23.

The right-hand side of Figure 8.16 shows the *percentages* of respondents who took part *at least once* in each activity. In this case, picnicking (47 percent) is well ahead of sightseeing, driving for pleasure, walking, and swimming at beaches, lakes, and rivers, which ranked second, third, fourth, and fifth, respectively. The numbers down the right-hand margin of Figure 8.16 are the estimated total number of activity days for each activity (each time a person takes part in an activity is counted as an activity day, irrespective of the time involved). On this basis, walking is first, followed by swimming at beaches, lakes, and rivers; picnicking; driving for pleasure; and sightseeing. Because the sample was relatively small, the data for the eleventh (nature walks) and succeeding activities is not as statistically reliable as the information for the first 10 activities. However, the general ranking of activities in terms of time spent and percent participating is probably reasonably accurate.

Recreation Fads and Gadgets. Although recreation fads and gadgets may not initially have a major effect on basic recreation participation patterns, they can be important. Fads often result in sudden unexpected pressures on recreation resources, which managers find difficult to accommodate. They may also have substantial, if short-lived, impacts. Sometimes what appear to be fads or gadgets are rapidly adopted by a large proportion of a population and turn out to be permanent and influential aspects of recreation— sea bathing, camping vehicles, and television are examples.

Fads and gadgets have played an important role in the development of recreation participation in the United States. With less social pressure to conform to set patterns of behavior and more discretionary income than people in most nations, Americans have developed and enthusiastically adopted a great variety of recreation innovations. When an interesting new activity or gadget is introduced, many people hurry to be among the first participants or owners. If the initial wave of converts reacts favorably to the innovation, a second larger group begins to adopt the fad or gadget. Commercial interests often become involved and try to convince the rest of the population that they should "keep up with the Joneses." If they are successful, a new craze begins. The card game, canasta; hula hoops; and miniature golf are examples of recreation innovations in the United States that became national crazes and then declined in popularity. Recent American recreation innovations, gadgets, and crazes include frisbees, skateboards,

Figure 8.16 **Estimated total participation by Americans 12 years of age and over and percentage of this population taking part in extraurban and selected urban recreation activities during the summer quarter, 1972. Total participation data for driving for pleasure, other activities, camping— developed sites, and camping— underdeveloped sites were not included in the tabulation. Walking included only walks of more than 30 minutes duration. (**Source: **U.S. Department of the Interior, Bureau of Outdoor Recreation,** Outdoor Recreation: A Legacy for America, Appendix A, and Economic Analysis, **Government Printing Office, Washington, D.C., 1974, p. 5.)**

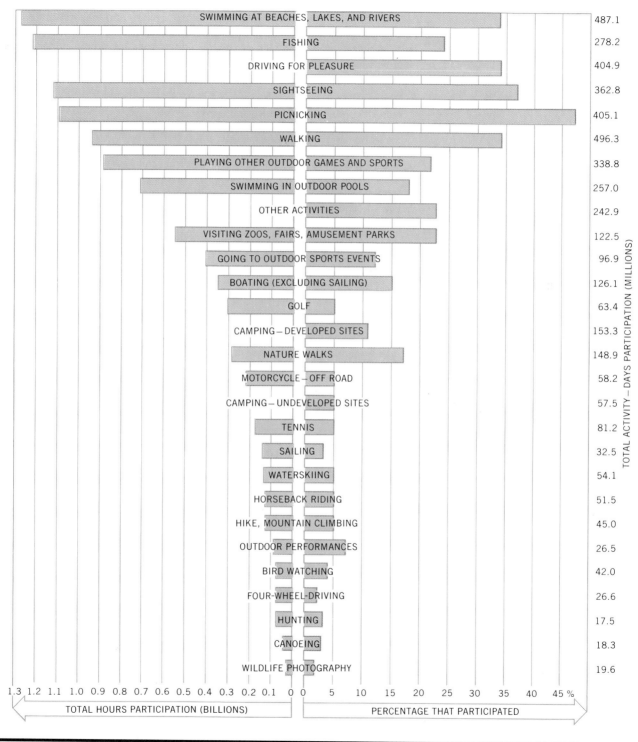

Activity	Total Activity – Days Participation (Millions)
SWIMMING AT BEACHES, LAKES, AND RIVERS	487.1
FISHING	278.2
DRIVING FOR PLEASURE	404.9
SIGHTSEEING	362.8
PICNICKING	405.1
WALKING	496.3
PLAYING OTHER OUTDOOR GAMES AND SPORTS	338.8
SWIMMING IN OUTDOOR POOLS	257.0
OTHER ACTIVITIES	242.9
VISITING ZOOS, FAIRS, AMUSEMENT PARKS	122.5
GOING TO OUTDOOR SPORTS EVENTS	96.9
BOATING (EXCLUDING SAILING)	126.1
GOLF	63.4
CAMPING – DEVELOPED SITES	153.3
NATURE WALKS	148.9
MOTORCYCLE – OFF ROAD	58.2
CAMPING – UNDEVELOPED SITES	57.5
TENNIS	81.2
SAILING	32.5
WATERSKIING	54.1
HORSEBACK RIDING	51.5
HIKE, MOUNTAIN CLIMBING	45.0
OUTDOOR PERFORMANCES	26.5
BIRD WATCHING	42.0
FOUR-WHEEL-DRIVING	26.6
HUNTING	17.5
CANOEING	18.3
WILDLIFE PHOTOGRAPHY	19.6

TOTAL HOURS PARTICIPATION (BILLIONS) 1.3 1.2 1.1 1.0 0.9 0.8 0.7 0.6 0.5 0.4 0.3 0.2 0.1 0

PERCENTAGE THAT PARTICIPATED 0 5 10 15 20 25 30 35 40 45 %

THE NATURE AND EXTENT OF RECREATION PARTICIPATION

CB radios, video games, nostalgia (an interest in the past that includes crafts, games, music, dances, and movies), the study of one's genealogy, and the conversion of tradesmen's vans into individualized recreation vehicles.

VARIATIONS IN PATTERNS

Although an appreciation of characteristic national participation patterns and the impact of widely adopted fads and innovations is important, recreation professionals must not lose sight of the many variations in recreation behavior that exist. As explained in earlier chapters, recreation is influenced by a great variety of personal and external factors. Recreation preferences and choices are very much a matter of individual circumstances and attitudes. Social and economic freedom coupled with opportunities to travel and use an extensive supply of recreation resources has produced a great range of recreation lifestyles, especially in Canada and the United States and to a lesser extent in some of the other developed nations. Therefore, although professionals must understand the dominance of some activities such as television viewing and picnicking, they should also be prepared to consider the needs of individuals and groups who prefer recreation lifestyles that differ substantially from those of the majority.

In some cases, the differences in one or more of the external factors are sufficient to produce distinct regional or national recreation behavior patterns. The ethnic origin or cultural background of the majority of the people are often the principal reasons for such differences, but religion, age structure, resource avail-

ability, climate, and even the main economic activity of the area may play a part. Some examples of special regional and national patterns are:

- Rodeos continue to be an important recreation activity in the ranchland areas of Canada and the United States but are generally of relatively little significance elsewhere.
- Tractor-pulling competitions for huge modified tractors that are never used for farming are popular at agricultural fairs throughout the large-farm cropland areas of the American midwestern and southeastern states.
- The centuries-old sport of bullfighting has remained largely confined to Spain, Portugal, southern France, and Latin America.
- Falconry persists as a favorite sport of prominent men in nations around the Persian Gulf; research is underway to prevent its demise because of inadequate supplies of suitable birds and appropriate game.
- The ritual of the sauna bath originated in Finland where it is still an essential part of the people's recreation lifestyle.

Differences such as these are often of great importance to national, regional, or ethnic groups. Preservation of unique recreation patterns are viewed as an important contribution to the perpetuation of a cultural identity. Unique crafts, sports, games, dances, festivals, and music can also be of considerable interest to tourists.

On the other hand, modern technology, mobility, communications, and education are tending to eliminate differences in recreation behavior among regions and nations. An outstanding example of this is the spread of soccer (association football). It originated in Britain, developed into that nation's principal winter team game during

the 1800s, and was exported by sailors, colonial administrators, and emigrants. It became quite well established in Canada and the United States in the late 1800s but gradually lost ground to another British import, rugby football. However, soccer gradually diffused through other countries and is now the world's most widely played sport. Practically every nation has a professional soccer league modeled after the British pattern. By 1970, the Federation Internationale de Football Association had more member countries than the United Nations.

In the United States and Canada, soccer was principally a game played among teams representing various ethnic groups until the 1960s. Then a grassroots movement started that increased interest and encouraged participation, especially by young people. Attempts to establish professional leagues, however, met with little success. Then Pelé—the famous Brazilian soccer player, who is said to be the single most recognized athlete in the world—accepted an offer to play for the New Jersey Cosmos. Owing partly to his international reputation and partly to his personal enthusiasm for soccer, Pelé was able to interest a large number of Americans of all ages and backgrounds in the game. By 1977, a playoff match between the Cosmos and Fort Lauderdale teams drew 77,691 spectators and, nationwide, the sport was attracting 6 million spectators each year. Meanwhile, 700,000 boys and girls under 19 years of age had begun to play soccer in programs sponsored by such groups as the American Youth Soccer Organization or the United States Soccer Federation.

TOURISM

Travel for pleasure is now an important and widely accepted recreation activity. Growing numbers of people throughout the world regard one or more trips each year as an essential part of their recreation lifestyles. As a result, international tourism is now one of the top items in world trade in terms of monetary value.

Who Is a Tourist? Professionals associated with international tourism define a tourist as someone who travels for more than 24 hours in a country where the individual is not a resident. Persons traveling on business, to meetings, or for health reasons are included in addition to those on pleasure trips. International tourist data is gathered on this basis and in some cases includes large amounts of nonrecreational travel.

In common usage, however, the term, tourist, is used to indicate anyone who travels many miles from home for pleasure whether or not an international boundary is crossed. The term is used in a very broad sense in the United States and Canada to include people traveling between, or even within, states and provinces. Some agencies suggest that a person must stay at least one night away from home in order to qualify as a tourist. An increasing number of organizations are indicating the business travel and local entertainment aspects of hotels, motels, restaurants, resorts, and other tourist facilities by using the phrase, tourism and hospitality industry.

Travel Motives. Although a few individuals have always taken trips for enjoyment, large-scale tourism is a modern development. A growing number of people began to travel for nonbusiness purposes in the early seventeenth century, but it was not until the middle of the eighteenth century that tours resembling today's travel vacations became common. Of course, such vacations were possible only for the rich and privileged. In addition, travel for pleasure alone was largely unheard of up to the middle 1800s. Until then, people said that they were going to the mountains, ocean, country, or spas for their health and that they were taking tours primarily for educational purposes. Following 1850, rising discretionary incomes, improved and cheaper transportation, and the growth of paid annual vacations gradually extended travel opportunity to the middle class. The process continues today as reduced air fares have made international travel possible for millions of people with quite modest incomes.

The reasons for recreational travel are also changing and are almost as diverse as the travelers themselves. Many people, especially those in the Soviet Union and the nations of eastern Europe, continue to vacation at spas whose activities are intended to be, first and foremost, physically and emotionally beneficial. Many people also continue to take their children abroad or send them for extended periods of time to foreign locations to develop the poise and cultural appreciation such journeys are said to confer. But health and education are no longer the primary purposes of long-distance trips. Most people today seem to travel as an escape, a quest, or a combination of both. Some of the more common travel patterns involve:

- Sightseeing at traditional or exotic locations to see the famous undeveloped or developed wonders of the world.
- Visiting friends and relatives, attending reunions, or exploring the ancestral home or country of origin.
- Seeking adventure, entertainment, excitement, or social experiences at resorts, camps, undeveloped areas, theme parks, or on tours and cruises to urban centers or exotic locations.
- Shopping expeditions to look for bargains, ethnic handicrafts, antiques, or merchandise characteristic of certain locations.
- Cultural trips (1) to visit museums, exhibitions, folk festivals, national celebrations, (2) to enjoy musical, theatrical and dance presentations, or (3) to become familiar with lifestyles of people in different regions and nations of the world.
- Educational trips to improve knowledge or develop special skills (1) through guided study tours to interesting locations or habitats, (2) through visits to historic sites and capitol cities, (3) by taking part in programs at camps for young people or adults, and (4) during participation in special programs offered during the summer at various college locations.
- Seeking relaxation and refreshment through visits to undeveloped areas, spas, retreats, resorts, or during cruises and prearranged tours.
- Participation as visitors in special events such as the Olympic Games, world's fairs, national exhibitions, color or blossom tours, the United States bicentennial celebrations, or Great Britain's silver jubilee festivities (Figure 8.17).
- Exploratory travel to enable a person to become acquainted with the positive and negative aspects of an area or way of life before deciding on a retirement community, a change of career, recreation lifestyle, or place of residence.
- Status travel that enhances the individual's social position through participation in world cruises, trips to

Figure 8.17 **One million men, women, and children of many different nationalities stand 20 or more deep along London streets to catch a glimpse of the British Royal Family on their way to St. Paul's Cathedral for the Silver Jubilee thanksgiving service in June, 1977. Tens of thousands took up their positions the night before in order to obtain a good view.**

exclusive resort areas, or travel to certain exotic or hard-to-reach locations considered desirable by a peer group.

In addition to these kinds of motives, another reason for travel is beginning to emerge, one that may not always be readily apparent to the participants themselves. As more and more ordinary people take long-distance trips, traveling for pleasure is becoming an accepted part of the culture, especially in such nations as Canada, the United States, and the more affluent countries of Europe. Many trips, therefore, are now as much the result of social conditioning and peer pressure as a keen desire to fulfill a specific goal. An actual decision to go on a trip no longer has to be made; only the choice of destination or activities are considered or discussed, since it is taken for granted that everyone with sufficient free time, adequate finances, and reasonably good health goes somewhere and does something at least once a year.

Peer pressure reinforces and perpetuates this new form of social conditioning. Children, for example, are asked by friends about their planned activities for the family vacation, and they, in turn, try to influence the parents to engage in some of the away-from-home activities considered most desirable among their friends. Adults feel an urge to "keep up with the Joneses" and, through participation in trips and activities away from home, show that they have the time, available cash, as well as the know-how necessary to be able to indulge themselves. And so, sometimes it is not the travel experience itself that is of the utmost importance but rather the act of going that really matters.

Destination Appeal. The nature and scope of tourism also varies considerably. For instance, all regions and nations are not equally appealing as travel destinations. There are several reasons for this. The occurrence of political unrest, a major natural disaster, an outbreak of disease, or a high incidence of crime affects tourism; even once-popular locations can quickly become areas that are avoided. Sometimes success destroys an area's attractiveness as overcrowding, overuse, and the resultant environmental and facility deterioration accompanied by rising costs causes people to become disillusioned and go elsewhere. Even the likelihood of success can sometimes scare visitors away. Concerned that overcrowding might mar their enjoyment, many families with young children, older people, and foreign visitors chose to avoid visiting the major American historical sites and cities during the bicentennial summer of 1976 and, as a result, many locations were disappointed by attendance figures far below expectations.

Some regions or nations could be popular travel destinations, but tourism is not encouraged. For instance, India, situated at the center of one of the world's main air routes between East and West is also blessed with beautiful beaches, magnificent Himalayan mountain scenery, the world-famous Taj Mahal, and a unique cultural environment that should make tourism both accessible and attractive. However, only 470,000 visitors from abroad, many of whom were business people or Indians visiting relatives, traveled to India in 1975. This seemed to be the direct result of a generally inhospitable attitude on the part of citizens toward foreign visitors coupled with a neglect of tourism publicity and facilities by both government and private enterprise. By 1977, however, tourism had risen to 640,000 foreign visitors, a substantial increase, which was attributed to the effects of an intensified government campaign to promote India as an exciting tourist destination and the development of a network of improved lodging, transportation, and entertainment facilities.

Finally, of course, there are some locations that simply do not possess much tourist appeal. For example, according to a recent study, the state of Kansas is perceived by most travelers as uninteresting, drab, and a pass-through region to be visited only when necessary to reach a better area beyond its borders. Because of this attitude, Kansas ranks near the bottom of the 50 American states in terms of numbers of tourists.

Attitudes Toward Travel. Another factor that affects the nature and scope of tourism is the attitude of people toward travel. Everyone does not share the same enthusiasm for travel. Some feel guilty about large expenditures of time or money on their own pleasure. Freedom to travel at will is also not enjoyed equally by all people. Some individuals are too poor, too busy, or physically unable to travel long distances. Many citizens of Communist nations are not allowed to travel outside their home community without official permission, and foreign travel is discouraged or forbidden. Certain segments of a population — such as the nonwhite residents of South Africa — are similarly restricted in their freedom of movement. Nations that have serious problems with their balance of payments often limit the amount of currency a citizen may take out of the country; as a result, foreign travel to some locations is effectively reduced and to other areas virtually eliminated.

However, for millions of people, travel is the ultimate recreation experience. It is no longer regarded as a luxury but considered a worthwhile investment of time and money with valuable educational, cultural, and recreational benefits. Middle-income families are giving travel a place in their budgets as they look on the experience not as a privilege, but as a right.

Travel Patterns. Although people's travel behavior differs considerably, many characteristic patterns of tourism emerge. Examples of these patterns are:

- In addition to the 12 million Canadian and 2 million Mexican visitors, 5.8 million foreign travelers visited the United States in 1978; the largest number came from Japan (886,000), but many were from Britain (757,000), West Germany (486,000), Venezuela (304,000), and France (260,000).

- In 1978, a high proportion of the 23 million Americans traveling to other countries visited Canada (12 million), but substantial numbers chose Western Europe (4 million), Mexico (3 million), and the West Indies (2 million) as their destinations.

- West Germans made about 25 million trips outside their country in 1977, making West Germany the nation with the highest proportion of the population taking foreign vacation trips.

- Of the half of the French population that takes vacations away from home (Figure 3.2), about 60 percent go abroad and, of these, more than half visit Spain.

- France has more foreign visitors than any other European nation.

- Foreign visitors to the United States favor certain locations. The Japanese like Hawaii because of its year-round summer climate; Latin Americans prefer Florida and the Southwest where Spanish is a second language in many areas; Europeans on a first trip most frequently visit New York with side excursions to Washington, D.C. and Niagara Falls; on a second trip, Europeans often fly directly to the West Coast to tour California and visit the Grand Canyon; the French tourist tends to be particularly interested in visiting the national parks and ranches in the West.

- In the Soviet Union, 47 million workers enjoyed state subsidized vacations at resorts or on cruises chosen by the government or unions in 1977.

- More than 1 million people from various parts of the British Isles and many foreign countries went to London to take part in the silver jubilee festivities in June, 1977. Of the 11.5 million foreign visitors who toured Great Britain during the jubilee year, almost 2 million were from the United States.

- In Brazil, the government discouraged both foreign and domestic travel in 1977 to slow the drain on hard currencies and reduce fuel consumption.

- Hawaii now attracts more visitors from the rest of the United States than go to either Mexico or the Caribbean.
- About 13 percent of the 32 million Britons who took a vacation in 1977 went abroad.
- In 1978, about 100,000 foreign tourists visited China; this was equal to the total number for the previous 23 years.
- The number of Japanese traveling abroad increased by 11 percent from 1976 to 1977, reaching a total of 3.2 million.
- About 4.4 million tourists, more than 1.5 million of them from the West, traveled to the Soviet Union in 1977, whereas 3 million Russians visited 135 foreign countries.
- Tourism is the leading industry in the states of Florida, Hawaii, and Nevada; some countries such as the island nations in the Caribbean, rely on tourism almost exclusively for their economic well-being.
- Tourism now accounts for 50 percent of Mexico's balance-of-payments income ($2.8 billion in 1978); of the 4 million annual foreign visitors, 85 percent are Americans and 5 percent are Canadians.

These examples indicate the scope and significance of tourism. However, it must be remembered that millions of individuals never leave their home environments. Many living in rural areas have not visited a major city, and large numbers of urban dwellers have never experienced an extraurban environment. For example, thousands of people residing in New York City have not seen the Atlantic Ocean.

RECREATION-ACTIVITY CLASSIFICATION

One of the basic tools used in scientific study is classification. Once appropriate classification systems have been developed, tested, and widely adopted, it is much easier for researchers, planners, and managers to make measurements and communicate among themselves and with others. Unfortunately, recreation professionals are having difficulty producing classification systems that are widely accepted. This is understandable, since recreation is such a complicated phenomenon and objective research in the area of recreation has been limited.

A basic problem has been lack of agreement on a definition of recreation. As mentioned in Chapter 1, some professionals believe in a much narrower definition than has been used in this book. The situation is complicated by the current tendency to use the term, leisure, instead of recreation, and the even narrower limits often suggested by advocates of that word. Obviously, it is impossible to produce a widely acceptable classification of recreation participation if there is no general agreement on which activities should be included.

Some of the difficulties associated with these definitional problems emerged earlier in this chapter. In the multinational time-budget study, for instance, an underestimation of the time spent on recreation resulted from the separation of recreation experiences from activities that can sometimes be recreational but were classified as duties. Mention has also been made of the problems produced when the term outdoor recreation is used in a special sense, and the manner in which some studies (such as the 1972 National Recreation Survey) concentrate on selected activities although this may not be readily discernible in the project title or the data tabulations.

Although terminology problems of this kind create difficulties, a number of attempts have been made to develop recreation activity or participation classifications. Some researchers have based classifications on the kinds of recreation resources involved such as land, water, or ice and snow (Figure 8.18). Although this approach is logical from the resource planning point of view, many activities involve combinations of resources rather than just one. The assignment of such an activity to only one type of basic resource can give an erroneous impression of its resource needs.

The majority of classifications attempt to group activities according to their general nature. For example, professionals associated with community recreation programs often classify activities as arts and crafts, clubs, dancing, dramatics, hobbies, music, outdoor activities (other than sports and games), social events, sports and games, and special events. A great variety of more detailed intuitive groupings have been used in recreation planning procedures. For example, the Michigan Department of Natural Resources recorded data for 209 different types of recreation activities in its statewide telephone survey. These were then grouped into 19 classes as follows:[7]

- *Swimming*—8 types, private pool to ocean.
- *Watercraft*—9 types, canoeing to tourist boats.

[7] Michigan Department of Natural Resources, Recreation Services Division, *Michigan Resident Recreation Activities and Providers: 1976 Telephone Survey*, Lansing, Michigan, 1977.

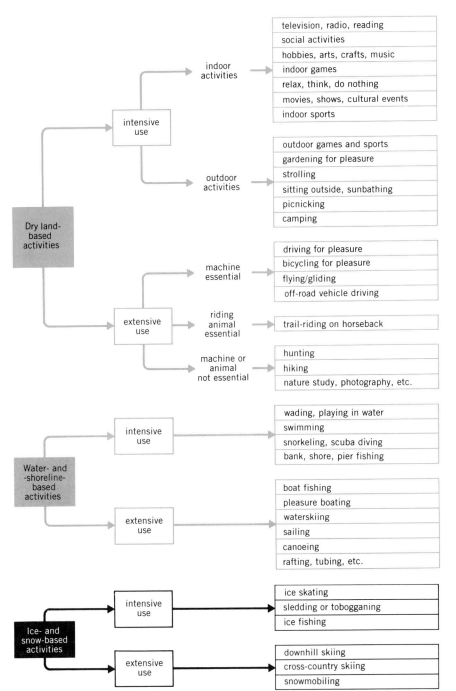

- *Land mobile*—10 types, bicycling to vehicle repair.
- *Air related*—9 types, parachuting to aircraft observation.
- *Food related*—4 types, picnicking to going out to eat or drink.
- *Viewing competitive events*—6 types, athletics to dog shows.
- *Viewing noncompetitive events*—10 types, live concerts to circuses.
- *Visiting sites*—9 types, parks to libraries.
- *Camping*—7 types, primitive to developed.
- *Miscellaneous*—10 types, sunbathing to shopping.
- *Nature related*—7 types, wildlife feeding to nature centers.
- *Attending meetings or centers for pleasure*—6 types, civic meetings to recreation centers.
- *Arts and crafts*—7 types, painting to weaving.
- *30 competitive sports*—60 types, badminton to karate.
- *Other games*—12 types, roller-skating to informal play.

Since classifications of this kind are not standardized, it is usually difficult or impossible to make comparisons among data compiled by different agencies or even among surveys made at different times by the same agency.

A number of authors have divided recreation into "active" and "passive" groupings. Such activities as driving for pleasure, picnicking, short walks, and seeing a sport as a

Figure 8.18 Classification of main groups of recreation activities based on the principal resource involved. Combinations of activities present problems in classification. (Source: Developed from Michael Chubb and Leslie M. Reid, "Activity Code Numbers," unpublished paper, Michigan Outdoor Recreation Demand Study, Department of Resource Development, Michigan State University, East Lansing, 1964.)

spectator have generally been considered "passive," whereas active games, sports, and long walks have been labeled "active." This type of approach has not proved particularly useful because of the arbitrary nature of the division and the different ways in which individuals participate.

Some researchers have suggested groupings based on various social or psychological aspects of activities or participation. In one approach, activities have been divided into groups based on people's propensities to take part in certain specific clusters of activities. For example, Burton found that in Great Britain, there were four relatively stable groupings: soccer, cricket, table tennis, and tennis; rugby football, athletics, basketball, physical conditioning, badminton, and cycling; roller-skating, ice skating, youth club activities, and horseback riding; and, picnicking, driving for pleasure, gardening, and dining out.[8]

In addition, a number of investigators have attempted to group activities that appear to involve the same type of psychological processes. For instance, McKechnie developed seven groupings that included these examples:[9]

- *Mechanics*— 22 activities, amateur radio to hunting.
- *Crafts*— 18 activities, ceramics and sewing to dancing.
- *Intellectual*— 16 activities, acting and politics to hiking.
- *Slow living*— 19 activities, gardening and television to dining out.

[8] Thomas L. Burton, *Experiments in Recreation Research*, Allen & Unwin, London, 1971, p. 209.

[9] George E. McKechnie, "The Psychological Structure of Leisure: Past Behavior," *Journal of Leisure Research, 61*, p. 33 (1974).

- *Neighborhood sports*— 14 activities, bicycling and kite-flying to baseball.
- *Glamour sports*— 15 activities, canoeing and motorcycling to tennis.
- *Fast living*— 4 activities, fraternal organizations to gambling, horseracing, and nightclubs.

McKechnie's classes were developed empirically from interview data.

Other investigators have developed sociopsychological groupings on a theoretical basis. One of the better known ones is a system developed by Dumazedier of the University of Paris and other sociologists involved in an international recreation study. Their classification has five major divisions, each of which has two subdivisions:[10]

- *I Physical:* (a) *Physical Play*— taking part in sports, games, spectator sports, and sex; (b) *Physical Travel*— tourism.
- *II Intellectual:* (a) *Intellectual Understanding*— obtaining knowledge through a teacher, book, field study, television program, concert, movie, play or lecture; (b) *Intellectual Production*— being creative as an amateur writer, scientist, or philosopher.
- *III Artistic:* (a) *Artistic Enjoyment*— listening to music; attending concerts, operas, and plays; visiting art galleries and museums; and reading about the arts; (b) *Artistic Creation*— taking lessons in the arts, singing, playing an instrument, painting, writing poetry or prose, dancing, acting, taking part in crafts as an amateur, or participating in community art programs and organizations.
- *IV Sociable:* (a) *Sociable Communication*— oral communication for pleasure between two or more people in person, on the telephone, or through written communications such as let-

[10] Max Kaplan discusses this system extensively calling it a leisure typology in *Leisure: Theory and Policy*, New York, Wiley, 1975, Chap. 13.

ters and diaries; (b) *Sociable Entertainment*— one-way communication from performers or the mass media to the consumer, as in movies, newspapers, television, magazines, and books.
- *V Practical:* (a) *Practical Collection*— personal hobbies that result in something to show for the effort and involvement in community collecting, preserving, and sharing, such as at museums, zoos, art galleries, historical sites, and historic homes; (b) *Practical Transformation*— activities that seek to change a thing (do-it-yourself projects and inventors), a person (gossips, advisers, amateur psychiatrists), or a social institution (political or service organization participants).

Classifications of this type are useful to behavioral scientists but are unlikely to be adopted by those interested in planning the development of recreation resources.

Many other methods of classifying recreation activities or participation have been suggested, but none have been widely accepted. This is partly because of the comparatively recent beginnings of objective recreation research and partly the result of the differing professional viewpoints of those involved. Land-managing agency planners favor classifications that distinguish among activities with different types of recreation resource requirements, whereas those involved in behavioral studies use classifications based on social or psychological differences. No doubt the variety of professions involved in recreation and its complex nature make it impossible for a single classification system to be widely acceptable. Nevertheless, standardization of the classifications used by the major groups of researchers and planners is possible and, once accomplished, improved communication and more useful data would result.

This completes the discussion of the factors affecting recreation participation and the mechanics of the recreation experience. In Part Three, the nature of recreation resources will be examined, including the extent, distribution, and management of both public and private amenities that are used for recreation.

DISCUSSION TOPICS

1. Using examples from your own or your family's recreation behavior patterns, explain how the amount of time spent on the various phases of the recreation experience varies from activity to activity. Is the amount of time devoted to the phases you describe an indication of their relative importance?
2. Do people normally take the four steps suggested in the decision tree when deciding to participate in a recreation activity? Support your answer by preparing decision trees for activities in which you have and have not participated.
3. Do the majority of people take part only in recreation activities that are their *real* preferences? Discuss, using examples from your own experience.
4. How do the percentages of time spent on various recreation activities by yourself and members of your family or others that you know differ from the percentages shown in Figure 8.12? If possible, keep time-budget diaries for a typical week to develop more accurate estimates of the time devoted to various types of recreation. What are the most probable reasons?
5. How does your participation in summer recreation activities and that of your family or people you know differ from the national pattern shown in Figure 8.16? Do you think that the people of the region in which you live exhibit a different pattern? What are the main factors contributing to these different personal, family, and regional patterns?

FURTHER READINGS

Marion Clawson and Jack Knetsch describe the five main phases that they feel are present in *every* recreation experience in Chapter 3 of their book *Economics of Outdoor Recreation* published in Baltimore by The Johns Hopkins University Press in 1966. John Neulinger's *The Psychology of Leisure* again provides additional perspectives on a number of matters discussed in this chapter. Parts of Chapter 1, "The Conceptualization of Leisure," and Chapter 3, "Some Leisure Facts," are especially relevant. Similarly, Chapter 5, "Selections: External, Internal, and Mediating Factors," and Chapter 6, "Functions: Manifest and Latent," in *Leisure Theory and Policy* by Max Kaplan contain many related ideas.

The lengthy report on the Multinational Comparative Time-Budget Research Project edited by Alexander Szalai and published in The Hague by Mouton under the title, *The Use of Time: Daily Activities of Urban and Suburban Populations in Twelve Countries* in 1972 contains much useful information concerning time-budget methods as well as thought-provoking data and discussions on recreation and related social behavior. Information on the methods used in the 1972 National Recreation Study is included in "*Appendix A, An Economic Analysis*" a supplement to the U.S. Department of the Interior report, *Outdoor Recreation: A Legacy for America* published by the U.S. Government Printing Office in 1974; unfortunately, there is little discussion of the survey results. Although the statistics are outdated, a number of the reports of the Outdoor Recreation Resources Review Commission published in Washington by the U.S. Government Printing Office in 1962 still provide helpful insights into the nature of participation. Report No. 19, *National Recreation Survey;* Report No. 20, *Participation in Outdoor Recreation: Factors Affecting Demand Among American Adults;* and Report No. 26, *Prospective Demand for Outdoor Recreation* are particularly useful. Many state, provincial, regional, and national recreation participation studies or comprehensive recreation plans contain pertinent statistics and discussions. *The Journal of Leisure Research* frequently contains reports of research concerning the nature of participation. However, whatever the sources consulted, it is necessary to know both the nature of the populations sampled, the survey methods used, and the actual questions asked to interpret recreation participation data correctly.

PART THREE

RECREATION RESOURCES

Waikiki, on the Hawaiian island of Oahu, has a unique blend of developed and undeveloped resources including excellent swimming beaches, a state park, a large city park, 150 resort and apartment hotels, and Diamond Head, the remains of a volcano.

9

THE NATURE OF RECREATION RESOURCES

Part Two of this book examined the human factors that affect recreation participation. Part Three explores the nature and distribution of recreation resources and shows how combinations of resources form a variety of recreation entities and systems.

Figure 9.1 **The Grand Canyon in Arizona is one of the world's best known resources because of its depth, width, erosional features, geologic formations, climatic zones, and changing colors. This photograph was taken from the South Rim at an elevation of 2100 meters (6850 feet) looking toward the North Rim which is more than 2400 meters (8000 feet) above sea level and 10 kilometers (6 miles) away.**

DEFINITIONS

What is a *recreation resource?* Many writers appear to think only of mountains, canyons, lakes, rivers and forests unmodified by human activities (Figure 9.1); they do not include highly developed areas used for urban parks or commercial recreation (page 285). No doubt this limited view of recreation resources reflects the common narrow interpretation of the term, "natural resources." Many only apply that term to largely undeveloped environments that are exploited primarily for minerals, timber, and water. Nothing in the dictionary meanings of natural or resources excludes human modification. Farm soils and woodlands are generally regarded as natural resources, even though they are often greatly altered by agricultural or forestry practices. To add to the confusion, some people attempt to distinguish between "natural" and "man-made" resources without defining either. Yet, it can be argued that there are no man-made resources, only natural resources that have been modified to a greater or lesser extent by humans.

Examples of landscape features used for recreation illustrate the gap between common usage in the recreation jargon and the dictionary definitions. Does the river Rhine cease to be a natural resource after it leaves the Alpine environments of its upper reaches and becomes progressively more channelized, urbanized, and polluted as it flows north through Western Europe's industrial heartland? How should New York City's Central Park with its artificial landscapes be classified? Are its soils, rocks, trees, and water no longer natural resources in peo-

ple's minds so that they do not think of its hills, woods, and lakes as recreation resources? Certainly, most recreation professionals will not immediately visualize the Rhine flowing through Düsseldorf or the boating lake in Central Park when natural resources or recreation resources are mentioned.

Because of such problems, the terms natural resource and man-made resources, are not used elsewhere in this book. It would be best to avoid recreation resource as well because of the limited interpretations mentioned earlier, but no suitable synonym for resource exists. Recreation resource will be used in its full dictionary sense to mean *a source of supply of recreation opportunities,* with no limitations on type or location. Books and television programs; postage stamps, and antiques; automobiles and aircraft; table games and puzzles; gardens and window boxes; golf courses and tennis courts; shopping centers and factories; homes and hotels; museums and libraries; restaurants and theaters; streets and roads, rivers and agricultural land; park naturalists, recreation program leaders, and professional athletes are all included. They all provide recreation opportunities.

Recreation resources have no common inherent characteristics; rather they derive that identity from human needs. A landscape feature or manufactured object does not become a recreation resource until someone perceives it as such. For example, ocean beaches provided comparatively little recreation until people's perceptions changed following the adoption of saltwater bathing as a health fad. Similarly, most people did not regard undeveloped landscapes as recreation

resources before Romanticism and urbanization began to alter perceptions. Conversely, something can cease to be a recreation resource when attitudes toward it change. The bicycle, for instance, ceased to be an adult recreation resource to most Americans as the privately owned motor vehicle became widely available. Adults have been taking up bicycling again in recent years but more as a source of pleasant exercise than as a basic recreation activity. Sometimes a significant change occurs in the object itself, making recreation experiences undesirable or impossible. Gross pollution of a lake or river, for example, may result in it no longer functioning as a recreation resource.

CLASSIFICATION OF RECREATION RESOURCES

Although recreation research and planning has flourished since the 1950s, no widely used method of classifying recreation resources has emerged. One approach is to define a number of broad landscape provinces (mountains, foothills, plains, coastal areas, etc.) and then use these provinces as units for inventory and analysis purposes rather than specific kinds of resources, such as potential swimming beaches, picnic areas, or campgrounds. This approach was used in some early recreation plans, but it proved to be too general for use in detailed planning situations in which specific sites had to be selected.

In the late 1950s, Marion Clawson proposed a three–class system. The three classes— "user-oriented", "resource-based", and "intermediate" — are summarized in Table 9.1. Again, the simplicity of

Table 9.1 Characteristics of Clawson's Recreation Resource Classification

Classes	Characteristics and Examples
User-oriented	Close to users; opportunities, such as golf, picnicking, zoo; typically used after work or school; 40 to more than 100 hectares (100 to several hundred acres); usually operated by cities, counties, or private agencies.
Resource-based	Has outstanding resources; may be distant from most users; major sightseeing, scientific, or historic values; hiking, camping, fishing, and hunting opportunities; used primarily during vacations; covers thousands of hectares; national parks, national forests and some state parks and private areas.
Intermediate	"Best" resources available at reasonable distances from users; picnicking, hiking, swimming, camping, hunting, and fishing opportunities; used during daylong and weekend outings; 40 to several thousand hectares (100 to several thousand acres); federal reservoirs, state parks, and some private areas.

SOURCE: Developed from Marion Clawson and Jack L. Knetsch, *Economics of Outdoor Recreation*, Baltimore, The Johns Hopkins University Press, 1966, p. 37.

the system had its disadvantages. Clawson himself identified several when he wrote:

> Although by far the greater number of areas and by far the greatest use falls into the general patterns described above, there is, in fact, a continuum from one extreme to the other, by any measure or characteristic that may be used. In size, for instance, some city parks will be larger than many state parks, but some of the latter will be larger than some federal resource-based areas. In the matter of timing of use, a few people will be located so near a national forest that they can use it for an after-work picnic, much like most people use a city park for this purpose. On the other hand, a few persons may be willing to spend their whole vacation going quietly each day to the local neighborhood park. In many other ways, some usage or characteristic outside the main pattern is possible.[1]

Because of these problems, Clawson's system has only been used to a limited extent in recreation research and planning. Unfortunately, however, the three class titles have become established, contributing to the general imprecision of recreation terminology. Clearly, all recreation activities from hiking in a wilderness area to strolling in an urban park are based on some type of resource. Clawson's term, resource-based, appears to stem from the narrow interpretation of the word, resources, discussed previously. It tends to deny the importance of good quality land and water resources in urban recreation systems. Perhaps more well-wooded parklands along urban rivers and more high-quality city beaches would

exist today if urban recreation opportunities had always been regarded as resource-based.

In 1962, the Outdoor Recreation Resources Review Commission (see p. 37) recommended another recreation resource classification system. The Commission hoped that it would provide a common framework for planning and also serve as an effective tool in recreation managment. Its summary report stated that it had:

> . . . developed a system encompassing the full range of physical resources needed for all kinds of outdoor recreation activity and specifying the types of management required for optimum recreation uses of each category. There are six broad classes, which include all types of outdoor recreation resources. They constitute a spectrum ranging from areas suitable for high-density use to sparsely used extensive primitive areas. In most cases an administrative unit, such as a park or forest, would include recreation areas of two or more classes.[2]

The six classes are described in Table 9.2.

The Bureau of Outdoor Recreation (see p. 37) further developed the ORRRC system and recommended it for inventorying and analyzing the supply of recreation opportunities in statewide comprehensive recreation plans. Many states tried the system in their early plans, but few found it really

[1] Marion Clawson and Jack L. Knetsch, *Economics of Outdoor Recreation*, Baltimore, The Johns Hopkins University Press, 1966, pp. 38–39.

[2] U.S. Outdoor Recreation Resources Review Commission, *Outdoor Recreation for America*, Washington, D.C., U.S. Government Printing Office, 1962, p. 96.

useful. It was difficult for planners to reach agreement on how to classify specific lands and to convert the areas in each class into numbers of recreation opportunities. Most agencies found it more satisfactory to record the number of facilities (campsites, picnic sites, boat launching ramps, etc.), since it is possible to establish a mathematical relationship between such units and the units commonly used in participation surveys and to estimate future participation (camper-days, picnicker-days, etc.).

Although the ORRRC-based system still appears in the planning manual of the Heritage Conservation and Recreation Service, it was not used in the first U.S. *Nationwide Outdoor Recreation Plan.*[3] Like many of the individual states, the Bureau of Outdoor Recreation found it more satisfactory to inventory and analyze recreation resources in general terms. First, there is a tabulation of the areas of different types of recreation lands (parks, forests, fish and game areas, etc.) under various levels of public administrative jurisdiction (federal, state, county, city, etc.). Then the same data are retabulated to give the total recreation land area in each of the nation's nine census divisions. These are followed by a general discussion of the availability of various types of recreation landscapes (shorelines, beaches, flood plains, wetlands, natural lakes, reservoirs, etc.).

No other widely recognized recreation resource classification system has emerged to date. Instead, each recreation planning agency has evolved a method of recreation resource analysis based on its own capabilities and needs. Most regional, statewide, and provincial comprehensive plans report and analyze recreation resources in terms of the area of recreation land under various jurisdictions and numbers of available facilities.

QUANTITATIVE MEASUREMENT

The supply of recreation opportunities provided by a recreation resource is usually expressed either in *facility-units* or in *use-units.* Examples of facility-units are a basketball court, a soccer field, a theater seat, a billiard table, a television set, a campsite, a picnic site, a kilometer of trail, or a square meter of swimming surface. A supply inventory using facility-units might report that a small state park has 75 picnic sites, 25 campsites, and a 50-hectare (124-acre) boating and fishing lake. User-units, on the other hand, express supply in terms of the number of experiences possible. Using this system, the state park might be reported to supply the following op-

Table 9.2 Characteristics of the ORRRC Recreation Resource Classification Method

Classes	Characteristics and Examples
Class I High-density recreation areas	Intensively developed; managed for mass use; generally close to major urban centers; usually city, county, or regional parks or parts of some state or national parks.
Class II General outdoor recreation areas	Developed for a wide variety of specific recreation uses; usually some distance from major urban centers; ski areas, developed state parks, relatively highly developed portions of forests.
Class III Natural environment areas	Various areas suitable for recreation in a natural environment, usually in combination with other uses; large, undeveloped areas in state parks, most state forest and national forest land, much of the national parks.
Class IV Unique natural areas	Outstanding scenic splendor, natural wonder, or resource of scientific importance; substantial areas such as a geyser basin in Yellowstone National Park.
Class V Primitive areas	Roadless areas, characterized by natural, wild conditions; large and remote enough to provide a wilderness experience; isolated sections of national forests and parks.
Class VI Historic and cultural sites	Sites of major historic or cultural significance, either local, regional, or national; historic buildings and archaeological sites; often part of state park systems. Many national and local park system units.

SOURCE. Developed from Outdoor Recreation Resources Review Commission, *Outdoor Recreation for America,* Washington, D.C., U.S. Government Printing Office, 1962.

---

[3] U.S. Department of the Interior, Bureau of Outdoor Recreation, *Outdoor Recreation: A Legacy for America,* Washington, D.C., U.S. Government Printing Office, 1973.

portunities each day— 75 picnicker-days, 25 camper-days, 10 boater-days, and 15 fisherperson-days.

Facility-units normally do not take into account the numbers of users who can enjoy the recreation resources during a given period. Therefore, an inventory using these units can be misleading or, at best, difficult to interpret. For example, a simple count of the number of ski centers in a region would reveal neither the tremendous differences in scope and lift capacity of the individual facilities nor variations in length of season caused by differences in latitude, elevation, or equipment. Clearly, the facility-unit approach is not satisfactory for precisely stating the supply of opportunities provided by resources that are developed and administered in a variety of ways by a number of different organizations. Neither will it work well if locations with considerable seasonal differences are included; a picnic site may provide three or four times as many opportunities in a warm climate as in a cold one. For such reasons, many planning agencies are changing from facility-units to use-units.

However, inventories using facility-units are relatively simple procedures that involve the counting of resources, such as campsites, billiard tables, or books, and the measuring of other items in spatial units, like square meters of beach, hectares of water, or kilometers of trail. In many cases, these data are already available from site plans and prior annual inventories of assets or can be obtained by measuring aerial photographs or maps. Even when the required information is not available from such sources, it is relatively easy to make an inventory if enough field personnel are

available. For instance, a state park agency can set up a simple inventory list with blank spaces for the number and size of facilities of each type and ask each park's manager to fill in the data.

In contrast, the measurement of use-units may be complicated by problems with definitions and lack of data. The question of what time unit to use is crucial. Inventories can be based on the number of opportunities resources are estimated to provide on average days, on peak-use days, or during the entire season. Approaches using a day as the time unit are satisfactory for such activities as camping if each user group is required to occupy a prepared site. The number of opportunities available is then the number of sites multiplied by the average number of people in a camping party at that facility and is expressed as a number of camper-days.

The situation is more complicated in the case of activities where user groups are not required to use a specific site. For example, in the case of a picnic area in an urban park, the patterns of use vary greatly from time to time. On a hot weekend day at the height of the summer season, it may be tightly packed with families and groups of young people who are relaxing in the shade and picnicking. In contrast, potential users may perceive the same area to be near its maximum capacity when less than half as many people are using it on a warm spring day for sunbathing, kite-flying, and playing informal games of softball and soccer. In such situations, the factors that influence the number of opportunities provided include the mix of activities undertaken, the *turnover rate*

(length of time spent by the average user or party of users) for each activity, and the maximum number of users who can enjoy the area before newcomers feel it is too crowded.

Each of these factors may vary both from day to day during the week, and seasonally. For instance, a city park picnic area may be used largely by office workers eating their lunches and reading books on weekdays but provide local residents with sunbathing, kite-flying, game playing, and picnicking opportunities on the weekends. The amount of time weekday and weekend users spend in the park will be different because many of the weekday users will have a limited lunch hour. Weekend users will tend to spend longer in the park during the warmer periods of the year than in the cooler months; the same number of picnic tables are therefore likely to provide more people with picnicking opportunities on cool spring days than on hot summer days because the turnover rate will be lower when people do not feel cold after sitting outside for some time. Many other factors may affect the number of opportunities a resource provides each day. These include the number of hours of daylight, whether or not artificial lighting has been installed, agency regulations setting the hours that an amenity is open for use, and the effects of budgets or union contracts on the number of hours essential employees are available.

Designing a satisfactory method of measuring the supply of opportunities provided by recreation resources can, therefore, be a difficult task. Most local government park systems and many state and provincial agencies use facility-unit methods and rely on their planners' and administrators' experience in interpreting these data as indicators of the actual numbers of available opportunities. Inventory techniques based on use-units are generally confined to large regional, state, provincial, and national agencies that are trying to use more sophisticated research and planning methods. The U.S. Forest Service, for example, developed a complex computer-based method known as the Recreation Information Management System (RIM) that employs use-unit measurement approaches for both making inventories of rec-

reation resources and recording actual participation.

CARRYING CAPACITY

Carrying capacity warrants special attention, since it is such a vital aspect of a recreation resource's productivity. The concept is not as well developed in recreation as it is in agriculture or wildlife management. The carrying capacity of a field or a range for grazing cattle or deer, for instance, can be stated with some confidence because the nutritional needs of the animals and available

food can be estimated with reasonable accuracy. Recreation professionals, on the other hand, are still experimenting with the concept, and opinions differ concerning its definition and potential usefulness. This is partly because the recreation situation is much more complex.

The carrying capacity of a recreation resource depends on two sets of factors. First, there are the basic physical and biological characteristics of the resource that determine productivity; for the beach development shown in Figure 9.2, for example, these characteristics include beach size, water quality,

Figure 9.2 The Huron-Clinton Metropolitan Authority built this artificial lake and swimming area at Stony Creek Metropolitan Park (50 kilometers or 30 miles) north of Detroit, Michigan. The beach has a high carrying capacity for swimming, sunning, and socializing because of its carefully designed slope, large area, intensively managed lawns, well laid-out food service-bathhouse building, and high quality maintenance.

Table 9.3 Examples of Factors That Affect the Recreation Carrying Capacity of a Resource

Selected Factors	Examples of an Aspect of Carrying Capacity that Is Affected
Site Characteristics	
Area of site.	Number of users that can be accommodated at any one time.
Length of season.	Number of days of use possible.
Arid climate.	Sparse, not easily regenerated vegetation.
Elevation above sea level.	Amount and persistence of snow for skiing.
Surface drainage.	Persistence of flooding after rain or snow melt.
Soil structure.	Ability to support use when wet.
Soil fertility.	Quantity and quality of vegetation.
Vegetation species.	Resistance to use and ability to regenerate.
Management of Resource	
Irrigation or fertilization of the soils.	Improves carrying capacity of vegetation.
Spraying to control annoying insects.	Increases use during infestation periods.
Treatment of water used for swimming.	More swimming can be safely accommodated.
Frequent collection of litter.	Fewer users are repelled by appearance of site.
Control of antisocial behavior.	Larger numbers of people can be accommodated without feeling of crowding.
Air-conditioning of buildings.	Encourages use by larger groups in hot weather.
One-way use of roads or trails.	More parties can use the resource without conflict.

water area of suitable depth for swimming, grass area, and parking lot capacity. Second, there are the psychological factors; for the beach users in Figure 9.2, enjoyment may depend on their attitudes toward the color of the water and type of sand as well as on the number, age, ethnic origins, and behavior of other users. As the photograph shows, people tend to disperse themselves evenly through an area, each group occupying a similarly-sized territory (see Chapter 7). Once the entire area is occupied with groups spaced in this manner, latecomers may go elsewhere because they have the perception that the resource is being used to capacity.

Therefore, a definition of carrying capacity must include consideration of both the site characteristics and psychological aspects. A useful definition of *recreation carrying capacity* is, the number of recreation opportunities that a specified

unit of a recreation resource can provide year after year without appreciable biological or physical deterioration of the resource or significant impairment of the recreation experience. Obviously, this definition contains a number of imprecise terms that express the basic concept but are inadequate for making empirical measurements. It is also clear from this definition that the carrying capacity of a resource is affected by a large number of factors; examples are given in Table 9.3.

If precision is required, the measurement units for each of the variables mentioned in the definition must be specified. For recreation opportunities, the most satisfactory unit is usually a use-unit rather than a facility-unit because the number of users that can be "carried" is what counts. For instance, in order to estimate wilderness backpacking capacity, a planner needs to know the number of backpacker-days that the wilderness

area can provide without deterioration of the resource or impairment of the experience. The next variable that requires definition is the unit by which the resource is measured—whether to use areal units such as hectares (as in the case of boating waters) or linear measurement (so many bicyclists per kilometer) as in the case of the capacity of a bicycle path. Where complex psychological and resource relationships are involved, as in use of a wilderness area by backpackers, it may be more appropriate to express capacity in terms of the total number of backpacker-days an entire wilderness area can provide rather than the average number per hectare or per kilometer of trail.

The phrase, *without appreciable biological or physical deterioration of the resource,* is more difficult to define in practical terms. The movement of users always has an effect of a greater or lesser magnitude on a recreation resource, depending on the resilience of the resource and the method of travel. Most biologic resources repair such damage given enough time. Physical resources, however, are a different matter. In an environment with fragile soils, walkers or vehicles may cause wind or water erosion that permanently damages the resource. Similarly, historical and archaeological sites may be irreparably damaged by foot traffic or touching. Therefore, the meaning of the word, *appreciable,* depends to a large extent on the management goals of the individual or organization concerned.

Finally, there is the problem of defining *significant impairment of the recreation experience.* At first, this appears to be a very subjective matter; each user is likely to have a different opinion concerning the degree of impairment produced by a certain level of use. Carefully structured interviews of both users and nonusers, however, can determine the proportion of people substantially affected. The managing organization must then decide what proportion is compatible with its objectives and set levels of use accordingly. For instance, a wilderness-managing agency might decide that no more than 25 percent of the backpackers using a wilderness should feel that their experience is significantly impaired. It would then devise questions to detect such feelings and limit the number of backpacker-days of use to a number that resulted in no more than 25 percent of the users giving affirmative answers to these questions. This number of backpacker-days would be the carrying capacity of that wilderness under those conditions.

INTERACTION OF RESOURCE COMPONENTS

Undeveloped resources and human resources do not function separately. Rather they interact in a variety of proportions at different locations. Society determines to a large extent how much of each will be made available for use, how they will be combined to form recreation opportunities, and how, when, where, and by whom they will be enjoyed.

Figure 9.3 represents, in a simplified manner, the basic ways in which society affects the supply of recreation opportunities. (Part Two, particularly Chapters 4, 5, and 6, showed that society also has a substantial effect on participation.) At the top left of the diagram is the relatively constant reservoir of undeveloped resources, namely, the undeveloped land, water, fauna, flora and air, together with the prevailing climatic assets and liabilities. At the top right is the more rapidly changing reservoir of human resources, consisting of people and their wealth of understanding, knowledge, skills, and financial resources.

At the first level of control, society decides in a multitude of ways at what rate both types of resources will be used for all kinds of human endeavors. For example, some societies favor rapid development of all their resources and try to stimulate it by eliminating obstacles or even providing incentives. Other societies are more conservative and limit development so that undeveloped resources will be available to meet future needs.

At the second level, the pro-

portion of each type of resource to be used for recreation is determined. Affluent societies are generally able to devote larger proportions of their resources to recreation than poor societies.

At the third level, recreation resources are divided between the public and private sectors. The division depends largely on the basic philosophy of the society. Does it favor predominantly private or principally public development or both more or less equally? Nations and political units within nations differ considerably on this question.

At the fourth level, the human resources allocated to recreation are divided among development of facilities, promotion (education and information services), recreation programs, facility maintenance, and protection. Different combinations of these resources produce a great variety of recreation opportunities from both the private and public sectors. The chapters that follow describe many examples of undeveloped recreation resources and summarize the characteristics of a wide range of public and private organizations that provide recreation through the allocation and management of these various resources.

Chapter 10 considers the nature and roles of undeveloped recreation resources. The various kinds and contributions of privately owned recreation resources are summarized in Chapters 11 and 12. Publicly owned resources are similarly described in Chapters 13, 14, and 15. Chapter 16 is devoted to a discussion of both public and private cultural resources. Chapter 17 concludes Part Three by presenting a brief summary of the vital contribution made by recreation profes-

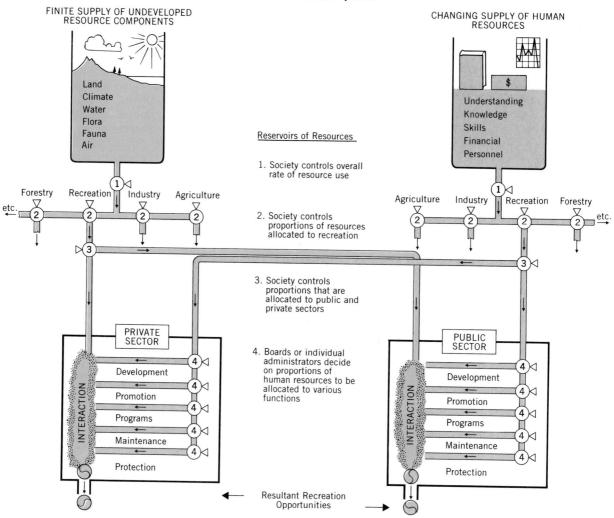

Figure 9.3 Diagram showing the interaction of the basic "supply" components of a recreation system.

FINITE SUPPLY OF UNDEVELOPED
RESOURCE COMPONENTS

Land
Climate
Water
Flora
Fauna
Air

Forestry   Recreation   Industry   Agriculture

etc.

CHANGING SUPPLY OF HUMAN
RESOURCES

Understanding
Knowledge
Skills
Financial
Personnel

Agriculture   Industry   Recreation   Forestry

etc.

Reservoirs of Resources

1. Society controls overall rate of resource use

2. Society controls proportions of resources allocated to recreation

3. Society controls proportions that are allocated to public and private sectors

4. Boards or individual administrators decide on proportions of human resources to be allocated to various functions

PRIVATE SECTOR

INTERACTION

Development
Promotion
Programs
Maintenance
Protection

PUBLIC SECTOR

INTERACTION

Development
Promotion
Programs
Maintenance
Protection

Resultant Recreation Opportunities

sionals as they manage resources to provide recreation opportunities.

As each of these components of the supply side of recreation systems is examined, remember that they do not exist independently. Instead, all of them overlap and interlock in a manner that makes it difficult to segregate and analyze them individually.

DISCUSSION TOPICS

1. Do you find it odd to apply the term, recreation resources, to such things as postage stamps, television sets, churches, highways, and recreation leaders? If so, can you suggest a better collective term for all of the supply factors?
2. Would an inventory of recreation resources that used the Clawson classification be helpful in planning recreation in your region?
3. How well does the ORRRC classification system work when applied to a range of recreation entities in the region in which you live? Would an inventory of the number of hectares in each ORRRC class be useful in planning recreation in your region?
4. Do you think an inventory of recreation resources that uses recreation facility-units would be more or less useful in regional planning than one using the six ORRRC classes?
5. Discuss the relative importance of the basic factors that determine the number of recreation opportunities that a recreation site can provide.
6. Can we accurately measure the carrying capacity of a recreation resource?

FURTHER READINGS

A basic discussion of the nature of resources is contained in Zimmerman's *World Resources and Industries* by W. N. Peach and James A. Constantin, published in New York by Harper & Row in 1972. Brockman's well-known book, *Recreational Use of Wild Lands* (C. Frank Brockman and Lawrence C. Merriam, Jr., New York, McGraw-Hill, 1979), contains only a short chapter on resources (''Nature of Wild Land Recreational Resources''), but examples of such resources are discussed in the chapters describing specific agencies. The ORRRC classification system is presented in detail in Chapter 6 of the Commission's summary report, *Outdoor Recreation for America,* published by the U.S. Government Printing Office in Washington, D.C., in 1962.

Recreation carrying capacity is developing a substantial literature, as indicated by the publication in 1973 by the U.S. Forest Service Intermountain Forest and Range Experiment Station in Ogden, Utah, of a technical report entitled, *Recreational Carrying Capacity: An Annotated Bibliography* compiled by George H. Stankey and David W. Lime. A good introduction to the subject is the *Recreational Capacity of the Quetico-Superior Area* by Robert C. Lucas, published by the Lakes States (now North Central) Forest Experiment Station, St. Paul, Minnesota, as Research Paper LS–15 in 1964.

10

UNDEVELOPED RECREATION RESOURCES

Most recreation occurs at developed locations. Even wilderness experiences often depend on human modification of the environment. Hikers and horseback riders generally follow trails created by the pas-

Figure 10.1 A rider stops to admire the scenery as he crosses a U.S. Forest Service bridge built for equestrian and foot traffic over Cottonwood Creek in Inyo National Forest, California. Most riders and hikers would find that any extensive exploration of such an area was impractical or impossible without the development of appropriate trails and bridges.

sage of hundreds of previous users or built with axe, saw, shovel, and (in some cases) dynamite. Such trails are also maintained; landslide debris and fallen trees are removed, trail drainage improved, and garbage picked up. One has only to try cross-country hiking with a heavy pack through rugged terrain (like that shown in Figure 10.1) or across boggy moorlands to discover that travel off the trail can lose its appeal after a few miles.

Recreation in remote areas is facilitated by a host of other developments — modern canoes and constructed portages permit trips down wild rivers, four-wheel-drive vehicles facilitate visits to distant beach and desert areas, and trailered powerboats and light aircraft bring remote hunting and fishing areas within the reach of millions. Animal, bird, and fish populations (important to sightseeing, hunting, fishing, and nature study) are greatly influenced by human activities. Forests are managed in ways that produce more deer; fish hatcheries and rearing facilities are used to bolster or create fish stocks. Some remote mountain lakes that are unable to sustain a native trout population on a long-term basis are periodically stocked with hatchery trout dropped from aircraft. Many other human actions affect remote recreation resources. Pesticides and other chemicals contaminate fish and game. Lake, river, and ocean quality is affected by sewage, agricultural practices, and industry. Dust, smoke particles, and fumes reduce hours of sunlight, increase precipitation, and even kill vegetation at distant locations.

Clearly, the dividing line between *developed* and *undeveloped* depends on one's perception of the meaning of these terms. We have found it useful to regard amenities as *undeveloped resources* if they are still in a reasonably unaltered state, irrespective of where they are located or who is responsible for their administration. Thus undeveloped recreation resources can be found anywhere — from the urban core to the wilderness.

This chapter explores the nature of undeveloped recreation resources. Such an exploration is possible only if each of the major components of a resource is examined separately. Seven components — geographic location, climate and weather, topography and landforms, surface materials, water, vegetation, and fauna — are included in the discussion. Separate consideration presents some difficulties because all the components interact, for example, an attractive picnic site is composed of just the right combination of climate, soils, slope, ground cover, tree cover, foreground vegetation, and scenic vistas. It is also clear that a specific physical or biological resource is not intrinsically *good* or *bad* for recreation. The discussion that follows focuses on attributes that have positive relationships with particular recreation activities. However, the same attributes may have negative effects on other activities. For example, a bay surrounded by bluffs and facing a strong prevailing wind may be good for sailing, difficult for fishing, dangerous for swimming, fine for beachcombing, too cold for picnicking, and exceptionally beautiful for the sightseer.

It should also be remembered that the manner in which users perceive[1] a recreation activity and the

[1] See Chapter 7.

depth of their involvement in it partly determines the role that a particular resource component plays in the experience (Figure 5.8). Therefore, it is dangerous to look at recreation resources with just the narrow viewpoint provided by one's own limited recreation preferences or experiences. Because a particular resource was used for certain types of recreation in the past does not mean it must only be used in that manner in the future. Rather, recreation professionals should see undeveloped recreation resources as a group of raw materials from which a wealth of different recreation opportunities can be produced. These raw materials must be managed as wisely as possible to provide both an increasing number and a greater diversity of recreation experiences now and in the future.

LOCATION, CLIMATE, AND WEATHER

Location on the earth's surface, climate, and weather are examined first, since they are so significant. Direct atmospheric influences such as temperature, precipitation, hours of sunshine, and wind are discussed in this section; secondary effects such as streamflow and vegetation are considered later.

Many factors combine to create the *climate* (long-term average weather conditions) at a particular place. Major factors are *latitude* and *elevation* as well as the location's position relative to large landmasses, high mountain chains, major ocean currents, and high-altitude air currents. Most of these factors are fixed for a given location; even ocean-current patterns are generally stable. High-altitude air currents, however, shift substantially from time to time. This is the major cause of changes in regional weather conditions.

The fundamental relationship between latitude and climate is generally recognized, but the basic reasons for this situation should also be understood. The higher the latitude, the greater the distance the sun's rays must travel through the earth's atmosphere and the more acute the angle at which the rays strike the earth's surface. *Less* radiation, therefore, is spread over *larger* areas as distance from the equator increases. In addition, a seasonal effect is produced by the earth's movement in its orbit around the sun. The earth's axis maintains a fixed orientation in space, resulting in a constant change of relationship to the sun's axis; it tilts away from the sun during the northern hemisphere's winter period and toward the sun during the summer. As a result, the farther a location is situated from the equator, the cooler is its climate and the shorter its summer season.

This basic pattern is modified by three other major influences. If a location is in the center of a large landmass, its summer and winter temperatures will tend to be more extreme than at a coastal location because land heats up and cools more quickly than water. Many coastal locations are also influenced by major ocean currents. For example, this is why the people in Western Europe can enjoy spring wildflowers while winter sports enthusiasts are still skiing and skating at the same latitude in parts of North America and the Soviet Union. The Gulf Stream and the North Atlantic Current (Figure 10.2), consisting of warm waters flowing north from the equatorial regions of the Atlantic Ocean, make the region's winters shorter and milder than other places at such a northerly location. In addition, major mountain chains can exert considerable influence on climate, depending on the direction of the prevailing winds. The classic ex-

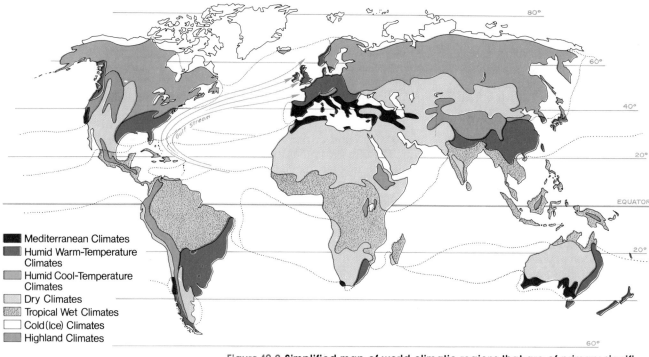

Figure 10.2 **Simplified map of world climatic regions that are of primary significance to recreation. Mediterranean climates encourage participation in the majority of common outdoor activities throughout the year. (**Source: **Developed from climatic regions map in Glen T. Trewartha,** Elements of Physical Geography, **McGraw-Hill, New York, 1957.)**

Mediterranean Climates
Humid Warm-Temperature Climates
Humid Cool-Temperature Climates
Dry Climates
Tropical Wet Climates
Cold (Ice) Climates
Highland Climates

ample is the rain-shadow effect: places downwind from mountains often have drier and sometimes warmer climates than similar areas without sheltering. This is because air masses lose their moisture when forced up over mountains and are warmed as they are compressed again on dropping to lower elevations on the other side.

CLIMATIC REGIONS

Table 10.1 summarizes the main features of the seven *climatic regions* shown in Figure 10.2 and gives examples of their significance to recreation. In examining each of these regions, remember that there are no sharp boundary lines like those shown on the map. Instead, each region is a continuum, extending from climatic conditions that represent one extreme of the region's characteristics to conditions that are typical of the other extreme. *Highland climates* are included as a group, since they consist of a complicated mixture of small climatic zones corresponding to altitude and exposure.

At locations with a *tropical wet climate,* the sun is high in the sky throughout the year so that incoming solar radiation is consistently high and so are air temperatures. About half of this region has a *tropical rain-forest climate* with average temperatures of close to 27°C (80°F) year round and between 150 and 500 centimeters (60 and 200 inches) of rainfall distributed throughout the year. The remainder has a *tropical savanna climate* that experiences similar average annual temperatures but slightly higher temperatures in the summer and slightly lower temperatures in the winter. Rainfall is between 75 and 150 centimeters (30 to 60 inches) and is concentrated in the summer. Southern Florida and most of the resort areas of the Caribbean have tropical savanna climates. These areas are coolest and driest and, therefore, best for recreation, when large numbers of people living in the northern United States and Canada are anxious to escape winter snow and ice (Figure 15.11).

The certainty of experiencing hot weather and warm water for swimming is a major factor in attracting people to tropical locations. Air-conditioning has reduced the discomfort of high temperatures and humidity. It allows people to retire to a comfortable environment at night and during the hottest period of the day, yet take advantage of the climate at other times for the enjoyment of outdoor activities, especially those involving beaches and water.

Dry climates are suitable for many recreation activities because these regions experience high numbers of hours of sunshine and low precipitation (Figure 10.3). Relative humidities are low so that high air temperatures do not feel as hot as in more humid climates. Even during the summer, outside activities are frequently feasible in the evening and early morning because of the ready escape of heat into the clear atmosphere and the consequent rapid cooling at night. The clear atmosphere also results in excellent visibility, which enhances photography or sightseeing from high vantage points. Air-conditioning is making some of the hotter locations in this region more attractive to tourists, especially where there are good opportunities for beach and other water-related activities.

Mediterranean climates are really a subdivision of the humid warm-temperature climatic class, which is described later. However, these regions are so important recreationally, they merit separate treatment. Mediterranean climates have many days each year with clear skies, light winds, and moderate to hot temperatures. Sheltered bodies of water are normally warm enough for swimming and other water sports. Clear skies and low humidity in the summer produce cool nights. Year-round participation in most sports is possible although some discomfort from chilly temperatures or rain may be experienced during one or two of the cooler months (Figure 10.3). Many older people, especially those who garden, prefer these disadvantages to the extreme summer heat of retirement communities in dry climates. Unfortunately, the world is not well provided with Mediterranean climates. Besides the areas around and to the east of the Mediterranean Sea, there are only four other regions with this type of climate—two sections of southern Australia, an area in California, a portion of central Chile, and, the western tip of South Africa.

A major portion of the world's population lives in locations where the two remaining types of *humid warm-temperature climate* prevail; they are the *humid subtropical climate* and the *marine west coast climate.* Included in these regions are the highly populated areas of most of western Europe, the northern part of the Indian subcontinent, major portions of China, the southern half of Japan, and most of the southeastern United States from New York City almost to the Mexican border. These humid areas

Table 10.1 Summary of Characteristics and Recreational Significance of Main Climatic Regions

Climatic Region	Location	Temperature	Precipitation	Recreational Significance
Tropical wet (no real winter)	Low-elevation coastal plains and interiors, up to lat 25° N and S of the equator.	Hot. Close to 27°C (80°F) year round. Savanna areas have slightly cooler "winter."	Generally heavy and spread through the year. Drier in "winter" in savanna areas.	High temperatures and humidities tend to discourage prolonged strenuous activity. Frequent cloudiness and heavy rain in wetter locations disrupt activities. Outdoor swimming year round. The southern Florida, Caribbean, Pacific islands, Brazilian, and West African resorts in this region enjoy either a cooler, drier "winter" or cooling sea breezes.
Dry	Larger area than region above, lat 15° to 50° N and S of the equator.	High maximum temperatures, especially in portions nearer equator. Cool to cold nights. Cold winters in more northerly portions.	Low to very low. Majority of region receives 25 centimeters (10 inches) or less. Low humidity.	Warmth and sunshine are favorable where temperatures are not extremely high. Outdoor swimming in hot and warm months. Resort areas in U.S., Southwest, parts of the Middle East and Soviet central Asia.
Mediterranean	Scattered; small; primarily on the southwest sides of continents between about lat 30° and 40° N and S.	Hot summers and moderately warm winters.	Moderate to low; concentrated in winter	Moderate temperatures, enough precipitation for trees and shrubs, and plentiful sunshine make this region particularly favorable to recreation. Outdoor swimming for most of year. Resort areas along coast of Mediterranean Sea, southern California, and southern Australia.
Humid warm-temperature	Subtropical eastern margins of continents and windward midlatitude west coasts between lat 20° and 60° N and S.	Temperate with moderately hot to cool summers depending on the latitude and continentality.	Rainy. Frequent cyclonic storms. Often humid in summer in hotter portions of region.	Portions nearer the equator are hot and humid enough to discourage some types of active recreation in midsummer, whereas those farthest away are cold enough to restrict winter activities. Swimming comfortable for from four to eight months. Indoor activities become increasingly important.

Climatic Region	Location	Temperature	Precipitation	Recreational Significance
Humid cool-temperature (snow)	Broad zones across North America and Eurasia between lat 35° N and 70° N; none in Southern Hemisphere.	Wide annual temperature range from below freezing in the winter to more than 21°C (70°F) in summer.	Moderate; concentrated in warmer months. Snow in winter.	Relatively short summer. Outdoor swimming comfortable for one to four months. Long, cold-to-very-cold winters make winter sports possible for from a few weeks to four months. Ice may be thick enough for ice fishing and other winter sports. Low-altitude ski resorts, especially in eastern North America. Maximum participation in indoor activities, especially in winter in northern portions of zones.
Cold (ice)	Narrow zones across northern Canada, Soviet Union, Greenland, and Antarctica.	Summer short or non-existent. Warmest month average is below 10°C (50°F); very cold in winter.	Low precipitation, but low temperatures result in little evaporation.	Virtual absence of summer means little opportunity for summer activities such as fishing or boating. Severe climate and brevity or absence of daylight in winter puts emphasis on indoor activities.
Highland (consists of various mixtures of the climates described above)	Mountainous areas, particularly the cordillera of North and South America and the central highlands of Asia.	Temperatures characteristic of any of above regions may be present, depending on latitude, elevation, and exposure of location.	Precipitation amounts and patterns characteristic of any of the above climates may be present, depending on latitude, elevation, and exposure of location.	Many climatic zones may be present in a small area, particularly on high mountains and in deep canyons. Temperatures and precipitation vary considerably in short distances, offering variety of opportunities. Particularly significant for temperature relief, skiing, and nature study.

have relatively mild winters and warm to moderately hot summers (Figure 10.3). They are suitable for a wider range of outdoor activities during more of each year than any other climatic type, except the Mediterranean climate.

Humid cool-temperature cli- *mates* are also known as snow climates because snow normally remains on the ground for extended periods. However, quite hot periods occur in the summers so that a primary feature is the wide range of mean temperatures experienced during the year, typically from below freezing in the winter to more than 21°C (70°F) during the summer months (Figure 10.3). Cold, snowy weather for several months reduces the opportunities for warm-weather activities but adds variety because of skiing, skating, ice hockey, snowmobiling, to-

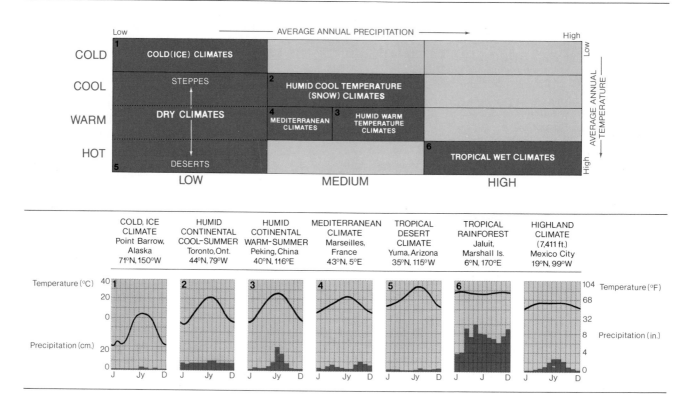

Figure 10.3 Diagram indicating how temperature and precipitation interact to form the six basic climatic regions mapped in Figure 10.2. The climographs show long-term monthly precipitation and temperature averages for sample stations in these regions and for a highland station. (Source: Data for climographs from Glen T. Trewartha, An Introduction to Climate, McGraw-Hill, New York, 1954.)

bogganing, ice fishing, and other cold-weather activities (Figure 10.4). Unfortunately, many of these activities take place at locations that require travel as well as the purchase of special clothing and equipment (Figure 4.1) so that the urban poor cannot participate as readily as in many summer activities.

At higher latitudes, shorter days during the winter leave little or no free time during daylight hours (except on weekends) for most people with full-time employment. Artificial lighting of ski facilities and

skating rinks is now fairly common, but it does not solve the problem of the substantial decreases in temperature and the resulting discomfort that often comes with nightfall. Summer recreation opportunities at higher latitudes are limited by the short season but are increased because of the additional daylight hours. Swimming is generally comfortable only in shallow rivers, streams, lakes, or bays where the sun has an opportunity to warm the water.

The cold climates, composed

of the subarctic, tundra, and ice cap regions, are characterized by generally low temperatures and very short summers (Figure 10.3). During the winter, areas poleward of the arctic and antarctic circles experience periods of varying length when the sun does not rise and temperatures may be very low although not as low as at some interior snow-climate locations. Recreation outside is impossible for extended periods. During the short summer, limited hunting, fishing, and nature study opportunities may be present, depending on the location and the weather. Few people currently live in the cold climates of the arctic and antarctic regions although the number is increasing with oil exploration in North America and Soviet development along the Arctic Ocean.

The preceding summary of the earth's main climatic regions is only an indication of the basic climatic conditions affecting recreation in different parts of the world. The climate at specific locations will differ from these generalizations, depending on a number of factors. Places that are centrally located in a region are more likely to be typical than those at the extremities. Locations at higher elevations, near bodies of water, or close to mountains may be atypical.

FAVORABLE AND UNFAVORABLE CONDITIONS

What, then, are the climatic features that are favorable and unfavorable to participation in recreation out-of-doors? The preceding summary of climatic regions introduced some of the important factors; this section examines them systematically.

Temperature. The desirable temperature for recreation depends on the humidity, the nature of the activity, and the individual. If both temperature and humidity are high, body temperature-control processes are inhibited and strenuous physical activity becomes more taxing. A hot, humid climate, therefore, is less suitable for vigorous recreation. However, in the case of swimming and associated beach activities, very dry air may make quite respectable temperatures uncomfortable because of the cooling effect of rapid evaporation. The amount of radiation received is another factor that affects temperature relationships. At mountain, polar, and some high-latitude, dry-climate locations, low levels of atmospheric dust and humidity permit the sun's radiation to penetrate more easily. This is why skiers can sunbathe at alpine locations and some of the dry-climate locations well outside the tropics are popular winter resorts.

Temperature and humidity at one location can affect participation at another. For example, Canadian tourist officials feel that a correlation exists between early summer conditions in the major urban centers of the United States and the number of American visitors to Canada. If

Figure 10.4 **Citizens in Ottawa, Canada's capital, skate on the Rideau Canal near the Parliament Buildings. They call the canal "the world's longest skating rink." Ottawa is in the humid cool-temperature climatic zone and has a winter sports season of four or five months.**

these cities experience hot, muggy weather in the early summer, then more people decide to go north for a vacation in a cooler, less humid area. For those who are unable to leave, the only possible relief from the long, hot summer may be visits in the evenings to waterfront or hilltop parks, where breezes and less reradiation of the sun's energy from buildings and paved surfaces result in somewhat lower temperatures. This is an important factor to be considered in the planning and operation of urban park systems.

At the other extreme is the problem of temperatures being too low for comfortable or safe participation. Beach activities, for instance, are highly sensitive to temperature changes, but acceptable temperatures vary considerably with geographic location. People who live in cooler climates will tolerate much lower air temperatures and stronger cooling breezes than those accustomed to warmer climates. Hikers, skiers, hunters, and others who participate in outdoor activities during cool or cold weather run the risk of injury or even death from frostbite or hypothermia.

The most widespread threat is that of hypothermia—the lowering of internal temperature when the body loses heat faster than it can produce it. This occurs when inadequately protected individuals are subjected to cool or cold air or water for appreciable periods. The body uses up its reserve energy trying to maintain normal temperature, then, the body starts to malfunction as its temperature drops. Uncontrollable shivering is followed by impaired judgment, memory lapses, incoherence, lack of muscle control, drowsiness and, eventually, death. Hikers and hunters who set out on

a warm sunny day and, then, become lost or caught in a storm are frequently the victims of hypothermia, even if the temperature does not drop any lower than 10°C (50°F). Many agencies, especially those that manage readily accessible highland areas, warn users of the dangers of hypothermia in their public education programs.

There is a multitude of other ways in which recreation is affected by temperature. In some cases, it is important that temperatures remain moderate or low. This is particularly true in connection with winter sports, where a generally warm season or even a few warm periods may not permit an adequate snow base to build up for skiing, tobogganing, and snowmobiling and

the ice on ponds, lakes, and rivers will not become thick enough for skating, travel by automobile, or ice fishing. In 1973, ski areas in Europe and the central and northeastern portions of the United States had what was described as their "worst season ever" because of unseasonably warm weather. Many slopes were completely bare and, in some cases, snow was trucked in to provide a small area for instruction or competitions.

Sun, Rain, and Winds. Sunshine is a primary ingredient for many kinds of recreation experiences (Figure 10.5). The number of hours of sunshine and the intensity of radiation not only play a major part in determining how comfort-

Figure 10.5 Two fugitives from Michigan's rigorous winter soak up the sun, establish the fact they are driving a much-coveted Corvette sportscar, and remain available (in an extension of their home territory) for social contacts while parked on an oceanside street in downtown Fort Lauderdale, Florida.

able participants feel physically but also affect people psychologically. Overcast days tend to have a depressing effect; colors do not appear to be as bright and visibility is often diminished. The number of hours of sunshine, however, is not necessarily inversely proportional to total precipitation. There are tropical locations that have twice as much rain as some places in warm temperature climates, yet they record much more sunshine because the rain comes as intense storms, which rapidly dissipate. In the United States, there are areas in the Northeast, Midwest, and Northwest where clouds obscure the sun at least 50 percent of the time, whereas the sun shines more than 90 percent of the time in parts of southeastern California and southwestern Arizona.

The amounts, periodicity, and variability of precipitation can also present problems for recreation. People who have planned outdoor activities may become despondent when rain spoils their plans. Many become exasperated if a succession of summer weekends are rainy or if their vacation includes an unseasonable number of rainy days. In some arid climates, sudden floods can sweep down dry watercourses and endanger unsuspecting campers, hikers, and rockhounds at places considerable distances from where the rain fell. Periods of drought may adversely affect fishing, canoeing, or wildfowl reproduction, and limit the supply of wild berries and mushrooms. Even with the assistance of irrigation, golf courses, sports fields, and lawns are difficult to maintain in dry regions or during periods of drought in more humid areas. Prolonged dry weather may make it necessary to

close forest, scrub, and rangeland areas to recreation because of fire danger. Large areas of North America and Western Europe had a prolonged dry period in 1976 and 1977. Its effects ranged from no swimming or boating on empty reservoirs in California and an economically disastrous low snowfall in the Rocky Mountain ski areas to an abnormally long, hot summer vacation period in Europe. Similarly, in the winter of 1979–1980, abnormally low precipitation coupled with several unseasonably mild periods had a disastrous effect on the winter sports industry in many areas of the American Midwest and Northeast, and adjacent areas of Canada. Only the ability to produce artificial snow allowed the XIII Winter Olympic Games to proceed as planned at Lake Placid, New York.

Air movements can have a positive or negative effect on recreation, depending on circumstances. Kite-flying, hang gliding (Figure 7.4), soaring, and sailing all depend on suitable wind or air currents. The great ocean waves, so important to the surfer, may originate hundreds of miles away as a result of wind action during ocean storms. Resorts situated on large bodies of water in tropical regions enjoy cooling breezes in the daytime as the lower layers of air over the land warm faster than the air over the water and convection currents develop. At night, the air over the land cools more rapidly and the breezes blow toward the water.

Strong winds frequently inhibit recreation participation in temperate coastal areas. Rough waters prevent swimming and sailing and, if the weather is cool, may drive people from the beaches completely. In ad-

dition, some locations have serious *climatic hazards.* Some of the world's major ocean resort areas lie along the paths often taken by ferocious storms. Hurricanes, which develop in the Atlantic Ocean above the equator, frequently pass through the Caribbean area and up the Atlantic coast of the United States. They sometimes cause great damage to resort buildings, beaches, and vegetation because of high waves and winds up to 325 kilometers (200 miles) per hour. In August of 1979, for example, a hurricane devastated parts of the island of Hispaniola to such an extent that tourism was impossible the following winter; in spite of a massive cleanup operation, not one of the Dominican Republic's 16 resort developments was in a condition to receive guests. Even more powerful tropical storms, known as typhoons, produce similar effects in parts of the Pacific Ocean. In some highland regions, certain valleys and adjacent areas are subjected to damaging wind storms generated in the nearby mountains as dense cold air sinks rapidly to lower elevations.

Optimal Climate. Clearly, it is not easy to designate a particular climate as being the best for recreation. Each person's interpretation of *best* will depend on which activities he or she feels are most important (Figures 10.4, 10.5). Many locations enjoy climates that are quite satisfactory for some activities but largely preclude others, and one climate or weather factor can facilitate one activity while hindering another (Table 10.2). From the viewpoint of the majority of the world's people, however, the most important consideration is the suitability of the climate for everyday pursuits close to

Table 10.2 Examples of the Effect of Climate and Weather on Recreation

Climate or Weather Factor	Effect on Recreation	
	Positive	**Negative**
Sunshine	Encourages outdoor activity, especially sitting outdoors, sunbathing, photography. Dries out clothes and camping equipment. Produces thermal currents for sailplane flying.	Produces sunburn and skin cancers. Glare may be annoying or unbearable. May cause headaches or eye damage.
High temperature	Warms water for swimming. Makes water-dependent activities more pleasant.	Too hot for strenuous activities. May lead to dehydration and heat exhaustion. Snow and ice melt at winter sports areas.
Late spring frost	Reduces mosquito populations.	Destroys spring blossoms in undeveloped areas, gardens, and orchards. Damages fruit crops and early vegetables. Delays morning golf starts.
Early fall frosts	Kills pollens, helping hay fever sufferers.	Discourages campers. Damages late garden crops and flowers.
Low temperature	May permit winter sports activities in areas that do not normally have them.	May make some activities unpleasant or impossible. Increases risk of frostbite or hypothermia.
Clouds	Scattered clouds improve scenic views and photographs.	Curtails sunbathing. Can discourage other activities in cool weather.
Rain	Maintains streamflow and levels in swamps and lakes. Waterfalls more spectacular. Desert flowers bloom. Wild mushrooms and fruits develop.	Outdoor events may be canceled. Wrecks plans of those who engage in outdoor activities. May produce mud slides or flooding that will interrupt travel. Makes dirt roads impassable.
Drought	No rain to prevent participation or spoil vacations.	Damage to flora, fauna (especially fish and waterfowl), golf courses, and sportsfields. Favors forest and range fires. Swimming and boating in reservoirs may cease.
Moderate winds	Sailing, kite-flying, and hang gliding favored. Cooling effect during strenuous activities in hot weather.	May make it too cold for some activities, especially near water.
Strong winds; storms	Good waves for surfing and scenic appeal. May deposit or uncover interesting materials on beaches.	Boating, swimming, and many other activities prevented. Boats, aircraft, camping equipment, shoreline resorts, and parks damaged. Snow blows off hills and blocks highways. Death or injury from lightning or wind action.
Heavy snow	Usually improves winter sports and scenic appeal. Can close roads giving people extra time off from work and school.	Travel slowed or blocked. Urban commercial recreation participation cut. Causes cancellation of many concerts, sports, and social events. Deer and game birds starve. Fish killed in lakes. Avalanches.
Fog	Sometimes has aesthetic appeal.	Hampers road, air, and water travel. Reduces temperatures and hours of sunshine.

home. An *optimal recreation climate* can, therefore, be defined as one that will permit participation in comfort for a maximum number of days each year in walking, playing games, or sitting out-of-doors relaxing in the sun. On that basis, Mediterranean climates have the most favorable year-round combination of moderate temperatures and clear skies. The remaining humid warm-temperature climates come next, with reasonably mild temperatures but less sunshine. The tropical and dry climates tie for third place; heat, humidity, and heavy rains are the disadvantages of the former; heat, aridity, and (in some cases) cold are the shortcomings of the latter. Snow and ice climates occupy fifth and sixth place respectively.

A knowledge of the different kinds of weather conditions that may be encountered in various climatic regions is especially important for travel agents and others involved in arranging travel. They must be able to advise travelers when optimum weather conditions exist at specific destinations and what problems will be encountered at other times. For example, they must know about the extremely high temperatures encountered in Death Valley National Monument, California, in midsummer; the East African rainy season in April and May, which often makes roads impassable; or the favorable early summer period in the Caribbean when the ocean is usually calmer, clearer, and therefore better for sailing, snorkeling, or scuba diving.

TOPOGRAPHY AND LANDFORMS

In Australia, at the center of its vast subtropical desert, lies a colossal rock; it is 348 meters (1143 feet) high, 3.2 kilometers (2 miles) long, and 1.6 kilometers (1 mile) wide. Alice Springs, the nearest town, is 450 kilometers (280 miles) away, across a rolling, largely uninhabited plain. Known as Ayers Rock, it is the world's largest inselberg (island mountain) and forms the main attraction in Ayers Rock–Mount Olga National Park. In spite of its remote location, the park is visited by an ever-increasing number of people. Ayers Rock, regarded by Australians as a symbol of national significance, is also attractive because of its visual appeal. Rising out of the arid landscape like a giant whale, its bare, gullied, gently rounded form is aesthetically pleasing in the light of the midday sun but has a special beauty when it appears to change color at sunset.

Ayers Rock is just one example of the many ways in which *topography* (the general shape of the surface of the earth) and *landforms* (particular surface structures) contribute to recreation. Frequently, the topography or a particular landform is not the sole attraction. In the case of Ayers Rock, it is a combination of landform, topography, and atmospheric conditions, but elsewhere vegetation and water may also be involved.

GENERAL TOPOGRAPHY

Highlands seem to hold a particular fascination for people in modern times. No doubt much of the attraction of such areas is their general appeal as completely different environments, the very antithesis of the crowded, hot, smoggy, flat, and treeless city. But there appears to be much more to it than that. Most people seem to have an urge to ascend to the highest point in an environment, whether it be the knoll in the middle of a city park or the highest point in a wilderness area. For many, heights give a feeling of exhilaration, a "king of the mountain" effect. Public agencies and private entrepreneurs accommodate these needs with various types of overlooks, observation towers, cable cars, ski lifts, and mountain railways.

Highlands also provide an attractive range of climatic zones. More radiation reaches ground level at higher elevations because the layer of insulating atmosphere is thinner and the air is less dense. Therefore, people, buildings, and other objects in sheltered locations are warmed rapidly by the sun's rays. However, radiation can also escape more readily back into the atmosphere. As a result, air temperatures drop approximately 2°C for every 300 meters increase in elevation (3.5°F per 1000 feet). Highlands therefore provide relief from summer heat, and, prior to the introduction of air-conditioning, movement to higher ground was one of the most satisfactory solutions to oppressive heat and humidity. Summer migration of rulers, governments, and the affluent to higher elevations began thousands of years ago and is still practiced to some extent. In the United States, many early Appalachian Mountain resorts were developed, at least partly, because of the climatic relief afforded at those locations. In winter, higher elevations and lower temperatures result in the snow accumulations so attractive to winter-sports enthusiasts. Climatic changes associated with different elevations also produce a variety of life zones that are especially interesting to people who live in other climatic regions.

Upland areas also supply excellent opportunities for aesthetic appreciation and photographic expression as well as strenuous recreation, such as hiking and climbing. In countries where mountains have a special religious significance, such activities can provide varying levels of spiritual fulfillment. A good example is Mount Fuji, which lies 120 kilometers (75 miles) southwest of Tokyo and is the focus of much religious as well as recreational activity.

The challenge of reaching a particular summit can be of great importance to hiking and climbing enthusiasts. Ascent routes are ranked according to difficulty and climbers often travel great distances for an opportunity to test their skills. Summit elevation, shape, sheer size, or a combination of all three may result in a mountain becoming a special attraction. However, unusually jagged formations such as the Matterhorn in Switzerland or the Grand Tetons in Wyoming have special appeal to the photographer, and sightseer as well as the climber. Where mountains are not part of the local landscape, quite low hills can become significant attractions, as is the case with the Downs of southeastern England, the Ardennes in Belgium, and the Irish Hills near Detroit, Michigan.

Highland landscapes may be excellent for sightseeing, camping, hiking, nature study, mountain climbing, and skiing, but there are some drawbacks. Many sites are over 2500 meters (8000 feet), the height at which the discomforts of altitude sickness often begin to appear. The most frequent symptom is a continuous headache, which

aspirin may not relieve; other effects may be insomnia, irritability, lassitude, nausea, and (sometimes) vomiting. Age and physical condition do not seem to be determinants. Most of those afflicted become acclimatized within a few days as their systems adapt to breathing oxygen at lower pressures. A greater proportion of recreation participants is affected now than in the past because air transportation and new highways make the ascent from lower elevations increasingly swift.

Automobiles also have difficulties at higher altitudes but, unlike humans, will not automatically adjust. In addition to the winter hazards of reduced traction and poor visibility, rarified air can result in poor carburetion. In summer, cooling-system failures may occur on long inclines, especially with vehicles towing trailers. Highland locations are frequently reached by tortuous mountain roads that make transportation of visitors, equipment, personnel, and supplies both difficult and expensive. Avalanches and landslides, fairly prevalent in mountain areas, create further problems and hazards for recreation use.

About 25 percent of the earth's surface is upland (Figure 10.6) and, of this, one-tenth lies above the snow line. Since the world's population is concentrated in food-producing lowland areas, most mountain regions are sparsely settled. Therefore, many nations have been able to set aside relatively undeveloped scenic uplands for use as national parks. However, the remaining areas of this type are rapidly disappearing as a result of economic development; exploitation of timber and mineral resources is in-

creasing as well as both summer and winter resort and second home construction.

Plateau areas (Figure 10.6) provide the next most varied landscapes for recreation. Sometimes plateaus are comparatively flat, resulting in little topographic variety; others are deeply dissected with immense, steep-sided valleys, producing an aesthetically pleasing mountainous effect. Generally, plains have even less topographic variety than plateaus, but changes in elevation that do occur assume special significance. Even a small hill can become a popular scenic lookout and busy winter sports area. River valleys, with their water associated landforms, such as bluffs and sand bars, can also be attractive recreation environments.

Even relatively flat plateau and plains areas can produce many recreation opportunities. The rolling landscapes of the Great Plains of North America or the veld areas of Africa (Figure 15.8) have aesthetic appeal because of their immensity and the contrasts they provide. Distant mountains, an approaching thunderstorm, a clump of trees, or a group of plains animals stand out vividly. Some recreation activities such as light aircraft or sailplane flying are favored by plateau and plains areas.

LOCAL LANDFORMS

In addition to the influence of a region's general topography, many kinds of local landforms are important recreation resources. Those associated with water bodies are usually the most significant. As explained later, water is an extremely powerful attraction, and the most popular recreation sites are those where good-quality water resources are combined with a variety of suitable landforms to create interesting shorelines.

A desirable shoreline for many water-oriented recreation activities has protruding headlands, deeply indented bays of various sizes and a good sprinkling of islands. Such environments provide opportunities for a great variety of activities, including sightseeing, picnicking, swimming, beachcombing, fishing, and boating. The critical area is the boundary between land and water; generally, the more interface there is between the two environments, the more opportunities are available. Of course, other factors play a part; if the shoreline is swampy or

has cliffs rising straight out of the water, some recreation opportunities are severely reduced. The best shorelines for recreation have a variety of features including high, rocky headlands to provide shelter from winds and waves and bays with reasonably wide sandy beaches backed by protective cliffs or sand dunes. Long sandy beaches may provide excellent swimming and sunning opportunities for large numbers of people but they are usually less favorable for boating or fishing.

Shorelines with many islands generally have good recreation potential if the waters are not too rough and users have ready access to boats. Small islands have special

appeal. Like mountain summits, they present a challenge that is hard to resist. Despite access difficulties, people enjoy reaching or possessing them; they are frequently the sites chosen for picnics, camping, and the construction of seasonal homes. Water areas between islands are often sheltered and interesting for boating. Many ocean islands are the tops of submerged reefs or ridges and are productive fishing and pleasant snorkeling locations. Generally, both the amount of shoreline and favorable climatic modifications tend to be maximized on islands, making them especially valuable as recreation environments. Examples of island groups with special recreational sig-

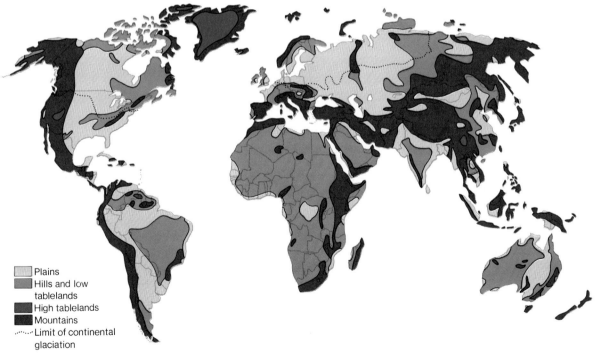

Plains
Hills and low tablelands
High tablelands
Mountains
Limit of continental glaciation

Figure 10.6 Map of world topographic regions. Upland (hills and mountains) and plateaus (tablelands) that have been spectacularly eroded are often preserved in parks or reserves. (Source: Adapted from "Landforms of the World," a map by **Richard E. Murphy,** Annals of the Association of American Geographers, 58, **1, March 1968.)**

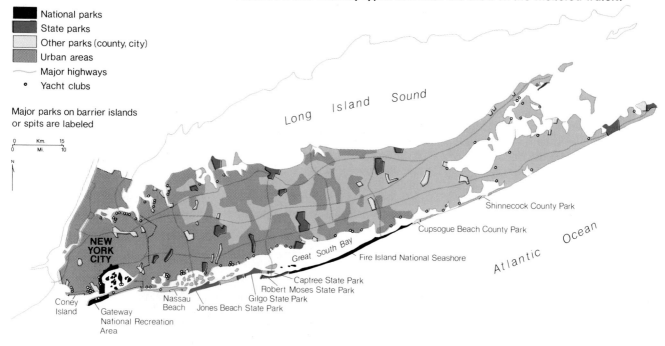

Figure 10.7 Long Island, New York, has an almost continuous chain of barrier islands and spits along its south side, which supports a series of elongated resort communities and public parks. Other parks and private recreation developments, including a large number of yacht clubs and commercial marinas, line the mainland shoreline and take advantage of the protected bays and inlets. Pleasure boats of many types and sizes are used on the sheltered waters.

Legend:
- National parks
- State parks
- Other parks (county, city)
- Urban areas
- Major highways
- Yacht clubs

Major parks on barrier islands or spits are labeled

Km. 0 — 15
Mi. 0 — 10

N

Long Island Sound

Atlantic Ocean

Shinnecock County Park
Cupsogue Beach County Park
Fire Island National Seashore
Great South Bay
NEW YORK CITY
Captree State Park
Robert Moses State Park
Gilgo State Park
Coney Island
Nassau Beach
Jones Beach State Park
Gateway National Recreation Area

nificance are the Hawaiian Islands (p. 285) and the South Seas Islands of Polynesia and Micronesia, the Caribbean islands, the San Juan Islands northwest of Seattle, the Florida Keys, the Thousand Islands in the St. Lawrence River, the Balearic Islands (Ibiza, Majorca, and Minorca) in the western Mediterranean Sea, and Greek islands such as the Cyclades.

Small peninsulas are another landform with considerable recreation potential not unlike that of islands. Being approachable by land, however, they are more suitable for heavily used resort and park developments. Barrier islands and spits

are a third type of coastal environment providing significant recreation opportunities. Waters sheltered by such landforms often are excellent for boating and sailing.

In Europe, there are many resort towns on the barrier islands along portions of the Baltic Sea coasts of Poland, Germany, and Denmark; along the North Sea shorelines of Denmark, Germany, and the Netherlands; and along sections of France's Mediterranean and Bay of Biscay coasts. The United States is blessed with a remarkable number of fine barrier islands and spits on its Atlantic and Gulf of Mexico shorelines. Many

national, state, and local parks, commercial resorts (Figure 3.11), and private seasonal homes are located on them. In New York State, Long Island has an almost continuous chain of barrier islands for 145 kilometers (90 miles) along its south-facing Atlantic shore. More than half are publicly owned recreation areas, including units of the Gateway National Recreation Area (Figure 10.7). These excellent beaches, the extensive lagoons behind them, and the mainland shoreline, constitute one of the most intensively used combinations of recreation resources in the world because of their high capacity and nearness to large populations. Swimming, nature study, hunting, and fishing opportunities abound and the sheltered waters of the lagoons are excellent for many kinds of boating activities.

Estuaries are especially important for the production of marine life and provide rich opportunities for nature study, fishing, crabbing, gathering shell fish, and all kinds of boating. A classic example is the 300-kilometer (190-mile) long Chesapeake Bay in Maryland and Virginia, with its thousands of smaller bays and estuaries. Unfortunately, such sheltered waters are also attractive for commercial harbors and, hence, to industry. All over the world, invaluable recreation opportunities have been lost and continue to be lost as estuaries are subjected to unplanned development and pollution.

Cliffs and other erosional shoreline features can be important scenic attractions. Sightseers appreciate the white cliffs of southeastern England and the magnificent coastline of Oregon's Pacific shore. Subsurface formations are important for fishing, snorkeling, and scuba-diving activities. The Great Barrier Reef, running for more than 1600 kilometers (100 miles) along Australia's northeastern coast is the world's most famous example of a subsurface formation.

A great variety of inland landforms are important recreation resources. Many are significant because of their spectacular size or shape, whereas others present important evidence of the earth's geologic history. The Grand Canyon, 1600 meters (5300 feet) deep and more than 320 kilometers (200 miles) long, is America's most popular natural attraction (Figure 9.1).

It is appreciated not only aesthetically but also for its great geologic significance. Highly eroded landscapes that feature such structures as mesas, natural bridges, spires, and pinnacles are the main attractions in areas such as Arches National Park and Bryce Canyon National Park in Utah, and the Badlands National Monument in South Dakota.

Volcanic landscapes are intriguing to visitors, particularly if they still show some volcanic activity; Hawaii Volcanoes National Park, for instance, is visited by almost 2 million people a year. The majority of the world's 600 active volcanoes are in a belt around the Pacific tectonic plate and people visit such areas in many countries from Chile at one end of the belt to New Zealand at the other. There are also active volcanic areas in Indonesia and the Middle East. In the Mediterranean, Mounts Vesuvius, Etna, and Stromboli are well-known attractions. Geysers, hot springs, mud pots, and fumaroles draw visitors to some locations. The most famous example of thermal activity is in Yellowstone National Park in Wyoming. It contains Old Faithful, a geyser that shoots a column of hot water some 45 meters (150 feet) into the air about once every hour; 200 other geysers; Mammoth Hot Springs, consisting of five mineral deposit terraces flooded by steaming water; and numerous mud pots and fumaroles. Iceland, New Zealand, and Italy also contain major areas of thermal activity.

Volcanic landforms in presently inactive areas are also of interest. Unique volcanic rock formations, such as the columnar structures at the Giant's Causeway in Northern Ireland and Devils Tower National

Monument in Wyoming are good examples.

Caves are fascinating to many people. The opportunity to experience a sense of adventure and enjoy the beauty of water-deposited formations motivates participation in tours of both publicly and commercially operated caves. Increasing numbers of people are taking up spelunking as a hobby. Caves are most commonly found in limestone areas where water has dissolved the rock along cracks and fissures. The National Speleological Society maintains records of some 23,000 noteworthy caves in the United States alone, and it is estimated that there may well be a total of 60,000 altogether. Carlsbad Caverns National Park, New Mexico, contains the largest cave discovered to date anywhere in the world, and it is famous for the size of its main cavern, which extends for more than 37 kilometers (23 miles).

Sand dunes are another important type of recreation landform. In shoreline areas, they create an aesthetically pleasing backdrop to beach activities and may also make the beach warmer by reflecting sun and providing shelter from winds. Owners of dune buggies and four-wheel-drive vehicles like large areas of rolling sand dunes on which to operate. Several areas in the United States, such as White Sands National Monument in New Mexico, have been set aside as parks primarily to protect spectacular sand dune environments.

Finally, a variety of recreationally significant landforms created by the great ice age glaciers cover extensive areas of Europe, the Soviet Union, and North America. Consisting of morainic ridges and hills, and sometimes dotted with small lakes and swamps, these glacial landscapes are not particularly suitable for agriculture. Nevertheless, they are valuable for recreation because of their rolling nature and great variety of land, swamp, stream, and lake habitats. They provide good opportunities for: pleasure driving and viewing the colors of the autumn leaves; fishing, hunting and nature study; cross-country skiing or snowmobiling; and contain many attractive sites for seasonal dwellings.

SURFACE MATERIALS

The nature of the materials making up the earth's surface layers is also significant (Figure 5.8). Many people collect specimens of rocks from beaches, river beds, and highland areas or multicolored sands from such places as Alum Bay in England. Colorful petrified wood is still a popular souvenir and the U.S. National Park Service is finding it difficult to protect the remaining material in Petrified Forest National Park, Arizona, from damage and theft. Dinosaurs and other prehistoric animals fascinate people, especially children, so that areas with fossil remains are often developed for public or commercial purposes. A remarkable example is Dinosaur National Monument in Utah, where visitors can watch technicians cutting away the rock to expose giant fossil bones on a cliff face protected from the elements by a unique exhibit building (Figure 16.8).

The serious collecting of rocks, minerals, and fossils for study and display and the cutting, polishing, and mounting of semiprecious materials have become popular hobbies in the last 30 years. There are more than 100,000 serious rockhounds in the United States and

participation is growing in Great Britain and Australia. The geological history of an area determines the availability, nature, and quantity of rock and gem materials. Much of northern Europe is not well provided with desirable surface material, but North America, particularly the United States, has a great variety of collecting opportunities. In North Carolina and some adjacent states, diamonds, rubies, sapphires, and emeralds can be found (Figure 10.8). Areas around the Great Lakes produce fossilized coral, copper nuggets, amethyst, and brightly colored agates. But the West is still the rockhound's paradise, contain-

ing an immense variety of materials such as turquoise, jasper, jade, opal, topaz, gold, ruby, agate, petrified wood, and fossils. Some restrictions on digging and collecting are now in force on certain public lands, but vast areas are still open. Many landowners and commercial enterprises provide improved sites for a fee, and a number of parks, such as the Crater of Diamonds State Park in Arkansas and Rockhound State Park in New Mexico have been developed by public agencies.

The surface materials that have the greatest effect on recreation experiences, however, are the various

Figure 10.8 At Crater of Diamonds State Park, Arkansas, as many as 1000 rockhounds a day pay a fee to search a regularly plowed, 32-hectare (78-acre) field for precious stones either by sifting through the surface materials or screening pails of dirt at the sluice boxes provided at the edge of the digging area. Although the search is a pleasant experience in itself, some people (about 60,000 to date) find genuine diamonds and many more find semi-precious stones and minerals such as amethyst, opal, and agate.

soils and sands encountered at every park, open space, and beach on which the users camp, sit, stroll, picnic, play games, and sunbathe (Figure 9.2). Intensive use of this type requires appropriate soil conditions. To grow good turf, for example, the soil should be deep, high in humus and nutrients, fairly well drained, and reasonably light so that it will not compact unduly under the impact of many feet. Unfortunately, few park sites have such soils, since recreation areas are seldom developed on prime agricultural lands. Where good soils do occur on North American recreation sites and in residence yards, they are often buried under poor material by large-scale regrading, spreading of basement excavation spoil, filling, or road-building operations. Consequently, recreation area developers and homeowners frequently find it difficult to grow grass, flowers, or trees without removing such materials and replacing them with good soil. This procedure is becoming increasingly expensive in urban centers so that many park agencies and homeowners either give up their attempt to produce good turf and other kinds of vegetation or they fight a losing battle against poor soils with costly and repetitive applications of fertilizers, weedkillers, pesticides, and fungicides. Good soils should be treated as an endangered resource from the recreational as well as the agricultural point of view.

There are many other important relationships between surface materials and recreation. Trails built on clay soils are slippery in wet weather and less satisfactory for hiking, riding, or motorcycling, especially in rolling or mountainous country. Heavy soils are unsuitable for weeping-tile sewage disposal systems and may either make it impossible to develop a desirable recreation site intensively or necessitate the building of much more expensive systems. Campgrounds built on heavy soils are not completely satisfactory, since they drain poorly in the spring and the aftermath of rainstorms is often wet tent sites and stuck vehicles. Areas with sandy or gravelly shoreline materials are generally more satisfactory for swimming, fishing, and boating because such soils cause little discoloration of the water, provide a solid bottom for wading and shallow-water activities, and form banks that are easy to negotiate when wet. The color and texture of swimming-beach materials are significant attributes of resorts and other types of recreation areas. Color is surprisingly important to many beach visitors and white sugar-like sand and pink coral sand have special appeal. The importance of sand is well demonstrated by the number of times it is mentioned in resort advertising. Sand of a reasonably coarse texture that is not readily windblown, is firm underfoot when wet, and brushes easily from feet and clothes is ideal.

WATER

Water is an amazing substance. It plays a remarkable role, not only in the essential biological, physical, and chemical aspects of human survival but also as part of many recreation experiences. Water is unique as a recreation resource because people appear to have a strong, innate need to relate to it and by reason of its ubiquitous involvement in recreation activities.

Human psychological involvement with water is not well understood but appears to be rooted in the distant past. Perhaps its origins lie in human evolutionary history or in our reliance on water as a biologic necessity, as a source of food, and later as a transportation medium. Whatever the origins, water has an extraordinary charisma. Children love running through it as it spurts from a city fire hydrant or garden hose on a warm summer day. Adults savor its sounds as it pounds on a beach or tumbles from a fountain and feel refreshed when walking or sitting by it in hot weather (Figure 4.11). Millions are awed by its power at Niagara Falls and thousands challenge its fury in flimsy kayaks and canoes as it foams down rocky channels. By viewing it, photographing it, painting it, and including it in architectural designs, individuals celebrate its unique everchanging visual values. For some, a special kind of inner peace may come through the contemplation of still waters, particularly at dusk. And, in some locations, people are still able to refresh both body and soul as they delight in a long, cold drink of water directly from a spring or stream.

Because of the increasingly numerous and complex recreational relationships with water, it is difficult to summarize its significance as a resource. Besides the many recreation activities that are directly dependent on water, there are many others that are frequently water-related (Table 10.3). Both must be taken into account when considering the significance of water for recreation (Figure 5.5).

The optimum and most intensive utilization of water resources for recreation occurs where land and water meet. Water is usually both warmer and calmer near the

Table 10.3 Examples of Water-dependent and Water-related Recreation Activities

Water-dependent Activities

Aesthetic appreciation of water	Powerboat racing
Beachcombing	Rafting
Canoeing	Sailing
Crew racing	Shell collecting
Driftwood gathering	Shellfish gathering
Fishing	Small boat cruising
Houseboating	Snorkel or scuba diving
Ice fishing	Surfing
Ice hockey	Swimming
Ice skating	Voyages in cruise ships
Ice yachting	Wading
Model boat sailing	Waterfowl hunting
Playing in water	Waterskiing

Activities That Are Frequently Water-related

Beach games	Pleasure driving
Birdwatching	Relaxing
Camping	Rock or fossil collecting
Hiking	Seasonal homes
Nature study	Sightseeing
Painting and sketching	Snowmobiling
Photography	Sunbathing
Picnicking	Walking

shore, and the majority of wading and swimming activities takes place in the shallows. Most fishing is done over productive shallows and reefs. Birdwatchers and waterfowl hunters find their quarry in shallow ponds and marshes. Agate and shell hunters prowl the waterline where the waves constantly turn over materials, and wetness more readily reveals patterns and colors. Artists, photographers, and sightseers generally find water most aesthetically pleasing where it interacts with land. In fact, few extraurban recreation activities are currently undertaken far from a shoreline, and, even ocean, lake, and river cruises are enhanced by the proximity of land and the scenery it provides. Therefore, the water-land interface is of primary concern in the production of recreation experiences, but large bodies of deep water also play vital roles in climatic, biologic, and other systems that are significant components of recreation systems.

OCEANS AND SEAS

A number of unusual attributes make the world's oceans and seas especially valuable recreation resources. First, their waters are saline although the salt content varies. Enclosed seas with substantial inflows of fresh water and relatively low evaporation are less salty than the open ocean; for example, the Baltic Sea is only one-fifth as salty as an average ocean area. On the other hand, the Red Sea, with little fresh inflow and high evaporation, is 50 percent saltier than average. Some people like to swim in saltwater because of its buoyancy, which makes it easier to stay afloat; extremely salty waters, such as those in the Dead Sea between Israel and Jordan or the Great Salt Lake in Utah are novelty attractions for tourists. Many consider saltwater and the salty atmosphere clean and invigorating. Others, however, accustomed to freshwater swimming and lakeshore environments, do not like the taste of saltwater, its effect on their eyes, or even the smell of a typical seashore.

The second unusual feature of the oceans is their appreciable tides. All water bodies are affected to some extent by the varying pull of the sun and moon, but a sizable cyclic rise and fall of water levels only takes place on the oceans and connected waters. Tides vary greatly from place to place, both in periodicity and height. The east coast of North America and the shores of Western Europe experience semidiurnal tide patterns with two high tides and two low tides of approximately similar heights in each 24-hour period. At resorts in the Gulf of Mexico, the tides are diurnal with only one high tide and one low tide. The Pacific and Indian Oceans and much of the rest of the world experiences various mixtures of these two types.

The situation is complicated because tidal height goes through a cycle. The range is greatest when the sun and moon are both pulling the earth's waters in the same direction so that the high tides are very high and the low tides are very low; these are known as spring tides. When the sun and moon are pulling at right angles, the displacement is minimal; these are called neap tides. The time a tide occurs is also constantly progressing. Each high tide and each low tide is approximately 50 minutes later than its predecessor because the moon takes more than 24 hours to circle the earth.

Tides have both positive and negative effects on recreation. Where tidal differences are considerable, the inflow and outflow of water may set up strong currents that are dangerous to both swimmers and boats. Currents are particularly hazardous when strong ebb tides run through narrow bay mouths or harbor entrances because careless swimmers and disabled or underpowered boats can be swept out to sea. In a few places, so much water is funneled through a narrow channel, it actually builds up as a visible wall of rapidly moving water that is known as a tidal bore. Two spectacular bores attract tourists in New Brunswick, Canada. The one on the Petitcodiac River at Moncton is particularly dramatic, reaching 1.8 meters (6 feet) in height as the water rises 2.4 to 3.4 meters (8 to 11 feet) per hour. Another sizable bore known as the Mascaret occurs in France on the river Seine below Rouen.

The major recreation problems with tides are experienced in areas that are used extensively for swimming or boating. Tidal currents can be hazardous at swimming beaches, where conditions change radically at different periods during the tidal cycle. So called *riptides* (fast outflowing currents) and *undertows* (subsurface currents that tend to pull the swimmer down) can be fatal to children, the nonswimmer, or the inexperienced. The tidal range may contribute to these problems; young or unobservant swimmers may return at high tide to a beach that was quite safe when the water was lower and suddenly find themselves in water well over 2 meters (6 feet) deep; surf and undertows may add to the danger in such situations. Conversely, where the undersea portions of beaches have a very gentle slope, the water may be so shallow at low tide that swimming is not feasible. On the other hand, such conditions may also produce expanses of sand and shallow warm water, which can be excellent for young children, playing games, or driving vehicles on the beach.

Where the tidal range is great, boat-launching ramps, mooring facilities, and boat-servicing structures are difficult to build and operate. Boat operators also require additional skills and need sophisticated charts, tide tables, and other navigational aids when in tidal waters. Several of the more heavily used boating areas in the world have substantial tidal ranges; parts of eastern North America and southwest England record maximum ranges of more than 12 meters (40 feet). Extremes are found at Truro in Nova Scotia, Canada, with over 30 meters (100 feet) and at the mouth of the Severn River near Bristol, England, where the range is more than 18 meters (60 feet).

Shoreline erosion is another problem connected with tides, currents, and waves that has serious recreation implications, especially where recreation-land ownership is limited or structures have been built close to the water. Unfortunately, many seasonal homes, resorts, and park facilities have been constructed where radical changes in shorelines take place. Barrier islands, spits, and other low-lying sandy shorelines are particularly vulnerable, especially in areas subject to hurricanes and typhoons. Owing to unwise land use and construction practices, large sums have been invested in protective works and beach restoration at such locations.

However, if humans learn to understand and live within the constraints of coastal environments, the effects of tides, currents, and waves can enhance recreation opportunities. The coastal zone offers a wider range of experiences than any other environment and the possibilities are constantly changing. This may be frustrating to those wishing to undertake one specific activity, but, for persons seeking variety, there is no resource complex that can equal an ocean shore. Opportunities for swimming, diving off rocks or breakwaters, sailing, or fishing occur at high tide; activities such as driving vehicles, hiking (Figure 15.1), playing games, building sand castles, exploring rocks and tidal pools, studying birds or marine creatures, beachcombing, digging for shellfish, or setting crab traps are possible at low tide. Even storms may be considered an asset, providing opportunities to view, photograph, or paint spectacular seascapes and, in their aftermath, to enjoy the tumultuous surf, as well as the treasures of shell, marine, and plant life or the semiprecious stones uncovered or deposited on the beach.

One of the best features of ocean shorelines in this age of heavy recreation use is their ability to erase the results of each day's activities. Below the high-water mark, a beach is fresh and clean after every tide. A good storm, coinciding with spring tides, can have a similar effect far up on the beach. In contrast, freshwater beaches usually undergo little self-cleaning, except during winter storms on larger lakes. There is also evidence that there is less risk of diseases produced by human pollution because ocean water is not as hospitable to pathogens as freshwater.

Ocean shorelines and estuaries are thus some of our most valuable recreation assets and should be treated accordingly. Recreation should be considered the highest and best land use of many coastal areas and other uses should be kept to the absolute minimum. Permanent developments such as overnight accommodations, campgrounds, and parking areas should be set well back and greater use made of public transportation and temporary types of structures to reduce human impact on these resources.

Examination of a world population map (Figure 4.13) reveals that some nations and population concentrations are better supplied with ocean shoreline opportunities than others. The majority of the world's nations have access to the sea, but there are several in Africa, Europe, and South America that do not. Some with ocean access have comparatively little shoreline in proportion to their area. The nations with the best ratios are those that are insular, peninsular, or elongated in shape, such as Great Britain, Italy, and Chile. The potential of a nation's coastline for recreation depends on the proportion of rocky shores, sandy beaches, marshes, and sheltered inlets as well as the lengths of shoreline, climatic conditions, and ocean currents.

INLAND WATERS AND WETLANDS

Lakes are widely distributed throughout the world, but they tend to be less frequent in arid areas and more frequent at higher latitudes, particularly in recently glaciated regions. As in the case of the oceans, it is the shallow waters adjacent to the lakeshores that are used most extensively for recreation. Offshore waters in wide lakes tend to get little recreation use unless they have shallow areas or islands in the middle. The most useful type of large lake, then, is elongated in shape with many long inlets so that there is a large amount of shoreline in proportion to its area. However, very large lakes of any type are valuable components of the recreation system because they modify climates, produce fine beaches, are part of significant fish ecosystems, serve as water-supply reservoirs for other waterways, or have special scenic appeal.

A number of regions of the world are famous because of the variety and amount of lake-oriented recreation they provide. The largest concentration of lakes in Europe is in the glaciated area comprised of southern Scandinavia (particularly southern Finland), portions of northern Germany, and the Baltic areas of the Soviet Union. Some of these lake areas are readily accessible from population centers and are heavily used. A second cluster of lakes is in Switzerland and the adjacent Alpine areas of France, Germany, Austria, and Italy. They are predominantly large, elongated lakes lying in valleys scooped out by glaciers. Pollution is a problem, but the appeal of these lakes and their mountain environments continues to make these regions and their resorts prime tourist destinations. The British Isles have similar, but smaller, lakes scattered through the northwestern part of Scotland and the northwestern part of Ireland. A cluster of smaller lakes forms the famous Lake District of northwestern England. The rest of Europe has comparatively few natural lakes.

The most remarkable lake region in the world occupies the recently glaciated northeastern portion of North America and is some 4800 kilometers (3000 miles) long and over 1900 kilometers (1000 miles) wide. Not only does this region contain tens of thousands of small lakes (Figure 10.9), it also includes the series of five large, connected bodies of water known collectively as the Great Lakes. The uppermost lake in the chain, Lake Superior, has an area of 82,400 square kilometers (31,820 square miles) and is the largest freshwater lake in the world. In addition, there are scores of lakes that are larger than 260 square kilometers (100 square miles). The region's potential for water-dependent and water-related recreation is limited, however, by its northern location, insect problems, and relative inaccessibility. The rest of North America, particularly the southwestern arid region, is not well provided with natural lakes, but there are a growing number of reservoirs.

There are no major lake regions in South America although there are several small groups of lakes in the southern Andes along the Argentine-Chilean border and several scattered medium-sized lakes. Central America is limited to a number of isolated, medium-sized lakes, except for Lake Nicaragua, which is 8300 square kilometers (3190 square miles) in extent. Africa has no major lake concentration, but a chain of elongated, large

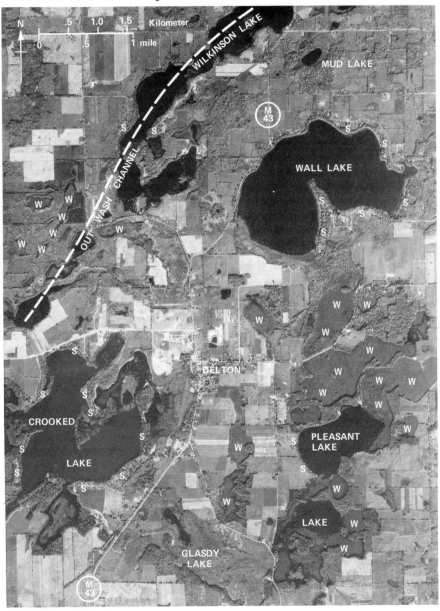

Figure 10.9 Two lobes of the glaciers that covered most of Michigan 14,800 years ago came together in this area of Barry County. The chain of lakes (upper left) was probably a melt water channel; other lakes were formed by the melting of huge ice blocks left buried in the deposited sands and gravels. Second homes (S) were built to take advantage of the resultant recreation resources but many are now used as permanent residences. Wetlands (W) created when lakes became filled with silt and vegetation are important wildlife habitats.

lakes runs down the Rift Valley in the eastern part of the continent; Lake Victoria, the second largest lake in the world, lies to the east; and Lake Chad lies between Chad and Nigeria. The Ethiopian mountains contain a number of smaller lakes.

Compared to North America, Asia has few lakes. The Asian portion of the Soviet Union has no comparable lake region and sizable lakes are rare even in the Siberian lowlands. Lake Baikal is 31,500 square kilometers (12,000 square miles) and by volume is the world's biggest lake. It lies close to the Mongolian border in southeastern Siberia. China has an extensive lake region in the lower portions of the valley of the Yangtze (Ch'ang Chiang) River. However, many of the water bodies have been modified and should be considered reservoirs. The Indian subcontinent, the arid Middle East, and Australasia have comparatively few lakes.

Like oceans, many freshwater lakes are well suited for such recreation pursuits as swimming, fishing, and beach and shoreline activities. Sailing and waterskiing are especially enjoyable and are usually safer on placid lake surfaces than in the less sheltered waters of coastal areas or in narrow rivers. In the winter, a great variety of activities takes place on lakes, including ice skating, ice hockey, ice boating, and ice fishing. Lakes are particularly favored locations for resorts, public parks, and privately owned seasonal homes because of their considerable recreation potential.

Rivers are much more widely distributed than lakes and, therefore, are accessible to larger numbers of people. Unfortunately, river valleys are often important transportation routes so that commercial centers and industries tend to be concentrated along them and urban blight, pollution, and lack of public access to the water reduce their recreation potential. Rivers can provide a wide range of recreation opportunities depending on their size, bottom and bank characteristics, flow patterns, water quality, and surrounding land uses. Again, it is the varied nature of the interfaces between the land and water that creates so many different opportunities.

Estuaries where freshwaters and saltwaters meet, have a diversity of biologically productive environments, both in and out of the water. A great variety of fish and other marine organisms reproduce in estuarine waters and marshes. Many birds and animals find the consequent variety of food, the intermittent tidal exposure of pools and marsh bottoms, and the shelter provided by marsh plants an ideal habitat. Estuaries and the tidal portions of rivers, therefore, often produce numerous fishing and hunting opportunities. The broad lower reaches of large rivers are also frequently used extensively for waterskiing and many kinds of boating.

Farther upstream, where rivers are still wide and generally have higher, less marshy banks, the environment is frequently ideal for more intensive recreation. Here there may be sites suitable for regional as well as major city parks. Regrettably, these locations are often already occupied by ports, industrial areas, railroad yards, or other urban developments. In addition, water quality is frequently poor so that people look upon the river as a liability rather than as an asset. In

some of the industrial nations, the building of expensive sewage-treatment systems and the stricter enforcement of pollution laws is beginning to improve the quality of river water with consequent beneficial effects on recreation. Unfortunately, riverbank use for commercial, industrial, or residential purposes is not easily changed, except when such areas have decayed to an extent that they are abandoned. Riverside resources set aside for recreation in intensively farmed rural areas are also rare. When such land was first settled, it seemed unnecessary to set aside areas for this purpose, and property of this type is now expensive. In headwater areas, public access to rivers is often more extensive, but even in predominantly publicly owned areas such as American national forests, much land immediately adjacent to rivers is privately owned farms, seasonal homesites, or hunting and fishing club areas.

These public access problems are unfortunate because rivers offer such a variety of opportunities. At inland locations where lakes are scarce or nonexistent, lands adjacent to rivers and major tributary streams can be an area's most valuable recreation resource. Swimming, fishing, boating, sailing, and canoeing are often feasible, and the potential for nature study is usually good in riverine environments. Not only are riverbank environments attractive to animals and birds, people in a boat or canoe on a waterway usually have a better chance of seeing and enjoying them. Convoluted rivers are particularly useful, especially if the banks are well vegetated, because numerous river bends make canoeing and boating

experiences more exciting and pleasurable. Fisherpersons, hikers, and picnickers can also enjoy a greater sense of solitude, even on quite intensively used stretches. In addition, foot trails, bridle paths, parkways, scenic lookouts, picnic areas, zoos, and botanical gardens will be more aesthetically attractive and offer more secondary opportunities when located in, or immediately adjacent to, river valleys.

In spite of access and pollution problems, rivers play an important part in recreation at many locations. In urban areas, they are frequently the sites of small parks and public promenades that are much appreciated by local strollers, fisherpersons, and picnickers. They are also considered prime locations for restaurants, luxury apartments, and residences. Some rivers are famous mainly because of their size, but others have great cultural, historical, or sentimental significance, for example, the Danube, Mississippi, Potomac, Rhine, Seine, and Thames rivers. Millions visit these rivers every year and many enjoy commercial boat tours on them. At the other end of the spectrum are the upland rivers, which characteristically tumble over rocky beds and attract the more adventurous canoeists, fisherpersons, and backpackers.

Many other types of water features are of significance to recreation. Small streams are important habitats for fish. Swamps, marshes, and ponds are essential to the survival of numerous animal and bird species, particularly waterfowl. Waterfalls, like mountains and islands, have a special appeal; Niagara Falls is third in popularity among the biological or physical attractions of the United States. Iguaçu Falls on the

Argentina-Brazil border (Figure 10.10) and Victoria Falls on the Rhodesia-Zambia border are major international tourist attractions. However, a waterfall does not have to be huge to be attractive. Even a narrow ribbon of water dropping from a cliff face or a series of rapids exert a special magnetism.

Water resources do present some problems when used for recreation. Water is always a hazard and, depending on a particular society's attitudes, fencing, patrols, life-guards, or rescue boats, may be considered necessary. Recreation shorelines that are eroding may be expensive to protect and low-lying land around water features may be difficult and costly to manage, especially if park sewage systems, buildings, and other improvements have to be built. Facilities built on shorelines may be difficult to protect from intruders and vandalism unless the shoreline is fenced; this is usually functionally and aesthetically undesirable.

VEGETATION

Recreation is dependent on vegetation in many ways. In some cases, it is the primary component. California's giant trees, the sequoias and the redwoods, are rated as the United States' fifth most popular biological or physical tourist attraction. In the autumn, the changing colors of various tree species create a third tourist season for the New England states, parts of the Midwest, and certain other areas of the

Figure 10.10 Iguaçu Falls on the border between Brazil and Argentina is a largely undeveloped attraction of major significance in both domestic and international tourism. They are four times as wide as Niagara Falls, plunging from both sides into a narrow gorge, The Devil's Throat, that is 75 meters (240 feet) deep and 3 kilometers (2 miles) long.

United States and Canada. Some plants serve as symbols of specific recreation environments and the presence of just a few specimens can cause travelers to stop and even take pictures. For example, palm trees are associated with tropical vacations, cacti with deserts, and sagebrush with the American West. Of particular appeal are some high mountains and deep canyons where it is possible to travel quite rapidly from one climatic life zone to another, seeing corresponding changes in the vegetation. Grand Canyon National Park, for example, possesses five of the seven botanical life zones that are found in the Northern Hemisphere. Then there are the various kinds of wild berries, fruits, nuts, and edible fungi that people gather. A great variety of plant materials such as driftwood, evergreen boughs and cones, seeds, and grasses are collected for decorative and craft-project purposes. Increasing numbers of outdoor enthusiasts are exploring wild plants as a source of interesting and nutritious foods. And, for many nature lovers, the identification of trees, flowers, shrubs, and fungi is a constant challenge and delight.

Many parks and reserves around the world have been set aside primarily because of the exceptional beauty or scientific value of their vegetation. Several units of the U.S. national park system are in this category and have names that clearly indicate the primary reason for their dedication; these include Redwood National Park in California, Saguaro National Monument in Arizona, and Everglades National Park in Florida.

Although vegetation is of considerable direct value where recreation activities are focused on the viewing or collecting of one species or group of species, the indirect significance to recreation is even greater. In the case of many recreation activities that take place out-of-doors, vegetation is an important aesthetic ingredient. It forms the backdrop against which many experiences take place or is an active component in the activity itself. Many plants that would otherwise be quite unremarkable become impressive when seen in groups or particular settings. Clusters of white or silver birches are generally more appealing than a solitary tree and when viewed beside water or in contrast to the dark greens of spruce in summer or the reds of maples in autumn can become truly spectacular. Artists, photographers, and naturalists delight in such landscapes. Isolated specimens or clumps of characteristically shaped acacia trees combine with grasses to form a dramatic backdrop against which the tourist views lion, giraffe, and the other veld ungulates in Africa's national parks (Figure 15.8). Without them, the experience would still be memorable, but with their unobtrusive presence, the effect is enhanced and heightened.

There is a host of other relationships between vegetation and recreation, many of which are usually taken for granted. Trees and grass play an important role in providing shade and relief from reflected heat in all manner of recreation environments, from a park bench in a city square to a campsite in a wilderness. Trees shelter ski runs from wind, thus helping to maintain snow depths. Vegetation is also closely related to fish and wildlife production; for instance, stream temperatures may become too high for trout if shading vegetation is removed. Deer-herd size is directly related to the amount of available browse. Grasses form ideal surfaces on which to run, play, stroll, and camp; they also are important for stabilizing areas where overuse or construction have caused erosion. Vegetation even provides a bonus in the form of fragrances, which may enhance recreation experiences; these range from the scent of a wild rose to the smell of a pine forest or the aroma of sagebrush.

Finally, vegetation can have negative relationships to recreation. Millions of people are allergic to pollens of one or more species and may be restricted in their recreation participation or enjoyment by the presence of these plants. Thorny, prickly, and spiny plants; toxic species such as poison ivy; or irritating plants such as nettles can be troublesome in some areas, especially to the uninitiated. Generally, however, it is the overabundance of vegetation in undeveloped areas that serves as a major deterrent to participation in hunting, off-trail hiking, and streambank fishing.

FAUNA

Animals, birds, and fish also play a variety of roles in recreation experiences. Many people, especially in North America and some less developed parts of the world, are primarily interested in fauna because of participation in hunting and fishing activities. In Canada and the United States, hunting and fishing have become popular forms of recreation with all levels of society and have greatly affected the course of conservation work, particularly that undertaken by provincial and state governments. Rabbits, ducks, partridge, geese, and deer are all hunted extensively and a wide range of freshwater and saltwater fish species—from carp to salmon—are avidly sought by anglers.

Much of the hunting and freshwater fishing in North America and elsewhere can scarcely be said to be based on undeveloped resources. Farming, ranching, and forestry have altered wildlife environments and resulted in substantial changes in the nature and range of animal populations. In the Great Lakes region and in many southern farming areas of the United States, white-tailed deer are prolific and large in size, whereas their populations are declining and individual deer are becoming smaller in more northerly areas where cutover forests are getting too mature to produce good browse. Sportsperson's groups and conservation organizations sometimes feed deer during severe winter conditions by putting out grain or cutting trees and shrubs to provide browse. Exotic species or subspecies of game animals, birds, and fish have been introduced in certain areas to provide increased and varied recreation opportunities, and active programs of game management and predator control have had considerable effects on animal populations. Only in some remote locations, such as wilderness areas and parts of the ocean, do game and fish populations still exist in a relatively unaltered state.

Having an opportunity to see a wild animal, bird, or fish is increasingly important to a growing number of people, especially those living in urban environments. "Bear jams" have become a familiar traffic hazard in national parks, such as Yellowstone (Figure 10.11) or Great Smoky Mountains, as motorists stop to watch bears. Many visi-

Figure 10.11 Brown bears eating food thrown to them illegally, often cause traffic jams on the main roads in Yellowstone National Park, Wyoming. Careful management of habitat, people, garbage, and vehicles is necessary if wild animal populations are to be maintained in substantially their original state yet be viewed by large numbers of people.

tors, particularly those with children, consider the viewing of wild animals their primary reason for visiting such areas. Large numbers of people congregate to see the migrations of the grey whales in California or the Canada geese in Wisconsin. Thousands of visitors from Europe and North America spend considerable amounts of money every year traveling to African national parks principally to view and study the unique and diversified wildlife (Figure 15.8). Participation in birdwatching and many forms of nature study and photography is increasing rapidly with growing memberships in related organizations. And, then, there are the less tangible values derived from fauna that provide atmosphere for a variety of recreation experiences; these include the song of a thrush in a city park, the eerie call of the northern loon on a Canadian wilderness vacation, a whiff of skunk odor in a campground at night, a bright feather on a woodland path, or fresh animal tracks in the mud along the shore of a lake or stream.

There are also negative aspects of fauna that can discourage participation in some types of recreation. Poisonous snakes, scorpions, and other venomous creatures are discouraging or even frightening to the uninitiated. Stinging jelly fish can be numerous enough to deter swimmers. Sharks are particularly troublesome in some Pacific Ocean waters and many Australian beaches have protective nets. Piranhas are a problem at some freshwater beaches in South America. The large animals that people enjoy seeing so much, such as bears and lions, can become dangerous, especially where their natural response to man has been altered because of familiarity or feeding. Thousands of automobile accidents involving deer, some resulting in human deaths, occur each year, especially in more populated areas of eastern North America.

However, it is usually the small organisms, particularly the insects, that have the most significant impact on the recreation participation of the greatest numbers of people over a wide area. The mosquito can make outdoor activities unpleasant or even hazardous—from the tropics to within the arctic circle and from the urban core to the wilderness. Multitudes of black flies often discourage early season fishing and canoeing in northern areas, and wasps, hornets, ants, and ticks can be detrimental or dangerous when picnicking or camping.

ASSOCIATIONS OF RECREATION RESOURCES

These components—climate, topography, landforms, surface materials, water, vegetation, and fauna—combine to form the undeveloped resource aspects of recreation environments. In some cases, recreation activities may focus on just one of these resources. However, most involve several and many touch on all of these components.

Generally, the undeveloped areas that are most popular or offer the greatest potential for participation in a broad spectrum of activities are those that have a good mixture of high-quality undeveloped resources; in other words, they show great landscape diversity. Yellowstone National Park with its mountains, gorges, rivers, waterfalls, geysers, forests, wildlife, and fishing opportunities, is an unparalleled complex of resources, which well deserved to be chosen as the world's first national park. Other national parks and reserves cannot approach the diverse excellence of Yellowstone, but they often include single resources or resource combinations of superlative quality or uniqueness. In addition, many state, provincial, regional, and commercial recreation areas are based on complexes of undeveloped resources of exceptional quality that can provide numerous excellent recreation opportunities (p. 285). And, it must not be forgotten that lands not designated as parks or reserves (especially public and private forest and range lands) include many tracts which contain resources that should be preserved for recreation use. Any remaining enclaves of relatively undeveloped high-quality recreation resources are of prime importance to society today, particularly in the densely populated parts of the world. In such regions, undeveloped sections of river valleys, wooded hills, sheltered estuaries, sandy seashore and lake beaches, high-quality wetlands, and natural streams must be looked upon as immensely valuable recreation resources and reserved for this purpose. Unfortunately, few developed nations have land-use planning and regulation procedures that do this effectively.

The number and type of recreation experiences that people obtain from a particular association of undeveloped resources depend on many factors besides the nature of the resources themselves. The controlling factors include ownership of the land, accessibility, the policies of the owners or controlling agencies, and the degree of development. In the chapters that follow, various ways of developing and administering recreation resources are discussed. Chapter 11 examines the nature and role of recreation resources that are operated by private individuals or organizations for personal, family, or private-group enjoyment.

DISCUSSION TOPICS

1. How much of your own time spent on recreation involves undeveloped recreation resources? Do you expect this pattern to change during your lifetime? Explain your response.
2. What constitutes an ideal recreation climate? Can you suggest an approach to classifying world climates that would be based on recreation participation rather than plant growth?
3. Which type of topography is ideal for intensive recreation use by large numbers of people? Justify your answer.
4. Is a high quality ocean shoreline better for recreation than a good freshwater-lake shoreline?
5. What is the best combination of undeveloped recreation resources you have experienced? Would other people think it is a good combination?

FURTHER READINGS

The relationships between recreation and undeveloped resources have not been systematically discussed in any readily available sources although there are theses and research reports dealing with a particular type of resource or resources at specific locations. Some statewide or provincial recreation plans have sections concerning recreation resources, which may be helpful, but most tend to give only a listing of resources (number of miles of shoreline, acres of forest, amount of snowfall) and not explore the relationships between the resources and recreation participation. A good physical geography book, such as Arthur N. Strahler and Alan H. Strahler's *Modern Physical Geography*, published in New York by John Wiley in 1978 will provide more information concerning climatic regions, topography, landforms, soils, and vegetation classes, but give few indications of their significance to recreation.

11

PRIVATE RECREATION RESOURCES

In Part Two, recreation resources are divided into three main groups. Those administered by governments are called *public recreation resources* and will be described in Chapters 13, 14, and 15. *Cultural*

Figure 11.1 Residences are often used as recreation environments in which to entertain friends. The piano adds to the recreation potential of this young couple's apartment but many amenities not usually regarded as recreation resources, including the stove on which a meal is prepared and the table on which it is served, also enhance its value as a recreation facility.

resources— both public and private —will be examined in Chapter 16. The remaining *private recreation resources* (owned by private individuals or private organizations) are discussed in this chapter and in Chapter 12.

Private resources will be described first, since they provide the majority of recreation experiences (Figure 11.1). This extremely important fact is frequently overlooked by students, professionals, and others interested in recreation. The significance of the private sector is often ignored and people's recreation environments are perceived as consisting primarily of the more conspicuous city, regional, state, and national parks. However, in western nations, between 80 and 90 percent of people's recreation time is spent on activities at home and 5 to 10 percent involves commercial recreation facilities (Table 8.4); only about 10 to 15 percent occurs on public lands. In addition, remember that even in the United States with its vast areas of public lands, the majority of the land (60 percent or about 930 million hectares or 2.3 billion acres) is privately owned. In non-Communist European nations, the proportion of private land is much higher and it plays an even more dominant role in recreation. The proportion of private land is generally highest where populations are densest. The nature and extent of privately owned resources is thus of primary significance when considering recreation opportunities that are readily accessible and used most often by the majority of people.

On the other hand, recreation experiences are often dependent on the use of both private and public resources. Sometimes the two kinds of resources are completely separate and recreation use of each remains distinct. More frequently, however, public and private resources are intermingled and in many cases interdependent. The majority of the most heavily used recreation destinations, including major resort areas, are places where people are able to enjoy a wide range of experiences because a variety of public and private recreation resources are available at one location. Users are often unaware of this intermingling and interdependence.

THE NATURE OF PRIVATE RESOURCES

Privately owned recreation resources range from the humblest amenities in people's homes to multimillion-dollar developments such as Disney World in Florida. Included are such diverse resources as backyard facilities, table games, restaurants, commercial theaters, private marinas, hotels, flying club aircraft, and guest ranches. Information on the nature, magnitude, and distribution of private resources is, therefore, fragmented and often incomplete. Frequently, the only information sources are manufacturers' (trade) organizations or facility managers' associations. Generally, there are no nationwide comprehensive estimates of the magnitude and use of private recreation resources like those available for public recreation resources.

Table 11.1 outlines the classification system used in this chapter and Chapter 12 to organize private resources. Private personal resources are discussed first, since they provide over 80 percent of most people's recreation opportunities. Other kinds of private resources are then described.

PERSONAL RESOURCES

Personal recreation resources are owned by individuals, families, or household groups and used primarily for their own pleasure or for entertaining friends and relatives. Groups that own private personal resources share these amenities in a casual manner as members of a household, a group of relatives, or an unorganized group of friends rather than as members of an organization.

The nature and extent of private personal recreation resources vary greatly, depending on the culture, discretionary income, and desired lifestyle of the people concerned. As explained in Chapters 4 and 5, many social and economic factors affect recreation lifestyles. Generally, the affluent spend more money on private recreation resources and consequently enjoy the greatest range of opportunities. Limited supplies of recreation goods and services or controls on the construction of private facilities may restrict the role of personal resources in some societies. In the Soviet Union, for example, individuals who wish to purchase personal recreation resources, such as vehicles, certain books, television sets, or residences with more space in which to entertain, may be unable to do so because of shortages or government policies. Similarly, building regulations, water-use controls, and energy restrictions may discourage the building of recreation resources, such as sports facilities and swimming pools on private property in some parts of the United States.

Table 11.1 Classification of Private Recreation Resources

Main Groups	Subgroups	Examples of Resources
**Personal, Organization, and Industrial Private Resources**		
Personal resources	Primary residences	Living room, recreation room, den, garage; audio equipment, card table and chairs; front porch, patio, garden, balcony, flat roof; basketball hoop, swimming pool.
	Second homes	Cottage, trailer, condominium; shoreline, woodland; time-share facility.
	Dual-purpose homes	Beach house, house on waterway, farmhouse near city, houseboat in harbor.
	Other personal resources	Operating farmland, woodland, hunting lands.
Private organization resources	Private recreation organizations	Social club, sports or athletic club, sportsperson's club, boat, or vehicle club, hiking or travel club: clubhouse, sports ground, workshop.
	Nonrecreational organizations	Residential management association; tribal council; religious, service, or benevolent organization: swimming pool, recreation center, lodge.
Quasi-public organization resources	Youth-oriented organizations	Group-program-oriented agencies—Scouts, 4-H, Camp Fire Girls: meeting hall, resident camp, adventure camp. Facility-based agencies—Ys,[a] CYOs,[b] Boys' Clubs: center with gym, pool, gameroom, meeting room; resident camp; hostel.
	Social welfare organizations	Settlement house, community center, camping organization: meeting room, playground, drop-in center, resident camp.
	Preservation organizations	Preservation trusts—historic, natural history, or farmland: unique ecosystem, scenic landscape, historic property, museum, agricultural land.
Industrial resources	Resources used by general public	Farm and ranch resources; agricultural landscape, farm animals, farm buildings; hedgerow, woodland, pond, wildlife. Industrial and forest-industry land: road, trail, campground; wildlife; quarry, pit; reservoir, boat ramp; powerline easement. Industrial tours: auditorium, exhibit park. Community programs: meeting room, gym, pool, park, sportsfield, community center.
	Resources for employees	Multipurpose room, basketball court, picnic area, sportsfield, activities center, campground, golf course.
**Commercial Private Resources**[c]		
Shopping facilities	Conventional stores	Small store, specialty store, department store, shopping mall.
	Other retailers	Mail-order, flea-market, auction sale.
Food-and-drink services	Food-and-beverage stores	Delicatessen, ice cream parlor, specialized bakery.
	Fast-food establishments	Hamburger stand, fried chicken, pizza parlor.
	Cafés and coffee houses	Neighborhood café, tea shop, coffee bar.
	Restaurants	Steak house, seafood restaurant, revolving restaurant.
	Bars and nightclubs	Pub, beer hall, tavern, bar, cabaret.
	Refreshment services	Concession at sports event, theater, or park.

Table 11.1 Classification of Private Recreation Resources (Continued)

Main Groups	Subgroups	Examples of Resources
	Personal, Organization, and Industrial Private Resources	
Participatory facilities	Dancing establishments	Dancehall, discotheque.
	Sports and games establishments	Bowling center, billiard parlor, roller rink, golf driving range.
Amusement parks	Traditional parks	Roller coasters, ferris wheels, penny arcades, shooting galleries, food services, etc.
	Theme parks	Experience and thrill rides, shows, landscaping, food services.
Stadiums and race tracks	Stadiums and arenas	Single or multipurpose structure, Madison Square Garden.
	Race tracks	Churchill Downs, Indianapolis Motor Speedway.
Camps, hotels	Campgrounds and marinas	Kampgrounds of America (KOA), camping resort, marina resort.
	Hotels and boarding houses	Hotel, motel, cabin, boarding house, pension, castle.
	Self-contained resorts	Warm-weather resort; ski, health and beauty, sports resorts; cruise ship.
	Farms and ranches	Vacation farm, dude ranch, private estate.
	Rental units	Cottages, cabins, condominiums.
	Camps and schools	Resident, sports, family, adult, nudist camps.
Shows, tours, and exhibits	Traveling shows	Circus, ice shows, carnivals.
	Exhibits and tours	Cave, miniature city, boat tour, viewing tower.
Commodities and people	Commodities	Fishing rod, playing cards, tent, book, swimsuit, ice cream.
	People	Entertainer, manufacturer, entrepreneur, instructor, repairperson.
	Delivery systems	Rental, charter, guided or package tour.

[a] Young Women's Christian Association (YWCA), Young Men's Christian Association (YMCA), Young Women's Hebrew Association (YWHA), Young Men's Hebrew Association (YMHA).
[b] Catholic Youth Organization.
[c] See Chapter 12.

PRIMARY-RESIDENCE RESOURCES

Recreation resources at people's residences provide more hours of pleasure than any other type of private or public resource; often they involve large monetary investments. Nevertheless, comparatively little quantitative information is available describing the nature and use of these resources. Research concerning primary-residence resources seldom occurs (except in the form of market research by manufacturers), since their use does not appear to affect public lands or policies directly, and investigation of such resources is difficult and expensive.

Many individuals and families depend almost exclusively on resources at their homes or at the homes of their friends and relatives for their recreation. The poor, the elderly, the handicapped, the socially maladjusted, and those who are isolated by fear, cultural differences, or climatic conditions, are especially dependent on home resources. People living in more remote rural areas, particularly in less developed nations, often have little opportunity to do otherwise than rely on their own resources, since no other developed recreation resources—private or public—are accessible to them.

In the past, the most heavily used personal recreation resources have been those that helped people enjoy simple solitary and social activities such as resting, eating, conversation, singing, dancing, playing games, or just watching other people or the environment. In less developed societies, the resources involved may still be minimal—the space around a cooking fire, the sheltered area inside a hut, or a bench positioned near a window or in front of the house that provides a view of the street. A few homemade or purchased resources like dice, cards, or musical instruments may play a prominent role.

In developed societies, however, the extent and complexity of residence recreation resources has steadily increased under the impact of higher discretionary incomes and changing technology. The introduction of comfortable chairs near the fireplace was followed by development of special rooms where recreation was a primary activity. Separate dining rooms permitted meals to become more socially and recreationally significant and less a matter of basic survival. Similarly, parlors, living rooms, sitting rooms, or lounges were developed as places where friends or acquaintances were entertained. Over the years, a succession of innovations was added to the home's recreation resources—table games of various kinds, pianos, stereopticons, radios, phonographs and, more recently, television sets, elaborate stereo sound systems, and large hot tubs.

Indoor Personal Resources. In modern times, the proportion of residence space devoted partially or completely to recreation has increased substantially. Many middle-class homes in developed societies now have one or more largely recreation-oriented rooms in addition to the dining and living rooms. The most common is the family room or recreation room. These range from relatively small rooms used for entertaining guests, viewing television, listening to music, reading, chatting with other members of the family, playing table games, and working on hobbies to entire basements equipped with comfortable furniture, billiard tables, pinball machines, Ping-Pong tables, dance floors, stereo equipment, large-screen television sets, and well-stocked bars. In addition, homes frequently contain dens—rooms usually equipped with a desk, easy chairs, shelves, and books that are suitable retreats for naps, quiet contemplation, letterwriting, reading, conversing with friends by telephone, music practice, hobby projects, and television-viewing as well as for personal and job-related paperwork. Many homes also have workshop areas where much or all of the activity is hobby-related and, therefore, considered recreational. In addition, some have solariums or built-in greenhouses, which are used for growing plants and enjoying the warmth of sunny days during the colder months of the year. Such rooms usually perform several functions not all of which are recreational.

Some homes have highly specialized rooms designed for a specific recreation activity. Such specialization was once the prerogative of the rich, who included music rooms, small movie theaters, gymnasiums, bowling alleys, indoor swimming pools, and rifle ranges in their residences. Now some quite modest residences have rooms containing expensive video and audio equipment; these rooms are used almost exclusively for watching television, seeing movies, and listening to music recordings. Specialized hobby rooms are also becoming more common. These range from rooms devoted to extensive model railway layouts to photographic darkrooms and lapidary workshops. Saunas are popular in some areas; these Scandinavian steam baths are being incorporated into a growing number of residences or built as separate outbuildings. Garages and other attached or separate buildings are frequently used as hobby workshops, art studios, or storage for recreation equipment, materials, and vehicles.

Outdoor Personal Resources. The number and variety of recreation experiences that involve residence exteriors are also increasing. Many older houses and some newer ones have front porches or verandas. Sitting on the front porch is an important recreation activity, especially in older neighborhoods and less developed regions. Sometimes, where there are no porches, people sit on their front steps (Figure 3.1) or even take over part of the public thoroughfare for their chairs and activities. Seated on the steps, in rocking or easy chairs or in a swing suspended from the porch ceiling by hooks, people enjoy the fresh air, read a newspaper or book, entertain friends, watch or greet passersby, or just sit and relax. Young people find porches are great places to play games or socialize with friends, especially on rainy days or when the house itself is filled with guests or other members of the family. The custom of using porches for recreation has largely disappeared, however, in modern single-family housing developments. This is largely because the residences are dispersed and set back from the road on large lots; in addition, there are few pedestrians to provide interest and opportunities for conversation.

In more affluent residential areas, recreation out-of-doors tends to be concentrated at the rear or side of the house where there is more privacy and space for facilities. At one time, amenities, such as attractive landscaping, swimming pools, and patios equipped with garden furniture, were limited to the wealthy. Now, higher discretionary incomes, mass production of goods, and changing aspirations have resulted in a variety of recreation facilities being found in the backyards of most middle-income and many lower-income households. The most common facilities are a patio area, equipped with chairs and a table used for relaxing, conversing with others, playing games, and eating meals. The patio may be just a level, paved area on which to set the furniture. It can also be roofed to provide shade or shelter from the rain or carpeted and screened to make a porch suitable for use on rainy days, during the early evening when the mosquitoes are bothersome, or as sleeping quarters on hot summer nights. The advent of moderately priced charcoal grills has made outdoor cooking of steaks, hamburgers, and other meats a widespread practice, particularly in the United States and Canada.

Similarly, relatively low-cost, aboveground, portable swimming pools make aquatic activities possible for the less affluent (Figure 3.12). Residence yards and gardens provide a great variety of other opportunities, depending on the size and nature of the area and its amenities, and the attitudes and interests of the owners. Areas may be flooded in winter to create ice skating rinks. Children and youth can participate in a variety of group games and social activities on grassed areas during the warm-weather months. And, if the yard is big enough, they can practice such sports as softball, touch football, and soccer. Adults may play with

their children or pets; sunbathe; watch birds; practice golf; play volleyball, badminton, or croquet; or undertake a wide range of landscaping and gardening activities, many of which may be perceived as recreational.

Although more than 85,000 swimming pools continue to be built in yards of American residences each year, there is also a growing interest in other recreation facilities. Golf enthusiasts are using the space for putting greens, avid tennis players are installing tennis courts, and sports-minded families are building multipurpose facilities called sport courts. The sport court is cheaper than most tennis courts or in-ground swimming pools and can be used for more than 15 sports and games such as basketball, shuffleboard, and volleyball as well as for practicing such sports as tennis, soccer, and racquetball. Nets and attachments are adjustable and removable, and lights permit use at night. It can even become an ice rink by freezing water on top of a heavy plastic covering during the winter months.

The extent to which people make recreational use of the land around residences depends to a large extent on the culture of their society and the customs of the community in which they live. Many Americans, for example, especially those in newer residential areas in the western two-thirds of the nation, limit landscaping to a few shrubs planted close to the house. The remainder of the yard is usually lawn with no boundary hedges or fences. Cultivated areas for flowers or vegetables are small or absent. In contrast, shade trees, fruit trees, extensive areas devoted to the cultivation of flowers and

vegetables, and substantial boundary hedges, fences, or walls are much more common in older parts of the United States, Canada, Europe, and other places where European horticultural influences have been greatest.

Because of such differences, the recreational use of residence yards varies considerably. As Table 11.2 suggests, minumum-maintenance yards generally provide fewer and less varied opportunities than more developed properties. Only in the case of games and sports requiring considerable open space does the less developed yard system offer substantial advantages. If the property is reasonably flat as well as unobstructed, it can be used as a rudimentary putting green, for an archery range, or as a place to pitch horseshoes. Net installations can be purchased that catch practice golf drives and tennis serves. Sloping properties may provide children with opportunities for sledding and skiing practice during the cold winter months. However, uses of these kinds may have a detrimental effect on neighbors if they dislike noise, fear for their windows and shrubbery, or have to put up with frequent intrusions by participants as they retrieve balls or complete a toboggan run on their property.

There are many other situations beside the conventional house yard where recreation activities take place out-of-doors. House and apartment-building balconies often function as miniature yards. Residents use balconies for relaxing, reading, sunbathing, entertaining, eating outside, growing plants, or just watching what is going on below. Flat roofs are frequently used in a similar manner. Extensive

Table 11.2 Recreation Features and Advantages of Private-Residence Yards

Features	Main Recreation Advantages[a]
Low-maintenance design (no hedges, fences, cultivated areas, fruit trees, or high-quality grass)	Less free time and money spent on maintenance; fewer worries about damage by weather, insects, disease, thieves, or vandals; allows several adjoining unfenced yards to form one large semipublic play area if the owners do not object; permits space-demanding activities like frisbee; touch football, croquet, volleyball and badminton— or storage of large boats or recreation vehicles.
Fences, hedges, or walls	Provide privacy for personal activities such as relaxing, sunbathing, swimming, reading, entertaining guests, and eating out-of-doors; protect residents, plants, and facilities from uninvited guests, thieves, vandals, and other people's dogs; provide shelter from winds and trap sun's heat; eliminate need to pen or tie up pets.
Large trees and shrubs	Obstruct views of surrounding buildings and streets; lessen noise intrusion; provide shade and reduce temperatures; produce a more aesthetic and relaxing environment; encourage birds and other forms of wildlife; may be suitable for climbing and installing swings, tree houses, and hammocks.
Flowers, vegetables, and fruits	Produce pleasurable experiences during growing process, followed by sense of accomplishment if all goes well; enhance appearance of property; provide gratifying experience of being able to harvest and consume home-grown produce.
Recreation equipment and facilities	Attract wildlife for observation (birdfeeders, birdbaths); entertain guests and encourage family togetherness (tables and chairs, swimming pools, barbecue grills, sandboxes and play equipment); increase aesthetic appeal (ornamental pools, fountains); provide opportunities for exercise and play (basketball hoops, tennis courts).
Any yard with a number of interesting features	Encourages periodic tours to observe seasonal changes taking place; provides opportunities to show and discuss yard with others; enhances area for social activities and entertaining.
Screened patio or sunporch facilities	Provide privacy and shelter from sun, rain, wind, and insects; protect equipment and furniture; often have electrical outlets, which facilitate use of electrical appliances such as coffee percolators, stereo equipment, and television sets; encourage enjoyment of table games and hobbies in a fresh air setting; may be used for entertaining and overnight campouts.

[a] Disadvantages are not listed, since the advantages of the low-maintenance design tend to be the disadvantages of the more highly developed yard and vice versa. There are also special disadvantages connected with specific features such as the safety and maintenance problems associated with swimming pools.

flower or vegetable gardens are often developed on roofs, and some people build specialized hobby facilities on them such as greenhouses, aviaries, or pigeon coops.

In many cities, balconies and roofs are the only personal open space available to large numbers of residents. House and apartment-building yards are often minute or completely absent; where they do exist, they frequently lack privacy and are undesirable environments

for recreation because of the presence of litter; pollution by noise, dust, or automobile exhausts; and the threat of lawlessness and vandalism. Many children play on balconies or roofs because they or their parents consider these locations safer than any of the street-level alternatives. The use of balconies and roofs for general outdoor-living space and recreation purposes is most common in cities in warm and hot climatic regions; architectural styles are often modified

to provide residents with a maximum amount of usable balcony or roof-top space.

SECOND-HOME RESOURCES

At one time, only the wealthy could afford to buy a *second home* that was primarily for recreational use. Now, people from a wide range of income levels own recreation dwellings. In the United States, it is estimated that about 3 million families or about 5 percent of all households have second homes. Only about one-third of these are fully equipped houses or apartments similar to primary residences. Most are relatively small cottages or cabins, and many are not suitable for occupancy during cold weather. Approximately 7 percent are shared between two or more families to reduce maintenance problems and costs. The owners of another 8 percent lease their properties when they are not using them to help defray expenses.

Water-Oriented Homes. In Canada and the United States, the relative availability of sites on ocean shorelines, estuaries, rivers, the Great Lakes, and inland lakes has resulted in the majority of second homes being water-oriented. The typical summer cottage found in the New England states, the Midwest, and Canada is a one-story, wooden structure built on a wooded shoreline. Such homes are normally used intensively in July and August and only for occasional weekends during the late spring and early fall. Similar shoreline cottages and use patterns are found in Scandinavia and some of the lake regions in other parts of Europe.

Many concentrations of American second homes are situated farther south, especially along sandy shoreline areas of the Atlantic, Gulf of Mexico, or California coasts. The majority are modest cottages, but an increasing proportion are more elaborate houses. Some are the seasonal homes of the wealthy with all the features of expensive primary residences. A number of communities that are composed largely of this type of dwelling are located in Florida and the desert resort

areas of Arizona and California. Recreation behavior at desert second homes tends to be similar to that at the coastal sites, except that horseback riding is more common, swimming and sunbathing activities take place at residence swimming pools, and other aquatic activities are enjoyed at nearby reservoirs. In Europe, similar concentrations of the affluent's seasonal residences are found around the lakes in Switzerland and northern Italy and at the more fashionable Mediterranean shoreline locations.

Ocean and desert-oriented second homes in the southern part of the United States were formerly used primarily in the winter months by owners who resided in northern cities. The spread of air-conditioning and rapid air travel has encouraged many owners to make periodic use of such homes throughout the entire year. Economic growth and population expansion in these locations have also increased the proportion of owners who live nearby and use their second homes on a regular rather than intermittent basis. Recreation participation at water-oriented second homes focuses on aquatic activities such as relaxing or sunbathing on the beach, swimming, boating, waterskiing, sailing, canoeing, fishing, digging for clams, and beachcombing. Visiting with friends, photography, reading, nature study, and taking part in various kinds of social gatherings are also important pastimes.

Homes in Agricultural Areas. Second homes are not necessarily located on water-oriented sites. In Europe, in particular, many second homes are scattered through the countryside or located

in small villages far from rivers, lakes, or ocean beaches. Several factors have contributed to this situation. Large numbers of the middle class started to emulate the aristocracy by acquiring "a place in the country" during the late 1800s. Cities became crowded and less environmentally desirable as a result of the industrial revolution. Migration of laborers and others to manufacturing centers left many homes in rural areas available for purchase or lease at reasonable prices. Most river, lake, and ocean shorelines were already part of operating farms or the estates of the wealthy. No great reserves of undeveloped private shorelines and low-cost public lands similar to those in Canada and the United States existed. In addition, second-home acquisition was motivated more by images of the aristocracy's landscaped country homes and the idyllic pastoral scenes of the romanticists than by a desire for the rugged hunting, fishing, and canoeing lifestyle associated with the North American "wilderness." In more recent times, stringent land-use and building regulations have prevented or discouraged new second-home developments in many European nations.

Europeans who own second homes in agricultural areas participate in a broad range of recreation activities while on their weekend or vacation visits. Some concentrate on the property itself, spending much time restoring or modernizing the dwelling or working in the garden. Others use their second homes primarily for social purposes, inviting friends for the weekend and holding frequent parties. Many use their properties as retreats where they can escape the pressures of city life; they spend their time resting and relaxing; reading; working on a favorite hobby or crafts project; going for walks along public footpaths through the farms and woods; gathering craft materials, nuts, and berries; or engaging in nature study activities. Others become involved in the life of the community, attending church services, taking part in the activities of local organizations, and enjoying the convivial atmosphere of the bistros, pubs, or beer gardens.

Second homes in agricultural areas of Canada and the United States are comparatively few in number. Some are owned by people who have family ties to a particular region or by those who wish to keep horses or other large animals.

Homes in Forest Areas.
Second homes are also located in forest areas away from rivers or lakes. A good number are used primarily during the hunting season and range from the relatively primitive deer-hunting camps found throughout much of Canada and the United States to the elaborate lodges of the wealthy, which occur in many nations. Woodland cabins are quite widespread in Europe, particularly in many of the eastern nations, including the Soviet Union.

Forest-oriented second homes are numerous in the United States and Canada, especially in areas with few lakes or where lakeshore property is becoming difficult to obtain. People who use these homes in the summer spend much time relaxing and enjoying the surrounding forest environment. Some fish extensively in forest streams. Others go hiking or motorcycle riding on woodland roads and trails. Such homes may also be used extensively at other times of the year as

base camps for mushroom gathering, hunting, snowmobiling, and cross-country skiing activities.

Homes in Highland Areas.
For centuries, affluent residents of nations with hot climates have migrated during the summer months to second homes situated at higher elevations. Such seasonal residences are often used more as a means of escaping the heat than to facilitate participation in specific outdoor activities. Nevertheless, the owners derive much pleasure from the change of location and social contacts. Many Americans with second homes in the Appalachian Mountains or highland regions of the West use their properties as weekend and vacation retreats or for the entertaining of friends and relatives. In many cases, such mountain sites are also attractive because of their forest environments and fine vistas, and some of the people who own them pursue outdoor activities such as backpacking, mountaineering, hunting, fishing, rockhounding, and nature study.

The growth of participation in skiing has resulted in the rapid expansion of second-home developments in certain highland regions. Large numbers of homes have been built since World War II in the vicinity of most of the major ski areas in both Canada and the United States as well as around many of the largest ski centers in Europe (Figure 11.2). Indeed, these developments are so extensive in some locations that they are causing serious environmental problems. Owners of these homes tend to combine downhill and cross-country skiing with entertaining, and they often engage in an active social life

at nearby restaurants, discotheques, nightclubs, and bars. Some also use their second homes at other times during the year for the kinds of activities described in connection with homes in forest locations.

Homes in and near Cities.
In the past, wealthy landowners and industrialists often spent the warmer months at their country estates or manufacturing locations and moved into their *town houses* for the winter social season. Some affluent people still maintain secondary residences in one or more cities for business and recreation purposes. Today, these are frequently apartments, which are used periodically as a home base when the owner or renter attends theater or other performances, sports events, or social occasions in the city.

A very different type of urban second home is found in and near many cities in West Germany, eastern Europe, and the Soviet Union. These consist of small cabins on tiny plots of land— often one-tenth hectare (one-quarter acre) or less— which are located in areas of previously unoccupied lands (especially strips along railroads). In eastern Europe and the Soviet Union, the plots are often located considerable distances from urban centers. Less affluent city residents, most of whom live in apartments or row houses that have no garden space, purchase or lease these plots, traveling to them by bicycle or public transportation.

Like residence yards, these small second homes are used for a wide range of purposes. Some are largely lawn, others are devoted almost exclusively to growing vegetables, fruits, flowers, or various com-

Figure 11.2 Most people buy a condominuim unit in a highland area such as this one at Colorado's Copper Mountain resort because of the winter social and skiing opportunities. Attractive living areas encourage entertaining and the ski lifts, restaurants, and other places of entertainment are all within walking distance. However, more owners are using such second homes year-round because highland resort areas are offering a growing number of sports and cultural opportunities during warmer months.

binations of these items. Many have recreation amenities such as patios, lawn furniture, ornamental ponds, or children's play equipment. In areas of eastern Europe and the Soviet Union where fresh fruit and vegetables are hard to obtain, plots tend to be more utilitarian; in some cases, people use them as miniature farms. But even where food production is a primary objective, plot users obtain many recreation benefits. Sometimes the owners stop after work for a few hours of fresh air and sunshine while hoeing their vegetables or sitting in lawn chairs. Other uses are sunbathing, playing with children, picnicking, entertaining friends, or staying overnight. Al-

most 10 percent of Moscow's residents spend vacations at such plots.

Second-Home Ownership.
A great variety of second-home arrangements exists in addition to individual or family exclusive ownership of a building and the parcel of land on which it stands. High land values and the need to control development often result in second-home sites being leased rather than sold. Public organizations such as Parks Canada (the Canadian national park agency), the U.S. Forest Service, the Tennessee Valley Authority, and certain state park agencies have leased land for second homes in the past. Most have now

severely curtailed or stopped this practice because second-home developments provide limited recreation opportunities for comparatively few citizens and also create numerous management problems. On the other hand, private land owners — especially corporations — often favor leasing because it allows them to obtain revenues from the land while retaining ownership for possible future redevelopment. In addition, private groups do not have the political problems experienced by public agencies when lease terms have to be enforced legally or when the renewal of a lease is denied.

An alternative to individual or family ownership of second homes involves *property-sharing,* an arrangement by which people can enjoy most of the amenities of a personal second home without having to bear the full costs of ownership and maintenance. Property-sharing is an excellent idea, since the majority of people are only able to make use of a second home for short periods of time in any given year. It also decreases the time a property is vacant and untended; this reduces the risk of loss from vandalism, burglary, and undetected damage resulting from bad weather or the failure of water and heating systems. Many second homes are being shared by two or more individuals or households under informal or formal agreements. This kind of arrangement is called a *shared whole ownership.*

Another alternative is provided by condominium developments in which second homes can be owned on a *time-sharing* basis. (A *condominium* is a type of ownership not a kind of building; a purchaser obtains ownership of one housing unit within a multiple-unit complex plus a share in the common facilities.) There are two types of time-sharing plans. Under the *interval-ownership plan,* a buyer receives title to one of the housing units for a particular period. During this period, the sharer is entitled to the full use of the housing unit and any associated recreation facilities such as pools, tennis courts, golf courses, gymnasiums, lounges, and saunas. This housing unit along with a share of the common amenities is the sharer's property for that period. The interval may involve more than one time; purchasing a period in the peak season and another during the off season is fairly common. Each share may be used, leased to someone else, or sold at the owner's discretion.

Under the other approach, called the *membership plan,* an individual purchases a share in a resort property for a specified period of time. This share does not include ownership of the unit or land, which remains in the hands of the developer. What it does is provide a guaranteed, paid-in-advance use of a particular housing unit and the resort facilities for a specified period each year during a given number of years. These may vary from 12 to 40 years. In addition, resorts under either of these plans often belong to a computerized international exchange program. For a small fee, time-sharers may exchange their time for a stay of comparable value at another resort, thereby making it possible to enjoy a water-oriented vacation one year and a skiing vacation at a different resort the next. One of these exchange programs lists 105 participating resorts in the United States, Canada, Mexico, the Caribbean, Central America, and Europe. In Europe, the time-sharing

resorts are referred to as club hotels, aparthotels, or multipropriété hotels.

Initial purchase prices range from $600 to $10,000 for a minimum interval, depending on the season involved, the housing unit's size and location on the property, and the resort's location, clientele, condition, and facilities. All time-share facilities have maintenance fees, which are usually collected annually. These fees tend to rise as the building ages and needs repairs. However, many people feel that time-share purchases are good investments because they are protected from inflation, an important consideration when hotel charges are rising at an annual rate of 7 percent or more. To date, some 500,000 Americans have purchased a share in one of the 500 time-share complexes situated in 26 states. The major areas are Colorado, Florida, Hawaii, and South Carolina. Some of the most attractive developments with time-sharing arrangements are to be found on Hilton Head Island, South Carolina, on South Padre Island, Texas, and at Vail, Colorado.

A number of luxury hotels are also being sold room by room in much the same way as the condominiums. Marriott's Camelback Inn in Scottsdale, Arizona, for instance, will sell an individual a guestroom in a limited partnership arrangement. The partner is then entitled to a maximum of 28 days of use per year with the room being rented by management the rest of the time under a rental pool program. End-of-year profits are shared by all such partners after maintenance expenses are deducted. The partner also has the option of spending the allotted 28

days at any of the other Marriott resorts or on any of their Sun Line cruises. Other such rooms are available at Mexico's luxury hotel, Las Hadas, and in numerous hotels in Hawaii and along the French Riviera. Similarly, the S.S. *United States,* a cruise ship, is selling one-sixth of its staterooms as time-share units, with investors having exclusive use of the staterooms two weeks each year for 20 years.

Trailers and Boats. An increasing number of people are using travel trailers and boats as second homes. They purchase or lease a site or berth, bring in their trailer or boat, and then seldom move it away from the chosen location. Some leave trailers and boats year-round at a campground or marina; others take them to their primary residence or to a storage area for the winter. A small proportion of travel-trailer owners lease, purchase, or obtain permission to use building lots, small farm properties, or parcels of undeveloped land to have a permanent private location at which to stay. Both small and large travel-trailer parks devoted primarily or entirely to the sale or long-term leasing of sites are growing in number. Some are informal family operations in rural areas. Others are large, sophisticated corporate enterprises in heavily used resort areas. Similarly, boat owners secure permanent moorings for their boats through a variety of arrangements, ranging from the purchase of their own waterfrontage to the long-term leasing of a marina berth. A growing number are using travel trailers or boats as recreation-oriented primary residences. In North America, for example, some retired persons move their trailers or boats from locations in the southern states or Mexico, where they live in the winter, to more northerly locations, where they spend the summer.

People use travel trailers and boats as second homes for a variety of reasons. Many find it is the only way they can afford to have a second-home type of experience. The average cost of a summer cottage is now $30,000, but a trailer or boat suitable for use as a residence can still be obtained for under $15,000. Even houseboats, which make attractive, comfortable second homes, can be purchased for $15,000 to $20,000. In addition, owning a boat or trailer makes it possible to move to another location if one place proves unsatisfactory or a change is desired. However, in some regions, a scarcity of trailer sites and boat berths has encouraged campground and marina owners to charge higher fees. In addition, some local governments have begun to limit severely or ban completely long-term occupancy of boats or travel trailers, tax boats and trailers as if they were permanent dwellings, or require the installation of costly site or berth facilities. These requirements and restrictions together with the scarcity of sites and increasing site rentals are making this kind of second-home arrangement less attractive or even impossible for a number of existing as well as potential boat or trailer owners.

DUAL-PURPOSE HOMES
Instead of purchasing and maintaining two separate residences, a growing number of individuals and families spend more than they would otherwise on just one home

site and buy a *dual-purpose home* at a location that provides the features of a primary residence as well as some of the attributes of a second home. In this way, they have second-home recreation opportunities available every day. They also avoid the trips to and from second homes that are often costly, time-consuming, and frustrating for people who maintain two separate residences. However, this advantage is frequently offset by regularly having to travel considerable distances to reach places of work, schools, shopping areas, and other service facilities.

Wealthy people began to acquire dual-purpose residences in the late 1800s when the development of trains, streetcars, and better roads made it possible to live at one location and work at another. Since that time, the radius of commuting has gradually expanded, especially in areas served by convenient high-speed train service or good highways. The type of individual who can afford this lifestyle has also changed. Nowadays, people from all walks of life reside in dual-purpose residences in or around urban areas. These include beach houses, lakeshore cottages, riverside apartments, small farms, condominiums at ski or beach resorts, homes next to golf courses, houseboats in harbors, and large travel trailers parked in forest areas. At such sites, the owners spend much of their free time on outdoor activities commonly associated with second homes or extended vacations. These include sunning, swimming, surfing, fishing, powerboating, canoeing, sailing, waterskiing, golfing, playing tennis and other sports, horseback riding, motorcycling, hunting, snowmobiling, and down-

hill and cross-country skiing.

The growing market for dual-purpose residences has been reflected in rising prices and a boom in dual-purpose home construction. Existing homes with dual-purpose potential are purchased and remodeled by entrepreneurs who make improvements that increase the recreation opportunities on the properties. Such homes rise steadily in value as the region's commuter facilities and economic conditions improve. Some builders specialize in individual homes or residential complexes designed expressly for people seeking the opportunity to live where they play.

A common type of American dual-purpose development is the single family-home subdivision built along a river, around a lake, or on canals connected to a lake, river, estuary, or ocean bay (Figure 4.12). Many such developments have been constructed in Florida as either second or retirement homes. Substantial numbers in or near urban areas are occupied by people who commute to work. Similar projects are found along the bays and estuaries of the Atlantic Ocean and the Gulf of Mexico coasts. Some have been built at freshwater locations, including metropolitan areas like Detroit. However, environmental problems, such as depreciation of water quality, vulnerability to flooding, negative reaction to the destruction of wetlands, and opposition to using water resources in excess of their carrying capacity, are discouraging this type of development in some areas.

The number of types of residential developments with dual-purpose features continues to increase. Examples include housing integrated with golf-course or tennis-court facilities (Figure 7.11), subdivisions with large lots and municipal regulations that permit owners to keep horses at their homes, and developments built around runways so that private-aircraft owners can keep planes in hangars behind their houses.

OTHER PERSONAL LANDS

Many people recreate on or from lands that are not owned primarily as sites for their principal residences or second homes. Farm and ranch owners, for instance, often use their cropland, pastures, woodlands, ponds, streams, swamps, and laneways for such activities as walking, horseback riding, hunting, fishing, swimming, boating, and snowmobiling. Some increase the available recreation opportunities by digging ponds for swimming, boating, and fishing or by managing agricultural lands and woodlands for optimum wildlife production (Figure 11.3). Some landowners go to con-

Figure 11.3 When properly constructed, farm ponds can be valuable recreation resources as well as a source of water for agricultural and domestic purposes. This family uses their pond for a variety of activities including boating, waterskiing, swimming, and fishing.

siderable trouble to preserve such opportunities for themselves by fencing and posting their properties against trespass.

Many people own personal recreation lands that include no permanent structures. Some tracts were acquired for the purpose of erecting a second or retirement home, but construction has been delayed indefinitely by economic constraints. In other cases, the lands remain undeveloped because owners have unwittingly purchased swamp, desert, or mountain land that proved largely inaccessible or too expensive or difficult to develop. On the other hand, a growing number of individuals and families, especially American and Canadian city dwellers, purchase extraurban land with no intention of ever developing it. These woodlands, marshes, and derelict farmlands are used for hunting, fishing, camping, snowmobiling, cross-country skiing, motorcycling, or nature study activities. In some cases, the land may also have sentimental value because it is part of a family farm that the individual has inherited or is in an area where the individual or a relative once lived. As in the case of second-home and dual-purpose properties, much of the enjoyment associated with such lands appears to be psychological. Owners may not be able to visit these resources nearly as often as they would like, but they derive constant satisfaction from knowing that such lands are theirs.

PRIVATE ORGANIZATION RESOURCES

Another complex array of recreation resources is owned by private organizations. These consist of people who form informal or formal associations for a variety of purposes and in the process provide recreation for themselves. In contrast to the private personal recreation resources, these amenities are owned by a number of unrelated individuals or households and are operated primarily for their benefit.

Providing recreation for members is the main objective of some of these organizations; examples are social clubs, sportsperson's clubs, hobby clubs, and noncommercial musical groups. Other groups are formed primarily for different purposes but provide varying kinds and amounts of recreation for members, depending on the nature of the organization and the goals and interests of participants. These organizations include churches, service clubs, professional associations, political parties, and labor organizations. The nature of the programs offered and the behavior of the members of many such groups indicate that recreation is a more important organization goal and member objective than is usually acknowledged.

The nature and magnitude of the contributions made by this major segment of the recreation resource system are largely unknown. Governments generally do not compile information on the recreation role of private-organization resources and the complex, fragmented nature of the groups discourage comprehensive studies by independent researchers. Isolated studies concerning individual private recreation organizations have been undertaken and some estimates of membership numbers, extent of participation, and resources are made by national associations or magazines that serve certain of these groups. Data are even more incomplete, however, for organizations that are not formed expressly to provide recreation for members. In the cases of religious organizations, service clubs, professional associations, business organizations, and political parties, for example, there is the added problem of identifying the reason individuals join and participate. Some of these groups are also reluctant to admit that their activities are partly or largely recreational because of the possible effects to their public image or tax status.

Although comprehensive data concerning the nature and significance of private-organization recreation are not available, it is clear that these groups make a substantial contribution. Few people are not members of one or more private organizations that provide them with recreation opportunities. In developed societies, the number of memberships per individual appears to increase with personal income. Some persons find recreation opportunities offered by organizations to be well attuned to their personal needs and, consequently, they join several groups. There are probably several million private organizations in the United States providing a great variety of opportunities for their members.

In the paragraphs that follow, the features of resources that private groups provide for their members are summarized. However, many organizations do not own land or facilities but obtain the necessary resources by means of leases or donations from members, other persons, corporations, or governments. Private associations frequently provide extensive programs for members that are partially or completely recreational yet involve few tangible resources.

The division into recreation organizations and nonrecreational organizations shown in Table 11.1 is somewhat arbitrary. It is based primarily on the intended principal activity as stated or implied by the name of the organization. However, groups are often formed with one stated purpose, whereas most of the members' interests, efforts, and activities are focused in another direction. For example, social activities frequently occupy much of the time members devote to a group's programs even though the organization's main objectives may be stated to be of a political, business, or public service nature. There are also individual groups within a particular class of recreation organization that spend much of their time on activities that do not appear to be purely recreational. For example, a number of citizens band radio groups in the United States concentrate on assisting motorists with travel problems and helping communities during emergency situations.

PRIVATE RECREATION ORGANIZATIONS

Organizations that are formed primarily to provide recreation experiences for their members range from small groups of individuals with similar interests to complex associations involving many thousands of people. These *private recreation organizations* do not fall neatly into a series of mutually exclusive classes. Rather, such groups exhibit a seemingly infinite variety of characteristic combinations.

Social Clubs. Organizations formed mainly to provide social activities for their members range from small informal groups that meet to play games, hold discussions, or have parties to legally incorporated clubs with hundreds of members. Although activities are often conducted on the property of members or other individuals or at facilities owned by public, quasi-public or religious organizations, many groups have their own facilities. Some of the world's most extensive and sophisticated recreation resource complexes are owned by private social clubs.

Small urban social clubs often lease one or two rooms or perhaps a disused store. Larger, more affluent groups may lease or construct an entire building. Social clubs formed by particular ethnic groups (such as people of Italian, Polish, or Scottish ancestry) frequently have large halls, where dances, concerts, parties, and banquets are held. Traditional men's clubs patronized by the wealthy and socially prominent have some of the most elaborate private-organization facilities found in urban areas. Some contain all of the amenities of deluxe hotels, including overnight guestrooms, dining rooms, bars, cocktail lounges, libraries, and smoking and reading rooms as well as billiards and other gamerooms, gymnasiums, swimming pools, squash courts, handball courts, and steamrooms. Such clubs are found primarily in major business and commercial centers, like New York, but appear to be declining because of rising costs and changing lifestyles. In London, for example, the number of gentlemen's clubs has dwindled in the last 30 years from 120 to about 40. Of those remaining, many have merged with other clubs or admit-

ted women in an effort to increase membership and pay the bills.

In Canadian and American suburban areas, country clubs are usually the most conspicuous of the property-owning private, social, or recreation organizations. Some function primarily as golf facilities, but many offer a wide variety of opportunities. They may contain snack bars, lounges, bars, dining rooms, party rooms, dance floors, bowling alleys, exercise rooms, patios, and swimming pools, which members use for informal and formal social activities. In addition, country clubs sometimes provide tennis, polo, horseback riding, cook-out, and winter-sports facilities. Although belonging to a particular class in society no longer remains a prerequisite for membership in many country clubs, members often tend to be of one race, religion, or income level. Therefore, many individuals consider affiliation an important sign of status. Thus it is not unusual for people to belong to several country clubs in their lifetimes, dropping out of one and joining another more exclusive club every time their position in life improves sufficiently to warrant it.

Sports and Athletic Clubs. Thousands of private sports and athletic clubs were formed in the late 1800s, mostly in the larger cities. Many developed extensive facilities, including outdoor areas for team sports and track and field events in addition to clubhouses equipped for athletic conditioning and indoor sports.

Today, many new sports and athletic organizations, together with some of the original clubs, provide a substantial and increasing number of recreation opportunities. Most tend to focus on one or a cluster of related sports. Some specialize in either indoor or outdoor activities; others provide a combination of the two. The most frequently encountered types of clubs in Canada and the United States are golf, tennis, badminton, racquetball, squash, softball, baseball, bowling, swimming, ice skating, skiing, and track and field clubs. Curling clubs are common in Canada, Scotland, and a few locations in the northern United States. Soccer clubs are widespread in Europe and many other parts of the world. Cricket clubs are found in most communities in England, Wales, Australia, New Zealand, and most of the other former British colonies.

The amenities owned by private sports clubs vary considerably. Many have no property and either lease land and buildings or use public facilities. This is particularly true of groups that play a single team sport, such as soccer. On the other hand, there are numerous private clubs that own extensive properties. Racket clubs with several courts and some form of clubhouse can be found in most of the larger and more affluent urban and suburban communities in Canada, the United States, Western Europe, and those parts of the world where tennis and racquetball are well-established sports. In the United States alone, for example, there are about 950 indoor tennis clubs and almost as many clubs devoted exclusively to racquetball. By providing indoor courts or installing large vinyl bubbles over some or all of their outdoor courts, these private clubs enable members to play in comfort throughout the year. Some of the racket clubs provide other amenities, including exercise equip-

ment, saunas, dining facilities, elaborate lounges, swimming pools (Figure 11.4), and extensive social programs reminiscent of country clubs.

Similarly, some private ski clubs own ski slopes, lifts, snow-grooming equipment, and clubhouses that contain pro shops, restaurants and, occasionally, swimming pools and other après-ski facilities. About 40 of these clubs are in operation in the United States in major ski resort areas; the majority, however, are located near urban centers. These near-urban clubs usually have small hills suitable for beginners, but more experienced skiers often use them regularly for practice. They can ski on the lighted slopes in the evenings and at other times when only short periods of free time are available. Others join private ski or tennis clubs to escape the crowded conditions and accompanying long waits so often found at commercial or public facilities.

Sportsperson's Clubs. A great variety of recreation resources is owned or leased by hunting, fishing, or shooting associations. Some clubs in the United States and Canada are made up of small informal groups of middle-income individuals who purchase a few acres of land that contain hunting or fishing cabins at locations that provide easy access to public lands or waters. In other cases, such groups may own several hundred acres of forest or marsh, where members do much of their big-game, small-game, or waterfowl hunting. Affluent individuals often create informal or formal associations to purchase or lease prime hunting or fishing areas, such as land surrounding high-quality waterfowl habitats or famous trout

and salmon streams in Quebec or Scotland. Such groups usually employ gamekeepers or wardens to protect their interests; in some cases, club personnel also undertake game- or fisheries-management activities.

There are also thousands of private sportsperson's clubs with little or no recreation resources that are open to virtually anyone willing to pay the modest membership fees. These range from large organizations with hundreds of members to small groups of 10 or a dozen people. Some have modest clubhouses, where the members attend meetings, talks, or movies on hunting or fishing topics, and gather on a regular or occasional basis to enjoy each other's company or to take part in planned social events. Some clubs have sufficient land for rifle or skeet-shooting ranges or for various kinds of demonstrations and competitions.

Boat and Vehicle Clubs. Many groups in this class own few resources. Some have neither land nor equipment and hold their meetings and events on public lands or on property owned by members and friends.

Boat clubs generally own or lease waterfront property, where boats may be moored or stored on land. Some have extensive marina and boat-servicing facilities. A large proportion have some form of clubhouse; these range from simple storage and shelter buildings to elaborate complexes that resemble sophisticated country clubs. Sailing and yacht clubs commonly have club-owned boats of various sizes. In some cases, these boats are only used for instructing the children of club members. At other clubs, adult

Figure 11.4 The East River Tennis Club in Queens, New York, provides its members with a 21-meter (70-foot) outdoor swimming pool, a sun deck, and 22 Har-Tru tennis courts protected by Irvin Air structures in winter. An elegant clubhouse contains a bar, lounge with fireplace, saunas, and locker rooms. The club operates a regular mini-bus service from Manhattan.

members may use the boats, making sailing feasible for those who cannot or do not wish to acquire their own vessels.

Similarly, private flying clubs normally purchase or lease facilities at an airport. Some have their own flying fields. Most have some form of clubhouse or headquarters. Since aircraft are fairly expensive, one of the main purposes of forming such

clubs is to obtain access to group-owned aircraft so that most clubs own one or more planes. Clubs frequently own or lease aircraft-storage hangars and some have maintenance facilities. Glider and sailplane flying are also usually club activities because more than one person is required to launch one of these aircraft. Some glider and sail-plane clubs own airfields, launching

winches, and powered tow aircraft. Others purchase or lease suitable hilltops from which gliders can be launched.

Private motorized-vehicle organizations vary greatly in their objectives and resources. Many do not own or lease any recreation resources for members' use, whereas others provide extensive facilities. Snowmobile clubs frequently have clubhouses. In some areas, especially Wisconsin and Quebec, snowmobile clubs own, lease, or are assigned responsibility for maintaining extensive snowmobile trail systems on public or private lands (Figure 5.2). In Quebec, officially registered clubs are legally empowered to receive government grants and collect fees from nonmembers who use the trails that the clubs maintain.

Motorcycle clubs range from the youthful, leather-clad, gang-type organization to groups of families and older people who ride small relatively quiet machines on backcountry roads and trails. Some have their own clubhouses and a few own or lease land that is used for racing or hill climbs. Off-highway vehicle clubs have rather similar characteristics. There are many other kinds of private-vehicle organizations—jeep clubs, dune buggy clubs, sports car clubs, antique car clubs, racing clubs, and van clubs, for example—but few have resources other than a clubhouse or meeting room leased for their business, educational, and social functions.

Hiking and Travel Clubs.
Another major group is the hiking, bicycling, mountaineering, camping, and travel clubs. Particularly in Europe, such clubs own or lease overnight accommodations that enable students and others of moderate means to travel widely. Some of the hiking and mountaineering organizations have built shelters in remote mountain areas. These structures are usually simple huts that provide shelter from low nighttime temperatures and bad weather. Such facilities make mountain resources available to hikers and climbers who do not

have the equipment, skills, or inclination to camp in exposed locations. Huts of this kind are common in parts of Europe, especially the Alps, but are generally absent in North American mountain regions.

A more elaborate kind of shelter is provided by some types of hiking and mountaineering clubs. The Appalachian Trail Conference, for instance, is composed of 93 affiliated clubs located along the 3200–kilometer (2000-mile) Appalachian Trail from Maine to Georgia. Its biggest affiliate is the Appalachian Mountain Club, headquartered in Boston. Founded in 1876, this 23,000-member organization focuses its efforts on supplying opportunities for hiking, camping, rock-climbing, canoeing, ski-touring, and bicycling. It owns and operates nine fair-sized lodges known as huts, which are situated about a day's hike apart along the Appalachian Trail in the White Mountains region of New Hampshire.

During the hiking season, each hut is staffed by a group of paid employees who backpack food and other supplies to the hut, cook the meals, and maintain the structure. The hut staffs also maintain 560 kilometers (350 miles) of trails and 18 trailside shelters in the surrounding White Mountains National Forest. Other activities of the club include the operation of several residential summer camps, cabin developments, and tent campgrounds at lower elevations along the Saco River in New Hampshire and along the Maine coast. The Boston chapter operates a large lodge in Gorham, New Hampshire, near the Wildcat ski area. The New York chapter runs a dormitory-style camp on Fire Island.

Several organizations have sim-

ilar, although not as elaborate programs. The Adirondack Mountain Club owns and operates two lodges in the Adirondack Mountains of New York State. The Alpine Club of Canada has a clubhouse near Canmore, Alberta, and high-altitude mountain shelters in Alberta and British Columbia.

In contrast, the 180,000-member Sierra Club concentrates on offering a wide range of supervised outings. By providing the human resources necessary to organize and lead expeditions, the club provides canoeing, backpacking, scuba diving, bicycling, sailing, rubber-rafting, and cross-country skiing experiences suitable for members with a wide variety of capabilities. These excursions range from one-day hikes and canoe trips to six-week expeditions in remote foreign areas. Of course, the Sierra Club has also contributed greatly to everyone's recreation opportunities by stimulating and facilitating the creation of many national park system units and wilderness areas.

Many other types of resources are provided by private hiking, camping, or travel organizations. The Nomad Travel Club of southeast Michigan, for instance, has two jet airliners, its own flight and aircraft maintenance crews, and a hangar-terminal building at Detroit's Metropolitan Airport. The club offers trips at cost to destinations decided on by the members. Another travel association turns members' homes into club recreation resources by arranging residence exchanges between members in different locations, thereby enabling participants to enjoy the facilities of each other's homes while visiting the attractions in the surrounding area.

Cultural and Hobby Groups. Although many cultural, artistic, and hobby programs are provided by local government agencies, private organizations are major suppliers of opportunities for participation in drama; opera; music; arts and crafts; games, like bridge and chess; and technical and collecting hobbies. Such groups frequently use public meeting rooms, auditoriums, or classrooms for their activities, but a substantial number purchase or lease facilities. Amateur drama groups often acquire old buildings such as barns, mills, churches, or schools and convert them into theaters. Arts and crafts organizations sometimes operate studios and galleries. Orchestras and bands provide their own practice and storage spaces. Model-railroad clubs often obtain large rooms or entire buildings for cooperative layouts and workshop areas. Similarly, many camera clubs have darkrooms and rock clubs maintain their own lapidary workshops.

NONRECREATIONAL ORGANIZATIONS

Several kinds of private organizations contribute substantially to the supply of recreation opportunities even though their primary purpose is not recreational. Indeed, some groups would probably object to their organizations being regarded as recreation providers. Nevertheless, such organizations do provide pleasurable experiences for their members and, in many cases, for the public at large. Many members obtain considerable satisfaction just from belonging and taking part in business meetings, carrying out administrative duties, performing social services, or attending religious

observances as part of a group. But organizations of this type also devote portions of their programs to social activities such as teas, banquets, picnics, and parties. Some have extensive recreation resources or other resources that receive substantial amounts of incidental recreational use.

The proportions of time and money that nonrecreational private organizations devote to recreation facilities and programs appear to be increasing, especially in affluent areas. Many groups are expanding the recreational aspects of their programs to survive. Some organizations that previously have refused to do so, are now renting facilities to nonmembers for recreational purposes to balance their budgets. Others have found that more and better recreation programs attract new members, who, then, contribute to the organization's financial support. In growing numbers these organizations are permitting and even encouraging nonmember participation in their recreation programs as another means of paying for programs or earning money for other projects, including the construction of new facilities. Recreation facilities and programs provided by some groups may be so extensive that they satisfy many of the recreational needs of an entire community. Such groups are, in effect, providing services that are usually supplied by municipal park and recreation systems.

Residential Management Associations. For many years, owners of houses, apartments, and second homes have formed associations to maintain and manage the roads, shared recreation resources, and other services in exclusive pri-

vate communities. This approach to the provision of local services is now being used extensively for middle-income residential and second-home communities.

The *planned-unit development* (PUD) is becoming increasingly common in the United States and Canada. Where municipal regulations permit this approach, developers may build residential housing units in tight clusters instead of the traditional dispersed single-family pattern. However, developers are usually required to compensate for the lack of individually owned open space by providing appropriate landscaped areas to which all the residents have access.

Many PUDs consist entirely of condominiums, whereas others include rental units. Some contain clusters of small or large apartment buildings. Others have only semidetached or detached units. A few are comprised of large, expensive units with many bedrooms and most of the amenities of homes in high-income single-family developments. Some of the larger PUDs consist of a number of different housing types — various sizes of condominiums, where some units have fenced patio areas; several kinds of apartments with no occupant-controlled outdoor space; and single-family dwellings with conventional private yards.

The recreation resources owned by condominium, conventional residential subdivision, and private second-home development associations vary greatly. Sometimes they are limited to lawn areas planted with a number of trees and shrubs. In other developments, the amenities include playgrounds, picnic areas, swimming pools, tennis courts, fishing and boating lakes, beaches, and recreation buildings with facilities for sports, games, meetings, and parties; in some cases, the amenities are so extensive that the units may function as dual-purpose residences.

Tribal Resources. Property owned by Eskimos and North American Indian tribes is a significant recreation resource in parts of Canada and the United States. Although some books and maps give the impression that such reservations are public lands, these areas are private. Persons who are not members of the specific native group concerned have no more right to use tribal land without permission than any other type of private land.

In the United States, there are 267 Indian reservations totaling more than 20 million hectares (50 million acres). Most of the 1 million people who belong to the 493 tribes have a legal interest in some reservation lands but only about 650,000 of them actually live on or near a reservation. The majority of reservation lands lie in the northern Great Plains or west of the Rocky Mountains (Figure 11.5). The states containing the largest reservation areas are Arizona, Montana, New Mexico, South Dakota, and Washington. However, large new areas are currently being turned over to the native peoples of Alaska. Some reservation lands are productive farms or forests, but a large proportion is arid rangeland and desert.

The most important recreation role of reservation lands is their use by the native peoples themselves. In addition to the recreation opportunities offered by the various churches, schools, and assortment of small-town commercial facilities, like

stores, cafés, and billiard parlors, various kinds of recreation opportunities are provided by the tribal councils. Facilities constructed by the councils include community centers, cultural centers, sports fields, parks, plazas, fairgrounds, racetracks, and rodeo grounds. Among the amenities contained in these facilities are meeting rooms, gymnasiums, swimming pools, museums, libraries, cooperative arts and crafts shops, and learning centers for the teaching and preservation of tribal history, culture, and skills. A number of the councils are also involved in game and fish management activities although such projects may, in some cases, be more important for food production than for recreation.

Although reservation lands are

private resources, recreation experiences are often made available to nonresidents. Some Indian lands include highly scenic areas such as Monument Valley on the Navajo Reservation in northern Arizona. Many non-Indians enjoy the beauty of such areas while passing through on public highways or during tours of the reservation. More than 400 annual Indian celebrations and events that are held on reservation lands are open to the public. These include the powwows (traditional tribal or intertribal festivals and family reunions). Powwows usually last several days and feature ceremonial dances and songs, rodeos, athletic competitions, sports contests, traditional games, special foods, and exhibits of native arts and crafts. Visitors are sometimes invited to pitch

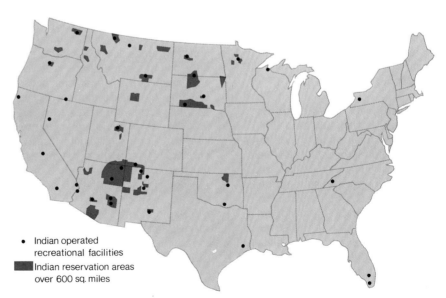

- Indian operated recreational facilities
■ Indian reservation areas over 600 sq. miles

Figure 11.5 **Map showing location of Indian tribal lands in the United States.**

their own tents among the Indian tepees at some of the ceremonial encampments and intertribal expositions. This opportunity is especially valuable because it enables non-Indian visitors to feel less like outsiders, and it creates many opportunities for guests and hosts to converse and get to know each other.

Arts and crafts guild shops are located on many of the reservations. These centers provide visitors with opportunities to observe skilled Indian craftspersons at work and ask questions about handicrafts with which they are not familiar. A number of traditional settlements on some of the reservations welcome visitors, offering them fascinating glimpses into the residents' unique lifestyles. The inhabitants of a chain of 19 traditional Pueblo villages in the Southwest, for example, allow visitors, but they do so strictly on their own terms. They invite guests only on certain feast days and reveal only those aspects of their lives that they wish to share. Nevertheless, by taking advantage of such opportunities, observant people are able to acquire considerable knowledge about, and understanding of, Indian history and culture.

Religious Organizations.
Christian, Jewish, and other religious groups provide a wide range of recreation experiences for their members. Such organizations may also offer opportunities to nonmembers, either as a public service or to encourage people to become members. The nature and scope of religious-group recreation facilities depends to a large extent on the attitude of the religious organization toward various forms of recreation as well as on the affluence of the

Figure 11.6 Weekly bingo games are often held in the multipurpose rooms of churches, synagogues, and other structures built primarily for the holding of religious services. When kitchen facilities are also available and the furnishings are movable, such rooms serve as recreation centers both for members and other groups that rent the space for limited or extended periods.

congregation. More conservative groups tend to develop fewer facilities for such recreation activities as dances; games, like bingo; and indoor or outdoor adult sports. However, even some of the most conservative groups develop young people's recreation facilities and programs to provide viable alternatives to what are considered less desirable recreation opportunities in the surrounding community.

Religious-organization facilities that are most commonly used for recreation are auditoriums, meeting rooms, and other multipurpose rooms (Figure 11.6). Depending on their size and the attitudes and desires of the religious group, such amenities are frequently used for banquets, wedding receptions, par-

ties, dances, games nights, concerts, movies, plays, shows, and club meetings as well as for sports such as basketball, volleyball, badminton, and table tennis. In many cases, an auditorium and a number of smaller meeting rooms are built adjacent to the main religious structure so that they may be used for either religious or more secular purposes as the need arises. Some groups with limited resources only have one room or hall and use it for secular activities as well as for religious services.

Religious facilities are also used extensively by other organizations that provide recreation opportunities. Quasi-public groups, such as Scout troops, are often affiliated with religious organizations, which provide them with facilities for their meetings, sports, and social activities. Hobby clubs, social clubs, orchestras, drama groups, and other cultural organizations with no connection to the religious group frequently rent such facilities for their meetings. In some communities, religious facilities provide most of the noncommercial recreation experiences enjoyed by citizens while away from home. This is especially true in rural communities, where all or the majority of the people belong to one religious group. For instance, Catholic parish halls function as community recreation centers in many parts of the world.

Many religious groups also own or lease lands and buildings in rural or resort locations. These range from campground areas with few facilities and camps with cabins, meeting halls, and dining rooms to elaborate resort- or hotel-type complexes. Generally, such resources are used for religious meetings, retreats, or summer youth programs. Nevertheless, many participants obtain much enjoyment from the change of scenery, the respite from daily routines and anxieties, and the opportunities for socialization. In addition, a good proportion of such camps or resorts have facilities for swimming, boating, fishing, hiking, riding, team sports, or indoor recreation activities. On the other hand, some religious-organization camps and resorts are operated primarily to provide vacation experiences for members, and religious activities occupy a relatively small part of the program.

Benevolent Organizations.
Another large group of private organizations that provide many recreation opportunities is comprised of the various **benevolent organizations.** These include labor unions and other employee groups, fraternal organizations, veterans' organizations, retired persons' associations, and many smaller special-interest groups. The primary objective of these organizations is to promote the general welfare of their members. They achieve this goal in a number of ways, ranging from negotiating wage and pension agreements to providing direct assistance for needy members and their families. Many benevolent organizations are also committed to helping others, and some of their funds are used to finance national projects such as college scholarships, hospitals, or homes for disadvantaged children and retired people. Local units often initiate fund-raising projects to enable them to sponsor community programs, such as summer camps for disabled children, support youth-organization programs, provide recreation experiences for special populations, or help construct recreation facilities for their use.

Another important function of these organizations, however, is having fun, and they do so in many different ways. The majority of the fraternal and veterans' organizations own or lease meeting halls. Their meetings, especially in the case of the fraternal organizations, may contain secret rituals that draw the members closer together and make the business part of the meetings more enjoyable. These facilities are also used for after-meeting social periods and special events such as banquets, dances, card-game tournaments, and bingo parties. A few are elaborate complexes with bowling alleys, golf courses, gamerooms, and bars.

Many of these groups also organize picnics, baseball and golf leagues, group outings to nearby sports and cultural events, and long-distance excursions. In addition, many of the organizations' fund-raising ventures — suppers, dances, card parties, shows, and circus performances — provide recreation opportunities, both for members and nonmembers who pay to attend. Retiree associations, parents-without-partners groups, clubs for the handicapped, and similar organizations generally own few resources of their own. Instead, they rely on public agencies or religious organizations to provide them with suitable facilities in which to hold their meetings and social activities.

The labor unions are the benevolent organizations that have the most extensive recreation resources. Like many industrial organizations, they are interested in providing recreation opportunities for workers. In addition, many unions strive to provide community-assistance programs or assist public agencies in their development. Some local units sponsor recreation programs for their members at whatever facilities are available in the community. Most have union halls, which are used for business meetings and social events. Larger locals, however, often acquire more elaborate facilities where all of their activities including meetings, social events, and a great variety of sports and other recreation programs take place. Other unions enter into agreements with management, the union taking responsibility for developing recreation facilities and programs and the company providing the land or space inside plant structures.

Most major unions also have regional or national recreation facilities. Some, like the International Ladies Garment Workers Union with its multimillion-dollar vacation center (Camp Unity in Pennsylvania), have invested in elaborate resorts. More often, unions operate centralized recreation facilities in major urban centers and unpretentious camps at attractive extraurban locations, which are used by members from many different local units. These camps are used extensively for conferences, workshops, and children's summer camp programs. A growing number of unions provide recreation centers for retired members, places where a diversity of educational, cultural, and social events are offered.

Most unions sponsor athletic teams and sports competitions. Many conduct classes and organize special-interest clubs so that members may learn skills needed for participation in a wide range of recreation activities. The majority hold regular meetings and arrange special events such as excursions, parties, and family picnics. Since many unions have a policy of supplementing existing community programs rather than duplicating them, union programs tend to be unique and unavailable from any other nearby source.

Service Organizations.

Groups such as the Rotary, Lions, Jaycees, and Kiwanis clubs are committed to raising funds for public service projects and to the giving of members' time and energy in the service of others. Many of these *service organization* programs involve building recreation facilities or sponsoring recreation activities for special populations. Individual service clubs provide funds for the construction of libraries, museums,

arenas, community centers, tennis courts, swimming pools, park toilet buildings, pavilions, playing-field bleachers, and numerous recreation facilities at residential homes, schools, and drop-in centers for youth and special populations.

Service clubs also pay for thousands of less costly recreation resources that facilitate or enhance the opportunities provided by a variety of public, quasi-public, and private organizations. Examples include uniforms for bands, sports teams, and scouts; art supplies, musical instruments, and athletic equipment; large-print books and children's reading materials; trees and zoo animals; city benches, picnic tables, barbecue grills, trash receptacles, wading pools, playground equipment, and ice resurfacing machines; and, furniture, television sets, and record-playing equipment. Some clubs prefer to supply the necessary materials and manpower themselves when undertaking the construction of playing fields, picnic areas, playgrounds, park shelters, swimming areas, zoo exhibits, fishing piers, and parks and nature trails for the physically handicapped.

Programs commonly provided by service organizations include the sponsorship of Scout troops, other youth clubs, young people's sports leagues or clinics, and recreation activities for the elderly. Clubs often organize picnics, parties, outings, and sports programs for the disadvantaged and handicapped. They also contribute to the safety of holiday weekends by providing weary drivers with coffee at highway rest areas and to the attractiveness and safety of recreation experiences by conducting park, playground, and river cleanups.

Many fund-raising projects like formal dances, barbecues, pancake breakfasts, auctions, rummage sales, shows, bingo games, card parties, carnivals, festivals, and street fairs are well-attended events that give pleasure to members as well as to the public. The haunted houses that 5000 Jaycee chapters operate each Halloween are a good example. Some attract sufficient paying customers to pay for almost all of the sponsoring chapter's service projects for the following year. Young people in particular are drawn to the houses, often returning several times in an attempt to discover how the special effects are created. At the same time, members who work on the project have great fun and their enjoyment is infectious; showing people through their haunted houses is one of the Jaycees' best methods of recruiting new members. Similarly, races, marathon contests, competitions, and tournaments often involve many local people as participants, spectators, sponsors, and organizers.

Some projects require total dedication by club members. The Newhall-Saugus Club of southern California, for instance, constructed a free day-use area for handicapped individuals, groups, and their families on a 4.5-hectare (11-acre) site in the Angeles National Forest near Los Angeles. Aided by other-area Lions clubs, the members raised and donated the money needed, persuaded others to provide materials and expertise, and gave thousands of hours of free labor. As a result, $80,000 raised in cash produced a facility valued by Forest Service officials at $500,000 (Figure 11.7).

Obviously, service clubs require members to donate substantial amounts of time, money, and materials. This does not mean, however, that they obtain no recreation benefits from their participation. Much pride and satisfaction can be derived from the successful completion of projects. Much pleasure can be obtained from helping others through one of the club-sponsored programs or fund-raising events. Regular meetings, often luncheon or dinner affairs, held at local restaurants or hotels, provide many opportunities for camaraderie. And, special events such as outings, parties, appreciation banquets, conferences, and conventions give members opportunities to become better acquainted while participating in a variety of recreation activities.

Figure 11.7 Wide, gently sloping paths, picnic tables with parts of the benches cut away to provide space for wheelchairs, railed bridges and fishing docks, and specially designed restrooms, make the recreation opportunities offered at the Los Cantiles day-use area accessible to handicapped visitors. Built by members of the 49 Lions clubs of District 4-LI and operated by the U.S. Forest Service, Los Cantiles Handicamp receives over 50,000 visitors a year.

CONTRIBUTION OF PRIVATE ORGANIZATIONS

The preceding examples show the scope and diversity of the recreation resources provided by private organizations. However, assessing the contribution of these resources is difficult. Occasionally, trade associations estimate the number of members in certain clusters of organizations. For example, membership in more expensive clubs such as country, social, athletic, military, and university faculty clubs in the United States is now said to be about 18 million. Some individual organizations have been studied in detail, but, generally, there are no comprehensive data for a city, region, or the nation.

An impression of the number of private organizations that provide recreation can be obtained from the classified advertising section of a city telephone directory. Entries under headings such as associations, clubs, fraternities, and sororities, as well as under organizations—athletic, business and trade, fraternal, labor, military, political, professional, religious, social service, veterans, and youth—indicate their frequency. Some groups listed do not turn out to be private organizations that own or lease recreation resources, but a surprising number, especially in affluent areas, prove to be in that category. Of course, directory listings are incomplete, since many private groups are too small to maintain a full-time office with a telephone. An impression of the number and nature of smaller associations can be gained by obtaining lists from city recreation departments, watching for advertisements and notices of meetings, reading newspaper accounts of organization events, and talking to people in the community.

Investigations of this type indicate that there are probably between 10 and 20 organizations per 1000 population in the larger American cities. As has been demonstrated, some of these groups do not have substantial recreation resources, but many of them do. Therefore, private organizations collectively make a major contribution to the supply of recreation opportunities—a fact that should not be overlooked in recreation planning and programming.

RESOURCES OF QUASI-PUBLIC ORGANIZATIONS

The resources discussed so far in this chapter are those controlled and financed by groups of private individuals. Some individual units such as church recreation centers or service clubs may receive help from a government agency in the form of a small grant or contribution of materials but, by and large, these organizations are self-supporting and have no continuing close relationships with any public body. In contrast, there are a number of private organizations that depend on public donations or government grants for a substantial part of their financial support; other groups are closely allied with government because their organizations undertake projects in cooperation with government agencies. Organizations of these two types are generally called *quasi-public organizations,* meaning that they tend to resemble public agencies.

The dividing line between quasi-public agencies and other private organizations is not clearly defined. Generally, a quasi-public organization has several of these characteristics:

- Most people feel the organization is responsible for providing services to society as a whole rather than to one or more special groups.
- A major part of the organization's financial support is from charitable donations, either collected by combined fund-raising appeals such as United Way, or through community-wide campaigns by the agency.
- Much of the organization's work is carried out by volunteers whose main or only connection with the agency is their voluntary work. (This contrasts with club situations where membership in the organization is of primary importance and volunteer service is secondary. Because volunteer assistance is essential for many quasi-public agencies, they are often called *volunteer organizations.*)
- The organization's policies are controlled by a board of directors composed largely or exclusively of prominent civic-minded citizens who are invited to serve and do so voluntarily. (Other types of organizations are usually controlled by elected officers and committees.)
- Virtually all of the organization's work involves service to society, and little or no effort is expended on social events or other programs for long-term members.
- The programs of the organization are primarily concerned with the outlook,

behavior, health, or general welfare of the strata in society that the agency seeks to serve.

As a result, the majority of programs conducted by quasi-public agencies are primarily in the field of social services; activities that appear to be largely recreational are usually included because of their educational or character-building values. For these reasons, it is sometimes difficult to determine precisely what aspects of the programs are recreational, although there is little doubt that millions of people rely on quasi-public agencies for some or many of their away-from-home recreation experiences.

YOUTH-ORIENTED ORGANIZATIONS

Of all the quasi-public agencies, the *youth-oriented organizations* provide the most recreation programs. Each organization in this group originally developed a unique program designed for a certain segment of the youth population — for example, girls [Girl Scouts of the United States of America, Camp Fire Girls, Girls Clubs of America, Future Homemakers of America (FHA)], boys (Boys' Clubs of America, Boy Scouts of America), rural youth (4-H Clubs[1]), the urban disadvantaged [Police Athletic League (PAL)], young Christian adults (YWCA, YMCA), young Jewish adults (YWHA, YMHA), or Catholic youth (CYO). However, they all strive to develop character and provide what the agency con-

[1] Sponsored by the U.S. Department of Agriculture, this youth program is designed to develop the *H*ead (mind), *H*eart (willingness to help others), *H*ands (skills), and *H*ealth (physical fitness and nutrition knowledge).

siders to be wholesome free-time activities.

Actually, the differences in programs and membership policies that originally distinguished these organizations are beginning to disappear. The YMCA, for instance, began in London in 1844 as a Protestant-oriented religious group for young men dedicated to building Christian character. Today, it welcomes people of both sexes, all ages, and of any or no religious affiliation. Similarly, Boys' Clubs of America are accepting girls, 22,000 of the 500,000 members of the Future Homemakers of America are boys, 4-H programs have been started for urban and suburban youth, and a number of senior citizen Girl Scout troops have been formed. As their participants become more diversified, these organizations are broadening their programs and becoming less distinguishable from each other. Nevertheless, there are differences and youth agencies can be divided roughly into two groups according to their operational philosophies.

Group-Program Agencies. *Group-program agencies* include club-type organizations, such as 4-H, Camp Fire Girls, and Boy Scouts and Girl Scouts. These organizations put much time and effort into developing and refining programs that are made available to as many young people as possible. To achieve this goal, they rely heavily on volunteers to organize groups of young people at the neighborhood level. It would be impossible to provide facilities for all the local units; therefore, the organizations usually only offer assistance with administration and running programs. Leadership-training courses and the instructional materials provided help familiarize volunteers with the general style and goals of the organization's programs. Publications and workshops keep leaders informed of changes in policy and help them develop appropriate programs.

The neighborhood units try to be as self-sufficient as possible, making use of whatever facilities are available to them. Few facilities are actually owned by individual clubs or troops. Instead, they meet in members' homes, schools, churches, space provided by local public agencies or businesses, empty stores, or community centers. Field trips are taken to nearby facilities of interest, such as public playgrounds and parks, zoos, museums, nature centers, places of business, and commercial-recreation developments.

However, units often acquire an assortment of possessions. Businesses, churches, and service organizations commonly sponsor clubs and troops and provide them with a place to meet, needed supplies, equipment, and uniforms. Occasionally, donations of land or materials provide a neighborhood unit with permanent facilities of its own, but usually the donor expects the facilities to be shared by several units. In this way, many clubhouses and camps are acquired and used by all of the troops or clubs in a particular district or region. Once acquired, such facilities are the responsibility of local councils (units chartered by the national organization to administer and develop programs in a specific geographic area) that maintain the properties and direct their development and use. Neighborhood units may be expected to contribute toward the upkeep of such facilities by paying user fees and performing maintenance and development tasks.

Boy Scout organizations in 100 nations continue the emphasis on vigorous group activities in undeveloped environments, an emphasis formulated in 1908 by Robert Baden-Powell, the movement's British founder. Access to suitable extraurban resources is therefore essential. Most of the 58,569 troops in the United States have access to at least one of the 600 camps operated by 417 local councils. In addition, the national office administers 6 high-adventure camps. These provide older Scouts and Explorers with outstanding camping and learning opportunities at locations in Minnesota, Florida, Kentucky, Maine, Wisconsin, and New Mexico. The New Mexico site consists of the Philmont Scout Ranch and Explorer Base, a 55,685-hectare (137,493-acre) area that provides thousands of young people with trail hiking, camping, horseback riding, burro-packing, and wilderness-survival experiences.

The Girl Guide or Scout movement was also started in Great Britain by Baden-Powell, but it is a separate organization. There are 93 other nations that have developed their own associations. These organizations form the World Association of Girl Guides and Girl Scouts (WAGGGS). It is a loosely knit federation but maintains world centers in Switzerland, England, Mexico, and India. These centers offer Girl Scouts and Guides opportunities to meet members of scouting movements in other countries and share ideas and each other's cultures.

In the United States, the first Girl Scout troop was formed in 1912 in Savannah, Georgia, by Juliette Gordon Low. Like the Boy Scouts, the Girl Scout movement has day- and resident-camp properties that are shared by troops for their outdoor programs and for leader-training sessions. The American organization operates national centers in Wyoming, New York, Maryland, and Georgia. Like the high-adventure camps for Boy Scouts, Girl Scout National Center West in Wyoming provides a wide variety of outdoor-living opportunities for older scouts. The Rockwood Girl Scout National Center is a year-round 38-hectare (93-acre) facility in Potomac, Maryland, that serves as a hostel for Girl Scouts from the United States and Girl Guides from other nations during visits to the nation's capital. One lodge has been adapted for wheelchair use and is heavily used by handicapped groups. The center is also used for a variety of programs concerning nature, conservation, and the visual arts.

Facility-Based Agencies. This group includes the YMCA, YWCA, YMHA, and YWHA organizations as well as some of the club-type organizations such the the Police Athletic League, Boys' Clubs of America, and Girls Clubs of America. Most of the *facility-based agencies* rely less heavily on volunteers than the group-program agencies. Instead, they hire trained professionals to operate their facilities, direct their programs, and supervise the volunteers who are generally needed to make the programs a success.

Some Camp Fire Girls and 4-H Clubs should be included in both the group-program-oriented and facility-based agency classifications because they have traditionally operated group programs led by volunteers but have also started facility-based operations in inner-city locations where the group-program approach had not worked well. Activity centers have been established in urban core areas either by constructing new buildings or, more often, by taking over disused buildings like schools, churches, stores, or old youth centers. Parts of buildings such as apartment complexes, community centers, or schools are also used to make the programs readily accessible. Many programs, especially in the case of the Camp Fire Girls, are conducted on a casual basis but are supervised by trained professionals and volunteers. Young people are encouraged to come and go as they wish, either taking part in group activities or using the facilities on an individual basis as their mood dictates.

That type of open program has always been the policy of the Boys' Clubs of America. It has encouraged the development of activity centers for underprivileged urban boys since 1906 when 50 established clubs formed a national association. There are now 1100 of these centers. Each usually contains a gymnasium, library, gameroom (Figure 11.8), well-equipped workshop, meeting rooms, and, less frequently, an indoor swimming pool or outdoor playing field as well as sports courts. These centers are open daily and are run by a professional staff. Most offer tutoring, family counseling, and help with personal problems as well as a wide range of recreation activities. Hot lunches are also provided. Yearly dues are charged, but they seldom exceed $5 a year. Once paid, a member is free to visit the club and

Figure 11.8 Members of the Boys' Club of Royal Oak, Michigan, have a wide range of opportunities from which to choose in the well-appointed gameroom. Sports and arts and crafts are also offered. About 200 boys (one-quarter of the total membership) use the facilities each day. A staff of 10 full-time professionals and many volunteers supervise the activities, teach skills, and help boys needing tutoring or counseling services.

use its facilities every day or several times a day, a situation that is a common occurrence. These low charges combined with the policy that staff members and volunteer assistants should always try to greet each member by name make the Boys' Clubs very attractive to many youths. Boys often regard the centers not just as a place to go, but as a substitute home.

A separate organization, Girls Clubs of America, operates in a similar manner and is now the parent organization for 258 Girls Clubs located in 128 cities. Each club is an independent unit and designs its facilities and programs around the needs and interests of the girls it serves. Generally, however, the clubs provide programs in sports, gymnastics, arts and crafts, creative dramatics, ecology and nature, cooking and sewing. Cur-

rently, there are more than 220,000 Girls Clubs members, over 90 percent of whom are from families with incomes of less than $10,000.

In a similar manner, the Police Athletic League provides sports, cultural, and service programs for disadvantaged youth in more than 100 cities. These programs take place at drop-in centers similar to the Boys' Clubs and Girls Clubs, but the centers are directed by police officers on special assignment from municipal law-enforcement agencies. However, the programs are not confined to the centers; they are just as often held on the streets, in vacant lots, or anywhere that is convenient for potential participants and where they are most likely to feel comfortable. The Catholic Youth Organization is another agency that operates well-equipped recreation centers in large cities, but the programs are designed expressly for Catholic youth. Like the Camp Fire Girls and 4-H clubs, such special facilities are considered necessary only in the urban core. In smaller communities, the CYO programs are operated by parish priests using church halls and other regular parish facilities.

The quasi-public organizations that provide the most varied opportunities in the greatest number of communities, both large and small, are the agencies often referred to simply as the Ys— the YMCA, YWCA, YMHA, and YWHA. Although they continue to be broadly affiliated with specific religious faiths, and were originally designed to serve the youth of just one sex and not necessarily every race, all of these organizations now accept members without restrictions based on religious affiliation, age, sex, or ethnic origin. Some programs are religiously oriented but most are not. Many are primarily intended for young people so that the Ys are very important youth-serving organizations. But the facilities are also used heavily by others, including preschoolers, the handicapped, and adults of all ages. Thus the Ys now tend to function as privately owned community centers that provide some of the best and, occasionally, the only facilities for a wide variety of recreation and social service programs. Most of the larger Ys contain swimming pools (Figure 18.13), gymnasiums, exercise rooms, sports courts, running tracks, large auditoriums, clubrooms, small meeting rooms, kitchen facilities, workshops, children's nurseries, lounges, gamerooms, libraries, cafeterias, snack bars, and rooms for residents and overnight guests.

These overnight accommo-dations are especially useful to students and others traveling on limited budgets. To encourage less affluent travelers from abroad, 44 YMCAs in 39 American cities formed a coast-to-coast network in 1978 as part of a cooperative program called, "Visit U.S.A." Some 12,000 low-cost rooms were made available (to Americans as well as foreign tourists), either by prepaid vouchers or at a slightly higher rate on a pay-as-you-go basis. Most of the participating Ys accept both men and women and have pools, gyms, and a variety of other recreation facilities that overnight guests may use during their stay.

Most of the Y associations also own extraurban properties that have been developed as day camps or resident camps. The Ys also conduct some programs at community facilities such as school gyms, pools, playgrounds, playing fields, churches, or public parks, to reach people in outlying areas.

Of these organizations, the YMCA is the oldest and largest. Founded in Boston in 1851, the U.S. National Council now consists of more than 1800 member associations across the country. These YMCAs employ some 6000 professionals to operate facilities and organize programs for almost 10 million members. The World Alliance of YMCAs, of which the U.S. National Council is a part, is made up of YMCA organizations in 65 countries.

In 1976, there was a total of 9414 local associations in these 65 nations, serving over 22 million members. Data concerning age and sex was available for only 56 percent of the members, but, of these, 35 percent were female, 51 percent were under 18 years of age, and 29 percent were over 30. The 9494 associations vary greatly in number of members and scope of facilities. Some new associations have only a handful of members and no land or buildings. Well-established metropolitan associations, on the other hand, often have several large fully equipped centers, some smaller less elaborate branch buildings, and one or more camps at extraurban locations. In 1976, the facilities owned by the associations around the world included 680 hotels or hostels with a total of 71,615 beds for permanent residents or travelers, 1000 cafeterias or restaurants, 1364 swimming pools, 1621 gymnasiums, and 715 camps with residential facilities.

A very different type of recreation resource is provided by the International Youth Hostel Federation. Originally conceived as a system of low-cost overnight accommodations for young hikers and cyclists, hostels are used now by people of all ages, however the majority are in their teens or early twenties. In Europe and some small nations elsewhere, it has been possible to develop extensive systems of hostels, which are located so that hikers and cyclists can easily travel from one hostel to another in a day. This is not as easily achieved in the United States, Canada, and other large nations because of greater distances and a comparative lack of footpaths and bicycle paths. More than 60 nations have youth hostel organizations, which are either members of the International Youth Hostel Federation or honor its membership cards. The 50 nations that are members have a total of more than 4500 hostels.

Many hostels are interesting old buildings such as mansions, churches, castles, mills, or coast guard stations that have been converted into dormitory, lounge, and kitchen facilities. Paid, or in a few cases, volunteer resident managers maintain the hostels. At some locations, they also prepare morning and evening meals. Members may make their own meals and are responsible for cleaning any facilities they use. Some European hostels located at high elevations in isolated areas function as storm refuges. At the other end of the spectrum are hostels in or near cities that are popular tourist destinations. Besides assisting individual travelers, hostel associations organize and lead low-cost group trips for hikers, campers, bicyclists, and canoeists.

The youth hostel movement began in Germany in 1909 and is now well developed in Europe, including Communist Poland, Bulgaria, Czechoslovakia, Yugoslavia, and Hungary. There are also hostels in Africa, Australia, New Zealand, India, and the Philippines. Japan has more than 500 hostels, most are modern structures located in some of the nation's major tourist regions. The movement is gaining a foothold in Latin America with a few hostels in Argentina, Bolivia, Chile, Mexico, and Uruguay. At present, the more than 240 American hostels are concentrated in the Northeast, the Great Lakes region, and central Colorado.

Hostel systems permit millions of youth, lower-income adults, and people who like traveling under their own power, to enjoy hiking and cycling through the countryside or to visit places of historic and cultural interest. Promoters of hosteling also feel it develops self-reliance, social maturity, cultural appreciation, geographic knowledge, and in-ternational understanding. In the past, hostel associations generally were supported by donations of buildings and money supplemented by annual fees and overnight charges paid by members. More recently, various levels of government have recognized the social and educational values of hosteling and have begun to provide direct financial aid. Many national governments give regular grants. The Canadian government, for instance, provides about $600,000 a year to assist the nation's 100 hostels that stretch from St. John's, Newfoundland, to Whitehorse in the Yukon Territory. Legislation introduced in the U.S. Congress in 1980 called for a $5 million program to encourage the development of the American youth hostel system by authorizing the use of excess federal property as hostels and by providing grants to nonprofit organizations for the improvement or creation of hostels. In 1977, California began a $1.9-million project to build a chain of hostels along the Pacific coast; similar state programs have been started in Alaska, Washington, and Maryland.

The preceding summary demonstrates that the recreation resources of quasi-public youth organizations are important components of most recreation systems, especially those of large urban areas. In many cases, these agencies only supplement the extensive opportunities offered by local governments. Sometimes, however, where local government programs are inadequate, youth organizations are the principal suppliers of many kinds of recreation opportunities.

SOCIAL WELFARE ORGANIZATIONS

Besides the youth-oriented agencies, there are a number of quasi-public *social welfare organizations* that provide recreation opportunities as a subsidiary, yet important, part of their services. Of major significance in this group in the United States are the 250 settlement houses and quasi-public community centers. Many were established around the turn of the century and have not only survived but have expanded in recent years. No longer entirely dependent on charity, these independent operations now receive some funding from local, state, and federal governments. Located in the hearts of large cities, settlement houses and quasi-public community centers tend to serve the needs of the disadvantaged residents of both sexes and all ages. Since they are usually not equipped with extensive indoor sports facilities or outdoor playgrounds and playing fields, the recreation opportunities tend to be less physically active and more social, educational, and cultural in nature. Many of these organizations also own extraurban properties that provide camping experiences for adults as well as children.

No agency is more successful in providing extraurban vacation experiences than the Fresh Air Fund. Founded in 1878, this organization is dedicated to providing disadvantaged New York City children with summer vacations away from their crowded neighborhoods. By 1980, some 1.4 million children, ranging in age from 5 to 16 years, had spent two weeks or more living with host families in one of the Fund's 353 "Friendly Towns" in 13 nearby states or at one of the agency's four summer camps. These camps are located on the Sharpe Reservation, a 1215-hectare (3000-acre) tract near Poughkeepsie, New York. One camp is for 9- to 12-year-old girls, another for 11- and 12-year-old boys, a third for 13- and 14-year-old boys, and the fourth is a special facility that caters to boys and girls from 8 to 12, half of whom are handicapped. During the four two-week camping periods held each summer, almost 2700 children take part in sports, excursions, and overnight camping trips. They explore a model farm to become familiar with common vegetables and farm animals. They learn to boat, fish (Figure 11.9), and swim (more than 90 percent of the children cannot swim when they arrive) as well as try a variety of activities such as arts and crafts, cooking, sewing, ceramics, and photography. The camper-to-counselor ratio is kept at about four-to-one in order to assure ample opportunities for individual attention. The 14,000 other youngsters who stay in private homes are also made to feel wanted and important. Frequently, the relationships established between hosts and guests last for entire lifetimes rather than one or even a few summers.

Another group of quasi-public organizations that provide valuable recreation opportunities are the various agencies formed to meet the needs of special populations. These societies, associations, and foundations such as the American Cerebral Palsy Association, the Children's Aid Society, United Service Organization (USO), the Red Cross, the National Association for Retarded Citizens, and the Joseph P. Kennedy, Jr. Foundation usually own few facilities of their own, at least at

the national level. Instead, they tend to provide the leadership and funding for programs that are carried out at the local level by using such facilities as hospitals, community centers, churches, parks, and schools. They also encourage other organizations to provide suitable programs and facilities, and they promote the acceptance of the disadvantaged individuals with whom they are concerned into the regular programs of these organizations.

One such organization—the Joseph P. Kennedy, Jr. Foundation

Figure 11.9 **Under the guidance of a counselor, two campers at the Fresh Air Fund's Sharpe Reservation experience the thrill of catching a fish for the first time. The success of this program stems as much from the availability of many enthusiastic and knowledgeable leaders as from a variety of resources inner-city children seldom have the opportunity to enjoy.**

—operates no facilities of its own, but, through sponsorship of programs at the local level, it has become one of the world's leading instigators of recreation for the mentally retarded and physically handicapped. With its guidance and financial support, hundreds of day camps and year-round activity programs are operated throughout the United States. The foundation has also established an international program of physical fitness and sports competition called the Special Olympics; these events take place in each of the 50 states and in 19 foreign countries. Over 650,000 participants and almost as many volunteer helpers are involved in this well-designed sports program that gives many individuals their first or only opportunity to experience the thrill of friendly competition.

Many of the local units of these social welfare organizations do own facilities. These include drop-in centers, day-care centers, halfway houses, shelters, rehabilitation centers, group homes, and well-organized summer camps where the kinds of people with whom the organization is concerned can go to get help with problems, make new friends, or enjoy a wide range of recreation activities. Many local agencies also purchase specially equipped vans and buses so that they can offer these people transportation to and from their facilities, take them on organized field trips and outings, and help individuals reach other facilities in the community.

PRESERVATION ORGANIZATIONS
Another major group of private associations that owns substantial

numbers of recreation resources is the *preservation organizations.* The main goals of these organizations are the preservation of natural history or historic resources and the provision of educational or research opportunities. However, many permit their resources to be used for recreation. In some cases, this produces much-needed revenues and encourages public support.

The majority of these organizations are small local associations with no land or buildings. Such groups concentrate on promoting the preservation of natural history or historic resources owned by others and on assisting the owners financially or with volunteer labor. A much smaller cluster consists of associations that own one or a few properties and only operate in a limited geographic area. A few major organizations have large-scale nationwide programs that involve many tracts and buildings.

The status of these organizations in terms of government recognition and funding varies considerably. Some are completely independent; they receive no public moneys and have no special government relationships. Others enjoy a quasi-public status; they have cooperative arrangements with public agencies and receive substantial government grants. Some even carry out certain projects for governments. Several major national organizations are in this category.

The National Trust. The world's leading private preservation organization is Great Britain's National Trust. In spite of its name, the National Trust is not a government agency, although its contributions to the preservation of landscapes, coastlines, and historic

buildings is equivalent or superior to those made by the national park agencies or the governments in many countries. It is a private charity, operating on an annual budget of about $24 million, over 50 percent of which comes from donations, the dues paid by its 500,000 members, and the admission fees collected from 4 million visitors to Trust properties. (Many additional millions visit the Trust's scenic areas, but these are free-of-charge; therefore, the users are not counted and do not contribute toward maintenance costs.) National and local government grants are received for special projects but constitute only a little over one-tenth of the operating budget.

The Trust owns and operates more than 200 important historic buildings that contain priceless collections of furniture, porcelain, and paintings. Its properties include 2000 farms that are part of significant landscapes or historic estates; 485 kilometers (300 miles) of unspoiled coastline; dozens of ornamental gardens; many nature preserves including islands and marshes; numerous prehistoric or Roman structures and artifact collections; and extensive resources from the industrial revolution such as canals, watermills, and manufacturing sites. Seventeen complete villages belong to the Trust, making it possible to preserve them in a rustic condition.

Altogether, the National Trust owns 162,000 hectares (400,000 acres), which is equal to 1 percent of England, Wales, and Northern Ireland. Examples of some of its more notable properties are:

- The 32,000 hectares (79,000 acres) of Lake District landscape that comprises England's most scenic combi-

nation of lakes, hills, and sheep farms (Figure 11.10).
- The meadow alongside the Thames River at Runnymede where King John signed the Magna Carta in A.D. 1215.
- A 5.6-kilometer (3.5-mile) section of Hadrian's Wall and several of the milecastles built by the Romans in the second and third centuries A.D. to keep Scottish raiders from entering England.
- Chartwell, Winston Churchill's former country home, which contains his library and many other personal items.

Many of the organization's other properties are of similar significance.

A number of factors enable the Trust to do so much with a modest budget. Many properties are donated to it because of its charitable status and public image. The establishing legislation permits the Trust to declare its lands to be "inalienable" so that donors are assured that their cherished property will never be altered unless Parliament decides it is essential. In addition, some donors and their heirs are permitted to live in parts of their historic houses while the Trust maintains the remainder and manages public use. The Trust also leases farms and buildings wherever this complements its programs, charges modest admission fees at developed sites, sells brochures and books, solicits special donations for unique projects, and uses volunteers for a wide range of tasks.

The National Trust for Scotland is a similar organization founded in 1931. It has 100,000 members and owns 32,400 hectares (80,000 acres) comprised of some 80 different holdings. No estimates are available of the number of people who enjoy the Trust's unsupervised scenic areas but more than 1.25 million people are counted annually at those properties where a charge is made.

The Nature Conservancy.

The largest provider of recreation opportunities among American private preservation organizations is the Nature Conservancy. This organization has some 60,000 members and an annual budget of about $20 million derived from gifts and individual or corporate memberships. Its main goal is to preserve ecologically significant land by investigating potential areas and protecting them from development. This is achieved through donation, purchase, or government action; by carefully managing lands it retains; and by conducting programs to increase public awareness. Since 1954, the Conservancy has acquired some 0.6 million hectares (1.5 million acres).

The Conservancy resells many of its properties to government agencies for park or wildlife purposes. Usually, it buys such lands under a prior arrangement with an agency, which then purchases the property from the Conservancy when the necessary funds become available. However, about 60 percent of the purchased properties are retained and managed by the Conservancy. Currently, it owns some 200,000 hectares (500,000 acres) valued at more than $110 million. Many of the Conservancy's close to 700 tracts are undeveloped parcels of less than 40 hectares (100 acres); most are cared for by some of the 3000 volunteers belonging to local chapters. Other parcels are much larger and tend to be developed to some degree. For example, the 14,175-hectare (35,000-acre) Virginia Coast Reserve consists of 13 barrier islands and their attendant tidal marshes. It is the largest privately owned wildlife reserve in the world. The Conservancy is developing an interpretive center and research facilities so that the area can be used for educational and scientific purposes.

In 1978, the Nature Conservancy purchased 90 percent of Santa Cruz Island, which lies 25 miles off the coast of southern California. It plans to operate the 22,275-hectare (55,000-acre) property as a wilderness preserve. The environment still looks much as it did in 1542 when Juan Rodriguez Cabrillo discovered it and includes many rare or endangered species. The Conservancy plans to build an interpretive center, provide group overnight accommodations, and conduct shoreline boating and hiking expeditions.

Figure 11.10 A visitor to Derwentwater in England's Lake District National Park enjoys the scenery in an area largely owned and maintained by the National Trust. Trust holdings in this photograph include the land on which the woman is standing, the woods below it, the shoreline in the background on the right, the islands, and half the lake bed.

Other Preservation Groups.
There are many other private preservation organizations which own lands that are used for recreation. In Great Britain, for example, 39 counties in England and Wales have county nature trusts; regional branches of the Scottish Wildlife Trust perform similar functions in Scotland. These groups manage more than 1080 nature reserves, totaling some 36,500 hectares (90,200 acres) which provide extensive nature study and related opportunities for their 120,000 members and the public.

In the United States, the National Trust for Historic Preservation was established in 1949 by Congressional charter. Its goal is to further the federal policy of preserving historic sites, buildings, and objects that are of national significance. Although the Trust owns and operates 9 museums and 10 historic properties, its main objective is to encourage and assist other agencies, corporations, and individuals in undertaking historic preservation. It does this by providing educational programs, demonstration projects, and technical assistance as well as by purchasing properties for resale to individuals or groups that will restore and protect them. The Trust spends about $13 million a year. Its funds come from federal government matching grants, donations, investments, admissions, the sale of books, and the annual fees paid by its 160,000 individual and corporate members. More than 250,000 people visit the Trust's museums and historic properties annually; most of its properties are located in the Northeast.

The National Audubon Society manages 64 wildlife sanctuaries, totaling 81,000 hectares (200,000 acres); about 34 percent of these lands are owned by the Society and the remainder are leased. Most refuges are located in the northeastern states, in Florida, and along the Texas coast. The main emphasis of this 400,000-member organization is protecting wildlife populations (especially birds), encouraging nature study, and providing environmental interpretation programs. Some of its refuges have trails, boardwalks, interpretive centers, and permanent staffs. In Great Britain, the 300,000-member Royal Society for the Protection of Birds fulfills a similar role. It manages 56 reserves, totaling more than 14,200 hectares (35,000 acres) and conducts extensive education and recreation programs.

Besides such national groups, there are many local associations that acquire and manage nature reserves or historic properties. Some are established to preserve one specific site. In combination, these national, regional, and local preservation organizations ensure that many different recreation opportunities are available to their members and the public.

FARM AND INDUSTRIAL RESOURCES

Another important group of private recreation resources consists of properties used for agricultural, forestry, manufacturing, or business purposes. These resources fall into two main categories — those used by the general public and those provided by many businesses for use by their employees.

RESOURCES USED BY THE PUBLIC
Private lands used for the production of crops, livestock, timber, manufactured goods, and services frequently provide large numbers of recreation opportunities for the general public. Some of these opportunities are sold commercially and will be discussed in Chapter 12. The majority occur informally; in many cases, the landowner is not even aware that a recreation experience has taken place.

Farm Resources. Agricultural lands and the animals, buildings, and woodlands associated with them provide many of these experiences. In the United States, 405 million hectares (1 billion acres), or about 44 percent of the land area, is occupied by the country's 2.3 million farms. Agricultural lands are, therefore, the nation's largest single recreation resource. In a few states, such as Iowa and Ohio, most of the extraurban land is used for agriculture so that farmlands are the principal source of many recreation opportunities, particularly hunting and fishing. This is also the case in many other states where land-use patterns are such that the majority of the residents have to travel for several hours to reach any sizable areas of nonagricultural land. Similar situations occur in the more intensively cultivated regions of many other nations.

Farmlands play a major role in providing landscapes that are attractive to travelers and sightseers. Most pleasure-driving takes place in agricultural regions. Each spring, tens of thousands flock to see the orchards in blossom in fruit-growing areas. Similarly, the vivid color contrasts that occur each autumn in fields, hedgerows, and farm woodlands delight many sightseers, especially in the New England and Great Lakes regions. The patchwork pastoral scenery and villages of Europe—immortalized by poets and painters like Wordsworth, Constable, and Gainsborough— continue to attract numerous pleasure-drivers, walkers, cyclists, and tour participants. Indeed, entire vacations or bus tours are devoted to seeing famous rural landscapes, like the Cotswolds, a rolling range of hills in western England. Many European national parks have been established to protect scenery that is largely composed of privately owned farmlands.

Agricultural areas provide many other kinds of recreation experiences for the public. Some take place as people travel along public roads, pathways, or waterways. Others occur as people use private farmlands, either with or without permission. Among the more important experiences are:

- Seeing, watching, and (in some cases) petting farm animals.
- Watching agricultural operations or seeing unfamiliar crops or farming practices.
- Photographing, sketching, or painting farm scenes.
- Swimming or fishing in farm streams or ponds; the "old swimming hole" is still a well-used resource in many rural communities.
- Gathering nuts, berries, mushrooms, and edible plants.
- Skating on ponds and tobogganing and skiing down hills.
- Birdwatching and other forms of nature study, especially near water, in woods, and around wetlands.
- Collecting arrowheads, geologic or biologic specimens, or materials suitable for nature crafts and lapidary projects.

In some regions, especially where croplands or ranchlands have few fences, farmland is often used extensively for horseback riding, motorcycling, and snowmobiling.

Hunting is also a major public activity on some private farmlands, but the situation varies greatly from place to place. In Canada and the United States, there are still many areas where hunting by the public on private agricultural lands without payment of a fee or even requesting permission is a common custom. In fact, private agricultural lands still provide more public hunting experiences than any other type of land in the United States. However, this custom is becoming increasingly unpopular with landowners because of the growth in the number of hunters, a decreasing proportion of whom are local residents or personal acquaintances, and the increasing incidence of littering, vandalism, and carelessness with firearms. As a result, more lands are being fenced and posted against trespass and hunting. Some states are attempting to preserve access to farmland by leasing private agricultural lands for public hunting. Landowners receive a per-acre fee for permitting public hunting; the money is recovered by raising state hunting-license fees or requiring the purchase of a special permit. The wildlife productivity of some agricultural lands is also declining because of hedgerow removal and changing farming methods.

The recreational use of private farmlands by the public is clearly of great value to society. This has already been recognized by the adoption of several other types of public programs in addition to leasing land for hunting. Many master

plans for major cities include broad greenbelts composed of private agricultural and forest lands. In Europe, such belts have often been created by the imposition of stringent land-use controls. In the United States, tax inducements are being offered in some states to encourage landowners to continue farming lands near cities. Scenic easements involving agricultural lands have been purchased alongside parkways and the visual value of roads through rural landscapes has been recognized by the restriction or removal of roadside billboard advertising. The U.S. Congress has also supported public use of private farmland by providing grants for a number of agricultural programs designed to increase recreation opportunities, particularly hunting and fishing. As urbanization continues, society is likely to try to preserve larger proportions of the remaining private cropland and woodlands for the production of food, fiber, and recreation experiences by means of leasing and easement programs, by the imposition of land-use controls, and through the creation of agricultural parks.

Industrial Lands. Properties owned by businesses and industries also sometimes function as important recreation resources for the general public. Woodlands owned by forest industries constitute the largest acreage of this type. In the United States, forest-industry lands total about 28 million hectares (70 million acres), an area over twice the size of the national park system prior to the addition of the new Alaska units in 1978.

Forest-industry lands are widely distributed. Some are intermixed with public lands along the Pacific coast and in the Rocky Mountain area. There is a major concentration of such lands in upper Wisconsin, Michigan, and Minnesota, and some scattered tracts can be found in central Ohio and western Pennsylvania. The eastern shore area of Maryland and Virginia together with northern New York and northwestern Maine contain substantial areas. An extensive belt runs across the South, from the Atlantic coast in Georgia and Florida to eastern Texas. Scattered industrial forests are also found in Kentucky, Oklahoma, and Arkansas.

Most of these lands are open for public recreation, except when fire conditions, logging operations, or other hazards make it inadvisable. The majority of the lands are open to the public without permit or fee. As in the case of state forests, national forests, and forests belonging to private individuals, forest-industry lands are used primarily by individuals, families, and small groups for the following dispersed recreation activities— pleasure-driving, fishing, hunting, berrypicking, wildlife-viewing, walking, swimming, camping, boating, canoeing, snowmobiling, and cross-country skiing. The resources that are most significant for recreation, therefore, are company-built and company-maintained roads and trails; the untold miles of streams, rivers, and shoreline; and the lands adjacent to these travel routes. In some regions, industry-lands also contain ponds and lakes, which are used extensively for swimming, fishing, and boating.

Some American forest-industry companies have developed facilities expressly for public recreation. A number have built small parks, picnic areas, or campgrounds. The parks tend to be located near forest communities and, in some cases, function as if they were local government parks. Some charge fees in order to control use and help pay for maintenance costs. Others use free permits as a method of regulating use and discouraging vandalism. Companies also lease land to hunting clubs and to individuals for recreational purposes, such as use as second-home sites or campsites.

Forest industries are involved in a variety of planning and management programs intended to increase recreation opportunities. Some employ recreation planners and have drawn up long-range recreation plans. A small but significant portion of company lands is designated as wildlife-management areas, either under cooperative agreements with a state agency, through a lease to a state agency, or in the firm's own management plans. Of course, the methods used to manage all the lands are important factors in determining the variety and size of wildlife populations found on industry lands.

Sand and gravel pits, quarries, and mines are another important type of industrial recreation resource. An increasing number of companies prohibit or place severe restrictions on public use of such areas because of vandalism, liability, and insurance problems. Nevertheless, many thousands of small, remote, or disused workings are utilized for recreation, usually without the permission of the owners. Depending on the nature of the extracted materials, the presence of water, the age of the workings, and the degree to which vegetation has become established, quarries and pits are often used for nature study, berrypicking, swimming, fishing, boating, hunting, shooting practice, motorcycling, snowmobiling, collecting fossil and mineral specimens, or teenagers' adventurous play activities. Some owners lease or give permits to organized groups of individuals who wish to use such lands on a long-term basis for rifle ranges, sportsperson's clubs, or vehicle-competition areas. The passage of environmental regulations are also forcing many owners to rehabilitate their lands following open-pit operations. In some cases, this results in the creation of attractive recreation areas that are open to the public under the management of the company, a concessionaire, a private group, or a local government agency.

Powerline rights-of way owned by electric power companies are often used by hikers, motorcyclists, hunters, snowmobilers, and cross-country skiers. Growing numbers of local government recreation agencies and community groups are making arrangements with power companies to use powerline corridors for community gardens or various kinds of trails.[2] Power company reservoirs are frequently used for a wide variety of water-oriented activities. In some cases, companies lease reservoir properties to public recreation agencies; elsewhere they may develop and operate their own facilities.

The development of recreation facilities by the power companies has been stimulated in the United States by Federal Power Commis-

[2] For a discussion of the possible hazards of using powerline rights-of-way for recreation, see Eric Meves, "Watts Up Must Come Down," *Parks & Recreation, 12,* (10), 29–31, (1977).

sion regulations that require a company to submit a plan for full public recreational use of a project's waters and adjacent lands before the necessary reservoir construction permit is issued. The Pacific Gas and Electric Company, for example, has developed recreation facilities in the Pit, Feather, Yuba, Mokelumne, and Fresno River valleys, which drain westward from the Cascade Mountains and Sierra Nevada into California's Central Valley. Their facilities consist of family and group picnic sites, family and group campsites, roadside rest areas, scenic overlooks, historic sites, and boat-access sites for fishing and waterfowl hunting. Many other companies provide recreation resources of a similar nature, although few are as extensive as those listed above. Even where facilities are minimal or absent, power company lands are often extremely important because the public uses them to gain access to streams and lakes. In many cases, these lands would probably not be open to the public if they had been purchased by any other type of private owner.

Industrial Tours. Each year, millions of people visit the lands and buildings of over 3500 American companies while taking part in industrial tours. Firms that offer tours tend to be those that manufacture consumer goods. Food-processing, newspaper-publishing, automobile-manufacturing, and beverage-producing (breweries, distilleries, and wineries) industries are the most heavily visited, but many other kinds of enterprises are involved. Nonmanufacturing and service organizations also offer tours; some of those most frequently visited are horse farms, broadcasting and recording studios, mines, stock exchanges, and the fields of the major producers of flower seeds and bulbs.

Most industrial tours are free. About two-thirds of the visits are made during the summer by vacationers or local residents accompanied by out-of-town guests whom they are entertaining. Some tours consist of a few introductory remarks by an employee followed by a walk or drive through parts of the facility where the more interesting, safest, or less obnoxious processes are taking place. Other companies provide special facilities to add to the visitors' enjoyment; these may include formal gardens, park-like grounds, comfortable assembly lounges, and auditoriums where films and demonstrations are presented. A few have exhibit areas, some of which contain outstanding collections and displays (see Chapter 16). A number of companies attempt to please visitors by giving them samples of the firm's products at the end of the tour. This practice is becoming less common because growing participation in the tours is making such gestures increasingly expensive.

A few industrial tours have become major tourist attractions. In some cases, special facilities developed for a tour and not used for any other purpose have become as important or even more important than the ordinary features of the establishment being toured. For example, the Universal Studios tour near Hollywood, California, now spends little time explaining actual film studio operations. It concentrates instead on providing carefully staged entertainment that includes exposing visitors to famous special effects from recent movies (Figure 11.11), showing several of the best known sets and movie "streets," and giving demonstrations of spectacular stunts and make-up techniques. The studio charges admission and draws around 4 million people a year to these costly exhibits.

Even more famous and elaborate are the gardens developed by the Anheuser-Busch Company adjacent to their breweries. The two largest Busch Gardens—The Old Country in Williamsburg, Virginia, and The Dark Continent in Tampa, Florida—have become admission-charging theme parks at which the brewery tours play a relatively minor role. The Dark Continent, Florida's most popular attraction after Disney World, for instance, is a 122-hectare (300-acre) zoological garden, which not only contains 2500 exotic birds and some 100 different species of animals but also features a variety of rides, restaurants, and animal shows. Over 2 million people visit The Dark Continent every year, but, with so many other things to do and see, comparatively few tour the brewery.

The Anheuser-Busch Company has always promoted its product by operating breweries in exotic garden-like settings and public use of these amenities has obviously engendered much good will. However, such public relations projects are becoming extremely expensive to build and maintain, especially now, when so many people are currently making use of them. As a result, Anheuser-Busch recently closed its gardenparks at the Houston, Texas, and Los Angeles, California, breweries. It is currently experimenting with a new program that seeks to derive maximum revenues from public use of the remaining parks.

Figure 11.11 People who take the Universal Studios Tour in Los Angeles, California, suddenly get a close-up view of the 7-meter (24-foot) animated white shark model used in the film "Jaws" as it lunges at the tram taking them through the area that demonstrates some of the studios' best known and most exciting special effects.

Community Programs.

Some firms contribute to a community's recreation opportunities by allowing outsiders to use facilities provided for employees. A few have developed resources specifically for the public's enjoyment. In most cases, enterprises follow such policies because they believe it promotes sales of the firm's goods or services either directly or through the positive image it creates. However, some companies have found it difficult to justify paying the full cost of such programs as advertising or public relations expenses and, therefore, charge user fees.

The Flick-Reedy Corporation in Bensenville, Illinois, is an example of a firm that opens its employee facilities to the public. Its indoor swimming pool, gymnasium, auditorium, and lunchroom are arranged so that they are accessible from outside the plant as well as from work areas. Only a few hundred employees and business visitors use these facilities for recreation, but thousands of people from the surrounding community take advantage of the amenities. They swim in the pool, attend social dances in the gym, see films and hear talks in the auditorium, and use the lunchroom for banquets and parties. The management also sponsors a variety of instructional programs as a community service. "Learn-to-swim" classes for adults, children, and the handicapped, for instance, are attended by more than 1000 individuals every year.

Another approach was adopted by a textile manufacturer in South Carolina. Since local governments at that time had neither park and recreation departments nor budgets for recreation programs and facilities, the Springs Cotton Mills Company set up a special corporation to supply recreation opportunities in each of the three communities where it has plants. During the 23 years following this action, the corporation acquired park lands, beaches, swimming pools, and golf clubs worth $10 million. The programming and maintenance staff grew to a total of 81 full-time employees and the annual operating budget reached $2.4 million. Community participation finally exceeded 1 million user-occasions a year. The facilities continue to expand; the latest addition is a $2-million recreation complex developed on a 16-hectare (40-acre) site. Its major features are a 3700-square-meter (40,000-square-foot) community center with gymnasium and indoor-outdoor swimming pool, two softball fields, six tennis courts, a football field, and a picnic area as well as hiking trails. Various forms of membership—unlimited use, limited use, family, adult, and student—are available for moderate monthly fees. Facilities and programs are operated under the guidance of a series of citizens committees with a company-management employee acting as chairperson.

The contribution of firms to the provision of community recreation resources can, therefore, range from situations such as the examples cited above to instances where businesses and industries provide no assistance. The latter is most common, but many companies play a minor role.

RESOURCES FOR EMPLOYEES

Employers have been providing recreation opportunities for their workers' enlightenment or enjoyment for more than 100 years. The number of firms making more than a minor contribution was very small, however, until the last few decades. Now, it is estimated that about 50,000 American companies sponsor some type of recreation program and spend more than $3 billion on such programs each year. This is only a small proportion of the nation's employers, but some of these firms are large companies with many workers.

Business efficiency and employee loyalty rather than worker welfare are the primary motives for employer-provided recreation. The vice-president of the Minnesota Mining and Manufacturing (3-M) Company made this clear when he declared,

> Value from our recreation program shows up in our financial statements. It shows up directly in the quality of employees we attract, train, and retain. It shows up in the productivity of our workers and in the attitude of our work force.[3]

At the Dallas plant of Texas Instruments Incorporated, the recreation programs are initiated and managed by the Texins Association, a nonprofit corporation operated by the employees. The association raises over two-thirds of its operational budget by charging annual membership dues and activity fees, collecting revenues from a number of vending operations, and opening its golf center to the public. It reimburses the company for the use of company lands, buildings, and employee time involved in the operation of association facilities and programs. In fact, long-range plans call for the eventual elimination of all company support and the association will become a private recreation organization. This approach requires extensive contributions of time by volunteers. Of the 250 people involved in the day-to-day operation of the recreation programs, only a nucleus of 35 to 45 are paid association employees.

The Texins Association programs include an intramural sports program with bowling, softball, flag football, volleyball, and basketball offered on a women's, men's, and mixed league basis. Courses on topics such as tennis, speedreading, crafts, and belly dancing are conducted in response to members' requests. Members may also join a variety of clubs, for example, the camera, rod and gun, flying, gem and mineral, camping, and amateur radio clubs. These and other activities are offered at the company-owned facilities, which consist of:

- An air-conditioned activities center and athletic complex, consisting of a gymnasium; steambaths and saunas; staff offices; a snack bar; fitness, game, meeting, and club rooms; and outdoor facilities that include a lighted softball field, two tennis courts, and a jogging track (Figure 11.12).

Figure 11.12 Built on company-owned land close to the Texas Instruments plant in Dallas, Texas, the 3-hectare (8-acre) recreation complex known as the Activities Center receives heavy use by company employees and family members both as individuals and as participants in organized sports leagues and hobby clubs. The facility and programs are the responsibility of the employees themselves who determine policies and provide much of the operating revenues through membership in a nonprofit association.

[3] "Should Your Company Have a Golf Course," *Golf Digest*, *25*, (3), 70 (1974).

- A 20-hectare (50-acre) property for the rod and gun club, which contains a clubhouse, two lakes used for swimming and fishing, a children's playground, picnic areas, and complete facilities for target shooting.
- A 3-hectare (8-acre) archery range with a pavilion and 14 regulation targets.
- A golf center, consisting of a miniature golf course, a 50-tee driving range, a large putting green, and a pro shop.
- The 27-hectare (66-acre) property of the Texoma Club on Lake Texoma, which is a 90-minute drive from Dallas. This family recreation park contains a developed campground, boat ramps, docks, a boat-storage building, children's playgrounds, and facilities for softball, volleyball, croquet, and horseshoe pitching.

Almost 7000 Texas Instrument Corporation employees and members of their families take part in the activities of the Texins Association each year.

The scope of employer-provided recreation is indicated by a 1975 national survey of 151 American organizations.[4] Although not an unbiased sample of all employers, the study involved a broad cross section of the nation's more progressive enterprises. It included manufacturing companies (54 percent), nonmanufacturing businesses (23 percent), and nonbusiness enterprises such as hospitals, educational institutions, and government agencies (23 percent). Some of the most important conclusions were:

- About 10 percent of the enterprises did not provide recreation opportunities.
- The majority (58 percent) offered limited programs that involved the spon-

[4] *Social, Recreation and Holiday Programs,* The Bureau of National Affairs, Washington, D.C., 1975.

sorship of one or more sports and one to three other activities.
- A large recreation area or building and extensive programs were provided by about 19 percent of the enterprises.
- The most common facilities were outside picnic areas, basketball courts, table tennis and gamerooms, lunchrooms with limited recreation equipment, shuffleboard courts, and horseshoe pits.
- Only about 13 percent had sports programs. The sports offered, in order of decreasing frequency, were bowling, softball, golf, basketball, baseball, tennis, volleyball, shooting, football, hockey, fishing, table tennis, horseshoes, archery, and skiing.
- The most frequently provided activities other than sports were, in descending order, attending sports events, picnics, dinner parties, group tours, theater parties, concerts, bridge, fashion shows, dancing, checkers or chess, crafts, photography, bingo, glee clubs, amateur radio, and stamp-collecting clubs.
- The most frequently reported extensive facilities were multipurpose centers that contained a gymnasium, swimming pool, meeting rooms, gameroom, and cooking and dancing areas; outdoor developments, consisting of picnic areas, group barbeque-cooking facilities, and pavilions for bingo, shows, and dances; and sportsfields, which usually included a swimming pool and a children's play area.

Only about one-third of the enterprises had employee associations that were involved in the operation of the recreation programs. Half of these association-run programs were completely or partially supported by participant fees.

Nonmanufacturing firms and nonbusiness organizations were found to have extensive programs more frequently than manufacturing companies. Enterprises in the heart of large metropolitan areas pro-

vided extensive opportunities more often than enterprises in small cities, suburban areas, or rural locations. The survey also indicated that the amount of money spent on recreation programs was increasing and added emphasis was being placed on providing opportunities for women workers.

Provision of recreation opportunities by employers is becoming increasingly common in other nations, although methods vary considerably. In Japan, for instance, many firms have always practiced extremely paternalistic policies, which include substantial social and recreational benefits. The latter often include extensive facilities and programs at the place of employment plus subsidized opportunities at nearby commercial recreation facilities. Most of the major corporations own from 15 to 20 guesthouses in mountain and seaside locations where employees and their families can sleep and eat cheaply. Others arrange subsidized rates at private inns.

In Communist nations, the government is ultimately both everyone's employer and the owner of all recreation resources other than those owned personally by individuals such as radios, bicycles, and (in some nations) second homes. However, the recreation resources provided for workers in Communist nations are included in this section rather than in the chapter on national government resources because many of the arrangements closely parallel the private company and employee situations just described.

In the Soviet Union, for example, a considerable proportion of people's recreation opportunities are provided through their place of work. Factories and worker unions sponsor extensive education and recreation programs to build morale, promote physical fitness, and increase productivity. Every major industry, commune, and union maintain their own recreation facilities and many also operate camps, spas, and vacation resorts at other locations for the exclusive use of their workers and dependents. Enterprises and unions that do not have their own vacation facilities send workers to central government operated spas, resorts, or cruise ships. Vacation privileges of these kinds are generally awarded on the basis of work performance and political reliability, with all or most of the cost being paid by the enterprise or union.

About half of all Soviet citizens who go away for a vacation use tour bases operated by trade-union supported tourism councils. These bases range from chalet or motel resort complexes to simple tent campgrounds with dining room, recreation hall, and shower facilities. In addition to the camping experience, tour bases offer many activities, including swimming, boating,

fishing, hiking, mushroom gathering, berrypicking, bicycling, motorcycling, mountain climbing, ski instruction, excursions to nearby museums, and evening lectures, movies, and dances. Some bases operate year round.

However, competitive sports and athletics usually receive the highest priority in Communist place-of-work-oriented recreation programs. The development of physical fitness, athletic ability, and esprit de corps is considered of great national importance because of its direct connection with productivity, military preparedness, and the prestige gained by winning international competitions. Factories and unions are therefore required to provide sports opportunities. Most of East Germany's 8000 sports clubs, for example, are operated by enterprises or trade unions. Clubs are located in rural hamlets as well as urban centers. Residents of the surrounding community are eligible for membership as well as workers and their families. Facilities vary from club to club, but, usually, they include a gymnasium, training rooms, swim-

ming pool, skating rink, sportsfield, and running track. Most funds for the clubs come through sponsoring enterprises or unions; the balance consists of a combination of direct government grants and monthly membership fees. The latter are small and entitle adult members to appropriate sports clothing, equipment, instruction, insurance, and the use of all club facilities.

The types of facilities and programs offered at sports clubs are controlled by the national government and not the members or sponsoring organization. Generally, a policy of providing the maximum number of opportunities for the greatest number is followed. Olympic sports are favored as are activities that involve mass participation. Over 2.5 million East Germans (15 percent of the population) belong to these clubs.

This completes the review of the principal types of noncommercial private resources that provide substantial numbers of recreation opportunities. The next chapter outlines the kind of recreation resources operated primarily to produce a profit for their owners.

DISCUSSION TOPICS

1. Summarize the differences that exist between the personal recreation resources available to you at your present primary residence and the primary-residence personal recreation resources accessible to two or three relatives or acquaintances who live under considerably different conditions. Discuss the reasons for the different patterns that you mention. What are the relationships between these different patterns and the recreation lifestyles of the individuals concerned?

2. Are private recreation organizations significant providers of recreation opportunities in communities with which you are familiar? Compare the contributions that private recreation organizations make to your recreation lifestyle and to the recreation lifestyles of two or three of your relatives or friends. Explain the differences.

3. Have your perceptions of religious and quasi-public youth organization recreation resources changed since you were young? Do you feel that these resources complement, duplicate, or compete with local govern-

ment recreation resources in communities with which you are familiar?

4. Are quasi-public preservation organizations performing a valuable service for society or are they reducing the effectiveness of government agencies by diverting potential support, resources, and funds from public preservation programs?

5. Are employer-provided recreation resources a sufficiently desirable part of a community's recreation system to justify public assistance with the planning, construction, and operation of such resources?

FURTHER READINGS

In spite of the dominance of recreation participation at home, most textbooks provide little information on personal recreation resources. Newspapers and magazines publish articles concerning trends in contemporary lifestyles, but these are usually based on interviews with a few individuals rather than broadly representative surveys. Government agencies and university researchers publish reports on home-interview surveys that include questions concerning recreation, but most are representative of relatively small populations and focus on television-viewing or participation away from home. A number of special reports concerning second homes have appeared, but the emphasis is usually on the economic or environmental concerns of developers or government agencies rather than on the resources involved.

The situation is similar in the case of most private organizations. Newspaper and magazine feature articles provide scattered impressions but little broadly representative data. Commercial magazines concerning special interests such as hunting, fishing, camping, arts and crafts, hobbies, and various sports (tennis, golf, running) sometimes describe individual organization facilities and programs. Organization periodicals—service club magazines for example—often include information on specific resources and programs but seldom any aggregate data. The latter can sometimes be found in promotional brochures and annual reports produced by an organization's national office. Trade journals, like *Institutional Management,* sometimes feature articles on organization facilities such as country clubs.

Descriptions of the recreation resources of religious organizations, quasi-public youth groups, and social welfare organizations are included from time to time in the *Journal of Health, Physical Education and Recreation, Parks & Recreation,* and other recreation journals. Background information can be found in some textbook chapters such as "The Quasi-public and Private Recreation Services" in *Leisure Services: The Organized Recreation and Park System* by Sessoms, Meyer, and Brightbill published by Prentice-Hall in 1975 or "Recreation in Other Settings" in Kraus' *Recreation and Leisure in Modern Society.* Similarly, most general recreation textbooks contain references to industrial recreation resources. However, *Recreation Management,* a monthly journal published by the National Industrial Recreation Association is devoted to facilities and programs provided by employers. The spring 1975 edition of *Outdoor Recreation Action* (a former Bureau of Outdoor Recreation periodical) was devoted to the recreation use of forest-industry and power-company lands as well as private farmlands.

12

COMMERCIAL PRIVATE RECREATION RESOURCES

Figure 12.1 The Crystal Court in Minneapolis' IDS Center offers downtown visitors a variety of recreation opportunities. Linked to 32 other buildings in a 12-block area by a series of second floor, glass-enclosed walks, it functions as a climate-controlled, year-round gathering place for shoppers, tourists, and workers from nearby offices. They walk around, shop, eat their lunches, dine at one of the restaurants, or people-watch from the benches, balcony, or observation platform.

This chapter describes those privately owned recreation resources that are developed and operated primarily for commercial purposes. It is a large and important group, which includes a variety of resources from shopping malls to ski centers (Figure 12.1). Some individuals rely on commercial resources for most of their away-from-home recreation experiences. Others, by choice or because of financial constraints, use commercial recreation facilities sparingly. Nevertheless, most people regard certain experiences such as a restaurant dinner or a theme-park visit as special occasions that add zest to their recreation lifestyles. Recreation enterprises are major employers in some urban areas and tourist regions. Commercial recreation is the principal industry in a number of regions, states, and nations; frequently, it also plays a vital role in maintaining a balance of payments or in producing essential foreign currencies.

SHOPPING FACILITIES

Many people enjoy visiting shops. Some find even routine trips to buy necessities are pleasurable because of the change in environment and interaction with people. Others dislike this kind of shopping intensely but enjoy shopping for items of special interest such as gifts, party clothing, records, books, sports equipment, or hobby items. A few perceive shopping as a challenge and obtain satisfaction from finding sale items or superior merchandise. In fact, in some societies, it is customary for merchants and potential buyers to approach each transaction as a friendly contest during which rituals are carefully observed and much mutual pleasure derived. Finally, many people enjoy browsing without any intention of buying; window-shopping is a common pastime, even when shops are closed.

CONVENTIONAL STORES

Separate small shops, department stores, and shopping centers all function as recreation resources. Older people and those who grew up in small towns and villages often prefer shopping at small family-operated businesses where the proprietors and employees try to become well acquainted with their customers. Shopping at such establishments can be important social events during which news is exchanged or good-natured banter takes place. Country stores and gasoline stations still serve as social focal points for many rural communities; local residents stop for chats with the proprietors or other residents whether or not they need to make purchases. Chairs, benches, and perhaps a table or two may be provided for those who wish to stay awhile. Friendly games of cards, checkers, or horseshoes often take place on a more or less regular basis. Some family-run establishments in older urban neighborhoods function similarly with facilities such as tables and chairs, television sets, or outdoor boccie[1] courts provided for the use of the customer-guests.

Specialty shops such as pet, music, hobby, sporting goods, book, antique, toy, and arts and crafts stores frequently provide recreation opportunities. People stop to hear recorded music being played at record stores and are introduced to unfamiliar artists or compositions (Figure 16.6). In the

[1] An Italian form of lawn bowling.

same way, musicians, backpackers, and amateur radio enthusiasts enjoy visiting music stores, camping outfitters, and electronic stores because they can discover and discuss new merchandise and get to know people with similar interests. Specialty shops often assist people with their hobbies by providing such services as repairs, individual and group instruction, advice on how to get help with product-related problems, and bulletin boards for the exchange of information and news about hobby clubs, upcoming shows, concerts, or special events.

Some establishments are designed primarily for people who shop and make purchases as a recreation experience. These range from the gift and souvenir shops found in tourist areas to coordinated shopping centers that specialize in one kind of product or a certain type of atmosphere. The latter may consist mainly of antique stores, arts and crafts shops, or establishments with a particular ethnic emphasis. For instance, the small town of Frankenmuth in Michigan has only 3000 residents, but 1.3 million people visit its business district every year. Developed around a Bavarian theme, it draws people from considerable distances to enjoy a distinctive environment as they shop for gift items like candles, glassware, wood carvings, and Christmas ornaments or as they sample German foods at one of the family-operated restaurants.

Department stores and modern, enclosed shopping malls usually lack the personalized service and opportunities for social interaction between customers and store personnel that are offered by smaller separate stores. However, large stores and malls do offer other advantages. Shoppers and browsers alike welcome the greater variety of merchandise and the reduced feeling of obligation to buy. Many feel free to visit such shopping facilities just for a respite from inclement weather, loneliness, or boredom.

Older people frequently choose to walk, sit, and observe passersby; read their newspapers; or eat their lunches in department store lounges or in shopping center courts because protection from harassment or robbery tends to be better than on city streets or in public parks. Many parents also perceive large department stores and malls as protected environments where children are safe from traffic hazards and the antisocial behavior of strangers. While they shop or enjoy a special event, their children are allowed to roam at will, looking at the merchandise that interests them or engaging in some recreation activity such as playing hide and go seek or watching television in an appliance department. In some cases, especially when a promotional event designed to attract young people is taking place, large retail complexes are used as free babysitters. Parents take their children to a mall or department store and then go elsewhere for their own business or pleasure returning to pick the children up at a prearranged time.

Young adults often spend their lunch hours and many of their after-work hours in shopping malls, using the courts as substitutes for the town squares and plazas that are absent in many suburban communities. In some areas, the courts function as community centers, particularly for teenagers, who gather there to talk, make new acquaintances, and plan group activities either at the mall or at other loca-

tions. Finally, a few use the facilities as suitable sites for specific recreation activities; they go for long walks up and down the enclosed mall (especially in inclement weather) or they make use of parking areas for jogging, bicycling, skateboarding, drag racing. or cruising in their cars.

Many developers enhance the recreation potential of their malls by including special features, facilities, and programs. Most provide public benches as well as aesthetic features such as pools, fountains, sculptures, and plantings for customers to enjoy. Courts are often used for art, antique, craft, and hobby shows as well as for a wide range of special-interest exhibitions, demonstrations, and programs. The latter usually include events with particular appeal to children — petting zoos, puppet and magic shows, or appearances by Santa Claus around Christmas time. A growing number of mall developers permit after-hour use of this valuable covered space; some allow youth groups to hold overnight "campouts" there. At least one, the Great Northern Shopping Center near Cleveland, Ohio, opens the mall to joggers on Sunday mornings during the winter months. Paved parking areas at malls are also used for the staging of carnivals, circuses, concerts, art exhibits, flea markets, and other community events. Large malls with extensive programs employ a professional staff to initiate, coordinate, and supervise these special events in cooperation with interested local groups. So numerous and popular have such events become that it is now estimated that nearly one-third of all mall visitors do not go with the intention of shopping but rather

to see what is going on.

Major department stores also provide experiences of a recreational nature. These include art exhibits, demonstrations, workshops, seminars, fashion and flower shows, concerts, celebrity appearances, and special shows and seasonal activities for children. Some sponsor community events such as Fourth-of-July fireworks displays and annual parades featuring numerous marching bands, elaborate floats, and the ubiquitous Santa Claus. These events are enjoyed by millions of people, either in person or on television. Major stores also present traditional Christmas-window displays, which provide hours of viewing pleasure for passersby as well as for persons who make special trips just to see them.

An increasing number of department store owners and mall developers are committed to community involvement. As a result, more stores and malls include facilities such as meeting and activity rooms, classrooms, auditoriums, exhibition areas, and space designed specifically to accommodate various activities and events. A good example is Woodfield Mall near Schaumberg, Illinois. This three-level, 240-store complex contains a Greek amphitheater designed to complement the shopping experience. Dancers, bands, choral groups, musicians, and actors perform here regularly, sometimes before large numbers of people. A crowd of 50,000 attended a Chicago Symphony concert presented in 1974 as the highlight of the center's third-anniversary celebration.

Finally, malls function as important recreation centers because of the kinds of commercial establishments they contain. A high proportion of the retail outlets at larger malls are specialty stores featuring merchandise that is largely recreational in nature. These include toy, hobby, arts and crafts, plant, flower, pet, sporting goods, camera, electronic equipment, jewelry, gift, book and magazine, record, and musical instrument stores as well as art galleries, travel agencies, and a number of food-and-drink establishments selling such items as ice cream, cheeses, wines, pastries, candies, nuts, and popcorn. Such stores not only supply goods that people buy to enhance their recreation lifestyles, they also display interesting merchandise that people enjoy viewing, discussing with friends, trying out, listening to, or tasting— even if they have no intention of buying. In addition, many malls contain a number of entertainment, sports, and dining facilities that turn the complex into a recreation destination for people who neither wish to shop nor browse. These facilities include restaurants, snack bars, movie theaters, discotheques (primarily for children and teenagers), pinball arcades, ice- and roller-skating rinks, bowling alleys, swimming pools, gymnasiums, and miniature golf courses.

The recreation potential of such stores, facilities, and mall-sponsored events is likely to increase in the future if malls broaden the kinds of services they provide. For instance, a shopping center in San Diego now contains a children's activity center. Designed to provide children with interesting things to do on a short-term basis, it features art, woodworking, make-believe activities, games, story hours, and educational films. Some of the stores pay part of the fee if

the parents make a purchase. The service is appreciated by parents whose children do not like to shop and by those who wish to use certain facilities without their children at times when they are unable to find babysitters. However, parents who do not come to shop or engage in another mall activity are also using the service because they feel it is beneficial for their children to have this type of social and learning experience on a regular basis.

America's 19,000 shopping malls account for almost 50 percent of retail sales, excluding building and automotive products. Many malls are small neighborhood complexes that are primarily intended to fulfill the shopping and social needs of nearby residents. Others are large regional operations which are usually located just off main highways close to major cities. Many are 40 kilometers (25 miles) or more away from the city's central core. Of these, over 1000 are climate-controlled, enclosed complexes. Two hundred are huge developments with more than 93,000 square meters (1 million square feet) of retail space. Many of the latter feature several levels and most contain three or four major stores. These are generally the malls that contain a variety of recreation enterprises and feature large-scale promotion events designed to draw people from considerable distances and encourage them to stay for substantial periods of time.

More than 30 regional shopping centers have been constructed annually in recent years. Malls are also beginning to emerge as important components of urban renewal programs. Some are being created from existing downtown streets that

are closed to traffic, landscaped, and in some cases, fully enclosed (Figure 12.1). Others are new developments that have adapted regional mall concepts to urban environments. The Market, in the Citicorp Center in New York City, for example, features verticality, with its retail space arranged on three floors around a seven-story, glass-roofed, tree-dotted atrium. Cities like Toronto and Montreal in Canada, and the larger cities of Japan have developed underground shopping areas that allow people to escape the discomfort of winter weather and urban street traffic. More than 70 of these complexes have now been constructed in Japan, featuring parklike settings complete with fountains, streams, and recorded bird songs.

OTHER RETAILERS

People purchase items from a number of other types of retailers and the experiences are often recreational.

Catalog Sales. Mail-order catalog systems are a source of pleasure in a number of ways. Lavishly illustrated catalogs provide hours of escapist entertainment for some. While browsing through the pages, they fantasize about what it would be like to own a particular item or take part in some activity that the product brings to mind. These people may never actually place an order, but dreaming about what they *could* buy is in itself a recreation experience.

Catalogs make it possible for children, the elderly, the severely handicapped, the sick, and those who live at remote locations to savor some of the joys of window-shopping or of making their own selections, even though they may not be able to visit a retailer in person. Catalogs are also important because they introduce people to recreation goods and activities with which they are not familiar. Finally, for many, especially young people, mail-order buying may be more enjoyable than making a purchase at a store. The decision-making process can be drawn out and anticipation builds as the order is completed and mailed. Then there is the element of surprise when the package finally arrives and is unwrapped.

Catalog purchases are increasing in number and diversity; they now account for about one-fifth of all general merchandise sales in the United States. It is possible to shop by mail or telephone for seeds, bulbs, and plants; craft and hobby materials; a variety of food and gift items; phonograph records, books, and magazines; toys; clothes; all kinds of boating, camping, sports, and automotive equipment; and many other recreation-oriented items from 10,000 different mail-order companies. Some enterprises provide valuable free advice to customers seeking information about merchandise and how to use it. Recreation Equipment of Seattle, a $20-million-a-year cooperative, includes helpful articles in its catalogs and employs a traveling demonstration team that lectures on camping, skiing, mountaineering, and wilderness ethics. Even better known is the L. L. Bean Company of Maine, which annually sells outdoor gear worth more than $120 million to 9 million customers in 50 states and 70 foreign countries. The Bean staff is renowned for assisting customers with a wide variety of recreation problems. Mail-order

companies of this type do much to make opportunities accessible to those who live in small communities or rural areas.

Markets and Sales. Markets and special events where new or used goods are sold provide recreation experiences in many countries. The reasons people enjoy such events as flea markets, street fairs, liquidation sales, garage sales, and auctions differ. The less affluent, for instance, may visit them strictly because they hope to obtain desired goods for less money. In this way, they may be able to own recreation items or engage in recreation activities that they otherwise could not afford. However, whether the items are basic essentials or recreational in nature, such people often obtain considerable satisfaction from finding a bargain.

On the other hand, many participants are fairly affluent; they attend such sales primarily for the experience itself. Some simply like to buy things and find it costs less to satisfy such urges at these kinds of events. There is also the anticipation involved in hunting for certain items or the thrill obtained from finding something unexpected. The risk element attracts many participants to auctions. So does the excitement of competition, particularly if the individual specializes in searching out a special kind of less common item such as old records, books by a specific author, or a particular type of antique. The social aspects of these events are also recreational, especially for those who go to flea markets regularly or attend rural auctions in areas where they are well known. Some people obtain so much enjoyment from sales that they turn participation

into a lifelong hobby. Even vendors sometimes spend a good part or all of their take on purchasing items from other sellers, counting their profits largely in terms of the pleasure derived from the social aspects of the transactions.

There are no comprehensive data on the recreational nature and scope of flea markets and sales, but the sheer number of people who attend and their attitudes and behavior during participation indicate the importance of these events. Some cities have even developed permanent sites for flea markets and, where the climate is suitable, large ones operate on a year-round basis. The most famous example is the Marché aux Puces at Porte de Clignancourt on the north side of Paris (Figure 12.2). Often attracting 300,000 visitors a week, the market consists of more than 2500 open-air stalls and 100 stores in the surrounding meandering alleyways. The merchandise, ranging from valuable antiques and unusual souvenirs to useless junk, provides pleasant shopping experiences for every taste and pocketbook.

The farmers' market is another kind of retail outlet that provides recreation experiences. Trips to such markets are often enjoyable because of the variety of attractive produce, mouthwatering foods, and colorful vendors they include. Tourists find them exciting destinations where unfamiliar agricultural products and handicrafts may be seen and purchased.

Another form of market is the show arranged by manufacturers, retailers, or hobbyists to display and sell their products. These range from sidewalk sales of artists' paintings and hobby shows at malls and civic centers to huge manufacturers' exhibitions held in major cities. Some offer experiences of the flea-market-type, but others present a range of very different opportunities. For example, at art and hobby shows, there are usually demonstrations, exhibits, films, and, occasionally, opportunities to try out materials and equipment. Boat, camping, and vehicle exhibitions usually feature a variety of live entertainment. Many people come only to see these shows and have little intention of buying anything. Once there, however, they cannot avoid being exposed to the delights of the activities concerned; sometimes this introduction is all that is needed to initiate participation in a new recreation activity.

FOOD-AND-DRINK SERVICES

From the time that humans first began to share the proceeds of their hunting, fishing, and food-gathering expeditions, meals have been social occasions rather than just a means of assuaging hunger. In fact, the word, companion, literally means *one with whom to break bread*. Even today, when people do so many things by themselves and meals often consist of quickly eaten convenience foods, people still speak of *eating alone* in a negative manner. Meals are expected to be times of fellowship and enjoyment.

Associating the act of eating with sociability and pleasure also works in reverse; social and recreation events are expected to include eating and drinking. For many people, a recreation experience would be incomplete without the consumption of food and beverages although, in many situations, the items consumed may be of little or

Figure 12.2 **So many residents and tourists visit the Marché aux Puces at Porte de Clignancourt, Paris on fine summer Sunday mornings, it becomes almost impossible to shop. Although some have specific merchandise in mind, most Sunday visitors choose the market primarily because it is an interesting destination for an outing; the crowded conditions and noise create an exciting atmosphere that adds to the recreation experience.**

no nutritional value. A cup of coffee, a soft drink, a glass of beer, an ice cream cone, a candy bar, or a box of popcorn have become part of the rituals associated with recreation activities.

Status is also involved. From earliest times, people have equated an abundance of food — especially meat — with success and high living standards. In most societies, *eating well* continues to enhance people's sense of well-being, power, and position. Many persons, therefore, not only enjoy fulfilling their social obligations by providing sustenance to guests but also derive considerable pleasure from being able to do so in an expansive manner.

Because of these factors, most societies have evolved diversified systems of commercial food-and-

drink establishments that emphasize the recreational aspects of eating and drinking. These systems include establishments such as delicatessens, cafés, teashops, bars, nightclubs, restaurants, and food services at sports stadiums and places of entertainment.

FOOD-AND-BEVERAGE STORES

Grocery, baked-goods, dairy-products, meat, liquor, and other kinds of stores all contribute to recreation experiences because they are sources of products used for meals, parties, and celebrations. There are a number of establishments, however, that play a special role in recreation; of these, the delicatessen is one of the most important. Unlike grocery stores that sell the basic ingredients from which ordinary meals are made, a delicatessen provides many prepared foods. The emphasis is on gastronomic enjoyment, not just nutrition. Displayed attractively in large pans, the prepared foods are a pleasure to see and smell, let alone taste.

To some customers, a delicatessen is merely a convenience—a place to obtain ready-to-eat foods when preparation time is short. For others, it provides opportunities to convert mealtimes into memorable occasions. Since prices are higher, many people only buy fully prepared foods as special treats. Such foods are particularly popular for picnics, parties, weddings, and other celebrations. Delicatessens also sell many other ingredients from which meals can be prepared at home. They stock foreign and regional items considered to be special delicacies. Usually, there is a great variety of rolls, breads, cheeses, cooked meats, wines, coffees, teas, and dried or canned goods from which to choose. Many customers habitually buy the same kinds of special foods because of taste preferences or ethnic, religious, or sentimental influences. Others are gastronomic explorers and periodically or continually sample unfamiliar foods in a search for new taste experiences. In both cases, the delicatessen may be the best or only source of the foods these individuals seek.

A number of shops specialize in high-quality foods or drinks of just one kind or several related kinds. Examples are the Baskin-Robbins chain of ice cream parlors that regularly stock 31 flavors or wine stores that specialize in the higher priced domestic and im-ported brands. In some cases, a visit to a specialty food or drink store becomes an established part of people's recreation patterns. For instance, there is a bakery in the theater district of Montreal called, The Bagel Factory, which has been widely adopted as a desirable after-the-show destination. Even on frosty winter nights, theater patrons wait in long lines to purchase a bag of hot bagels to eat on their way home.

FAST-FOOD ESTABLISHMENTS

America's fast-food industry had its beginnings in 1921. A short-order cook in Wichita, Kansas, squashed a meatball into a flat patty in order to cook it faster and served it in a bun so that it was easier to eat. The idea caught on and the small hamburger stand expanded eastward into a chain of establishments called, White Castle restaurants. By limiting the menu to a few low-priced items, such as hamburgers, coffee, soft drinks, and french fries, and by remaining open 24 hours a day, the little restaurants soon became popular, especially with young people on dates. Today, there are 149 White Castle restaurants. More than 15 percent of American restaurant meals involve hamburger fast-food establishments. The fast-food industry has expanded however, to include chains that specialize in other quickly prepared foods such as fried chicken, pizza, and fried fish. A total of more than 65,000 units produce revenues of over $25 billion annually.

Not all of this business involves eating for pleasure, but the development of a nationwide craving for pop food, as it is sometimes called, has turned eating for survival into eating for fun. For young people, fast-food restaurants function as neighborhood social centers. They have replaced the vanished ice cream parlor or corner drugstore as places to go to see and be seen, to feel a part of the community, and to make new friends. For families, they are often a reason for togetherness; the only time some households get together is to share a meal at a fast-food establishment.

Although the fast-food restaurant was largely a North American phenomenon until recently, it is rapidly becoming a way of life for residents in many large cities throughout the world. Tokyo, for instance, has more than 1100 pizza parlors, hamburger stands, fried-chicken outlets, and coffee-and-donut shops. U.S.-based fast-food chains like McDonald's, Kentucky Fried Chicken, Denny's Pizza Hut, and Dairy Queen account for more than half of this fast-food business.

CAFÉS AND COFFEEHOUSES

Like the fast-food establishments, cafés serve not only as sources of reasonably priced snacks and meals but also as social centers. Throughout the world, unpretentious little eating places provide a variety of recreation opportunities. To some, they are places to relax with friends over a hot beverage or a cold drink and exchange news of local interest. Others go to play checkers, cards, or pinball or to listen to the juke box (automatic record player). Some like to sit at an outdoor table on a warm, sunny day and observe the passing scene. In many small towns and rural communities, there is only one café; often it serves as the hub of the area's social life. In the Great Plains region of the United States, for instance, many cafés do most of their business at lunchtime during the week when farmers in from the fields and businesspersons from nearby shops and offices get together to relax and talk. Another busy period occurs on Sundays when many families congregate in the café after church services to eat lunch and exchange the news of the week. In such situations, the café, whatever its size or appearance, can be the single most important recreation resource in the entire community.

Teashops and coffeehouses also function as social or cultural centers where people congregate for the recreation experience as much as for the refreshments. These establishments differ considerably from one nation to another and, for this reason, are valuable destinations for tourists seeking a different cultural experience. Residents in some areas enjoy them for the same reason. In Japan, for instance, although tea remains a central ritual of Japanese life, coffee has become the drink of the active city dweller. It is often consumed in exotic little shops called kissaten, of which there are now 20,000 in Tokyo alone. Offering a surrogate foreign experience, these shops serve a wide range of unusual coffees in environments symbolic of France, Italy, Spain, or Latin America. An essential element is music, with some kissaten featuring live performances. However, most shops rely on recorded music played through elaborate sound systems. Some present popular music of Japan, but the majority cater to the Japanese infatuation with the symphonic music of the

West. Regular patrons often spend hours sipping coffee, listening to the music, talking quietly, or studying.

RESTAURANTS

People in the developed nations are increasingly willing to spend money on meals away from home. In the United States alone, over 130 million meals are purchased every day, and it is expected that one of every two food dollars will soon be spent on prepared meals. Although the fast-food establishments now claim over one-third of this $70-billion annual expenditure, the full-service restaurant is still the place most people choose when they have enough time and money. Until recently, most people considered a meal at a good restaurant to be a luxury reserved for very special occasions. This is no longer the case; growing numbers of middle-income individuals feel that the expense is justified. After all, a restaurant meal offers not only a change of menu but also an opportunity to relax and experience the feeling of being pampered. The very word, restaurant, has evolved from a French word meaning to restore. It is this ability to provide a soothing respite from the pressures of everyday life that makes restaurants so attractive and such important recreation resources.

Many of the 350,000 restaurants in the United States are little more than higher priced, sit-down versions of fast-food outlets. These family restaurants appeal to older adults who desire more comfortable surroundings, a more varied menu, and more personalized service than the fast-food establishments provide. Many outlets are part of a national or regional restaurant chain

that caters to diners with special gastronomic interests; these include pancake houses, steak houses, and seafood restaurants. Some of the more expensive establishments feature ethnic foods or smorgasbords, which appeal strongly to people wanting to enjoy new and different foods.

However, for many people, the facilities as well as the food must be just right if the experience of dining out is to be truly recreational. Restaurant designers and proprietors go to great lengths to create pleasurable dining environments. They use a variety of techniques which include:

- Constructing opulent interiors with comfortable seating and lighting arrangements.
- Displaying interesting antiques, works of art, or hobby collections.
- Playing recorded music or providing live entertainment, such as pianists, vocalists, strolling musicians, bands, or orchestras.
- Choosing a suitable location and providing large windows through which a high proportion of the diners can enjoy the beauty of ocean or mountain scenery or watch people engaged in sports or other interesting activities (Figure 14.16).
- Constructing revolving restaurants at the top of tall hotels or office buildings so that patrons are afforded spectacular and constantly changing views of a city's skyline.
- Cantilevering restaurants out over sidewalks in central locations so that customers can watch the activity taking place up and down a busy street.
- Locating restaurants in boats or historic structures such as old mills, mansions, or railroad stations.
- Developing theme restaurants that offer customers a glimpse of past environments, either real or imagined.
- Providing facilities for private parties and celebrations.

Involving the patrons in the food's preparation. Some restaurants encourage guests to create their own salads or supervise the cooking of their entrees, whereas others—especially ethnic restaurants—have chefs prepare the food at the patrons' tables.

Of course, exotic environments do not automatically produce an exceptional customer experience, even when accompanied by good food. Only a few establishments are able to transform a restaurant meal into a truly memorable occasion. This occurs when a combination of many factors—surroundings, cuisine, service, entertainment, even the patrons themselves—somehow creates an atmosphere that is special in every way.

A relatively recent development has been the proliferation of dinner theaters. These establishments provide a full-course meal or buffet followed by a play or musical review performed by a resident professional troupe (Figure 12.3). They attract patrons who have previously not seen or felt comfortable attending live theater in addition to regular theatergoers. As a result, dinner theater has flourished. Only seven existed in the entire United States in 1969; today, with 500 dinner theaters in operation, some larger metropolitan areas have half a dozen or more and even small cities often support more than one. Over 50 percent of the actors and actresses presently employed in the United States work in dinner theater productions.

BARS AND NIGHTCLUBS

Of all the kinds of food-and-drink enterprises, those that are primarily in business to serve alcoholic beverages vary the most. Affected by dif-

Figure 12.3 **An audience enjoys a play after their meal at a dinner theater in Montgomery, Alabama. By positioning the stage in the center of the restaurant and designing the sets and action for a theater-in-the-round audience, all patrons are afforded an intimate theater experience.**

ferences in licensing regulations, and variations in drinking customs associated with geographic location, ethnic background, and the economic level of the clientele, these establishments range from tiny stand-up bars with almost no furniture to immense, elaborate nightclubs accommodating thousands of people at one time. Depending on local attitudes and the type of establishment, drinking places can serve as community centers where a wide variety of people meet, drink, eat, and play games. On the other hand, they can be places where only those who tend not to fit into society pass the hours commiserating with one another and getting drunk. Most establishments fall somewhere between these two extremes.

The classic example of the community-center-type of facility is the traditional British public house, or pub. Romanticized in literature,

songs, movies, and the memories of tourists and military personnel, it can be, under ideal circumstances, almost as perfect as its image. Such conditions occur most often in smaller communities where strong traditions prevail concerning use of the pub and at establishments where the proprietor is a good manager and host. In such situations, a substantial proportion of the local population may frequent the pub. Men and (to a lesser extent) women as well as young adults and older people enjoy the social atmosphere as they drink beer, eat snacks, gossip, discuss important issues, play darts, and sing songs. Music is a particularly important part of pub activities in Ireland; some establishments in Dublin have rooms where local musicians congregate to sing and play almost every day.

At the other extreme, there are large pubs in industrial cities where the clientele is mostly male workers and the emphasis is on hard drinking. Many suburban pubs are beginning to resemble American taverns as they install juke boxes, operate as disco dance spots for several evenings a week, and expand food services to include extensive lunch and dinner menus. In fact, many British pubs are providing eating-out opportunities similar to those supplied by fast-food establishments in the United States.

English and Irish pub traditions have been exported, especially to former colonies like Australia and New Zealand. In the United States and Canada, however, a very different pattern has emerged. Because of the great variety of strong ethnic influences, there are drinking establishments that resemble those in many countries, not just those of England and Ireland. In some parts of Canada, for instance, there are large beer parlors reminiscent of German beer halls. But these are exceptions, confined to neighborhoods and communities that contain high proportions of residents who share the same ethnic background. Generally, the effects of an early Puritan negative attitude toward alcoholic beverages and stringent licensing laws have resulted in the development of a quite different kind of establishment. Known as a tavern, this establishment is a hybrid development that consists of a bar equipped with stools as well as a number of sets of chairs and tables. Light snacks or full meals are usually served in addition to both beer and mixed drinks. Often, there is a television set over the bar and a juke box in the table area. Magazines and games like backgammon, darts, chess, and Monopoly may be available; gameboards are sometimes built into the table tops.

The entertainment provided in American taverns depends on the characteristics and affluence of the customers whom the owners are attempting to attract. Many proprietors are satisfied with a regular, if limited, clientele drawn from the surrounding neighborhood, and they provide nothing but a regular-size television set and a juke box. Some permit customer dancing and set aside a space for it. Generally, the juke box provides background music as well as music for dancing. Most tavern owners lease the juke box and the distributor supplies current or older records appropriate to the tastes of the clientele. Some indulge their own tastes in opera, jazz, folk music, the classics, or big hits of earlier times, thereby attracting steady customers who share their musical preferences. Proprietors of taverns in ethnicly distinct neighborhoods often feature appropriate minority-group music, which not only comforts homesick local patrons but also provides a foreign atmosphere that makes the establishment a tourist attraction for people with other backgrounds.

Live music in American taverns usually involves paid performers rather than customer volunteers. Many engage a single musician or small group to play in the evenings or during their busiest periods — usually Friday and Saturday nights. Larger taverns have dancefloors and well-equipped stages and sound systems. In fact, about half of the American establishments calling themselves discotheques are really glorified taverns with dancefloors and live bands.

Where many potential customers are keenly interested in sports events, larger taverns often install large-screen television projection systems. These are so popular with patrons that many have little hope of seeing major programs such as championship sports events unless they make reservations weeks in advance or arrive hours before the telecast is scheduled to begin. During these programs, the establishment often operates like a private social club with regular patrons participating in a betting pool organized by the bartender. This adds to the excitement of the telecast as patrons crowd around the television screen yelling for their favorite team or athlete. Even losers find solace in the big after-the-game parties with lots of free food and drink that most proprietors provide with part of their gain from the wagered money.

Some cities have a variety of establishments that specialize in certain types of alcoholic beverages. The cocktail lounge, for instance, features mixed drinks served in plush surroundings. Originating in the United States, it is found on the main streets of cities, in most sizable hotels, and as part of many larger higher priced restaurants. It has not proven successful in Europe, but most larger hotels still have one (called the American Bar) for the convenience of American guests. Another specialized establishment, the wine bar, recently became popular in London, England, and is currently trying to gain a foothold in Canadian and American cities. Wine bars serve no beer or liquor but offer a wide range of wines along with good food and coffee. They are sophisticated gathering places for younger people, couples on dates, and light drinkers who visit them before or after the theater, for dining, and for late-night refreshments.

Nightclubs and cabarets are essentially taverns with a floor show consisting of singers, comics, or other performers, and, in some cases, an area for dancing. These types of establishments are increasing in Canada and the United States as larger numbers of people appear to be seeking a more intimate relationship between performer and audience. Some nightclubs at resort hotels accommodate hundreds of people and resemble large concert halls in everything but seating arrangements. By featuring artists with dynamic personalities and relaxed, informal styles of presentation, however, they still are able to provide an intimate kind of theater experience. Smaller cabarets that present comic monologues, short plays, and a variety of revues and musical entertainments have a similar appeal because the performers often mingle with the audience during and after the show; these establishments are particularly popular with young people.

REFRESHMENT SERVICES

Eating and drinking has always been a secondary recreation experience at spectator events. Since few bring their own refreshments, most spectators rely on refreshment stands or vendors for their food and drink. Many refreshment services are provided by private companies, known as concessionaires, which pay the facility management for this privilege. Some privately owned and government-owned facilities prefer to operate their own food services. In either case, profits from refreshment sales are often an important source of revenue.

The competition for franchises at stadiums and arenas is particularly fierce; the providing of simple snacks at sports events is now a multimillion dollar industry. At Super Bowl XII, for example, a crowd of 75,000 people consumed more than $250,000 worth of food and beverages, including 80,000 quarter-pound superdogs, 100,000 beers, and 500 gallons of frozen daiquiris. To serve these snacks, 1500 employees operated 22 main concession stands, 20 portable snack bars, 30 beer bars, 8 cocktail stands, 3 main restaurants, and 64 private sky suites— at the same time hundreds of roving vendors carried food and drink directly to fans in the stands.

Although more people prefer to bring their own refreshments to parks, concession stands and vendors are still important suppliers of snacks and meals. Children, in particular, look forward to buying something to eat or drink during visits to parks and zoos. For adults, an ice cream product or cold beverage is a welcome pick-me-up on a hot summer afternoon, and a steaming cup of coffee on a cold or damp day is equally inviting. Food services are especially appreciated by tourists who find it difficult or impossible to bring their own food; concessions allow them to remain at a recreation resource all day without having to go hungry. Similarly, sightseers can make maximum use of the available daylight hours if they can pick up snacks from vendors in the vicinity of major tourist attractions instead of taking time to leave the area, find a restaurant, and wait for service.

The refreshment business is in a constant state of change. Until the 1940s, for instance, American

movie theater owners were reluctant to serve food items, not only because of the litter but also because they were convinced the sound of munching would drive noneating customers away. Since then, of course, proprietors have accepted the fact that most customers regard refreshments as an indispensable part of their movie-going experience. Now, they continually improve their refreshment stands and introduce new items. Some theaters have even installed bars so that patrons can drink beer or sip cocktails while watching a movie.

PARTICIPATORY FACILITIES

Another broad group of commercial enterprises that provide numerous recreation experiences are those at which patrons take part in dancing, games, or sports. These range from discotheques and pool halls to bowling centers, riding stables, and golf courses.

DANCING ESTABLISHMENTS

Enterprises that are primarily concerned with providing opportunities for dancing are now common, following a period when they were comparatively scarce. Commercial dancehalls were numerous during the ballroom dancing era of the 1930s and 1940s. Urban areas in the United States and Canada usually had one or more dance palaces where several hundreds or even thousands of couples danced one or more times a week to the music of a band. Dances were held regularly in urban and resort hotels; dance pavilions in resort areas or locations close to urban centers did a brisk business during the summer months. People flocked to listen and dance to the sound of the big-name bands, which made regular circuits of the larger establishments. Then rock music and other forms of dancing became dominant and most of the large ballrooms and dancehalls were demolished or converted to other uses. Dancing at commercial enterprises became largely a secondary activity at a few hotels and eating or drinking establishments.

Although some reawakening of interest in ballroom dancing has occurred during the last decade, the major change has been the emergence of disco dancing as a recreation activity. To accommodate the dancers, around 20,000 discotheques are presently in operation. Since the music is recorded and therefore basically the same everywhere, discos compete with one another in terms of the elaborateness of sound systems and decor and variety of secondary activities provided. Major discos have spent as much as $2 million on their facilities and equipment and some are total-entertainment complexes, with movie projection facilities, boutiques, bars, restaurants, and extensive gamerooms.

Naturally, such expenditures are the exception rather than the rule. However, since much disco dancing is done as a form of escapism with considerable sums of money being invested in dancing lessons and costumes, customers expect discotheques to have a certain amount of glamor as well as adequate dancing facilities. This means the provision of hard, semi-slick dancefloors, good sound systems, the right kind of music played by personable deejays, and enough trappings such as mirrors, flashing lights, and special effects to transport dancers into the fantasyland they seek.

SPORTS ESTABLISHMENTS

Although private clubs and publicly owned facilities are conspicuous providers of opportunities for people to play sports and games, the commercial sector also offers substantial numbers of opportunities (Figure 4.8). Activities commonly available at commercial enterprises include horseback riding, bowling, billiards, pinball, roller-skating, skateboarding, motocross *bicycle* racing, and golfing. Many so-called sports clubs, especially those providing racket-sports facilities, are actually profit-making commercial enterprises rather than private associations, although they require annual memberships of their customers.

Bowling centers are a good example of commercial suppliers of sports opportunities. They are often the best or only facilities of their kind, but, as is the case with all commercial enterprises, they can only be located in areas where they are likely to make a profit. Therefore, although there are 8500 bowling establishments in the United States, most are concentrated in the suburbs of the larger industrial cities. The Detroit area, for instance, has 140 commercial bowling centers. Some, such as the Thunderbowl Center with 94 lanes and amphitheater facilities, are huge complexes. Each week, more than 2 million games are played at these establishments by 325,000 bowlers who belong to leagues as well as by thousands of other people who bowl as families or groups of friends. Some of the centers operate 24 hours a day because evening- and night-shift workers prefer to play when they finish work, and there is insufficient capacity during normal afternoon and evening hours to satisfy the needs of all the potential customers.

A contrasting example of a commercial recreation enterprise is the riding stable. Riding stables are found in both suburban and rural areas. Some provide stabling for privately owned horses and also rent horses by the hour or for longer periods. Most stables have a small paddock for instruction, and some own larger areas equipped for jumping. However, the majority of commercial stables rely on public lands to provide the trails used by more experienced customers. Therefore, they are usually situated near public parks or forests that have extensive trail systems. Some commercial stables are operated as concessions inside public parks under rules established by the park agency.

One of the most innovative sports facilities of recent times is the wave pool. Invented in Europe and introduced into the United States by commercial interests, these facilities contain machinery that creates waves resembling natural shoreline surf. One of the earliest wave pools – Big Surf, near Phoenix, Arizona – has a large pool that can produce waves big enough for surfing. Wave size is adjustable, however, and this and similar pools usually alternate periods without waves with periods when waves of different intensities are generated.

Wave pools are now being incorporated into elaborate commercial complexes that feature a variety of aquatic opportunities. An ex-

Figure 12.4 A variety of water-oriented facilities comprise the Wet 'n Wild complex at Orlando, Florida. On the left is the giant water slide, the water playground is in the foreground, the wave pool is at the rear right, and the six-story-high slide is on the far right.

ample is Wet 'n Wild near Orlando, Florida. It consists of a series of heated pools on a 5-hectare (12-acre) site (Figure 12.4). One large pool is constructed so that children may play in low waves at the shallow end while older and better swimmers can body-surf farther out in the ocean-size waves. A giant 120-meter (400-foot) water slide deposits riders into another large pool. Other pools contain water play equipment for youth of various ages. A sandy beach for sunning and relaxing lies on the shores of a small lake equipped with paddleboats, sailboats, and miniature speedboats.

The multipurpose recreation center is another commercial sports complex that appears to be gaining favor. As in the case of shopping centers, entrepreneurs are finding it profitable to group a number of recreation facilities at one location. In southern California, for example, a chain of enterprises has been established under the name of Family Recreation Centers. Each center contains trampolines, minibowling facilities, snack bars, tennis- and baseball-practice machines, several well-maintained miniature golf courses, and a gameroom filled with pool tables and pinball machines. At least one miniature golf course is indoors, making play in bad weather possible. These centers are open every day from 9:00 A.M. to midnight and attract all kinds of people, including the elderly.

Other innovations that currently appear to be quite successful are:

- Roller-discos that enable customers to combine the activities of roller-skating

and disco dancing. Many of America's 1600 roller-skating rinks have reduced noise and increased maneuverability with the introduction of plastic floors and skate wheels. They have also created a discotheque atmosphere by adding deluxe sound systems, disc jockeys, and multicolored lights synchronized to pulsate with each high and low musical note.
- Indoor golf-o-tron practice machines that simulate playing golf on one of several famous golf courses by showing hundreds of color slides stored in a computer-operated carousel. As the player drives the ball at a picture of the course, the ball's trajectory is visually simulated and the appropriate picture for the next shot is then projected.
- Indoor tennis practice machines that enable players to improve their strokes by hitting 200 to 250 balls in a 15-minute period. Some machines can be adjusted to match a player's ability or to provide certain kinds of shots.

Such facilities not only provide recreation experiences but also frequently expand participants' involvement in the sport. For instance, individuals who use the facilities described above may be encouraged to: take roller-skating or disco dancing lessons to perform better; spend a golfing vacation at one of the resorts where the famous courses shown by the golf-o-tron are located; or play tennis with friends more frequently because of improved skills.

AMUSEMENT PARKS

Amusement parks are collections of mechanical rides, sideshows, games, and food stalls that provide a variety of activities at one location. More than 375 of these parks are now in operation in the United States. There are two main types:

the traditional amusement parks, which have changed very little during the past century, and the theme parks, which are a comparatively recent development. Such facilities form an exciting part of many people's recreation environments; about one out of four Americans visits an amusement park each year, staying an average of four hours and spending $12.

TRADITIONAL PARKS

Introduced in the late 1800s, the traditional amusement park—with its roller coaster, giant Ferris wheel, and strings of bright lights—had become a familiar and well-attended recreation resource in the United States by the 1930s. Amusement park companies constructed them along waterfronts and on the outskirts of urban areas. Street-railroad companies built their own parks just outside cities to increase the number of weekend passengers on their lines. A few of the earlier parks are still in operation.

One of the most famous of the traditional amusement parks is at Coney Island, located on the south side of Brooklyn in New York City (Figure 6.11). It has survived a series of setbacks caused by fires, economic depressions, profound population changes, subway-fare increases, urban renewal projects, the advent of television, and the development of more sophisticated amusement parks. Today, more than 1 million people swarm into the area on hot summer days, drawn by the readily accessible amenities of ocean, public beach, and amusement park (Figure 12.5). Once there, they swim, lounge on the beach, walk along the ocean front, eat snacks, attend concerts,

Figure 12.5 **The amusement park, beach, extensive array of other public and commercial recreation resources, and ready accessibility by public transportation draw thousands of New York area residents to Coney Island on fine summer days.**

buy souvenirs, go dancing, ride on the Ferris wheels and roller coasters, and patronize the penny arcades, gamebooths, shooting galleries, and sideshows. Some new attractions have been added recently, including the publicly owned New York Aquarium and a giant toboggan water slide, but, basically, the area and its appeal remain the same.

A special type of amusement park, the oceanside resort pier, had its origins in Great Britain during the early 1800s. Suspended above the waves on columns embedded in the ocean floor, the pier was originally a seaward extension of a resort's promenade and was used primarily for boarding coastal passenger vessels. However, people

liked to stroll and to sit on piers while enjoying the breeze and view. Pier companies, therefore, started charging admission, providing more amenities, and making the structures larger and more elaborate. Several were major developments covering as much as 9300 square meters (100,000 square feet) and containing theaters, concert halls, dance pavilions, restaurants, bars, seafood stands, slot machine arcades, and other amusements. Piers were also used extensively for fishing and for a variety of special events, ranging from performing animal shows to diving exhibitions.

More than 80 piers of various sizes were built in Great Britain between 1813 and 1957. About 50 are still in existence (Figure 5.5), but high maintenance costs and changing patterns of recreation behavior are resulting in their gradual demolition. Some have been purchased and are being operated by local governments.

Elaborate piers were not as numerous in North America, and only a few survive. Even the best known — Atlantic City's 686-meter (2250-foot) long Steel Pier — faces an uncertain future. Built in 1898 as a major attraction on the famous boardwalk, the pier was recently purchased by Resorts International, operators of the city's first gambling casino. Their plans for the pier have not been revealed but, currently, its only use is for the staging of sports events. Other piers along the boardwalk continue to offer a variety of mechanical rides and games of chance. Central Pier contains a new sky needle that provides visitors with a panoramic view of the resort area.

Few traditional amusement parks in the United States, except Coney Island, continue to be major recreation resources. Most are finding it difficult to survive in the face of increasing costs and growing competition from other forms of entertainment. Many function primarily as low-cost gathering places for young people, and some are no longer viewed as appropriate destinations for family outings.

THEME PARKS

The lion's share of amusement park attendance and profits is now going to several dozen recently constructed theme parks that differ considerably from the traditional amusement parks. The latter are haphazard clusters of unrelated rides, games, shows, souvenir vendors, and refreshment stands. *Theme parks* contain all of these kinds of amenities, but they are cleverly tied together and promoted as a coordinated package of attractions developed around a single theme. The theme may be a period of history, the world of nature, an imaginary land, or a certain type of music.

Traditional amusement parks are usually located on the edge of cities. Theme parks are built between major metropolitan areas and near the intersections of two or more interstate highways so that as large a population as possible lies within a 160-kilometer (100-mile) radius. Visitors pay separately for each activity at traditional parks, whereas theme parks charge an admission fee that covers the cost of all rides, shows, and exhibits (exclusive of food and merchandise). The older traditional parks usually try to keep going in their drab settings with a minimum of maintenance and redevelopment. In contrast, the theme parks provide lavishly and imaginatively landscaped environments, maintain them immaculately, and constantly improve the facilities or add new attractions. Motley crews of unskilled workers and fast-talking hucksters are often employed to run traditional parks. Theme parks are staffed by clean-cut, uniformed young people who have been selected and trained to be friendly and helpful.

The pioneer in the field of theme parks is, of course, Walt Disney Productions. Inspiration for the first park is said to have come to Walt Disney when he took his granddaughter to an amusement park and wondered why such places could not be cleaner, more wholesome, and more interesting to adults as well as to children. The result was Disneyland, a 60-hectare (150-acre) fantasy park opened in 1955 at Anaheim, California. Originally developed around five theme areas — Fantasyland, Tomorrowland, Frontierland, Adventureland, and Main Street, U.S.A. — the various attractions are marvels of imaginative thinking and technological ingenuity. But the way the park was designed and operated was equally remarkable. The shutting out of the surrounding urban environment and emphasis on spaciousness, cleanliness, wholesomeness, and friendliness, creates an inviting, secure landscape that enables people to forget the outside world temporarily. It provides family groups in particular with an ideal destination for major outings.

Disneyland's success quickly led to the building of other theme parks. Walt Disney World, a second development by Walt Disney Productions, was constructed on a 1000-hectare (2500-acre) site in central Florida. Here the concept was expanded to include hotels, campgrounds, and facilities for a wide range of outdoor activities such as golf, tennis, swimming, boating, hiking, fishing, and horseback riding (Figure 12.6). The magnitude of Disney World and its effect on tourist flows had an almost immediate impact on Florida's economy. The Miami region in the southeastern portion of the state suffered a severe drop in tourism, whereas the area around the theme park experienced a land and building boom.

By 1978, a total of 18 *superparks* (theme parks attracting over 2 million customers a year) were in operation. In addition, a number of smaller theme parks were in busi-

Figure 12.6 This aerial view of Disney World shows the Magic Kingdom with its 6 themed areas in the foreground. The features visible include the river boat ride (1), Space Mountain thrill ride (2), Cinderella's Castle (3), Flight to the Moon space exhibits (4), America the Beautiful 360° movie theater (5), Main Street nostalgia shops and rides (6), and Frontierland Western town (7). In the background are Bay Lake (8), the Contemporary Resort Hotel (9), Fort Wilderness Resort Campground (10), and the monorail transportation system (11).

ness at locations between lesser urban centers or close to large metropolitan areas. Since these parks rely less on tourists and more on repeat visits from residents of the immediate region, they tend to be more thrill-ride oriented because experience rides are interesting only once.

Theme parks are very expensive to construct and operate so that they all face the challenge of attracting more customers, including repeat customers and, if possible, customers from other parks. This has led to an "arms race" in the development of thrill rides. Family-owned-and-operated Knotts Berry Farm achieved a 52 percent increase in peak season attendance by adding thrill rides. Even Disneyland, after reaching a plateau of about 10 million visitors a year, improved its attendance sharply by adding an enclosed roller coaster (Space Mountain) in 1977.

Any competitive advantage a park gains is usually short lived. No sooner has the steepest, largest, longest, highest, fastest, or scariest ride been introduced at one park than a "better" one is opened at another and the race continues. However, these facilities are so expensive that the economic viability of the parks is threatened. The average cost is $3 million, but Space Mountain at Disneyland cost $17 million—more than it took to build the entire complex in 1955. Substantial increases in admission charges do not appear to be a viable solution, since even customers who are enthusiastically awaiting each new attraction are complaining about price increases.

The zenith of the theme-park building in North America may have passed. Higher construction,

promotion, maintenance, and labor costs plus the fear that the industry may have already reached market saturation are discouraging developers. Attendance at existing parks is already equal to about 45 percent of the total Canadian and United States populations between the ages of 5 and 64.

In the future, if new amusement parks are built, they are most likely to be modest regional developments. The large parks have whetted people's appetites for this form of recreation and, as a result, there is a market for smaller parks if they are readily accessible. However, those that are successful usually have one or two special features that set them off from the major parks. Otherwise, such developments run the risk of being regarded (and avoided) as cheap imitations.

One regional attraction of this type is Old Chicago. This $46 million, 54,500-square-meter (586,500-square-foot) development in one of Chicago's southwestern suburbs, consists of a small theme park in a 100-store, fully enclosed shopping center. The park has 30 major rides, including a corkscrew roller coaster. It also has a split-level, supervised play-equipment area for children, numerous permanent exhibits that explain Chicago's past, and a 300-seat theater featuring almost continuous circus, magic, puppet, and multimedia sight-and-sound shows. Disco dances are held on weekends and special events are scheduled throughout the year to encourage repeat visits. Old Chicago entertains 3 million people a year.

Although several other countries have shown considerable interest in developing major theme

parks, this kind of recreation resource remains largely an American phenomenon. The only sizable coordinated amusement park in Europe is the 9-hectare (22-acre) Tivoli Gardens in Copenhagen, Denmark. However, it is not a recent development; although the attractions have been updated many times, the park itself was first opened in 1843. Medium-size theme parks have been constructed in Hamburg, Germany; Lagos, Nigeria; and in Sydney and Brisbane, Australia. They are also being built as one means of sharing oil profits with the peoples of Abu Dhabi, Bahrein, and Kuwait—citizens will be admitted free. Walt Disney Productions is presently providing design and management services for a Disneyland-type park to be built near Tokyo with Japanese financing.

MUSEUMS, GARDENS, AND PARKS

Although most of the world's better museums, botanical gardens, unique landscapes, and zoological parks are publicly owned and managed, there are many commercial developments that provide recreation experiences of this type. A few of these enterprises are resources offering experiences that cannot be obtained elsewhere. Many, however, are not particularly noteworthy and some are so inferior that it is surprising they manage to remain in business. The accessibility of such attractions and the way in which they are advertised are often the main reasons for their success.

Commercial enterprises of this type are commonly located along highways frequented by tourists. Sometimes such roadside attractions are used as interesting rest stops on long drives, especially by vacationing families with young children. Tourists often visit privately owned areas that contain caverns, interesting vegetation, or beautiful landscapes instead of nearby public lands with similar features because the private areas have been more extensively developed. For example, people may have to hike considerable distances along trails to see the special features of a public park, whereas they can view similar attractions at a nearby commercial enterprise either from their own cars or from boats, trains, or aerial tramways. Such rides are often attractions in themselves.

The availability of frequent guided tours and an assortment of snack bars, restaurants, souvenir stands, picnic facilities, children's playgrounds, and special exhibits may also increase the appeal of commercial attractions. Visitors may also choose commercial resources when they find nearby public areas closed, overcrowded, or too restrictive. Absence of restrictions is of particular importance to individuals who wish to collect materials as souvenirs or for hobbies. Several commercial operations in Arizona near the Petrified Forest National Park, for example, allow visitors to pick up fossilized wood and take it away with them for a fee, whereas collecting specimens is forbidden in the national park.

Of all the reasons for visiting one of the commercial attractions, however, curiosity seems to be the most common. People like to see unfamiliar or unusual things. Entrepreneurs are adept at presenting an attraction in such a way that potential customers are convinced they are being offered a rare opportunity

to be mystified, frightened, or entranced. Some of the more heavily visited establishments of this nature include:

- Wax museums, like Madame Tussaud's in London, that contain collections of lifelike figures representing well-known people, past and present.
- European miniature parks, such as Madurodam in Holland, that contain scale models of real cities or well-known historic structures; these are especially interesting to young children and to adults who make models as a hobby.
- Exhibitions like Ripley's Believe-It-or-Not museums, that feature bizarre or unusual exhibits.
- Roadside attractions that feature employees handling animals considered dangerous; the most common are the reptile farms that offer exhibitions of alligator-wrestling or the milking of venom from poisonous snakes.

Many people find such attractions irresistible and consider them essential components of a successful vacation.

Although most are small-scale enterprises, some commercial gardens and animal parks are extensive developments costing millions of dollars and having an appeal similar to theme parks. In fact, some developments such as the marine-life parks and drive-through animal parks are sometimes described as theme parks, although they are not nearly as broad-based and lack many amusement park features such as thrill and experience rides. Nevertheless, many of the larger gardens and animal parks are well-known tourist attractions receiving over 1 million visitors a year.

These major developments contain extensive plant and animal collections, but much of their allure lies in the innovative ways in which

they are displayed. Showmanship is apparent in every aspect of the operation, from promotion and park design to the special exhibits, demonstrations, programs, and shows. The amenities often include imaginative children's playgrounds, picnic areas, petting zoos, shops, restaurants, and boat, train, or animal rides — all of which provide interesting secondary recreation opportunities. Such gardens and parks are not merely places where people go when they wish to see flora and fauna with which they are unfamiliar, they are also attractive as places of entertainment.

Some of the most elaborate and best-known commercial parks are:

- Garden parks, such as the 25-year-old Florida Cypress Gardens which features 11 internationally themed gardens; it also offers live-animal exhibits, a huge aviary, an overhead walk-through aquarium, a spectacular water-ski show, guided canal tours of the cypress area in electric boats, speedboat rides on a large lake, and an area featuring theme-park-type rides, shows, and food stands.
- Natural wonders parks such as those developed at the sites of major springs; these parks provide views of fish and marine plantlife by glass-bottom boat, boat cruises along the waterways and, sometimes, as is the case at Weeki Wachee in Florida, they present underwater swimming shows that are viewed through large windows.
- Marine-life parks like the Sea World complexes that feature performances by trained dolphins, sea lions, and killer whales and that provide opportunities for visitors to see, touch, feel, and feed a wide variety of marine creatures. The Ohio Sea World development includes adventure playgrounds, ponds for fishing, and lumberjack and water-ski shows.

- Wildlife parks where visitors drive through fenced enclosures in their automobiles to view wildlife (usually animals of the African veld) roaming freely in settings landscaped to resemble their native habitat; tape recorders enable the visitors to hear about the animals and points of interest encountered along the way.
- Underwater observatories like the $2.5-million Coral World Underwater Observatory and Marine Park on the island of St. Thomas in the Virgin Islands; this development consists of an offshore submerged tower that permits close observation of life around a coral reef; a large onshore aquarium, a restaurant, and a discotheque.

Several of these kinds of attractions are being developed as chains of enterprises owned by the same company. For instance, Sea World has built parks in California, Florida, and Ohio; Lion Country Safari Parks are now located in California, Florida, Georgia, and Texas.

In Europe, several large-estate owners have turned parts of their properties into commercial wildlife parks to earn money for property maintenance and taxes. In 1966, Lord Bath began the safari park trend in England when he turned 90 hectares (200 acres) of his estate at Longleat into an African wildlife park. It now attracts over 500,000 visitors each year. In France, the owners of the Chateau de Thoiry near Paris spent $3 million to establish a wild-animal park, which includes a vivarium, baby-animal zoo, picnic area, restaurant, and gift shop. This proved to be a sound investment. Less than 20,000 individuals toured the museum-like castle each year prior to construction of the new amenities. The number increased to well over 1 million once

the wild-animal park was in operation, making the Chateau de Thoiry one of France's major tourist attractions.

SHOWS, TOWERS, AND TOURS

There are several kinds of commercial entertainment enterprises that do not fit into the categories described above or those that follow. These include traveling shows, viewing towers, and other resources that provide interesting sightseeing opportunities.

TRAVELING SHOWS

The proportion of the population that attends traveling shows has decreased substantially. Reasons for this decline in interest include the advent of movies and television as popular free time activities, changes in the general population's level of sophistication and expectations, and the marked increase in the number of people who are able and prefer to travel to large urban centers to attend major productions and events. As a result, the arrival in a smaller community of a traveling show such as a circus is no longer considered an important event. Indeed, buying tickets for such attractions is now often a matter of duty rather than a recreation ritual, since charities often sponsor them to raise money.

The shows themselves have also changed. Some major circuses, for instance, still go on tour but perform only in indoor arenas in cities large enough to guarantee full houses for extended periods of time. Ringling Bros. and Barnum & Bailey Circus, long billed as "the greatest show on earth," spends

two months in New York City's huge Madison Square Garden while on tour. Unfortunately, the sheer size of the crowds and the lack of audience contact remove much of the original magic of the circus. Nevertheless, it is one of the most popular of the remaining traveling shows, playing to 7 million people at the 1000 performances presented annually by its two units in 80 American cities. Many of the 18 American circuses that still perform in tents, on the other hand, have become little more than shabby carnivals. However, there are a few noteworthy exceptions that serve as vivid reminders of the time when the annual visit of the traveling circus was the high point of many children's summers.

There are a number of other types of traveling shows that continue to provide high levels of excitement for the people who are attracted to them. Ice-skating extravaganzas star some of the world's finest skaters and feature elaborate sets and costumes; these continue to appeal to a wide range of people. Carnivals still travel from town to town, but many are little more than collections of children's rides. They are often hired by shopping centers and used as promotional events to encourage family visits. Rodeos are staged regularly or occasionally at a variety of indoor and outdoor locations throughout the country and attract both local residents and tourists (Figure 17.5). Many are traveling shows in the sense that the necessary livestock and much of the equipment is often owned by entrepreneurs who organize rodeos at several locations. The major participants, however, are not paid employees but independent professionals or semiprofessionals who take part in rodeos of their choice. Commercial motocross events (motorcycle races run over an obstacle-filled figure-eight course) are organized in a similar manner, with the entrepreneur bringing in the equipment and constructing the track. Riders may be independent professionals, manufacturer-sponsored professionals, or amateurs. These races are taking place in many of the larger cities that contain suitable arenas. Automobile thrill shows are traveling shows in the full sense of the word; owners provide all the equipment as well as the drivers. Thrill shows, rodeos, and carnivals are often hired as major attractions at local and regional fairs.

TOWERS AND TOURS

Another group of entrepreneurs make scenic or historic places more accessible or enjoyable by providing views from overlooks, towers, the top floors of tall buildings, aerial tramways, airplanes, airships (blimps), or helicopters. In some cases, these viewing facilities are criticized because they are not considered environmentally compatible with the related resource.

One of the most controversial is the structure that was given the rather deceptive name of National Gettysburg Battlefield Tower. Opened in 1974, it is built on land within 450 meters (500 yards) of the site where President Lincoln delivered his short speech now known as the Gettysburg Address. Advertised as "The Classroom in the Sky," this 90-meter (300-foot) observation tower offers a panoramic view and a multilingual audiovisual interpretive program. Critics express dismay that such an obtrusive struc-

ture should spoil this historic landscape. The attitude is not shared by tens of thousands of people who pay to ascend the tower every year. Most regard it as a valuable asset because the high viewpoint and explanatory program provide a perspective and understanding of the far-flung battlefield that they cannot achieve at ground level on their own.

Entrepreneurs also take advantage of people's willingness to pay for panoramic views of urban areas. The Eiffel Tower in Paris, visited by 60 million people since its opening in 1889, was the first major commercial structure built primarily for viewing. Most famous urban commercial overlooks built subsequently have been part of tall buildings such as the Empire State Building in New York City or Sears Tower in Chicago.

Similarly, commercial interests capitalize on people's desire to see cities or scenic areas by taking guided tours through, around, or over them by bus, train, boat, helicopter, or airplane. For example, it is rare to find a large city located beside a major lake, river, or estuary that does not have at least one company providing commercial boat tours. The three-hour 56-kilometer (35-mile) Circle Line trip around New York Harbor has been called "America's favorite boat ride." Since the service began in 1945, more than 30 million passengers have taken the trip to enjoy the famous skyline from many different angles and to see the advertised "170 notable sights," including the Statue of Liberty and the United Nations complex. Some sightseeing cruise vessels are equipped with bars, restaurants, ballrooms, or theaters. Evening

cruises are often offered to provide romantic views of twinkling onshore lights, moonlit water, and shoreline silhouettes together with opportunities to dine, socialize, attend a concert, or dance under the stars.

STADIUMS AND RACETRACKS

Although the majority of America's giant stadiums, small-town arenas, and playing fields are publicly owned, there are still a considerable number of commercial developments that provide additional or, in some cases, the only available sports facility of a particular kind. Often, these are modest multipurpose structures that can be rented by local teams for practice sessions and games; leased for a variety of shows, exhibitions, and club or community events; and used by the general public at specified times if they contain such facilities as swimming pools or skating rinks. Occasionally, they are huge complexes and major suppliers of a great variety of recreation experiences.

One such complex—New York's Madison Square Garden—contains a 20,000-seat arena, an amphitheater, several restaurants, a bowling center, and an art gallery; in fact, it has enough space and facilities to accommodate seven fair-sized events simultaneously. An almost continuous series of events is scheduled in order to make a profit for the parent company, Gulf & Western Industries. These include basketball and hockey games (both the Knickerbockers and Rangers are company-owned teams), boxing and wrestling matches, tennis tournaments, horse shows and rodeos, motocross competitions, ice-skating extravaganzas, circuses, and a variety of concerts, shows, and entertainment spectaculars that attract large audiences.

An individual, group of individuals, or a corporation sometimes owns a professional sports team and also provides playing facilities built or adapted expressly for the sport. This is most common in the case of hockey and baseball clubs. Such arrangements can result in many benefits, not only for team members but also for spectators. For example, when the Dodgers baseball club was moved from Brooklyn to Los Angeles in 1958, it played in the vast saucer-like Coliseum. Because it is primarily a football facility, many baseball fans were seated so far from home plate that they had trouble seeing what actually took place.

Dissatisfied with the situation, the owners built Dodgers Stadium in 1962. Except for an annual mobile-home show and an occasional rock music concert, it is used for nothing but Dodgers games. Designed specifically for baseball, it provides the best possible view from each seat rather than accommodating the largest possible number of spectators as some of the giant stadiums tend to do. In accordance with the owners' wishes, ticket prices have been kept low to make the games accessible to as many people as possible and to permit more frequent attendance by the less affluent fans. A giant $3 million color television screen has been constructed to show replays, close-ups and highlights of other games and events. This combination of good facilities and moderate prices appears to have been highly successful for all concerned. The club has enjoyed over a decade of

seasons when there were more than 2 million paid admissions and, in 1978, they exceeded 3 million for the first time.

Of course, it is not just the facilities that make stadiums and arenas such significant recreation resources. It is the management and professional players who attract the large crowds (over 70 million a year) and involve many million more in the telecasts of the games. Most important in terms of the total hours of pleasure provided are the 28 professional teams of the National Football League, followed in descending order by the 26 teams of the National Baseball League, the 21 teams of the National Hockey League, the 24 teams of the National Basketball Association, and the 24 teams of the North American Soccer League.

Other commercial sports developments in the United States are small, single-purpose facilities. Some are built by individuals who have a personal interest in a particular sport and are motivated to provide such a facility for themselves as well as for the general public (at a fee), because no other organization has shown an interest in doing so. Many begin as shoestring operations; the people concerned pool their resources, lease or buy a property, and, as finances allow, proceed to develop it for a specific purpose, such as dirt bike racing or stock car racing. Others are elaborate developments like the Trexlertown Velodrome in Pennsylvania. Built by a wealthy publisher who wanted to encourage public interest in bicycle racing, this track is comparable in quality to the best European velodromes. Special-events races are open to the public and training programs are held there

each summer.

Some single-purpose facilities are developed strictly for profit. Frontons, buildings to accommodate the playing and viewing of the sport of jai alai, are a good example. Located throughout Florida and, to a much lesser extent, in Connecticut, Rhode Island, and Nevada, these special arenas contain large spectator facilities and the three-walled courts on which the handball-like game of jai alai is played. Since frontons feature pari-mutuel betting on the outcome of seven-point games with eight teams involved in each game, some people are attracted to jai alai events in much the same way others are drawn to horseracing.

In the United States, 4 of the 10 sports events with the greatest total number of spectators involve racing (Table 8.7). Total attendance at thoroughbred, harness, greyhound, and auto races now exceeds 150 million people a year. The recreational significance of these races is considerably greater than this figure suggests, since large numbers of people who seldom or never attend an actual race read about races in newspapers and magazines, listen to descriptions of them on the radio, watch them on television, discuss them with relatives or friends, or participate in off-track betting activities. A new type of commercial recreation facility, the wagering amphitheater, is now appearing in the United States. These developments permit people to make legal bets and then watch live telecasts from one or more of New York's five racetracks. Teletrak, the New Haven, Connecticut, facility, accommodates 1800 people in its theater and an additional 400 in the clubhouse and restaurant area.

Although some races are held at publicly owned tracks, the majority take place at privately owned facilities; this includes most of the major events that capture the imagination of the public as well as ardent racing fans. For example, the three horseraces that constitute the unofficial American championship known as the Triple Crown (the Kentucky Derby, Preakness Stakes, and Belmont Stakes) are run at private tracks—Churchill Downs, Pimlico, and Belmont Park. However, these tracks are ill equipped to handle the huge crowds that wish to attend.

For instance, of the 130,000 individuals who gain admittance to Churchill Downs to see the Kentucky Derby, only 48,000 can watch from grandstand seats. The rest, crammed into the grassy area in the center of the track are unlikely to see any of the two-minute-long race unless they climb onto someone's shoulders. Similarly, the Indianapolis Motor Speedway gives spectators the chance to be part of an event considered by many to be the ultimate sporting experience—the running of the Indianapolis 500. Since 1911, millions of fans have traveled to this privately owned racetrack to watch the world's best racing-car drivers compete for money and honor. Over 235,000 spectators can be accommodated in trackside grandstand seats. An additional 100,000 mill about the infield, seeing little of the race but, like the spectators at Churchill Downs, are apparently content to enjoy the social aspects and excitement of the occasion.

Unlike the thoroughbred tracks mentioned above, which hold many other races during the year, the only race run on the Speedway is the annual 500-mile race. However, there is a lot of prerace activity, including daily practices and time trials, which are well attended. People also visit the Speedway at other times in the year to tour the museum and hall of fame, go for a ride around the famous 4-kilometer (2.5-mile) track on one of the official tour buses, or use its golf facilities.

CAMPS, HOTELS, AND RESORTS

Another major group of recreation opportunities provided by commercial resources involves the participant staying overnight in accommodations that are connected with or close to a recreation resource. This group is particularly important to tourist industries, since people who stay overnight in a tourist region generally spend considerably more money than those who only stay a few hours. Accommodations are also significant because many resources discussed in this chapter and the next four chapters are accessible to participants living some distance away only if they are able to spend one or more nights at commercial campgrounds, motels, hotels, or resorts. In addition, of course, the overnight stay may in itself be an important part of the recreation experience.

CAMPGROUNDS AND MARINAS

Although public campgrounds are usually less expensive and are frequently located in more pleasing environments, many campers stay at commercial campgrounds. There are several reasons for this. Commercial campgrounds are often the only choice, since public campgrounds are far less numerous. Of the 1 million individual campsites available in the United States in 1978, for example, 700,000 were located in commercial campgrounds. In addition, of the nation's 15,000 campgrounds, the 3000 operated by 20 commercial campground chain organizations and many independently owned campgrounds are large-scale operations located close to the most popular tourist areas (Figure 12.7). Most of these facilities are capable of accommodating much larger numbers of campers than nearby public campgrounds. In fact, government agencies often encourage the development of large commercial campgrounds near public parks and forests because this reduces the need to build more campgrounds on valuable undeveloped landscapes.

Public campgrounds are also sparse or completely absent in or near most American and Canadian cities. Consequently, urban residential trailer parks that reserve a number of sites for transients are valuable recreation resources for trailer, truck-camper, and motor-home travelers. The situation is different in Europe. Numerous overnight campgrounds, many commercially operated, are located close to or actually within cities. In Paris, for instance, one campground is located in a residential suburb on the banks of the river Seine. Camping tourists can easily commute by train to the center of Paris in just 15 minutes.

One reason for many European campgrounds being located in urban areas is that fewer people have automobiles so that a greater proportion of campers arrive by bus or train. In addition, it is still com-

Figure 12.7 **This Kampgrounds of America camping resort includes a large adult recreation center. The KOA system consists of 850 privately owned campgrounds throughout Canada and the United States. Most have a recreation hall containing a gameroom, lounge, and snack bar and many provide opportunities for swimming, boating, fishing, hiking, bicycling, and horseback riding.**

mon for young people and families to spend their vacations at campgrounds located in their own communities if they seek camping rather than travel experiences. Western Europe has more than 10,000 campgrounds so that finding a place to camp is usually easier than in the developed portions of the United States and Canada.

Commercial campgrounds in North America often have a number of facilities or services that are considered highly desirable by many campers but which are seldom provided at public campgrounds. These include:

- Acceptance of advance reservations, thus making it possible to plan an itinerary that includes a series of popular destinations without constantly worrying about campsite availability.
- More amenities, such as electric, water, and sewer hookups; paved camping spaces; bathhouse and laun-

dromat facilities; recreation halls; and well-lit, patrolled campsite areas.
- A policy of remaining open in the off-season, thus making it possible for people to camp while enjoying such activities as snowmobiling, ice fishing, hunting, and cross-country skiing.
- Providing some campsites containing fully equipped tents or recreation vehicles so that campers traveling by air and others not wishing to bring their own equipment may still enjoy the advantages of camping. This also allows noncampers to try camping and see how they enjoy the experience before investing in equipment of their own.

Although some campers consider it a bad feature, the tendency to build campsites close together at commercial campgrounds is regarded as an asset by others. They find it creates more opportunities for becoming acquainted with other campers. In addition, the town-like setting provides a sense of familiar-

ity and security that is comforting to those who are not used to extraurban environments.

Of course, commercial campgrounds differ widely, ranging from primitive to luxurious. In Europe, campgrounds intended primarily for transients may consist of little more than a large open field and minimal washroom facilities. On the other hand, many function as destination resorts where people spend entire vacations; these may contain grocery stores, bars, restaurants, dance pavilions, recreation halls, swimming pools, and well-equipped utility buildings. Similarly, in North America, some camp resorts feature high-amenity, deluxe campsites and a variety of recreation facilities and programs. Sometimes guests have access to golf courses, tennis courts, playing fields, ski slopes, riding stables, and park-owned lake frontage with beaches, fishing piers, boat-launching ramps, and marina facilities. A wide range of rental equipment (boats, horses, bicycles, sports equipment) and instructional programs may also be available.

In both Europe and North America, there are many commercial campgrounds where owners leave their trailers on a site for the entire season or year round. In this way, they enjoy many of the advantages of a second home without some of its costs and responsibilities. They also avoid some or all of the expenses and problems of towing a trailer and storing it at or near their residence.

Commercial marina developments offer similar services for boat owners. Most provide the boater with a berth in a protected harbor and the use of a number of onshore facilities—restrooms, showers, grocery stores, and boat-maintenance facilities. Marinas enable people who do not live on property with water frontage to own and enjoy the use of larger boats. These may be kept at the marina year round. Some individuals with trailerable boats rent marina space during the boating season, thereby avoiding the inconvenience of having to transport, launch, and load their boats each time they are used. A few berths are usually reserved for overnight guests, making it possible for boat owners to use their vessels for short or extended trips. Marinas, therefore, function much like campgrounds with a greater or lesser proportion of short- or long-term users, depending on the marina's location, features, and nearby amenities. Unfortunately, the number of marinas, both public and private, is limited because suitable shoreline resources are scarce and development is costly.

HOTELS AND BOARDING HOUSES

Hotels, motels, cabins, boarding houses, and other overnight accommodations play a vital role in making recreation experiences available to people who live some distance from a resource. Lodging establishments with significant recreation resources on the same site function as primary recreation destinations and will be discussed in the next section. Others are used primarily as a place for people to stay while traveling or using recreation resources at nearby sites.

Overnight Accommodations. Hotels and motels are essential components of many recreation systems (see p. 285). They are especially important in cities that are major tourist or overnight visitor

destinations. In New York City, for example, the majority of people from other cities, states, and nations who visit the downtown attractions spend at least one night in a hotel. Even Broadway theatergoers from nearby communities often stay overnight at a hotel so that they can enjoy a leisurely evening and not have to drive home afterwards. Airlines offer short, package excursions, which include accommodations at major hotels, for people wishing to visit large cities to shop, attend the theater, or see special exhibitions, sports events, or cultural attractions.

Hotels are also crucial resources in some of the less developed nations where the majority of tourists travel by public transportation and there are few other types of accommodations. China, for instance, set a limit of 100,000 visas for visitors from abroad in 1979, although it was anxious to expand foreign tourism to earn hard currencies needed to buy vital imports. The limit was imposed because of a serious hotel-space shortage. In an effort to solve this problem quickly, the government undertook an emergency hotel-construction program in 30 cities. It involved foreign contractors and investors and included importing prefabricated two-story motels to provide interim accommodations in the six most heavily visited cities.

Motels fulfill the function of hotels in many Canadian and American cities. Some have been built in downtown locations, but many occur in suburban clusters adjacent to airports or the intersections of two or more major highways. Sometimes, clusters of hotels or motels are constructed close to major recreation attractions such as

theme parks or national parks to take advantage of the demand for rooms. Elsewhere, clusters built primarily to serve business travelers have stimulated construction of eating and drinking places, shopping centers, golf courses, and other entertainment resources that collectively form new and important recreation complexes.

Large hotels and motels are, therefore, significant components of recreation systems, both by reason of the accommodations they provide and because of the impact their construction can have on development patterns. Accommodations of this type also make it possible for certain kinds of recreation activities to take place. For example, airlines and tour businesses either limit or do not organize package tours to locations that lack adequate first-class hotel capacity. Similarly, organizations will not hold major sports events, conventions, and meetings in communities that have inadequate overnight facilities.

Smaller, less pretentious accommodations also play a vital role. Indeed, there are many situations where such establishments are more important than first-class hotels and motels. In Canada and the United States, the majority of noncampers who vacation away from home and do not stay with relatives or friends, rely on a variety of less expensive lodgings, including cabins, tourist homes, boarding houses, and budget motels and hotels. The proportion of travelers and vacationers using modest overnight facilities is even greater in Europe where discretionary incomes are lower. In Great Britain, for example, the majority of vacationers going to ocean resorts (Figure 5.5) stay in boarding houses or private homes that offer bed and breakfast. In France and some other nations on the continent, pensions—rooming houses for transients—are important tourist accommodations in cities as well as in resort areas.

Recreation Facilities. Overnight accommodations often provide on-site recreation resources. Such facilities are becoming more elaborate as competing enterprises add amenities to attract customers. For instance, North American hotels and motels have progressed from providing in-room radios to black-and-white television sets, to color television sets, to stereo equipment, and to opportunities to watch special programs and recent movies on closed-circuit television. Similarly, competition for customers has led most higher priced and many medium-priced establishments to install swimming pools and attractively furnished sun decks or patio areas.

Except in resort areas, such facilities were intended as a customer service; they were supposed to provide short periods of relaxation for transient guests, but owners did not expect them to play a major role in people's recreation environments. Now, some hotels and motels are offering such elaborate recreation facilities that they are serving a dual purpose. Besides being a source of diversion for traveling tourists and business guests, these amenities are drawing customers who stay overnight just to use them. Holiday Inns, for instance, now attract both kinds of guests to the 100 motels in their nationwide system that contain recreation complexes called Holidomes. These complexes, used annually by over 10 million people, contain multipurpose areas (for wedding receptions and parties), swimming pools, exercise machines, whirlpool or sauna facilities, snack bars, children's play areas, and facilities for a variety of activities like shuffleboard, pinball, table tennis, badminton, volleyball, and miniature golf. In some locations, people who are not overnight guests are also allowed to use these facilities on a fee basis.

Other ways in which hotels and motels function as recreation resources for guests, local residents, and tourists include:

- Renting space for parties, dances, banquets, shows, and club meetings.
- Renting rooms at reduced rates to air travelers with long daytime waits between planes and permitting them to use facilities such as television sets, indoor or outdoor swimming pools, sports facilities, saunas, bars, and restaurants.
- Constructing atrium-type lobbies containing bars, restaurants, "sidewalk" cafés, boutiques, and large open areas in which dances and a variety of special events are held to entertain guests and attract visitors; some of these lobbies are so architecturally spectacular that they are major tourist attractions.
- Providing rental equipment such as tennis rackets, golf clubs, and bicycles so that guests can participate in activities they would otherwise be unable to enjoy.

Some large hotels also contain an assortment of elaborate recreation facilities such as theaters, nightclubs, discotheques, and gambling casinos. For example, the $131-million, 26-story MGM Grand Hotel in Reno, Nevada, contains a casino that is as long as 2 football fields, a 2000-seat fronton where 12 jai alai games are played every night, a shopping mall with more than 40 stores, a huge 1800-seat nightclub, 7 restaurants, numerous bars, 2 movie theaters, a children's entertainment center, 5 indoor tennis courts, a 50-lane bowling center, and health spas for both men and women. Also on the property are a 19-hectare (46-acre) lake, 3 tennis courts, a gigantic swimming pool, and a campground with 292 spaces for casino users who wish to live in their recreation vehicles.

SELF-CONTAINED RESORTS

Some hotel, motel, villa, and cabin developments include such extensive on-site recreation resources that many guests spend most of their time enjoying the amenities and seldom leave the grounds. Few stay for only one or two days; most come for a vacation of a week or more. Such establishments are usually situated at extraurban sites that are readily accessible to appropriate market areas.

These *self-contained resorts* are of four main types. The majority feature warm-weather recreation—particularly beach and water-oriented activities, golf, horseback riding—and offer the aesthetic enjoyment of relatively unspoiled environments. Some are winter resorts that focus primarily on skiing but provide a variety of other outdoor and indoor activities. Another kind stresses activities that promote health and beauty. A fourth group concentrates on providing rigorous sports instruction and practice opportunities.

Warm-Weather Resorts. Like campgrounds, warm-weather resorts range from primitive to luxurious. A good example of a primitive resort is Maho Bay Camp in the Virgin Islands. Situated on a heavily wooded hillside overlooking a secluded beach, the facilities consist of 14 tent-cottages, a small office-commissary, and a communal bathhouse and toilets. The various amenities are connected by wooden steps and walkways. Bedding and towels are provided and the tents contain basic utensils, propane stoves, iceboxes, tables, chairs, sofas, and beds. There is no piped hot water and even the use of the cold-water showers has to be restricted to conserve the only water supply, rain.

There are no restaurants, bars, recreation halls, or owner-initiated activity programs at Maho Bay Camp. Some equipment is available for the guests' use, including a net that is sometimes erected on the beach for impromptu volleyball games. In spite of an apparent lack of amenities, this resort is very popular. It is appreciated by people who seek a temporary hideaway in which to unwind, loaf, read, sun, swim, scuba dive, go for walks, and enjoy some magnificent scenery.

At the other end of the spectrum is the Mauna Kea Beach Hotel. This lavishly landscaped resort is located on a sheltered cove containing one of Hawaii's most beautiful white-sand beaches. Besides the luxury 310-room hotel with its gourmet restaurants, gift shops, nightclubs, discotheques, and ballrooms, the resort provides an outdoor swimming pool, nine all-weather tennis courts, and a fine 18-hole golf course. Guests have access to stables and miles of horse trails at nearby Parker Ranch. Special activities and organized programs abound, including lawn games, snorkeling, scuba diving, sailing, deep-sea fishing, catamaran cruises, and a well-organized chil-

dren's day camp. Instruction in golf, tennis, and scuba diving as well as guided hunting trips for upland game birds, bighorn sheep, and wild boar are also available. This resort is also very popular. It is enjoyed by people who seek outstanding social and physically active outdoor experiences.

Ski Resorts. Another kind of self-contained resort that is highly dependent on the nature and extent of undeveloped resources is the winter-sports facility. Such resorts are particularly challenging to develop and operate because of the complex relationships that exist between resources and users and the critical roles played by weather conditions and transportation systems. Many North American winter-sports resorts not only have a maximum season of 135 days but may only be used to capacity on weekends and holidays. In addition, a relatively small proportion of the world's population ski so that resorts depend heavily on repeat customers. Even in the United States, there are less than 11 million people who ski regularly, despite high discretionary incomes, extensive advertising, and the heavy promotion of downhill skiing as a socially desirable activity.

Nevertheless, there are over 1300 American ski developments located in 41 states, ranging from small ski hills in metropolitan areas to self-contained alpine winter sports towns with ski runs on several mountains. Of these centers, about 50 are regarded as world-renowned major resorts; all of these, as well as most smaller resorts, are situated in one of four principal skiing regions commonly referred to as the East, Midwest,

Rockies, and Far West. As Table 12.1 shows, these regions are distinctive and offer a great variety of skiing conditions and recreation opportunities.

Many ski resorts in the eastern half of the United States own all of the land used by their guests for downhill as well as for cross-country skiing. Western resorts, however, generally own just the land on which their ski villages are built and lease the surrounding slopes for ski runs and trails from state or federal agencies. Most major resorts are located in hilly or mountainous areas that provide excellent skiing opportunities; yet extensive terrain alterations are often necessary to produce safe, attractive runs. In a few cases, artificial hills have been constructed making it possible to develop a ski resort in an area devoid of suitable topography.

At Scotsland Resort in Wisconsin, for example, a hill was formed on flat terrain with materials excavated during the construction of a hotel and artificial lake. Although it is one of the smallest ski-resort hills in the Midwest, it is heavily used for several reasons. Since it was designed specifically for skiing, it includes a steep headwall at the top, which challenges experienced skiers. Further down, there are two open bowls that are well suited to intermediate skiers. Long, gentle runs that are just right for beginners lie at the bottom. In addition, an underground drainage system permits melted water to drain away rapidly under the snow. This prevents the slopes from becoming slushy and retards melting during thaws. An extensive snow-making system, two double chairlifts, two rope tows, and lighting for night skiing increase the resort's capacity.

Table 12.1 Characteristics of U.S. Ski Regions

Characteristics	The East	The Midwest	The Rocky Mountains	The Far West
Range	Northern Georgia and western North Carolina to Maine.	Michigan, Wisconsin, Minnesota, parts of Illinois, Ohio, and Indiana.	Mountain areas of New Mexico, Colorado, Utah, Idaho, and Montana.	Pacific coast mountain areas of California, Oregon, Washington, Alaska.
Elevation (above sea level)	Modest; 460–1400 meters (1500–4500 feet).	Minor; glacier-produced hills reach 490 meters (1600 feet) at most.	High; between 1500–3300 meters (5000–11,000 feet); some resorts at 2400 meters (8000 feet).	Similar to Rocky Mountains region.
Skiing opportunities	Enormous variety; some of the most interesting and stimulating skiing; most trails are carved through forests and are narrower than elsewhere; good cross-country skiing opportunities.	Less variety; ideal learner and intermediate slopes; runs are often cut through woods; lacks rugged terrain; drops of 60–180 meters (200–600 feet) at most; excellent slalom course and ski jump facilities; competitions numerous; exceptional cross-country skiing.	Best skiing for expert skiers; some runs are through forest; many open slopes are 300 feet or more in width; satisfying long runs; greatest vertical drop in United States; status-skiing opportunities; some gentle slopes permit use by less than expert skiers.	Exceptional bowl and panoramic skiing; excellent opportunities for learners as well as experts; sheer scale of High Sierra skiing unsurpassed; some ski areas are close to urban centers in Northwest.
Major resort areas	Intensive development along mountainous spine of Vermont; most challenging areas are in New Hampshire; one big mountain area (Whiteface) is in New York along with 100 smaller areas; Sugar-Loaf area in Maine is well known and impressive; several popular resorts in Pennsylvania.	Clusters of centers ideal for learners around Detroit, Chicago, Milwaukee, Minneapolis-St. Paul metropolitan areas; chain of resorts bordering Great Lakes from Lusten, Minnesota, across Wisconsin to Boyne City, Michigan; Boyne Country ski development is leader in Midwest—first in world to install a quadruple chairlift.	Contains nation's most prestigious resorts (Colorado in particular); even small resorts match largest resorts elsewhere in skiable area but not necessarily in facilities; subregional differences not substantial, but southern resorts have drier powder snow, whereas northern areas have greater snow depths.	Two concentrations in southern California—areas within 160 kilometers (100 miles) of Los Angeles and the High Sierra resorts of Lake Tahoe region; prime ski area in northern California is Mt. Shasta; three areas on flanks of Mount Hood near Portland, Oregon; three areas in Snoqualmie Pass near Seattle, Washington; more than 30 areas in Oregon and Washington designed primarily as day areas.
Advantages or disadvantages	Closest to heaviest concentrations of potential skiers; most areas readily accessible by car; best areas seriously overcrowded at times; many areas have distinctive atmospheres and many loyal users.	Many resorts within a 1- or 2-hour drive of large urban centers; midwestern skiers known for their enthusiasm and dedication; excellent ski services and instruction opportunities.	Many resorts not readily accessible; cost and altitude problems for non-Westerners; some of the most beautiful settings in the world; great diversity of winter sports and après-ski opportunities.	Access often difficult in Sierra Nevadas; evening and weekend opportunities excellent in other areas; best areas are away from usual vacation routes; same cost and altitude problems for skiers from the East; exotic settings available on highest slopes.

Table 12.1 Characteristics of U.S. Ski Regions (continued)

Characteristics	The East	The Midwest	The Rocky Mountains	The Far West
Length of season	Usually 3 or 4 months; extended and made more reliable by heavy use of snow-making equipment; occasional mild winter can be disastrous, especially in the South.	Similar to the East but colder temperatures an asset; adequate skiing almost a certainty throughout season where snow-making equipment is used.	Longer season than East or Midwest; depends on latitude and elevation.	Longest season; year-round skiing possible in some high northern locations.
Skiing conditions	Winds occasionally strong.	Often extremely cold temperatures, sometimes accompanied by strong winds.	Most comfortable climatic conditions; mostly skiing below timberline, which provides wind-protected trails; more sunny days than other regions.	Threat of storms; risk of being snowed in.
Snow and trail conditions	Unpredictable; extreme cold periods alternate with devastating thaws; snow on trails often packed hard because of heavy use.	Heavy snowfalls supplemented by use of snow-making equipment; has most uniform conditions of all regions.	Large quantities of snow in average season; dry-air conditions produce snow that rarely packs into hard snow or ice; best consistency in world—better even than in European Alps; danger of avalanches; problems with whiteouts and flat light.	Heavy snowfalls—often too much; reaches depths of 5 meters (15 feet) in Sierra Nevadas in average season; snow very persistent—comes early and stays late; unfortunately often damp, sometimes quite wet conditions.
Examples of major resort developments.	Stowe, Vermont considered by many to be the ski capital of the East; steep, narrow trails provide challenge; 660-meter (2150-foot) vertical drop; 58 different lodge facilities.	Boyne Country, Michigan, largest privately owned ski development in United States; foremost complex in the Midwest; best racing slopes in region; 190-meter (625-foot) vertical drop; can accommodate 1500 people in deluxe lodge, inn, and villa facilities.	Aspen, Colorado, considered by many to be the ski capital of the world; includes 4 huge mountain slopes; one just for beginners; 1160-meter (3800-foot) vertical drop; 95 places to stay, providing 1608 rooms and 1469 condominium facilities.	Heavenly Valley, California-Nevada border, largest ski area in the world; 5200 hectares (20 square miles) of lift-served terrain; 1100–1200-meter (3600–4000-foot) vertical drop; 24 places to stay.

An adequate quantity of good quality natural snow for a reasonable length of time each season has generally been regarded as essential for a ski resort to be successful. The recent development and installation of expensive snow-making systems, however, has, to a large extent, overcome possible deficiencies in both snow quantity and quality. Snow-making equipment was first used extensively in the East and Midwest regions as a means of improving snow conditions, providing skiing during midwinter thaws, and extending the length of the season.

Prompted by an economically disastrous season of severe drought, many western resorts have also invested in snow-making machines to ensure an adequate depth of snow on the main slopes and to keep the most heavily used trails in good condition.

In an effort to attract cross-country skiers[2] as well as provide additional recreation opportunities for the downhill skiers, many resorts have added extensive cross-country trails. There are now close to 900 American resorts with ski-touring facilities. Some resorts are intended exclusively for cross-country skiers. Amenities usually include equipment rentals, instruction programs, guided tours and outings, and a network of training areas and trails that are carefully laid out, regularly patrolled, and groomed with a machine that leaves straight, parallel tracks in the snow. The Trapp Family Lodge in Vermont maintains a staff of 12 instructors and 120 kilometers (75 miles) of groomed trails. It also provides a swimming pool, restaurant, bar, television, and fireplace-lounge at a 60-room inn.

The Telemark Lodge, a multimillion dollar, year-round resort in Wisconsin, successfully combines the two sports. Each season it accommodates 70,000 downhill and 15,000 cross-country skiers. It has 93 kilometers (60 miles) of trails and hopes eventually to gain recognition as the world's leading cross-country ski resort (Figure 12.8). In pursuit of this goal, the management is conducting extensive programs including a full-term school for high school and college students. Telemark also hosts the American Birkebeiner mass citizens' race that is held on a specially designed 55-kilometer (34.2 mile) course. It attracted over 4000 skier-participants in 1980.

To lure the maximum number of users—both skiers and nonskiers

[2] Although many of the 7 million cross-country skiers are also downhill skiers, the majority have either abandoned or have never tried the sport of downhill skiing.

Figure 12.8 Telemark in northwestern Wisconsin, began as a downhill skiing facility. A 115-meter (370-foot) glacial moraine (1) has been extensively developed to provide skiing opportunities for novice and intermediate skiers on 10 different slopes. A $6 million lodge (2) provides overnight accommodations and a variety of après-ski facilities including indoor and outdoor swimming pools, a skating rink, a theater, and a nightclub featuring big-name entertainment. An airstrip (3) makes the remote area more accessible. More recently, Telemark has become a well-patronized cross-country ski center; carefully designed machine-groomed trails take advantage of the surrounding area's undulating terrain with its attractive combinations of woodland, lakes, rivers, and marshes.

—commercial ski resorts supply a variety of services, facilities, and programs. These include:

- Lighted slopes and trails (especially at resorts close to metropolitan areas) to extend the skiing day and accommodate after-work skiers.
- Reasonably priced equipment rentals and ski schools with ample beginners' slopes to attract new participants.
- Rope tows, chairlifts, gondolas, and trams to transport skiers rapidly and effortlessly to the skiing areas.
- Snow-cat or helicopter transportation and guide services to make skiing in back-country areas feasible.
- Ice-skating rinks, toboggan runs, sleigh rides and heated swimming pools to provide other outdoor activities and attract nonskiers.
- Indoor swimming pools and tennis courts to attract nonskiers and please the skiers, most of whom swim and about 65 percent of whom play tennis.
- Apres-ski programs, including movies, live entertainment, and parties involving the use of resort-provided lounges, gamerooms, discotheques, restaurants, bars, and nightclubs.

Most resorts also provide children's nurseries and ski lessons to encourage continued attendance by skiers after they become parents.

Such services and facilities are not unique to North American ski resorts. In fact, at many of the 16 major ski resorts in the alpine regions of Austria, France, Germany, Italy, and Switzerland, a greater proportion of development money has been spent on hiring highly professional resort personnel, constructing more and bigger lifts, developing superior ski schools and children's nurseries, and providing luxurious accommodations with ample facilities for nonski activities, such as swimming, skating, playing tennis, horseback riding, promen-

ading, and terrace sitting. This was possible because less money had to be used to improve slopes, cut trails, build access roads, and install essential services.

For the same reason, sophisticated après-ski programs involving first-rate entertainment, fine cuisine, and glamorous special events are more economically feasible at most European ski resorts. Consequently, many are not just excellent sports facilities, they also function as deluxe social centers, especially for the affluent. It is estimated, for example, that less than 50 percent of the winter guests at Cortina d'Ampezzo—one of Italy's most prestigious winter resorts—ever ski. Skiing may be the excuse but not necessarily the reason for going there. Many vacation at Cortina primarily to see friends; to entertain guests in an exotic environment of exclusive shops, restaurants, hotels, nightclubs, and discotheques; or to be seen by others and recognized as one of "the beautiful people." The glittering social atmosphere of Cortina and other major resorts in the Alps is unequalled anywhere else in the world.

Spas and Beauty Resorts.
Although visiting a hot springs resort is not now considered by many North Americans to have the same recreational potential as a ski vacation or a relaxing cruise, it is still a viable choice. In fact, a spa is one of the few recreation resources that gives individuals an opportunity to spend free time exclusively on themselves. All kinds of people— men and women, young and old, stout and slim, married and single, sick and well—go to spas and most come away revitalized. No other recreation facilities can produce the

same kinds of beneficial results.

European spas have always emphasized health or more precisely, the *Kur.* This word does not literally mean a cure, although individuals often take treatments for specific ailments and receive considerable relief. Rather, the word describes the total relaxation and renewal of vitality that can take place in spa environments; these results are considered as beneficial as any changes that might occur in a guest's physical condition. Water therapy always plays an important role. The mineral-rich waters are taken internally and are administered externally in the form of mud baths, thermal tubs, and hydromassages.

Many European spas are very old, having been in more or less continuous use since the Romans first developed them 2000 years ago. The construction of modern spa facilities and elegant hotels, however, have converted many of them into luxury resorts. The usual stay is three weeks, with some affluent people returning to the same resort several times a year. Weekend visitors seeking a respite from their hectic lives are also numerous.

Typical of such resorts is Bad Pyrmont in West Germany. The large Kurhotel-Kurhaus contains a casino, a diet kitchen to supplement haute cuisine in the grand dining room, and a block-long café facing a 80-hectare (200-acre) park. Six tennis courts in the park and a nearby nine-hole golf course are available to hotel guests. Hiking trails and jogging paths wind through the park and into the surrounding forest. Concerts are held three times a day in the park or in the concert hall and theatrical shows are presented each evening.

Around the park are modern bath-houses where guests drink or bathe in the spring waters. A huge enclosed, heated wave pool is used for recreation, supervised exercise, and therapy. At the gymnasium, guests can exercise under the guidance of an instructor or participate in group activities.

In the Soviet Union, spas and sanitariums are so highly regarded as vacation destinations that every factory and collective farm provides access to one as part of the workers' benefits. Some units build their own facilities; others are constructed and operated by the state. These establishments are a combination of hospital and resort hotel where specially trained doctors and nurses oversee each carefully regulated day. Rest, good food, and medical care are provided along with opportunities for a wide variety of recreation experiences. Over 2345 sanitariums containing 510,000 beds in hotel-like rooms are presently available. Many are located on the ocean or in mountain areas and are not associated with hot springs.

The spa concept in North America is entirely different. Many Americans regard European spa treatments as disagreeable; they find the waters to be too hot, too salty, and generally distasteful, and most dislike the odor produced by springs containing sulphur. In addition, some American physicians challenge the effectiveness of mineral-water therapy. As a result, modern American spas emphasize beauty treatments. Daily facials, massages, manicures, and pedicures are provided in opulent surroundings that pamper and soothe. More recently, American spas have begun to stress fitness, promoting themselves as health and beauty resorts.

The most recent trend in American spas is the resort-spa, an enterprise that offers a combination of health and recreation opportunities. An example is La Costa Spa Resort Hotel and Country Club that sprawls over 2800 hectares (7000 acres) of hilly terrain near San Diego, California. The facilities include tennis courts, golf courses, gourmet restaurants, and bars. The atmosphere is amiable and casual with the responsibility for adherence to a recommended personalized diet and activity schedule resting entirely on the individual.

Sports Resorts. Resorts that provide sports instruction and practice facilities are a growing part of the resort industry, especially in the United States. Tennis and golf are the sports primarily involved. Some resorts are expanding their programs to include a second or even third sport without adversely affecting the quality of their original area of specialization. Most have a number of auxiliary recreation facilities and programs. These provide a change of activity for the sports enthusiast and enable spouses and other family members who are not interested in the featured sport to share in a sports-resort vacation.

North Carolina's Pinehurst Country Club is an example of a sports resort. Pinehurst was originally a golfing resort highly regarded for its six courses—especially the "Number 2" course, which rates as one of the world's finest courses. Guests usually played several rounds of golf a day and watched instructional golfing films in the evenings. Today, however, Pinehurst is almost as well known for its 20-court tennis club and instructional program or its extensive horseback riding facilities. The latter include 320 kilometers (200 miles) of trails winding through the 3900-hectare (9700-acre) property. Most Pinehurst guests still go for a quality golfing experience, but growing numbers are tennis or riding enthusiasts. Some guests participate in all three sports. It is not unusual, however, for guests to take part in none of these activities. The presence of a health club and spa, trap- and skeet-shooting facilities, an Olympic-size outdoor swimming pool, and a lake for boating is tending to turn Pinehurst into a self-contained resort with activities to suit every taste.

Club Mediterranee. For people seeking respite from their everyday problems and desiring ample opportunities for social interaction, Club Mediterranee resorts have special appeal. Starting in 1950 as a group of people wishing to go on organized tenting holidays, this 1-million member organization now operates 82 resort villages in 29 nations. Today, its resorts provide comfortable indoor accommodations for over 600,000 guests a year, but the emphasis is still on group activity and sports.

Most Club Mediterranee resorts are ocean-beach-oriented developments in locations with Mediterranean or tropical wet climates. However, to provide opportunities for downhill and cross-country skiing, 20 villages have been built in alpine areas during the last few years. The first Club complex in the United States is a year-round resort presently being constructed on a site at the base of Copper Mountain in Colorado. It will accommodate 450 people and feature skiing, tennis, a discotheque, and a theater.

To ensure as carefree a vacation as possible, distractions are intentionally eliminated at Club Mediterranee. There are no radios, television sets, telephones, or newspapers. Most of the costs are covered in the weekly rate so that money is largely unnecessary. Dress is casual and the lifestyle is communal, with guests sharing rooms and dining family-style at tables seating eight. Although the program is informal, guests are enthusiastically encouraged to socialize and take part in a busy schedule of sports, games, outings, evening entertainments, parties, and dances. Those who do not crave physical activity are also made welcome. Instruction is available in many activities, such as crafts, photography, bridge, and backgammon, and the library is well stocked with books for quiet reading. A music room is used for the presentation of daily concerts and is always open for the use of guests.

To encourage interaction among guests, the resorts are completely self-contained and usually located in isolated places. Consequently, guests spend nearly all of their time in each other's company on Club property, leaving only as a group for occasional excursions. Each resort has a distinctive appearance, constructed (at least superficially) as a reflection of the local culture. This allows guests to enjoy what they perceive as an exotic environment although, in reality, experiences are carefully planned and controlled to make sure no one feels uncomfortable or out of place.

Although promoted primarily as a mecca for young, active, single adults, Club Mediterranee vacations are also enjoyed by married couples and older individuals. Attitude rather than age determines whether or not a person enjoys the Club Mediterranee experience. Several dual-purpose resorts have recently been developed to attract families; they contain special mini-club facilities for the children who, separated by age and capabilities, attend their own day-long programs of sports, nature study, excursions, and crafts classes. The largest group of guests (47 percent) is still from France, but participants come from many other countries, including Canada and the United States (17 percent). Americans and Canadians go to Clubs in the Western Hemisphere primarily, where they comprise 80 percent of the patrons.

Locations and Seasons.
Until recently, many resorts operated on a seasonal basis. Warm-weather resorts in locations with cool or cold winters only operated during the brief summer period. In locations, such as Florida, resorts of this type offered full services in the traditional winter season but operated on a limited basis or closed completely during the rest of the year. Ski resorts usually closed as soon as spring thaws seriously affected the snow and did not open again until sufficient snow accumulated at the beginning of the following winter. Now, changing participation patterns and technology together with economic pressures are often making it feasible or desirable for resorts to stay open longer or year round.

Such changes have been made possible partly by changes in participation patterns. A much smaller proportion of resort users adhere to the traditional social seasons. More are single or couples without children who, therefore, do not need to comply with school schedules. An increasing proportion are retired people without any pressing time commitments. Finally, improved air transportation together with increased automobile ownership and better highway systems have made many resorts more accessible to larger numbers of people, especially those with more modest incomes or less free time. Consequently, resort customers are coming from a broader spectrum of society than ever before.

Because of these and other factors, many resorts are changing their operational patterns. Air-conditioning of resort rooms, restaurants, bars, stores, movie theaters, and cars has helped make it possible for resorts in tropical wet climates to attract visitors during the hot, humid summer months. Reduced rates and vigorous advertising campaigns have also assisted. In Florida, the opening and year-round promotion of Walt Disney World and other attractions have been major influences. A number of warm-weather resorts in locations with cold winters have developed winter-sports programs so that they can operate for several months in the winter as well as three months in the summer. Some with suitable topography but marginal climatic conditions have managed to become downhill skiing resorts by installing extensive snow-making equipment. Others with adequate climate but no suitable slopes have attracted winter visitors by providing opportunities for cross-country skiing, skating, or snowmobiling.

Similarly, many ski resorts are now year-round operations. This has been achieved by adding or expanding warm-weather facilities, including golf courses, racket sports courts, playing fields, swimming pools, and riding stables. Snowless bobsled-type alpine slides or monorail-type mountain coasters have been installed on the slopes of 40 winter resorts in the United States and Canada to encourage summertime use of the chairlift facilities. These slides and coasters have proved most effective, attracting 3 million users a year. A few ski resorts, like Steamboat Springs, Colorado, have initiated grass-skiing programs. Many have developed distinctive warm-weather programs. For instance, at Montana's Big Sky Resort, the emphasis is on outdoor activities (backpacking, horseback riding, fishing, river rafting) and, at Vermont's Killington Resort, a number of wilderness instructional programs (mountaineering, canoeing, backpacking) are featured.

Many resorts and hotels within one or two hours of metropolitan areas have improved occupancy rates substantially by promoting their establishments as *getaway resorts.* These enterprises tend to be smaller resorts without a major attraction, such as an extensive beach area, downhill skiing facilities, or good fishing opportunities. Instead, they offer a variety of facilities like skating rinks, swimming pools, sports courts, and dancefloors along with a well-organized series of programs that include movies, card games, lectures, workshops, parties, and different live shows every night. Such amenities can be very attractive to people wishing to break away from the pressures or boredom of daily routines for short periods of time.

The busiest period for getaway resorts is usually the weekend, with guests arriving after work on Friday and departing for home early Sunday evening. However, by offering discounted rates and special programs, some establishments have also developed a steady, if smaller, midweek clientele composed primarily of older retired people. Most of the resorts try to attract repeat customers and lure new visitors by sponsoring an almost continuous series of special events, including sports clinics, winter carnivals, and themed weekends.

CRUISE SHIPS

For some, a cruise ship is the ultimate getaway resort. Once the ship leaves shore, the passengers are in relative isolation without ready access to telephones, newspapers, or incoming mail. This situation provides excellent opportunities for privacy and freedom from the responsibilities of home and work. At the same time, most of the facilities usually found at large resorts are available on board. In addition to comfortable sleeping accommodations, these may include lounges, activity rooms, restaurants, bars, nightclubs with live entertainment, discotheques, ballrooms, cinemas, libraries, gamerooms, casinos, shops, swimming pools, sun decks, bowling alleys, jogging tracks, gymnasiums, saunas, putting greens, golf and tennis practice areas, and facilities for billiards, pool, table tennis, shuffleboard, and skeet shooting (Figure 12.9). On the Cunard line's new ship, *Countess,* for instance, over 2300 square meters (25,000 square feet) have been allocated for public rooms of this type and five of the passenger decks have open-air sections, including a large protected pool and

Figure 12.9 **Passengers aboard Sitmar Cruises T.S.S. Fairwind have a wide range of recreation opportunities from which to choose on their floating resort. For many people, however, the pools and sun decks are the main attraction.**

sun deck.

Of equal importance are the organized recreation programs, social activities, and special events that provide opportunities for passengers to meet and become well acquainted. With a trend toward shorter cruises, however, there is a need to accelerate this process. Therefore, an increasing number of cruises are being organized around one special interest like bridge, photography, golf, films, gourmet cooking, classic or contemporary music, backgammon, or archaeology. Passengers assemble several times a day for informal lectures, classes, films, and live performances or demonstrations concerning the featured topic. Sharing a common interest to begin with, participants tend to strike up conversations and share experiences almost immediately, producing a congenial atmosphere and a more enjoyable vacation experience.

Ocean and coastal cruises vary greatly in length and destination. Some last only part of a day and usually focus on viewing a particular coastal region. Weekend party cruises and three-day trips to "nowhere" from metropolitan ports, such as New York, are increasing in number. Cruises lasting one or two weeks in the Caribbean, along Mexico's west coast, through the Panama Canal, or around the Mediterranean Sea draw large numbers of participants. Air-sea package arrangements under which passengers fly at reduced rates (or in some cases at no extra charge) to board cruise ships at various domestic or foreign ports make it possible for many more people with limited budgets or vacation time to enjoy cruises. Cruises lasting many weeks or several months may also be re-

turning to favor, following a period when air travel appeared to have completely eliminated long-distance voyages.

One important aspect of longer cruises is the number and kinds of ports included in the itinerary. In some cases, the visits are just a few hours in duration and passengers can only do a little sightseeing and shopping. On other cruises, ships may stay in port for one or more days while passengers enjoy such organized shore activities as playing golf, visiting historic sites, and traveling extensively—sometimes to other cities and inland areas of special interest.

Worldwide, there are currently about 140 cruise ships in service, 75 of which sail from U.S. ports. A high proportion of the vessels are privately owned and operated, primarily by Greek (32), Soviet (18), Italian (18), British (13), Norwegian (12), and Panamanian (11) shipping lines. Most enjoy some form of government support. Although there are still 4 American ocean-going ships that carry passengers, the last 2 regular-service cruise ships were taken out of service in 1978 when the expiration of federal subsidies made it impossible for them to compete with foreign vessels. However, United States Cruises plans to operate a one-class cruise ship accommodating 1200 passengers between Los Angeles and Hawaii starting in 1980. Very few of the present ships were built expressly for cruise ship service; most are older ocean liners that have been extensively renovated. Several vessels have been cut in half and fitted with new midsections to increase capacity. Some cargo vessels have been transformed into cruise ships by adding new decks to in-

crease the public space and by completely refurbishing their interiors. This may be changing however. The high passenger volume during the last few years (over 1 million people annually have been taking cruises from North American ports alone and most cruises have been sold out six months in advance) has encouraged five cruise companies to begin construction on new vessels despite building costs of over $100 million. These ships are expected to enter service in late 1981 or early 1982.

Although more and more cargo-carrying shipping lines are terminating passenger services, some 275 American and 100 foreign cargo vessels sailing out of U.S. ports still accept passengers, as do many of the vessels operating from foreign ports. Trips vary from 12 days to 7 months in length and are especially attractive to retired people with more time to spend or to travelers who are seeking realistic seagoing experiences. Few of the recreation facilities commonly found on cruise ships are available, but there are advantages. These include opportunities to rest and relax, explore ports of call on one's own, and get to know the crew and understand the way a ship operates.

In contrast to the lack of new ocean-going cruise ships, many inland waterway passenger ships have been built recently. This is particularly true in Europe where the main rivers and canal systems are used extensively for both day excursions and overnight cruises. Boats used on inland waterways are smaller and contain few recreation facilities compared to their ocean-going counterparts, but some still provide the same kind of leisurely getaway experience. Most river cruises stop frequently to allow passengers to disembark for sightseeing activities. The boats also tie up each evening to provide a quiet night's rest and avoid passing interesting scenery in the dark.

Barges that transport passengers along the canals of France and England are even plainer and smaller than the riverboats. Few facilities on these barges have been specifically designed for recreation, but the small dining room usually serves as lounge, gameroom, and bar, and an outdoor area is used as a sun deck. The latter is the most important feature of these boats; passengers spend most of their time there lounging in deck chairs while they watch the passing boats and changing countryside. Sometimes, bicycles are carried on board or one member of the crew accompanies the barge in a motor vehicle so that transportation is always available for side trips to shops, historic sites, or other places of interest.

Similar experiences are provided by American passenger vessels on the Erie Canal waterway in the northeastern United States, on the Great Lakes and the St. Lawrence River, and aboard two sternwheelers on the Mississippi River. One of these—the *Mississippi Queen*—is a modern, $24-million vessel built in the shape of a nineteenth-century paddlewheeler but containing a swimming pool, movie theater, sauna, and gymnasium. The other—the *Delta Queen*—lacks such amenities but offers a unique opportunity to enjoy a trip aboard a carefully preserved sternwheeler.

OTHER MOBILE RESOURCES

Several other kinds of mobile resources are being used as traveling bases from which to enjoy interesting recreation experiences. Since they are not as self-contained as cruise ships, most rely heavily on the surrounding environment to provide the necessary opportunities and services. However, unlike conventional tours where seeing several specific destinations is the primary goal, the emphasis is on experiences that are an integral part of the travel phase.

One of the best examples of this kind of mobile resource is the river raft—a rubberized, nylon craft constructed of individually inflated chambers so that it is virtually unsinkable and almost untippable. Built in various sizes to accommodate from a few to as many as 15 persons, these rafts are used to transport passengers down scenic waterways. Most of these boats are oar-powered but some of the larger ones have stern-mounted outboard motors that function as rudders in rapids and propel the craft through slow-moving stretches. During expeditions that last anywhere from a day to two weeks, the passengers camp out along the river. The outfitters supply most of the equipment and food and provide professional guides who know the area intimately and are prepared to handle emergencies. The guides describe the history and geology of the river and often do all of the work, including the preparation of meals and the frequent loading and unloading of the rafts. On participatory trips, however, the passengers are expected to do their share of the work and are encouraged to learn how to control the craft in both still and white water.

Such trips are available in many countries, including Australia, Canada, Chile, Ethiopia, New Guinea, New Zealand, Norway, Peru, Sweden, Turkey, and Yugoslavia. In the United States, many rivers are suitable for commercial river-rafting expeditions. Western rivers are used most often, however, because of the availability of long stretches of navigable waterways, challenging rapids, and an abundance of wildlife and spectacular scenery. These rivers include the American, Stanislaus, and Tuolumne in California; the Rogue, Selway, Snake, and Salmon in the Northwest; and, the Green, Yampa, and Colorado in Colorado, Utah, and Arizona. By far the most popular is the 320-kilometer (200-mile) section of the Colorado River that runs through the Grand Canyon. Twenty-two commercial outfitters presently offer Grand Canyon river expeditions that take from five days to two weeks to complete. Use of this waterway became so intense by the middle 1970s that it was necessary to limit its use.

Not all mobile resources are water dependent. Several outfitters in Kansas, the Oklahoma Panhandle, and Wyoming take tourists on horse-drawn covered wagon tours that simulate the experiences of pioneer families as they migrated westward in the late 1800s. Passengers spend several days traveling along rough trails, some of which still show signs of the ruts made by the migrant's wagons. They relive the experiences of the pioneers by eating similar food, helping with the chores, sleeping in the wagons or in the open, and hearing anecdotes about the earlier journeys.

In contrast, entrepreneurs in

France are offering two-week, deluxe hot-air balloon vacations. These combine the thrill of seeing countryside selected for its natural beauty and cultural interest from professionally piloted hot-air balloons with the pleasures of meals at gourmet restaurants and accommodations at prestigious hotels.

Railroad operators, like shipping line owners, are also beginning to recognize the full recreational potential of their systems. Trains are being converted into attractive recreation resources by adding special facilities and programs. The Trans-Canada Show Train is one such venture. During the 10-day trip, passengers enjoy the use of a gameroom and library and attend live performances in a specially equipped theater car. At overnight stops, passengers stay in first-class hotels and see a variety of plays, ballet performances, and concerts at local theaters. As in the case of vacation cruises, the trip is an end in itself; participants spend little time in Vancouver, the destination city, since most of them fly back to Toronto, the departure point, just a few hours after arrival.

FARMS AND ESTATES

Very different types of experiences are provided by the various kinds of farms, ranches, and rural estates that are used as commercial recreation resources. In most cases, the owners entertain paying guests in order to supplement their income rather than provide their principal means of support. Their guests enjoy observing agricultural activities, exploring the unfamiliar environment, or participating in the establishment's social events.

Farms. Throughout much of the world, rural property owners play host to paying guests. The farms may be large or small, suburban or remote, mechanized or hand operated, rustic or contemporary. The United States alone has more than 500 vacation farms; most are concentrated in New York and Pennsylvania. There are more in Europe; England alone has 1000 farms that take paying guests and Ireland and Denmark each have 250.

Some farms accept only a few visitors at a time and provide no special facilities or programs. Instead, the guests are given whatever accommodations and meals are normally available and are treated as friends or relatives. Sleeping quarters may be spacious and well appointed or spartan and dormitory-like. There is a fixed menu and meals are usually plain but wholesome farm cooking. Because the farms are active profit-making concerns, those who wish can usually take part in at least some farm operations.

Apart from occasional trips into town, guests are left to their own devices during the day. They are encouraged to use nearby resources for activities, such as swimming, boating, fishing, hunting, horseback riding, cross-country skiing, specimen-collecting, or nature study. Visitors are informed of recreation opportunities in the surrounding area but will not be taken to them unless going to such events or destinations is part of the household's normal routine. However, many guests sightsee on their own by foot, by bicycle, by public transportation, or by using their own automobiles. Others prefer to rest and relax in the pleasant surroundings of the farmhouse sitting room, veranda, or yard.

Evenings and Sundays are usually more organized. Hosts may initiate group activities such as hayrides, outdoor picnics and barbecues, singalongs, or games of chess, checkers, and cards during their own free time. Guests may also be invited to attend family parties, community dances, and church services, or accompany the hosts on visits to neighbors' homes, local markets, fairs, auctions, shops, pubs, or bars.

Ranches. Some livestock ranches that take paying guests operate in a similar manner to the vacation farms. The majority, however, have replaced such informality with organized programs which involve specially constructed facilities and additional staff as well as the regular ranch resources.

For example, each of the more than 100 ranches that make up the Authentic Western Ranches Accepting Guests organization continues normal ranching activities so that visitors obtain an accurate impression of life on a working cattle ranch. Guests are housed in separate cabins or rustic lodges, but they share family-style meals and may take part in cattle drives, branding sessions, and routine chores such as mending fences or milking cows. They are also encouraged to participate in a wide range of recreation activities. Fishing and swimming can often be enjoyed in the ranch's lakes and streams. Salt licks are placed so that deer or elk attracted to them are in full view of the guest cabins. Planned activities include rodeos, square dances, horseback riding instruction, all-day rides, packhorse and jeep trips, chuckwagon dinners, guided fishing trips, scenic automobile excursions, and big-game hunting expeditions.

Guest ranches, on the other hand, are no longer working establishments and provide little true cattle ranch atmosphere. Most are primarily in the outfitting and guiding business, providing backcountry hunting and fishing trips. The majority offer ranch-oriented activities similar to the Authentic Western Ranches, but the meals are more elaborate, accommodations more luxurious, and many facilities not found on working ranches are usually present. These often include cocktail lounges featuring name entertainment, heated swimming pools, tennis courts, golf courses, rifle ranges, and fly-fishing ponds. Movies, organized children's programs, teen social events, and adult dances and parties are also arranged.

At least 10 states and several Canadian provinces contain ranches that accept guests, but the majority are in Colorado, Wyoming, and Montana. Most guests are families from urban centers in the eastern industrialized portions of the United States and Canada. Growing numbers are foreign tourists, especially families from West Germany and Japan.

Other Rural Enterprises.
Several other kinds of rural establishments offer recreation experiences to overnight guests. In Alabama and Georgia, for instance, some plantations specialize in providing game-bird-hunting opportunities. Comfortable lodgings, meals, guides, jeeps, and well-trained bird dogs are furnished. However, Europe has the greatest variety of opportunities. For example, in Great Britain, there are more than

500 historic homes accepting paying guests, ranging from the manses of country clergy to ornate castles. A number of titled landowners open their ancestral estates to overnight guests to produce badly needed revenue. Visitors are taken on tours of the residence and grounds, eat their meals with the owners, and often are asked to take part in social, religious, or sports events as if they were family or friends. Many castles and large estates also offer golf, swimming, fishing, hunting, and horseback riding opportunities.

NATIVE PEOPLE'S ENTERPRISES

North American Indian tribal organizations in the United States and Canada own and operate a substantial number of commercial recreation resources that include overnight accommodations. Many tribes have constructed campgrounds, trailer parks, lodges, and motels for the use of visitors and travelers. More than 300 such developments are now in operation; some are sizable resort complexes.

One of the most elaborate is the Inn of the Mountain Gods, a resort on the Mescalero Reservation in south-central New Mexico. This $15-million tribal business enterprise consists of a 134-room hotel, full convention facilities, four bars, a heated swimming pool, tennis courts, an 18-hole golf course, and an 85-hectare (210 acre) man-made lake. The latter is well stocked with trout and provides sailing and canoeing opportunities. Since the 187,000-hectare (461,000-acre) reservation is largely undeveloped wildlands and includes five ecological zones, from desert to

alpine, it is an interesting environment in which to hike, ride, and study nature. During the winter, the tribe operates the adjacent Sierra Blanca ski area. Its cable car system runs year round so that tourists can always reach the glass-walled observation tower on 3480-meter (11,400-foot) Signal Peak.

The Mescalero reservation is also used extensively for hunting elk, deer, and antelope. The tribal council reintroduced elk in 1967; the 167 animals purchased at that time have, with careful management, developed into a herd of 1500. Outsiders may purchase a variety of hunting opportunities, ranging from permits to shoot a particular kind of game to elaborate *package hunts*. The latter include several days and nights at the hotel, guide service, packing out the game, and the processing and shipment of the meat. Although the elk-hunt package costs $2000, the tribe receives hundreds of applications each year. Most cannot be accepted, however, because only 50 elk permits are issued annually to non-Indians (together with 50 for members of the tribe) to maintain the size of the herd.

Although most of the reservations are located in the western half of the nation (Figure 11.5), the largest single concentration of Indian-provided tourist facilities is found in North Carolina, home of the eastern band of Cherokees. Their facilities are well patronized by motorists traveling the north-south corridor to Florida and include 40 motels and 25 campgrounds. The tribe also has a history museum and a full-size operating village depicting Cherokee life in 1750. Two developments — Frontierland/Funland and Santa's

Land—offer many of the thrill rides and fantasy experiences typical of theme parks. During the summer months, *Unto These Hills*—a drama depicting 300 years of Cherokee history—is presented to large audiences in an outdoor amphitheater.

CAMPS AND SCHOOLS

Residential camps, clinics, and schools, operated as commercial ventures, provide a range of recreation opportunities for children. Recently, similar enterprises intended for families and adults have been increasing in number. However, the individual's perceptions and attitudes determine whether or not such experiences are recreational. This is especially true in the case of children who are sent against their wishes and may have to take part in activities they dislike—for them the camp, clinic, or school experience may be far from recreational!

Children's Camps. Each year, tens of millions of young people around the world are sent to some form of residential camp or school. Although many of these are operated by governments or quasi-public agencies, a large number of such establishments in Western Europe, Canada, the United States, and other democratic nations are private enterprises. In the United States alone, some 10 million children spend at least part of their summer vacation at one of the nation's public, quasi-public, private-organization, or commercial camps. There are four main types of camps—day, residential, special, and travel.

Few day camps are operated on a commercial basis; most are run by church, community, welfare, or youth-serving organizations. Lo-

cated in or near urban areas, the primary recreation resource is usually the land itself. The better quality camps have on-site opportunities for swimming, nature study, hiking, boating, and fishing. Essential facilities are toilets, a shelter building, and picnic tables, but day camps frequently provide a swimming pool and a sportsfield.

Commercial residential camps are common, especially in the northeastern United States. These camps vary greatly in the availability, size, and nature of both their undeveloped and developed resources. They can be large or small, primitive or highly developed, co-educational or single sex, specialized or general, and have a structured or free-form type of program. Accommodations and meals may be spartan or they can rival a good resort. Activities offered often include some or most of the following: swimming, canoeing, boating, sailing, fishing, scuba diving, waterskiing, horseback riding, hiking, rock-climbing, canoe and backpacking trips, team sports, gymnastics, golf, tennis, archery, riflery, fencing, ice skating, bowling, go-carting, and a wide range of programs in the creative arts. Children may attend sessions lasting a few weeks or the entire summer.

Special camps have similar resources and programs but are operated for children with special needs or interests or for those whose parents wish them to receive special help or instruction. Such camps usually require additional facilities and staff to provide individualized programs. Some special camps are designed to help individuals who are overweight, physically handicapped, emotionally disturbed, mentally retarded, or learning

disabled. Others feature programs for children of one particular culture, ethnic group, or religion. Many function as schools or clinics, providing intensive action-learning programs in one or more of the performing arts, lifetime activities (e.g., swimming, golf, tennis, gymnastics, horseback riding, sailing, skating), or team sports (e.g., soccer, hockey, football, basketball).

Sports-oriented camps are often conducted on private-school or small-college campuses, where appropriate athletic and dormitory facilities are available, instead of on camp-owned lands. Some of these clinics are operated by the colleges themselves, but many are private operations that pay rental fees to obtain the use of superior training facilities. Each camper usually stays only one week; consequently, these programs are the most intensive and highly specialized of all summer camp programs. Participants usually concentrate on one sport, practicing for up to five hours a day and spending most of the remaining time performing conditioning exercises, attending coaching clinics, or seeing instructional films.

Travel camps provide children with opportunities to experience new environments. Some strive to develop resourcefulness, skills, and endurance with long-distance canoe, horse, backpack, bicycle, or sailboat trips. In the United States and Canada, the majority of this travel takes place on public lands; base-camp lands and facilities, however, are frequently privately owned. At the base camps, participants acquire the skills needed for mountaineering, river-running, or wilderness survival. Most equipment is provided and the ratio between participants and leaders is small.

Other travel camps are conducted as guided tours with staff members taking small groups on cycling trips through scenic areas or by motor vehicle to places of interest at home and abroad. These "focus trips," as they are called, usually concentrate on one area of interest so that participants learn much about one aspect of natural history, art, drama, music, or a certain culture, geographic area, or religion in a short period. Participants may camp along the way; stay in hostels, hotels and motels; or be billeted in private homes.

Family and Adult Camps.
Until recently, summer camps (except those operated as religious gatherings, retreats, and programs for special populations) were mainly for young people. This is no longer the case; adults are now acquiring new skills and insights or simply enjoying a chance to relax in a variety of structured camp environments. Many camps are spartan; others resemble comfortable resorts. And, in some cases, luxury resorts function as camps. Club Mediterranee resorts, for instance, with their structured programs, casual lifestyle, and atmosphere of camaraderie operate like summer camps despite their exotic settings and elaborate sports facilities. Like children's camps, some camps for adults offer a wide choice of recreation experiences, but the majority specialize in providing one type of experience or producing one kind of result for a certain clientele. For example, there are self-improvement centers, nudist camps, swinger retreats, diet camps, senior citizen camps, yoga and fitness centers, wilderness camps, vacation schools, and sports clinics of many kinds.

Recently, many children's residential camps have started to reserve several weeks for family use. A few are now operating exclusively as family camps. These camps offer all the usual resident camp activities on a take-it-or-leave-it basis, producing a relaxed vacation experience. Campers have the choice of taking part as a family or of splitting up and participating with people who are the same age or who have similar interests. Such camps can result in satisfying, carefree vacations and strengthened interpersonal relationships for families (including single-parent ones) whose previous, more conventional vacations have proven boring or stressful.

Many summer school programs are offered by public colleges. A substantial proportion, however, are commercial operations that offer a variety of courses and many other recreation opportunities in resort-like environments. Guests stay in cottages, bunkhouses, or dormitories, attend classes in the creative or performing arts in well-equipped learning centers, and get together after classes for team sports, boating, fishing, swimming, tennis, golf, or horseback riding. In the evenings, music appreciation lectures, discussion sessions, and various social events take place. Some of these resort schools provide facilities and programs for families; others only accept adult guests.

PRODUCTS AND SERVICES

Up to now, this discussion has been limited to the kinds of recreation resources that are owned by private individuals or corporations and operated as profit-making ventures.

However, most recreation experiences depend to some extent on products and services provided by other kinds of commercial enterprises. In some cases, these enterprises produce or provide nothing but recreation goods or services; examples are sporting goods manufacturers, talent agencies, and motion picture studios. Other businesses provide goods or services that may or may not be recreational, depending on how thay are used; examples include automobile manufacturers, newspaper publishers, and airline companies. Both types are essential components of people's recreation environments.

RECREATION PRODUCTS
People can and do recreate without making use of any manufactured article. Activities like resting, sunbathing, dancing, talking, singing, making love, meditating, yoga, and playing word games are some examples. However, even if they do not require them, these experiences might be made more carefree, pleasurable, or successful by the availability of such products as hammocks, sunscreen lotions, recorded music, park benches, guitars, contraceptives, candles, instruction manuals, or paper and pencils. Even medications, which seem to have nothing to do with recreation, may be an essential part of a recreation experience for people who depend on them to control pain or to reduce the side-effects of a disease or disorder. Without them, participation in recreation activities might be completely impossible for some.

The multitude of commodities that form the support system for recreation activities cannot be readily described because they are so numerous and changeable. Every day in fact, some products are discontinued because they have outgrown their usefulness, others are improved, and new ones are introduced. Nevertheless, an indication of the significance of products can be obtained by considering the functions of manufactured commodities. The majority of them fall into one of the two basic categories.

Those goods that play a major role in recreation and are most commonly thought of as recreational form one group; these will be referred to as *primary recreation commodities.* Without such products, many recreation activities either could not take place or would be so drastically affected that many people would no longer consider them to be recreational. Examples of primary recreation commodities grouped into major categories are listed above at right.

Obviously some of these products are not essential for the experience to take place. For instance, some people spend considerable time living out-of-doors without any gear manufactured specifically for camping. For a few, the challenges involved in this kind of undertaking make participation exhilarating. For the majority, however, it would not be a recreation experience at all but an exercise in endurance and survival that should be avoided if possible.

Many other products do not play a major role but, nevertheless, are commonly used for recreation purposes; these make up the other group that will be called *secondary recreation commodities.* Were these kinds of products not available, related recreation activities or events would still be possible for

Primary Recreation Commodities

• Sports equipment	—Baseballs, skis, skateboards, fishing gear, racing car.
• Games	—Monopoly, playing cards, frisbees, pinball machines, chess sets.
• Camping gear	—Tents, trailers, sleeping bags, basic survival and housekeeping equipment.
• Printed matter	—Novels, comic books, crossword puzzle books, hobby magazines.
• Toys	—Dolls, wagons, gym sets, kites, beach pails and shovels, electric trains.
• Hobby supplies	—Model kits, stamps, cameras, film, woodworking tools, paints, flower seeds.
• Musical instruments	—Pianos, harmonicas, guitars, violins, drums, saxophones.
• Electronic entertainment equipment	—Television sets, radios, record players, record albums.
• Pets	—Tropical fish, dogs, birds
• Clothes and sportswear	—Swim suits, formal attire, some kinds of protective clothing and shoes.
• Travel accessories	—Knapsacks, suitcases, backpacks, tote bags, passports, maps.

the majority, although, for many people, they would be much less enjoyable. Such commodities tend to make activities and events better, easier, safer or more comfortable.

Examples of products that play a supportive or optional role and are therefore secondary commodities include:

The fact that these products are not absolutely necessary does not mean that they are uncommon, seldom purchased and used, or of less importance than primary products to some individuals. People are often willing to take on extra work or scrimp on basic necessities so that they can afford to buy them. Once

Secondary Recreation Commodities

• Sportswear	—Warmup suits, clothing designed specifically for skiing, jogging shoes.
• Foods and beverages	—Beer and snack foods for parties, dried foods for backpacking.
• Furniture and accommodations	—Lawn furniture, card tables, and folding chairs, an extra bedroom for overnight guests.
• Accessories	—Disposable picnic supplies, ice chests, barbecue grills, binoculars, boat motors, patios, family rooms, battery-operated fish locators, golf carts, light meters.
• Options	—*Color* television, *stereo* record-playing equipment, *padded* seating at stadiums and auditoriums, air-conditioning, *electric* tools, *pedigreed* dogs and cats, souvenirs.

purchased, such items may be much admired and used almost constantly. In fact, some of these secondary recreation commodities have become so well accepted that they are purchased and used as essentials, even though they are not.

PEOPLE

Just as there are many recreation activities that involve commercially produced commodities, so there are numerous activities that require the direct or indirect services of one or more individuals. Some of these services are commonly provided by public employees as described in Chapters 13, 14, 15, 16, and 17. An even greater variety of recreation services is provided by individuals and groups who supply recreation opportunities commercially. Frequently, how much a participant enjoys a recreation experience largely depends on the understanding and skill of these professionals. In some cases, the recreation experience consists primarily of enjoying the creative talents of such people (Figure 12.10). Without their contribution, the experience would not take place; they either create tangible recreation resources or function as recreation resources themselves.

The individuals and groups involved in providing commercial recreation services and producing recreation experiences include:

- Entertainers who brighten and enrich the lives of many people—actors, musicians, singers, dancers, writers, film makers, professional athletes, comedians, magicians, circus performers, radio deejays, and television talk-show hosts.
- The people behind the entertainers without whom the show could not go on—producers, set and costume designers, directors, joke-writers, sound-and-lighting experts, stagehands, make-up artists, television-camera technicians, coaches, grounds-keepers, and custodians.
- Creators who are responsible for designing or producing recreation resources—inventors, manufacturers, craftspersons, engineers, factory workers, architects, artists, brewers, horse breeders, highway construction workers, petroleum product refiners, chefs, and typesetters.
- Service personnel who operate, maintain, and repair recreation-oriented businesses and commodities—television and telephone repair-persons, sales personnel, ticket sellers, ushers, concession-stand workers, airline pilots, automobile mechanics, gas station attendants, hotel managers, maids, travel agents, and cruise ship personnel.
- Persons who help individuals acquire the attitudes, perceptions, knowledge, or skills necessary for participation in or full enjoyment of recreation activities—psychiatrists, scuba diving instructors, piano teachers, writers of travel guides or do-it-yourself manuals, camp or resort program directors, film critics, and product demonstrators.
- Individuals who are directly responsible for bringing resources and consumers together—talent agents, distributors, store (or hotel, theater, or sports-facility) owners, advertisers, television-station employees, entrepreneurs, and publicists.

In addition, there are people who perform an ancillary function by in-

Figure 12.10 Dolly Parton, talented singer, song-writer, and actress, performs some of her own compositions before an appreciative audience at New York's City Hall. The informal lunch-time concert occurred at the close of a welcoming ceremony during which Ms. Parton was presented the keys to the city.

directly bringing consumers and resources together. In many cases, the involvement of such persons may be incidental but, without their contribution, participation in a specific recreation activity would, for some people, be unlikely or completely impossible.

Paid babysitters, taxi drivers, bus operators, and airline pilots often fall into this category when individuals make use of their services to take part in a particular recreation activity or reach a certain recreation resource. Everyone involved in the production and distribution of newspapers, telephone books, radio programs, and magazines would also fall into this category; many people learn about upcoming recreation events, services, or products through the use of these resources. However, it is also possible for such people to perform a primary recreation function. For example, babysitters often provide recreation experiences for children under their care. Taxi drivers frequently entertain clients with their chatter and anecdotes or even turn a trip into an important recreation experience in itself by pointing out and explaining the significance of interesting sights along the way. And, the people who produce newspapers usually provide a variety of recreation opportunities such as crossword puzzles and comics along with information regarding events, services, or products.

RENTAL ARRANGEMENTS

Finally, enterprises that provide equipment or personnel on a short-term basis are playing an increasingly important role. There used to be a slight social stigma attached to renting rather than buying goods.

But inflation, coupled with a growing concern for conservation of natural resources and an increase in the number of people who want to do things for themselves or try new activities, has contributed to a positive attitude toward renting. Americans now spend $2 billion a year to rent goods including almost every type of recreation equipment.

Examples of recreation resources that can be rented from concessionaires, recreation en-

terprises, and rental firms are shown in Table 12.2. The availability of these resources can expand people's recreation environments in many ways. Persons who cannot afford or do not wish to acquire the resource can still take part in an activity occasionally. For instance, lower-income people can rent a canoe, rowboat, or small outboard-powered boat to use for an afternoon's excursion on a river or lake (Figure 8.7). Similarly, more afflu-

Table 12.2 Examples of Recreation Equipment That May be Rented

Transportation equipment	—Automobiles, motorcycles, bicycles, four-wheel-drive vehicles, pack animals, boats, aircraft, snowmobiles.
Sports equipment	—Rollerskates and ice skates, golf clubs, tennis rackets, fishing rods, scuba diving gear, waterskiing equipment, downhill or cross-country skis, hunting rifles, rowboats, cabin cruisers, riding-horses, snowmobiles.
Camping equipment	—Tents, sleeping bags, cooking gear, coolers, backpacks, camping trailers, motor homes, houseboats.
Television, movie, and music equipment	—Television sets, movie projectors, films, stereo equipment, recordings, juke boxes, pianos, other musical instruments.
Hobby equipment	—Movie and still cameras, woodworking or automotive tools, power-operated garden equipment, spray-painting equipment, sewing machines, metal detectors.
Works of art; furnishings	—Paintings, sculptures, mobiles, plants, stocked aquariums, sofas, lamps, desks, roll-away beds, cots.
Equipment for entertaining	—Chairs, tables, dishes, tablecloths, bar equipment, coat racks, canopies, striped party tents, dancefloors, disco sound systems, hot tubs, grills, rotisseries, outdoor lighting systems.
Clothing	—Formal attire, sports clothing, costumes for parties.
Equipment for amateur performances	—Sound and lighting equipment, stage properties, scenery, costumes, portable stages.
Aids for participants	—Wheelchairs, walkers, strollers, cassette tape guides, golf carts, binoculars, deck chairs, lockers, car top carriers.
Amusements	—Games, pinball machines, billiard tables, cassette tapes of novels, films, video cassettes, records, toys.

ent people can charter a fully equipped houseboat or one of the world's 10,000 live-aboard power or sailing vessels to use for a vacation cruise.

Rental equipment also enables people to sample one or a variety of activities and equipment before purchasing equipment of their own. For example, persons who are thinking of becoming tent campers can rent a complete outfit and go camping to see how much they enjoy the experience. Others try different kinds of camping equipment to find out which is most suitable for their needs. Rentals also enable vacationers and those traveling on business to participate in many recreation activities that would otherwise not be open to them. Rental cars, for example, allow people to visit out-of-the-way golf courses, parks, beaches, cultural resources, and other tourist attractions that would otherwise be inaccessible to them. Resorts, clubs, and rental companies make it possible for travelers to take part in sports activities by renting skis, golf clubs, tennis rackets, firearms, and scuba diving gear. Entrepreneurs in East Africa lease complete safari outfits, including a vehicle and camping equipment, to tourists who wish to visit the game preserves on their own.

People also function as resources that can be rented. They sell their knowledge, skills, or physical attributes to those who do not possess these attributes but need them to make participation in a recreation activity possible or more pleasurable. Frequently, people who provide services for hire are associated directly with a specific item of rental equipment. Fishing guides and charter-boat captains, for example, usually include the use of a boat with their services. For a fee, the customer obtains both the temporary use of a boat and someone who is knowledgable in its operation. This enables someone who is not familiar with a particular waterway or type of boat to take a boating or fishing trip safely. Usually, the charter-boat captain or the guide will also show the client where and how to fish successfully, turning what might otherwise be an unproductive, frustrating outing into a successful fishing experience. Other rental commodities, the value of which can be similarly enhanced by the presence of a knowledgable individual, include automobiles, four-wheel-drive vehicles, horses, scuba diving equipment, and African safari gear. The services rendered by such individuals are especially valuable for people who are nervous about using such rental items in an unfamiliar environment.

In some cases, it would be foolhardy, impossible, or against the law for inexperienced people to rent recreation commodities and undertake a particular activity alone. The services of qualified professionals are then essential rather than optional. Rental commodities that often require the services of an operator, guide or instructor include hang gliders, packhorses, aircraft, and large rubber rafts used for white-water river-running. The availability of such professionals allow people to try unfamiliar activities without undergoing prolonged instruction or take part in activities that they would not dare to undertake alone.

Another group of people sell their services for recreation purposes but neither possess rental commodities nor work for someone who does. They rent only their time and expertise and expect the customer to provide the necessary equipment or facilities. At customers' homes or other prearranged locations, these tutors, teachers, and coaches will help people learn to dance, play a musical instrument, sing, paint, sew, speak a foreign language, play chess, swim, play tennis, and so forth. Private escorts and tour guides accompany people who hire them to social events or on sightseeing excursions. Caterers and bartenders are available to prepare and serve food and drink at formal dinners, wedding receptions, or informal parties at private residences or in rented space. Another group of professionals will provide entertainment at private events. Their services range from conducting games and presenting magic shows at children's birthday celebrations to performing comedy routines, playing the piano for dances, or organizing social activities at adult parties.

HIERARCHY OF ENTERPRISES

Publicly owned recreation resources tend to be irregularly distributed because of local and regional differences in attitudes toward public involvement in recreation and the relatively random occurrence of such key resources as lakes and rivers. In fact, some local and regional governments have adopted acquisition and development programs to combat such irregularities and bring their systems closer to nationally accepted standards for the spacing and scope of recreation resources.

Commercial recreation resources, on the other hand, are generally distributed in proportion to population. This is because such enterprises must be able to attract enough customers to make a profit. Normally, only part of a population will participate in any given recreation activity. Therefore, the threshold population needed to support a particular enterprise will have to be considerably larger than the required number of customers.

The size of this population varies with the kind of commercial recreation resource. Some enterprises, such as small bars, cafés, and fast-food establishments, require relatively small threshold populations so that these resources occur quite frequently. In contrast, movie theaters, bowling alleys, and amusement parks require much larger threshold populations and, therefore, occur less often. An example is the trap- and skeet-shooting range. According to the Winchester Division of the Olin Corporation (a firm that has begun a shooting-range franchise operation) such a facility can only make a profit if it can draw from a population of at least 500,000 people. Consequently, all of the 21 centers developed to date by this company are located in large metropolitan areas; a population of 500,000 or more is required for all future franchise sites.

Of course, the threshold population needed for a specific recreation enterprise can vary depending on a number of factors. These include the capital and operational costs of the establishment, the profit level its owner is willing to accept, and the participation rate of the population concerned. Nevertheless, the various kinds of commercial recreation resources do tend to form a definite ranking, or *hierarchy,* based on population as shown in Figure 12.11.

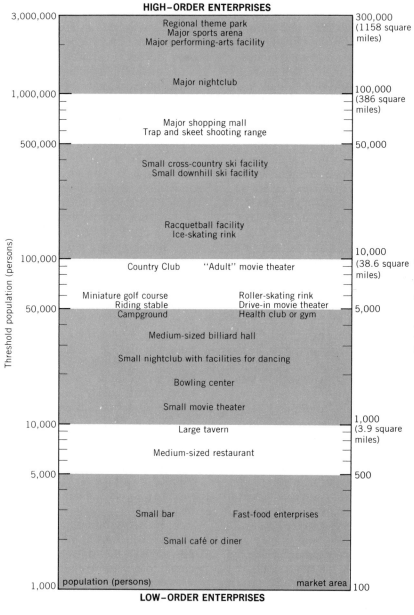

Figure 12.11 **Tentative hierarchy of commercial recreation enterprises for urban areas in the American Midwest developed from telephone directory listings.**

Hierarchical influences produce important distributional patterns. Within large cities, commercial recreation resources are spaced approximately in accordance with this hierarchy and population distribution. *A market area* from which it draws its customers lies around each establishment. Businesses with small threshold populations (*low-order enterprises*) have small market areas and form relatively dense systems. Superimposed on these systems is a series of more open networks formed by the *high-order establishments* and those that have intermediate thresholds.

In urban areas, recreation establishments are sometimes clustered together, forming a recreation-oriented enclave, such as a *restaurant district* or *theater district.* This occurs most readily where the population is highly mobile and is often encouraged by planning regulations that require the grouping of establishments with similar uses. In such cases, the clustered enterprises draw from much larger mutual or overlapping market areas. Recreation districts are powerful attractions and give cities that possess them a special allure for those who enjoy urban commercial recreation.

The fact that a commercial recreation resource requires a minimum threshold population before it can be profitable is particularly important in less densely populated areas. If a small town in a rural area does not have sufficient population to support a higher order commercial enterprise, then the residents may have to do without that type of recreation opportunity, unless it can be provided for them by a non-profit agency. It may also be unable to support more than one of the lower order establishments. Thus both the number and variety of recreation enterprises present in relatively isolated communities varies with population size.

CONTRIBUTION OF COMMERCIAL RECREATION

This chapter has demonstrated the magnitude and diversity of opportunities provided by commercial recreation resources. These opportunities are often unique so that commercial enterprises tend to complement rather than duplicate the experiences offered by publicly owned recreation resources. In many instances, commercial enterprises make it possible for ordinary people to try activities that otherwise are available only to the rich or a select few. For example, very few individuals are ever in a position to become directly involved in sports car racing; yet anyone with a driver's license and a little money can rent a small imitation Grand Prix car and experience the thrill of handling such a vehicle on one of the scaled-down racetracks built as commercial enterprises during the last few years.

Another of the commercial sector's characteristics is its ability to respond quickly to current trends. Entrepreneurs are often willing to invest considerable sums of money in constructing new kinds of facilities long before public agencies are in a position to do so. An excellent example of this is the contribution commercial recreation made to the development of skateboarding as an activity for young people. Within one three-year period, the number of skateboard parks in the United States rose from 0 to 200, and nearly all of them were built as commercial enterprises. Without the private developer, there would have been few safe, well-designed facilities for skateboarders to use.

Sometimes entrepreneurs are also willing to provide opportunities on a speculative basis. By taking risks, they give new activities the support systems and exposure they need to prove their worth and appeal. This happened in the case of the wave pool. Private developers not only introduced it into the United States but illustrated its value in comparision to the conventional swimming pool or beach. It quickly became apparent that wave-pool users stayed longer, returned oftener, and were willing to pay substantially higher admission charges than those paid at conventional pools and beaches. In addition, establishments in locations where attractive public pools and beaches were readily available proved that a high proportion of potential users preferred wave-pool facilities. The success of these commercial developments convinced several public agencies that wave pools can function not only as attractive family recreation resources but also as effective revenue producers. As a result, wave pools have now been constructed by a number of city and county park and recreation departments and at least one state park agency.

Sometimes the commercial sector experiments with ideas that lead to the development of new recreation products or facilities. It then proceeds to use its skillful marketing techniques to actually create a demand for the new resource. In this way, commercial enterprises function as important trend setters.

Of course, the appeal of many of the innovations is short lived, but some are highly successful, becoming permanent components of the recreation system. In both cases, however, they provide people with new and exciting recreation opportunities that not only encourage people to participate but also produce a heightened sense of pleasure for those who like to try novel activities.

This ability to generate high levels of participant enjoyment is one of the most important contributions of commercial resources. Offering new recreation experiences is only one of the ways in which commercial resources achieve this effect. Many provide opportunities to take part in activities that are exciting no matter how often people participate. Examples include thrill rides, gambling casinos, and spectator sports, such as horseraces and professional hockey or football games. Others provide an enchanting or glamorous atmosphere, which greatly enhances the participant experience. Examples of resources that may exhibit some of these intangible qualities are discotheques, nightclubs, circuses and ice shows, and experience rides at major theme parks.

Commercial recreation also provides a variety of cultural experiences not usually offered by the public sector. These include opportunities to sample unfamiliar foods in delicatessens and ethnic restaurants, experience life on farms and large estates, and become acquainted with areas of the world where no public or quasi-public campgrounds or lodgings exist.

Commercial enterprises are also able to specialize, supplying opportunities that strongly appeal to limited segments of the population. In contrast, public recreation agencies try to offer facilities and programs that are of interest to a large cross section of the populations that they serve. And, finally, the commercial sector, within the limits imposed by laws and regulations, provides a variety of recreation opportunities that the public sector, for one reason or another, tends to avoid.

Because of its special contributions, commercial recreation plays a tremendously important role in expanding and enriching our recreation environments. Variety is said to be the *spice of life;* for many people, most of this variety comes from experiences provided by commercial recreation enterprises.

DISCUSSION TOPICS

1. Do commercial recreation resources expand your recreation environment and the environments of people with whom you are familiar? Explain your response.
2. Merchants are encouraging people to think of shopping malls as community centers by constructing recreation facilities and incorporating events, such as hobby shows, concerts, and carnivals into mall programs. Is this socially desirable?
3. Should private enterprise be encouraged to provide more urban and rural campgrounds or should the number of local, intermediate, and national government campgrounds be increased?
4. Prepare a list of products that are never used in one way or another for recreation purposes; justify your selections.
5. Use the telephone directory advertising pages for an area with which you are familiar to examine that area's hierarchy of recreation enterprises. Does the pattern appear to be typical of other areas with similar-sized populations? How does it differ from areas with larger and smaller populations?

FURTHER READINGS

Commercial recreation receives little attention in most general recreation textbooks. Information will sometimes be found indexed under headings such as commercial, farm, or private recreation. Usually, such references mention the historical development of commercial recreation and a few specific resources such as theme parks, recreation farms, and resorts. An interesting introductory reading is "The Leisure Industries: Investigations of Commercial Recreation and Tourism," a *Leisure Today* supplement to the November–December 1975 issue of the *Journal of Physical Education and Recreation.*

Arlin F. Epperson's pioneering book, *Private and Commercial Recreation: A Text and Reference,* published in New York by John Wiley in 1977, concentrates on tourist-oriented extraurban recreation enterprises. The first half of this book provides a valuable overview of the nature of commercial recreation. It also contains useful lists of pertinent references. Another basic source is *Tourism Principles, Practices and Philosophies* by Robert W. McIntosh published in Columbus, Ohio, by Grid, in 1972.

National census reports such as the U.S. Bureau of the Census periodic publications, *Census of Business* and *Census of Selected Service Industries,* contains statistics concerning the number and economic impact of various kinds of businesses, but it is often difficult to obtain separate data for a particular group of recreation enterprises. Special national studies like the Bureau of Outdoor Recreation's *1975 Nationwide Inventory of Publicly Owned Recreation Areas and Assessment of Private Recreation Enterprises* and the National Association of Conservation Districts publication *Inventory of Private Recreation Facilities 1977* must be used with discretion because they include only selected kinds of primarily extraurban commercial enterprises.

Most of the more detailed information on commercial recreation enterprises is found in specialized publications. For example, business magazines such as *Business Week, Forbes, Fortune,* and *Nation's Business* periodically publish general articles on major segments of the recreation industry or descriptions of specific recreation enterprises. More detailed information on segments of commercial recreation is published in the trade magazines, for example, *Amusement Business, Tourist Attractions and Parks Magazine, Bowling Proprietors Magazine, Skiing Area News, Campground & RV Park Management, Club Operations, Resort Management Magazine,* and *Restaurant Hospitality.* These and dozens of other similar publications are not available in many libraries, but recent copies can sometimes be consulted by contacting the managers of appropriate enterprises. There are also many how-to-do-it books and pamphlets intended to assist professionals involved in the planning, development, and management of specific kinds of commercial recreation resources. Some are published by trade associations, government commerce departments, and university tourism, extension, or hospitality industry departments.

Unfortunately, the average person searching for information concerning the recreation industry in a specific geographic area will most likely find it in the promotional material published by chambers of commerce, tourist organizations, and government commerce departments or in tourist-oriented articles published in automobile association and travel magazines. This type of material should be used with great caution. Usually only selected information that projects a positive image is included. Listings and data frequently exclude enterprises that do not belong to the sponsoring organization and quantitative information may be guesses rather than the results of reliable surveys.

13

PUBLICLY OWNED RECREATION RESOURCES: LOCAL AND REGIONAL AGENCIES

CONCEPTS & PROBLEMS

Small Portion of Free Time Is
  Spent at Public Resources
Vital Role of Public Resources
Highly Diversified Involvement
Acres Are Not Opportunities
Use of Local Parks Dominates
Resource-Population Imbalance
Local Roles Vary Greatly
Some Parks May Not Fit Classes
Center Designs Must Be Flexible
School-Park Plan Has Benefits
Uniqueness of Each Local System

Figure 13.1 By providing swimming pools and beach parks, governments make it possible for large numbers of people to enjoy water-dependent recreation experiences. Many people would never have these opportunities if they had to provide their own facilities or pay the fees charged by private enterprises that operate water-oriented amenities as profit-making ventures.

Publicly provided recreation resources are of great significance even though only a relatively small portion of people's free time involves use of such resources. Many away-from-home urban recreation experiences are furnished by public parks, recreation centers, sports facilities, and cultural amenities. In fact, most people would seldom picnic in a parklike environment, go swimming, visit a zoo, borrow a book from a library, or explore the wonders in a fine museum if governments did not provide these kinds of opportunities (Figure 13.1). Similarly, many extraurban recreation experiences such as hunting, fishing, canoeing, and visiting largely unspoiled areas would no longer be possible for a wide range of people if public ownership did not provide access to extensive lands containing the appropriate resources.

Generally, commercial enterprises are unable to duplicate these kinds of opportunities, at least not at prices middle- and lower-income people can readily afford. The initial costs of acquiring and developing the necessary resources combined with continuing expenses such as taxes and maintenance are usually too high in proportion to possible returns to make a profitable business feasible. In contrast, governments can frequently offer opportunities of this nature free or for a nominal charge.

There are several reasons for this. Taxes can be used for resource purchase, development, and maintenance. Public park and recreation agencies generally do not pay taxes on their lands and buildings. They may also have the economic advantages of large-scale operations and the contributions of other gov-

ernment organizations. National, state, and provincial forest agencies, for example, often use their employees and equipment for a variety of timber, range, and water projects as well as for recreation resource management.

Publicly owned resources also contribute substantially to recreation on private lands. Public parks, forests, waters, and mountain ranges are often important positive components of environments in which people choose to build private residences, luxury apartments, condominiums, hotels, restaurants, resident camps, second homes, resorts, and sports complexes. Even if they never set foot on the public lands, private-facility users enjoy the scenic views provided by them and find the relatively unspoiled environment relaxing. Moreover, public-agency management activities that preserve or enhance recreation environments on public lands frequently increase the use and monetary values of adjacent private resources.

Finally, public recreation resources produce important social benefits. Urban parks form green space that enhances the psychological and physical environments of city residents and visitors whether they use the areas or not. Civic or national pride is often associated with government-operated museums, art galleries, and parks. Widespread citizen support for national park systems in Canada and the United States is a case in point. A large proportion of the population derives pleasure from these systems although a much smaller number of people have an opportunity to enjoy national park amenities in person. Many have to be content with pictures, articles, or other peo-

ple's accounts of visits to these areas; nevertheless, they obtain satisfaction and pride just from knowing that such resources exist and are protected as part of the national heritage. Often there are strong feelings of personal ownership. Such feelings cannot be derived from similar resources under private ownership irrespective of the philosophy and management skills of the owners or developer'

THE SCOPE OF PUBLIC INVOLVEMENT

Governments provide a wide range of recreation opportunities. Table 13.1 indicates the diversity of this involvement, but only a few examples can be listed. Many other kinds of resources are involved at each level. In addition to this chapter, Chapters 14–17 are largely devoted to descriptions of these resources.

The nature and extent of the recreation resources provided by political units vary greatly. One municipal, regional, state, provincial, or national government may make extensive provisions for public recreation, whereas an adjacent government unit of the same kind may supply comparatively few such opportunities. The degree of involvement depends on the interaction of a number of factors; the main influences are shown in Figure 13.2.

Some cities and counties have extensive park and recreation systems because settlement patterns, wealthy donors, or philanthropic organizations contributed to the preservation of open space, and, subsequently, local citizens supported the development of recreation facilities and programs. Other

Table 13.1 Examples of the Diversity of Government Involvement in Providing Recreation Opportunities

Level of Government	Kinds of Resources Administered	Resultant Recreation Opportunities
Municipal government	Recreation centers.	Games, swimming, arts and crafts, socials.
	School gyms, pools, and sportsfields.	Sports,[a] athletics,[a] swimming,[a] plays,[a] concerts,[a] dances, carnivals,[a] exhibitions.[a]
	Civic and cultural centers.	Plays,[a] concerts,[a] shows,[a] exhibitions.[a]
	Beaches and parks.	Swimming, boating,[a] sunbathing, picnicking, attending special events.[a]
	Libraries.	Borrowing books, recordings, artwork; seeing films.
	Nature centers.	Hiking on trails, seeing wildlife, hearing talks.
	Cemeteries.	Walking, jogging, birdwatching.
County government	Parks.	Picnicking, swimming,[a] sports,[a] boating,[a] fishing.
	Fairgrounds.	Agricultural fairs,[a] horseracing,[a] rodeos,[a] folk festivals.[a]
	Airports.	Recreation travel, flying,[a] gliding.[a]
	Historic records and sites.	Geneological study, sightseeing.
	Reservoirs.	Swimming, fishing, boating, waterskiing.
State or provincial government	Highways, roadside parks.	Pleasure driving, sightseeing, picnicking.
	Forests.	Sightseeing, hiking, nature study, hunting, camping.
	Fish hatcheries.	Raising fish for anglers, sightseeing.
	Parks.	Picnicking, swimming, sightseeing, camping, fishing.
	Rivers and lakes.	Fishing, boating,[a] sailing,[a] swimming, canoeing, scuba diving.
	Schools, hospitals.	TV, games, sports,[a] swimming, arts and crafts.
National government	Museums.	Exhibits, studying, attending talks, films.
	Parks.	Sightseeing, camping, hiking, nature study, skiing.[a]
	Historic buildings and battlefields.	Sightseeing, photography, reliving history.
	Canals and harbors.	Boating,[a] sightseeing, fishing.
	Military bases and ranges.	Sightseeing, hunting, nature study.
	Forests.	Hunting, fishing, camping, motorcycling, snowmobiling.
	Multiple-use desert and mountain areas.	Dune buggies,[a] four-wheel drive vehicles,[a] sand sailing, rock climbing, collecting rocks, sightseeing.

[a] Include both taking part in and attending such activities.

local political units may offer few recreation opportunities because such influences were minor or absent. Sometimes it is the influence of one political leader, planner, or recreation professional that has been the major factor.

In the case of states and provinces, great differences often exist even between adjacent units. For example, Indiana with its preponderance of cropland, largely agriculturally oriented population, and conservative political atmosphere has generally been less involved in recreation at the state level than neighboring Michigan. The latter, with a high proportion of its area in woodlands or wetlands, the majority of its population in manufacturing and service employment, a large tourist industry, and generally more liberal political traditions, has been a leader in state involvement in recreation. Sometimes just one factor can be largely responsible for the degree of government involvement. Colorado, for instance, had only a small undeveloped state park system until comparatively recent times. This was mostly because so many recreation opportunities were provided by huge areas of federal government land and private rangelands. The growth of urban population and a desire to provide more attractions for out-of-state tourists finally provided the impetus to develop and expand Colorado's state park system.

At the national level, the form of government plays a dominant role in determining the nature and extent of involvement. Governments of Communist nations, for example, are usually deeply involved in a great variety of recreation opportunities ranging from urban hotels and restaurants to camping facilities in remote forest

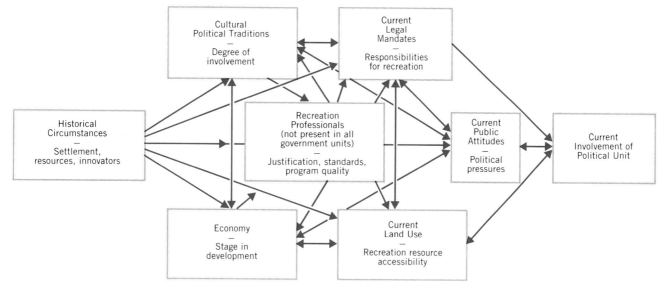

Figure 13.2 **Main factors influencing the nature and extent of political unit involvement in recreation.**

Cultural
Political Traditions
–
Degree of
involvement

Current
Legal
Mandates
–
Responsibilities
for recreation

Historical
Circumstances
–
Settlement,
resources, innovators

Recreation
Professionals
(not present in all
government units)
–
Justification, standards,
program quality

Current
Public
Attitudes
–
Political
pressures

Current
Involvement of
Political Unit

Economy
–
Stage in
development

Current
Land Use
–
Recreation resource
accessibility

areas. However, the nature and extent of these recreation opportunities still varies from country to country within the Communist bloc depending on other factors such as the kind of Marxist philosophy being followed or the nation's level of economic development. Similarly, socialist governments such as Sweden's generally play a larger role in providing recreation than the governments of nations that are politically more conservative. Democratic nations with governments based on the British system often have extensive recreation involvement at all government levels.

Because of the great differences in each government's recreation involvement, it is difficult to provide a comprehensive overview of public-agency-provided recreation in just a few pages. Nevertheless, the following information gives an indication of the general nature and scope of government involvement in recreation by presenting a general summary and a number of examples. These examples should not be regarded as typical. No two city park and recreation systems are exactly alike and national parks tend to be substantially different because preservation of uniqueness is usually a prime objective. The units and systems discussed should, therefore, be considered as indicators of the nature and scope of public-agency recreation resources rather than as representative of average units or systems.

Factor	Determines:
Historical circumstances	Patterns of settlement; attitudes toward resources, development, conservation, and planning; effects of innovative politicians, planners, entrepreneurs, and citizen groups.
Cultural-political traditions	Form of government and degree to which political unit is expected to be involved in public welfare or tourism promotion.
Economic situation	Political unit's stage of economic development and current level of prosperity; determines priorities and funds available for recreation.
Legal mandates	Constitutional or legislative assignment of responsibilities for park and recreation services.
Recreation professionals and organization	Scope and quality of involvement by assisting with justification; standards, financing, design, operation, maintenance, and public relations.
Current land use	Land use feasibility especially the accessibility of various types of recreation resources relative to population concentrations.
Current attitudes of public	Interest in and political pressure for government provision of recreation opportunities.

PUBLIC RECREATION LAND DISTRIBUTION

One indicator of the involvement of governments is the amount of public land dedicated to recreation. However, area data have to be interpreted carefully. A hectare in an urban park may provide far more recreation experiences annually than a national park containing thousands of hectares. Similarly, a small piece of high-quality lakeshore in a forest may be capable of supplying many more recreation opportunities than vast areas of desert or high-altitude mountain lands.

AMERICAN PUBLIC PRIMARY RECREATION LANDS

A major problem in understanding the contribution of public resources to recreation opportunity supply is the variety of lands involved. This situation is particularly complex in the United States where recreation opportunities occur on many kinds of government lands — city, township, county, state, and federal[1] — as well as on lands controlled by special park districts and regional park authorities. The relative areas of the different kinds of public lands on which recreation is considered to be a desirable primary activity are shown in Figure 13.3. Of course, on some of these lands, uses other than recreation are regarded as equally important, especially in the case of state and national forests.

As Figure 13.3 indicates, over 108 million hectares (267 million

acres) or more than four-fifths (83.5 percent) of America's publicly owned lands on which recreation is a primary activity are under federal government control. State governments administer 17 million hectares (42 million acres) or about one-eighth (13.1 percent) of the national total. Lower levels of government have only 3.4 percent of these lands or a total of 4 million hectares (10 million acres). However, the total amount of recreation that occurs on these lands varies considerably. On state lands, for instance, recreation use is probably two to three times larger than the total use on federal lands. Similarly, the total number of recreation experiences provided by lands administered by cities, townships, and counties is certainly many times larger than the total number of recreation experiences taking place on state lands.

Unfortunately, the amount of recreation use that these lands receive is often not known. No accurate figures on the total recreation use of government lands exist, since reliable estimates are generally available only where paid admissions, entrance controls, traffic counters, or registration procedures make it possible to gather the necessary data. Information is usually lacking on the number of people who informally use many kinds of urban and rural public lands for activities such as strolling, sitting in the sun, bicycling, playing with children, sightseeing, hunting, fishing, nature study, berrypicking, pleasure driving, or off-highway motorcycling.

Throughout this discussion, remember that the lands being described are only a portion of the total lands under public ownership; lands on which recreation is consid-

ered to be a secondary activity will be discussed separately. For example, the federal government lands included in Figure 13.3 are only part of the total area administered by the National Park Service, U.S. Forest Service, U.S. Fish and Wildlife Service, Bureau of Land Management, Bureau of Reclamation, Corps of Engineers, and the Tennessee Valley Authority.

As shown in the top section of Figure 13.3, city, township, county, and regional government primary recreation lands constitute 3.4 percent of America's land of this type. Only one-fifth (20.9 percent) of the city, township, county, and regional government lands actually consists of parks and recreation areas. This represents a mere 0.7 percent of the total supply of primary recreation lands administered by all three levels of government. Nevertheless, these are the areas that are more heavily used for recreation that any of the other kinds of local, state, or federal government primary recreation lands.

On the other hand, city, township, county, and regional recreation agencies provide surprisingly large amounts of forest, fish and game, and nature preserve areas, which are classified as public primary recreation lands. The public is often largely unaware of these lands, however, since they are relatively undeveloped and are, therefore, less appealing for playing games, picnicking, swimming, and other activities commonly undertaken in urban parks. Nevertheless, these three types of areas constitute more than three-quarters of the recreation lands provided by local forms of government.

In examining the bottom section of Figure 13.3, it will be seen

---

[1] In the United States, lands administered by the national government are usually called federal lands.

City, Township, County, District, and Regional Government Primary Recreation Lands		Percent of Total for Each Level of Government	Percent of Total for All Levels of Government
4 million hectares (10 million acres)	Parks and recreation areas	20.9%	0.7%
	Forest areas	46.0	1.6
	Fish and game areas	15.8	0.5
	Historical and cultural areas	0.2	0.0
	Wilderness and nature preserves	15.7	0.5
	Other	1.4	0.1
		100.0	3.4

State Government Primary Recreation Lands			
17 million hectares (42 million acres)	Parks and recreation areas	10.6%	1.4%
	Forest areas	45.6	6.0
	Fish and game areas	37.7	4.9
	Historical and cultural areas	0.1	0.0
	Wilderness and nature preserves	3.4	0.5
	Other	2.6	0.3
		100.0	13.1

Federal Government Primary Recreation Lands			
108 million hectares (267 million acres)	Parks and recreation areas	7.2%	6.0%
	Forest areas	60.0	50.1
	Fish and game areas	12.3	10.3
	Historical and cultural areas	0.5	0.4
	Wilderness and nature preserves	10.5	8.8
	Other	9.5	7.9
		100.0	83.5
			100.0

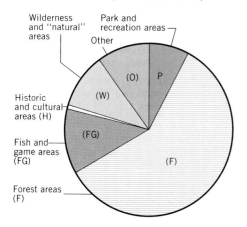

Figure 13.3 Administrative responsibility for public lands in the United States on which recreation is a primary activity. Playgrounds and playfields are included in the parks and recreation areas category. Areas of circles and their subdivisions are drawn to scale. SOURCE. U.S. Department of the Interior, **Bureau of Outdoor Recreation,** Outdoor Recreation: A Legacy for America, **U.S. Government Printing Office, Washington, D.C., 1973. Table 3-1.**

that only 7.2 percent of the federally administered lands on which recreation is considered a primary activity is actually classified as parks or recreation areas. These include the intensively developed portions of the national forests, national park units, and the Corps of Engineers' reservoir lands. Such lands together with the historic and cultural areas (0.5 percent of the federal primary recreation lands) carry the bulk of the recreation activity that occurs on federal government lands.

Federal forest lands are also used extensively; the most common activities are hunting, fishing, camping, pleasure driving, and picnicking. These lands constitute 60.1 percent of the federally administered primary recreation lands and 50.1 percent of the total primary recreation lands controlled by all three levels of government. Such lands are largely areas in the national forests or portions of Bureau of Land Management properties.

State government lands on which recreation is considered a primary activity are shown in the middle section of Figure 13.3; they are also largely forest lands. However, fish and game areas are much more significant, areally, comprising 37.7 percent of state primary recreation lands compared to 12.3 percent at the federal level. State parks and recreation areas contain less than one-quarter as much primary recreation land as the federal parks and recreation areas, although the former receive considerably more recreation use.

The regional distribution of federal, state, and local government primary recreation lands is shown in Figure 13.4. Since the census regions themselves differ substantially in size, caution is required

when making areal comparisons. (The Mountain Region, for example, is 13 times larger in total area than the New England Region.) Nevertheless, the public primary recreation lands are asymmetrically distributed, the majority being located in the western third of the nation. The imbalance is even more pronounced when the area of these lands is related to population distribution (see Figure 4.15) as shown in the right-hand column of Figure 13.4 (area per 1000 population).

The Mountain Region contains the largest amount of public primary recreation land, totaling 53 million hectares (131 million acres). This is equal to just over one-quarter of the region's total area. The Pacific Region is next with 44 million hectares (109 million acres), which is equal to 18.5 percent of its total area. As will be shown later, these two regions contain many large units of the national park system, numerous developed recreation sites (both in the national forests and on the desert and range lands of the Bureau of Land Management), and a number of federal reservoir recreation areas.

At the present time, the federal lands in these two regions alone comprise three-quarters of the nation's total supply of public primary recreation lands. The proportion of public primary recreation lands in the West will be even higher if Congress decides to add large areas of Alaska to the various national land reserve systems. It was possible to establish these huge land reserves primarily because the western portion of the United States was not extensively settled until after the adoption of the first federal park and forest reserve legislation.

Until then, these lands had been preserved by their relative inaccessibility and general unattractiveness to early settlers who were mostly farmers or ranchers.

The middle third of the United States contains almost one-tenth of the nation's public primary recreation land. The West North Central Region has the largest share, partly owing to the factors mentioned in the previous paragraph. In addition, state-government administered primary recreation lands are extensive, covering a larger area than the region's federal lands. In the West South Central Region, the early Spanish land grants, comparative accessibility of the region, and generally more conservative attitudes of its citizens resulted in less land being set aside for federal or state parks, forests, and wildlife reserves. Only 2.9 percent of the region's total area is public primary recreation land.

Fifteen percent of the nation's supply of public primary recreation land is located in the remaining five census regions that make up the eastern one-third of the country. However, each of these regions is much smaller than any of those farther west; therefore, several have quite high proportions of public recreation land. The highest is the

Figure 13.4 **Distribution by census regions of public lands in the United States on which recreation is a primary activity. (Note that the Pacific Region includes Alaska and Hawaii and that "local" lands include city, township, county, district, and regional government primary recreation lands.) SOURCE. Developed from Bureau of Outdoor Recreation,** Outdoor Recreation: A Legacy for America. **U.S. Government Printing Office, Washington, D.C., 1973, Table 3-2.**

Census Regions	Area of Public Recreation Lands	Percent of Nation's Total Public Primary Recreation Lands				Hectares (Acres) per 1000 Population			

1 PACIFIC Includes Alaska and Hawaii
A: 43,993,000 (108,623,000)
P: 18.5%
RT: 34.0 | F: 31.7 | S: 2.1 | L: 0.3
RT: 1558 (3850) | F: 1449 (3579) | S: 94 (232) | L: 15 (37)

2 MOUNTAIN
A: 53,167,000 (131,277,000)
P: 25.1%
RT: 41.1 | F: 40.5 | S: 0.4 | L: 0.2
RT: 5513 (13,623) | F: 5429 (1341) | S: 56 (138) | L: 28 (69)

3 WEST NORTH CENTRAL
A: 9,048,000 (22,341,000)
P: 6.7%
RT: 7.0 | F: 2.9 | S: 3.6 | L: 0.5
RT: 542 (1339) | F: 223 (551) | S: 282 (697) | L: 37 (91)

4 WEST SOUTH CENTRAL
A: 3,332,000 (8,226,000)
P: 2.9%
RT: 2.6 | F: 2.0 | S: 0.4 | L: 0.2
RT: 159 (393) | F: 126 (311) | S: 22 (54) | L: 12 (30)

5 EAST NORTH CENTRAL
A: 5,801,000 (14,323,000)
P: 9.0%
RT: 4.5 | F: 1.6 | S: 1.7 | L: 1.2
RT: 141 (348) | F: 50 (124) | S: 54 (133) | L: 37 (91)

6 EAST SOUTH CENTRAL
A: 2,950,000 (7,283,000)
P: 6.2%
RT: 2.3 | F: 1.4 | S: 0.6 | L: 0.3
RT: 217 (536) | F: 129 (319) | S: 61 (151) | L: 27 (67)

7 SOUTH ATLANTIC
A: 7,611,000 (18,792,000)
P: 10.5%
RT: 5.9 | F: 3.1 | S: 2.3 | L: 0.5
RT: 225 (556) | F: 117 (289) | S: 89 (220) | L: 19 (47)

8 MIDDLE ATLANTIC
A: 2,420,000 (5,975,000)
P: 9.1%
RT: 1.7 | F: 0.2 | S: 1.6 | L: 0.1
RT: 65 (161) | F: 6 (15) | S: 55 (136) | L: 4 (10)

9 NEW ENGLAND
A: 973,000 (2,403,000)
P: 5.6%
RT: 0.8 | F: 0.3 | S: 0.4 | L: 0.1
RT: 80 (198) | F: 34 (84) | S: 40 (99) | L: 6 (15)

A - Area in hectares (acres)
P - Percent of region's total land area

RT - Regional total   F - Federal   S - State   L - Local

PUBLICLY OWNED RECREATION RESOURCES: LOCAL AND REGIONAL AGENCIES

South Atlantic Region where 10.5 percent of the region is public primary recreation land. This region contains extensive national forests, large national parks system units, and more state primary recreation lands than any other region except the West North Central Region.

Clearly, the eastern portion of the United States has a much smaller supply of public primary recreation land than the West. However, the full impact of this imbalance only becomes apparent when the supply is related to population size. This has been done in the right-hand column of Figure 13.4 by dividing each region's area of public primary recreation lands by its population. In spite of its large area, the Mountain Region is relatively sparsely populated so that it enjoys the highest ratio, namely, 5513 hectares (13,623 acres)/1000 population. The Pacific Region has a much larger total population so that its ratio is less than one-third that of the Mountain Region.

The rest of the nation has much lower ratios. The Middle Atlantic Region has the lowest value, 65 hectares (161 acres)/1000 population, even though public primary recreation lands occupy 9.1 percent of its area. This is because the region contains a large portion of the huge population centered around New York City as well as another densely populated area to the west that extends from Pittsburgh, Pennsylvania, to Buffalo, New York. The region with the next lowest ratio is the New England Region—80 hectares (198 acres)/1000 population. It has only 973,000 hectares (2.4 million acres) of public primary recreation lands (40 percent of the Middle Atlantic Region total), and it contains the New York-Boston urban area.

The East North Central Region has a high percentage of public primary recreation lands (9 percent), but it also has large populations in the Milwaukee-Chicago and Detroit-Cleveland urban areas. It is third lowest in area ratio with 141 hectares (348 acres)/1000 population. In fourth position is the West South Central Region. It has a relatively small population compared to its area, but only 2.9 percent is public primary recreation land. Therefore, its ratio of 159 hectares (393 acres)/1000 population is only slightly higher than the ratio for the East North Central Region. The East South Central, South Atlantic, and West North Central regions occupy intermediate positions. The South Atlantic Region has a substantial population, but this is balanced to some extent by its 7.6 million hectares (18.8 million acres) of public primary recreation lands.

The preceding discussion provides a general indication of the availability of public primary recreation lands to the people living in the various regions. However, the resources or population are unevenly distributed in a number of cases so that many people enjoy even fewer opportunities than the data indicate. For instance, most of the population of the Pacific Region is concentrated in southwestern California and the Portland-Seattle area, but much of the public recreation land is located in more remote parts of the region. Similarly, a substantial proportion of the public primary recreation lands in the East North Central Region is either national forest, state forest, and state park areas located in northern Michigan and Wisconsin or national forest and state park units located primarily in southern Illinois, Indiana, and Ohio. On the other hand, the majority of the residents live elsewhere in the region and can make use of most of these resources only if they undertake an overnight trip by private vehicle. Therefore, there may still be a need to expand the area of public primary recreation land in and near metropolitan areas, even where the regional hectares per 1000 population ratio is reasonably high.

AMERICAN PUBLIC SECONDARY RECREATION LANDS

The 129 million hectares (319 million acres) of public primary recreation land discussed in the previous section are only part of the public lands that are used for recreation in the United States. Many other areas provide numerous recreation experiences, although recreation is not a primary management objective. For instance, government agencies often permit the general public or selected groups to use parts of military bases, wildlife refuges, and water-supply catchment areas for recreation activities when such use does not interfere with the primary goals of these areas. Recreation is also an important component of the use of public roads, municipal airports, and public school facilities.

Much of the recreation on these secondary recreation lands is informal, dispersed, or difficult to identify (e.g., pleasure driving). Quantitative data are therefore generally absent and the relative recreation significance of these lands is largely unknown. Obviously, public primary recreation lands provide the majority of the opportunities for most activities on public lands, but secondary lands do play an important subsidiary role in many cases.

Only about one-third of the public lands in the United States are classified as primary recreation land. Since recreation is completely banned on only a small proportion of the remainder, about 234 million hectares (578 million acres) are secondary recreation lands. Currently, in addition to providing substantial recreation opportunities, these secondary lands form a valuable reserve, since they include many areas that have the potential to become public primary recreation lands in the future. Distribution of these public secondary recreation lands among the three levels of government is shown in Figure 13.5.

Similar information concerning the overall distribution of public primary and secondary recreation

lands in other countries is generally not available. Differences in the roles of government agencies also make quantitative comparisons misleading. However, some examples of specific kinds of recreation lands in other nations will be included later when we discuss various types of public recreation resources.

The remainder of this chapter describes local government and regional recreation resources. These are the lands and facilities that produce the majority of the recreation experiences provided by the public sector.

LOCAL AND REGIONAL RECREATION AGENCIES

Governments below the national and state or provincial levels are

generally present in several forms in developed nations. In the United States and Canada, local government services are usually provided by incorporated townships, villages, towns, or cities. However, county or parish governments often provide selected public services such as the police, main roads, principal drainage ditches, and health programs. Where urban development is limited and rectangular municipalities predominate (e.g., in parts of the United States laid out under the Congressional Survey System), the geographic distribution of local government jurisdictions is generally relatively easy to understand (Figure 13.6). In other parts of Canada and the United States as well as in Europe, municipal boundaries may be quite irregular, since they may follow traditional political, religious, or land-settlement boundaries.

Other levels of local government exist at some locations. In some urban areas, metropolitan governments or special authorities have been created by amalgamating either all the government functions of a number of adjacent municipalities or by centralizing one or more of their primary functions such as parks, sewage, highway, police, or public transportation. Regional governments may be similarly responsible for most or a few services over a much larger area. Such regional authorities usually have jurisdiction over several rural government units as well as several urban units. Sometimes a regional government may be responsible for many counties.

Metropolitan and regional forms of government have not flourished in the United States because citizens or local business interests generally wish to maintain

Figure 13.5 Distribution of public primary and secondary recreation lands among levels of government in the United States. SOURCE. Developed from Bureau of Outdoor Recreation, Outdoor Recreation: A Legacy for America, **U.S. Government Printing Office, Washington, D.C., 1973, Table 3-1; and Bureau of the Census,** The Statistical Abstract of the United States, **U.S. Government Printing Office, Washington, D.C., 1977, Table No. 337.**

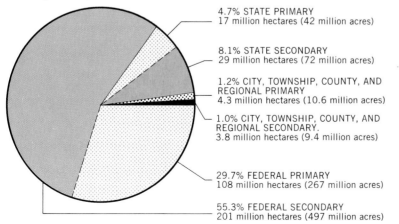

4.7% STATE PRIMARY
17 million hectares (42 million acres)

8.1% STATE SECONDARY
29 million hectares (72 million acres)

1.2% CITY, TOWNSHIP, COUNTY, AND REGIONAL PRIMARY
4.3 million hectares (10.6 million acres)

1.0% CITY, TOWNSHIP, COUNTY, AND REGIONAL SECONDARY.
3.8 million hectares (9.4 million acres)

29.7% FEDERAL PRIMARY
108 million hectares (267 million acres)

55.3% FEDERAL SECONDARY
201 million hectares (497 million acres)

Figure 13.6 **Local government jurisdictions in the Lansing region of southern Michigan. Within the 448,000 hectare (1728 square mile) three-county area, there are 11 cities, 16 villages, 48 townships, and 3 counties each governed by a separate elected body that can provide recreation opportunities.**

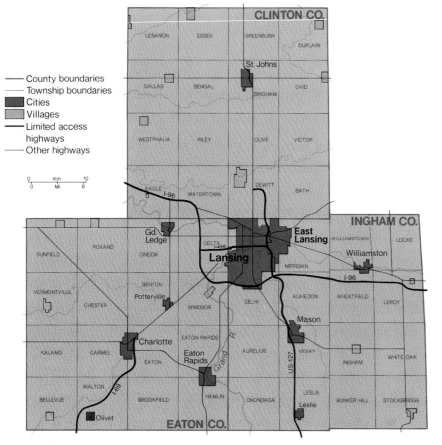

governments is less likely to have large regionally significant parks or a good zoo than a similar area administered by a metropolitan or regional government. The range of local government opportunities also depends on tradition, taxpayer attitudes, economic conditions, undeveloped resource availability, and the amount of financial assistance provided by other levels of government. Consequently, the kinds and scope of public recreation services offered by municipal governments vary considerably.

This variation makes it difficult to describe local government recreation facilities and programs. Every political unit is different and broad generalizations concerning municipal recreation tend to give an erroneous impression of uniformity. The fact that no city, township, county, metropolitan, or regional government is really typical of its class must be kept in mind in considering the descriptions and examples that follow.

The wide range of recreation experiences supplied by local and regional government agencies can be divided into two main groups. The first consists of opportunities provided intentionally by public bodies that operate facilities such as libraries, schools, parks, and recreation centers. The second group is comprised of experiences that occur incidentally because of agency-provided facilities that are not intended to produce recreation opportunities, for example, enjoying a trip on a municipal bus or subway train, playing games or walking for pleasure on city streets, or fishing in a metropolitan reservoir. Such opportunities occur because of the activities of a wide range of local or regional government organizations

the autonomy of smaller political units. Consolidation of the planning and provision of public services has been much more prevalent in Canada, Great Britain, and some other European nations. In Canada, for example, many functions of the 13 municipalities in the Toronto urban area were amalgamated in 1953 with the creation of Metropolitan Toronto. More recently, the Ontario provincial government set up large

regional governments covering the entire southern portion of the province that, together with Metropolitan Toronto, provide many of the basic public services.

The nature and extent of local government recreation opportunities available in a given area depends to some extent on the kinds of government involved. An urban area that is under the jurisdiction of a number of small independent city such as street departments, transportation commissions, water departments, and boards of education.

CITY AND DISTRICT AGENCIES

City, township, county, metropolitan, and regional recreation resources can be the responsibility of several different types of government agencies. Originally, the responsibility for town squares, small parks, and boulevards was normally assigned to the street department or to an agency with wider duties often called the department of public works. Such departments are still in charge of parks in many small towns, villages, and less populated townships and counties. Quite extensive systems of sizable parks are operated by the road departments of several urbanized counties in the United States and Canada.

As urban park systems developed, some governments formed separate park departments. Later, municipalities began to provide recreation programs; these were generally placed under existing educational or social agencies or under a specially created separate recreation department. Early park departments and other agencies charged with operating local parks were usually directed by engineers or horticulturalists who had little interest in providing organized recreation programs. Agencies in charge of recreation programs were generally staffed with people dedicated primarily to promoting physical fitness and providing sports or arts and crafts programs.

Thus the division between the park and the program aspects of publicly provided recreation became firmly established. Subsequently, the two functions often competed with one another for financial support and control of resources. The absence of cooperation was particularly unfortunate where the park department was responsible for developing and maintaining sportsfields and other facilities that the recreation department used for its programs.

Many urban municipalities in the United States and Canada eventually brought the two functions together by forming combined departments. About two-thirds of all American cities with more than 10,000 inhabitants now have this arrangement; only one-fifth still have separate recreation departments. The remaining 15 percent have a variety of other administrative arrangements. Combined departments are comparatively rare outside Canada and the United States. In other nations, departments of public works are generally responsible for the development and maintenance of municipal parks, and local government and quasi-public agencies (such as schools, athletic clubs, and private cultural organizations) are given public funds for the operation of specific recreation activity programs.

Other types of recreation agencies have been formed in some areas. Illinois, for instance, has legislation enabling local governments to establish two types of special agencies known as *park districts* and *forest preserve districts*. In both cases, all or part of a number of political units may be placed under the jurisdiction of a single agency for park and recreation or forest preserve purposes. The Cook County Forest Preserve District is the most famous example. It ad-

ministers 24,300 hectares (60,000 acres) in the Chicago urban area and complements the resources offered by the Chicago Park District and numerous other park agencies (Figure 13.7). The district's main goal is to preserve extensive areas of woodland as public green space. In doing so, it also provides many facilities for picnicking, hiking, horseback riding, and fishing as well as maintaining large open grassy areas, which are heavily used for a great variety of recreation activities. In total, 160 park departments or districts, 5 forest preserve districts, and 1 conservation district serve the 7 million people living in the 262 municipalities that make up the six-county, northeast Illinois region.

In contrast, the seven-county urban area in southeast Michigan around Detroit does not have a series of autonomous park or forest preserve organizations. Instead, the city of Detroit has a large and active recreation department, about 130 local governments have their own park and recreation departments, and each of the counties has one or more county government agencies responsible for the provision of recreation opportunities. However, there is a regionwide public recreation resource-administering agency called the Huron-Clinton Metropolitan Authority, which has jurisdiction over five counties. Formed originally to conserve the areas along the Huron and Clinton rivers, the authority has developed a series of large, water-oriented regional preserves rather than a broad spectrum of urban park and recreation facilities. However, many of its *metroparks* contain highly developed and intensively used beaches, picnic areas, and sports facilities (Figure 9.2).

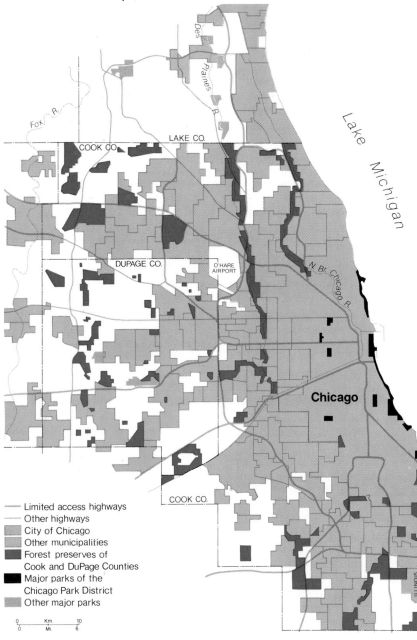

Figure 13.7 Map of the Chicago metropolitan area showing the principal municipalities, parks, forest preserves, and limited access highways. The Cook County Forest Preserve lands are now almost completely surrounded by urban development and are, therefore, all the more valuable as nearby greenspace for the area's 7 million people.

Limited access highways
Other highways
City of Chicago
Other municipalities
Forest preserves of Cook and DuPage Counties
Major parks of the Chicago Park District
Other major parks

The 4.5 million people of southeast Michigan are therefore served primarily by a total of approximately 150 local government park and recreation agencies. Some people argue that this situation—each government unit having a separate department of parks and recreation—is highly desirable because it permits local citizens to maintain control over recreation policies and programs. Others contend that consolidating some or all park and recreation functions under district or regional park authorities improves recreation opportunities. They suggest that consolidation can result in the avoidance of duplication, development of programs that meet the needs of special groups, *economies of scale* (lower costs because of volume buying and the capability to purchase special equipment), and the ability to maintain a more skilled and experienced professional staff.

COUNTY AGENCIES

Traditionally, American county parks have been viewed as intermediate between extensively developed city parks and less developed state parks. This image is still substantially correct, since most county parks tend to be larger than city parks; contain a resource such as a woodland, lake, or river; and include facilities that are limited to picnic areas, swimming beaches, boat-launching sites, campgrounds, nature centers, and hiking and riding trails. County park systems of this traditional type do not usually employ professionals to conduct recreation activity programs other than those involving environmental interpretation.

However, there are many exceptions, especially in the case of more affluent urbanized counties, particularly if no regional park agency has been formed. Some counties bordering large cities provide extensive, highly developed recreation resources and conduct comprehensive recreation programs. In a few cases, where a single county contains a major city and its surrounding suburbs, the county park system may function as a metropolitan system. The Milwaukee County system is an example of this arrangement. Its role is broader than most metropolitan systems in that it is the sole provider of parks and the principal supplier of public recreation programs for all the municipalities in the county. Even areas that were originally city-of-Milwaukee parks have been incorporated into the county system. It includes resources ranging from downtown squares, recreation centers, and playgrounds to a major zoo and large extraurban parks.

County government involvement in park and recreation programs generally decreases with distance from major urban centers. A typical American rural county that contains little or no suburban development may have two or three small parks, a few historic sites or roadside parks, and a fairground. The parks usually are 10 to 20 hectares (25 to 50 acres) in extent, feature a locally important recreation resource such as a picnic grove or swimming beach, and contain limited amenities such as parking areas, picnic tables, and pit or vault toilets. Rural county fairgrounds typically have a horse racetrack with grandstands in addition to buildings and open spaces that are used for the annual fair exhibits.

There are many exceptions, however, including both urban and rural counties that provide neither parks nor recreation programs.

In other nations, counties (or their equivalents) have generally not been as involved in providing developed recreation resources as in the United States. In Great Britain, for example, there was less need for publicly owned parks at a level between those provided by the urban municipalities and the resources administered by the national government. Most people were able to enjoy swimming, walking, picnicking, cycling, and aesthetic appreciation in less developed environments by going to urban beaches, using traditional public footpaths and common lands, or by visiting privately owned parklike estates or woodlands. Only in more recent times have major increases in levels of recreation participation, travel by private car, and participation in certain space-demanding activities such as golf, horseback riding, and sailing made the large-scale development of county parks a necessity. A number of county governments now have several quite extensive parks.

Many of these county recreation areas have been designated *country parks* by the Countryside Commission. This arm of the British government is responsible for a number of recreation and preservation programs, including national parks and long-distance trails. Under the Countryside Act of 1968, the commission can make grants to local governments of up to 75 percent of the cost of acquiring, developing, and managing country parks. The goal of the program is to provide urban residents with more recreation opportunities at nearby rural sites without substantially adding to highway congestion, depreciating experiences at sites that have high remoteness and solitude values, or causing additional damage to agricultural and other rural interests. The resultant country parks are filling the gap between the urban park systems and more remote areas of national significance such as the national parks. In many instances, they function in a manner similar to the more accessible and highly developed state or provincial parks in the United States and Canada.

At present, Great Britain has more than 120 designated country parks. About half are operated by county governments; the remainder are administered by other levels of local government and various private organizations and individuals. The county-operated country parks vary considerably in size, some being less than 20 hectares (50 acres) and others exceeding 400 hectares (1000 acres); the average size, however, is about 75 hectares (185 acres). Opportunities commonly provided include sightseeing, picnicking, walking, nature study, fishing, and horseback riding. Some also offer swimming, boating, camping, and the viewing of historic sites. The majority of these country parks are clustered around London and major industrial cities such as Birmingham, Liverpool, Manchester, and Nottingham.

TOWNSHIP AGENCIES

Recreation resources provided by lesser units of local government such as townships and parishes also vary greatly. In Canada and the United States, township governments are generally most highly developed in certain eastern and midwestern states and provinces such as Michigan, New Jersey, New York, Pennsylvania, and Ontario. Some townships in these areas have their own parks and a few also conduct recreation programs. In most other states and provinces, township governments are limited in number and concerned mostly with building and maintaining minor roads. In sparsely populated regions, township governments have often not even been formed, although the township names and boundaries assigned by the original land or settlement surveys may appear on maps. In such cases, higher levels of government normally carry out all local government functions.

Generally, the number of recreation opportunities provided by a township government is small in comparison to the number generated by a city or county. However, this contribution may be significant where the population is also small or no other resources are available. On the other hand, some suburban townships have extensive park and recreation programs and are major providers of recreation opportunities not only for their own residents but also for people from nearby communities.

In rural areas of Great Britain, district councils are the functional equivalent of township governments, although some districts are considerably larger than the 93 square kilometers (36 square miles) of a regular township under the U.S. Congressional Survey System. Like their North American counterparts, rural district councils are becoming more involved in the development and operation of designated recreation resources, especially in areas that have growing populations or attract substantial

numbers of visitors from other regions. A few have established country parks similar to those operated by county councils. Some have built recreation centers and swimming pools in areas with more concentrated populations. Many continue to provide or assist in the maintenance of traditional recreation resources such as village greens, village halls, and roadside parks.

From this summary, it is evident that local park and recreation resources differ considerably from one place to another. Not only are there many kinds of local government recreation organizations that may or may not exist but also the degree to which government units participate in such programs varies greatly. Especially in the case of counties and townships, involvement may range from the provision of virtually no parks or recreation opportunities to the development of extensive resources and programs. The situation is further complicated by irregular municipal boundaries and overlapping jurisdictions.

Consequently, it is often difficult for recreation professionals, let alone the general public, to understand fully the nature and extent of the local recreation facilities and programs available in a given area. This is particularly true when financial support has been obtained from higher levels of government; then situations become so confusing the average recreation resource user often cannot tell which level of government is primarily responsible. In some cases, where facilities and user fees are similar to those provided by commercial enterprises, users may not even realize such resources are publicly owned. These problems are of little consequence

to users who do not care which organization provides the recreation opportunity as long as it is available at an affordable price. But it is discouraging to the public agencies concerned when their funding is dependent on the good will and affirmative vote (in tax-rate setting elections) of the same users. In large urban areas, the complex jurisdictions) of the same users. In large ferent governmental agencies frequently make regional recreation planning and coordination difficult.

LOCAL RECREATION LANDS DISTRIBUTION

Differences in the factors that affect local government involvement in recreation (Figure 13.2) result in geographic variations in the amount of designated recreation resources provided. In terms of total area of local government primary recreation lands, the East North Central Region of the United States, with over one-third of the national total, has more than twice as much of these lands as the next highest region (Figure 13.8). The South Atlantic and West North Central regions are next with 15.0 and 14.4 percent respectively. The New Eng-

Figure 13.8 **Distribution by census regions of city, township, county, district, and regional government lands in the United States on which recreation is a primary activity. (Note that data for district governments includes regional government lands.) SOURCE. Developed from Bureau of Outdoor Recreation,** Outdoor Recreation: A Legacy for America, **U.S. Government Printing Office, Washington, D.C., 1973, Table 3-2.**

Census Regions	Total Local Recreation Lands in Hectares (Acres)	Percent of Nation's Local Government Primary Recreation Lands		Hectares (Acres) per 1000 Population	
1 PACIFIC Includes Alaska and Hawaii	413,000 (1,021,000)	RT	9.5	RT	14.6 (36.1)
		CO	7.0	CO	10.7 (26.4)
		D	0.6	D	0.9 (2.2)
		T	0.0	T	0.0
		C	2.0	C	3.0 (7.4)
2 MOUNTAIN	273,000 (675,000)	RT	6.3	RT	28.3 (69.9)
		CO	4.9	CO	22.2 (54.8)
		D	0.0	D	0.2 (0.5)
		T	0.0	T	0.0
		C	1.3	C	5.8 (14.3)
3 WEST NORTH CENTRAL	624,000 (1,542,000)	RT	14.4	RT	37.4 (92.4)
		CO	8.5	CO	22.2 (54.8)
		D	0.3	D	0.9 (2.2)
		T	1.9	T	4.8 (11.9)
		C	3.6	C	9.5 (23.5)
4 WEST SOUTH CENTRAL	251,000 (620,000)	RT	5.8	RT	12.1 (29.9)
		CO	3.1	CO	6.3 (15.6)
		D	0.5	D	1.0 (2.5)
		T	0.0	T	0.0
		C	2.3	C	4.7 (11.6)
5 EAST NORTH CENTRAL	1,526,000 (3,771,000)	RT	35.1	RT	37.3 (92.2)
		CO	29.7	CO	31.5 (77.8)
		D	1.5	D	1.6 (3.6)
		T	1.9	T	2.0 (4.9)
		C	2.1	C	2.2 (5.4)
6 EAST SOUTH CENTRAL	368,000 (909,000)	RT	8.5	RT	27.2 (67.2)
		CO	7.9	O	25.2 (62.2)
		D	0.0	D	0.0
		T	0.0	T	0.0
		C	0.6	C	1.9 (4.7)
7 SOUTH ATLANTIC	653,000 (1,614,000)	RT	15.0	RT	19.2 (47.4)
		CO	13.4	CO	17.2 (42.5)
		D	0.2	D	0.0
		T	0.0	T	0.0
		C	1.5	C	2.0 (4.9)
8 MIDDLE ATLANTIC	161,000 (398,000)	RT	3.7	RT	4.3 (10.6)
		CO	1.4	CO	1.6 (4.0)
		D	0.1	D	0.0
		T	1.2	T	1.4 (3.5)
		C	1.2	C	1.4 (3.5)
9 NEW ENGLAND	76,000 (188,000)	RT	1.8	RT	6.2 (15.3)
		CO	0.1	CO	0.2 (0.5)
		D	0.1	D	0.2 (0.5)
		T	0.9	T	3.3 (8.2)
		C	0.7	C	2.5 (6.2)

RT - Regional total   CO - County   D - District   T - Township   C - City land and Middle Atlantic regions have the lowest totals (1.8 and 3.7 percent, respectively) but they were settled first and are smaller in total area.

The West North Central Region has the largest share of city primary recreation space followed by the West South Central and East North Central regions. The West North Central Region also leads, along with the East North Central Region, in area of township primary recreation land. District and regional primary recreation lands are only substantial in the East North Central and Pacific regions. In contrast, the area of county government lands is highly significant in most of the regions, particularly the East North Central, South Atlantic, and West North Central regions. This is primarily because of large areas of county forest lands that are used extensively for recreation.

The right-hand column of Figure 13.8 shows the amount of local primary recreation land per 1000 population in each region. The four regions in the western two-thirds of the nation have the best ratios for city government primary recreation land. Two of them, the Mountain and West North Central regions, also have high county recreation land area to population ratios. The best overall pattern of ratios is in the West North Central Region which has a good balance of city, township, district or regional, and county lands. The Middle Atlantic Region has the poorest ratios with only 1.4 hectares (3.5 acres)/1000 population for city recreation lands and just 4.3 hectares (10.6 acres)/ 1000 population for all types of local government recreation lands (this region also has the lowest ratio of federal government primary rec-

reation land to population—see Figure 13.4). The New England Region has the second lowest ratios, but township recreation land is of more significance in this region than in any other eastern region. Clearly the need to expand local government primary recreation space is greatest in the Northeast. The West South Central Region is third lowest with 12.1 hectares (30 acres)/1000 population and comparatively low ratios for federal and state government lands (Figure 13.4). This region's position will probably deteriorate even further as the population continues to grow in areas that form a portion of the Sunbelt unless substantial new primary public recreation lands are designated.

KINDS OF LOCAL RESOURCES

City, township, district, county, and regional governments administer many kinds of designated recreation resources. The following discussion summarizes these resources, starting with those that are most common. A number of specific recreation facilities and systems are also described. However, each of these systems consists of a distinctive combination of various kinds and sizes of resources. Therefore, no one system or resource can really be regarded as typical.

In addition, local government resources do not always fit neatly into the categories described. In newer, tightly planned communities, the division into playlots, neighborhood parks, playfields, and other groups is often clear because planners have purposely created a hierarchy of units that meets professionally recognized standards. Most

systems, however, have a number of resources that do not fit readily into such classes. Sometimes parks function as more than one type of resource; for example, a downtown city square may serve shoppers, tourists, and other out-of-town visitors during the day but function as a neighborhood park in the evenings and on weekends. Other resources are atypical in terms of their size or the absence or presence of certain facilities. Nevertheless, the categories shown do provide a useful method of describing and comparing systems.

Most of the resources described here can be found in some township, district, county, and regional park and recreation systems as well as in city systems. Such resources are generally more extensive and diverse in large urban centers than in small towns or rural areas. Nevertheless, there are some smaller communities and townships that have comparatively large and diversified systems. Indeed, resources such as elaborate recreation centers and swimming pools that formerly were found only in major urban park and recreation systems are now included in many small city and township systems.

SQUARES, PLAZAS, AND MALLS
Since earliest times, areas of public open space in urban centers—known variously as *squares, plazas,* or *malls*—have been essential components of city recreation systems. Many were originally intended to be market places, military parade grounds, gathering places for civic functions, or areas where livestock and other essential possessions could be assembled and pro-

tected in case of siege. Religious festivals, fairs, circuses, concerts, plays, and dances were also held in these areas. Such events still take place at such locations today and are facilitated in some places by the provision of toilets, storage structures, and permanent or temporary stages and seating facilities. In one instance—Detroit's $30-million Philip Hart Plaza—underground kitchens provide working space for the groups involved in the many ethnic festivals that are staged there during the summer months (Figure 17.8).

Squares and Plazas. Many of the squares in small towns in Canada and the United States consist of open grassy rectangles with trees lining the edges or scattered within; a public building, war memorial, or small fountain often occupies the center. Children may play on the sculptures or in the area around the fountains in such squares, but frequently the recreational experiences enjoyed by users are primarily aesthetic. Some American and Canadian town squares are not even equipped with benches, which might encourage people to use them for recreation. Even so, they are sometimes used for public celebrations, festivals, band concerts, and demonstrations of various kinds. In some locations, especially in parts of Europe and places influenced by European culture, simple urban squares have evolved into elaborate parks (Figure 13.9). These parklike squares are often extensively landscaped areas containing fountains, statues, ornamental plantings, walkways, and benches on which people may sit to enjoy the amenities, special events, or the passing scene.

Larger towns and cities, especially those designed by landscape architects and urban planners, often have a series of squares and similar areas of open space. Cities with streets that run obliquely or radially from central locations (such as in Paris, London and Washington, D.C.,), frequently contain triangular "squares," which are formed where such streets cut corners off rectangular parcels of land. Some urban areas also have traffic circles at important intersections. A growing number of cities are constructing new plazas as part of their urban renewal programs. These facilities are often intended to enhance a business district or waterfront area, or complement and provide a focal point for a complex of cultural facilities or government buildings. Unlike squares, such areas are often circular or linear, are usually paved, and are frequently abutted by buildings on part or most of their perimeters rather than by streets and roads. In contrast, many of the older plazas are open to vehicular traffic and originated as central market areas, or as open space in front of an important building (church, palace, city hall), or around a community's well.

Squares, plazas, triangles, and traffic circles are often used extensively for recreation, especially when they occur in downtown locations frequented by large numbers of workers, shoppers, or tourists. Their primary use may be aesthetic or historic appreciation when they contain ornamental plantings, water features, monuments, or sculptures. But many are also excellent locations for strolling, sitting on benches, or lying on the grass. Shoppers and tourists seek them out in order to sit and rest their feet.

Workers congregate at midday to eat their lunches and enjoy the sun and fresh air. Families, friends, and lovers find them convenient meeting places. Many combine these activities with conversation, listening to portable radios, reading newspapers or books, writing postcards, planning the next part of sightseeing or shopping expeditions, or watching the passing scene. Where accessibility, facility design, social constraints, and climatic factors provide optimum conditions for the use of these areas, they are among the most heavily used public recreation resources.

Some squares and plazas have considerable potential for active recreation in addition to their historic, aesthetic, or less vigorous recreation values. A growing number of sculptures, for instance, are designed so that children may play on them. Water features in major plazas are often developed as elaborate, innovative recreation structures, which are not only attractive to look at but also enjoyable to walk through, perch upon, wade in, climb on, or listen to. Some larger reflecting pools, which are restful to sit beside in warm weather, are constructed so that they can be used as outdoor skating rinks during the winter months.

Unfortunately, the contribution of squares, plazas, and similar areas can be seriously affected by the behavior of the people who use them. In some cases, attractive squares or plazas containing many amenities function as no-man's-lands. Even during daylight hours, they are used as rendezvous for persons involved in muggings, drugs, prostitution, and other illicit activities. Such places are generally avoided by other people, except for an occa-

Figure 13.9 In 1908, this square in Saint John, New Brunswick, Canada, containing grass, trees, and flowerbeds was transformed into an entertainment center by the erection of a bandstand and the paving of the surrounding area. Musical performances attracting as many as 10,000 people were held there regularly for many years until the bandstand fell into disrepair. However, in 1977, the two-story bandstand (reportedly the only structure of its kind) was refurbished and King Square is once again the site of a series of Recreation and Parks Department summer programs. At other times, the square with its walkways, benches, ornamental plantings, and shaded areas is an attractive gathering and resting place for residents and visitors.

sional derelict and a few tourists who make use of the amenities unaware of the area's reputation. Perceptive and vigorous police action is usually needed to make such resources accessible to the public again.

Pedestrian Malls. A fairly recent trend has been the development of linear "squares" or plazas known as *pedestrian malls.* The idea is not new; some of the fashionable shopping streets in older cities have wide sidewalks, shade trees, ornamental plantings, and seating arrangements similar to those found in the most highly developed modern pedestrian malls. Since World War II, however, the growing impact of motor vehicles, urban decay, and the building of privately owned mall-type suburban shopping centers, have prompted many cities to create public malls in downtown shopping districts. This is done either by reducing the number of traffic lanes or by completely closing a street to traffic and providing the resultant pedestrian area with appropriate landscaping, sculpture, and seating facilities.

About 100 developments of this kind have been completed in the United States and Canada. Most are located in medium-sized cities, but a growing proportion are being developed in major metropolises. Pedestrian malls are encountered more frequently in Europe, especially West Germany, where one or more malls have been built in each of 350 different urban areas.

Of course, the primary motive for converting public streets to malls is economic gain; businesspersons wish to encourage shoppers to visit their stores and city officials hope to stabilize or improve tax bases in downtown areas. However, the changes improve the recreation environment for shoppers and non-shoppers alike. Noise and air pollution levels drop substantially so that walking, window-shopping, relaxing, or conversing are more enjoyable. There is more room for walkers to proceed at their own pace and for those relaxing on benches to doze, read, enjoy the sun, or watch passersby. Opportunities for recreation experiences are enhanced or increased in malls that contain facilities such as playgrounds, open-air restaurants, and amphitheaters suitable for the presentation of concerts or other performances.

The degree to which pedestrian malls can be considered primary public recreation space depends, therefore, on the extent of the facilities and programs provided. Some are really little more than wide sidewalks, and thus offer few recreation opportunities. Others are elongated public parks that attract people who have no intention of visiting any of the stores. Such malls are usually designed, operated, and maintained by local government park and recreation departments as part of city park systems.

PLAYLOTS AND MINIPARKS

Two other public recreation resources that may receive intensive use are playlots and miniparks. Usually less than half a hectare (one acre) in size, most are located in the more densely populated parts of urban areas where space is at a premium. In fact, advocates argue that such resources are needed as substitutes for the missing back-

yards of tenement and apartment buildings. Many have been created in the past 30 years as society became aware of the need for recreation space close to home and as urban streets became less suitable for play because of parked cars and speeding traffic. The availability of vacant lots in the war-damaged communities of Europe and in the decayed inner-city areas of the United States also stimulated the development of playlots and miniparks.

Playlots (also called totlots) are normally developed in one of several special situations. Some are built in large housing projects, especially publicly funded developments intended for less affluent families. Many inner-city playlots occupy part or all of a piece of land from which a house or tenement has been removed. Others are located on readily accessible sites at the edge of larger parks, an arrangement preferred by park professionals because it facilitates protection and maintenance services.

The emphasis in playlots is on play equipment for children, including sandboxes, swings, climbers, and slides. Usually, some benches are provided so that adults can sit and converse while supervising their children's play. Well-designed playlots have injury-reducing sand or wood chips beneath the play equipment and hard surfaces around the seating to withstand foot traffic and facilitate the use of baby carriages and children's wheeled toys. Grassed areas are usually impractical because of heavy use.

The term *minipark* (or vest-pocket park) is used to describe areas similar in size to playlots but that are not primarily intended for children's play. A high proportion

do include play equipment, but the emphasis is usually on providing recreation experiences for a broad range of people. Typical miniparks include shade trees and benches for sitting, ball-game facilities such as full or partial basketball courts, and small amphitheaterlike areas used primarily by teenagers as places to meet and socialize or stage informal entertainments. A few have been built in downtown shopping areas to provide green and tranquil environments in which workers and shoppers can relax or eat lunch. The majority of miniparks and playlots, however, are intended to provide recreation opportunities for people living within the block or housing-development unit where the facility is located.

Miniparks and playlots built on vacant inner-city residential lots have not proved to be the panacea for lack of conventional public and private recreation space that some professionals expected. Many receive little or no use. According to some observers, this is because highly developed miniparks and playlots are inappropriate for these locations. They feel that residents want simple amenities suited to their interests and needs rather than elaborate facilities. For example, they suggest that older children need opportunities for creative play and such experiences would best be provided by *adventure play-grounds.* Introduced in Great Britain and Sweden and now quite common in Europe, these playgrounds contain a supply of boards, logs, old tires, and other relatively inexpensive materials that children are allowed to use for creative play with a minimum of supervision. However, such facilities have not been popular with recreation agencies in the United States because of their appearance, the question of liability, and the problem of providing adequate supervision; only 19 American cities currently have adventure playgrounds.

In many instances, however, it is the minipark's location that is to blame for lack of use. Frequently, such parks have been constructed on one vacant lot in the middle of the block. Consequently, the windowless walls of remaining buildings rise on two or even three of its sides. Since visibility is limited to those standing right in front of the park or living in the building immediately opposite, persons involved in antisocial acts are not readily observed. As a result, illicit activities tend to proliferate. Children and older users alike are frequently intimidated, molested, assaulted, or robbed. At many sites, structures and landscaping have been completely destroyed; some parks have been transformed into a shambles of broken equipment, smashed glass, dumped trash, and scrawled obscenities within days of their completion.

For these reasons, corner lots are preferred locations for miniparks because they are more readily observable. In addition, street corners are the normal gathering places for young people, thus a corner location fits existing social patterns. Irrespective of location, the greatest success with inner-city miniparks has been achieved where the surrounding community has been involved in the planning and development as well as the operation and maintenance of the park. Although such involvement does not preclude vandalism and other antisocial behavior, it usually reduces it substantially.

NEIGHBORHOOD PARKS

As the name suggests, a *neighborhood park* is intended to serve a cluster of blocks or streets that constitutes a small social unit. Cities are divided into neighborhoods by physical or social boundaries such as main streets, nonresidential areas, railroad tracks, highways, rivers, or differences in the residents' economic, ethnic, or religious backgrounds. A typical neighborhood contains 2000 to 5000 people and is 0.75- to 1.5-kilometers (0.5- to 1-mile) wide. Planners usually try to locate a park and an elementary school near the center of each neighborhood so that residents can readily reach them on foot. Sometimes the park and school occupy adjacent or contiguous sites.

Neighborhood parks vary considerably in size and function. Generally, they tend to be smaller in older areas, ranging from less than 0.5 hectare (1 acre) to 2 or more hectares (5 or more acres). In newer communities, planners try to ensure that they are at least 2 hectares (5 acres) in size and many are in the 5- to 10-hectare (10- to 25-acre) range. Small sites are commonly devoted to children's play and teenagers' sports, especially when located next to a school; such parks are then called neighborhood playgrounds. On larger sites, park and recreation agencies normally provide opportunities for as many age groups as possible. Typical facilities include a children's playground; one or more courts or fields (sometimes of junior size) for basketball, softball, tennis, volleyball, soccer, or football; a separate multipurpose area equipped with benches or picnic tables; and various sized areas of grass and shade trees (Figure 13.10). Sometimes neighborhood parks are equipped with children's spray pools, shuffle-

Figure 13.10 **Peter's Park in Boston is typical of many medium-sized neighborhood parks in older areas. The children's playground with its heavily used equipment is in the foreground. The park also contains a baseball field, tennis court, and three lighted basketball courts.**

board courts, ice-skating and hockey rinks, ornamental flower-beds, a toilet building, and some form of storage shed or office. Park and recreation departments conduct most of their children's activity programs in neighborhood parks and school playgrounds.

COMMUNITY PARKS

The term *community park* is used to describe units that serve a number of neighborhoods; some agencies call them district parks. There may be considerable differences in size, depending on the way the park system has evolved. Ideally, each community of 10 to 20 neighborhoods (50,000 to 100,000 people) should have at least one large central park and a series of satellite community playfields distributed throughout the area so that each group of 5 or 6 neighborhoods is served by a playfield. Under these circumstances, all residents only have to travel about 1 kilometer (0.6 mile) to reach a playfield and no more than 4 to 6 kilometers (3 to 4 miles) to visit the large central park. In practice, however, community parks and playfields are not necessarily well distributed. Large parks are often at the edge of older communities because centrally located land was not set aside early enough. Frequently, the central portions of older communities are also inadequately supplied with playfields.

Community playfields are normally between 4 and 10 hectares (10 and 25 acres) in extent. Their main purpose is to provide opportunities for a variety of athletic and sports activities for youths and adults. Usually, there are outdoor facilities for basketball, baseball,

softball, tennis, soccer, and football. Many include some form of bleachers to accommodate spectators; toilet buildings with changing rooms, showers and lockers; and an office and storage building from which sports activities can be administered. Lighting installations that permit events to take place in the evening are becoming increasingly common. Some playfields contain an outdoor swimming pool, a fieldhouse with indoor facilities for basketball and similar sports, or a complete community recreation center. If the site is sufficiently large, the sports activities may be clustered in the interior of the playfield with playlots, neighborhood park facilities, and landscaping forming a buffer around the edge. In this case, the playfield may function as a resource at the block and neighborhood levels as well as at the community level.

Community parks can be from 20 to more than 80 hectares (50 to more than 200 acres) in size; the larger the community served, the more land that is required. Usually, park and recreation departments try to obtain a site that contains at least one major, largely undeveloped resource such as a small lake, a stretch of river, a stand of mature trees, or an area with interesting topography. Where such a site is not available, existing resources may be enhanced by excavating ponds, damming streams, building artificial hills, or by extensive tree planting.

Community parks provide recreation opportunities that most people do not experience every day. They contain family and group picnic areas suitable for outings lasting several hours on weekends or special occasions. Many have swimming beaches, small-boat rental fa-

cilities, fishing opportunities, hiking trails, nature centers, small zoos, special horticultural displays, golf courses, toboggan runs, or modest ski facilities. Special amenities such as day camps, open-air theaters, and museums are sometimes included. Community park sites may also contain playfields and units from other levels in the hierarchy such as playlots or neighborhood parks. Normally, both community parks and playfields are located on or near public transportation routes and include considerable parking space because most users travel several miles.

REGIONAL PARKS

Large cities commonly have one or more major parks located near their outskirts. Typically, such parks are 200 hectares to more than 1000 hectares (500 to more than 2000 acres) in extent and include a fair-sized lake, shoreline area, or woodland. These parks provide opportunities for picnicking, swimming, hiking, fishing, and nature observation in less developed environments and for longer periods than is usually the case in community parks. Most use occurs on weekends or holidays when families and groups of friends can travel some distance to spend several hours or a full day at such resources.

Parks of this type are called *regional parks* because they attract users from a wide area to enjoy features not usually found in community parks. Many are units in city park systems. Others are components of county, regional, or special authority park systems (Figure 9.2). Not all large urban areas have regional parks; in some locations, city park systems do not include parks of this type and adjacent county or regional park systems have not provided such resources close to the cities.

Regional parks are generally less developed than community parks in terms of the variety of facilities and the proportion of the site devoted to constructed resources. Most have extensive picnic facilities comprising a series of units strategically distributed around a lakeshore or through a wooded or rolling landscape so that the feeling of being in an undeveloped rural environment is maximized. Each unit usually consists of a parking area, toilet building, and a number of picnic tables and grills scattered at advantageous spots along the shoreline or among the trees. Areas around and between picnic units are left in a largely undeveloped state. Other typical resources in regional parks include scenic roadways, swimming beaches with appropriate service buildings, extensive walking and riding trails, boat-rental and boat-launching facilities, fishing opportunities from bankside and boats, group camps and day camps, *environmental interpretation centers,* and winter sports facilities. In some systems, regional parks contain swimming pools, marinas, golf courses, family campgrounds, and a variety of sports courts and playing fields.

Not all public open spaces that function as regional recreation resources are called parks; some are named preserves or reserves. Many units of the county forest preserves in Illinois, for example, act as regional parks. Such units often contain developed areas equipped with picnic facilities, trails, and fishing lakes. On the other hand, increasing numbers of city, county,

and regional park agencies are acquiring sizable areas primarily dedicated to nature preservation. Some of these may also function as regional parks, since opportunities for nature study, picnicking, hiking, fishing, or boating are provided. However, this is not always the case; use is limited to interpretation and nature study in some areas. In addition, several cities in the western United States own extensive mountain or desert properties outside their built-up areas; some of these are called parks, but they are largely undeveloped at present and do not function as regional parks.

LINEAR PARKLANDS
The types of open space just described—squares, plazas, pedestrian malls, playlots, miniparks, neighborhood parks, community parks, and regional parks—are the main kinds of units making up park systems administered by city, county, district, and regional park and recreation agencies. In addition, urban systems usually have one or more types of linear recreation resources such as promenades, parkways, valley parks and trail parks. These resources consist of pleasing environments that are intended to provide recreation experiences for people as they travel through them.

Promenades. An important type of linear park is created when a lengthy walkway or *promenade* is built so that people can stroll and enjoy a special resource. The most common form is a promenade located along a river, lake, or ocean shoreline. Some of the largest and most elaborate beach-oriented promenades have been built at European seaside resorts (Figure 13.11). Such developments consist

of broad, paved walkways (often at several levels) along the beach, benches both outside and within shelters, ornamental plantings, toilet buildings, and a number of kiosks selling food, drink, and souvenirs. Promenades often connect small or large parks that contain other local government recreation facilities such as swimming pools, boat ponds, band shells, and concert halls. Public-operated, concession-operated, and privately owned recreation resources associated with promenades commonly include restaurants, boat-rides or other excursion businesses, amusement parks, and recreation piers. Highly developed beach areas of this type attract huge crowds of vacationers and day users during the summer. They are probably more intensively used for a greater number of recreation activities than any other public recreation resource.

Beach promenades are not as intensively developed in Canada and the United States. Atlantic City, New Jersey, and some of the early resort cities in the Northeast have boardwalks or paved promenades, but the public facilities are less elaborate. Elsewhere, public beachfront development has been minimal, usually consisting of little more than a normal city sidewalk, some parking bays, and limited ornamental plantings. Such areas may contain neither publicly provided benches nor toilet facilities. In many American coastal cities, the amount of publicly owned land abutting the ocean is very small because original settlement patterns permitted private ownership of waterfront lots. In addition, hotels, motels, private homes, and seasonal residences sometimes even control the beach above the high-water line. In such

Figure 13.11 The highly developed promenade in the French Mediterranean year-round resort of Juan-les-Pins on the Côte d'Azur near Cannes provides a variety of recreation experiences for large numbers of people. Lighting encourages evening use and changing cubicles (foreground) facilitate swimming, sun-bathing, and boating.

cases, public use is limited to street allowances that run down to the ocean. Large multipurpose piers are also less common in North America; however, fishing piers are being built, especially in warmer locations that have many retired residents or substantial tourist flows.

Promenades built along lake and river shorelines are also important public resources. Lakeshore developments are typically less elaborate than oceanfront promenades, but a few exceptions occur where popular resort towns became established at an early date. Riverside promenades are famous in cities such as Budapest, London, Moscow, and Paris, but most cities have been rather prodigal with their riverfronts, using them primarily for industrial and transportation purposes. However, in the last two decades, many urban areas have started major recreation-oriented waterfront redevelopment programs. Old warehouses, factories, railroad spurs, and docks are being removed and replaced with promenades, malls, parks, and boating and fishing facilities. Where appropriate, old buildings are being renovated or converted to create multipurpose commercial-retail-recreation complexes (Figure 18.4).

Parkways. Originally, *parkways* were curving, land-scaped roads along which people could take relaxing drives in their horsedrawn carriages. A number of city park systems designed in the late 1800s and early 1900s consisted of a series of large parks connected by a ring of parkways. In some cases, the connecting links were in the form of broad boulevards divided into two carriageways by a landscaped strip down the middle. The idea was for people to travel slowly from one large park to another enjoying the beauty of the scenery en route. Later on, with the advent of the automobile era, some parkways were developed that resembled elongated community parks with periodic parking lots, picnic areas, and playfields. Today, some of these parkways and parklike boulevards are important parts of the recreation systems of urban areas such as Boston, Chicago, Kansas City, and Minneapolis.

Unfortunately, growth in motor vehicle traffic and use for routine travel have often completely negated the original intent. Frequently, boulevards and parkways have become the most direct and least interrupted routes leading into or around cities. Resultant high-traffic volumes cause depreciation of recreation experiences in several ways. They result in bumper-to-bumper traffic patterns that fray nerves, cause air pollution, increase the risk of accident, and make leisurely pleasure driving impossible. Heavy traffic also contributes to damaged road surfaces and injury to vegetation from dust, exhaust fumes, salt spray, or accidents. Increasing traffic flows may even lead to loss of landscaped areas when extra vehicle lanes are added to accommodate greater volumes of traffic.

Responsibility for such arteries has sometimes been transferred from park and recreation departments to street or public works departments, making the change from scenic parkway to busy highway virtually complete. The term, *parkway,* may be retained but most of its original meaning has been lost. *Parkway* is also used incorrectly as a name for some modern, controlled-access highways intended primarily to carry large volumes of relatively high-speed traffic. Although some of these expressways may run through attractive landscapes, the recreation benefits obtained are usually minimal because of high speeds and the inability of

drivers to either pull over and stop to enjoy the scenery or drive directly into any adjacent parks.

Valley Parks. Another type of linear resource is the *valley park* created when river or stream valleys are preserved as public open space. This practice is increasing with the adoption of regulations prohibiting construction of buildings on flood plains and the stricter enforcement of regulations concerning water pollution and dumping on bottom lands. Some local governments are obtaining control of such lands by easements or by gradual purchase. Others are using their condemnation powers. For instance, heavy loss of life and property damage caused by flooding resulting from Hurricane Hazel in 1954 prompted the Toronto Region Conservation Authority to expropriate 16,200 hectares (40,000 acres) of valley lands along the eight rivers draining the area. Thousands of acres of this land are now operated as conservation authority recreation areas or local government parks under agreements with the authority. A number of special facilities such as the Ontario Science Center and the Metropolitan Toronto Zoo have also been built on suitable parts of these lands.

In other situations, planning departments and park and recreation agencies seek to create valley parks because of their intrinsic value for recreation. Many urban valleys are remarkably scenic in spite of their proximity to development. This is particularly true where cities have been built on tableland dissected by deeply cut valleys. Road and building construction in such depressions is more difficult, thus their environments often re-

main relatively unaltered. In fact, waterways, patches of woodland, and plant and animal species may actually be reminiscent of presettlement conditions in some valley locations.

Trail Parks. Hiking, bicycling, and horseback-riding facilities in the form of narrow *trail parks* are becoming increasingly important components of urban public recreation systems. Most resources of this type in the United States and Canada have been developed recently. The impetus has come from a resurgence of recreation walking, bicycling, and horseback riding; the general unsuitability of city streets for safe walking and bicycling; and the availability of various rights-of-way. Such trails are being built along abandoned railroads, on the banks of old canals, along powerline rights-of-way, and on linear purchases or easements. In many cases, these trails are designed so that they lead to or connect other kinds of public recreation resources. As a result, trail parks provide not only satisfying physical and aesthetic experiences but also significantly improved access to public recreation sites, especially for individuals who have no motorized transportation. Unfortunately, urban trail parks, like some shoreline and valley parks, are usually more difficult to administer, manage, and protect than parks consisting of compact parcels.

RECREATION CENTERS

The term *recreation center* is used to describe a building or collection of buildings where opportunities for several broad groupings of recreation activities are available (Figure 13.12). As in the case of parks, rec-

Figure 13.12 **The Butzel/Adams Playfield and Community Center is part of the City of Detroit park and recreation system. It consists of a recently completed community center building together with the ice arena, bathhouse, field house, playground, and outdoor sports facilities that existed previously. The ice arena is the only indoor rink in the system but the remaining amenities represent the Department of Recreation's concept of a desirable community recreation center.**

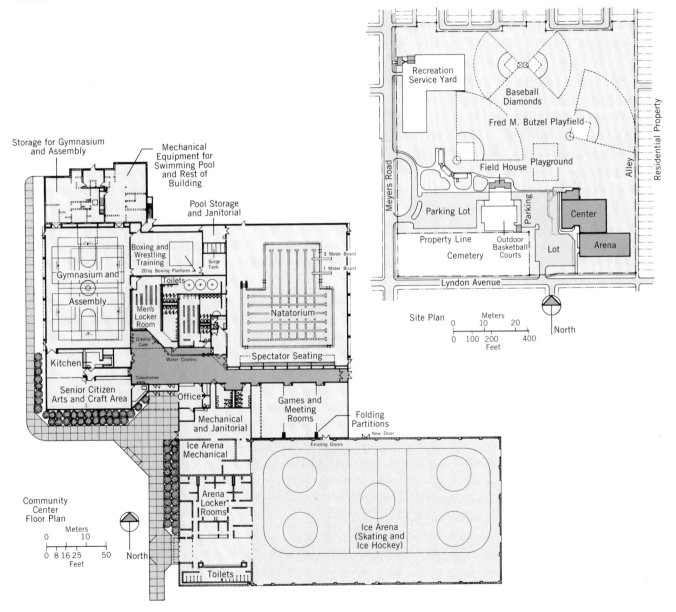

reation centers vary in size and in the quantity and quality of the amenities provided. Usually, they are divided into two groups—*neighborhood recreation centers* and *community recreation centers,* depending on size and function. No well-established dividing line exists, rather, there is a continuum from small simple structures to large elaborate complexes.

Neighborhood Centers. Like neighborhood parks, *neighborhood recreation centers* are intended to serve an area with a radius of from 0.75 to a maximum of 1.5 kilometers (0.5 to 1 mile). The ideal situation occurs where a center is located within or adjacent to a neighborhood park so that both indoor and outdoor activities are provided at the same site. This is not always feasible in older sections of cities so that park and recreation departments are often forced to adopt other approaches. Sometimes a recreation center is built on a small property, which leaves little space for outdoor activities. Under other circumstances, disused shops, old houses, or older public buildings such as obsolete schools and fire stations are converted into neighborhood centers.

Sometimes store and school sites include fair amounts of paved parking or playground space, but usually there is little or no grassed areas suitable for games such as football or baseball. In neighborhoods where a single comprehensive recreation center has not been feasible, a number of separate buildings may be used instead; a renovated house becomes a senior citizen center, a converted store functions as a teenage drop-in center, and an old fire station provides space for arts and crafts programs

and a variety of club activities.

Ideally, a neighborhood recreation center should contain a large mulitpurpose room, a smaller room for arts and crafts, a similar sized room for meetings, kitchen space connecting into the large room and meeting room, an office for the staff, washrooms, and adequate storage space for the necessary games, equipment, chairs, and supplies. Such a center is of maximum value when designed so that each of the three main rooms can function independently of the other two. Three different programs can then take place at the same time without interfering with each other. If the center is located in a neighborhood park, it is advantageous for some toilets to be constructed so that they are accessible at times when the rest of the center is closed. Sports teams and the general public may then use these facilities without gaining entry to other parts of the building. Where the adjacent park is used for winter sports, one room should be directly accessible from the outside so that it can function as a warming room for participants and spectators.

Multipurpose rooms in neighborhood centers are normally too small and do not have sufficient ceiling height for indoor sports such as basketball, volleyball, or badminton (gymnasium-sized rooms are usually too expensive to be included in neighborhood facilities). Active programs are, therefore, limited to children's games, table tennis, some kinds of physical conditioning, various forms of dance instruction, and social or square dancing. At other times, furniture may be brought in or rearranged so that a multipurpose room is suitable for a club meeting, film show, party

or social, talent show, concert, theatrical presentation, banquet, hobby exhibit, card party, or a variety of instructional programs.

The most desirable feature of a multipurpose room is complete flexibility so that it can be rapidly converted from one use to another. Floor-to-ceiling storage space built into one or more walls is usually provided so that folding or stacking chairs and other equipment can easily be set up or put away. A movable stage, portable projection screen, piano on casters, folding card tables, a record player, and a public address system are other basic requirements. Lighting, electrical outlets, doors, windows, and other features should be distributed so that a maximum number of room arrangements is possible. For example, it should be possible to place the stage at one end of the room, in the center, or on one side, depending on the nature of the event. If the room is large, folding partitions that divide it into two or more separate rooms increase its usefulness.

Usually, a second smaller room in a neighborhood center is devoted primarily to arts and crafts. Again, flexibility is desirable so that it is not only an appropriate environment for classes in drawing, painting, sewing, ceramics, and similar activities but also may be used when needed for lectures or meetings involving small groups. If there is a third room, it generally is equipped with folding chairs and tables to make it suitable for a variety of activities such as lectures, club meetings, music instruction or practice, drama rehearsals, and children's programs.

Community Centers. A *community recreation center*

(sometimes called a district center) usually provides neighborhood-type opportunities for people living nearby and more specialized experiences for those residing in all the neighborhoods that lie within the group of neighborhoods that it serves. Therefore, it contains neighborhood center facilities plus amenities that are either used infrequently or that are financially possible to provide only at a few locations. The latter usually consist of an auditorium and a gymnasium with sufficient room for at least one full-sized basketball court. Indoor swimming pools are now becoming more common in community centers, especially in locations where use of outdoor pools without water-heating equipment is limited and where no public school in the community has an indoor pool.

Community center gymnasiums must also be carefully designed to be fully effective. The layout should make it possible to have several practice sessions, informal games, and different kinds of sports or gymnastic activities taking place at the same time with minimum interference. When sports such as basketball are to be played in competitive leagues, an appropriate amount of space must be available for spectators. Male and female locker-room and shower facilities are necessary and should be separate from the locker rooms and toilets serving spectators and other indoor or outdoor areas. Adequate storage space for equipment and seating is also essential.

Similarly, auditoriums in community centers are constructed so that they can serve several functions. If quite elaborate concerts and dramatic presentations are planned, there is usually a fixed stage equipped with wings, curtains, and lighting. Dressing rooms, washrooms, and scenery storage are also required backstage. However, less elaborate space can be suitable for infrequent presentations when the design permits the use of adjacent meeting or craft rooms and toilet facilities are nearby. As in multipurpose rooms, community center auditoriums are equipped with removable seating, partitions, and folding tables so that many different kinds of performances, meetings, exhibitions, and banquet arrangements are possible. In some cases, budget limitations require that a combined gymnasium-auditorium be built, but this is usually undesirable because fewer recreation opportunities can be provided because of design compromises and scheduling conflicts.

Other Center Functions. Neighborhood and community recreation centers also perform a number of important functions that facilitate participation in local government recreation programs. Centers are nearby locations where people may readily obtain information about recreation programs and special events, both in their own neighborhood and at other sites. Young people, the less educated, the less affluent, and those who, because of their ethnic background, have difficulty understanding the language used by most people in the community usually become aware of self-improvement programs and sign up for them much more easily when friendly community center staff members are available to help them. These individuals are much less likely to become involved if participation requires reading a newspaper advertisement, writing a letter, filling out and mailing in a form, or making a telephone call. When located in parks, centers can improve recreation opportunities because the staff provides protection to the facilities and encouragement, assistance, and supervision for the users.

Recreation centers can also help bring about, develop, and maintain a strong sense of community. Individuals in the open space of a park setting tend to recreate beside other people rather than with them. When the same individuals take part in an activity inside a building, however, they more readily begin to talk and exchange ideas with other participants. For this reason, a recreation center can be of great social significance, especially in racially mixed neighborhoods or other locations where it is socially desirable for residents of two or more neighborhoods to meet and become acquainted. A center that provides an interesting variety of facilities and programs can bring people of different backgrounds together and give them many opportunities to understand and appreciate each other.

Distribution of Centers. Not all local governments have recreation centers. In communities where public school systems provide recreation-center-type opportunities, recreation agencies often feel it is either unnecessary or undesirable to build and operate separate recreation centers. Centers are also considered unnecessary in some affluent communities because families have so many recreation amenities at their places of residence. However, home facilities, no matter how extensive, seldom meet all the social, competitive, and physical needs of family members, especially young people. Therefore, the operation of recreation centers is justified even in upper-income communities.

Large-scale development and operation of multipurpose recreation centers by local governments are primarily American and Canadian phenomena. About two-thirds of all cities in the United States with more than 10,000 people have 1 or more centers. The mean number of centers per city is 5 and the median is 2 but some cities have as many as 150 centers. The frequency is somewhat lower in Canada. In Europe, there are virtually no government-operated multipurpose centers. In many nations, local and county-level governments are involved primarily in the provision of a variety of separate facilities such as parks, sports centers, libraries, museums, and art galleries. Their involvement in recreation programs is seldom direct. It generally takes the form of financial aid to other recreation organizations; these include quasi-public sports groups, youth groups, and arts organizations. Some local governments operate centers for youth or older people, but the programs tend to be largely social in nature and other kinds of recreation opportunities are obtained elsewhere.

RECREATION AT SCHOOLS

Local, county, and regional school systems can be major providers of recreation experiences. The number and type of experiences and the clientele served vary greatly from system to system.

Administrative Arrangements. The circumstances under which recreation experiences occur at schools may be divided into several groups. These consist of situations where enjoyment is experienced by:

- Students undertaking activities that are part of their school's normal instructional program.
- Students taking part in extracurricular activities provided for them by their school.
- People of various ages participating in educational sessions that are not part of regular daytime instructional programs.
- Individuals taking part in recreation programs for the general public that are provided by school agencies.
- Members of the general public participating in recreation programs conducted by local government park and recreation agencies using school-system facilities (Figure 8.11).
- People attending programs conducted by quasi-public or private organizations using school facilities, for example, youth organizations, sports groups, and hobby clubs.
- Individuals using school facilities in an informal manner such as groups getting together to play games on a school playground outside school hours or passersby stopping to watch informal play or school sports events.

The number of these kinds of experiences provided by a school depends on the type of resources available, the location of those resources, the policies and programs of both the school agency and local government, and the attitudes and needs of the population.

In some cases, experiences may be limited to those obtained by students during the regular school day because the school agency provides no extracurricular programs, does not permit other agencies or organizations to use its facilities, and only allows use of its playgrounds and sportsfields by its own students during regular school hours. At the other extreme, there are school systems that provide all of the various types of experiences listed above (Figure 13.13). In some locations, boards of education are the sole providers of local government-funded public recreation programs.

The most common arrangement, however, is for education agencies to give priority to in-school, extracurricular, and night-school programs for enrolled students and once those needs are filled to permit limited use of school facilities by other government agencies and quasi-public groups. The amount of use by nonschool groups tends to depend on the traditions of the community and past experiences with arrangements of this kind. Many school agencies are reluctant to permit outside agencies or groups to use school buildings or expensive outdoor facilities because of the difficulties involved. The latter include disrupting normal maintenance schedules, establishing responsibility for the proper use and protection of facilities, paying for extra maintenance and supervision services, and solving the many additional administrative problems that occur.

As a result, nonschool use is often limited to well-established youth groups (such as the Scouts) and local-government-conducted summer recreation programs for children. Not that these concessions are unimportant; many youth groups would never be formed and many park and recreation agencies would find it difficult or impossible to obtain suitable space for their programs if the use of school facilities was not permitted. This is particularly true in many inner-city locations, especially those that are

Figure 13.13 **Members of a ceramics class enjoy opportunities provided by the Pender County Board of Education, North Carolina, in cooperation with the county Recreation Department, the Cape Fear Technical Institute, and other organizations. Opportunities ranging from classes in the arts, music, and square dancing to youth group, volleyball, and basketball programs are offered under a community schools program designed to make optimum use of school facilities. Three-quarters of North Carolina's 156 school districts offer such programs often stimulated by the state's Community Schools Act of 1977 that provides $25,000 grants to participating districts.**

Obviously, more education and recreation opportunities can be provided with greater efficiency if schools and recreation departments cooperate. This principle was jointly adopted as a policy by the American Association for Leisure and Recreation, the National Recreation and Park Association, and the National Community Education Association in 1976. These organizations, representing some 25,000 educators and recreation professionals, issued a joint statement adopting as their common goal the mobilization of the:

> . . . *total available community resources to provide services that offer opportunities for education, recreation, and social services to citizens of all ages, in order to cultivate and enhance the human and environmental potential of our society.*

The statement further declared:

> *We jointly recommend that all communities and states engaged in community school programs, establish a strong formal system of interagency communication, coordination, and cooperation between and among the school systems, existing recreation and park agencies, and other community service agencies. This would provide for the joint planning, development, and operation of all programs, facilities, and services, and would aid in preventing duplication.*[3]

However, although the number of recreation departments and school

inadequately supplied with playlots and neighborhood parks.

In the United States, almost all recreation departments in cities with over 10,000 inhabitants use local school facilities to some extent.[2] Even so, only about 60 percent have formal, written agreements covering such arrangements. This suggests that the use is relatively limited and does not involve highly developed facilities such as gymnasiums and swimming pools in the other two-fifths of the cities. Eighty percent of all cities over 10,000 population (both those with and

without agreements) use school-grounds for recreation department programs. Almost 90 percent use school buildings to some degree. About 45 percent of the city recreation departments are involved in cooperative planning and development of joint facilities.

School authorities and local government recreation departments have many areas of common interest, including arts and crafts, drama, music, sports, and environmental interpretation. In addition, most schools and recreation departments follow policies of providing opportunities for people of all ages; therefore, they share a concern for more than just young people's programs.

[2] Roger A. Lancaster, "Municipal Services," *Parks & Recreation*, 11(7), 18–27 (July 1976).

[3] The National Joint Continuing Steering Committee, *The Ultimate – To Serve*, National Recreation and Park Association, Arlington, Va., 1976, p. 12.

agencies that coordinate their planning, development, and operations is growing, they are still comparatively few.

School Resources. Just as the administrative arrangements under which school facilities are used for recreation differ from place to place, so school-owned resources used for recreation vary considerably. In the case of costly resources that are used extensively for recreation as a secondary use (e.g., theatrical stages and swimming pools), the presence of such facilities depends largely on the affluence of local residents and businesses where school budgets are tied to local property taxes. Similarly, schools generally have more elaborate resources that may be used for recreation in prosperous industrialized nations.

The age of an individual school can also affect the scope of such facilities. Schools built at suburban locations in the last few decades tend to have larger sportsfields and a greater proportion of their building space devoted to recreation-oriented activities than schools built in earlier times. As a result, school-owned resources that could be used for recreation are usually most limited in older, less affluent inner-city areas where the need to supplement private, commercial, and local government park and recreation facilities is greatest. Conversely, school recreation facilities in affluent suburban areas are often exceptional; however, they may be underused because there is a more than adequate supply of similar resources provided by other public agencies or by private and commercial enterprises. These other facilities often seem more attractive,

especially to young people because they are not linked to a public-education facility.

Generally, the school resources used most frequently for recreation are the hard-surfaced play areas. Schools use them for physical education and sports activities during and after school, especially in schools with limited indoor facilities and in regions with warm climates. Schools, recreation agencies, and quasi-public groups commonly make use of school resources for a variety of special extracurricular activities, including sports, children's summer programs, community carnivals and celebrations, arts and crafts instruction, and movable-equipment events, which range from concerts on portable stages to environmental interpretation programs using mobile nature centers.

School-aged children play on these hard-surfaced areas during recess and at other times if such use is allowed. Preschoolers from the immediate area also enjoy using the hard surfaces for their games and for riding their wheeled toys, unless their presence is discouraged. Young adults use them for informal basketball games and other sports, both when it is permitted and often when it is forbidden. Frequently, such areas are also the focus of social activities for the young people of the surrounding neighborhood.

In many systems, middle school and high school properties include athletic fields. Usually, these range in size from as little as 2 hectares (5 acres) to 10 hectares (25 acres) or more, depending on the school size. Senior high schools tend to have more athletic field area per student than middle schools or junior high schools be-

cause of the space needed for full-sized facilities and the larger number of athletic opportunities offered. Middle school facilities usually consist of one or two football or soccer fields, which may also be used for other sports such as softball and field hockey.

High school athletic fields generally have three or more football-soccer-softball fields plus tennis courts and track and field facilities. Some communities have elaborate stadiums used for interschool athletic meets and football or soccer games. Again, the degree to which school athletic fields are used for events administered by park and recreation departments or other groups depends on which agency controls the facilities and what policies it has established. The use of extensively developed athletic fields is usually tightly controlled to avoid damage from improper use, overuse, or vandalism.

The recreation potential of school buildings also tends to increase with academic level. Elementary schools typically have few specialized facilities. Most have a small multipurpose hall with a stage; this room is used by the school for physical education, concerts, and special events. Where permitted, such halls can also be important places for recreation departments and other groups to sponsor concerts, film shows, dramatic presentations, socials, dances, indoor sports, game nights, and classes in gymnastics, dance, or other activities that need space for physical movement. Classrooms may also be used for instructional programs, meetings, and presentations involving small groups.

High schools usually have the most extensive facilities that can be used for recreation. Most high schools contain bigger auditoriums with more elaborate stages than lower level schools, making it possible to accommodate larger audiences and produce more sophisticated shows. In fact, a high school auditorium is often the best publicly owned facility available to a community for the presentation of plays, concerts, lectures, and film shows. The majority of high schools have a series of rooms equipped to facilitate the teaching of classes in creative and industrial arts, music, homemaking, and typing, which can be valuable resources for extracurricular and adult recreation programs.

High schools also frequently possess extensive indoor sports facilities. Large modern school complexes may even include a separate multipurpose building (sometimes called a fieldhouse), which contains a number of courts for activities such as basketball, volleyball, badminton, handball, paddleball, and tennis; a running track; a swimming pool; rooms for gymnastics, wrestling, and weight training; and appropriate teaching, changing, shower, and storage space. Major facilities of this kind generally have a large main gymnasium that can be divided into several smaller activity areas or used as one large hall for special sport and gymnastic events that attract many spectators. The average high school has at least some of these amenities, usually in association with a medium-sized gymnasium.

The potential for recreation opportunities offered by these various school resources is obviously great, but, as mentioned earlier, it is seldom fully realized. In some communities, unselfish cooperation between school and recreation agencies results in optimum educational and recreational benefits for citizens of all ages. The ideal situation is achieved when joint committees that represent both the park and recreation department and the school authorities work together on planning and operational matters of mutual concern.

School/Park Complexes. A number of excellent *school/park complexes* have been constructed and operated under the direction of the joint committees described above. The main objective is to provide the optimum number and kind of education and recreation opportunities for students during school hours as well as for citizens of every age at other appropriate times.

The most frequently encountered school/park facility combines a neighborhood school with a neighborhood park and recreation center (Figure 13.14). Construction details and operating arrangements vary but facilities often call for:

- School use of the recreation center and park facilities for physical education classes and extracurricular activities.
- Recreation department use of the school gymnasium, auditorium, craft rooms, certain other classrooms, and storage space.
- Building features that permit easy access from the outside to rooms used by both organizations and appropriate inside doors, which can be locked to control entry to parts of the building that are not being used.
- The hard-surface playground to be adjacent to the school and designed so that it can be used for physical education activities, play during recess, and play at other times.
- Use of facilities, provision of supervision, and payment of expenses to

be divided on the basis of an equitable formula.

When similar arrangements are made for building and operating school/park complexes that involve high schools, the advantages to the community can be even more spectacular, although not necessarily of greater significance. The use of schools for recreation and other purposes will be increasingly common in the next decade as school enrollments continue to decline. Some school/park facilities are already being used to provide social services in addition to education and recreation. These are known as *community complexes.*

SPORTS FACILITIES

In addition to sports facilities in various types of parks, recreation centers, and schools, the majority of local government recreation systems include one or more specialized sports developments. These provide opportunities to participate in or watch one or several kinds of related activities. They include large stadiums, horseracing tracks, golf courses, ski areas, and marinas.

Stadiums. Although many large stadiums were built by private interests in the past, the current trend is for major facilities to be constructed by city, county, or regional governments. This is largely because of the great cost of the kind of facility that is now considered essential. Competition between major cities to attract professional sports teams and the desire to achieve national or international status through them have been largely responsible for the escalation in the elaborateness of public stadiums. In some cases, costs have be-

Figure 13.14 Beverly Farms Park-School in Montgomery County, Maryland, was developed cooperatively by the county public school board and The Maryland-National Capital Park and Planning Commission. The school uses the gymnasium and ballfield for physical education classes and maintains the area around the building. The park and planning commission maintains the park area and issues permits for afterschool, weekend, and vacation use of the ballfields and gymnasium (which is designed for separate use). The Montgomery County Recreation Department has first call on these amenities and schedules children's softball and soccer, boys' club sports, adult softball, and children's summer programs in the park, and basketball, floor hockey, karate, and jujitsu programs in the gymnasiums. Other parts of the school building are used by school, scout, and religious groups and for recreation department crafts programs.

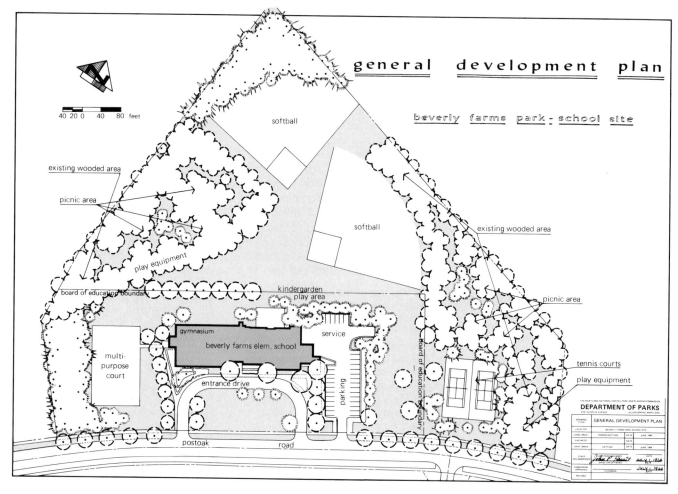

come so high that it has been necessary for state or national governments to become involved in building or financing stadiums.

Currently, there are some 50 new or recently enlarged government-owned major stadiums in the United States. Building or renovating these structures has cost the taxpayers more than $6 billion plus another $1 billion for sewers, access roads, and other services. Some have been constructed in the belief that their presence will bring economic gains to adjacent commercial areas or entire communities. Unfortunately, some of these stadiums are so expensive to operate that the managers are fortunate if they can pay half of the annual operating costs let alone any of the construction costs and the interest on loans. Local or state taxpayers are, therefore, subsidizing most of these ventures, even where one or more major professional sports teams use the stadium.

The majority of the large new stadiums are domed structures, which permit football, basketball, and other sports to be played indoors in air-conditioned comfort before crowds of 70,000 to 90,000 spectators. They are also used for concerts, traveling shows, political meetings, conventions, religious crusades, and trade shows. Part of the high construction cost comes from enclosing and controlling the environment of such huge spaces. The inclusion of elaborate facilities is another major expense. Large sums are spent on cushioned seats, artificial playing surfaces, restaurants and cafeterias, lavish private suites, and giant-screen television systems, which provide spectators with simultaneous and instant-replay pictures of events taking place on the field.

Many of the new public stadiums have been constructed to accommodate owners of teams who have threatened to move elsewhere unless new facilities were built to their specifications. In this way, teams are provided with excellent facilities, which their owners were unwilling or unable to build and, in many cases, the owners benefit substantially from new leases that subsidize their operations at taxpayer expense. Nevertheless, many politicians and taxpayers continue to regard such arrangements as desirable. Supporters of stadium projects feel that a large city must have at least one major league sports team to project a national image, which, in turn, encourages industrial, business, convention, and tourist activity. They see stadiums as symbols of prosperity and sources of civic pride and renewed community spirit. Some regard them as important catalysts for urban renewal programs.

In Pontiac, Michigan, for example, the construction of the Silverdome (Figure 17.5) raised property values and instigated the building of new hotels, restaurants, and bars. On the other hand, city taxpayers are now being assessed a substantial amount each year to pay for the Silverdome indebtedness and to cover its operating deficits. For middle-income homeowners, this is amounting to an additional $50 to $100 on their annual property taxes. At the same time, tickets for sports events, concerts, and traveling shows are sold at high prices in an effort to make the facility self-supporting. Therefore, less affluent taxpayers are contributing substantially to a facility that many of them cannot personally afford to use. Nevertheless, the domed stadiums do provide substantial recreation opportunities, both for more affluent taxpayers and residents of the surrounding communities who are able to attend the various events and for tourists who enjoy guided tours of the facilities.

Although not quite as spectacular or versatile as the domed facilities, most publicly owned stadiums are open-air structures. In New York City, the municipal government owns both Yankee Stadium, which houses the New York Yankees baseball club, and Shea Stadium, home of both the New York Mets baseball club and the New York Jets football team. All of these teams are profit-making commercial enterprises. In an effort to modernize and improve the facilities at Yankee Stadium, the city recently spent $48 million on renovations (this will grow to a total of $240 million by the time all of the interest is paid).

The Los Angeles Memorial Coliseum is administered by a nine-person committee with representatives from the city, county, and state governments. It consists of a 95,000-seat open-air stadium and 20,000-seat indoor arena. The complex is the home of the University of Southern California and the University of California at Los Angeles sports teams. This facility, unlike so many others, has been able to pay its own way through astute management. Whether this continues to be the case remains to be seen, since one of its biggest clients, the Los Angeles Rams professional football team, decided to move to nearby Anaheim. The proposition that lured the Rams away included Anaheim's promise to undertake a $22-million stadium-enlargement project and provide a more favorable lease, which almost guarantees a multimillion dollar profit for the team's owner. Los Angeles, meanwhile, is determined to find a new tenant and to make the stadium more competitive. To do so, the city council sought $9 million in federal funds to modernize the Memorial Coliseum facilities.

Only a short distance from the

Memorial Coliseum is the Rose Bowl. Built and operated by the city of Pasadena, it is the largest facility of its kind, seating 106,900 spectators. Constructed primarily for the annual play-off game between the Big Eight Pacific coast college football championship team and the Big Ten eastern college football championship team, the Rose Bowl is largely unused during the rest of the year. This policy may be changing however; the Super Bowl professional football final was played there in 1977 and it has recently been used for several bartering events known as swap meets.

Not all cities have major facilities like either the Pontiac Silverdome or the Los Angeles-Memorial Coliseum. Even so, most have some form of municipal stadium, large sportsfield, or indoor ice arena where a variety of the community's important sports events and entertainments are held.

Golf Courses. The golf course is another sports facility that involves sizable amounts of money and caters to only a relatively small proportion of an area's citizens. About 14 percent of American golf courses are owned and operated by local government agencies. However, some 5 million people, or approximately 40 percent of the nation's regular golfers, play primarily on these courses. In addition, much of the golf played by the 4 million casual golfers also takes place on municipal courses.

Approximately one-third of the cities in the United States have municipal golf courses. The majority have only one or two courses; 40 percent are 9-hole courses, the remainder are 18-hole courses. Publicly owned golf courses are some-

times included as part of large city or regional parks, but they are also constructed as separate entities.

The city of Los Angeles has what is probably the largest municipal golf course operation in the world. Its 10 full-sized and 4 par-three courses are managed by a special Golf Branch in the Recreation and Parks Department. The region's mediterranean climate makes it possible to play golf during all seasons of the year and more than 1.25 million rounds of golf are recorded annually.

Other Sports Facilities. Local government park and recreation agencies own a great variety of other, less frequently encountered sports facilities. Many have developed boating resources such as launching ramps, docks, and marinas with appropriate landscaping, parking, and washroom facilities. Some of the major marinas on tidal waters, inland rivers, and the Great Lakes are municipally owned.

In northern and mountain locations, local government recreation agencies frequently own and operate winter sports complexes. Most are quite modest, consisting of beginner's ski slopes, toboggan runs, natural ice-skating rinks, and minimal user services. A few are more elaborate and resemble commercial developments. The city of Duluth, Minnesota, for example, spent $6.6 million constructing the Spirit Mountain complex. It has 14 ski runs, 4 chairlifts, 11 kilometers (7 miles) of cross-country trails, and all the snow-making, slope-grooming, lodging, restaurant, and ski school services normally found at a major winter resort.

Local governments sometimes have special spectator facilities in

addition to the conventional stadiums and arenas used for football, soccer, baseball, or hockey. Such facilities may be commercial resources, which have been acquired to prevent severe economic losses in the community. For example, the city of Hialeah purchased Hialeah Park, the famous Florida horseracing track, when the owners experienced major financial problems. It is now being operated on a long-term lease so that the city continues to receive economic benefits from the racing programs as well as from the thousands of tourists who annually pay to see the track's tropical birds, fish, and vegetation.

In some cases, cities have obtained sports resources because private organizations constructed facilities for national or international competitions. In 1978, for example, the city of New York and the U.S. Tennis Association built a major tennis center on city parkland at Flushing Meadow in Queens. The association spent $9.5 million on the development (sale of television rights to the U.S. Open for three years, however, contributed $6.5 million toward the construction costs). The complex contains a 19,500-seat stadium court where major tournaments such as the U.S. Open and the Davis Cup are played, a 6500-seat grandstand court, 40 other indoor and outdoor courts, and appropriate supporting facilities. The association pays substantial rental fees for use of the site during tournaments, but, at other times, the courts are available for use by the public.

Other specialized sports resources found in some municipal park systems include skateboard parks, softball complexes, ice-skating and hockey arenas, bicycle tracks, motorcycling areas, and automobile racetracks. The variety of such facilities appears to be increasing as people's interests and capabilities become more extensive and recreation agencies seek to serve a wider spectrum of the public.

One new type of facility, which is being widely adopted, is the outdoor *parcourse* or *exercise trail.* Patterned after a Swiss fitness program called the *vita parcours,* it provides people of all ages and capabilities with 15 to 25 exercise stations along a running trail. Each station includes a sign explaining the exercise and prescribing the number of repetitions that should be undertaken at varying levels of fitness so that supervision is not essential. Participants set their own pace and perform or skip exercises as they see fit.

Over 1000 courses have been built in Switzerland and southern Germany since the first *vita parcours* was developed 10 years ago. They can now be found in the public parks of almost every sizable community and in rest areas along the busiest autobahns. Introduced into the United States in 1973, parcourse facilities are now provided by over 300 municipalities. Many companies and institutions have also constructed parcourse trails for the use of their employees or students.

MOBILE RESOURCES
Another kind of resource that has been adopted by many local government agencies to provide more evenly distributed and diversified opportunities is the *mobile recreation unit.* Such facilities can be purchased from specialized manufacturers, but many agencies construct

their own, either to save money or to obtain a unit designed for specific needs. The city of San Pablo, California, for instance, converted a schoolbus into a mobile senior citizens center. It goes to places where many older people live, providing them with regular opportunities to see movies, play games, or take part in a variety of social activities or arts and crafts programs.

Most mobile units are designed to supply just one kind of recreation experience. Some are sports and game mobiles. They can be driven to a vacant lot or neighborhood park where the accompanying personnel conduct clinics or programs using the portable equipment. Such units make it possible for young people to enjoy a variety of play-

ground equipment, learn basic sports skills such as boxing, become acquainted with a number of games, develop physical fitness, go swimming, or have fun using roller skates or skateboards (Figure 13.15):

Mobile units are sometimes used to support roving-leader programs designed for children and teenagers. These vehicles are equipped with the items needed to quickly begin games such as softball, baseball, or basketball without extensive organization or special facilities. Leaders drive a van to wherever youths naturally congregate—whether it be on street corners, in parking areas, or on vacant lots—and they initiate impromptu games or social activities.

Figure 13.15 A mobile swimming pool sponsored by a local television station and operated by the Department of Recreation provides children in the City of Detroit with much-needed opportunities to cool off and enjoy playing in the water on a hot summer afternoon. Department staff fill the swimmobile from hydrants and supervise its use. When feasible, they teach the rudiments of swimming to those who wish to learn.

In some places, these programs have proven very successful and have largely replaced the organized activities formerly provided at neighborhood parks. The park programs they replace have been poorly attended but this was not because of a lack of interest but because many would-be participants were too intimidated to take part. In these locations, the neighborhood parks have become "home turf" to young people of the immediate area and, as a result, they are considered off limits to anyone living outside an invisible but nevertheless well-established boundary.

Other mobile units include cultural facilities that allow people to see movies, watch puppet and magic shows, attend plays and concerts, borrow books, or take part in arts and crafts activities. A few function as traveling zoos, nature centers, or museums, making zoo or farm animals, specimen collections, scientific or historical exhibits, and many other educational experiences more readily accessible. In Milwaukee, Wisconsin, for example, the recreation department has constructed a mobile observatory-planetarium facility with technical assistance from the local astronomical society. This mobile unit makes it possible to conduct astronomy programs anywhere in the city.

OTHER RESOURCES

This section has provided a general overview of many of the designated recreation resources that are commonly administered by local governments. Discussion of culturally oriented resources such as theaters, museums, and libraries, is deferred until Chapter 16. Similarly, local government amenities that provide recreation opportunities but that are not designated or managed as recreation resources—these include roads, airports, and reservoirs—are examined at the end of Chapter 15.

EXAMPLES OF LOCAL SYSTEMS

It is impossible to understand the diversity of recreation areas, resources, and programs involved in local government systems unless specific examples are examined in some detail. This can be a never-ending task for the dedicated recreation professional because of the infinite variety of such systems. They form a continuum extending from simple rural township park systems—consisting of only one or two small areas maintained by road crews—to huge urban systems with hundreds of parks, dozens of buildings, and thousands of employees.

This great diversity is produced by variations in the controlling factors shown in Figure 13.2. Ways in which these factors have affected the nature and scope of local systems include these examples:

- Early settlement patterns, survey systems, and political influences produced small irregularly shaped cities, townships, and counties in some regions and large, predominantly rectangular political units in others, thereby affecting the availability and shape of lands that were later set aside for recreation.
- Lakes, swamps, ravines, mountains, flood plains, and deep river valleys often hindered settlement and preserved landscapes that later became valuable recreation resources; conversely, where such features did not prevent settlement, few potential park sites remained available for subsequent designation and use.
- Influential politicians, businesspersons, philanthropists, civic organizations, or recreation professionals persuaded some communities to develop extensive recreation systems early in their histories; other communities, lacking the influence of such innovators, developed few or no recreation resources.
- Some communities have traditions that certain kinds and numbers of recreation opportunities are the responsibility of the local government; for instance, some give special emphasis to cultural or sports facilities, whereas others specialize in landscaped parkways, ornamental gardens, or multipurpose recreation centers.
- More affluent local government units often have a wide range of modern, well-kept recreation facilities, whereas economically depressed communities may have only a few, deteriorating resources.
- Extremely affluent communities may provide few or no local government recreation resources because residents believe that the existence of extensive personal and organization recreation resources make public programs unnecessary.
- Regions with the necessary enabling laws have district or regional park agencies, whereas places without such legislation have no such organizations.
- Municipal recreation facilities may be relatively accessible in well-planned modern suburbs but quite difficult to reach in some inner-city areas where railroads, expressways, main thoroughfares, industrial zones, dilapidated neighborhoods, and other physical or psychological barriers limit or discourage use.
- Public willingness or reluctance to pay taxes or fees for recreation amenities result in well-funded or inadequately financed systems.

It is not surprising that no two local government recreation systems are exactly the same, since influences of these kinds vary extensively from place to place and interact in a variety of ways.

BASIC CHARACTERISTICS OF 17 SYSTEMS

The uniqueness of each local government recreation system makes it impossible to illustrate adequately the nature and scope of such systems in a limited space. However, the basic characteristics of 17 different city, township, county, special district, and regional systems have been compiled in Table 13.2 to indicate the range of agencies and jurisdictions that are involved and the great variety of resources that they provide. The table also illustrates the problems encountered when attempting to compare systems by means of such information. Since it only includes a few basic statistics concerning each system, three systems are later described in some detail to more fully demonstrate the scope of the recreation facilities and programs administered by local and regional governments.

The systems summarized in the table include several kinds of agencies. In the cases of Cheyenne, Wyoming; Sioux City, Iowa; Evansville, Indiana; Kansas City, Missouri; Delta Township, Michigan; Terrebonne Parish, Louisiana; Gaston County, North Carolina; and Dade County, Florida, the agency is called the *parks and recreation department* or some similar name. The Riverside County, California, and Metropolitan Toronto, Ontario, Canada, agencies are both called a *parks department,* indicating that their primary responsibility is the provision of park facilities. The Milwaukee County, Wisconsin, department's name indicates it also administers cultural resources.

Wooded open-space protection is the primary purpose of the Forest Preserve District of DuPage County, Illinois, but it also provides extensive recreation facilities. As explained earlier, the Huron-Clinton Metropolitan Authority, Michigan, has concentrated on developing a dozen fair-sized regional parks (Figure 9.2). Flood control by means of dams, reforestation, and improved agricultural methods is the primary objective of the Muskingum Watershed Conservancy District, Ohio; however, it has established extensive picnicking, swimming, boating, fishing, and camping facilities on its impoundments.

The first three columns of Table 13.2 indicate the magnitude of each agency's overall responsibilities in terms of the total area, total population, and average population density of the jurisdiction being served. The total area ranges from 2800 hectares (6900 acres) for Cheyenne, Wyoming, to 1,866,000 hectares (4,608,000 acres) in the case of Riverside County. (The latter is a huge, elongated area extending across most of southern California from Los Angeles County to the Colorado River on the Arizona border.) Populations vary from the 14,000 citizens of Madison to the Huron-Clinton Metropolitan Authority's 4,453,000 people. Similarly, population densities vary from 0.2 person/hectare (0.1 person/acre) in Terrebone parish to 33.3 persons/hectare (13.5 persons/acre)/ in Metropolitan Toronto.

Clearly, such differences in the numbers, areas, and densities to be served greatly affect the design, operation, and use of these recreation systems. However, average population densities do not tell the whole story because some munici-palities include large industrial or undeveloped areas that make the averages much lower than the actual densities in the main residential areas. Similarly, some townships, parishes, and counties include densely populated sections near cities but have much lower average densities because other sections contain few people. In addition, many local government recreation systems receive heavy use by residents of other jurisdictions so that total population and average density values do not necessarily indicate the number of people being served.

The next three columns of Table 13.2 express the amount of land managed by the recreation agency as a total area, as a percentage of the government's total jurisdiction, and as an average area per 1000 population. Generally, city park and recreation agencies manage 5 to 10 percent of their jurisdictions, whereas townships and county park and recreation agencies control a much smaller proportion. Milwaukee County's Department of Parks, Recreation and Culture is an exception among the township and county park and recreation agencies since it manages 6.7 percent of the county; this high proportion occurs because the county is small and the system includes both the former city of Milwaukee park system and extensive flood-plain lands.

The Terrebonne Parish Parks and Recreation Board and the Gaston County Recreation and Parks Department manage no lands directly because both use facilities controlled by other agencies. The Terrebonne Parish board offers most of its programs at recreation centers and parks that are developed, administered, and maintained by the parish's eight recreation dis-

Table 13.2 Examples of Local Regional Government Recreation Systems

Type of System	Government Unit or Agency	Jurisdiction Contains — Thousands of Hectares (Acres)	Thousands of Persons	Persons per Hectare (Acre)	Lands Managed — Total Area in Hectares (Acres)	Percent of Jurisdiction	Hectares per 1000 Population (Acres)	Number of Units (Percent of Area) — Square or Mall	Playlot, Minipark	Neighborhood Park	Community (District) Park or Playfield	Regional or Metropolitan Park	Linear Park or Parkway	Budgets in Dollars — Capital in Thousands (per 1000 Population)	Other in Thousands (per 1000 Population)	Number of Employees — Permanent (per 10,000 Population)	Part-time (per 10,000 Population)
Town or city system	Town of Madison, Conn.	9.5 (23.4)	14	1.5 (0.6)	93 (230)	1.0	6.7 (16.4)	2 (1.8)	1 (1.5)	2 (2.6)	1 (23.5)	0 (0.0)	1 (0.4)	45 (3,229)	225 (16,101)	6 (4.3)	195 (13.9)
	City of Cheyenne, Wyo.	2.8 (6.9)	55	19.6 (8.0)	223 (550)	8.0	4.1 (10.0)	38 (4.6)		8 (6.7)	1 (7.3)	2 (35.5)	0 (0.0)	114 (2,074)	863 (15,691)	7 (1.3)	75 (13.6)
	Sioux City, Iowa	13.3 (32.9)	89	6.7 (2.7)	1,049 (2,591)	7.9	11.8 (29.1)	0 (0.0)	11 (0.55)	18 (7.0)	7 (3.9)	12 (79.3)	0 (0.0)	1,069 (12,045)	1,152 (12,975)	82 (9.2)	420 (47.2)
	City of Evansville, Ind.	8.9 (22.0)	134	15.2 (6.1)	882 (2,178)	9.9	6.6 (16.3)	4 (0.02)	16 (0.73)	19 (4.9)	8 (28.2)	2 (47.8)	6 (18.4)	3,015 (22,500)	2,340 (17,466)	179 (13.4)	550 (41.0)
	Kansas City, Mo.	81.8 (202.0)	473	5.8 (2.3)	3,764 (9,293)	4.6	8.0 (19.7)	2 (0.02)	6 (0.08)	131 (17.4)	13 (19.8)	4 (41.2)	108 (21.2)	898 (1,899)	11,002 (23,259)	630 person/years	
Township system	Meridian Township, Mich.	8.3 (20.5)	34	4.1 (1.7)	133 (329)	1.6	3.9 (9.7)	0 (0.0)	4 (1.7)	3 (53.5)	5 (14.4)	1 (30.4)	0 (0.0)	0 (0)	0 (0)	0 (0)	0 (0)
	Delta Township, Mich.	9.1 (22.6)	27	3.0 (1.2)	141 (349)	1.5	5.2 (12.9)	0 (0.0)	1 (0.3)	0 (0.0)	5 (99.7)	0 (0.0)	0 (0.0)	488 (18,074)	221 (8,185)	7 (2.6)	25 (9.3)
County or parish system	Terrebonne Parish, La.	463.0 (1144.0)	86	0.2 (0.1)	33 (81)	0.01	0.4 (0.9)	1 (1.2)	0 (0.0)	0 (0.0)	0 (0.0)	2 (98.8)	0 (0.0)	0 (0)	382 (4,463)	4 (0.5)	52 (6.1)
	Riverside County, Calif.	1866.0 (4608.0)	585	0.3 (0.1)	7,543 (18,625)	0.4	12.9 (31.8)	0 (0.0)	0 (0.0)	0 (0.0)	0 (0.0)	22 (69.8)	1 (26.8)	1,250 (2,137)	1,500 (2,564)	70 (1.2)	75 (1.3)
	Gaston County, N.C.	93.1 (230.0)	170	1.8 (0.7)	0 (0)	0.0	0.0 (0.0)	0 (0.0)	0 (0.0)	0 (0.0)	0 (0.0)	0 (0.0)	0 (0.0)	420 (2,471)	180 (1,059)	6 (0.4)	40 (2.4)
	Dade County, Fla.	570.0 (1408.0)	1500	2.6 (1.1)	4,437 (10,955)	0.8	3.0 (7.3)	0 (0.0)	32 (0.24)	63 (3.1)	53 (7.1)	17 (48.7)	77 (12.4)	13,000 (8,667)	34,409 (22,939)	849 (5.7)	1,055 (7.0)
	Milwaukee County, Wis.	87.8 (217.0)	1655	18.8 (7.6)	5,881 (14,520)	6.7	3.6 (8.8)	9 (0.06)	12 (0.26)	29 (2.5)	26 (6.3)	37 (37.1)	13 (52.5)	2,325 (1,405)	37,035 (22,381)	990 (6.0)	1,745 (10.5)
Park district	Willamalane District, Oreg.	4.5 (11.2)	45	10.0 (4.0)	166 (409)	3.7	3.7 (9.1)	0 (0.0)	0 (0.0)	9 (7.3)	8 (19.3)	1 (61.1)	0 (0.0)	289 (6,422)	2,332 (51,828)	4.2 (9.3)	300 (66.7)
Forest district	DuPage County, Ill.	85.5 (211.0)	720	8.4 (3.4)	6,234 (15,393)	7.3	8.7 (21.4)	0 (0.0)	0 (0.0)	0 (0.0)	0 (0.0)	32 (100.0)	0 (0.0)	2,800 (3,888)	2,600 (3,611)	94 (1.3)	100 (1.4)
Metropolitan	Metropolitan Toronto, Ontario, Can.	62.6 (154.6)	2086	33.3 (13.5)	3,196 (7,892)	5.1	1.5 (3.8)	1 (0.01)	0 (0.0)	0 (0.0)	0 (0.0)	24 (100.0)		3,610 (1,731)	6,521 (3,126)	160 (0.8)	450 (2.2)
Regional	Huron-Clinton Metropolitan Authority, Mich.	858.0 (2119.0)	4453	5.2 (2.1)	6,867 (16,955)	0.8	1.5 (3.8)	0 (0.0)	0 (0.0)	0 (0.0)	0 (0.0)	11 (100.0)	0 (0.0)	5,800 (1,303)	11,101 (2,493)	183 (0.4)	592 (1.3)
Conservation	Muskingum Conservancy District, Ohio	*	*	*	1,052 (2,598)	*	*	0 (0.0)	0 (0.0)	0 (0.0)	0 (0.0)	5 (100.0)	0 (0.0)	1,500 (*)	2,252 (*)	14 (*)	156 (*)

SOURCE: Compiled from park system brochures, annual reports, and correspondence with agencies. Most data are for 1978–1979. Similar data were requested from New York City but were not forthcoming. *Indicates data were not supplied.

tricts. These districts are distinct units of the parish government; separate capital improvement and maintenance taxes are levied in each district to provide funds for the development and operation of the district's recreation facilities. Gaston County Recreation and Parks Department, on the other hand, currently provides most of its programs at public schools or municipal parks. However, it plans to acquire its own lands in locations where these amenities are inadequate or absent.

Among the special agencies (those having jurisdiction over functions other than recreation or areas larger than a county), the Forest Preserve District of DuPage County manages the highest proportion of the land within its jurisdiction (7.3 percent) followed by the Municipality of Metropolitan Toronto Parks Department (5.1 percent). Much of the property managed by the latter is river-valley land acquired to reduce future flood damage following Hurricane Hazel's devastation in 1954. In contrast, the Huron-Clinton Metropolitan Authority controls only 0.8 percent of its five-county area around Detroit; however, it has neither the Canadian department's broad recreation responsibilities nor access to large areas of publicly owned floodplain.

The value in the column showing how much agency land there is per 1000 persons is an index of how well a jurisdiction is supplied with recreation lands of this type. Sioux City and Kansas City appear to be better supplied than the other municipalities listed. However, the degree to which the lands are developed and the nature of the facilities affect the number of opportunities created. The Forest Preserve

District of DuPage County, for example, has given priority to land acquisition so that it has a high area-per-1000-persons figure (8.7) but provides limited facilities. Nevertheless, area-to-population ratios are commonly used as one index of recreation opportunity supply. The National Recreation and Park Association recommends that urban communities have a minimum of 8 hectares (20 acres) of regional parks and 4 hectares (70 acres) of other kinds of urban parks per 1000 persons.

The next six columns of Table 13.2 list the number of different kinds of park units in each system and the percent of the system's area that each kind occupies. Generally, the city park systems have the widest distribution of units and area among the various types. Evansville has a fairly typical distribution pattern but unusually high proportions of the Kansas City system's units and acreage consist of neighborhood and linear parks. Most of the latter are parkways. Riverside County exhibits a pattern characteristic of many county systems—most of the system's area consists of a relatively few regional parks. The Milwaukee County system functions as a combined city and county system and therefore has numerous squares, playlots, neighborhood parks, and district parks as well as regional and linear parks. The Dade County Metropolitan Park and Recreation Department, Florida, functions similarly in the unincorporated areas, but most cities situated within Dade County have their own park systems.

Agency budgets are divided into funds spent for capital improvements (buying land or constructing facilities) and all other ex-

penditures (administration, operations, and maintenance) in the next two columns of Table 13.2. In each case, the amount spent per 1000 persons is also shown. During the period concerned, the Sioux City, Evansville, Delta Township, Dade County, and Willamalane, Oregon systems spent more per capita on new amenities than the other agencies. On the other hand, all of the cities together with the Madison, Dade County, Milwaukee County, and Willamalane District systems made much larger expenditures per person on administration, operations, and maintenance. This is primarily because they provide extensive recreation facilities and programs on a year-round basis, which require numerous employees and substantial expenditures for supplies and services. In contrast, the Riverside County, DuPage County, Metropolitan Toronto, and the Huron-Clinton systems provide few organized recreation programs and only have large numbers of users during limited periods each year; thus their per capita operating costs are lower. The Meridian Township, Michigan, system currently has no staff or formal budget. Administration and maintenance are provided by planning and public works employees on an ad hoc basis.

The last two columns of Table 13.2 show the actual number of permanent as well as seasonal and part-time employees together with the number of employees per 10,000 citizens. Usually, agencies that offer extensive organized recreation programs have the highest ratios of employees to citizens. Some have comparatively few permanent employees and many seasonal or part-time staff members.

For example, the Beach and Recreation Department in Madison has only 6 permanent personnel but it employs almost 200 seasonal and part-time staff. A good number of the latter only teach or lead one activity for a few hours each week. However, a park department that provides only a few organized programs may also have substantial numbers of seasonal and part-time workers if it has numerous beaches requiring many attendants and operates its own rental and food services. Park agencies may also temporarily hire considerable numbers of persons for seasonal construction or maintenance projects under government programs designed to reduce unemployment. For instance, 15 of the 25 seasonal or part-time employees of the Delta Township Department of Parks and Recreation were paid with federal employment assistance funds. Therefore, the number of persons that an agency employs is not a clear indicator of the scope of its various programs.

THE EVANSVILLE SYSTEM

Evansville is an important regional center for a farming, coal-mining, and oil-producing area in southwestern Indiana and adjacent areas in Kentucky. Its industries include manufacturers of steel products, foods, plastics, furniture, and pharmaceuticals. Although the city only has a population of 134,000, a total of about 300,000 people live in the five-county metropolitan area.

The Evansville Department of Parks and Recreation is headed by an executive director who is responsible both to the mayor and a four-person board of park commissioners. The department has an an-

nual budget of between $3 and $6 million, depending on the amount of funds obtained from outside sources. In 1977, for example, the $5.3 million budget included $850,000 from the U.S. Army Corps of Engineers for construction of boat-launching ramps on the Ohio River, $705,500 in U.S. Economic Development Administration funds to carry out extensive renovations and development of department facilities, $400,000 in U.S. Department of Labor grants for zoo improvements, $185,000 from the U.S. Department of Housing and Community Development for park rehabilitation and land acquisition in the central city, and $75,000 in federal grants from the Land and Water Conservation Fund to assist with development of the 13-kilometer (8-mile) long Greenbelt Park. Another $94,000 came from smaller grants, donations, and bequests. The balance of the money expended consisted of city taxes and user fees.

Facilities. The Evansville park system's 55 individual units occupy 882 hectares (2178 acres). The 12 largest parks account for 86 percent of this area, the remaining units being mostly 2 hectares (5 acres) or less in extent. All but one of the larger parks are located well away from the downtown area. Most units in the older parts of the city are small, many being 0.4 hectare (1 acre) or less in size. The southeastern sector has the fewest facilities—it contains no large parks and the small parks are widely spaced so that several school sites are used for department programs.

Picnicking facilities are provided at 35 locations and consist of 450 picnic tables and 11 picnic

shelters. Some of the shelters are simple open-sided structures; others are screened or totally enclosed and equipped with kitchens. They may be rented at modest rates for group picnics involving from 30 to 250 persons. The more elaborate shelters and a number of meeting rooms, banquet rooms, or lounges in other park buildings and golf-course clubhouses are available for more formal meals and other social events. Two-thirds of the picnic areas have adjacent play space and most include children's play apparatus.

Evansville is better provided with public swimming pools than most cities of its size. The department has 12 aquatic complexes, 9 of which have a children's wading pool in addition to a swimming pool. One is a modern indoor complex containing a spectator lounge, sun deck, snack bar, children's play pool, and an eight-lane, 50-meter Olympic pool with a 3.7-meter-deep (12-foot-deep) diving area. User fees are charged at only 2 of its 12 pools.

The city has 56 public tennis courts; 30 are located in parks and the rest are at elementary or high schools. The department operates three 18-hole golf courses, two lighted par-three courses, and one miniature golf course. Other sports facilities provided by the department include 25 softball diamonds, 2 football fields, 16 horseshoe courts, and 4 volleyball courts. An ice arena with a regulation 26-by-31-meter (85-by-100-foot) ice surface, a snack lounge, and supporting facilities was opened in 1979. Bosse Field, a 5265-seat stadium and home of the Evansville Triplets minor league baseball team is also the department's responsibility.

The system includes a number of other special facilities such as the Mesker Park Zoo, which attracts more than 250,000 visitors each year. Near the zoo is an outdoor music theater. Another park contains a roller-skating rink with modest entry fees and low skate-rental charges. A modern nature center is located in an 80-hectare (200-acre) virgin hardwood forest traversed by signed interpretive trails.

The city has a modest system of recreation centers consisting of two department community centers and five senior citizens centers provided by the Evansville Housing Authority. However, the department uses many other facilities for its programs including schools, churches, commercial health clubs, racquetball clubs, and bowling centers, as well as their own nature center and park shelters. The department's programs are, therefore, much more accessible than the distribution of city-operated recreation centers would indicate.

Programs. The Department of Parks and Recreation estimates that informal use of the system amounts to some 2 million user-occasions annually compared to about 500,000 user-occasions for instructional programs, organized sports, and special events. However, some informal use such as walking, jogging, and aesthetic appreciation is not included in the estimates. The major groups of organized programs and the estimated participation in user-occasions are:

- Swimming programs—informal swimming (254,000), swimming instruction (32,000), and competitive team swimming (8000).
- Softball and baseball programs—informal play (87,000), 425 competitive slow-pitch league teams (212,000), and eight sites where no-cut junior baseball is played (667).
- Basketball programs—informal play (22,000) and 103 competitive league teams (19,000).
- Golf programs—informal play, tournaments, leagues, and championships (142,000); there are also 10 instructional classes (667) and individual instruction by the golf pros who manage the golf courses.
- Tennis programs—informal play, a series of formal tournaments (34,000), and 45 instructional classes (3600).
- Zoo programs—regular attendance (221,000) and "Children's Day," "Christmas at the Zoo," and "Halloween at the Zoo" (18,000).
- Unorganized use—picnicking (276,000), use of play apparatus (113,000), use of open-field and play areas (132,000), walking on trails (113,000), and visits to scenic overlooks (19,000).
- Nature programs—informal visits to the nature center and reserve (52,000), nature clubs for children (550), junior naturalist programs, family presentations on Sundays (9600), and guided walks and field trips.
- Children's activities—summer playground programs involving sports, games, music, nature study, arts and crafts, and special events (52,000) and nonresidential camping (800).
- Senior citizens' programs—informal use of the senior citizens centers (65,000) and participation in special monthly events (24,000).
- Programs for special populations—drop-in participation in games and exercises and day-camp experiences such as sports, games, swimming and field trips (420).
- Special musical events—"Bluegrass Sunday," a six-hour program of music and refreshments, (15,000); "Mid-Day Mid-Town Music Series," downtown lunch-hour presentations, (1200); Mesker Music Theater concerts (15,000); and "American Music in the Parks" (950).
- Arts and crafts and self-improvement programs for all ages—more than 140 classes are offered, including classes in guitar, disco dancing, oil painting, photography, ceramics, theater, baton twirling, slimnastics, bowling, weightlifting, contract bridge, interior decorating, house plants, and landscaping (10,600).
- Recreation center programs—informal participation in center activities (87,000) and drop-in programs (19,000).

Many other unique or smaller programs are provided such as a Riverfront Park Craft Fair (12,000), a traveling show wagon featuring amateur talent (1800), an "Almost Anything Goes" competition in which teenagers take part in a series of unusual relay-type events (6500), an adult football program (2600), and volleyball, racquetball, archery, soccer, jogging, and running programs.

The department has developed an extensive mechanism for keeping in touch with citizen attitudes and desires. There are 12 advisory committees and independent societies that make suggestions concerning the zoo, cultural arts, nature education, bikeways, and golf, tennis, aquatic, teenager, and senior citizen programs. A continuous evaluation of department facilities and programs is carried out, using telephone interviews and clip-out questionnaires in brochures and local newspapers. The telephone survey contacts half of the participants in each season's programs. The findings help staff members evaluate their performance, judge the appropriateness of programs, and discover new ways in which to serve the citizens. The department has also attempted to contact both users and nonusers by means of questionnaires mailed to metropolitan-area households or completed by students in city high schools.

The park commissioners keep informed of conditions throughout the system by holding regular board meetings at departmental facilities in various parts of the city and encouraging citizen participation. It appoints task forces and holds public hearings when evaluating special problems. The annual program-planning procedure consists of a zero-based budgeting approach so that no activity is automatically continued. Instead, 19 separate program budgets are prepared and evaluated on the basis of how effectively each will contribute to the achievement of departmental goals.

THE NEW YORK CITY SYSTEM

New York City has one of the world's most complex local government recreation systems. It consists of more than 1150 individual properties, a number of which are large areas containing a wide variety of resources. A geographically fragmented urban structure and multilayered political and administrative systems add to the complexity of the situation.

Administration. Local government recreation resources in New York City are managed by the Parks, Recreation & Cultural Affairs Administration (PRCA). It is one of the super agencies that report directly to the mayor under the city's strong-mayor form of government. The mayor selects the agency's head and a number of other employees are also political appointees. The mayor's office prepares the city's budget, which is reviewed by the Board of Estimate. This board consists of the mayor, the comptroller, the president of the city council, and the presidents of the five boroughs. A weighted voting system makes it possible for the mayor, comptroller, and council president to outvote the five borough presidents.

In these ways, the mayor, various political leaders associated with the mayor, and members of the mayor's administrative staff can exert considerable influence on both the staff and budget of the PRCA administration. However, the city council also has a measure of control because it has to approve the budget and all city laws. The 37-person council is composed of 27 members elected from specific districts plus 2 elected at large from each of the five boroughs. The mayor may veto council decisions, but the council may override the veto by means of a two-thirds majority.

Although the days of blatant corruption are long gone, political organizations are still strong in New York City and staff members of the PRCA administration are still subject to direct political pressures. Some people feel that this is an essential part of the democratic process. Other believe it is more desirable for agency administrators to be protected from direct pressure by insisting that everything except routine matters be decided by a group of elected or appointed officials such as a city council or park and recreation board.

Political influence may be applied through the mayor's office or by means of a number of intermediaries, including city council members and borough presidents. With their own offices and administrative staffs, the presidents act to some extent as if they were borough mayors. They do not have direct control over the major operating agencies but frequently make their wishes known to agency administrators, especially the district managers within their boroughs. In addition to the traditional political organizations, New York City also has a large number of strong ethnic, neighborhood, and special-interest groups that use these various administrative channels to influence city agencies.

New York City is not the only community where the management of recreation resources is directly affected by political pressures. However, there is no other city where recreation administrators operate such a large and diversified system under such complex political and administrative structures. The situation is further complicated by the extremely heavy use and resultant deterioration of many of the recreation resources and the difficulty the city has been experiencing lately in raising sufficient funds to pay for even the most basic public services.

Facilities. The division of the city into a complex system of subcities, smaller communities, and neighborhoods has had a profound effect on the supply of recreation opportunities. This fragmentation partly results from the fact that the city is split into many separate geographic units by its bays, inlets, and wetlands (Figure 6.11). Only the Bronx is part of the mainland and it is surrounded on three sides by water. Richmond (Staten Island) and Manhattan are both islands. Brooklyn and Queens occupy the western end of Long Island.

The New York City recreation

system occupies 15,110 hectares (37,300 acres), an area more than two-and-a half times the size of Manhattan Island and equal to 18 percent of the city's total area.[4] These lands are not uniformly distributed among the five boroughs. Queens has 44 percent of the total area and only 7 percent is in Manhattan. Each of the other three boroughs has 16 percent.

On the other hand, the distribution is more equitable when the area of each borough is taken into account. The Bronx and Queens both have 22 percent of their area in city recreation lands compared to 18, 17, and 12 percent respectively for Manhattan, Richmond, and Brooklyn. However, Richmond is in a much better position than any of the other boroughs if the area of parkland per 1000 population is calculated. It has 7.6 hectares (18.8 acres) per 1000 persons, whereas Queens, the Bronx, Brooklyn, and Manhattan have 3.5, 1.8, 1.0, and 0.7 hectares per 1000 respectively.

Although many of the system's components are small squares, neighborhood parks, or playgrounds, a surprising number are large parks (Figure 13.16). There are 43 parcels that are more than 40 hectares (100 acres) in extent; 11 of these are in Queens, 10 on Staten Island, 8 in Brooklyn, 7 in Manhattan, 5 in the Bronx, and 2 straddle the Brooklyn-Queens boundary. Several occupy more than 400 hectares (1000 acres). Among the largest are Pelham Bay Park in the Bronx occupying 860 hectares (2125 acres) and Marine

Park in Brooklyn occupying 740 hectares (1829 acres). Parts of these and some of the other large parks have not been developed.

The properties of the New York City recreation system are classified into three main groups— parks and park strips, major playgrounds, and squares and miscellaneous public places. The system contains 592 park or park strips; some of these are large irregular tracts divided by waterways and highways. Others such as Bryant Park behind the New York Public Library are only a few hectares in extent, consisting of all or part of one or more city blocks. A number are linear parks; one of the longest is Riverside Park, which extends for almost 10 kilometers (6 miles) along the Hudson River. The PRCA administration also develops and maintains landscaped areas along 160 kilometers (100 miles) of city parkways; these include extensive plantings of flowering shrubs.

The administration has over 230 major playgrounds under its care, excluding those that are part of a park. Each one is equipped with basketball courts and other sports facilities as well as children's play equipment. In addition, the city has more than 260 playgrounds owned by the Board of Education or the Housing Authority, which are operated jointly by these organizations and the PRCA administration. Finally, the PRCA administration is responsible for more than 60 city squares, 145 triangles, and 110 plazas, malls, promenades, and other public places. These resources are particularly difficult to maintain because many contain less durable amenities such as monuments, fountains, or floral displays; are heavily used; and are often subject

to severe littering and vandalism.

The New York City recreation system offers a wide range of sports resources. Among the most significant are:

- Its eight stadiums which include the 55,000-seat Shea Municipal Stadium and the 54,000-seat Yankee Stadium.
- More than 380 turf softball diamonds, 230-hard-surfaced softball diamonds, and 180 baseball diamonds; about one-third of the turf fields are little-league-sized diamonds and a similar proportion of the baseball fields have spectator seating.
- Its 330 volleyball courts, 400 paddle tennis courts, 2000 handball courts, and 480 tennis courts.
- Jogging trails at 20 locations, 25 running tracks, 7 cross-country courses, and 40 playground, boardwalk, park, and parkway areas designated for bicycling—either daily or periodically.
- Its 13 full-sized golf courses (averaging 5440 meters or 5950 yards), of which 4 are open year-round, 2 are pitch-and-putt courses, 1 is a miniature course, and 2 are driving ranges.
- A total of nearly 900 shuffleboard courts, 350 horseshoe-pitching courts, 100 boccie courts, and 20 lawn-bowling greens.
- Bridle paths in 10 parks with a combined total length of more than 65 kilometers (40 miles); horses and riding instruction are available from concessionaires in two of the parks or from nearby commercial stables.
- Ice skating during suitable weather on many park lakes where the ice is tested and maintained by PRCA administration personnel; the system also has 5 outdoor and 2 indoor artificial ice rinks and 20 locations where skiing or sledding is permitted.
- More than 100 American football fields and 40 soccer fields.

In addition, a substantial portion of the city's 930 kilometers (580 miles) of waterfront is suitable for

[4] All data in this section are for 1970 unless otherwise indicated. The PRCA administration was unable to supply more recent information.

BRONX

1 Bronx Park
2 Claremont Park
3 Crotona Park
4 Ferry Point Beach Park
5 Macomb's Dam Park
6 Pelham Bay Park
7 Riverdale Park
8 St. Mary's Park
9 Sound View Park
10 Van Cortlandt Park

BROOKLYN

11 Coney Island Beach & Boardwalk
12 Dyker Beach Park
13 Fort Greene Park
14 Manhattan Beach Park
15 Marine Park*
16 McCarren Park
17 Prospect Park
18 Red Hook Recreation Area
19 Shore Road Park
20 Sunset Park

MANHATTAN

21 Battery Park
22 Central Park
23 East River Park
24 Fort Tryon Park
25 Fort Washington Park
26 High Bridge Park
27 Inwood Hill Park
28 Randall's Island Park
29 Riverside Park
30 Ward's Island Park

QUEENS

31 Alley Park
32 Baisley Pond Park
33 Brookville Park
34 Clearview Park
35 Cunningham Park
36 Flushing Meadow Park
37 Forest Park
38 Highland Park
39 Juniper Valley Park
40 Kissena Park

RICHMOND (STATEN ISLAND)

41 Barrett Park (zoo)
42 Clove Lakes Park
43 Conference House Park
44 Fresh Kills Park
45 LaTourette Park
46 Silver Lake Park
47 Willowbrook Park
48 Wolfe's Pond Park

*Part of this park is now in the Gateway National Recreation Area

Former major New York City parks now part of the Gateway National Recreation Area:

Canarsie Park
Great Kills Park
Jamaica Bay Wildlife Refuge
Rockaway Beach Park
South Beach Park
Spring Creek Park

Principal City of New York parks ●
Gateway National Recreation Area
Limited access highways ——
Major streets ——

Figure 13.16 **A map of the five boroughs of New York City showing the distribution of the larger areas managed by the Parks, Recreation, & Cultural Affairs Administration. These lands are only part of a system that includes over 1150 individual properties. Although the larger parks are quite well distributed throughout the city, many residents do not have ready access to these resources or smaller parks and playgrounds.**

recreation. To increase the recreation potential of this resource, the PRCA administration has provided 40 places where people can fish from beaches, piers, or the banks of waterways and seven marinas with boat-launching and mooring facilities.

Resources for family recreation are also extensive. Picnic areas are available at 30 locations and contain some 2700 picnic tables. The city's eight beach parks include 30 kilometers (18 miles) of beach; amenities include rental lockers, chairs, and umbrellas. Residents may also cool off at four types of inland facilities. About 300 sprinkler showers or spray pools are provided for small children and 60 minipools are maintained for older children. Adults and older children can use 28 full-sized outdoor swimming pools and 11 indoor pools. Concessionaire-operated facilities include nine locations where rowboats or pedal boats can be rented, 15 cafeterias or restaurants, and dozens of food counters and pushcarts.

The PRCA administration operates eight recreation centers. In addition to the indoor swimming pools already mentioned, these centers contain gymnasiums, boxing and exercise rooms, gamerooms, auditoriums, meeting rooms, arts

and crafts rooms, and woodworking shops equipped with power tools. Six golden-age centers are provided for senior citizens. Golden-age groups also meet at 13 other properties that have suitable facilities. In some parks, families or individuals may use small garden plots to grow their own vegetables or flowers.

Finally, the PRCA administration provides many culturally oriented opportunities. The administration has complete control of the resource in some cases; in others, a city-owned resource (such as an art museum or zoo) may be operated by a nonprofit organization with the PRCA paying for some or all of the maintenance and services. Examples of the various resources involved include:

- Zoos in Central Park, Prospect Park, and Flushing Meadow Park; the Bronx Zoo; and the New York City Aquarium at Coney Island, all of which are—or soon will be—operated by the New York Zoological Society with PRCA administration assistance; similarly, the Staten Island Zoological Society operates the Barrett Park Zoo.
- The New York Botanical Garden, the Brooklyn Botanic Garden, the Queens Botanical Garden, the Wave Hill Center for Environmental Studies, and the Conservatory Gardens in Central Park.
- Seven city museums, including the Metropolitan Museum of Art, the American Museum of Natural History, and the Museum of the City of New York.
- New York City libraries consisting of 10 central or special libraries, 178 branch or regional libraries, and a number of bookmobiles; the PRCA administration provides liaison and budgetary review between the system's three units.
- Fourteen theaters, concert halls, and outdoor areas used for concerts, in-

cluding Carnegie Hall, the Delacorte Theater in Central Park (Figure 16.3), and the New York State Theater at Lincoln Center. The administration owns the land and the buildings in nearly all cases and is often the source of much of the funding, but the operation of major facilities is directed by trustees.
- More than 750 statues, columns, and other sculptures or memorials in various parks and squares, including the Army and Navy sculptured groups in Brooklyn's Grand Army Plaza, the Hans Christian Andersen statue in Central Park, and Grant's Tomb in Riverside Park. The PRCA administration has a separate division that cleans, preserves, and repairs these amenities.
- Historic landmarks designated under the Landmarks Preservation Commission of the PRCA administration, including city-owned structures such as the Poe Cottage and the Bartow-Pell Mansion.

The New York City recreation system also contributes to the cultural life of the city by providing seven areas that may be used for band practices, 10 band shells, 23 designated "troubadour areas" where people may play guitars and other stringed instruments, and 19 "forum areas" where political meetings and speeches may take place.

Programs. The organized recreation programs provided by the PRCA administration are as diverse as the city's recreation resources. Programs are organized on a borough basis and adjusted to meet the needs of the populations involved. Many are similar to those described earlier for Evansville, Indiana. Others are special programs adapted to the rather different conditions existing in some sections of the city.

One of the PRCA administration's most successful special programs is its mobile unit service.[5] Started in 1971, over 40 units now create more than 3000 events every year. Each unit consists of a large semitrailer truck with the requisite equipment stored or built into the trailer. The 11 types of mobile units and their functions are as follows:

- Playmobiles equipped with climbers, sliding poles, rocking horses, and basketball hoops that provide play opportunities for children under 10.
- Sportsmobiles that permit young people to enjoy trampolines, volleyball, soccer, shuffleboard, golf, chess, checkers, backgammon, and table tennis.
- Swimmobiles that become mobile swimming pools when their long tanks are filled with water from street hydrants.
- Arts and crafts units that provide opportunities for ceramics, wood sculpture, collage, tie-dying, mask-making, and bead work.
- Cinemobiles equipped with rear-projection screens that show full-length feature films.
- Showwagons that contain movable stages and sound systems used for rock, soul, country, jazz, and magic shows.
- Puppet and marionette vehicles that present shows produced by the administration's professional puppeteers.
- Zoomobiles that contain various animals—ranging from rabbits, lambs, goats, and cows to monkeys, parrots, and snakes.
- Skatemobiles equipped with 120 pairs of roller skates and a music system that make it possible to turn any suitable hard surface into a roller-skating rink.
- Tennismobiles that contain all the equipment needed (including rackets and balls) to transform a city street

[5] Cathie Behrend, "Recreation at Your Doorstep," *Parks & Recreation, 12, 6* (June 1977).

into temporary tennis courts.
- Boxingmobiles that consist of portable boxing rings, complete with dressing rooms, mats, gloves, and headgear used for demonstrations as well as for amateur bouts.

Appropriately trained leaders always accompany each unit.

Mobile units are not used on a casual basis. Instead, community meetings are held in each sector of the city to discuss needs and possible sponsors. Units are then scheduled according to need, support, and the past record of neighborhoods or organizations as sponsors. Depending on the situation, a unit may be set up on a city street, in a park or playground, or on space owned by another agency or organization. The PRCA administration considers all block associations, hospitals, therapeutic centers, quasi-public youth organizations, churches, and museums to be potential sponsors.

THE DADE COUNTY SYSTEM

Dade County occupies the southeastern corner of the Florida peninsula and includes the Florida Keys together with about half of the Everglades National Park. Most of the county was originally part of the huge Everglades freshwater swamp. Now, much of it has been drained and converted to agricultural and urban uses or is operated as part of a large-scale flood-control, drainage, and water-conservation project. Most of the county's urban development and 1.5 million inhabitants are concentrated in a strip along the county's eastern edge. The principal cities are Miami, Miami Beach, Hialeah, and Coral Gables. Its economy is based primarily on tourism, convention business, seasonal residents, retirees, and agriculture.

Administration. The Metropolitan Dade County Park and Recreation Department is administered by a director who reports to the Dade County Parks Board; it, in turn, is responsible to the Dade County Board of Supervisors. As Figure 13.17 shows, the department is divided into seven main units in addition to the director's office. The three divisions in the upper part of the chart are responsible for research, planning, and administration. The remaining divisions are primarily involved in the operation of facilities and programs.

The department had a total budget for 1978–1979 of $47.4 million, of which $13 million was used for capital expenditures such as land acquisition, new facilities, and major reconstruction. The remaining $34.4 million was spent on administering, operating, and maintaining the system. About $17.4 million of the money for these noncapital expenditures came from the county's general fund and was allocated as shown in Figure 13.17; the balance consisted of revenues from user fees and the sale of food, drink, and other items. Unlike some county and regional park systems, Dade County devotes a considerable proportion of its budget to providing a wide range of recreation services, including organized programs.

Facilities. The 3931-hectare (9706-acre) Dade County park system is comprised of the 180 units shown in Table 13.2 and another 33 units that do not fall into any of the categories in that table. The latter include an ornamental garden, a

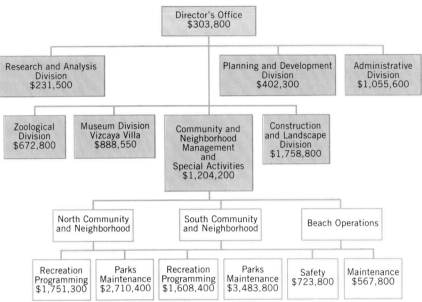

botanic garden, an historic mansion and grounds, a shooting sports range, a family campground, an organization camp, and a campground and beach that can only be reached by boat. These 33 units occupy a total of 1266 hectares (3127 acres) or 28.5 percent of the system.

The department divides its facilities into four categories. Large parks, which consist primarily of relatively undeveloped resources (such as ocean beaches), that provide a range of family-oriented opportunities are classified as metropolitan parks. Major parks with a primary emphasis on extensive developments for sports such as softball, racquetball, tennis, football, firearms shooting, or equestrian activities are called regional parks. Community parks are generally larger than 2

hectares (5 acres) in size and contain facilities that require constant supervision, for example, recreation centers and swimming pools. Neighborhood parks are smaller and have no constantly supervised facilities.

Dade County's community and neighborhood parks are located in the unincorporated urbanized communities that surround the metropolitan area's 16 incorporated municipalities. These small parks are used primarily by the residents of the unincorporated communities. Each incorporated municipality has its own neighborhood parks, swimming pools, and recreation programs; many also have larger parks and specialized facilities such as beaches, golf courses, and stadiums. However, the Dade County metropolitan and regional parks are

used extensively by residents of these municipalities as well as by those who live in the unincorporated areas. Some major county facilities are also important tourist attractions.

Examples of the large parks and special facilities in the Dade County system are:

• Crandon Park—the county's largest park—occupies two-thirds of Key Biscayne, a barrier island reached by a causeway across Biscayne Bay. Amenities in the park include 4 kilometers (2.5 miles) of beach, 102 beach cabanas, a zoo, a narrow-gauge railroad, an amusement park, a miniature golf course, a roller-skating rink, play areas, a marina, and extensive picnic areas in an attractively landscaped setting.
• Dade County Auditorium—a 2500-seat facility with excellent acoustics—is used for ballet, opera, concerts, and stage shows.
• Vizcaya Museum and Gardens—built to resemble an Italian Renaissance villa—consists of a 70-room mansion full of artwork and antiques surrounded by gardens containing numerous pools, fountains, and sculptures.
• Trail Glades Ranges—a large rifle-, pistol-, skeet-, and trap-shooting facility—is used for practice and competitions by individuals, a number of local clubs, and several state organizations.
• Thompson Park—located on the edge of the Everglades and designed primarily as a family camping park—contains three fishing lakes.
• Elliott Key Boating Park—a destination for day-long boat, fishing, and overnight camping trips—is accessible only by boat and consists of a small campground, marina, and park on another of Biscayne Bay's barrier islands.

Altogether, six of the larger county parks have beaches on either Biscayne Bay or the open Atlantic Ocean.

Programs. Supervised activity programs for children and adults are offered at more than 30 parks and school playgrounds. A well-developed athletic program consists of softball, volleyball, basketball, and other team-sport leagues together with opportunities for tennis and archery. Southern Florida's warm climate makes it possible to undertake these activities year-round, but a number of programs are expanded during the summer months, especially those intended for school-age children. These latter programs include camping, outdoor education, contests, special events, and supervised trips. Painting, ceramics, dance, music, drama, and other cultural activities are offered throughout the year.

DIVERSITY AND UNIQUENESS

These examples scarcely begin to indicate the diversity that exists in the nature and extent of municipal, township, county, district, and regional government recreation systems. Altogether, there are over 78,000 units of lower level government in the United States consisting of 18,517 incorporated municipalities, 16,991 townships, 3044 counties, 23,885 special districts, and 15,781 school districts.[6] Not all of these units operate recreation resource systems, but many do so and each one is different.

In studying the scope and contribution of these recreation agencies, it is important to appreciate the similarities that the various systems exhibit but, at the same time, recognize the uniqueness in function that often exists. If the functions

of all the lower level government recreation agencies in a region are considered, a hierarchical system emerges. Somewhat like commercial recreation enterprises, lower level government recreation systems function as regional, subregional, or community resources in terms of the size of the area from which most of their users emanate. Such hierarchies exist within larger hierarchies that include various kinds of intermediate (state or provincial) and national government-administered recreation systems. Intermediate level recreation systems will be described in Chapter 14.

[6] U.S. Department of Commerce, Bureau of the Census, *The Statistical Abstract of the United States,* U.S. Government Printing Office, Washington, D.C., 1977, Table No. 479.

DISCUSSION TOPICS

1. How significant have the recreation opportunities provided by lower levels of government been in your life and the lives of people with whom you are familiar? Have such resources provided any experiences that would probably not have occurred otherwise?
2. What form of local government administrative structures and arrangements are involved in the provision of public parks, schools, and recreation programs in the urban area with which you are most familiar? Would changes in these structures and arrangements improve people's access to recreation opportunities?
3. Prepare a concise summary of the recreation resources, informal recreation opportunities, and formal recreation programs provided by a local government with which you are familiar. Are these resources, informal opportunities, and programs adequate, well balanced, and satisfactorily distributed?
4. Examine the facilities, location, and clientele of several public parks or recreation centers in a city with which you are familiar. How do the resources you select fit into the classifications suggested in this chapter (playlot, neighborhood park, neighborhood center, community center, etc.)?
5. Should county and regional park agencies provide organized recreation programs?

Since many periodical articles and most recreation textbooks concern themselves with the recreation facilities and programs provided by lower levels of government, there are many sources of additional information. However, many of these sources tend to focus on the how-to-do-it aspects of facility management and activity programming. Often there is little mention of the nature and distribution of lower level government recreation resources.

The Fourth Edition of Doell's well-known textbook, *Elements of Park and Recreation Administration* (Charles E. Doell and Louis F. Twardzik, Burgess, Minneapolis, 1979), contains much useful information in the chapters concerning city, suburban, metropolitan, and county park systems. Similarly, additional insights can be obtained from Richard Kraus's introductory chapter, "The Role of County and Local Governments," in *Recreation and Leisure in Modern Society* or from Chapter 3, "Structure and Organization of Recreation and Park Agencies," in *Creative Administration in Recreation and Parks* by Kraus and Curtis, published in St. Louis by Mosby in 1977. Discussion of the role of schools in providing recreation opportunities appears in appropriately titled chapters in *Public Administration of Recreational Services* by George Hjelte and Jay S. Shivers, published in Philadelphia by Lea & Febiger in 1978, and in *Public Recreation Administration* by Jesse A. Reynolds and Marion N. Hormachea published in 1976 by Reston Publishing of Reston, Virginia.

Articles describing recreation resources administered by lower levels of government are often included in recreation journals, especially *Parks & Recreation.* However, it is usually necessary to consult materials prepared by individual agencies if comprehensive reviews of facilities and programs are desired. A few agencies have excellent summary material of this kind. Sometimes, an organization's annual or biennial report provides an adequate overview. In many cases, however, it is necessary to piece together information from a number of reports, lists, and conversations to obtain a complete picture of an agency's resources. Personal visits to recreation systems, continuous monitoring of articles in newspapers, and periodic attendance at agency meetings are also necessary if one wishes to obtain an in-depth understanding of facilities, programs, and problems.

14

PUBLICLY OWNED RECREATION RESOURCES: STATE AND PROVINCIAL AGENCIES

CONCEPTS & PROBLEMS

Special Roles of Intermediate and National Parks
Preservation or Use Conundrum
System Comparison Is Not Easy
Great Variety of Intermediate Park Resources
Classifications Differ Widely
Resources, Settlement, and Goals Affect Nature of System
Acceptability of Lodges, Logging, or Hunting in Parks
Forest Programs Vary Greatly

Figure 14.1 **Lake Barkley State Resort Park** in western Kentucky offers users a wide range of amenities including overnight accommodations at a modern lodge (foreground) or campground (across the inlet), tennis courts and an activities center (near lodge), and a sand beach, boat ramp, picnic area, and playground (top left). A recreation director and a park naturalist supervise an extensive program of organized recreation activities.

This chapter describes the main recreation resources administered by *intermediate governments* such as individual states in the United States and the provinces in Canada (Figure 14.1). Chapter 15, which follows, is primarily concerned with resources controlled by national governments but concludes with a summary of institutional and undesignated resources administered by all three levels of government. Generally, the intermediate and national government cultural resources will not be discussed until Chapter 16 except where they are integral parts of park systems used as examples.

SIGNIFICANCE OF INTERMEDIATE AND NATIONAL RESOURCES

Most recreation resources administered by intermediate and national governments are used less than those under local governments. Nevertheless, intermediate and national resources are equally significant components of our recreation systems for several important reasons. First, such resources offer recreation opportunities that are not available in most people's home communities. These opportunities range from seeing exceptional scenery or famous historic sites and taking camping vacations on picturesque lakeshores to backpacking in undeveloped wilderness areas. Second, many intermediate and national government resources extend over much larger areas than local government lands. Users can, therefore, undertake more expansive activities such as hunting and off-highway vehicle driving.

Third, intermediate and national government recreation resources are generally some distance from users' homes so that visiting them involves travel. Whether the journey is short or long, the anticipation, preparation, travel, and recollection phases are likely to be longer and provide more pleasure than most visits to local government resources. Such experiences are often perceived as special occasions because the resources are not as accessible or visited as frequently as those closer to home. Fourth, there is often an element of excitement involved in going to intermediate and national government areas because they are less familiar or completely unknown. These resources provide a special kind of excitement for those who visit them to take part in higher risk activities such as rock climbing, white-water canoeing, or downhill skiing. Finally, the uniqueness or remoteness of some intermediate and national resources gives them a special allure; some people dream about visiting them for months, years, or even their entire lives.

Although the total recreation use of intermediate and national government resources is generally much smaller than the use of local government parks, there are some state, provincial, and national resources that are major suppliers of opportunities. For example, state parks on Long Island in New York State (Figure 10.7) draw huge crowds of beach users on fine weekends and holidays during the warm months; Jones Beach State Park, for instance, frequently has 250,000 visitors at one time. Similarly, large numbers of users visit intermediate and national government resources such as Illinois Beach State Park near Chicago,

Huntington State Beach near Los Angeles, Point Pelee National Park in southern Ontario, or the various units of the National Capital Parks in Washington, D.C. Such areas are often similar to local government parks in appearance, use, and operation. Some critics contend that these areas should be developed and managed by local governments and not by intermediate or national agencies. Others feel that there is a need for higher levels of government to share the responsibility of providing areas for heavy use by urban residents to an even greater extent.

Some intermediate and national government resources are of great importance to society because of their roles in environmental and heritage preservation. Not that local governments are inactive in these areas. Indeed, some contribute substantially to historic preservation, whereas others maintain significant undeveloped environments. Nevertheless, most local governments have neither the mandate nor the resources necessary to make major contributions in these areas. Responsibility for preserving famous historic sites, spectacular geologic formations, unique fossil beds, declining wildlife populations, and vanishing ecosystems, therefore, falls primarily on the higher levels of government.

Society places a special value on parks that preserve resources such as the prehistoric cliff dwellings of Mesa Verde National Park in Colorado, the underwater flora and fauna of Florida's John Pennekamp Coral Reef State Park, the heather moors and red deer herds of Exmoor National Park in southwestern England, the unique animal communities in East African reserves like Tanzania's Serengeti National Park, or the active volcanic peaks, snowfields, glaciers, lakes, forests, grasslands, and desertlike areas of Tongariro National Park in New Zealand. These and hundreds of similar reserves around the world are not just places where people enjoy themselves; they are also the bank vaults in which humanity is attempting to preserve many irreplacable aspects of its heritage.

Many of these resources are also of great scientific value. In addition to providing opportunities to study various species and ecosystems, they are also reservoirs of increasingly rare biologic materials, which may prove invaluable to human welfare in the future. As a result, some individuals and agencies give priority to preservation and scientific study and consider public use of scientifically significant parks and reserves to be undesirable. This is often the case in less developed or totalitarian nations where public use of such areas is still minimal or where widespread public support is not required to assure adequate government funding. In such nations, national parks and reserves are often not open to everyone. Limitations may range from restricting use to a small number of guided tours on specified roads to allowing only a few scientists with special permits to enter. Deciding how to manage resources for both the preservation of heritage values and public use is the most difficult problem facing many state, provincial and national agencies.

Finally, recreation resources administered by intermediate and national governments are often of more direct economic significance than resources controlled by local governments. Some local agency

resources that draw participants from throughout a region (for example, major beaches, zoos, stadiums, and marinas) increase local business revenues; however, most local government resources have relatively small direct economic impact. In contrast, many intermediate and national recreation resources produce substantial seasonal or year-round economic benefits for the areas in which they are located. This is often the main reason communities wish to be the site of major intermediate or national level recreation developments. In some cases, government agencies select sites for major recreation developments to promote economic advancement at locations where it is most needed.

INTERMEDIATE RESOURCES

Intermediate governments established at a level between local governments and national governments are found primarily in the larger nations. The most extensive and highly developed intermediate government recreation resources are in the United States and Canada where state and provincial governments play a major role in providing recreation opportunities. They acquire, develop, and manage a wide range of recreation resources, pass a variety of far-reaching laws affecting recreation, and often provide extensive financial and technical aid to local government park and recreation programs.

AMERICAN STATE PARKS
The more than 4000 individual units comprising state park systems in the United States have a total area of over 4.5 million hectares

(11 million acres). This is almost equal to the combined area of Massachusetts and New Hampshire. Thus state parks are a significant part of the nation's landscape. Attendance at state park systems exceeds 600 million user-days per year, which is well over twice that of the national park system. State park systems, therefore, are significant suppliers of recreation opportunities in spite of the highly seasonal nature of much of their use and the relative inaccessibility of many units.

Comparing Park Systems. Each of the states has state-administered parks, but there are considerable differences in the nature, extent, and facilities of the 50 systems. Although the National Association of State Park Directors periodically compiles nationwide state park data, objective comparison of systems is difficult because such statistics do not necessarily indicate a system's scope.

Comparison of the number of units in one state park system with the number in another can be misleading. For example, Oregon is listed as having 242 parks and therefore appears to have a more extensive system than Michigan with only 93 units.[1] However, Oregon's system is administered by the Highway Division of the State Department of Transportation and includes 30 wayside parks, which are less than 8 hectares (20 acres) in extent; Michigan's system is

[1] Most statewide data in this section are from the National Association of State Park Directors report, *State Park Statistics — 1975,* compiled primarily from 1975–1976 statistics and published by the National Recreation & Park Association, Arlington, Va., in 1977. More detailed information is from individual listings or brochures issued by the various state park systems.

under the Department of Natural Resources and contains no roadside parks. Oregon has 80 parks—one-third of its units—under 40 hectares (100 acres) in area, whereas only 10 Michigan parks—11 percent of its units—are that size.

Development in many of the smaller Oregon state parks is limited to basic picnicking facilities and only one-fifth (53 parks) have camp-grounds. Most of these camp-grounds are small; just 7 units (3 percent of the parks) have camp-grounds with more than 100 sites. On the other hand, the majority of Michigan's units contain a full range of facilities and 90 percent (83 parks) include campgrounds. More than half of Michigan's state parks (52 units) have campgrounds con-taining over 100 campsites and 37 percent have 200 or more sites. Sim-ilarly, state park systems that in-clude many small historic sites may appear to be more extensive than those that do not if only the num-ber of units is considered.

Another commonly used com-parative measure is the total area of a park system. This yardstick also fails to distinguish between systems that are small in area but have been extensively developed and systems that have large areas but contain comparatively little develop-ment. For example, North Carolina has 34 quite extensively developed units totaling some 28,000 hectares (69,000 acres), whereas Nevada's 16 units, containing 58,500 hect-ares (144,500 acres), are relatively lightly developed. In a number of cases, state park systems contain one or more huge wilderness-type parks that distort the impression ob-tained when the areas of such sys-tems are compared to data for sys-tems without such expansive

Figure 14.2 Two staff members in addition to the person in the contact station (left), greet users entering Michigan's Dodge #4 State Park on a busy summer weekend. Like many of the other highly developed systems, Michigan's state parks monitor use by limiting access, installing traffic counters, and recording information concerning the number of days people camp in the park.

undeveloped units. Area statistics can be particularly deceptive in some western state park systems where large tracts of desert are in-cluded. Such lands produce limited recreation opportunities because of high daytime temperatures, aridity, limited vegetation, and environ-mental fragility.

The number of persons using a state park system is another indica-tion of its relative significance, but this criterion also has its problems. Some systems have tight entry con-trols and accurate counting proce-dures at each park (Figure 14.2); others have little control on where or when people enter the parks and estimate attendance by rather crude methods. In addition, the majority of use in some systems is by long-term campers and day-users who stay many hours, whereas much of the attendance recorded by other systems may consist of people mak-ing brief sightseeing visits or using readily accessible parks for nonre-creational rest stops. As a result,

use estimates can vary considerably in both accuracy and meaning.

The amount of money a state park agency spends on operations and maintenance is also a potential index of the number of opportuni-ties a system provides. Unfortu-nately, the amounts expended de-pend partly on the kinds of activities involved, the nature of the facilities, the quality of the services provided, and the location of the units. Operating a modern resort-type park is much more expensive per user-day than running a rela-tively undeveloped woodland campground. Park systems that try to keep washrooms spotless, beaches clean, buildings and walk-ways in good repair, and grounds free of litter obviously spend more moneys than systems that accept lower maintenance standards. Re-cently built, high-quality paved roads cost less to keep in good con-dition than older, patched, bi-tuminous surfaces or gravel roads that must be frequently graded. Finally, units in urban areas usually pay more for labor and many basic materials than parks in rural locations.

There are a number of other park features that may be useful in comparing systems such as their goals and policies, the number and quality of facilities, and the size and nature of staffs and programs. However, it is even more difficult to obtain comparable data on a nationwide basis for these kinds of characteristics.

Regional Differences. Figure 14.3 shows the regional differences in the basic characteristics of number of units, area, expenditures, and use. The right-hand section of the diagram presents these data related to the size of each region's population; this indicates the relative adequacy of state park system lands and operational budgets and also provides an impression of the participation rates for each region. However, these rates must be interpreted with caution because considerable numbers of users go to parks in regions other than the region in which they live and some regions attract larger proportions of outsiders to their parks than others. The population actually served by a region's parks, therefore, may differ considerably in size from the region's population according to the census.

The Pacific Region and the Middle Atlantic Region are clearly the leading regions in terms of total area, size of budgets, and amount of use (left-hand section of Figure 14.3). The Pacific Region accounts for approximately 20 percent of the parks, 25 percent of the area, 17 percent of the budgets, and 21 percent of total national usage. In com-

parison, the much smaller Middle Atlantic Region accounts for approximately 11 percent, 36 percent, 26 percent, and 17 percent of each of these categories respectively. The Pacific Region's leading position is primarily the result of the large number of state parks in California, Oregon, and Washington; the extensive areas in the Alaska and California systems; the substantial budget in California; and the considerable attendance in California, Hawaii, Oregon, and Washington. In the Middle Atlantic Region, New York State's approximately 1.2 million hectares (3 million acres) of parklands is the main reason for this region having more area than any other. Both New York and Pennsylvania have large budgets and high attendance.

The Pacific and Middle Atlantic regions are ahead of other regions even when their substantial populations are taken into consideration. The former has 34.7 hectares (85.7 acres) and the latter 38.3 hectares (94.6 acres) per 1000 population (right-hand section of Figure 14.3); both figures are well ahead of the national average of 18.8 hectares (46.5 acres) per 1000. However, much of the land involved is relatively inaccessible to the large urban populations so that high ratios do not necessarily mean that more opportunities are available to the majority. The Middle Atlantic Region spent $2210 per 1000 population compared to the $1986 figure for the Pacific Region. Both values are greater than the national average ($1512) but less than the East South Central Region's $3064 figure; however, this latter value is largely a result of the high cost of operating modern resorts in the Kentucky and Tennessee systems.

The participation rate in the Pacific Region (4228 user-days per 1000 population) is higher than any other. This is to be expected because of the long park-use seasons experienced (especially in California and Hawaii) and the large number of tourists who visit units in these and the other states in the region.

At the other extreme is the West South Central Region; it has only 4.7 hectares (11.7 acres) of state parkland per 1000 population or 2.5 percent of the national total. This region also had almost the lowest expenditure on operations and maintenance—just $938 per 1000 population or 62 percent of the national average. (Only the West North Central Region is lower with a value of $936.)

Degree of Development. Individual state park systems differ considerably in degree of development and the range of activity programs offered. Some provide a minimum of facilities and services. Such systems are mostly in the less populated wooded parts of the nation. Often these parks offer recreation facilities similar to those provided by state forests in the more highly developed states.

A typical state park in one of the less developed systems consists

Figure 14.3 **Distribution by census region of U.S. state park units, area, operations and maintenance budgets, and attendance. The right-hand set of histograms relates these data to the regional populations. SOURCE. Developed from National Association of State Park Directors and Missouri Division of Parks and Recreation,** State Park Statistics—1975, **National Recreation and Park Association, Arlington, Virginia, 1977.**

Census Regions	Regional Values as Percentages of National Totals		Regional Values per 1000 population	
1 **PACIFIC** Includes Alaska and Hawaii	U	19.5	U	27.0 units
	A	24.5	A	34.7 ha (85.7 acres)
	B	17.4	B	$1,986
	ATT	20.6	ATT	4,228 users
2 **MOUNTAIN**	U	9.0	U	36.4 units
	A	7.8	A	32.3 ha (79.8 acres)
	B	3.6	B	$1,186
	ATT	5.4	ATT	3,259 users
3 **WEST NORTH CENTRAL**	U	10.8	U	25.3 units
	A	5.5	A	13.2 ha (32.6 acres)
	B	4.9	B	$936
	ATT	7.8	ATT	2,740 users
4 **WEST SOUTH CENTRAL**	U	6.2	U	11.5 units
	A	2.5	A	4.7 ha (11.7 acres)
	B	6.1	B	$938
	ATT	7.2	ATT	2,004 users
5 **EAST NORTH CENTRAL**	U	12.7	U	12.1 units
	A	9.0	A	8.8 ha (21.7 acres)
	B	13.0	B	$1,019
	ATT	18.0	ATT	2,549 users
6 **EAST SOUTH CENTRAL**	U	4.4	U	12.8 units
	A	2.2	A	6.5 ha (16.1 acres)
	B	12.9	B	$3,064
	ATT	8.8	ATT	3,769 users
7 **SOUTH ATLANTIC**	U	9.6	U	11.2 units
	A	6.5	A	7.8 ha (19.3 acres)
	B	10.9	B	$1,041
	ATT	10.1	ATT	1,739 users
8 **MIDDLE ATLANTIC**	U	11.1	U	11.6 units
	A	35.6	A	38.3 ha (94.6 acres)
	B	25.6	B	$2,210
	ATT	17.2	ATT	2,675 users
9 **NEW ENGLAND**	U	16.6	U	53.1 units
	A	6.4	A	21.1 ha (52.1 acres)
	B	5.9	B	$1,547
	ATT	4.8	ATT	2,281 users

U - Units   A - Area   B - Budget   ATT - Attendance

PUBLICLY OWNED RECREATION RESOURCES: STATE AND PROVINCIAL AGENCIES of a beach area on a small lake or impoundment, an adjacent picnic area, a campground with 40 to 50 sites, and a number of hiking trails running through the hinterland of the 40- to 200-hectare (100- to 500-acre) property. Buildings are usually limited to modest toilet buildings with running cold water at the beach and picnic area; one or more toilet buildings with hot water, showers, and clothes-washing facilities in the campground; a small office (sometimes combined with a superintendent's residence); and a garage for maintenance vehicles with adjoining workshop and storage space. Roads, parking areas, and campsite spurs are usually gravel rather than hard surfaced in such systems and services are limited to basic facility maintenance and ranger patrols. The goal is to provide a relaxed experience based largely on a relatively undeveloped woodland or aquatic environment.

At the other end of the state park spectrum are highly developed systems consisting primarily of large, intensively managed beaches or resorts. Parks in these systems frequently have many of the features of small cities, including extensive paved roads and parking lots, a detachment of full-time law enforcement officers, residential areas (for the staff), and a variety of food-service establishments and small shops. Additional amenities usually include large toilet buildings and changing rooms together with a number of specialized facilities such as marinas, recreation halls, waterfront promenades, equipment rentals, and large campgrounds that often provide electrical, water, and sewer connections at each campsite. Other commonly encountered amenities are picnic shelters, chil-

dren's play equipment, swimming pools, golf courses, riding stables, sportsfields, recreation halls, boat rentals, boat-launching ramps, marinas, stocked fishing ponds, hotels, motels, cabins, and wintersports facilities such as ice-skating rinks, toboggan runs, and ski developments. Parks of this type, especially those with major beaches, may have more than 10,000 visitors on a hot weekend day. Like a small city, a major park of this type needs hundreds of service personnel, a fleet of vehicles, and a variety of specialized equipment, ranging from tractor-mounted mowers to snow-making machines.

The nature and extent of each system's facilities depend on a number of factors. Some states have adhered closely to the concept promoted in the 1920s that state parks should be established primarily to preserve areas that are of statewide significance because of their outstanding scenic, geologic, botanical, or wildlife features. In these cases, parks tend to vary in size depending on the magnitude of the resources involved, and they generally contain limited facilities that are oriented toward viewing and studying these resources. Features commonly protected and displayed include waterfalls, river gorges, picturesque coastlines, beautiful lakes, cave systems, mountain peaks, remnants of original ecosystems (such as mature forests or undisturbed swamps), paleontological sites, geologic phenomena, and important historic sites or buildings.

Other states have concentrated on acquiring sites with the potential to accommodate large numbers of picnickers, beach users, or winter sports enthusiasts. Parks in such

systems are generally developed on the best available resources within reasonable distances of large population centers. The majority of systems tend to be a compromise between these extremes with some parks managed primarily for resource preservation and viewing, whereas others are developed and operated for intensive recreation use.

About 10 percent of the states have several units that contain hotels or lodges. Some were constructed in the 1920s or 1930s when accommodations inside state and national parks were often considered essential because automobile travel was slow and many units were not near commercial hotels. Since that time, better roads and the widespread construction of motels along highways have made hotels and lodges in parks less necessary. Nevertheless, a number of states have followed a policy in recent years of renovating old lodges or constructing new resort hotels or cabins. These include Alabama, Arkansas, Kentucky (Figure 14.1), Missouri, Ohio, Oklahoma, Tennessee, and West Virginia. In several states, the primary motive has been to encourage tourism in economically depressed areas.

Almost half the states operate overnight cabin accommodations in at least a few parks. States that have substantial numbers of rental cabins in their parks include Kentucky, Montana, Ohio, Pennsylvania, South Carolina, Texas, and Washington. As in the case of hotels and lodges, cabins were first constructed in the early days of state parks. Large numbers were also built under the make-work programs of the Great Depression. However, comparatively few have been constructed in the last two decades, except during expansion programs intended to promote economic development. Many authorities feel that hotels, lodges, and cabins are not desirable in state parks because such developments are expensive, offer unnecessary competition to nearby commercial developments, and represent an inappropriate use of valuable public resources for the benefit of a comparative few.

Attempts have been made to clarify the nature and purpose of various kinds of state park units by adopting classification systems. The National Conference on State Parks (now the National Society of Park Resources) established specifications for six types—state parks, state monuments, state recreation areas, state beaches, state parkways, and state waysides. However, the system has not been widely adopted because of differing circumstances. For example, the conference recommended that the term, *state park,* be applied only to relatively large units of outstanding scenic or wilderness character, many of which also contain significant scientific or historic features. Obviously, this would severely limit the number of units that could qualify, especially in states where large tracts of outstanding scenic or wilderness lands are scarce or have already been preserved as federal reserves.

Since the term, state park, has more status and economic significance than the other suggested names, changing a unit's name from state park or giving a new area a name other than state park is unlikely to occur because of public and political opposition. As a result, most systems call the majority of their units state parks. A few

apply the term, state recreation area, to units that are used by large numbers of people primarily for activities that do not focus on enjoying scenic, geologic, or biological resources.

Although campgrounds and lodgings are often prominently featured in pictures of state park facilities, the great majority of users do not remain overnight. On a national basis, only about 9 percent of visits involve an overnight stay. Day-use in state parks consists largely of picnicking and taking part in beach activities with lesser amounts of time devoted to playing games, sightseeing, pleasure driving, fishing, boating, walking, hiking, nature study, and waterskiing. Some park units also provide opportunities for horseback riding, golf, archery, rifle shooting, hunting, winter sports, or snowmobiling.

The summaries that follow describe the main features of six contrasting state park systems, namely those of California, Colorado, Kentucky, Michigan, New York, and Texas. Since every system tends to be somewhat different, none can be said to be typical of a distinct type of system. Rather, the selected examples illustrate the great variety of amenities and programs offered. The basic characteristics of the six systems are shown in Table 14.1. The California, Kentucky, Michigan, New York, and Texas systems are generally extensively developed and heavily used. Colorado does not experience as great participation pressures as the other five states and has only recently developed its system.

California's System. Although the federal government gave Yosemite to the state in 1864,

the present system had its origins in the creation of the California Redwood Park at Big Basin in 1902. Now, it ranks among the nation's top systems in terms of excellent resources, number of intensively used sites, total attendance, and budget size. The various units are classified into nine groups as shown in Table 14.2.

In developing the system, the California Department of Parks and Recreation has concentrated on providing picnicking, swimming, family camping, group camping, fishing, hiking, horseback riding, nature study, and interpretive opportunities. Facilities are functional but not elaborate. Only a few units have fully equipped campgrounds with water, electricity, and sewer connections at each site. There are no hotels or lodges and only a few rustic or motel-type cabins. Park stores and food services occupy modest facilities.

The majority of the units classified as state parks are concentrated in the southern coastal ranges, in the north central portion of the Sierra Nevada, and along the western side of the coastal ranges in the northern half of the state (Figure 14.4). State recreation areas, on the other hand, occur mostly on the Central Valley's lakes and water-storage reservoirs. Most of the state beaches are grouped in four clusters located within relatively short driving distances of the state's major population centers—San Francisco, Los Angeles, and San Diego. However, the smaller number of state beaches at other locations is partly because of less suitable conditions. Especially north of San Francisco, there are few good swimming beaches and *water-contact activities* (such as swimming,

Table 14.1 Basic Characteristics of Six State Park Systems in 1975

State	Number of Units	Area in Thousands of Hectares (Acres)	Attendance During Year — Total in Millions of Visits	Attendance During Year — Percent of Overnight Visits	State Expenditures During Year (in millions of $) — Land and Capital Improvements	State Expenditures During Year (in millions of $) — Operations and Maintenance	Total State Park Expenditures for Year — Per Capita Dollars	Total State Park Expenditures for Year — Per User Dollars	Revenues During Year Other than Appropriations (in millions of $) — Fees to Park or Enter	Revenues During Year Other than Appropriations (in millions of $) — State Operated Facilities	Revenues During Year Other than Appropriations (in millions of $) — Privately Operated Facilities
National mean (50 systems)	78	80.1 (197.9)	11.6	11.5	6.4	6.5	3.33	1.24	0.8	1.6	0.2
California	230	341.5 (843.1)	48.6	10.7	53.0	37.8	5.17	2.22	5.0	3.5	0.6
Colorado[a]	44	64.4 (159.1)	9.4	6.3	1.1	1.9	1.38	0.79	na[b]	0.4	0.0
Kentucky	45	16.4 (40.6)	28.8	4.1	8.4	22.2	9.58	1.12	nc[c]	13.4	0.3
Michigan	93	90.6 (223.7)	20.4	28.5	0.0[d]	10.6	1.17	0.52	2.4	3.5	0.2
New York	209	1206.8 (2977.7)	54.6	5.3	14.1	53.5	3.59	1.38	2.5	8.7	2.8
Texas	87	41.4 (102.2)	14.2	14.2	23.3	7.9	3.18	2.69	1.2	1.0	0.3

[a] Includes state historical societies.   [b] na = not available.   [c] nc = no charge.   [d] Usually about $4 million, special circumstances resulted in no capital expenditures in 1975.

SOURCE: Developed from National Association of State Park Directors and Missouri Division of Parks and Recreation, *State Park Statistics— 1975,* National Recreation and Park Association, Arlington, Va., 1977.

Table 14.2 California State Park Classification System

Classification	Description	Total Units — Number	Total Units — Percent
State parks	Relatively undeveloped areas with outstanding scenic, resource, cultural, or ecological values. Most are large with a full range of facilities and services.	61	25.4
State recreation areas	Provide experiences such as camping, picnicking, swimming, and fishing in environments that do not qualify for state park status. Most are on inland water bodies. Many are quite small with fewer facilities than state parks.	34	14.2
State beaches	Ocean beaches used primarily for beach activities and fishing. Some have campgrounds; many are less than 40 hectares (100 acres) in area.	71	29.6
Wayside campgrounds	Small roadside campgrounds.	3	1.3
State vehicular recreation areas	Areas for individual or competitive off-highway vehicle riding.	2	0.8
Historical units	Places and objects of statewide historic significance; includes historic sites and buildings in urban areas.	37	15.4
State reserves	Contain outstanding or unusual resources or scenic values. Usually much smaller than state parks; some very small. Limited development.	14	5.8
State wildernesses	Large areas that have retained their primeval character. May be within other large units. Undeveloped except for trails.	2	0.8
Nature preserves	Small areas (often within other units) that contain items of scientific interest, rare or endangered species, or unique geologic or topographic features.	16	6.7

SOURCE: Developed from California Department of Parks and Recreation, *Statistical Report 1975–76 Fiscal Year,* Department of Parks and Recreation, Sacramento, Calif., 1977.

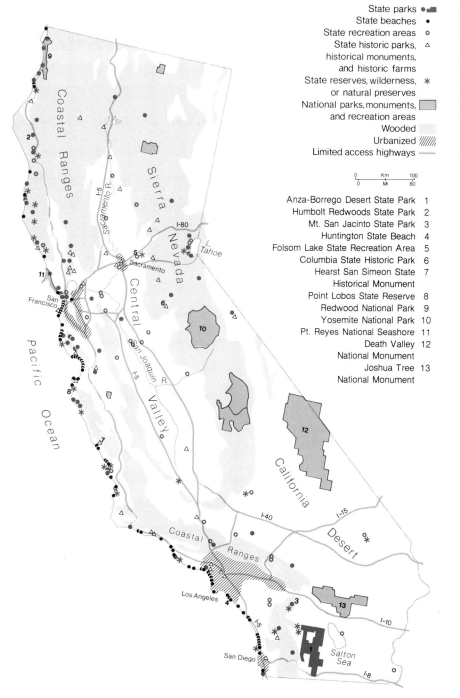

State parks   •▬

State beaches   •

State recreation areas   o

State historic parks,   △
historical monuments,
and historic farms

State reserves, wilderness,   ✳
or natural preserves

National parks, monuments, ▨
and recreation areas

Wooded

Urbanized ▨

Limited access highways ——

Anza-Borrego Desert State Park   1
Humbolt Redwoods State Park   2
Mt. San Jacinto State Park   3
Huntington State Beach   4
Folsom Lake State Recreation Area   5
Columbia State Historic Park   6
Hearst San Simeon State   7
Historical Monument
Point Lobos State Reserve   8
Redwood National Park   9
Yosemite National Park   10
Pt. Reyes National Seashore   11
Death Valley   12
National Monument
Joshua Tree   13
National Monument

Figure 14.4 Map of California state park system.

surfing, and scuba diving); these are less pleasurable or even hazardous because of cold water and strong currents. Historic units are concentrated in the gold-mining region of the Sierra Nevada, the San Francisco area, and the southern areas originally occupied by the Spanish missions.

Eight examples of California state parks are described in Table 14.3. These and the other units in the system contain a total of 324 kilometers (201 miles) of ocean shoreline, 808 kilometers (502 miles) of lakeshore, and 140 kilometers (87 miles) of river frontage. Developments include 13,854 campsites of various types, 7584 developed picnic sites, and 2410 kilometers (1498 miles) of trails. The state has spent a total of $187 million on land acquisition and received other property worth $77 million in gifts, transfers, and exchanges. Development has cost more than $130 million. Annual operating expenses were $32 million in 1975–1976, of which 34 percent was offset by receipts from fees and concession revenues.

In addition to the state-managed areas, there are 24 units totaling 2996 hectares (7398 acres) that are operated by local governments. These state-owned areas usually have the word, state, included in their names. A number of state beaches and 2 state recreation areas are in this group. The data for these units are not included in the statistics given above, but their locations are shown in Figure 14.4.

Colorado's System. Like several other states in mountainous and desert regions of the West, Colorado had only a few small, relatively undeveloped state parks until

Table 14.3 Examples of California State Parks (1975–76 Data)

Unit Name	Area in Hectares (Acres)	Main Features and Annual Use
Anza-Borrego State Park	207,102 (511,362)	Largest U.S. state park.[a] Parts of several mountain ranges interspersed with valleys, "badlands," and flatlands. Ecosystems range from desert to pinyon pine and juniper forest. 142 developed campsites. Primitive camping, pleasure driving, hiking, nature study, interpretive programs. (775,900)
Columbia State Historical Park	100 (246)	Restoration of a gold-rush town. Exhibits, tours, gold-panning, stagecoach rides, old-time theatrical performances, square dances. Picnicking, stores, restaurants, hotel. (526,940)
Folsom Lake State Recreation Area	764[b] (1,886)	Encompasses 193 km (120 miles) of shoreline, 80 km (50 miles) of trails. Picnicking, boat camping, tent and trailer camping, swimming, boating, waterskiing, fishing, horseback riding, nature study, hiking. (2,241,500)
Hearst San Simeon State Historical Monument	60 (149)	Vast Hispano-Moresque castle filled with works of art and surrounded by pools, fountains, statuary, gardens, and guesthouses built by newspaper magnate, William Randolph Hearst, between 1919 and 1951. Conducted tours. (799, 220)
Humboldt Redwoods State Park	18,143 (44,798)	Largest of the 18 units in the system that contain sizable stands of coast redwood, *Sequoia sempervirens*. 3240-ha (8000-acre) main stand contains trees over 90-m (300-ft) tall and 2000 years old. 34 km (21 miles) of streams. 257 developed campsites, 80 km (50 miles) of trails. Picnicking, horseback riding, swimming, fishing, nature trail, interpretive program. (768,386)
Huntington State Beach	64 (159)	7 km (4.3 miles) of ocean beach serving the Los Angeles metropolitan area. Heavily used for such beach activities as swimming, picnicking, sunning, surfing, fishing, clamdigging. 550 fire rings. Contains nesting sanctuary for the California Least Tern. (1,599,527)
Mount San Jacinto State Park	5,474 (13,515)	Great block of mountain terrain covering more than 20 townships. Much is over 1800 m (6000 ft) in height, including 3295-m (10,804-ft) San Jacinto Peak. Surrounded on three sides by even larger areas of national forest. Much of park and forest is state- or federal-designated wilderness. 83 developed campsites, primitive camping, hiking, horseback riding, picnicking, interpretive program. A 4-km (2.5 mile), $8-million aerial tramway provides access from Palm Springs area by which visitors ascend through five major climatic and life zones to a lookout-restaurant complex. (388,617)
Point Lobos State Reserve	517 (1,276)	7.3 km (4.5 miles) of rocky, deeply incised ocean shoreline with offshore islands and rocks. Magnificent vistas. Sea lions, the once-almost-extinct sea otter, thousands of sea birds, Monterey cypress trees, wildflower meadows. Includes 304 ha (750 acres) of submerged land (nation's first underwater reserve). Interpretive program, guided tours, trails, picnicking. (292,050)

[a] Although often referred to as the nation's largest state park, the Adirondack Forest Preserve in New York State is not a state park in the usual sense, despite the fact it is called the Adirondack Park in the legislation that established it.
[b] In addition there are 6356 hectares (15,693 acres) leased from the U.S. Bureau of Reclamation.
SOURCE: California Department of Parks and Recreation, *The California State Park System Guide*, 1976; plus individual park brochures, undated; California Department of Parks and Recreation, Sacramento, Calif.

quite recently. Most citizens and legislators saw no need to spend money on state parks because vast areas and many unique resources were open to the public in nearby national parks, forests, and public-domain lands. This attitude changed in Colorado during the 1960s when rapidly growing urban populations demanded more nearby recreation opportunities and the state sought to increase economic benefits from tourism.

Although *State Park Statistics —1975* lists 44 areas in the Colorado park system (see Table 14.1), only 31 units are developed and open to the public. Of these units, 26 are classified as state recreation areas and 5 as state parks. The recreation areas generally offer a range of activities that include camping, swimming, waterskiing, powerboating, horseback riding, hiking, rock climbing, snowmobiling, and hunting. Many are located around water-supply reservoirs; eight of these impoundments are over 400 hectares (1000 acres) in size. Some of the units classified as state parks are not substantially different from the state recreation areas, but the emphasis is more on appreciation of undeveloped environments and less on recreation involving developed facilities and mechanical equipment.

One-third of Colorado's state parks are located in its high-plains region, which extends eastward from the Rocky Mountains (Figure 14.5). Landscapes in this region range from rolling hills to relatively flat grasslands. Rainfall averages between 25 and 50 centimeters (10 and 20 inches) annually, so that the environment is comparatively arid and trees occur naturally only at springs and along waterways. With limited topographic relief, no woodlands, and few natural water bodies, good state-park-system sites were virtually nonexistent until water-control reservoirs began to be constructed. Nearly all of the 11 state recreation areas in the high-plains region include flood-control impoundments built by the Corps of Engineers or irrigation reservoirs constructed by the Bureau of Reclamation. Of these plains parks, 9 occur along a narrow corridor running north and south through the Denver area from Pueblo to Fort

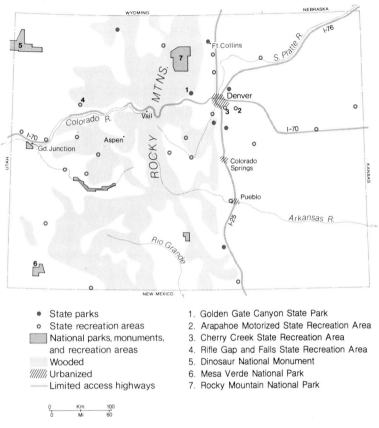

Figure 14.5 Map of the Colorado state park system in 1979. At that time, there were 7 state parks and 24 state recreation areas.

- State parks
- State recreation areas
- National parks, monuments, and recreation areas
- Wooded
- Urbanized
- Limited access highways

1. Golden Gate Canyon State Park
2. Arapahoe Motorized State Recreation Area
3. Cherry Creek State Recreation Area
4. Rifle Gap and Falls State Recreation Area
5. Dinosaur National Monument
6. Mesa Verde National Park
7. Rocky Mountain National Park

Collins; this corridor contains the majority of Colorado's population. The other 2 units lie further east toward the state's boundary with Kansas.

The parks in this region are used predominantly for water-oriented activities. As in many other previously lakeless areas of the Great Plains, the construction of extensive impoundments has resulted in large-scale participation in swimming, fishing, powerboat cruising, waterskiing, and sailing. The reservoirs have also attracted many waterfowl; most stop briefly while migrating, but a good number spend the winter and some are year-round residents. Several of the plains parks are used extensively for hunting waterfowl, small game, and deer. Fish species and fishing quality vary considerably, depending on the nature of the impoundment and summer flow conditions. Cherry Creek State Recreation Area is the most highly developed of the plains parks (Table 14.4).

Another group of parks is situated in the foothills of the Rocky

Table 14.4 Examples of Colorado State Parks (1977–1978 Data)

Unit Name	Area in Hectares (Acres)	Main Features
Arapahoe Motorized State Recreation Area	243 (600)	Special plains park for motorcycles and off-highway vehicles. Includes motocross, time-trial, perimeter-ride, hill-climb, and minibike areas. No campground or water resources. 13 km (8 miles) east of Denver on former U.S. Department of Defense bombing range.
Cherry Creek State Recreation Area	1586 (3915)	356-ha (880-acre) South Platte River flood-control reservoir on Denver's outskirts. System's most heavily used unit with more than 1.5 million annual visits. 165 campsites, group campsites, flush toilets, 20 picnic shelters, horseback-riding concession, swimming, marina, boat ramps, boating, sailing, shooting range, fishing for 7 different species, ice fishing, and ice skating. Interpretive walks and displays, amphitheater, evening programs, nature trail, prairie dog observation area. 10 km (6 miles) of paved bicycle trail. Model airplane area. Dog-training area. Special swimming, picnicking, camping, and fishing facilities for the handicapped. Problem with low water levels in drought periods. Elevation 1610 m (5280 ft).
Golden Gate State Park	3391 (8372)	Third largest unit in the system. One-hour drive northwest of Denver in Front Range. Elevation 2776 (9100 ft). Forested. Fine views of more than 160 km (100 miles) of mountain peaks along Continental Divide. Developed campground with 135 sites, picnicking, flush toilets, hiking, backpacking, nature trails, horseback-riding concession, rock climbing, cross-country skiing, snowmobiling.
Rifle Gap and Falls Recreation Area	885 (2185)	One of the cluster of western parks around Grand Junction. Consists of two sections. Main area contains 142-ha (350-acre) Bureau of Reclamation reservoir. Smaller section has waterfalls and caves. Camping, picnicking, hiking, rock climbing, boating, fishing, swimming, waterskiing, scuba diving, nature study, interpretive programs, hunting, ice fishing, and ice skating, snowmobiling. Elevation 1830 m (6000 ft).

SOURCE: Colorado Department of Natural Resources, Division of Parks and Outdoor Recreation, park system and individual park brochures, Colorado Department of Natural Resources, Denver, Colo., 1977 and 1978.

Mountains' eastern ranges. Several are in the northern part of this region near the Denver-Fort Collins urban area. Three are located about 100 kilometers (60 miles) west of Colorado Springs and one is much further south.

These units differ considerably from the plains units. Set in mountainous environments with more adequate moisture conditions, they generally provide a wider range of recreation opportunities. Most sites are 600 meters (2000 feet) to 1200 meters (4000 feet) higher than the plains parks. Vegetation ranges from grasslands at lower elevations to forests of poplar, ponderosa pine, and Douglas fir farther up the slopes. Appreciation of scenic values, hiking, backpacking, horseback riding, rock climbing, nature study, cross-country skiing, and snowmobiling are important activities in many of these parks. The majority also include water supply or flood-control reservoirs so that some or a full range of water-oriented activities may be undertaken depending on the characteristics of the impoundment and the quality of the water.

The remainder of Colorado's state park units are located on the western slopes of the Rocky Mountains. Most are clustered in the upper portions of the Colorado River watershed near Grand Junction. The rest are scattered to the north and south. The features and activities in the western parks are similar to those of the parks on the eastern slopes of the mountains. However, these western parks are too far from the Denver-Fort Collins population centers to permit short-term visits. Most participants are residents of nearby small towns or people on camping vacations.

Kentucky's System. The first tangible steps toward creating a park system for Kentucky occurred in the 1920s when a state park commission was formed.[2] The legislature appropriated little or no money for parks during the commission's early years, but some sites were acquired through bequests or by local fundraising appeals. By 1936, the system consisted of 14 parks valued at over $1.5 million and occupying 2617 hectares (6461 acres). Extensive developments, including the construction of picnic areas, trails, and lodges, were carried out during the 1930s under various federal make-work programs. In 1939, the system contained 20 parks worth some $3.3 million. A new expansion program emphasizing the development of lodges and cottages was started in 1946 to attract more tourists and produce economic benefits in less developed parts of the state. Approximately $8 million was spent between 1948 and 1955.

In 1960, a separate Department of Parks was created and voters approved a $10-million bond issue for state park expansion and development. Altogether, some $25 million was expended between 1960 and 1965, much of the money being used for expansion of resort facilities. The Department of Parks also started to provide environmental interpretation programs and other kinds of supervised recreation opportunities in an effort to induce lodge and cottage patrons to stay longer. A separate Division of Recreation was created within the department in 1961.

The present system consists of 45 units totaling 16,443 hectares (40,600 acres). They are divided into three classes for design and management purposes. Out of the total, 15 are classified as *major resort parks* and have names ending in the words, *state resort park*. These units are mostly between

---

2 Data for this section is primarily from Clara Wootton, *The History of the Kentucky State Parks,* Blue Grass Press, 1975.

400 hectares (1000 acres) and 1500 hectares (3700 acres) in extent and more than half of them are located on the shores of major reservoirs. All contain a motellike lodge and most also have a number of cottages or larger vacation homes which are rented on a nightly basis. Other amenities include meetingrooms, gamerooms, swimming pools, campgrounds, beaches, golf courses, tennis courts, bicycle rentals, marinas, riding stables, and supervised recreation programs. These resort parks resemble moderate to higher priced commercial resorts, except that the guests have access to much larger areas of lakeshore and woodland than are available at most private developments. Thirteen of these resorts are open year round. The most heavily used state resort parks are Cumberland Falls (Table 14.5), Kentucky Dam Village (Table 14.5), Lake Barkley (Figure 14.1), and Natural Bridge.

Kentucky has 18 units that are classified as *recreation parks* and have names ending in *state park*. These areas emphasize day-use activities; only 1 park has a few cottages but 13 include campgrounds. Recreation parks range in size from 10 hectares (20 acres) to 1400 hectares (3500 acres), but the average unit is about 280 hectares (700 acres) in extent. Less than one-third of these parks include access to a sizable body of water; 10 have no lakes within their boundaries. About half of the sites were selected because of historic connections and contain historic buildings or exhibits. The majority offer opportunities commonly found in state parks such as picnicking, swimming, fishing, children's playground activities, hiking, and camping (Table 14.5).

Nine units are classified as *state shrines* and consist of monuments, museums, or historic buildings located on sites generally ranging from less than 1 hectare (2.5 acres) to 6 hectares (15 acres) in size. Amenities, other than the historic attraction, are usually limited to conducted tours, a gift shop, and picnic facilities.

Finally, one unit—the Kentucky Horse Park—is unlike all the others and really belongs in a class by itself. Opened near Lexington in 1978 and described as a *theme park,* it is dedicated to fostering an understanding and appreciation of horses and riding through exhibits, demonstrations, and competitions (Table 14.5).

One of the early state park commissioners adopted the goal of locating a state park within an hour-to an hour-and-a-half-drive of all Kentuckians. This objective has now been achieved, largely through making improvements in highways and vehicles rather than improving the distribution of state parks. As Figure 14.6 shows, almost 60 percent of the units are concentrated in a 120-kilometer (75-mile) wide corridor that lies between the Cumberland Gap and Cincinnati and constitutes less than one-third of the state's area.

This corridor resulted largely from recognition in 1750 that the Cumberland Gap (a natural pass through the Cumberland Plateau section of the Appalachian Mountains) was the best route from Virginia into the Ohio Valley. Most early upper valley settlers traveled through the Gap along the route marked initially by Daniel Boone. The area "downstream" from the Gap became the focus for agricultural and political activity in Ken-

Table 14.5 Examples of Kentucky State Parks (1977 Data)

Unit Name	Area in Hectares (Acres)	Main Features and Annual Use
Cumberland Falls State Resort Park	727 (1794)	Forested upland and gorge; 18-m (60-ft) waterfall, which is next highest in the east after Niagara Falls. 60-room lodge, 47 cottages, 210-seat dining room, coffee and gift shops. Swimming pool open to all park users, supervised recreation program, 40-seat recreation room, playground, trails, tennis courts, fishing opportunities. Interpretive program, 100-seat ampitheater. 70 campsites, picnic areas. Second to Kentucky Dam Village in attendance. (2,222,000)
Kentucky Dam Village State Resort Park	486 (1200)	Resort overlooking 52,125-ha (128,800-acre) Lake Kentucky. 92-room lodge with swimming pool; 49 ordinary cottages; 20 two-story, three-bedroom *executive cottages,* 300-seat dining room; coffee, gift, and handicraft shops. Airstrip, beach, 18-hole regulation golf course, supervised recreation program, 300-seat recreation room, playground, tennis courts, shuffleboard courts, fishing opportunities. 225 campsites, picnic areas. Boat dock, 52 open slips, 148 covered slips, boat ramps, paddle boats. Horseback riding. (6,675,000)
Fort Boonesborough State Park	75 (184)	Reconstruction of the fortified settlement built in 1775 by Daniel Boone. 16 eighteenth-century crafts are demonstrated by people in pioneer dress using functioning antiques. Museum, gift and handicraft shops. Interpretive program. Beach, playground, fishing opportunities. 187 campsites, picnic areas. Boat dock, 10 open-boat slips, launching ramp. (1,300,000)
Jefferson Davis Monument State Shrine	6.5 (16.0)	107-m (351-ft) concrete obelisk overlooking the farm where Jefferson Davis, President of the Confederate States of America, was born. Gift shop. Playground, picnic areas. (181,000)
Kentucky Horse Park	418 (1032)	Former stud farm converted at a cost of $27 million into a theme park dedicated to the horse. Visitor center features 20-minute film about horses and their relationship to the human race. Museum traces history of the horse. Walking tour shows how a horse farm operates. Events area includes a 0.5-mile training track, dressage and jumping ring, 1-mile steeplechase course, cross-country course, and polo field. Riding trails. Picnic area around a 3-ha (7-acre) lake. Restaurant, bookstore, art gallery, gift shop, 263 campsites, grocery store, swimming pool, playground. Special events and competitions throughout the year. (Anticipated attendance: 1,500,000)

SOURCE: Kentucky Department of Parks, "Facilities Guide—Kentucky State Parks and Shrines," April 1977; *Kentucky State Parks Recreation & Naturalist Operation Manual, 1977;* plus individual undated park brochures, Department of Parks, Frankfort, Ky.

tucky. Eventually, the state capital was established at Frankfort some 200 kilometers (125 miles) to the northwest. The downstream region, therefore, contains a greater concentration of historically significant sites and buildings than areas of comparable size elsewhere in the state.

Most of the state park system units in the Cumberland Gap-Cincinnati corridor were established at least partly because of historical significance. Six state shrines are clustered within a 80-kilometer (50-mile) radius to the south and southwest of Lexington. Six state recreation parks of historical importance ring Lexington within a similar radius; these include Fort Boonesborough State Park (first fortified settlement in Kentucky), Blue Licks Battlefield State Park (last battle of the American Revolution), Fort Hill State Park (Civil War fortifications), My Old Kentucky Home State Park (1818 mansion that is said to have inspired Stephen Foster to write the ballad "My Old Kentucky Home"), Lincoln Homestead State Park (boyhood home of Abraham Lincoln's father), and Old Fort Harrod State Park (first permanent pioneer settlement west of the Allegheny Mountains). Other units in the belt that have historical significance are General Butler State Resort Park (1859 mansion), General Burnside State Park (astride two early trails from the Cumberland Gap), and the Dr. Thomas Walker State Shrine (site of the first cabin erected

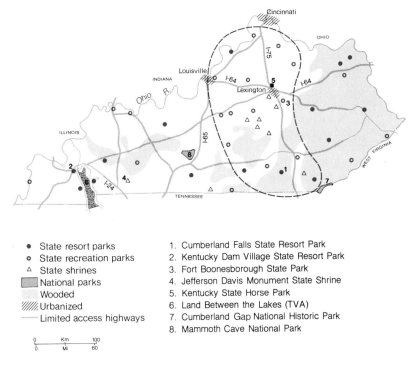

Figure 14.6 Map of the Kentucky state park system in 1979. At that time, there were 20 state recreation parks, 15 state resort parks, and 9 state shrines. Dashed line indicates corridor that contains majority of units.

- ● State resort parks
- ○ State recreation parks
- △ State shrines
- ▨ National parks
- ░ Wooded
- ▨ Urbanized
- — Limited access highways

1. Cumberland Falls State Resort Park
2. Kentucky Dam Village State Resort Park
3. Fort Boonesborough State Park
4. Jefferson Davis Monument State Shrine
5. Kentucky State Horse Park
6. Land Between the Lakes (TVA)
7. Cumberland Gap National Historic Park
8. Mammoth Cave National Park

primarily for historical reasons. Since many Kentuckians tend to be somewhat conservative and oriented toward the work ethic, parts of the state outside the corridor would probably have even fewer park units if economic arguments had not been used.

Kentucky's state park recreation-activity program is currently unique. No other state park system offers such a wide range of supervised activities at such a high proportion of its units. Recreation programs (other than interpretive activities) are operated on a year-round basis in 13 of the resort parks and on a seasonal basis in the other 2 resort parks and 11 of the state recreation parks. The organized programs focus on sports and games, arts and crafts, music, dance, drama, nature study, social activities, and special events. Examples of the supervised scheduled activities provided are volleyball tournaments, sandcastle-building contests, full-length film shows designed for families, bingo games, square dances, concerts by musical groups, and automobile tours of nearby places of interest. The Department of Parks currently employs 24 full-time and 61 seasonal persons to supervise and conduct its recreation programs in addition to its 7-member interpretive staff. Many amenities are also used extensively on a casual basis; these include swimming pools, golf courses, tennis courts, rental bicycles, riding horses, and gamerooms.

in Kentucky by a white man). The remaining units in the Cumberland Gap-Cincinnati corridor are located there primarily because of specific physical resources such as one of the major waterfalls in the eastern part of the nation (Cumberland Falls State Park), and a 40-kilometer (25-mile) long flood-control reservoir (Lake Cumberland State Resort Park).

Kentucky's adoption of a state resort-development policy helped establish units outside the Cumberland Gap-Cincinnati corridor. This policy is contained in the objectives of the Department of Parks:

To encourage and stimulate the tourist industry in Kentucky by leading the way in resort park development in areas of low tourist importance with emphasis on stimulating and creating demand to be served by private enterprise development . . . [and] To provide quality recreation and leisure to the citizens of the Commonwealth [of Kentucky] as well as to out-of-state visitors.[3]

More than half of the units outside the corridor are state resort parks, whereas only one-quarter of the extracorridor units were established

[3] Kentucky Department of Parks, *Kentucky State Parks: Recreation & Naturalist Operation Manual, 1977,* Department of Parks, Frankfort, Ky., 1977, p. 13.

Michigan's System. Although Michigan is less than 320 kilometers (200 miles) from Kentucky, its state park system is entirely different in terms of both the resources and programs provided.

Unlike Kentucky, the Michigan system has no lodges, modern cottages, restaurants, or organized recreation programs. Its cottages are limited to a few rustic trailside cabins located in relatively remote parts of two of the more northerly and less developed parks. Food establishments consist of concession-operated refreshment stands in some of the larger beach-oriented parks and a modest cafeteria at the ski development in Porcupine Mountains State Park. Highly developed facilities such as golf courses, miniature golf, tennis courts, and recreation rooms are absent. Only one park has a swimming pool and it was built because water at the park beach on Lake Erie became too polluted for swimming.

In some ways, Michigan's state park system resembles the California system. The emphasis is on large-scale use for picnicking, swimming, and camping in moderately developed environments. Most of the parks are located either at sites with fair to excellent natural sand beaches or at locations where woodlands and water combine to form attractive recreation environments. Only eight units were created primarily to preserve or display resources of historic significance. Two of these—Mackinac Island State Park and Fort Michilimackinac—are administered by a separate commission and are not considered part of the state park system. The relatively limited role of the system in historic restoration and historic interpretation is mandated by a state policy that assigns responsibility to the History Division of the Michigan Department of State.

A major difference between the Michigan and California systems is the contrasting patterns of use. A much smaller proportion of use at Michigan state parks consists of visits lasting only a few hours. Most of the parks are considerable distances from major population centers so that the majority of users arrive by car and stay most of the day, overnight, or a number of days. The California system, on the other hand, has many swimming, picnicking, and sightseeing resources that are close to, or even within, urban areas so that much of the use is of comparatively short duration. Michigan has contributed to the development of use patterns that involve longer stays by providing 14,000 developed campsites; this is more than any other state park system in the nation. Camping accounts for 29 percent of the use of state parks in Michigan compared to 11 percent of the use of state parks in California.

Many of the differences in the nature and distribution of the Michigan and California systems are the result of the circumstances under which the two systems evolved. In California, the early establishment of national parks and national forests in the Sierra Nevada region made state acquisition of conservation or recreation lands appear less essential. Many unique resources of statewide significance in the eastern part of the state were already protected by federal ownership. On the other hand, very few of Michigan's potential state park sites enjoyed federal protection because most of the state had been settled earlier and national park system units and national forests were not established until much later. In addition, much of the eastern part of California was perceived as relatively remote and inhospitable during the early days of the state park movement.

Conversely, residents regarded waterfront locations in Michigan's northland as desirable camping and seasonal home sites so that automobile associations, car manufacturers, and road builders did their best to improve accessibility. Unlike California, few good state park sites close to population centers were readily available in Michigan because nearly all the land in the southern third of the state was being farmed. The only exceptions were sand-dune areas along the Great Lakes shorelines. Finally, the incentive to create historic parks was not as strong as in California with its Spanish mission and gold-rush regions. It was, therefore, both desirable and feasible to establish early state parks in the northern two-thirds of Michigan, whereas the creation of state parks in the interior of California was initially neither needed nor particularly practical.

Because of these circumstances, Michigan has generally followed a policy of acquiring sizable areas containing good quality undeveloped resources for its state park units. Wherever possible, these have consisted of areas of 200 hectares (500 acres) or more that include water frontage suitable for substantial numbers of people to take part in a range of water-dependent and water-related activities. In some cases, units have been created primarily to preserve unique or high-quality resources such as a waterfall, spring, virgin woodland, or scenic landscape. However, the system includes units that are less than 80 hectares (200 acres) in extent. A few units contain rather mediocre resources and were included only because of political pressure.

The current Michigan state park system consists of 93 units with a total area of 90,700 hectares (224,000 acres). About two-thirds of the units are over 80 hectares (200 acres) and one-third are over 400 hectares (1000 acres). The three largest parks have areas of 23,500 hectares (58,000 acres), 8500 hectares (21,000 acres), and 6900 hectares (17,000 acres). The first two are in relatively remote areas of the Upper Peninsula, but the third (Waterloo Recreation Area) is in the densely populated southern region.

At present, the Michigan Department of Natural Resources classifies its state park system units as either *state parks* or *state recreation areas*. The latter are usually substantial tracts of land, but they do not include the extensive high-quality undeveloped resources characteristic of the system's larger state parks. Most consist of blocks of land that were at one time farmed and contain patches of open fields and woodlands of various ages intersected by rural roads and farm lanes. As a result, state recreation areas are more oriented toward dispersed uses such as exploring, nature study, horseback riding, hunting, fishing, snowmobiling, and cross-country skiing. There is less emphasis on the preservation and nonconsumptive use of a single high-quality resource as is usually the case in a major state park. However, most state recreation areas also have swimming beaches, picnic areas, campgrounds, and other facilities normally found in units designated as state parks.

Michigan's current two-group classification system makes it difficult to present a useful analysis of the distribution of units. However, a new system has been developed by planners in the Parks Division of the Department of Natural Resources and, since it is more appropriate for our purposes, it will be used even though it has not yet been adopted by the department. Under this system, a total of 23 units that are not typical state parks are removed from the state park category. Of these, 8 are termed *state urban parks* because they are close to, or within, urban areas (Figure 14.7) and have use patterns that are more characteristic of city parks than extraurban state-operated parks. Generally, the focus at these parks is on short-term use for picnicking or beach-activity purposes. Family camping is

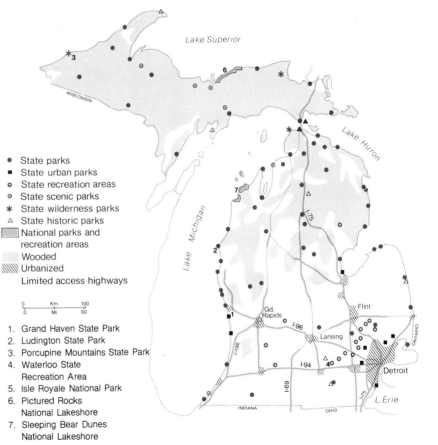

1. Grand Haven State Park
2. Ludington State Park
3. Porcupine Mountains State Park
4. Waterloo State Recreation Area
5. Isle Royale National Park
6. Pictured Rocks National Lakeshore
7. Sleeping Bear Dunes National Lakeshore

- State parks
- State urban parks
- State recreation areas
- State scenic parks
- State wilderness parks
- State historic parks
- National parks and recreation areas
- Wooded
- Urbanized
- Limited access highways

Figure 14.7 Map of Michigan state park system. Two well-known resources—Mackinac Island and Fort Michilimackinac (marked with solid triangles) are operated separately by a commission.

not always provided. Another 6 units are designated *state scenic parks* because the main attraction is a unique geologic formation or landscape. Usually, development of these units is limited because of the small size of the site or proximity of another unit with developed facilities. Most of these parks are in the interior of the Upper Peninsula. The third new class consists of *state wilderness parks*. There are 3 large parks in northern Michigan that are recommended for this group. Finally, 6 units are suggested for inclusion in a *state historic park* category.

The dominant factor influencing the distribution of Michigan's state park units has been the location of suitable undeveloped resources. As Figure 14.7 shows, 41 percent of the units are state parks, state urban parks, or state scenic parks located on Great Lakes shorelines. The majority of these sites were selected because they provide good opportunities for both the aesthetic and physically active enjoyment of sandy shorelines.

In the southern third of the state, all but 1 of the 15 state recreation areas as well as some of the state urban parks are arranged in a southwestward slanting horseshoe-shaped region extending from north of Detroit to northeast of Grand Rapids. This region outlines the limit of travel of the Saginaw Lobe of the last glacier that pushed across Michigan. Successive advances and retreats of the ice produced a maze of morainic ridges and valleys, many of the latter containing lakes or wetlands. The gravelly or sandy nature of many of the soils and the rolling nature of the landscapes make much of this region unfit for modern agricultural

operations. However, such landscapes are often suitable sites for state recreation areas, particularly where lakes and rivers are present. Michigan began to obtain park sites in the region in the 1930s. Following World War II, a program to acquire and develop a series of state recreation areas near Detroit produced the cluster of more than a dozen units that forms the eastern arm of the horseshoe.

Finally, the distribution of the state park units located in the interior of the northern half of Michigan's Lower Peninsula is tied primarily to the location of undeveloped resources. More than half the units are located on major lakes. The Hartwick Pines site preserves one of the few remaining uncut white pine stands in the state. The remaining units are situated on smaller lakes or impoundments.

Table 14.6 describes four well-known Michigan state park system units. Grand Haven is a city of 15,000 inhabitants on Lake Michigan in the southwestern part of the state. The park located there is a typical small-city lakeshore park, except that it is operated as a state park and has family camping facilities. It is packed with young people and families on hot summer weekends. Ludington State Park is far enough north to avoid the extremely heavy day-use pressures experienced by the Grand Haven park. However, its campgrounds are full most of the summer and weekend day-use is substantial. Porcupine Mountains State Park is a symbol to preservationists and a perpetual target for those who see economic benefits in logging its forests or building a shoreline highway and more extensive recreation facilities. The Waterloo Recreation

Area provides a great variety of year-round recreation opportunities to people in urbanized southern Michigan.

New York's System. This is one of the largest state park systems in terms of area, number of units, size of operating budget, and amount of use. It is also one of the oldest. A precedent for state ownership of property with important heritage values was established in 1850 when the Hasbrouck House (Washington's headquarters during the Revolutionary War) was acquired, thus creating the nation's first publicly operated historic site. Five years later, the state purchased the Niagara Reservation.

In 1900, an Interstate Park Commission was formed cooperatively with New Jersey. It established the Palisades Interstate Park to preserve the lower Hudson River's scenic west shore. State involvement in parks grew with the creation of Bear Mountain and the adjacent Harriman state parks in 1915 and 1920 and the purchase of two passenger vessels to transport New Yorkers up the Hudson River to this complex. In 1924, a separate state park section was formed in the New York Conservation Department. Expansion was particularly rapid in the 1930s and after the passage of state parkland acquisition and development bond issues in the 1960s.

The system now consists of more than 200 units. About one-third are named *state parks,* one-fifth are called *state historic sites,* and the rest are *canal parks, marine parks,* or relatively undeveloped *reservations.* Their size, nature, and degree of development vary greatly so that the name is often not a

Table 14.6 Examples of Michigan State Parks (1978 Data)

Unit Name	Area in Hectares (Acres)	Main Features and Annual Use
Grand Haven State Park (state urban park)	19 (48)	Lake Michigan shoreline park in the city of Grand Haven. Good swimming beach, 170 campsites, picnic area, playground, food service, store. Pier fishing for perch. Fifth in order of total use. (756,000)
Ludington State Park (state park)	1,684 (4,157)	Rolling sand dunes along Lake Michigan. Forested. 3 campgrounds with a total of 398 campsites. 2 good beaches—one on Lake Michigan, the other on Michigan's largest impoundment. 8 separate loop hiking trails, totaling 29 km (18 miles). Interpretive center. Youth-group outdoor center. Boat ramp. Good fishing. Wildlife. Great variety of environments. (763,000)
Porcupine Mountains State Park (state wilderness park)	23,625 (58,332)	One of Michigan's three *wilderness* parks and its largest state park. One of the few large "wild" areas left in the Midwest. Rocky uplands, patches of virgin forest, 4 secluded lakes, many streams, 35 km (22 miles) of rugged Lake Superior shoreline. 2 campgrounds with 199 sites, 4 rustic campgrounds, 9 hike-in cabins, trailside shelters. Boat ramp, picnic area, interpretive program. Ski area, 180-m (600-ft) vertical drop, 9 ski runs, chairlift, T-bar lift, rope tow. Hunting permitted during fall season. (344,000)
Waterloo State Recreation Area	7,065 (17,445)	Largest state recreation area in system. Wooded glacial moraines studded with lakes. Some private inholdings, including lakefront homes. Network of paved and graveled rural roads. 2 campgrounds with 378 campsites; 50 rustic sites, 11 picnic areas. 2 swimming beaches. Interpretive center and trails. Boat ramps on 8 lakes, walking access to many other lakes; good fishing. 2 youth-group outdoor centers; 1 group camping area. Hiking trails. Much wildlife. Hunting in fall and winter. (934,000)

SOURCE: Michigan Department of Natural Resources, Parks Division, "Michigan State Parks" (folder), plus individual park brochures, Michigan Department of Natural Resources, Lansing, Mich., undated.

good indicator of the amenities offered. For example, units with the name, state park, range from large, extensively developed and highly accessible areas such as Jones Beach State Park to Waterson Point State Park, which is a 2.4-hectare (6-acre) picnic area on the St. Lawrence River reached only by boat. The New York Office of State Parks and Recreation recently developed a state park classification system based on environmental and management factors as well as the physical features of the sites. However, the unit's great diversity and problems involved in changing existing names have made it difficult to apply the classification to the existing system.

Since the new system has yet to be implemented, only three categories of units have been used in Figure 14.8, namely state historic sites, state canal parks, and state parks. The latter group has the great diversity mentioned above and includes some units called reservations, recreation areas, camping areas, and arboretums. Parks that provide 100,000 or more use-periods a year are shown by special symbols. Generally these are units that have extensive amenities or unique scenic or historic attractions.

Most state historic sites are concentrated along the Mohawk River and the lower Hudson River at places that played important roles in the Revolutionary War or the development of early industry and transportation. The majority are buildings of historic significance, but several are battlefields or forts. Most

of the state canal parks are on the Erie Canal, which runs from near Albany to the Niagara River. These parks usually provide sightseeing, picnicking, and fishing opportunities as well as pleasure-boat berthing and sewage pumpout facilities.

The units designated as state parks are concentrated on western Long Island and along the lower Hudson River, Niagara River, Lake Ontario, and St. Lawrence River shorelines. Most others are scattered through the six state park regions that comprise the central portion of the state (Figure 14.8). The northeast is almost devoid of state parks; as explained later, this is largely because the Adirondack Region is the responsibility of the forest-recreation-oriented Department of Environmental Conservation.

Figure 14.8 Map of New York State showing the state park system and two forest preserve parks.

■ ● State parks with over 100,000 visits
○ Other state parks
△ State historic sites
▲ State canal parks
— Adirondack and Catskill park boundaries
🦋 State-owned lands in forest preserves
▒ Wooded
▨ Urbanized
— Limited access highways

```
0        Km        100
0        Mi        60
```

1. Allegany State Park
2. Bear Mountain State Park
3. Jones Beach State Park
4. Letchworth State Park
5. Niagara Reservation State Park
6. Roberto Clemente State Park
7. Saratoga Reservation State Park

A. Adirondack Park (Forest Preserve)
B. Catskill Park (Forest Preserve)

STATE PARK REGIONS
1. Niagara Frontier
2. Allegany
3. Genesee
4. Finger Lakes
5. Central New York
6. Adirondack and Catskill Parks
7. Taconic
8. Palisades
9. Long Island
10. Thousand Islands
11. Saratoga-Capital District
12. City of New York

network of controlled-access roads (Figure 10.7).

The second most heavily used part of the system is the Niagara Region. It has only 9 percent of the units, 2 percent of the system's area, and 7 percent of the state's population; yet it experiences more than 16 percent of the use. This is largely because Niagara Falls is an internationally famous sightseeing attraction; over half the region's use takes place at the Niagara Reservation. The next most heavily visited location is the Palisades Region on the west side of the Hudson River above New York City. It receives 8 percent of the use and contains 11 percent of the units, 29 percent of the area, and 4 percent of the population. Use is lower than in the Long Island Region because it does not include high-capacity ocean beaches and its parks are less accessible. The other 9 regions contain 64 percent of the units, 59 percent of the area, 74 percent of the population (43 percent in New York City), but provide just 27 percent of the use.

New York state park system units are generally larger than most state parks in the eastern part of the United States. Of these units, 56 percent are more than 200 hectares (500 acres) and 28 percent are over 400 hectares (1000 acres). Amenities vary from region to region because of differences in resources, needs, and operational problems. The period when the development took place and the formerly largely autonomous nature of each regional park commission also contributed to these differences. Most parks in regions that are near the state's larger urban areas have few or no overnight accommodations. For example, the 17 state

The Long Island Region carries the bulk of the system's user load. Although it has only 16 percent of the units designated as state parks, 10 percent of the acreage, and 14 percent of the state's population, it provides 49 percent of the recorded state park system use—almost 23 million user-days in 1977. This is because the region has 15 state parks within 65 kilometers (40 miles) of the center of New York City, and it contains 43 percent of the state's population. Several of these parks are highly developed beaches with large capacities. In addition, the Long Island parks are accessible by means of an extensive

Table 14.7 Examples of New York State Parks (1977 Data)

Unit Name	Area in Hectares (Acres)	Main Features and Annual Use
Roberto Clemente State Park	9 (22)	First major urban state park. Olympic-size swimming pool, diving pool, wading and fountain-spray pools for toddlers; bubble cover to permit winter use. Recreation building with gym, lounges, senior citizen and youth centers, gameroom, classrooms, meeting rooms, arts and crafts facilities. Plazas, picnic areas, food services, supervised playgrounds, outdoor sports facilities. Organized programs. Special programs for the elderly, handicapped. Open year round. Shows, concerts, and special events during the summer months. (374,000)
Jones Beach State Park	977 (2413)	Supervised surf, bay, and pool swimming. Over 10 km (6 miles) of white sand beach. Floodlit swimming and diving pools. 3-km (2-mile) boardwalk, 4 large restaurants, 14 other food-service pavilions, picnic areas, parking for 23,000 cars. Band concerts, shows, and free outdoor dancing every night at music shell during summer. Nightly musical productions at 8200-seat Marine Theater. Outdoor roller-skating, 18-hole pitch-and-putt golf course, archery range; softball, shuffleboard, paddle tennis facilities. Rowboats, bait and tackle; piers extend into bay to facilitate fishing. Areas reserved for surf fishing. Playgrounds. Organized children's programs. (14,131,000)
Saratoga Spa State Park	811 (2002)	Extensive family and group picnic facilities, 2 swimming pools, playing fields, 2 golf courses, miles of hiking and bicycle paths. Skating, sledding, tobogganing, snowmobiling, and cross-country skiing. Park contains commercially operated facilities, including the famous Gideon Putnam Hotel and 4 health pavilions with mineral baths. Also in the park are two important nonprofit cultural facilities—the 500-seat Houseman Theater and the Saratoga Performing Arts Center (5100 seats plus lawn space). The latter is the summer home of the Philadelphia Symphony and the New York City Ballet. A variety of cultural experiences are offered daily throughout the summer season. (911,000)

SOURCE: New York State Office of Parks and Recreation, individual park brochures, New York State Office of Parks and Recreation, Albany, N.Y., undated.

parks in the Long Island Region have no cabin, family, or group camping facilities except for family campgrounds at 2 parks in the eastern part of the region. Cabin and camping opportunities are also few or absent in the Niagara, Palisades, Saratoga-Capital District, and City of New York regions. Elsewhere, the majority of state park units have cabins, tent sites, and trailer sites. Similarly, there are considerable differences among regions in the proportions of their parks that have swimming pools, golf courses, boating developments, softball or baseball fields, interpretive trails, or winter-sports facilities.

Most New York state parks are similar to those in California or Michigan, except that they tend to be larger and sometimes include amenities such as swimming pools, golf courses, and sports facilities. Table 14.7 summarizes the features of three parks that have rather different features. The first one, Roberto Clemente State Park, is a small, intensively developed urban recreation facility in the Bronx, a borough of New York City. It is part of the City of New York State Park Region's urban recreation program developed in response to criticisms that many city residents are unable to take advantage of state park amenities. The second example is Jones Beach, the state's best-known and most heavily used state park. Saratoga Spa State Park is the third example; originally established to protect extensive mineral springs, it is now used for a wide variety of cultural and outdoor activities and as a health spa.

Finally, it is important to understand the special status and contribution of the Adirondack and Catskill preserves. Although legislation and maps refer to these areas as *parks*, they are not state parks administered by the New York Office of Parks and Recreation. Rather, they are forest preserves operated by the New York Department of Environmental Conservation, the agency responsible for state forests, fish, wildlife, land resources, water, and air pollution. The principal difference between the forest preserves and state forests is that no logging or other timber-management practices are carried out in accordance with the legislative requirement that the preserves be kept "forever wild." The department refers to the Adirondack and Catskill areas as *forest preserves* and manages them along with its state forests, wildlife-management areas, and fish hatcheries through a system of regional and district offices. Administration and management of the Adirondack Preserve, for example, is divided among several districts in two separate regions. Unlike most state parks, there is no central headquarters.

The recreation facilities provided in the Adirondack and Catskill forest preserves also differ from those found in the state parks. Campgrounds (called campsites by the department) are less developed than in state parks. Only one preserve campground has electrical outlets and most do not have showers. However, the majority do have lifeguards at beaches and sewage-dumping stations for trailers. Like New York state park campsites, many forest preserve campsites may be reserved in advance through the commercial Ticketron system. The most highly developed of the department's recreation sites in the preserves are three ski resorts equipped with lifts, lodges, ski shops, and ski schools. The most famous is the Whiteface Mountain Ski Area near Lake Placid, which was one of the sites used for the 1980 Winter Olympics. It has 6 lifts, 28 downhill slopes or trails, snow-making equipment, and 2 lodges.

Only parts of the areas within the Adirondack and Catskill forest-preserve boundaries are state owned; much is still private property (Figure 14.8). In the case of the Adirondacks, 930,000 hectares

(2.3 million acres) or 38 percent is state owned. The remaining 62 percent is private property used for forestry, agriculture, private personal recreation, organization recreation, residential housing, and commercial purposes (including recreation enterprises). Many property owners are nonresidents who use their holdings as weekend or seasonal retreats. Nevertheless, the park has 125,000 year-round residents, most of whom live in its 92 villages and towns.

Until recently, there was little or no control on private structures and land-use practices within the forest-preserve boundary. Urban sprawl and substandard buildings were beginning to have a substantial negative impact on traditional aesthetic values. To counter this trend, the legislature created the Adirondack Park Agency in 1971. It was charged with drawing up a land use and development plan for the state land and controlling development on private lands. Many bitter political and legal battles developed as the agency assumed its responsibilities.

Some authors refer to the Adirondack area as "America's largest park" or "the largest wilderness area in the East." Certainly, the land within the legal boundaries is one of the largest areas so designated, since it is almost three times as large as Yellowstone National Park. It also contains exceptional resources, including 46 peaks over 1220-meters (4000-feet) high — all of which are on state lands. Other resources within the boundaries are 2300 lakes, 1930 kilometers (1200 miles) of rivers, and 48,300 kilometers (30,000 miles) of streams. Facilities include 5700 campsites and 340 picnic areas operated by the

state and more than 1600 kilometers (1000 miles) of hiking trails. However, the area within the designated boundary does not currently have the contiguity of public ownership, centralized administration, or kinds of recreation facilities and programs usually associated with a major *state* park. Perhaps this situation will change with accelerated land acquisition and the development and implementation of new management plans. In the meantime, the two New York State forest preserves are in a class by themselves.

Texas' System. Although Texas began to set aside historic sites in the 1880s and created a State Parks Board in 1923, the financial support necessary for a comprehensive state parks system was not forthcoming until the 1970s. Most early park sites were donated and some reverted to the donors when the state failed to make use of them. Many of the early parks were developed in the 1930s under federal government make-work programs; however, any state expenditures for land purchase, construction, or maintenance had to be repaid from park revenues. By 1958, the Parks Board managed 58 parks, but revenues were not sufficient to pay for operations and maintenance. Facilities built in the 1930s and 1940s were deteriorating rapidly. An investigation of the situation resulted in the Department of Park Administration at Texas Technological College being engaged to produce the state's first long-range plan for its park system. In 1963, the administration of the system was strengthened by combining the state's park, fish, and game functions under a new Parks and Wildlife Department.

A constitutional amendment passed in 1967 authorized the sale of $75 million in state bonds for the acquisition and development of new state parks. However, repayment was to come from entrance fees and these revenues did not grow sufficiently to justify more bond issues. An added problem was that the bond money could not be used for renovations of established parks. In 1971, the state legislature established the Texas Park Fund and financed it with a special one cent per package tax on cigarettes. This produces some $12 million annually for park planning, acquisition, and development. Thus Texas has many state park sites acquired decades ago, but the system has only recently been placed on a reasonably secure financial footing.

The Texas Parks and Wildlife Commission adopted a state park classification system in 1975. The characteristics of the classes in this system and the current number of each type of unit are summarized in Table 14.8. The Texas state park system differs from the systems previously described in a number of ways. Although Texas has more than 600 kilometers (370 miles) of Gulf of Mexico shoreline, including many fine barrier-island beaches and lagoons, there are only three state parks and two small state recreation areas along the coast (Figure 14.9). California, Michigan, New York, and a number of other states with ocean or Great Lakes shorelines have been much more active in acquiring and developing major beach parks. In Texas, reliance on land donations, lack of appropriations for property purchases, the high cost of gulf-coast shoreline, and accessibility problems have

contributed to the comparative scarcity of coastal state park units.

Historic units are much more prominent in Texas than in most other state park systems. The three kinds of historic units occupy only a little over 5 percent of the system's area but comprise 37 percent of the units. Except for several forts established by the U.S. Army in the 1860s to protect transportation routes and frontier settlements, the historic units are concentrated in the region of initial large-scale settlement in the southeastern quarter of the state. The units classified as state historic parks differ from typical historic units in other state park systems in that they are much larger [average area 187 hectares (462 acres)] and include extensive recreation opportunities of other kinds.

As in California and Kentucky, the Texas state park system units are concentrated in the more densely populated regions. Figure 14.9 shows that about three-quarters of the units are in the eastern half of the state. This is partly because of the clustering of historic units. However, about 75 percent of both the state parks and state recreation areas are also located in east Texas. In the case of state recreation areas, this is to be expected because the guidelines recommend that they be within one-and-a-half-hours' driving time of urban centers (Table 14.8).

State park sites, on the other hand, have traditionally been selected primarily because of the presence of outstanding undeveloped resources or scenic values. Therefore, one might expect them to be more widely distributed with several in the less developed western half of the state. On the

contrary, most of the state parks tend to be clustered within 120 kilometers (75 miles) of eastern urban centers; especially noticeable is the group of eight state parks (more than one-quarter of the total number in the state) that are within 120 kilometers (75 miles) of the city of Austin, the state capital. This pattern started in the early days of the system as donors, politicians, and administrators favored readily accessible sites in the attractive Hill Country of east Texas. There was little incentive to establish parks in west Texas. It was so far from most of the population and had neither the numerous outstanding resources nor the high flows of tourists, seasonal home owners, and other recreation users that stimulated state park establishment in more remote areas of states such as Michigan. More recently, the concentration of state parks in east Texas has been favored by the department's policy of establishing these parks where they will best meet existing high-priority recreation needs or where the resource values will produce substantial participation when developed. Assurance of federal protection has not been a significant influence on the distribution of state parks, since the state has comparatively few national parks or forests.

Texas state park developments are similar to those in the state parks of California, Colorado, or Michigan; the emphasis is on picnicking, camping, and swimming facilities of a relatively modest nature dispersed in rustic environments. Therefore, two special units will be described rather than giving detailed examples of each type of unit in the system.

Classified as a state historical park, the Texas State Railroad is a

Table 14.8 Classification, Characteristics, and Number of Units in the Texas State Park System

Classification	Main Features	Site Size and Location	Development Guidelines and Limits	Total Units Number	Total Units %	Total Area Hectares (Acres)	%	Number of Units Currently Developed
State parks	Spacious; outstanding undeveloped resources or scenic values; also often have historic, ecological, archaeological. or geologic values; selected compatible recreation activities.	405 ha (1000 acres) is minimum size recommended. Enough area to provide buffer zone around resource and space for facilities and use. Located where park will meet priority recreation needs of state or where values create substantial demand.	Activities oriented toward undeveloped resources. No playfields, golf courses, or swimming pools. Development limited to 20% of site.	29	28	36,796 (90,853)	70	20
State recreation areas	Relatively undeveloped; best available scenery; usually associated with water resources; provide a variety of resource-oriented opportunities.	203 ha (500 acres) is minimum size recommended. Readily accessible from one or more major urban centers—within 1-1/2 hours' driving time.	Meet priority needs of state according to state plan. Used by large numbers of people. Development limited to 25% of site.	31	30	9,401 (23,211)	18	23
State fishing piers	Pier projecting into ocean or lagoon.	Site too small for extensive recreation developments. Located to provide fishing opportunities for a region.	Ample parking space; essential sanitation and control facilities.	3	3	6 (15)	—	3
State historical parks	Primarily for preservation and interpretation of prehistoric or historic site, event, person, or object but includes other recreation opportunities.	Large enough to include all of historic feature, yet permit substantial recreation facilities.	Recreation developments only if there is demonstrated demand or they complement historic appreciation. Usually no swimming pools, etc.	15	15	2,807 (6,930)	5	14
State historic sites	Preservation and interpretation of sites, events, persons, or objects.	Usually limited in size. May be within another type of unit.	Limited to facilities needed for historic appreciation.	18	18	177 (437)	—	10
State historic structures	Preservation of structures with architectural characteristics of a particular period, style, or method.	Very limited or no surrounding lands included. May be within another type of unit.		4	4	2.2 (5.4)	—	1
State natural areas	Areas of outstanding ecological, biological, geologic, or scenic value with largely undeveloped characteristics that are important for perpetual preservation, study, and dispersed recreation enjoyment.	Large enough to protect the integrity of the primary resource, provide adequate access, and offer wilderness-type experiences where feasible.	Low-density developments as needed for access, control, safety, sanitation, and interpretation.	3	3	3,470 (8,568)	7	0

SOURCE: Texas Parks and Wildlife Department, *Texas Parks and Wildlife Commission Policy for the Administration of the Texas State Park System,* September 1975; and "Texas State Parks" (mimeographed), November 1978, Texas Parks and Wildlife Department, Austin, Tex.

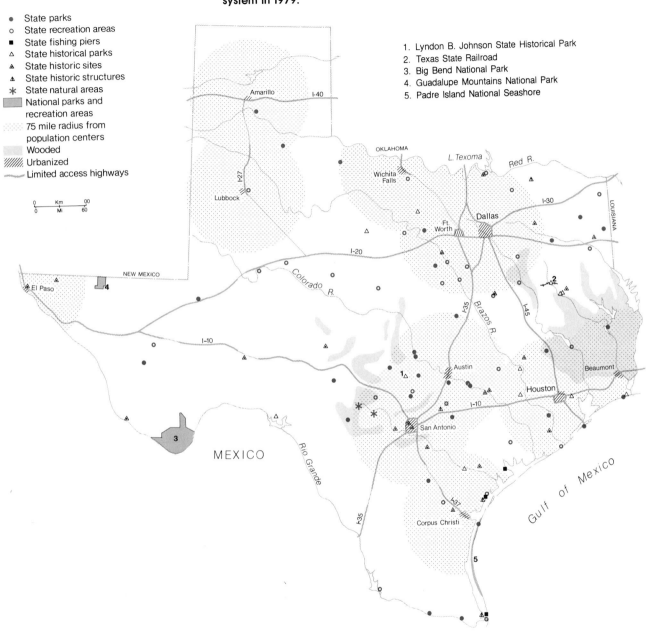

Figure 14.9 **Map of Texas state park system in 1979.**

State parks
State recreation areas
State fishing piers
State historical parks
State historic sites
State historic structures
State natural areas
National parks and recreation areas
75 mile radius from population centers
Wooded
Urbanized
Limited access highways

0 Km 00
0 Mi 60

1. Lyndon B. Johnson State Historical Park
2. Texas State Railroad
3. Big Bend National Park
4. Guadalupe Mountains National Park
5. Padre Island National Seashore

Amarillo   I-40
OKLAHOMA
L. Texoma   Red R.
Wichita Falls
I-27
Lubbock
I-30
LOUISIANA
Dallas
Ft. Worth
NEW MEXICO
El Paso
Colorado R.
I-20
I-35
Brazos R.
I-45
I-10
Austin
Beaumont
Houston
I-10
San Antonio
MEXICO
Rio Grande
Gulf of Mexico
I-37
Corpus Christi

40-kilometer (25-mile) railway operating between the small cities of Rusk and Palestine in northeastern Texas. Built in 1896 to serve the iron smelter and other industries at the Rusk State Penitentiary, the line was transferred to the Parks and Wildlife Department in 1972. The department renovated the track, rolling stock, and two Victorian train stations. Railroad exhibits, snack bars, and gift shops were incorporated in the stations. Now, summer visitors enjoy one-and-a-half-hour one-way trips or three-and-a-half-hour round trips in a turn-of-the-century railroad car drawn by a steam locomotive built between 1896 and 1917. The line runs through rugged, well-forested terrain, crossing rivers and gullies on wooden trestles. Each depot is in a city or county-owned park, which provides picnicking, camping, and other recreation opportunities.

The Lyndon B. Johnson State Historical Park lies 100 kilometers (60 miles) west of Austin. It is an unusual development both because it was created when the person commemorated was still alive and because of its symbiotic relationship with the adjoining Lyndon B. Johnson National Historic Site. The National Park Service is responsible for the national historic site, which consists of the Johnson ranch house, ranch buildings, cemetery, schoolhouse, and reconstruction of the house in which President Johnson was born. The service conducts bus tours of the ranch, but the house is not open to the public at present because Mrs. Johnson has a life lease.

The visitor center at the state historical park provides introductory interpretive experiences both for people visiting the state facility and for those who are primarily interested in touring the national historic site. It has exhibits of photographs, documents, and other items connected with the Johnson family, particularly from the presidential years. An indoor auditorium and outdoor amphitheater are used for film shows and a variety of live presentations. A nearby pioneer cabin and cluster of restored farm buildings demonstrate the impact of various ethnic groups on the Hill Country. The center provides experiences similar to those at National Park Service interpretive centers.

Since this 292-hectare (720-acre) unit is classified as a state historical park, it offers other kinds of recreation opportunities. Facilities include family and group picnic areas, an Olympic-size swimming pool, a children's wading pool, a lighted baseball diamond, tennis courts, and a trail that leads past enclosures containing native wildlife, Texas longhorn cattle, and several exotic animals.

Other Systems and Parks. Although the state park systems discussed above differ greatly in their characteristics, they do not reflect all the variations in systems and parks found in other states. Most of the other systems are smaller in terms of number of units, area, and scope of development. Several northeastern states have few state parks because of their early settlement patterns, small geographic areas, and limited number of suitable sites. Such states generally have less than 30 units, most of which are small and equipped with only the most basic facilities. However, several large western states have even more modest facilities even though the total area of their systems is much larger.

Arizona, for example, has 15 units totaling 9923 hectares (24,500 acres).[4] The Nevada state park system consists of 7 state parks, 6 state recreation areas, and 3 historic monuments, which occupy 58,515 hectares (144,481 acres); 1 unit, The Valley of Fire State Park, is 13,851 hectares (34,200 acres) in extent, thus most of the other units are quite small. In North Dakota, the 5823-hectare (14,378-acre) state park system is composed of 18 units. All of these states have relatively small populations and limited economies; Arizona and Nevada also contain substantial numbers of federal recreation resources. Such states have, therefore, felt less need for extensive state park systems and have been less financially able to support extensive facility development.

There are also many individual state parks that offer resources and opportunities that are very different from those described earlier. Examples of some exceptional units are:

- Crater of Diamonds State Park in Arkansas where the state periodically turns over a 32-hectare (78-acre) field to give visitors fresh chances of finding diamonds from the only known diamond-bearing peridotite intrusion in North America. About 200 diamonds are found in the park each year as are numerous specimens of 100 different kinds of semiprecious stones and minerals (Figure 10.8).
- Will-a-Way Recreation Area in Georgia's Fort Yargo State Park designed expressly for the handicapped. The visitor center, cottages, group camp shelter, rental boat facility,

[4] Data in this paragraph are from National Association of State Park Directors and Missouri Division of Parks and Recreation, *State Park Statistics—1975.*

swimming area, sports facilities, playground, and trail system are constructed without steep slopes, uneven surfaces, steps, or narrow entrances, and include special devices such as paved ramps and water chairs at the swimming beach.

- Charles Towne Landing State Park in Charleston, South Carolina, a 270-hectare (667-acre) exposition park located on the site of the state's first English settlement; features reconstructed fortifications, a replica of a seventeenth-century trading ship, a 1670-style experimental crop garden, an English-style formal garden, a historical pavilion, and an animal exhibit (Figure 14.10).
- Hennepin Canal Parkway State Park, a linear park occupying 2397 hectares (5918 acres) in northwestern Illinois, utilizes 380 hectares (939 acres) of canal waters and the adjacent tow paths or lands for picnicking, boating, fishing, wheelchair fishing, hiking, bicycling, horseback riding, trapping, snowmobiling, and historic or nature interpretation.
- John Pennekamp Coral Reef State Park and the adjacent 47,220-hectare (116,600-acre) Key Largo Coral Reef Marine Sanctuary at the north end of the Florida Keys contain beautiful coral reefs and marine life, which may be viewed by going out in one's own boat, taking glass-bottom-boat tours, renting boats, snorkeling, or scuba diving.
- The Ozark Folk Center built by the town of Mountain View with federal funding, but operated, under lease, by the Arkansas State Parks Division. The $3.4-million complex consists of a 1060-seat music auditorium, which features Ozark Mountain music and dance programs every night; a 24-building forum where craft and music techniques are demonstrated; a continuing education center; a traditional foods restaurant, and a 60-unit lodge with gameroom and swimming pool.

Clearly, the diversity of opportunities offered by state park systems is

Figure 14.10 Visitors to Charles Towne Landing board a replica of a seventeenth century trading ketch, one of the state park's many exhibits that represent life in South Carolina during its first hundred years. This and two other exposition parks were developed to celebrate South Carolina's Tricentennial; the Midlands Exposition Park shows life during the state's second century and the Piedmont Exposition Park portrays the many changes that have taken place in recent times.

increasing as states realize the social and economic values of serving a wide range of needs and interests.

PROVINCIAL PARKS

Canada's provincial parks resemble American state parks in many ways, but there are also a number of important differences. Like state parks, they are in an intermediate position between local, county, or regional government parks and national government recreation resources. However, many areas in Canada have few or no parks at the township, county, or regional level, so

that provincial parks are often expected to bridge a somewhat wider gap than their American counterparts.

Several Canadian provinces have established huge provincial parks that resemble some Canadian national parks in scope, resources, and management. State parks of this magnitude are seldom feasible or necessary in the United States because of the comparative lack of suitable undeveloped sites, the wide geographic distribution of national parks, federal government control of the majority of the nation's less developed lands, and the federal government's superior financial capability. In Canada, the establishment of large provincial parks has been favored by:

- Provincial control of the great majority of the unsettled public lands (*Crown lands*) within the 10 provinces; the national government only has direct control of the national parks, certain experimental areas, defense bases, and other federal installations.
- The large proportion of most provinces that consists of these provincially managed Crown lands; much of the nation is not particularly suitable for agriculture because of soil conditions, topography, or climate so that most of the population and the main agricultural areas are concentrated in a narrow belt running along Canada's southern border, whereas the northern two-thirds of most provinces are largely undeveloped provincial woodlands, wetlands, or tundra.
- Sites selected for the earlier national parks were concentrated in the Rocky Mountain region and in the Maritime (Atlantic) Provinces. Until the last decade, there were no sizable national parks in the woodland and lake regions of Ontario and Quebec, the areas closest to the majority of the Canadian population.
- The Canadian form of confederation under which the provinces play a major role in policy making and taxation; most of the provinces are less dependent on the national government for financial aid than are their American counterparts.

Consequently, Ontario, Quebec, and some of the other large provinces have found it comparatively easy, both politically and financially, to set aside huge areas of provincially controlled Crown land as provincial parks. This is the reverse of the American situation where many national parks have been created exclusively or largely by redesignat-ing portions of the one-third of the nation that is federally controlled public land.

The Ontario System. Ontario was one of the first intermediate level governments anywhere in the world to make a substantial financial commitment to public parks. In 1885, the legislature allocated $435,000 (almost 20 percent of its budget) to purchase property adjacent to Niagara Falls. Two years later, the land was formally dedicated as Queen Victoria Park. It is now part of the system administered by the Niagara Parks Commission, an autonomous provincial agency that is not connected with the agency that administers provincial parks.

At present, the Niagara Parks Commission system consists of a 1134-hectare (2800-acre) chain of landscaped garden parks extending 56 kilometers (35 miles) along the Niagara River between Lake Erie and Lake Ontario. Beside affording views of the Niagara cataract, Whirlpool, Niagara Glen, lower river, and Niagara Plain areas, the parklands contain a number of historic monuments, fortifications, battlefields, and cemeteries. Facilities range from an outdoor amphitheater, picnic areas, playing fields, tennis courts, and a golf course to gift shops, restaurants, shelters, and pavilions. In addition, the commission operates a school of horticulture and maintains an extensive system of nurseries and greenhouses. Many millions of people from dozens of countries visit these parklands each year to see the horticultural displays and view the falls by daylight and after dark when they are illuminated by commission-operated colored floodlights.

The province-wide provincial park system had its origins in the establishment of Algonquin Provincial Park in 1893. The system grew as new parks were added—Quetico in 1913, Long Point and Presqu'ile parks in 1921, Ipperwash in 1938, and Sibley and Lake Superior parks in 1944. Nevertheless, a systematic large-scale program for extending, developing, and managing the system did not come into being until after The Provincial Parks Act was passed in 1954.

Ontario's system is now the largest in Canada in terms of number of units, number of developed facilities, and amount of use. It consists of 130 officially established units covering some 4.1 million hectares (10 million acres) or about 5 percent of the province's land area. Among the system's resources are over 20,000 campsites accessible by automobile, 3000 wilderness campsites at interior locations, 118 kilometers (73 miles) of beaches, 4825 kilometers (3000 miles) of canoe routes, and 1610 kilometers (1000 miles) of designated trails. Annual attendance is more than 11 million visits, of which about 3.7 million involve overnight camping.

Provincial parks in Ontario are administered by the Ministry of Natural Resources. It is probably the world's most influential resource-managing intermediate-level government agency. An area of about 93 million hectares (230 million acres) representing almost 90 percent of the province's land and water surface (almost equal to the combined area of Texas, Oklahoma, and Maine) is administered by the ministry. Consequently, many provincial parks are adjacent to or surrounded by other Crown lands controlled by the ministry.

This reduces the problems associated with establishing new parks and maintaining appropriate environments in and around park units.

The Ministry of Natural Resources uses a provincial park classification system with six classes. *Primitive provincial parks* are large undeveloped areas where natural forces have free reign and users can enjoy solitude, experience challenging situations, and commune with nature while exploring park environments by nonmechanized means. Units containing undeveloped ecosystems or land forms distinctive of the province that should be preserved for educational or research purposes are called *nature reserve provincial parks.* Parks with outstanding recreation landscapes and sufficient undeveloped or historical resources to provide high-quality recreation and education experiences are designated *natural environment provincial parks. Recreation provincial parks* are units that offer a wide range of activities for large numbers of users. Finally, water routes with significant undeveloped and cultural resources that provide outstanding canoeing or boating experiences are classified as *wild river provincial parks.*

The system currently has 3 primitive parks, 11 nature reserve parks, 37 natural environment parks, 71 recreation parks and 5 wild river parks. Primitive parks are relatively inaccessible (Figure 14.11) and during a short summer season are used by small numbers of people for canoe trips, backpacking, fishing, and nature study. Natural environment parks are widely dispersed at locations where high-quality historical or undeveloped resources are present. They are ab-

sent from the intensively farmed southwestern portion of southern Ontario, except for some Great Lakes shoreline locations. Elsewhere, the sites developed for such parks are generally close to main highways. No doubt, there are other suitable sites in the interior of the southern part of northern Ontario, but the absence of suitable roads makes such sites impractical at the present time. Recreation parks are also widely distributed. About 25 percent are beach-oriented units on Lake Ontario, Lake Erie, or Lake Huron. Another group forming an east-west belt north of the populated strip along Lake Ontario is based largely on inland lakes. The remainder are largely camping parks spaced along the Trans-Canada Highway in the northern portion of the province.

Ontario's provincial parks tend to resemble the less developed state parks in the United States. Campgrounds, picnic areas, and beaches are like those classified as state parks in the California or Michigan systems. Algonquin is the province's best known park because of its early formation, large size, fame as a canoe area, and role as a weekend-drive destination or place to take visitors (Table 14.9). The province is experimenting with a new type of urban day-use park at Bronte Creek. It combines traditional picnicking, hiking, and nature study with features usually found in local government regional parks. Another recent innovation is Polar Bear Provincial Park, a vast, largely inaccessible area on the shores of Hudson Bay. It is likely to be visited in the immediate future only by a few affluent fisherpersons, hunters, naturalists, canoe campers and backpackers.

The British Columbia System. Like several of the state park systems in the western United States, the British Columbia system consists of numerous units ranging from small roadside parks to extensive undeveloped areas. Starting with the creation of Strathcona Provincial Park on Vancouver Island in 1911, it has grown to more than 340 units. British Columbia provincial parks resemble Ontario provincial parks in basic development style but differ in the classification system used, the number of huge parks, and the proportion of small parks.

The British Columbia Park Act lists six classes of park land. *Class A* parks preserve outstanding biological, geologic, scenic, or historic resources for public enjoyment, and no commercial or industrial activities are permitted except as needed to facilitate such use. The main reason for creating *Class B* parks is to provide public recreation opportunities. Resource preservation is not the main purpose and other resource uses may be permitted where not detrimental to the park's recreation potential. *Class C* parks are intended primarily to provide recreation for nearby residents and are managed under the direction of a board composed of local citizens. Commercial and industrial use is not permitted except where needed for such purposes.

Units in the fourth group are called *recreation areas.* Like Class B parks, they are intended primarily for recreation use, but other uses are permitted; however, recreation areas do not have the wider range of undeveloped resources necessary for inclusion in one of the three park classes. This classification appears to be replacing the Class B

Figure 14.11 Map of Ontario provincial park system. Inset map shows Ontario Ministry of Natural Resources administrative regions.

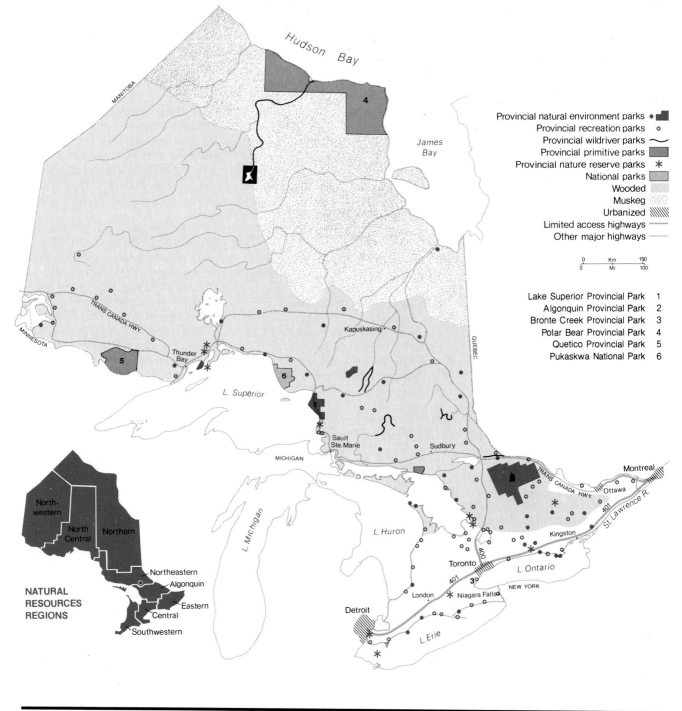

Provincial natural environment parks • ■
Provincial recreation parks ○
Provincial wildriver parks ⌒
Provincial primitive parks ▰
Provincial nature reserve parks *
National parks ▨
Wooded
Muskeg
Urbanized
Limited access highways
Other major highways

Lake Superior Provincial Park 1
Algonquin Provincial Park 2
Bronte Creek Provincial Park 3
Polar Bear Provincial Park 4
Quetico Provincial Park 5
Pukaskwa National Park 6

NATURAL RESOURCES REGIONS

Table 14.9 Examples of Ontario Provincial Parks (1978 Data)

Unit Name and Classification	Area in Hectares (Acres)	Main Features and Annual Use
Algonquin (natural environment) Provincial Park	754,272 (1,862,400)	Created in 1893. Ontario's second largest unit. Lakes, streams, wetlands, forests, and rocky uplands on the southern edge of the Canadian Shield. Only the strip along Highway 60 is accessible by road and is used for sightseeing, picnicking, swimming, vehicle camping (1345 sites), and enjoying interpretive exhibits and programs. Lakes, streams, and portages form over 1600 km (1000 miles) of canoe routes; heavily used by individuals and groups. 75% of the park is periodically logged. (600,000)
Bronte Creek (recreation) Provincial Park	448 (1,107)	First unit to provide a mixture of traditional day-use activities and regional park type opportunities for an urban population. 40 km (25 miles) from Toronto. Farmland and deep winding ravine of Bronte Creek. 0.6-ha (1.5-acre) artificial swimming or ice-skating lake, 8 lighted tennis courts, multipurpose ballgame and square-dance court, toboggan hill, picnic areas, children's farm and playloft, operating old-time horse-powered farm, hiking and interpretive trails, visitor center, archaeological displays, tractor-train. (250,000)
Polar Bear (primitive) Provincial Park	2,408,734 (5,951,900)	South shore of Hudson Bay. As large as New Hampshire; almost three times the area of Yellowstone National Park. Nearest highway connecting to southern Ontario is 362 km (225 miles) from park. Access usually by rail to Moosonee and then air. Lowland transition forest, tundra, and subarctic environments. Cold summers with frequent light rain. Permafrost, muskeg, small lakes. Important habitat for survival of polar bear and woodland caribou. Lynx, moose, walrus, seals, whales, snow geese, and other waterfowl. Archaeological, historical, and present-day Cree Indian cultural values. Limited canoe trips, backpacking, fishing, scientific study, and goose hunting. No roads. Travel on foot or by watercraft; aircraft flights to specified places. Primitive campsites, portages, trails, and interpretive services. (na[a])

[a] na = not available.
SOURCE: Ontario Ministry of Natural Resources; individual park brochures, planning proposals, policy reports, and information publications; Ontario Ministry of Natural Resources, Toronto, Ont., 1975–1978.

park category, since no Class B parks have been established for several decades. *Wilderness conservancies* constitute the fifth group and are defined as roadless tracts in which environments are preserved intact and no development is permitted except when needed to protect the natural processes. Finally, lands in the sixth category are termed *nature conservancy areas.* These are roadless tracts inside provincial parks that are intended to preserve representative unaltered ecosystems and landforms. Development is not allowed unless needed for preservation and wilderness use.

As Table 14.10 shows, Class A parks are the most numerous comprising two-thirds of the system's units. Class B parks, on the other hand, are few in number but very large in size so that they constitute almost one-third of the system's total area. The locally administered Class C parks are quite small (by British Columbia standards) and represent less than 0.1 percent of the system's area in spite of their large number. Seven tracts within the Class A and B parks totaling 657,122 hectares (1,623,726 acres) have been designated nature conservancy areas; almost two-thirds of this land is in Class B parks.

As in Texas, intermediate level park location in British Columbia has been strongly influenced by settlement patterns and accessibility. More than two-thirds of the system's units are concentrated in the populated southern quarter of the province (Figure 14.12). The northern three-quarters of the province contains eight largely undeveloped major units and a series of smaller parks located primarily along the few main highways.

The absence of large parks protecting typical sections of the coast's fiordlike landscapes found from just north of Vancouver to the Alaskan border is quite noticeable.

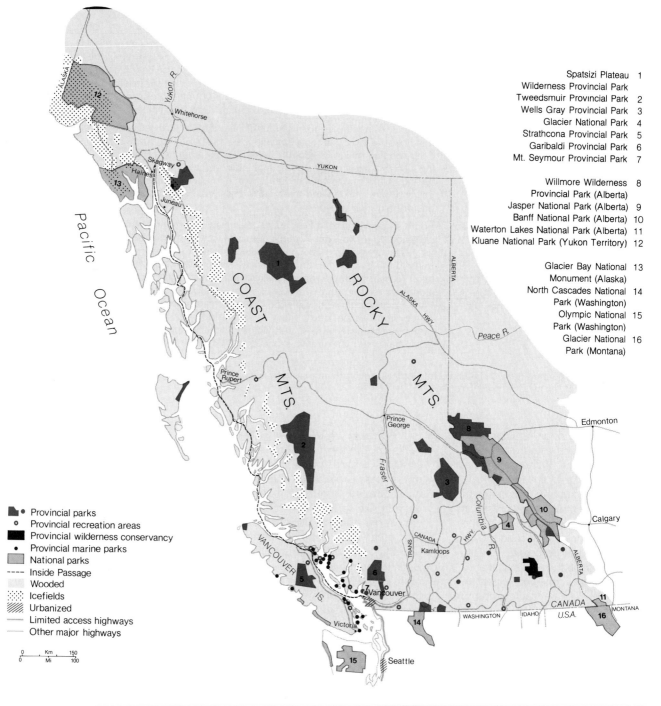

Figure 14.12 Map showing major British Columbia provincial parks and related national parks and travel routes.

Spatsizi Plateau 1
Wilderness Provincial Park
Tweedsmuir Provincial Park 2
Wells Gray Provincial Park 3
Glacier National Park 4
Strathcona Provincial Park 5
Garibaldi Provincial Park 6
Mt. Seymour Provincial Park 7

Willmore Wilderness 8
Provincial Park (Alberta)
Jasper National Park (Alberta) 9
Banff National Park (Alberta) 10
Waterton Lakes National Park (Alberta) 11
Kluane National Park (Yukon Territory) 12

Glacier Bay National 13
Monument (Alaska)
North Cascades National 14
Park (Washington)
Olympic National 15
Park (Washington)
Glacier National 16
Park (Montana)

Legend:
- Provincial parks
- Provincial recreation areas
- Provincial wilderness conservancy
- Provincial marine parks
- National parks
- - - Inside Passage
- Wooded
- Icefields
- Urbanized
- Limited access highways
- Other major highways

Km 150
Mi 100

Table 14.10 Numbers and Areas of British Columbia Provincial Parks (Data for 1978)

Type of Unit	Units Number	Units %	Area Hectares (Acres)	Area %	Average Area of Unit Hectares (Acres)
Class A parks[a] (outstanding undeveloped or historic resources)	260	74.9	2,818,378 (6,964,116)	62.2	10,840 (26,785)
Class B parks[a] (regional recreation opportunities)	6	1.7	1,343,860 (3,320,633)	29.6	223,977 (553,439)
Class C parks (recreation for local populations)	55	15.9	2,270 (5,608)	0.1	41 (102)
Total for established parks	321	92.5	4,164,508 (10,290,357)	91.8	12,974 (32,057)
Recreation areas	25	7.2	238,066 (588,252)	5.3	9.523 (23,530)
Wilderness Conservancies	1	0.3	131,528 (325,000)	2.9	131,528 (325,000)
Total for all lands in system	347	100.0	4,534,102 (11,203,609)	100.0	13,067 (32,287)

[a] Class A and B parks include seven tracts that have also been designated as nature conservancy areas.

SOURCE: Developed from British Columbia Ministry of Recreation and Conservation, "Summary of All Provincial Parks to December 31, 1978" (mimeographed), Ministry of Recreation and Conservation, Victoria, B.C., 1979.

These landscapes are one of the main attractions for tourists and cruise-ship passengers who travel the Inside Passage. Elsewhere, such panoramas of water, rugged shorelines, forests, and mountains would be considered priority sites for intermediate level or even national parks. The highest peaks and huge icefields of the Coast Mountains are similarly unprotected except for Atlin Provincial Park, which lies just north of Juneau. According to the Ministry of Recreation and Conservation, numerous sites in the coastal region have been designated for possible inclusion in the provincial park system but inaccessibility by road has prevented the establishment of any units. However, lack of road access has not always stopped the creation of intermediate level preserves in other jurisdictions. A possible alternative explanation is that the presence of great softwood forests and potential mining, hydroelectric, and industrial sites creates economic and political environments that do not favor the establishment of large preserves.

The largest unit in the British Columbia system is Tweedsmuir Provincial Park on the eastern slopes of the Coast Mountains about 480 kilometers (300 miles) northwest of Vancouver. It is a little larger than Yellowstone Park, and, like Yellowstone, contains a wide range of mountain, hill, valley, river, and lake environments. Special resources protected by the park, at least to some degree, include the brightly colored peaks of the Rainbow Mountains, some of the eastern peaks of the Coast Mountains, magnificant alpine flower communities, a variety of forest types, Cariboo Plateau grass-

lands, 366-meter-high (1200-foot-high) Hunlen Falls, and a wide variety of animal species such as moose, mountain caribou, and mountain goat. Two nature conservancy areas protect almost one-third of the park's lands, precluding any use of the resources except by backpackers and canoeists. However, hunting is permitted seasonally in other parts of the park and all game species, including grizzly bear and mountain goat, may be shot.

Tweedsmuir Park is much less accessible than its position on a map indicates. No paved roads lead to it. From the north, access from Highway 16 is by way of many kilometers of gravel roads followed by a trip in a good-sized boat across a huge reservoir considered too dangerous for canoes or small boats. The south part of the park can be reached by driving 370 kilometers (230 miles) along gravel-surfaced Highway 20, but many potential users are discouraged by the narrow winding road, its frequently dusty condition, and its unsuitability for travel trailers or larger motor homes. Facilities consist of a headquarters, two campgrounds with a total of 32 campsites, and two privately operated camps. There are no roads within the park other than a short stretch of Highway 20. The trail system is rudimentary and visitors frequently enter and leave the park by chartered float plane.

Many large provincial park system units are located in the more populated southern quarter of British Columbia. Three parks lie just west of the Continental Divide, abutting Jasper, Banff, and the other national parks clustered in that region. Other major parks are scattered through the succession of mountain ranges that run from the northwest to the southeast throughout this southern region. Most of these large mountain parks are relatively undeveloped, with few or no interior roads and campgrounds. Some of the more accessible units have several picnic areas and campgrounds, extensive trail systems, and substantial interpretive programs.

Mount Seymour Provincial Park is one of the more highly developed units. Located only 15 kilometers (10 miles) from downtown Vancouver, it occupies 3509 hectares (8670 acres) of mountain terrain overlooking the city. Facilities include a paved highway leading to the 1000-meter (3300-foot) level, four picnic areas, several lookouts, and a chairlift that operates seven days a week during the summer if the weather is suitable. This lift is

part of an extensive winter-recreation development comprised of another chairlift, four ski tows, two cross-country ski trails, a toboggan run, and the usual array of service facilities. The ski area is also open in the evenings when conditions are suitable.

Most of the dozens of smaller units in the southern region are located near main highways in the river valleys. A typical unit consists of a small beach on a river or lake equipped with 10 to 30 picnic sites and a similar number of campsites. Some are larger and contain sizable campgrounds with more than 100 campsites. More than 40 units are located on Vancouver Island; most are relatively small picnic and camping areas. There are 24 shoreline units on the mainland, Vancouver Island, and islands in the Strait of Georgia that have been designated as provincial marine parks; the numerous islands and comparatively sheltered water form an excellent cruising environment for large and medium-sized boats. These marine parks will eventually provide safe anchorages, mooring buoys, docks, campgrounds, fresh water, and toilets wherever feasible, but many are presently undeveloped.

INTERAGENCY PARKS
A number of intermediate level governments have worked together to establish parks that complement each other. An early attempt was the Palisades Interstate Park project initiated by New York and New Jersey. It now consists of a 16-kilometer (10-mile) stretch of Hudson River shoreline in New Jersey but no immediately adjoining lands in New York. However, there are now

a number of separate state park units adjacent to the border in both states that might not have been created without the impetus provided by the Palisades Interstate Park idea.

In some cases, agencies have succeeded in acquiring lands astride a common boundary and operate their lands in a complementary manner. New Jersey and Pennsylvania, for example, have established Washington Crossing State Park on the Delaware River to mark George Washington's famous surprise attack on the Hessian troops at Trenton on Christmas night, 1776. The interpretive programs are coordinated so that the New Jersey unit's narrative completes the story begun in the Pennsylvania park. A reenactment of the crossing with participants in appropriate dress takes place every Christmas Day.

Perhaps the best-known adjoining intermediate level parks on an international boundary are the Peace Arch provincial and state parks on the Canada-United States border near Vancouver, British Columbia. They are used extensively by sightseers, photographers, and groups holding international meetings and picnics. Started with donations from school children in the state of Washington and in British Columbia, the jointly managed parks now contain lawns, ornamental plantings, formal gardens, picnic areas, and a large ceremonial arch. Inside the arch are two wide open gates and the inscription, "May These Gates Never Be Closed."

Intermediate level parks, therefore, are remarkably varied. Some are tiny historic sites in urban areas consisting of a single house or monument. Others are campgrounds in remote locations, which are smaller and less developed than many intermediate level forest camping facilities. A few are huge, largely undeveloped wilderness areas with few users because of their inaccessibility. Others are units that resemble large local government parks or commercial resorts with manicured lawns, flower beds, playgrounds, golf courses, recreation centers, and employees conducting recreation programs. Management policies are equally diverse. Use of some units is limited to hikers or canoeists who may be required to travel certain routes and camp at specified locations. Less restrictive policies of other agencies permit a wide range of uses, including snowmobiling, dune buggy driving, hunting, the holding of major sports competitions, privately owned seasonal homes, and logging of forests in selected areas. Understanding the nature and appropriateness of these various resources and policies often challenges the objectivity of recreation professionals.

FORESTS

Intermediate level forest resources play a major recreation role in most of Canada and many parts of the United States. Much of the recreation use of these forests involves activities such as pleasure driving, picnicking, fishing, hunting, hiking, berrypicking, and motorcycling. These activities disperse the users over large areas. Recreation use of forests also tends to be distributed more evenly through the year than the use of resources such as state and provincial parks. As a result, politicians, the general public, and many recreation professionals are often unaware of the numerous ex-

periences intermediate government forests provide.

The recreation use of intermediate level and other public forests continued to increase during the middle 1970s. Larger populations, more private vehicles, better highways, and improved roads into forests contributed to this growth. Greater availability and social desirability of trail bikes (off-highway motorcycles), four-wheel-drive vehicles, and snowmobiles resulted in many forest areas being used in ways and at times during the year that were previously unknown.

No doubt television and advertising also had an effect. Many of today's adults grew up in an era when Lassie, the children's canine heroine, was involved in weekly television adventures while associated with people who worked for the U.S. Forest Service in what were purported to be western national forests. The locations chosen for filming were usually aesthetically attractive. They were also portrayed as potentially dangerous but this only added to their appeal as far as young viewers were concerned, since Lassie and her human companions always managed to survive their confrontations with floods, fires, rambunctious wildlife, and other hazards. During the same period, the public was also exposed to extensive forest conservation advertising featuring the U.S. Forest Service's media personality Smoky Bear. Television and magazine advertising also showed a wide range of products in use in forest environments. Most of these advertisements tried to give the promoted products a glamorous or rugged image but, in so doing, such campaigns also portrayed nonurban environments as exciting, socially de-

sirable destinations for adventure-seeking individuals.

No matter how North Americans acquired a personal interest in forest areas, there is little doubt that many now view public forests as attractive recreation environments. Forests are often regarded as places where one can race around the roads and trails in specialized vehicles, use firearms more or less indiscriminately, fish and camp where one wants to, and end a day drinking with companions around a roaring campfire. Renewed interest in natural history and a growing concern for the environment have also encouraged people to seek out public forests for periods of quiet contemplation and nature study or for backpacking, canoeing, camping, and cross-country skiing activities.

A forest's recreation potential depends on the nature of the undeveloped resources and on human impact. Extensive flat areas covered with even-aged woodlands are used comparatively little. If the stand consists of large overmature trees, people may enjoy viewing it from the perimeter but few will penetrate very far—fallen trees make travel difficult, there is comparatively little wildlife (at least of the kinds people hope to see), flowers and edible berries may be largely absent, and camping in deep shade is undesirable, especially in more humid climates. Young stands produced by fire or timber-cutting are often difficult to penetrate although they can show more environmental diversity. Plantations, especially coniferous plantations on sandy soils, are facetiously called *biological deserts*. Continuous woodlands of these kinds usually provide few opportunities for the sightseer, hunter, or naturalist.

In contrast, a rolling or dissected terrain covered with a variety of forest types and stands of different ages can be a recreation cornucopia when developed appropriately. Locations with a good mixture of different kinds of environments are especially productive because ecosystem interfaces produce the largest numbers of opportunities. Forest openings form vistas, campsites, places to pick berries, and good environments for wildlife. Streams, rivers, and lakes in a forest greatly enhance its recreation potential by adding scenic appeal, increasing biologic diversity, providing water-oriented experiences, and acting as access routes. Finally, carefully located developments such as roads, trails, lookouts, campsites, water-access sites, and portages can make it possible for people with many different interests to enjoy forests.

Little information is available about the kinds and amounts of recreation that occur in forests, especially those administered by intermediate level governments. The reasons for this include multiple access points, dispersed activities, relatively low priorities given recreation management, and limited resources available to measure recreation use. Some agencies have camping data because they use a permit system. Information on other activities is usually absent, except where fishing and hunting behavior has been investigated by fish and game agencies.

State Forests. In the United States, forests administered by state governments[5] occupy 8.7 million

[5] In other nations, the term, *state forests,* is sometimes used to denote forests administered by the national government.

hectares (21.5 million acres), an area about the size of Maine or one-tenth of the area included in the national forests. However, *state forests* play a disproportionately important role in recreation because several of the largest systems are much more accessible to people living in major urban areas than most national forests. As Table 14.11 shows, the majority of the acreage is located in the Pacific, West North Central, East North Central, and Middle Atlantic regions. The West South Central, East South Central, South Atlantic, and New England regions have comparatively little state forest land.

Most state forest lands are concentrated in comparatively few states. The 10 states with the largest area have 74 percent of the national total. Four of these states — Michigan, Minnesota, Pennsylvania, and Washington — alone account for 57 percent. The states with the largest forests are generally those that experienced much abandonment of marginal farmlands or cutover woodlands during the 1920s and 1930s and that, subsequently, developed strong conservation programs. Alaska is an exception. It was recently granted large tracts of federal land under terms of its statehood agreement and is presently organizing some of these into what may eventually be the nation's largest state forest.

Michigan currently has the largest state forest. It is 1.5 million hectares (3.8 million acres) in extent, most of which is located in the northern two-thirds of the state (Figure 14.13). Almost 40 percent was originally state game refuges or deer yards managed by the state's wildlife agency; about half of those lands were purchased with hunting

license fees. All are now administered as state forests, but wildlife considerations play a major role in management. A multiple-use approach is followed that not only emphasizes timber and wildlife production but also recognizes the importance of other forms of recreation and watershed protection.

Not all of the land within the Michigan state forest boundaries (shown in Figure 14.13) is state owned; about 40 percent still belongs to individuals or companies. This complicates management and can lead to conflicts when people recreating on state lands cross onto private property. The state continually tries to consolidate its holdings by buying or exchanging lands, but the growing value for private recreation of almost any kind of land in these areas makes acquisition increasingly difficult.

State constructed recreation facilities in Michigan's state forests consist of 177 campgrounds containing 3440 campsites; 65 trails, designated specifically for hiking and cross-country skiing, with a total length of 1231 kilometers (765 miles); and 97 trails, totaling 4560 kilometers (2834 miles), that are used extensively for snowmobiling as well as for hiking, motorcycle riding, and cross-country skiing. The state uses grooming machines to maintain 4340 kilometers (2700 miles) of the snowmobile trails.

A typical Michigan state forest campground lies on the shores of a small wooded lake and contains about 20 campsites spaced among the trees along a graveled access road. Drinking water comes from drilled wells fitted with hand pumps. Waterless vault toilets are pumped out periodically by private contractors using tank trucks. About half

Table 14.11 Distribution of State Forest Land in the United States (1977 Data)

Region	Largest State Forest Systems in Region in Thousands of Hectares (Acres)		Percent of National Total	Total State Forest Area in Thousands of Hectares (Acres)	Percent of National Total
Pacific	Washington	806 (1992)	10.6	1,479 (3,655)	19.4
	Hawaii	327 (808)	4.3		
	Oregon	318 (785)	4.2		
Mountain	Utah	583 (1440)	7.6	904 (2,234)	11.9
	Idaho	199 (491)	2.6		
	Montana	81 (199)	1.1		
West North Central	Minnesota	1214 (3000)	15.9	1,308 (3,231)	17.1
	Missouri	79 (195)	1.0		
West South Central	Arkansas	8 (19)	0.1	13 (32)	0.2
East North Central	Michigan	1527 (3772)	20.0	1,830 (4,521)	24.0
	Wisconsin	181 (446)	2.4		
East South Central	Tennessee	66 (164)	0.9	91 (225)	1.2
South Atlantic	Florida	124 (307)	1.6	310 (767)	4.1
	Maryland	53 (130)	0.7		
Middle Atlantic	Pennsylvania	809 (2000)	10.6	1,174 (2,900)	15.4
	New York	293 (724)[a]	3.8		
New England	Maine	369 (912)	4.8	521 (1,287)	6.8
Total				7,629 (18,852)	100.0

[a] Excluding the Adirondack and Catskill forest preserves.
SOURCE: National Association of State Foresters, unpublished table entitled "Resource Summary," provided by the association.

the campgrounds have small sandy or gravelly beaches that provide limited swimming opportunities. Most have a one-lane graveled boat ramp suitable for launching small boats and canoes. None of the campgrounds have resident staff; mobile units check that campers have registered, undertake protective patrols, and carry out routine maintenance. Statewide campground use is about 1.2 million camper-days per year.

Michigan's state forests are also used by large numbers of firearms and bow hunters. Many of the state's more than 1 million white-tailed deer use these forests as all or part of their range. Several other animals and a number of game birds are also hunted extensively in

Figure 14.13 **Map showing areas in Michigan that have been designated as state and national forests. These boundaries were established by state or federal laws but much of the land has not been acquired by the respective governments. In some parts of the forests, more than half of the land is still privately owned.**

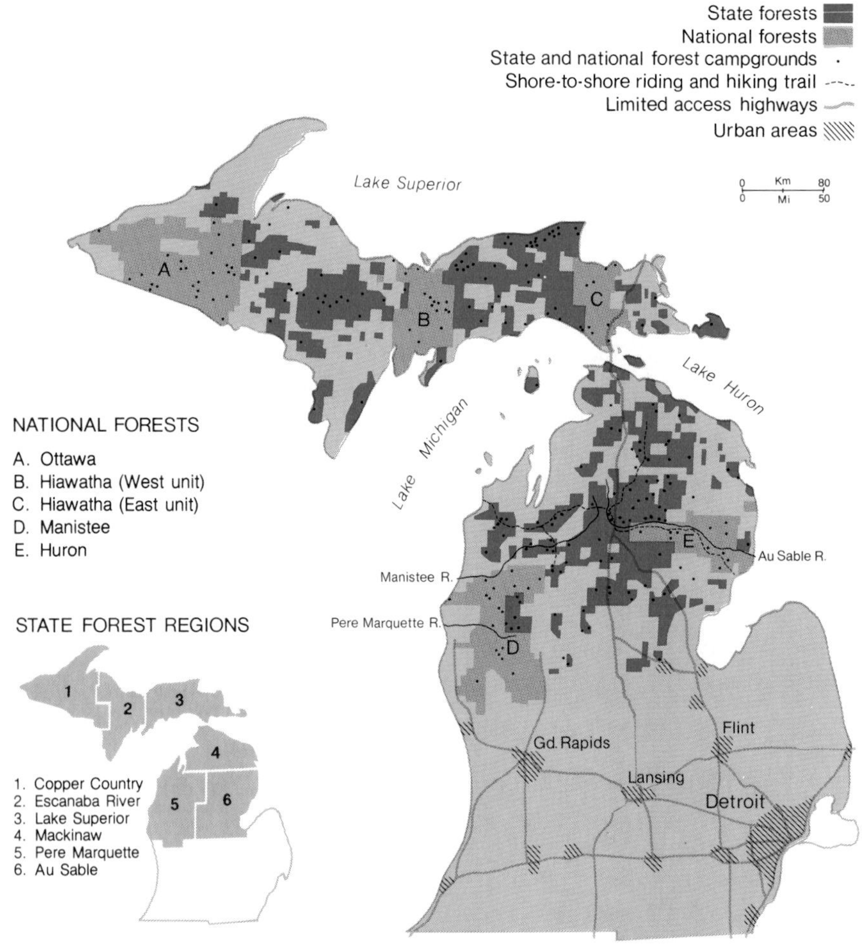

State forests
National forests
State and national forest campgrounds
Shore-to-shore riding and hiking trail
Limited access highways
Urban areas
Lake Superior
0 Km 80
0 Mi 50
Lake Huron
Lake Michigan
A
B
C
D
E
NATIONAL FORESTS
A. Ottawa
B. Hiawatha (West unit)
C. Hiawatha (East unit)
D. Manistee
E. Huron
Au Sable R.
Manistee R.
Pere Marquette R.
STATE FOREST REGIONS
1. Copper Country
2. Escanaba River
3. Lake Superior
4. Mackinaw
5. Pere Marquette
6. Au Sable
Gd. Rapids
Flint
Lansing
Detroit

state forests. Whenever possible, management is designed to improve wildlife environments. For example, logging is often located and timed so that it is beneficial to the production of deer browse. Wildlife habitat is also improved by noncommercial timber cuts, burning vegetation, applying herbicides, making openings in the tree cover, and by planting the seeds of desirable herbaceous species.

State forest roads and trails are used by hikers, horseback riders, and motorcyclists in the warmer months and by snowmobilers, skiers, and snowshoers in the winter. The 354-kilometer (220-mile) Shore to Shore Riding-Hiking Trail (Figure 14.13) is a cooperative venture running across state forests, national forests, and private lands. State and national forests complement one another in many other locations by providing large areas of continuous public ownership. Renowned rivers and streams such as the Au Sable, Manistee, and Pere Marquette continue to provide good canoeing and fishing opportunities, primarily because large proportions of their watersheds are protected as either state or national forests.

Pennsylvania's 782,000 hectares (1.9 million acres) of state forests are even more accessible to large numbers of people than Michigan's forests. As in Michigan, pleasure driving, hunting, fishing, and trail use are the major recreation activities. Camping is less prominent because no developed campsites are administered by the Division of State Forest Management. Instead, sites in the state forests that are suitable for more intensive recreation have been developed as part of the state park system. Only primitive and backpack camping is usually allowed on state forest land and a permit must be obtained in advance. Pennsylvania's forests also contain more than 4200 small tracts that have been leased to state residents as cabin sites. New leases have not been granted since 1970, but previous leases are renewed if sites and cabins have been properly maintained.

The Division of State Forest Management is also responsible for 4180 kilometers (2600 miles) of roads. These include some of Pennsylvania's most scenic roads and improve access for fisherpersons, hunters, and others involved in recreation. Some forest roads are designated as scenic drives and particular care is taken to protect their aesthetic qualities. However, the scenic values of all forest roads are protected or improved by creating vistas, by making only well-designed selection cuts near roads, or by not cutting at all in some critical areas.

There are 4000 kilometers (2500 miles) of foot trails in the Pennsylvania state forests of which some 1125 kilometers (700 miles) are long-distance hiking or skiing trails. In addition, 4000 kilometers (2500 miles) of marked snowmobile routes follow little-used roads and designated trails. The state also designates and protects *natural* and *wild* areas within the forests. To date, 44 natural areas occupying 23,500 hectares (58,000 acres) and 15 wild areas totaling 43,340 hectares (107,000 acres) have been established. These include a wide range of ecologically and geologically significant sites that will be managed so that their pristine characteristics may be enjoyed by hikers, fisherpersons, hunters, and those interested in nature study.

Other American state forest systems offer similar recreation opportunities, but most have neither the extensive developments nor the heavy use characteristic of the Michigan and Pennsylvania systems. If forest-oriented recreation participation continues to expand, state forest opportunities will continue to grow in importance as public parks become more crowded and private landowners limit or prevent public use of their properties.

Provincial Forests. As explained earlier, most Canadian provinces control large areas of land because all unsettled public lands that are not national reserves,

experimental areas, or defense establishments are a provincial responsibility. In the larger provinces, land suitable for agriculture is limited so that large areas have not been extensively settled. These regions contain some small communities but are mostly woodland changing into tundra in the north and mountains in the west. British Columbia, Ontario, and Quebec have particularly high proportions of provincial land. These lands are often used for hunting, fishing, canoeing, camping, and other forms of dispersed recreation, especially when readily accessible to population centers. Some people use air transportation to reach areas with good hunting, fishing, or canoeing opportunities.

The southern portion of Ontario's 89 million hectares (220 million acres) of provincially managed forest and tundra[6] is used extensively by southern Ontario's 8 million residents and the millions more living across the border in the surrounding states. At least 75 million recreation-use periods occur on provincial forest and tundra lands each year or about four-and-one-half times as many as take place in Ontario's provincial parks.[7] This estimate is probably conservative because most of the use is dispersed and occurs at undesignated and unsupervised sites.

The proportion of Ontario that is provincial land varies from none in the extreme south to almost 100 percent in some northern areas. In

6 In Canada, these lands are usually called *Crown lands.*

7 Data in this section is from Hough, Stansburg & Associates Ltd. and Jack B. Ellis and Associates Ltd., *Crown Land Recreation Study,* Ontario Ministry of Natural Resources, Toronto, Ont., 1977.

the Ministry of Natural Resource's five northern administrative regions — Northwestern, North Central, Northern, Northeastern, and Algonquin (see Figure 14.11) — which occupy 95 percent of the province, only 7 percent of the land is privately owned, 5 percent is provincial parks, and 1 percent is national government property. The remaining 87 percent is provincial government administered forest, tundra, and water. This vast expanse totaling 77.3 million hectares (191 million acres) is larger than the entire national forest system in the United States before the addition of the new Alaskan national forests in 1978. Its resources include dozens of river systems, hundreds of miles of coastline on the Great Lakes, James Bay, and Hudson Bay, and thousands of lakes sprinkled through a largely wooded environment.

The Ontario Ministry of Natural Resources is currently reviewing the role of recreation in the management of these provincial lands. In the past, timber, mineral, and waterpower production have been the main management objectives. Recreation has generally not been given much consideration except in connection with fish and game production or in areas designated for sale or lease as private cottage sites. Indeed, many managers of ministry lands, like their counterparts in other intermediate and national forest agencies, have tended to resist the use of land, personnel, and funds for recreation purposes. They believe recreation diverts resources from timber production, which they regard as their primary mission. The 75 million recreation experiences provided each year by the provincial forest lands are, therefore, largely a matter of people using private facilities, undeveloped resources, and developments that were not primarily intended to provide recreation opportunities. For example, roads, water-access sites, portages, and campsites constructed for management and fire protection purposes are often important components of people's fishing, hunting, and canoeing experiences.

Thirty percent of the recreation experiences currently produced by Ontario's provincial forests are estimated to occur at people's cottages. Until recently, the province sold lakeshore cottage sites to individuals who wished to construct vacation homes for themselves. Now sites may only be leased and a system giving priority to Ontario residents has been introduced. However, even where the sites have been sold, cottage owners depend on the amenities of the surrounding provincial forest lands for many of their recreation experiences (Figure 14.14). In fact, cottagers often feel they have a right to exclusive use of provincial lands near their cottages and object to the public using these areas.

Camping is the next most important activity. It involves some 13 million user-occasions annually or about a quarter of the total provided by provincial forests. To date, the Ministry of Natural Resources has not provided extensively developed campgrounds except in provincial parks. However, there are hundreds of rudimentary campsites scattered through the forests. Some, located along canoe routes, are only accessible by water. Most are clearings that are large enough to accommodate several camping parties and have been equipped with fireplaces and, in some cases, picnic

Figure 14.14 Most of this part of northern Ontario near Sudbury, Canada, is provincially administered public forest. An extensive network of rivers and lakes makes it an ideal environment for water-based recreation so many shoreline parcels have been sold or leased to individuals for second home purposes.

tables. Usually, no toilet facilities are provided and the only source of water is a nearby lake or stream.

Campers may also set up tents or trailers at any other forest location they choose, except on lands bordering public roads or specifically posted against camping. Like other forest agencies, the ministry is finding that overuse and misuse of designated campsites and self-chosen sites are creating environmental and maintenance problems. However, an experimental program that prohibited self-choice camping within a half mile of public roads and required campers to pay a small fee to use prepared campgrounds equipped with pit toilets and garbage receptacles was not considered successful.

The other main recreation uses of Ontario's provincial forests are fishing (15 percent of participation), swimming (8 percent), boating (6 percent), hiking (6 percent), snowmobiling (5 percent), hunting (3.5 percent), and canoeing (2 percent). Managing resources for these activities plus camping and cottage use is taking about 22 percent of the ministry's staff time in the five northern regions; another 9 percent is devoted to operating provincial parks. On the other hand, only 19 percent of the budget for these regions is spent on provincial forest recreation, whereas 14 percent is used for provincial parks. The *Crown Land Recreation Study*[8] suggested that

[8] Hough, Stansburg, and Ellis, *Crown Land Recreation Study.*

the much greater number of recreation experiences provided by the provincial forests justifies substantial increases in funds for forest recreation management.

OTHER RESOURCES

Intermediate governments administer a wide variety of other types of recreation resources. Not all states and provinces have each of the kinds of resources mentioned below, but many have several of them. Sometimes these amenities are administered by separate agencies with names that clearly indicate the nature of the resources. In other cases, these resources are managed by organizations with very different titles and purposes.

Fishing Resources. Fishing opportunities are usually highly dependent on intermediate level resources in both the United States and Canada. In many cases, the state or province manages the bed of the stream, river, lake, or ocean over which the fishing takes place. In addition, intermediate governments usually have primary responsibility for controlling water levels, protecting water quality, establishing fishing regulations, and introducing hatchery-raised fish. State and provincial forests also contribute to fishing opportunities by protecting watersheds from erosion, stabilizing flows, reducing water temperatures, and providing public access to waterways.

A number of intermediate governments operate facilities that are primarily intended to produce recreation fishing opportunities. Some acquire and develop fishing access points so that fisherpersons can reach streams, rivers, lakes, and ocean shorelines. Often these are only narrow corridors from the nearest public road that provide just enough space to launch a car-top or trailered boat. Larger, heavier watercraft and more intensive use have prompted some agencies to develop quite elaborate fishing-access sites. These facilities usually consist of one or more concrete boat-launching ramps, parking spaces for vehicles and trailers, and a toilet building. A concession-operated tackle, bait, boat-rental, and refreshment stand may also be included.

An increasing proportion of fish caught by anglers in Canada and the United States come from state and provincial fish hatcheries. Some species cannot reproduce in the environments into which they are introduced so that the hatcheries function almost like factories that manufacture recreation commodities. Originally, hatcheries were designed without much thought for their secondary role as interesting places to visit. Now they are often equipped with visitor reception centers that contain exhibits, fish-viewing facilities, picnic areas, and large parking lots. Similarly, appropriately designed fish ladders (devices to help fish travel past obstructions when migrating) can be significant as sightseeing resources as well as components of fish management programs.

Intermediate level agencies also build fishing piers. These make it possible for those without boats or who find it difficult or impossible to fish from a small boat or the shore to enjoy fishing experiences. In some cases, fishery agencies arrange with highway departments or other organizations to construct fishing and viewing walkways on the sides of or underneath road bridges. Artificial reefs—consisting of concrete blocks, old automobile bodies, or strings of old tires chained together—are built by fishery agencies to produce sheltered environments where fish will congregate and be more readily caught.

Boating Resources. Prior to World War II, boating facilities administered by intermediate governments were limited or absent. After the war, growth in the pleasure-boat fleet, development of specially designed boat trailers, and the greater use of larger boats for cruising, deep-water fishing, and sailing resulted in boating-facility needs exceeding the capacities of commercial and local government marinas. Intermediate governments reacted in a variety of ways to this situation. Many improved fishing-access sites on important boating waters or developed launching sites at state or provincial parks. Some also developed extensive systems of special boating facilities, including channels, harbors, marinas, and canals.

Michigan has the largest and most sophisticated intermediate level boating-facilities program involving both inland launching sites and a system of harbors on the Great Lakes. The latter consists of 65 harbors-of-refuge administered by the Waterways Division of the Department of Natural Resources complemented by 18 harbors controlled by other agencies. These harbors are located so that people cruising or fishing along the state's 3590 kilometers (2230 miles) of Great Lakes shoreline seldom have more than 25 kilometers (15 miles) to travel to reach a harbor. The U.S. Army Corps of Engineers cooperates with the state in building and maintaining these harbors by dredging and constructing breakwaters. The state either develops and operates the necessary launching ramps, piers, berths, and toilet buildings itself or assists a local government to do so.

Although most artificial waterways used for pleasure boating are administered by national governments, a growing number are being operated by intermediate governments. In the United States, for example, several state agencies have restored canals that were built in the 1800s or early 1900s for the transportation of raw materials and manufactured goods. Such resources can be costly to restore and manage because of their extensive facilities, lengthy boundaries, and the numerous places people may enter or leave the property. Nevertheless, old canals can be valuable multipurpose recreation resources. Depending on the circumstances, a canal and its adjacent lands may provide opportunities for powerboat cruising, canoeing, walking, hiking, bicycling, skiing, snowmobiling, ice skating, fishing, hunting, camping, environmental interpretation, and rides on horsedrawn or muledrawn canal boats. Many canals run through scenic pastoral or wooded areas; yet they are reasonably accessible to residents of nearby urban communities. To some extent, North American canals can provide the kinds of walking, hiking, bicycling, fishing, and nature study experiences enjoyed by Europeans who use traditional public footpaths across private lands. Old canal rights-of-way are often the only routes by which boaters, canoeists, hikers, and bicyclists can pass through urban areas in a rea-

sonably pleasant environment.

Canal rights-of-way are often owned by intermediate governments or can be acquired by them at reasonable cost. Several portions of canals have been converted into state parks such as the Illinois Hennepin Canal Parkway State Park and the White Water State Memorial in Indiana. In Ohio, the state still owns almost 645 kilometers (400 miles) of old canal, thousands of hectares of canal reservoirs, and many associated dams, lift locks, and aqueducts. Nine state parks include elements of the state canal system. A number of canal sections have been transferred to local government park authorities, but not all recipient agencies are using them as waterways.

Fairs. Many states and provinces operate fairs or exhibitions that are now primarily recreation events. The most common type is the annual agricultural fair. Such fairs usually include a wide range of entertainment in addition to exhibits of farm products and equipment. Most offer outdoor performances by nationally known entertainers together with concerts by high school bands and other local groups. The majority have a carnival or midway consisting of games of chance, shooting galleries, souvenir stands, refreshment booths, and a variety of mechanical rides. Other common attractions are horse shows, horseraces, and automobile-thrill shows. The majority of fairgoers usually come from urban neighborhoods rather than rural communities.

Thirty-five states have permanent state fairgrounds usually located in or close to the state capital or a major city. The size and quality

of the facilities vary greatly. Some states have constructed extensive modern buildings; others continue to use small facilities built many years ago. Most state fairgrounds, especially the modern ones, operate throughout the year. In some cases, the grandstands and racetracks are used for a succession of horse shows and horseraces. Pet, hobby, sporting goods, and automobile shows are staged in the exhibit halls.

Some intermediate governments are now developing permanent exhibition parks as places of entertainment rather than agricultural fairs. An outstanding example is Ontario Place, located in the city of Toronto on 40 hectares (100 acres) of artificial islands in Lake Ontario (Figure 14.15). Built by the Ontario Ministry of Industry and Tourism, it is intended to be a focal point for visitors and residents alike. The main features are:

- Cinesphere — a spherical theater equipped with the world's largest curved screen on which remarkably realistic movies of Canadian scenery are shown.
- The Forum — a large outdoor amphitheater with an asymmetrical pylon-supported roof that seats 8000 people for performances ranging from symphony and rock concerts to tribal dance exhibitions and circuses.
- The Pods — five modernistic structures built over the interior lake, which contain restaurants, boutiques, and exhibits, including one featuring a multimedia history of the province.
- Children's Village — a large play area for children up to 14 years of age, which contains a great variety of unusual equipment.
- The Ontario North Now Pavilion — a series of silo-shaped buildings linked by canvas tunnels containing participatory exhibits that introduce the visi-

Figure 14.15 The Lake Ontario waterfront and adjacent areas in Toronto, Ontario, contain a wealth of recreation resources including: (1) Exhibition Park (site of the Canadian National Exhibition), (2) Exhibition Stadium (home of the Blue Jays major league baseball team), (3) the Maritime Museum, (4) Old Fort York historic site, (5) commercial buildings with observation decks, (6) Coronation Park, (7) Canadian National Tower (a 533-meter—1815 foot—free-standing structure containing observation decks, a discotheque, and a revolving restaurant), (8) private yacht clubs, (9) Toronto Island Airport (sightseeing and pleasure flying), and (10) the ferry to Toronto Island Park. In the foreground is the provincial government operated recreation complex known as Ontario Place; its principal attractions are: (11) Ontario North Now Pavilion, (12) the Pods, (13) Cinesphere, (14) the Forum, (15) Children's Village, (16) the Marina, and (F) food concessions.

tor to different aspects of Northern Ontario environments and culture.

The development also offers a marina, refreshment stands, several bars and specialty restaurants, picnic areas, a beach, paddle boats, and boat tours. Ontario Place complements the Canadian National Exhibition (CNE) grounds, which are located immediately adjacent to it on the lakeshore. Now over 100 years old, the CNE started as a provincial agricultural fair and gradually expanded to become the world's largest annual exhibition.

Sports Facilities. In the past, intermediate governments have generally not been involved in the development and operation of sports facilities except when a major event such as the Olympic Games has taken place in their jurisdiction. Now the trend is toward increased participation by states and provinces as facilities become more costly and local and county governments find it more difficult to persuade their taxpayers that additional levies for such purposes are desirable.

The most remarkable state government sports facility to date is the Meadowlands Sports Complex in New Jersey. The state first became involved in the development of the 8100-hectare (20,000-acre) marshy site immediately across the river from Manhattan in 1968. The marsh was a major environmental and planning problem because of the 50,000 tons of garbage dumped there every day, pollution created by scattered small industries, negative attitudes toward building large structures there because of drainage and foundation problems, and the fact that control of the area was divided between 14

Figure 14.16 More than 75,000 spectators enjoy a professional football game in Giants Stadium (foreground), part of the Meadowlands Sports Complex in New Jersey (above). Also shown is the Meadowlands Racetrack (background), that includes an enclosed, climate-controlled grandstand containing a dining area (below) which overlooks the track and provides spectacular views of the New York skyline. The 325 events held at the complex each year currently draw more than 6 million people, a figure that will increase considerably once the 20,000-seat Meadowlands Arena is in operation.

municipalities. Therefore, the New Jersey legislature created the Hackensack Meadowlands Development Commission and charged it with producing appropriate plans and programs.

Seeking a psychological and functional focal point for the project, the legislature then established the New Jersey Sports and Exposition Authority and authorized it to build a regionally significant sports complex at Meadowlands (Figure 14.16). It stipulated that a major league baseball or football franchise had to be secured before public tax-free bonds could be sold to finance the project. The promised facilities and greater crowd potential tempted the New York Giants professional football team to abandon Yankee Stadium and sign a 30-year lease.

Now, the Meadowlands Sports Complex consists of a 238-hectare (588-acre) site containing two major facilities. Giants Stadium is lavishly equipped and seats 78,000 spectators. Nearby, Meadowlands Racetrack contains a 1-mile track designed for both thoroughbred and harness racing; it offers nighttime racing events, accommodates 40,000 bettors, and has clubhouse, restaurant and cocktail lounge facilities. Excellent expressway connections, large parking areas, and special trains make the complex one of the most accessible facilities of its size. The authority is currently constructing a 20,000-seat arena for professional basketball and ice

hockey games and a variety of ice shows, circuses, rock concerts, and other special events.

Intermediate governments are involved in sports facilities in many other states. In Louisiana, for example, the state government spent $163 million on the Superdome, the world's largest multipurpose stadium and convention complex. Located in downtown New Orleans, this 83-meter-high (273-foot-high) structure can seat between 63,500 and 95,500 spectators, depending on the type of event. The lower seating sections can be rearranged to accommodate football, basketball, baseball, conventions, trade shows, and a variety of concerts and shows. In New York State, the famous Aqueduct, Belmont Thoroughbred Park, and Saratoga racetracks are owned by the New York Racing Association, a state-controlled corporation whose stock cannot pay dividends or be traded.

Financial and Technical Resources. Many intermediate governments make substantial financial and technical contributions to local government recreation systems. States and provinces provide grants to assist lower level agencies in planning recreation amenities, acquiring land, constructing facilities, or rehabilitating existing developments. Some of these moneys are national government funds, which are given to intermediate governments for distribution. In the United States, for instance, federal grants

to local governments arising from the Land and Water Conservation Fund Act are administered by state government recreation or fiscal agencies. Many intermediate governments also make grants to local governments. These range from general fund grants to assist with urban park development or the operation of a major sports arena to appropriations from gasoline taxes or license fees to help build special facilities such as pleasure-boat berths or launching ramps.

Intermediate governments also make important technical contributions to local government recreation systems. State and provincial recreation agencies often carry out largescale research and planning studies that benefit local systems. In some cases, intermediate government recreation staffs directly assist local governments with their research, planning, grant-application, policydevelopment, and programorganization activities. Other intermediate agencies provide aid ranging from advice on the public health aspects of swimming-pool design to consultation on the best methods of operating children's summer camps.

The contribution of intermediate governments to recreation is, therefore, much more extensive and diverse than most people realize. Chapter 15 will show that the same is true about national government contributions.

DISCUSSION TOPICS

1. Is intermediate government involvement in recreation an undesirable duplication of programs that could better be provided by local or national government agencies?
2. Is the idea of a universally applicable state or provincial park classification system an impossible dream?

3. Should state or provincial park systems include elaborate developments such as restaurants, lodges, swimming pools, golf courses, or ski lifts? Are hunting, off-highway vehicle driving, rock collecting, and organized sports or arts and crafts programs appropriate in such systems?
4. Which of the eight intermediate level park systems described in this chapter appears to be providing the citizens of the state or province with the most desirable and best distributed range of recreation opportunities?
5. Should state or provincial forests be more extensively developed and managed for recreation or would it be better to create new intermediate level parks in such forests and concentrate recreation use at such facilities as much as possible?

FURTHER READINGS

Several basic textbooks include sections describing the role of intermediate governments in recreation, but most emphasize administration rather than describe the resources involved. Useful resource-oriented discussions include: Chapter 7, "The Role of State Agencies," in the third edition of Clayne R. Jensen's *Outdoor Recreation in America: Trends, Problems, and Opportunities,* published in Minneapolis by Burgess in 1977; the first part of Chapter 11, "State and Local Recreation Lands," in Brockman and Merriam's *Recreational Use of Wildlands;* and Chapter 4, "The States" in Doell and Twardzik's *Elements of Park and Recreation Administration.* The third chapter in the Bureau of Outdoor Recreation publication *Outdoor Recreation: A Legacy for America* is entitled, "Recreation Resources: The Places for Action," and contains tables comparing the areas of federal, state, and local government recreation resources; Chapter 4 in that report includes brief summaries of the state and federal roles.

Unfortunately, data concerning intermediate recreation resources tend to become outdated rapidly, especially if governments are expanding their recreation resource systems or changing policies and programs. Therefore, it is always advisable to seek recent publications by the specific agencies concerned if up-to-date information is required. Many agencies revise their basic summaries annually. Usually, a listing of all units in the system showing location, size, and amount of use is issued. Some governments also publish brochures for each of their parks and forests. Comprehensive recreation plans can also provide extensive information concerning resources. Promotional articles concerning specific state or provincial recreation resources appear frequently in the travel or outdoors sections of many major newspapers, especially the *New York Times.*

15

PUBLICLY OWNED RECREATION RESOURCES: NATIONAL AND MULTILEVEL RESOURCES

CONCEPTS & PROBLEMS

Only America Has Highly Developed Systems at All Levels

U.S. National Park System Is Unique

Park Developments Are Both a Bane and a Blessing

National Park Criteria Vary Widely from Nation to Nation

Multiple-Use Management Is Difficult to Achieve

Incidental Resources Supply Many Kinds of Opportunities

Most of this chapter describes the various kinds of recreation resources that are administered by national governments. These include parks, forests, wildlife reserves, water-resource developments, and tourist facilities (Figure 15.1).

Figure 15.1 Olympic National Park in the state of Washington is one of the many resources maintained by national governments that provide exceptional opportunities for sightseeing, hiking, and nature study in spectacularly scenic environments.

The last part of the chapter summarizes the roles of resources that occur in essentially the same form at all levels of government. These consist of recreation amenities provided by institutions and resources that are not designated as recreation amenities such as streets, roads, railroads, airports, and buildings.

NATIONAL RESOURCES

Recreation resources controlled by national governments vary greatly in nature and extent. Some countries have no national parks, no national forests used extensively for recreation, and few or no nationally operated historic, cultural, sports, or resort facilities. Others such as Canada occupy an intermediate position with limited national government involvement in recreation because of the strong role of the provinces. National recreation resources are prominent in nations that have very strong central governments such as the countries of Eastern Europe. The United States is unique in that it has extensive, highly developed recreation resource systems administered by the national government as well as large systems operated by both intermediate and lower levels of government.

U.S. FEDERAL LANDS

One reason for the U.S. Government's large-scale involvement in recreation is the high proportion of the nation that is still federal land. A total of 300 million hectares (741 million acres) or 32 percent of the country is administered by national government agencies. Federal ownership is highest in the West. About

two-thirds of the Pacific and Mountain regions is federally owned, the proportion being highest in Alaska (96 percent),[1] Nevada (86 percent), Idaho (67 percent), and Utah (65 percent). In contrast, less than 5 percent of the rest of the nation is federal land. States with small proportions include Connecticut (0.3 percent), Iowa (0.6 percent), Maine (0.7 percent), and New York (0.8 percent).

Federal land distribution, its principal uses, and its managing agencies are shown in Table 15.1.[2] The Bureau of Land Management controls the largest area; it administers 182 million hectares (450 million acres) or 61 percent of all federal land and 20 percent of the nation's area. As Figure 15.2 shows, most of the Bureau's lands are located in Alaska and 10 other western states. The second largest area is under the U.S. Forest Service, which has 76 million hectares (188 million acres) or 25 percent of all federal land and 8 percent of the nation's area. The U.S. Fish and Wildlife Service has the third largest holdings with 4.2 percent of federal land and 1.4 percent of the nation's area. The fourth largest area is managed by the National Park Service, which controls 3.5 percent of federal land or 1.1 percent of the nation's area. As the table indicates, most federal lands are used primarily for forest or wildlife management purposes. Domestic livestock grazing is the second most preva-

lent primary land use, followed by dedication as national park system units.

NATIONAL PARKS

Park systems operated by national governments are often the most conspicuous and best known extraurban recreation resources available at the national level. The names of national parks such as Yellowstone, Banff, and Serengeti are not only household words in the countries concerned but also are internationally famous. However, the nature and extent of national park systems vary greatly. Some nations have done little more than mark a few national park boundaries on their maps. At the other end of the spectrum is the U.S. national park system with its hundreds of almost fully protected park units, thousands of full-time professionals, and millions of users each year.

United States. The dream that began with the romanticists and became reality because of the efforts of individuals such as Hedges, Langford, Clagett, and Theodore Roosevelt,[3] has now grown into the world's most remarkable national park system. Of course, the United States has had the advantages of affluence, a strong central democratic government, a comparatively well-educated population, and much largely unsettled land containing exceptional landscapes. Most important perhaps, it just happened to include one remarkable area known as Yellowstone. Had this unparalleled group of resources been discovered in another country, it

---

[1] Alaskan data are changing as the state and native peoples receive land under the statehood agreements.

[2] The figures in Table 15.1 do not reflect the Carter Administration's 1978 emergency transfers of Alaskan lands or any subsequent congressional action.

[3] See Chapter 2, pp. 25–26 and p. 29.

Table 15.1 Distribution of Principal Federal Lands Among Agencies in 1977

Area in Millions of Hectares (Acres) and Percent of All Federal Lands

Department	Agency	Parks & Historic Sites	Forestry[b] & Wildlife Lands	Flood Control & Navigation	Reclamation & Irrigation	Power Generation & Distribution	Grazing	Military, Including Airfields	Other Uses	Total
Interior	All agencies	10.7 (26.3) 3.5%	127.4 (314.6) 42.4%	a	2.5 (6.1) 0.8%	0.3 (0.8) 0.1%	58.8 (145.1) 19.6%	—	10.6 (26.2)[c] 3.5%	210.2 (519.1) 70.0%

National Park Service 10.7 hectares (26.3 acres) 3.5%
Bureau of Land Management 182.3 hectares (450.2 acres) 60.7
U.S. Fish and Wildlife Service 12.6 hectares (31.2 acres) 4.2
Bureau of Reclamation 2.7 hectares (6.7 acres) 0.9
Other Interior agencies 1.9 hectares (4.7 acres) 0.6

Department	Agency	Parks & Historic Sites	Forestry & Wildlife Lands	Flood Control & Navigation	Reclamation & Irrigation	Power Generation & Distribution	Grazing	Military, Including Airfields	Other Uses	Total
Agriculture	All agencies	a	67.8 (167.5) 22.6%	—	—	—	8.0 (19.7) 2.7%	—	0.3 (0.8) 0.1%	76.1 (187.9) 25.3%

U.S. Forest Service 75.9 hectares (187.5 acres) 25.3%
Other Agricultural agencies 0.16 hectares (0.4 acres) 0.05

Department	Agency	Parks & Historic Sites	Forestry & Wildlife Lands	Flood Control & Navigation	Reclamation & Irrigation	Power Generation & Distribution	Grazing	Military, Including Airfields	Other Uses	Total
Defense	All agencies	a	0.04 (0.1) 0.01%	2.9 (7.2) 1.0%	a	0.3 (0.7) 0.09%	a	8.2 (20.2) 2.7%	1.1 (2.6) 0.4%	12.5 (30.8) 4.2%

Civilian functions, U.S. Army Corps of Engineers 3.2 hectares (8.0 acres) 1.1%
Other defense services and agencies 9.2 hectares (22.8 acres) 3.1

Department	Agency	Parks & Historic Sites	Forestry & Wildlife Lands	Flood Control & Navigation	Reclamation & Irrigation	Power Generation & Distribution	Grazing	Military, Including Airfields	Other Uses	Total
Tennessee Valley Authority (independent agency)		0.08 (0.2) 0.03%	a	0.3 (0.7) 0.09%	—	a	—	—	a	0.4 (0.9) 1.2%
All other departments		a	a	a	—	—	—	a	1.0 (2.5) 0.3%	1.1 (2.6) 0.4%
Grand total		10.8 (26.5) 3.6%	195.2 (482.2) 65.0%	3.2 (8.1) 1.1%	2.5 (6.1) 0.8%	0.6 (1.5) 0.2%	66.8 (164.8) 22.2%	8.2 (20.2) 2.7%	13.0 (32.1) 4.3%	300.3 (741.3) 99.97%

[a] Less than 0.1 million.
[b] Forestry lands are generally managed under multiple-use policies for a variety of purposes, including wilderness.
[c] Largely oil and gas reserve lands.
SOURCE: Developed from General Services Administration, *Summary Report on Real Property Owned by the United States Throughout the World as of September 30, 1977*, U.S. Government Printing Office, Washington, D.C., August 1978; plus GSA supporting data.

might very well have inspired the creation of a national park system there, even if the nation's circumstances were quite different.

The U.S. *national park system* consists of some 280 separate areas totaling 13 million hectares (32 million acres) located in 49 states, the District of Columbia, Puerto Rico, and the Virgin Islands. Vermont is the only state currently without a unit. At first, it is a little difficult to understand the characteristics of the various kinds of units. The naming process has been occurring for more than 60 years and has not followed a consistent pattern. In some cases, units were transferred to the system complete with inappropriate names. At other times, legislation establishing units was passed without ensuring that names were used consistently. Recently, the National Park Service and drafters of congressional legislation have been more successful in limiting and standardizing unit

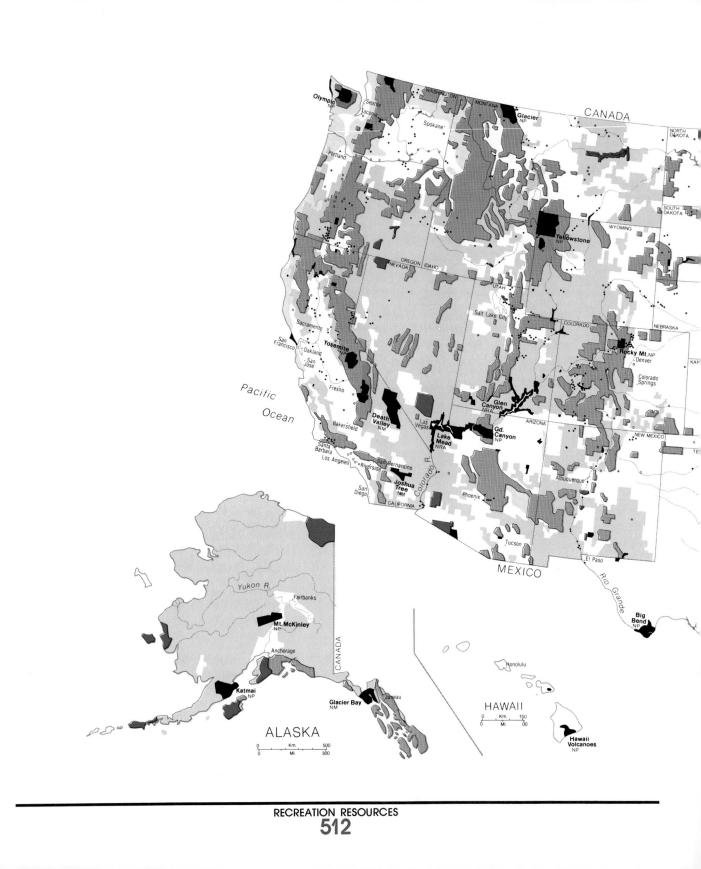

CANADA

NORTH DAKOTA

WASHINGTON

Seattle
Tacoma

Spokane

MONTANA

Glacier
NP

SOUTH
DAKOTA

Portland

Olympic
NP

WYOMING

Yellowstone
NP

Sacramento

OREGON   IDAHO
NEVADA

San
Francisco   Oakland

San
Jose

UTAH

Salt Lake City

COLORADO

NEBRASKA

Yosemite
NP

Fresno

Denver

Rocky Mt. NP

KAN

Colorado
Springs

Pacific

Ocean

Bakersfield

Death
Valley
NM

Las
Vegas

Glen
Canyon
NRA

ARIZONA

Santa
Barbara

Lake
Mead
NRA

Gd.
Canyon
NP

NEW MEXICO

Los Angeles
Riverside

San Bernardino

San
Diego

Joshua
Tree
NM

CALIFORNIA

Phoenix

Albuquerque

TE

Tucson

El Paso

MEXICO

Big
Bend
NP

Yukon R.

Fairbanks

Mt. McKinley
NP

Anchorage

CANADA

Honolulu

Katmai
NP

Glacier Bay
NM

Juneau

HAWAII

ALASKA

Km.   500
Mi.   300

Km.   150
Mi.   00

Rio Grande

Colorado R.

Hawaii
Volcanoes
NP

RECREATION RESOURCES

512

Figure 15.2 Map of the United States showing the distribution of the principal recreation lands administered by the national government.

National parks, monuments, seashores, lakeshores, and recreation areas (National Park Service)

National wildlife refuges (U.S. Fish and Wildlife Service)

National forests and grasslands (U.S. Forest Service)

Forested land outside of designated areas

Areas of major BLM holdings (Bureau of Land Management)

Dams and reservoirs (U.S. Army Corps of Engineers, Tennessee Valley Authority, and International Boundary and Water Commission)

Dams and reservoirs (Bureau of Reclamation)

names. Redesignation of many long-established units is desirable but unlikely because of the political problems involved.

To date, 19 different names have been applied to U.S. national park system units. They are park, monument, preserve, lakeshore, seashore, river, wild and scenic riverway, historic site, historical park, military park, battlefield park, battle-field site, battlefield, memorial, memorial grove, recreation area, parkway, center for the performing arts, and park for the performing arts. In most cases, these terms are preceded by the word, *national,* but there are a few units in the District of Columbia that have names that omit this word. For purposes of analysis, the various kinds of units will be arranged in eight groups.

The first group consists of units that bear the name, *national park.* Ideally, a national park in the U.S. system is a largely undeveloped area with a unique combination of several outstanding resources that make it a major part of the nation's heritage. It should be of sufficient size to ensure adequate protection of those resources and their enjoyment by substantial numbers of

Table 15.2 Number, Size, and Type of Units in U.S. National Park System[a]

Group	Units in System		Thousands of Hectares and (Acres)			Budget in 1979		Permanent Positions in 1979		Use in 1977	
	Number	Percent	Total	Mean	Percent	Millions of Dollars (Mean)	Percent	Number (Mean)	Percent	Millions of User-days (Mean)	Percent
National parks	37	13.3[b]	6,414 (15,837)	173 (428)	50.7	79.5 (2.2)	30.7	1,765 (47.7)	26.1	62.0 (1.7)	24.1
National monuments	81	29.1	4,002 (9,881)	49 (122)	31.6	22.5 (0.3)	8.7	619 (7.6)	9.1	18.1 (0.1)	7.0
Historic units	108	38.8	89 (219)	1 (2)	0.7	50.5 (0.5)	19.5	1,563 (14.5)	23.1	68.8 (0.6)	26.7
National seashores, lakeshores, and recreation areas	29	10.4	1,713 (4,229)	59 (146)	13.5	46.8 (1.6)	18.0	1,047 (36.1)	15.5	54.5 (1.9)	21.2
River units	4	1.4	98 (243)	25 (61)	0.8	3.9 (0.4)	1.5	89 (22.3)	1.3	2.3 (0.6)	0.9
Parkways	5	1.8	65 (161)	13 (32)	0.5	13.1 (2.6)	5.1	386 (77.2)	5.7	37.5 (7.5)	14.6
Preserves	2	0.7	265 (655)	133 (328)	2.1	1.0 (0.5)	0.4	25 (12.5)	0.4	—	—
Washington D.C. area units											
(a) National capital parks	7	2.5	5 (13)	1 (2)	[c]	37.4 (5.3)	14.4	1,184 (169.1)	17.5	12.0 (1.7)	4.7
(b) Other units	5	1.8	11 (26)	2 (5)	0.1	4.6 (0.9)	1.8	96 (19.2)	1.4	2.5 (0.5)	1.0
Total for park units	278	99.8	12,662 (31,264)	45.5 (112)	100.0	259.3 (0.9)	100.1	6,774 (24.5)	100.1	257.7 (0.9)	100.2
Other administrative services and functions	14	—	—	—	—	5.9	—	144	—	—	—
Total	292	—	12,662 (31,264)	43.4 (107)	—	265.2 (0.9)	—	6,918 (23.7)	—	257.7 (0.9)	—

[a] Excludes data for Virgin Islands, Puerto Rico, and Washington, D.C., administrative offices. Budget and staff are 1979 fiscal year estimates.
[b] Boldface entries are three highest values in the column.
[c] Less than 0.1.
SOURCE: Calculated from Department of the Interior, National Park Service, computer print-out "NPS State-by-State Budget and Staffing, FY79" dated August 8, 1978.

Figure 15.3 Map of the U.S. national park system showing the general distribution of the principal types of units. (Space constraints made it impossible to include all units or show their exact location, especially in the northeast.) SOURCE. Developed from U.S. Department of the Interior, "National Park System," 1977 and other U.S. National Park Service maps.

• ▮ National park
○ ⬚ National monument, scientific reserve
▰▰ National seashore, lakeshore, recreation area
△ National historical park, battlefield, memorial, cemetery
〰 National scenic river
— Parkway
⋯⋯ Appalachian Trail

people. Most national parks, therefore, consist of a complete landscape unit such as an entire mountain or mountain range, a major portion of a large valley, or a large peninsula or island and extensive surrounding waters. Presently, there are 37 national parks with a total area of 6.4 million hectares (15.8 million acres) or just over half of the system (Table 15.2).

The number of units named national park would likely be smaller and the average size of such units would likely be much larger if all units were classified by today's standards. A number of parks, especially the 10 that are smaller than 40,000 hectares (98,800 acres), would probably be named differently if established now. For example, Hot Springs National Park in Central Arkansas, is only 2350 hectares (5800 acres) in extent and is primarily a spa with most of the amenities operated by private concessionaires. Other small national park units that do not have two or

more major resources of national significance include Carlsbad Caverns in southeastern New Mexico; Mammoth Cave in Central Kentucky; and Mesa Verde in southwestern Colorado. Mesa Verde is also the only U.S. national park in which the major resource is archaeological (Figure 3.7).

Yellowstone, the area that is famous not only as America's but also the world's first national park, is the largest unit designated as a U.S. national park. Located in the northwest corner of Wyoming (Figure 15.3), its area, 0.9 million hectares (2.2 million acres), is larger than Maryland and Rhode Island combined. The park consists of a series of high, rolling plateaus intersected with small mountain ranges and surrounded by the higher main peaks of the Rocky Mountains. Its main features are:

- The world's largest geyser area, which includes Old Faithful, a geyser that erupts about every 65 minutes. There are also 10,000 other geysers, hot springs, and mud pots.
- The 39-kilometer (24-mile) long, 366-meter (1200-foot) deep Grand Canyon of the Yellowstone River, a spectacular combination of lemon yellow to orange rock, evergreen forests, and rushing water that includes the Lower Falls, which is almost twice as high as Niagara Falls.
- More than two dozen mountains over 2450-meters (8000-feet) high, several of which have quite easy trails to their summits where visitors may enjoy panoramic views of the park.
- 32-kilometer (20-mile) long Yellowstone Lake at an elevation of 2358 meters (7731 feet) which provides excellent boating, canoeing, fishing, and wildlife observation opportunities amid a panorama of forested slopes and snow-covered peaks.
- Large wildlife populations, including moose, bison, elk, black bear (Figure 10.11), deer, pronghorn antelope, and bighorn sheep. Many of these animals can be seen quite readily by visitors because of the manner in which the landscape forms a series of relatively small and accessible ecological units.

Dozens of other features and the particular way in which they are intermixed make Yellowstone a resource without parallel.

The facilities provided in Yellowstone are both a bane and a blessing. The original roads through the park were built by the U.S. Army for the horses, stagecoaches, and wagons of the early park users and patrols. Naturally, these roads connected the main features of the park and tended to follow the valleys. Hundreds of kilometers of two-lane, paved roads now twist through the center of the park, including a 233-kilometer (145-mile) Grand Loop, which passes close to all the most famous sights. In July and August during the last two decades, these roads often became jammed with cars and camping vehicles as the bulk of each year's 2.5 million visitors tried to see the park on brief visits during the height of the summer season.

Despite substantial increases in the price of gasoline, considerable numbers of people are still visiting the park during the summer season. Many are disappointed because slow traffic, jammed parking lots, and full campgrounds (Figure 18.3) make it impossible to achieve their purpose in the short time available. Some find the numerous vehicles on the roads and in the parking lots and campgrounds completely incompatible with their expectations of this remote park. They advocate complete replacement of private vehicles with public transportation or even the actual removal of roads. However, the Yellowstone road system does enable the average urban family, elderly people, the disabled, and others who are unable or unwilling to hike long distances to experience this unique heritage firsthand (Figure 10.11). Other facilities in the park include an extensive trail system, six visitor centers, 16 developed campgrounds, and the following concession-operated facilities—three hotels, six cabin complexes, four automobile service stations, seven grocery and curio stores, and two medical centers.

Each of the other major national parks has its own special features and problems. Examples of well-known units with contrasting resources are:

- Grand Canyon National Park—a 500,000-hectare (1.2 million-acre) linear park in Arizona. Contains more than 480 kilometers (300 miles) of the world's most famous gorge; its primary features are the visual impact of the canyon's vast scale (Figure 9.1), the range of scenic views produced by a wide variety of erosional forms and lighting conditions, and the scientific values of the 2 billion years of geologic history and five botanical life zones (ranging from the subarctic Hudsonian to the Sonoran Desert zone) that are encountered on descending into the canyon. (Annual use—2.9 million.)
- Everglades National Park—a 566,500-hectare (1.4 million-acre) subtropical wilderness at the southern tip of Florida. Preserves portions of the half-land, half-water Everglades area, which contains many rare plants (sawgrass, wild orchids, West Indies mahogany), birds (wood ibis, spoonbills, bald eagles), reptiles (alligators, crocodiles), and mammals (manatee, bobcats, key deer). These are nonexistent or seldom observable anywhere else in the nation. (Annual use—1.1 million.)
- Great Smoky Mountains National Park—a 209,500-hectare (517,400-acre) mountain park in North Carolina and Tennessee. Contains a section of some of the oldest mountains on earth; its primary features are diverse mountain and valley ecosystems, extensive hiking opportunities, preserved pioneer buildings and landscapes, and beautiful views—especially in the autumn when the deciduous trees change color or in the late spring when hundreds of species of flowering plants come into bloom. (Annual use—11.6 million.)

- Hawaii Volcanoes National Park—a 92,800-hectare (229,200-acre) park on the island of Hawaii. Includes several intermittently active volcanoes; its many miles of roads and 240 kilometers (150 miles) of foot trails (sometimes closed because of eruptions) enable visitors to see an unfamiliar terrain that includes the 4172-meter (13,680-foot) Mauna Loa, over a dozen craters (some with recent lava flows), a variety of unusual lava formations, many fine ocean views, and a number of contrasting vegetation types, some of which contain dense stands of tree ferns or other unusual plant species. (Annual use—1.8 million.)
- Olympic National Park—a 365,000-hectare (901,200-acre) mountainous area in the state of Washington. Its primary features are centuries-old temperate rain forests containing lush plant growth—ranging from abundant fungi, mosses, and lichens to four species of coniferous trees, which often reach heights of 76 meters (250 feet); abundant wildlife, including the rare Roosevelt elk; ruggedly shaped mountains; numerous active glaciers; and 80 kilometers (50 miles) of scenic ocean coastline (Figure 15.1). (Annual use—2.7 million.)

Only 13.3 percent of the system's units are national parks, but they receive almost 31 percent of the field budget, employ about 26 percent of the permanent field staff, and attract almost 25 percent of the users.

The second main group of U.S. national park system units consists of areas called *national monuments*. This name causes confusion because only two of these units—the Statue of Liberty in New York Harbor and Cabrillo National Monument in San Diego—are actually *monuments* in the most frequently used sense of the word (a statue, column, carving, or mausoleum-type building commemorating a famous person or event). The system contains many other major statues, columns, and mausoleum-like buildings, but they are usually classified as *national memorials* or are part of a unit included in one of the other historical classifications.

The majority of the 81 national monuments are primarily historical (28 percent) or archaeological (27 percent). The remainder are geologic (27 percent), biological (10 percent), paleontological (6 percent), or large areas containing a diversity of resources (3 percent). Some historical and archaeological monuments are less than 40 hectares (100 acres) in extent and are similar to units classified as historic sites. However, many other historical and archaeological national monuments cover several hundred hectares or contain such extensive ruins that a sizable staff is required for preservation and interpretation duties.

Ideally, a unit included in the national monument group should contain a resource that is of national park caliber but lacks the diversity of resources or the size required for national park status. Table 15.3 lists examples of monuments that are of this type.

Currently, two vast national monuments are of national park quality and size. One is Glacier Bay National Monument located in the panhandle area of Alaska (Figure 14.12). It is the largest single unit in the national park system occupying more than 1.1 million hectares (2.8 million acres) of land and water. Its main features are 16 glaciers pushing down into tidewater inlets; towering ice cliffs from which great masses fall away and form icebergs; several mountain ranges, including a number of peaks over 3000 meters (10,000 feet); many vegetation types, ranging from sites just colonized after glacial retreat to mature forests; and a great variety of wildlife, including whales, porpoises, bears, seals, mountain goats, and more than 200 bird species.

The other unit that is of national park caliber is 1.1 million-hectare (2.8 million-acre) Katmai National Monument in southwest Alaska. It is the second largest unit in the system and contains the site of one of the greatest volcanic eruptions in history, which took place in 1912. Katmai's main attractions are its volcanic features; more than 241 kilometers (150 miles) of a scenic coastline that includes many fiords; a series of large inland lakes; extensive wildlife populations, including many brown bears; and excellent fishing.

Another unit that has features to justify national park status is Death Valley National Monument. This 850,000-hectare (2.1 million-acre) unit consists of most of the 180-kilometer (110-mile) long valley, including the bordering mountain ranges. Elevations range from 86 meters (282 feet) *below* sea level to more than 3300 meters (10,800 feet). The monument protects environments, ranging from marshes, salt flats, sand dunes, and desert scrub to several kinds of forest. Consequently, it contains a great diversity of life forms including 650 plant species, 21 of which are endemic (only grow in the monument).

No doubt Glacier Bay, Katmai, and possibly Death Valley, like many previous monuments, will eventually be redesignated as national parks. Areas such as these have often been protected from commercial development by using

Table 15.3 Examples of U.S. National Monuments

Major Theme	Name (Location)	Area in Hectares (Acres)	Main Features and Annual Use 1977
Geologic	Devils Tower National Monument (Wyoming)	546 (1,347)	Solitary 264-m (865-ft) high pillar of rock. Remnant of large volcanic intrusion. First national monument. Featured in movie *Close Encounters of The Third Kind*. (156,000)
	Great Sand Dunes National Monument (Colorado)	14,915 (36,827)	Huge wind-blown sand deposit trapped by the Sangre de Cristo Mountains. Some dunes are 210 m (700 ft) high. Unique landscapes and biological communities. (229,000)
	Jewel Cave National Monument (South Dakota)	516 (1,275)	Series of limestone caverns with attractive quartz, calcite, and gypsum deposits. Guided tours during summer months. (105,000)
Paleontological	Dinosaur National Monument (Utah/Colorado)	85,476 (211,051)	Rock formations containing well-preserved dinosaur fossils. Yielded 26 complete dinosaur skeletons now on exhibit in major museums. Visitor center incorporates quarry face allowing public to watch workers exposing fossils (Figure 16.8). Scenic canyon and Green River landscapes. (413,000)
Botanical	Saguaro National Monument (Arizona)	33,848 (83,576)	Excellent examples of botanical communities, ranging from Sonoran desert scrub at 600 m (2000 ft) through grassland, oak, oak-pine, ponderosa pine, to the Douglas fir/white fir forest at 2600 m (8500 ft). Giant saguaro cactus forest contains specially adapted insect, bird, and mammal species. (422,000)
Archaeological	Bandelier National Monument (New Mexico)	14,973 (36,971)	Cliff and open-pueblo dwellings of a fifteenth century Indian community along a 3-km (2-mile) long canyon. Other sites in the wild plateau, canyon, and forest backcountry. 97 km (60 miles) of trails. (137,000)
Historical	Fort Jefferson National Monument (Florida)	19,086 (47,125)	At west end of Florida Keys island chain. Largest all-masonry fort in the Western World. Built in 1846 as coast defense. Exceptional coral reef communities and bird life. Marine reserve. (21,000)

SOURCE: U.S. Department of the Interior, National Park Service: brochures for individual units.

the Presidential power of establishing monuments by proclamation rather than attempting the lengthier and less certain process of establishing a national park by Act of Congress. In the meantime, the inclusion of such vast units distorts the national monument data. These three monuments cover 3.1 million hectares (7.6 million acres) or almost 78 percent of the monument group's total area. If they are removed from the statistics listed in Table 15.2, the other 78 national monuments occupy 7 percent rather than 32 percent of the system's total area and the mean area is reduced to 11,505 hectares (28,408 acres).

Most national monuments are not extensively developed. The majority are limited to one combination headquarters and interpretive center building, a limited number of trails, a few modest picnic areas, and one or two small campgrounds. Very few have any other recreation facilities. Some of the historic monuments are completely undeveloped or consist of only one or two historic structures.

Less developed or more remote monuments often have no ranger-led activities, interpretation being carried out by signs, small displays, or self-guiding trails. Monuments have an average of less than 8 permanent staff positions per unit compared to almost 48 and 15 per unit for national parks and other historic units respectively, and 36 for seashores, lakeshores, and recreation areas. Similarly, the average budget and total number of users is substantially smaller at the monuments than at each of these other three groups (Table 15.2).

The third main group consists of the remaining historic units. These areas have the following names (preceded by the word, national) — *historic site, historical park, military park, battlefield park, battlefield site,* and *battlefield.* The 108 areas in this group comprise 39 percent of the units in the system but only 0.7 percent of its area since most are small.

Many of these units are located in the populated eastern portion of the country and a good number are regarded as essential sightseeing destinations, since they are vital parts of the national heritage. Consequently, the historic units, although small in area, receive almost 27 percent of the system's total use. This high level of use coupled with the large number of individual units and the substantial resources needed to develop, protect, and interpret many of the areas, results in almost one-fifth of the budget and one-quarter of the permanent staff positions being allocated to the historic units group.

The group includes a wide range of areas and structures, which can be divided into three subgroups based on the characteristics of the main features. The most numerous are units that preserve structures or building sites that are important be-

cause of sustained use for a historically significant activity. These include fortifications, canals, industrial sites, settlements, and seats of government. Three examples of this subgroup are given in Table 15.4. Approximately 40 percent of the areas in the group, 43 units, fall into this category; 14 of these are forts.

The second subgroup contains sites that commemorate an event rather than preserve a specific historic structure or ruin. Of the 33 units in this subgroup, 25 are the sites of important battles during the Revolutionary War, the War of 1812, or the Civil War. Others commemorate peaceful relationships with Canada and Mexico, the territorial growth of the nation, and similar events.

The last subgroup commemorates specific individuals. Many of these units contain buildings in which the person was born or lived. Some are memorials erected on sites that have little or no connection to the individual concerned. Persons honored include presidents, statesmen, explorers, inventors, writers, poets, and sculptors. Half of the 32 units commemorate presidents. One area, Mount Rushmore National Memorial in South Dakota is an anomaly in that it consists of the top of a mountain that has been carved into the colossal likenesses of four presidents — Washington, Jefferson, Lincoln, and Theodore Roosevelt (Figure 4.9). It is hardly in keeping with modern national park principles of protection or historic site authenticity, but it was added to the system some years ago because of political pressure. Nevertheless, the memorial is a nationally known attraction, which annually provides inspiring experi-

ences for many of its 1.25 million visitors.

The fourth main group of units consists of *national lakeshores, seashores,* and *recreation areas.* Each of these kinds of units usually includes extensive stretches of shoreline on a major water body or river. Water-dependent and water-related recreation activities are important aspects of the development and management of these units. However, protection of high-quality shoreline environments is given priority in the case of seashores and lakeshores. Recreation facilities are usually more varied and extensive in the case of recreation areas.

Currently, there is a total of 29 lakeshores, seashores, and recreation areas constituting just over 10 percent of the units and almost 14 percent of the system's total area. Use is heavy, especially in the case of some of the recreation areas. This group produces about 21 percent of the experiences provided by the system and has a relatively high average use value. It also absorbs 18 percent of the budget and has a relatively high average number of permanent staff members per unit.

Recreation areas are the most numerous of these water-oriented units; 15 have been established to date. More than two-thirds lie west of the Mississippi River and all but 1 of these are located on reservoirs. The 10 national seashores, on the other hand, are concentrated in the East; 7 lie along the Atlantic shoreline, 2 on the Gulf of Mexico, and 1 on the Pacific coast. Of the national lakeshores, 2 of the 4 are on Lake Michigan and the other 2 are on Lake Superior's southern shore.

National lakeshores, seashores, and recreation areas are generally of medium size, averaging about

Table 15.4 Examples of Historic Units in U.S. National Park System[a]

Types of Units	Name (Location)	Area in Hectares (Acres)	Main Features and Annual Use 1977
Historic structures or building sites	Independence National Historical Park (Pennsylvania)	15 (37)	Buildings and sites in downtown Philadelphia prominent in the Revolution and at the nation's founding. Includes the Liberty Bell and Independence Hall where the Declaration of Independence and the Constitution were signed. (3,452,000)
	Fort Larned National Historic Site (Kansas)	291 (718)	U.S. Army frontier post begun in 1859. Protected eastern part of Santa Fe Trail. Base of operations against Plains Indians. Original sandstone buildings. (21,000)
	Ford's Theatre National Historic Site (Washington, D.C.)	0.1 (0.25)	Authentically restored theater where President Lincoln was shot in 1865. Includes museum and house opposite where he died. Both period and modern plays performed. (562,000)
	Chesapeake and Ohio Canal National Historical Park (Maryland, District of Columbia, West Virginia)	8,197 (20,239)	One of the longest—296 km (184 miles)—and most intact stretches of early 1800s canal. Almost 500 locks, aqueducts, and other structures. Hiking, bicycling, camping. Muledrawn barge trips. (2,636,000)
Units commemorating events	Wright Brothers National Memorial (North Carolina)	175 (431)	Coastal sand dunes where Wilbur and Orville Wright made first flight in a heavier-than-air machine. Monument. Replica of aircraft in visitor center. (535,000)
	Gettysburg National Military Park (Pennsylvania)	1,572 (3,882)	Civil War battlefield where the Union Army repulsed the second Confederate invasion of the North and more soldiers died than in any other North American battle. President Lincoln gave his famous 296-word address in dedicating the cemetery. Many monuments and memorials. Extensive interpretive facilities and programs. (1,602,000)
	Jefferson National Expansion Memorial National Historic Site (Missouri)	37 (91)	192-m (630-ft) stainless steel Gateway Arch with special elevator cars to observation deck. Museum, courthouse (1839), and cathedral (1831). Park on Mississippi River in downtown St. Louis. Commemorates nation's westward expansion. (3,611,000)
Units commemorating people	Adams National Historic Site (Massachusetts)	3.2 (8.0)	House and furnishings used by four generations of the Adams family, including the two presidents. 14,000-volume library and beautiful English-style garden. (31,000)
	John Muir National Historic Site (California)	3.7 (9.0)	House in which conservationist John Muir lived while writing some of his best known works and founding the Sierra Club. (30,000)

[a] Excluding historic areas and buildings included in the other seven groups listed in Table 15.2
SOURCE: U.S. Department of the Interior, National Park Service: brochures for individual units.

59,000 hectares (146,000 acres). The largest is Lake Mead National Recreation Area along the Arizona-Nevada border near Las Vegas (Figure 15.3). It consists of 547,000 hectares (1.35 million acres) of land surrounding 60,750 hectares (150,000 acres) of water contained in two Colorado river reservoirs. Nine service complexes have been developed at intervals around the lakes. Most of these contain a ranger station, campground, marina, boat ramp, store, and restaurant. Some also have a swimming beach, amphitheater, lodgings, and picnic shelters. Although the recreation area is about 400 kilometers (250 miles) from Los Angeles, many residents of that area have in the past driven regularly to Lake Mead for weekend camping, boating, swimming, and fishing. Annual use has exceeded 6.5 million.

The most used unit in this group is Gateway National Recreation Area which produces more than 9 million experiences each year. This 10,166-hectare (25,100-acre) development is made up of three separate areas situated around the large Atlantic Ocean bay, which lies between Long Island, New York, and Sandy Hook, New Jersey. The Jamaica Bay and Breezy Point area is the largest; it consists of the western part of the Rockaway Peninsula with 7 kilometers (4.5 miles) of ocean beaches, and most of Jamaica Bay, including many islands and marshes (see Figure 10.7). Another area consists of some 11 kilometers (7 miles) of Lower Bay shoreline and an area around Great Kills Harbor, Staten Island (see Figure 6.11). Another area consists of the Sandy Hook Peninsula and the surrounding

ocean and bay waters.

Not only does Gateway National Recreation Area receive more use than any other unit in the national park system, it also presents the most formidable array of problems ever faced by a recreation land managing agency. Much of the area has been radically changed by filling, dredging, water pollution, use of land and waters as garbage dumps, and the building of airfields, military bases, and roads. Decisions must be made concerning such matters as what should be done with the aircraft hangers, concrete gun emplacements, missile silos, 1.8-meter (6-foot) thick concrete runways, live artillery ammunition (remaining from former use as an Army proving grounds), and a great variety of decaying buildings. The situation is complicated by the high costs of demolition and the desires of various public and private groups to use or preserve certain structures and areas. This unit also contains many recreation facilities developed previously by city or state agencies, some of which were already in poor condition or are now considered inappropriate. Intermixed with these military structures and recreation facilities are a surprising number of undeveloped areas, including ocean beaches, beach dunes, freshwater and saltwater marshes, meadows, and holly forests. More than 300 resident and migratory bird species use portions of Jamaica Bay for feeding, resting, and nesting. Designing and implementing a development plan that appropriately balances all the pressures to use these lands with the need to preserve and interpret the historic and undeveloped resources is an extremely difficult task.

The national park system's four

remaining groups constitute only 8.2 percent of the total number of units and 3.5 percent of the total area (Table 15.2). Nevertheless, they contain many unique and important resources. The river units, consisting of *national rivers* and *wild and scenic riverways,* preserve resources along free-flowing streams and provide opportunities for canoeing, rafting, boating, fishing, hiking, hunting, nature study, and related activities. Parkways were originally intended to be aesthetically pleasing routes for pleasure driving through scenic landscapes. Although there are only five parkways (Baltimore-Washington; Blue Ridge; George Washington; John D. Rockefeller, Jr.; and Natchez Trace) occupying 0.5 percent of the system's area, these units record 37.5 million user occasions or 14.6 percent of the national total. However, some parkways are now used extensively by nonrecreational traffic that cannot be readily excluded from use data. National preserves are areas set aside to protect special environments that do not merit designation as one of the previously mentioned types of units. Big Cypress National Preserve in Florida provides part of the freshwater supply crucial to the environment of adjoining Everglades National Park.

Finally, the eighth main group of units consists of a variety of areas in and around Washington, D.C. It is not appropriate to include these units in the previously described groups because they have not been given any of the standard names mentioned.[4] In addition,

---

[4] Except Ford's Theatre National Historic Site, which is included in the historic units group.

most are unusual in both their characteristics and the kinds of use that they receive. This group can be divided into two subgroups—those units that are inside the capital and the five units that are outside the federal district.

The units inside Washington (in addition to Ford's Theatre) are:

- The White House and its grounds—official residence and office of presidents since 1800. It receives more than 1.3 million visits each year.
- The National Mall—a landscaped area extending from the Capitol building to the Washington Monument.
- The National Visitor Center—consists of parts of Union Station. It features programs and facilities that help people obtain information about and gain an appreciation of the National Capital.
- The John F. Kennedy Center for the Performing Arts—contains the Eisenhower Theater, a concert hall, and an opera house (Figure 16.1).
- Theodore Roosevelt Island—a 36-hectare (89-acre) wooded tract and monument in the Potomac River.
- The Lyndon Baines Johnson Memorial Grove—a landscaped area further down the Potomac River.

More than 300 other parks, parkways, monuments, memorials, and fortifications that are known collectively as the National Capital Parks comprise the rest of the Washington subgroup. The best known of these are the Washington Monument, the Lincoln Memorial, the Jefferson Memorial, the Tidal Basin with its Japanese cherry trees, and Rock Creek Park.

Although these resources comprise less than 0.1 percent of the national park system's area, the buildings and monuments in them provide more than 12 million user-occasions annually. In addition,

many millions of people enjoy the landscaped areas and buildings from the outside but are not counted. Because of the large amount of use, the involvement of many individual properties, and the need for large-scale interpretation, maintenance, and protection services, the units in this subgroup have 1184 permanent staff positions (17.5 percent of the national total) and a combined budget of more than $37 million or 14.4 percent of the nationwide operating budget. Over $15.5 million of this amount is needed for the 627-person U.S. Park Police force, which is primarily responsible for patrolling the District of Columbia units.

The other subgroup in the Washington area consists of a cultural park and four areas that function as regional parks. These are located from 20 kilometers (12 miles) to 100 kilometers (60 miles) from the city. The best known of the regional parks is Catoctin Mountain Park, a 2430-hectare (6000-acre) wooded mountain area that contains Camp David, the presidential retreat. The cultural park—Wolf Trap Farm Park for the Performing Arts—features an outdoor theater used in the summer for the staging of a variety of cultural events.

The foregoing summary illustrates the wide range of resources and programs offered by the national park system. However, as Figure 15.4 shows, there is considerable regional variation in the number and kinds of units. The Mountain and Pacific regions have the largest total area and substantial portions of the units, nationwide budget, permanent staff, and total use. On the other hand, the South Atlantic Region has the largest share

of the budget, the greatest number of staff, and more users than the Pacific and Mountain regions combined. This is because that region has more heavily used historic units than any other region; is close to, and includes part of, the nation's most populated area; and contains a number of units such as the National Capital Parks, Great Smoky Mountains National Park, and the Blue Ridge Parkway, which have widespread appeal. The other six regions have many fewer national park system resources. Although the five census regions east of the Mississippi River only include 15 percent of the system's area, they contain 47 percent of the units, receive over 60 percent of the use, and are assigned about 54 percent of the budget and 58 percent of the permanent staff positions.

Use of the national park system continues to grow (Figure 15.5). However, this is not just a manifestation of increased per capita participation resulting from more free time, higher discretionary income, and increased mobility. It is also the result of more units, greater acreage, and expanded facilities at both new and older units. Approximately 55 percent of the use occurs in connection with overnight stays

Figure 15.4 Distribution by census region of U.S. national park system units, budget, staff positions, attendance, and land area. Budget and staff are 1979 fiscal year estimates. (Excludes data for Virgin Islands, Puerto Rico, and administrative offices in Washington, D.C.) SOURCE. Developed from Department of the Interior, National Park Service, "NPS State-by-State Budget and Staffing, FY79," computer print-out dated August 8, 1978.

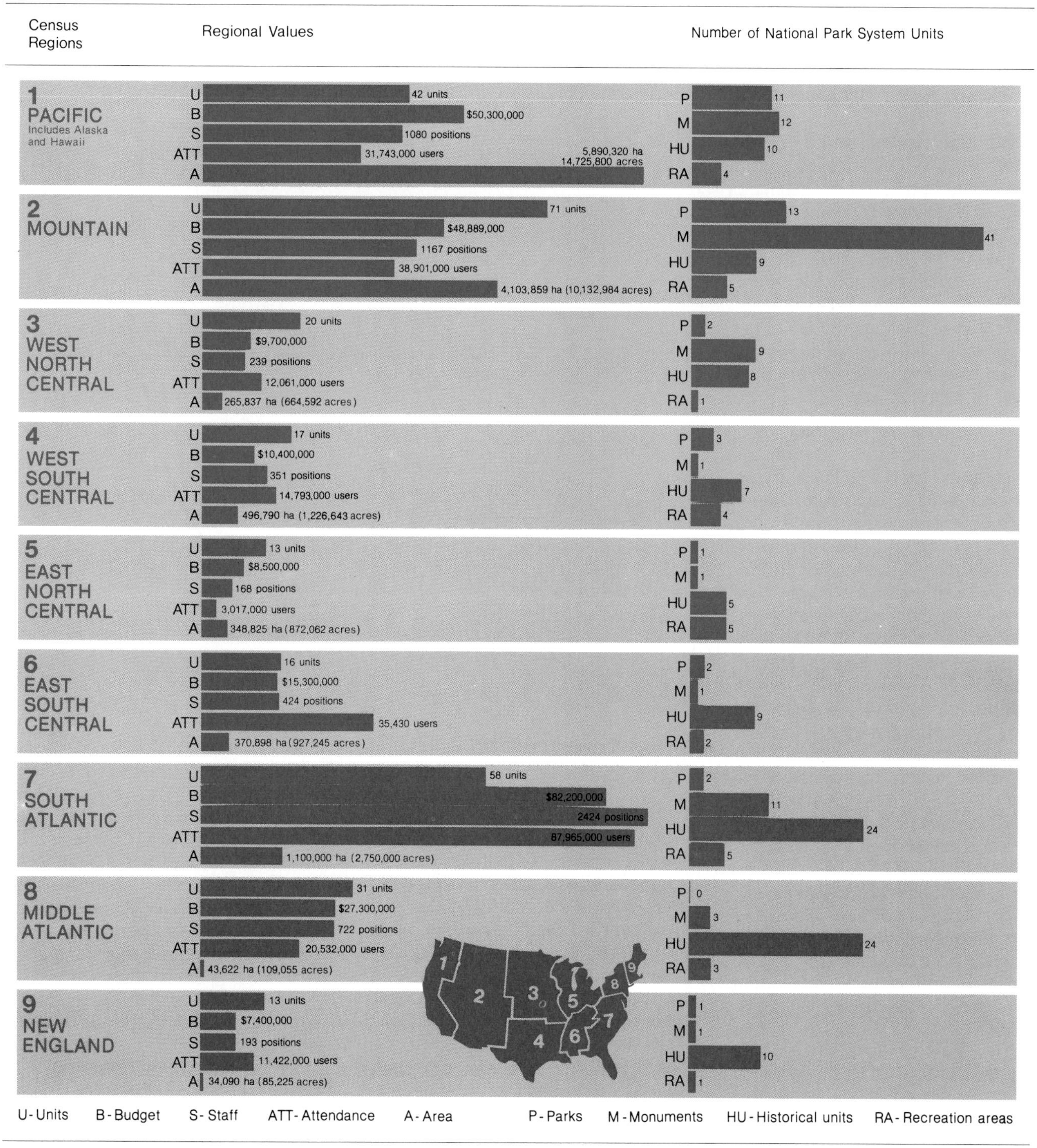

Census Regions	Regional Values		Number of National Park System Units	

1 PACIFIC Includes Alaska and Hawaii
- U: 42 units
- B: $50,300,000
- S: 1080 positions
- ATT: 31,743,000 users
- A: 5,890,320 ha 14,725,800 acres
- P: 11
- M: 12
- HU: 10
- RA: 4

2 MOUNTAIN
- U: 71 units
- B: $48,889,000
- S: 1167 positions
- ATT: 38,901,000 users
- A: 4,103,859 ha (10,132,984 acres)
- P: 13
- M: 41
- HU: 9
- RA: 5

3 WEST NORTH CENTRAL
- U: 20 units
- B: $9,700,000
- S: 239 positions
- ATT: 12,061,000 users
- A: 265,837 ha (664,592 acres)
- P: 2
- M: 9
- HU: 8
- RA: 1

4 WEST SOUTH CENTRAL
- U: 17 units
- B: $10,400,000
- S: 351 positions
- ATT: 14,793,000 users
- A: 496,790 ha (1,226,643 acres)
- P: 3
- M: 1
- HU: 7
- RA: 4

5 EAST NORTH CENTRAL
- U: 13 units
- B: $8,500,000
- S: 168 positions
- ATT: 3,017,000 users
- A: 348,825 ha (872,062 acres)
- P: 1
- M: 1
- HU: 5
- RA: 5

6 EAST SOUTH CENTRAL
- U: 16 units
- B: $15,300,000
- S: 424 positions
- ATT: 35,430 users
- A: 370,898 ha (927,245 acres)
- P: 2
- M: 1
- HU: 9
- RA: 2

7 SOUTH ATLANTIC
- U: 58 units
- B: $82,200,000
- S: 2424 positions
- ATT: 87,965,000 users
- A: 1,100,000 ha (2,750,000 acres)
- P: 2
- M: 11
- HU: 24
- RA: 5

8 MIDDLE ATLANTIC
- U: 31 units
- B: $27,300,000
- S: 722 positions
- ATT: 20,532,000 users
- A: 43,622 ha (109,055 acres)
- P: 0
- M: 3
- HU: 24
- RA: 3

9 NEW ENGLAND
- U: 13 units
- B: $7,400,000
- S: 193 positions
- ATT: 11,422,000 users
- A: 34,090 ha (85,225 acres)
- P: 1
- M: 1
- HU: 10
- RA: 1

U- Units   B- Budget   S- Staff   ATT- Attendance   A- Area   P- Parks   M- Monuments   HU- Historical units   RA- Recreation areas within units. This is composed of 12.7 percent developed-site tent camping, 17.1 percent recreation vehicle camping, 8.2 percent backcountry camping, 4 percent group and boat camping, and 12.9 percent stays in concessionaire-operated hotels, lodges, cabins, or tents. Backcountry camping in particular has shown rapid growth rates; in the early 1970s, the number of participants more than doubled. As a result, a limit on the number of backcountry travel permits that will be issued at any one time has been instituted in a number of overused areas.

Canada. At first, the Canadian national park system does not appear to be especially large. It contains some 112 units compared to the approximately 280 units of the U.S. system, and these parks are widely spaced, particularly in the more northern areas (Figure 15.6). However, the Canadian system's 13 million-hectare (32 million-acre) area makes it the largest national park system in the world unless the Carter administration's additions to the American system in late 1978 are confirmed by congressional action or inaction. Its magnitude tends to be concealed by Canada's size[5] and the fact that so much of the system's total area is contained in just a few parks.

One unit—Wood Buffalo National Park in northern Alberta and southern Northwest Territories—occupies 4.5 million hectares (11.1 million acres) or an area five times the size of Yellowstone National Park. Alone it constitutes one-third of the entire Canadian park sys-

[5] Second largest nation in the world. Canada has an area 6.5 percent greater than the United States.

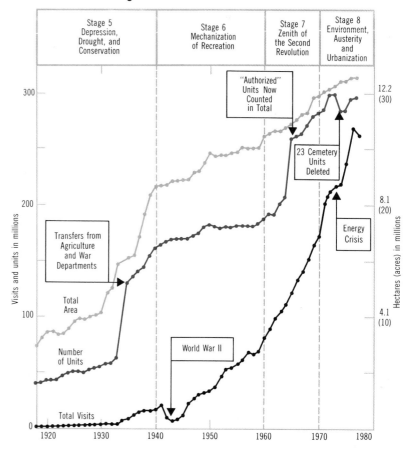

Figure 15.5 Graph showing growth of U.S. national park system units, area, and annual visits. SOURCE. Typed table "60 Years' Growth of National Park Systems," National Park Service, August 8, 1978.

tem's area. If the next four largest parks (Kluane, Auyuittuq, Jasper, and Banff) are added to Wood Buffalo's area, the total becomes 10.6 million hectares (26.1 million acres) or almost 82 percent of the system's lands.

Canada's national park units are divided into three separately administered groups. The largest group consists of a number of relatively small units that have been established primarily because of their historic resources; these are called

either *national historic parks* or *national historic sites* depending on the size and scope of the amenities. There are now over 75 national historic sites that are operated like parks. In addition, Parks Canada (the name given to the agency that administers the system) is responsible for more than 600 lesser historic sites, most of which consist of little more than a commemorative plaque. The second group is comprised of 29 large units bearing the name, *national park,* where the

Figure 15.6 Map of the Canadian national park system showing distribution of the national parks and the majority of the national historic parks. SOURCE. Developed from several maps provided by Parks Canada.

■ National parks
▲ National historic parks

preservation and enjoyment of relatively unaltered landscapes is the main objective. Finally, Parks Canada is developing a number of linear parks under a new cooperative program involving local and provincial governments. These can be of four types—*historic waterways, wild rivers, historic trails,* or *parkways.* The first units established under this program are historic canals including the heavily used Rideau-Trent-Severn Waterway in Ontario.

About half of the system's lands are located in the three Prairie Provinces (Alberta, Saskatchewan, and Manitoba), 20 percent is in the far west (British Columbia and the Yukon Territory), and another 20 percent is in the Northwest Territories. The Atlantic Provinces contain 3.2 percent of the lands and Ontario and Quebec have even less—just over 2 percent. Therefore, only a small fraction of the system's lands is reasonably accessible to the populated areas of Ontario and Quebec where close to two-thirds of all Canadians live. On the other hand, the majority of the historic parks and larger historic sites are grouped in Ontario, Quebec, New Brunswick, and Nova Scotia within or close to populated regions (Figure 15.6).

Canadian national park system units vary greatly in the degree to which they are developed. Some of the older units include extensive resort and residential areas because early policies encouraged park use by allowing the building of hotels, businesses, private-organization facilities, seasonal residences, and homes and services for workers. Banff National Park, for example, contains two large resort hotels, a sizable winter-sports complex with skiing, skating, curling, and to-

bogganing facilities; swimming pools using hot sulphur waters; a military cadet camp; and a School of Fine Arts. It also includes a permanent town of more than 3200 people that has both year-round residences and seasonal homes as well as a variety of stores, restaurants, and other urban amenities. Currently, much of the management effort and budget are devoted to administering the park's urban aspects, including the townsite street, water, and sewer systems. Parks Canada is attempting to reduce the impact of such developments by terminating or buying out leases where appropriate and emphasizing day-use and short-term camping wherever possible.

At the other extreme are some of the newer and more remote parks that have little or no development. Five are inaccessible by road or rail and have to be reached by boat or aircraft. Nearly all the national parks include campgrounds, hiking trails, fishing opportunities, and nature trails. At least two-thirds contain museums or interpretive centers. About one-half have concession-operated overnight lodging.

Since Canada does not extend across as wide a range of latitudes as the United States, its national parks do not include as great a variety of environments as the U.S. parks. Nevertheless, the diversity is substantial, as shown by the following examples:

- Banff National Park is a 648,100-hectare (1.6 million-acre) area that contains a number of magnificent snow-capped peaks, large glaciers, deep valleys, clear alpine lakes, and an abundance of wildlife. It is the system's oldest national park.
- Wood Buffalo National Park occupies 4.5 million hectares (11.1 million

acres) and is, therefore, the world's largest national park. Established to protect the last remaining herd of wood bison, this vast section of the Great Plains also contains over 8000 mixed-breed bison and the nesting ground of the last wild flock of whooping cranes.
- Point Pelee National Park is a 1600-hectare (3950-acre) section of an 18-kilometer (11-mile) long peninsula and its adjacent marshlands that projects into Lake Ontario; it is the southernmost point on the Canadian mainland. This warm, productive site has good sand beaches and a wide range of environments attracting more than 300 bird species, over 100 of which nest within the park.
- Cape Breton Highlands National Park is a 95,200-hectare (235,000-acre) coastal tableland that rises 520 meters (1700 feet) above the Atlantic Ocean. It consists of thickly forested hills, 300-meter-high (1000-foot-high) cliffs, and large lonely coves; these features form exceptional seascapes which may be viewed from many points on a 296-kilometer (184-mile) highway encircling the park.

Total use of the Canadian national park system exceeds 20 million occasions annually, about one-fifth occurring at historic units.

Great Britain. Older, more densely settled nations in Europe were unable to establish large publicly owned national park systems like those in Canada and the United States. By the time the national park idea began to diffuse around the world, nearly all the land in Europe had long been the property of private individuals or organizations. Most was in use for agricultural, grazing, forestry, residential, commercial, or industrial purposes; there were no great reserves of unoccupied public lands from which national parks could be created.

Great Britain's first national park was not designated until 1950. By then, postwar recreation participation expansion was beginning to affect the countryside as growing numbers of city dwellers sought weekend cottages or places to walk, picnic, camp, and boat. It became clear that famous scenic areas such as Dartmoor, the Peak District, and the Lake District would not continue to be as aesthetically attractive unless development was stringently controlled. In 1949, national government legislation established the Countryside Commission for England and Wales with authority to designate exceptionally scenic areas as national parks and make arrangements for appropriate planning controls, management procedures, and financial support. A similar organization for Scotland was created in 1967. Five areas were selected as potential national parks but none have actually been created because, so far, the need is not as great; Scotland currently has a population of only 6 million, is relatively remote, and has not yet experienced the high level of recreation use and development pressures that have occurred in England and Wales.

Nearly one-tenth of England and Wales is now designated as national parks (Figure 15.7). Unlike most North American national park system units, however, the land remains predominantly in private ownership. After centuries of timber cutting, clearing, animal grazing, and cultivation, little of the original ecosystems remains; most of the lands within the boundaries are either rough grazing or fenced pastures. Consequently, none of Great Britain's units qualify for designation as *national parks* according to

Figure 15.7 Map of national parks and other areas in England and Wales designated as being of national significance by the Countryside Commission. The majority of these lands are privately owned and continue to be used for agricultural or forestry purposes. SOURCE. Developed from a map "Countryside Conservation: Designations and Definitions as at 1 September 1975," in The Countryside Commission, Countryside Commission. The Commission, Cheltenham, 1975.

National parks
Areas of outstanding natural beauty
Defined and potential heritage coasts
Long-distance footpaths and bridleways
Limited access highways
Urban areas

NATIONAL PARKS

1. Northumberland
2. Lake District
3. Yorkshire Dales
4. North York Moors
5. Peak District
6. Snowdonia
7. Pembrokeshire Coast
8. Brecon Beacons
9. Exmoor
10. Dartmoor

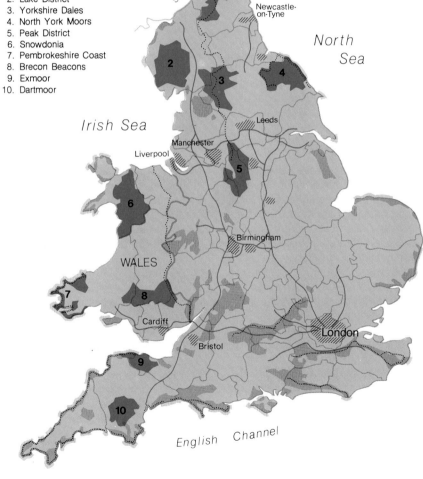

the specifications adopted by the New Delhi conference on national parks.[6] Nevertheless, they do preserve some of Great Britain's most scenic landscapes and annually provide millions of recreation experiences.

The seven national parks in England and three units in Wales occupy 1.4 million hectares (3.4 million acres) or an area a little over one-sixth the size of Yellowstone National Park. Most of the land is *open country* as defined in the National Parks and Access to the Countryside Act of 1949, meaning it is mountain, moor, heath, hill, cliff, or foreshore. Agricultural land, other than pasture and rough grazing, is usually not included. The majority is hill or plateau grasslands produced by the early removal of forests and subsequent grazing. Some remnants of the original hardwood forests remain on steep slopes and in other places protected from grazing. Extensive Forestry Commission plantations are located in several of the parks, contributing to the managed appearance of the landscape, especially where conifers have been planted in large even-aged blocks. Some mountain tops in the Snowdonia and Lake District units consist of steep rocky peaks surrounded by areas of alpine vegetation.

Valleys and other lower sections of the parks usually consist of rectangular pasture fields enclosed with fences, hedges, or stone walls. Farmhouses and barns are scattered across the landscape. In some

[6] The International Union for Conservation of Nature and Natural Resources (IUCN) at its 1969 meeting in New Delhi defined national parks, in part, as areas that include one or several ecosystems that are not materially altered by human exploitation and occupation.

cases, sizable villages and even small towns lie inside park boundaries. Rural roads, most of them paved, connect these settlements and sometimes cross intervening areas of mountain or moor. Portions of parks are also crossed by main highways, railroads, and powerlines. In addition to farming and forestry, limited areas within the parks are used for quarrying, light industry, and military exercises.

The National Trust, a private organization dedicated to the preservation of landscapes and historic sites (see Chapter 11), owns many important parcels in national parks, but most are quite small. The majority of the trust's lands are open without charge throughout the year and make a significant contribution to preservation and public access, particularly in the Lake District National Park (Figure 11.10). Similarly, the parks contain a number of national nature reservations that are owned and managed by the Nature Conservancy, another private organization. Some of the parks contain extensive areas that are owned or leased by the Forestry Commission and managed as *state forests,* the equivalent of U.S. national forests. State forests inside parks include some areas designated as forest parks that have been developed to provide pleasure driving, walking, picnicking, and camping opportunities. Most of the remaining state forest lands in national parks are used extensively for walking, horseback riding, fishing, and special activities such as car rallies and **orienteering** (using a map and compass to follow a given course on foot). In addition, the public has access to a number of areas within the parks that are owned or leased by the govern-

ment for defense purposes.

Nevertheless, the bulk of the property in the national parks of England and Wales is privately owned. This land plays a major role in providing recreation opportunities when it includes campgrounds, riding stables, food services, grocery stores, souvenir shops, and automobile-service facilities. More important, this private land contains most of the farms, villages, hills, moors, and mountains that visitors come to view, photograph, sketch, or paint. It forms the backdrop for much of the pleasure driving, picnicking, walking, hiking (Figure 6.6), bicycling, horseback riding, camping, and second-home use that occurs within the parks. Walkers, hikers, horseback riders, and those interested in nature study use ancient or recently acquired public rights-of-way along lanes and pathways on private lands. Private lands also provide landowners, their guests, or those who lease the rights with opportunities for fishing and rabbit, pheasant, grouse, or deer hunting. Such opportunities are not open to the casual visitor, except where hunting and fishing clubs offer guest memberships for a fee.

Obviously, this mix of predominantly private resources—many of which are used for recreation contrary to the desires of the owners—together with limited public lands does not lend itself to administration by a large centrally controlled bureaucracy like the National Parks Service or Parks Canada. Instead, the parks are managed by committees comprised of two-thirds local representatives and one-third members appointed by the national government. Eight parks are under the care of committees that are part of a county government administrative structure, whereas the other two (Peak District and Lake District) are managed by special national park boards. The committees and boards attempt to reconcile the often conflicting interests of local landowners and the general public while carrying out their main tasks of preserving the resources and providing access for recreation. Much of this work involves controlling the location and nature of new developments or the materials and methods used to repair or modernize existing structures.

Most of the routine administration of the parks is carried out by county planning-department personnel. They develop the park plan, prepare reports on proposed changes in buildings or land use, issue permits, secure access agreements, and investigate proposals for new public facilities. In some cases, land for the latter is purchased or leased by the park committee, which then constructs the desired footpaths, parking area, information center, picnic area, or campground. However, publicly owned and operated facilities are few and far between; most campgrounds for instance are commercial ventures. Park committees also employ small operational staffs consisting of interpretive and service personnel at information centers as well as wardens who patrol the roads to assist visitors and detect infractions of regulations. Three-quarters of approved planning, administrative, and management costs are paid by national government grants from the Countryside Commission; the remaining 25 percent come from the county concerned.

The largest unit in the British system is 224,470-hectare

(554,240-acre) Lake District National Park (Figure 15.7). It includes several of England's highest mountains, 17 of her largest lakes, and many picturesque landscapes (Figure 11.10). Boating and fishing are more common in this park than in the others because most of the parks do not contain sizable water bodies. The smallest park is the 58,320-hectare (144,000-acre) Pembrokeshire Coast National Park. It consists of a chain of parcels around the tip of the peninsula that forms the southwestern corner of Wales. Some of the nation's most spectacular coastal scenery and a wealth of prehistoric and historic sites lie within this park.

Unlike the National Park Service and Parks Canada, the Countryside Commission does not have primary responsibility for nationally significant historic sites and buildings. Instead, the Department of the Environment (formerly the Ministry of Public Buildings and Works) manages more than 700 sites and buildings, a number of which are located in the national parks. Some, like the Tower of London (Figure 16.12), have long been Crown properties, but most are formerly privately owned resources that have been transferred to the department by gift, purchase, legacy, or in lieu of death taxes. Resources include Stonehenge; dozens of Roman structures; numerous abbeys and chapels; many fortifications, including Edinburgh Castle; and a variety of bridges, crosses, and other historic structures and sites.

Still, the Countryside Commission's responsibilities do not end with the national parks. It has designated areas of outstanding natural beauty, proposed long-distance footpaths and bridleways, and rec-

ommended areas for preservation as heritage coasts (Figure 15.7). As in the case of the national parks, these programs involve protection and modest development by local government agencies with grants and technical assistance provided by the commission. However, since local governments do not have to participate (as in the case of the national parks), commission involvement tends to be more limited.

Other Nations. The preceding examples of national park systems show that national park resources and management approaches vary considerably from nation to nation. International agencies attempting to develop worldwide listings of areas called *national parks* have found this variation to be a continuing problem. Many units so designated do not meet the requirements of basically unaltered resources and protective management established by the 1969 IUCN New Delhi meeting. Among the resources that have been inappropriately named national parks are:

- Extensively developed parks in metropolitan areas that are only of regional significance.
- Towns, villages, factories, farms, rivers, and forest plantations that are currently functioning and that do not contain any appreciable areas of undeveloped landscape.
- Scientific reserves to which the general public is not admitted or only admitted on a very restricted basis.
- Parks that only exist on maps and have no master plan, staff, budget, facilities, means of user access, or prospects for obtaining these attributes.

The examples that follow illustrate the diversity of resources included in national park systems around the world.

New Zealand claims to have been the second nation to establish a national park. Fifteen years after Yellowstone National Park was created, paramount chief Te Heuheu Tukino gave the Maori's sacred Tongariro mountain area to the nation "for the purpose of a national park" to prevent division and sale to private interests. Established as Tongariro National Park by Act of Parliament in 1894, the area has gradually been expanded so that it now contains more then 69,000 hectares (170,500 acres). In addition, nine other units have been added to the New Zealand system; currently, it comprises 2.2 million hectares (5.3 million acres) or about 8 percent of the nation's area.

More than three-quarters of these lands are contained in four parks located in the southwestern quarter of South Island. The largest of these units, and one of the world's major parks, is 1.3 million-hectare (3.1 million-acre) Fiordland National Park. This mountainous area includes an extensive coastline that includes many fiords, a number of large lakes, 581-meter (1904-foot) Sutherland Falls, many vegetative types, and the greatest number of native New Zealand bird species found at any one location.

New Zealand national parks are comparatively lightly developed. Most have one or two complexes consisting of one or more hotels, motels, lodges, youth hostels, motor vehicle campgrounds, visitor centers, and park administrative buildings located at or near the edge of the park. Generally, park interiors are only accessible by hiking trails or by boats or amphibious aircraft. There are no developed campgrounds in the interiors, but camping is permitted everywhere except in a few especially sensitive areas. The parks also contain a substantial number of simple trailside huts for hikers, hunters, and climbers. Many were built in the early days of the system when the relative inaccessibility of the parks, considerable public interest in exploring remote areas, and high risk of encountering dangerous mountain weather conditions made their construction necessary. Others were erected more recently in an attempt to reduce the impact of informal camping at fragile or scenic locations. Some of the mountain parks contain ski developments. Recreational and commercial hunting of introduced species such as chamois, goats, red deer, and wild pigs is allowed under permit. Because of extensive environmental damage, a policy has been adopted that calls for the eventual extermination of all exotic browsing animals. Even commercial hunting from helicopters is encouraged. Sheep and cattle grazing, prospecting, mining, and hydroelectric power-generation take place in some of the parks.

In addition to the 10 national parks, there are two *maritime parks* consisting of areas owned by the national government interspersed with private land. The National Parks Authority and the Department of Lands and Surveys provide policy, administrative, and technical support for the national parks at a national level. However, each national park and maritime park is managed by a local national park board. Both the authority and the individual boards include representatives of private groups such as naturalists' and climbers' organizations as well as personnel from government resource and tourism agencies.

In Australia, the status of *national parks* is completely different. As in Canada, unsettled public lands are controlled by the six states (the equivalent of Canadian provinces) and the national government only has direct jurisdiction over the remaining Crown lands in the Northern Territory. Unlike Canada, the *national* parks in the Australian states are designated or acquired and managed by the *state* governments. The state agencies that administer national parks are also responsible for parks, nature reserves, and historic sites that do not have the word, national, in their names. Thus national parks in the Australian states are similar to provincial parks in Canada and technically do not meet the IUCN guideline that national parks be under the jurisdiction of a nation's "highest competent authority."

New South Wales, Australia's most populous state, has the most extensive system. It consists of 45 national parks, 119 nature reserves, and 9 historic sites administered by the state National Parks and Wildlife Service. The national parks occupy about 83 percent of the system's 2 million hectares (5 million acres). One-fifth of these national parks are relatively inaccessible and have no facilities or staff. Most of the remainder have picnic and camping facilities. Swimming is available at 23 parks, 6 have cabins or survival huts, and 1 contains a ski development. The largest unit is Kusciusko National Park which occupies 640,700 hectares (1.6 million acres) southwest of Canberra in the Australian Alps section of the Great Dividing Range. The majority of New South Wale's national parks are located along this range or the Tasman Sea coastline.

African national parks that contain large numbers of the larger native animals are especially valuable resources. Such populations are of worldwide significance because they are the last remnants of the great herds that roamed extensive portions of the world 10,000 years ago during the Pleistocene epoch. Elsewhere, environmental change and human activity have virtually eliminated the large populations and many individual species. Only in Africa is it still possible to see animal communities composed of huge herds of ungulates (hoofed animals), substantial numbers of pachyderms (elephant, rhinoceros, and hippopotamus), and many carnivores (lion, leopard, and cheetah). Preservation of such communities for future generations appears to depend primarily on the successful management of a comparatively small number of national parks and reserves.

Most of the parks with the outstanding large animal communities are located on the plateau lands of East and South Africa at an elevation of from 450 meters (1500 feet) to 1525 meters (5000 feet). Some are relatively flat tablelands; others contain hills, mountains, or deep valleys. The majority are situated near the boundary or just outside the boundary of the hot, wet climatic region (Figure 10.2). Rainfall ranges from moderate to low and there is a pronounced dry period during the winter. Vegetation varies from dry, relatively open woodlands in locations with moderate rainfall to low grass savanna in drier areas. Parks with the low grass savanna-type of vegetation are particularly suitable for wildlife observation.

Since seeing the larger animal species is the main goal of users, facilities differ considerably from those in most North American or European national parks. A number of the parks have hotels or lodges that overlook watering places so that visitors may watch the animals when they come to drink. Some parks have concessionaire-operated cottage villages or campgrounds with basic facilities where people visiting the parks on their own or as part of a guided safari may set up tents. Airstrips are frequently located near hotels or campgrounds so that the more affluent or short-term users may fly to the parks and avoid long drives over rough roads. Park roads generally have graded dirt surfaces and there are many informal tracks developed by the passage of many vehicles to off-road locations where wildlife commonly congregates. Important resources in most parks are the fleets of concessionaire-operated, roof-hatch-equipped vehicles that enable users to see and photograph wildlife at close quarters.

The best known and most vi-sited African national parks are in Kenya, Tanzania, and South Africa. Nairobi National Park in Kenya is unique because it is only 6.4 kilometers (4 miles) from the downtown area of a city of 850,000 persons; yet it contains substantial numbers of the commoner ungulates and carnivores (Figure 15.8). Kenya's largest unit, Tsavo National Park, occupies 2.1 million hectares (5.1 million acres) and contains some 20,000 elephants. Tanzania's system includes Kilimanjaro National Park with its famous 5899-meter (19,340-foot) mountain; Serengeti National Park, consisting of vast grassland areas traversed by enormous herds of ungulates at certain seasons of the year; and a number of large game reserves. Kruger National Park in South Africa covers 2 million hectares (4.9 million acres) and is more intensively managed than most of the African parks. It contains seven overnight accommodation complexes with 3000 beds, a number of campgrounds, restaurants, and

Figure 15.8 Abutting the outskirts of a major city, Nairobi National Park in Kenya provides excellent opportunities for observing and photographing many of the typical East African veld animals against a scenic backdrop of visually pleasing topography (Ngong hills) and vegetation (acacia trees).

shops, and 8000 kilometers (5000 miles) of paved roads.

Kruger National Park is visited by almost 400,000 people annually, 25 percent of whom are from overseas. In other African nations where populations of relatively affluent white residents are smaller, the great majority of park users are from abroad. Most black Africans do not get a chance to visit their national parks and large numbers have never seen a lion or elephant. Many regard the parks as undesirable vestiges of colonial rule, but some tolerate them because of their vital role in attracting foreign tourists, a valuable source of much-needed hard currencies.

National parks in other nations exhibit a great variety of resource characteristics and management programs. The diversity of the amenities and policies involved is illustrated by the following examples:

• Japan has designated 23 areas as national parks that comprise 5.3 percent of the nation's area; however, nearly all of the land is privately owned, development controls are minimal, commercial exploitation is widespread, and publicly operated facilities are extremely limited.
• In the Soviet Union, restricted nature reserves called *zapovedniki* conserve resources that are similar to North American national park resources; however, their primary purpose is utilitarian scientific research rather than heritage protection for citizen enjoyment so public use is generally limited and, in some cases, forbidden.
• Several nations have established units intended to protect the way of life of relatively undeveloped societies; Peru, for instance, created Huascarán National Park in a high mountain area, which has been occupied by Indian farmers for centuries.
• In Europe, an increasing number of park administrators are attempting to

reduce human impact by limiting users' activities; for example, visitors are not permitted to leave the trails in Czechoslovakia's Tatra National Park or in the Swiss National Park in Switzerland.

Many other variations exist among the more than 1500 national parks or equivalent reserves that have been created by some 100 nations. Another 30 countries have taken the initial steps necessary to establish a national park system and will, no doubt, add to this diversity of resources and approaches. Only about 40 nations currently have no national parks.

NATIONAL FORESTS

As in the case of national parks, there is great variation among nations in the extent and role of national forests. Some countries have little or no woodland under the jurisdiction of the national government because the forests are privately owned or because public forests are the responsibility of lower levels of government. However, even where national governments do manage large forests, it is unusual for them to provide extensive recreation facilities. In most cases, there are no developed picnic areas, campgrounds, or swimming beaches, and the majority of the recreation use involves such dispersed activities as walking, fishing, hunting, or camping at self-selected sites.

United States. The large area and extensive facilities of the U.S. national forests result in these resources playing a prominent role in extraurban recreation. The system occupies an area of 76 million hectares (188 million acres) that com-

prise 8 percent of the nation's area and 25 percent of federal government lands. This is equal to the combined areas of France and the United Kingdom. More than three-quarters of the system's lands lie in the Pacific and Mountain census regions (Table 15.5). Especially large tracts are located in the Sierra Nevada, Cascade, and Rocky mountains and in the southeastern coastal areas of Alaska (Figure 15.2). Most of the national forests in the eastern two-thirds of the nation are concentrated in the Appalachian Mountains, northern Great Lakes, and the Quachita Mountains-Ozark Plateau regions.

When the distribution of national forest land is related to population, the Mountain Census Region is in the lead with almost 3895 hectares (9615 acres) per thousand population (Table 15.5). The Pacific and West North Central regions follow with 926 hectares (2286 acres) and 188 hectares (465 acres) per thousand population respectively. National forest land is least available in the Middle Atlantic Region which has only 6 hectares (15 acres) per thousand residents.

National forest system lands are located in 44 states, Puerto Rico, and the Virgin Islands. Only Delaware, Iowa, Maryland, Massachusetts, New Jersey, and Rhode Island have no national forests. Connecticut, Indiana, Kansas, Maine, New York, Ohio, and Vermont have comparatively little. The largest blocks of forest are located in Alaska, California, and Idaho, each of which contains more than 8 million hectares (20 million acres) — an area slightly larger than South Carolina. States with the largest proportion of their areas designated as national forest are Idaho (38 per-

Table 15.5 Distribution of National Forest Lands, Wilderness Areas, and Recreation Use by U.S. Census Regions

Census Region	Total Area — Thousands Hectares (Acres)	%	Hectares per 1000 Population	Designated Wilderness — Thousands Hectares (Acres)	%	Hectares per 1000 Population	Recreation Use at Developed Sites[a] — User-days in Thousands	%	User-days per capita	Dispersed Recreation Use[a] — User-days in Thousands	%	User-days per capita
Pacific	26,573 (65,613)[b]	35.0	926 (2286)	1,654 (4,085)	31.7	57.6 (142.3)	31,190	42.3	1.1	48,369	36.9	1.7
Mountain	38,261 (94,472)	50.3	3895 (9615)	3,057 (7,549)	58.5	310.9 (768.2)	26,392	35.8	2.7	46,219	35.3	4.7
West North Central	3,160 (7,802)	4.2	188 (465)	422 (1,042)	8.1	25.1 (62.0)	2,485	3.4	0.2	5,999	4.6	0.4
West South Central	1,675 (4,136)	2.2	79 (195)	10 (25)	0.2	0.5 (1.2)	1,447	2.0	0.1	4,402	3.4	0.2
East North Central	1,947 (4,808)	2.6	48 (119)	3 (7)	0.1	0.1 (0.3)	3,165	4.3	0.1	7,581	5.8	0.2
East South Central	1,239 (3,060)	1.6	91 (225)	10 (26)	0.2	0.7 (1.7)	1,877	2.5	0.1	4,564	3.5	0.3
South Atlantic	2,540 (6,271)	3.3	75 (185)	52 (129)	1.0	0.0 (0.0)	4,863	6.6	0.1	10,457	8.0	0.3
Middle Atlantic	211 (520)	0.3	6 (15)	— (−)	—	— (−)	669	0.9	0.0	1,345	1.0	0.0
New England	405 (999)	0.5	33 (82)	18 (44)	0.3	1.5 (3.7)	1,687	2.3	0.1	2,087	1.6	0.2
	76,011 (187,681)	100.0	354 (875)	5,227 (12,907)	100.0	24.3 (60.0)	73,775	100.1	0.3	131,023	100.1	0.6

[a] A U.S. Forest Service user-day is a total of 12 person-hours.
[b] Numbers in parentheses are equivalent values in acres.
SOURCE: Developed from area data, U.S. Department of Agriculture, Forest Service, "Land Areas of the National Forest System as of September 30, 1977," U.S. Department of Agriculture, Washington, D.C., 1978; and use data in "National Forest Recreation, State Summary of Recreation Use, CY 1977."

cent), Oregon (25 percent), Colorado (22 percent), Washington (21 percent), and California (20 percent).

The vast area and wide distribution of the national forest system result in these lands providing a broad spectrum of recreation opportunities. Environments include tropical forests growing in the hot, wet conditions of the Virgin Islands; cypress swamps and oak-pine forests in the warm, humid Southeast; maple-beech-hemlock and spruce-fir woodlands in the cool, snowy Northeast and the Great Lakes regions; oak-bunch grass and broadleaf evergreen vegetation in the warm, dry Southwest; parklike pine and grass areas in the cool, dry Rocky Mountains; and dense stands of tall fir, hemlock, and spruce in the cool, moist Northwest. The system also contains 1.5 million hectares (3.8 million acres) designated as national grasslands, which are located primarily in the high-plains area just east of the Rocky Mountains.

In addition to various types of forests and grasslands, the system includes many other resources. In some cases, entire mountain ranges have been incorporated in the national forests so that they contain large areas of rocky peaks and alpine tundra. Many nationally known landmarks such as 1918-meter (6288-foot) Mt. Washington in New Hampshire, 4304-meter (14,110 foot) Pikes Peak in Colorado, and glacier-clad 3290-meter (10,788-foot) Mt. Baker in Washington are largely national forest land. So are hundreds of other peaks throughout the nation, including many that are well-known for their exceptional scenic qualities. Often the appeal of such landscapes is heightened by the presence of picturesque streams, rivers, waterfalls, and lakes. High-quality lakes and waterways are not confined to mountainous regions however; they are located in many other forests, particularly those in the Great Lakes area that contain large numbers of lakes and ponds.

The great range of environments encompassed by the national

forest system includes many resource combinations that have special appeal. Some examples of the diverse environments present in the forests are:

- Dozens of major springs, hundreds of lakes, and many clear-flowing streams in a subtropical setting in the Ocala National Forest, Florida.
- Thirty-five kilometers (22 miles) of Hells Canyon, the deepest river gorge, 1.6 kilometers (1 mile), in North America together with more than 150 lakes, 2400 kilometers (1500 miles) of streams, and an abundance of large animals, including bear, elk, mountain goat, and bighorn sheep in the mountainous Payette National Forest of central Idaho.
- Rocky ridges, deep valleys, sandstone cliffs, natural bridges, limestone caves, springs, 800 kilometers (500 miles) of streams, and 400 kilometers (250 miles) of reservoir shoreline in the Daniel Boone National Forest of eastern Kentucky.
- A rugged coastline with hundreds of islands and fiords, excellent freshwater and saltwater fishing, and a substantial population of brown and grizzly bears in the Tongass National Forest of Alaska's panhandle. It also contains the Mendenhall Glacier— one of the world's largest glaciers accessible by road—with a massive face that is 2.5-kilometers (1.5-miles) wide and 30- to 60-meters (100- to 200-feet) high.
- Volcanic landscapes, including extensive lava fields and a steep 150-meter (500-foot) high volcanic cone, together with the southern part of the Cascade Mountain Range in the Deschutes National Forest, Oregon.
- More than 5000 lakes surrounded by rugged shorelines intermixed with sand beaches and dotted with islands set in a .4 million-hectare (1 million-acre) largely uncut forest of pine, spruce, and white birch in the Superior National Forest, Minnesota.
- Fine sand beaches, rocky shorelines, and forested Coastal Range mountains along 55 kilometers (34 miles) of the Pacific Ocean coast in the Siuslaw National Forest, Oregon; includes 90-meter (300-foot) high sand dunes in the Oregon Dunes National Recreation Area, beautiful displays of rhododendrons and azaleas in the spring, and opportunities for clamming as well as ocean, lake, and stream fishing.

Many such combinations of high-quality resources are present in the national forests. Often these areas rival national park system units in terms of uniqueness, recreational potential, and scenic appeal.

The national forest system is managed by the U.S. Forest Service for timber production, livestock grazing, water supply, recreation, and fish and wildlife purposes. In the Multiple Use-Sustained Yield Act, the United States Congress specified that management for these purposes should be coordinated so that the resources are used "in the combination that will best meet the needs of the American people." The goal is perpetual production of "crops" of timber, livestock, water, recreation opportunities, and fish and wildlife rather than the preservation of undeveloped environments. However, some areas may be left in a largely unaltered condition because they are important as part of the national heritage or as resources for wilderness recreation.

Most national forest lands are actively managed. This involves operations such as constructing roads, logging, fighting fires, controlling insect infestations, salvaging fire- or insect-damaged timber, revegetating burned watersheds, thinning timber stands, reseeding grasslands, improving habitat for fish and wildlife, and building recreation facilities. The amount of time and money that is spent on the various aspects of management depends on a particular forest's resources and the needs of society in the area that it serves. A remote forest with no recreation resources of regional or national significance will usually devote most of its budget and personnel time to timber and range management; comparatively little time and money may be used for water, recreation, or fish-and-wildlife-habitat management. On the other hand, a forest that has extensive, regionally significant recreation resources and is readily accessible to major population centers will probably use a substantial proportion of its appropriations for the development, operation, and maintenance of picnic areas, scenic roads, boat-launching sites, campgrounds, and various kinds of trails.

As a result, the number of intensively managed recreation resources in a forest and the degree to which they are developed vary greatly. A remote, little-used forest may contain 20 to 30 small recreation developments, each of which consists of 10 to 20 picnic or camp sites. Roadways are normally not paved. Water may be available from a hand pump but is often not provided in more arid locations. Toilets will usually be of the concrete vault variety, which have to be pumped out periodically. There may be a small beach and graveled boat-launching ramp if the site includes a sizable body of water. Usually, no charge is made for the use of any of the facilities. Although facilities of this nature may be limited, all of the roads and trails constructed by the U.S. Forest Service may function in themselves as important recreation resources. Such roads and trails often provide numerous opportunities for recreation activities such as pleasure driving, sightseeing, backpacking, hunting, fishing, berrypicking, motorcycling, snowmobiling, and cross-country skiing.

At the other extreme are national forests that contain more extensive and more highly developed recreation facilities. These usually are forests that are located within 500 kilometers (300 miles) of large urban areas or forests that contain an exceptional resource such as a major water-body or mountain area. In these cases, the forest frequently has a number of picnic areas and campgrounds that include 50 or more sites; some campgrounds may have over 100 sites. Picnicking and camping facilities of this type often resemble small state parks with paved roads and parking areas, toilet buildings with flush toilets and electric light, a pressure system delivering water to faucets throughout the area, and an office or contact station where an attendant is on duty during the day or at least at peak periods. Picnic areas and campgrounds at lake or ocean shoreline locations frequently have highly developed swimming facilities, including maintained beaches, lifeguard stations, bathhouses, and concessionaire-operated food services. In some cases, there are concrete boat-launching ramps, docking facilities, boat rentals, and bait shops.

The largest concentrations of extensively developed recreation facilities occur at national recreation areas and ski areas. There are now seven national recreation areas administered by the U.S. Forest Service with a total area of some 770,000 hectares (1.9 million acres). The seven are Whiskeytown-Shasta Trinity (California);

Hells Canyon (Idaho-Oregon); Sawtooth (Idaho); Oregon Dunes (Oregon); Flaming Gorge (Utah-Wyoming); Mount Rogers (Virginia) (Figure 15.9); and Spruce Knob-Seneca Rocks (West Virginia). These developments provide large numbers of opportunities for activities such as picnicking, camping, swimming, waterskiing, boating, sailing, fishing, and hiking. In the case of ski areas, the ski slopes and lift facilities are developed on leased national forest land by commercial interests working under U.S. Forest Service supervision. Resort facilities are usually built by private enterprise on private land at the base of the slope.

In summary, the national forests contain more than 6400 developed picnic areas and campgrounds, 320 swimming beaches, 850 boat-launching sites, and 210 winter-sports areas. National forest system lands contain 730,000 hec-

Figure 15.9 This campground at the Mount Rogers National Recreation Area in the Jefferson National Forest, Virginia, includes paved roads and camping spurs, and modern washrooms equipped with flush toilets and warm showers. The U.S. Forest Service operates a total of five campgrounds of this type in the recreation area and many similar facilities in other recreation areas and forests across the nation.

tares (1.8 million acres) of lakes, 365,000 hectares (900,000 acres) of artificial reservoir water surface, and 134,000 kilometers (83,000 miles) of forest streams. About half the nation's population of large wild animals (deer, antelope, elk, moose, bear, mountain lion) live in the national forests, which are also the prime habitat of many fish, birds, and smaller animals, including a number of endangered species.

Total annual recreation use of the national forest system is estimated to exceed 200 million visitor-days, about 64 percent of which is dispersed recreation. The great majority of this use takes place in the Pacific and Mountain census regions. Together, these regions accommodate 78 percent of the developed-site recreation and 72 percent of the dispersed recreation (Table 15.5). California national forests receive about 23 percent of the total nationwide developed-site and dispersed-recreation use. The next states, in order of total use, are Colorado (9 percent), Oregon (8 percent), and Washington (6 percent). In the eastern half of the nation, the most heavily used national forests are in Michigan (2.7 percent), North Carolina (1.7 percent), and Florida (1.7 percent).

As would be expected, camping is the activity that occupies the greatest proportion of the time visitors spend in national forests (Table 15.6). The second largest amount of time is spent on mechanized recreational travel (pleasure driving, including off-highway vehicle use). These two activities take up half of the users' time. Hunting and fishing are next in importance, followed by hiking and picnicking. The remaining 13 activities occupy only a

Table 15.6 Estimated Proportion of National Forest Users' Time Spent on Various Activities

Activity	Percent of Total Annual Use[a]
Camping	25.7
Mechanized recreational travel	24.1
Fishing	7.8
Hunting	7.1
Hiking and climbing	5.0
Picnicking	4.1
Winter sports	4.0
Viewing landscape or sports events	3.9
Using recreation residence (cottage)	3.3
Boating	2.9
Swimming and scuba diving	2.2
Resort use	2.0
Use of organization camp	1.9
Seeing U.S. Forest Service interpretive exhibits or programs	1.8
Horseback riding	1.4
Gathering forest products	1.4
Nature study	0.6
Games and team sports	0.5
Waterskiing and other water sports	0.4
	100.1

SOURCE: Developed from U.S. Department of Agriculture, Forest Service, "National Forest Recreation, State Summary of Recreation Use, CY 1977."
[a] Statistics based on the time spent on an activity tend to exaggerate the relative significance of camping as a recreation activity.

quarter of national forest users' time but involve many people's most memorable experiences.

Other Nations. No nation has national forest system recreation facilities that are as highly developed and extensive as those in the United States. In most countries, national forests are open for walking, picnicking, pleasure driving, nature study, and similar activities, but facilities developed specifically for recreation are minimal or absent. Where such amenities have been constructed, they are usually limited to graveled parking areas, foot trails, and a few picnic tables located at places with special attractions such as overlooks, scenic

areas, and beaches.

One exception is the recreation facilities system developed by the British Forestry Commission. The commission was established in 1919 because World War I had shown it was strategically and environmentally unwise for Great Britain to rely on imports as the main source of wood products. The primary goal was to increase the nation's forest resources by planting large areas in fast-growing timber and pulpwood species.

The commission now manages some 1.2 million hectares (3 million acres) or about 5 percent of Great Britain's area. Most of this *state forest* land is covered with plantations, the majority of which are pure stands of coniferous species planted on former grasslands or heaths. Unlike U.S. national forests, only a small proportion contain relatively unaltered original forest. Many people criticize the plantation program because it has radically altered the appearance of numerous pastoral landscapes. The commission is attempting to soften the impact by planting mixtures of species, by leaving some areas unplanted, and by avoiding straight-line plantation boundaries.

Originally, the Forestry Commission discouraged recreation in planted areas because of the threat of fire. Now, most of the state forest lands are open to pedestrian use. Vehicles are prohibited on forest roads and lands, except for six scenic drives and where access to parking areas, picnic groves, or campgrounds is provided. The commission's policy is to concentrate on providing opportunities for day-users to park their cars, have a picnic, and take short walks in the forest.

The principal recreation facilities in British state forests currently consist of:

- 426 picnic areas, usually comprised of a parking area and a dozen or so picnic tables but lacking in water or toilet facilities.
- 358 marked forest trails and 114 labeled interpretive trails.
- 2 major arboretums (collections of specimen trees) and 25 less extensive arboretums.
- 25 permanent or seasonal information and interpretation centers.
- 12 Class A campgrounds that feature flush toilets, hot showers, a campground store, and a resident attendant.
- 15 Class B or woodland campgrounds that are only equipped with piped water and facilities for campers

to empty their own chemical toilets.
- 44 group campgrounds for use by youth organizations.
- 49 cabins and 39 houses, which can be rented for vacation purposes.

The commission has also established facilities or programs that encourage participation in special activities at specific sites. The principal activities and number of sites designated are orienteering (113), rock climbing (20), horseback riding (100), pony trekking (52), motor vehicle events (94), archery (10), small game hunting (18), deer hunting (66), fishing (41), swimming (11), sailing (7), boating (7), and canoeing (15).

Many of these amenities and much of the recreation use are concentrated in seven forest parks. These are sizable blocks of forest land with considerable recreation potential. Most are in mountainous locations and unplanted areas. Four of these parks are in Scotland, another is on the border between Scotland and England, one is in North Wales, and one is on the border between Wales and England. By establishing special forest-access facilities and other developments at these locations, the Forestry Commission has created recreation areas that provide a broad range of opportunities but can be managed more easily than if the same amount of use was widely dispersed.

OTHER LAND-MANAGING AGENCIES

A number of other national government agencies administer substantial areas of land that are used extensively for recreation. Such resources are most expansive in the United States where they include

lands controlled by the Bureau of Land Management, the U.S. Fish and Wildlife Service, and the Department of Defense.

National Resource Lands. The largest area of federal land administered by one U.S. government agency is under the jurisdiction of the Bureau of Land Management. This area, known as the national resource lands, consists of the public domain remaining after lands for agriculture, settlements, commercial forests, transportation routes, national parks, national forests, national wildlife refuges, military bases, and other purposes have been removed. As a result, most of the natural resource lands in the 48 contiguous states is poorer quality rangeland, desert, and mountain. Only about 2 percent is commercial forest land. Some of the natural resource lands in Alaska are of better quality, but much of the northern portion is tundra.

About one-fifth of the United States is national resource land. This is a total of 183 million hectares (452.7 million acres) or an area equal to western Europe excluding Switzerland and Italy. Nearly two-thirds of this land is in Alaska; most of the rest (in descending order by total area) is in Nevada, Utah, Wyoming, Oregon, California, New Mexico, Arizona, Colorado, and Montana (Figure 15.2). More than 68 percent of Nevada and 41 percent of Utah are national resource lands.

This huge resource has great recreation potential. Much of the national resource lands that lie in the 48 contiguous states is within the dry climatic zone and has a very high proportion of sunny days. Some areas are sufficiently warm to be good locations for winter resorts. Others are high enough to provide relief from summer heat and skiing opportunities during the winter. Many locations in the Southwest have deeply eroded landscapes that provide interesting vistas of canyons, spires, and mesas. Environments range from alpine tundra on some mountain ranges to salt flats in the bottom of dry desert lakes. Since most of the national resource lands in the 48 contiguous states are in dry regions, permanent swamps, lakes, and streams are generally absent, but many rivers (including the Colorado) flow through Bureau of Land Management lands. Vegetation is often limited to desert or dryland shrub communities.

Like the national forests, the national resource lands are managed on a multiple-use basis. However, the proportion of time and money spent on the various uses differs markedly in the more arid areas where the majority of the bureau's efforts involve managing rangelands for livestock grazing purposes. Supervising grazing leases, processing land sales and ownership disputes, and administering petroleum, natural gas, and other mineral leases are also major activities of the bureau. Timber management is the bureau's most prominent activity in western Oregon and on some of the higher national resource lands in the other northwestern states. Unfortunately, Congress until recently did not recognize the necessity of providing substantial legislative and monetary support for these management procedures. As a result, the bureau has been chronically understaffed and inadequately funded considering the magnitude of the resources it man-

ages. The Federal Land Policy and Management Act of 1976 provided much more substantial legal mandates and financial support for active management of the national resource lands.

Developed recreation resources on national resource lands are limited for several reasons. The best recreation sites have often been transferred to other federal agencies or to state or local government park agencies. The majority of the bureau's lands are considerable distances from major population centers so that there is less pressure to develop facilities. Water features are scarce and environments are often fragile, so that sites suitable for intensive development are limited. Where artificial reservoirs have been built on national resource lands, the policy in the past has been to place resultant recreation developments under the jurisdiction of other agencies. Finally, limited personnel and budgets have restricted bureau involvement in recreation resource development and management.

Nevertheless, the national resource lands are estimated to provide more than 60 million user-days of recreation each year. Most of the bureau's 215 developed recreation sites are small picnic areas and campgrounds with amenities similar to less developed picnic and camping facilities in the national forests. A few are larger picnic areas and campgrounds with piped water and flush toilets. Recreation use patterns tend to be like those of the national forests, except that an even larger proportion is dispersed recreation and some activities such as off-highway vehicle driving, camping at dispersed locations, and collecting rocks and minerals are more promi-

nent. Off-highway use of motorcycles, four-wheel-drive vehicles, and dune buggies is now the principal recreation activity at a number of Bureau of Land Management areas. Heavy vehicle use takes place in parts of the California Desert, along the Lower Colorado River, near Las Vegas in Southern Nevada, in the Phoenix-Tucson region of Arizona, in portions of the Front Range mountains in Colorado, near Boise in Idaho, in eastern Oregon, and in the Little Sahara area of Utah.

National Wildlife Refuge System. Another important source of recreation opportunities is the federal government wildlife refuge system administered by the U.S. Fish and Wildlife Service. It consists of some 390 wildlife refuges occupying 14 million hectares (34 million acres) or an area equal in size to the state of Arkansas. The refuges are of five types. Most numerous are the migratory waterfowl refuges established to protect habitats essential to ducks, geese, and other waterfowl during their seasonal migrations. Approximately 280 or three-quarters of the refuges are of this type, but they constitute only about 12 percent of the system's area. Most are relatively small wetlands located primarily along the four waterfowl migration routes—the Pacific (Puget Sound-Central Valley), Central (High Plains), Mississippi, and Atlantic flyways (Figure 15.2).

The second most numerous are the refuges established to aid other kinds of migratory birds. There are about 70 of these; they also occupy about 12 percent of the system. Some are small rocky islands along the Pacific and Atlantic coasts, which are significant nesting sites for sea birds. Others are more extensive habitats that are important to a number of species; an example is the Okefenokee Swamp Refuge in Georgia. The third type of refuge is called a waterfowl production area. These are scattered through the prairie pothole portion of the North Central Region. For administrative purposes, they are grouped into 20 Wetland Management Districts, but there are hundreds of individual wetlands. These vital duck-breeding areas amount to about 4 percent of the system's total area.

Big-game refuges are the fourth most numerous type of unit. There are 16 of these totaling 3.1 million hectares (7.7 million acres) or 23 percent of the system's area. Refuges of this type are created to protect and manage large animals such as moose, bison, elk, caribou, pronghorn antelope, reindeer, and bear. Examples are the 7500-hectare (18,500-acre) National Bison Range in Montana and the 690,000-hectare (1.7 million-acre) Kenai Moose Range in Alaska. Big-game refuges are scattered through nine western states; the only noticeable concentration is the four units in the coastal region of southwestern Alaska.

The fifth kind of unit is the wildlife or game range. These are national resource lands that are administered by the U.S. Fish and Wildlife Service under an Executive or Public Land Order. Game ranges are managed jointly with the Bureau of Land Management. There are four wildlife ranges and four game ranges with a total area of 6.5 million hectares (16.1 million acres) or 47 percent of the system. Distribution of these units is similar

to the big-game refuges. Examples are the 650,000-hectare (1.6 million-acre) Desert Wildlife Range in southeastern Nevada and the 346,000-hectare (855,000-acre) Charles W. Russell Game Range in northeastern Montana.

Although these units are referred to as national wildlife *refuges* and the national wildlife *refuge* system, they are managed on a utilitarian rather than a purely preservation basis. Conserving wildlife for hunting purposes is emphasized and much financial support for land acquisition, research, and management has come from hunters in the form of federal migratory-bird-hunting stamp fees and excise taxes on firearms and ammunition. Refuge system lands are used for hunting, cutting hay, growing agricultural crops, logging, and trapping fur-bearing animals when such uses are compatible with wildlife conservation. In recent years, almost half the units in the system have been opened to some form of hunting and about 15 percent are used for migratory-bird, big-game, and upland-game hunting. Other management practices include building dikes and water-control structures [there are more than 16,000 kilometers (10,000 m es) of dikes in the system]; prescribed burning of vegetation; shooting or trapping and removal of excess animals; reintroducing species; spraying to control insect pests or vegetation; and digging or blasting ponds. On the other hand, there are many parts of refuges and ranges that are virtually unaltered and rival areas in national parks in terms of pristine condition and beauty.

The facilities provided for recreation vary greatly. Some units have no visitor facilities, but people

may view wildlife from roads passing through or near the refuge. Many have loop roads or trails (often on the crest of dike systems) that are open to vehicles or walkers. Interpretive services such as signs, exhibits, interpretive trails, museums, guided tours, and audiovisual programs are common. A number of refuges include picnic areas, swimming beaches, boat-launching sites, and campgrounds. There have been no recent surveys of the recreation use of the national wildlife refuge system units, but it is estimated that approximately 20 million visits are made to them annually or about one-fourteenth the number of visits to national park system units. About 5 percent of this use is hunting and almost one-third is fishing. The remaining two-thirds is predominantly general sightseeing as people come to observe the birds and animals. However, recreation use that is not related to fish and wildlife has been growing steadily and is now estimated to be more than 20 percent of the total use. The dominant unrelated activities are picnicking, swimming, camping, and boating. The U.S. Fish and Wildlife Service is attempting to reduce the proportion of unrelated recreation because it diverts resources and funds from fish and wildlife conservation activities.

Military Lands. Military organizations often have control of large areas of land containing extensive recreation resources. Sometimes these resources are accessible only to military personnel but, in other cases, dependents and the general public may use them. Such lands may also be valuable reserves of potential public recreation land that can become available when areas are declared surplus to military needs.

In the United States, the Department of Defense controls 433 military installations with a total area of 9.2 million hectares (22.8 million acres). Bases with large numbers of personnel generally have considerable recreation facilities, including movie theaters, recreation centers, sportsfields, golf courses, and libraries. Some bases are used extensively by military personnel for hunting, fishing, camping, and off-highway vehicle driving. In 1978, the secretaries of Defense and Interior signed an agreement authorizing the Heritage Conservation and Recreation Service to assist military units and state agencies to develop programs for public use of recreation resources at defense installations.

In addition to the 433 bases in the United States, the Department of Defense administers another 300 military installations in other nations. Altogether, the department operates almost 7000 individual recreation facilities at home and abroad. These include about 600 sports complexes, over 500 craft and photography workrooms, 670 bowling centers, 310 golf courses and driving ranges, 383 youth centers, and dozens of other indoor and outdoor facilities. About 35,000 civilian and 8000 military personnel are employed in operating these amenities. Operation and maintenance cost approximately $500 million annually, about 45 percent of which comes from user fees and profits from operating military exchanges (shops for military personnel and their dependents).

WATER-RESOURCE PROJECTS

Although many water-dependent and water-related recreation opportunities occur on national resource lands and in national parks, forests, and wildlife refuges, large numbers of freshwater associated experiences take place at artificial bodies of water controlled by other agencies. Lakes produced by damming rivers for flood control, irrigation, or industrial and municipal water-supply purposes often receive heavy recreation use. This is especially true where such bodies of water have been created near population centers in regions that previously had inadequate supplies of accessible water surface.

Nevertheless, such projects are also criticized because other kinds of recreation opportunities are destroyed when they are built. Opportunities lost often include trout fishing in streams and rivers, boating and hiking along meandering rivers, canoeing down white-water streams, hunting in riverside wetlands or around valley agricultural lands, and enjoying scenic landscapes in valleys or canyons.

In the United States, three federal agencies have played a prominent role in constructing water-control projects and providing recreation opportunities. They are the Corps of Engineers, the Bureau of Reclamation, and the Tennessee Valley Authority.

Corps of Engineers Projects. The Corps of Engineers is the branch of the U.S. Army responsible for constructing military roads, bridges, camps, fortifications, and other permanent or temporary structures. In 1824, the corps' responsibilities were extended for commercial and strategic reasons to include the construction of civilian harbors and associated canals and ship channels. Since these facilities were also used for pleasure boating and tourist travel, the corps was the first federal agency to contribute substantially to recreation opportunities at extraurban locations. Subsequently, the corps was instructed to build navigation dams and locks on the Ohio River (1836) and the Mississippi River (1879). In 1917, its duties were expanded to include major flood-control projects, and funds were provided for flood-control structures on the Mississippi and Sacramento rivers.

The corps was not authorized to include recreation considerations in projects until 1932. Then it was instructed to modify navigation improvements where appropriate to accommodate pleasure craft. Its role in flood control was given national scope in 1936 and the Flood Control Act of 1944 authorized, but did not require, the construction of purely recreation facilities at Corps of Engineers impoundments. Now its projects receive over 400 million user-visits a year, which is more than the national park system, the national forest system, or any other federal lands. However, use-data for the various agencies are not directly comparable because of different measurement situations and methods.

Recreation resources available to the public at the more than 400 Corps of Engineers projects, each of which provide over 5000 recreation occasions annually, include:

- More than 2.3 million hectares (5.6 million acres) of land, 2 million hectares (4.9 million acres) of impoundment water surface, and 75,600 kilometers (47,000 miles) of impoundment shoreline.

- Approximately 1200 day-use areas and 1000 campgrounds or other overnight facilities at recreation areas developed and administered by the corps itself (some of the facilities in such areas are operated by concessionaires under the corps' supervision).
- More than 460 day-use areas and 270 campgrounds or other overnight accommodations at recreation complexes developed by other federal agencies and state or local government agencies; similarly some of these amenities are concessionaire-operated.
- Some 130 day-use areas and 50 overnight areas at other locations that are concessionaire-developed and concessionaire-operated.

In addition, there are 200 fish and wildlife areas managed by other federal agencies or state agencies and a number of undeveloped areas that are managed for fish and wildlife purposes.

Corps of Engineers impoundments are usually managed for a number of purposes, although a multiple-use approach is not required by law. Water-storage capacity is usually used in a manner that provides the best compromise between the various needs of the valley, including flood storage, hydroelectric power generation, navigation, low flow augmentation, fish and wildlife management, and participation in various kinds of recreation activities. On large reservoirs, there may be several sizable recreation developments, including one or two complexes constructed by the Corps of Engineers; a state park; and one or more county or city parks (Figure 15.10). Other Corps of Engineers land around a reservoir is often managed for various

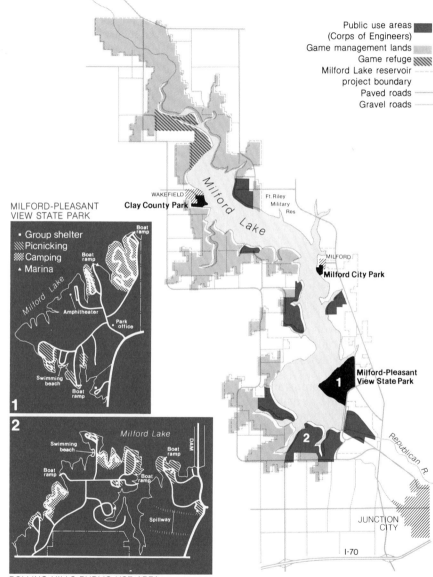

Figure 15.10 Milford lake is a 6500-hectare (16,000-acre) flood control impoundment built by the U.S. Army Corps of Engineers on the Republican River, 210 kilometers (130 miles) west of Kansas City. Its 260 kilometers (160 miles) of shoreline include 10 developed public recreation areas—7 operated by the corps and 3 leased to the state, Clay County, and the City of Milford. The Kansas Forestry, Fish and Game Commission is responsible for operation of the game management lands and the fishing and boating aspects of the lake. SOURCE. Developed from U.S. Army Corps of Engineers map "Milford Lake, Kansas," 1974.

combinations of hunting, agricultural, and forestry purposes. Areas with special resources may be designated as *natural areas* and managed to protect their scientific, ecological, historic, archaeological, or aesthetic values.

Public facilities constructed by the Corps of Engineers at larger impoundments are generally grouped at several locations around the shoreline in order to disperse use and reduce conflicts. At more elaborate dams with electric power generators, there are usually parking lots, viewing areas, and interpretive facilities such as an exhibit, visitor center, or self-guiding tour of the structure. Boating amenities are often elaborate. Typically, there is a dredged boat basin or harbor created with rock-fill breakwaters that is equipped with a multilane, concrete boat ramp; a large parking lot for vehicles and boat trailers; and a concessionaire-operated boat-service and fishing-supplies establishment. Boat-berthing facilities may range from a few finger piers to elaborate floating boathouses. At intensively used locations, beaches, picnic areas, and campgrounds generally have paved roads, flush toilets, picnic tables, and fireplaces. Since many projects are near urban centers, much of the recreation use consists of relatively brief evening or weekend day visits. National averages for the percent of users undertaking various activities at Corps of Engineers impoundments are sightseeing (34 percent), fishing (26), boating (18), picnicking (16), camping (11), swimming (10), waterskiing (4), and hunting (3 percent).

Navigational developments built and maintained by the Corps of Engineers also provide a wide range of opportunities. Dredged and protected harbors along the ocean and Great Lakes shorelines provide calm waters for seasonal moorings or refuge from storms. Dredged and marked channels in estuaries and along rivers make it possible for larger pleasure boats (especially deep-keeled sailing vessels) to enter harbors and travel through waterways that would otherwise be unnavigable. Interconnecting systems such as the Gulf Intracoastal Waterway, the Atlantic Intracoastal Waterway [2000 kilometers (1240 miles) from Norfolk, Virginia, to Key West, Florida], the New York State Barge Canal, and the Illinois Waterway make it possible for quite small boats to cruise long distances (Figure 15.2). Some owners move their boats north in the summer to cruise the Great Lakes or northeastern estuaries and then go to a Gulf of Mexico location for the rest of the year. The system of coastal and inland waterways also provides many opportunities for cruising, fishing, and other boating activities by local people, especially where dams have been built to raise water levels. Finally, watching commercial shipping is an important recreation activity at some of the corps' principal locks. In some cases, the Corps of Engineers provides viewing stands, visitor centers, interpretive programs, and picnic facilities.

Because the corps' main civilian responsibilities are flood-control impoundments and waterways for commercial shipping, its developments exhibit a unique distributional pattern. Navigational projects are concentrated along the main rivers and coastal waterways that serve ports and industrial cities. These include the Mississippi and adjacent portions of its tributaries, the St. Lawrence Seaway, many lesser rivers along the Atlantic and Gulf coasts, and the Columbia and Sacramento as well as a number of small rivers on the Pacific coast.

Multiple-use flood-control impoundments are most frequent in upstream and headwater regions of rivers that periodically flood urban areas or valuable croplands. Sizable clusters of impoundments occur in California around Los Angeles and the east side of the Central Valley; in Oregon on the upper Willamette River; in the hill country of north central Texas; along the Arkansas River and its tributaries in Kansas and Oklahoma; on the headwaters of the Mississippi River in Minnesota; in Kentucky, Ohio, Pennsylvania, and West Virginia on tributaries of the Ohio River; in the Southeast between Atlanta, Georgia, and Columbia, South Carolina; and in New England in the Connecticut and Merrimac river valleys (Figure 15.2). There is also a series of huge impoundments on the upper Missouri River in South Dakota, North Dakota, and Montana. Four of these lakes are more than 160 kilometers (100 miles) long. The largest is the Oahe Reservoir which is 372 kilometers (231 miles) long, has a surface area of 152,280 hectares (376,000 acres) and includes 3620 kilometers (2250 miles) of shoreline available for recreation use. Corps of Engineers projects are generally absent in the Great Basin and in the Rocky Mountain regions. More than 80 percent of the impoundments are within 80 kilometers (50 miles) of an urban area so that the Corps of Engineers projects are likely to receive an even larger share of use in the future.

Bureau of Reclamation Projects. The Department of the Interior's Bureau of Reclamation was established in 1902 for the purpose of building irrigation systems in the arid areas of the western United States. Originally, the bureau's work was to be financed by the sale of public lands but, later, a system of congressional appropriations plus charges to water users was instituted. Most of the early impoundments were built in relatively sparsely populated areas so that there was little demand for recreation facilities. In addition, the lands involved were usually national resource lands or national forest system properties. Therefore, it was logical for the Bureau of Land Management or the U.S. Forest Service to manage any public recreation facilities developed on the shores of Bureau of Reclamation reservoirs. Later, when larger scale recreation complexes became appropriate at some impoundments, the National Park Service, the bureau's sister agency, provided the necessary design and management skills. In contrast, most Corps of Engineers projects require the acquisition of private land so that management of recreation developments by other federal agencies is not as logical as in the case of reclamation impoundments.

For these reasons, the Bureau of Reclamation is much less directly involved in recreation resource management than the other federal agencies mentioned previously. It administers less than 20 percent of the developed recreation areas located on its reservoirs and most of these are quite small. State agencies are responsible for about 30 percent of reservoir recreation areas, followed by the U.S. Forest Service

with 18 percent, water-user organizations with 14 percent, and the U.S. Fish and Wildlife Service, the National Park Service, county park agencies, and local recreation districts with between 4 and 7 percent each. However, some of these are large complexes of national significance such as the Lake Mead National Recreation Area at Hoover Dam and the Glen Canyon National Recreation Area above Glen Canyon Dam, both of which are in Arizona and operated by the National Park Service.

The Bureau of Reclamation has constructed 220 reservoirs with a shoreline of more than 15,607 kilometers (9700 miles). All are situated in the 17 western states or in Alaska. Sizable groups of reservoirs are located in the Central Valley of California, western Oregon, central Washington, Southern Idaho, western Colorado, central Kansas, and central Nebraska. The remainder are scattered in the other 10 states. Recreation participation patterns tend to be similar to those at Corps of Engineers reservoirs.

Tennessee Valley Authority Projects. The third major federal water resource managing agency is responsible for a much smaller geographic area than the Corps of Engineers and the Bureau of Reclamation. It is the Tennessee Valley Authority, a federal corporation charged with water control, power production, and economic development in the 207,000-square-kilometer (80,000-square-mile) valley of the Tennessee River. The valley runs along the west side of the Appalachian Mountains from Virginia to Alabama and then turns northwest across Tennessee (Figure 15.2).

The authority was created under President Roosevelt's New Deal program to improve the physical, social, and economic environments of valley residents by controlling floods, generating power, providing water transportation, manufacturing fertilizer, improving agriculture, and in other ways stimulating development. Today, The Tennessee Valley Authority operates 30 major dams. Of these, 9 on the main river create an almost continuous series of reservoirs extending 1050 kilometers (650 miles) through five states. Altogether, the authority's impoundments have a total water-surface area of more than 200,000 hectares (500,000 acres) and a shoreline of over 16,000 kilometers (10,000 miles). The agency also owns some 365,000 hectares (900,000 acres) of land located primarily around its reservoirs and along its waterways.

Recreation was not specified as one of the primary purposes of the Tennessee Valley Authority when it was established. Nevertheless, the authority's planners made sure that recreation was taken into consideration in planning land use around the new reservoirs. Appropriate areas were set aside and transferred to the National Park Service, the U.S. Forest Service, and the U.S. Fish and Wildlife Service or sold or leased to state agencies, commercial enterprises, private organizations, and private individuals. Today, the reservoir shorelines contain a vast array of recreation facilities, including 19 state parks, more than 500 public-access sites, 90 county and municipal parks, dozens of private clubs and quasi-public youth group camps, some 13,000 second homes, and over 340 commercial fishing camps, marinas, and resorts.

Thus the authority has usually not participated directly in providing recreation opportunities on its reservoirs by developing and managing its own recreation sites. Instead, it has provided leadership by planning and promoting the construction of a variety of public and private facilities. The corporation has also aided directly in the provision of opportunities by supplying technical assistance to other recreation providers and conducting demonstrations.

The authority's most ambitious demonstration project is the 69,000-hectare (170,000-acre) Land Between the Lakes multiple-use area in western Kentucky and Tennessee. Consisting of a 65-kilometer (40-mile) long, partially wooded peninsula between a Corps of Engineers impound and a Tennessee Valley Authority reservoir, the area is being used to develop and exhibit recreation facilities and management methods. It has three campgrounds containing a total of 800 campsites; each campground is equipped with swimming areas, boat-launching ramps, electricity, and flush toilets. Land Between the Lakes also contains a large day use area, four picnic areas, a conservation education center, a group campground, and 20 water-access sites, most of which have picnicking and camping facilities. Emphasis is on camping, fishing, hiking, horseback riding, hunting, and environmental education in surroundings that are actively managed to produce wildlife and forest products. The authority is experimenting with a wide range of facilities, management procedures, and activity programs in cooperation with a number of agencies, universities, and schools.

TOURIST FACILITIES

In the majority of the nations with strong private enterprise systems, national governments seldom undertake the construction and operation of tourist-oriented accommodations and restaurants. Even in situations where regions or specific recreation entities lack appropriate commercially operated amenities, the usual procedure is for national governments to stimulate private-enterprise development by providing them with incentives such as low cost loans or tax advantages. Nevertheless, there are some situations where non-Communist governments do feel justified in actually building or operating tourist facilities.

The most common situation is where a government believes that the development or expansion of tourism will improve economic conditions in an underdeveloped region or in the nation as a whole but sees no possibility of achieving the desired scale or quality of development by providing incentives to private enterprise. The other frequently encountered situation is where a major recreation resource of national or international significance is at a remote location that discourages private development of tourist amenities. In this case, the government may justify its direct involvement on the grounds that its facilities will help make the resource accessible. However, economic benefits—especially the attraction of foreign tourists and the resultant balance of payments advantages—are often the primary stimulant even in these cases.

Among the non-Communist nations, Mexico has developed the largest and most sophisticated national government-controlled system of tourist facilities. In 1969, it established INFRATUR (now FONATUR, a Spanish acronym for National Fund for the Promotion of Tourism), which uses computer-assisted location-modeling methods to select sites for new government-controlled resorts. Locations in poorer parts of the nation that have few employment opportunities are given preference. FONATUR then buys the land and installs all of the basic services (power, water, sewage, road, airport) and townsite facilities (medical, school, housing) with the assistance of matching loans from international lending institutions. Lots are then sold to private developers who build and operate hotels, restaurants, shops, and other facilities under tight government control. The international loans are repaid from the taxes produced by the economic expansion.

The largest Mexican government-developed resort to date is Cancún located on a 23-kilometer (14-mile) long barrier island in the Caribbean Sea just off the tip of the Yucatán Peninsula. Still in the construction phase, it will eventually have some 10,000 hotel rooms and attract more than 1 million people a year (Figure 15.11). Cancún is already producing more than 10 percent of all tourist expenditures in Mexico.

A similar development with a 1-million-visitor-per-year potential is now underway at Ixtapa, a 40-kilometer (25-mile) stretch of sugar-sand beach on the Pacific Ocean 240 kilometers (150 miles) north of Acapulco. Already completed are 5 luxury hotels, the 18-hole Robert Trent Jones golf course, 12 lighted tennis courts, a shopping center, and an airport. A Club Mediterranee is about to open and 14 more

Figure 15.11 Cancún, one of several government-planned resorts in Mexico, provides a variety of warm-weather resort-type recreation opportunities such as golf, tennis, sunbathing, sailing, deep-sea fishing, skin diving, and pool swimming. Because of a hazardous undertow, the use of offshore waters along the beach facing the Caribbean is not encouraged. Most of the winter visitors are Canadians and Americans seeking a few days in a tropical savanna climate as a respite from their home region's cold, snowy weather.

hotel sites have been approved. Two more major resort complexes of this type are planned for Baja California.

FONATUR has also designed and constructed five two-story, 42-room *archaeological villas* to make some of Mexico's best known pre-Columbian ruins more accessible to the less adventurous traveler. Each heated and air-conditioned villa includes a swimming pool and tennis courts and is located within walking distance of the historic site. Three, more elaborate villas are being built at other locations. Club Mediterranee operates these facilities for the government. The Mexican government supports its resort, villa, and commercial tourist-facility programs with extensive promotional activities abroad. It also attempts to negotiate

improved airline service and reduced border-crossing formalities.

A somewhat different approach to government involvement in tourist facilities occurs in Spain and Portugal. These two nations have developed systems of moderately priced overnight accommodations and eating places that were originally intended to make travel feasible for less affluent citizens. Sometimes these facilities are modern buildings constructed expressly for the purpose, but usually they are renovated historic structures such as castles, forts, or monasteries. Often, they are developed in out-of-the-way places that previously had few tourist amenities, thereby stimulating tourism in less visited regions. Some are in localities that provide opportunities for skiing, fishing,

hunting, horseback riding, and mountain climbing.

The fact that most of the buildings are old and the charges are moderate does not mean that the facilities and services are substandard. All Portuguese and Spanish government hostelries are equipped with comfortable beds and modern plumbing. Amenities vary but most contain valuable antique furnishings, include dining rooms featuring well-prepared regional dishes, and are located in beautiful formal gardens or scenic rural settings. Some offer Olympic-size swimming pools or a secluded beach on a Mediterranean cove.

Twenty-five of these establishments, known as *pousadas*, are maintained by the Portuguese government and more are being developed. Scattered throughout some of the nation's most scenic and historic regions, they provide guests with ready access to a variety of recreation resources, including forests, reservoirs, mountain lakes, ocean beaches, the Peneda-Geres National Park, museums, historic sites, fairs, and festivals. The Spanish system began in 1928 when the king opened his hunting lodge near Madrid to paying guests. The government now owns and operates 71 *paradors* (similar to Portugal's pousadas), 8 *albergues* (strategically located roadside inns), 3 *hosterias* (restaurants decorated in the region's traditional style and specializing in its cuisine), *2 refugios* (lodges in scenic mountain areas), and one 122-room privately managed seaside hotel. These establishments continue to be well patronized by both Spaniards and foreign visitors, most being full from April to October. About 40 percent of the guests are from other nations, primarily Germany, France, Switzerland, and Great Britain.

In the majority of the Communist nations, most—if not all—of the tourist facilities are public property managed by a national, regional, or local government organization. Often special systems are operated for foreign tourists in order to make it easier to provide separate and different services and also to charge higher rates than those paid by citizens. In Cuba, for instance, a government agency named Cubatur operates all the hotels, restaurants, tour buses, resorts, fishing boats, and other facilities used by foreign tourists. Intourist, the Soviet Union's travel agency, has a billion-dollar-a-year budget and manages 56 hotels, 30 motels, and numerous campgrounds, which contain restaurants and other service facilities. Hosting 4.4 million tourists a year, Intourist assumes total responsibility for their welfare; it makes reservations, arranges transportation, furnishes rooms and meals, and provides guides. But there are exceptions to the Communist government-monopoly policy. In Yugoslavia, for example, private ownership of businesses has been permitted since the middle 1960s and about 250,000 citizens are self-employed; at least 20,000 of the establishments that provide meals and accommodations for foreign visitors are now privately owned.

MULTILEVEL RESOURCES

This section describes resources used for recreation that are basically the same in purpose, form, and management methods at all three levels of government. These re-

sources will be considered in three groups—*institutional recreation resources* (colleges, correctional institutions, and health care facilities), *undesignated recreation resources* (streets, roads, highways, airports, and other public amenities not intended primarily for recreation), and trails (walking, horseback riding, or vehicle trails).

INSTITUTIONAL RECREATION RESOURCES

Facilities that provide recreation opportunities for people in public institutions are especially important. When individuals are away from their home environments for long periods, recreation can be a powerful antidote for homesickness, loneliness, boredom, anxiety, or despair. The significance of institutional recreation resources depends on a number of factors, including the needs and attitudes of the individuals concerned, the nature and extent of the resources, and the accessibility of other opportunities.

For instance, if students at a college have no transportation and off-campus forms of recreation are not within easy walking distance, they will probably regard the recreation resources provided by the college as vital components in their recreation environments. In contrast, many students attending a college located in a city may not feel the college's recreation resources are particularly important, especially if they live off-campus and commute to classes each day. The accessibility of the institution to relatives and friends is also of great significance. Many public institutions—correctional facilities and state psychiatric hospitals in particu-

lar—have been built in out-of-the-way locations that are poorly served by public transportation. The difficulty of reaching these institutions discourages visits by families and friends, thereby decreasing or eliminating social contacts and increasing the inmates' isolation and dependency on social opportunities within the institution.

College Facilities. Although some are supported extensively by private funds, the majority of colleges and universities in the United States, Canada, and many other nations are dependent primarily on grants from local, intermediate, and national governments. Therefore, recreation resources offered by institutions of higher learning are included in this chapter, recognizing that there are many private colleges that also supply recreation opportunities.

Like elementary and high schools, colleges often provide recreation experiences for the general public as well as for their students and staffs. The degree to which college recreation resources are used by the general public depends on the college's location, the nature of the resources, and the institution's policies. In many cases, college resources are used heavily by students and employees both during the day and in the evenings so that there is little or no unused capacity that can be made available to the general public. In fact, many institutions are unable to meet student needs for some kinds of opportunities in spite of substantial investments in sportsfields, stadiums, swimming pools, tennis courts, fieldhouses, ice arenas, all-events buildings, student unions, and residence hall lounges and gamerooms.

A common practice is to give priority to scheduled classes, followed by the meetings, practices, and games arranged by organized student groups and teams. Any remaining time is then assigned to informal use by students or employees on either a reservation or a first-come/first-served basis. Facilities may operate around the clock if participation greatly exceeds daytime and evening capacity.

On the other hand, there are numerous situations where even high-demand college-sports facilities are used extensively by outsiders. A good example is the Cortland campus of the State University of New York.[7] There, the 40 hectares (100 acres) of physical education, athletic, and recreation facilities, including the multimillion dollar Physical Education/Recreation Education Center (Figure 15.12), are used extensively for instructional purposes during the day. From 4:00 P.M. to 10:00 P.M. daily and on weekends, however, the facilities are shared with off-campus groups and individuals who are charged a modest fee. Classes open to the general public are conducted in many sports, including wrestling, racquetball, squash, and ice skating. Off-campus organizations such as a youth hockey association, a community square dance club, and a figure skating club use the resources on a regular basis. The City of Cortland Youth and Recreation Commission conducts summer tennis clinics, slow pitch and baseball leagues, and track and field programs at the outdoor facilities. The commission also leases the ice arena during the

[7] Vince Gonino and Thomas Steele, "Multipurpose Facility," *Journal of Physical Education & Recreation, 48*(9), 1977, pp. 35–37.

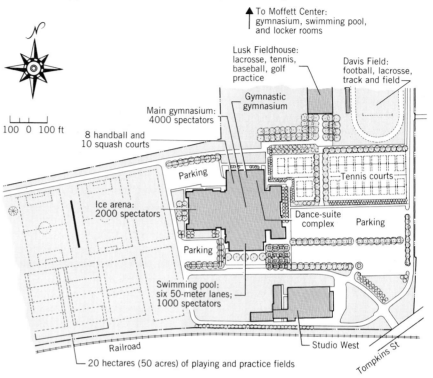

Figure 15.12 **The Physical Education/Recreation Center and adjacent facilities on Cortland campus of the State University of New York. These resources provide many recreation experiences for residents of the surrounding area as well as recreation opportunities for students, staff, and faculty.**

Christmas vacation to provide free skating opportunities for the entire community. In addition, special community events not connected with the university are held at the center, including contests, swim-a-thons, clinics, tournaments, and championship games. Many individuals from the community use the center regularly for personal recreation.

Colleges also provide extensive spectator opportunities for students, employees, and the public. In the United States, many colleges actively promote spectator and television-viewing of sports events to obtain revenues from ticket sales and to promote alumni, public, and po-

litical support for the institution and its programs. A number depend on revenues from major intercollegiate sports to pay for intramural and individual sports programs. College football, for instance, has become a major source of both public entertainment and college revenue; annual attendance now exceeds 33 million and millions more watch games on television or listen to them on the radio. Four-year colleges with football teams have built more than 600 stadiums to accommodate spectators (Figure 8.14). Some are huge; the largest at the present time is the University of Michigan stadium at Ann Arbor, which seats more than 100,000 persons.

Similarly, intercollegiate basketball draws nearly 30 million spectators each year to college arenas and fieldhouses. To accommodate the crowds, colleges, during the last decade, have built over 40 new sports facilities, each seating 10,000 or more spectators.

Although the contribution of sports resources is extensive, recreation opportunities provided by other college resources are equally important. Many college campuses are parklike areas used for walking, jogging, bicycling, relaxing, people-watching, sunbathing, picnicking, nature study, photography, sketching, painting, boating, and cross-country skiing. Some institutions facilitate these kinds of activities by providing amenities such as bicycle paths, benches, picnic tables, and boat rentals. Large open grassy areas are used for informal games, outdoor concerts, and special events. The University of Massachusetts, for instance, is the site of an annual three-day "Toward Tomorrow Fair." Over 200 exhibits are placed around the campus ponds and workshops and discussion groups are conducted in the nearby 2000-seat Fine Arts Center. Each year, this event attracts some 30,000 off-campus visitors.

Other college-owned properties, including woodlots, ponds, and experimental farms, also supply recreation opportunities, especially if amenities such as trails, picnic tables, or viewing areas are provided. Special events—open houses, conducted tours, and farmers' days at agricultural colleges—can be pleasurable as well as instructive. The University of Georgia's Marine Institute, for example, opens its research facility on Sapelo Island, an Atlantic coastline barrier island, to

visitors on selected Saturdays. Interested persons are taken by ferry to the island and bused to the institute's preserve for a close look at marine life and a tour of the small museum.

Some colleges provide restaurant, lodging, and vacation opportunities, which can be pleasurable for those on business as well as for tourists and relatives or friends of students. Universities with instructional programs in hotel, restaurant, or tourism management often have facilities of this kind. A growing number of educational institutions are keeping some residence halls, cafeterias, and instructional facilities open in the summer vacation period to offset fixed costs. Frequently, such accommodations are used to house young people taking part in educational, cultural, or sports programs. But a number of colleges also offer programs for families, the elderly, single adults, or special-interest groups; these combine learning experiences and recreation opportunities and are promoted as a low-cost alternative to the traditional vacation. Currently, more than 150 colleges sponsor family-oriented summer programs and 230 offer special "Elderhostel" programs for persons 60 and over; the latter include a full week of classes, room, and board at a cost of $150 or less. Although accommodations are often spartan and the food is usually plain, the change of environment, new social contacts, access to recreation facilities, and interesting educational programs combine to produce a far more stimulating experience than participants could obtain elsewhere for the same cost.

College dormitories also provide reasonably priced summer

lodgings for tourists. This practice started fairly recently in Canada and the United States, although it has been common elsewhere for decades. Currently, 200 educational institutions in the United States and 350 in 47 other nations make lodgings available to the public.

Besides using instructional facilities for summer programs, many colleges offer courses during the regular school year that are intended to interest people who are not within the academic community. Often held during evening hours so that working people can take advantage of them, a variety of subjects is offered on a credit or noncredit basis. Some courses are similar to those developed as part of the college curriculum, but many are special offerings designed to help nondegree enrollees acquire new knowledge, skills, or insights that will be useful in the pursuit of certain hobbies, interests, or activities. Similar enrichment programs are conducted either during the day for preschool children or in the late afternoons, during weekdays, or on Saturdays for school-age boys and girls. Sports, athletics, and classes in music, dance, theater, and art are some of the most common and most heavily attended programs for youth. Colleges are also major suppliers of many other kinds of cultural experiences that are not a part of an organized program; these experiences will be discussed in Chapter 16.

Although college resources often provide many recreation opportunities for the general public, usually their primary purpose is to satisfy the education and recreation needs of the students. They fulfill the latter role with varying degrees of success, depending on the nature of the facilities and the kinds of programs offered. Resources commonly available to students living in college residence halls are lounges and television rooms; small libraries; gamerooms; spaces suitable for meetings, parties, or dances; outdoor areas for sitting and sunning; basketball courts; and grassy spaces for playing games such as softball or touch football. Facilities often provided on a campuswide scale are gymnasiums, saunas, physical conditioning rooms, swimming pools, sportsfields, racket sports courts, running tracks, golf courses, canoe rentals, winter-sports developments, bowling alleys, and rooms and auditoriums suitable for the showing of movies and the presentation of concerts and plays. Where colleges provide a wide range of readily accessible facilities and programs, participation may be high. Students find that such opportunities help them make new friends and acquaintances, overcome bouts of homesickness, relieve boredom, and release tension while providing physical activity, low-cost entertainment, skill development, or new knowledge and fresh insights.

Correctional Institutions.
Unlike the situation at colleges, recreation resources at correctional institutions or detention facilities are seldom accessible to either employees or the public. But this does not make them less important. Individuals under temporary or prolonged periods of confinement often find that such resources provide the best or only opportunities for physical activity, social experiences, and relief from the boredom, anxieties, and pressures of incarceration. The value of these opportunities to the

institution and society are also widely recognized. Well-designed programs managed by persons who are able to establish rapport with participants can have positive influences on their attitudes and behavior and be an effective means to rehabilitation. Besides shortening the length of time some individuals are confined, successful recreation programs may also make the work of the institution employees easier and safer. Such programs can help raise morale and alleviate despair, thereby reducing the incidence of vandalism and violence.

Obviously then, with its worth firmly established, the provision of adequate recreation facilities should be a priority at all correctional institutions. Unfortunately this is not the case. Overcrowding and underfunding are common and produce explosive situations where, in spite of need, recreation opportunities are reduced rather than increased. Existing recreation facilities, already inadequate, are frequently allowed to deteriorate for want of maintenance funds, or are removed entirely to provide more housing space for new inmates. Such situations are common where prison populations are continuing to expand, but governments and taxpayers are unwilling to increase facilities accordingly. In the United States, for example, there are currently about 300,000 prison inmates in the nation's 200 long-term and 1000 minimum and medium security institutions. This population is now undergoing a net increase of between 200 and 400 persons each week. In addition, there are some 225,000 individuals in local jails awaiting trial or serving short sentences.

According to federal government guidelines, recreation facilities

at American local and county jails (structures designed primarily to function as temporary holding facilities) must be sufficient to provide all inmates with at least two hours of exercise or recreation outside their cells each week. At some of these jails, filled to the point of overflowing, this is a physical impossibility because no appropriate facilities exist. At many others, the facilities consist of two types of resources: (1) small, walled-in outdoor areas with no special provision for recreation activities other than walking and (2) small sparsely furnished rooms equipped so that only a handful of inmates at any one time can watch television or play pool, table tennis, or a few other table games. However, prisoners may remain confined in their cells even when such facilities are available because there are too few guards to supervise the movement of inmates from place to place.

In some jails, cell or dormitory doors are opened to provide access to the corridors and give inmates a place to exercise. This is often done when inclement weather prevents outdoor exercise. Additional space may be provided for weekly religious services or for a small lending library. There is increasing pressure to permit contact visitation, but this usually requires structural changes to create open areas where inmates and visitors can meet without intervening barriers. This arrangement also demands adequate supervision and many jails have too few staff and insufficient funding to make visitor contact feasible.

Facilities at state prisons are also often severely limited. In fact, prison recreation directors, especially those at older institutions, frequently cite the lack of available space as their most serious problem. Programs must be drastically curtailed, not because of lack of inmate interest or cooperation, but rather because so many of the limited facilities must be used for many purposes.

At Michigan's Marquette State Prison, for instance, the softball diamond doubles as the football field and a little auditorium is used simultaneously for music classes and weightlifting programs. Although there are 250 inmates in the weightlifting program (the prison's most popular organized recreation activity), the available space can accommodate only 25 individuals at one time. Many more inmates would like to take part, but the recreation staff has stopped accepting new enrollees since there would be no possibility of participation. Similarly, many inmates who wish to play basketball cannot do so, since the court is generally used by groups of individuals who have been playing together for years. Obviously, there is no chance for an individual to take part in a variety of activities; those who gain access into just one of the programs are considered fortunate. Neither is there any opportunity for an individual to engage in a recreation activity on an occasional or spur-of-the-moment basis.

In many institutions, the problem of inadequate space is compounded by the fact that the recreation facilities themselves are extremely poor. This is the case at Marquette Prison where, to give just one example, the basketball court consists of an eight-year-old asphalt surface with cracks running through it. It is also too small for a 5-on-5 game. To make matters worse, it is located outdoors in the center of the prison's open courtyard. Rather than miss their games for part of the year, basketball players bundle up, shovel snow off the court, and play as best they can in the below-freezing temperatures of an Upper Peninsula winter.

The underlying reason for these kinds of circumstances—a common situation at many state prisons—is lack of funding. At Marquette, for example, an extremely tight budget makes proper maintenance impossible and funds available for improvements seldom cover the costs of more than one project in any one year. In 1978, for instance, a decision had to be made between resurfacing the handball-paddleball court or constructing a boxing ring. Although boxing is very popular, the cement floor in the handball area had not been resurfaced since its construction as part of the outdoor recreation yard some 40 years before. It seemed more important to restore this area to use than to install a new facility, no matter how welcome it would be. Such improvements are much appreciated but do little to solve a problem situation of such magnitude. The prison desperately needs a large, enclosed athletic building, a need that was first recognized years ago when the facility was placed at the top of the building-priority list. For one reason or another, however, it was never built. Now, with overcrowding at an all-time high, a new dormitory has top priority and an administrative building is considered next in importance.

Designated recreation facilities are not the only institutional resource that influence the nature and scope of inmate recreation opportunities. The characteristics of living quarters and regulations governing the use of these areas play a major role in determining how most of the inmates' free time will be spent (Figure 3.4). United Nations' prison standards suggest that each inmate be given 6 square meters (65 square feet) of living space. Many prisoners at both the local jails and state and federal prisons have 2.3 square meters (25 square feet) or less. Cramped quarters and the fact that few inmates are fortunate enough to have single cells often prevent prisoners enjoying many everyday recreation experiences, even in institutions where the possession of books, hobby materials, radios, and television sets are allowed. Work opportunities would also be welcomed as relief from boredom and despair, but, in many prisons, there are jobs for less than half the population. As a result, inmates frequently do little but lie on their bunks, smoke, and go to and from the dining halls for meals. They find it too crowded to exercise or move around and so noisy that it is difficult to read or sleep.

Not all correctional institutions are quite this grim. As new buildings are constructed or funds are provided to improve obsolete prisons, recreation needs are being given more consideration. In some cases, swimming pools, gymnasiums, saunas, bowling alleys, tennis and handball courts, team-sport facilities, classrooms, recreation halls, television and music rooms, libraries, and arts and crafts shops are provided. The gymnasium is often a multipurpose facility designed to function as a movie theater, hall for social events, or auditorium with stage for concerts, lectures, and dramatic presentations.

Facilities of this kind are included at all of the eight new minimum-security camps built as part of the U.S. federal penal system to provide more humane incarceration for nonviolent prisoners. Located in attractive landscaped grounds, these camps have few of the exterior features usually associated with prisons such as armed guards and high walls. Instead, a wide variety of recreation facilities are provided, including tennis courts, nine-hole golf courses, driving ranges, jogging tracks, handball courts, and patios equipped with resort-type furniture for the entertaining of friends and relatives.

In spite of the resortlike appearance of these camps, inmates maintain that life in some of the more progressive maximum-security institutions is preferable. Instead of the 50 men-to-a-room dormitory arrangement found at the minimum-security institutions, inmates at prisons like the new Federal Correctional Institution in North Carolina have private living quarters with big windows and wooden doors with locks to which inmates have their own key. Although these doors are locked from the outside at 9:30 P.M., prisoners are free to do as they please for as late as they wish inside their own roomlike cells. According to inmates, access to this much privacy and space for the safe storage of personal belongings provides the most valuable kind of recreation opportunity that could be offered within a prison environment. Although elaborate facilities like golf courses are absent at these institutions, there are better and larger hobby, trade, education, and rehabilitation programs. According to inmates, opportunities of this kind can change prisons from

human storage areas into rehabilitation centers with livable, creative, helpful environments.

Facilities at women's prisons have generally been superior to men's prisons until recently. Most women's institutions were not only newer, better designed, and constructed with relatively open grounds, but also the majority were far less crowded. Inmates often had single rooms and considerable freedom to furnish them as they wished, including the installation of radios and television sets. At some institutions, technical and academic courses, which could lead to college degrees, were offered in classrooms not unlike those found in colleges. Parklike grounds, some containing swimming pools, provided a more pleasant environment and were heavily used for recreation activities. Weekend movies and a much broader range of recreation facilities made lifestyles closer to those experienced by inmates before they were imprisoned, thereby helping them retain a sense of personal identity during their incarceration. However, this situation has changed rapidly as more women have been convicted and given longer sentences. The number of women inmates in U.S. federal prisons doubled during the last 10 years to a total of more than 1300, and there are now about 15,000 women imprisoned in local and state jails and prisons. Crowded conditions and inadequate recreation facilities and programs are the result.

Health Care Institutions.

The previously common custodial-care type of facilities that provided shelter for special populations such as the elderly, the chronically and incurably ill, the severely retarded,

or the physically disabled, are gradually disappearing and being replaced by institutions with a more therapeutic orientation. Halfway houses and other residential shelters or training centers have been developed to provide all the necessary care and protection services while also encouraging maximum levels of independence and participation in community life. Their main purpose is to prepare as many patients as possible for full-time existence in the outside world. Many centers rely heavily on community resources, both private and public, to provide recreation experiences. Developing extensive facilities of their own would only encourage the residents to remain isolated. However, basic facilities such as lounge areas containing recreation amenities commonly found in private homes (comfortable furniture, newspapers, magazines, books, pianos, television sets, radios, record players, hobby materials and equipment, games, and table tennis and pool tables) are usually provided.

An increasing proportion of nursing homes for the elderly or severely incapacitated are dedicated to rehabilitating people who have been allowed to deteriorate physically or mentally. The goal is to create stimulating environments that prolong independence, encourage socialization, and promote physical activity. Attractive lounges, libraries, meeting rooms, hobby and craft workshops, gamerooms, indoor and outdoor conditioning and sports facities, and pleasant grounds with places to sit, walk, or have a picnic are provided where residents can enjoy each other's company and engage in a wide variety of activities (Figure 15.13). But, as in all institutions, the effectiveness of these re-

Figure 15.13 **Women at the Daughters of Jacob Geriatric Center in the Bronx take part in a weaving program with the help of a qualified therapist. Such programs not only provide satisfying, creative recreation experiences, they also encourage the elderly to use their hands and intellects.**

sources depends on the adequacy of financial support and staff performance. Having sufficient, well-qualified, and dedicated recreation professionals to organize a wide range of individualized and group programs, encourage participation, supervise the activities, and see that the facilities are suitably maintained is essential.

The recreation needs of patients in general hospitals were given little attention until quite recently. Because hospitalization was expected to be quite brief for the majority of patients, the provision of recreation facilities or programs did not seem necessary. Even in military veterans' hospitals, institutions

for the mentally ill, or clinics specializing in the treatment of specific diseases, where a higher proportion of patients remain for extended periods, the emphasis was on medical and directly therapeutic programs. Gradually, however, the important role that recreation can play in building patient morale, developing cooperative attitudes, assuaging fear, and encouraging wholehearted participation in activities that can further the healing process has been recognized (Figure 3.5).

Therapeutic recreation programs in many hospitals now take place in attractive surroundings typical of noninstitutional recreation environments and are conducted in as

relaxed an atmosphere as possible. Facilities include weight-lifting rooms, gymnasiums, swimming pools, children's indoor playrooms and outdoor playgrounds, bowling alleys, craft and hobby workshops, outdoor areas and indoor lounges, all adapted or designed to make them accessible to patients with special needs. Games, athletic equipment, toys, puzzles, hobby kits, craft supplies, musical instruments, and playground equipment are utilized whenever appropriate to make the program as pleasurable as possible at the same time that it contributes to the patient's recovery or rehabilitation. These and other facilities such as picnic areas, gamerooms, ballfields, sports courts, auditoriums, and dayrooms may also function as recreation centers where patients can go at different times. Easy access to such amenities enables patients to be with other people; make friends; enjoy sunshine and fresh air; see a movie; attend a concert, dance, show, or party; take part in sports or a game; or engage in some solitary recreation activity. In doing so, patients have an opportunity to release pent-up emotions and excess energy, find an outlet for self-expression, or obtain relief from anxiety, boredom, or loneliness.

Opportunities for social contacts and recreation are also receiving greater emphasis for short-term patients at general hospitals. Gamerooms, dayrooms, lounges, and television rooms are being provided where ambulatory patients can go to enjoy books, magazines, games or puzzles; watch television; attend a show or party; participate in a discussion group; meet other patients; or entertain visitors. For those who are confined to bed but who are well enough to welcome some diversion or entertainment, rental television sets are available in many hospitals and volunteers provide bedside opportunities to borrow books, puzzles, toys, games, and magazines or to purchase a limited number of recreation items. Sometimes, just the chance to carry on a few moments' conversation with someone not professionally involved in the treatment of the illness is the patient's most needed kind of recreation activity. In response to this need, some hospitals support programs in which volunteers make bedside visits. Such programs are especially helpful to those who have few visitors of their own and to children who have never been away from home before.

TRAILS

In the past, the majority of government operated trail systems in Canada and the United States were located entirely on public park or forest lands and managed by one agency. Only a few major trails, such as the Appalachian Trail, crossed a variety of public and private lands and were managed by a number of public and private organizations. Recently, there has been increased support for expanding government sponsored trail systems outside existing public lands. This support has resulted from increased participation in all kinds of trail use from walking to off-highway motorcycling as well as consequent problems with overuse and conflicts between different types of users. Energy supply problems and the need to expand trail resources that are readily accessible to cities has also focused attention

on potential trail resources in rural areas near cities where public parks and forests are often limited or absent. In the United States and Canada, the lack of bicycle paths and public rights-of-way across private land make government provision of independent trail systems all the more desirable.

All levels of government have become involved in developing new and expanded trail systems. The nature and degree of involvement vary considerably, however, and it will be many years before it is possible to assess accurately the degree to which various public agencies are committed to the concept of building and operating trails outside public parks and forests. The situation is confusing in that the publicity regarding new independent trail programs makes it appear that intermediate or national government agencies are planning to actually develop and manage extensive systems of this kind.

For instance, publicity concerning the National Trails System Act of 1968 and subsequent amendments gave some people the impression that the U.S. government would acquire, develop, and manage a nationwide trail system in a manner similar to the national park system. This impression has been reinforced as the designation of dozens of fairly short local and intermediate government-administered trails as part of the national trails system has been announced by the Heritage Conservation and Recreation Service. In reality, the federal government has no intention of assuming any additional responsibility for most of the trails that are designated as national trails. Federal grants may assist in acquisition and development in

many cases but ownership and management usually remain with the local or state governments and private individuals or groups concerned.

Generally, local or state governments are responsible for the detailed design, acquisition, development, operation, and maintenance of national trails that are not on federal land; designation as a national trail only indicates that the amenity meets specified functional and construction standards. There are three exceptions to date—the Appalachian Trail, the Continental Divide Trail, and the Pacific Crest Trail. The National Trails System Act requires the National Park Service to administer the first and the U.S. Forest Service the last two of these trails. Under this mandate, the two agencies are taking the initiative in planning, land or easement acquisition, and coordinating private-group involvement, but they will not assume all the maintenance and policing responsibilities.

The Appalachian National Scenic Trail extends some 3300 kilometers (2050 miles) connecting the highest parts of the Appalachian Mountain Range from Mount Katahdin in Maine to Springer Mountain in Georgia. Almost half of the trail is on federal lands, just over an eighth is on state lands, and the remainder is privately owned. More than half of the private sections are protected by legal agreements granting development and access rights. The trail came into being and continued to exist primarily because of the tenacity of the large number of private groups and individuals who negotiated with private landowners, made arrangements with public agencies, and, in many cases, actually did the physical work involved in development and maintenance. These groups formed the Appalachian Trail Conference in 1925 to coordinate their efforts.

The Pacific Crest National Scenic Trail runs approximately 4025 kilometers (2500 miles) along the Sierra and Cascade mountain chains between the Canadian and Mexican borders. About 85 percent of the trail is on federal land and just over 13 percent is privately owned. The Forest Service provided the initial impetus with its Sierra and Cascade trail surveys in the early 1920s, but the adoption of the idea of a trail running the full length of the crest and the formation of a Pacific Crest Trail Conference did not occur until the following decade.

The Continental Divide National Scenic Trail will also run between the Canadian and Mexican borders. Its 5000-kilometer (3100-mile) route follows the crest line of the Rocky Mountains in a southeasterly direction from Montana across Wyoming to Denver and then in a more southerly direction through Colorado and New Mexico. Most of the route is across federally managed national forest, national park, or national resource lands so that land acquisition will not be a major problem. There is no continuous existing trail or organized trail association as in the case of the Appalachian and Pacific Crest trails, but segments of existing federal trails have been incorporated in the route.

Prospects for the addition of new lengthy trails to the national system do not appear good. Some of the major trails shown on the original maps of the proposed system were rejected following study of their potentials and problems.

The proposed 5223-kilometer (3246-mile) North Country Trail, which will follow a winding route around the Great Lakes from northern New York to its junction with the Lewis and Clark Trail in North Dakota, has not been enthusiastically received by all the state and local government jurisdictions through which it would run. In fact, some government units have expressed negative attitudes. The main reasons for these appear to be a desire to avoid overuse of resources by nonresidents and the problems and costs state and local governments expect to face if they are responsible for acquisition, development, maintenance, and law enforcement.

On the other hand, a number of intermediate and local governments have made considerable progress in establishing their own independent trail systems in recent years. In some cases, the creation of state and local trails has been encouraged by the Railroad Revitalization and Regulatory Reform Act and other federal legislation that has facilitated or subsidized the conversion of abandoned railroad rights-of-way into bike paths, hiking trails, or multipurpose trails. Elsewhere, special funding such as snowmobile or motorcycle license fees and gasoline taxes have been used to help finance trails for such vehicles.

Many of the new intermediate and local government trails that are announced run through public parks or forests and, in some instances, involve the rebuilding or improved maintenance of old trails. As in the case of the proposed national trails, there is a tendency to avoid the costs and problems associated with trail corridors that run

through private lands. However, a number of intermediate and local governments are developing extensive systems of independent trails by using roadsides, powerline rights-of-way, and abandoned railroad or canal properties. In some cases, intermediate governments are providing grants to local governments for this purpose. Sometimes, these funds are given directly or indirectly to local user organizations that undertake trail construction and maintenance.

UNDESIGNATED RESOURCES
In addition to the great variety of public lands, waters, and structures that are managed to some degree for recreation purposes, there are many other kinds of public areas and buildings that provide recreation opportunities. Included in this group are sidewalks, streets, public bus systems, rural roads, highways, bridges, railroads, airports, public buildings, and cemeteries. These undesignated recreation resources provide a wide range and considerable number of opportunities. Their contribution is infrequently acknowledged and seldom investigated.

The most important group of undesignated recreation resources are those involved in travel or transportation. These resources have already been mentioned as playing an essential role in the participation process by providing access to recreation sites, events, or facilities. But frequently, they also act as recreation resources themselves. In some cases, such resources provide incidental enjoyment to people who are using them to reach specific destinations.

At other times, they may be the primary recreation resource.

Usually, undesignated resources are used informally for recreation without permission being sought or specifically granted by the administering agency. Sometimes such use is planned and managed by a public agency. Or a private club, neighborhood association, quasi-public organization, or commercial enterprise may make use of an undesignated resource for recreation after securing permission from the controlling government organization.

Urban Sidewalks and Streets. The network of streets, sidewalks, and alleys in urban residential areas is the undesignated resource that receives the heaviest recreation use by the greatest number of different kinds of people. Besides being used for intended travel and transportation purposes, streets and sidewalks are the scene of a great range of sports, games, and social activities (Figure 4.17). In fact, there is little doubt that this public space provides more recreation experiences than any other public resource, including schoolyards and public parks.

During favorable weather conditions, children and teenagers use streets and sidewalks as play space. The younger ones often find that public sidewalks in front of their homes are the best or only suitable place to enjoy playing with wheeled toys such as doll carriages, wagons, tricycles, and pedal cars. Older children use longer stretches of sidewalk for rollerskating, skateboarding, riding scooters, and learning to ride bicycles. They also make good use of these paved surfaces for games such as jump rope, jacks,

marbles, hopscotch, and bouncing balls. In the older neighborhoods of cities like Chicago and New York where there are no front yards and the houses adjoin the sidewalks, a number of highly structured games have evolved that make innovative use of all the available street features, including the walls of buildings, the stoops; the curbs and uniform squares of concrete sidewalks; the gutters; and the asphalt roadways. Some of these games such as stoopball, boxball, and box-baseball require little or no additional resources other than a rubber ball and a group of players.

Such other games as "Red Rover," "Red Light," "May I," and a number of ball games make greater use of the street itself. Stickball is a common street game in the old neighborhoods—it is played with a bat (or a broom or mop handle) and a ball. Wiffle bats and balls made of light plastic make it possible to play a street version of baseball without damaging windows or vehicles. Street pool—known as skelsy or skelly in some neighborhoods—is a popular game with teenagers; it involves the use of a "court" that is marked out on the street with a piece of chalk (Figure 15.14). Streetball is a version of basketball played anywhere that a small open area is available. When schoolyards are full or closed, a street or alley is used. A garbage can often takes the place of the hoop (streetball is usually played with only one basket) and specific parked cars and streetside trees are designated as boundaries.

Figure 15.14 Teenagers in Brooklyn use bottle caps to play a game of street pool (skelsy) on a court they have marked out on the street near their homes. In urban neighborhoods where open space close to residences is scarce or nonexistent, sidewalks and streets are heavily used for recreation purposes.

During the colder months, participation in street games is usually reduced and the nature of the activities changes. In snowy locations, streets become convenient places to practice ice hockey. Where snow accumulations are sufficient, roads —especially in hilly areas—are often used (albeit illegally) for sliding, skiing, sledding, and tobogganing.

To many casual observers, use of streets and sidewalks as substitute recreation open space seems both inappropriate and inadequate. Admittedly, they can be dangerous playgrounds with the everpresent possibility of a child being struck by a vehicle. They are certainly devoid of all the sophisticated amenities generally considered essential features of properly designed city parks and school playgrounds. Nevertheless, through the ingenuity of many generations of young people, these resources are used intensively by adapting old games and developing new activities to suit a neighborhood's particular characteristics. Children raised in these environments often prefer streets to well-equipped playgrounds when given the choice. Some playground designers are now duplicating "street facilities" to attract youth and enable them to play their favorite street games in the less hazardous environments of neighborhood parks.

The use of streets and roads as recreation facilities is not confined to children. Young adults use the downward sloping curves of hilly streets, parking ramps, and paved drainage ditches alongside busy thoroughfares as skateboard areas. People of various ages stroll through their neighborhoods on foot or cruise on their bikes or in their cars with no specific destination in mind; their main purpose is to see what is going on, to exchange greetings with people they already know, or to make new acquaintances. Joggers and cyclists of all ages use the streets. Older adults see the sidewalks and streets adjacent to their homes as available open space for a variety of activities. Some sit on stoops, walls, or the curb and watch the world go by. Others set up chairs and maybe a table, which they use for entertaining friends, for relaxing and enjoying a little sun or a cool breeze, for playing a game, for working on a hobby, or for eating outside.

Finally, in response to requests by special-interest groups or government agencies, streets are periodically closed to vehicular traffic and used for the staging of neighborhood block parties (Figure 7.10), street recreation programs (Figure 13.15), and other organized events. Sanctioned by the appropriate governments and sponsored by service clubs, private organizations, or commercial enterprises, these activities include running marathons (p. 85), soapbox derbies, bicycle tours and races, on-street sports car races, street dances, carnivals, festivals, fairs, concerts, shows, children's activity programs, Easter Sunday promenades, parades, flea markets, sidewalk sales, arts and crafts exhibits, and a variety of special rituals such as the December 31 gathering of people in New York's Time Square to greet the arrival of the New Year. Use of streets for such purposes[8] often inconveni-

ences nonparticipants, but it also brings events to the attention of a great many people who stop and take part, thereby enjoying recreation experiences they would likely have missed had the event been held in a less public location.

Public Transportation. In addition to providing inexpensive transportation, public transit systems also function as recreation resources themselves or as essential components of more complex recreation resources. Even the most mundane system can provide recreation experiences for people who like rides. The landscapes through which the conveyance travels are of little or no interest to such people; it is the ride that counts. Sometimes it is largely a matter of novelty; many individuals—children in particular—eagerly anticipate their first ride on a streetcar, subway, ferry boat, bus, or commuter train. On the other hand, there are persons who use public transportation systems frequently and still enjoy the ride or derive pleasure from observing the equipment and operating procedures.

Some transportation systems attract pleasure riders and observers because of their modernity and technical innovations; others are of nostalgic interest. The former includes monorail systems, recently constructed subway systems in cities like Washington, D.C., and high-speed trains such as Japan's. The latter includes London's double-decker buses and San Francisco's cable cars. Such public conveyances are often retained for their historic and recreation value long after they have ceased to function as efficient movers of people or goods.

---

[8] In New York City alone, there are 12 major parades and around 5000 street events a year, some of which involve the use of many blocks and the services of 11 city agencies.

For example, San Francisco's cable cars—introduced in 1873 and the only vehicles of their kind left in the world—are now considered the city's best known landmark and favorite tourist attraction. The system carries about 12 million passengers a year, 90 percent of whom are tourists. People watch and photograph the cars as they lurch by, then climb aboard and try to sit or stand near the driver (gripperson). Those who are close enough watch in fascination as he or she pulls back the lever that tightens the grip on the cable running constantly in a slot beneath the street; in this way, the car is pulled up the city's steep hills. Passengers also compete for the right to help rotate the cars on the turntables located at the end of two of the three runs and line up to tour the carbarn that contains historic exhibits and houses the huge cable drums that operate the system. The cable-car system is so recreationally and historically significant that it was given national historic landmark status in 1964. Protected since 1955 by legal mandate that guarantees perpetuation, the system is now undergoing a $40-million overhaul that will make the operation safer without altering its appearance and will extend one of the routes into the heart of Fisherman's Wharf.

The majority of recreation experiences obtained by riding on public transportation systems, however, are primarily a matter of the user having an opportunity to see the passing panorama of people and places. The less affluent and those who do not wish to drive their own vehicles frequently take trips on city bus, subway, or streetcar systems purely for recreation purposes. Guidebooks often recommend public transportation as a reasonably priced, interesting way for tourists to familiarize themselves with a city, region, or nation. By means of public transportation, tourists not only see well-known landmarks, but they can also see many aspects of the everyday lives of the local people; this can be a valuable learning experience, especially for those from an entirely different culture. The public transportation system in these cases acts as one very important component of a complex recreation resource.

Rural Roads and Highways. Like urban streets, rural roads are used for a number of recreation activities. These include walking, jogging, hiking, pleasure driving, and horseback, bicycle, and motorcycle riding. Although not developed with such uses in mind, roadsides often contain resources that make them attractive locations for relaxing, picnicking, photography, nature study, berrypicking, nut gathering, and rock collecting. Where it is not prohibited, they are also used as convenient places to camp. In winter, snowmobilers often make use of rural roadways; in many jurisdictions, snowmobiling is permitted on the shoulders of roads or on the roads themselves where they are left unploughed and impassable to wheeled vehicles.

Major highways provide fewer recreation opportunities of these kinds not only because they tend to be busier and contain less interesting roadsides but also because many of these forms of transportation and types of activities are prohibited. Even stopping (except in emergencies) is not permitted on many main thoroughfares. There is one amenity located along highways, however, that is often used for recreation. It is the roadside rest area, a facility constructed primarily for the comfort and convenience of travelers, which also reduces highway accidents by providing safe and readily accessible places where drivers can stop to rest their eyes and stretch their legs.

These goals could be achieved with the construction of restrooms and off-highway parking lots, but rest areas frequently offer much more. Wherever possible, scenic locations are selected as rest area sites. Sufficient land is included to provide space for the development of picnic facilities and play areas and still leave some undeveloped areas for visitors to explore. Not only does this type of facility encourage more drivers to stop, but it also allows them to enjoy the area much as they would a park. Local residents often use nearby roadside rest areas as destination parks for picnics or Sunday outings. Many travelers spend not just a few minutes, but several hours, at rest areas relaxing, picnicking, and walking about. Moreover, although overnight parking is forbidden at 38 percent of the rest areas in the United States and is allowed only in emergency situations at another 38 percent, no restrictions whatsoever are imposed at the remaining 24 percent. These rest areas frequently function much like small-scale state or provincial parks, receiving considerable use as campgrounds, picnic areas, play areas, and gathering places for the young and other groups.

Bridges. Apart from their utilitarian role, bridges serve as recreation resources in a number of ways. They often span scenic environments so people frequently use bridges as vantage points from which to see or photograph such features as rivers, waterfalls, gorges, or wetlands containing unusual plants and wildlife. Their location also provides unobstructed views of photogenic or interesting developed landscapes such as busy harbors and city skylines. Many bridges are built over bodies of water that are productive fishing grounds, making them attractive sites for anglers who fish from, alongside, or underneath them. Some rural bridges function as diving platforms (Figure 15.15).

Bridges can be recreation resources in their own right. A number are important tourist attractions because of their size, age, beauty, or structural characteristics. Some, such as San Francisco's Golden Gate Bridge, have become world famous landmarks attracting millions of visitors a year. Others, like picturesque old covered bridges, may be less impressive or individually identifiable but still provide many recreation opportunities for the casual tourist, amateur photographer, or history buff specializing in bridge design and ornamentation. In Vermont alone, there are 86 covered bridges still in use. They are considered so important that a law has been passed protecting them as part of the state's heritage.

However, the recreation potential of a bridge is dependent on more than the scenic or utilitarian values of the location or its photogenic qualities. Accessibility and policies regarding pedestrian and cyclist use of the structure are major factors affecting recreation use. Some controlled access-highway bridges have no sidewalks and pedestrians and cyclists may be prohibited. In other cases, special walk-

Figure 15.15 Many bridges serve as undesignated recreation resources for swimmers, fisherpersons, and sightseers. Governments and companies often discourage such uses because of liability problems.

ways are provided, thereby encouraging people to visit the bridge on foot and enjoy its amenities in comparative comfort and safety. Where bridges cross rivers or estuaries with productive fisheries, walkways are often installed in a manner that will make them most useful as fishing locations. Parking lots and other amenities aid in converting the bridge into the equivalent of a fishing pier.

Even bridges on which pedestrian or cyclist traffic is prohibited are occasionally used for recreation. For example, bridges are sometimes officially closed to vehicular traffic to allow the temporary use of the roadway for marathons, bicycle tours, or organized walks. Perhaps the best known of these is the an-

nual Labor Day walk across the 7.2-kilometer (4.5-mile) long Mackinac Bridge between the Upper and Lower Peninsulas of Michigan. Starting at 7:30 A.M., cars are restricted to the two west lanes, thus allowing some 30,000 pedestrians a once-a-year opportunity to trek across the bridge in a north-south direction. This community walk is now a well-established ritual with the Governor of Michigan traditionally walking with the first group of participants.

Railroads. Although rail passenger service has been declining in North America, many people continue to have a nostalgic affection for trains. They may have lost much of their appeal as a means of fast, comfortable transportation, but many people continue to travel periodically by train because of the recreation experiences that they provide. Trains are being chartered with increasing frequency by special-interest groups to provide transportation to and from events such as college football games or winter-sports rallies for snowmobilers and their families. In many cases, most of the participants would find it faster, cheaper, and easier to use an alternative form of transportation. Some of them travel considerable distances out of their way to reach the point of departure and a few actually come from the destination site itself just to be able to take part in the trip. Obviously, it is not the transportation that these passengers seek but rather the special atmosphere and camaraderie that is traditionally associated with group excursions by train.

A number of trains that have almost or completely outlived their economic usefulness in regularly scheduled passenger service are being operated as tourist attractions. Where the novelty of a ride on a vintage train is supplemented by interesting scenery, the appeal becomes even greater. In some nations such as Mexico, these lines are operated as part of the national railway system because they promote tourism. In others—Switzerland for example—lines that were previously operated by the national government have been taken over and maintained by associations of railway enthusiasts. But in the United States, the best known of these historic railroads continue to operate as commercial enterprises. One—the Silverton Railroad in southwestern Colorado—is the last regularly scheduled narrow gauge railroad in the United States. Operating between the small communities of Silverton and Durango, the trip has become so popular with tourists that it is virtually impossible to get a ticket without a reservation and the train makes two runs a day during the summer period.

Airports. Airports attract a considerable number of non-traveling visitors. The majority are drawn to the airport to watch aircraft taking off and landing. At some airports, this is facilitated by specially designed visitor observation decks, many of which contain coin-operated telescopes. Others go to people-watch, take guided tours, or enjoy short airplane rides just for the experience or scenic view. Some attend special events like air shows or the arrival or departure of celebrities.

Passengers and the people who come to see them off or meet them often spend long periods of time waiting in airport terminals. Airports usually provide amenities for their convenience, comfort, or entertainment; these include lounges; reading rooms; rows of arm-chair mounted coin-operated television sets; art displays; small museums or special exhibit areas; chapels which offer periodic religious services; snack bars, coffee shops, and restaurants; bars and cocktail lounges; newsstands; and a variety of shops. Finally, for anyone who can afford the cost of membership, there are the VIP clubs. Operated by 11 different airlines and located in most of the larger cities on their routes, these comfortably furnished lounges provide a quiet oasis in which to rest, visit with friends, enjoy a drink or light snack, read, relax, watch television, play cards or other table games and, at many locations, sit and watch the airfield activity from large picture windows.

Buildings. Many public buildings erected and used primarily for nonrecreational purposes also provide pleasurable experiences. Often the managing agency makes no special provisions for recreation use. In many cases, individuals or small groups just take advantage of a building characteristic or facility in an informal manner and no special management procedures are required. Activities include visiting buildings for sightseeing purposes, people-watching in the lobbies, or attending sessions of courts or legislative bodies.

There are also situations where public buildings are managed in a manner that is complementary to recreation, although the structures were not necessarily intended to perform a recreation function.

Some common examples are:

- Rooms and auditoriums in city halls, state buildings, and federal buildings being used for meetings of special interest groups or for the staging of cultural events.
- Holding of community events in the lobbies and courtyards of federal buildings (under terms of the Cooperative Use Act of 1976); the most common uses of such facilities have been for fine arts exhibitions and concerts, dance recitals, and theatrical presentations.
- Display and sale of stamps in post office buildings; U.S. Post Office philatelic sales total about $90 million a year.
- Use of municipal fire stations or adjacent open space for community events such as ice cream socials or square dances.
- Holding concerts, pageants, rallies, dances, sports competitions, rifle programs, rummage sales, and a variety of shows and exhibitions in Department of Defense armories.

In these situations, the public agency's primary (or only) expense is the cost of maintenance and, in many cases, this is paid by the user-group involved.

Finally, many public buildings contain a variety of special facilities, which are intended for the casual visitor. These include information desks where people can learn more about the building and the activities taking place in it, small exhibit areas, publication sales rooms, gift shops featuring appropriate items, exhibition halls, elaborate reception centers, and observation galleries from which visitors can watch activities without interfering with them. Personnel are often available to answer questions, point out interesting exhibits or architectural features, and escort visitors through those areas of the building open to the public. Buildings with visitor services of this type include the United Nations Headquarters in New York, many city halls, most state and provincial capitals, the United States Capitol, the Canadian Parliament Buildings, the Federal Mints, the Bureau of Engraving and Printing, the Federal Bureau of Investigation in the Department of Justice Building, and many other federal department buildings such as those housing the Departments of Interior, Agriculture, and Commerce.

Other Resources. Many other publicly owned structures and facilities are used officially and unofficially for recreation purposes. Parking ramps in downtown areas are often used informally by skateboarders, kiteflyers, and sightseers; they are also being used more by recreation departments and cultural organizations for the staging of community concerts and special events. Municipal reservoirs and water-filtration and sewage-treatment plants are often open to visitors and jogging, hiking, bicycling, ice skating, boating, fishing, and picnicking are sometimes permitted on the grounds and at the reservoirs or ponds. Fire towers and lighthouses built for utilitarian purposes are considered by many individuals as interesting structures to look at, sketch, and photograph. Towers and lighthouses often admit visitors who enjoy the challenge of climbing them and appreciate the opportunity to examine the inside facilities, view the surrounding countryside from the top, and talk with employees about their duties

and experiences. Water-associated structures such as dams, locks, and harbor installations are important tourist destinations. Viewing facilities, guided tours, or visitor information centers are often provided to help sightseers understand the workings and purposes of such structures.

Public cemeteries, especially in parts of the world where people see nothing sacrilegious about using them for recreation purposes, are sometimes the nicest or only places where urban people can go to walk, enjoy quiet relaxation, get some fresh air, sit or lie in a cool place under a tree, have a picnic, observe birds and other wildlife, or be alone with a friend or lover. Such use is not as common in North American communities, although activities such as bicycling, jogging, cross-country skiing, model-plane or kite flying, fishing, and practicing golf strokes are being mentioned more frequently in newspaper articles. This may indicate a changing attitude on the part of a growing number of citizens but it does not necessarily mean that the use of cemeteries for recreation is being encouraged or even condoned by the administrators concerned. Quite the opposite is true in fact; most of the reports point out that the individuals caught taking part in such unseemly activities were evicted from the premises and, in some cases, given stiff fines.

However, with over 800,000 hectares (2 million acres) of public and private land set aside for interment purposes in the United States and the demand for open space ex-

ceeding the supply in many communities, this negative attitude toward the multiple use of cemetery lands is likely to change. In some instances, it already has. A number of cemeteries are permitting more extensive public access and allowing what are considered appropriate recreation activities to take place in certain areas or at certain times. Others are leasing unused land to municipal recreation departments for interim use as picnic areas, playgrounds, sportsfields, golf courses, and nature study sites until such time as it is needed for burials.

Some cemeteries are tourist attractions. Large numbers of people take pleasure in visiting cemeteries of historic or national significance as well as cemeteries where they can see the burial sites of famous people. Many individuals seek and explore old abandoned graveyards. A growing number of these individuals are interested in acquiring rubbings of individual gravestones because of their interesting or artistic designs. Some cemeteries are so beautiful that people visit them just to enjoy the fountains, plantings, or landscapes. Others include such a variety of ostentatious tombstones and memorials that they function as outdoor art museums filled with hundreds of beautifully carved and elaborately decorated urns, busts, statues, memorials, and mausoleums.

This completes the review of public recreation resources, except for those that are primarily sources of cultural experiences. Both public and private cultural resources will be discussed in the next chapter.

**DISCUSSION
TOPICS**

1. What contributions have national government recreation resources made to your enjoyment of life and to the enjoyment of people with whom you are familiar?

2. Is it desirable for national government recreation resource managing agencies to construct and operate highly developed recreation areas in or adjacent to large urban centers?

3. Is the supply of extraurban recreation opportunities provided by intermediate and national park system units adequate in the region where you live? Consider geographic distribution and accessibility as well as the type and amount of opportunities supplied.

4. Is a policy of preservation coupled with limited recreation facility development better than a policy of multiple-use management in terms of providing a good supply of recreation opportunities to a broad spectrum of the public?

5. Summarize the features of two institutional recreation resource systems with which you are familiar and suggest changes that could be made to improve the nature and supply of recreation opportunities provided.

6. Do undesignated resources supply more or fewer recreation opportunities for you than for other people you know? Explain, mentioning ways in which changes in age, lifestyle, or place of residence increase or decrease the recreation importance of undesignated resources.

FURTHER READINGS

As in the case of intermediate resources, textbooks tend to concentrate on national government recreation system administrative matters and provide little information concerning the resources involved. Some resource-oriented material is included in Chapter 5, "Federal Government Involvement" in Jensen's *Outdoor Recreation in America,* and, in Chapter 8, "The National Park System," Chapter 9, "The National Forests as Outdoor Recreation Areas," and Chapter 10, "Other Federal Agencies" in Brockman and Merriam's *Recreational Use of Wildlands.*

General articles on national government recreation resources are published periodically in a number of recreation journals. Good sources of national park system information are *National Parks and Conservation Magazine,* published monthly in Washington, D.C., and *Parks,* a quarterly publication of the International Union for Conservation of Nature and Natural Resources. *Parks and Recreation* and *Recreation Canada* occasionally include articles concerning national level recreation resources.

Up-to-date information on national government managed recreation resources usually has to be obtained directly from the agency concerned. Again, the emphasis in agency reports and statistics is generally on administration rather than the resources, but data on the latter can often be obtained from brochures or user guides for individual units.

Information on specific institutional resources appears regularly in *Parks and Recreation* and the *Journal of Physical Education and Recreation.* However, summary data are seldom published and generally have to be compiled from information supplied by individual institutions. It is virtually impossible to find useful information concerning the nature and extent of undesignated resources because recreation is not normally recognized as a management objective so that agencies do not record the location and extent of recreation use.

16

CULTURAL RESOURCES

This chapter describes the various kinds of cultural resources that commonly supply recreation opportunities. These consist of facilities

Figure 16.1 The Grand Foyer of the John F. Kennedy Center for the Performing Arts in Washington, D.C. links the 1150-seat Eisenhower Theater, the 2750-seat Concert Hall, and the 2200-seat Opera House. More than 6 million people visit it each year; only 2 million of these visits involve attending a concert, play, ballet, opera, film, or other performance for which admission is charged. The majority of users are participants in one of the center's many free cultural programs or tourists who come to view the facility and its art works.

and programs that provide pleasurable artistic, dramatic, literary, and musical experiences or facilitate enjoyable exploration of our environment, including materials pertaining to the characteristics, achievements, and history of the human race. Although cultural experiences can take place at any location under a variety of circumstances, the amenities most likely to provide recreation opportunities of a cultural nature are museums, libraries, broadcast and film resources, individual artists, and performing arts organizations and facilities (Figure 16.1). Unlike the various recreation resources described earlier, which were divided into a number of separate chapters based on ownership, public and private cultural resources will be treated as a single group; there are several reasons for this approach.

First, discussing cultural resources as a group avoids duplication since there are generally no substantial differences in the experiences provided by public and private cultural resources. Second, the differences among the roles of various levels of government and those between government and private organizations are much less distinct in the case of cultural resources than for other types of recreation resources. This is especially true in the United States where all levels of government usually assume a supportive role rather than take full responsibility for the development and operation of cultural amenities. As a result, most American cultural institutions that are commonly regarded as publicly supported, seek and receive substantial aid from private sources. On the other hand, some private facilities that appear to be public operations receive no government support. Commer-

cial resources are usually more easily identified; however, many nonprofit cultural resources are perceived as commercial enterprises by the public.

Third, cultural resources should be examined as a group because individual components of the system are closely related and often dependent on each other for survival. In addition, these resources have a much greater impact on people as a system than they do as separate resources. Collectively, cultural resources form environments that effect the way individuals (and the societies to which they belong) feel, think, communicate, and act; in fact, culture is one of the essential foundations and principal shapers of civilization.

It is important for recreation professionals who are not directly involved in cultural programs to understand the nature, values, and problems of cultural resources. Cultural institutions can often assist recreation agencies in providing recreation opportunities. For example, libraries and museums sometimes supply space, staff, and materials (books, films, pictures, records, exhibits) to facilitate or enrich recreation agency programs such as arts and crafts classes, musical activities, environmental interpretation presentations, and meetings of various hobby and social clubs. In many communities, cultural institutions are a prime source of expert assistance with public and quasi-public programs involving music, dance, and drama. Conversely, public and quasi-public recreation organizations often manage the plazas, malls, parks, playgrounds, nature centers, meeting rooms, halls, auditoriums, and gymnasiums in which cultural organizations conduct their regular

or outreach programs. Understanding and cooperative attitudes by both groups of professionals lead to socially beneficial, symbiotic arrangements.

To appreciate the complex nature of cultural resources and the special challenges facing providers of cultural experiences, it is necessary to have a basic understanding of the peculiar manner in which cultural resources are funded. Therefore, the various sources of financial support for cultural resources will be examined first.

SUPPORT FOR CULTURAL RESOURCES

The arts in the United States have blossomed during the last 25 years. Once considered culturally backward, the nation now has many world-renowned cultural resources, including museums, artists, writers, orchestras, and dance companies. Professional arts organizations are flourishing. Between 1965 and 1979, their numbers rose dramatically—from 58 to 144 orchestras; from 27 to 65 opera companies; from 37 to 300 dance companies; and from 23 to 270 theater companies. Folk arts and crafts have shown similar rapid growth rates. Currently, it is estimated that at least 50 percent of the American population takes part in some form of cultural activity on a more or less regular basis. And, in eight of the nation's largest cities, attendance at cultural events and museums now exceeds paid sports attendance.

Much of the increased interest stems from changes in perception and opportunities. Until recently, most Americans thought of cultural activities mainly in terms of the concert stage, classical theater, and galleries filled with paintings—usually Western European. Now the arts are perceived as including a much greater variety of resources ranging from symphonies, opera, and ballet to jazz, folk music, handicrafts, ethnic festivals, films, and puppet arts. Today, cultural resources appeal to a broad spectrum of the population, including many who were previously intimidated or disinterested.

This *popularization of the arts* has its critics as well as its supporters. Some find it disturbing that major cultural institutions are striving to attract wider audiences; they believe attempts to develop programs with broad appeal can only lead to a lowering of standards. Others object to public funding of organizations or projects that do not, in their opinion, provide what they consider to be a quality arts experience. They believe that grants should be reserved for developing the fine arts and supporting prestigious cultural institutions.

Many people, however, welcome popularization because it is making the arts more accessible. Supporters praise institutions for broadening, modernizing, and glamorizing their presentations and exhibits. *Outreach programs* are encouraged because they make cultural experiences available both to segments of the population that have been largely ignored in the past and to communities that have been culturally deprived because of size or geographic location. Although supporters admit that all of the offerings do not attain the same degree of excellence, they approve because the broader programs provide the large-scale exposure that is necessary for the development of a

widespread appreciation of the arts. Involvement on the part of large numbers of people, they argue, will help develop a more knowledgeable and sophisticated populace; as this occurs, there will be a growing demand not only for more but also for better cultural resources.

Unfortunately, the supply of cultural opportunities has not been able to keep up with the demand. Although the increase in participation is heartening to providers of cultural experiences, it is also placing great pressures on existing programs and creating an urgent need for new or improved facilities. Since high-quality cultural experiences are costly to provide, the increased revenues from fees and ticket sales, though substantial, are seldom sufficient to cover even the operating expenses. As a result, cultural programs often take place in inadequate, understaffed facilities and most are dependent for survival—sometimes quite heavily—on charity of one kind or another. Of course, this situation is not unique. Many other public and quasi-public programs, including city-sponsored park and sports programs, also rely heavily on donations of money, time, and resources.

THE PRIVATE SECTOR

Many cultural resources owe their existence to donations by private individuals, foundations, or corporations. Usually these gifts are in the form of money but sometimes they may be donations of land, facilities, or services.

The majority of North American cultural resources are the result of donations by individuals. The fact that philanthropy of this magnitude is primarily found in Canada

and the United States is often attributed to favorable tax laws. Existing laws on tax write-offs certainly encourage philanthropy, but the wealthy in Canada and the United States have followed a tradition of providing the public with exceptional cultural opportunities from the earliest days. Some built museums, opera houses, libraries, or theaters; others contributed land, books, works of art, or museum specimens. This pattern of generosity continues today. In recent times, land for the Wolf Trap Farm Park for the Performing Arts (a unit of the national park system) was donated by Catherine Filene Shouse and nearly all of the cost of one of the most expensive public buildings ever constructed in America—the $95 million East Building of the National Gallery of Art—was donated by one person, Paul Mellon; 40 years earlier, his father, Andrew Mellon, provided funds for the gallery's main building.

Although wealthy individuals make many large donations of this nature, most private assistance for the operation of cultural institutions comes from families with modest incomes. On the average, Americans donate around 2.3 percent of their before-tax income to charities and nonprofit organizations of their choice. Over $3 billion of this amount supports cultural resources.

Americans also donate much free time to cultural organizations. This contribution is substantial as the following examples show:

- Volunteer workers now form over half the work force at public museums and art galleries.
- A growing number of public libraries depend on volunteers to remain open on more than extremely limited schedules.

- Public television stations rely heavily on volunteers, a reliance that is likely to increase now that an amendment to the Telecommunications Act of 1978 permits stations to use the value of this labor as matching money when applying for federal grants. Since stations are required to raise $2 in private donations for every $1 in federal aid (a challenge that is impossible for many stations to meet), this new provision may earn public television as much as $20 million a year in additional federal funds.
- Much of the administration and maintenance for nonprofit performing arts organizations is undertaken by volunteers. These behind-the-scene workers help stretch the available revenues by performing such tasks as typing, answering telephones, producing newsletters, cleaning up after rehearsals and performances, repairing equipment, and preparing sets and costumes.

So important have the services of these volunteer workers become, it is doubtful that any nonprofit cultural resource could thrive or perhaps survive without them.

Another method of distributing private wealth for social purposes is to establish a philanthropic foundation. Such organizations are mainly an American phenomenon although a few exist in Canada and several nations of Western Europe including Great Britain. Although America's 22,000 foundations support a great variety of public services, a substantial portion of their funds go to cultural resources. Among the cultural amenities supported by foundations are the Smithsonian Institution, Colonial Williamsburg (see Figure 16.13), and many libraries, repertory theaters, art galleries, and zoos. However, foundations' contributions to the arts have declined recently because of the effects of inflation,

government regulations, higher taxes, and an accompanying desire to maintain high support levels for other areas such as education, health, and social welfare.

Contributions from corporations also play a significant role in supporting cultural resources. American companies donated a total of $256 million for such projects in 1979. The largest portion of these funds went to public museums, followed by public radio and televi-

sion, symphony orchestras, theater, opera, and dance companies (Figure 16.2).

One of the biggest contributors is the Exxon Corporation. Annually it spends around $7 million of its $35 million charities budget on the support of projects such as the "Great Performances" public television series and the "Treasures of Tutankhamen" traveling exhibition. Exxon also develops new talent by sponsoring programs to train con-

Figure 16.2 As this advertisement explains, the Texaco Corporation has made it possible for Canadians and Americans to listen to live radio broadcasts of Metropolitan Opera Company performances since 1940. Recently, Texaco expanded its support to include live telecasts over PBS stations and, in 1980, it donated $5 million to the Metropolitan Opera Company's Centennial Endowment Campaign.

ductors, writers, painters, and sculptors and by featuring regional theater companies in their television series. Assistance of this magnitude is not unique, however. There are at least 14 American corporations that currently give more than $1 million annually to the support of the arts.

The level of corporate philanthropy is not necessarily in direct proportion to the size of the company. In fact, the largest corporations actually give the least in terms of percentages of their profits. One of the most generous American corporations (more than 5 percent of profits or $7.9 million in 1979) is the Dayton-Hudson Corporation. It has been among the top 15 corporate philanthropists in the nation for 32 years although some 200 corporations are larger in terms of revenues. Unlike most companies, Dayton-Hudson concentrates on only two areas—social action and the arts—and spends most of its money in communities where company operations are located. In Minneapolis, site of the firm's headquarters, for instance, virtually every cultural institution owes either its existence or financial well-being to Dayton-Hudson support.

Although much aid is in the form of grants to organizations, corporations assist the arts in several other ways. Many encourage art appreciation and sales by purchasing and displaying art works in their buildings. Some firms provide their employees with reduced-rate or free admission to cultural facilities or events. Such programs benefit cultural resources by providing some assured financial support and expanding audiences by encouraging individuals to attend who otherwise might never do so. At least 29 companies including Gulf Oil, Bank of America, Lever Brothers, Quaker Oats, and Xerox encourage their workers to support the arts by matching employee donations to cultural institutions. Public broadcasting stations have benefited most so far, but these programs are also an important source of revenue for other cultural organizations that are located in the same communities as the participating corporations. Other companies help cultural organizations develop sound business management, public relations, and fundraising programs by offering free professional assistance.

In contrast to decreasing support of the arts by foundations, assistance from corporations has been growing rapidly. Contributions increased tenfold during the last decade and, in 1979, corporations for the first time displaced foundations as the primary patron of the arts. This change in corporate behavior is partly because present tax laws encourage corporate philanthropy, but mostly it results from the realization that support of cultural resources is a good business practice. Promotion of the arts can enhance a corporation's image, increase sales, generate good will, and improve employee morale. Development or improvement of cultural opportunities within the community where a company is located makes it a more desirable place in which to live. This can be of direct benefit to a corporation since it helps attract and retain employees, especially the highly educated personnel on which the management of a successful business often depends.

Corporate support has advantages and disadvantages. Many cultural organizations prefer aid from companies because it is more dependable than small donations from many individuals and generally involves far less red tape than government grants. If the right contacts have been developed, donations from corporations can usually be obtained more quickly, easily, and cheaply than donations from any other source. However, it is often difficult or impossible for smaller, less prestigious organizations and experimental programs to attract corporate support. In fact, there is a tendency for corporations to avoid funding projects that could prove to be controversial or that might reflect views in conflict with those of the company or its most conservative stockholders. Some cultural organizations do not seek corporate funding because they feel it is impossible to retain the integrity of their programs or cultivate high levels of creativity while under obligation to please a corporate sponsor.

THE ROLE OF GOVERNMENT

Despite substantial contributions from the private sector, many cultural resources would find it impossible to survive without some form of government aid. Financial assistance from governments is also desirable for a number of reasons. Generally, private donations are only directed toward organizations, programs, and artists that appeal to the donors. Commercial operations are financed only if there is a good chance of adequate profits. But governments—especially in democratic nations—may neither require the subsidized cultural organizations to make money nor please a majority of either the politicians or the taxpayers. This provides many organizations and artists with the freedom they need to experiment and develop new art forms.

Government support is also necessary if people are to see major cultural attractions from other nations. Traveling international exhibitions of cultural resources are made possible today largely through grants from corporations, but supplementary government grants are almost always needed and government agency assistance is usually required to make the necessary arrangements. In the case of the performing arts, the chances of making a profit from tours by foreign artists were once very good so that productions were usually backed by private impresarios. Now that the profit margin is disappearing, generous subsidies from domestic or foreign governments are needed to make such tours financially feasible.

Federal Government Role.
The establishment in 1965 of two independent agencies—the National Endowment for the Arts and the National Endowment for the Humanities—formally committed the U.S. Government to the support of cultural resources. Annual budgets for these two agencies rose from the original $2.5 million to over $300 million in 1980; about 50 percent of these funds provide aid to specific arts projects and artists. Since their establishment, more than $1 billion has been distributed, and the endowments are now major forces in American cultural development.

The endowments' impact has been felt in every state and in both large and small communities. Grants have subsidized traveling exhibitions, inner-city arts groups, large institutions (such as New York's Metropolitan Opera) and the production of public broadcasting television programs (e.g., the widely acclaimed "Adams Chronicles"). New orchestras, theaters, and dance and opera companies have been established. Subsidies have helped develop the talents of musicians, painters, sculptors, dancers, writers, poets, and film makers. Many grants have been highly successful although the amounts provided were small. This is partly because the funding is usually in the form of challenge grants; recipient institutions must raise as much as $3 in new donations or local taxes to qualify for $1 of federal endowment. Such grants cannot begin to finance projects in their entirety nor are they intended to do so. Rather, they serve as catalysts by providing the impetus needed for local fundraising drives or encouraging public and corporate support at the community level. Sometimes an endowment grant is the "seed money" that is so desperately needed to get a project started.

Unfortunately, endowment appropriations are inadequate. Only one in four applicants considered deserving of help actually receives funds. Currently, a budget of at least $700 million would be necessary to satisfy the overall need. Nevertheless, the endowments are a significant beginning and, most important, they proclaim that cultural resources are now a legitimate concern of the federal government.

State Government Role.
State government support for cultural resources is also growing. In contrast to 1967 when only 10 states had such agencies, every state now has a state arts council. These councils distribute funds appropriated by state legislatures to help deserving cultural resources that range from major art museums to small community arts and crafts programs. State appropriations have risen from a total of $4.8 million in 1967 to $97 million in 1980. Appropriation growth rates in some states are truly remarkable. In Michigan, for example, the annual appropriation rose from $572,000 in 1976 to over $6 million in 1980, a tenfold increase.

Support of cultural resources varies considerably from state to state. In 1980, for instance, New York was the most beneficent in total appropriations ($32 million) and second in per capita spending ($1.87 per person). These funds were distributed by the State Council on the Arts in three categories—the performing arts (music, dance, theater), the communication and visual arts (museums, planetariums, film makers, writers), and special programs (mostly ethnic arts group projects). During the same year, Alaska's appropriation was much smaller ($1 million), but it represented an expenditure of $2.52 per person, placing that state in first place on a per capita basis. A total of 22 states contributed $1 million or more and 6 spent at least $0.75 per capita. On the other hand, some states provided very little support for the arts. Although the average appropriation in 1980 was $0.44 per capita, 12 states contributed less than $0.15 per person and 4 states provided less than $100,000. Like the federal endowments, most of the state grants are small, but they often mean the difference between life and death for a facility or program.

Local Government Role.
The most extensive changes in gov-

ernment involvement in the arts have taken place at the local level. Interested citizens have banded together to work for the establishment of community arts councils. Such agencies are becoming quite common in small towns as well as large cities. They are responsible for promoting cultural programs throughout the community and for providing technical and financial assistance to resident artists and local arts organizations. Public pressure has also resulted in substantial increases in local government expenditures for operating these arts councils and for funding cultural facilities and programs. In a few communities, these expenditures occasionally exceed $100 million in a single year. Collectively, the annual contribution of local governments in the United States to cultural resources is now estimated to be approximately $1100 million.

The local government cultural agency with the largest budget at the present time is the Cultural Affairs Department of New York City, a remarkable achievement for a community that is experiencing severe financial problems. Although not nearly sufficient to answer all the community's needs, the agency's annual budget of $27.5 million represents a commitment to culture that is unequalled even by most higher level governments (only the National Endowment for the Arts and the New York State Council on the Arts have larger budgets).

With a staff of about 60 persons, the department provides maintenance funds for 25 major cultural institutions such as the Bronx Zoo and the Metropolitan Museum of Art. It also awards numerous small matching grants to a

Figure 16.3 An audience enjoys a New York Shakespeare Festival performance as part of New York City's free summer cultural presentations. This performance is in Central Park's Delacorte Theater, built expressly for this purpose with funds from the city and George Delacorte, president of the Dell Publishing Company.

wide range of community-based arts groups, supports the activities of individual borough arts councils, and helps to finance cultural presentations throughout the city. The latter include performances each summer in the city's parks by such prestigious organizations as the New York Philharmonic, the Metropolitan Opera, and the New York Shakespeare Festival (Figure 16.3). The department also develops programs in cooperation with other municipal agencies and works with a mayoral task force to locate and open up unused space in city-owned buildings for cultural purposes. Another major function is to obtain additional public and private funding for the arts and to act as a liaison between these sources and an appropriate artist or cultural institution.

The Crucial Role of Public Funding. Although overall financial support increased substantially in the 1970s, many American cultural institutions and programs were in jeopardy by the end of the decade. Rapid increases in operating costs, cutbacks in some forms of government assistance, and higher levels of participation placed numerous cultural organizations in a precarious position. Existing budgets would not permit programs to continue as in recent years, yet reductions in the opportunities provided were undesirable if community interest and involvement were to be sustained. Many organizations were forced to take drastic steps just to survive. These included operating on reduced hours, turning almost exclusively to volunteer labor, lowering the quality of programs or maintenance, and deferring urgently needed facility repairs. When these measures proved inadequate, some organizations used endowment fund principal to pay debts; others sold irreplaceable assets to avoid bankruptcy. Some organizations eliminated one or two programs or productions; a few canceled whole seasons. For example, the New York Shakespeare Festival's Public Theater did not present its traditional free summer Shakespeare productions in Central Park in 1980; New York City's Department of Cultural Affairs was unable to provide its customary level of funding and no other government source of funds could be found. Despite all efforts to economize, however, a few institutions found their financial problems insurmountable and discontinued operations entirely; for instance, the Carriage Harness Museum in Cooperstown operated by the New York State Historical Association was closed in 1978 and its collection of horse-drawn conveyances (considered to be the finest in the country) was dispersed at public auction.

When public funding for cultural resources is lacking, all providers of cultural experiences are affected to some extent. As a rule, however, two kinds of institutions rely on public funding more than others and, therefore, they suffer the worst effects when public funds are not available. One kind presents art forms that are nontraditional or avant-garde. Such programs are often enthusiastically received by a small segment of the public but, usually, they confuse, intimidate, or even alienate large numbers of people, at least until they are better un-

derstood. As a result, these institutions seldom attract adequate levels of support from audiences or private benefactors; they need public funding to survive. The other group of institutions that is usually severely affected when public funding is inadequate consists of organizations involved in the preservation or presentation of art forms often collectively referred to as *high culture.* These include fine arts museums and symphony orchestras together with opera, repertory theater, and classical ballet companies. Unlike the institutions that protect and encourage the nontraditional art forms, these organizations often receive considerable financial support from corporations as well as substantial numbers of individuals. Nevertheless, these organizations seldom attract mass audiences and require public funding to survive because they are usually so expensive to operate.

However, both kinds of institutions are vital components of a society's cultural resource system. Nontraditional programs often produce major breakthroughs in the arts, establishing new directions or providing a renewal of vitality. Great art, in fact, often begins by opposing tradition. Because risks are taken, an art form is able to grow and become not only a celebration of the past but also a reflection of the society in which it is found. On the other hand, high-culture programs preserve and protect the world's irreplaceable heritage. Such programs keep the cultural legacies of the past not only safe but alive so that people now and in the future can know of their existence and be enriched. For these reasons, neither kind of institution can be dismissed as unimportant just because it fails

to attract a large audience or appeals mainly to one kind of audience. Both kinds of cultural resource are essential to the well-being of civilized society and, therefore, the public funding that will allow them to flourish can be justified as a sound investment rather than a foolish expenditure on what some critics call "frills."

Other Nations. Major cultural resources in other countries have usually developed as the result of government or royal patronage rather than because of private initiative and donations. Per capita government financial support of the arts in many nations, especially West Germany, Austria, Sweden, Canada, and Great Britain, is also far more extensive than in the United States. For example, Great Britain and West Germany provide seven and ten times more support, respectively.

In Communist nations, most cultural resources are established, financed, and controlled by the governments. The quality and nature of these amenities, therefore, are often dependent on the attitudes of those in power and the finances at their disposal. This arrangement has advantages and disadvantages. Where there has been reasonable freedom for artistic expression and adequate funding has been provided, museums, orchestras, and theatrical and ballet companies have evolved that are undoubtedly among the finest in the world. On the other hand, absolute government control over cultural institutions frequently curtails freedom of self-expression, a condition generally considered essential for creativity. Consequently, cultural programs in Communist nations are often limited in scope.

However, approved cultural opportunities are usually numerous and provided free or at much lower fees than those charged in countries where patrons are expected to defray much or all of the operating costs.

THE DEVELOPMENT OF AN AUDIENCE

Up to this point, only the financial aspects of support for cultural resources have been discussed. However, most of the value of these resources to society—and, therefore, the reason for supporting them—is lost if individuals fail to show any interest in the opportunities offered. Therefore, audience development is as important as providing the funds necessary to sustain such resources.

Some cultural resources have little difficulty in attracting large numbers of people either because they provide experiences that arouse people's curiosity or because they are highly entertaining. Zoos, children's museums, and many forms of literary and theatrical expression fall into this category. Other forms, however, require a certain level of public sophistication to be appreciated. These are unlikely to acquire substantial audiences unless sufficient numbers of people have developed a taste for them—examples include fine arts museums, opera, poetry, and the classical forms of literature, drama, music, and ballet. Frequently, individuals develop a liking for these resources quite effortlessly simply by being exposed to them at an early age in the company of friends or family members who are knowledgeable and enthusiastic. Otherwise, the desire and ability to benefit from cultural resources usually originate in some type of educational program.

The most accessible programs of this nature take place in the public schools either as part of the school curriculum or as afterschool activities. Such programs can develop appreciation of cultural resources and teach skills that permit personal involvement in cultural pursuits such as reading books, singing in choral groups, writing poetry, acting in plays, painting pictures, playing musical instruments, or performing in dance ensembles. Many school programs use resources in the surrounding area. These may involve field trips to cultural events and facilities or they may consist of community artists visiting the schools. One such program, Young Audiences—a nationwide nonprofit organization with 38 chapters—provides varied experiences in the visual and performing arts for 2.5 million public school children each year. Cooperative programs of this kind can produce a lifelong interest in going to museums, libraries, nature centers, symphony orchestra concerts, or ballet, opera, or theatrical productions.

Even if individuals decide not to pursue these interests in later life, exposure to such experiences during the early years may still have lifelong beneficial effects. Exposure to cultural programs can help young peple develop their imaginations and sensitivity. It can assist them in learning how to express their feelings and it can improve perceptiveness, expand outlooks, and develop a willingness to try new things. Unfortunately, these kinds of benefits are not as tangible as those produced by other school programs so that it is sometimes difficult for some people to recognize their worth. Consequently, cultural programs are often considered nonessential extras and, therefore, are either not included in school curricula or are the first programs to be terminated when funds are limited.

The other group of programs that provide large numbers of individuals with cultural experiences are those offered by the cultural organizations themselves and a wide range of community groups. However, these are seldom as effective as the school programs for several reasons. First, they must be sought out, so that only people who are already somewhat motivated are likely to take part. Second, many programs involve fees that discourage participation by the less affluent. Third, adult programs are disadvantaged because higher percentages of the potential participants may have developed negative attitudes or a reticence to try new things.

Nevertheless, such programs form a very important part of the support system for cultural institutions. They include: classes in the arts at community recreation centers, free performances at downtown malls, lectures on books or films at public libraries, workshops at local opera guilds, television programs about exhibitions or artists, trips to museums or theaters arranged by church groups or quasi-public organizations, outreach programs operated by museum and performing arts organizations, city recreation-department-sponsored exposure programs such as ethnic or music festivals, and the many credit and noncredit cultural courses offered for enrichment purposes by schools and colleges.

Unfortunately, as in the case of school cultural activities, cultural programs offered by local government recreation departments are often given low priority when funds are allocated. As a result, sports programs frequently have better facilities and more staff. When expenditures must be reduced, cultural programs are usually the first to be curtailed. Often there are only the most rudimentary arts and crafts programs or no cultural programs at all in communities where much of the population is economically disadvantaged and local government funds are limited. This is unfortunate since recreation departments are usually in the best position of any of the nonschool organizations to reach large numbers of people. Moreover, they frequently provide the only cultural opportunities that are available to some segments of the population, especially the elderly, the handicapped, and the economically disadvantaged.

PERFORMING ARTS RESOURCES

The United States has been experiencing a *performing arts* renaissance. More people than ever before are attending classical concerts, operas, plays, poetry readings, and dance presentations. Increasing numbers are actively involved in opera societies, dance classes, amateur theatrical productions, and musical groups of all types and sizes. More young people are interested in developing their artistic talents and using them not just as a hobby but in a lifelong career. And, larger numbers of people are finding it possible to work full-time in the arts because there are more facilities and professional companies with which to perform and bigger audiences willing to pay

higher prices for the privilege of watching and hearing them.

Governments are becoming more involved in the provision of performing arts opportunities in response to this increased participation and interest. However, the policy of partial assistance rather than complete subsidization persists in the United States, especially at the state and federal levels. As yet, there are no officially recognized national performing companies or facilities, at least none that are similar to the national institutions established by most other nations. Nevertheless, as the following discussion indicates, there are several organizations that receive considerable federal assistance and fulfill many of the functions of national arts institutions. In some ways, this situation is preferable because many rather than a few resources have gained national status, and they are able to represent and reflect the diversity of American performing arts far more effectively than a single organization.

NONPROFIT THEATER

The theater is the most popular form of the performing arts in the United States; paid admissions for dramatic presentations exceeded 62 million in 1979. Many of these performances take place in nonprofit theaters. These range from large, specially built theaters in elaborate cultural complexes that are heavily subsidized with state and federal money to small privately operated theaters that receive minimal grants from state and local arts councils.

This network of nonprofit theaters houses 175 professional acting companies. One-third of these are located in New York City and the

remainder are scattered throughout the country in 83 different communities. The latter are especially important because they make a wide variety of theatrical experiences regularly and readily accessible to people far removed from New York City's extensive performing arts resources. In 1979, 13 million individuals attended plays at these theaters alone.

Regional Theater. About 50 of the larger, well-established resident theaters function as *regional theaters.* Located in cities such as Houston, Texas; Los Angeles; Louisville, Kentucky (Figure 16.4); Minneapolis; New Haven; San Francisco; Seattle; and Washington, D.C., these theaters have developed superior acting companies and are raising American theatrical standards with high-quality presentations of revivals and the classics. However, some are also sources of new, exciting productions. Regional theaters often cooperate with one another, thereby sharing the costs and risks involved in staging new plays and expanding the opportunities for a new work to be refined and seen. The best of these works are being adopted for production in commerical theaters on Broadway with increasing frequency and some become major successes. The latter are often exported to other nations and occasionally are incorporated into the repertoires of touring companies that play in commercial theaters, civic centers, and college auditoriums in communities throughout the country.

Regional theaters are, therefore, contributing to the overall growth and vitality of theater not only in their own particular localities but also elsewhere in the United

States and abroad. As a group, they already occupy equal rank with the theaters of Broadway and, to a large extent, are supplanting Broadway as the major force in developing new directions in American theater arts. Indeed, these non-profit companies have long outgrown their original role of cultural experience-providers for hinterlands residents. Instead, regional theater now functions as if it were America's national theater by supplying the nation with a steady flow of new plays, actors, directors, and designers.

The New York Public Theater. The New York Shakespeare Festival's Public Theater has been selected as an example of a non-profit resident theater because it is well known and shares many of the problems faced by similar theaters everywhere. It is a complex consisting of a cabaret and several small theaters under one roof. Often, as many as seven different productions are in performance or in some state of preparation at the same time. These include everything from workshops to large-scale productions like *A Chorus Line*. However, the theater is more than just a facil-

ity for the staging of plays. It is also an attractive place to meet, drink, eat, buy a book, and enjoy miscellaneous musical offerings. A number of reduced-price tickets are always available to facilitate attendance by the less affluent. The theater has a total of 700 employees, making it the largest American acting company.

The Public Theater was started in 1954 by a group of actors who wanted to make classic plays available to the public free of charge. Initially, they had no external financial backing and presented plays in a church. In 1956, their producer, Joseph Papp, persuaded the New York City Parks Department to let the company give free Shakespearean performances in a neglected Lower East Side amphitheater. The reviews were good and so was audience support. In 1959, the group began to perform Shakespearean plays in Central Park with the help of a $40,000 municipal grant. When the Parks Commissioner forbade the use of park facilities unless admission was charged, a theater was provided with funds contributed by a publisher and the city government (Figure 16.3).

In 1966, Papp raised $500,000 from private sources to buy the Astor Library, which is still the home of the Public Theater. The innovative rock musical *Hair* was their first major production in the new building. It was an enormous success and has since earned the Public Theater organization over $1 million. During 1973, Papp and the Public Theater were invited to present plays at the prestigious Lincoln Center. At the same time, three Public Theater productions were playing to packed houses on Broadway and the budget increased

Figure 16.4 The Actors Theatre of Louisville, Kentucky, consists of a restored and modified Victorian warehouse (insert, left) and a Greek Revival style bank (insert, right) plus a modern addition in the rear called the Pamela Brown Auditorium (above). Designated as the state theater of Kentucky, ATL currently presents a 7-play Off-Broadway Series in the smaller Victor Jory Theatre, a Festival of New American Plays, a 5-week tour of communities in Kentucky and West Virginia, and free workshops, Saturday morning Children's Theatre, and programs for senior citizens and schools. Over 225,000 persons a year see one or more performances.

to $11.3 million.

This did not assure the theater's future. In 1975, with no Public Theater company playing on Broadway, the budget fell to $6.2 million. A deficit of $1 million rapidly accumulated and the theater was in danger of closing. Just in time, another production—the musical *A Chorus Line*—became a great success first at the Public Theater and later at a Broadway commercial theater. By 1977, the budget had expanded to $30 million.

Unfortunately, such financial security can last only as long as the Public Theater is able to produce plays that appeal strongly to mass audiences, but this has never been the purpose of the institution. *A Chorus Line,* presently being staged by three separate companies, consumes a large proportion of the Public Theater's budget; at the same time, however, it subsidizes 50 percent of the Public Theater operation. Box office earnings at the Public Theater's own building pay less than 20 percent of the $4 million needed to cover basic expenses. Even with its many successes and nearly capacity audiences, the theater continues to lose heavily. Of course, many of its activities are not expected to produce revenues. Some, like the presentation of Shakespearean plays in Central Park during the summer are available to the public without charge. Many, like the experimental workshops that give artists a chance to work together, try out new material, and develop their talents happen behind the scenes and are never performed before a paying audience. Yet, these activities are vital to the survival and growth of theater arts. In spite of these cultural contributions, however, little help has come from government sources. Subsidies remain at a level equal to about 15 percent of the basic Public Theater budget.

Community and School Theater. A number of groups besides resident theaters provide theatrical opportunities for people in smaller communities or offer experiences not available at other theaters. Some 2600 community theater organizations currently exist in the United States and usually concentrate on better known classical dramas and recent commercial theater successes. Local residents are often responsible for the formation of such groups, which provide some of the best opportunities for nonprofessionals to become directly involved in theater productions. Few of these organizations can afford their own theaters; most make use of auditoriums in schools, churches, and civic and cultural centers.

An estimated 200 experimental acting companies perform offbeat and avant-garde plays in lofts, basements, store fronts, and converted industrial buildings as well as conventional theaters. These groups usually exist away from the theatrical mainstream (in New York City, they are referred to as *Off Off Broadway*) and operate on low budgets that make it a challenge just to survive. But these circumstances also provide a special kind of freedom that permits participants to take chances and explore new forms of theater. At the same time, low ticket prices allow audiences to take chances in search of new and stimulating cultural experiences.

In smaller communities without community theaters of their own, outreach programs give residents an opportunity to attend a play. These programs are often a part of the activities of resident theater organizations. For example, the Meadow Brook Theater Company, located on the campus of Michigan's Oakland University, has been conducting an outreach program for several years. During a typical tour, this resident theater company gave 20 performances before 6000 persons in 16 small communities from southern Michigan to the Upper Peninsula. This particular tour was made possible, in part, by state government grants of some $164,000.

Auditoriums in schools are often used to stage the productions of community theater organizations. They are also used by groups of high school students who produce plays either as part of the school curriculum or as participants in afterschool drama clubs. There are about 30,000 of these groups in the United States. Productions are often well attended by the general public, but their greatest value lies in the opportunities provided for the development of skills on the part of the performers and stage crews and the appreciation of theater such presentations can foster in student audiences. At the college level, use of theater resources by nonstudents is often minimal. However, colleges with superior auditorium facilities are frequently the largest suppliers of theater arts opportunities in their areas. Over 1600 American colleges now have theater arts instructional programs and most of the resultant student productions are open to the general public.

In response to growing enrollments in performing arts courses and increased interest by students and the public in attending cultural presentations, many colleges are building modern facilities designed expressly for presentations by drama, music, and dance departments. Others make use of multipurpose structures like gymnasiums, dormitory kivas, and large lecture halls. Some presentations are held outdoors at sites equipped with portable stage, sound, lighting, and seating facilities. In addition to student and faculty presentations, many colleges provide exposure to a broad spectrum of cultural experiences by sponsoring programs featuring touring professional performing arts companies, renowned guest artists and lecturers, and by presenting film festivals and travelogues. Attendance is sometimes restricted to students, but frequently the presentations are also available to the general public for relatively low admission fees.

COMMERCIAL THEATER

Although a high proportion of America's finest theatrical productions now originate at nonprofit theaters, the outstanding ones are eventually featured at one of Broadway's 36 commercial theaters. Some exceptional plays and musicals are still being created on and for Broadway, but Broadway producers cannot afford to take the chances they once did since new productions now cost as much as $1 million to develop. However, to most theatergoers, Broadway still means the biggest, most lavish productions played by the most experienced performers and staged by the nation's leading directors and producers. So, despite escalating ticket prices, Broadway theater remains New York City's premier attraction

with a total of 9.8 million paid admissions during the 1978–1979 season.

Most of the other major American cities also contain commercial theaters. The largest of these sometimes initiate shows of their own or are chosen as the location for pre-Broadway tryouts of new productions. Generally, however, these theaters feature major touring theatrical productions, thereby providing local residents with opportunities to see Broadway-type shows. The organizations responsible for the planning, casting, and transporting of these shows are usually committed to providing performances that are as similar to the original production as possible. A recent road show of *The Wiz*, for instance, involved 65 persons, three buses, and two large tractor-trailers at a daily operating cost of $17,500. In addition, there are over 500 dinner theaters that present Broadway-type shows and revues. Sometimes, especially in smaller communities, these are the only sources of professional theater experiences (see Chapter 12).

Commercial summer theater used to be a few weeks of stock musicals performed in the open air or canvas tents in city parks or at major resorts in less urbanized areas. Now, it often involves highly professional productions of Shakespearean plays, American classics, recent Broadway shows, Las-Vegas-type musical productions, or original dramas and revues, staged in heated and air-conditioned permanent structures. Where populations are sufficient to support them, some of these theaters operate year round although the nature of the stage offerings may change with the seasons. This does not mean that

the concept of summer theater has disappeared. About 250 small playhouses, located primarily in popular tourist-destination areas, continue to operate only during the height of the tourist season. Mostly they present frivolous comedies and musicals starring well-known stage personalities. Such productions are considered *safe plays* that are, therefore, guaranteed to attract overflow audiences. This is not necessarily the type of material the operators of these theaters would like to present, but many face such serious financial problems that they have no choice.

Finally, discussion of the American theater resources would be incomplete without mention of the 30 commercial theaters located in London's West End — the British equivalent of Broadway. Without the extensive exchanges of personnel and productions that take place between Broadway and the West End, neither the New York nor the London stage would be as powerful a creative force. In fact, neither would probably survive long in its present form without the inspiration, competition, and contributions of the other. But London's theaters also function directly as cultural resources for Americans.

Foreign visitors are occupying an increasing proportion of theater seats in London; by 1977, over half of London's theatergoers were from abroad. Of these foreign patrons, more than 50 percent — or at least one-quarter of the total audience — were from the United States. It is now fairly common for Americans to make short trips expressly to enjoy one or more productions at London theaters. There are several reasons for doing so. Tickets are generally cheaper and more easily obtainable than on Broadway. Staggered performance schedules allow visitors to attend more than one production on a given day. And, most important, major differences in acting styles, types of shows, and a special emphasis on professionalism make attending a West End production a high point in the life of those who appreciate good theater.

SYMPHONY ORCHESTRAS

Substantial growth in American orchestral music both in terms of audience support and in the number of individuals involved in its presentation has also occurred in recent years. There are now over 1500 American symphonic groups providing regularly scheduled performances; these include 144 full-fledged orchestras, of which 31 are major professional symphony orchestras. Annual attendance at concerts by these groups exceeds 25 million people.

Orchestras are no longer found only in the half-dozen largest cities where major high-quality ensembles have existed for many years. Seattle, for example, with a population of 500,000, has constructed a cultural center to house a symphony orchestra, opera company, art museum, and repertory theater company. Recently, the voters approved a $19 million bond issue to build a second theater, another art center, and a rehearsal wing for the opera and the symphony orchestra. In spite of the many cultural experiences available, the Seattle Symphony Orchestra more than holds its own, regularly enjoying sold-out seasons.

Many orchestras share auditoriums and rehearsal facilities with other performing arts groups, but a substantial number now use facilities built expressly for their needs. The Denver Symphony Orchestra is a good example. For 44 years, it survived and showed moderate growth in spite of performing in a hall with terrible acoustics. Today, the orchestra has a new $13 million, 2700-seat concert hall with 360-degree seating around the orchestra (Figure 16.5). The first such structure in the United States (Mexico City and Berlin have similar facilities), Boettcher Concert Hall was financed with both municipal bonds and private funds.

OPERA COMPANIES

Until recently, opera was considered by many Americans to be an exclusive art form patronized mostly by intellectuals and wealthy socialites. In the last decade, however, people from all backgrounds began to realize that opera can be a thoroughly enjoyable, exhilarating form of entertainment. As a result, attendance rose from 2 mi lion in 1950 to more than 10 million in 1979. There are now over 900 American organizations that produce operas, presenting a total of more than 7000 performances each year. Of these, 70 have annual budgets of $100,000 or more and are considered major opera companies. Together, these 70 organizations spend some $80 million each season. Now, it is no longer necessary for opera enthusiasts to travel to New York City when they wish to see a first-rate production. Chicago and San Francisco both support international opera houses and there is important operatic activity in smaller metropolitan centers such as Boston, Seattle, and Houston, Texas.

Through the efforts of local opera guilds and because of the in-

Figure 16.5 The Denver Symphony Orchestra performing in the $13 million Boettcher Concert Hall. The 360-degree seating arrangement provides a more intimate acoustical and visual experience for larger numbers of people.

creased availability of suitable facilities, many communities host full-scale productions by major touring companies. In 1978, for instance, the Metropolitan Opera (the Met) included Philadelphia on its spring tour for the first time in 10 years because the city had acquired a theater that was both acoustically satisfactory and large enough to make an engagement financially feasible.

Performances were staged at the Robin Hood Dell West amphitheater, which was built as a summer home for the Philadelphia Orchestra but designed to accommodate opera and ballet as well. There, the Met drew the largest audience ever to attend one of its out-of-town performances—a total of 15,000 people. Because of the nature of the facility, 5000 people paying $10 and $20 per seat were able to see the opera from the covered portion of the theater almost as they might have done in an opera house. Benches were set up outside this area to accommodate another 5000 people and 5000 more watched from the sloping lawn on blankets or chairs brought from home. None of these 10,000 people were charged admission. If properly designed, such amphitheaters can, therefore, serve two purposes. Quality cultural experiences can be provided for those who can afford them. But it is also possible to expose large numbers of people to performances they might otherwise miss because they are either unable or insufficiently motivated to pay for a ticket.

Opera is the most expensive of the performing arts. Each new production requires at least $200,000 to develop and the fixed costs are usually higher than the box-office receipts. For example, the Met, although it currently plays to audiences averaging 95 percent capacity, spends some $85,000 a night and only receives ticket revenues of $70,000. There is no easy solution to this problem. Ticket prices will no doubt continue to rise but at the present rate of up to $50 a seat, there is already concern that they have reached their limit. If prices go still higher, attendance may drop as fewer people feel they can afford to attend. The opera cannot readily increase productivity; performances already take place before sell-out audiences and opera can scarcely be performed properly in less time, with fewer artists, or without sets or costumes.

In the case of the Met, government subsidies totaling $2 million are received from the National Endowment for the Arts, the New York State Arts Council, and New York City. This does not begin to cover the $40 million budget or even the operating deficits of $12 million or more that have plagued the Met in recent years. However, increased support from individuals, corporations, and foundations have permitted the Met to meet its expenses during the last three seasons. Whether private sources will continue to contribute at such levels (around $10 million a year) remains to be seen. Meanwhile, many of the other opera companies are reducing their staffs and numbers of productions as their financial situations deteriorate.

DANCE COMPANIES

When the New York City Ballet first performed in Washington, D.C., 30 years ago, just 5 people were in the audience. Now the company attracts a capacity crowd of 2300 people every night for three weeks during its annual appearance at the Kennedy Center for the Performing Arts. Other American dance companies are enjoying similar success; attendance at performances of the approximately 125 ballet companies and 725 other dance companies now exceeds 20 million, making dance the fastest growing of all the performing arts. One of the classic ballets, the *Nutcracker,* has become especially popular; more than 200 performances are presented each Christmas season.

There are several reasons for the increased popularity of dance. These include the development of ballets with American themes and modern dance works, the emergence of dance superstars, a growing interest in fitness with an accompanying admiration for the athletic ability and movement personified by dancers, and the more effective promotion of dance as an attractive art form. One additional reason that is often overlooked is the availability of more and better facilities. Dancers require well-built stages; prior to the late 1970s, there were not enough of them to make major dance company tours financially feasible or to encourage the establishment of more than a few resident dance troupes.

As recently as 1969, 70 percent of the nation's dance activity took place in the New York City area. Just six years later, following the building of many suitable stages, fully 70 percent of the dance audience were attending performances elsewhere in the country. This occurred despite the fact that there was a marked increase in dance activity in New York City during the period. This does not mean, however, that dance is flourishing financially; most ballet companies earn little more than 50 percent of their operating expenses. Like other art forms, dance must rely heavily on private sponsors and government grants to survive.

CULTURAL CENTERS

The majority of U.S. dance activity takes place in the nation's *cultural centers*. This type of facility is a fairly recent innovation that evolved after World War II. Cultural centers usually consist of a cluster of two or more stages under one roof or in a number of closely connected buildings and contain both participant and audience facilities for all the performing arts. As the advantages of this type of facility became apparent, the idea quickly spread. More than 100 cultural centers were built between 1960 and 1970 at a total cost of over $1 billion in government funds and private donations. There seems little doubt that within the next decade, every sizable community will either have a cultural center in operation or be actively engaged in the planning or fund-raising stages.

One such community is San Francisco. Over $20 million in private donations and $9 million in municipal funds were recently spent on a new 3000-seat Performing Arts Center and the expansion or renovation of nearby existing facilities. The complex makes it possible to stage over 200 major performances a year, providing much needed additional space for audiences, touring groups, and local companies. No longer do the San Francisco opera, symphony orchestra, and ballet companies share one facility, a situation that previously

hampered rehearsals, limited the number of performances, and prevented all three organizations from growing in size and quality. Completion of the center is enabling San Francisco to once again assume leadership in the performing arts. Traditionally recognized as the West's cultural center, its position was being challenged by Los Angeles and Seattle, both of which had developed fine cultural centers.

Lincoln Center. One of the first cultural centers to be constructed was New York City's $160 million Lincoln Center for the Performing Arts. Opened in 1962, the center consists of six major buildings containing 13 auditoriums with a total seating capacity of 12,000. Although beset with financial difficulties and criticized both for its architectural design and program choices (as are many such centers), it has brought a wide variety of cultural experiences to New York residents and visitors. The center now houses the Metropolitan Opera, the New York City Opera, the New York City Ballet, and the New York Philharmonic. Its programs include: operas; dance productions; symphony concerts; new plays, classic plays, and revivals; special appearances by some of the world's most talented performing artists; and an 18-day summer series of free outdoor concerts, plays, and special events. Each year, a special training program helps some 400 teachers from public schools in the three-state area to develop appreciation courses in the arts. In addition, performers annually stage hundreds of presentations in the 87 participating schools before about 30,000 children, many of whom

have never experienced live performances of ballet, opera, or plays.

Kennedy Center. Another cultural center that has received criticism as well as praise, is the John F. Kennedy Center for the Performing Arts in Washington, D.C., (Figure 16.1). It was originally envisioned as a major arts facility that would be constructed on federal lands, financed primarily by private donation, and maintained with revenues from ticket sales. The intention was for the center to function as a viable, privately operated enterprise requiring little or no support from public funds. However, after President John F. Kennedy was assassinated, the U.S. Congress gave the center his name along with the mandate to become a ''living memorial.'' This was done without fully considering either the financial or administrative implications of such a decision.

Built at a cost of $78 million, $53 million of which came from federal grants or loans, the facility has been continually beset with problems. After years of contending with major leaks in the roof and structural deterioration, Congress appropriated $4.5 million in 1977 to pay for extensive repairs. By this time, the center had accumulated a $1 million deficit in its operating budget and had failed to set aside any funds to pay the interest on the construction bonds held by the U.S. Treasury. It had not even been able to pay its full share of routine maintenance costs so that the National Park Service (which is responsible for presidential memorials) had gradually assumed a larger share of this burden ($4.2 million in 1980).

The inadequacy of Kennedy Center revenues cannot be attributed to a failure to seek private funds. Sponsors have been actively sought and a large part of the costs ($2.5 million in 1979) of the presentations are underwritten by corporate, foundation, or individual donations. Nor can the financial crisis be blamed on a lack of public interest. On the contrary, over 2 million patrons a year fill 85 percent of the available seats—the best attendance record of any American performing arts center. The problem is that performing arts complexes—especially such grandiose edifices as the Kennedy Center—cannot become self-sufficient because of the extremely high and continually escalating costs of operation. Virtually all major performing arts centers in other countries are heavily subsidized.

Irrespective of how the Kennedy Center is financed, it has proved to be a major recreation resource. In 1976, 6.3 million people visited the complex just to see the art works donated by over 34 foreign governments or to take the theater and roof-top sightseeing tours; only the Smithsonian's Air and Space Museum draws more visitors. On nights when its four halls are sold out—a frequent occurrence—nearly 7000 people enter the complex to enjoy theater, opera, dance, or concert presentations. Since its opening in 1971, attendance at performances for which admission was charged has exceeded 10 million. At about 900 of these presentations each year, 15 percent of the seats are available at half-price to students, senior citizens, the handicapped, and low-income groups. In addition, an average of 1500 free events a year have been presented; these are heavily attended by residents as

well as tourists.

The Kennedy Center has also had a significant effect on Washington, transforming it into a center of influence that will greatly affect the future of American performing arts. It has sponsored numerous music and dance festivals, hosted the annual American College Theater Festival, encouraged a new generation of American playwrights, served as a showcase for the best of American ballet and motion pictures, and imported some of the finest foreign performing arts companies. Dozens of plays, concerts, and musicals have originated at the center and then diffused across the nation. It has established a performing arts library, a workshop for original musicals, a resident theater company, and a summer opera company. A national conservatory of music, dance, and drama is planned for the future. This wide variety of programs is offered in the belief that the center's mission is to create opportunities for a diversity of American artists and to promote presentations of a wide range of the performing arts in all regions of the nation.

Wolf Trap Farm Park. Although not a year-round cultural complex like those just described, Wolf Trap Farm Park for the Performing Arts warrants special mention because of its national significance. Operated as part of the national park system, this facility is located on a 40-hectare (100-acre) tract of rolling land in the foothills of the Blue Ridge Mountains, 24 kilometers (15 miles) west of Washington, D.C. The park's main feature is the Filene Center, an open-sided amphitheater that can accommodate almost any type of produc-

tion on its 30-meter (100-foot) wide by 20-meter (64-foot) deep stage. It seats 3500 people under cover and another 3000 on the surrounding lawn.

During a 12-week summer season, the center offers the National Folk Festival, the International Children's Festival, and a number of famous national and international artists performing programs of classical music, opera, ballet, modern dance, and many kinds of folk, jazz, and popular music. A diversity of other activities take place on the grounds, including workshops, lectures, band concerts, free programs for children, and numerous informal performances by a wide range of artists. Concession stands, a tent where buffet dinners and box lunches can be obtained, and numerous picnic tables encourage people to come early and enjoy a meal in the park. By providing such a varied program, Wolf Trap Farm Park attracts individuals from every walk of life and functions as a family recreation park as well as a performing arts center.

OTHER NONPROFIT FACILITIES

Many other types of nonprofit and public facilities are used for the arts besides major cultural complexes. Park band shells and amphitheaters are used for summer performing arts presentations. One of the best known of these structures is the Hatch Memorial Shell located in a riverside park in Boston (Figure 2.5). In July, members of the Boston Pops and the Boston Symphony join in presenting free, open-air concerts at the Hatch Shell before large audiences seated informally on the grass. Since it began in 1928, this traditional program has provided thousands of hours of pleasure for Boston residents and visitors.

Auditoriums, concert halls, and town halls provide stages for a wide variety of cultural presentations. Some, like Carnegie Hall (which was originally operated by a private company but is now owned by the City of New York) are venerable, prestigious institutions whose fine acoustics make them ideal for presentations by soloists and small ensembles. Many civic, convention, and community centers serve as multipurpose facilities that provide space for meetings, discussions, workshops, lectures, and performing arts presentations that appeal to smaller audiences. In addition, such centers often contain auditoriums or gymnasiums that are used for performances by local groups and for commercially sponsored plays and concerts.

Ethnic centers also often offer programs designed to promote the dance, music, and arts and crafts of a particular cultural group. Such facilities frequently serve as learning centers for young people who are interested in discovering and taking part in aspects of their unique cultural heritage. They also function as social centers for individuals and family groups. Some act as visitor centers where other community residents or tourists may go to learn about an unfamiliar culture.

OTHER COMMERCIAL FACILITIES

In addition to the theaters, coffeehouses, cabarets, and nightclubs that may regularly or occasionally schedule concerts, there are a variety of privately owned facilities built expressly for commercial performing arts performances. Some are music halls and pavilions that attempt to appeal to all tastes and ages and offer a diversity of programming, ranging from children's theater and puppet shows to classical music or dance performances, rock or pop music concerts, and shows featuring well-known variety acts or comedians. A number operate only during the summer, presenting a series of programs that appeal strongly to particular segments of the population. In this way, they can depend on the continued support of a substantial number of subscribers who buy season tickets year after year. Typical of these establishments are the 10 outdoor music theaters such as the Greek Theater (near Los Angeles) and Pine Knob (near Detroit) that are operated by the Nederlander family. Over 100 concerts that feature well-known music acts of special appeal to young adults are held at each of these complexes during the summer months. At Pine Knob, a huge stage is the focal point for a 5800-seat open-air pavilion bordered by a lawn-covered artificial hill. The lawn area, serviced by a good sound system, can accommodate another 4500 people who pay about 25 percent less than those in the pavilion. This particular Nederlander complex is apparently filling a local need for big-name entertainment in an informal setting. The renewal rate for season tickets is 94 percent, almost all of the concerts attract sell-out crowds, and attendance totaled 4.5 million during its first five years of operation.

Some commercial music halls are unique facilities used exclusively by one particular group or for one type of music. Preservation Hall in New Orleans, for example, was originally an art gallery where jazz enthusiasts assembled to hold informal jam sessions when the gallery was closed. Eventually, the art dealer moved and the musicians became the sole proprietors. The *rehearsals,* as they were called, attracted visitors and Preservation Hall became well known as the place to hear the best traditional jazz. Today, potential customers line up well in advance of the 8:00 P.M. nightly opening. But it is the music and not the hall that attracts the sell-out crowds. The building remains unchanged; it is a run-down, dingy hall that is neither air-conditioned nor equipped to serve food or drink. Early arrivals may sit on backless benches, but most customers have to stand or sit on the floor. The musicians play just a few feet from the audience without benefit of special stages, lighting, or sound systems.

Perhaps the single most famous institution of this kind is Nashville's shrine to country music, the Grand Ole Opry. Actually, the "Grand Ole Opry" is a radio program—America's oldest continuous radio show—and now one of the nation's biggest live entertainment spectacles. It started quite by accident in 1925. A radio announcer introduced his country music show that followed a classical music program with the words, "For the past hour, you've listened to Grand Opera, now you're going to hear some grand ole opry." The name stuck, the program grew in popularity, and local fans began dropping into the studio to see what their favorite performers looked like. The show was moved several times to bigger and better facilities to accommodate expanding audiences. Finally, in 1943, it moved into the 3000-seat Ryman Auditorium.

However, demand for seats continued to grow so the Grand Ole Opry took up residence in the new, specially designed, $15 million, 4400-seat Opry House in 1974. It is part of a major entertainment complex that includes a TV production center, a 600-room hotel, and a $37 million theme park called Opryland. Today, when the "Grand Ole Opry" is broadcast live to hundreds of thousands of homes in 38 states and Canada, turn-away crowds gather to watch the program. Almost 1 million people attend the Opry broadcasts every year. Nor have devoted fans forgotten the original 85-year-old home of Opry. Open to the public and carefully preserved, the Ryman Auditorium is visited by thousands who still want to see where the original country music stars once performed.

BROADCAST, RECORDING, AND FILM RESOURCES

Currently, the most significant cultural resources in terms of total impact on society are the broadcast, recording, and film resources. Their influence is great because of the variety of opportunities they provide, their unmatched accessibility, and the large amount of time that people devote to them (Figure 8.12). Listening to radio broadcasts, hearing musical performances on records or tapes, watching television programs, and going to the movies have become primary activities in the recreation lifestyles of people all over the world. These activities often supplant the reading of printed materials or attendance at live concerts and plays. Such activities are of tremendous importance because they can affect the way people think and act. As far as recreation is concerned, exposure to these resources can influence people's decisions concerning the use of their free time and alter their attitudes toward other recreation resources, including the cultural resources described elsewhere in this chapter.

RADIO BROADCASTING SYSTEMS

Radio broadcasting is a comparatively recent invention. It began in the United States in 1920 when the first commercial radio station was developed in Pittsburgh. Within two years, 564 broadcasting stations had been licensed, broadcasting was recognized as an advertising medium, and the sale of advertising was adopted as the primary means of financial support. Eventually, four commercial radio networks emerged, but their influence was to prove greatest in the area of television.

Today, these corporations are no longer dominant in radio although they continue to own a few stations and maintain small systems of affiliated stations. The majority of America's more than 9000 radio stations are privately owned and operated for the most part without government interference. Of these, 51 percent are still amplitude modulation (AM) stations, but the proportion of frequency modulation (FM) stations is increasing rapidly, permitting more listeners with FM receivers to enjoy a clearer, static-free sound. Most stations adopt a distinctive format (one particular kind of popular music, classical music, or news). Some radio stations in small towns and rural areas offer substantial amounts of news and local interest programming to attract a wide range of local listeners. Others, in larger communities, concentrate on attracting one segment of the population. Some 200 black-oriented stations, for example, broadcast programs featuring prominent black personalities and present newscasts, music, and commercials tailored to the interests of black citizens.

Noncommercial radio broadcasting is also increasing. Some stations broadcast largely educational programs and are supported by municipal or state governments, colleges, or donations from foundations and listeners. A network of some 220 of these noncommercial stations has been loosely organized under the name National Public Radio (NPR). Although currently aided by congressional appropriations amounting to some $10 million a year, these stations continue to depend heavily on nongovernment support. National Public Radio is still relatively limited in scope; it covered only 60 percent of the country and was able to reach only one-third of all potential listeners in 1979.

Over 450 million radio sets were in use in the United States in 1979; 166 million adults were said to listen regularly for an average of three hours a day. Although, to most people, radios are primarily a handy source of light entertainment, sports broadcasts, and basic information, they are also valuable cultural resources. Much of the programming on the NPR stations consists of classical music, opera, folk music, and a variety of literary and dramatic presentations that appeal to a small but appreciative audience of about 5 million people. One series, "Masterpiece Radio Theater," offers dramatizations of classics; like its television counterpart, this program is made possible by a grant from the Mobil Corporation.

Before the advent of television, commercial radio stations broadcast many more documentaries and dramas than they do now, but this is beginning to change again. In 1973, the Columbia Broadcasting System (CBS) radio network introduced "Mystery Theater," a nightly series of one-hour dramatic presentations; in 1979, it added a second series, "Sears Radio Theater," which consisted of original plays featuring well-known actors. Nevertheless, music has always been the principal program offering of radio. Through radio, people are able to keep up with trends in contemporary music; some also become interested in learning to sing or play a musical instrument. Listeners are also exposed to unfamiliar forms of music and, in the process, some acquire a liking for it. This is especially true of opera (Figure 16.2) and other types of classical music. Now that high quality FM broadcasting has been developed, radio audiences' appetites for such music seem to be growing more rapidly.

No major nation is now without radio broadcasting in some form. Altogether, there are some 820 million radio sets in use around the world, served by over 15,500 stations. In the United States and Latin America, most stations are under private management. In India and most Communist nations, broadcasting systems are state owned and operated. Other systems such as the British Broadcasting Corporation (BBC) and the Canadian Broadcasting Corporation (CBC) enjoy substantial independent powers but operate as public authorities, deriving most of their income from parliamentary grants (CBC) or from license fees on all radio receivers (BBC). Less often, systems operate as a partnership between private interests and public authorities (as in Switzerland, Italy, and Sweden, for example). These systems also receive much of their financial support from radio-receiver license fees.

One broadcasting system that merits attention because of its major cultural role is the West German system. Private radio and television broadcasting is prohibited by the Constitution. Neither is there an extensive federal network of stations, only a single station broadcasts nationwide. Instead, each state operates stations of its own that feature distinctive programming. This approach encourages the continuance of vigorous regional cultures. Although functioning independently of each other, these state radio stations can, when desired, be linked together for national programs.

Major symphony orchestras are maintained by seven of the nine West German state stations. The best known and most prestigious are the Bavarian Radio Orchestra in Munich and the North German Radio Symphony in Hamburg. Besides presenting numerous concerts that are broadcast statewide and sometimes nationwide, these orchestras regularly tour the states that they serve and occasionally perform concerts abroad. Fees collected monthly by the Federal Post Office from each listener support the stations and their orchestras.

RECORDING INDUSTRY

People raised in environments where first-class long-play record albums (LPs) and magnetic tape recordings are readily available and relatively cheap (Figure 16.6) may find it hard to realize that LPs and tapes were only introduced in 1948 and that high fidelity recordings and compact stereo equipment were not available until the early 1960s. However, in the United States, making recordings had developed into a $3 billion-a-year industry by 1978. By that time, major companies like the WEA conglomerate (Warners/Elektra/Asylum labels) and the CBS Records Group (Columbia and Epic labels)—which together account for 40 percent of all the discs sold in the United States—along with 70 independent pressing facilities were producing more than 4 million LPs a day. And this was not nearly enough to keep up with the demand.

Although classical music was originally the nucleus around which the recording industry evolved, it now constitutes less than 5 percent of the total recordings being manufactured. However, this does not mean that there are fewer people purchasing such recordings; rather, it is a matter of so many others buying recordings of contemporary works. The range of materials now available is vast. Through recordings, people are able to enjoy all the treasures of Western music, explore non-Western musical forms, listen to historic performances, and explore the early beginnings of folk music, jazz, and other types of musical expression. They can also listen to plays and poetry recorded by some of the world's finest actors or, in some cases, by the authors themselves.

Figure 16.6 Record stores like this one that play selections from recent releases and allow customers to browse through hundreds of long-play record albums are found in almost every sizable North American community. The invention of the phonograph has made it possible for people of even modest means to have access to music of their choosing whenever and as often as they wish.

People with visual impairments are able to listen to recordings of books and magazines. A growing number of people are purchasing or renting tape-recorded readings of dramatizations of best-sellers or classics so that they can listen to them on portable recorders at the beach, while traveling on public transportation, or on their own automobile tape decks as they commute or drive long distances to reach vacation destinations.

Many of the recordings sold today are contemporary music that is unlikely to be remembered long. Nevertheless, the increased accessibility provided by recordings to music of all kinds has had a tremendous impact. Recordings no longer merely mirror the musical scene; they now mold it, affecting the musical tastes and extending the musical horizons of millions of people. Recorded music has in-

creased people's interest in going to concerts. It has also raised the expectations of concert audiences because music enthusiasts are now accustomed to hearing the finest performances reproduced under ideal acoustical conditions when they listen to their own high-fidelity radios and record players.

TELEVISION BROADCASTING SYSTEMS

Although technically feasible since 1931, television developed slowly until the end of World War II. Then the broadcasting of television programs started in earnest in Great Britain and the United States. Many other countries followed suit in the early 1950s. By 1959, 52 nations had established television systems and were broadcasting programs to some 75 million receivers, two-thirds of which were in American

homes. By 1979, television had spread to 123 of the world's 156 nations and there were almost 400 million television sets in use, 146 million of which were in the United States. Color sets were available in almost 80 percent of the American homes and another 19 percent were said to contain at least one black-and-white television set in working order. Other nations with substantial numbers of television sets in 1979 included: the Soviet Union (75 million), Japan (26.4 million), West Germany (20.5 million), Great Britain (18 million), Brazil (15 million), France (14.7 million), Italy (12.6 million), Canada (10.2 million), Spain (7.4 million), Poland (7 million), Mexico (5.5 million), East Germany (5.2 million), the Netherlands (5.1 million), Australia (5 million), and Argentina (4.5 million).[1] In all, about 6700 television stations were in operation, more than 1000 of which were in the United States.

Commercial Television. Since radio and television stations are both part of a nation's broadcasting system, their ownership, operation, and relationship to government is usually similar. In the United States, the majority of television stations are commercial ventures operating with only minimal control and entirely without government financial support. Unlike radio, however, 88 percent of the more than 720 commercial television stations are either owned by, or closely affiliated with, one of the three major broadcasting networks. Many of the daytime and almost all of the eve-

[1] Rufus W. Crater, "Television and Radio," in *1980 Britannica Book of the Year.* Encyclopaedia Britannica, Inc., Chicago, 1980.

ning programs broadcast by these stations are supplied by one of these commercial networks, which, therefore, control most of what the public sees on television.

The proportion of time devoted by American commercial stations to various types of programs during the 1978–1979 season's prime-time hours were: general and family dramas 30.3 percent; motion pictures 21.2 percent; situation comedies 20.5 percent; action, adventure, and mystery shows 18.2 percent; news 2.3 percent; sports 3 percent; and special features 4.4 percent. Although some of these programs were high-quality productions that were largely educational or cultural in content, the majority were light entertainment whose primary function was to attract the largest possible number of viewers.

The commercial networks in the United States are convinced that the majority of people wish to watch these kinds of programs and, generally, this seems to be true. Vast audiences regularly tune in to these shows and, with a few exceptions, ignore programs that are more intellectually demanding. It has been suggested, however, that the majority of viewers do not select their programs carefully nor do they necessarily watch programs that they like. Rather, they choose television viewing as an activity and then watch whatever program is easiest to tune into or is the least objectionable during that time period.

However, the networks may be underestimating the tastes of their audience. On several occasions in recent years, large numbers of people have passed up escapist entertainment to watch serious programs like "Roots" and "The Holocaust."

Growing numbers of viewers are criticizing shows that they feel contain inane plots, prurience, or excessive violence. And, for the first time since television became a widely adopted recreation activity, there has been a slight reduction in the total time-prime television audience. There are signs that viewers may have begun to mature and television-watching is becoming less a matter of habit and more a case of specific program selection.

If these trends continue, the networks will probably change programming policies and commercial television will become a more culturally stimulating medium. Certainly, if viewer-operated television recording equipment is purchased by sufficient numbers of people, the present network approach will no longer be viable. Prime time will lose much of its meaning because a large proportion of the viewers will record shows and see them at their convenience. Counter programming (scheduling the best programs at the same time to prevent any network from acquiring a huge audience) will no longer be effective; people will tape one special program for later viewing while watching another as it is broadcast. Large numbers of people will also be able to substitute nonnetwork materials during their viewing hours by using videotape recorders and videodisc players. (The latter replays prerecorded programs through the owner's television set but does not have the videotape recorder's capability of recording programs. However, its lack of versatility is offset by the fact that the machine and discs are much cheaper and, therefore, are likely to be accessible eventually to almost all segments of the population, much as phono-

graphs and records are now almost universally enjoyed.)

Four other sources of television programs are expected to further reduce the size of audiences for the three major American commercial networks. These are:

- Pay-cable-television systems that provide subscribers with a variety of program choices; this form of competition is a real threat since one in every five American television sets now receives some type of cable programming.
- The 85 independent television stations that are drawing larger shares of the television audience by pooling their resources and producing attractive offerings such as the novels-for-television programs.
- Special networks such as the Spanish International Network and the Black Entertainment Network that are seeking to satisfy the special viewing needs of ethnic audiences in the United States.
- The Public Broadcasting System that is increasing its audience by presenting a greater variety of costlier productions and by mounting a more aggressive promotion campaign.

With the availability of so many viewing choices, the mass audience for which the commercial networks compete so vigorously is bound to disappear. In its place will be a number of smaller but sizable audiences, each of which will be more homogeneous in interests and backgrounds. Naturally, sponsors will wish to support programs that will attract the group or groups of people most likely to be interested in buying their particular products or services. This should create a demand for more programs with appeal to the more affluent (often better educated and more discriminating) segments of the television-viewing population.

This is already happening to a limited degree and its success to date is likely to encourage more sophisticated programming in the future. For example, after NBC's April, 1980 prime-time telecast of the contemporary drama, "The Oldest Living Graduate," NBC's president Fred Silverman announced a commitment to four more first-rate live drama productions for the 1980–1981 season. "The Oldest Living Graduate" was watched by 25 million people—a relatively small but appreciable audience. Not that sports, comedies, or adventure shows are likely to disappear; there is a need for all kinds of programming and a variety will continue to be offered. However, the fact that more programs will be intelligently written, deal honestly and sensitively with controversial social issues, or be high in cultural content will mean that commercial television may become a more positive social and cultural force. Already, considerable numbers of people who feel intimidated by live presentations of an educational or cultural nature or who are bored by similar offerings on public television are enjoying and relating to programs on commercial networks that contain stimulating subject matter, feature talented artists, or present cultural material and ideas with which they are unfamiliar. By making such programs available as well as palatable, commercial television is helping develop an American population that is more tolerant, better informed, and more discerning, the kind of population that is essential for the well-being of all the cultural resources.

Public Television. In contrast to most other nations, the concept

of a nationwide public television network is relatively new in the United States. The system that has developed is not like those in other nations in organization or funding. The PBS is not really a network in the sense that NBC, CBS, and ABC are networks. Rather, it is a loosely knit organization of some 260 locally controlled independent stations. Each pays dues to support a central agency that investigates, plans, and schedules programs. Naturally, PBS wishes as many stations as possible to use these programs and broadcast them at the same time, just like the commercial networks, but such decisions are made by each individual station based on priorities and perceptions of local audience preferences. The PBS obtains programs from many sources; many are produced by member stations and a high proportion are imports made originally by foreign companies—mostly British—for their public television networks.

The U.S. system is complicated by the presence of the Corporation for Public Broadcasting (CPB), an agency established by the Public Broadcasting Act of 1967 when Congress first decided to provide funds to assist in the development of public broadcasting. A board appointed by the President governs CPB and is responsible for distributing the appropriated funds. The PBS operates the electronic interconnection and transmits programs to member stations under a contract with CPB.

Although federal subsidies for public television now total some $100 million a year and may reach $200 million by 1983, the level of support is small compared to other nations. Grants amount to only

$0.37 per capita in contrast to more than $5 in Great Britain and over $6 in Japan. Federal aid is also meager in terms of the system's needs. It is estimated, for instance, that PBS requires at least $1 billion a year if the dream of building a first-class noncommercial television service is to be realized. In reality, PBS receives less than half of this amount or about 7 percent of the combined budgets of the commercial networks. Approximately one-quarter of its funds comes from federal grants, another one-quarter from state government subsidies, just over one-tenth from 2 million individual donors, and somewhat less than one-tenth from about 40 corporate sponsors. The remaining funds come from a variety of sources, including local governments, foundations, small businesses, and station money-making projects that include on-the-air auctions.

Public television is at a disadvantage when competing for viewers with the commercial networks because of its limited budget. Funds are desperately needed for promotional purposes. The average public television station attracts no more than 4 percent of the available audience, partly because its existence is barely visible. Money is also needed for the system's improvement and expansion; two-thirds of the stations still broadcast over UHF channels that cannot be received by many households and some areas still have no PBS programming. In fact, for one reason or another, only about 75 percent of the potential television audience is presently able to receive PBS broadcasts. Additional funds are also essential if more sophisticated programs are to be produced in the

United States; so far, most of the prestigious shows on PBS have been imported British productions.

Nevertheless, PBS achievements have been considerable. It was responsible for developing the single biggest technological advance in television program distribution—its satellite transmitting system. This system not only reduces transmitting costs but permits four different programs to be distributed at one time, providing member stations with an unprecedented choice of programs. The PBS prime-time audience is steadily increasing; an estimated 46 million households now view PBS programs for an average of over 8 hours a month.

The PBS programs have enhanced or expanded the cultural opportunities of millions of Americans. Ballet, classical music, stage plays, award-winning movies, dramatized books, art exhibits, and opera are available to anyone with access to a television set that receives a public television station signal—whether they be rich or poor, urban or rural, semiliterate or well educated, highly mobile or housebound (Figure 16.7). Such presentations widen the cultural horizons of all who watch. There is also evidence that increased attendance at live performances—at opera and ballet in particular—is partly the outcome of people seeing and enjoying televised performances. The increased exposure to the arts that public television provides is sometimes phenomenal. Over 10 million people, for example, watched a live broadcast of the Metropolitan Opera's production of *La Bohème*. Or, looked at another way, the San Francisco Ballet's appearance on the "Dance in America" series reached an audi-

Figure 16.7 A production crew from WGBH (Boston's public television station) prepares to tape a scene for the $2.5 million four-part dramatization of Nathaniel Hawthorne's "The Scarlet Letter." This play, shown nationwide over PBS stations in 1979, was funded by the National Endowment for the Humanities, the Corporation for Public Broadcasting, Exxon, and the Mellon Foundation. WGBH, with its 400 employees and annual budget of over $25 million, is responsible for up to 25 percent of all PBS programming, including plays, documentaries, children's shows, science programs, and symphony and pops concerts.

ence that would take 34 years to equal if the group performed to capacity houses every single day.

PBS has also shown it can contribute to the development of U.S. television. By making alternative programming available during a period when commercial television programs are largely escapist enter-

tainment, it has demonstrated the existence of an audience that desires more sophisticated fare. This encourages at least a few sponsors to support commercial programs designed for smaller but more selective audiences. Public television also functions as a conscience for the commercial networks, prodding them into producing more programming of a public service or cultural nature.

COMMERCIAL FILM RESOURCES

Motion pictures and the theaters in which they are shown are important recreation resources for two main reasons. First, they are usually accessible to many people because of theater locations and relatively low prices. Second, they offer a variety of entertainment opportunities that appeal to a wide range of people. As a result, moviegoing is a frequent and favorite free-time activity for people in most of the world's nations. Of course, a high proportion of these films contain little material of lasting cultural value. But many high-quality films have been produced and have earned for the motion picture recognition as an art form on a par with the more traditional cultural resources.

Motion Picture Theaters. In the more affluent nations, where television is a widespread free-time activity, movie theater attendance has dropped considerably. For instance, an average of 80 million Americans went to the movies every week in 1946 compared to only 22 million in 1977. Some researchers predict that movie theaters will almost disappear in the United States when pay cable television becomes even more widespread, videodiscs or videotapes of old and recent movies are readily available, and more individuals are able to afford such services and equipment. Not everyone shares this opinion, however, because going to a movie theater can provide the opportunity for a much-needed outing and is often regarded as an important social occasion, especially by families and young couples. Nevertheless, movie attendance patterns are changing and, as a result, facilities and programs are changing too. Local movie theaters, once found in every urban neighborhood and small community, have largely been forced out of business by rising operating costs and declining revenues. Those that remain can seldom afford the high rentals of new films so that they struggle to survive by showing older films in ill-maintained theaters that are seldom more than half-full. Many of the very large, elaborate theaters built in the centers of major cities have also closed or been converted to other uses because of low attendance. Potential customers have become increasingly reluctant to pay high parking fees or use public transportation after dark, especially to watch movies that can be seen at theaters closer to home.

Even though the loss of the large downtown theaters and the little neighborhood, smalltown, and village movie houses is unfortunate, especially for millions of inner-city and rural people who depended on them, it has not meant the end of the American movie theater business. At least 20,000 commercial movie screens are currently in operation at 16,000 theaters in the United States, but locations have

changed substantially in response to economic pressures and the needs of potential customers. About 3500 drive-in movie theaters continue to flourish on the outskirts of communities with populations big enough to support them or in areas with substantial numbers of summer tourists. They attract an audience composed mostly of young couples on dates; parents who take their children, thereby avoiding the costs and problems of finding a babysitter; and people who find a drive-in more convenient because it eliminates the need to dress up, hunt for a parking space, and walk some distance — activities that usually accompany seeing a movie at a downtown theater.

Playground facilities are often provided at drive-ins for the pre-show entertainment of children, and extensive snack bar facilities enable customers to have a meal or supplement food items brought from home. In-car heaters are often available to encourage attendance during colder weather. At theaters featuring sound played through the car radio, films can be presented in several languages; this is of great importance in areas with large numbers of non-English speaking residents because it allows them to hear first-run movies in their own language as part of the general moviegoing population rather than having to wait until such films have completed their first runs and are distributed to foreign language neighborhood theaters. This system had its American premiere at a Los Angeles drive-in where the audience was able to tune in *Star Wars* in either English or Spanish.

Since most Americans prefer to use their own cars to reach a movie theater, the availability of ample

free parking close to a theater is a great asset. For this reason, most new theaters have been constructed at large shopping centers rather than in downtown business districts. Suburban shopping centers have been viewed as ideal locations in recent years because the majority of potential movie patrons live in suburban areas.

Many of these new developments contain not one but a number of minitheaters, each of which features a different film. These complexes are proving successful for a number of reasons. They have fewer seats, making them more economical to operate and more attractive to filmgoers who tend to feel lost in large downtown theaters if attendance is low. People also prefer having a selection of films at one location. Families often come as a group but the parents attend an adult movie in one theater and the children go to a general audience film at another. Moviegoers who detest line-ups also appreciate the opportunity to choose another film rather than return home disappointed or endure a long wait. When a film is especially popular, it may be shown in more than one of the minitheaters but at staggered times; this makes it easier for people to fit seeing the movie into their schedules.

The Films. Not all theaters show the same kinds of films. Some feature award-winning foreign films, famous silent and sound movies from earlier times, short subjects, art films, or documentaries either as regular fare or as part of special film festivals. About 780 U.S. theaters feature pornographic films, which are seen by some 2 million people a week. Foreign language films may be shown occasionally or regularly at theaters in neighborhoods containing many non-English speaking residents. A few exhibitors have even formed production companies to make films for specific groups. The owner of a chain of movie houses in Los Angeles, for example, makes and shows films that appeal strongly to a predominantly young, black, urban audience.

Most American theater owners, however, do not cater to any special interest group; instead, they try to attract as large and diversified an audience as possible. To accomplish this, they offer as full a range of the most recent American-made films as they can afford.

Until the early 1970s, the major American film companies served as the world's primary suppliers of screen entertainment, producing between 190 and 250 feature films each year. By 1971, over half their films were losing money and several firms were near bankruptcy. Since then, almost every company has undergone major managerial changes, sought financial stability through diversification, and adopted a policy of making fewer but "better" (often meaning more profitable rather than higher quality) films. In 1977, only 118 films—the fewest ever—were released, but during the same period, U.S. motion picture box office receipts reached a record $2.4 billion. A few of the recent movies like *Jaws* and *Star Wars* have had such widespread appeal that they have become special audiovisual events, drawing huge audiences over long periods of time with many people returning to see them again and again (Figure 5.10).

This new trend in filmgoer behavior is believed to be attributable to the fact that the first generation of people reared on visual forms of communication have now come of age. Their orientation is primarily toward images, but television is not able to satisfy them as adults because its small picture and mediocre sound system fails to envelop the viewer in the action. So, in large numbers, they are turning to movies like *Star Wars* to satisfy their desire for sensational, highly visual experiences. Much to the delight of the film industry, such experiences can be just as—or possibly even more—enjoyable on repeat viewings.

Blockbuster movies (the name given to films that attract large audiences) are becoming more and more common. From the early days of films until 1970, only a dozen or so movies grossed as much as $25 million. Since 1970, however, at least 25 films have produced revenues of this magnitude with a few like *Star Wars* earning over $500 million in worldwide rental fees. By gauging customer interest carefully and marketing films aggressively, producers are now able to distribute movies that more people either wish to see or are manipulated by advertising into believing they ought to see. Large promotional budgets —occasionally reaching 60 percent of production costs—are now considered essential. Although the film companies are more cautious, the tendency is to produce large-budget films. The risks are exceptionally high of course; only 1 film in 10 makes substantial profits. But then, the stakes are also very high; if the film really succeeds, the earnings can be enormous.

Although Canada and the United States continue to be an important market, fewer films are being produced with this audience as the primary target. Since other countries are now generating $600 million per year in film rentals (compared to $700 million for American and Canadian rentals), many films initiated by American studios are being given a worldwide orientation. Such films are frequently financed by backers from several countries and are sold to distributors controlling particular regions, often before the film even goes into production. They are usually action pictures involving war, disasters, monsters, or period adventures with a minimum of dialogue that will complicate translation. Casts generally include big-name stars, usually of several nationalities, to appeal to the widest possible audience and indicate a certain size and class of production to potential buyers. Unfortunately, although many of these films are not appreciated by the more sophisticated Canadian and U.S. filmgoers, they comprise a growing proportion of the available major films because of Hollywood's limited productivity.

Other Nations. Although film-making techniques, styles of presentation, and subject matter may differ considerably from one nation to another, the motion picture has evolved into an art form with worldwide appeal. Total annual attendance at movie theaters around the world exceeds 13 billion. However, people in some nations rely on films for recreation much more extensively than those living elsewhere.

Soviet citizens, for example, attended movies an average of 15.4 times in 1979. With fewer choices for evening recreation activities, films are a favorite and relatively cheap form of entertainment. They are also very accessible; with 340,000 public movie houses nationwide (one for every 750 citizens), there are few places where people are out of easy reach of a cinema. Other nations that had a per capita attendance of 10 or more visits to a movie theater in 1979 were: Brunei, Bulgaria, Cuba, Grenada, Guam, Guyana, Hong Kong, Iceland, Ireland, Lebanon, Mauritius, Singapore, and Taiwan. Americans during the same period attended movies an average of 4.8 times.[2]

In Western Europe, there is a total of 27,000 movie theaters (or one theater for every 4100 homes) selling some 1.5 billion tickets a year. The theater density varies greatly from country to country, examples are: 1 theater for each 2000 homes in Italy, 1 for each 3000 in France, and 1 for each 7300 in West Germany. In Great Britain, where 60 percent of the nation's movie theaters have closed in the last 15 years, it is 1 for each 11,700 homes. In Europe, the number of times people visit movie theaters is inversely proportional to the number of films shown on television. In Great Britain and West Germany, for instance, where over 1000 motion pictures are televised each year, people go to the movies an average of twice a year. In Italy, on the other hand, where only about 120 movies are shown annually, attendance is still nine times a year per person, the highest participation rate of any European country.

As far as the films themselves are concerned, Hollywood pictures

[2] Thomas W. Hope, "Motion Pictures," in 1980 Britannica Book of the Year. Encyclopaedia Britannica, Inc., Chicago, 1980.

— especially the blockbusters like *Star Wars* — are heavily attended although some 700 films are being produced each year by the various European film studios. Even in Italy where 220 films are made each year, American films account for 30.4 percent of all box-office revenues. Elsewhere in the world, Japan and India are important film producers, completing about 300 films a year. Film attendance on a per capital basis is 1.4 films a year in Japan and 3.8 in India. The Indian participation rate is quite low but, because of the large population, it is second only to the Soviet Union in total attendance with 2.4 billion paid admissions every year.

GOVERNMENT FILM RESOURCES

Unlike most other developed nations, government support for motion pictures has been severely limited in the United States. Until recently, it consisted primarily of the making of public relations films for the various government agencies. In 1976, however, the National Endowment for the Arts established The American Film Institute as an independent nonprofit organization in an effort to advance the state of American film and television arts. This institute preserves films; operates an advanced institute for film makers through grants and internships; publishes film books, periodicals, and reference works; supports basic research; and operates a national film repertory exhibition program.

In addition, special programs that encourage independent film makers are now being sponsored from time to time by the National Endowment for the Arts. One of

these, the Short Film Showcase program, which was started in 1977, awards a $2500 honorarium to independent makers of short films that have been judged outstanding by a panel of film directors, critics, and theater owners. In return, the film makers allow their works to be distributed free to commercial movie houses nationwide. More than 2000 theaters now take part in this program. By showing these films as part of their regular schedule of feature movies, the theater owners are providing exposure for the film makers and are developing an appreciation for a cinematic form of expression that was almost extinct in the United States.

In other developed nations, the creation of a distinctive national film industry is generally considered culturally important. As a result, national film institutes have been created in all of the Communist nations and most of the world's other countries. These institutes are either heavily or completely subsidized by the government. Such national film agencies are responsible either directly or indirectly for the production not only of educational films and documentaries but also of full-length feature films. The latter often explore or glorify certain aspects of national life, thereby providing citizens and foreign viewers alike with cultural information that could not readily be obtained in any other way. The institutes also provide artistic encouragement and economic support to the nation's writers, performing artists, and film makers.

One such institute was founded in Sweden in 1963 and has since become the driving force behind 80 percent of that country's film production. The National Swedish Film Institute is based in an ultramodern

$11 million building in Stockholm, which houses two professional studios, three theaters, and extensive film archives. Funds totaling more than $6 million are distributed annually by the institute to film projects selected on the basis of merit. Once an award is granted, the director is guaranteed full production costs. The national government presently provides $2.1 million of these funds from general revenues; the rest are raised by a 10 percent levy on cinema receipts. With this kind of support, Swedish film makers have increased in number, many have broadened their outlook, and some have begun tackling more universal themes. The rate of production has also increased; about 25 feature films are now being completed each year.

A quite different program exists in Australia where British and American movies were virtually the only films that were shown for almost 50 years. Television was also saturated with imported American programs or imitations of successful American shows. In an effort to change this situation and develop an Australian film industry, the government established both a film school and a film commission in 1975. Through this program, young people—mostly from the television industry—are obtaining the guidance and financial security that they need to develop their talents as film makers. The Australian Film Commission now distributes about $10 million a year, first advancing money to develop scripts and then providing one-half the estimated production costs of those judged to have artistic merit. Such large-scale subsidies permit film makers to enjoy a level of artistic freedom unknown to most directors. As a re-

sult, the 80 feature films produced so far are highly personal works that explore new ideas and innovative techniques. The best of these films have earned international acclaim and are being enjoyed in many other nations including the United States.

DEVELOPMENT OF ARTISTS

Of all the kinds of components that must come together to make cultural experiences available, the one that is absolutely essential is the artists themselves. Although many professional companies and arts facilities receive government funding to help them survive, this aid would be of little consequence if no skilled artists were available. Government attitudes toward talented individuals and their development vary. In many countries, especially the Communist nations, state arts schools have been established where gifted children may receive free training in the arts from an early age. If they are good enough, they may eventually earn a position in one of the specialized state-supported schools or professional organizations. Other nations encourage the development of talent through systems of scholarships and grants that enable gifted individuals to pursue programs of intensive study.

In the United States, there is a tendency for artists to develop their talents on their own, using whatever help their family or friends can provide at least until they are at a stage where their abilities are apparent. At this point, there is a limited amount of government support available in the form of grants or low-interest loans that may help

them continue their training. Some professional arts schools and college departments, many of which are partially funded by tax moneys, may also award fellowships that alleviate the high cost of advanced study. These scholarships and grants are often privately funded. Unfortunately, under such a system, many children never have an opportunity to develop their talents or fulfill their artistic potential because, at the critical stage, there is insufficient money for instruction. Adults are usually faced with the need to support themselves and continue their artistic training at the same time so that many find it too arduous and give up in despair. Even accomplished artists often find it impossible to make a living from artistic activities and have to supplement their income in other ways.

However, there is a growing appreciation of creative ability in America, and with it has come a genuine desire to help creativity develop and thrive. Privately endowed retreats are making it possible for gifted writers, artists, and composers to temporarily escape the demands of everyday life and concentrate on new works of art. Many arts centers and schools with art programs are being better funded so that they can provide the instruction and equipment needed to foster talent more successfully. Local and state arts councils as well as the National Endowment for the Arts and Humanities are at least partially supporting numerous artists as they struggle to perfect their talents and gain public recognition.

The nonprofit performing arts organizations are also supplying a growing number of opportunities for young performers, playwrights, and directors to polish their skills.

Many of these programs are joint efforts. For instance, the Arts Connection is a New York City program that finds disadvantaged children with artistic potential and gives them an opportunity to develop their talents. Open auditions are held at the public schools, and those who are chosen are bussed once or twice a week to the Alvin Ailey Dance Studio or the New York School for Circus Arts to take part in free classes in dance or acrobatics. Although the arts schools are making major contributions to this program, the Arts Connection would not be possible without the cooperation and financial backing of many other agencies, including New York City's Department of Cultural Affairs and Board of Education, the New York State Education Department, the U.S. Office of Education, and the National Endowment for the Arts. It is expected that this program, which has already reached 4000 elementary school children, will be expanded in the near future to include students in the junior high schools and to provide similar opportunities for instruction in the theater arts.

In a program reminiscent of depression-era projects, the federal government has also become involved in the encouragement of artistically gifted individuals. It recently organized a coast-to-coast mobilization of out-of-work artists by using Comprehensive Employment and Training Act (CETA) funds to provide employment on 600 arts projects for at least 10,000 actors, musicians, dancers, poets, writers, film makers, painters, teachers, and administrators at over 200 locations.

MUSEUMS AND COLLECTIONS

Museums are operated by a wide variety of public and private organizations. According to the American Association of Museums, a *public museum* is a nonprofit, permanent establishment that is open to the public, administered in the public interest, and exempt from federal and state income taxes. The association states that a public museum's purpose is the conserving, preserving, studying, interpreting, enhancing, organizing, and exhibiting to the public for its instruction and enjoyment objects and specimens of educational and cultural value. These objects include artistic, scientific (animate as well as inanimate), historical, and technological materials. Worldwide, there are currently about 24,000 establishments of this kind including over 6000 in the United States.

In addition to the public museums, there are a large number of privately owned and commercially operated museums. Most of these preserve and display materials similar to those included in public museums but, generally, they tend to feature collections limited to just one subject or area of interest.

As Table 16.1 shows, museums fall roughly into four general groupings. These, in turn, include numerous kinds of collections, containing an almost infinite variety of materials.

THE NATURE OF MUSEUMS

Although each museum is unique in some way, all share common goals. One of these—a desire to more effectively serve the needs of the casual visitor—has received special

emphasis recently and, as a result, museums are changing rapidly. Once modeled almost exclusively after Greek temples, Gothic churches, or Italian Renaissance palaces, museums are now modern, attractive structures that are less architecturally intimidating to the nonscholar. Some, like the Solomon R. Guggenheim Museum in New York City designed by Frank Lloyd Wright, with its six-story spiral descending ramp, draw visitors as much to see the structure as to view the exhibits. Unfortunately, such unconventional buildings sometimes prove more satisfactory as works of art than as museum facilities and curators find that designing effective displays is difficult.

More often, however, new structures are functional in design and are carefully planned so that they are well-suited both to their site and intended purposes. A good example is the museum constructed by the National Park Service in Dinosaur National Monument that lies astride the Utah-Colorado border (Figure 16.8). This structure, built with glass-paneled walls, encloses a section of a world-famous fossil quarry. It permits people to see the dinosaur remains as part of an on-site exhibit and, at the same time, provides shelter both to the visitors and the exposed fossils in the quarry wall.

Museum exhibits are also changing extensively. The traditional rows of dusty cases crammed with labeled objects are giving way to innovative displays that focus on interpretation and maximum visitor involvement rather than sheer volume of materials. Again, the Dinosaur National Monument is a good example. Supplementary displays help the visitor assimilate basic facts

Table 16.1 Types and Contents of Museums

Type	Examples of Kinds of Museums	Examples of Kinds of Exhibits
Art museums	Fine arts; contemporary; modern; twentieth century; decorative; folk; primitive; textile; ethnic; crafts institutes and centers	Paintings, prints; drawings; lithographs; sculptures; glass; pottery; jewelry; photographs; rare books; furniture; period rooms; rugs and tapestries
Science museums	Botanical gardens; nature centers; zoological parks; aquariums; insectariums; trailside museums; on-site museums; planetariums; observatories; museums of natural history, paleontology, science, and health; many children's museums	Live plants and animals; mineral, fossil, shell, mammal, plant, and insect specimens; reconstructions of environments; aeronautics exhibits; automated science exhibits; exhibits concerning human physiology and anatomy
History museums	Historical society museums; historic houses and sites; restored villages; preserved or reconstructed forts, structures, and vessels; national monuments, cemeteries, battlefields, and historic parks; museums of anthropology and archaeology; outdoor museums (archaeological sites)	Early newspapers; portraits; old photographs; journals; original documents; military relics; furniture; clothes; decorative objects; vehicles; toys; utensils; models of forts, ships, and battle sites; chronological presentations of the human experience in a particular geographical area; prehistoric materials.
Specialized museums	Ethnic, sports, transportation, circus, hobby, military, industrial, and maritime museums; ghost towns; some children's museums; halls of fame; presidential libraries; national archives	Collections of objects (stamps, antiques, cars, dolls, coins); sports memorabilia; maritime and military relics; scale models; presidential papers and memorabilia

about the age of dinosaurs and the species found in the quarry. Others explain the quarry's history and the purposes and techniques of paleontology. But the primary exhibit is the quarry itself. A second floor gallery gives visitors an excellent view of the bones exposed in the quarry wall and the workers chiseling around certain bones to bring them into clearer relief.

Museum programs and services are also being expanded and improved to attract wider audiences. Administrators are more conscious of the need to reach visitors effectively on a person-to-person basis and to be responsive to individual needs and interests. A naturalist

center, for example, has been opened in the Smithsonian Institution's National Museum of Natural History in Washington, D.C. The facility and its services are free and open to anyone; amateur naturalists may seek information by telephone or bring a specimen in for identification and study. To help users, the center maintains specimen collections in seven areas of natural history, a stock of equipment such as microscopes and plant presses, a comprehensive library, and an audiovisual laboratory. Classes in such fields as taxidermy and scientific illustration are conducted and a free newsletter informs subscribers of new materials and programs.

Lectures, films, demonstrations, classes, concerts, dance programs, poetry readings, children's theater, puppet shows, seasonal events, and guided tours (Figure 16.11) are some of the opportunities frequently provided by museums for the enjoyment and enrichment of visitors. Gift shops, restaurants, cafeterias, and informal rest, play, and picnic areas are commonly available at larger museums, creating a more hospitable environment and encouraging people to come more often and stay longer.

In an effort to involve still larger numbers of people, many museums have developed excellent traveling exhibitions that are sent to

Figure 16.8 **Visitors to the Quarry Visitor Center in Dinosaur National Monument can see why this cliff in northeastern Utah is considered the world's richest deposit of dinosaur fossils. So far, over 1200 fossilized bones of many kinds of dinosaurs and other reptiles have been exposed on the relatively small quarry face that forms the north wall. Watching technicians bring bones into relief develops an understanding of the techniques used to free fossils from the surrounding matrix and adds to visitor enjoyment.**

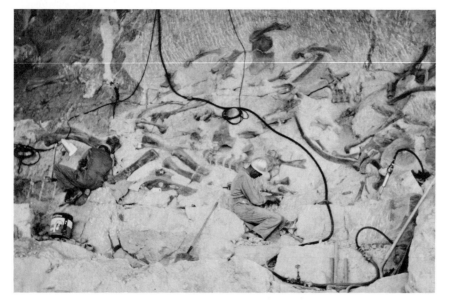

distant communities on loan or taken to suitable locations (schools, libraries, shopping malls, office building lobbies, and cultural or community centers) in the immediate area. The Smithsonian Institution Traveling Exhibition Service (SITES), for instance, sends out more than 200 exhibitions a year that are seen by over 8 million people. These exhibitions arrive ready to be displayed on panels complete with interpretative graphics. Advance promotional material is also provided.

THE ROLE OF PUBLIC MUSEUMS

Public museums are major suppliers of cultural experiences. They provide access to many specimens and materials that otherwise would only be available to a privileged few. Prior to their establishment, only the wealthy could hope to savor the beauty of a great work of art by purchasing it or enjoy the wonders of nature by traveling to different parts of the world. No doubt commercial establishments could have provided such opportunities by acquiring valuable or unusual resources and making them accessible to the general public for a fee. As explained later, some commercial museums have done so on a moderate scale in the past and are doing so today. However, the high costs associated with acquiring and protecting extensive collections and providing appropriate facilities for them make it impossible to operate museums of the caliber of many of the world's public museums as profit-making ventures. Of course, it might be feasible to do so if visitors could be charged exorbitant admission fees, but, in that case, few people would be able to afford the experience. Public museums, however, are able to offer visitors access to all that lies within, free of charge, or for a modest fee.

Public museums preserve and make vast quantities of culturally significant materials accessible to the public. Whether they are also recreation resources, however, depends on the users' attitudes. A museum trip may be involuntary and can be nonrecreational for some participants if, for instance, it is part of a school field trip or mandatory family outing. Nevertheless, the majority of users enjoy going to museums. Public museums provide some of the most satisfying recreation experiences available anywhere because they offer opportunities to socialize, explore, learn (Figure 16.16), understand, think, experiment, appreciate, enjoy, and, in some cases, feel awed, inspired, or renewed. The 1500 largest American public museums currently receive over 200 million visits a year.

PUBLIC ART MUSEUMS

Many art museums are prestigious cultural resources that have tended in the past to appeal to a relatively small, affluent, and well-educated segment of the population. As recently as 1975, a survey of summer visitors to the New York Metropolitan Museum of Art[3] revealed that 50 percent of the 85,000 people who visited it during the survey period were not residents of New York City. Half of the nonresidents were adults, 56 percent were college graduates, and 58 percent had

family incomes of $20,000 or more. Approximately 22 percent were professionals (executives, artists, writers), 22 percent were housewives (most of whom had better than high school educations), 19 percent were students, 14 percent were white-collar workers, and 11 percent were teachers; only 8 percent were retired or unemployed and just 4 percent were blue-collar workers. Of these visitors, 38 percent were from out-of-state locations and 6.5 percent came from abroad.

Such statistics make it difficult for art museums to obtain government support. Many legislators regard them as costly institutions maintained at taxpayer expense for the pleasure of a small, exclusive group of people, many of whom do not even pay taxes to the community or state that supports the facility. However, the Metropolitan Museum of Art survey was able to justify municipal and state funding (at that time making up 18 percent of the museum's total operating budget) for several reasons.

First, the sheer numbers of visitors to the museum showed it to be one of the city's most important recreation resources, outdrawing supposedly better known attractions. During the year of the survey, the museum recorded 3.5 million visitors[4] in comparison to the Empire State Building's 1.5 million, the Statue of Liberty's 1.1 million, and the United Nation's 1 million. Moreover, according to two out of three of the visitors surveyed, seeing the museum was either a very or fairly important reason for their going to

New York. Even more persuasive were the statistics regarding the visitors' economic impact. During that summer, the out-of-town museum visitors were estimated to have spent $2.1 million *each week* on restaurants, hotels, entertainment, and transportation plus an additional $1.6 million *per week* on shopping. The survey concluded that government support was well justified because of both the substantial economic benefits and the prestige the museum bestows on New York City, the State of New York, and the nation.

Today, art museums are appealing to a much broader audience than was indicated by the Metropolitan Museum of Art's 1975 study. There are many reasons for this change, but the museums themselves have much to do with it. Methods used by art institutions to broaden their appeal and become more accessible include:

• Promoting intensive use of outreach programs so that thousands of people are given an introduction to, or fresh perspective on, the field of fine arts; for instance, the National Gallery of Art in Washington, D.C., annually sends touring art shows to 4000 communities as part of its extension services.
• Remodeling to produce a less formal atmosphere; most art museums now contain cafés, gift shops, and comfortable areas in which to sit and relax.
• Creating dynamic exhibits that make art collections more meaningful and interesting to the nonscholar; many art museums are installing electronic guide-and-lecture devices and some have introduced motion stations that use color film, videotapes, and sound recordings to provide information concerning works of art and their creators.

[3] The largest museum in the Western Hemisphere, covering four city blocks and containing 7 hectares (17.5 acres) of floor space.

[4] Attendance at the Metropolitan Museum of Art has risen dramatically in recent years; 4.2 million people visited the museum in 1979.

- Adopting more aggressive promotion tactics; newspaper articles and television programs on major art shows have proven particularly effective in increasing public interest in art in general as well as in specific exhibitions.
- Presenting spectacular touring shows such as the Tutankhamen exhibition on loan from Egypt, which drew 8 million visitors to art museums in eight American and Canadian cities between 1976 and 1979.

Touring exhibits have proved to be an ideal way to reach individuals who have previously been disinterested in museums of any kind. For instance, over 25 percent of the visitors to the Tutankhamen exhibit reported that it was their first museum experience.

Of course, only a small proportion of these new participants become regular museumgoers, but many gain an appreciation for museums that results in a changed attitude toward public funding of these institutions. Even those who do not attend a special exhibition often develop an increased appreciation of a museum from the publicity surrounding such events and take pride in living in a community where such cultural opportunities exist. Conversely, people who live in areas lacking facilities that make these opportunities possible are often motivated by such publicity to work for the expansion or creation of local museums.

Like public libraries in the late nineteenth century, art museums are now regarded as symbols of a progressive community. As a result, since 1950, over half a billion dollars has been spent in the United States on the construction of new art museums or the enlargement of existing ones. Of course, many of these facilities are quite small.

About 44 percent of the approximately 1000 American public art museums have annual budgets of under $50,000. However, 5 percent now spend $1 million or more each year, and governments at all levels are being asked to provide better financial support.

Art Museums Elsewhere.
The art museums of Europe were rich storehouses of culture long before the first colonists settled in America. World War II had a severe impact on these institutions; many museums and collections had to be reconstructed following the war. The last few years have seen a renaissance in European museum development, including the emergence of many modern exhibition centers and the construction of neighborhood, regional, open-air, and modern art museums.

It is really unfair to single out one European art museum from the many hundreds of world-famous facilities that are presently enriching the lives of both residents and foreign visitors. However, a unique, contemporary art complex called the Centre National d'Art et de Culture de Georges Pompidou deserves special attention. Opened in Paris in early 1977, Centre Beaubourg as it is familiarly called, is a controversial, six-storied structure that cost $200 million to build, requires a staff of 900, and has an annual budget ($26 million) that is greater than the combined budgets of the 30 other French national museums.

Its vast 10 hectares (25 acres) of floor space accommodates four major departments—literature, music, art, and film. It includes: the National Museum of Modern Art; a three-story library (the largest in

France, with 1 million books covering every field of knowledge; one of the nation's few public libraries); a children's library; a museum of graphics, design, and architecture; a movie theater; rooftop gardens; child-care facilities; bars; and a restaurant. An acoustic music research institute is located in a separate building beneath the 1 hectare (2.5 acre) plaza in front of the center, leaving the street-level space available for open-air concerts, informal street theater performances (Figure 16.9), and the enjoyment of the public. This plaza is the largest and almost the only new open space to be created in central Paris since the beginning of the twentieth century.

Although controversial in design and criticized on political and economic grounds, the Centre Beaubourg seems well on its way to fulfilling its purpose—to stimulate public interest in the arts by reaching as many people as possible. The building stays open until 10:00 P.M. every evening to make it more accessible to workers, homemakers, and students. Unlike many art museums that intimidate visitors with gloomy exteriors, formal galleries, and stern-faced, uniformed guards, it is a bright, friendly place. Children feel free to sprawl in the library aisles engrossed in a book or to laugh, talk, and play almost anywhere without fear of censure. Families from the provinces enjoy the center's atmosphere; they say they feel welcome and at ease. Most do not enter the art gallery although they are using the library facilities in large numbers. Typically, they watch a concert or street theater entertainment in the plaza, ride the escalator to look out over the Paris rooftops, and have lunch at the cafeteria. However, they come

Figure 16.9 **A street musician entertains a crowd of visitors at Centre Beaubourg in Paris, France. The many activities that take place in the plaza, the unconventional architecture of the building, and the friendliness of the staff encourage people who have never visited a museum before to make evening and weekend outings to Centre Beaubourg.**

back again with a positive attitude that leads many to explore some of the educational and cultural opportunities that they missed on their first visit. Over 20,000 people visit Centre Beaubourg daily; 50,000 visit there on Sundays.

Elsewhere in the world, only a few countries have been able to afford art museums comparable to the great European institutions. Some nations such as Japan and China, possess a rich heritage of national art treasures that are accessible to the public in outstanding museums. Japan, for example, has the Tokyo National Museum, which contains over 86,000 exhibits associated with the history and fine arts of Japan, China, and India, and the National Museum of Western Art, which is home to several Rodin masterpieces. As in Europe and North America, Japanese art museum facilities are being improved or constructed in response to public demand. For instance, a new national museum of art was opened in Osaka in 1977 and contains more exhibition space than any other museum in Japan.

PUBLIC SCIENCE MUSEUMS

Of all the types of public museums, science museums appeal to the greatest diversity of Americans. Although science museums constitute only 18 percent of the nation's museum facilities, they draw 45 percent of the visitors. No matter how small, science museums are appreciated by those who wish to become better acquainted with unfamiliar locations, concepts, or materials. The majority of the nation's science museums include an assortment of historical and artistic as well as natural science materials to reflect many aspects of the region or state they represent.

Some science exhibits consist of little more than a case or two of interesting local materials set up in a hallway of a public building; nevertheless, they often function as museums attracting considerable numbers of viewers—tourists as well as residents. Many science museums are unpretentious establishments eking out a precarious existence in dilapidated storefronts or other makeshift facilities and are supported by small government grants and donations from visitors and local residents. Some are well-supported showplaces that rank among the finest museum facilities in the nation; these are often the result of the generosity of private donors. One such facility is the George C. Page Museum of La Brea Discoveries located on land owned by the County of Los Angeles. Mr. Page, fascinated from the time of his arrival in Los Angeles in 1918 by the La Brea tar-pit fossils, donated almost $4 million to the county to build an underground interpretive center. It and the adjacent land contain the pits from which fossils are being recovered, dramatic fossil exhibits, a gift shop, three theaters showing films on the history of the tar pits and dinosaur discoveries, and a glass-walled laboratory where scientists can be seen cleaning and assembling fossil animal remains. It is operated as part of the Los Angeles County Natural History museum and is open to the public without charge.

Finally, there are a few science museums, such as the Smithsonian Institution in Washington, D.C., that are immense museum complexes. The Smithsonian, irreverently nicknamed the *nation's attic,* is actually 11 separate museums (some of which are not science oriented) and a worldwide network of research sites. Besides the original museum,

it includes the National Collection of Fine Arts, the National Portrait Gallery, the East Building of the National Gallery of Art, the Freer Gallery of Art, the National Museum of Natural History, the National Museum of History and Technology, the Hirshhorn Museum and Sculpture Garden, the National Zoological Park, the Cooper-Hewitt Museum of Design and Decorative Arts (located in New York City), and the National Air and Space Museum. The latter, opened on July 1, 1976, is a $40 million facility with 23 major exhibits in three great halls. It has become Washington's biggest single attraction, drawing 20 million visitors in its first two years.

Begun with a $500,000 bequest from an English scientist, James Smithson, the Smithsonian Institution was officially launched in 1846 by an act of Congress. It is set up, not as a federal agency, however, but as a unique semiprivate institution under the jurisdiction of a board of regents composed of private citizens as well as representatives from the three branches of government. Since that time, gifts of money, buildings, and exhibit materials from private individuals together with donated collections from other institutions and gifts presented to the United States Government have expanded the facilities and collections. Even so, about 90 percent of the $100 million annual operating expenses comes from federal funds and 75 percent of its 4600 employees are federal civil servants. Therefore, it is generally recognized as America's national museum.

Nature of Exhibits. Except perhaps for some specialized facili-

ties such as children's centers (most of which are science oriented), science museums are the museums that offer users the greatest opportunity for active involvement. No other type of museum has made as much progress in improving presentation techniques. Natural history museums, in particular, are abandoning the unimaginative scholarly collection approach that tried to inform through exposure to a maximum number of specimens. Instead, dramatic dioramas, working models, and displays incorporating films, slides, and tape recordings, provide stimulating information concerning the complexities of the natural world.

Although expensive to maintain, touchable and moving exhibits turn passive observers into active participants and make otherwise inanimate presentations come alive. At the Museum of Science and Industry in Chicago, for example, visitors can take a trip through a coal mine, walk into a 5-meter-high (16-foot-high) model of the human heart, watch baby chicks hatch, explore the narrow passageways of an actual German World War II submarine, stroll along an 1890s Main Street, and start a miniature sawmill operating with the push of a button. This 6-hectare (14-acre) complex of 75 halls containing 2000 exhibit units, attracts over 4 million visitors a year. Opened in 1933, its popularity encouraged the development of similar science museums in many other locations. One of its offspring, the Ontario Science Centre in Toronto, excels in its ability to stimulate visitor participation. Not to be outdone or outdated, however, the Chicago Museum is adapting its older exhibits to provide more opportunities for visitor involvement and is changing more than 10 percent of its exhibits each year to keep pace with changes in science and technology.

Children's Museums.

Nowhere is the blending of education and entertainment more complete than in modern children's museums. These are stimulating, exciting places where the "please-touch" spirit produces a kind of amusement-park atmosphere. Such museums are not dedicated to preservation; rather, their primary goal is helping children feel comfortable in the world around them, particularly with the complexities of science and technology. Exhibits are specifically designed to kindle children's imaginations and help them develop new interests.

Although children's museums are increasing in number, the concept itself is not a recent development; the world's first children's museum—the Brooklyn Children's Museum—was opened in 1899. From the outset, it was not intended to be just a miniature adult museum; instead, it was planned as a special place where children could come to satisfy their curiosity. Cases were not locked and children were encouraged to handle the specimens. Displays were designed for touching, exhibits developed with movable parts, and live animals provided for the children to handle.

These policies were highly controversial at the time (and to some extent, they still are), but the museum was an immediate and continued success. In 1977, the principal exhibits were moved into a free-form, $4 million structure that was designed to function primarily as an effective teaching environment. Programs at the old museum

building continue; they include films, demonstrations, instructional classes, clubs, workshops, field trips, story hours, planetarium shows, and junior curator opportunities, all of which specifically exclude parents so that the children may relax and explore in an environment of peers. A collection of mobile exhibits is available for use in area schools.

Currently, children's museums are rapidly expanding with several hundred in operation throughout Canada and the United States. However, the concepts introduced by the Brooklyn Children's Museum and others like it have not been confined to this type of institution. Other facilities that now emphasize visitor involvement in many of their exhibits include libraries, zoos, and interpretive centers. Adults (once they overcome the inhibitions produced by years of exposure to the "be quiet—don't touch" philosophy of traditional museums) are also seeking visitor-involvement museums where they can take part and have fun as well as acquire knowledge and develop fresh perspectives.

These innovative museums are bridging the gap that many people feel exists between resources that are labeled as cultural (i.e., educational, but not much fun) and those that are regarded as recreational (a lot of fun, but not very informative). Unfortunately, because of the uninhibitedly enthusiastic clientele and the absence of a traditional museum atmosphere, some people fail to see the serious purpose and great value of user-participation museums. As a result, many of these facilities have difficulty attracting long-term foundation support or substantial government aid.

Living Collections.

The group of science museums with the most widespread appeal are those that contain living collections. These include nature centers and preserves, many trailside and on-site museums, botanical gardens, conservatories, insectariums, aquariums, some of the national parks, and a variety of zoological gardens and parks. The latter—known familiarly as zoos—attract over 130 million visitors a year in the United States alone.

Most nations maintain at least one zoo. They range in size from small municipal zoos with a few specimens to the huge African game parks teeming with wildlife (Figure 15.8). Size, however, is not nearly as important as the quality of the exhibits and viewing experience, the rarity of the animal species, and the resource's accessibility to potential users. In the United States, some 200 urban zoos offer large numbers of people their only direct exposure to wild animals and, for a growing proportion of urban populations, their only contact with the domesticated animals that they never take the time or have the opportunity to see on farms in rural areas. Petting zoos provide settings in which close contacts between animals and people can take place and walk-through aviaries allow people to enter temporarily an environment that contains many birds.

Zoological gardens and parks are changing rapidly as the needs of the creatures and human visitors are better recognized. Not only is it more aesthetically and educationally satisfactory to see animals in settings resembling their natural habitats, it is healthier for the creatures themselves. As a result, bare cages full of pacing animals located in dimly lit, poorly ventilated buildings are being replaced by appropriately landscaped tracts of land in which social groups of the various species are free to roam and interact in viewing range of visitors. Emphasis is also being placed on fostering natural reproduction by keeping sufficient numbers of creatures in environments that are conducive to normal social behavior. This replaces the former stamp-collection-type approach in which zoos tried to obtain and exhibit single specimens of as many different species as possible. Unfortunately, natural habitat exhibits are expensive to build and maintain, and also require much larger tracts of land than traditional buildings and cages. Such exhibits are beyond the capabilities of many older urban zoos. These zoos usually face severe space limitations in addition to serious difficulties in maintaining present collections and facilities in the face of rapidly rising costs.

In the new types of social habitat exhibits, animals are separated and protected from the visitors (and each other where appropriate) by unobtrusive devices such as moats and natural barriers. Some visitors complain that they cannot get as close to the animals nor see as many kinds as they used to at traditional zoos. Most people, however, realize the value of seeing animals living in a relatively normal physical and social environment much as they do in the wild.

An outstanding example of this kind of resource is located in Southern California. The 38-hectare (93-acre) San Diego Zoological Garden not only has the largest collection of animals in the world (5500 specimens), but the majority are exhibited in natural habitat settings. The zoo's environment is enhanced by the region's mild Mediterranean climate that provides about 330 days of sunshine a year. This permits most of the animal-visitor encounters to take place outdoors and also makes it possible to grow many kinds of exotic flora (3000 different species) on the grounds. This zoo has contributed substantially to the development of the design of mixed-animal exhibits and walk-through aviaries.

In 1972, a large extension of the zoo was opened on 730 hectares (1800 acres) of land located some 48 kilometers (30 miles) north of downtown San Diego. The San Diego Wild Animal Park (Figure 16.10), as it is called, is dedicated primarily to the study and preservation of endangered species. However, it is proving to be successful in both areas. Of the 19 endangered species presently established in the park, 14 have reproduced. In addition, as many as 40,000 people a week spend many happy hours watching 2000 animals of 186 species living under conditions somewhat similar to their native habitats.

Recreation opportunities at the San Diego Wild Animal Park are rich and varied. Visitors can see the six ecological sections of the park

Figure 16.10 **The large exhibit areas and tour-by-train arrangements at the San Diego Wild Animal Park remove opportunities for close contact between animals and visitors. However, this system permits species to live together much as they would in the wild. Visitors can observe animals engaged in behavioral patterns that are far more natural than in traditional zoos where movement is limited by lack of space and behavior is modified by proximity to large numbers of people.**

by taking a 1-hour monorail train ride around the park's perimeter. The animals have sufficient room to maintain their instinctual flight distance so that observers can see the animals at ease and reacting in a reasonably natural manner to the stimuli of their surroundings. This tour also operates in the evening, providing visitors with an unusual experience since zoological parks usually close at dusk. A paved 2-kilometer (1.25-mile) hiking trail brings people closer to some of the animals seen only from afar while on the monorail. A botanical garden and tour for the visually handicapped have been developed. A huge walk-through aviary housing some 100 species of East African birds provides additional opportunities for closer contact with the zoo's inhabitants. The Animal Care Center includes windows arranged so that visitors can see some of the problems involved in providing special diets or medical attention for wild animals.

Unfortunately, the facilities at the two San Diego zoological parks are far from typical. As popular and desirable as such modern, spacious facilities may be, they are so costly to build and maintain that few municipalities can afford them. The two San Diego facilities, for instance, shared a $21 million budget in 1978. However, these zoos are exceptional in another way; they manage to be self-supporting. This is largely because relatively high admission fees are charged ($5.25 for adults and $2.50 for children at the wild animal park and $3.00 for adults and $1.00 for children at the zoological garden) and because the parks are able to draw large numbers of paying visitors. Both sites are relatively accessible to the large

urban population of southern California and the many tourists who visit that region year round. Total annual attendance currently exceeds 5 million.

More typical of American urban zoos is the Detroit Zoological Garden, a 50-hectare (126-acre) facility containing 600 mammals, 700 reptiles, and 100 birds displayed in 40 exhibits. This zoo also maintains a second facility—a small children's zoo at Belle Isle, a large island park in the Detroit River near downtown. The Detroit zoo operated on a $4.5 million budget in 1978, only 70 percent of which was self-generated. This zoo is heavily used during the summer (an average of 20,000 visitors a day) but receives few visitors (several hundred to an occasional 2000 a day) during the rest of the year. Its entrance fees are relatively modest—$2.00 for adults and $0.75 for children.

Until 1979, when the city appropriated $7.7 million for the zoo (including $2.1 million for construction projects), most new exhibits and renovation work was financed by contributions from private donors and the 1800-member Detroit Zoological Society. An innovative "Adopt an Animal" program has been producing $80,000 in private donations to cover the annual feeding costs of creatures ranging from small reptiles and amphibians ($15) to big cats ($900) or gorillas ($1200). Nevertheless, the Detroit Zoo, even with the substantial increase in municipal funding just received, continues to postpone many needed repairs and high-priority improvements.

Most municipal zoos operate under similar conditions, making do with existing grounds and structures, carrying out repairs and reno-

vations whenever additional public funds can be obtained, and waiting for private donations to make major changes possible. Because of the high cost and difficulty of obtaining more extensive sites in urban areas, major zoological parks in the future are likely to be built outside cities and financed largely or entirely by intermediate or national governments. The Minnesota Zoological Garden is one such facility. This 194-hectare (480-acre) park, located south of Minneapolis, was built by the state government at a cost of $40 million. Opened in 1978, it contains over 250 species of animals and 2000 varieties of plants exhibited in groupings named The Tropics, Sea Life, The Northern Trek, Minnesota Wildlife, and The Children's Zoo.

In a similar fashion, many different types of parks and facilities are introducing people to unfamiliar or exotic flora. Outstanding opportunities of this kind are available at some of the sites set aside by state or national governments to preserve certain plant habitats or species. Unfortunately, most of the more remarkable plant communities occur in less accessible locations so that relatively few people are able to see them. Therefore, formal gardens, greenhouses, and conservatories in urban areas and labeled nature trails and interpretive centers in regional parks are the principal resources that provide opportunities for people to see and appreciate less common types of vegetation.

By walking through the almost 4000 square meters (1 acre) of glass-enclosed environments at the Enid A. Haupt Conservatory of the New York Botanical Garden, for example, people can experience desert, fern forest, or tropical forest environments or step back in time to see a topiary or medieval herb garden. Children can find out what the plants look like that produce much of their food and learn to love and properly care for plan taking parts in classes conducted at the conservatory's "Greenschool," which is operated in cooperation with the city's public schools.

These experiences have only just become available to the people of New York through the generosity of private citizens. Built originally in 1902 with donations from Carnegie, Vanderbilt, and Morgan, the conservatory deteriorated as the city found it increasingly difficult to pay for its upkeep. By 1971, the structure was being considered for demolition. However, Mrs. Enid A. Haupt, an ardent horticulturalist and member of the botanical garden's board of directors, provided funds for a $5 million restoration and the building was saved.

An aquatic exhibit is another kind of living museum that is available in many locations, some of which are more accessible than others. Such exhibits come in many forms. At a few—often called underwater parks—visitors enter the marine environment on specially marked trails using scuba or skin diving equipment. Others permit visitors to feel they are sharing the environment with its marine inhabitants by floating over it in glass-bottomed boats.

However, most people still gain firsthand knowledge of the aquatic world by having marine life brought to them at traditional public aquariums. These may contain numerous exotic species exhibited in large tanks in a specially built facility such as Chicago's John G. Shedd Aquarium. It features a coral reef exhibit that provides a close-up view of more than 10,000 fish and other organisms native to the Caribbean Sea. Some aquariums are not separate institutions but occupy buildings within zoological gardens. Nature centers frequently contain a number of tanks holding fish and other organisms that are common in nearby bodies of water. All of these resources provide valuable opportunities to understand and enjoy a world with which relatively few people are familiar.

Observatories and Planetariums. Although high-powered telescopes are accessible to the public through membership in astronomy societies and occasionally at university or other publicly owned observatories, the number of people who take advantage of these opportunities is limited. Even Kitt Peak National Observatory in Arizona (home of the U.S. ground-based astronomy research and development center), which is open to the public, contains excellent exhibits, and conducts hour-long tours, only receives 76,000 visitors a year.

But now that it is possible to "bring the heavens indoors" by simulating the appearance of the universe with lights projected onto the dome of a planetarium, more people can satisfy their desires to know more about astronomy. Many planetariums—over 850 in the United States alone—are built in conjunction with science museums. Others are separate facilities with exhibits and displays of various instruments and specimens. Some also have observatory facilities that are devoted entirely to public use.

Anthropology and Archaeology Exhibits. Some of the most heavily visited science museums are those that contain evidence of early man or highly developed ancient civilizations. Because most people are curious about the past, anthropological and archaeological exhibits attract a high proportion of casual visitors, many of whom are not regular museumgoers. Many of the world's major excavated sites and ruins such as Stonehenge in England have become well-known, primary tourist attractions. Nations that contain large numbers of these sites often function as vast outdoor museums in which visitors travel from one important site to another, either on their own or as part of a tour, to gain an impression of an earlier civilization or to achieve social status.

One such nation—Greece—contains the remains of one of the world's most famous buildings, the Parthenon. The Acropolis, the hill on which it stands, is located in Athens and is visited annually by over 2 million tourists. This is more people than are said to have visited the temple in all the centuries of ancient Athenian supremacy. However, this is just one of hundreds of important archaeological sites in Greece. From Athens alone, one-day trips can be made to several other sites of major importance, and special exhibits such as those found in the National Archaeological Museum in Athens provide additional glimpses of the civilization from which much of our present culture has evolved.

In the Western Hemisphere, no nation surpasses Mexico in the number or diversity of archaeological discoveries. More than 15,000 different sites containing the remains of a dozen or more independent civilizations that flourished in the region during the last 3000 years have been discovered so far. The government has excavated and preserved many of these sites as outstanding outdoor museums.

Not all of these sites are located in out-of-the-way places. In 1978, while digging in a downtown street to install an underground transformer, power company workers unearthed a gigantic circular monolith, now judged to be the most important Aztec sculpture ever found. The site was immediately barricaded off and a full-scale archaeological dig, involving the removal of several adjacent buildings, was begun. Since that time, scientists have uncovered the complete foundations of the Great Temple—the most important pyramid in the Aztec civilization—and the area is being developed as an historic zone. When the work is completed, visitors will be able to tour the Aztec site as well as nearby buildings representative of later periods and visit a restored nineteenth century edifice that will house the many exquisite objects and interesting artifacts now being found around the temple site.

The finest single source of information and understanding of ancient civilizations in Middle America is also found in Mexico City. This is the world-renowned National Museum of Anthropology and History located in Chapultepec Park (Figure 8.7). Its immense, dramatically illuminated galleries, filled with large numbers of artifacts, dioramas, and life-size reconstructions, offer users —whether scholars or casual visitors —a museum experience that is unequalled anywhere else in the world (Figure 16.11).

In the United States, museums of anthropology and archaeology usually feature a display of North

Figure 16.11 Members of two tour groups at Mexico City's National Museum of Anthropology and History view some of the ground floor exhibits including the massive Aztec calendar carving known as the Sun Stone (rear wall). Although exhibit explanation cards are written only in Spanish, some of the tours are led by English-speaking guides.

American Indian artifacts and emphasize the early history of the human race in the Americas, but some include material on humanity's early beginnings. Authentically re-created Indian villages and carefully preserved archaeological sites are especially attractive to casual visitors. Some, like Mesa Verde National Park, site of a concentration of 2800 cliff dwellings inhabited by an Indian civilization around A.D. 1100 (Figure 3.7), are outstanding archaeological discoveries that attract visitors from all over the world. At some sites still under development, the public may watch the work in progress or even take part in a dig.

PUBLIC HISTORY MUSEUMS

People have always been curious about their roots and enjoy looking at relics that are representative of things their forebears might have owned or that reflect the conditions under which they lived. Most families also treasure at least a few possessions that have been handed down from generation to generation as reminders of the past. However, people seldom have room to store many inherited items so that they have to part with memorabilia and valuables that they do not wish to discard but cannot keep. Fortunately, individuals and organizations are often available to accept these materials and provide space for their protection and display. This is the way most history museums not only originated but continue to expand their collections, particularly in North America. Of all the types of museums, history museums are the most abundant and varied.

Historical Society Museums.
Starting in the late 1700s, Americans interested in studying and preserving historical items banded together to form county or state historical societies. These groups frequently started small museums, some of which became major institutions. Some societies were fortunate in establishing close relationships with their county or state governments almost from the beginning. Wisconsin was the first state to provide substantial aid to a historical society, spending $620,000 for a museum building. This support has continued over the years with the state helping to renovate the original museum facilities, purchasing a historymobile to take exhibits to communities throughout the state, and financing the acquisition of several historic houses and the development of a museum village.

One of the exhibits operated by the Wisconsin Historical Society is the Circus World Museum complex at Baraboo. Designated as national historic landmarks, the weathered buildings were once the winter headquarters of the Ringling Brothers Circus. Preserved as they were originally, the buildings along with the displays they now contain provide an impression of this circus community in its heyday. In addition, the actual sights, sounds, and smells of a turn-of-the-century

smalltown circus can be experienced through the demonstrations and performances that take place daily on the 13-hectare (33-acre) grounds. Visitors can watch the entire circus operation as it was then, including the arrival of the baggage wagons on railroad flatcars, their unloading, the parade, the raising of the Big Top, informal practice sessions, and the one-ring show itself. Through living museums such as this one, historical societies safeguard the historical heritage of a particular region and, at the same time, make it accessible to the public as an enjoyable, educational experience.

In addition to state historical societies, many smaller organizations were founded to protect and study local materials of historical interest. Because of their efforts, there are few communities in the United States that do not own and display at least a few relics of the area's past. Some local historical societies make do with limited facilities and survive on budgets of a few hundred dollars obtained from memberships, donations, and small government grants—surviving only because of the hard work and dedication of volunteers.

Other local societies are more fortunate. Some own spacious museum buildings and operate on substantial municipally provided budgets that make it possible to maintain a full-time paid curator and staff. These institutions are sometimes the only—and usually the best—preservers of an area's historical heritage. They also help people trace their family origins. This is a challenge that they are often well equipped to meet because of their extensive collections of documents. Resources provided

by state and local historical societies are usually complemented by the facilities and programs provided by private preservation organizations and various government park systems as described in Chapters 11, 13, 14, and 15.

Kinds of Historical Exhibits.
History museums take many kinds of forms and some of the most enjoyable and frequently visited are not buildings containing displays of assorted relics. For example, the state of Ohio (through the leadership of its historical society) maintains 15 prehistoric sites, 3 natural history areas, 13 historic houses, a grist mill, a Quaker meeting house, 7 fort sites, 4 battlegrounds, 3 monuments, the tombs of 2 presidents of the United States, a reconstructed log fort of the Indian Wars period, a sternwheel steamboat, and the remains of an iron furnace in addition to 3 state historical museums.

People enjoy visiting sites that help them relate to earlier times, events, or persons. Many regard them as primary destinations for short outings or vacation trips. Each year, for example, more than 1 million people, representing the 50 states and many foreign countries, visit Abraham Lincoln's tomb in Oak Ridge Cemetery at Springfield, Illinois, and 500,000 tour the house where he lived during his days as a lawyer. The reconstructed pioneer village of New Salem where Lincoln spent six years of his youth is one of Illinois' most visited state parks.

Historic buildings of this kind are important educational and recreation resources. They reveal so much more about people and their times than displays in museum cases. Visitors to historic buildings can sense how the original inhabitants lived, whether the structures be pioneer cabins, plantation mansions, royal palaces, forts, stores, taverns, sawmills, manufacturing plants, schools, or churches. They can gain a better understanding of crucial events or feel close to famous people whose lives were connected to the building being visited. When a number of such preserved, restored, or reconstructed structures are grouped together on one site—such as has been done at the New Salem State Park in Illinois —the effect is even more dramatic, especially if suitably attired employees assume the roles of original residents.

National and International Roles. History museums occur in most countries of the world. They are operated or supported by governments not only in the highly developed but also in the less developed nations because of their usefulness in raising national consciousness or maintaining a sense of cultural and historical unity. As a result, many national history museums strive through their exhibits to outline the nation's outstanding scientific and artistic achievements as well as describe important historical events.

Such exhibits are seldom seen by more than a small portion of the population. This is especially true in large countries with widely scattered populations and in poor nations where most people have neither the time nor the money for traveling to capital cities to tour museums. For this reason, many national museums conduct active outreach programs. An outstanding example is currently occurring in Canada. In 1977, the National Museums of

Canada—with the assistance of private foundations, the provinces, and the railroads—purchased the train used in the United States to carry historical displays from one region to another during the nation's bicentennial celebration. It was completely refurbished and filled with innovative exhibits depicting Canadian geography, history, and culture. The Canadian Discovery Train, as the museum-on-wheels is called, began a five-year journey in 1978, which will eventually take it within reach of 90 percent of the population. Although the government decided against naming it the Unity Train in case such a move might be seen as propaganda, it is hoped that the traveling museum will be a unifying force that provides Canadians with a stronger sense of national pride and identity.

Often, seats of government are located in historically significant structures that contain many treasures of a nation's past. Such buildings may, in turn, be surrounded by memorials, monuments, and clusters of buildings that house other historic materials. The Kremlin complex in Moscow is one of the best examples. In addition to the Grand Kremlin Palace that houses the Supreme Soviet (the national legislature), there are the Alexander Gardens (that now contain the eternal flame), the Kremlin Armoury (a public museum containing the relics of czardom), and five cathedrals that have been restored and preserved as monuments of artistic and architectural merit. Of great national significance are the more recent additions to the complex—the Tomb of the Unknown Soldier, the Monuments to the Hero Cities of World War II, and the Lenin Mau-

soleum where the father of the revolution lies in state. A visit to Lenin's tomb is an important event in the lives of the Russian people and, every day, citizens line up patiently for as long as four hours to enter the tomb and file by the glass coffin. A Lenin Museum has also been constructed at the edge of Red Square to house Lenin photographs and memorabilia.

Specific events or periods of history are also featured at history museums to help keep their memory alive and give the citizenry cause for pride in the heroism or accomplishments of their forebears. Again, the Soviet Union serves as a good example. In a nation that suffered 20 million casualties during World War II, there is a reverence for the deeds and sacrifices that made survival possible. The government has erected numerous war museums and memorials that function as primary destinations for vacationing Russian families and are also visited frequently by local citizens. These visits are not completely happy occasions, especially for those who lost relatives in the war. In that sense, the experience is not recreational. However, many visitors leave the memorials with a deepened sense of pride that enables them to return to their daily tasks with renewed dedication and vigor. For many people, this kind of emotional experience *is* recreation in its purest and most valuable form.

Finally, history museums provide an excellent means of attracting, impressing, and enlightening foreign visitors. Countries that have enjoyed a colorful past and have managed to preserve and protect many vestiges of their history, are often very attractive to tourists.

Great Britain is a good example. Unlike the United States, where there has been (at least until recently) a tendency to neglect and replace outdated structures, Great Britain contains large numbers of old buildings. Many have been well cared for and continue to be used as private homes, municipal buildings, churches, schools, and commercial establishments. As a result, entire communities sometimes function as history museums and guided or self-conducted walking tours of such locations are popular activities for tourists wishing to gain an appreciation of Great Britain's past.

Historic buildings that are no longer used for their intended purposes are frequently maintained by nonprofit organizations or government agencies and opened to the public. One such structure is the 900-year-old Tower of London, which for generations has been the biggest single tourist attraction in Great Britain (3 million people visited it in 1977). Much of this fortress remains as it was, but major additions have been made over the years—such as the Jewel House, which was built in 1967. The 7-hectare (18-acre) Tower complex includes The National Museum of Arms and Armour, a gallery depicting the history of the tower, bookstalls, and gift shops. It continues to be used as the official repository for the Crown jewels, which are on public view and protected by some of the most sophisticated electronic devices in the world.

Since the fortress still technically belongs to the Royal Family, it continues to be guarded—as it has been for centuries—by 36 yeoman warders. Each night, these guards in traditional uniforms perform the Ceremony of the Keys

Figure 16.12 **Limited numbers of visitors to Britain's Tower of London may attend the Ceremony of the Keys by prearrangement. Held nightly just before 10:00 P.M. as part of the regular duties of the Chief Yeoman Warder, the 700-year-old ceremony involves locking the fortress gates and delivering the keys for safekeeping to the resident governor.**

(Figure 16.12). Continued observance of such longstanding traditions heightens history museum experiences, not just at the Tower of London but at many other places throughout Great Britain. Such ceremonies are not carried out as performances solely for the benefit of tourists but rather as routine duties.

The interests of the British people extend far beyond their own historical heritage, however. Sir Hans Sloane collected all kinds of items concerned with every facet of history at a time when there were no public museums. When his huge collection was bequeathed to the nation in 1753, the government began the London institution that is now one of the world's greatest history museums. The British Mu-

seum, as it is called, contains many thousands of exhibits illustrating some 6000 years of human history. It is a remarkable resource, which people seldom tire of revisiting since it is impossible to see all of its exhibits during one or, indeed, a whole series of visits.

PUBLIC SPECIALIZED MUSEUMS

Specialized museums are designed specifically for one type of visitor or contain materials of one particular kind. Besides the children's museums (described in the section on science museums), there is a wide variety of other museums that fall into this category. Comparatively few, however, are operated by public agencies; the majority are private organization or commercial museums.

Museums Commemorating Individuals. A small but important group of public specialized museums commemorate the deeds of individuals. Sometimes these are separate galleries within larger museums. A number are structures built especially for the purpose or are complexes containing buildings associated in some way with the person being honored. The Edison National Historic Site in New Jersey, for instance, is composed of Thomas Edison's laboratory and the nearby Edison family estate. Within this museum complex, which is now part of the national park system, are many of Edison's early inventions, his personal collection of books and correspondence, and a comprehensive exhibit on his life and achievements.

Similarly, the Ringling Museum Complex at Sarasota, Florida, consists of John Ringling's home and the Italian-style villa that he built to house his personal collection of art. Upon his death, these buildings and the treasures they contained, along with 15 hectares (37 acres) of landscaped grounds, were bequeathed to the state of Florida. The state now maintains the complex and has added another 13 hectares (31 acres), on which it has constructed The Museum of the Circus.

Another group of publicly operated commemorative museums consists of presidential libraries. Most of the earlier presidents were honored by the preservation of their homes or by the construction of memorials. Now the tradition of establishing extensive libraries has developed. Six have been completed and two more are in the planning stage. Since a 1955 law forbids using federal funds for construction, these institutions are built with private donations and then turned over to the federal government for operation. In addition to files of official papers, these museums contain exhibits of presidential memorabilia that range from childhood homes and replicas of White House offices to personal possessions and gifts from foreign heads of state. Attendance at these museums has been steadily increasing. The Lyndon B. Johnson Library in Austin, Texas, for instance, with 700,000 visitors annually is one of the biggest tourist attractions in the southwest second only to the Alamo. The John F. Kennedy Library, opened in Boston in 1979, is expected to attract well over 1 million visitors a year.

Federal Museums. Of the specialized historical museums that are entirely funded by the U.S. Government, the National Archives,

with its 93,000 square meters (1 million square feet) of documents dating back to earliest colonial times, is one of the most important and heavily used. As many as 2000 Americans bent on tracing their family history visit the main facility in Washington, D.C., each month and many more request information by mail or through 11 regional branches. In addition, the National Archives is a premier tourist destination because it houses and keeps on public view such national treasures as the original copies of the Declaration of Independence, Washington's Farewell Address, and the U.S. Constitution.

Museums have also been developed by several federal government agencies to inform the public about the nature and purpose of their activities. The American Museum of Atomic Energy at the Atomic Energy Commission's Oak Ridge research facilities in Tennessee, for example, traces the history, development, and adaptations of atomic power, using models, movies, and demonstrations to make the program enjoyable as well as educational. By far the most impressive of the agency museums is the facility developed by the National Aeronautics and Space Administration at the John F. Kennedy Space Center, Cape Canaveral, Florida. Over 1.3 million tourists a year are taken by bus on one of two different tours. They see huge rockets and space capsules, enjoy exhibits and film presentations at the visitor center, tour the Air Force Space Museum, and visit historic buildings where sound-and-sight shows explain the main features of the space program or re-create some of the program's most exciting moments.

MUSEUM GIFT SHOPS
Once little more than postcard counters, museum gift shops have now been expanded into extensive retail operations. One of the most successful — the retail shop and mail order division of New York's Metropolitan Museum of Art — grosses more than $10 million a year, thereby contributing over one-third of the museum's income. These stores are appreciated by casual buyers and collectors as reliable sources for authentic, fairly priced merchandise. They also function as extensions of the museums in which they are located.

Books, native crafts, art reproductions, musical instruments, jewelry, toys, games, and natural history specimens that relate to museum exhibits are featured. Such items allow visitors to buy and enjoy materials that remind them of their museum experience, expand their knowledge, or increase their involvement. Children can be encouraged through such purchases to pursue an interest in a topic that fascinated them during their museum visit.

Some critics suggest, however, that the gift shops have become so attractive that they actually supplant the museum experience; many visitors spend so much time browsing through the gift shops that they have neither the time nor inclination to tour the museum exhibits. On the other hand, it is argued that a well-designed gift shop display can arouse people's curiosity and send them in search of the gallery where the original or related materials are exhibited.

COLLEGE MUSEUMS
Although college museums are usually open to the public, they are

primarily facilities built to house materials collected by scholars affiliated with the museum, collections accumulated by instructors in the various departments, and exhibits of materials purchased as teaching aids. Some have extensive public exhibits; others have relatively few, using most of the available space for research, storage, and workshops. Some are highly specialized museums with exceptional collections. The University Museum at the University of Pennsylvania, Philadelphia, for example, is one of the leading anthropology museums in the United States.

Schools with specialized programs of study also tend to develop unusual collections that are of interest to nonstudents as well as students. The U.S. Military Academy at West Point, for instance, contains the country's largest military museum. Some like the Florida State Museum on the Gainesville campus of the University of Florida have been chosen as the official repository of state-owned collections and function, therefore, in two capacities — as a university teaching facility and an official state museum. Such institutions contain comprehensive exhibits of state flora and fauna as well as displays depicting life as it existed in various parts of the state in both historic and prehistoric times.

Colleges with departments of horticulture often have greenhouse, arboretum, conservatory, and outdoor garden facilities that contain labeled specimens, both native and exotic. Although developed primarily for educational purposes, these facilities are often open to the public and staffed by knowledgeable persons who are willing to answer questions. Many campuses include planetariums with permanent exhibits and regularly scheduled public shows and lectures. College observatories are fairly common; most hold occasional open sessions when the public is invited to tour the facilities and observe celestial phenomena through the telescopes.

College art galleries and art museums are numerous. They usually contain permanent collections of paintings and sculptures, hold shows of student and faculty art works, and present special exhibitions, lectures, guided tours, and concerts. Such activities may be of considerable interest to the public, but these facilities often function primarily as teaching museums with collections displayed to coincide with what is being taught in the institution's art departments.

PRIVATE NONPROFIT MUSEUMS

Despite the high costs of acquisition and maintenance, there are a considerable number of privately funded museums in the United States. Some of these such as Southern California's Palm Springs Desert Museum — a $5.5 million art and natural science facility — easily match and sometimes surpass the finest public museums. The J. Paul Getty Museum near Malibu, California, is a spectacular fine arts museum made possible by a gift of $45 million from J. Paul Getty, the oil billionaire. Upon Getty's death in 1976, the museum received a bequest of $700 million. This provided an endowment six times larger than that of the nation's wealthiest public museum, the Metropolitan Museum of Art, and an annual budget twice the size of the total budgets of all the units comprising the Smithsonian Institution.

Under such favorable circumstances, these kinds of private museums can develop outstanding facilities, exhibits, and programs. They can also make their exhibits highly accessible to the general public should they wish to do so. The Palm Springs Desert Museum, for instance, is open to all members, students, and children without charge and free admission is extended to the other residents of the community several times a month. The J. Paul Getty Museum is free to everyone at all times; about 1500 people a day visit this amenity.

Colonial Williamsburg. A very different kind of private nonprofit museum is Virginia's famous history museum complex called Colonial Williamsburg. This painstakingly accurate reconstruction is intended to resemble Williamsburg as it was during the eighteenth century revolutionary period when it was the capital of Virginia. Acquisition and development of this nonprofit institution was financed by an $11 million grant from John D. Rockefeller. Until recently, it was maintained with the income from a $60 million endowment (also a Rockefeller gift) plus the sales of admission tickets, souvenirs, and hotel and restaurant services. Since these resources no longer meet more than 50 percent of its $54 million a year operating costs, the institution now depends heavily on donations from individuals and corporations. It has also received its first assistance from the federal government in the form of a $450,000 grant from the National Endowment for the Humanities.

The 32-hectare (80-acre) town,

Figure 16.13 Young visitors to restored Colonial Williamsburg ride in an ox-drawn cart driven by one of the role-playing employees. Despite the presence of large numbers of people, the meticulous attention to historical detail is so effective that many visitors to the museum town actually feel transported to another time and place and become caught up in the activities of the "inhabitants."

with its authentic colonial streets (Figure 16.13) and gardens, 211 exhibition rooms, 36 craft shops, 3 hotels, and 7 restaurants, employs 600 persons who function as village inhabitants. Colonial Williamsburg attracts more than 1 million visitors a year, and its influence as the first museum town is widespread. It has inspired many other authentic reconstructions both in the United States and other nations. It has also been used as a model for many pseudohistoric re-creations.

Industrial Museums. A wide variety of museums have been developed by business and industry either as part of existing company buildings or as separate entities. These amenities are usually open to the public without charge. Generally, they pertain to the company's product or service in some way and, quite often, contain priceless exhibits. The Corning Glass Center in western New York, for instance, is a first-class museum dedicated to the human uses of glass. It is supported by annual company grants of more than $1 million. One of its main features is a display of glass artifacts and objects representative of civilizations from the time of ancient Egypt. Another well-known industrial museum—The George Eastman House of Photography in Rochester, New York—uses working exhibits and movies to describe the history of photography and contains several galleries in which collections of cameras and famous prints are displayed.

Other museums illustrate the manufacturing process and many complement or even supplant a tour of the factory. For example, in 1973, the Hershey Foods Corporation of Pennsylvania built a separate, simulated chocolate factory when visitor traffic through the plant began to interfere with normal operations. Chocolate World, as the facility is called, traces the process of chocolate production from the cacao bean plantation to the wrapped candy bar and attracts over 1.5 million visitors a year.

Some industrial museums are the result of special interests of the owners and may be only superficially related to the company product if at all. The John Woodman Higgins Armory in Worcester, Massachusetts, for instance, traces the development of military armor. A former president of the Worcester Pressed Steel Company admired metal craftsmanship and personally collected many of the articles on display.

Perhaps the most famous example of this kind of museum is the community of 85 historically significant structures that Henry Ford moved to and restored on a 105-hectare (260-acre) site near his automobile manufacturing plant in Dearborn, Michigan. Greenfield Village, as it is called, was never meant to be an authentic re-creation of one particular village; rather, Ford wished to preserve buildings or objects that were representative of times past or important contributors to the nation's industrial development. In addition, Ford only selected items that had special meaning to himself. Therefore, the complex contains buildings in which he personally lived or worked; several structures associated with one of his closest friends, Thomas Edison; and buildings or exhibits related to earlier Americans whom he particularly admired like Abraham Lincoln and the Wright brothers. Today the village and adjacent museum are one of the top historical attractions in the nation, drawing over 1 million visitors a year.

Religious and Special Interest Museums. Another group of museums of interest to the public are those operated by religious organizations, ethnic societies, and hobby, athletic, and special-interest associations. Many of these specialized museums are small, consisting of no more than a few cases of materials displayed in the reception area of a building used by the organization. Sometimes, however, entire rooms are set aside and developed as museum facilities. A good example is the several exhibit rooms containing displays of 600,000 coins and medals that are maintained by the American Numismatic Society at its headquarters in New York City. The society also has a library that is the most comprehensive of its kind in the United States.

In some cases, separate buildings have been constructed to provide storage space for large collections of materials as well as for informative exhibits. Many religious and ethnic museums are of this type. An example is the Maurice Spertus Museum of Judaica in Chicago, which includes exhibits concerning Jewish history, culture, and art. In a few locations, major complexes have been constructed for people who wish to learn more about a particular society's way of life—past or present. One such complex—the Amish Homestead, Farm, and Village—has been developed by the Amish people in Lancaster County, Pennsylvania, to help visitors appreciate Amish culture. These facilities, along with the area's markets, restaurants, inns, and guided tour services, have made the region one of the top-10 tourist destinations in the nation, attracting more than 5 million people every year.

Halls of Fame. One group of private museums that is largely a North American phenomenon, consists of regional and national halls of fame. These specialized museums are developed to assemble and preserve significant materials relating to a particular sport (basketball, skating, auto racing), group (cowboys, farmers, surgeons), or activity (country music, aviation). Exhibits are included to explain the history and illustrate various aspects of the subject, and libraries are maintained to preserve records, books, historic documents, and photographs. Since most of these museums are closely affiliated with related clubs or professional organizations, they also serve as a means of honoring persons who have been outstanding participants or have contributed to the development or status of the group or activity.

Halls of fame are often located in communities where the activity had its origin or first began to flourish. Devotees of the activity frequently regard a tour of the community as a pilgrimage that is as important as a visit to the museum. One of the first established and among the most heavily visited (200,000 paid admissions a year) of these amenities is the National Baseball Hall of Fame and Museum. It is located in Cooperstown, New York, the small town where the game of baseball was said to have been invented by a student at a nearby military academy. (This is now regarded as legend rather than fact; a baseball-type game is known to have been played by the ancient Egyptians, adopted and developed by the English, and refined into roughly its present form by a New York City fireman in 1848.) The museum was initiated by some of the town residents and built with funds or materials donated by fans and members of baseball leagues throughout the nation. Opened in 1939, the complex gets about 90 percent of its funding from admission fees and has been expanded several times. It now includes displays of nostalgic or historic significance to baseball, the National Baseball Library (the world's largest collection of books and printed materials on baseball), and the Hall of Fame gallery containing plaques for each of the players so honored. Films and recordings are used to re-create exciting moments in the sport's colorful history.

Although most of these halls of fame are controlled by groups of interested persons and operate without any government funding or endorsement, a few enjoy varying degrees of government support. One, the Aviation Hall of Fame in Dayton, Ohio, has the unique distinction of being founded by an Act of Congress (PL 88–372). However, like the others, it is entirely funded by membership dues and private contributions.

COMMERCIAL MUSEUMS

Although most of the commercial museums attract customers for their entertainment value—and have, therefore, been described in Chapter 12—some also function as significant cultural resources. Careful reconstructions of the past; the exhibits at wildlife parks and botanical gardens; the privately owned and displayed collections of materials such as crafts, art works, antiques, artifacts, natural history specimens, and vintage automobiles; and the exhibits maintained by restaurants, retail outlets, and commercial greenhouses and nurseries all provide people with enlightening recreation experiences. Commercial museums are also culturally important because they often attract people who feel intimidated or bored by public museum facilities, programs, and exhibits. People who might otherwise never be reached can have their interest roused and may be prompted to visit other kinds of museums or take part in programs and activities related to the materials displayed.

LIBRARIES

Public funds generally support local, state, and national libraries and maintain collections for use in schools, universities, hospitals, prisons, recreation centers, and various government departments and agencies. Private collections of books are maintained by individuals and families, private and quasi-public organizations, schools, museums, religious institutions, business enterprises, and industrial firms. Commercial enterprises such as summer camps, resorts, hotels, cruise ships, and bars often provide library materials for the use of their employees and guests. Over 2 billion books are contained in the libraries of the United States alone.

PUBLIC LIBRARIES

Although modern public libraries owe their existence to the generos-

ity and dedication of a great many individuals and agencies, one person—Andrew Carnegie—played such an important role in the evolution of public library systems that he deserves special mention. In 1881, he began to encourage the development of free public libraries by paying for one to be built in Pittsburgh where his steel plant was located. In the years that followed, Carnegie and the foundation, which he formed, constructed libraries in any municipality in Great Britain, Canada, or the United States that would agree to maintain free library services for its citizens.

By 1920, numerous community and county libraries throughout England, Scotland, Wales, and Northern Ireland had been established as a direct result of Carnegie's philanthropy. Similarly, 125 libraries were constructed in communities and on campuses throughout Canada. In the United States, more than 2500 libraries were built, including 65 branch library facilities for New York City, which alone cost over $5 million. Unfortunately, the philanthropist's zeal was not always matched by the local governments. Many of these facilities were poorly maintained, seriously understaffed, and stocked with mediocre collections. Nevertheless, most of the 3000 Carnegie libraries have survived, providing easy access to a wide variety of printed materials that have enriched the lives of millions of individuals. Besides being an important source of comfort and entertainment, they have helped large numbers of aspiring individuals to improve their economic situation, develop their intellectual capabilities, and explore their cultural heritage.

Like the public museums, pub-

lic libraries are committed to preserving and providing access to materials—books in particular—that otherwise would be beyond the means of all but the wealthiest individuals, at least in any quantity. Most nations recognize the need for good public libraries although not all countries provide library services of an equally high standard nor feel able to support them with similar levels of funding. Nations that currently maintain particularly well-developed public library systems include Canada and the other Commonwealth countries, Great Britain, the United States, and the Scandinavian nations.

The Role of Local Public Libraries. Of all the kinds of libraries—private or public—the tax-supported library facilities operated at either a municipal or county level are the most accessible to the largest number of people. Although their basic function is still the preservation of material by collection, such libraries now provide a wide range of services that greatly increase their ability to satisfy the cultural, educational, and recreational needs of the people they serve (Figure 16.14). Besides the basic reference, instructional, and educational materials, a wide selection of fictional works are provided to suit all kinds of tastes and accommodate all levels of reading ability. A diverse assortment of other materials may also be available, including periodicals, newspapers, catalogs, sewing patterns, sheet music, pictures, talking books and large-print materials for the visually impaired and, if circumstances warrant it, a collection of foreign language materials. Collections of materials of local interest are often exhibited, and

Figure 16.14 Modern libraries offer a wide range of services designed to help people use their free time effectively. This advertisement by the American Library Association points out that people can obtain help in planning a trip, garden, or construction project; borrow films and recordings to enjoy at home on their own equipment; secure assistance with diverse recreation activities such as belly dancing and genealogical research; attend craft classes, lectures, book discussions, or puppet shows; and, if they are unable to visit the library in person, receive materials by mail.

You could plan a trip,   borrow a classic film,   get help finding a job,   join a book discussion group,

plan a garden,   attend a concert,   get fast answers,   learn to do-it-yourself,

trace your family tree,   stay in shape,   earn a diploma,   learn English,

take record albums home,   see a puppet show,   check out paperbacks,   learn to belly dance,

register to vote,   hear a lecture,   attend a crafts class,   or get your books by mail.

AT THE LIBRARY?
At the library.

Come see what's new besides books.

tables and bulletin boards are used to display community-related publications and notices about upcoming programs and events. These help old as well as new residents become more knowledgeable about their community.

Films, records, cassettes, art prints, paintings, gardening and woodworking tools, typewriters, sewing machines, pets, toys, games, and puzzles may be borrowed at many libraries and are attracting segments of the population that did not previously use libraries. These resources are also welcomed by people who use libraries more as social centers than book-lending facilities. For example, the municipal library in Maryland's Brooklyn Park solved the problem of how to control the large numbers of young people who congregated in the air-conditioned reading room on hot summer days by providing recreation equipment. They are now able to play pool or table tennis in the basement, enjoy games like checkers and Monopoly, or borrow equipment such as tennis rackets and kites. Of course, these young people are also encouraged to borrow books and the staff is gratified to see a marked improvement in book circulation. This innovative library system now ranks fourth nationally in per capita circulation.

Few library systems are now content to limit the use of their collections to individuals who can come to a centrally located facility. Sophisticated extension services have been developed that extend the benefits of the library resources to a wider range of potential users. These services include:

• Opening small branch libraries in outlying areas to improve accessibility.

- Establishing limited library facilities in locations where special populations are found. These include hospitals, schools, nursing homes, jails, neighborhood centers, and community centers.
- Operating bookmobiles on a regular schedule to carry a selection of materials to convenient locations where large numbers of potential users tend to congregate (e.g., children's playgrounds, community parks, and shopping centers), or to designated stops in rural areas, thereby shortening travel distances for scattered populations.
- Providing mail delivery service and outreach programs to bring books and other library materials to the homes of confined individuals, including the elderly, the disabled, and the sick.
- Using the broadcast media to tell adults about programs, services, and interesting books and to offer children the opportunity to hear stories read aloud; one innovative program — Dial-A-Story, which is offered by the Washington, D.C., public library — provides taped stories that children can request and listen to over the telephone.

In addition, many libraries expand their collections by cooperating with other libraries. Information or materials may be shared or exchanged between branch and main libraries or libraries in adjacent communities. Additional materials may be borrowed by interlibrary loan from state or national libraries.

A growing number of libraries are choosing to function as community centers. They are doing so by providing a variety of amenities including:

- Rooms that may be used by members of the community for meetings and special events.
- Comfortably furnished lounge areas suitable for casual reading, quiet con-

versation, or informal group discussion.
- Play areas for children.
- Activity rooms for young people, which can be used on an informal basis or as the location for workshops, demonstrations, discussion groups, parties, and club meetings.
- Parklike grounds for public use and enjoyment, including those who are not regular library users.
- Display cases and wall space that can accommodate special exhibits of general interest.

Auditoriums and workrooms are also being incorporated into libraries where finances permit. These make it possible for libraries to sponsor a wide range of community programs and events such as travelogues, lectures, craft demonstrations and workshops, cooking classes, literature discussions, puppet and magic shows, concerts, poetry readings, dramatic presentations, film festivals, and adult education programs.

Unfortunately, libraries that contain these amenities and provide an extensive range of opportunities are not common. Dependent as they are on local tax moneys for over 80 percent of their budgets, many of the 14,000 American public libraries and branch facilities operate in makeshift, inadequate, or unpretentious surroundings and count on private donations of time, money, and books to prosper or, in some cases, even survive. These struggling institutions are usually in economically depressed communities, rural areas, and less affluent neighborhoods in large cities where the absence of other recreation facilities and the low incomes of many of the residents combine to increase the potential value of good library services.

In a few areas, this potential is being realized. At the Detroit Public Library's Duffield Branch, located in an inner-city neighborhood, which was the scene of riots in 1967, the librarian has been able to turn the facility into the life-enrichment center of the community. In 1976, with the help of a $1900 grant from United Community Services, a recreation and nutrition summer program was initiated. It provided many malnourished youngsters with a good lunch, but it also encouraged use of the library and restored the connection between the library and community. The summer program was only the beginning. The librarian went out into the community to contact potential users, parading through neighborhood streets announcing afterschool programs with a megaphone and taking interesting materials into school classrooms. A bookmobile service was developed to deliver materials to nursing homes and the residences of older people and shut-ins.

Meanwhile, the library itself was altered to be more attractive and more responsive to user needs. The book collection was improved to accommodate local interest in sports, black heroes and heroines, Afro-American poetry, and stories for teens. The library atmosphere was made more inviting through the addition of colorful, frequently changed posters and eye-catching displays that told young people about "neato books" they could borrow. Innovative programs were implemented, including Saturday afternoon movies and afterschool events, which consisted of parties, lively book discussions, games and contests.

By 1978, the Duffield Branch

Library had become an "in" place to be. Numerous young people, including some who had formerly been involved in street muggings, harassment of the library staff, and even the lighting of fires in the library, were enthusiastic users. Many children were regularly doing their homework at the facility. The eight-week summer recreation program had grown so that it not only served 8000 lunches but stimulated the circulation of more than 10,000 books. Best of all perhaps, the results of tests at the neighborhood elementary school revealed that, for the first time in 10 years, reading scores were up.

Actually, this is the most important role of public libraries today. Modern forms of communication and education are largely dependent on the ability to read and comprehend and libraries can provide the impetus needed to start people reading and supply the materials that will keep them reading, no matter what their reading comprehension levels, personal interests, or economic situation may be.

Unfortunately, cutbacks in funding and, therefore, in services rather than expansion of financial support and programs, is now the rule and library closings are not uncommon. The Duffield Branch Library itself was threatened with closure as recently as 1975, a year in which four other Detroit branch libraries were closed. These libraries, like the Duffield Branch, seemed expendable at the time because their circulation of books had become almost negligible. It was generally supposed that this was the result of the neighborhoods being peopled by individuals who could not or would not read rather than some type of resource inadequacy.

Sadly, the former may well be the case now that the last and potentially the best resources for correcting this situation have been permanently removed.

At first glance, many library systems serving large metropolitan areas such as those in Buffalo, Jersey City, Newark, Denver, Washington, D.C., and Minneapolis appear better housed, better equipped, and better staffed than many cities, but, in reality, they too are operating in a state of crisis. As government aid is reduced or eliminated, such facilities have no choice except to curtail services, close less heavily used facilities, and trim purchases, programs, and maintenance. Even in New York City, where the nation's largest library system operates more than 200 branches on a budget of $70 million a year, the facilities are seriously understaffed and operating on reduced hours. Funds are inadequate to provide needed book acquisitions, maintenance, or protection for library materials or users.

The situation is not entirely bleak, however. Voters in many communities like Youngstown, Ohio; Emporia, Kansas; and Huntington, West Virginia continue to increase tax support for their libraries and, in a number of cases, give them top priority. Atlanta voters recently turned down several other projects in favor of spending $19 million on the improvement of their library system. And, despite the fact that it places further strain on existing facilities, libraries are heartened by the fact that library resources in communities all across the country are being used more intensively by increasing numbers of people. Library usage is climbing by 8 percent or more a year and book circulation since 1968 has increased by over 40 percent.

National, State, and Regional Libraries. Throughout the world, almost every nation maintains or is striving to develop some form of national library whose primary purpose is to collect and preserve the country's literature. Since most national libraries automatically receive a free copy of every book and periodical that is published in the country and many of them also try to acquire the most important materials published in other nations, the collections are often both extensive and comprehensive in scope. Unlike the collections at the local public libraries, however, these materials are either inaccessible or available to the public only on a limited basis. Some of the world's finest national libraries include the Bibliothèque Nationale in Paris, the British Museum Library in London, and the State V.I. Lenin Library in Moscow.

The largest and most accessible national library is the U.S. Library of Congress, which also functions as that body's legislative reference library. It receives about 15 percent of Congress' operating budget to maintain its facilities and services. The collections include copies of almost all of the important materials that have ever been printed, not only in the United States but in the entire world. Its more than 75 million items range from books, magazines, and maps to films, photographs, recorded music, and objects of historic significance. Everyone is welcome to visit the Library of Congress. Individuals are free to explore at will or tour the premises as part of a guided tour. Exhibition halls contain fine prints, rare books, and interesting public documents, including Thomas Jefferson's rough draft of the Declaration of Independence and Abraham Lincoln's drafts of the Gettysburg Address. On weekday evenings during the winter, concerts and literary programs are offered without charge to all who wish to attend.

Although visitors can make use of Library of Congress materials, they may not remove them from the premises. Residents of other parts of the country, however, may borrow materials by applying through their local public libraries for an interlibrary loan. A fine collection of braille and talking books and magazines is also available and requested items are mailed without charge to citizens with impaired vision.

In many countries, the national library function is shared (and sometimes fulfilled entirely) by state, provincial, or large city libraries. In the United States, each state maintains a state library, which is located in the capital city and offers services at a state level similar to those offered by the Library of Congress at the national level. These libraries serve as state government reference and research libraries and all but one (Michigan permits its residents to visit the facility and select and borrow books) make books available to the general public only when requested to do so through interlibrary loan. They are also responsible for providing library services to people in state-operated institutions such as prisons and hospitals.

On a lower level, there is a growing tendency for cities and counties, two or more counties, or public libraries and school libraries to pool their resources and form combined library systems. Such arrangements are often more economical and efficient and result in the provision of better and less expensive library services. In New York State, for instance, most municipal libraries belong to one of 22 regional library systems. Each system has a headquarters library that is responsible for acquisition and processing of library materials and provides improved accessibility to all the materials on a regionwide basis.

Regional libraries have been particularly successful in bringing library service to small towns and rural areas in Canada. Most of the provinces make extensive use of this type of system so that library services now reach well over 75 percent of all Canadians. Most of the larger municipalities continue to operate their own libraries with the regional systems covering the remainder of the provinces through a network of headquarters, branch libraries, and small library stations, financially assisted by provincial government grants. As in the United States, however, the municipal and regional libraries remain heavily dependent on local tax moneys.

COLLEGE LIBRARIES

Although they are intended primarily for student and faculty use, most of the 4000 college libraries in the United States are open to the public and are used by individuals seeking a wider range of materials than the local public library provides. Some college libraries allow books to be taken out by nonstudents; others only permit them to use books on the premises. Some larger college libraries are similar to national libraries in the quality and scope of their collections. The Harvard University Library in Boston, for example, is not only the largest university library in the world, it also ranks in size with the British Museum Library and France's Bibliothèque Nationale.

PRIVATE LIBRARIES

Although generally less accessible and less interesting to the public than the tax-supported local libraries, a number of private libraries, most of them limited to one particular subject, provide certain segments of the population with exceptional educational and recreation opportunities. Some of the 10,000 specialized libraries are maintained by private bodies such as the National Academy of Sciences or the various halls of fame. Materials in these libraries are seldom loaned to individuals but can usually be examined by people who make arrangements to visit the library in person. Very small but useful libraries are often maintained by private organizations such as hobby clubs. These materials help members increase their skills and knowledge. Finally, the small libraries maintained by businesses and resorts for their employees, visitors, or guests are often well-used, much-appreciated resources.

MULTIPURPOSE CENTERS

Most of the cultural facilities described above offer only one or two groups of cultural opportunities. Even those called cultural centers generally provide experiences that are limited to the performing arts. A new type of complex is now being

Figure 16.15 The cultural center in Port Charlotte, Florida. The complex on the left consists of the administrative building, library, classrooms, senior lounge, and theater (3 stories). Workrooms and shops are on the right.

built that includes a much broader range of opportunities.

The people of Port Charlotte, Florida, have developed a $3 million complex of this type. It combines the attributes of several kinds of singlepurpose cultural, recreational, and educational structures (Figure 16.15). The main components are:

- A 40,000-volume library with the largest per capita circulation of any library in the state.
- A 418-seat theater that schedules community variety shows, public forums, concerts, travelogues, opera, plays, revues, and feature films either free or at low admission prices (the annual deficit is covered by donations).
- Sixteen classrooms arranged in a square around a courtyard with a gazebo in the center where a variety of entertainment programs are held.
- A large Senior Lounge where inexpensive lunches are served and

where people gather informally or take part in a seven-day-a-week program of organized activities, including games, dances, informal concerts, and song fests.
- Workrooms where a corps of nearly 2000 volunteers produces handicrafts and restores donated items for fundraising purposes.
- A series of shops where the center's merchandise is displayed and sold.

Plans call for an addition to the library and the construction of two more buildings to provide better facilities for the center's numerous arts and music programs.

The complex acts as library, senior citizens center, cultural center, community center, and school. The library is operated by the county and is the only building that regularly receives direct tax support. It caters to the needs of older citizens by providing a wide selection of records and large-print books, a

talking-book service, and a home book-delivery service for shut-ins. The educational programs, which are largely recreational for the majority of the students, consist of more than 200 classes offered during each 10-week term. The courses include instruction in boating, bridge, ballet, art, music, foreign languages, mathematics, television repair, woodworking, and world affairs. They are available to everyone for a modest donation-type fee; entrance examinations are not required and, unless requested, homework assignments, examinations, and credits are not given. Since Port Charlotte currently has the highest ratio of elderly residents of any American community (more than 50 percent of the population is over 65), there is considerable emphasis on programs for older citizens. However, people of all kinds, including young children and the handicapped, make use of the center and participate in its many programs.

The Port Charlotte Cultural Center is the result of cooperative action by citizens, local government, and private enterprise. Constructed on 3.5 hectares (8.5 acres) of land donated by the developers of Port Charlotte, the complex was built in stages as funds became available. An initial grant of $446,000 by the county government from its share of state racetrack taxes helped start the project after local fund-raising drives and attempts to secure foundation or federal support proved inadequate. An $82,500 grant under the federal Library Construction Act also assisted in the early stages. The majority of the funds, however, have come from donations by local residents and from the earnings of center volunteers.

THE SIGNIFICANCE OF CULTURAL RESOURCES

The recreation significance of the great range of cultural resources described in this chapter is not easy to assess. Obviously, some of the resources, especially those that make up the group known as *mass culture* (Hollywood films, commercial television programs, best-selling novels, and popular music and magazines) are perceived as highly recreational by vast numbers of people. There are also people who feel that these resources are so low in cultural content that they should not be regarded as cultural resources at all but simply as sources of light entertainment.

Neither view is necessarily correct; experiences obtained from these resources often give individuals fresh insights into their own or other people's behavior or introduce ideas and provide information that help them understand and appreciate certain aspects of their environment or cultural heritage. In addition, almost all of these resources, regularly or occasionally, include material that is immediately or will eventually be accepted as a cultural resource even by the purists. On the other hand, certain material is considered so boring or distasteful by some individuals that exposure to it will never provide them with recreation experiences.

When the resources that form the group known as *high culture* (art films, fine arts museums, classical music and literature, opera, and ballet) are considered, the situation becomes even more complicated. These resources are avoided by many people because they are convinced that such activities provide few if any pleasurable experiences. Even the people who regularly make use of these resources do not always consider their experiences recreational. In some societies, these resources have gained a reputation that encourages many individuals to become involved with them to acquire sophistication, achieve status or social recognition, grow intellectually, show their support for an organization that has acquired considerable prestige, or please a teacher, employer, friend, or relative. Participants with these kinds of motivations may obtain little or no enjoyment from their involvement. However, exposure to the resources can alter perceptions and eventually some of these participants may acquire a liking for the experience that these resources provide.

There is another aspect of cultural resources that makes their recreation potential tenuous. Whereas many other resources occur in environments that provide many opportunities for secondary recreation experiences even if the principal resource is not particularly well liked, cultural resources like books, concerts, and museum exhibits stand largely on their own. If they fail to rouse a person's interest sufficiently to make involvement pleasurable, there is less likelihood of participation being enjoyable for other reasons (Figure 16.16).

Figure 16.16 Visitors listen intently to the guide during a tour of the Louvre in Paris. Since there are few opportunities to engage in social conversation or other kinds of secondary activities, the recreational benefits derived depend largely on the participants' attitudes toward the cultural resource consisting of both the guide's presentations and the art works. For many participants, learning about the paintings and the artists who created them is a satisfying recreational experience.

It is this close relationship between attitude and enjoyment that makes evaluating high-culture resources so difficult. Their recreation value seems to be directly proportional to the level of appreciation possessed by participants, and this is impossible to gauge simply by tabulating the size or even observing the behavior of audiences. Nor is it a relatively stable relationship; appreciation for a cultural resource can easily be negatively affected or destroyed by exposure to a series of poor experiences, just as it can be developed or nurtured by contacts with fine performances and exhibits or by increased knowledge. Assigning a recreation value to these resources is made even more difficult by the fact that the esteem in which they are held fluctuates, not only from country to country but also from time to time as the attitudes of populations are affected by changes in society and in the resources themselves.

Unfortunately, relatively small proportions of most populations take full advantage of the varied opportunities offered by cultural resources. However, the importance of such resources is more extensive than the total recreation experiences provided. Some people obtain considerable satisfaction just from knowing specific cultural resources exist or from hearing about them from people who do make use of them. Exposure to cultural resources can also produce a chain reaction causing changes in the way a person thinks, feels, and acts. Because the arts are intermingling more, a considerable *cross-stimulation effect* is also being produced. Television with its enormous audiences plays a major role in this phenomenon. While watching a television program, a person can enjoy a recreation experience and, at the same time, be introduced to literature, art, music, dance, a museum exhibit, or a natural wonder. This exposure, in turn, often stimulates a desire to participate directly in the activity or undertake a related activity such as seeing a live performance, reading a book, listening to a recording, or visiting an exhibit.

At the same time, there can also be a *ripple effect.* Watching a television program, reading a book, seeing a museum exhibit, or attending a lecture or concert can stimulate an urge to explore areas that have little or nothing to do with the resource that inspired the action. Unintentionally, the resource can trigger a thought pattern that encourages a person to take a trip, join an organization, try a new activity, acquire a new skill, or alter a lifestyle or pattern of behavior.

Cultural resources are also important on a less personal level. They can enhance a community's or nation's image and be major sources of civic and national pride. Houston, Texas, for instance, has become well known for its ability to provide outstanding cultural experiences. In fact, it is one of the few cities in the United States that can lay claim to having all four of the performing arts—opera, ballet, theater, and symphony—represented by fully professional companies. The citizens recognize the value of these resources to the city's well-being and show their appreciation not only by attending performances in large numbers but also by providing high levels of financial support.

The fact that cultural resources can also function as major economic resources for a community, state, or nation is also being recognized. Although relatively poor revenue generators for themselves, cultural resources often play a key role in the economic growth of a community since many businesses prefer to locate in an area that contains a diversity of such resources. Tourism is also encouraged by cultural resources, thereby producing additional income for transportation systems, hotels, restaurants, parking facilities, and various manufacturers and retailers whose businesses may or may not be directly related in any way to the cultural resource. Additional tax moneys accrued by such means are usually considerable and sometimes can be enormous; these funds can be used to provide essential services and maintain or improve the living environment of the citizens, including supplying more and better recreation opportunities.

The economic significance of cultural resources was illustrated a few years ago when the Stanford Research Institute made a study for the city of San Francisco of the probable effects of the proposed Performing Arts Center. It reported that the city would receive major economic benefits starting with the construction payrolls and leading eventually to the benefits from the sale of 500,000 admissions, increased employee payrolls of over $1 million, and increased business revenues of $4 million each year. It also predicted that the center would stimulate expansion of other organizations and facilities resulting in additional economic benefits. This report succeeded in changing the attitudes of many of the proposed center's critics, including several key political figures, and the city committed $9 million in public funds to the $33 million project.

Such economic benefits can accrue to all communities that possess interesting cultural resources, but some places have been more successful than others because they better appreciated the potential value of these resources and accepted responsibility for promoting their attractiveness. For instance, many of the poorest urban neighborhoods in the United States—Boston's Roxbury, Chicago's West Side, Los Angeles' Watts, and New York's Harlem—often contain unusual cultural resources, but many outsiders regard them as potentially dangerous areas that should be avoided. Such neighborhoods are only now awakening to the fact that they are interesting places for nonresidents to visit and are beginning to encourage tourism as a means of increasing revenues, rebuilding residents' pride, lessening outsiders' negative attitudes, and prompting city government improvement of basic services, including police protection.

One of the most aggressive programs of this nature currently being undertaken is in Harlem. The Uptown Chamber of Commerce's tourist map and brochure is being distributed to travel agents and New York City hotels. Describing over 70 things to do, it points out that the area contains more than a dozen theaters and fully one-quarter of the city's museums. A black-owned sightseeing company is showing busloads of visitors the cultural resources of general interest such as the Morris-Jumel mansion (George Washington's revolutionary headquarters), the Schomburg Library (containing the nation's largest collection of black history and literature), and the house where the singer Paul Robeson once lived. More New Yorkers are beginning to feel at home in the area and appreciate Harlem for its great contributions to American culture, particularly in the fields of music, literature, and theater.

New cultural resources can also be catalysts for the redevelopment of entire areas. A good example of this is the 42nd Street Theater Row in Manhattan, a $1 million experiment in urban redevelopment. In 1975, when a theater company moved into a former burlesque house on West 42nd Street, the street was a tawdry, unsavory strip containing massage parlors, pornographic movie theaters, empty buildings, and sleeping derelicts. By 1978, it was transformed into a blossoming, legitimate theater district containing a cluster of eight small theaters and a new French restaurant. Paid for by member companies, the artists themselves, grants from the Ford Foundation, cooperating labor unions, the 42nd Street Local Development Corporation, and the City and State of New York, the project is already considered only the initial step. The second phase—costing $9 million and involving the revitalization of adjacent streets—is under way.

And finally, cultural resources are important in their own right because they protect and preserve ideas, art forms, and materials that together comprise the heritage of the human race. In addition, they nurture new ideas and art forms. In so doing, cultural resources influence society and shape the ways that people live and think whether they personally make use of them or not.

DISCUSSION TOPICS

1. Do cultural resources enrich your recreation environment and the environments of people with whom you are familiar? If so, describe these resources and identify their primary sources of revenue.
2. Cultural resources in the United States differ from those in other nations in several important ways. Discuss the differences and the resulting advantages or disadvantages.
3. Since lack of adequate funding is now a constant source of anxiety for almost all of the cultural resources, it would seem likely that many of these resources are destined to deteriorate or even disappear. Can you suggest any possible solutions to this problem?
4. Government funding of cultural resources is a controversial issue in the United States. What are your opinions on the opposing viewpoints?
5. In your opinion, is popularization of the arts a good or a bad trend? Use examples to support your viewpoint.

Few recreation textbooks or journals devote more than a few lines to cultural resources although some include several pages on the performing arts. *The Encyclopaedia Britannica* includes extensive information on the development and nature of the world's major cultural resources. The development of American museums is outlined in *Museums U.S.A.: A History and Guide* by Herbert and Marjorie Katz, published in Garden City, New York, by Doubleday in 1965. Monro MacCloskey's *Our National Attic,* published in New York by Richards Rosen Press in 1968, describes The Library of Congress, The Smithsonian Institution, and The National Archives. Nicholas Zook's *Museum Villages USA,* published in Massachusetts by Barre Publishing in 1971, and Bernard Livingston's *Zoo: Animals, People, Places,* published in New York by Arbor House in 1974, are highly readable discussions of these two special types of cultural resources.

The development and value of libraries are explored in a book by Elmer D. Johnson, *History of Libraries in the Western World,* published in Metuchen, New Jersey, by the Scarecrow Press in 1970. Two other books that discuss library services are *A Century of Service* edited by Jackson, Herling, and Josey, published in Chicago by the American Library Association in 1976, and *The Library Reaches Out* edited by Coplan and Castagna, published in Dobbs Ferry, New York, by Oceana in 1965.

In *Leisure and Popular Culture in Transition* by Thomas M. Kando, published in St. Louis in 1975 by Mosby, several chapters are devoted to assessing the quality of cultural life in America. The chapters, "High Culture," "Mass Culture: The Printed Media," and "Mass Culture: Cinema," provide good background material on specific cultural resources as well as summarizing their present position. *The Performing Arts in America,* edited by Diana Reische and published in New York by H. W. Wilson in 1973, explores the status and problems of the performing arts. Two sources that discuss the role of cultural activities in recreation programs are *The Interrelated Arts in Leisure* by Nellie D. Arnold published in St. Louis by C. V. Mosby in 1976, and Ann Satterthwaite's report "Art and Culture: A New Priority in Urban Recreation" published in 1977 by the Heritage Conservation and Recreation Service, U.S. Department of the Interior, as part of Volume II of the *National Urban Recreation Study.*

Each *Yearbook* published by Encyclopaedia Britannica includes reports on the past year's major events of a cultural nature, including art exhibitions, the opening of new museum or theater facilities, and important happenings in literature, music, theater, dance, and the motion picture, television, and radio broadcasting industries. Periodicals that often have articles on cultural resources and are commonly available at public and college libraries include *Americana, American Education, Americas, Archaeology, Art in America, ARTnews, Dance Magazine, The Journal of the Film and Television Arts—American Film, Opera News,* and *Smithsonian.* Many of the related professional associations and individual institutions publish useful bulletins, reports, and newsletters. Newspapers often report on cultural events or facilities and some, like the Sunday editions of the *New York Times,* occasionally feature in-depth articles on topics such as government funding or the significance of a certain kind of cultural resource.

17

PROFESSIONAL RESOURCES: ADMINISTRATION, MANAGEMENT, AND PROGRAMMING

CONCEPTS & PROBLEMS

Professionals Are Resources
Good Administration Is Crucial
Financing Provides a Firm
    Foundation
Increasing Complexity Requires
    Careful Research and
    Planning
Good Design Aids Maintenance
Variety of Programs Is Huge
Fun Not Win-at-all-costs
Encourage Lifetime Activities
Balanced Programs Include Five
    Kinds of Activities
Therapeutic Recreation's Role

Figure 17.1 A U.S. Forest Service ranger discusses the features of various trails with hikers who are about to enter a national forest wilderness. His knowledge of the attractions and exigencies of each trail will help them choose a route that will best suit their interests, physical capabilities, and time constraints.

Although tangible recreation resources such as playgrounds, athletic fields, community centers, parks, campgrounds, libraries, and museums make major contributions to recreation, these amenities would not exist and are often of little use to the average citizen unless certain professional services are provided. Even wilderness areas may provide comparatively few recreation opportunities unless trails and bridges are developed and maintained. Prudent wilderness users also depend on other services such as maps, weather forecasts, and advice from an area's managers (Figure 17.1). In contrast, there are many situations where tangible recreation resources may be minimal, absent, or overlooked and where experiences are created largely or entirely through the services provided. For example, nature study experiences in national parks or recreation programs at undesignated sites (city streets, church halls, hospitals) depend largely on the ideas, leadership, and skills provided by recreation professionals.

This chapter discusses the contribution made by professionals to the provision of recreation opportunities. It has been placed last in this recreation resource section because it is easier to appreciate the role of various kinds of professional services if the nature and extent of tangible recreation resources are already understood. The space devoted to this topic is purposely limited because most students in preparatory programs for recreation professionals take a number of courses that examine the methods and problems of providing recreation services. Thus the position and space given to this chapter should in no way be considered indicative

of the relative importance of professional services. On the contrary, the knowledge and leadership of recreation professionals and others employed in recreation agencies and organizations are essential components of most recreation systems.

The contributions of recreation professionals can be divided into two broad areas. The first, *administration,* involves the organization of recreation systems, the development of policies, and the provision of financial support. The second area, *management,* includes research and planning; the design, construction, operation, maintenance, and protection of inanimate resources; and the use of human resources in conjunction with inanimate resources to provide organized recreation programs. (This latter activity is often referred to as *programming.*) The bulk of this chapter is devoted to these two topics.

ADMINISTRATION

The nature and quantity of recreation opportunities offered by a recreation system depends to a large extent on the manner in which it is administered. One urban park system, for example, may have extensive, well-constructed recreation facilities, good maintenance, and excellent recreation programs, whereas a similar system elsewhere may have substandard facilities, poor maintenance, and inadequate programs. Such differences may largely be the result of differences in administrative structure and skills.

ORGANIZATION
A key factor in the administration of recreation systems is the manner in

which the administrative structure is organized. In the past, many public and private recreation agencies were organized in an autocratic manner. An individual, sometimes without any background or training in recreation, was put in charge and allowed to administer the agency with little or no direction from the individual or group that made the appointment. Now, most recreation agencies have more sophisticated administrative structures that involve democratically operated controlling boards and a number of advisory committees.

The typical modern city park and recreation department, for example, is controlled by a board or commission composed of citizens appointed by the mayor or city council. Usually the board members have an interest in recreation and knowledge of the local system but no related professional experience or training. Such boards generally rely on the director of the department and the supporting staff for technical information and recommendations. Budgets and major development proposals are prepared by the staff, modified (if necessary) by the board, and recommended to the city council. Some boards have standing or special committees consisting of board members, professional advisors, and citizens who act in an advisory capacity. Frequently, citizen involvement is encouraged by publicizing board meetings and holding public hearings on major projects and controversial issues.

There are many other kinds of urban park and recreation organizational structures. Municipalities with a city manager form of government usually authorize the manager to carry out much of the coordination and supervision that might otherwise be performed by the mayor or park and recreation board chairperson. Some municipalities still have a park department that is separate from the recreation department, each having its own director and controlling board. Others have a department that constructs and maintains parks but undertakes no recreation programming because that is a responsibility of the board of education. Where the park and the recreation functions are in separate departments or recreation programming is provided by the board of education, a wide variety of relationships exists. In the best situations, harmonious cooperation between departments results in mutual benefits and better service to the public. At the other extreme are cities where acrimonious relationships between staff members of different departments result in little or no cooperation and a reduction in the quality or quantity of public recreation opportunities.

Similarly, the administrative organization of intermediate-level government agencies responsible for recreation resources and programs differs widely. Some states, for example, have consolidated most recreation functions[1] at a state level in one large department, often called a department of natural resources. Others still have separate agencies to administer the state's park, fisheries, wildlife, boating, forestry, and tourism programs. Such independent agencies are often controlled by separate boards, each reporting independently to the state governor and legislature. Administrative structures of this type do not

[1] The term recreation function is used to include all types of park and recreation programs.

encourage integrated cooperative programs. In some cases, small agencies of this type have proven to be particularly susceptible to pressures from political leaders or special interest groups.

The organizational status of the recreation function within a government or private organization can profoundly affect the nature and scope of the opportunities provided. In urban areas, for example, the best supplies of municipally provided opportunities are usually found in communities that have a combined park and recreation department that has equal status with other major functions such as public safety, streets, and sewer and water services. Recreation professionals, both as individuals and through professional organizations, sometimes have opportunities to influence the administrative status of the recreation function. Such opportunities occur when constitutions or charters are being prepared or when internal administrative reorganizations take place. Individuals and professional organizations then encourage legislative groups and administrators to give the recreation function equal status with other primary public services and appoint an appropriately qualified recreation professional as the department head.

POWERS AND RESPONSIBILITIES

Legislative constitutions and municipal charters are also important in that they often specify the powers and responsibilities of recreation organizations. In some cases, special legislative acts or municipal ordinances are passed that set out in detail the purposes, powers, and

proposed scope of operations of recreation organizations. States, for example, have passed acts that either establish specific recreation agencies (like the Michigan act setting up the Huron Clinton Metropolitan Authority) or provide a legal framework within which agencies (such as park districts or county park systems) may be formed if sufficient local support is forthcoming.

Participating in the drafting of acts, charters, and ordinances that legally establish the powers and responsibilities of recreation agencies provides recreation professionals with the chance to improve the administration of recreation systems. A document of this type often establishes a wide range of guidelines for the agency, including:

- The geographic area and kinds of resources over which it has jurisdiction.
- The types of recreation facilities and programs that it may develop.
- The structure and method of appointment of any controlling and advisory boards or committees.
- Procedures for establishing policies, developing budgets, raising funds, acquiring land, and developing facilities.
- Powers to create and enforce regulations intended to protect users and resources from antisocial behavior.

In some instances, agencies supplement legislative guidelines of this kind with internal administrative rules that describe responsibilities and procedures in more detail.

The powers given to recreation agencies by founding or permissive legislation vary greatly. Some regional park agencies and park districts have the power to set and collect an annual tax levy. City, district, county, and regional park systems sometimes have their own police or law-enforcement rangers equipped with patrol cars, radios, and other standard police equipment. Many systems are empowered to conduct recreation programs on a wide range of public and private lands; other departments may only operate on their own property. Important attributes are the degree to which an agency may produce revenue by operating profit-making facilities and the extent to which it can accumulate and borrow money. Developing legislation that will permit recreation agencies to be fully effective in the manner intended is a complex and specialized professional responsibility.

POLICY DEVELOPMENT

The recreation professional and any controlling board or commission must establish more detailed policies and procedures within the framework created by the founding legislation. Again, there is great variation in the manner in which this is done. Many agencies rely almost completely on their professional staff to develop policy recommendations, which are usually adopted with little modification. Other recreation organizations develop many of their policies through committee or board discussions (Figure 17.2). When a problem arises, it is referred to the appropriate group for consideration and, then, is solved when a suitable course of action is recommended and adopted.

Recreation professionals frequently have a major impact on the number, quality, and diversity of recreation opportunities available in an area because of their skill in developing and recommending administrative policies. Examples of policy issues that can have consid-

Figure 17.2 Members of the Lansing (Michigan) Parks Board and Director of Parks and Recreation Douglas Finley (fifth from left) listen as residents complain about antisocial behavior in the city's most heavily used park. Meetings are held in various neighborhoods on a rotation basis so that the board and director can learn directly about citizen concerns. This information along with staff recommendations and suggestions from organized groups is taken into consideration when formulating policies.

erable effect on recreation opportunity supply are:

- How much money to charge various age groups for admission to swimming pools or for fishing licenses.
- Whether to offer organized summer recreation programs on the streets and in parking lots or only at school playgrounds and parks.
- How many benches to include when renovating downtown parks and squares, which have been experiencing problems with drunkenness and vagrants.
- What action to take when powerboat enthusiasts and waterskiers interfere with the enjoyment of fisherpersons.
- Whether to permit private and quasi-public organizations to use public parks or recreation centers for their organized recreation programs.
- How to react to the proposed donation of a large mansion that would be expensive for the agency to repair and maintain.
- Where to locate new parks and recreation centers in developing suburban areas.

There are usually no simple solutions to such problems. Often it takes much investigation and negotiation to develop policies that appear to be the best compromise.

The competent recreation professional undertakes such investigations well in advance of policy-setting meetings and attempts to negotiate appropriate compromises where this is feasible and proper. The extent to which professionals can do this depends on the agency's customary policy-making procedures. In some cases, the staff is expected to undertake all of the preparatory work and present policy recommendations in a virtually finished form. Other organizations expect the staff to obtain information but leave policy development to the board. Sometimes board chairpersons or advisory committee chairpersons are extensively involved on a day-to-day basis in policy formulation and only expect the professionals to serve a staff function.

There are also situations at all levels of government where elected officials (mayors, city councilpersons, county supervisors, legislative representatives and senators) take part directly in deciding policy. This is often the case where decisions are politically significant. For example, questions such as where to build a new recreation center or swimming pool frequently become the subject of bitter battles between city councilpersons. They may investigate potential sites, issue public statements, and enter into protracted debates in attempts to secure a facility for a particular constituency. Under such circumstances, recreation professionals may find it difficult to avoid becoming personally involved in the conflict. Considerable skill and tact are usually required to retain the goodwill and respect of the various factions involved.

Policy making is further complicated by direct citizen involvement and the influence of special interest groups. Previously, it was expected that citizens' desires would be expressed primarily through elected representatives. Now there is a growing reliance on public hearings at which both individuals and organized groups are encouraged to give opinions. Such hearings can provide much useful information for an agency and result in a better informed public. They can also be extremely time consuming especially if many hear-

ings are held to cover a large geographic area and all the proceedings have to be tape recorded and transcribed. Where citizen-organization and special-interest-organization involvement is high, the recreation professional may find it difficult to maintain a stance that is respected by all four groups to which he or she owes some allegiance — the controlling board, elected representatives, the general public, and special interest groups.

Although great diplomacy and restraint are generally required if recreation administrators are to keep the respect of all factions in policy disputes, it is also necessary for professionals to provide leadership. They must point the way toward decisions that are likely to be most socially satisfactory in the long run. Often this leadership has to be provided unobtrusively so that board members and elected representatives do not feel the administrator is usurping their responsibilities. Some of the most effective recreation professionals are those who make it a habit of being relatively inconspicuous in public, but who are able to exert a strong guiding influence behind the scenes.

FINANCIAL SUPPORT

Another area in which recreation professionals make a major contribution is in finding ways to provide financial support for facilities and programs. Considerable fiscal knowledge and experience is needed to operate a large recreation system such as a major city park and recreation department successfully. A good administrator must be familiar with all of the possible sources of funding and know their advantages, disadvantages,

and limitations. Generally, the most significant financial support sources are tax levies, revenue from the sale of goods or services, donations, and government grants.

Direct Taxation. Perhaps the most critical source of money for recreation is direct taxation where a uniform tax rate is levied on the population at large specifically for this purpose. This money is important because it is often the primary source of support, especially in the case of federal systems and less sophisticated local systems. It is also necessary for a certain amount of locally raised funds to be available to match grants made under various government programs where regulations require that the recipient agency contribute a certain percentage of the funds.

Most local governments adopt budgets that include a small levy for recreation purposes and collect this money as part of the general property taxes. Where community leaders and recreation professionals have managed to develop strong public support for municipal recreation programs, the amount of money coming from property taxes may be considerable. However, funds from this source may also be quite niggardly, especially in rural municipalities and those that are economically disadvantaged. Inflation and tax-limitation measures have also been reducing the value or level of funds provided by property taxes in numerous communities. As a result, many recreation professionals are waging a continuous battle just to maintain existing levels of funding for municipal recreation facilities and programs.

Most of the national recreation resources in the United States are operated by using funds from direct taxation. The majority of the money used to run the national parks, national forests, and other federal amenities comes from the general fund. Revenues from admission and other fees are returned to the general fund rather than being used by the agency that collected them.

Fees and Charges. There are two opposing schools of thought regarding the desirability of relying on extensive revenues from the sale of goods and services at recreation developments. One group believes that recreation opportunities ought to be accessible to as many citizens as possible so that fees and charges should be kept to a minimum or avoided altogether wherever possible. The other group sees the operation of revenue-producing activities as a good method of producing much-needed money for a diversity of recreation facilities and programs. They argue that it is only fair for those who use the recreation resources to pay more than those who do not.

Some recreation systems produce substantial revenues by charging admission to all their developments and making a reasonable profit on the operation of amenities such as refreshment stands, vending machines, gift shops, restaurants, tour trains, rental boats, campgrounds, and winter sports areas. Those agencies that wish to produce maximum revenues usually operate as many amenities as possible with agency employees rather than contracting with concessionaires. As a result, such organizations have substantial numbers of service employees and systems for purchasing, storing, and transporting foods and other heavily used

items. Where profits are substantial, agencies are able to finance non-revenue-producing activities as well as the operation and maintenance of the facilities that produce the revenue.

Many recreation programs operated by intermediate-level governments are financed by revenues received from users rather than general tax funds. State fish-rearing programs and stream-improvement projects are usually supported largely or entirely by state fishing-license fees and federal grants from the Dingell-Johnson fund, which are produced by the 10 percent excise tax on fishing tackle. Similarly, state wildlife management programs are funded by state hunting-license fees plus federal grants from the Pittman-Robertson fund, which result from the 11 percent federal excise tax on guns and ammunition. Other examples of indirect payment for services-through-license-fees are the provision of boating facilities and safety patrols with boat-license funds or the construction and grooming of trails with the proceeds from snowmobile licensing.

This type of *earmarking* of funds has distinct advantages where readily identifiable groups of users undertake activities that require special resources. However, recreation professionals are now analyzing such arrangements more carefully because they can cause problems concerning the subsequent use of the resource. For example, some hunters are demanding that non-contributing groups such as hikers, cross-country skiers, snowmobile operators, and birdwatchers should be prohibited from using lands purchased with hunting fees and Pittman-Robertson funds because their activities interfere with the

management of these areas for hunting and wildlife production.

Donations. Gifts are usually a small proportion of recreation agency revenues except in the case of special facilities. Zoos, botanical gardens, and art galleries often depend to a great extent on donations for constructing buildings and developing exhibits. Some undertake periodic fund-raising drives to provide money for specific projects. Such drives are frequently conducted by volunteers or by a corporation as a public service, but recreation professionals often are involved in administration and use of the proceeds.

Gifts are essential for the operation of many programs. As explained in Chapter 16, few cultural opportunities would exist without corporate and private donations. Even prestigious organizations like New York City's Metropolitan Opera are attempting to secure more support from individuals by a variety of methods that include offering special privileges to persons who join the Metropolitan Opera Guild.

Government Grants. During the past two decades, the number of state and federal government programs for financially aiding recreation agencies have rapidly increased in number, and the variety of projects eligible for assistance has grown substantially. The federal Land and Water Conservation Fund Act, for instance, supplies millions of dollars each year to state and local government recreation projects. Congress provides these funds from the sale of federal property, federal powerboat fuel-tax receipts, and Outer Continental Shelf mineral receipts. Matching grants (one federal dollar for every state or local dollar) are made for recreation land acquisitions and facility developments that are compatible with the state's comprehensive recreation plan. Grants have been given for a variety of projects, including the development of state parks, inner-city miniparks, swimming pool complexes, roadside parks, hiking trails, and bicycle paths.

Other federal and state assistance programs are available through organizations such as the Department of Housing and Urban Development, Department of Commerce, the Corps of Engineers, and state boating agencies. A recreation agency's professional staff must be aware of these various assistance programs and know how to apply successfully for funds.

Budgeting. Recreation professionals play a major role in providing opportunities when they prepare budgets. This involves estimating the cost of carrying on all of the continuing projects of the agency, predicting the expenses connected with planned new projects, and suggesting the combination of direct tax levies, revenues, donations, and grants that will most satisfactorily balance the budget. Usually an agency will borrow money during the year to carry out its projects pending the receipt of tax moneys and grants so that some provision has to be made for bank loans. Major projects may be financed by revenue bonds issued by the agency's parent municipality or state; the bonds are then repaid from user fees.

The budget for a large recreation system is usually a complex document composed of separate sections for each of the agency's major projects and areas of operation. Work on the following year's budget usually begins early in the current year and continues through a series of committee meetings, board sessions, and meetings with the parent organization until agreement is reached. Again, much depends on the technical and diplomatic skills of agency professionals. They must have a thorough knowledge of both the agency's financial situation and the budgetary processes of the parent organization. Often they are required to appear before municipal council or higher level finance committees and defend agency requests for appropriations. Sometimes such proceedings become enmeshed in party politics and decisions are not made objectively. Then, the recreation professional may be able to prevent arbitrary appropriations cuts by presenting cogent justifications that are hard to refute.

OTHER ADMINISTRATIVE ACTIVITIES

Recreation professionals are frequently involved in many other administrative duties that can have substantial impacts on the supply of recreation opportunities. An organization's land-acquisition program requires special skills and attention to detail, whether negotiations are carried on by agency personnel or outside firms. A good administrator will establish procedures that will enable the agency to identify desirable lands and, where possible, buy them as they come on the market well in advance of actual need. Advance purchase usually results in lower prices, more opportunities to arrange advantageous exchanges, easements, or leases, and less chance of becoming involved in expensive legal actions such as condemnations (compulsory purchase).

Maintaining good relations and communications with the general public is another critical task for professionals at all levels. Some large agencies employ public relations firms to carry out the basic work of supplying the media with news items and photographs. Most do it themselves or through the parent organization's information office. Whatever the mechanism, the effective recreation administrator is likely to spend many hours giving talks at meetings of organizations such as parent-teacher associations and service clubs, working with the broadcast media, and initiating or actually preparing news releases, slide shows, movies, and exhibits. The cultivation of good personal relationships with media personnel is particularly helpful. An effective public relations and information program is important because it helps make recreation opportunities more accessible to people and increases citizen understanding and support at the ballot box, during the budgeting process, and when controversies occur (Figure 17.3).

Finally, recreation professionals can affect the supply of opportunities by the way in which they administer the internal operations of their agency. Personnel selection and management are especially significant. Administrators should constantly strive to use procedures that result in the best qualified person being given a job and, then, being continually stimulated to provide the best possible service. Recreation professionals also contribute administratively to the success of their

Figure 17.3 Public recreation agencies use a variety of programs to inform citizens of their activities, encourage participation, and solicit support. The Oakland County (Michigan) Parks and Recreation Commission exhibits a display of photographs and informational literature prepared under the direction of Janet Pung, its public communications officer, at shopping malls and fairs (top). The East Bay Regional Park District (California) holds dedication ceremonies for a 90-hectare (220-acre) restored marsh at the Hayward Regional Shoreline Park (bottom). The district's landscape architect, Peter Koos, explains the park's master plan to citizens and media representatives as the dike in the background is breached to let in the waters of San Francisco Bay.

systems in establishing and maintaining efficient purchasing and record-keeping procedures.

MANAGEMENT

The contributions that professionals make to recreation resource management are generally more visible than those made in administration. The recreation center leader conducting a craft program, the lifeguard supervising a resort swimming beach, and the national park interpreter leading a hike are well-known components of recreation resource-management systems. But for every employee who is readily visible to the public, there are usually others who contribute their skills and experience behind the scenes. This section outlines the human resources and activities involved in the research, planning, design, construction, operation, maintenance, and protection procedures involved in recreation system management. Procedures that primarily involve running activity programs are discussed in the next section.

RESEARCH AND PLANNING

Some recreation professionals have always undertaken a certain amount of research and planning before developing and operating recreation resource systems. They have had the gift of being able to evaluate objectively complex situations in their heads, weigh the evidence in favor of various conclusions, and, then, select the conclusion and course of action that would be most beneficial. Such gifted people often have the vision necessary to anticipate trends so that, usually, their plans for the future turn out to be most appropriate.

However, as recreation systems and behavior have become more complex, it has been increasingly difficult for administrators and managers to make objective decisions and plan ahead purely on the basis of personal intuition. Sometimes, completely new situations have arisen such as the advent of the snowmobile or the problems with gasoline prices and supplies. The rate at which changes take place has also increased and the magnitude of the impact of such changes has grown radically now that such large sums are spent on the provision of recreation opportunities. In other words, it is costing more both economically and socially when recreation professionals guess incorrectly. Mistakes become obvious sooner and are more embarrassing in terms of expensive developments or elaborate programs being criticized as inappropriate. There is a growing interest, therefore, in using more sophisticated research and planning methods to ensure that appropriate administrative and management decisions are made at the right time.

Research. High-quality scientific research is still comparatively rare in the recreation field. This appears to be the result of a number of interlocking factors. First, remnants of the work ethic encourage many people to regard recreation as a subject unworthy of serious academic study. In spite of the obvious significance of recreation (especially in the social, psychological, and physical health areas), recreation research is seldom considered as important as other kinds of applied investigations. Research funds are harder to obtain and few outstanding researchers are attracted to the field. In addition, many recrea-

tion problems, especially those involving human behavior, are complex and change rapidly, making them difficult to investigate. In combination, these problems of attitude, funding, personnel, and complexity produce a vicious circle that tends to perpetuate the situation.

The world's largest coordinated recreation research program continues to be the one conducted by the Forest Service, U.S. Department of Agriculture. There are now some 30 full-time researchers located around the nation at various offices of the Service's eight forest experiment stations. In addition, there are over 100 university-based investigators who work part-time on cooperative recreation research, which is partly funded by the Forest Service. In the past, most of the investigations have been concerned with wilderness and campground carrying capacity, camping behavior, river-dependent recreation, and the nature of littering and vandalism. Recently, a forest service urban research unit was established in Chicago. It is providing funds for a number of cooperative studies concerning the recreation use of urban areas.

Several other American federal agencies sponsor recreation research. The Department of Health, Education, and Welfare provides funds for studies in sports medicine, therapeutic recreation, and recreation programming methods. Investigations of urban recreation problems have been funded by the Department of Housing and Urban Development. The Corps of Engineers has undertaken studies of recreation participation patterns and preferences both on its reservoirs and along major rivers, and the Coast Guard has sponsored boating

surveys. The majority of this work is done by universities, the remainder by consulting firms.

The National Park Service undertakes extensive research in connection with the management of its system, but the majority of projects concern archaeological, historical, wildlife, or vegetation problems. Generally, the Service has made comparatively few investigations of the human behavioral aspects of management, except for work on the environmental impact of float trips down the Grand Canyon. The Park Service has also sponsored a number of studies on the economic impact of park use.

When the Bureau of Outdoor Recreation (now Heritage Conservation and Recreation Service) was originally created by act of Congress in 1962, the drafters of the legislation intended the new agency to be a focal point for federal recreation research, continuing the nationwide surveys and methodological studies undertaken by the Outdoor Recreation Resources Review Commission. However, Congress has provided comparatively little money for this purpose so that the agency's research activities have been limited to a few participation surveys and a handful of methodological investigations.

The various state governments in the United States have conducted many surveys in the past two decades. Most have been intended primarily to provide participation data for statewide comprehensive recreation plans. Consequently, little attention has been paid to analyzing the data in order to discover causal relationships and, in some cases, the data do not appear to be particularly reliable. In addition, many state agencies have carried out studies of the behavior of special groups such as fisherpersons, hunters, state-park users, boaters, snowmobilers, and skiers. Again, the objective has usually been to provide participation data for planning purposes and little analysis of an explanatory nature has been attempted. The total amount of recreation participation data gathered by federal, state, and local government recreation surveys is immense, but its usefulness in terms of increasing understanding of recreation behavior has been limited by methodological problems and lack of coordination.

Although much recreation research has been completed in the past several decades, it has tended to be concentrated in five main areas. First, there has been a large number of physical education and sports medicine studies that examine the physical or psychological aspects of participation in various games and sports. These are mostly university faculty or graduate student thesis-research projects, and the subjects studied are usually university students, high school students, or residents of institutions rather than the general public. The second large group of research projects involves investigations of methods of conducting recreation programs and the impact of such programs, including, in some cases, their therapeutic values. Again, most studies have been carried out by university faculty or graduate students; the subjects are generally students, institution residents, or participants in municipal recreation programs.

The third large group is resource-management oriented investigations performed for or by land-managing agencies. Most of these studies have concerned national forest, national park, or less developed state park problems because the majority of the university researchers have been interested in the more remote resources, and much of the funding has come from forest-oriented sources. The fourth area is national, state, or specific agency studies of participation in outdoor activities, which were mentioned earlier. Finally, there have been a number of economic impact studies; most have been done by or on behalf of tourist- or economic-development agencies. Recreation professionals and researchers in related fields have obviously been making considerable contributions to our understanding of recreation through these studies, but some significant gaps exist.

One of the most serious of these gaps is the lack of information concerning people's recreation lifestyles. As noted above, there is considerable data on participation in certain kinds of activities (especially those that involve public agencies) and on the use of specific public resources. But apart from the time-budget studies mentioned earlier, very little is known about individuals' recreation lifestyles. It is impossible to obtain these data by integrating information from a selection of separate participation surveys. Continuous study of the recreation lifestyles of a representative panel of individuals is necessary. This makes it possible to monitor not only time-budgets but also to examine critical areas such as the interaction of changing external factors (Chapters 4–6) with personal factors (Chapter 7). To help individuals find personally and socially satisfactory recreation lifestyles, it is necessary to examine the psycholo-

gical, social, economic, and accessibility aspects of participation in the context of everyday living.

Another major omission has been the relative absence of research concerning recreation opportunities in urban areas. In the United States, there have been numerous evaluations of individual municipal recreation programs and a national study of urban recreation sponsored by the federal government. However, these investigations usually examine the problem from the viewpoint of those who administer and use existing municipal recreation services. Very few studies have examined the supply of urban recreation opportunities from the viewpoint of the average citizen. To provide urban recreation environments that are more responsive to the needs of all citizens, it will be necessary to develop mechanisms for more extensive community involvement, including studies that integrate data provided by facility managers with information obtained by interviewing on-site users and nonusers at their places of residence (Figure 17.4). In particular, continual investigation of ways to provide more opportunities in people's immediate neighborhoods is needed. Recreation researchers can make an even greater contribution in the future if they can provide more information concerning recreation behavior patterns as a whole and suggest ways of developing more satisfactory urban recreation supply systems.

Planning. Recreation professionals make significant contributions to the supply of recreation opportunities in their resource-planning activities. At one time, planning was regarded as a fairly simple task. It was seen as primarily a matter of producing a list or map showing the location of suitable physical resources. For example, state park system planning involved identifying suitable undeveloped resources that were of statewide significance; accessibility to population centers, carrying capacity for recreation activities, development potential, and location relative to other recreation resources were generally not considered. In the United States, the National Park Service provided leadership and technical assistance with a number of state and regional park system plans of this type during the 1930s.

Following World War II, state and regional park planning procedures gradually became more *people oriented*. This process accelerated when states were required to prepare statewide comprehensive recreation plans to receive grants from the Land and Water Conservation Fund. At first, these plans consisted mainly of inventories of publicly owned physical resources such as acres of forests, numbers of campsites, and miles of hiking trails. Most of the planners were foresters, landscape architects, or wildlife management or fisheries specialists. Few had any urban recreation or social science experience.

Slowly, the space in the state comprehensive plans devoted to the demand aspects expanded. Initially, more sophisticated analyses of population size, age structure, and growth were presented. Then, there was a period when many states conducted surveys of participation by state park users, fisherpersons, hunters, skiers, and other readily identifiable groups. Following this, a number of states undertook extensive telephone interviews

Figure 17.4 Terry Westover, doctoral candidate in recreation geography at Michigan State University, interviews urban park users concerning their perceptions of the incidence and impact of antisocial behavior in a methodological study funded by the U.S. Forest Service. Carefully designed and executed surveys of both users and nonusers are needed to understand complex problems such as the effects of deviant behavior and law enforcement policies on participation patterns.

or interviews in the home to determine statewide participation patterns in a wide range of recreation activities.

The ultimate goal was to develop a planning method that predicted future levels of demand for recreation opportunities and related those values in a quantitative fashion to the probable supply of op-

portunities. Comparing the estimated demand to the probable supply would then indicate the magnitude and location of supply deficits and surpluses. Recreation resource development projects could then be adjusted to provide more opportunities of the appropriate kinds at the locations with predicted deficits.

Unfortunately, the relationships between participation and the various external and personal controlling factors are complex and it proved much more difficult to develop methods of accurately predicting future recreation demand than had been anticipated. Indeed, a mathematical model that is statewide in scope and that can estimate future recreation participation with some degree of accuracy has largely turned out to be an impossible dream. Only in comparatively simple situations have reasonably accurate predictions been achieved. However, many statewide recreation planning agencies have not had sufficient funds to attempt the large-scale data gathering and analysis necessary for the estimation of future recreation demand on a geographic basis. Recently, the Heritage Conservation and Recreation Service has been encouraging states to spend less time on detailed supply-and-demand analysis and more time on identifying, analyzing, and recommending solutions to their main recreation problems.

Good comprehensive recreation planning requires the services of professionals with a wide range of training and skills. The topics that should be addressed in a typical local, regional, or intermediate level plan include:

• The nature, location, accessibility, and recreation capacity of both public and private developed and undeveloped resources.

- Existing recreation programs (public and private) and changes in them that are likely to occur in the future.
- The size, distribution, socioeconomic characteristics, and growth patterns of the population.
- Existing and anticipated transportation modes and networks.
- Existing patterns of recreation participation, trends in participation, and changes in constraints and stimuli.
- The essential issues such as lack of specific opportunities, user conflicts, inaccessibility, antisocial behavior, absence of coordination, and the need to provide opportunities for special segments of the population such as the disadvantaged, the handicapped, and the elderly.
- Possibilities of making innovative policy or program changes so as to address these issues and provide more and better recreation opportunities for the entire population.

An interdisciplinary team or several people with interdisciplinary training are necessary for this type of planning. Depending on the circumstances, the assistance of individuals with a knowledge of sociology, demography, transportation, forestry, fish and wildlife management, geographic analysis, tourism, and land-use planning may be needed to supplement the expertise of those with a recreation background.

Obtaining a good balance among the various components of a comprehensive plan is a desirable but difficult goal. Often it is impeded by imbalances in the skills and data available as well as lack of funds to correct these problems. It should also be recognized that some plans are treated as an end in themselves. For instance, statewide comprehensive recreation plans are sometimes regarded primarily as a means of qualifying for federal

grants. Consequently, some state recreation programs such as the state park system, state forest recreation developments, and boating-facilities programs are planned, developed, and operated with little or no reference to the guidelines established in the state's comprehensive recreation plan.

Few local governments have had either the staff or the funds to undertake sophisticated analyses of resources, population, transportation, and participation. Instead, many have relied on what are known as *recreation standards.* These are specific numerical values for various measures of the adequacy of recreation systems that have been agreed upon by professional organizations. For example, the current National Recreation and Park Association standards include the following suggested values:

- Ten acres (4.1 hectares) of urban parks per 1000 population.
- Twenty acres (8.1 hectares) of regional parks per 1000 population.
- One softball diamond per 3000 population.
- One 18-hole golf course per 25,000 population.

Such standards are intended as guidelines and not absolute values. To date, these standards have been developed by agreement among panels of practitioners rather than by empirical research. A number of authors have pointed out that some of these standards are becoming less appropriate, especially when applied to areas with large, dense populations.

DESIGN AND CONSTRUCTION

Another major factor that determines the number and nature of

recreation opportunities available to people is the quality of the amenities provided. This is controlled by both the design of the facilities and the way in which they are constructed. Developments are usually designed by consulting architects, landscape architects, engineers, and interior designers working under the supervision of recreation professionals. However, some large organizations employ their own specialists, some of whom become almost as well versed in recreation as recreation professionals. In other situations, the converse is true; recreation professionals in charge of small park systems or commercial recreation developments often become familiar with the relevant aspects of building, design, landscaping, engineering, and interior decorating and only call in consultants when it is obligatory.

Landscape design plays an important part in many kinds of recreation experiences from the wilderness to the city park or square. In wilderness areas, trails must be located so that the best balance is achieved among such requirements as ease of hiking, safety, low maintenance costs, taking people where they want to go, providing superior aesthetic experiences, and causing the least disturbance to fragile environments. In the United States, national forest landscape architects are laying out the boundaries of areas to be logged so that the cut-over patches are as inconspicuous as possible. Boundaries are designed to follow the natural shape of the land, avoiding straight lines, abrupt vegetation height changes along skylines, and unsightly areas along roads used for pleasure driving. In state parks, careful landscape design is used to separate uses and minimize user conflicts while enhancing aesthetic values. Perceptive shaping of the terrain and the selection and placing of vegetation in city parks can create beautiful vistas, make areas feel larger, provide shade, give a feeling of privacy, direct pedestrian traffic, protect fragile slopes, screen ugly sights, and provide surfaces suitable for activities ranging from football to sunbathing.

Ensuring that buildings are designed so that they produce an optimum number of the desired opportunities is an equally important responsibility of recreation professionals. But it is also important to devise ways to provide these opportunities at the lowest possible costs. Since the numbers of users at many recreation facilities vary according to the event, time of day, day of the week, or season of the year, buildings should be designed to adapt to considerable fluctuations in user demand. Proper design can ensure that a restaurant, theater, recreation center, museum, or sports facility will not only be able to accommodate large crowds when necessary but also adjust to the needs of one or more smaller groups. Not only does this reduce operating costs, it can also make users feel more comfortable and, in the case of revenue-producing facilities, it can increase the earning power of the building.

A good example is the Silverdome stadium in Pontiac, Michigan. Some events such as the Detroit Lions football games are able to draw huge crowds, but others, including traveling shows (Figure 17.5) and the Detroit Pistons basketball games, seldom use the 73,000-seat stadium to capacity. By installing a mammoth curtain across

Figure 17.5 Half of the Pontiac (Michigan) Silverdome becomes a rodeo arena for a single performance of the Longhorn World Championship Rodeo as the promoters assemble pens and stalls and over 2100 cubic meters (2800 cubic yards) of soil for the 90 ranked competitors and the award-winning livestock. Such events are economically feasible because the dividing curtain permits Pistons' professional basketball games to be played during the four days of preparations. Traveling shows make it possible for people to enjoy recreation experiences usually not available in their area.

the 50-yard line, the managers of the Silverdome can create two areas, thereby allowing a revenue-producing event to take place in one area while preparations are being made for a show in the other or permitting two events to be staged at one time. Not only is this a much better arrangement financially, it also is appreciated by both the spectators, who prefer a more intimate atmosphere for concerts and other shows, and by the entertainers, who like to perform in a full house.

All aspects of a structure's design can affect its performance as a recreation resource. For example, the position of a building on the site may influence its utility. Placing a building such as a library or community center in the middle of a wooded urban site so that it cannot be readily seen, will not encourage drop-in participation by pedestrians, especially during evening hours if crime is a problem in that vicinity. On the other hand, placing a performing arts building too close to a busy highway or rapid transit line can be a serious mistake unless funds are available for completely soundproof construction.

The circulation of all kinds of traffic, both inside and outside the buildings, also requires careful attention. Parking areas, public transportation stops, porticos, walkways, ramps, and doorways should be located and constructed so that access is as easy and as safe as possible, especially during periods of bad weather. This is not to say that roadways and parking spaces have to be crowded around a building with no regard for aesthetic considerations. But it is important to ensure that the handicapped, elderly, people in party clothes, or those carrying young children or artwork can gain access with a minimum of difficulty. In the past, the handicapped and the elderly have often been virtually denied the use of recreation buildings by long walks, innumerable steps, steep slopes, slippery surfaces, revolving or narrow doors, doors that are too hard to open, or inadequate provision of places to sit and rest.

Circulation between facilities and within buildings at a recreation development also requires thoughtful design. Walks, lobbies, and hallways should be of adequate size to accommodate the planned numbers of users. The principal destinations of users must be arranged so that people reach them easily by following the natural flow. Important service functions such as information booths, ticket offices, and toilets should be strategically placed and readily visible along the main circulation routes. In many situations, the best circulation designs are those that encourage one-way flows and avoid the abrupt intersection of two major flows. Circulation design is especially significant in theme parks, zoos, art galleries, and sports stadiums.

The design of recreation buildings often requires special knowledge and skills so that it is important for recreation professionals to make sure that consulting architects and engineers have the necessary qualifications and experience. Many

recreation facilities present special technical problems. For instance, acoustics, lighting, stage design, storage space, rehearsal and dressing rooms, and audience comfort all have to be taken into consideration in the case of halls and theaters. Other facilities that involve special technical expertise include swimming pools, ice arenas, art galleries, libraries, restaurants, discotheques, and exhibit buildings for zoological gardens. But even the design of small buildings should be given close attention; neighborhood recreation centers that must be intensively used for a wide range of activities are a special challenge (Figure 13.12). Recreation administrators and the responsible committee or board members should also ensure the best possible facility by examining and comparing the attributes of a number of structures already in service elsewhere; by taking into consideration the special requirements for their facility, as seen by both staff members and potential users; and by developing guidelines from these investigations that will help the consultant develop an appropriate plan.

In many cases, the materials and construction methods are just as important as the circulation and general layout of a facility. For example, materials and workmanship must complement space allocation and circulation if a heavily used campground toilet building is to be attractive, durable, and convenient to maintain. Walls, partitions and doors should be easy to wash down, fast-drying, and resistant to graffiti and other forms of vandalism. Toilet bowls, washbasins, and other fixtures must be as securely installed and as damage-resistant as possible; all valves, pipes, and tanks

should be accessible only from a locked plumber's alley. The selection of the appropriate size, construction, and location of doors, windows, skylights, and ventilators affects lighting, temperature, humidity, rates of drying, safety, and the degree to which problems are encountered with insects, birds, and antisocial acts. Concrete and tile floors must be laid without depressions, cracks, or corners where water or dirt can accumulate or penetrate.

These and other design and construction guidelines are important if recreation structures are to fulfill their purposes with as few difficulties as possible. Recreation professionals who make sure that good design and construction methods are followed save their organizations money and also reduce the amount of time that services are not available because of facility breakdown or vandalism.

OPERATIONS AND MAINTENANCE

Recreation professionals have a saying—"Don't build it if you can't maintain it." This means that an organization should not construct a facility (or accept a gift of one) unless it is reasonably easy to maintain, and the money, staff time, and skills necessary to keep it in good condition are available. It goes without saying that the organization must also be able to operate the facility. That is, it should have the resources needed to keep the development open during normal hours and protect it from damage at all times. Unfortunately, administrators and controlling bodies do not always adhere to these principles. Sometimes they proceed with a favorite project despite the fact that existing financial trends indicate adequate operations and maintenance funding will likely be unavailable; they place their faith in the belief that, somehow, once the facility is in use, a source of funding will automatically materialize. Unfortunately, this faith is not always realized and a facility either never fulfills its potential or quickly deteriorates through lack of care and protection.

Well-designed operations and maintenance programs are essential if a recreation system is to produce high-quality experiences. In some situations, the money and staff time needed to operate and maintain the system may be relatively small. For example, a somewhat remote and lightly used forest may be able to maintain its overlooks, picnic areas, and campgrounds very adequately by using a system of daily inspection and biweekly maintenance. To do this, a self-administered registration and fee-payment system is set up at the developed campgrounds. It enables the campers to pay their fees by completing the registration information on a prepared envelope, putting their money in it, and dropping it in a special box. A forest employee living nearby visits the campground each evening, checks to see that all is in order, including an appropriate registration for each occupied site. Garbage collection, toilet-building cleaning, and other maintenance is carried out by a traveling crew that visits each site twice or three times a week. Such a system can work well where use is moderate and antisocial behavior is rare.

In elaborate, heavily used systems, operations and maintenance programs often involve hundreds of employees, extensive equipment, and numerous buildings. A major city park system may routinely undertake the following operations and maintenance procedures:

- Snow ploughing, salting, and repairing parkways and park walks, roads, and parking lots.
- Grooming ski slopes and toboggan runs; spraying water on outdoor ice rinks during freezing weather.
- Pruning trees and shrubs and removing dead specimens in parks and squares and along city streets and parkways.
- Spraying trees and shrubs for insects and diseases; aerating, fertilizing, mowing, and spraying lawn areas, sports fields, and golf courses.
- Preparing beds, planting, and maintaining perennial and annual flower displays.
- Emptying trash baskets, picking up litter, cleaning buildings, removing graffiti, and repairing the damage caused by vandalism.
- Repairing and painting benches, fences, bridges, fountains, swimming and wading pools, picnic tables, playground equipment, toilet buildings, community centers, athletic stadiums, vehicles, and other park buildings and equipment.
- Removing excessive accumulations of algae or flotsam from beaches, grading the surface, and periodically running the sand through a beach cleaner to remove glass, bottle caps, and other undesirable objects.
- Putting markings on athletic and sports fields; installing special sports equipment and seating.
- Setting up and staffing facilities at which attendants are required; periodically picking up and checking cash receipts.
- Obtaining and distributing supplies needed for operations and maintenance, including fuels, food, drinks, paper products, equipment, and new and laundered uniforms.
- Patrolling park areas, parkways, recreation centers, and other facilities to assist users, detect maintenance problems, and discourage antisocial behavior.

Some systems may undertake other operations and maintenance procedures connected with special facilities such as zoos, aquariums, museums, theaters, marinas, and children's camps.

Supervising a large operations and maintenance program, whether it be for a city, theme park, ski resort, or major state park such as New York's Jones Beach, is a complex undertaking. The recreation professionals who manage such programs have to be versatile individuals who can successfully handle mechanical, biological, and human problems. Now that costs are increasing much faster than funds appropriated for operation, maintenance managers are having to change their procedures. Some are reducing the number of staff assigned to specific locations and using mobile maintenance crews instead. Greater attention is being given to analyzing operations and setting performance standards so that resources can be more efficiently used. More local, intermediate, and national government recreation agencies are contracting with private firms or even community groups for routine maintenance services.

In spite of rising costs, the operations and maintenance programs cannot be neglected. Recreation professionals have long believed that problems increase unless reasonable standards are maintained. They contend that it is more efficient to pick up litter frequently than let it accumulate because users drop less litter in a clean environment. Similarly, they argue that vandalism is reduced if graffiti and

Legend

Proportion of systems or units with programs[a] | Relative contribution in terms of opportunities[a]

Most have — — High
Many have — — Medium
Some have — — Low

Providers of Organized Programs

	Private Organizations						Commercial Enterprises							Public Organizations — Government Recreation			Institutions			Public and Private Cultural Organizations			
Examples of Groupings of Organized Programs[b]	Club	Property Management	Religious/Service	Quasi-public (Youth)	Quasi-public (Preservation)	Industry (for Employees)	Shopping (including malls)	Food and Drink	Dancing	Participatory Sports	Park/Show/Tour	Stadium/Racetrack	Camp/Hotel/Resort	Local	Intermediate	National	Higher Learning	Correctional	Health Care	Performing Arts	Broadcasting	Museum/Art Gallery/Zoo	Library
	1	2	3	4	5	6	7	8	9	10	11	12	13	14	15	16	17	18	19	20	21	22	23
I Physical Activity Programs																							
(a) Physical play:																							
Team sports (basketball, volleyball, soccer)																							
Dual sports (bowling, tennis, boxing)																							
Individual sports (fishing, skating, swimming)																							
Fitness activities (exercise, jogging, aerobics)																							
Active games (billiards, New Games, dodgeball)																							
Spectator sports (baseball, auto races, regattas)																							
(b) Physical travel:																							
Outings (bicycle tours, canoe and hiking trips)																							
Tourism (tours, cruises)																							
II Intellectual Programs																							
(a) Intellectual understanding:																							
Field study (interpretation or research)																							
Lectures, exhibits (museums, TV)																							
Courses (adult education)																							
(b) Intellectual production:																							
Participatory (discussions, workshops)																							

[a] Absence of indication of "some" systems or units with programs or absence of a "low" relative contribution of opportunities does not mean programs or contributions are never provided by that group.

Classification was developed from the Dumazedier system (see Kaplan, *Leisure: Theory and Policy,* Chapter 13).

	Providers of Organized Programs																						
	1	2	3	4	5	6	7	8	9	10	11	12	13	14	15	16	17	18	19	20	21	22	23
III Artistic programs (a) Artistic enjoyment:																							
Organized performances (concerts, TV)																							
Interpretive programs (tours, courses)																							
(b) Artistic creation:																							
Instructional programs (courses, workshops)																							
Participatory programs (guilds, societies, clubs)																							
IV Sociable programs (a) Sociable communication:																							
Personal interaction (socials, parties)																							
(b) Sociable entertainment:																							
One-way communication (nightclubs, movies)																							
V Practical programs (a) Practical collection:																							
Personal hobbies (shows, swaps, workshops)																							
Community collections (museums, historic sites)																							
(b) Practical transformation:																							
Do-it-yourself assistance (courses, clubs)																							
Personal development (courses, workshops)																							
Help others (assist social agencies)																							
Cause change (neighborhood, political action)																							

other forms of damage are promptly removed or repaired. In any event, the average user's recreation experience is depreciated or even made impossible if operations and maintenance programs do not provide a satisfactory recreation environment.

ACTIVITY PROGRAMS

Although all the contributions of all kinds of recreation professionals are important, none is of greater significance than that of people who conduct recreation activity programs. They are constantly *in the front line* where the users interact with the resources. Only when program personnel successfully use their knowledge, skills, and personalities to help prospective participants obtain desired recreation experiences is the goal of the recreation agency or enterprise fully achieved.

Personnel Involved. The number of different kinds of supervised recreation activity programs offered by various government, quasi-public, commercial, and private organizations is immense. Figure 17.6 attempts to give an impression of the main groupings of such programs and shows how they are widely distributed throughout the recreation organization spectrum. The listing in the left-hand column follows the Dumazedier approach mentioned in Chapter 8; the organizations are arranged in the order in which recreation resources were described in earlier chapters. Even from this simplified and condensed tabulation, it is evident that very large numbers of people are involved in organizing, supervising, presenting, and leading these programs.

Many of the individuals who help with supervised recreation activities are not full-time professionals. A number of organizations have numerous part-time employees who assist with recreation programs. These include lifeguards, sports coaches, playground program leaders, community center supervisors and class instructors, library aides, tour guides, camp counselors, seasonal rangers, and cruise program directors. A large proportion of this group consists of students, some of whom intend to become recreation professionals when their training is complete.

Another sizable group is comprised of people in other professions whose duties include involvement in recreation programs. Examples are teachers, librarians, historians, hospital staff, social workers, industrial public relations personnel, farmers, forest rangers, and retail-mall managers. Some of these individuals become expert at assisting with specific recreation programs through studying pertinent literature or receiving help from recreation professionals. Finally, many recreation programs make use of the services of volunteers. The exact nature of these arrangements varies considerably. Some individuals volunteer their services primarily for the pleasure it brings them and the organization may regard involv-

ing such people in their programs as another way of providing recreation opportunities. On the other hand, there are thousands of volunteers who help operate programs mainly as a public service or as a personal duty. In many instances, supervised recreation programs would be cancelled or severely curtailed without their assistance.

The main impetus and technical contribution usually comes from the full-time recreation professionals, however. In the United States and Canada, these are predominantly people who have graduated from a college or university and majored in community recreation, physical education, park administration, or recreation resource management. This is especially true in the case of municipal governments and quasi-public organizations. Nevertheless, there are many people employed primarily to supervise or conduct recreation programs who do not have this type of training. They are generally found in organizations that are not concerned solely with providing recreation as a social service. Examples are biologists conducting programs at nature centers, religious leaders running social events and recreation centers at churches, hotel management personnel organizing recreation programs at resorts, farmers operating trail rides and campfire programs at vacation farms, and professional athletes providing social activities at sports schools.

Types of Programs. As Figure 17.6 demonstrates, many different types of organizations provide supervised recreation opportunities. Each of the groups of programs listed in the figure represents a number of separate activities

as the examples indicate. All of the activities can be made available to participants in several different program formats. Therefore, the total number of relatively distinctive programs offered by various organizations is huge.

Currently, there are no data available that make it possible to quantitatively describe the overall patterns of recreation program provision. About all that can be said is that there are certain providers that appear to be major suppliers of certain kinds of programs and that there are some that offer a greater variety of programs than others. The groups of providers thought to have the most extensive programs are marked by the most continuous shading of the column squares in Figure 17.6.

The types of programs provided by an organization depend on a number of factors. A primary factor is the goals of the organization. A commercial recreation enterprise, for example, only provides programs that will produce a profit directly or may increase the overall profits by attracting a crowd of people, some of whom are likely to become customers during their visit. On the other hand, a religious organization may be interested in providing more self-actualizing recreation experiences for its participants and encouraging esprit de corps; their program choices may also be influenced by a desire to attract new members, encourage young people to take part, and, in some cases, produce revenues to help finance organization projects and programs (Figure 11.6).

It is usually much harder to agree on desirable goals in the case of public recreation programs because there are so many different opinions concerning the relative value of the different kinds of recreation and the roles governments should play in providing opportunities. Basically there are two schools of thought. One group of recreation professionals believe it is their responsibility to decide what kinds of programs will best suit the needs of the people they serve. This group contends that recreation professionals know the value of the various kinds of recreation programs and should prescribe them for their clients in much the same way that doctors prescribe medication for their patients. This philosophy often results in the adoption of programs that are limited in scope. For instance, some professionals in this group feel public programs should help people improve themselves and not just provide amusement. Consequently, they may recommend that only programs that (in their judgment) are highly educational should be provided. Others in this group emphasize sports and other physically active programs because they believe physical fitness is of paramount importance to the well-being of both the individual and society. In both these situations, potential participants may have a say in which activities are to be featured, but they have little influence on the general orientation of the program.

The other group of recreation professionals believe the choice of programming is not so much a responsibility as a privilege that should be shared with the people being served. This philosophy may also lead to the adoption of programs that are limited in scope, but there is a major difference—the programs are more likely to represent what the participants wish to do rather than what professionals permit them to do. By undertaking telephone and home-interview surveys and by asking special interest groups, neighborhoods, or the community as a whole, what programs should be offered, recreation professionals devise programs based on the preferences of potential participants. Sometimes they follow a policy of scheduling a wide variety of activities and then canceling those that do not draw sufficient participants. In such cases, the programming decisions are made by those who are in the habit of taking part together with some new participants who were attracted to the program for one reason or another.

The best programs are usually those that emerge after a combination of approaches has been used to develop goals and objectives. A competent professional will:

- Examine existing and previous program offerings and participation patterns to identify trends and determine their causes.
- Talk to both staff and participants to become better acquainted with participation constraints and possible solutions.
- Consult with professionals in other agencies, both in the community and elsewhere, to obtain their opinions concerning existing programs and possible innovations.
- Conduct studies of community residents' recreation lifestyles and attitudes with special attention to people who have not participated in the community's public recreation programs.
- Examine the participation patterns and needs of special target groups such as teenagers, the elderly, the handicapped, the less affluent, and non-English speaking residents.
- Experiment with a variety of new ideas to develop innovative programs.

He or she will then interpret these data and use professional judgment to draw up recommendations for appropriate goals, objectives, and programs.

The recommended goals, objectives, and programs resulting from such a procedure will normally be a compromise. They will provide opportunities for a range of programs, including some in each of the five main divisions—physical activities, intellectual activities, artistic activities, social activities, and practical activities. Emphasis will be given to programs that produce opportunities for moderate to large numbers of participants; yet, a good selection of more exclusive activities that interest quite small numbers will be included. Similarly, programs that serve the age groups, economic groups, and ethnic groups with the greatest needs will receive preference; yet, provision will be made for some activities that appeal to all strata of society. Of course, these plans have to fit the constraints imposed by budgets, staff size and abilities, available physical resources, and seasonal or daily limitations on usable time.

Examples of Programs. To understand the scope and impact of supervised recreation, it is necessary to be acquainted with the various types of programs that are offered by different organizations. The great diversity of such programs makes it impossible to provide a truly representative summary. Rather, a selection of typical and exceptional programs that indicates the range of opportunities offered will be mentioned.

Physical activity programs are probably more numerous than any other kinds of program. Certainly

Table 17.1 Examples of Physical Programs

Program	Primary Agencies Offering Programs	Target Groups	Locations	Supervision Provided
Learn to swim	Park and recreation departments, schools, colleges, institutions, quasi-public organizations, private clubs, commercial camps	All ages from tots (0–6 yr) to senior citizens	Recreation centers; schools; institutions; clubs; camps; YWCAs and YMCAs, YMHAs and YWHAs; park pools	1 instructor for each 7 to 10 students, lifeguards
Basketball	Same as above. Churches, industries and businesses, institutions, apartment complexes	10-year-olds and over	Same as above. Parks, playgrounds, parking lots, apartment facilities	Referee or instructor, only scheduling of league games in some cases
Bowling	Park and recreation departments, colleges, institutions, quasi-public organizations, private clubs, commercial enterprises, benevolent organizations	Mostly teenagers and older	Recreation centers, student unions, commercial centers, lodge halls	Mostly scheduling of games and supporting activities; instruction in some cases
Shuffleboard	Park and recreation departments, private clubs, industries, retirement complexes, resorts, camps	Mostly older people	Parks, recreation centers, resorts, cruise ships, retirement centers	Mostly scheduling
Canoe tripping	Park and recreation departments, schools, colleges, quasi-public organizations, private clubs, commercial camps, outfitters	Primarily youth and young adult. Some for families and senior citizens	Interurban or more remote river or lake areas	Scheduling, making arrangements, basic instruction, leadership and supervision
Long-distance running	Park and recreation departments, schools, colleges, institutions, quasi-public organizations, private clubs	Teenagers and older	Streets, parks, golf courses	Scheduling, course marking and supervision, officials, emergency services

this appears to be correct according to the schedules provided by most local government and quasi-public organizations. Table 17.1 lists six examples of this type of activity and the kinds of organizations that sponsor such programs. Additional examples that illustrate the range of activities involved are: team sports such as flag football, floor hockey, lacrosse, water polo, softball, and volleyball; dual sports such as fencing, golf, judo, and table tennis; individual sports such as archery, fishing, gymnastics, target shooting, and weight lifting; fitness activities such as jogging, gymnastics, aerobic dancing, and exercise classes; and active games such as croquet, rope jumping (skipping), and billiards.

The number of people taking part in physical activity programs has grown rapidly in recent years. No doubt this has been the result of a number of influences, including a greater proportion of young people in the population, increased interest in physical fitness, exposure to large doses of sports on television, and society's adulation of sports personalities. In addition, school and local government recreation programs have often neglected other types of activities in favor of sports.

In recent years, many organizations that provide physical activity opportunities have taken steps to change the composition of their programs in this area. The dominance of competitive league sports for males has been reduced in favor of more nonleague instruction and participation by people of all ages and both sexes. Problems in youth sports programs with poor sportsmanship, abusive coaching, and failure to help less talented players have been reduced by more closely supervising volunteer coaches or replacing them with paid staff. Additional or new opportunities for males and females to take part together in sports such as basketball, softball, and volleyball are being provided. Efforts to replace the win-at-all-costs attitude with a desire for everyone to enjoy participating have included the introduction of New Games[2], wherein competition is replaced with cooperation (Figure 17.7). Emphasis has also been placed on introducing people to sports and games that they can play throughout their lifetimes.

Intellectual programs have increased in variety and number during the past few decades and are provided by a wide range of organizations (Figure 17.6). There are two kinds of intellectual programs— those that only involve the receipt of intellectual stimulation and those that require the participant to make a definite personal contribution to the program. Of course, whether or

[2] Started in 1973 by Stewart Brand of San Francisco, the concept of group games in which everybody wins is now promoted by the New Games Foundation.

Figure 17.7 Participants at a New Games event work together to keep the earthball moving smoothly around the edge of the parachute. Such games require concentration and some manipulative skill but the emphasis on having a good time and attaining a common goal encourages people to participate regardless of their age or degree of coordination.

not participation in such programs is recreational depends on the goals and perceptions of the participant. Many people obviously obtain much pleasure from experiences of this type.

Examples that illustrate the range of intellectual activities and the diversity of sponsoring organizations involved in programs of this kind are:

- Outreach programs conducted by museums, zoos, planetariums, and historic preservation organizations with the intention of providing intellectual stimulation for the general public.
- Environmental interpretation programs operated by private clubs, quasi-public preservation organizations, colleges, museums, forestry agencies, and local, intermediate, and national park agencies; such pro-

grams involve lectures, films, self-guiding trails, field study, and various combinations of these approaches.
- Great books or great issues discussion groups organized by public libraries.
- Elderhostel programs whereby older people spend one week at a college taking intellectually stimulating courses on topics such as religion, philosophy, international issues, and race relations; more than 230 colleges in over 40 states now participate.
- Public affairs and other informative programs broadcast by radio and television stations.
- College and university adult education courses intended for people who do not wish to take classes for credit; courses include historical, scientific, political, and philosophical topics.
- Educational tours to study historic areas such as Greece, natural history in Europe and Latin America, or for-

mal gardens in Britain and Japan that are organized by major museums and botanical gardens.

Accessibility to such programs is generally best for those who live in major cities and poorest for residents of small towns and rural areas.

Although there is clearly a need for more intellectual opportunities because of higher levels of education, larger numbers of retired citizens, and a general increase in the sophistication of people's recreation behavior, there are a number of problems that may limit expansion of such programs. The main constraint is lack of funds. Appropriations for intellectual programs are generally small and the current movement towards limiting taxes is reducing them even further. Intellectual programs are often not considered as important as other activities so their budgets tend to be cut first. In the case of colleges and universities, rising costs are resulting in fee increases that are making it more difficult for people with moderate incomes to take evening and off-campus classes intended primarily for intellectual enjoyment.

Artistic activity is another major division of organized recreation. Although organizations throughout the spectrum of providers supply artistic experiences, the majority of opportunities are provided by public and private cultural organizations and other types of public agencies (Figure 17.6). Artistic programs fall into four main groups—art, dance, drama, and music.

Art activities are frequently combined with crafts in local government, quasi-public youth organization, and private youth camp programs. In small organizations, this is usually logical in terms of

working space and staff assignments but can result in artistic expression being neglected. Often programs for younger participants are called "arts and crafts," and, in many cases, the emphasis is primarily on the crafts. Leaders who are not particularly creative tend to feel most secure with prepared craft projects that can be completed in the scheduled time by everyone following the same steps. More talented and experienced staff and smaller groups are needed to provide individualized opportunities for artistic development. Some organizations are achieving these conditions by securing the volunteer or paid services of professional artists.

The principal programs involved in art activities are sketching, painting, graphics, photography, sculpture, and the printing of designs. Sketching includes the use of charcoal, pastels, and other media as well as pencil. Watercolor, oil, acrylic, and other paints are used on a variety of materials in painting. The graphic arts involve the design of artistic works that are intended to convey a specific message to a definite audience. They include greeting cards, posters, and murals. Photographic programs range from an introduction to black-and-white photography to advanced workshops in the production of color motion pictures complete with sound track. In the case of sculpture, the medium may be clay, wood, stone, glass, metal, or plastic, and the technique being used may range from molding clay with the fingers to cutting and welding steel with oxyacetylene torches. Printing designs on cloth or other materials may be done with silk screen techniques, stencils, or blocks carved from wood or other materials.

Dance programs of an artistic nature have expanded both in scope and number in recent years. Classical and modern ballet, modern dance, jazz dance, folk dance, and other forms of movement are offered in a wide variety of programs for different age groups and levels of ability. Dramatic programs include plays, musicals, street theater, pantomime, puppetry, and television and motion picture performances. There is also a great range of musical programs available such as choir, orchestra, band, and group and solo instrument activities, extending from classical music through folk and jazz to disco and rock.

In addition to various art forms and styles of artistic expression, there is a variety of ways in which each of these areas can be approached in designing a program. Some consist of performances or exhibitions by professionals or highly regarded amateurs without any opportunity for interaction with the audience. Then, there are purely instructional programs in which the participant learns primarily from a teacher. In other programs, such as little theater groups and choral societies, the emphasis is on production and the participants learn through interaction and by rehearsing and giving actual performances. Appreciation programs involve exposure to a variety of artistic works together with instruction concerning their production and discussions about their merits (Figure 16.16). Workshops in which one or more established artists or the group as a whole react to participants' work is another common approach. In the case of the performing arts, there are also instructional, appreciation, practice, and workshop programs in supporting areas such as composing, conducting, scenery construction, costume design, lighting, and directing.

This wide range of artistic activities, program formats, and sponsoring agencies creates an almost infinite variety of program combinations. The diversity that exists is illustrated by the following examples:

- Local government recreation agencies, YMCAs, YWCAs, YMHAs, YWHAs, and community colleges provide classes and workshops in such activities as tole painting, ceramics, guitar playing, modern dance, photography, and puppet arts.
- Volunteer dance groups like the Chicago Dance Council or the Winston-Salem Dance Forum sponsor demonstrations, children's classes, workshops, and a variety of dance events, including folk and square dances and dance movies.
- Using both public and corporate funds, New York's Lincoln Center for the Performing Arts presents a summer outdoor program that includes country, chamber, band, and symphony music concerts, opera, several kinds of theatrical productions, and a variety of dance performances.
- Commercial enterprises selling music, musical instruments, or art supplies commonly arrange recitals, concerts, demonstrations, exhibits, and instructional classes.

Other important suppliers of artistic experiences are schools, clubs, libraries, and museums.

The fourth major division of recreation programs provides opportunities for people to be sociable. Of course, many people take part in physical, intellectual, artistic, and practical activities primarily because they wish to make social contacts, but the emphasis in the organization and presentation of the programs is on the activity and not on social interaction. Sociable activities may involve communication between two or more individuals or consist of an entertainment-type format with little or no interaction between the performer and the participants.

Sociable programs are provided by a broad spectrum of private organizations, commercial enterprises, public organizations, and cultural groups (Figure 17.6). In fact, it is difficult to find an organization that does not sponsor some type of activity of this kind. Examples of sociable programs are:

- Organized parties, outings, and picnics arranged by neighborhood associations, hobby clubs, retirement complexes, church groups, employee associations, resorts, and local government recreation departments.
- Fund-raising events such as dinner dances, ice cream socials, fashion shows, card parties, and bingo nights, which are commonly sponsored by service clubs, churches, parent-teacher organizations, political parties, charities, and organizations that support cultural resources.
- Youth parties, games nights, and other social events run by organizations such as the Scouts, Boys' Clubs, the Catholic Youth Organization, Camp Fire Girls, and 4-H.
- Entertainment, games, and other social opportunities provided for military personnel and their dependents at the 120 units of the United Services Organization (USO), which are maintained at bases, cities, and airports around the world.
- Performances and programs provided by entertainers on records, in movies, on radio and television shows, at nightclubs, and at other commercial facilities like theme parks and outdoor music centers and pavilions.

As indicated in Figure 8.12, taking part in sociable programs is a relatively important recreation activity.

The final main category of programs consists of practical activities; it is divided into two groups — practical collection and practical transformation. Programs of this kind are primarily provided by private clubs, quasi-public youth organizations, and public organizations (Figure 17.6). Local government recreation agencies and quasi-public youth organizations have conducted practical craft programs for many decades. Private clubs have developed into major suppliers of practical opportunities more recently.

The range of practical activity programs that are currently available is illustrated by these examples:

- Local government recreation departments, public schools, and community colleges offer courses on a wide range of hobby topics from carpentry, electronics, and automobile repair to gardening, sewing, and microwave cooking.
- Hobby clubs (stamp, coin, rock, antique car, etc.) organize programs for their members, including lectures, demonstrations by experts, workshops, shows, and field trips; such clubs may be separate private organizations, clubs sponsored by churches or quasi-public youth organizations, or clubs operated by local government recreation agencies.
- Service clubs, community associations, and environmental groups organize programs through which members and others become involved in improving social or environmental conditions.
- Self-improvement programs that help people modify their behavior or develop new recreation interests or skills are offered by many clubs, religious groups, quasi-public youth organizations, commercial enterprises, local government recreation departments, schools, colleges, correctional institu-

tions, and television networks.

- Many libraries, museums, zoos, and historical societies arrange for interested students and adult volunteers to help with the collecting, care, or display of their materials.
- Over 100 field schools and many privately or government-sponsored projects are employing thousands of volunteers to assist with archaeological investigations.
- Government natural resource agencies, sportsperson's clubs, boating organizations, and snowmobile clubs provide officially sanctioned training and safety courses for hunters, boaters, and snowmobilers.
- Over 500 schools, quasi-public organizations and private groups in the United States conduct experiential education or risk recreation programs in wilderness areas for individuals who wish to develop self-awareness, confidence, and concern for others.

It appears likely that the number and variety of practical programs will continue to increase as more people become involved in environmentally oriented living and do-it-yourself activities.

There are also a number of special programs that are combinations of a variety of activities and, therefore, do not fit neatly into any one of the five categories described above. These smorgasbord experiences are also difficult to classify under this system because participants' goals and perceptions vary considerably. Of course, one of the organizer's main objectives in arranging a program of diverse attractions is to appeal to as many people as possible.

Special events vary in size from neighborhood affairs to celebrations that involve an entire city, metropolitan area, or region. Some of the smallest of the neighborhood events are playground fairs or carnivals

organized by local government recreation departments as part of their summer playground programs. Such fairs usually include a range of physical, intellectual, artistic, sociable, and practical events. Some stalls at the fair, for instance, may be exhibits of playground-program participants' artistic or practical work achievements. There is generally an emphasis on events that can be enjoyed by both program registrants and nonregistrants. Activities commonly included are simple contests and games; dramatic, dance, or vocal performances by the children; demonstrations by artists and musicians; and an assortment of sideshow attractions operated wherever possible by the children themselves.

On a larger scale, many of the special events are organized by community organizations, commercial interests, or local government recreation agencies. Examples are street fairs sponsored by local associations or merchants, celebrations of a local sports team's achievements arranged by a service club or booster group, and special events held to mark the opening of a major public or commercial facility, which usually involves a coalition of public and private sponsors. Again, the objective is generally to offer a range of opportunities, including entertainment, demonstrations, exhibits, and participatory events.

Large-scale special events are becoming increasingly popular as a method of providing variety in local government recreation programs, as a means of revitalizing downtown areas, or as an attraction for tourists. Some events are continuations of traditional festivals and fairs that developed originally from religious or agricultural celebrations.

Many others are of recent origin, but traditional festival names or themes may be used to lend authenticity to the occasion. In these cases, the activities offered tend to be similar although the names and themes of the events may vary.

In the United States, large-scale special events tend to fall into six main groups. Early in the year there is a variety of special events that carry the name of an attractive, locally common, flowering plant, shrub, or tree. Examples are cherry-blossom, azalea, dogwood, and tulip festivals. Some feature tours of the areas where the trees and plants are most abundant, but, generally, the theme is of more significance in advertising and decorations than in specific activities. A number of special events use food products native to the area as the main attraction; these include the cherry, cranberry, maple syrup, peanut, pumpkin, shrimp, and watermelon festivals. In these cases, there is usually considerable emphasis on consuming and taking home various foods associated with the featured product.

Ethnic festivals are another important group; in this case, the music, dances, and handicrafts of a culture are featured as well as its foods (Figure 17.8). A variety of events are promoted as folk or music festivals. Some consist largely of music performances, but others include a wide range of artistic, craft, dramatic, sociable, and gastronomic activities. A number of small towns have adopted historical themes and call their celebrations pioneer, frontier, or gay-nineties days. Winter carnivals are held in many locations where winter sports are important activities, but, generally, these events lack the diversity

Figure 17.8 Located on Detroit's riverfront near the Renaissance Center (right background), the Philip A. Hart Plaza is crowded with people enjoying the Polish Ethnic Festival. It is only one of a series of festivals offered in the plaza by the city each summer under the supervision of Betty Lloyd, Superintendent of Recreation. Continuous musical, dance, and theatrical presentations take place in the amphitheater, ethnic foods and cultural displays are available in the lower level's kitchens and exhibition gallery, and crafts are demonstrated and sold from booths on the upper level.

of opportunities and attractions characteristic of festivals and fairs held in warmer weather.

Recreation professionals fre-quently become involved in special events of these various kinds. A number of park and recreation de-partments in major cities are re-sponsible for organizing and operat-ing festivals and recreation professionals play leadership roles in such cases. A more common situation is where recreation professionals sit on committees composed of representatives from various organizations that are cooperatively managing a special event. Such assignments can be difficult if the recreation professional has to speak against proposals that would use and possibly damage park areas or facilities or that would interfere with the regular recreation activities that take place at these public resources.

PROGRAMS FOR SPECIAL POPULATIONS

An increasingly large proportion of recreation professionals are involved in managing programs for *special populations.* These are people who cannot participate in recreation activities to the same extent or in the same manner as the majority of the population because of a physical, mental, emotional, or social problem or handicap. In some cases, people's disabilities are being treated by medically supervised participation in recreation activities. Such treatment is known as *therapeutic recreation* and will be discussed later in this chapter.

The portion of the population that is faced with special problems and challenges when attempting to participate in ordinary recreational programs consists of several groups of disadvantaged people. Some are partially or profoundly deaf, others are partially or completely blind. A substantial number have movement problems because of the effects of age, disease, birth defects, or accidents. Some are mentally retarded. Another group is handicapped by a mental illness or personality problem. Many others are disadvantaged by language, racial, sexual, or economic dif-

ferences. A growing number have difficulty fitting into regular programs because of their special family or marital status. And finally, there are considerable numbers of people who cannot take advantage of ordinary programs because they are institutionalized.

Providing accessible and appropriate recreation opportunities for such special populations is a challenge to recreation professionals and to society as a whole. Considerable progress has been made toward achieving equality of recreation opportunity for special populations in the last few years. Commonly accepted ideas about what different special populations want to do, ought to do, or are able to do for recreation are undergoing rapid change. However, most of the credit for this belongs not to the recreation providers but to the special populations themselves. Although recreation professionals have generally been slow to recognize either the capabilities or the desires of their special clients, a growing number of individuals within the special populations have refused to accept arbitrary restrictions and have insisted they have the right to enjoy life more fully.

In response to these demands and to a growing awareness that disadvantaged populations have for many years been repressed and recreationally deprived by the rest of society, programs are being introduced that are gradually freeing special populations from the restraints of the past. The right to take risks and suffer defeat traditionally has been denied special populations, the mentally retarded and physically handicapped in particular. Because they have been overprotected, many have never

experienced the joy of challenge or competition in their recreation activities. But this is changing. Ski programs are introducing the blind, mentally retarded, and amputees to the excitement of downhill skiing. Blind youths are being exposed to the challenges and thrills of rock climbing and skating. Children with a variety of disabilities are enjoying a wide range of outdoor experiences at summer camps; they are learning how to fish, swim, handle boats, and ride horses. They are also having the opportunity to experience victory and live with the disappointment of defeat in competitive sports that range from participation in softball and hockey leagues to competing in Special Olympics track-and-field events.

Because of the interest and determination of disabled World War II veterans, wheelchair sports have become a worldwide movement involving 10,000 disabled men and women, 2000 of whom live in the United States. Activities range from bowling, archery, weight lifting, and track-and-field events to team sports such as softball and basketball. Insisting on adherence to the original versions of the activities in every possible way, the sports allow the participants to judge their abilities by the same standards that apply to other athletes, thereby providing the same kinds of psychological benefits. This is considered by the disabled to be a great improvement; previously, they were only encouraged or allowed to take part in physical activities that were so modified that they were almost unrecognizable and, in many cases, were little more than juvenile games.

Special populations are also showing interest in a wide variety of activities that the *temporarily able bodied*[3] used to think would be uninteresting or impractical for people with certain handicaps. As a result, special programs are being developed to facilitate their participation. By using various devices (for example, baseballs that emit sound), blind people are enjoying games like softball and golf and are able to jog with friends or take part in competitive track. Deaf people and those who are confined to wheelchairs are enjoying all types of dancing as a social activity. Older people, too, are rejecting sedentary activities like crafts and bingo, which have been staples of every senior citizens program for years. Instead, if health permits, they are choosing to take part in programs that offer opportunities to enjoy a wide range of outdoor activities such as bicycling, hiking, and camping.

Special populations are also struggling to free themselves from the limitations of the unrealistic sexual roles that society has expected them to play for so long. Apparently, it is difficult for some people to believe that age or a disability does not remove sexual drives and the need for close personal relationships. But, gradually, society is recognizing these needs and providing supportive programs. These range from counseling and sex education classes for the mentally retarded to a variety of programs for the elderly and handicapped that provide the same opportunities for the two sexes to meet and develop meaningful relationships that usually occur in programs for youth and

the nonhandicapped.

On the other hand, there are still some situations where separation of the sexes is justified in terms of providing an adequate experience for a special population. One example is outdoor-activity skill-development programs such as those offered by the Girl Scouts and National Outdoor Women organizations, which only admit females. These organizations feel that females need opportunities to learn skills, take risks, perform tasks, and assume leadership roles that have been traditionally left to males. If males are allowed to participate, they argue, many females tend automatically to assume dependent roles and the whole point of the program is lost. Conversely, of course, males learn to assume nurturing roles in similar programs where females are absent. But, because males usually have many opportunities to participate in challenging outdoor activities without females, there is less need for these kinds of programs to exclude females. However, this situation may change as more females take up activities and use facilities and programs traditionally reserved for males.

Although physical barriers are gradually disappearing and the number and variety of recreation opportunities suitable for special populations are increasing, participation by the handicapped is still low. A year-round activity program for mentally retarded and physically disabled residents of three midwestern communities, for instance, attracts no more than 60 of the 3000 persons who are eligible to take part. The main reason for this low attendance does not seem to be a lack of awareness, transportation, or

money to pay for the program on the part of potential participants. Nor is it a reflection on the nature of the program itself; it has the reputation of being an exciting, innovative, well-organized, and enthusiastically led program that provides many interesting recreation opportunities, including trips to zoos, concerts, and sporting events.

The main problem in this and similar cases appears to be the anxiety of both the potential participants and those who care for them. Many of the latter wish to protect the handicapped persons in their care and shield them from any risk of physical harm or emotional hurt. They feel the only way to accomplish this is to keep them at home. The potential participants, on the other hand, are often afraid of both the challenges they may have to face in taking part and the unkind treatment they may receive from people they will meet. Overcoming such fears is a major challenge for the people who are in charge of supplying recreation opportunities for special populations. It is not an easy task because it involves not only the reassuring of the potential participants and their families but also the education of the members of the community with whom the handicapped individuals are likely to come into contact.

Nevertheless, there are some people who are incapable of taking part in recreation programs outside their own homes. The recreation needs of these special individuals are also being taken into consideration and many agencies are developing outreach programs to alleviate the loneliness and boredom of their isolation. Special radio services have been established in several communities (often under the aus-

---

[3] A thought-provoking term that is used by those society labels handicapped to describe people who currently *appear* to have no debilitating characteristics.

pices of public radio stations using volunteer help) to broadcast newspapers, books, periodicals, information of local interest, and discussions on a wide range of subjects to the homes of the visually impaired and physically disabled. The equipment needed to receive these broadcasts is often supplied free of charge. Telephone and citizens band (CB) radio services are being organized so that homebound persons have a regular opportunity to talk to someone who cares. Shut-ins are also being visited in person by librarians, performing artists, social workers, the clergy, members of youth groups, and adult volunteers who deliver books, hot meals, craft materials, and requested items, and who stay to read to them, entertain them, play a game with them, help them with chores and minor repairs and, most importantly, to visit with them. These friendly contacts with people from the outside world are often the best and sometimes the only recreation experiences some of these homebound people have.

There are also individuals who need special attention because they live in social situations that set them apart from the general population. Examples include children in single-parent homes, unmarried older adults, recently divorced or widowed persons, parents of children with special problems, and parents without spouses. Programs designed especially for these groups can provide appropriate recreation experiences. At the same time, an attempt can be made to help some of the participants solve personal problems common to people in their situation. In some cases, just providing opportunities for individuals with similar backgrounds to meet, share anxieties, and ex-

change views produces beneficial results. Special programs like the Big Brother/Big Sister and Adopt-a-Grandparent programs provide valuable opportunities for personal interaction among individuals of different age groups. Many of the participants in these programs enjoy a variety of recreation experiences together and develop warm and lasting friendships that resemble the mutually supportive relationships found among members of close-knit families.

Unfortunately, the idea of providing specially designed programs for various types of special populations has its drawbacks. In far too many cases, such programs only help to isolate the participants and set them apart from the rest of society. In an effort to involve special populations more fully in community life, a growing number of programs are being designed initially for general audiences and, then, modified so that persons with special needs are also able to take part. In this respect, all programs that remove physical barriers at commercial and public recreation facilities or make transportation to recreation opportunities available for the disadvantaged are, in themselves, recreation programs for special populations. In fact, they are considered by many people to be some of the very best programs because they integrate persons with special needs into the recreation lifestyles of the wider world. Other programs that help bring special populations into the recreation mainstream include simultaneous broadcasts of television programs for the hearing and the hearing-impaired, the provision of touchable exhibits and cassette tape explanations at museums for the benefit of the visually impaired,

and the installation of a few specially built picnic tables at parks to accommodate groups and families whose members include persons in wheelchairs.

THERAPEUTIC RECREATION

Although all recreation professionals hope that the experiences they supply will have some therapeutic value to participants, there are some whose work primarily involves using recreation as a tool for healing ailing minds and bodies. These are the recreation therapists who work in institutions such as hospitals, schools, prisons, convalescent and old-age homes, rehabilitation centers, halfway houses, daycare centers, special camps, and group homes.

In the beginning, therapeutic recreation consisted primarily of diversional types of activities provided for the entertainment of groups of hospitalized patients. Many of these programs were developed and administered by such organizations as the American Red Cross and the U.S. Veterans Administration. Now, therapeutic recreation has a much more extensive purpose. It was defined by a 1969 task force of the National Therapeutic Recreation Society as "a process which utilizes recreation services for purposive intervention in some physical, emotional, and/or social behavior and to promote the growth and development of the individual."[4]

Therapeutic recreation pro-

[4] Unpublished paper presented at the Ninth Southern Regional Institute of Therapeutic Recreation, University of North Carolina at Chapel Hill, 1969; cited in Viki S. Annand, "A Review of Evaluation in Therapeutic Recreation," *Therapeutic Recreation Journal, 11*(2), 1977, p. 43.

grams are still conducted in many military hospitals under the auspices of the American Red Cross; responsibility for therapeutic recreation programs in Veterans Administration hospitals has now been transferred to the hospital staffs. Other hospitals that provide therapeutic recreation services include general, children's, and state psychiatric hospitals. In addition, programs now take place in many locations that are not hospitals. These include prisons, reformatories, detention homes, state schools for the retarded, senior citizens centers, clinics, recreation centers, community mental health centers, centers for the retarded, senior citizens, centers, clinics, public schools, colleges, halfway houses, retirement communities, nursing homes, mobile recreation units, and private homes. A wide variety of public and private agencies are involved in providing these services.

No longer diversionary in nature, programs are usually conducted by, or under, the direction of professionally trained therapeutic recreation specialists. They make use of innovative techniques and equipment to help individuals retain present levels or regain lost levels of physical or mental health and social adjustment, overcome disabilities, and reach their full potential as individuals as well as functional members of society. Current programs are designed to accommodate the special needs of every age group from infants to the elderly. They are intended to help a wide variety of people, including alcoholics, drug addicts, juvenile and adult offenders, the socially maladjusted, the retarded, the economically and culturally deprived, and the mentally ill. A major goal is to assist

people who are temporarily or permanently incapacitated in various ways and degrees by the effects of birth defects or disorders, diseases, accidents, and old age. The latter include the physically disabled, the elderly, individuals with hearing and visual impairments, and persons suffering the debilitating effects of such conditions as cerebral palsy, asthma, muscular distrophy, cystic fibrosis, diabetes, and arthritis.

Therapeutic recreation programs are also reaching many people who do not have special needs or handicaps. This is because mainstreaming and rehabilitation of special populations is now a primary goal. Wherever feasible, programs are conducted in ordinary community settings rather than in isolation and are arranged so that partici-

pants from the community at large are included or involved. In this way, it is expected that the people with disabilities will become more self-confident and eventually be drawn into the wider world of the community. At the same time, it is hoped that more people in the community will learn to understand their afflictions and disabilities and come to accept the disadvantaged as co-workers, neighbors, and friends.

A wide variety of activities are included in therapeutic programs. Of course, every conceivable recreation experience can have beneficial results and, therefore, could be used for this purpose. However, art, crafts, pets, horticultural projects (Figure 17.9), hobbies, music, rhythmic activities, dance, games,

Figure 17.9 A participant in a therapeutic horticulture program sponsored by South Carolina's Clemson University prepares a flower bed under the guidance of hortitherapy masters degree candidate Joyce Berry. Working with plants helps the participants forget their problems, gain new interests, build self-confidence, and develop marketable skills. Graduates of the eight American hortitherapy curricula are conducting programs in a variety of institutions including prisons, hospitals, senior citizens homes, and schools for the handicapped.

athletics (including jogging and wheelchair sports), creative-play opportunities, and a wide range of social events (picnics, parties, outings, etc.) are commonly used to reach and help people with special needs. Group-living experiences in challenging wilderness settings have proven particularly useful in developing self-esteem and altering the attitudes and behavior of troubled young people.

Many new or innovative adaptations or existing programs are being developed to better suit the needs of different individuals. An example is the CB radio station now in operation at West Paces Ferry Hospital in Atlanta, Georgia. Installed for the use of the paralyzed patients in the Shepherd Spinal Center, it has become a valuable therapeutic tool. The radio provides new patients with the challenge of learning to operate the equipment. It also expands their horizons during long confinements by allowing them to communicate regularly with people in the outside world. The resultant wide-ranging contacts appear to help patients overcome the trauma caused by the sudden loss of personal mobility. Even after discharge, the Center's CB radio functions as a support system, providing ex-patients with a means of keeping in touch and reporting problems whenever they arise.

Recreation therapists have very demanding jobs. They must develop good working relationships with clients, otherwise there is little chance that their programs will succeed—no matter what is included or where they are held. The responsibility of assessing their clients' problems and capabilities rests on their shoulders. Then, they must choose activities that will be interesting and enjoyable and at the same time produce beneficial effects that bring the clients one step closer to achieving some long-range goal.

Professional training can provide much of the technical knowledge that will help recreation therapists make appropriate assessments and decisions. It can also help them acquire the skills and knowledge of techniques necessary to running effective, enjoyable programs. But empathy—the personal trait that enables people to reach and help others—is a talent that is seldom acquired through academic study but should be part of the qualifications of every recreation therapist.

This completes a brief review of the way in which the knowledge and skill resources of recreation professionals contribute to the creation of desirable recreation environments. In the final chapter, which follows, the major changes taking place in the factors that affect recreation behavior and resource supply will be examined to suggest possible future recreation patterns and problems.

DISCUSSION TOPICS

1. Outline the administrative structure of one local government recreation agency and one intermediate level government recreation agency with which you are familiar. Do these structures appear to be administratively efficient?

2. Summarize a major recreation policy issue that has recently been of concern to a local government or intermediate level government with which you are acquainted. List the arguments for and against the principal solutions recommended.

3. Outline the sources of revenue used by a local government recreation agency with which you are familiar. What portions of its budget come from fees and charges and what impact do these appear to have on participation patterns?

4. Discuss the manner in which a large recreation development that you know is designed. Does the design provide the desired recreation opportunities with minimal operational and maintenance problems?

5. Summarize the recreation programs that are provided by the government of a city in which you are familiar in terms of the approximate number of opportunities offered in each of the five areas described in this chapter. Does this supply of opportunities appear adequate to meet the needs of the different kinds of people living in various parts of the city?

The majority of recreation literature is concerned primarily with techniques for administering and managing recreation resources and programs so that there is no lack of references for this chapter. The textbooks by Doell and Twardzik, Kraus and Curtis, Hjelte and Shivers, mentioned at the end of Chapter 13, are useful sources. Other basic references are George Butler's *Introduction to Community Recreation* published in New York by McGraw-Hill in 1976, *Productive Management of Leisure Service Organizations* by Christopher R. Edginton and John G. Williams published in 1978 by John Wiley in New York, and *Leisure Services: The Organized Recreation and Park System* by Sessoms, Meyer, and Brightbill. Discussions of various aspects of administration and management can be found in each of these sources by consulting the index.

Interesting examples of recent research reports are summarized in a *Parks and Recreation* monthly column, "Research Update." Detailed discussions of research methods and results appear primarily in the *Journal of Leisure Research, Leisure Sciences, Journal of Travel Research, Therapeutic Recreation Journal,* and *Research Quarterly* published by the American Alliance for Health, Physical Education, and Recreation. Joseph J. Bannon's *Leisure Resources: Its Comprehensive Planning,* a 1976 Prentice-Hall book published in Englewood Cliffs, N.J., and *Outdoor Recreation Planning* by Alan Jubenville published the same year in Philadelphia by Saunders, provide information on some aspects of recreation system planning. Three basic books on facility design are *Park Planning Handbook* by Monty I. Christiansen published in New York by John Wiley in 1977, Albert J. Rutledge's *Anatomy of a Park* published in New York by McGraw-Hill in 1971, and the AAHPER report, *Planning Facilities for Athletics, Physical Education and Recreation,* published in Washington, D.C., in 1980.

Dozens of publications are devoted to specific aspects of administration and resource management. Examples are *The Process of Recreation Programming* by Patricia Farrell and Herberta M. Lundegren published in New York by John Wiley in 1978, *Recreation and Special Populations* by Thomas A. Stein and H. Douglas Sessoms published in Boston in 1977 by Holbrook Press, and Elliott M. Avedon's book published in Englewood Cliffs, N.J., by Prentice-Hall in 1974 entitled, *Therapeutic Recreation Service: An Applied Behavioral Science Approach.* There are also a number of specialized periodicals such as *Recreation Management* and *Park Maintenance* or the Park Practice Program of the National Recreation and Park Association, which includes three publications entitled *Trends, Design,* and *Grist.*

Providing adequate recreation opportunities for the future requires foresight, imagination, and time. Several years ago, planners in Toronto, Ontario, took advantage of large volumes of material being excavated for new downtown buildings to build a series of artificial islands and peninsulas in Lake Ontario. The resultant recreation resources such as Ashbridge's Bay Park (foreground) are now helping meet the need for more close-to-home, water-oriented recreation opportunities.

651

18

PROBLEMS, TRENDS, AND THE FUTURE

The preceding chapters have emphasized that recreation behavior (and its attendant sociologic, economic, and land-use impacts) is controlled by a wide range of per-

Figure 18.1 **Many Americans were forced to curtail use of their motor vehicles in 1979 when gasoline shortages suddenly occurred in several parts of the nation. In southern California, some individuals tried to preserve their vehicle-oriented recreation lifestyles by lining up at service stations whenever gasoline was available, storing extra fuel in whatever containers were on hand, and then using it during the weekends for recreation purposes, leaving just enough in the tank to get to work on Monday.**

sonal and external factors. Since most of these influences are constantly changing and these changes are often rapid and unexpected, some aspects of recreation are highly ephemeral (Figure 18.1). Consequently, it is virtually impossible to predict with any certainty what new directions recreation is apt to take either in the next decade or in the more distant future. Yet, it is essential that individuals and organizations involved in providing recreation opportunities be aware of existing trends and the challenges they are likely to present. To a large degree, the actions of recreation providers today determine the nature and extent of recreation opportunities for years to come (p. 651). Whether facilities and programs will satisfy the needs of tomorrow's citizens depends largely on how well providers are able to assess the impact of current trends on future environments and lifestyles. This chapter examines the factors that are most likely to alter recreation behavior patterns in the future. It will also explore the changes that may have to be made by various recreation opportunity providers to ensure the survival and appropriateness of their programs.

However, as we take a look at the future, remember that there are many aspects of recreation that are neither changing nor are likely to change. This fact is often overlooked in the chapters and articles that discuss the future of recreation. It is tempting to become so infatuated with the highly visible, spectacular changes in some aspects of recreation behavior that the timelessness of other aspects is forgotten. The continuing dominance of recreation in and around the place of residence and the perpetual ap-

peal of the simple pleasures such as lying in the sun, watching the world go by, chatting with friends, reading magazines and newspapers, or playing cards and ball games should always be kept in mind. Although radical changes take place from time to time, recreation in many ways steadfastly remains the same.

This chapter is divided into four sections. The first considers resource trends including energy, land use, user conflicts, and carrying-capacity problems. Economic influences resulting from international trade imbalances, the effects of inflation and recession, and changes in government roles are examined in the second section. The third section discusses the social implications of inflation, the effects of unemployment and poverty, and population and demographic trends. Finally, the probable overall effects of these and other factors on recreation behavior and resources in the future are assessed.

RESOURCE TRENDS AND ISSUES

One group of issues that is already having considerable impact on recreation and is likely to have an even greater influence in the future concerns the availability and desirable use of the world's remaining undeveloped resources. Until recently, little thought was given to the majority of these resources since there seemed to be an endless supply and their attributes, including the characteristics that made them attractive for recreation, appeared to be more or less indestructible. Today, most people are beginning to realize that the earth's resources can no longer be taken

for granted. Generally, they are either nonrenewable or more sensitive to abuse than had been previously suspected. In both cases, they are disappearing at an alarming rate because of the sheer numbers of people wishing to use them and because of the deleterious effects of modern technology. Obviously, the best solution is to reduce population levels and abandon practices that harm the resources. Unfortunately, the former is not easy to accomplish and the latter is impractical as long as people cling to current lifestyles. Therefore, while attempts are being made to encourage a worldwide adoption of population controls, individuals and governments are trying to cope with a growing number of serious resource problems. This section concentrates on resource problems that are most likely to have a substantial impact on recreation.

ENERGY-SUPPLY IMPLICATIONS

Of all the resource problems, those that are energy related have the greatest potential for altering the way large numbers of individuals spend their free time, especially in automobile-oriented societies (see Chapter 6). The people who are most likely to be profoundly affected are those who live in developed nations that consume large amounts of fossil fuels as their primary source of energy and depend heavily on other nations as sources of supply. At the present time, these include Japan, the United States, and most of the nations of Europe. However, unless major new sources of energy are developed, the lifestyles of almost everyone in the world will eventually be affected as fossil fuels, a nonre-newable resource, become increasingly scarce or costly because, in one way or another, most of today's lifestyles depend to some extent on fossil fuels, petroleum in particular.

Situation in the United States. Americans are especially vulnerable because they are the world's heaviest oil users; the United States is also one of the world's major importers of crude oil (see box). This situation is unlikely to improve since most of the potential sources of oil now appear to lie outside the United States. Therefore, unless its need for oil diminishes, the United States will become increasingly dependent on foreign sources. This will make it increasingly susceptible to the debilitating effects of oil embargoes, oil production interruptions, and intentional cutbacks in the nations from which it obtains oil, and the escalating prices that accompany shortages. The rising cost of foreign oil is just as serious a threat to American lifestyles as the possibility of long-term oil shortages. Already, it is contributing to the nation's growing trade deficit, depreciation of American currency abroad, and inflation. This situation must be brought under control if the country is to prosper.

WORLD'S MAJOR CONSUMER

In 1978, the United States, with 5 percent of the world's population, used almost 18 million barrels of oil a day (1 barrel of oil produces about 42 gallons of gasoline) or 36.2 percent of the world's total petroleum supply. For comparison, the other major consumers were the Soviet Union (8 million barrels a day or 13 percent of the world total), Japan (5.1 million barrels or 10 percent of the world total), and West Germany (2.6 million barrels or 5 percent of the world total). Using less are France, Canada, Great Britain, and Italy, each of which have a consumption rate of around 2 million barrels a day (collectively accounting for 13.8 percent of the world total).

Although the United States was the world's second largest crude oil producer in 1978, it still imported an average of 8.4 million barrels a day, making it dependent on outside sources for about 45 percent of its annual oil supply.

Since the United States is said to use more oil for nonessentials than it imports, reducing oil consumption to more reasonable levels should not be impossible nor should it impose undue hardships on most citizens. According to industry sources, for instance, 6 percent of the nation's petroleum supply is used to produce single-use items like plastic cups, containers, and trash bags; in 1978 alone, 733,000 tons of petroleum-derived plastics were used and discarded. Unfortunately, although industry has accepted the need to conserve and has effectively reduced its energy use by 10 to 15 percent over the last few years, efforts to convince the general public of the seriousness of the present energy situation have, until recently, met with limited success. In 1978, for example, in the midst of the Iranian oil crisis and dire predictions concerning America's energy future, daily consumption actually went up,

reaching 21 million barrels a day, an all-time high.

Since that time, however, use has begun to decrease. There are two reasons for this. Some Americans responded to the urgings of government leaders to help reduce America's dependency on foreign oil. They assumed personal responsibility for their own patterns of energy consumption and made efforts to conserve. Voluntarily, they restricted use of appliances, added insulation to their homes, kept inside temperatures warmer in summer and cooler in winter, purchased less powerful automobiles, made greater use of car pools and public transportation, observed the 55-miles-per-hour speed limit, and reduced the use of their automobiles, powerboats, and recreation vehicles. For others, the decision to curb levels of energy consumption has not been voluntary. Many have had no choice but to conserve as they faced the effects of rising inflation and escalating prices—not only for gasoline and the products that are derived from petrochemicals (sports clothes, photographic film, phonograph records, fiberglass boats, etc.) but also for heating, cooling, and lighting their places of residence and for all types of merchandise that are becoming increasingly expensive to manufacture and transport because of rising energy costs. Together, these two groups of citizens have helped produce a drop in American energy consumption in 1979 to 18.3 million barrels a day; this includes a 5 percent decrease in gasoline usage.

Despite this improvement, it appears unlikely that Americans will conserve energy on a large scale until doing so becomes absolutely unavoidable. For the majority of citizens, this point has still not been reached. Therefore, the government eventually will have to risk public outrage and enforce energy conservation. Exactly what form this enforcement will take is still not clear, but it is bound to include measures that affect people's present automobile usage since gasoline accounts for 40 percent of total oil consumption. These measures will likely include stricter enforcement of lower speed limits; increased regulations concerning the size, power, and fuel efficiency of automobiles; reduced construction of new high-speed highways; limitations on downtown parking; restrictions on where or when owners may use their automobiles, powerboats, and recreation vehicles; and, if nothing else works, controls that will limit the availability of gasoline. Whether these controls consist of higher gasoline taxes to discourage nonessential use, some kind of gasoline rationing, or the periodic closing of gas stations (especially on weekends and holidays when most of the nation's travel-for-pleasure takes place), the end result will be a loss of mobility, a situation that is bound to have a considerable effect on recreation behavior patterns.

Alternative Transportation Modes. Before a nation as large as the United States can drastically reduce automobile use, other forms of transportation must be provided. Most Americans, including the affluent, will probably agree to curtail use of private automobiles for everyday transportation, especially if, by so doing, they are assured of their use for recreation purposes. To adopt this lifestyle, however, decent walking surfaces, safe bicycle paths, and inexpensive, efficient

systems of public transportation are needed. Where adequate systems exist, particularly in large urban centers, ridership has already shown substantial gains. In 1978, ridership reached 6.4 billion passenger-trips (this still represented a ridership that was considerably less than half of the 1950 level), and the use of mass transit continued to climb during 1979 as many Americans sought to minimize the effects of escalating gas prices, spot shortages, and long line-ups at gas station pumps.

At the present time, however, relatively few communities contain adequate public transportation systems. Most are committed to the development or extension of such systems, but escalating costs are making it difficult to maintain present systems, let alone improve or extend them. This is especially true in some of the older cities faced with severe budgetary problems and in sprawling suburban communities where dispersed populations make it impossible to operate extensive systems without incurring heavy deficits (Figure 18.2). This situation may ease somewhat as $16.4 billion in federal funds are distributed to urban areas to subsidize operations and help pay for new projects.

Many people may also be willing to use public transportation rather than the family car for some or all of their recreation excursions and vacation travel, provided the chosen recreation resources or destinations are accessible by public transportation. For example, extraurban bus ridership increased 20 percent in 1979 and rail travel rose by about 6.5 percent. However, to be energy efficient,[1] trains, buses, and airplanes must have high seat-

occupancy rates; unfortunately, the majority of people will not be willing or able to use these modes of transportation unless they offer good service at reasonable prices. To achieve such service, the U.S. Government will have to commit itself wholeheartedly to the development of extensive extraurban transportation networks. Extraurban transportation systems that attempt to serve a wide range of people will never be able to turn a profit in a country covering so huge an area.

Nevertheless, the federal government so far continues to expect systems to be self-sufficient and is still more concerned about avoiding additional costs to the taxpayer than developing adequate extraurban transportation services. Even when the United States was facing serious oil shortages in 1979, it was proposed that 43 percent of the Amtrak rail passenger system be eliminated[2] to save taxpayers $300 million in annual federal subsidies and higher fares and reduced service be implemented on the remaining routes to hold down the operating deficit. If such policies continue, it is predicted that Amtrak will eventually only serve the busy corridors such as Boston to Washington and a few of the more lucrative long-distance routes. Similarly, there is resistance to giving bus systems the financial support they need to maintain adequate levels of service in less heavily populated areas. Residents of much of rural America who do not have cars are

[1] With adequate ridership, trains can produce 400 passenger-miles, buses 250 passenger-miles, and airplanes 77 passenger-miles per gallon in comparison to the 44 passenger-miles per gallon for private automobiles.

[2] Included were trains serving such national parks as Yellowstone, Grand Canyon, and Yosemite.

Figure 18.2 The city of Los Angeles (excluding any of the numerous surrounding cities) contains 2.9 million people dispersed over 1199 square kilometers (463 square miles). The majority live in single-household homes, commute to jobs in widely scattered businesses and industries, and travel considerable distances in all directions to reach a great variety of recreation resources. In such circumstances, the development of an adequate mass transit system is virtually impossible and access to a private vehicle almost mandatory.

facing virtual isolation as more and more routes are eliminated in an effort to control operating losses.

Until recently, air transportation in the United States seemed to be thriving; passenger traffic rose 13.4 percent in 1978 and an additional 13.5 percent for the first nine months of 1979. A high proportion of the increased use involved recreational travel. This expansion was mainly a result of the 1978 airline deregulation law and the ensuing rapid expansion of air service and substantial reductions in fares. However, business has dropped in the last few months and profits are decreasing (e.g., $500 million less in 1979 than in 1978) despite traffic gains. It is expected that lower air fares will continue, but there is also little doubt that periodic upward price adjustments will occur as competing airlines reach their load capacities and fuel and other operating costs soar. Additional revenues will also be needed to pay for $100 billion in equipment that American airlines say will have to be purchased by 1990. Whatever happens, it is unlikely that air service will ever function as a primary means of intercity transportation. Even now, the costs of air travel are still out of reach for most Americans except on an occasional basis. Frequent delays and frustrations associated with outdated, overcrowded airport facilities are also discouraging many potential customers from using airplanes instead of private automobiles for shorter trips.

Role of the Automobile.

Since it is doubtful that a viable alternative will be available to the majority of Americans for years to come, it is fairly certain that the private automobile will remain the predominant mode of personal transportation in the United States, at least for the remainder of the century. Its role, however, will alter in response to changes in the energy situation.

Most people will not be able to afford the luxury of driving a car on a day-to-day basis. Car and van pools will increase and probably become the accepted method of solving public transportation problems in suburban communities and rural areas. Already ride-sharing is being encouraged in many locations by the establishment of special state-monitored or employer-sponsored programs and the provision of reserved traffic lanes, reduced toll rates on bridges, and special parking arrangements for shared vehicles. Less affluent households will tend not to own automobiles at all, not only because of the prohibitive

costs of vehicles and gasoline but also because of the proportionately larger impact that higher energy costs will have on their budgets generally.

The rest of the population will cling to their automobiles as long as it is feasible to do so. Middle- and high-income Americans have grown accustomed to being able to go where they wish, when they wish, and for as long as they wish in their own private vehicles, and this is not the kind of freedom that will be given up easily (see Chapter 6). However, most moderate-income Americans will have to compromise. Already changes in lifestyles are taking place. Many people are exchanging their big automobiles for smaller, less comfortable but more fuel-efficient models. They are replacing heavier camping vehicles and trailer-borne boats with models that use less gasoline and require less powerful towing vehicles. They are buying sailboats and canoes instead of power-driven watercraft. And they are becoming more selective about the places they choose to go to by private automobile.

If present trends continue, extraurban trips in the future will likely cover shorter distances, be less frequent, and involve one rather than a series of destinations. People will also choose to travel by the most direct route instead of by the most scenic (and often circuitous) route. Wheelspoke trips will become popular—vacationers will select destinations where a variety of recreation opportunities are available within close proximity of each other, choose a central location in which to stay, and, then, spend their vacation time exploring the nearby attractions. Urban areas will also be enjoyed in this manner, and cities

with good public transportation systems will be especially attractive. During weekend excursions, few people will drive distances of more than 100 miles; most will settle for destinations of 50 miles or less.

Impact on Recreation.

Changes of these kinds will have a widespread effect on recreation. Tourist developments in out-of-the-way locations will probably be unable to survive, especially if most of their customers come only for weekends, live over 100 miles away, and travel by private car. However, weekend establishments that can alter their facilities and programs sufficiently to appeal to people on extended vacations may find business improved since they will then have an advantage over more distant resort areas. A sustained change in people's mobility could have a catastrophic effect on regions and states whose travel trade is presently economically significant and is almost completely dependent on automobile traffic. For example, the American tourist industry was reported to have suffered losses of $717 million during a three-month period in 1973 following the Arab oil embargo. At that time, the government labeled tourism "nonessential to the nation's economy" and ordered gasoline stations closed on weekends to reduce the amount of fuel being used for pleasure travel. Large numbers of people were unable to make weekend trips to resort areas and extraurban recreation facilities, or they were discouraged from taking longer trips because they were unwilling to make adjustments in their itineraries.

Closer to large population centers, the situation is likely to be reversed. Commercial recreation resources that are within easy driving distance or accessible by public transportation will probably thrive. Private campgrounds that are less than a tankful of gas away from metropolitan areas will be especially popular, particularly if they provide a variety of recreation opportunities. During the summer of 1979, such facilities enjoyed turn-away business in many areas. A large proportion of the customers leased and set up their large trailers for the entire season, driving back and forth on weekends in smaller, more fuel-efficient cars. Use of local government recreation resources will undoubtedly escalate. Considerable pressure will be placed on governments at all levels to provide more and better opportunities for people to engage in activities like camping, swimming, boating, and fishing in areas closer to home. Local government recreation programs are likely to have considerably more participants. If public recreation agencies do not begin to prepare for such an eventuality in time, the management problems involved in operating all types of public recreation resources in and near cities could become serious. The need for all kinds of neighborhood commercial recreation resources will also grow and there will be increased interest in local shopping and cultural resources. Traveling shows and exhibits will be appreciated by larger numbers of people and community special events will be well attended.

In many cases, however, use will depend on the resource's location and its access by public transportation, especially if people face gasoline rationing or local shortages. During the spring of 1979, this was illustrated in urban areas in southern California and, to a lesser extent, in several other large metropolitan areas scattered across the country. In these communities, many people temporarily became more conservative in their driving habits with noticeable effects on some of the local recreation resources. Out-of-the-way theaters, night clubs, restaurants, movie houses, major-league baseball parks, museums, and amusement parks all experienced reductions in attendance. Beaches, shopping centers, and other facilities and locations that had functioned as popular gathering places for youth became less crowded as teenagers' use of family vehicles was curtailed.

Obviously, situations that may arise as a result of a less mobile society could cause numerous problems. Certainly, such situations will present many challenges. But not all of the effects will be negative. Many of the urban parks that presently have a high incidence of crime might actually become safer when there are more people using the facilities during evening as well as daylight hours. They may also be subjected to less acts of vandalism and littering as the proportion of the population that uses and cares about the parks begins to grow. The fact that increased use of local government parks, sports facilities, zoos, recreation programs, libraries, and museums is likely to come during a period of austerity when public agencies are having to face rising costs and make do with limited budgets,[3] may have positive results. When a high enough proportion of a population demands a certain amenity, a way is usually found to provide it, and the taxpayers are much more likely to vote for higher levels of funding for them. It has always proved an asset, either at the polls or during budget hearings, for an item to be considered an essential resource or service rather than a frill.

Providers of recreation opportunities may also find that larger numbers of individuals wish to take part in the planning, development, protection, and maintenance of local recreation resources. Grass roots campaigns to arouse interest or raise funds for needed recreation facilities and programs may also become more numerous and successful. Conversely, of course, the reduced accessibility of many intermediate and national government recreation resources may cause a lessening of interest and a drop in levels of support. But, to some degree at least, this would be offset by the reduction in management problems associated with present high levels of use (Figure 18.3).

Finally, if more and better recreation resources are provided at the local level and public transportation systems are improved, many people who presently have limited recreation opportunities will benefit. For the poor, the handicapped, the elderly, and the unemployed, the energy crisis and the loss of personal mobility may cause additional hardships, but it could actually expand their personal recreation environments. If, on the other hand, they reside in areas where opportunities are not increased, public transportation systems are not developed, and costs for existing opportunities are not kept down, they may be left with little more than the recreation experiences they can provide for themselves.

---

[3] To be discussed later in this chapter.

Figure 18.3 Starting in the late 1960s, many of the better-known but more distant national parks, such as Yellowstone, began to be used by increasing numbers of people who appreciated them more for the resort-type experiences they could provide than for their outstanding undeveloped features. Higher gasoline prices and inflation are now beginning to discourage this kind of use, but many people who are primarily interested in interacting with the undeveloped resources are continuing to visit these parks because they are willing to economize in other ways to make such trips feasible.

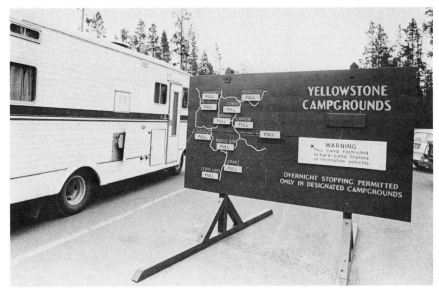

Besides the problem of decreased mobility, there are many other effects of a sustained widespread energy crisis that would change the nature of people's recreation needs. Some of these, including changes in where people live, introduction of staggered work schedules and shorter work weeks, and increases in levels of inflation, will be discussed later under appropriate headings.

LAND AND WATER PROBLEMS

A second important resource problem that is having a growing impact on recreation opportunity availability is the manner in which land[4] is used. In the past, land has been viewed as a virtually inexhaustible resource by many of the world's peoples. This has been especially true in Canada and the United States where there always appeared to be ample room for the activities of more and more loggers, miners, farmers, manufacturers, merchants, resort developers, and home-builders. Since World War II, however, demands on finite land resources have increased and converged to such an extent that land-use conflicts have become the rule rather than the exception.

Recreation has become a central issue in a growing number of these conflicts. In other cases, the

[4] In this section, land is used in its fullest economic sense and includes all the attributes of a site.

number and kind of recreation opportunities provided by a given area may be greatly affected by a land-use change although recreation use may not even be mentioned in the controversy. This section discusses current land use trends and issues and their possible effects on recreation opportunity supply in the future.

Agricultural and Urban Lands. Up to now, recreation opportunities in agricultural areas have remained fairly constant. Generally, farmers and ranchers have continued to tolerate visits from outsiders who have wanted to fish, hunt, and engage in other recreation activities on their lands, even when their numbers began to escalate in the 1950s and 1960s. Now, however, a number of factors are combining to produce rapid changes in rural areas, particularly where they adjoin cities or major transportation corridors, and these are beginning to have a considerable effect on recreation-opportunity supply.

Farms on poorer soils, in hilly areas, and in locations with climatic conditions that are less hospitable to good crop production are being converted to ranching, forestry, or recreation uses. In some cases, this is causing a loss of recreation opportunities as lands are closed to visitors or no longer suited to certain recreation activities. In other cases, especially on lands that have been developed for recreation purposes, opportunities are expanded for some activities such as camping, skiing, rockhounding, snowmobiling, fishing, and hunting.

Meanwhile, the mechanization of agriculture and the application of business methods to farming are concentrating agriculture on the most productive lands. These are the large, level areas that have reasonably good soils, drainage, and climatic conditions. Many of these lands have been purchased by investors and are being farmed as large corporate operations. These tend to provide fewer recreation opportunities than small family farms. The landscape becomes less interesting to sightseers as hedgerows, patches of woodland, and old buildings are removed and replaced with large continuous fields. The areas also become less productive of wildlife, but activities such as hunting and fishing are often discouraged anyway because of vandalism and liability problems (except where a concessionaire leases hunting or fishing rights).

Unfortunately, many of the most productive agricultural lands lie in regions that are rapidly being urbanized. About 1.2 million hectares (3 million acres) a year of America's prime farmlands are currently being converted into highways, airports, military bases, water-control reservoirs, and a wide range of commercial, industrial, and residential developments. Another 800,000 hectares (2 million acres) are losing their usefulness as cropland after being isolated by scattered highway and urban development. Since these lands are becoming an increasingly scarce commodity, the value of the remaining lands is rising rapidly. This is making it harder for owners of smaller farms in near-urban areas to meet the costs of rising taxes and still operate their farms at a reasonable profit. It is also encouraging speculators to purchase farms in the path of urban development and hold the land (often making no attempt to farm it) until a developer

makes an acceptable offer. As a result, rural land-use patterns now include belts of idle lands around cities.

This situation affects recreation in a number of ways. Idle land held by speculators generally tends to increase the number of certain types of recreation opportunities available near urban areas (Figure 4.12). On the other hand, the higher prices paid for land and the disruption of the market by speculators, makes it more difficult for public recreation agencies to purchase land near urban centers.

The loss of prime agricultural land to development and speculation has caused much concern, but measures introduced so far have done little to slow the process. Attempts have been made in Congress to pass a national land-use bill, but negative attitudes by business interests have made it politically impossible. Most of the states have some type of legislation intended to discourage the conversion of prime agricultural land to other uses, but, generally, these measures have been ineffective. Stronger action may be encouraged, however, as agriculture products become even more significant as food for a growing population, earners of hard currencies, and possibly as energy sources.

If the loss of agricultural lands and other adverse effects of urban sprawl eventually result in the adoption of effective land-use controls, some of the recreation effects mentioned above may be reduced or eliminated. Limiting the outward expansion of cities will also have an impact on recreation inside urban areas. New residential areas will generally consist of higher density town house or apartment develop-

ments built on the remaining vacant tracts or on areas cleared of old buildings. The renovation of existing buildings and use of airspace for residential construction will also be encouraged. The proportion of the population living in smaller residences with little or no private open space at their disposal will increase. With less personal space to both use and maintain, people will probably participate more often in recreation activities at away-from-the-place-of-residence facilities. This will place an added load on local public and quasi-public recreation resources, making it necessary to renovate and expand facilities.

Since space will be at a premium in redeveloped areas, both public and private recreation resources will make use of presently unused space such as roofs, piers, and areas under or over streets. City parks will be under added pressure from both municipal and private interests; proposals to locate or expand structures such as schools, libraries, theaters, museums, and municipal service buildings in parks will become more frequent. Redeveloped parks will have to be designed so that larger numbers of different kinds of recreation opportunities can be obtained from the limited space. This may mean placing some facilities underground, creating terraces and other multi-level structures, and using a variety of devices to make it possible for activities to take place in closer proximity or for an area to be converted to different uses as the occasion arises.

Water, Wetlands, and Coastlines. Water-quality problems caught the public's attention some years ago in the United States and Canada and resulted in great efforts to halt various forms of pollution. Already considerable improvement is evident. People are swimming at Lake Erie beaches when it had been unsafe to do so for 17 years, and game fish are being caught in rivers that were once virtually devoid of normal aquatic organisms. Since water-quality improvement appears destined to continue, more water resources will again be usable and attractive for many kinds of recreation. Cities that have access to such resources will relocate roads and clear away old warehouses, factories, and residential areas to develop lakefront and riverfront parks and programs; a number of municipalities have already completed projects of this type (Figure 18.4). A resurgence of participation in water-dependent and water-related activities from swimming and sailing to the enjoyment of moonlight cruises and waterfront cafés will follow. Energy-supply problems and land-use legislation to control urban sprawl may supply added incentives for waterfront redevelopment.

An issue related to water quality that has been receiving increased attention is wetlands preservation. Bogs, swamps, tidal marshes, and other forms of wetlands are of direct importance to recreation because they are important habitats or food sources for many species of wildlife, which are sought by hunters, fisherpersons, and seafood gourmets. They also function as interesting environments for naturalists, sightseers, photographers, painters, and boaters. Wetlands also contribute indirectly to recreation by storing water, filtering out silt, neutralizing

Figure 18.4 **Downtown San Antonio's 4-kilometer (2.5-mile) Paseo del Rio (River Walk) area is an example of what can be accomplished when the private and public sectors jointly develop an urban water resource. The once neglected and flood-prone San Antonio River is now an attractive, meandering waterway. Its banks are landscaped with subtropical plants and lined with a variety of recreation resources including walkways, parks, restaurants, shops, an outdoor theater, and a convention center containing a theater and a sports arena. Work on the waterway and the arched, limestone bridges began during the WPA era.**

contaminants, and providing a more evenly distributed year-round flow for springs, streams, and rivers. Unfortunately, wetlands in the past have generally been considered liabilities rather than assets, at least until they were drained and filled; as a result, nearly half of America's original wetlands have been obliterated.

Today, however, the ecological significance and practical values of wetlands are being recognized and a variety of private as well as international, national, and intermediate level government programs have been initiated to preserve the wetlands that remain. Support for such action appears to be growing so that it is likely that wetland conversion will cease in many U.S. jurisdictions within the next few years. This will be beneficial to recreation in the ways previously discussed, but it will also have negative effects, especially in the case of boating.

Wetlands along rivers and estuaries are the favored locations for small-boat harbors and marinas because, generally, it is both cheaper and easier to produce boat basins and berths by driving sheet piling and dredging in a marsh than it is to build breakwaters in deep water or excavate solid ground. Not being able to use wetland sites for such purposes is bound to affect the nature and scope of recreation boating. In coastal California, for instance, where most of the remaining potential marina sites are wetlands that are being protected, there is already a severe shortage of boat berths. Charges for the existing berths and moorings are rising quickly and most marinas have long lists of potential customers hoping for a vacancy. This situation, which is unlikely to improve, is encouraging prospective boaters to turn to other activities or make do with smaller, trailer-borne boats, which are not ideal craft for ocean use.

Wetland preservation will have similar effects on the expansion of boating facilities in other states, especially the southern ones with shorelines on the Gulf of Mexico or the Atlantic Ocean. It will also prevent or limit the construction of many recreation-oriented residential developments. In particular, the dredge-and-fill operations where every lot backs onto a canal will become much less common. Buildable waterfront property will become even more valuable, especially if a fair-sized boat can be accommodated without dredging. Similarly, the development of both public and private fishing-access sites, campgrounds, cottages, and other facilities at waterfront locations may no longer be possible in locations requiring wetland dredging or filling.

Another water-related issue that will have a growing impact on recreation concerns the practice of building large dams for flood-control and water-supply purposes. For many years, American and Canadian environmental organizations have been suggesting that the gains in terms of construction jobs, flood control, water supply, and reservoir-based recreation often have not

been worth the losses resulting from flooded agricultural land, destroyed river recreation, inundated aesthetic and cultural values, and the social and psychological damage suffered by those whose lands were affected or whose lives were disrupted. In the West, some irrigation-storage reservoirs have also been criticized for losing too much water by evaporation, filling with silt too rapidly, serving limited numbers of farmers, or depreciating downstream environments. And, in 1978, the Carter administration denied funds to a number of water projects on the basis that they were fiscally or environmentally unsound. It therefore appears likely that the great dam-building-era is drawing to a close; only reservoirs that clearly have social, environmental, and economic benefits that considerably exceed the attendant costs will be built.

Accompanying these changes in attitudes and policies toward reservoir construction is a growing awareness that the best way to protect human settlements from flood damage is to move them out of the flood plain wherever possible and prevent further building in flood-prone areas. An increasing number of local governments are passing laws that prohibit the construction of any type of residential or high-value commerical or institutional structures in flood-plain locations. In some cases, virtually all structures are forbidden except essential nonresidential service buildings such as golf clubhouses for which permits may be issued if certain flood-protection specifications are met. The net result of these two trends is that the supply of new reservoir recreation opportunities is unlikely to continue to rise as rapidly as it has since World War II. At the

same time, fewer existing recreation opportunities will be lost to reservoir construction. In many cases, flood-plain zoning will encourage the conversion of riverside lands into parks, parkways, "natural areas," golf courses, and other recreationally valuable amenities.

These changes may prove particularly significant if problems with energy supplies seriously limit extraurban travel. The building of fewer reservoirs in remote areas would not be a problem; in fact, many of the more sparsely populated areas will have an oversupply of reservoir-oriented recreation opportunities if travel is restricted. However, failure to build new reservoirs near well-populated areas could result in a variety of much-needed water-dependent and water-related recreation opportunities never being available to some large urban populations. On the other hand, the protection of flood plains in urban areas will undoubtedly increase the supply of recreation opportunities for many urban residents.

Finally, changing attitudes and regulations concerning the management of coastal lands will have a considerable effect on the future recreation use of the 58,000 kilometers (36,000 miles) of shoreline in America's 48 contiguous states. More than 75 percent of the U.S. population and most of the larger cities are located in states bordering an ocean or Great Lake. Providing more recreation opportunities in coastal regions is, therefore, particularly important in view of the deepening energy crisis and accompanying loss of mobility for most Americans.

Until recently, most coastal developments in the United States proceeded with little government interference as long as construction remained above the high-water mark. As a result, hundreds of thousands of permanent residences, seasonal homes, hotels, and other commercial structures have been built as close to the ocean or Great Lakes as possible to take advantage of their shorelines' aesthetic qualities and recreation amenities. Generally, where the shorelines are solid rock, this has not caused serious problems other than the reduction of aesthetic values of a previously undeveloped stretch of rugged coastline and the greater difficulty of constructing sewage systems. On the other hand, where shorelines are composed of sand or clay, there are many instances where erosion or flooding have resulted in extensive property damage and even loss of life.

Unfortunately, individuals and developers usually inspect property and plan developments on attractive sections of the 26,000 kilometers (16,000 miles) of coastline that is susceptible to serious erosion problems during salubrious summer weather. They do not see what happens to these shores during periods of high water and gale-force winds. When hurricane-driven or winter-storm-driven waves surge inland tearing away beaches and smashing buildings or undermining their foundations, it has been considered an "act of God" rather than part of a normal and continuous process of erosion and deposition. Insurance companies, local governments, and federal agencies rally round to repair the damage, restore services, and provide aid that will enable people to rebuild in the same locations. Huge sums have been spent on building seawalls,

groins, and jetties as well as pumping vast quantities of sand from offshore areas onto badly eroded beaches (Figure 3.11). In some cases, these efforts have proved futile (Figure 18.5); in others, satisfactory results have been achieved, but the actions taken have initiated or accelerated erosion at another location.

Although many of the problems resulting from the abuse of coastal wetlands and the development of beachfront properties in unstable areas have been apparent for decades, little was done until the middle 1970s. Up to that time, these problems were viewed primarily as the responsibility of local governments since most of the land involved was privately owned. Accelerated coastal development in

the late 1960s accompanied by increased pressures to preserve remaining coastal resources for use as publicly owned recreation areas eventually led to changes in attitude and the adoption of appropriate legislation. In 1972, Congress passed the Coastal Zone Management Act. It authorized federal grants to assist with coastal problems but specified that a state must develop a comprehensive coastal zone management plan before funds would be made available. Half of the thirty coastal states have now passed companion legislation. One example is the California Coastal Act of 1976 that provided agencies with extensive powers to protect, to maintain, and to restore coastal resources because they are of vital and enduring interest to all

Figure 18.5 Broken concrete and twisted steel sheet pilings are all that remain of a seawall built to protect property from shoreline erosion along this section of the Long Island coast. Once the forebeach is gone, even large expenditures on massive protective devices often prove futile because of the tremendous power of storm-driven waves. Careful investigation of erosion potential before development takes place followed by the establishment of appropriate setback and land-use regulation is a more sensible approach.

the state's citizens.

Governments are also beginning to realize the economic implications of continued development of vulnerable coastal areas. Although land speculators and developers are reaping huge profits, the protection of these resources is costing taxpayers millions of dollars a year. For example, about $65 million in local and federal funds are currently being spent on replenishing the sands in front of the barrier-island resort developments at Miami Beach, $135 million in flood claims were paid by the Federal Insurance Administration to property owners in storm-damaged coastal areas in 1978, and, in the years 1975 to 1977, federal aid to the development and protection of barrier islands totaled over $500 million. It is doubtful that the public will continue to support such expenditures for the benefit of a relatively few Americans, particularly when there is no guarantee that the expenditures will not have to be repeated over and over again in the most fragile areas.

Future changes in attitudes, policies, and programs will gradually produce a different combination of recreation opportunities in many coastal areas. Especially in flood-prone areas on barrier islands, there will be movement away from developed recreation facilities toward leaving the shorelines in their undeveloped state. The federal government will likely assume responsibility for most of the remaining unprotected and undeveloped barrier-island areas. (Currently, a bill is in the House of Representatives' National Parks and Insular Affairs Subcommittee that proposes to include all such areas on Atlantic coast and gulf coast barrier islands

in national parks.) The imposition of strict building codes and limitations on federal disaster aid and flood insurance programs will discourage rebuilding of areas damaged repeatedly by major storms. New residential and commercial construction in hazardous locations will also be forbidden or discouraged by curtailing government programs that facilitate the construction of roads, bridges, and water and sewage systems. Where allowed, seasonal homes and resorts will have to be set back farther from the water and concentrated on higher, less vulnerable sites. Public agencies will reduce their efforts to restore beaches and prevent erosion or flood damage in locations where positive results are unlikely to be more than temporary.

As the value of these more hazardous areas as building sites is reduced—by legal restrictions, absence of public services, lack of protective works, or problems in obtaining insurance—they are more likely to be used for public recreation purposes. Public park and recreation agencies will minimize storm damage to their resources by restoring natural sand movement to the area or island, reestablishing and preserving protective vegetation, locating permanent park facilities as far inland as feasible, and using portable toilet buildings and other service structures as much as possible so that they can be removed and stored inland during periods when damaging storms may occur. Beach access will be by tractor trains running along the beach from centralized parking lots rather than by paved roads and parking lots located just behind the dunes. These changes will result in a larger proportion of the nation's shoreline

recreation experiences being of the day-use and primitive-camping types and a smaller proportion being of the type currently enjoyed by occupants of on- or near-shore residences, condominiums, hotels, resorts, and campgrounds.

Deserts and Forests. Future recreation opportunities will also be influenced by attitude and policy changes regarding the use of deserts and forests. Many people still perceive these resources as virtually indestructible. In the past, this attitude was not a serious threat since these resources were relatively inaccessible and only lightly used. However, the situation began to change about 20 years ago. Increases in free time and discretionary income, the building of high-speed highway systems, and a recognition of the recreation value of less developed environments combined to produce completely new use patterns. Technology also contributed by developing a series of new or modified products that altered many people's perceptions of and relationships to less developed environments. These include the elaborately outfitted van, the truck-mounted camper, the snowmobile, the all-terrain vehicle, the motorcycle designed for off-highway use, the four-wheel-drive vehicle, the dune buggy, the horse trailer, and the half-ton pickup truck, which is equally at home on high-speed highways and potholed back-country roads.

As a result of these changes and developments, desert and forest recreation use began to increase dramatically and also become more diversified. No longer did the users consist almost exclusively of small parties of hunters or fisherpersons, family or youth organization groups of tent campers, and avid backpackers and naturalists. Instead, a growing proportion were motorcyclists and four-wheel-drive vehicle owners looking for exciting trails to travel and challenging hills to climb. People with dune buggies sought out areas to use as weekend playgrounds. Growing numbers found the areas attractive destinations for horseback riding activities. Individuals and clubs explored the areas in their campers and pickup trucks searching for and collecting a variety of plants, animals, fossils, mineral specimens, lapidary materials, historic relics, and artifacts. And, a growing number came, not to use or remove any specific resource, but simply to enjoy the freedom from restraint and urban law enforcement practices that these remote, undeveloped areas provided. Soon, the residents and more traditional types of visitors were complaining about all-night drinking parties, the noise made by off-highway vehicles and in-van hi-fi systems, and vandalism and other antisocial acts.

All of these newer activities had a greater environmental impact than the earlier and limited hunting, fishing, backpacking, and old-style tent-camping expeditions. Many motorcyclists and four-wheel-drive vehicle owners particularly enjoyed pitting their machines against difficult terrain; therefore, they started to make regular use of the poorest roads and trails and take off through woodland and across grassland and desert where no vehicle had ever gone before. Some collectors began extensive diggings to obtain more and better materials, and a few made use of power-driven

equipment or explosives. Many people banded together in clubs and began to organize and participate regularly in scheduled activities such as off-highway vehicle races, hill-climb competitions, organized trail-rides on horseback, and group campouts and field trips. Certain favored locations became heavily used both on weekends and during vacations. Eventually, there were more than 10 million off-highway vehicles in use.

Initially, the impact was not particularly noticeable but, as the numbers of users and the frequency of use increased, environmental changes became obvious. Deserts, grasslands, and tundra are particularly susceptible to damage. Once the vegetation or surface materials are disturbed, wind erosion, run-off erosion, or melting of permafrost may rapidly result in the formation of deep gullies, which permanently scar the landscape.

One of the most profoundly affected regions was the California desert. It is an area of 9.7 million hectares (24 million acres) extending from the Sierra Nevada and Peninsula Range mountains in the west to the Mexican border in the south and to the state line in the east and north (Figure 14.4). The northern two-thirds of this desert is relatively high. Much of it is over 900 meters (3000 feet) in elevation with many mountains rising to more than 1500 meters (5000 feet). Precipitation averages no more than 25 centimeters (10 inches) annually with some places receiving less than 10 centimeters (4 inches). The region receives an average of 80 percent sunshine but cools down rapidly at dusk because of the clear air and elevation.

Intensive agriculture occurs on

two small irrigated areas in the Imperial Valley and some of the more heavily vegetated highlands are grazed. Several large military bases are used for testing and training. Outside the irrigated areas, the population is sparse except for a few towns and hamlets associated with military installations, transportation centers, and mining operations.

In the past, the California Desert received comparatively little recreation use. But starting in the 1950s, this situation changed. The population of the Los Angeles-San Diego urban region increased from 5.9 million in 1950 to 11.6 million in 1970 and southern Californians began to feel more crowded at home and at play. Construction of interstate highways 8, 10, 15, and 40 substantially reduced the travel time and aggravation of getting through the mountains and into the desert. It became possible to reach even the more remote desert areas for a camping weekend. At the same time, and partly because of the increased interest in desert recreation, the technological innovations mentioned earlier flourished. The development and availability of reliable and relatively cheap Japanese motorcycles played a major role; increasing numbers of people perceived these machines as ideal vehicles for desert recreation.

The Bureau of Land Management controlling two-thirds of the region (6.5 million hectares or 16 million acres) is the principal land-managing agency in the California Desert. In the past, its activities were largely restricted to the supervising of grazing, mining, and settlement permits. Limited budgets and staff meant that little recreation planning, construction, or management could be undertaken. The new mechanized desert users found they were able to do what they liked on the plains, hills, canyons, and mountains of Bureau of Land Management lands because there was virtually no supervision. For many people, this meant freedom to explore and enjoy the varied environments without paying fees or being directed by signs, fences, and rangers to stay on the roads or camp only at designated locations. Enjoy it they did — by engaging in a wide range of activities from partying, hunting, target shooting, sand sailing, motorcycling, and dune buggy driving to hiking, photography, specimen collecting, and nature study. Campers ranged from those with just a motorcycle and a sleeping bag to families with $30,000 motor homes.

The fragile, largely unsupervised desert and its resources soon began to show signs of abuse. Lawless individuals vandalized old buildings, road signs, and the few camping and picnicking facilities. Archaeological treasures were damaged or removed. This included desecrating ancient Indian sites; painting over, shooting at, or trying to chip or blast petroglyphs out of the rock; and purposely driving vehicles around and around on intaglios (huge designs constructed of stones), even where they had been fenced for protection. However, the most serious problem involved the environmental changes being produced by the widespread use of off-highway vehicles.

Most of the vegetation disappeared in the heavily used locations because of abrasion by many wheels, soil compaction, and the use of any woody material for campfires. Areas surrounding these gathering places and around most established campgrounds became a mass of intersecting tracks. Biologists issued warnings about the possible loss of rare species of plants and animals. Newspaper and magazine articles that included photographs of large numbers of motorcycle riders taking part in cross-desert races drew public attention to the situation. Preservationist groups called for a ban on off-highway vehicles or the establishment of larger wilderness areas. Many of the off-highway vehicle users and organizations contended they were not doing any permanent damage. Grazing, mining, industrial, and power company interests became worried that wilderness or other restrictive designations might stop them from using the desert as freely as they had in the past.

National interest in the off-highway vehicle problem reached a peak in the early 1970s and resulted in a Presidential order requiring regulation of such vehicles on all federal lands across the nation. Concurrently with other federal agencies, the Bureau of Land Management began a review of off-highway vehicle regulations that placed all lands in one of five classes. The four main classes were: lands where vehicles may travel anywhere; areas where vehicles must stay on previously existing roads and trails; lands where vehicles may only travel on certain roads and trails designated by the bureau; and areas where all off-highway vehicle travel is prohibited. Lands in a fifth class were designated for possible development of access roads, campgrounds, and other facilities for the use of all kinds of recreation participants. The regulations also designated a number of areas or corridors for use in competitive vehicle events.

In 1976, Congress passed the Land Policy and Management Act. Besides providing the first consolidated legislative directive for multiple-use management of all the bureau's lands, the act required it to complete a $10 million comprehensive long-range management plan for the California Desert by October 1980. Some 80 studies were carried out to obtain data for this plan, which includes consideration of all types of recreation. The act also gave the bureau authority to appoint rangers with full law enforcement powers (Figure 18.6), and Congress provided additional funds for ranger patrols and other recreation management procedures. However, the additional resources provided to date are small in comparison to the problems involved. For example, there are currently only 15 rangers to patrol all the bureau's California Desert lands and enforce the off-highway vehicle regulations.

The California Desert problems of overuse and antisocial behavior are extreme but not unique. Other lands administered by the Bureau of Land Management, the U.S. Forest Service, and other federal, state, and local government agencies often experience similar difficulties. Unauthorized vehicular use of private lands (especially by snowmobiles and motorcycles) is also an issue in some regions. Snowmobiles can cause harm by compacting the snow, damaging young trees, and disturbing wildlife. Motorcycles damage forested areas by destroying ground cover, compacting soils, tearing up hillsides that cause erosion and result in the death of trees when their roots are exposed, and the destruction of trout spawning

Figure 18.6 Bureau of Land Management Ranger Lynell Schalk assists a desert user while on routine patrol in the El Centro Resource Area of southern California. Her four-wheel-drive vehicle is equipped with full police equipment, including firearms, and she has completed an eight-week training program at the Federal Law Enforcement Training Center in Glyncoe, Georgia.

beds and aquatic habitats when the disturbed soils are washed into rivers and lakes. However, four-wheeled off-highway vehicles generally present less of a problem in wooded areas than on grasslands, deserts, or tundra because trees discourage a high percentage of drivers from leaving established roads or trails. In addition, forest areas, if caught in time and given a chance, generally recover from abuse and usually do so more rapidly than deserts or tundra because replacement vegetation is able to grow much faster to stabilize damaged areas and cover the scars. Forest agencies also usually have more management personnel per areal unit than the Bureau of Land Management and, therefore, have been able to maintain much tighter control over their lands. For these reasons, forest agencies are often

able to place fewer restrictions on off-highway vehicle use — at least in certain areas.

The problems connected with off-highway vehicle use and associated antisocial behavior may have reached their peak. In the next few years, the increased price of gasoline, the higher cost of vehicles, the general effects of inflation, and the smaller proportion of young people in the population will tend to reduce the growth of off-highway vehicle ownership and usage. Current procedures of designating public lands as being open, partially open, or completely closed to off-highway use and the providing of more ranger personnel to enforce these regulations are also beginning to bring the problem under control. In some locations, agencies are leasing private lands for off-highway vehicle use to provide needed opportunities

and, thereby, reduce trespass and damage on closed public as well as private lands. Future off-highway use will probably be confined largely to parks developed especially for that purpose, designated sand-dune areas, and backroads and trails that can accommodate the traffic with minimal environmental impact and maintenance.

Wilderness. Although off-highway vehicles and overall planning for recreation use of fragile environments have received much attention in the 1970s, two larger land-use issues that will affect recreation opportunities in the future have been emerging. These are the future ownership and future management of federal lands. Involved in these issues are controversies concerning the desirability and, in some instances, the legality of federal ownership of extensive tracts of land as well as the role the federal government should play in their protection and development. A major component and sometimes the cause of these controversies is the question of how much land should be preserved and managed as permanent wilderness.

The federal lands issues are coming to a head in the West where the states contain large areas of federally controlled lands. Although there have been many disputes concerning the management of these lands in the past, these have generally been small-scale skirmishes regarding the use of specific areas. Now the right of the federal government to decide which lands should remain in federal ownership as well as how they should be managed is being challenged.

The main battle at present concerns the future of federal lands in

Alaska. The 1959 Statehood Act and the 1971 Alaska Native Claims Settlement Act specified how the 99 percent of the state which was federally owned was to be allocated. The state government was to choose 41.6 million hectares (104 million acres) or about one-third of Alaska to be used for settlement or management by the state; this is an area a little larger than California. The state was also to control all navigable waters and the coastline, which is longer than the entire coastline of the 48 contiguous states. Native Aleut, Eskimo, and Indian tribes were to receive 17.6 million hectares (44 million acres) and $962 million in cash settlements. The Department of the Interior was to select up to 32 million hectares (80 million acres) to be set aside as national park system units, wildlife refuges, and wild and scenic rivers. Land not selected by the end of 1978 was to be managed by the Bureau of Land Management on a multipurpose basis as national resource lands.

Selection proceeded slowly until 1968 when the first major oil discoveries were made on the north slope. The process then accelerated as the various groups tried to pick the lands that were most desirable from their particular viewpoints. In 1973, the Secretary of the Interior recommended specific lands for the proposed parks and refuges, but Congress failed to take action on the required legislation until 1978. Then a bill to designate 50.6 million hectares (125 million acres) as national parks, national wildlife refuges, wild and scenic rivers, and national forests was passed in the House of Representatives by a vote of 277 to 31. This would have placed over one-third of Alaska

under fairly restrictive federal management programs or in a state of complete preservation in the case of wilderness areas.

Prodevelopment groups were incensed because they had expected much more of the federal lands to be managed as national resource lands and, therefore, be available for exploitation to a large extent. The size and location of the areas proposed for wilderness designation were also seen as detrimental to state and national interests. Those supporting less restrictive plans argued that the nation needs all the oil, gas, uranium, coal, timber, scarce nonenergy minerals, and accessible recreation it can obtain. Alaska's senators fought the proposed bill vigorously and prevented it coming to the floor for a vote. President Carter, then, signed a proclamation under the Antiquities Act designating 23 million hectares (56 million acres) as national monuments and Secretary of the Interior Andrus withdrew an additional 16 million hectares (40 million acres) from development under the Federal Land Policy and Management Act until 1981 or until Congress could reach an agreement on how the lands should be used. A new but basically similar bill was approved by the House of Representatives in early 1979, but it and a compromise bill proposed by the Senate Energy and Natural Resources Committee had still not been debated in the Senate by year's end. When it became clear in February, 1980 that the Senate intended to delay action until after the July 4 recess, Andrus ordered the acreage on which he had previously imposed temporary restrictions to be turned into 12 wildlife refuges and 4 natural resource

areas, thereby affording them 20-year-protection from exploitation and placing them under the care of the U.S. Fish and Wildlife Service and, in the case of the natural resource areas, the Bureau of Land Management and the National Park Service.

Alaskan political leaders, meanwhile, are conducting a sophisticated campaign to sway public opinion in favor of less restrictive Alaska-lands legislation. Their arguments are based on states' rights; the nation's future energy, timber, and mineral needs; potential unemployment in Alaska; and the right of the public to use publicly owned lands for such activities as operating off-highway vehicles, hunting, and fishing. The state legislature appropriated more than $2 million for the campaign, which included advertisements in national newspapers as well as newspapers in the home states of the members of the Senate Energy and Natural Resources Committee. A number of legal actions have also been started challenging various aspects of the federal government procedures.

Principal support for the proposed establishment of large, well-protected national parks, refuges, wild and scenic rivers, forests, and wilderness areas has come from the Alaska Coalition. It consists of 31 organizations, including the Sierra Club, other conservation groups, and the United Auto Workers Union. Proponents point out that Alaska contains some of the most remarkable undeveloped scenic and wildlife resources left in the world and that Americans owe it to this and future generations to preserve the best of these environments in their original state. They maintain that 90 percent of the state's high-potential oil- and gas-bearing lands and over two-thirds of Alaska's mineral-rich areas would be outside the proposed reserves.

The Alaska land-allocation decisions are perhaps the single most important group of recreation resource decisions that have ever been made. If the final federal action follows the patterns suggested by the legislation currently approved by the House (but so far rejected by the Senate), it will provide a high degree of protection to 52 million hectares (129 million acres) of land. This is an area slightly larger than California. The reserves would consist of:

- About 18 million hectares (44 million acres) in 13 national park system units; this will more than double the size of the national park system.
- Some 32 million hectares (79.5 million acres) of new national wildlife refuges or extensions to existing refuges; this will more than triple the size of the national wildlife refuge system.
- Approximately 2.3 million hectares (5.8 million acres) in 16 wilderness areas in the Tongass National Forest.

A total of some 27 million hectares (67 million acres) of these park, wildlife-refuge, forest, and river-system lands would be designated as wilderness areas, thereby excluding virtually all possibility of development other than for hiking and riding trails.

Included in the proposed reserves are additions to the Arctic Wildlife Refuge, which contains the calving grounds of the nation's largest caribou herd. Another exceptional area is the Aniakchak Caldera National Monument, which contains the 10-kilometer-wide (6-mile-wide) crater of a collapsed volcano surrounded by a 600-meter-high

(2000-foot-high) rim (Figure 18.7). As in the case of Yellowstone, the wisdom and significance of these reservations will probably not be fully realized for at least a century.

If, on the other hand, those who favor fewer parks and refuges, less wilderness, fewer restrictions on the use of federal lands, and the transferring of more land to the state of Alaska are successful in their campaigns, recreation resource and behavior patterns will be affected both in Alaska and elsewhere. In Alaska, more roads, settlements, and tourist facilities will be developed in areas with good recreation opportunities. Landscapes at these locations will also show more evidence of mining and petroleum-extraction activities. Recreation opportunities of all kinds will become more accessible because of road construction, fewer restrictions on use of aircraft and off-highway vehicles, and the construction of on-site overnight facilities. At least initially, this will likely prove economically beneficial to the state as larger numbers and a broader range of people will be able to reach and enjoy Alaska's prime scenic, hunting, and fishing resources. In the long run, however, increased development will almost certainly have a harmful effect on some of the unique landscapes and fish and wildlife populations, which are now, and will continue to be, the main attraction for the majority of Alaskan visitors. Uniqueness is always a critical factor in attracting visitors to

Figure 18.7 **Located on the Alaska Peninsula, the Aniakchak Caldera is a spectacular landscape especially when viewed from an aircraft. The crater floor contains a 670-meter (2200-foot) mountain, the result of a later eruption, and Spirit Lake that empties through a rift in the rim as the Aniakchak River. Virtually inaccessible except by air, the area is currently visited by people who arrive by float plane to explore the caldera's many volcanic features and interesting plant life.**

remote locations, but it will be of even greater significance if fuel costs continue to rise and long-distance trips become increasingly expensive.

If a substantial change of federal policy toward parks, refuges, development, and state ownership of lands in Alaska occurs, repercussions are likely to be felt in many other states. Already Nevada has been encouraged by the large amount of land being transferred to Alaska and by Alaska's seeking jurisdiction over even more land and fewer restrictions on federal lands to take action on its own behalf. In May 1979, Nevada's legislature passed a law that declared that the state had sovereignty over the 20 million hectares (49 million acres) of federal land currently administered by the Bureau of Land Management. These national resource lands comprise 69 percent of the state and are essential to Nevada's ranching and mining industries. Those favoring this so-called sagebrush rebellion believe that the state should have the opportunity to direct its own destiny by exploiting these resources and using resultant revenues as it sees fit. Proponents argue that the federal government obtained the lands by blackmail; they allege that it made federal ownership a condition of statehood in 1864. Increases in grazing fees, attempts to reduce grazing intensity, tightened federal control on the exploitation of oil and other minerals, and the realization of the potential value of some of the lands by powerful real estate interests may have prompted Nevada's present annexation attempt.

The Nevada ploy appears to have no legal basis because the national resource lands never belonged to the state or to individuals; they had been part of the public domain from the time they were either acquired by purchase from or as a result of war with other nations or Indian tribes. Nevertheless, it has proven possible in the past for states to gain further concessions from the federal government in matters of land ownership and management by mounting persuasive public relations campaigns coupled with astute political maneuvering. And so, leaders of the movement hope to entice other states into the fray, broaden the attack to include the national forests, and eventually get 246 million hectares (607 million acres) or 80 percent of the nation's federal lands turned over to the states. So far, the Alaska legislature has passed a resolution commending Nevada's action. Arizona, Idaho, Utah, and Wyoming are all drafting or have introduced sagebrush-rebellion legislation of their own. And California has already passed a bill authorizing the attorney general to sue for state ownership of national resource lands. This bill, however, was vetoed by the governor in September 1979. Similar doubts about the efficacy of such legislation have been expressed by political leaders in Colorado and New Mexico.

If an alliance of several large western states occurs, it could wield considerable political power, especially if energy shortages and attendant economic and social dislocation continues. Should this happen, it is possible that a major transfer of federal lands to state control or the adoption of a cooperative management policy would result. This would likely mean more development of state-park-type facilities and commercial recreation enterprises on these lands. Conversely, there would probably be fewer opportunities for wilderness experiences, camping at small back-country campgrounds, and pleasure driving on well-maintained back-country roads. Considering that most of the western states' constitutions and laws mandate that state lands be managed for the highest financial return, it would also seem likely that some lands would be leased or even sold for single-purpose use. Recreation use in most of these cases would be discouraged or prohibited. It is also likely that some of the states would be unable to afford the high costs of proper management procedures, particularly if tax revolts continue to limit or reduce state budgets. In these states, recreation opportunities will be lost or become less attractive as resources are allowed to deteriorate and facilities are not provided. And, last but not least, the pressures of special interest groups and speculators on elected officials would be tremendous; some of the lands that are now prime recreation lands would almost certainly end up being leased or sold for uses that would preclude recreation by the general public.

The question of how much land should be designated as part of the wilderness system is one of the major issues that stimulated both the Alaska and Nevada attempts to obtain control of the federal lands within their borders. Business interests that have been providing so much support for these campaigns are generally strongly opposed to wilderness designation because it precludes new mining, oil extraction, grazing, and timber-cutting operations as well as prohibiting the construction of roads, reservoirs, and commercial recreation developments.

The wilderness issue is currently receiving considerable attention in the United States because Congress instructed the federal land-managing agencies to make a study of all their lands to determine which areas qualified for wilderness designation. This is a difficult task because of the vast areas involved, the comparative lack of pertinent data, the subjective nature of some of the criteria, and the fact that such evaluations have to be fitted into the regular duties of agency staff rather than assigned to employees or consultants hired especially for the job. Areas in the national park system and national wildlife refuge system have been recommended for wilderness status on a unit by unit basis. Such designations are not as likely to generate widespread opposition since access to these lands is already controlled, most areas are relatively small, and most people have already come to accept the need for fairly rigorous environmental protection policies in parks and refuges. However, heated controversies have arisen in some areas where there is strong local support for the construction of roads and facilities, the use of off-highway vehicles, or the manipulation of wildlife habitats through procedures such as clearcuts or the construction of water impoundments.

In contrast, the areas of national forests and national resource lands that are proposed for wilderness designation are often large and, in many cases, are viewed as regionally or nationally important as present or future sources of economic gain or personal recreation opportunities. For example, some

tracts in recently recommended wilderness areas have extensive forests on them so that residents of nearby communities, individual forest product enterprises, or national forest product organizations argue that designation will cause closing of businesses, loss of jobs, and an even more serious shortage of building supplies, which will result in fewer moderately priced homes for people to buy. It is true that some of these forests contain limited stands of better quality timber. But for the most part, the forests in these and existing wilderness areas are at relatively high elevations; as a result, they contain comparatively little marketable timber per hectare because of the slow growth and low density of the trees. In addition, many wilderness areas are largely rugged terrain dissected by deep mountain valleys or many lakes and wetlands. Small patches of timber scattered through such environments are seldom profitable to cut. Most of the wilderness areas are also remote. In only a few instances such as the Boundary Waters Canoe Area (a wilderness area in the Superior National Forest, Minnesota) are there substantial areas of relatively accessible marketable timber.

The majority of designated wilderness land is mountain peaks and ridges, snowfields and glaciers, alpine meadows, tundra, scrubby woodlands, sand dunes, and stony desert, so that comparatively little is good grazing land. Nevertheless, desert grazing is permitted where it was taking place prior to the 1964 Wilderness Act. Prospecting and mining can also occur in national forest wilderness areas up to 1983, following which time, mining will only be permitted at existing

mines or valid claims. However, there are indications that courts may rule that mining is inconsistent with the objectives of the Wilderness Act. Therefore, critics may have some basis for contending that wilderness designation will prevent mineral extraction. On the other hand, many of the wilderness areas do not appear to contain commercially significant mineral deposits.

A variety of other objections to wilderness designation are frequently raised. Some people believe wilderness only benefits the more affluent who have the time, equipment, and money to take extensive backpacking, horseback, or canoe trips. Others object because the wilderness designation tends to exclude less active, handicapped, and older citizens. Local residents who are accustomed to using mechanical transportation to explore areas that are proposed for wilderness status complain about their loss of personal freedom. Individuals, entrepreneurs, chambers of commerce, and local governments oppose the wilderness classification if they have been counting on economic benefits to be gained from developments such as roads, reservoirs, ski areas, or summer resorts.

The U.S. Forest Service presented a report on its Roadless Area Review and Evaluation (RARE) to Congress early in 1979. The report recommended that 6.2 million hectares (15.4 million acres) of the 25 million hectares (62 million acres) of roadless land that had been studied should be designated as wilderness. Another 4.3 million hectares (10.6 million acres) was suggested for further investigation, and 14.6 million hectares (35 million acres) was rejected as wilderness and returned to full-scale multiple-use management. As is to be expected, neither the forest industries nor the preservationist organizations were pleased with the report. The former contended that too much marketable timber was included in the recommended wilderness areas; the latter felt that many good areas were omitted. Surprisingly, even *Business Week,* the well-known industry-serving periodical, felt that more land should have been included in the further-study category.[5]

The Bureau of Land Management is to complete its review of possible wilderness lands within the next few months. Following that, Congress will finish its investigations of the reports received from all the federal agencies and prepare legislation for Presidential approval by late 1981. These deliberations will take place in an environment colored by energy problems, inflation, inadequate supplies of housing, the Alaska-lands issue, and the sagebrush rebellion. Nevertheless, if Congress continues to have a generally liberal attitude toward wilderness, it appears likely that the system will eventually consist of some 30 million hectares (75 million acres) or be about five times its present size. Although a substantial portion will be in Alaska, numerous wilderness areas will be scattered through the mountains and deserts of the west and two or three dozen will be located in the east. Added interest and participation in wilderness activities is likely to result from such large-scale designation and widspread distribution. Some losses of opportunities for pleasure driving, powerboating, off-highway ve-

hicle driving, downhill skiing, hunting, and fishing will occur in these areas because of restrictions on use or motorized access.

RECREATION CONFLICTS AND CARRYING CAPACITY

Although the use of the California Desert by off-highway vehicles and the question of how much wilderness is needed are basic land-use issues, they also involve two other important aspects of recreation resource management, namely, user conflicts and carrying capacity. Each of these topics is a major problem for recreation resource managers although, in many cases, the two are

interconnected; user conflicts often arise when carrying capacity is exceeded.

As recreation activities have become more numerous and complicated, the range of user conflicts has grown (Figure 18.8). It now includes a great variety of situations from problems in remote wilderness areas to difficulties in the family living room. Some examples that illustrate the scope of the problem are conflicts that occur between:

- People who wish to watch television or listen to recordings on their stereo equipment and careless citizens band or ham radio operators whose transmissions cause televison or stereo equipment interference.

Figure 18.8 **As this sign on a Maine community beach attests, unrestricted use of recreation resources is seldom possible because some activities are incompatible, some are considered inappropriate, and some are potentially harmful to the site or its users. When use increases, the number of regulations also tend to grow as managers try to minimize user conflicts and other problems. However, skilled managers will usually avoid highly negative signs such as this one and control behavior that is perceived as antisocial by using printed rules, a few site-specific signs, and prompt, friendly enforcement.**

[5] "A Rush to Cut, Dig, Drill," editorial, *Business Week, 2570,* January 29, 1979, p. 134.

- Those who wish to use public parks for parties, rock concerts, fairs, and other noisy, crowd-attracting events and those who wish to restrict park use to quiet, contemplative, individual, or small-group activities.
- Residents of a country or smaller political unit who feel they should have exclusive use of certain government resources because they pay taxes for the privilege and people from another nation or smaller political unit who feel it is their right to share these recreation resources.
- People who use powerful motorboats for towing waterskiers or racing back and forth on a small lake and others who use the lake for fishing from a rowboat, sailing, canoeing, swimming, relaxing on a moored pontoon boat, or scuba diving.
- Hikers on forest or desert trails and motorcyclists who produce noise and dust or people with horses who create problems with manure and rough trails.
- Dog owners who walk their unleashed pets in parks or residential areas and park users (especially those with young children), joggers, and property owners who take special pride in their unfenced lawns and flowerbeds.

Sometimes the conflict is complicated by legal ramifications. For example, in the case of the wildlife management lands purchased with Pittman-Robertson funds (see Chapter 17), it appears reasonable to expect that hunters would be given priority in using these resources over hikers, berrypickers, birdwatchers, snowmobilers, and cross-country skiers.

In other situations, there may be conflicts between persons undertaking the same activity. This may be the result of antisocial behavior on the part of one or more participants. More often, however, it is because the psychological carrying capacity of the recreation environment has been exceeded (see Chapter 9). In these situations, conflicts may sometimes be alleviated by improving the design of the facility or by adopting appropriate management procedures such as limiting the number of people admitted to a development at any one time.

There are bound to be more problems with user conflicts and carrying capacity in the future if population and levels of participation continue to increase. However, the locations where these problems occur are likely to be different as major changes in the population age structure take place and as the energy problem intensifies. For instance, fewer difficulties will likely be experienced at the more remote resources; there is apt to be less participation in backpacking activities in wilderness areas as the population ages and, if gasoline is more costly or harder to obtain (Figure 18.1), the numbers of powerboaters and campers may decrease at out-of-the-way reservoirs and national parks. On the other hand, more user conflicts and carrying capacity problems will likely be encountered at recreation resources that are in or near urban areas. If the uncertainty of being able to obtain gasoline is a major deterrent, for example, resources that are less than half a tank of gasoline away from urban centers will attract many more participants and experience difficulties associated with heavy use. However, recreation resource managers may be able to reduce the effects of higher intensity use by redesigning the facilities, changing operation policies, and upgrading maintenance procedures. The participants may also make heavier resource use possible by adapting their behavior patterns to suit a more crowded environment.

The management techniques that can be employed to mitigate the effects of overuse depend on the resource, the kinds of activities, and the patterns of use. Examples of methods that can be utilized to reduce user conflicts without necessarily decreasing the total number of opportunities provided by a resource are:

- Separating different kinds of users on a time basis; for instance, a lake may be reserved for fisherpersons during the early morning and evening hours and be available for use by powerboats and waterskiers during the rest of the day.
- Spatially separating less compatible uses by including buffer zones in a facility's design so that activities do not conflict or by zoning an area (such as a lake) so that incompatible activities do not overlap.
- Setting up one-way systems at exhibitions and on trails, drives, and canoe routes so that more people can enjoy the experience while having fewer contacts with other users.
- Providing alternative resources that will divert some of the users from an overused fragile environment to one that is capable of carrying the additional load, for example, people who are using unique scenic, biological, or cultural resources in state or national parks for activities typically undertaken at community and regional parks may be diverted to new county parks or commercial developments if they are placed at strategic locations and cost about the same.

If it is impossible to offer alternative opportunities of this kind or if sufficient people are unwilling to use the less fragile resources, it may become necessary to adopt some type of rationing system.

Rationing systems that seek to

reduce conflicts or keep use below maximum carrying-capacity levels are of three kinds. The first method is based on the premise that the supply is much too small to satisfy demand under any circumstances; therefore, only a portion of the potential participants will be served. In most cases, the selection of the individuals who will be allowed to take part is made by line-up, ticket, or reservation systems; the person who lines up, buys a ticket, or requests a reservation early enough gains access to an activity or facility such as an exhibition, theater, art class, restaurant, sports event, or ski hill. Currently, a number of states are using reservation systems for all or some of their state park campsites and the National Park Service and U.S. Forest Service are experimenting with reservation systems for the limited numbers of backpacker permits that are being issued for some heavily used wilderness areas. Such methods are criticized, however, because certain individuals (those who can plan ahead, those who can afford to spend long periods of time in line-ups, the more affluent, the ablebodied, or the better educated) usually have an advantage.

The alternative is to use some type of lottery system so that all who wish to participate have an equal chance of being allowed to do so. Currently, this is a common method of choosing participants for special hunting seasons during which limited numbers of animals or birds are available. Some professionals are predicting that many kinds of recreation opportunities will eventually be allocated by the lottery approach; they visualize the day when computer systems will not only make random drawings to

decide who will be allowed to undertake high-demand activities (such as visiting Yellowstone National Park) but also determine the date when they will be permitted to do so.

The second method is to try to make opportunities available to as many individuals as possible although this may affect the quality of the experiences. It is based on the premise that a limited experience is better than no experience at all. Local government recreation departments use this system when operating swimming pools on a fixed-time basis. At set intervals, everyone is required to leave the pool and stand in line to get a new admission ticket if they wish to enjoy the facility for another period. However, they may not get another chance that day if the line-up is already long. Some European national parks and natural history interpretive areas accommodate high volumes of users with minimum environmental damage by only opening up a small area of the park and insisting that all visitors remain on the trails. Other techniques for reducing the impact of large numbers include prohibiting campfires or the gathering of firewood, limiting the size of hiking or canoeing parties, or requiring campers to camp only at prepared sites that are designed to withstand heavy use. The Bureau of Land Management plan for establishing off-highway vehicle-use zones in the California Desert is another example.

The third method is to restrict use by making it more difficult for people to participate. Here the premise is that only the most enthusiastic potential participants will make the necessary effort and casual users or those who wish to take

part for dubious reasons will be discouraged from doing so. This is often the reason for the imposition of admission fees and reservation systems; organizations may also reduce the number of applicants by not accepting telephone or mail applications or by limiting the locations, dates, or hours when reservations or tickets may be obtained. Some agencies discourage certain groups of users by purposely creating hardships for them. For instance, heavy day use by fisherpersons that was causing environmental degradation of picturesque lakes in some wilderness areas was eliminated by moving road barriers and parking areas farther away from the lakes thereby making it necessary for people to walk longer distances to reach the fishing sites.

As recreation participation grows, recreation professionals of all kinds will be required to make an increasing number of decisions regarding user conflicts and overuse, especially in and near urban areas. It will be their responsibility to decide which type of approach will produce the best combination of social benefits. Meanwhile, the adoption of staggered work schedules and shorter work weeks to reduce energy use may become widespread and provide some relief; if a larger part of the work force has to work in the evenings, on weekends, and during holidays, then problems with user conflicts and overuse at traditionally busy times will be reduced. It may also prove possible to alter work schedules expressly to alleviate certain recreation resource problems. West Germany, for example, has already adopted a policy of staggering summer vacations thereby reducing the pressures on its most popular resort areas and spreading use more evenly throughout the summer season. If substantial midweek and out-of-season use can be encouraged (especially at recreation resources that are largely supported by user fees), another beneficial effect will be realized. The resultant increased revenues will permit improvements in facilities and maintenance programs that could further reduce user conflicts during peak periods and increase the overall carrying capacity of the resources.

ECONOMIC TRENDS AND ISSUES

The influences that economic factors have on people's ability to participate in recreation were summarized in Chapter 4. Economic conditions also affect the amount of money that is available for the development and maintenance of both public and private recreation resources. Other programs that have an impact on recreation such as pollution abatement, road maintenance, and public transportation are similarly dependent on the economic climate. It is, therefore, important when exploring the future to include consideration of probable economic conditions.

Unfortunately, forecasting the state of any one country's economy or the economic situation of the world as a whole, either on a short- or long-term basis, is a highly speculative activity. The factors that affect the well-being of regions, nations, and groups of nations are simply too numerous, complex, and unpredictable to make accurate forecasts possible. Assessing the effects such factors might have on

people's recreation environments (even if they were well understood and tended to remain constant over long periods of time) would still be difficult because all societies and geographic areas are not affected equally. However, there are likely to be certain basic changes in economic conditions in the future that will be the direct result of problems that are already apparent. Changes of this nature that will probably have the greatest effect on recreation environments will be emphasized in the discussion that follows.

INTERNATIONAL TRADE

It is impossible to predict the precise nature or effects of future trade relationships between nations. No one, for instance, could have fully anticipated the profound changes both in world trade patterns and the economic status of individual nations that have resulted from the growing importance and unequal geographic distribution of oil. However, a brief examination of some of the present trends will at least give some indication of the kinds of problems many nations may have to face and their likely effects on recreation.

Trade Deficits and Surpluses. The buying and selling of crude oil supplies is presently the single most important contributor to imbalances in world trade. Since there seems to be little hope for substantial changes, at least in the near future, the effects of these transactions on the economies of various nations are significant, both now and for years to come. Naturally, the nations whose need for oil imports produces large trade deficits are the most negatively affected,

and the poorest nations are affected worst of all. Forced to borrow money to buy oil, they have collectively accumulated debts of over $250 billion. In a few cases, this indebtedness is already so enormous that it threatens their ability to survive.

Turkey, for example, never recovered from the oil price hikes of 1973–1974; the nation has now run out of foreign exchange and is teetering on the edge of bankruptcy under the burden of a $17 billion foreign debt. The effects on living standards have been enormous. Because of its inability to pay for imports of raw materials, an industrial slump has occurred that has idled almost 60 percent of plant capacity and pushed unemployment levels to 25 percent. The annual inflation rate is close to 100 percent. Citizens face serious shortages of basic commodities and foodstuffs as well as daily blackouts of electric power. Worst of all, the deteriorating conditions are contributing to social and political chaos. The government, although it is a parliamentary democracy, has found it necessary to declare martial law in 20 of its 67 provinces. This is intended to help stop sectarian clashes among various Muslim groups and discourage terrorist gun battles and politically motivated killings that have claimed more than 2000 lives in an 18-month period.

Fortunately, few nations that suffer substantial trade deficits develop the severe problems of Turkey, but the threat of such difficulties occurring is cause for concern. Most nations struggle to reduce their trade imbalances because such debts help depress the value of a nation's currency in world markets and contribute to a rapid rise in domestic prices. This is presently the case in the United States whose trade deficit in 1978 — $28.45 billion — was the biggest in the nation's history. Oil imports were a major cause; of the $172.03 billion spent on imports, $39.5 billion was used for the purchase of foreign oil.

Obviously, it is much better for a nation to have a trade surplus than a deficit, but this does not mean that there are no problems attached to the accumulation of surpluses, especially if they are substantial and are obtained at considerable cost to the welfare of other nations. After all, the continued prosperity of a successful exporter country depends on the economic well-being of importer nations. In addition, when trade becomes disproportionately favorable to one nation, the other nation tends to panic, taking any actions it sees fit to restore a balance before its economy is seriously affected. These range from the adoption of measures that reduce the need for or use of the imported resources to the erection of trade barriers. The latter is accomplished by the imposition of quotas and tariffs that make it impossible or more difficult for imported goods to gain entry to a nation's markets or compete with domestic products. And finally, too much success can breed resentment among less trade-efficient nations and lead to world tensions and, in some cases, become a contributing factor to the outbreak of hostilities.

Effects on Recreation.
Besides the general impact trade imbalances can have on standards of living, employment, and political stability (effects that indirectly expand or reduce people's recreation participation potential), imbalances can directly affect recreation opportunities in a number of ways. Perhaps the way that is likely to have the greatest influence on worldwide recreation patterns in the future is the impact on travel.

One type of restriction is self-imposed. People living in nations with worsening trade deficits usually find that their money is worth less abroad. Provided that they are not blessed with unlimited discretionary income, they react in one of several ways. Some individuals cease to travel abroad. Others compromise and visit only those nations whose currency has depreciated even more than their own. However, the majority of would-be travelers tend to avoid only those nations with the strongest currencies (Switzerland, West Germany, and Japan at the present time) and otherwise choose their destinations much as they would under more favorable circumstances. This does not mean that their trip will be exactly the same. To make it economically feasible, they may shorten their trip, visit fewer countries, go to neighboring countries rather than distant ones, choose less expensive restaurants and lodgings, and either drastically curtail or eliminate visits to major tourist cities and resort areas where costs are likely to be highest.

At the present time, international tourism patterns are emerging that have been brought about mainly by a steady and rapid drop in the value of the U.S. dollar as measured against other currencies. So far, there has been little change in the number of Americans traveling abroad. Lured by cheaper air fares, they are continuing to visit foreign countries in record numbers, but their travel patterns are not the same.

In Switzerland, for example, American visits decreased by almost 25 percent in 1978, reducing that nation's tourist revenues from American sources by $50 million. This caused considerable hardship to many hotels, restaurants, and resorts. To counterbalance these losses, the Swiss tourist industry began to cultivate new clients such as the affluent citizens of Arab nations. At the same time, in an effort to revitalize American tourism, the Swiss National Tourist Office developed new marketing approaches. In their literature for distribution to Americans, they now deemphasize the attractions of the major cities and resort areas and, instead, point out the wonderful vacation opportunities that exist in locations that are less well known but cheaper to visit. Similar campaigns are being mounted in France, West Germany, Italy, Great Britain, the Scandinavian countries, and Japan. As more and more Americans follow their advice, there will be a growing need for less elaborate accommodations and out-of-the-way recreation resources of all kinds. The resultant changes in travel patterns could have considerable effects on regional economies and lifestyles.

Nations that have favorable currency exchange rates for American tourists are also determined to increase their revenues by providing attractive destinations. During the last two years, Canada has been promoting itself as an inexpensive foreign vacation choice. It is making it easier and cheaper for Americans to visit major tourist areas by providing prepaid packages through American travel agents. These include everything from transportation and accommodations to tickets to special events and car or camper rentals.

On the continent, Spain is currently one of the least expensive countries for Americans to visit. Besides aggressively promoting its many attractions (Figure 18.9), it has expanded its recreation resources to accommodate more and different kinds of visitors. This expansion program included the reopening of gambling casinos, the construction of nine new first-class hotels, and the development and operation of a nudist camp on the Costa del Sol. This program has proved very successful. Tourists spent $4.8 billion in Spain in 1978, a substantial increase from the $3.2 billion spent in 1977. The increased tourism has had a considerable effect on the Spanish economy as a whole, helping to reduce the nation's balance of payments to its lowest point in a decade and contributing to a fall in the annual inflation rate from 26.5 percent in 1977 to 16.5 percent in 1978.

The American tourist industry is also being affected by the devaluation of the dollar. Although it may be more costly for Americans to travel abroad, it has never been less expensive for Europeans and Japanese to visit the United States. Foreigners in increasing numbers (20 million in 1978) are spending their vacations in American cities and resort areas. They are also staying longer and spending more freely ($8.5 billion in 1978 in contrast to $7.2 billion in 1977). This is encouraging the expansion of tourist facilities in the United States. It is also challenging Americans in general—and tourist facility employees and operators in particular—to develop linguistic skills and learn enough about the customs of other

Figure 18.9 **By emphasizing the economic advantages of vacationing in Spain, the Iberia Airlines advertisement recognizes the fact that Americans still wish to travel to Europe and enjoy its diverse amenities but many cannot afford to do so in countries where their dollar has depreciated in value.**

nationalities to be able to make foreign visitors feel comfortable and welcome during their stay.

The role that increased numbers of foreign tourists could play in improving the nation's balance of payments is also being recognized in spite of the fact that Americans abroad are still outspending people visiting the United States by $2 billion. Although the President's proposed budget for fiscal 1980 deleted the $14 million U.S. Travel Service budget for the operation of six foreign promotional offices, thereby effectively abolishing the agency, the action has been challenged by Congress. It would now seem likely that a quasi-public corporation may be created to coordinate and greatly expand the government's role in promoting tourism abroad.

The other type of travel restriction that may be employed more frequently in the future if trade deficits warrant it, is government-imposed travel controls. Although such controls can take the form of complete bans on foreign travel, they are usually made more palatable by allowing people to travel abroad only if they can do so on limited funds. This is the present situation in most of the nations of eastern Europe.[6] Hungarian citizens, for example, are no longer forbidden to travel abroad nor are they confined to coach tours organized by the national travel agency. Every three years, they are free to apply for authorization to travel to capitalist countries. The nature and extent of their trip, however, will be gov-

erned by the fact that they are allowed to buy only $200 in Western currencies to cover the costs of everything, including transportation, overnight accommodations, food, and recreation.

Besides its impact on travel patterns, the need to maintain favorable trade balances also affects the recreation products people can buy and the prices they must pay for them. An example is the recent arrangement between Japan and the United States whereby Japan agreed to voluntarily limit its exports to America of many articles including automobiles and color television sets. It did this to avoid the imposition of formal trade restrictions and to help trim its huge trade surplus with the United States. At the same time, Japan has relaxed its quotas and tariffs on some items to make it easier for American goods to reach Japanese markets at more competitive prices. But this is an exceptional circumstance born of economic necessity. Generally, protectionist sentiment is growing (almost 50 percent of all world trade is now restricted to some extent by a tariff or quota), and it is likely that people's access to foreign goods and resources at reasonable prices will be lessened in years to come. This not only denies consumers the right of free choice but often necessitates their paying much higher prices for inferior domestic products. And, in the case of basic commodities like imported foodstuffs and gasoline, large numbers of people are going to be asked to get along without them or learn to get by with much less.

Finally, people who live in countries that are blessed with large trade surpluses are bound to be given additional recreation opportu-

nities. Often these opportunities will come from new urban and extraurban parks, major athletic facilities, playing fields and gymnasiums, concert halls, museums, and special developments such as theme parks constructed primarily as a means of enriching the lives of all the citizens. Elsewhere, new recreation experiences may result from a government program to establish a major tourist industry under a plan to develop a diversity of revenue-producing businesses. Sometimes new opportunities will be the result of a government's attempts to placate trading partners. Japan, for instance, set aside the equivalent of $7.7 million in late 1978 to be spent on the acquisition of Western cultural items for the nation's public museums.

INFLATION AND RECESSION

The two most common manifestations of economic instability—inflation and recession—are often considered the most serious kind of domestic problem a country can have. If either persists, a nation's economic as well as its social well-being can be threatened. The economic effects of inflation and recession will be discussed in this section, whereas their social effects will be included in the section on social issues.

Inflation and recession are not recent economic phenomena. National economies have always tended to fluctuate in response to major changes in government policies and actions, international trade relationships, productivity growth rates, domestic and worldwide harvests, supplies of raw materials, and availability of wanted or needed

---

[6] Eastern European nations wish to decrease their net indebtedness to the West that currently exceeds $50 billion following the accumulation of an $8 billion trade deficit in 1978.

kinds of consumer goods. What is different is that the causes and nature of present-day forms of inflation and recession are more complicated and, therefore, harder to combat. It is not uncommon, for instance, to find inflation coexisting with recession and high levels of unemployment. Current inflation also has a greater tendency to both accelerate and be unyielding, and these characteristics make it more frightening and dangerous than earlier forms of inflation, which tended to remain fairly constant and respond fairly quickly to efforts to control it.

Worldwide, a few nations such as Belgium, the Netherlands, West Germany, Switzerland, and Japan have annual inflation rates well below the 10 percent level. Most of the other countries including Canada, the United States, Great Britain, France, Italy, the Nordic nations, and Australia are currently experiencing inflation rates ranging from 9 percent to 20 percent. Some countries, especially those in South America, are suffering increases of 30 to over 100 percent. As for the future, most economists see little hope of change. The world's rate of productivity will probably grow more slowly than it has in the past, and above-normal inflation may persist indefinitely.

The Economic Impact. Unabated inflation affects a nation and its people in many ways. On the national level, a country that cannot maintain economic stability loses the respect of other nations and, as a result, its trade relationships and the international value of its currency deteriorates. This is most unfortunate because, in many cases, this only aggravates the problem of

inflation. For individuals, the most obvious effect of inflation is a loss of buying power. In nations with high levels of inflation and high percentages of poor people, this can mean a serious reduction in the standards of the population's health care, diet, housing, and general living conditions. But even in nations like the United States where inflation rates have been relatively modest, the effects are considerable.

Americans are now paying 100 percent more for purchases and services than they did just 10 years ago. Until very recently, however, average earnings kept pace with inflation so that, statistically at least, the population should have been able to maintain the same standard of living. In reality, this has not been the case for the majority of Americans. The main reasons many people's financial situations have actually deteriorated are:

- Tax rates are not immediately adjusted for inflation so that higher income usually means more taxes even though the higher income may be worth less.
- Average income figures give an erroneous impression because some people (for instance, unionized blue-collar workers and others who are protected against inflation by investments or contracts that include cost-of-living adjustments) have been keeping ahead of inflation; their gains balance the losses experienced by nonunionized blue-collar workers, white-collar workers, the self-employed, professionals, and people on pensions.
- The highest inflation rates have been in food, energy, housing, medical care, and transportation items,[7] which

[7] Although prices for other items rose at an annual rate of 5.3 percent in the first part of 1979, the prices for these necessities showed an 18.6 percent increase.

traditionally make up over 60 percent of the budgets of 80 percent of American households and consume most of the meager budgets of lower income groups, including large numbers of black, handicapped, and retired citizens.

- Certain portions of the population have been affected more than others, for example, homeowners who live in the Northeast and use oil for heating large older homes, retired people living partly on interest from bank savings accounts or U.S. Savings Bonds, and families with several children who are trying to save enough for a downpayment on a house.

In addition, a considerable number of people *feel* their economic situation has deteriorated although actually it has not. The reason for this pessimistic outlook is that most Americans have grown up in an environment of high expectations where an inability continuously to raise a standard of living is regarded as an indication of falling behind. Therefore, for the first time since the depression, the majority of Americans are either experiencing a declining standard of living or are convinced that they are doing so because they are simply "staying even" rather than "getting ahead."

Residents of the United States are also anxious because they are losing hope of the situation stabilizing, let alone improving, in the near future. Even if inflation does not worsen but simply continues at recent levels, it will only take six or seven years for the cost of living to double again! And, in the meantime, there is a good probability of incomes really falling behind, particularly if large numbers of people are asked to settle for smaller raises without any guarantee that prices will also be controlled. Then, there is the added threat of a recession. If this occurs (and most people feel it has already begun), the American people will face increased levels of unemployment, fewer opportunities for advancement at work, and even higher prices. Corporations will suffer diminishing revenues and governments will have to make higher welfare and unemployment compensation payments at the same time that substantial reductions in tax receipts occur.

People's reactions to inflation are not always predictable. Traditionally, individuals faced with spiraling prices and the possibility of unfavorable employment conditions try to save as much of their earnings as they can and, if possible, postpone making major purchases. But, during the current period of inflation, Americans generally are behaving quite differently. No less anxious about the future, they are nevertheless determined to acquire as many of the large items like houses, automobiles, home furnishings, and appliances as they can before prices rise even further. Even purchases of expensive recreation goods and experiences are showing no sign of abatement. Large numbers of Americans are investing in high-priced boats, audio and video equipment, resort holidays, ocean cruises, European vacations, or tickets to shows and concerts in the belief that if they do not do so now, they may never be able to do so.

These buy-in-advance or enjoy-in-advance philosophies, which have prevailed since 1977, are a growing cause for concern because so many of the middle and upper middle income individuals and families that would normally be protecting themselves against the ravages of inflation and unemploy-

ment are allowing themselves to become just as susceptible to economic ruin as poorer segments of the population who have no other choice. Only 3.4 percent of the national disposable income is currently being set aside as savings. Savings already accumulated are also being depleted; 4 out of 10 households are presently meeting expenses by using their savings and nearly one-fourth of American households no longer have any savings at all. Worse yet, Americans are going into debt at a record pace to maintain their high levels of spending.

During 1979, the total installment debt exceeded $300 billion and consumer and personal mortgage debts combined rose to $1.2 trillion. The debt outstanding now equals 83 percent of personal income after taxes although the availability of easy credit terms keeps the actual mortgage and consumer debt repayment level at around 25 percent. It may be that consumers have already overextended themselves; in 1978, the delinquency rate on consumer installment loans rose to 2.5 percent, 210,399 personal bankruptcy petitions were filed in 1979, and, during the first months of 1980, there were indications that Americans were easing up on their spending. However, the large-scale borrowing from the future that has already taken place cannot help but make life more difficult for millions of American families for years to come, especially if inflation continues to cause income to decrease in value and recession reduces overtime and increases layoffs. The latter can hardly be avoided if Americans in large numbers suddenly decide to retrench financially because consumer spending now

pays for over 60 percent of the goods and services produced in the United States.

Using savings, borrowing heavily, and buying on credit are not the only ways in which Americans are attempting to combat inflation. Large numbers of workers are regularly putting in overtime, and one out of every 20 workers has a second or even third job. More wives are seeking part- or full-time employment not because they seek personal fulfillment but because their families need the money or want to maintain their ability to buy extras. It is expected that two-thirds of all married women will be working part- or full-time within the next 10 years. Meanwhile, more than two-thirds of the population have made at least some change in their way of living to adjust to the effects of inflation. For poor people and individuals on fixed incomes, these adjustments are sometimes so severe that they endanger the lives of the people concerned.

For the majority of people, however, they include less drastic changes such as:

- Eliminating high-priced food items from their diets.
- Buying used clothing or making do with what they already have.
- Giving up owning more than one car or buying or keeping an older car instead of replacing it or buying a new one.
- Taking shorter, less expensive vacations or none at all.
- Canceling club memberships and season's ticket subscriptions to sports or cultural events.
- Purchasing durable items that promise to expand recreation opportunities in or around the place of residence.
- Moving closer to the place of work or finding accommodations that provide easy access to public transportation,

shopping, and recreation opportunities.

Some of the changes affect people's plans for the future. These include postponing early retirement; delaying marriage; turning down an opportunity to relocate in another community; choosing or changing a career because of its greater income potential; deciding against starting a family or having another child; abandoning a dream of providing college educations for all or, in some cases, any of the children; and lowering expectations on the size, location, or kind of residence that the family hopes to have.

Implications for Recreation. The most obvious result of persistent inflation or recession is a decrease in purchasing power. This situation has to be faced by governments and private suppliers of recreation products and experiences as well as by individuals. It is a particularly difficult situation for providers of recreation opportunities because the need for recreation increases rather than decreases during times of economic instability. Therefore, more opportunities should be provided at a time when there are less funds with which to provide them. Nor should the quality of the recreation products or experiences be allowed to deteriorate. People with less money to spend need their purchases (including items that provide recreation experiences) to last. They also find it is harder to forget their problems and enjoy themselves so that the situation demands programs that are even more interesting or entertaining than usual. Maintaining the quantity and quality of recreation resources at a time when the potential customers and participants are unable or unwilling

to pay very much for their production or operation is one of the greatest challenges recreation providers will ever have to face. But face it they must because failure often means abandoning large numbers of people to lives filled with loneliness, anger, and despair.

Although inflation generally affects the supply of recreation opportunities negatively, it can have some positive effects. Sharing the frustrations and problems produced by inflation and recession can sometimes bring people together. This may lead to individuals joining forces to increase the supply of recreation experiences at a family, neighborhood, or community level. This may also result in people banding together to help financially troubled public agencies, quasi-public organizations, or commercial enterprises to survive or expand their recreation programs. These people may not be able to provide much in the way of funds, but they can make substantial contributions through gifts of time and talent. Such cooperative endeavors can also instill a new vitality, friendliness, and cohesiveness into a household, a neighborhood, or an entire community.

During periods when economic growth lags, cities and states often become highly competitive, mounting aggressive campaigns to attract new industries, desirable businesses, higher proportions of more affluent citizens, and larger numbers of tourists. Since the availability of recreation opportunities is known to be an effective lure, recreation resources that make an area a more attractive place in which to live, work, or spend a vacation, are apt to receive reasonable levels of public funding in spite of tight government

budgets. Recreation resources that can be shown to be effective in reducing antisocial behavior or improving the mental or physical health of the citizens may also be given support.

Finally, periods of inflation and recession can serve a useful purpose because they tend to weed out resources and programs that have not been answering people's recreation needs particularly well. Hard times cause people who are involved in supplying recreation opportunities to take a more critical look at their products or operations and to examine more closely the needs of the people they serve. Later, when new products, resources, and programs are developed and introduced, they may be more appropriate, better designed, and more effective in achieving the goals for which they are intended because of this period of introspection.

Products and programs may also be provided at less cost both to the supplier and the consumer or participant. In times of prosperity, there is less incentive to economize. When funds are scarce, necessity encourages the development of new techniques and procedures, and the acceptance of simpler or cheaper kinds of projects and programs. In the long run, these may be better than the more elaborate or more pretentious alternatives they replaced. The decision to use existing facilities rather than construct new facilities is just one example. When budgets are tight, for instance, a recreation department may choose to convert a surplus school building or church into a community center thereby obtaining more space for less money. More important, the site may be far more hospitable and accessible to the people it is meant to serve than any of the sites or buildings that might have been provided. Similarly, the rehabilitation and conversion of older buildings into restaurants, theaters (Figure 16.4), recreation centers, cultural centers, libraries, and museums may do more than save around 30 percent of the costs of new construction. It may provide a facility in far less time and in a much better location. These structures may also be better built and far more interesting to see and visit because of their historic significance, distinctive architecture, or beautiful craftsmanship and ornamentation (Figure 18.10).

CHANGING GOVERNMENT ROLES

Since many recreation resources and programs are completely or heavily dependent on government funding, the amount of money a government has to spend and how it decides to spend it is very important to the future of recreation. Until recently, governments at all levels have tended to follow a pattern of acquiring and spending larger and larger amounts of money to provide an increasingly extensive variety of public services. This is particularly true in the case of Canada, the United States, and the major industrialized countries of western Europe where combined national government spending has increased from 28 percent of combined national output to 41 percent in the last 20 years.

This period of rapid government expansion appears to be coming to an end. Austria, Finland, Norway, and Sweden substantially reduced government spending in

Figure 18.10 (a) The restored Duluth, Minnesota, Union Depot (now known as the St. Louis County Heritage and Arts Center) includes a newly constructed performing arts wing on the right. It is the home of eight nonprofit historical and arts organizations, and provides a visually exciting, centrally located cultural center for the community. (b) The tracks behind the depot have been enclosed to create an all-weather transportation museum that features one of the nation's finest collections of antique railroad rolling stock.

1977, 1978, and 1979. The government in the Netherlands has introduced a plan (Bestex 81) designed to limit borrowing to 4.5 percent of the national income and cut spending by $5 billion over a three-year period. In Denmark, the antitax Progress Party has become the second largest party in Parliament. Antispending sentiment is not confined to Europe. Already several steps have been taken in the United States to lower taxes and limit government budgets. However, unlike European nations, where political leaders and their governments are taking the lead, the movements to reduce government spending in the United States are primarily instigated by conservative local politicians and businesspersons.

Tax Cuts in the United States. The tendency of the federal government to overspend its budgets is not a new phenomenon. As early as 1790, the U.S. Government amassed a national debt of $75 million, a considerable sum in those days. And, since 1961 (with the exception of a slight reduction in 1966), the debt has been climbing steadily every year. What is new, is the enormity of the present $900 billion federal debt, the ever more rapid increases in federal spending (the federal budget more than doubled in the 1973–1981 period from $247 billion to over $600 billion), and the widespread negative reaction to both. Growing numbers of federal government officials, economists, state legislators, and ordinary citizens are showing concern about the present spending habits of the federal government and its likely effects on the nation's well-being.

Although the national debt

cannot be held entirely responsible for the current magnitude of inflation (much of the blame must be shared by other factors such as a growing scarcity of key commodities, international financial forces, trade deficits, lowered productivity, consumer spending habits, and wage, price, and profit spirals), there is little doubt that it is a major contributor. Many economists feel it cannot continue much longer at its present size and rate of growth without disastrous effects on the nation's economy. Just like individuals, the nation borrows to pay its debts and the interest paid on money borrowed to finance federal expenditures now exceeds $80 billion a year. Obviously, taxpayers would prefer to see such large amounts of money used for more productive purposes. In addition, a large part of this sum is raised by taxes on individuals and corporations. With annual deficits increasing the debt at an alarming rate, federal taxes will have to be continually raised just to keep the nation solvent. Since Americans are almost as disturbed about rising taxes[8] as they are about inflation, it is doubtful that further tax increases to support larger budgets and the continued growth of the national debt will be tolerated.

It seems fairly certain, therefore, that the federal government is facing a period of budgetary restraint. Just how this change will be brought about is still unclear. At the moment, Congress and the President are reviewing government spending, but little progress has been made toward bringing it under

[8] Federal income taxes amounted to $982.59 per capita or $2523 per household in 1979, an 83 percent increase compared to 1974.

control. Unless this is achieved in the near future, it is likely that some type of action by the electorate will result in drastic measures being taken. In many ways, this is regrettable because sudden external action will be far more disruptive to government programs than any measures Congress might voluntarily adopt. One reform group, for instance, is pressing for legislation that would require the federal government to regulate its spending increases in accordance with the growth of the nation's productivity. Another group is advocating an amendment to the Constitution that would require a balanced federal budget. Congress must call a Constitutional Convention to consider the matter if the required number of state legislatures pass resolutions calling for this action.

State and local governments are also being pressured to reduce spending. In many cases, state and local government budgets were 10 times larger in 1979 than they were in 1960. Municipal income and property taxes reached a total of $68.1 billion and state income and property taxes were $35.3 billion in 1979, amounting to $466.39 per capita or $1202.31 per household. In 1978, local property taxes alone rose over 10 percent in many areas. This has caused real hardships for homeowners who live on small fixed incomes. In revolt against such rapid and, as far as many people are concerned, unwarranted increases, a growing number of citizens are banding together to support a variety of measures that promise tax relief.

Unlike the movement against excessive federal spending, which is only in the preliminary stages, the campaign to reduce taxes at state and local levels is already in full swing. It started in 1977 when a few states enacted modest ceilings on spending. Then, in June 1978, California voters overwhelmingly approved Proposition 13, a state constitutional amendment that drastically limits property taxes. The success of this referendum stimulated similar citizens' movements throughout the nation, and a record number of voter initiatives appeared on ballots the following November. The majority were approved, resulting in the imposition of tax cuts, spending limits, or both, on the governments of 12 additional states and one large county. Voters also showed their desire for frugality by rejecting 40 percent of the $3.5 billion in bond issues requiring voter approval.

The movement to limit public spending at state and local levels continues to gain support; tax relief measures currently are either in effect or are under consideration in 33 states. Many public officials (especially newly elected ones who promised as candidates to cut spending) are currently introducing tax relief measures and budgetary restrictions of their own. If all the proposals are adopted, it is expected that annual state government revenues in some 40 states will be reduced by $3.5 billion ($1.2 billion in California alone) within the next several years. This will result in substantial cuts in some existing programs and services and necessitate the postponement or abandonment of many new projects currently under consideration.

Implications for Recreation. Substantial cuts in taxes are bound to have negative effects on

the budgets of individual agencies that depend on government appropriations for all or part of their operating funds. These include many important providers of recreation experiences such as the National Park Service and other recreation agencies in the federal government, state park departments, state and local arts councils, state or municipally owned sports complexes, public art galleries, zoos, all kinds of museums, municipal parks and recreation departments, public libraries, and community schools and colleges. But the budgets of many departments and agencies that supply services considered essential to the functioning of society or the nation's security or economic stability are also funded from these taxes. Therein lies the most serious problem; budget cuts are seldom divided equally among all of the public functions but instead are nonexistent or minimal for agencies that are regarded as indispensable. Since recreation generally has not attained this envious position, organizations that provide recreation opportunities are among those bearing the brunt of efforts to reduce expenditures.

Events in California following the recent property tax cut are an indication of what may happen elsewhere during the next few years if similar measures are taken. However, California's situation is not typical in one significant respect. Unlike most other communities, states, or nations that are cutting taxes and spending, California's state legislature had a $6 billion surplus when Proposition 13 took effect. By using some of this surplus as a substitute for municipal taxes, many of the effects of the property tax cuts were postponed. Since cush-

ioning of this magnitude will not be available to most other governments, tax-cutting measures are apt to have far more serious implications for recreation in other jurisdictions as is bound to be the case in California if and when the surplus funds are depleted. This is now almost a certainty with the November 1979 passage of Proposition 4, another taxpayer-initiated measure. This amendment to the state constitution attempts to maintain current levels of spending by limiting state as well as local government expenditure increases to changes in population and the cost of living. If revenues in excess of such levels are received, they must be returned to the taxpayers.

The effects of Proposition 13 have already been considerable although such services as police and fire protection and basic programs at schools have been preserved virtually intact. Most of the lost revenue (about $1 billion) not covered by the $4.2 billion state surplus has been met by reductions in park, library, cultural, and street-maintenance programs. These cuts do not seem to have aroused much public outcry. Most complaints have come from people who were personally involved in the organizations concerned and a small minority of citizens who have always been staunch supporters or enthusiastic users of these facilities and programs (Figure 18.11). The general feeling appears to be relief that none of the so-called essential services have been seriously affected.

Unfortunately, the people who disagree with this kind of thinking are either not very influential or not particularly vocal. Actually there are many vital services that have been curtailed or eliminated. Schools have stopped many of their music, art, athletic, summer school, and extracurricular activity programs. Most joint activity programs between school districts and local government recreation departments have been cancelled. Community colleges have eliminated 20 percent of the 4600 noncredit courses previously scheduled and have begun to charge for those that are still offered. Most of the canceled courses were of a recreational nature or intended for senior citizens. Owing to the imposition of fees, attendance at the remaining noncredit courses has decreased by 26 percent. Libraries in California are now said to offer the poorest services in the entire country. Hours have been cut substantially and funding for staff, maintenance, and book acquisitions has been drastically reduced. Fines and other fees have doubled and tripled; many of the special programs and services have been eliminated. Since the poor, young, elderly, and disabled were major users of these kinds of resources and special services, such cuts have caused little hardship for most of the state's major taxpayers.

San Francisco is using income from its hotel tax (which was previously earmarked for community art projects, museums, and orchestras) to maintain basic municipal services, but the proportion of residents who really appreciate the neglected amenities is relatively small. Less pretentious cultural resources have been hard hit in almost every community throughout the state because the small grants on which they depended for survival have been canceled. Since these organizations generally served special segments of the population (special interest or minority groups,

Figure 18.11 **In 1979, volunteer instructors and students at the San Francisco Community College Fort Mason Art Center demonstrated in support of the center's arts program when it was threatened by Proposition 13-induced budget cuts. Expansion of the program was halted and the staff was reduced by one but the center survived. Since then, state financial support has grown from 25 to 85 percent, compensating for the loss of city funds. The center is part of the Fort Mason marina in the Golden Gate National Recreation Area.**

students, senior citizens), few politically powerful people were affected or incensed by their disappearance. Future prospects for these and indeed all kinds of cultural undertakings in California are poor. In an effort to project a conservative image at the state level following the passage of Proposition 13, the legislature cut the California Arts Council's 1979 appropriation by 60 percent to $1.4 million. This almost completely eliminated the Council's grants to local organizations and placed California in 49th position among the states in arts support on a per capita basis. Apparently, this went a little too far, however, because the governor strongly endorsed a 500 percent increase in the Arts Council budget for the 1980 fiscal year in spite of the fact that he is firmly committed to reduced spending at the state level. Unfortunately, this renewed support ($7.3 million) came too late for the organizations that had failed to survive the rigors of the post-Proposition 13 period.

The changes taking place in local park facilities and recreation activity programs is perhaps the most important effect of Proposition 13 because these changes are adversely affecting the recreation lifestyles of the largest number and widest cross-section of California's population. The extent and nature of the cutbacks in budgets and staff by local park and recreation agencies that occurred in 1978 as a result of the passage of Proposition 13 are shown in Table 18.1. Land acquisition and development budgets suffered the largest cuts. As would be expected, part-time staff was reduced more than full-time staff. Generally, special park districts experienced the most severe combined reductions in budget and staff with some having to merge to survive and a few being abolished. City park and recreation agencies were also hard hit.

Not all agencies have been affected equally since some of the local governments were more dependent on property taxes as a source of revenue than others. Therefore, the results of the cutbacks vary considerably from

Table 18.1 Percent Decrease in California Local Government Park and Recreation Agency Budgets and Staff in 1978 as a Result of Proposition 13

Item	Cities with Population of 50,000+	Cities with Population of 0–50,000	Counties	Special Districts
Total budget	−31%	−27%	−10%	−29%
Land acquisition budget	−24	−87	−59	−88
Land and facility development budget	−70	−58	−48	−57
Operations and maintenance budget	−19	−16	−10	−21
Programs and services budget	−25	−26	− 9	−28
Number of full-time staff	−21	−24	−15	−30
Number of part-time staff	−52	−53	−47	−52
Number of CETA staff	−33	−61	0	−59

SOURCE: "Survey of Proposition 13 Impacts, 1978," California Park and Recreation Society. (Reproduced in "The 1978 Nationwide Outdoor Recreation Plan, Review Draft," Heritage Conservation and Recreation Service, U.S.D.I., Washington, D.C., 1979.)

agency to agency and place to place in both nature and intensity. Some of the most common results are: the postponement or cancellation of capital improvements, the reduction of maintenance, the closing or reduction in operating hours of neighborhood recreation centers and municipal swimming pools, the termination or curtailment of sports and activity programs, the cancellation of special events, and the elimination of programs for the handicapped.

Even more significant, perhaps, are the widespread policy changes regarding fees; 85 percent of the state's park and recreation agencies raised their fees following Proposition 13's passage. Some of the additional $101 million needed to balance local government budgets was obtained by charging people from 30 to 400 percent more to swim in community pools, enter municipal parks, visit beaches and zoos, use campgrounds, play golf and tennis, participate in softball leagues, use facilities at community recreation centers, or take part in organized recreation programs. On the surface, this seems fair that the people who use public recreation resources pay for them. Unfortunately, many of the most frequent users — minority groups, low-income families, the elderly, the handicapped, the unemployed, children, students — are in no financial position to assume this responsibility. Sadder still is the fact that when these kinds of users are denied access to subsidized forms of recreation, they often have no other means of obtaining similar experiences.

Proposition 13 had some other, less obvious effects on people's recreation environments.

Rather than drastically reduce programs the first year, the state government decided to reduce the costs of their programs by insisting that all state agencies deny pay raises to their employees and not hire any additional personnel. The lack of pay increases together with the increased workloads resulting from the hiring freeze has led to a noticeable lowering of morale. A number of the state's younger employees are leaving to enter the private sector or find employment in other states and, in some departments, employee turnover has doubled. Already this is beginning to cause a deterioration in the quality of services, including recreation. The recreation lifestyles of government workers have also been affected because they are trying to live on incomes that are not keeping up with inflation.

But again, the citizens who are being affected the most are those who can least afford it. The government hiring freeze has reduced work opportunities for people who have trouble finding employment. Limitations on welfare benefits have forced 1.3 million welfare recipients to manage on the same benefits despite inflation. Public transportation services have been curtailed and, in some cases, terminated; these changes are hardest on the poor since they frequently have no private means of getting about other than walking. Unfortunately, a loss of transportation services can mean not only a reduction in people's recreation environments but also a decrease in employment opportunities. Finally, Proposition 13 (whose primary purpose was to make housing more affordable by eliminating excessive property taxes) now seems certain to drive housing prices even higher. The main reasons for this are local government reductions in the provision of municipal services and higher costs to developers. This will make it even more difficult for less affluent people to fulfill their dreams of owning their own homes.

Of course, certain segments of the population have benefited from Proposition 13. About 4 million homeowners have enjoyed decreases in their property tax bills with reductions often amounting to 60 percent or more. (However, loss of itemized deductions for property taxes has cost property owners increases in their state and federal income taxes.) Landlords and businesses have benefited substantially with 10 major companies receiving tax reductions of more than $10 million each. A number of landlords lowered rents somewhat, but the majority of renters only received a delay in rent increases. A few businesses passed savings on to customers and others donated all or portions of their windfalls to charity and community projects of their own choosing. Most businesses, including a few providers of recreation experiences, used the savings to keep prices from rising more than they would otherwise have done.

Although the California situation provides some indication of the circumstances under which many recreation providers may have to operate in the not-too-distant future, there is another factor that may make the situation even more difficult. The California recreation environment has yet to feel the impact of austerity at the federal government level. Since the drive to scale down federal spending has not yet begun in earnest, it is dif-

ficult to predict exactly what the impact will be. It is bound to be substantial, however, because of the unique nature of some of the federal programs and the high degree of dependency on federal funding that some of the lower level governments (particularly larger and older cities) have developed.

A high percentage—as much as 65 percent—of the federal budget is fixed, making it very difficult, if not impossible, to spread cuts equitably throughout the many federally funded projects and programs. Interest must be paid on the public debt (presently 12 percent of the annual budget). Commitments to other nations must be met and the national security maintained (currently 24 percent of the annual budget). Domestic programs such as the Coast Guard, the courts, the FBI, and the Weather Service can be trimmed somewhat, but cuts, if they occur, are likely to be minimal. In the federal budget 43 percent is currently designated for direct-benefit payments to individuals (social security retirement benefits, veterans' pensions, supplemental security income payments, medical aid, etc.). These may be reduced to some extent by more rigorous elimination of cheating and unnecessary administrative practices, but they are too politically and socially important to permit substantial cuts. It is probable that appropriations for such agencies and facilities as the national park system, the Smithsonian Institution, the National Endowment for the Arts, and public broadcasting will be subjected to close scrutiny and restrained as much as possible. Even so, it seems unlikely that the funding will be drastically reduced because of the major role such resources play in

the development and sustenance of national pride.

There are two areas, however, that are vulnerable and likely, therefore, to lose the most if Congress responds to demands for reduced federal spending. The first is social welfare programs operated directly by the federal government. Federal help is essential to meet the needs of a great many Americans, but it seems doubtful that even the programs now in effect will receive adequate funding in the future. Already many badly needed programs are threatened, including youth employment and training programs, programs to help poor people meet their energy needs, and the proposed national health care plan.

The second vulnerable area is aid to state and local governments. It currently comprises 20 percent of the federal budget. All lower levels of government (but cities in particular) have become increasingly dependent on federal aid. By 1978, for instance, communities with populations of 500,000 or more were receiving an average of $0.50 in federal funds for each $1 raised locally. Loss of some of these funds would mean layoffs of government employees and cutbacks in services. For cities that are already financially troubled and are located in states whose governments are reducing state aid in an effort to economize, the situation could easily become critical.

The challenges for recreation providers that such situations might produce will vary according to the severity of the funding cuts and the characteristics of the population served. Responsibility for the poor, sick, handicapped, unemployed, minorities, and elderly will fall more and more heavily on local governments. Communities with large numbers of disadvantaged people will be hard pressed to satisfy even their minimum needs and still maintain adequate levels of essential services. One of the needs of the disadvantaged will be for inexpensive, readily accessible recreation. However, it will be increasingly difficult for recreation agencies to provide such programs if they are operating deteriorating facilities with tiny budgets and skeletal staffs.

Possible Solutions. This is such a bleak forecast it is hard to see how publicly supported forms of recreation can hope to survive. However, the fiscal crisis, if and when it occurs, may not prove as devastating as it now appears. Generally speaking, governments at all levels have been expanding their programs for many years with little regard for cost and, in some cases, real need. Most supporters of tax reform are in favor of such measures because they wish to put an end to such wasteful practices. However, it is faster and easier to limit spending by reducing appropriations for specific programs and laying off employees than it is to consolidate services, streamline administrative procedures, find and eliminate program duplication, or investigate and stamp out incidents of fraud and abuse. For this reason, most government bodies that have suddenly had to start austerity programs in the last few years have taken the former course of action because it was able to produce immediate results. As time goes by and a demand arises for some of the lost programs, however, there will probably be less emphasis on dropping programs and more em-

phasis on learning how to provide a wide range of programs more efficiently.

Similarly, public recreation providers will discover ways to live with the new frugality. They will try to avoid relying on raising fees, abandoning sound maintenance practices, and eliminating all programs except the ones that appeal strongly to the most politically powerful taxpayers. How they do this will depend on the circumstances; each situation will require a different approach. Basically, like the governments on which they depend, providers will have to pay more attention to the development of efficient administrative and management practices.

Such practices may consist primarily of the internal reorganization and streamlining of all of the agency's operations. In other cases, the main thrust may be development of closer ties or even formal amalgamation with other public and quasi-public organizations to eliminate duplication, consolidate services, share expenses and resources, and better serve the recreation needs of all segments of the population. Sometimes it may be appropriate to turn to private enterprise to finance the construction and operation of specialized facilities such as marinas, golf courses, and swimming pools.

Agencies may also have to become more receptive to offers of outside assistance, whether it be in the form of individual volunteers or sponsorship of specific programs and projects by businesses, civic groups, private organizations, or groups of interested individuals. In fact, they may have to adopt policies of not merely accepting this help but actively soliciting it when

such assistance could be useful. Neighborhood associations and local sports clubs, for instance, could be of considerable help to recreation departments in planning and conducting activity programs or in constructing, supervising, and maintaining park, playground, and recreation center facilities. Such cooperative arrangements have not been unknown in the past, of course. But, there is little doubt that there could be many more such arrangements and, generally, they could be much better organized for the mutual benefit of all concerned. Volunteers cannot replace regular professional staff, but, certainly, they can supplement them and perform many valuable services. However, it is mandatory that organizations make sure that volunteers are assigned to suitable tasks and taught the skills needed to carry out their assignments in an effective manner.

Recreation providers will also have to use sound judgment in assessing programs and establishing new priorities. Too often, under the pressure to reduce costs quickly, decisions are made in haste that may indeed balance the budget but, at the same time, may create an imbalance in the overall program and the scope of the services it provides. Special consideration must continue to be given to ethnic groups and elderly, handicapped, and poor citizens. Each of these special groups may be numerically small, but they are often more dependent on the recreation opportunities provided by the agency than any of the larger groups. Every effort should be made to maintain and, if necessary, expand the programs that benefit the people in such groups and to protect them from the hardships imposed by the implementation of new policies, especially major fee increases. In California, many agencies have already found ways in which to achieve these goals. One approach is to secure outside funding or sponsorship for some of the programs threatened with cancellation. Another is to start various types of work programs whereby low-income people can earn the admittance fees for facilities or programs they can no longer afford.

Recreation providers will also have to develop successful fundraising techniques. Careful management policies and the cultivation of volunteers and sponsors will never completely eliminate the need for more money. This will be a new and difficult challenge for many recreation agencies, which, until recently, have been able to rely almost exclusively on government appropriations. It is equally difficult for many cultural institutions that, in times past, have tended to divorce themselves completely from any form of commercialism. But circumstances alter priorities and both kinds of recreation organizations will have to accept the fact that considerable time and energy will have to be used to find new sources of revenue and formulate innovative methods of earning or attracting additional income. That this is possible has already been demonstrated many times, particularly in the case of nonprofit cultural institutions. Such institutions have successfully applied aggressive marketing techniques to attract more paying customers, earn additional revenues from the sale of merchandise, and increase the number of donors and the size of their donations. Many artists and recreation professionals are

repelled by such methods, but they are surely preferable to closing facilities and abandoning programs in which one believes.

Finally, and perhaps most important of all, public recreation providers must sell themselves and the recreation experiences that they offer to the very people that are causing them anguish—the taxpayers, voters, and legislative bodies who have denied or are threatening to deny them adequate funding. Up to now, the political process has been able to supply funds for most programs considered worthwhile or indispensable by these groups. Although money may be less plentiful in the future, there is no reason to believe that it will not continue to be raised and distributed in reasonable amounts to deserving programs. To judge by present levels of support, providers of public recreation opportunities generally have not been doing an adequate job of convincing others of the worth of these opportunities! This does not mean that they are incapable of doing so or that those who control the public purse strings will not respond favorably if the arguments are sound.

SOCIAL TRENDS AND ISSUES

The nations of the world are beset by a great variety of social problems each of which threatens to alter, if not destroy, the framework of the society in which it is found. Some such as the need to control population levels or stamp out communicable disease are issues of worldwide concern and can only be dealt with effectively if all nations work together. Others, like racism, poverty, and crime tend to vary

considerably from nation to nation and are more of an internal problem that each country, within the limits of its resources, must solve for itself. Nevertheless, what happens in any of these areas in one nation can affect the well-being of adjacent nations or the entire world.

Because these problems are so complex, interdependent, and susceptible to change, it is impossible to predict their impact on future society with any certainty. Nor is it feasible to rank the issues accurately according to their potential to cause problems. Some that are major issues today will be of little consequence several years hence. Either they will have been partially or totally resolved or they will have been superseded by issues that seem minor now or have not even been recognized at the present time as possible sources of difficulty.

However, since social issues affect the way individuals live, think, and act, providers of recreation opportunities ought to be aware of current issues and the kind of effects they might have in the future if circumstances remain more or less the same. As people change in response to these effects, their recreation needs are going to change and recreation providers must be able to identify these needs as far in advance as possible so that they can prepare to meet them. A knowledge of social issues and their possible effects is also essential because, in many cases, the recreation providers can and do play a significant role in helping to resolve the issues or mitigate or prevent some of the effects. It is impossible to include all of the major social issues in this book, but a few that already have shown considerable staying power and appear most likely to affect or be affected by recreation resources will be discussed.

IMPACT OF INFLATION AND RECESSION

Although inflation and recession are economic issues, the social problems that they create are no less important, especially when they occur in nations like the United States that have traditionally enjoyed an upwardly mobile society. It is not easy for a population that expects each generation to live better than the last and each year to bring with it a marked improvement in living standards to accept the fact that this may no longer be feasible. For many Americans, of course, this kind of situation has never been a reality and a sizable number have abandoned the dream of ever rising above their own or their parents' level in society. A few have lost all hope and have given up struggling altogether. But the majority of citizens accept the inequalities inherent in the American economic system and keep trying to improve their lot in life because they remain firmly convinced that the "good life" is attainable for any American who is willing to work hard to achieve it.

One of the greatest dangers of persistent inflation or severe recession in the United States lies in the fact that their presence can rob large numbers of hard-working, aspiring people of their dreams of getting ahead. Furthermore, it can cause panic in the more affluent levels of society where people who are used to getting ahead suddenly find themselves making little or no economic progress. Inflation and recession do not have to be severe to have this effect; they can easily be

perceived as worse than they really are when sufficient numbers of people become frightened of losing what they have so recently achieved. These effects are heightened by the feelings of helplessness that inflation and recession produce. In nations where hard times are not unusual, people often develop a built-in patience and confidence that carries them through subsequent periods of economic instability. This is the case in the United States at the present time for those older citizens who experienced, survived, and recovered from the Great Depression. But, for the majority of Americans, the current economic situation is a new and, therefore, very stressful experience that is particularly hard to bear because it seems beyond anyone's control.

Another potentially dangerous effect of inflation and recession is that they often invalidate many of the long-standing rules by which a society lives. During the current period of inflation, for instance, Americans have found that the accepted ways of being a responsible citizen — being completely self-supporting, living within one's means, planning for the future, regularly setting aside portions of income as savings, avoiding going into debt or buying on credit — no longer apply. In fact, the situation seems to favor lifestyles and spending habits that traditionally have been considered detrimental to a household's or nation's stability and well-being. This has many unsettling effects: it confuses the individuals who have accepted and organized their living patterns around the old values; it produces guilt and anxiety feelings in those who feel obliged to change their established way of life despite

the fact that they continue to believe in the old values; and it creates resentment among those who cling to the old values but see others fare better by abandoning them.

The result of these effects can be social unrest and a loss of faith in the political system. If the effects are severe enough, widespread, and of long duration, civil disorder and even the overthrow of the government either at the polls or by force may follow. There is little threat of the latter occurring in the United States, but there is little doubt that the government's apparent inability to control inflation or take action to ward off a recession, which most people feel has already begun, is producing a general dissatisfaction with all levels of government. This, in turn, is contributing to a loss of public support. Few people mind paying taxes when things are going well. But, when they are feeling hard pressed themselves, they are often reluctant to give increasing portions of their dwindling income to pay for programs that do not seem to carry any assurance of solving the problem that worries them most — inflation. Therefore, it can be said that inflation is partially responsible for the tax revolt that is presently sweeping the country and making it so difficult for public recreation departments and nonprofit cultural resources to survive.

Inflation is also making it harder for governments to provide many of the social welfare programs that are even more urgently needed now that people are suffering a loss of spendable income. These range from government-created jobs and training programs designed to aid the nation's youth, minorities, and chronically unemployed to financial assistance for creating a barrier-free environment for the handicapped and grants to help revitalize the nation's cities. The curtailment of these programs will cause hardships for many individuals, but it will also lower the quality of American life in general because society is only as strong as its weakest parts.

On a personal level, inflation and the stress it creates are affecting people's lives and behavior in ways that are certainly not beneficial to the individuals concerned, their friends and relatives, or to society as a whole. Stress affects individuals differently; some seem to have higher levels of tolerance to stressful events and, as long as the anxiety-producing agents do not become severe or persist too long, they are able to cope with little or no adverse effects. But, for many people, the problems of dealing with the loss of buying power, changing or abandoning current lifestyles and future plans, or living with feelings of frustration, uncertainty, resentment, or personal failure, are already intolerable.

Some of these people are developing grave emotional problems; others are succumbing to a variety of minor or serious physical ailments. It has not yet been proven that stress actually causes sickness or death, but it is generally recognized that it can lower resistance and increase susceptibility to a wide range of illnesses from common colds to ulcers and fatal heart attacks. Some people are becoming prone to accidents. Others are increasing their reliance on alcohol, drugs, or high-risk activities as a way to gain relief from feelings of desperation. More people are parti-

cipating in gambling activities in a desire to get ahead again or recover lost ground. The readily accessible forms like lotteries, betting pools organized at work, or competitive games and sports played for money among friends are especially popular.

Larger numbers of people are developing antisocial behavior patterns (rudeness, aggressiveness, lack of self-control) that are not only damaging to themselves but also to those with whom they come in contact—strangers as well as acquaintances. A growing number of families are being adversely affected by these changes in behavior; troubles range from increases in the incidence or severity of quarreling, spouse beating, and child abuse to the complete break up of marriages. Children have personal problems of their own. They may suffer a loss of peer status and self-esteem when they are forced to curtail certain activities or economize on purchases considered desirable by the majority of their friends. They may also be troubled by a loss of parental companionship and guidance in homes where parents become preoccupied with money matters, the father takes on additional work, or the mother seeks outside employment to try to make ends meet.

The effects of inflation are not always negative, however. Some families seem less threatened than others over an inability to achieve or retain certain living standards. They are making the necessary adjustments to inflation and lowering their expectations without too much difficulty. In many cases, the ways in which they have chosen to alter their lifestyles are actually strengthening family ties and providing high

levels of personal satisfaction. Some individuals are finding the adversity a challenge that allows them to discover and develop talents and interests they never knew they had. Members of families who have accepted the need to economize are spending more time together and are discovering the joys of being a close-knit household and of taking part in simpler pastimes (Figure 18.12). Children in particular are benefiting from situations where they are encouraged to help and, in so doing, are made to feel that they are contributing in a meaningful way to the family's welfare. If inflation and recession persist, it is desirable for the good of society as well as individuals that larger numbers of Americans find ways to adjust to life in a downwardly mobile society and take heart in the fact that even if living standards generally cannot be quite as high as they had come to expect, life can still be very satisfactory and, in some ways, even better.

Implications for Recreation. Beyond trying to keep the costs of recreation experiences down and the number of employment opportunities up, despite steadily declining revenues, there is little that providers of recreation can do to control inflation or prevent recession. But they can play a major role in helping to mitigate their effects. First, recreation resources can and do offer people opportunities to escape reality and temporarily forget their worries. The private sector is particularly adept at providing this kind of opportunity and such resources as amusement parks, discotheques, professional sports facilities, and movies are much appreciated by the people

Figure 18.12 As inflation and gasoline shortages or price increases cause changes in recreation lifestyles, more families are rediscovering the recreation potential of their own homes and possessions. Although simpler pastimes may not be as glamorous or exciting as the more expensive, gas-consumptive outings to commercial enterprises or public parks, they often provide experiences that are more satisfying. Individuals have more chances to communicate in a relaxed atmosphere and these experiences can develop closer family relationships.

who can afford to make use of them. Unfortunately, there are already many Americans who find such places beyond their means, and this is a source of added frustration for those who once enjoyed them on a regular basis. Either the private sector must devise ways of making such experiences less expensive occasionally, if not regularly, or the public sector should provide similar escapist types of opportunities without charge or at low cost to fill the void.

A second way in which recreation providers can alleviate the effects of inflation or recession is to offer programs that can help people improve their situations. Such programs are not necessarily better than the resources that offer relief; for many troubled people, a short respite from anxiety is all they hope for and often all they need to help them survive. But, for those people who are determined to overcome the negative aspects of inflation and have some hope of being able to do so by their own efforts, they are most welcome and their value is enhanced by the fact that their positive effects may be long-lasting or permanent. These kinds of programs can often be provided most effectively by the public, quasi-public, or private nonprofit sector. They include classes that introduce people to hobbies, sports, or other activities that are less cost-intensive, thereby allowing people to discover and substitute new forms of recreation for ones they can no longer afford. Another important contribution is made by courses that help people acquire the skills or knowledge needed to do such things as make minor house or car repairs, grow and preserve fruits and vegetables, build furniture, or make clothes. It is unlikely that all such activities will be perceived as recreational. But many people are obtaining considerable satisfaction from becoming more self-sufficient and the money saved can help balance their budgets. This relieves some of the anxiety or, in some cases, saves enough money to finance some kind of recreation experience that the family or individual otherwise could not afford.

Finally, recreation providers may be able to help people abandon their belief that "more" is synonymous with "better." If inflation persists, it will become necessary for all but the most affluent to adopt a more frugal lifestyle. The transition will not be easy, especially in the United States where people are incessantly bombarded by advertising assuring them that buying a certain product or experience is the sure or only way to achieve happiness. Neither does it help to be exposed to articles in countless magazines giving details of celebrities living glamorous lives and to nightly television programs about supposedly average Americans having the kinds of experiences and living in the kinds of surroundings that people in similar circumstances in real life can never hope to attain. Perhaps advertising will gradually change and possibly television productions will begin to depict characters and situations that are more realistic. In the meantime, however, many people — consciously or subconsciously — expect their lives to be just like those they see on television. They feel cheated when their lives do not measure up to these expectations.

Providers of recreation are in contact with these people, especially the young, who are particularly susceptible to this form of brainwashing. Recreation professionals usually work with them in pleasant situations where they probably have a better opportunity than anyone to alter their perceptions — directly or indirectly — about what constitutes the good or the attainable life. Recreation leaders may be able to introduce young people to the pleasures found in simpler activities. They can also deemphasize the importance of winning or acquiring the finest equipment and most expensive materials so that having a good time or being fulfilled is not dependent on being the best performer or having the best of everything. In the case of adults, recreation professionals can provide the guidance that will help people alter their perceptions and develop satisfying recreation lifestyles that are not based on purchases they really do not need and may not even be able to afford. Leisure counseling may be the best recreation program any agency can offer in periods of economic depression.

EMPLOYMENT, INCOME, AND POVERTY

Chapters 4 and 7 include discussions of the effects on recreation participation of poverty, income levels, fringe benefits, hours of work, and other employment-related factors. The section that follows examines employment trends and their probable effect on recreation behavior in the future.

On a worldwide basis, unemployment continues to be a major problem. In spite of concerted efforts to create employment opportunities and eliminate poverty, at least 300 million workers in the developing countries are currently unemployed or seriously underemployed and about 15 million people in the developed countries are out of work. The United Nations classifies two-thirds of the world's people as poor since they have annual per capita incomes of $1375 or less. Almost half of this group (about 1.2 billion people) has yearly per capita incomes of $500 or less. Life for most of the world's inhabitants, therefore, (two out of every three people) consists of little more than an unending battle to survive. Illiteracy, malnutrition, disease, high infant mortality, low life expectancy, wretched living conditions, lack of vitality, and other manifestations of poverty are their common lot.

Society's struggle against poverty never stops and considerable progress has been made, especially in the last 25 years. But, since the battle must be waged simultaneously on so many fronts, it is a formidable task requiring vast expenditures and massive programs that must be implemented on an international scale to be truly effective. It seems unlikely that poverty will ever be completely eliminated, but society continues to try since the price of failure is too high in human terms ever to be acceptable.

Conditions in the United States. The situation in the United States is better in many ways than it has ever been before. During 1978, about 24.6 million persons or 11.3 percent of the population were living below the federal poverty level (determined at that time to be around $3000 for a single person and $6000 for a family of four). This compares to 39.5 million persons, or 22.4 percent of the population living under similar circumstances in 1959. In addition, the welfare system has been greatly expanded and altered so that it reaches more of the nation's needy in new and better ways; 10 million people currently are given financial assistance under the Aid to Families with Dependent Children (AFDC) program; 4.5 million elderly, poor, and disabled people obtain help with health care expenses through Medicaid; and more than 18 million people benefit from the food stamp program.

As far as employment opportunities are concerned, unemployment (hovering around the 6 percent level) is higher than it has been during most of the past 30 years. However, there is almost full employment of married men and the number of employed persons as a percentage of the entire population (59.4 percent in February 1979) is at an all-time high. The size of the labor force is also larger than it has ever been before — 102.5 million or 63.9 percent of the population is over 14 years of age and either employed or available for employment. About half the nation's families currently earn incomes that assure them of a moderate or better-than-moderate standard of living. These people generally enjoy lifestyles that include recreation possessions and opportunities available only to a small percentage of Americans in earlier times (Figure 4.9).

In spite of these achievements, however, the situation is discouraging. Although the impact of gross malnourishment has been appreciably reduced and, as a result, there are fewer infant deaths, hunger in America has not been eliminated and the problems of inadequate housing, education, medical care, and job opportunities for the poorest members of society are still largely unresolved. Nor are they likely to improve much in the near future. On the contrary, there are a number of factors that are currently either contributing to a deterioration in living standards for some or all of the nation's poor or threatening to jeopardize the expansion or continuation of the antipoverty programs.

Inflation is a particularly potent enemy of the poor because it can have a more devastating effect on them than on any other income group and, at the same time, it can make more affluent citizens less responsive to the needs of the disadvantaged. When this segment of the population is anxious about its own welfare and future, it is unlikely to support anything more than a mild expansion of any of the antipoverty programs. This can easily lead to an actual reduction in benefits owing to the effects of inflation. Currently, the future looks grim because governments at all levels are trying to appease this more affluent and politically important class of voters by curtailing expenditures.

Of equal significance is the present unemployment situation; the fact that 5.9 million people are out of work is not nearly as important as the characteristics of the un-

employed. Unemployment in the United States is not distributed evenly among all segments of the population; larger proportions of adult women (5.7 percent), blue-collar workers (6.4 percent), blacks and other minorities (11.9 percent), teenagers (16.1 percent), and minority group teenagers in particular (35.5 percent—if youths who have given up searching for work were counted, it would be much higher, possibly close to 60 percent) are out of work than other groups such as married men (2.6 percent), adult men (4 percent), whites (4.9 percent), or white-collar workers (3.4 percent). Again, like inflation, unemployment has the greatest impact on people who make up the least affluent segment of society. Should a severe recession occur, these groups will be affected even more.

What makes this situation dangerous to society is the widening gap it is creating between the nation's various economic groups. It is true that inflation affects everyone, but the more affluent generally have the advantage of savings, an accumulation of possessions, more energy-efficient cars and homes, and better educations in addition to the security of full-time, higher paying jobs to protect them. Unless inflation and recession worsens or persists for a long time, this group will not be affected as drastically as the lower income groups. In addition, the trend for more wives of men with relatively high incomes to seek full-time employment is threatening to increase substantially the economic inequities among the various strata of society. Not only are these women more likely to be in a position to obtain higher paying jobs, their money is much less likely to be needed for basic necessities

and so, in effect, affluent people are steadily becoming better off economically, whereas middle-income and poor people are falling further and further behind.

The large numbers of families who have only recently gained access to some of the cherished amenities (automobile, home, good educational opportunities for the children, and the chance to enjoy some of the recreation experiences that traditionally have been the prerogative of the rich) are becoming alienated from the economic groups that are both above and below them. Like the more affluent, these middle-income people also have a high incidence of spouses who work, but most do so just to hold onto what they have acquired. Therefore, they are beginning to resent the competition for jobs from a segment of the population that they feel does not need to work. They are also increasingly resentful of the lower income people receiving what they perceive as substantial amounts of public assistance, the cost of which they feel is borne disproportionately by their particular economic group. They do not dispute the need to help those Americans who are less fortunate than themselves, but they are angered by the unfairness of a system that they feel supports the poor and favors the rich but does little to make things easier or better for the hardworking middle class that forms the backbone of American society.

Meanwhile, it becomes increasingly difficult for the poorest members of society to keep faith in a system that not only seems unable to alleviate their suffering but also tends to deny them the educational and employment opportunities they need to improve living conditions for themselves. Most affected are the urban youth, particularly blacks who in some areas are more than 60 percent unemployed. This is a socially and politically explosive situation that is not likely to resolve itself, especially since the number of blacks of working age is going to increase much more rapidly over the next few years than the number of whites in this age group.[9] Competition is also increasing. More of the jobs suitable or accessible to black youths are being filled by illegal aliens and newly arrived immigrants who are willing to accept less pay and more difficult working conditions. Other potential jobs are taken away from blacks by better qualified people such as married women, persons trained as professionals who cannot find work at higher levels, and elderly persons seeking supplementary income.

There is little doubt that the issue of employment for black youth is a major problem facing American society. It is also apparent that it cannot be solved quickly or without massive expenditures of money and manpower. Although a strong economy has generated millions of new jobs over the last few years and the federal government has invested some $1.5 billion a year in various youth-employment programs, the rate of unemployment for this group continues to climb. But society must solve the problem, no matter how high the cost, if only because the costs to society if the employment situation is not resolved are almost beyond measuring. Crime is already one of America's most serious problems

[9] The black birth rate has risen steadily for a decade and is now almost three times that for whites.

and a high percentage of the antisocial acts are committed by individuals within this group, those who live without work or hope. The costs society pays for antisocial acts in terms of suffering of victims, damage to property, and expenditures for courts and prisons are tremendous.

But even more important is the fact that the very framework of American society is in danger of breaking down. These alienated youth are the parents of tomorrow and they are ill equipped (as many of their parents and friends already are) to pass on to the next generation any of the perceptions and skills that would enable them to compete in or even feel a part of American society. They are, in fact, becoming a separate distressed society detached from the labor force but dependent on the work-oriented prosperous society that surrounds them for whatever measure of charity it sees fit to provide. No nation can hope to thrive as a divided society, especially when the division is along racial lines, and the gulf is so wide culturally and economically (20 percent of the population currently earns 46 percent of the income). Every effort must be made to assimilate the disadvantaged into the mainstream of society, remove the causes of friction among all the various economic groups, and restructure the system so that no one group has an unfair share of either the system's rewards or responsibilities.

Implications for Recreation. Although providers of recreation cannot play a primary role in the accomplishment of these goals, they can make many valuable contributions. First, they can help as-

suage the despair of the disadvantaged. To do so, however, they must be certain that they develop programs in consultation with the people concerned so that the recreation opportunities they provide are appropriate. Second, they can help the disillusioned and defeated members of society regain hope, rebuild self-confidence, and develop pride, both in themselves and in their communities. This can be accomplished by continually involving people in the development of neighborhood and community recreation resources and by providing leaders who are sensitive to people's problems and able to provide the necessary encouragement to bolster participants' morale and self-esteem. Third, through programs and the incidental interactions that take place between leaders and participants, disadvantaged people can become better able to apply for and hold a job.

Many of the chronically unemployed—especially the young—lack the discipline, motivation, basic skills, positive attitudes, and kind of work habits that enable them to acquire and keep jobs. There are excellent opportunities within recreation settings for these skills and attitudes to be learned and developed. In addition, some recreation providers are able to offer employment opportunities. However, these jobs are often dead-end, make-work positions that fail to teach any marketable skills, give any feeling of accomplishment, or encourage good work habits. It is essential that there be adequate supervision and training, some degree of challenge, and opportunities for real involvement. Most importantly, an effort must be made to establish and maintain on-the-job performance and behavior standards to give those that stick with it the discipline and attitudes necessary to obtain a regular job. Such on-the-job training programs are neither easy nor inexpensive to design or operate, but they are very worthwhile if they restore even a small percentage of the participants to lives of economic independence within the mainstream of society.

Providers of recreation can also help increase understanding and tolerance among members of the different economic and subcultural groups. People who are responsible for the production of motion pictures, television programs, plays, magazines, newspapers, and books have excellent opportunities to provide the public with insights into the lives and needs of different kinds of subcultural groups thereby helping to bridge the gulf caused by ignorance. People involved in the development of recreation facilities, programs, and special events can provide opportunities that bring people of different backgrounds together and encourage them to interact and become acquainted (Figures 18.13, 17.8). Recreation professionals can also try to plan and operate their facilities and programs so that—to the greatest extent possible—no particular individual or group need be excluded strictly because of certain personal characteristics, or lack of transportation, equipment, or the price of admission.

In a country as affluent as the United States, recreation opportunities of all kinds should be accessible to all. Not only is it morally right that every citizen should have the benefits of a diversity of recreation experiences, it is socially expedient that recreation opportunities be

Figure 18.13 Children from diverse backgrounds become good friends while learning to swim in an aquatic program at a YMCA in San Francisco. Recreation programs of all kinds can provide opportunities for people of all ages to meet and learn to appreciate people with characteristics different from themselves.

fairly distributed. For most Americans, the right and opportunity to recreate represents one of the greatest rewards of living in the United States under its particular form of economic and social system. Ensuring that all members of the population have a fair share of recreation opportunity is one of the best proofs that the system is a just one that is worthy of everyone's support and loyalty.

THE CRUCIAL ROLE OF POPULATION

The relationships between recreation participation and population size, density, distribution, and migration are summarized in Chapter 4. Population growth rates on both a world and national scale will play a crucial role in determining people's future recreation patterns.

With the possible exclusion of nuclear war, no social problem appears to have a greater potential for radically changing the lifestyles of the majority of the earth's people than population growth.

The world's rapidly expanding population is exerting great pressures on its biologic systems and producing major increases in the number and extent of serious problems relating to the human condition—starvation, malnutrition, poverty, illiteracy, crowded living conditions, inadequate housing, ill health, urban slums, unemployment, rising inflation, and a shortage of essential goods and services. Unchecked, such conditions often lead to despair in individuals, family strife, and, if conditions are bad enough for long enough, to a severe rise in antisocial behavior or the outbreak of civil disorder or war.

Although all nations are not affected equally, overpopulation is every nation's problem because it threatens to destroy many of the earth's major biologic systems on which all life depends. Even the nations that presently are underpopulated or are reaching zero population growth have difficulty maintaining their way of life; they must compete for depleting resources, deal with the problems of emigration from overpopulated nations, and concern themselves with the possible effects of the environmental, social, political, and economic consequences of overpopulation in countries other than their own.

So far, attempts to develop a satisfactory global population policy have been disappointing and the world population continues to grow at a rate of 2.5 people per second, or about 250,000 people a day, or some 80 million people a year. This is an alarming situation, especially for those who believe that the population already exceeds its biologic limits and must be reduced rather than just stabilized. Latest estimates suggest that the earth will be supporting 6 to 6.8 billion people in 2000 with almost 80 percent crowded into the poorer nations. This prediction assumes, of course, that vigorous population control policies will be developed and adopted; otherwise, the population could exceed 10 billion by that date.

Whether the latter situation can be prevented from developing is not clear, but, obviously, life with dignity or perhaps life in any form for many people in the world depends on a solution being found. A recent announcement that the world population growth rate may

actually be declining for the first time in history (it is estimated to have fallen 0.5 percent in the last decade from 1.98 percent a year in the 1965–1970 period to 1.88 percent in 1975–1977) gives some cause for optimism. This optimism is reinforced by the knowledge that drops are occurring not only in the developed countries where birth rates have been low for some time but also in many of the undeveloped nations where birth rates have been traditionally high. The main exception is the continent of Africa; this has become the fastest growing area in the world with the annual growth rate increasing in the last 10 years from 2.6 to 2.8 percent. Even China, which accounts for some 25 percent of the world's population, is committed to achieving zero population growth. Although its population continues to grow by 10 million a year, the rate of growth has declined to 2 percent, a rate only a little above the world average.

Nevertheless, optimism must be tempered with caution. The challenges facing the world as it struggles with the problems produced by even the most conservative population growth estimates are tremendous. If zero population were attained tomorrow, world population would still increase for 50 years or more producing additional pressures on the environment, the food supply, and the ability of cities to support them. It is estimated, for example, that over 50 percent of the world's population will be crowded into urban areas by 2000. At least 22 cities will have populations of 10 million or more with many millions of people trying to survive in squalid slums and squatter settlements.

About 600 million people will be living in abject poverty in spite of advances in science, technology, and agricultural practices. The majority of the world's people will be spending their entire lives without adequate food supply, health care, clothing, housing, personal space, education, employment opportunities, or recreation experiences. A much smaller proportion of the world's population will enjoy the personal freedoms taken for granted today by the majority of people who live in the developed countries of Western Europe and North America. Such privileges will be luxuries few nations can afford. Obviously, every effort should be made to prevent the arrival of such widespread suffering and despair.

The Situation in the United States. The total population in the United States on January 1, 1979, was estimated to be 219,530,000. This represented an increase of 1.7 million people or a 0.8 percent growth rate over the preceding year consisting of 3.3 million births, 1.9 million deaths, and a net legal immigration of 347,000. If there had been no immigration, current birth and death rate trends would probably cause the population to stabilize within the next 50 years, perhaps at about 260 million. But with immigration — especially illegal immigration — there is almost certain to be continued population growth throughout the next century.

It is estimated that immigration now accounts for between 30 and 50 percent of the population growth. This proportion is likely to increase because the United States now serves as a safety valve helping relieve the pressure of the Mexican population explosion that is unequalled in all but a few countries. The population of this 97 percent Roman Catholic nation reached 66.9 million in 1979. It tripled during the past 50 years and, with a reduced infant mortality, an improved life expectancy (62 years), almost half of the population presently under the age of 15, and a current growth rate of around 2.8 percent, it is expected to double again by the year 2000. Almost 50 percent of Mexico's potential work force (12.5 million people) is currently either unemployed or underemployed. The inflation rate, until recently, was over 30 percent, and one-fifth of the fully employed Mexicans (1.3 million people) currently earn less than $75 a year. No wonder the United States is attracting larger and larger numbers of desperate Mexicans who enter the country legally or illegally in search of jobs and better living conditions.

It is virtually impossible to estimate with any degree of accuracy the size of this mass emigration, but an average of around 800,000 undocumented Mexican aliens are apprehended in the United States each year and sent back to Mexico. It is suspected that at least 4 million Mexicans are currently living illegally in America and that the number is growing by as many as 1 million persons a year. These people along with others from such nations as Jamaica, Haiti, Cuba, Colombia, Nigeria, the Philippines, Korea, Greece, India, and Iran form a significant subculture that exists in furtive isolation cut off from the mainstream of society. It also negates the nation's effort to achieve zero population growth.

The effects—particularly the economic effects—that this subculture is already having on American society are still largely unknown. Nevertheless, there is little doubt that there is a substantial impact that may grow in significance if the number of undocumented aliens increases. Undocumented aliens may contribute to problems of unemployment among unskilled American workers, mainly because they are willing to work for low wages and few benefits. However, this may not be as serious a problem (at least at the present time) as some contend since many of the menial jobs filled by undocumented aliens are unattractive to most Americans and might not get done at all if willing aliens were not available. In fact, many of the firms that regularly employ undocumented workers would probably go out of business if aliens were unavailable thereby eliminating the related skilled worker and administrative positions currently held by Americans.

There is also a widespread belief that undocumented aliens are seriously aggravating the fiscal problems of some of the nation's economically troubled cities. It is argued that since they do not appear to contribute substantially to the tax system and because they are not included in the population figures (on which some 40 percent of federal aid to cities is based), then, they must be a financial liability. Cities are said to spend much money (estimated, for instance, to be in the millions of dollars annually in New York City) on health, education, welfare, and other social services for undocumented aliens and receive little or no revenues from them to help defray the cost. Whether this is true or not is debatable. Recent studies indicate that the proportion of undocumented aliens making use of social services is much lower than most estimates suggest. They also indicate that their contributions through Social Security payments and income, property, and sales taxes are large enough so that they are probably subsidizing rather than depleting the nation's social service programs.

In any case, it appears likely that large-scale illegal Mexican emigration will continue to affect employment and the ethnic composition of the American population for many decades to come. The massive fencing and patrol system that would be necessary to stem the flow is unlikely to be installed because of negative reactions both at home and abroad. The pressures that stimulate this migration will persist into the foreseeable future. However, some improvements in the Mexican population situation have been reported. A $130 million-a-year free family-planning program was implemented five years ago, and government statistics indicate that it has helped reduce the growth rate from 3.6 to 2.8 percent. Even more encouraging for the future are indications of changing attitudes. The Catholic Church —although not openly supportive— is no longer actively opposing the program, and more husbands are agreeing to their wives' practice of birth control. The discovery of huge oil reserves in southern Mexico has been heralded as the first step toward eventual economic prosperity. In 1978, the growth rate of the nation's economy was 6 percent, almost twice that of the United States. To date, the boom has done little to expand job opportunities, but the inflation rate has slowed to 15 percent—a considerable achievement in itself.

Implications for Recreation. As long as human populations continue to grow, recreation resources will receive increasing amounts of use. Many resources are already showing the damaging effects of overuse, and some of these will develop serious problems, especially the ones that are in or near urban areas. The need to accommodate larger numbers of people over the next few decades will require the adoption of new and more efficient administrative practices and management techniques. Policies that provide the maximum number of quality recreation experiences at the lowest possible cost and least possible harm to the resource will need to be developed and enforced. To be effective, these policies—especially the ones that restrict use—will require the creation of forceful education and public relations programs to inform the public of the reasons for the new policies and restrictions and to elicit their cooperation and support. New and innovative facilities and activity programs will also have to be developed to assure that larger numbers of people have access to adequate supplies of recreation opportunities.

Population growth and size are not the only demographic factors that affect recreation behavior and the kind of recreation services needed to provide adequate opportunities. Other important aspects of population are: distribution and migration, age structure, ethnic composition, marital status, and family composition. Current trends in each of these areas in the United States will be discussed in the paragraphs that follow.

Energy problems, larger numbers of retirees, migration of busi-nesses and industries, and changing lifestyle aspirations will continue to result in migration from the northeast and north-central regions to the South and West. The South will grow fastest, adding 20 million people by the year 2000 and the West will increase by 13 million during that period. As a result, there will be increased demand for recreation opportunities in these fast-growing areas, whereas there will be less pressure on some resources in the regions that are growing slowly or not at all. Some people and industries will continue to move out of the larger cities, particularly the oldest ones, but the worst of the mass exodus is over. In fact, quite a few cities will reverse the flow to a limited extent as crime control, housing renewal, and redevelopment projects make them more attractive living environments. In those cities where the population continues to decrease significantly, recreation professionals will have to provide programs for a smaller, older, and poorer clientele using less money. Some of the fast-growing cities in the South and West will produce exemplary park and recreation systems, but others will face serious problems because of the effects of tax limitations.

As these migrations take place, the composition of many urban populations will change even where the number of people remains fairly constant. Many older middle-income families with children will still migrate from central cities to suburban areas unless the costs of housing, energy, or taxes become completely prohibitive. Central cities will continue to have high proportions of the poor, elderly, and minorities, but single people, young couples, and middle-aged couples without children will become more numerous in urban neighborhoods that become more attractive through extensive redevelopment. Recreation providers in the larger cities will, therefore, have to contend with substantial and fairly rapid changes in the kinds of people they serve and will have to devise programs appropriate for a wide variety of interests.

Although the movement of population to the South and West appears destined to proceed for several decades, there is likely to be a decrease in the movement of people between jobs or within regions. As a large proportion of the population becomes middle-aged or retired and employment and economic conditions make moving less feasible, Americans will probably spend longer periods living in the same residence. With less time devoted to moving and fixing up new living quarters, people will have more time to spend on recreation. Coupled with energy problems, this suggests more casual use of urban parks, sports and cultural facilities, and increased participation in community recreation activities such as sports leagues, special interest classes, hobby clubs, and all kinds of special events if suitable facilities and programs are provided.

Dramatic changes will occur in the ages of recreation participants because of the changing age structure of American society. The youth-oriented period is ending as those born in the postwar baby boom move out of their twenties, through their thirties, and, then, into their forties. Public and commercial recreation providers will have to devote more facilities and program resources to providing opportunities attractive to a less youthful group of clients. These will range from more opportunities for the younger adults to take part in activities providing high-risk, social, and glamorous entertainment experiences to opportunities for the more mature adults to enjoy cultural, dining, and travel experiences. Unlike earlier generations of people in this age group, older individuals in the coming decades are expected to be much less concerned about leaving an inheritance for their children and more oriented toward self-indulgence and spending freely on a wide variety of recreation experiences.

At the same time, the percentage of elderly will also increase as the smaller predepression, baby-boom group reaches retirement age. The proportion of older people will then remain at a higher level because of the impact of increased life expectancy. By 2025, the number of people over 65 will double from today's 24 million to an estimated 50 million. Again, this will require a considerable shift in facilities and programming; greater emphasis will be placed on activities that maintain health and provide social contacts (Figure 18.14).

The racial composition of the American population will also change. The proportion of blacks (currently 11.8 percent of the population) will increase because of a higher birth rate. The Chicano population (currently about 8 million citizens and legal residents and 4 to 10 million undocumented aliens) will grow even more rapidly as will the Puerto Rican (presently 2 million) and other Spanish-speaking populations (currently 2.4 million). In fact, by 1990, Hispanic peoples will form the largest minority group in the nation. The United States is

Figure 18.14 A group enjoys an evening of square dancing at a senior citizens center in Seattle, Washington. As larger proportions of the population become older and live alone, more organized programs will be needed that combine opportunities to socialize and exercise.

also committed to a policy of admitting larger numbers of the world's refugees and this along with the continued influx of immigrants and undocumented aliens from nations other than Mexico will further the cultural mix of the American population.

Most of the Hispanic population will continue to live in urban areas. The majority will remain concentrated in a few northern cities such as New York and Chicago and in communities throughout the South and Southwest, particularly those in California, Texas, and Florida. An increasing number of

recreation programs will have to be in Spanish and a higher percentage of staff will need to be bilingual (Figure 7.5). The various distinct ethnic groups (blacks, Hispanics, and various groups of Asians) are already becoming large enough and are gathering sufficient economic power in some locations to have an appreciable effect on the nature of commercial recreation enterprises and products. In the future, there will be a growing demand for more ethnic restaurants, nightclubs, musical groups, records, radio and television stations, newspapers, magazines, films, sports facilities, and other recreation resources. Minority groups will also continue to alter the tastes and expand the recreation environments of other Americans, especially in the areas of food, festivals, games and sports, music, dance, art, and theater.

Another major trend that will profoundly influence recreation is the change in the composition of households. Traditionally, the American family has consisted of husband, wife (not working outside the home), and one or more children living under the same roof. In 1979, however, only 17 percent of all households were of this type; by 1985, the proportion will drop to less than 13 percent. In other words, 9 out of 10 households will soon consist of unmarried individuals, married couples without children, married couples with children where the wife works, single or divorced parents with children, divorced individuals, widows, widowers, or various other nontraditional combinations. Clearly, the recreation agency or commercial enterprise that continues to plan and operate its programs on the assumption that it is serving the traditional American family will be totally out of touch with reality. Recreation will need to be more diversified and specialized to suit the needs and interests of so many kinds of households. Since the majority of households will not contain dependent children, the adults may have more discretionary time and income to spend on recreation away from home. The additional time, however, may be offset by a higher number of people working either full- or part-time.

Households will include even fewer children than at present as more couples decide to have only one child or remain childless. Therefore, there will be a smaller proportion of young people in the population to serve with community recreation programs. And many of the youth-oriented resources such as team sports and athletic equipment, rock concerts and records, fast-food restaurants and junk foods, certain kinds of movies and television programs, games and toys, will face a steadily shrinking market. Couples will have more years both earlier and later in their marriages when there are no dependent children in the household. A tendency to delay marriage and an even higher proportion of dual-career marriages will mean that larger numbers of adults can travel and take part in active and time-demanding recreation activities more frequently than they could in the past. This suggests more participation for this particular segment of society in activities such as weekend trips to cities or ski resorts, package tours to foreign countries, and cruise ship vacations.

On the other hand, wives will be working in a much higher proportion of households that contain children; by 1990, two out of every three mothers will be working full time. This will further decrease the amount of time spent on family recreation outside the home and mean less recreation time for larger numbers of married women unless husbands and children begin to assume a far greater share of homemaking responsibilities.

One of the greatest challenges for recreation professionals in the future will be to meet the needs of much larger numbers of people of all ages who will be living alone or as a single parent, or as the child of a single parent. An increasing proportion of these people will not have any close peer group or adult relationships to sustain them and will feel alienated from society. This situation will result from substantial increases in the proportion of single-parent families (currently 9.8 million or 12 percent of all households), the number of unmarried or divorced persons, widows, and widowers living alone (currently 16 million people or 20 percent of all households), and teenage pregnancies (1 of every 5 babies—600,000 a year—is currently born to a teen-aged mother, one-half of whom are unmarried). Special outreach programs and a variety of organized activities that provide opportunities for social interaction will be needed to help these people to make or retain contact with the outside world and to develop mutually beneficial friendships.

Therefore, although there are likely to be dramatic alterations in transportation patterns and economic conditions, the changes that will have the most far-reaching effects on recreation are the radical changes that are taking place in the characteristics of the population. Keeping abreast of these changes, understanding their implications, and adapting facilities and programs quickly and efficiently to meet new patterns of need will be a challenge for all recreation professionals. More sophisticated research, planning, and evaluation procedures will be required to ensure that the responses to social change are both appropriate and timely.

RECREATION TOMORROW

Until recently, the major influences affecting people's recreation environments appeared to be reasonably stable. The changes taking place seemed fairly straightforward and, most of the time, quite predictable. It appeared almost certain that, at least in the more affluent developed nations, recreation would evolve along well-established lines and assume a greater and greater importance in people's lives. For large proportions of the population in these countries, the trends indicated substantial and steady increases in both discretionary income and free time. These increases appeared to be leading to a situation that would allow the majority of citizens to enjoy lives filled with recreation possessions, travel and vacation experiences, and periods of ease that were previously attainable only by a wealthy minority. Although it was never expected that the poorer, less developed countries would attain the same high levels of living standards, it was optimistically assumed that there, also, many citizens would eventually be able to enjoy sophisticated recreation lifestyles including ownership of automobiles and television sets, and access to a wider variety of commercial recreation resources.

Today, such rosy predictions are obviously not warranted. As previous sections of this chapter disclosed, a number of serious problems have come to the fore that even a few years ago were considered (if they were thought about at all) to be minor difficulties that would have little effect or require nothing more than scant attention for years to come. And now, in many ways and with comparatively little warning as far as the general public is concerned, these problems have assumed gigantic proportions and are threatening to destroy ev-

eryone's dream of a better life.

The section that follows is confined to a short discussion of the probable overall direction recreation in the United States will take in the future. Although many of the developed nations of the world share a good number of America's problems and advantages, they are also dissimilar in some respects so the final outcome may be somewhat different for them. Nevertheless, the developed nations are so much alike in important ways that, basically, their recreation lifestyles should undergo fairly similar patterns of change.

Unfortunately, the changes in recreation environments that will take place in the undeveloped countries will bear little resemblance either to the ones that occur in the United States or to the changes that were predicted would take place as they began to develop. Many of these countries, especially those that are completely dependent on imports for their energy supplies, are in such serious economic difficulty that the majority of their citizens will find it impossible to retain many of the features of the simple recreation lifestyles they now possess let alone aspire to more expensive and technologically sophisticated ones.

CONFLICTING TRENDS AND NEW DEVELOPMENTS

Many current trends now run counter to each other making it difficult to assess the probable net result. For example, the trends toward longer vacations, shorter work weeks, the postponement of marriage and parenthood, increased longevity, and earlier retirements would all seem to indicate substan-

tial increases in free time for large numbers of people. But this may never happen. The desire and need for more education (including training in work-related skills), the removal of mandatory retirement laws, and the effects of rising inflation may actually decrease the total amount of time the population has available for recreation pursuits. Obviously, the control of inflation would be a decisive factor. Nevertheless, there are major trends (like the desire of a much larger proportion of women to follow a career) that are still likely to reduce the free time of considerable numbers of American citizens.

Similarly, it is difficult to estimate what will happen to another crucial factor affecting recreation lifestyles—the amount of discretionary income that tomorrow's citizens may have for recreation purposes. Previously, it seemed fairly safe to assume that salaries would continue to increase substantially and that living standards would continue to rise for the majority of citizens. The former still appears to be true, but there is now good reason to believe that most people are going to have to make do with less, especially in their recreation pursuits. Again, inflation is a primary contributing factor but other trends such as the growing need to conserve resources (including land and oil) are likely to encourage simpler, less materialistic recreation lifestyles even if inflation is brought under control and discretionary income begins to grow again. At the same time, a new group of Americans is emerging that is composed of couples with dual careers who have few or no children. This segment of the population is not only able to sustain an expansive recreation lifestyle but also shows every sign of being largely inflation-proof and capable of overcoming the limits imposed by the scarcity of resources. This relatively small group of people are likely to enjoy recreation lifestyles that are close to or surpass the most optimistic forecasts of the past.

The fact that several of the most recent changes in the United States are not like any that have gone before also makes it impossible to accurately forecast what will happen in the future and predict the changes in American society and recreation behavior patterns that will take place as a result. Examples of these developments include resource shortages, the aging of the population, the emergence of a postindustrial society, the growing dominance of the broadcasting media in everyday life, the changing roles of women, and the possible division of society into two or more separate economic or ethnic classes. Many of the immediate effects of these changes are already apparent and have been explored in this and earlier chapters. But many of the consequences and the possible ways that Americans will respond and react to them may not be known for many years.

Finally, any consideration of future recreation environments in the United States must take into account the many problems and changes taking place in other nations and regions of the world—a truly formidable task. Never has the world seemed so small and the events of even the tiniest or remotest areas so significant. Who would have predicted that events in Vietnam, Iran, or Afghanistan could have had such extensive effects on the American economy, psyche, or

recreation lifestyles? It is no longer sufficient for those who look into the future to be concerned with just the resource, economic, or social problems of their own nation.

PURGATORY OR PARADISE

In view of the many serious issues that now confront society and, in several instances, threaten its very survival, it is tempting to predict a gloomy future for people generally and for their recreation lifestyles in particular. Admittedly, people are going to face many challenges and suffer many disappointments as the United States (and other nations that have enjoyed similarly high levels of prosperity) pass through the transition stage from an era of rapid growth and seemingly unlimited resources to a new age of dwindling resources and lowered expectations. How they react and adjust during this traumatic period is of the utmost importance because they will be developing behavior patterns and ideals that will form the basis for society in the future.

Until recently, the behavior of the American people and their political leaders has not been very encouraging. They have exhibited a tendency to divorce themselves from society as a whole and regroup into small but aggressive factions that are committed to promoting their members' well-being and interests or retaining the status quo, no matter what the costs to other Americans or world society. Generally, they have seemed reluctant to adjust in any purposeful way to the demands that changing conditions are imposing. They have shown every sign, in fact, of holding on to old lifestyles and attitudes despite the growing evidence that such be-

havior is no longer feasible.

However, this does not mean that Americans cannot or will not adjust when circumstances warrant it. Growing numbers of citizens are beginning to face the need for change and many are doing so with grace, good humor, and ingenuity. There is little doubt that Americans are having to modify the materialistic attitudes that grew from the dream of a chicken in every pot to include a 24-inch color television set, two cars, a recreation vehicle, a large boat, and the best cuts of beef on the outdoor barbecue in front of the swimming pool at the air-conditioned ranch-style house. Aspirations of such magnitude will not die easily nor be abandoned without regret. But what the majority of citizens have not yet realized is that they are not being asked to sacrifice very much, at least for many, many years to come. Residents of the United States have enjoyed one of the highest standards of living in the entire world for a long time now and there is little doubt that they will continue to do so. As those who are already beginning to adjust to the new reality have discovered, there is still lots of room for *the American Dream,* but it may have to be modified somewhat so that it only includes a small television set, one lower powered car, a lightweight camper, a sailboat or canoe, smaller or less expensive cuts of beef, and a space-and-energy efficient condominium without a swimming pool.

It should also be remembered that nations such as the United States with extensive human, technological, and undeveloped resources at their command are fully capable of solving or mitigating many if not all of the problems that presently beseige them. People in the highly developed nations have successfully come through many difficult periods. In fact, the past era of tremendous productivity and prosperity is actually the exception rather than the rule even for the United States. There is no reason to believe that there has been either such a loss of national will or such a change in personal characteristics that present difficulties cannot be overcome. Already, many of the issues (such as the need for pollution and population controls) have been confronted and considerable progress is being made toward making urban areas better places in which to live. The very fact that the advanced nations are attempting to combat problems such as excessive energy use, run-away inflation, and alienation of segments of their populations leads one to believe they will eventually be solved.

As for the future of recreation itself, never have people everywhere needed it more. It is a field that is going to grow, not diminish, in importance as time goes by. Exactly what recreation's precise characteristics will be in future years is not clear but there are many indications of what its general form will

be like. From all indications, recreation will still be susceptible to change and yet as constant as ever. It will most certainly include a variety of recreation products and activities that have yet to be invented. Obviously, recreation is not going to be as closely dependent on costly material possessions. Apparently, it is also unlikely to be as automobile-oriented, and, as a result, recreation opportunities in or close to the place of residence are going to assume more importance and take up higher percentages of most people's weekday, weekend, and vacation time. It should be noted, however, that making the transition to a less energy-intensive and cost-intensive lifestyle does not necessarily mean a less satisfactory recreation lifestyle. It will only be a different one. As special populations (including women as well as ethnic minority groups, the elderly, and the disadvantaged) become more demanding and more distinguishable as separate clienteles, public and private recreation programs will deemphasize trying to be "all things to all people" and concentrate instead on serving the special needs and interests of individuals and specific groups. If present

trends continue, recreation is going to comprise larger proportions of some people's time (primarily unionized workers) and be squeezed into shorter time spans in other people's lives (particularly working wives with young children). Both types of people, however, will have one thing in common: each will demand greater levels of satisfaction from their recreation experiences.

This increased emphasis on satisfaction in recreation experiences is, perhaps, the single greatest change that will likely take place in the field of recreation. In turn, it will be the single factor that will contribute most to the elevation of recreation to a position of prominence. Much recreation will amuse and divert as it has always done in the past. However, recreation professionals will strive harder to satisfy the inner needs for self-fulfillment of the diverse people who take part in their programs. If public, quasi-public, and nonprofit recreation programs accomplish this goal more successfully, recreation will finally achieve its fullest potential and take its rightful place on a par with work as one of the activities that give purpose and meaning to people's lives.

DISCUSSION TOPICS

1. What effect do you think changing energy supplies and prices will have in the future on your recreation environment and the environments of others with whom you are acquainted?
2. Discuss the probable effects of land-use policies, user conflicts, and overuse on your recreation environment now and in the future.
3. How are current changes in economic conditions likely to affect the nature and scope of recreation opportunities in the city or region with which you are most familiar?
4. How can recreation professionals provide more appropriate recreation programs for the diversity of household types that are currently emerging?
5. How do you think people will view their future recreation environments? Will they think they are purgatory or paradise? Explain your answer.

FURTHER READINGS

Most recreation textbooks currently in use either omit mentioning the probable future nature of recreation or present information that is now outdated. Some of the recently published books still paint a picture of future Americans with higher discretionary incomes and more free time traveling extensively by private automobile to all types of extraurban recreation resources. No doubt editions of these books published in 1980 or later will begin to reflect the great changes that have taken place in the 1970s. The July and August 1980 editions of *Parks and Recreation* contained a special series of articles discussing a number of the current problems confronting recreation professionals and how these problems are likely to affect the nature and scope of recreation services in the future.

The best sources of up-to-date information on the probable future of recreation are newspapers and magazines. Sometimes they tend to be sensationalized, but most of the relevant feature articles appearing in major newspapers are reliable, especially those found in the *New York Times* and the *Wall Street Journal.* A number of the weekly magazines, particularly *U.S. News & World Report* and *Business Week* are good sources. Many of the useful articles are not primarily concerned with the future of recreation but include various aspects of it when discussing subjects such as population, energy, inflation, trade developments, taxes, unemployment, transportation, or business prospects. Recent editions of The Encyclopaedia Britannica *Book of the Year* are good sources of summary information concerning social and economic changes in the United States and elsewhere.

GLOSSARY OF TERMS

This glossary contains the recreation terms and technical words that are printed in color in the preceding chapters.

Accessibility The relative ease with which users can take part in a recreation opportunity. Often controlled largely by external factors such as resource availability and travel time, accessibility is also a function of personal factors such as personality, sex, age, attitude, and physical condition.

Administration Activities undertaken by recreation professionals that involve the organization of recreation systems, the development of appropriate policies, and the provision of the requisite financial support.

Adventure playgrounds Informal playgrounds for children and teenagers consisting of an open space containing an assortment of construction materials such as boards, logs, and tires and a supply of basic tools, nails, rope, and other items to facilitate the building of play structures. Participation is usually closely supervised.

Appropriation doctrine The legal approach to water resource ownership in the western United States that allows the rights to use water to be acquired by those who first own land along a waterway and declare their intention of using the water.

Asymmetrical distribution A situation where a phenomenon is unevenly distributed so that one or more areas have many, while others have few or none.

Availability The availability of recreation resources and opportunities depends on the nature of undeveloped resources present in an area, on resource ownership, on the degree to which resources are developed, on the carrying capacity of the resources, and on their distribution.

Balance of payments The difference between the total amount a nation spends abroad on all goods, services, and donations and the total amount it receives from abroad under these headings.

Benevolent organizations Associations such as labor unions, fraternal organizations, military veterans' groups, and retired persons' clubs that are formed primarily to promote the general welfare of their members.

Cafeteria system The arrangement by which some employers allow each of their employees to choose the particular mixture of fringe benefits that is most satisfactory for them.

Carrying capacity Recreation carrying capacity is the number of recreation opportunities that a specified unit of a recreation resource can provide year after year without appreciable biological or physical deterioration of the resource or significant impairment of the recreation experience.

Climate The climate of a location is its long-term average weather conditions and is described in terms of temperature, precipitation, humidity, and sunshine patterns.

Climatic hazards Aspects of a location's climate that create a substantial threat to human safety such as hurricanes, typhoons, tornadoes, or blizzards.

Climatic region A region of the earth's surface that has basically the same climatic characteristics throughout its area.

Choice An activity that a person chooses to do from among the various alternative recreation opportunities that are available. (Some authors use the term preference instead but this implies that the participant prefers the activity over all others rather than choosing only from among those that are available.)

Cold climates Regions that have generally low temperatures and short summers such as the subarctic, tundra, and icecap regions.

Community complex A facility consisting of a local government school constructed in or adjacent to a park, which provides social services in addition to recreation and education.

Community park A large park that provides 10 to 20 neighborhoods with the kinds of recreation experiences that most people only enjoy on weekends rather than every day. Facilities often include swimming beaches, golf courses, nature centers, and small zoos, in addition to extensive picnic and play areas (sometimes called district parks).

Community playfields A small to medium-sized park that provides a variety of athletic and sports activities for youths and adults from a group of five or six neighborhoods.

Community recreation center This provides neighborhood-type indoor recreation opportunities for people living nearby, together with facilities such as a large auditorium, a full-sized basketball court, or an indoor swimming pool that are intended to serve a number of neighborhoods.

Condominium A system of building ownership where a purchaser obtains ownership of one housing unit within a multiple unit complex together with part ownership of common facilities such as parking areas, grounds, and recreation amenities.

Country park A type of park developed in Britain to provide urban residents with recreation opportunities at nearby rural locations without substantially adding to highway congestion or depreciating experiences at exceptional sites such as national parks.

Cross-stimulation effect   Situations where people become interested in participating in a new type of recreation activity because they were exposed to it while taking part in a different activity. For example, a person may become interested in playing a musical instrument while enjoying a concert on television.

Crown land   The term used for public land administered by national or provincial government agencies in Great Britain, Canada, and other former British colonies. In Canada, the provinces administer vast areas of Crown lands.

Cultural center   A structure containing two or more stages and both participant and audience facilities for all of the performing arts.

Cultural resources   Facilities and programs that provide pleasurable artistic, dramatic, literary, and musical experiences or facilitate enjoyable explorations of our environment.

Discretionary income   Income left after people pay for what are regarded in their particular culture to be the basic essentials needed to operate an average household.

Discretionary time   Time that is left after an individual has attended to bodily necessities and essential work and social obligations; free time.

Drive to maturity   The stage in economic development when substantial growth occurs in all sectors of the industrial economy, but the emphasis gradually changes from heavy industry to highly diversified sophisticated manufacturing.

Dry climate   A climate that has a total annual precipitation of 25 centimeters (10 inches) or less. Warmth and many hours of sunshine favor outdoor activities except in extremely hot periods.

Dual-purpose home   A home that has all the features of a primary residence but also includes one or more key attributes of a second home acquired for recreation purposes.

Earned time   An employment system under which workers can go home as soon as they have fulfilled their production quotas and still be paid for a full day.

Elevation   The height of the land above sea level.

Environmental interpretation center   A special kind of museum that contains exhibits and demonstrations that help visitors understand and appreciate the surrounding environment (sometimes called interpretive center or nature center).

Exercise trail   See parcourse.

Experience phase   A distinctive portion of a recreation experience such as the anticipation phase, outward-travel phase, or recollection phase.

Facility-based agency   A quasi-public, youth-oriented organization that specializes in providing recreation programs in buildings that it owns and operates. Examples include the YWCA and the Boys' Clubs of America.

Facility-unit   A unit of recreation resource measurement such as a basketball court, campsite, or square meter of swimming surface. Facility-unit measurement does not necessarily reflect the number of opportunities the resource can provide.

Fish ladder   A series of interconnecting pools or channels built alongside a dam or waterfall so that fish may travel upstream past the obstruction.

Flexitime   A work-scheduling system under which employees arrange their own 40-hour weekly work schedule around a core period in the middle of the day by starting earlier or later or working only 4½ or 4 days.

Forest preserve district   A local or regional government unit established under state enabling legislation that acquires, manages, and protects forest lands in all or part of a number of political units.

Fourth World   The 45 extremely poor nations that are still in the traditional society stage of development.

Group-program agency   A quasi-public, youth-oriented organization that specializes in developing and refining programs that are made available to as many young people as possible by using volunteer leaders and donated space in private homes, schools, churches, or community centers.

Haves; have nots   The highly developed nations of the world are sometimes referred to as "the haves" and the remainder are called "have nots."

Hierarchy of commercial resources   The tendency of commercial recreation resources to form a ranking system and be distributed according to the size of the market area needed to support each type of resource.

High culture   The group of cultural activities that currently appeals to a relatively small portion of the population; includes art films, fine arts museums, opera, ballet, and classical music, plays, and literature.

Highland climate   The complicated mixture of climatic zones found in hilly or mountainous regions.

High-mass-consumption stage   The stage in economic development when the economy reaches its full potential, producing large quantities of consumer goods and services.

High-order enterprise   A commercial enterprise that requires a large number of potential customers in its market area. High-order enterprises are therefore spaced some distance apart and form an open network.

Humid cool-temperature climate
A climate that has an annual temperature range from below freezing to more than 21°C (70°F) and a moderate average annual precipitation, some of which falls as snow in the winter but most of which occurs in the warmer months.

Humid subtropical climate A temperate, rainy climate with moderately hot summers and cool winters.

Humid warm-temperature climates Temperate, rainy climates with moderately hot to cool summers and warm to cool winters. Included in this category are marine west coast climates and humid subtropical climates such as in the southeastern United States.

Institutional recreation resources Recreation amenities provided for the enjoyment of the inhabitants of public institutions such as colleges, prisons, and health care facilities.

Interdisciplinary An approach involving the knowledge and methods of several academic fields of study.

Intermediate governments Governments that function at a level between a national government and regional, county, or local governments such as the state governments in the United States and the provincial governments in Canada.

Interval ownership plan An ownership system whereby an individual receives title to a housing unit and a share in the use of common amenities for a specific period or series of periods each year.

Landform A particular kind of undeveloped surface structure such as a mountain, hill, canyon, or plain.

Latitude The distance a point on the earth's surface is located north or south of the equator expressed as a vertical angle from the equator to the point.

Leisure Time that is free of work, subsistence activities, or other duties; free time, spare time, discretionary time.

Low-order enterprise A commercial enterprise that requires a small number of potential customers in its market area. Low-order enterprises are therefore located quite close together and form a dense network.

Marine west coast climate A rainy climate with relatively mild winters and cool to warm summers.

Market area The area from which an enterprise draws its customers.

Mall A large, elongated urban public area, often lined with trees, that is used as a walk or promenade (see square and plaza). Streets in shopping districts that have been modified by the removal of some or all vehicular traffic and the addition of vegetation and street furniture are sometimes called pedestrian malls. Large self-contained shopping centers are often referred to as shopping malls in North America.

Management Activities undertaken by recreation professionals that produce recreation opportunities through research and planning; the design, construction, operation, maintenance, and protection of inanimate resources; and the use of human resources such as instructors, coaches, and artists.

Mass culture Widely enjoyed cultural opportunities such as commercial television programs, bestselling novels, commercial films, and popular music and magazines.

Mediterranean climate A subdivision of the humid warm-temperature climatic class that is characterized by relatively light annual precipitation, largely concentrated in the winter, and many days with clear skies, light winds, and moderate to hot temperatures.

Membership plan A system whereby an individual purchases the use of a particular housing unit and the accompanying resort facilities for a specified period each year for a given number of years. Ownership of the building and land remains with the developer.

Minipark A very small park that provides a variety of recreation experiences because it contains a range of amenities such as shaded sitting areas, limited ball game facilities, and children's play equipment.

Mobile recreation unit A recreation resource such as a small swimming pool, band shell, or library that is mounted on a truck or trailer and can be moved from place to place.

Motivations Inner urges that prompt an individual to behave in a particular manner.

Multiple-purpose trip Travel undertaken for several different purposes. Frequently recreation is combined with business travel or trips to visit relatives.

National park system All the units making up the network of recreation resources administered by a national park agency whether the units are called national parks, national monuments, national preserves, or a variety of other names.

Neighborhood park A park that is intended to serve 2000 to 5000 people living in a cluster of blocks or streets that comprises a distinct neighborhood. A wide range of facilities including a children's playground, many sports courts or fields, picnic tables and benches for sitting, and areas of grass and shade trees are usually included.

Neighborhood recreation center A building that provides indoor recreation opportunities for a population similar in size to that served by a neighborhood park (see neighborhood park).

Optimum recreation climate A climate that will permit people to participate in comfort for a maximum number of days each year in everyday activities such as walking, playing games, or sitting out-of-doors relaxing in the sun.

Orienteering   An educational recreation activity in which a topographic map is used to follow a given course across the landscape by identifying landmarks, taking compass readings, and measuring distances. It is often done on a competitive basis.

Outdoor recreation   Any type of urban, rural, or wilderness recreation activity that takes place outside a building including activities ranging from sunbathing, picnicking, jogging, and watching cultural and sports events to hunting, mountain climbing, and wilderness camping; urban outdoor recreation often occurs in backyards, on building rooftops, on the streets, and at commercial enterprises such as sidewalk cafés, go-cart tracks, and miniature golf courses.

Outreach programs   Programs conducted by libraries, museums, art galleries, performing arts institutions, and other recreation providers that make opportunities readily accessible to people by taking materials, exhibits, programs, demonstrations, or performances to residential neighborhoods, shopping centers, schools, or work places.

Parcourse   An exercise trail consisting of 15 to 25 stations along a running trail. Each station includes a sign explaining the exercise and prescribing the desirable number of repetitions; some have simple equipment.

Park districts   A local or regional government unit established under state enabling legislation that acquires, manages, and protects forest lands in all or part of a number of political units.

Parkway   As originally conceived, a parkway was a curving landscaped pleasure drive often built around the outskirts of a city to connect two or more major parks. In recent times, many parkways have become major

traffic arteries and largely have lost their value as recreation resources.

Participation patterns   The manner in which a population takes part in recreation either as a whole or in terms of particular activities or sites. Patterns are usually described by measuring how much time various kinds of people from different locations spend on specific types of activities at a variety of resources.

Paseo   The ritual in Spain and spanish-speaking nations whereby people promenade through the main part of town or around the central plaza during the early evening in order to meet friends or make new acquaintances.

Pedestrian mall   See mall.

Perceptions   The ways in which an individual sees a person, place, object, or activity. These mental impressions are based on personal interpretation of all the relevant stimuli received.

Performing arts   The wide range of activities known as the performing arts includes classical music, opera, drama, poetry reading, and dance presentations.

Perquisites   A special type of employee fringe benefit such as employer-provided vehicles, admission tickets to concerts and sports events, recreation centers, resorts, and entertainment and travel allowances.

Personal recreation resources   Buildings, rooms, yards, vehicles, equipment, books, films, clothing, animals, and other items owned by individuals or household groups and used primarily for their own pleasure or for entertaining friends and relatives.

Planned unit development (PUD)   A medium- to large-sized residential development in which the housing (detached, semidetached, apartment, or condominium units) and associated parking and recreation facili-

ties are grouped into fairly tight clusters thereby creating substantial areas of open space without increasing the overall population density beyond that usually found in conventional residential developments.

Playlot   A small park devoted primarily to play facilities for young children such as sandboxes, swings, climbers, and slides but usually there are some benches and shade trees where adults can sit while supervising their children's play.

Plaza   An urban open space ranging from traditional plazas in old Italian towns formed by the coalescence of several intersecting streets to courtyards incorporated in urban renewal projects. Plazas usually have buildings surrounding them rather than streets and have most of their surface paved.

Popularization of the arts   Attempts by cultural institutions to attract wider audiences by providing programs that are less traditional in content and presentation.

Preconditions for takeoff   The situation when new ideas and goals begin to gain a foothold in a traditional society and create an environment favorable to the beginning of economic development.

Preference   A recreation activity that a person likes to do (or would like to do) more than any other activity (see choice).

Preservation organizations   Private groups that have the preservation of natural history or historic resources and the provision of related educational and research opportunities as their primary goals.

Primary recreation commodities   Goods that play an essential role in recreation experiences such as sports equipment, games, camping gear, printed matter, hobby supplies, musical instruments, and certain vital articles of clothing.

Primary sector The portion of a nation's economy that consists of extractive industries—for example, agriculture, mining, fishing, and timber cutting.

Private recreation organizations Organizations that are formed primarily to provide recreation experiences for their members such as social, sportsperson's, boat, cultural, and hobby clubs.

Private recreation resources All kinds of recreation resources owned by private individuals and private organizations. This group ranges from personal backyard facilities and table games to youth clubs, preservation organizations, restaurants, private marinas, flying club aircraft, and guest ranches.

Programming The organization of human recreation resources in conjunction with recreation facilities to provide organized recreation programs.

Promenade A lengthy walkway built so that people can stroll along it and enjoy resources such as ornamental plantings or a river, lake, or ocean shoreline.

Property sharing A property ownership arrangement under which two or more individuals or households jointly own a recreation property such as a lakeshore cottage, houseboat, or ski resort condominium.

Public recreation resource A recreation amenity that is owned by a government and used by the public at large or specific segments of the public.

Quality experience A recreation experience from which the participant receives a high degree of satisfaction. Quality experiences occur most often when activities are spontaneously undertaken for sheer fun as an end in themselves and no pressures, ulterior motives, long-term goals, or preconceived expectations are involved.

Quasi-public organization A private organization that tends to be regarded as a publicly controlled agency because of characteristics such as community involvement in its policies and programs, reliance on public donations or government grants, projects undertaken in cooperation with government agencies, a majority of programs involving service to society with little or no effort expended on social events, and a primary concern with the welfare of the strata of society the organization seeks to serve.

Recreation Any type of conscious enjoyment that the participant perceives as recreational. It can include activities that are normally thought of as bodily functions, psychologically abnormal, or detrimental to objects, the individual, or society.

Recreation carrying capacity The number of recreation opportunities that a specified unit of a recreation resource can provide year after year without appreciable biological or physical deterioration of the resource or impairment of the recreation experience.

Recreation center A building or collection of buildings where opportunities for several broad groupings of recreation opportunities are offered such as indoor sports and games, arts and crafts, cultural programs, and social events (see neighborhood and community recreation center).

Recreation goods (or commodities) Usually includes only items that are generally recognized as being prominent ingredients of recreation experiences. However, almost all commodities can be recreation goods (see primary and secondary recreation commodities).

Recreation renaissance The period from 1840 to 1880 when social restrictions on recreation participation were reduced, opportunities were expanded, and governments began to become permanently involved in the provision of recreation experiences on a large scale.

Recreation resource A source of supply of recreation opportunities such as a book, television program, coin collection, automobile, garden, shopping center, museum, restaurant, road, farm, mountain, lake, musician, art instructor, or professional athlete.

Recreation services The range of recreation facilities and programs offered by a particular organization or commercial enterprise. Usually used as a collective term for all the recreation amenities provided by a local, county, or regional government agency.

Recreation standard Specific numerical value or range of values for a measure of recreation system adequacy that has been agreed upon by a professional organization; for example, the goal of having a minimum of 10 acres (4.1 hectares) of urban parks per 1000 population.

Regional park A large park with special amenities not normally found in community parks such as a fair-sized lake, shoreline area, or woodland that attract users from a number of communities. Regional parks may be part of city, county, district, or regionally organized park systems.

Regional theater A professional, noncommercial theater that provides theatrical experiences for a major metropolitan area, state, or combination of states and contributes substantially to national theatrical standards by producing superior acting companies and high-quality presentations of new plays as well as revivals and the classics.

Restaurant district A cluster of restaurants in close proximity to one another in a city center.

Riparian doctrine Laws and legal precedents that permit each landowner along a waterway to use water for normal domestic, agricultural, or industrial purposes provided the flow is not decreased sufficiently to interfere with similar uses downstream.

Ripple effect   The situation where seeing a television program, reading a book, or being exposed to some other type of performance or exhibit stimulates an individual to explore areas that have little or nothing to do with the resource concerned. As a consequence, the individual may take a trip, join an organization, try a new activity, acquire a new skill, or adopt a new lifestyle.

School/park complex   A situation where a school has been built in or immediately adjacent to a park, and the design and operation of the two amenities are coordinated so that the school's students benefit from the park's recreation and education resources while the park and recreation department uses school facilities to enhance its programs.

(The) seaside   A British expression meaning an oceanside resort location.

Secondary recreation commodities   Goods that do not necessarily play an essential role in recreation experiences but whose presence may make recreation experiences more enjoyable. Examples can include snack foods, golf carts, *color* television, and patios and family rooms.

Secondary sector   The portion of a nation's economy consisting of industries that manufacture goods for sale to others.

Second home   An individual's or household's second or other additional residence usually acquired because it makes specific recreation opportunites more accessible. Examples are lakeside cottages, ski resort condominiums, and apartments in cities that the occupants use periodically when they wish to entertain or go to performances or sports events.

Second recreation revolution   The dramatic changes in social attitudes toward recreation, recreation participation patterns, and the provision of recreation services that have taken place from 1700 to the present time and have resulted in the great majority of citizens in developed nations having access to a multitude of recreation opportunities that were previously the prerogative of the affluent.

Self-contained resort   A commercial hotel, motel, villa, or cabin development that includes such extensive onsite recreation resources many guests spend most of their time enjoying the resort's amenities and seldom if ever leave the grounds.

Sequential patterns   The situation where an individual, couple, or group frequently take part in two or more recreation experiences in a particular sequence. This sequence may be a socially accepted norm (eating out, going to a performance, having a snack or drink on the way home) or a group ritual (taking part in a particular sequence of activities on a special day such as a birthday or religious holiday).

Service organization   An organization that is committed to public service as its primary purpose. These groups contribute to community betterment by raising funds or donating their time to various kinds of improvement projects.

Shared whole ownership   An arrangement whereby two or more individuals or households share the ownership of a second home or other property under a formal or informal agreement.

Simultaneous experience   A recreation experience that a person enjoys at the same time as another recreation experience. For example, people often eat, drink, knit, or undertake some other type of hobby while watching television.

Social welfare organizations   Private organizations that are primarily concerned with the welfare of disadvantaged people. Many of these groups have a quasi-public status and provide extensive recreation opportunities.

Special populations   People who cannot participate in recreation to the same extent or in the same manner as the majority of the population because of a physical, mental, emotional, or social problem or handicap. Most people tend to think primarily of those who are obviously handicapped (the blind, deaf, retarded, and physically disabled) when the term special population is used. However, there are many other less obvious groups that also need special attention — the elderly, short people, single parents, prisoners, and people serving in the armed forces. Indeed, everyone is a member of a special population in one way or another.

Square   A rectangular urban open space usually bounded by four streets and containing one or more of the following features: lawn area, shade trees, statuary, a formal garden, a fountain, benches for sitting, and a public building such as a library, court house, or local government offices.

State forest   In the United States, a state forest is an area of land, owned by one of the 50 states, that has been designated as a state forest. In Great Britain and some other nations, a state forest is a forest managed by the national government.

Subcultural group   An identifiable group within a culture such as people who are united by place of residence, religion, ethnic origin, age, occupation, marital status, political affiliation, lifestyle, or recreation activity preference.

Takeoff stage   The stage in economic development when sufficient political and economic support has emerged to make the rapid development of the manufacturing and services industries possible.

Tertiary sector The portion of the nation's economy that consists of providing services to people including retail sales, education, health care, banking, and insurance.

Theater district A cluster of theaters in close proximity to one another in a city center.

Theme park Amusement parks that contain thrill rides, games, shows, souvenir vendors, and food service facilities cleverly tied together in a pleasing, efficient design based on a single theme. Usually these parks are owned and operated by one corporation, are promoted as a coordinated package, and involve a substantial entrance fee that prepays admission to a sampling of the majority of attractions.

Therapeutic recreation The treatment of a person's physical or mental disability by medically supervised participation in recreation activities.

Third World Originally, this term referred to all nations other than the highly developed Western nations and the Communist bloc nations. Now it is often used to denote all the world's less developed nations except the poorest 45 nations (see Fourth World).

Threshold population The number of people needed in the service area of a facility or program before it can be supported economically or justified administratively.

Time budget The manner in which an individual allocates time between bodily necessities, work, duties, recreation, and spiritual needs.

Time-sharing Arrangements by which the use of a condominium, apartment, or other recreational residence is shared among two or more individuals or households on a prearranged basis. For details of the two main approaches, see **interval ownership plan** and **membership plan.**

Topography The general shape of the surface of the earth in a particular area.

Traditional society A society that has remained comparatively unchanged for a long time with a landowning aristocracy, most people employed in agriculture and living a hand-to-mouth existence, and social, economic, and political activities dominated by traditional customs.

Tropical rain forest climate A climate that has a relatively uniform high temperature year round and heavy to very heavy precipitation well distributed throughout the year.

Tropical savanna climate A climate that has high average temperatures like the tropical rain forest climate, but the summer temperatures are slightly higher and the winter temperatures are slightly lower. Rainfall is generally less and is concentrated in the summer.

Tropical wet climates Areas that have tropical rain forest or tropical savanna climates.

Turnover rate Length of time spent by the average user or party of users on a particular activity.

Undesignated recreation resources Amenities that are used for recreation purposes but are not designated as recreation resources, such as streets, highways, and airports.

Undeveloped resources Lands that are still in a reasonably natural state irrespective of who is responsible for their administration or where they are located from the urban core to the wilderness.

Use-units Units used in quantitatively expressing the supply of recreation opportunities offered by a particular resource. This method takes into account the turnover rates for various activities and uses units such as picnicker-days, camper-days, or boater-days.

Volunteer organization A quasi-public organization that relies primarily on volunteers to lead and supervise its programs in contrast to a facility-based agency that relies primarily on paid staff.

Water contact activities Recreation activities where the user comes in direct contact with the water such as swimming, surfing, and scuba diving.

Youth-oriented organization An organization that is dedicated primarily to providing programs for one or more segments of the youth population, for example, Girl Scouts, Boys' Clubs, Police Athletic League, or Catholic Youth Organization.

SELECTED BIBLIOGRAPHY

A bibliography of major recreation publications is of great value to the beginning student or recreation professional. However, the vast amount of written material concerning various facets of recreation that has appeared in the past few decades makes it impossible to include a truly comprehensive listing. We have, therefore, concentrated on sources in English that are considered essential components of the recreation literature and can usually be obtained from larger college libraries. The entries are arranged in nine groups. The first group, recent basic textbooks, consists of the principal comprehensive textbooks published in the last decade that are concerned with recreation as a whole or with a major subdivision of the field. The next group is a large one consisting of sources that describe the historical development of recreation attitudes, behavior, and resources. It includes a number of older textbooks that are now superseded but show how recreation philosophy and management developed. The next five groups correspond roughly to the chapter sequence in this book. They are: factors affecting recreation behavior; recreation resources; general administration; research, planning, and design; and resource management and programming. The eighth group consists of books that are collections of general readings. Finally, there is a small group of publications concerning recreation careers.

RECENT BASIC TEXTBOOKS

Brockman, C. Frank, and Lawrence C. Merriman, Jr., *Recreational Use of Wild Lands,* McGraw-Hill, New York, 1979.

Bucher, Charles A., and Richard D. Bucher, *Recreation for Today's Society,* Prentice-Hall, Englewood Cliffs, N.J., 1974.

Butler, George D., *Introduction to Community Recreation,* 5th ed., McGraw-Hill, New York, 1976.

Carlson, Reynold E., Theodore R. Deppe, and Janet R. MacLean, *Recreation and Leisure: The Changing Scene,* 3rd ed., Wadsworth, Belmont, Calif., 1979.

Cosgrove, Isobel, and Richard Jackson, *The Geography of Recreation and Leisure,* Hutchinson Univ. Library, London, 1972.

Curtis, Joseph E., *Recreation: Theory and Practice,* C. V. Mosby, St. Louis, 1979.

Doell, Charles E., and Louis F. Twardzik, *Elements of Park and Recreation Administration,* 4th ed., Burgess, Minneapolis, Minn., 1979.

Douglass, Robert W., *Forest Recreation,* 2nd ed., Pergamon Press, New York, 1975.

Epperson, Arlin F., *Private and Commercial Recreation: A Text and Reference,* Wiley, New York, 1977.

Freeman, William H., *Physical Education in a Changing Society,* Houghton Mifflin, Boston, 1977.

Frost, Reuben B., *Physical Education: Foundations, Practices, and Principles,* Addison-Wesley, Reading, Mass., 1975.

Frye, Virginia, and Martha Peters, *Therapeutic Recreation: Its Theory, Philosophy, and Practices,* Stackpole Books, Harrisburg, Pa., 1972.

Godbey, Geoffrey, *Recreation, Park, and Leisure Services: Foundations, Organization, Administration,* Saunders, Philadelphia, 1978.

Godbey, Geoffrey, and Stanley Parker, *Leisure Studies and Services: An Overview,* Saunders, Philadelphia, 1976.

Graham, Peter J., and Lawrence R, Klar, Jr., *Planning and Delivering Leisure Services,* Wm. C. Brown, Dubuque, Iowa, 1979.

Haworth, John Trevor, and M. A. Smith, eds., *Work and Leisure: An Interdisciplinary Study in Theory, Education and Planning,* Lepus Books, London, 1975.

Hormachea, Marion N., and Carroll R. Hormachea, *Recreation in Modern Society,* Holbrook Press, Boston, 1972.

Ibrahim, Hilmi, and Fred Martin, *Leisure: An Introduction,* Hwong Publishing, Los Alamitos, Calif., 1977.

Jensen, Clayne T., *Leisure and Recreation: Introduction and Overview,* Lea & Febiger, Philadelphia, 1977.

Jensen, Clayne R., *Outdoor Recreation in America: Trends, Problems, and Opportunities,* 3rd ed., Burgess, Minneapolis, Minn., 1977.

Knudson, Douglas M., *Outdoor Recreation,* Macmillan, New York, 1980.

Kraus, Richard G., *Recreation Today:*

Program Planning and Leadership, Goodyear Publishing, Santa Monica, Calif., 1977.

⸺, Recreation and Leisure in Modern Society, 2nd ed., Goodyear Publishing, Santa Monica, Calif., 1978.

⸺, Therapeutic Recreation Service: Principles and Practices, 2nd ed., Saunders, Philadelphia, 1978.

McCall, Joseph R., and Virginia N. McCall, Outdoor Recreation: Forest, Park, and Wilderness, Bruce, Beverly Hills, Calif., 1977.

McIntosh, Robert W., Tourism Principles, Practices and Philosophies, Grid, Inc. Columbus, Ohio, 1972.

Mercer, David, ed., Leisure and Recreation in Australia, Sorrett Publishing, Malvern, Australia, 1977.

O'Morrow, Gerald S., Therapeutic Recreation: A Helping Profession, Reston Publishing, Reston, Va., 1976.

Sessoms, H. Douglas, Harold D. Meyer, and Charles K. Brightbill, Leisure Services: The Organized Recreation and Park System, 5th ed., Prentice-Hall, Englewood Cliffs, N.J., 1975.

Weiskopf, Donald C., A Guide to Recreation and Leisure, Allyn and Bacon, Boston, 1975.

HISTORICAL DEVELOPMENT OF RECREATION ATTITUDES, BEHAVIOR, AND RESOURCES

Addams, Jane, Twenty Years at Hull-House, New American Library, New York, 1960.

American Association for Health, Physical Education and Recreation, Goals for American Recreation, AAHPER, Washington, D.C., 1964.

Armitage, John, Man at Play: Nine Centuries of Pleasure Making, Frederick Warne & Co., New York, 1977.

Barlow, Elizabeth, Frederick Law Olmsted's New York, Praeger, New York, 1972.

⸺, The Central Park Book, Central Park Task Force, New York, 1977.

Bohn, Thomas W., and Richard L. Stromgren, Light and Shadows: A History of Motion Pictures, Alfred Publishing, Port Washington, New York, 1975.

Bridges, William, Gathering of Animals: An Unconventional History of the New York Zoological Society, Harper & Row, New York, 1974.

Brightbill, Charles K., Man and Leisure: A Philosophy of Recreation, Prentice-Hall, Englewood Cliffs, N.J., 1961.

⸺, The Challenge of Leisure, Prentice-Hall, Englewood Cliffs, N.J., 1963.

Brightbill, Charles K., and Harold D. Meyer, Recreation: Text and Readings, Prentice-Hall, Englewood Cliffs, N.J., 1953.

Burkart, A. J. and S. Medlik, Tourism: Past, Present, and Future, Pitman, London, 1974.

Butler, George D., Pioneers in Public Recreation, Burgess, Minneapolis, 1965.

Caillois, Roger, Man, Play, and Games, Glencoe Press, New York, 1961.

Clawson, Marion, Land and Water for Recreation: Opportunities, Problems, and Policies, Rand McNally, Chicago, 1963.

⸺, The Bureau of Land Management, Praeger, New York, 1971.

Clawson, Marion, and Burnell Held, The Federal Lands: Their Use and Management, Johns Hopkins Press, Baltimore, 1957.

Cowell, Charles C., and Wellman L. France, Philosophy and Principles of Physical Education,. Prentice-Hall, Englewood Cliffs, N.J., 1963.

Danford, Howard G., Recreation in the American Community, Harper, New York, 1953.

Doell, Charles E., and Gerald B. Fitzgerald, A Brief History of Parks and Recreation in the United States, Athletic Institute, Chicago, 1954.

Dulles, Foster Rhea, A History of Recreation: America Learns to Play, 2nd ed., Appleton-Century-Crofts, New York, 1965.

Everhart, William C., The National Park Service, Praeger, New York, 1972.

Fitch, Edwin M., and John F. Shanklin, The Bureau of Outdoor Recreation, Praeger, New York, 1970.

Fiztgerald, Gerald B., Community Organization for Recreation, A. S. Barnes & Co., New York, 1948.

⸺, Leadership in Recreation, A. S. Barnes & Co., New York, 1951.

Foss, Phillip O., Recreation: Conservation in the United States, A Documentary History, Chelsea House, New York, 1971.

Frome, Michael, The Forest Service, Praeger, New York, 1971.

Gerber, Ellen W., Innovators and Institutions in Physical Education, Lea & Febiger, Philadelphia, 1971.

Green, Arnold W., Recreation, Leisure and Politics, McGraw-Hill, New York, 1964.

Green, Thomas F., Work, Leisure, and the American Schools, Random House, New York, 1968.

Haun, Paul, Recreation: A Medical Viewpoint, Columbia Univ. Bureau of Publications, New York, 1965.

Hawkins, Donald E., Supply/Demand Study, Professional and Pre-Professional Recreation and Park Occupations, National Recreation and Park Association, Washington, D.C., 1968.

Heckscher, August, Open Spaces, Harper & Row, New York, 1977.

Hutchinson, John Lambert, Principles of Recreation, Ronald, New York, 1951.

Jackson, Sidney L., Eleanor B. Herling, and E. J. Josey, eds., A Century of Service, American Library Association, Chicago, 1976.

Johnson, Elmer Douglas, and Michael H. Harris, History of Libraries in the Western World, 3rd ed., Scarecrow Press, Metuchen, N.J., 1976.

Johnston, Nancy, Central Park Country, Sierra Club, San Francisco, 1968.

Jury, Mark, Playtime!: Americans at Leisure, Harcourt Brace Jovanovich, New York, 1977.

Kando, Thomas M., *Leisure and Popular Culture in Transition,* 2nd ed., C. V. Mosby, St. Louis, 1980.

Katz, Herbert, and Marjorie Katz, *Museums U.S.A.: A History and Guide,* Doubleday, Garden City, N.Y., 1965.

Kieran, John, Arthur Dailey, and Pat Jordan, *The Story of the Olympic Games: 776 B.C. to 1976,* J. B. Lippincott, Philadelphia, 1977.

Knapp, Richard F., and Charles E. Hartsoe, *Play for America: The History of the National Recreation Association: 1906–1965,* National Recreation and Park Association, Arlington, Va., 1979.

Kraus, Richard G., *Public Recreation and the Negro: A Study of Participation and Administrative Practices,* Center for Urban Education, New York, 1968.

La Gasse, Alfred B., and Walter L. Cook, *History of Parks and Recreation,* American Institute of Park Executives, Wheeling, W. Va., 1965.

Larrabee, Eric, and Rolf Meyersohn, eds., *Mass Leisure,* Free Press, Glencoe, Ill., 1958.

Lindner, Staffan Burenstam, *The Harried Leisure Class,* Columbia Univ. Press, New York, 1970.

MacDonald, J. Fred, *Don't Touch That Dial!: Radio Programming in American Life, 1920–1960,* Nelson-Hall, Chicago, 1979.

Madow, Pauline, ed., *Recreation in America,* H. W. Wilson, New York, 1965.

Mangels, William F., *The Outdoor Amusement Industry From Earliest Times to the Present,* Vantage Press, New York, 1952.

Meyer, Harold D., and Charles K. Brightbill, *State Recreation: Organization and Administration,* A. S. Barnes & Co., New York, 1950.

Miller, Norman P., and Duane M. Robinson, *The Leisure Age: Its Challenge to Recreation,* Wadsworth, Belmont, Calif., 1963.

Moss, Peter, *Sports and Pastimes Through the Ages,* Arco Publishing, New York, 1963.

Murphy, James F., ed., *Concepts of Leisure: Philosophical Implications,* Prentice-Hall, Englewood Cliffs, N.J., 1974.

Nash, Jay B., *Philosophy of Recreation and Leisure,* Wm. C. Brown, Dubuque, Iowa, 1960.

———, *Recreation: Pertinent Readings, Guide Posts to the Future,* Wm. C. Brown, Dubuque, Iowa, 1965.

Olmsted, Frederick Law, *Civilizing American Cities: A Selection of Frederick Law Olmsted's Writings on City Landscapes,* edited by S. B. Sutton, MIT Press, Cambridge, Mass., 1971.

Olmsted, Frederick Law, Jr., and Theodora Kimball, *Frederick Law Olmsted, Landscape Architect, 1822–1903,* Benjamin Blom, New York, 1970.

Parker, Stanley Robert, *The Future of Work and Leisure,* Praeger, New York, 1971.

Pieper, Josef, *Leisure: The Basis of Culture,* Pantheon Books, New York, 1963.

Reed, Henry Hope, and Sophia Duckworth, *Central Park—A History and A Guide,* 2nd ed., Clarkson N. Potter, New York, 1972.

Ruck, S. K., *Municipal Entertainment and the Arts in Greater London,* Allen & Unwin, London, 1965.

Siepmann, Charles A., *Radio, Television, and Society,* Oxford Univ. Press, New York, 1950.

Spears, Betty Mary, and Richard A. Swanson, *History of Sport and Physical Activity in the United States,* edited by Elaine T. Smith, Wm. C. Brown, Dubuque, Iowa, 1978.

Staley, Edwin J., and Norman P. Miller, eds., *Leisure and the Quality of Life: A New Ethnic for the 70's and Beyond,* American Association for Health, Physical Education and Recreation, Washington, D.C., 1972.

Thurston, Hazel, *Royal Parks for the People,* David & Charles, Newton Abbot, Devon, 1974.

Twentieth Century Fund Task Force on Performing Arts Centers, *Bricks, Mortar, and the Performing Arts,* The Twentieth Century Fund, New York, 1970.

Udall, Stewart L., *The Quiet Crisis,* Holt, Rinehart & Winston, New York, 1963.

U.S. Congress, Outdoor Recreation Resources Review Commission, *Outdoor Recreation for America,* U.S. Government Printing Office, Washington, D.C., 1962.

———, *Study Reports Nos. 1 through 27* (see listing of titles on pp. 199–203 in *Outdoor Recreation for America*).

U.S. Department of the Interior, National Park Service, *Parks for America,* U.S. Government Printing Office, Washington, D.C., 1964.

Van Doren, Carlton S., and Louis Hodges, *America's Park and Recreation Heritage: A Chronology,* U.S. Government Printing Office, Washington, D.C., 1975.

Vendien, C. Lynn, and John E. Nixon, *The World Today in Health, Physical Education, and Recreation,* Prentice-Hall, Englewood Cliffs, N.J., 1968.

Way, Ronald L., *Ontario's Niagara Parks,* Niagara Parks Commission, Niagara Falls, Ontario, 1960.

Weir, I. G., ed., *Parks: A Manual of Municipal and County Parks,* A. S. Barnes & Co., New York, 1928.

Yukic, Thomas S., *Fundamentals of Recreation,* Harper & Row, New York, 1963.

Zeigler, Earle F., ed., *History of Physical Education and Sport,* Prentice-Hall, Englewood Cliffs, N.J., 1979.

Zeigler, Joseph Wesley, *Regional Theatre: The Revolutionary Stage,* Univ. of Minnesota Press, 1973.

FACTORS AFFECTING RECREATION BEHAVIOR

Adler, Richard, and Douglass Cater, eds., *Television as a Cultural Force,* Praeger, New York, 1976.

Anderson, Nels, *Work and Leisure,* Glencoe Press, New York, 1961.

Cheek, Neil H., Jr., and William R. Burch, Jr., *The Social Organization of Leisure in Human Society,* Harper & Row, New York, 1976.

Cheek, Neil H., Jr., Donald R. Field, and Rabel J. Burdge, *Leisure and Recreation Places,* Ann Arbor Science Publishers, Ann Arbor, 1976.

Comstock, George, Steven Chaffee, Natan Katzman, Maxwell McCombs, and Donald Roberts, *Television and Human Behavior,* Columbia Univ. Press, New York, 1978.

de Grazia, Sebastian, *Of Time, Work and Leisure,* Doubleday-Anchor, Garden City, N.Y., 1962.

Dumazedier, Joffre, *Toward a Society of Leisure,* Free Press, New York, 1967.

———, *Sociology of Leisure,* Elsevier, New York, 1974.

Ellis, Michael J., *Why People Play,* Prentice-Hall, Englewood Cliffs, N.J., 1973.

Foundation Van Clé, *International Congress on Leisure Activities in the Industrial Society,* Foundation Van Clí, Antwerp, 1974.

Goldsen, Rose K., *The Show and Tell Machine: How Television Works and Works You Over,* Dial Press, New York, 1977.

Huizinga, Johan, Homo Ludens, *A Study of the Play Element in Culture,* Beacon Press, Boston, 1950.

Iso-Ahola, Seppo E., *The Social Psychology of Leisure and Recreation,* Wm. C. Brown, Dubuque, Iowa, 1980.

Iso-Ahola, Seppo E., ed., *Social Psychological Perspectives on Leisure and Recreation,* Charles C. Thomas, Springfield, Ill., 1980.

Kaplan, Max, *Leisure in America: A Social Enquiry,* Wiley, New York, 1960.

———, *Leisure: Theory and Policy,* Wiley, New York, 1975.

Kaplan, Max, with C. Attias-Donfut, *Educational and Leisure-Time Activities of the Elderly,* European Centre for Leisure and Education, Prague, 1973.

Kaplan, Max, and Phillip Bosserman, eds., *Technology, Human Values and Leisure,* Abingdon Press, Nashville, 1972.

Kaplan, Stephen, and Rachel, eds., *Humanscape: Environments for People,* Duxbury Press, North Scituate, Mass., 1978.

Katz, Elihu, and Michael Gurevitch. *The Secularization of Leisure: Culture and Communication in Israel,* Faber & Faber, London, 1976.

Kleemeier, Robert W., ed., *Aging and Leisure,* Oxford Univ. Press, New York, 1961.

Lee, Robert, *Religion and Leisure in America: A Study in Four Dimensions,* Abingdon Press, Nashville, 1964.

Levy, Joseph, *Play Behaviour: A Person-Environment Interaction Model,* Wiley, New York, 1978.

Little (Arthur D.) Inc., *Tourism and Recreation: A State-of-the-Art Study,* U.S. Department of Commerce, U.S. Government Printing Office, Washington, D.C., 1967.

Loy, John W., Barry D. McPherson, and Gerald Kenyon, *Sport and Social Systems: A Guide to the Analysis, Problems, and Literature,* Addison-Wesley, Reading, Mass., 1978.

Matley, Ian M., *The Geography of International Tourism,* Association of American Geographers, Washington, D.C., 1976.

Millar, Susanna, *The Psychology of Play,* Penguin Books, Baltimore, 1968.

Neulinger, John, *The Psychology of Leisure: Research Approaches to the Study of Leisure,* Charles C. Thomas, Springfield, Ill., 1978.

Neumeyer, Martin H., and Esther S. Neumeyer, *Leisure and Recreation: A Study of Leisure and Recreation in Their Sociological Aspects,* 3rd ed., Ronald, New York, 1958.

Oglesby, Carole A., *Women and Sport: From Myth to Reality,* Lea & Febiger, Philadelphia, 1978.

Parker, Stanley Robert, *The Sociology of Leisure,* Allen & Unwin, London, 1976.

Poor, Riva, ed., *4 days, 40 hours,* Bursk and Poor Publishing, Cambridge, Mass., 1970.

Rapoport, Rhona, and Robert N. Rapoport, *Leisure and the Family Life Cycle,* Routledge & Kegan Paul, Boston, 1975.

Robbins, Florence Greenhoe, *The Sociology of Play, Recreation, and Leisure Time,* Wm. C. Brown, Dubuque, Iowa, 1955.

Roberts, Kenneth, *Leisure,* Longman Green, London, 1970.

———, *Contemporary Society and the Growth of Leisure,* Longman Green, London, 1978.

Robinson, J. P., *How Americans Use Time,* Praeger, New York, 1977.

Romney, G. Ott, *Off the Job Living: A Modern Concept of Recreation and Its Place in the Postwar World,* McGrath Publishing Co. and National Recreation and Park Association, Washington, D.C., 1972.

Rooney, John F., Jr., *A Geography of American Sport: From Cabin Creek to Anaheim,* Addison-Wesley, Reading, Mass., 1974.

Sapora, Allen V., and Elmer D. Mitchell, *The Theory of Play and Recreation,* 3rd ed., Ronald, New York, 1961.

Shapiro, Stephen A., and Alan J. Tuckman, *Time Off,* Doubleday-Anchor, Garden City, N.Y., 1978.

Slavson, Samuel Richard, *Recreation and the Total Personality,* Association Press, New York, 1946.

Smigel, Erwin O., *Work and Leisure: A Contemporary Social Problem,* College & University Press, New Haven, Conn., 1963.

Sports Council and Social Science Research Council, *Public Disorder and Sporting Events,* Gavin Martin, London, 1978.

Stebbins, Robert A., *Amateurs: On the Margin Between Work and Leisure,* Sage Publications, Beverly Hills, Calif., 1979.

Szalai, Alexander, *The Use of Time: Daily Activities of Urban and Suburban Populations in Twelve Countries,* Mouton, The Hague, 1972.

Tuan, Yi-Fu, *Topophilia: A Study of Environmental Perception, Attitudes, and Values,* Prentice-Hall, Englewood Cliffs, N.J., 1974.

Tupper, Margo, *No Place To Play,* Chilton Books, Philadelphia, 1966.

Twin, Stephanie L., *Out of the Bleachers,* The Feminist Press, Old Westbury, N.Y., 1979.

U.S. Congress, Outdoor Recreation Resources Review Commission, *Study Reports Nos. 1 through 27* (see listing of titles on pp. 199–203 in *Outdoor Recreation for America*), U.S. Government Printing Office, Washington, D.C., 1962.

Vickerman, Roger William, *The Economics of Leisure and Recreation,* Macmillan, London, 1975.

Winn, Marie, *The Plug-in Drug,* Viking, New York, 1977.

Wurman, Richard Saul, *The Nature of Recreation,* MIT Press, Cambridge, Mass., 1972.

Zehner, Robert B., *Indicators of the Quality of Life in New Communities,* Ballinger, Cambridge, Mass., 1978.

Zeigler, Earle F., *Physical Education and Sport Philsophy,* Prentice-Hall, Englewood Cliffs, N.J., 1977.

RECREATION RESOURCES

American Association of Museums, *America's Museums: The Belmont Report* (Report to the Federal Council on the Arts and the Humanities), American Association of Museums, Washington, D.C., 1969.

Barlowe, Raleigh, *Land Resource Economics: The Economics of Real Estate,* 3rd ed., Prentice-Hall, Englewood Cliffs, N.J., 1979.

Brockman, C. Frank, and Lawrence C. Merriman, Jr., *Recreational Use of Wild Lands,* McGraw-Hill, New York, 1979.

Carnegie Corporation of New York, *A Public Trust: The Landmark Report of the Carnegie Commission on the Future of Public Broadcasting,* Bantam Books, New York, 1979.

Clawson, Marion, *America's Land and Its Uses,* Johns Hopkins Press, Baltimore, 1972.

Clawson, Marion, and Jack L. Knetsch, *Economics of Outdoor Recreation,* Johns Hopkins Press, Baltimore, 1966.

Conservation Foundation, *National Parks for the Future: An Appraisal of the National Parks as They Begin Their Second Century in a Changing America,* Conservation Foundation, Washington, D.C., 1972.

Dace, Wallace, *Proposal for a National Theater,* Richards Rosen Press, New York, 1978.

Dunn, Diana R., *Open Space and Recreation Opportunity in America's Inner Cities,* U.S. Department of Housing and Urban Development, Washington, D.C., 1974.

Ezersky, Eugene M., and P. Richard Theibert, *Facilities in Sports and Physical Education,* C. V. Mosby, St. Louis, 1976.

Finlay, Ian, *Priceless Heritage: The Future of Museums,* Faber & Faber, London, 1977.

Friedberg, M. Paul, and Ellen P. Berkeley, *Play and Interplay: A Manifesto for New Design in Urban Recreational Environment,* Macmillan, New York, 1970.

Gabrielsen, M. A., *Sports and Recreation Facilities for School and Community,* Prentice-Hall, Englewood Cliffs, N.J., 1958.

Hahn, Emily, *Animal Gardens,* Doubleday, Garden City, N.Y., 1967.

Harvey, Emily Dennis, and Bernard Friedberg, eds., *A Museum for the People, A report of proceedings at the seminar on neighborhood museums, held Nov. 20, 21, 22, 1969, at MUSE, the Bedford Lincoln Neighborhood Museum in Brooklyn, New York,* Arno Press, New York, 1971.

Head, Sydney W., *Broadcasting in America, A Survey of Television and Radio,* 3rd ed., Houghton Mifflin, Boston, 1976.

International Council of Museums, *The Museum in the Service of Man: Today and Tomorrow,* Papers from the Ninth General Conference of ICOM, Paris, 1971.

International Union for Conservation of Nature and Natural Resources, *Proceedings of a Regional Meeting on the Creation of a Coordinated System of National Parks and Reserves in Eastern Africa,* IUCN, Switzerland, 1976.

Johnson, Elvin R., *Park Resources for Recreation,* Charles E. Merrill, Columbus, Ohio, 1972.

Johnson, Warren A., *Public Parks on Private Land in England and Wales,* Johns Hopkins Press, Baltimore, 1971.

Kirchshofer, Rosh, ed., *The World of Zoos,* Viking, New York, 1968.

Livingston, Bernard, *Zoo: Animals, People, Places,* Arbor House, New York, 1974.

Lowry, W. McNeil, ed., and American Assembly, Columbia University, *The Performing Arts and American Society,* Prentice-Hall, Englewood Cliffs, N.J., 1978.

MacCloskey, Monro, *Our National Attic,* Richards Rosen Press, New York, 1968.

Mathews, Virginia H., *Libraries for Today and Tomorrow,* Doubleday, Garden City, N.Y., 1976.

Miller, Peggy L., *Creative Outdoor Play Areas,* Prentice-Hall, Englewood Cliffs, N.J., 1972.

Patmore, J. Allan, *Land and Leisure in England and Wales,* David & Charles, Newton Abbot, Devon, 1970.

Peach, W. N., and Constantin, James A., *Zimmerman's World Resources and Industries,* 3rd ed., Harper &

Row, New York, 1972.

Perrin, Richard W. E., *Outdoor Museums,* Milwaukee Public Museum Publication, Milwaukee, 1975.

Reische, Diana, ed., *The Performing Arts in America,* H. W. Wilson, New York, 1973.

Rosenberg, Bernard, and David Manning White, *Mass Culture: The Popular Arts in America,* Free Press, Glencoe, Ill., 1957.

Simmons, I. G., *Rural Recreation in the Industrial World,* Halsted Press, New York, 1975.

Smith, Anthony, *Animals on View: An Illustrated Guide to Britain's Safari Parks, Zoos, Aquariums, and Bird Gardens,* Weidenfeld and Nicolson, London, 1977.

Smith, Clodus T., Lloyd E. Partain, and James R. Champlin, 2nd ed., *Rural Recreation for Profit,* Interstate Printers & Publishers, Danville, Ill., 1968.

Strahler, Arthur N., and Alan H. Strahler, *Modern Physical Geography,* Wiley, New York, 1978.

Tilden, Freeman, *The State Parks, Their Meaning in American Life,* Alfred A. Knopf, New York, 1962.

United Nations Educational, Scientific, and Cultural Organization, *Museums, Imagination and Education,* UNESCO, Paris, 1973.

U.S. Department of the Interior, *Quest for Quality,* U.S. Government Printing Office, Washington, D.C., 1965.

Wittlin, Alma S., *Museums: In Search of a Usable Future,* MIT Press, Cambridge, Mass., 1970.

Zook, Nicholas, *Museum Villages USA,* Barre Publishing, Barre, Mass., 1971.

GENERAL ADMINISTRATION

Appenzeller, Herb, *Athletics and the Law,* Michie Co., Charlottesville, Va., 1975.

Artz, Robert M., and Hubert Bermont, eds., *Guide to New Approaches to Financing Parks and Recreation,* Acropolis Books, Washington, D.C., 1970.

Bannon, Joseph J., and Edward H. Storey, *Guidelines for Recreation and Park Systems,* Univ. of Illinois, Urbana, 1970.

Bucher, Charles A., *Administration of Physical Education and Athletic Programs,* 7th ed., C. V. Mosby, St. Louis, 1979.

Burdick, John M., *Recreation in the Cities: Who Gains from Federal Aid?,* Center for Growth Alternatives, Washington, D.C., 1975.

Colgate, John A., *Administration of Intramural and Recreational Activities: Everyone Can Participate,* Wiley, New York, 1978.

Ford Foundation, *The Finances of the Performing Arts, A Survey of 166 Professional Nonprofit Resident Theaters, Operas, Symphonies, Ballets, and Modern Dance Companies,* Ford Foundation, New York, 1974.

Hines, Thomas. I., ed., *Revenue Sources in Recreation and Park Management,* National Recreation and Park Association, Washington, D.C., n.d.

Hjelte, George, and Jay S. Shivers, *Public Administration of Recreational Services,* 2nd ed., Lea & Febiger, Philadelphia, 1978.

Howard, Dennis, and John L. Crompton, *Financing, Managing and Marketing Recreation and Park Resources,* Wm. C. Brown, Dubuque, Iowa, 1980.

Hyatt, Ronald W., *Intramural Sports: Organization and Administration,* C. V. Mosby, St. Louis, 1977.

Kraus, Richard G., and Joseph E. Curtis, *Creative Administration in Recreation and Parks,* 2nd ed., C. V. Mosby, St. Louis, 1977.

Meyer, Harold D., and Charles K. Brightbill, *Recreation Administration: A Guide to Its Practices,* Prentice-Hall, Englewood Cliffs, N.J., 1956.

Mueller, Pat, and John W. Reznik, *Intramural-recreational Sports: Programming and Administration,* 5th ed., Wiley, New York, 1979.

O'Morrow, Gerald S., ed., *Administration of Activity Therapy Service,* Charles C. Thomas, Springfield, Ill., 1976.

Reynolds, Jesse A., and Marion N. Hormachea, *Public Recreation Administration,* Reston Publishing, Reston, Va., 1976.

Rodney, Lynn S., *Administration of Public Recreation,* Ronald, New York, 1964.

Throsby, C. D., and G. A. Withers, *The Economics of the Performing Arts,* St. Martin's Press, New York, 1979.

van der Smissen, Betty, *Legal Liability of Cities and Schools for Injuries in Recreation and Parks,* W. H. Anderson, Cincinnati, Ohio, 1968.

Voltmer, Edward F., Arthur A. Esslinger, Betty Foster McCue, and Kenneth G. Tillman, *The Organization and Administration of Physical Education,* Prentice-Hall, Englewood Cliffs, N.J., 1979.

Weimer, David L., *Private Funds for Parks and Recreation,* Playground Corp. of America, Long Island City, N.Y., 1969.

RESEARCH, PLANNING, AND DESIGN

American Alliance for Health, Physical Education and Recreation, *What Recreation Research Says to the Practitioner,* AAHPER, Washington, D.C., 1975.

American Alliance for Health, Physical Education, Recreation, and Dance, *Planning Facilities for Athletics, Physical Education and Recreation,* AAHPERD and The Athletic Institute, Washington, D.C., 1980.

Appleton, Ian, ed., *Leisure Research and Policy,* Scottish Academic Press, Edinburgh, 1974.

Architectural Record (editors of), *Places for People: Hotels, Motels, Restaurants, Bars, Clubs, Community Recreation Facilities, Camps, Parks, Plazas, Playgrounds: Examples of Outstanding Achievement,*

McGraw-Hill, New York, 1976.

Athletic Institute, *Planning Areas and Facilities for Health, Physical Education and Recreation,* Athletic Institute, Chicago, 1966.

Baker, Mark Lee, Stephen G. Gang, and Gerald S. O'Morrow, *Prototypical Park Design, Access for the Handicapped,* Univ. of Georgia, Athens, 1979.

Bannon, Joseph J., *Leisure Resources: Its Comprehensive Planning,* Prentice-Hall, Englewood Cliffs, N.J., 1976.

Baud-Bouy, Manuel, and Fred Lawson, *Tourism and Recreation Development,* CBI Publishing, Boston, 1977.

Buechner, Robert D., ed., *National Park Recreation and Open Space Standards,* National Recreation and Park Association, Arlington, Va., 1970.

Burton, Thomas L., *Experiments in Recreation Research,* Allen & Unwin, London, 1971.

Burton, Thomas L., ed., *Recreation Research and Planning: A Symposium,* Allen & Unwin, London, 1970.

Burton, Thomas L., and P. A. Noad, *Recreation Research Methods: A Review of Recent Studies,* Univ. of Birmingham, Alabama, 1968.

Butler, George D., *Recreation Areas: Their Design and Equipment,* 2nd ed., Ronald, New York, 1958.

Christiansen, Monty I., *Park Planning Handbook: Fundamentals of Physical Planning for Parks and Recreation Areas,* Wiley, New York, 1977.

Clarke, David H., and H. Harrison Clarke, *Research Processes in Physical Education, Recreation, and Health,* Prentice-Hall, Englewood Cliffs, N.J., 1970.

Coppock, J. Terry, and Brian S. Duffield, *Recreation in the Countryside: A Spatial Analysis,* St. Martin's Press, New York, 1975.

Dattner, Richard, *Design for Play,* Van Nostrand Reinhold, New York, 1969.

Driver, B. L., ed., *Elements of Outdoor Recreation Planning,* Univ. of Michigan Press, Ann Arbor, 1975.

Fairbrother, Nan, *New Lives, New Landscapes: Planning for the 21st Century,* Alfred A. Knopf, New York, 1970.

Gearing, Charles E., William W. Swart, and Turgut Var, eds., *Planning for Tourism Development: Quantitative Approaches,* Praeger, New York, 1976.

Gold, Seymour M., *Urban Recreation Planning,* Lea & Febiger, Philadelphia, 1973.

Guggenheimer, Elinor C., *Planning for Parks and Recreation Needs in Urban Areas,* Twayne Publishers, New York, 1969.

Hatry, Harry P., and Diana R. Dunn, *Measuring the Effectiveness of Local Government Services: Recreation,* Urban Institute, Washington, D.C., 1971.

Heaton, Israel C., and Clark T. Thorstenson, *Planning for Social Recreation,* Houghton Mifflin, Boston, 1978.

Hubbard, Alfred, *Research Methods in Health, Physical Education, and Recreation,* 3rd ed., American Association for Health, Physical Education and Recreation, Washington, D.C., 1973.

Jubenville, Alan, *Outdoor Recreation Planning,* Saunders, Philadelphia, 1976.

Knetsch, Jack L., *Outdoor Recreation and Water Resources Planning,* American Geophysical Union, Washington, D.C., 1974.

Ledermann, Alfred, and Alfred Trachsel, *Creative Playgrounds and Recreation Centers,* rev. ed., Praeger, New York, 1968.

National Association of State Park Directors and the Missouri Division of Parks and Recreation, *State Park Statistics—1975,* National Recreation and Park Association, Arlington, Va., 1977.

Newcomb, Robert M., *Planning the Past: Historical Landscape Resources and Recreation,* Archon Books, Hamden, Conn., 1979.

Ontario Research Council on Leisure, *Analysis Methods and Techniques for Recreation Research and Leisure Studies,* Ontario Research Council on Leisure, Toronto, 1977.

Pelegrino, Donald A., *Research Methods for Recreation and Leisure: A Theoretical and Practical Guide,* Wm. C. Brown, Dubuque, Iowa, 1979.

Rouard, Marguerite, and Jacques Simon, *Children's Play Spaces: From Sandbox to Adventure Playground,* Overlook Press, Woodstock, N.Y., 1977.

Rutledge, Albert J., *Anatomy of a Park: The Essentials of Recreation Area Planning and Design,* McGraw-Hill, New York, 1971.

Shivers, Jay S., and George Hjelte, *Planning Recreational Places,* Fairleigh Dickinson Univ. Press, Rutherford, N.J., 1971.

U. S. Department of the Interior, Bureau of Outdoor Recreation, *Outdoor Recreation—A Legacy for America,* U.S. Government Printing Office, Washington, D.C., 1973.

U.S. Department of the Interior, Heritage Conservation and Recreation Service, *A Guide to Designing Accessible Outdoor Recreation Facilities,* U.S. Government Printing Office, Washington, D.C., 1980.

van der Smissen, Betty, ed., *Recreation Research,* American Association for Health, Physical Education and Recreation and National Recreation and Park Association, Washington, D.C., 1966.

Ward, Colin, ed., *Vandalism,* Architectural Press, London 1973.

Whitaker, Ben, and Kenneth Browne, *Parks for People,* Shocken Books, New York, 1973.

Williams, Wayne R., *Recreation Places,* Teinhold, New York, 1958.

RESOURCE MANAGEMENT AND PROGRAMMING

Amary, Issam B., *Creative Recreation for the Mentally Retarded,* Charles C. Thomas, Springfield, Ill., 1975.

American Association for Health, Physical Education and Recreation, *Programming for the Mentally Retarded,* AAHPER, Washington, D.C., 1968.

American Association of Museums, *Museums: Their New Audience* (a report to the Department of Housing and Urban Development), American Association of Museums, Washington, D.C., 1972.

American Camping Association, *Camp Standards with Interpretations,* American Camping Association, Martinsville, Indiana, 1976.

Anderson, Dorothy H., Earl C. Leatherberry, and David W. Lime, *An Annotated Bibliography on River Recreation,* U.S. Department of Agriculture, Forest Service, North Central Forest Experiment Station, St. Paul, Minn., 1978.

Anderson, J. M., *Industrial Recreation,* McGraw-Hill, New York, 1955.

Arnold, Nellie D., *The Interrelated Arts in Leisure,* C. V. Mosby, St. Louis, 1976.

Athletic Institute, *The Recreation Program,* rev. ed., Athletic Institute, Chicago, 1966.

Avedon, Elliott M., *Therapeutic Recreation Service: An Applied Behavioral Science Approach,* Prentice-Hall, Englewood Cliffs, N.J., 1974.

Avedon, Elliott M., and Frances B. Arje, *Socio-Recreative Programming for the Retarded,* Columbia Univ. Press, New York, 1964.

Bannon, Joseph J., *Problem Solving in Recreation and Parks,* 2nd ed., Prentice-Hall, Englewood Cliffs, N.J., 1980.

Bannon, Joseph J., ed., *Outreach: Extending Community Services in Urban Areas,* Charles C. Thomas, Springfield, Ill., 1973.

Bosselman, Fred P., *In the Wake of the Tourist: Managing Special Places in Eight Countries,* Conservation Foundation, Washington, D.C., 1978.

Brightbill, Charles K., and Tony A. Mobley, *Educating for Leisure-centered Living,* 2nd ed., Wiley, New York, 1977.

Burby, Raymond J., III, *Recreation and Leisure in New Communities,* Ballinger, Cambridge, Mass., 1978.

Carlson, Bernice W., and David R. Ginglend, *Recreation for the Retarded Teenager and Young Adult,* Abingdon Press, Nashville, 1968.

Chapman, Frederick M., *Recreation Activities for the Handicapped,* Ronald, New York, 1960.

Coplan, Kate, and Edwin Castagna, eds., *The Library Reaches Out: Reports on Library Service and Community Relations by Some Leading American Librarians,* Oceana Publications, New York, 1965.

Corbin, H. Dan, *Recreation Leadership,* 3rd ed., Prentice-Hall, Englewood Cliffs, N.J., 1970.

Corbin, H. Dan, and William J. Tait, *Education for Leisure,* Prentice-Hall, Englewood Cliffs, N.J., 1973.

Danford, Howard G., revised by Max Shirley, *Creative Leadership in Recreation,* 2nd ed., Allyn and Bacon, Boston, 1970.

Edginton, Christopher R., and John G. Williams, *Productive Management of Leisure Service Organizations: A Behavioral Approach,* Wiley, New York, 1978.

Epperson, Arlin F., Peter A. Witt, and Gerald Hitzhusen, eds., *Leisure Counseling: An Aspect of Leisure Education,* Charles C. Thomas, Springfield, Ill., 1977.

Fain, Gerald S., and Gerald L. Hitzhusen, eds., *Therapeutic Recreation: State of the Art,* National Recreation and Park Association, Arlington, Va., 1977.

Farrell, Patricia, and Herberta M. Lundegren, *The Process of Recreation Programming: Theory and Technique,* Wiley, New York, 1978.

Gunn, Scout Lee, and Carol Ann Peterson, *Therapeutic Recreation Program Design: Principles and Procedures,* Prentice-Hall, Englewood Cliffs, N.J., 1978.

Hall, J. Tillman, *School Recreation: Its Organization, Supervision, and Administration,* Wm. C. Brown, Dubuque, Iowa, 1966.

Hendee, John C., George H. Stankey, and Robert C. Lucas, *Wilderness Management,* U.S. Department of Agriculture, Washington, D.C., 1978.

Henkel, Donald, and Geoffrey C. Godbey, *Parks, Recreation, and Leisure Services—Employment in the Public Sector: Status and Trends,* National Recreation and Park Association, Arlington, Va., 1977.

Hoffman, Adeline M., *The Daily Needs and Interests of Older People,* Charles C. Thomas, Springfield, Ill., 1976.

Howard, Dennis, and John L. Crompton, *Financing, Managing and Marketing Recreation and Park Resources,* Wm. C. Brown, Dubuque, Iowa, 1980.

Hunt, Valerie V., *Recreation for the Handicapped,* Prentice-Hall, Englewood Cliffs, N.J., 1958.

Hyatt, Ronald W., *Intramural Sports: Organization and Administration,* C. V. Mosby, St. Louis, 1977.

Jubenville, Alan, *Outdoor Recreation Management,* Saunders, Philadelphia, 1978.

Kaplan, Max, *Leisure, Lifestyle and Lifespan: Directions for Gerontology,* Saunders, Philadelphia, 1978.

———, *Leisure: Perspectives on Education and Policy,* National Education Association of the United States, Washington, D.C., 1978.

Kleindienst, Viola K., and Arthur Weston, *The Recreational Sports Program: Schools . . . Colleges . . . Communities,* Prentice-Hall, Englewood Cliffs, N.J., 1978.

Kraus, Richard G., *Recreation Leader's Handbook,* McGraw-Hill, New York, 1955.

———, *Recreation and the Schools: Guides to Effective Practices in Leisure Education and Community Recreation Sponsorship,* Macmillan, New York, 1964.

———, *Social Recreation: A Group Dynamics Approach,* C. V. Mosby, St. Louis, 1979.

Kraus, Richard G., and Barbara J. Bates, *Recreation Leadership and Supervision: Guidelines for Professional Development,* Saunders, Philadelphia, 1975.

Lutzin, Sidney, G., ed., *Managing Municipal Leisure Services,* International City Management Association, Washington, D.C., 1980.

McCullagh, James C., *Ways to Play: Recreation Alternatives,* Rodale Press, Emaus, Pa., 1978.

Meyer, Harold D., Charles K. Brightbill, and H. Douglas Sessoms, *Community Recreation: A Guide to Its Organization,* 4th ed., Prentice-Hall, Englewood Cliffs, N.J., 1969.

Michel, Donald E., *Music Therapy: An Introduction to Therapy and Special Education Through Music,* Charles C. Thomas, Springfield, Ill., 1977.

Moran, Joan M., *Leisure Activities for the Mature Adult,* Burgess, Minn., 1979.

Mueller, Pat, and John W. Reznik, *Intramural-recreational Sports: Programming and Administration,* 5th ed., Wiley, New York, 1979.

Mundy, Jean, and Linda Odum, *Leisure Education: Theory and Practice,* Wiley, New York, 1979.

Murphy, James F., *Recreation and Leisure Service: A Humanistic Perspective,* Wm. C. Brown, Dubuque, Iowa, 1975.

Murphy, James F., and Dennis R. Howard, *Delivery of Community Leisure Services: An Holistic Approach,* Lea & Febiger, Philadelphia, 1977.

Murphy, James F., John G. Williams, E. William Niepoth, and Paul D. Brown, *Leisure Service Delivery System: A Modern Perspective,* Lea & Febiger, Philadelphia, 1973.

National Recreation and Park Association, *Creative Recreation Programming Handbook,* NRPA, Arlington, Va., 1977.

Neal, Larry L., ed., *Recreation's Role in the Rehabilitation of the Mentally Retarded,* Univ. of Oregon Press, Eugene, 1970.

Nesbitt, John A., Paul D. Brown, and James F. Murphy, eds., *Recreation and Leisure Service for the Disadvantaged,* Lea & Febiger, Philadelphia, 1970.

Newcomb, Robert M., *Planning the Past: Historical Landscape Resources and Recreation,* Archon Books, Hamden, Conn., 1979.

Olszowy, Damon R., *Horticulture for the Disabled and Disadvantaged,* Charles C. Thomas, Springfield, Ill., 1977.

Pomeroy, Janet, *Recreation for the Physically Handicapped,* Macmillan, New York, 1964.

Robinson, Frank M., Jr., ed., *Therapeutic Re-creation: Ideas and Experiences,* Charles C. Thomas, Springfield, Ill., 1974.

Sharpe, Grant W., *Interpreting the Environment,* Wiley, New York, 1976.

Shivers, Jay S., *Camping: Administration, Counseling, Programming,* Appleton-Century-Crofts, New York, 1971.

———, *Essentials of Recreational Services,* Lea & Febiger, Philadelphia, 1978.

Shivers, Jay S., and Clarence R. Calder, *Recreational Crafts: Programming and Instructional Techniques,* McGraw-Hill, New York, 1974.

Shivers, Jay S., and Hollis F. Fait, *Therapeutic and Adapted Recreational Services,* Lea & Febiger, Philadelphia, 1975.

———, *Recreational Service for the Aging,* Lea & Febiger, Philadelphia, 1980.

Smith, Julian W., Reynold E. Carlson, George W. Donaldson, and Hugh B. Masters, *Outdoor Education,* 2nd ed., Prentice-Hall, Englewood Cliffs, N.J., 1972.

Stein, Thomas A., and H. Douglas Sessoms, *Recreation and Special Populations,* Holbrook Press, Boston, 1977.

Sterle, David E., and Mary R. Duncan, *Supervision of Leisure Service,* San Diego State Univ. Press, San Diego, 1973.

Sternloff, Robert E., and M. Roger Warren, *Park and Recreation Maintenance Management,* Holbrook Press, Boston, 1977.

Stevens, Ardis, *Fun is Therapeutic: A Recreation Book to Help Therapeutic Recreation Leaders by People Who Are Leading Recreation,* Charles C. Thomas, Springfield, Ill., 1972.

Straub, William F., *The Lifetime Sports-Oriented Physical Education Program,* Prentice-Hall, Englewood Cliffs, N.J., 1976.

Theobald, William F., *Evaluation of Recreation and Park Programs,* Wiley, New York, 1979.

Tilden, Freeman, *Interpreting Our Heritage,* Univ. of North Carolina Press, Chapel Hill, 1967.

Tillman, Albert A., *The Program Book for Recreation Professionals,* National Press Books, Palo Alto, Calif., 1973.

U.S. Department of the Interior, Bureau of Outdoor Recreation, *How Effective Are Your Community Recreation Services?,* U.S. Government Printing Office, Washington, D.C., 1973.

———, *Federal Assistance in Outdoor Recreation,* U.S. Government Printing Office, Washington, D.C., 1975.

U.S. Department of Agriculture, Forest Service, *Proceedings: River Recreation Management and Research Symposium,* U.S. Government Printing Office, Washington, D.C., 1977.

U.S. Department of the Interior, *National Urban Recreation Study,* U.S. Government Printing Office, Washington, D.C., 1978.

van der Smissen, Betty, *Evaluation and Self Study of Public Recreation and Park Agencies: A Guide with Standards and Evaluative Criteria,* National Recreation and Park Association, Arlington, Va., 1972.

van der Smissen, Betty, and Helen Knierim, *Fitness and Fun through Recreational Sports and Games,* Burgess, Minneapolis, Minn., 1964.

Vannier, Maryhelen, *Recreation Leadership,* 3rd ed., Lea & Febiger, Philadelphia, 1977.

Young, George, *Tourism: Blessing or Blight?,* Penguin Books, Harmondsworth, Middlesex, 1973.

Zehnder, Leonard E., *Florida's Disney World: Promises and Problems,* Peninsular Publishing, Tallahassee, 1975.

Zeigler, Earle F., *Issues in North American Sport amd Physical Education,* AAHPER, Washington, D.C., 1979.

COLLECTIONS OF GENERAL READINGS

Fischer, David W., John E. Lewis, and George B. Priddle, *Land and Leisure: Concepts and Methods in Outdoor Recreation,* Maaroufa Press, Chicago, 1974.

Goodale, Thomas L., and Peter A. Witt, eds., *Recreation and Leisure: Issues in an Era of Change,* Venture Publishing, State College, Pa., 1980.

Gray, David E., and Donald A. Pelegrino, *Reflections on the Recreation and Park Movement,* Wm. C. Brown, Dubuque, Iowa, 1973.

Jensen, Clayne R., and Clark T. Thorstenson, *Issues in Outdoor Recreation,* 2nd ed., Burgess, Minneapolis, Minn., 1977.

Lavery, Patrick, eds., *Recreational Geography,* Halsted Press, Wiley, New York, 1974.

Loy, John W. Jr., and Gerald S. Kenyon, eds., *Sport, Culture, and Society,* Macmillan, New York, 1969.

Smith, Michael A., Stanley Parker, and Cyril S. Smith, eds., *Leisure and Society in Britain,* Allen Lane, London, 1973.

Van Doren, Carlton S., George B. Priddle, and John E. Lewis, eds., *Land and Leisure: Concepts and Methods in Outdoor Recreation,* 2nd ed., Maaroufa Press, Chicago, 1979.

RECREATION CAREERS

American Alliance for Health, Physical Education, Recreation, and Dance, *Opportunities in Recreation and Leisure,* AAHPERD, Washington, D.C., 1978.

Jensen, Clayne R., *Recreation and Leisure Time Careers,* Vocational Guidance Manuals, Louisville, Ky., 1976.

Photo Credits

15.11: Courtesy Mexican National Tourist Council. 15.13: Sepp Seitz/Woodfin Camp. 15.14: Fred R. Conrad/The New York Times. 15.15: Bill Hewitt/United Press International.

Chapter 16

16.1: Jack Buxbaum/JFK Center, Washington, D.C. 16.2: Advertisement Courtesy of Texaco, Inc. 16.3: Frederick Ohringer. 16.4: David Talbot/Actors Theatre of Louisville. 16.5: Fred Thumhart. 16.6: Joel Gordon. 16.7: William Baker for WGBH-Boston. 16.8: Michael Chubb/Recreation Resource Consultant. 16.9: DeSazo Kay Reese & Associates. 16.10: © Zoological Society of San Diego 1980. 16.11: Marc & Evelyne Bern-heim/Woodfin Camp. 16.12: British Tourist Authority. 16.13: Photograph by Colonial Williamsburg. 16.14: © Walt Disney Productions Courtesy, American Library Association. 16.15: Fred Haitz. 16.16: Jim Anderson/Woodfin Camp.

Chapter 17

17.1: U.S. Forest Service. 17.2: Michael Chubb/Recreation Resource Consultant. 17.3 (top): Oakland County Parks & Recreation Commission; (bottom): East Bay Regional Park District. 17.4: Michael Chubb/Recreation Resource Consultant. 17.5: The Detroit News. 17.7: Ed Buryn/Jeroboam. 17.8: Halstead/Stewart, Detroit. 17.9: Courtesy, Horticulture Department of Clemson University, South Carolina.

Part Four Opener: Les Baxter/Toronto Harbor Commission.

Chapter 18

18.1: United Press International. 18.2: George Hall/Woodfin Camp. 18.3: Bob Krueger/Rapho-Photo Researchers. 18.4: Photo courtesy San Antonio Convention and Visitors Bureau. 18.5: Joel Gordon. 18.6: Bureau of Land Management U.S. Department of the Interior. 18.7: M. Woodbridge Williams/National Park Service. 18.8: Frederick D. Bodin/Stock, Boston. 18.9: Courtesy Iberia International Airlines of Spain. 18.10: Bruce Ojard/St. Louis County Heritage and Arts Center. 18.11: Bob Clay/Jeroboam. 18.12: Joan Menschenfreund. 18.13: Jane Scherr/ICON. 18.14: Timothy Eagan/Woodfin Camp.

INDEX

(Page numbers in boldface denote a definition or basic description; (d)-discussion topic, (f)-figure (map, diagram, or photograph), (r)-further readings, (t)-table)

Carnegie, Andrew, 23, 24, 609
Carrying capacity, **292** (*see also* Recreation resources carrying capacity)
Carter, President Jimmy, 42, 43, 69, 70(f), 73, 668
Catholic Youth Organization (CYO), 348, 350–351
Cemeteries, recreation use of, 560
Central Park, New York City, 5(f), 23(t), **24–25, 25(f)**, 146–147, 164, 568(f), 572–573
Centre National d'Art et de Culture de Georges Pompidou (Centre Beaubourg), 594–595, 595(f)
Charter for Leisure, 49, 50(t)
Cheyenne, Wyoming, Parks and Recreation Department, 449, 450(t)
China, People's Republic of, 48, 69, 71, 128, 143, 167, 167(f), 168(f), 175, 176(f), 179, 280, 388
City and district park and recreation agencies, 423–424, 424(f) (*see also* Local and regional government recreation resources, kinds of)
Classification systems (*see* Recreation resources, classification of; Recreation activities, classification of)
Clawson, Marion, 35(t), 36, 287–288
Clawson's recreation resource classification, **287–288**, 288(t), 295(d)
Climate and weather, 153–154, **297**, 297–299, 303–307, 306(t), 469, 471, 473
    climatic hazards, 304, 305, 306(t)
    climatic regions, 298(f), 299–303, 300–301(t), 302(f), 303(f)
    impact on recreation, 298, 299, 300–301(t), 301–303, 303–306, 303(f), 304(f), 306(t), 396
    optimal recreation climate, 305, 307, 322(d)
    weather, effect on recreation, 1(f), 153–154, 299, 300–301(t), 303, 304, 305, 306(t), 307, 390–392, 395
Club Mediterranee, 395–396, 403
Coastal problems, 41(t), 42, 315, **662–664**, 663(f)
Colleges, as recreation resources, 546
    amenities for students, 546–547, 548–549
    sports facilities and spectator events, 269, 270(f), 546–548, 547(f)
    other amenities, 548, 605–606, 613
Colonial Williamsburg, 606–607, 607(f)

Colorado, recreation resources
    federal government resources, 463, 518, 533, 536, 537, 538, 543, 554, 601
    intermediate government resources, 469, 470(t), 471–474, 473(f), 474(t)
    other features, 391–392, 397, 575, 575(f)
Communist nations
    constitutions, 48–49
    cultural resources, 569–570
    factors affecting recreation participation, 120, 127–128, 167, 170, 210, 279
    recreation amenities, 69, 362–363, 395, 414
    spas and sanitariums, 395
    tourist facilities, 546
Community complexes, parks, playfields, 433
Community recreation center, 371–372, 373, 437(f), 438–439
Concessionaires, vendors, 375
Condominiums, 219–220, 220(f), **333**
Coney Island, 378, 378(f)
Connecticut, recreation resources, 385, 449–452, 532
Constitutions, national, 48–49
Conversations and writing letters, significance as a recreation activity, 225, 258, 261, 263, 264(f), **266**, 327, 329, 366, 367, 371, 372, 429, 431, 442
Cook County, Illinois, Forest Preserve District, 423, 424(f)
Corps of Engineers, U.S. Army, recreation facilities, 511(t), 512–513(f), 540–542, 541(f)
Correctional institutions, recreation resources, 55(f), 549–551
Country parks (*see* Great Britain)
Countryside Act and Commission (*see* Great Britain)
Countryside, use of term, 7
County park and recreation agencies, 27, 424–425
Cross-stimulation effect, 616
Cruise ships and cruises, 272–273, 397–399, 397(f)
Cultural and subcultural influences, effect on participation, 143–146, 208–209, 228(d), 329
    membership in religious organizations and political groups, 124–125(t), 209–210, 209(f), 222

minority ethnic and racial group membership, 210–211, 211(f), 371, 374
Cultural centers, 575, 576, 577–578
Cultural opportunities, recreational significance, 51, 52, 52(t), 61, 65, 66, 202, 203, 212, 269, 332, 342, 354–356, 367, 373, 373(f), 394, 400, 402–403, 410, 429, 431, 438, 439, 442, 448, 453, 458, 477, 483(t), 485–487, 489, 562, 563, 568, 568(f), 570, 571, 573, 584, 585, 590, 591, 593–594, 594–595, 595(f), 597–600, 598(f), 603, 604, 604(f), 605, 607(f), 611–612, 612–613, 614, 614(f), 640–641
Cultural resources (recreation), 562–564, 615–617, 617(d), 618(r)
    broadcast, recording, and film resources, 580 (*see also:* Film resources; Radio broadcasting systems; Recording industry; Television broadcasting systems)
    contribution of, 66, 71, 269, 562(f), 563, 593, 595, 597, 600, 603, 609, 612, 615–617, 617(d)
    development of an audience, 570–571, 593–594
    development of artists, 589–590
    means of support, 564
        government role, 76(t), 108, 566–567, 568, 588–589; federal government (U.S.), 32, 38(t), 567, 571, 577, 584, 588, 590, 596, 605; local governments (U.S.), 567–568, 602, 611–612, 614; state governments (U.S.), 567, 571, 599, 602, 605; other nations, 127–128, 569–570, 571, 581, 584, 588–589, 594–595, 597, 601, 603–604
        private sector contributions, 564–566, 565(f), 600, 605, 606, 608, 609, 614; corporations, 565–566, 565(f); foundations, 565; individuals, 564–565
    libraries, 23(t), 24, 32, 563, 609, 612–613, 618(r)
        public libraries, 609–612, 610(f), 614
    multipurpose centers, 613–614, 614(f)
    museums and exhibits, 448, 563, 590, 591(t), 618(r) (*see also:* Museums, commercial; Museums, private

private resources, 154, 162, 381, 383, 386–387, 388–389, 394–396, 398–399, 400, 401

tourism, 272, 279, 676

transportation, 163, 167, 169–170, 170(f), 172, 175, 176(f), 177–178, 178(f), 180, 181, 184, 186

other features, 101–102, 105–106, 653, 674

Evansville, Indiana, Department of Parks and Recreation, 449, 450(t), 451, 452–454

Exercise trail (*see* Parcourse)

External factors affecting recreation (*see* Participation, recreation)

Facility-units, definition of, **289–291**, 295(d)

Fads, 40, 141, 262, 274–276

Fairs, agricultural, 504, 642

Farm and industrial recreation resources

resources for employees, 103, 221, 361–363, 364(d), 613

resources used by the public, 107–108, 108(f), 357–360, 360(f), 364(d)

community programs, 360

farm resources, 155, 356–357

industrial lands, 357–359

industrial museums, 607–608

industrial tours, 359–360, 360(f)

Farms, ranches, and estates, use by paying guests, 383, 400–401

Fast-food establishments, 371, 408

Fauna, 320–322, 321(f), 401, 472(t), 473, 495, 498, 499–500, 503, 516–517, 526, 530, 531–532, 531(f), 534, 536, 538, 539

Film resources, 29, 30(t), 31(t), 32, 585

cultural aspects of films, 585, 587, 588–589

Fish Restoration and Management Act (Dingell-Johnson), 37, 624

Flexitime, 96–97, 221

Florida, recreation resources

cultural resources, 604–605, 606, 614, 614(f)

federal government resources, 516, 518, 521, 534, 536, 542, 664

local government resources, 449, 450(t), 451, 458–460, 459(f)

private resources, 377, 377(f), 379, 380(f), 382, 385, 396

tourism, 271, 272, 279, 280

other features, 119(f), 120, 123, 463, 489

Food and drink, recreation role of, 370–371, 375

bars and nightclubs, 373–375, 408

cafés and coffeehouses, 371–372, 408

fast-food establishments, 371, 408

refreshment services (concessionaires, vendors), 375

restaurants, full-service, 372–373, 373(f), 384, 411(r), 506(f)

Forest preserves or reserves, 27, 28, 30, 423, 424(f), 434, 449–451

Forest Preserve District of DuPage County, Illinois, 449–451

Forests (intermediate government), recreation use of, 497–498, 501, 508(d)

provincial forests, 501 (*see also* Ontario provincial forests)

state forests, 498–501, 499(t)

historical development of, 23(t), 27(t), **28**, 29, 30(t), 32, 36

(*see also:* Michigan, intermediate government resources; Pennsylvania, intermediate government resources)

4-H Clubs, 348–350

France, recreation resources

cultural resources, 594–595, 595(f), 615(f)

private resources, 369, 370(f), 383, 384, 386

other features, 18(f), 103, 167(t), 170, 170(f), 178, 252–260, 279, 435(f)

Free time, **7**, 253

Amount of, 28, 29, 30(t), 31(t), 35, 35(t), 38(t), 39, 41(t), 44(d), 96–100, 212, 225, 226, 227–228

Attitudes toward, 22, 144–145, 193–194

Fresh Air Fund, 352, 353(f)

Future of recreation, 701–702, 704(d), 705(r)

probable recreation patterns in the United States, 702–703

purgatory or paradise, 703–704

Gambling, 4, 6, 17, 19, 20, 26, 52(t), 54, 64, 68, 78(t), 88, 124(t), 127, 128(f), 135, 328, 344(f), 374, 385, 389, 397, 410, 691

Games, card, table, and other indoor,

significance as a recreation activity, 58, 202, 203, 225, **268–269**, 327, 328–329, 330(t), 366, 371, 373, 374, 377, 389, 438

Gardening and cultivation of house plants, significance as a recreation activity, 52(t), 62, 79, 202, 203, 223, 250, 263, 269, 328, 329, 330, 330(t), 331, 332–333

Gaston County, North Carolina, Recreation and Parks Department, 449, 450(t), 451

Georgia, recreation resources, 488, 539, 542, 548, 553, 648

Getaway resorts, 397

cruise ships, 397–399, 397(f)

Girls Clubs, 348, 350

Girl Scouts, 30(t), 348–349

Goals and lifestyles, effect on recreation participation, 142–143, 199, 201–203, 212–214, 221–222, 228(d)

Government involvement in recreation (*see:* Resources (recreation), publicly owned; Significance of recreation, degree of government involvement)

Government regulations and policies, 75, 76(t), 88, 98, 101, 104, 105, 108–110, **109(t)**, 117(d), 125–128, 128(f), 135, 136, 149, 154–155, 167, 201, 218, 219, 279, 325, 331, 335, 336, 357, 358–359, 398, 678 (*see also* Economic factors, government-imposed taxes, duties, licenses, and fees)

Grand Ole Opry, Nashville, 579–580

Great Britain, recreation resources

cultural resources, 574–575, 581, 604, 604(f)

history of recreation, 19(f), 27, 38(t), 425, 528

local government resources, 129(f), 425, 609

national government resources, 35(t), 129(f), 163(f), 248(f), 249(f), 355(f), 425, 463, 526–529, 527(f), 536–537, 581, 604, 604(f)

private resources, 19(f), 27(t), 129(f), 162, 332, 354, 355(f), 356, 373–374, 378–379, 382, 383, 388–389, 401, 528, 604

tourism, 95, 128–129, 129(f), 277, 278(f), 279, 280

transportation, 180, 181, 182, 182(f), 556

other features, 114, 126, 143, 276

traditions, rituals, customs, and habits, 97–98, 119, 128–130, 129(f), 150(d), 210, 226, 229(f), 230, 244, 558

Social status, desire for, effect on recreation participation, 95, 140–142, 230, 277–278, 370, 394, 615

Social trends and issues, recreation implications, 689
  employment trends and the struggle against poverty, 693
    conditions in the United States, 693–695; recreation implications, 695–696
  impact of inflation and recession, 690–691
    recreation implications, 691–693, 692(f)
  population trends and issues
    growth rates, worldwide, 696–697
    situation in the United States, 697; effect of changes in age structure of population, 699–700, 700(f); effect of changes in household composition, 701, 704(d); effect of changes in racial composition, 700–701; effect of larger population, 699; effect of movement of population, 699; immigration and its impact, 697–698

Social welfare organizations (see Quasi-public organizations)

Soils (see Surface materials)

South Africa, Union of, recreation resources, 27(t), 71–72, 146, 167, 167(t), 168(f), 175, 176(f), 279, 320, 321, 531–532, 531(f)

South Atlantic Region, U.S., 117, 276, 498, 499, 533

South Carolina, recreation resources, 468, 489, 489(f), 542, 647

South Dakota, recreation resources, 272, 518, 519, 542

Soviet Union, recreation resources, 112, 167, 167(t), 168(f), 175, 176(f), 179, 252–260, 277, 279, 395, 532, 546, 587–588, 603, 654

Spain, recreation resources, 130, 170, 170(f), 276, 279, 545, 677

Spare time, 7 (see also: Free time)

Spas and beauty resorts (see Resorts)

Special populations, 644–648 (see also: Activity programs, special population programs; Handicapped, recreation for)

Spectator events, 383–384, 385, 410

Sports and athletic clubs, 338–339, 340(f)

Sports events, recreation significance of, 32, 53(t), 62, 72, 75, 87, 203, 212, 229(f), 230, 260, 261, 269, 270(t), 270(f), 332, 374, 384, 385–386, 443, 445–446, 504, 506(f), 507, 547–548

Sports facilities, 326–327, 375, 376, 377, 384, 443, 506
  privately owned, commercial, 376–377, 384–386
  privately owned, noncommercial, 328–329, 331, 335–336, 338–339, 340(f), 342–343, 344–345, 350–351, 360–363
  publicly owned, 443–447, 506–507, 506(f)
    colleges, 546–549
    correctional institutions, 550–551
    health care institutions, 551–552

Sports, participation in, 24(f), 39, 40, 52, 52–53(t), 59, 60, 63, 79, 86(f), 87, 195, 196, 199, 202, 203, 212, 213, 222, 223, 258, 260, 261–262, 262(f), 263, 264(f), **267–268**, **268(t)**, 274, 275(f), 276, 329, 330(t), 335, 338–339, 340–341, 340(f), 366, 376–377, 390, 393, 394, 395–396, 397, 402, 409–410, 431, 432, 433, 434, 439, 442, 446, 455, 555

Sportsperson's clubs, 339

Sports resorts (see Resorts)

Squares and plazas, 19, 24, 26, 429–430, 430(f), 643(f)

Stadiums and arenas, 384–385, 443–446, 506–507, 506(f), 547–548

State forets (see Forests, intermediate government)

State park classifications, 469, 470(t), 475, 479, 480–481, 485, 491–492, 495

State parks, U.S., 464–466
  distribution, 466, 467(f)
  historical development, 23(t), 25, 27(t), 28, 29, 30(t), 31(t), 32, **33**, 35–36, 37–39, 38(t)
  nature and extent of facilities, 76, 466–469
(see also: California—; Colorado—; Kentucky—; Michigan—; New York—; Texas—; state park system)

Stores, department (see Malls, shopping and department stores)

Surface materials, 153, 291(f), 312–313

Sweden, recreation resources, 146, 170, 170(f), 588–589

Swimming, significance as a recreation activity, 53(t), 60, 63, 199, 203, 222, 223, 261–262, 263, 268, 274, 275(f), 309, 329, 330(t), 331, 335, 338, 339, 340(f), 358, 377, 377(f), 378, 379, 389, 390, 394, 397, 397(f), 400, 401, 402, 425, 433, 434, 439, 453, 457, 458, 463, 469, 473, 502

Symphony orchestras, 66, 563, 575, 575(f)

Television broadcasting systems, 35(t), 582–583, 584–585
  cultural aspects of programs, 584, 585, 616

Television, use as a recreation resource, 35(t), 52–53(t), 54, 56(f), 60, 64, 202, 203, 253, 256–257, 261, **263–264**, 264(f), 328, 366, 367, 374, 389, 547, 565, 580, 582–584, 585

Tennessee Valley Authority (U.S.), recreation use of projects, 511(t), 512–513(f), 543

Tennessee, recreation resources, 272, 466, 468, 516, 543, 544, 579, 605

Terrebonne Parish, Louisiana, Parks and Recreation Department, 449, 450(t)

Territories and residence, effect on recreation participation, 214, 292
  location of residence, 142, 217–219, 218(f), 220, 224–225, 225
  territories, 214–215, 448
    home territory, 194(f), 215–217, 216(f), 219, 291(f), 304(f)
    personal space, 215
  type of residence, 219–220, 220(f)
(see also: Personal recreation resources, primary residence resources)

Texas, recreation resources, 117, 220, 271, 272, 468, 470, 484–488, 486(t), 487(f), 542, 605

Texas, state park system, 484–488, 486(t), 487(f)

Texins Association, recreation programs, 361–362, 361(f)

Theaters, commercial, 375, 574–575

Theaters, nonprofit, 571
  community and school theater, 573–574
  New York Shakespeare Festival's

Public Theater, 568(f), 569, 572–573
  regional theaters, 571–572, 572(f)
Therapeutic recreation, 54–56, 55(f),
60, 552, 644, **646–648**, 647(f)
This book, purpose, organization, and
use, 3–4, 7–10, 8(f), 9(f)
Threshold population, **110**, 112, 117,
157, 407–409
Time and its use, perceptions of, 143–
145, 193–194, 194(f), 226, 227–228,
250
Time available for recreation, 50–51,
96–100, 225
  social obligations, 226–227, 228(d)
  use of discretionary time, 227–228
  work lifestyle, 225, 228(d)
(see also: Time and its use, perceptions
of)
Time-sharing, **333**
Title IX, Education Act of 1972, 41(t),
132–134
Tivoli Gardens (Denmark), amusement
park, 381
Topography and landforms, 153–154,
196(f), **307**, 308–312, 309(f), 322(d),
390, 351(f)
  canyons, mesas, caves, 286(f), **311**,
  474(t), 476(t), 516, 518(t), 534, 538
  glacial landforms, **311–312**, 316,
  317(f), 480, 517, 526, 534
  hot springs, 21, **311**, 515, 516, 526
  mountains, 86(f), **308**, 469, 472(t),
  474, 474(t), 484, 495, 496, 516–
  517, 526, 528, 529, 530, 533
  sand dunes, **311**, 481(t), 518(t), 534
  shorelines and islands, 77(f), 119(f),
  285(f), **309–311**, 310(f), 413(f),
  469–470, 472(t), 478, 481(t), 483(t),
  496, 509(f), 517, 521, 526, 529,
  530, 534
  volcanic landforms, 285(f), **311**, 517,
  518(t), 534
  water features (including reefs and
  waterfalls), 313, 314, **318–319**,
  319(f), 474(t), 476(t), 489, 490, 516,
  518(t), 533, 534
Toronto, Ontario, Metropolitan Parks,
Department, 449, 450(t), 451
Tourism, 22(t), 23(t), 34, 38(t), 39, 40,
53(t), 67, 70, 77–79, 77(f), 95, 99,
99(f), 102, 148, 150, 171–172, 178,
179, 246–247, 270–273, 273(f), **277–
280**, 285(f), 544–546, 616–617, 657,
676–678, 677(f)

Tourist facilities, national government-
developed, 544
  Communist countries, 546
  Mexico, 544–545, 545(f)
  Portugal, 545
  Spain, 545–546, 677
Tours, guided, 384
Township parks and recreation agencies, 425–426
Traditions, rituals, customs, and habits,
impact on recreation, 97–98, 119(f),
120, 128–130, 129(f), 135, 135(f),
150(d), 201, 208–209, 210, 226,
229(f), 230, 244, 329, 366, 370, 371,
440, 556, 558, 642
Trail parks, 436
Trails, government-sponsored (Canada
and U.S.), 165, 553, 554
  design and construction, 630
  historical development of, 38(t), 39,
  42
  national trails (U.S.), 553–554
Transportation availability, (see Recreation opportunity accessibility)
Transportation systems, public (urban),
172–175, 173(f), 655, 656(f)
  recreation use of, 556–557
Travel, for recreation, 22(t), 23(t), 34,
38(t), 39, 40, 41, 53(t), 70, 77–79,
77(f), 95, 99, 99(f), 102, 103, 104,
116, 202–203, 270–273, 273(f), 616–
617
Tribal resources, 343–344, 343(f)
  tourist facilities, 401–402

Undesignated resources, publicly
owned, recreation use of, 107–108,
108(f), 554–555
(see also: Airports; Bridges; Buildings;
Cemeteries; Railroads, Roads (rural)
and highways; Sidewalks and Streets
(urban); Transportation systems, public,
urban)
Undeveloped recreation resources (see
Resources (recreation), undeveloped)
United Nations, Universal Declaration of
Human Rights, 48
U.S. Department of Agriculture, Forest
Service (see National forests, national
forests and Forest Service, U.S.)
U.S. Department of Defense, recreation
resources (see Military resources, U.S.)
U.S. Department of Health, Education
and Welfare, 627

U.S. Department of Housing and Urban
Development, 627
U.S. Department of the Interior, Bureau
of Land Management, recreation use of
resources, 511(t), 512–513(f), 537–
538, 665–667, 667(f), 668–669, 670,
671–672, 674
U.S. Department of the Interior, Bureau
of Reclamation, recreation use of projects, 511(t), 512–513(f), 543
U.S. Department of the Interior, Heritage Conservation and Recreation Service (formerly Bureau of Outdoor Recreation), 7, 37, 627, 629
U.S. Fish and Wildlife Service (see National Wildlife refuges and Fish and
Wildlife Service, U.S.)
U.S. Forest Service (see National
forests, national forests and Forest Service, U.S.)
U.S. National Park Service (see National Parks and National Park Service,
U.S.)
Universal Studios Tour, 359, 360(f)
Urban park and recreation systems (see
Local and regional government re-
sources; Activity programs)
Use-units, definition of, **289–291**
User-conflicts, 66, 110, 672–673
User conflicts and carrying capacity
problems, future recreation implications
of, 672–675, 672(f), 704(d)
Utah, recreation resources, 117, 130,
518, 535, 537, 590–591, 592(f), 670

Valley parks, 436
Vegetation, 319–320, 472(t), 480,
516–517, 518(t), 531(f), 533–534
Vermont, recreation resources, 391–
392, 393, 397, 532, 558
Viewing facilities (towers, observation
decks, airplanes), 384
Visiting commercial establishments
(cafés, bars, dancehalls), significance as
a recreation activity, 52(t), 202, 203,
225, 264(f), **267**, 332, 368, 371–376
Visiting friends and relatives, entertaining, attending social functions, significance as a recreation activity, 202, 212,
213, 258, 261, 263, **264–265**, 264(f),
328, 329, 330(t), 331, 332, 333,
333(f), 394
Virginia, recreation resources, 535, 542,
543, 606–607, 607(f)